The Backbench Diaries
of Richard Crossman

THE
BACKBENCH DIARIES
OF
RICHARD CROSSMAN

edited by
JANET MORGAN

HAMISH HAMILTON
AND
JONATHAN CAPE

FIRST PUBLISHED 1981
© BY THE ESTATE OF R. H. S. CROSSMAN 1981

HAMISH HAMILTON LTD,
57–9 LONG ACRE, LONDON WC2
JONATHAN CAPE LTD,
30 BEDFORD SQUARE, LONDON WC1

BRITISH LIBRARY CATALOGUING IN PUBLICATION DATA

CROSSMAN, RICHARD HOWARD STAFFORD
THE BACKBENCH DIARIES OF RICHARD CROSSMAN
I. GREAT BRITAIN – POLITICS AND GOVERNMENT
1945–1964
I. TITLE   II. MORGAN, JANET
941.085'5'0924   DA 592
ISBN 0-241-10440-8
ISBN 0-224-01811-6

PRINTED IN THE UNITED STATES OF AMERICA

Contents

Illustrations

Editor's Introduction

A dozen files, rusting at the hinges, contain Richard Crossman's Backbench Diaries. They are closely typed on heavy foolscap, interleaved with crumbling newspaper cuttings — Crossman's weekly articles for the *New Statesman*, the *Sunday Pictorial* and, later, the *Daily Mirror*. These columns, on domestic and international politics and, for the *Statesman*, on books, were intellectually much alike whichever paper published them. Well-reasoned, closely argued, they were the product, in Crossman's own favourite phrase, of 'a bump of irreverence'. Stylistically, though, Crossman's contributions to the *Statesman* on the one hand the the *Pictorial* and *Mirror* on the other could not have been more different. For the thoughtful left-wing weekly, of which he had been an assistant editor since 1938, his sentences were longer, his allusions complex and his humour ironical. For the popular papers of the Mirror Group, whose star columnist he became in 1955, the sentences were short, his remarks blunt and his mockery direct.

Such facility for addressing people in whatever fashion would most quickly captivate and most painlessly inform them was arguably Crossman's greatest skill. He was primarily a teacher — a philosophy don who could fill the hall at Oxford University, a memorable lecturer to the Workers' Educational Association in the late 1930s, a popular columnist in mass-circulation newspapers, the lucid exponent of a complicated superannuation scheme or of the intricacies of parliamentary procedure to his Cabinet colleagues ('who, for a moment, believed they understood it') and, at the end of his life, the confident amateur analyst, for the benefit of an enraptured crowd of children, of the workings of his swimming pool.

Many of his fellow politicians were — and remain — puzzled by Crossman's desire to unravel, explain and criticize. Some of them found it irritating; some, as the *Backbench Diaries* show, condemned him for it. This is not wholly surprising. To start with, Crossman was not naturally tactful. He would assume that all those he met enjoyed nothing better than to have their assumptions questioned and their arguments challenged. Civil servants who worked with him were not the only ones to feel that he wished life to be one long seminar. But if much of his aggressiveness stemmed from intellectual joie de vivre, some of it was camouflage for personal diffidence. Crossman was at his easiest with his family; he could enjoy the company of old friends, particularly women. But, uneasy with small remarks and every-day artifice, he would often resort to provocative talk and tactless teasing, which the more sensitive found unbearable.

Not that Crossman was himself thick-skinned. For instance, while he shunned formal parties and celebrations, he liked to be invited. (His dislike of official occasions and formal dress is interesting. He certainly found them stuffy but his objection partly arose from his own shyness and fear of dis-comfort. He would begin to enjoy himself once he found the company congenial and an occasion festive. Of the State Opening of Parliament in October 1967, for example, he wrote with relief '... I sheepishly got into my morning suit and actually found it perfectly comfortable. I could wear my ordinary white shirt and didn't have the separate hard collar for which I'd carefully gone out and bought the collar studs for *1s. 3d.*') Crossman always noticed who wrote to and visited him during his various illnesses and which M.P.s had remarked on his absence from the House. He was particularly touched, as this volume indicates, by the kindness of his friends when his wife Zita died and by their efforts to entertain him in the months afterward. Crossman's special affection for 'the Israeli' sprang in large part from his admiration for people who could simultaneously enjoy intellectual disputation, where he was bold, and extravagant emotion, where he was tentative.

If some of Crossman's colleagues and associates in the Parliamentary Labour Party and, later, on the National Executive Committee resented the brusqueness of his manner, others were infuriated by his influence. Though he had spent six years in local government, as Labour councillor for Cowley and from 1934 to 1940 as Leader of the Labour Group on Oxford City Council, in 1951, when the *Backbench Diaries* open, he had been a Member of Parliament for only six years. His Amendment to the Address on the King's Speech in 1946 and his refusal, as a member of the Anglo-American Palestine Commission in the same year, to follow the Foreign Secretary's line were believed, not least in his own eyes, to have cost him office and the hope of it. In 1951 he was 43 and confined to the backbenches. Not that Crossman minded; to the politically ambitious his airiness was maddening. He disdained the trudging life of the Commons—only after 13 years in the House did he discover how to put down an Amendment to a Public Bill and bring himself to take part in Committee Stage proceedings. 'On Friday', he wrote in early February 1959, 'I went up to the Public Bill Room ... I was directed up in a lift to a room on the left and found a man in an armchair, with his feet up. I addressed him politely, assuming he was the official, but found he was the messenger. He took me into a fine room and there were three of my New College students—the whole Public Bill staff taught by me —and at the far end was a white-haired pundit, Mackenzie, who is five years younger than me and who looked as though he had been sitting there twenty years, waiting for my arrival!'

Nevertheless, to the chagrin of his colleagues, Crossman was famous. Neglecting what politicians believed or hoped to be the most spotlit of platforms, the House of Commons, he enjoyed instead celebrity as the regular columnist of a paper of immense circulation, authority as a staff writer for an influential left-wing weekly, popularity as a radio, and later a television, broadcaster and notoriety as one of the Labour Party's most prominent and effective rebels. What is more, when Crossman did choose to speak in the House on his own subjects of foreign policy and defence, the benches filled.

Crossman's life appeared altogether enviable. He was very able and, though he never ceased to remind younger colleagues of the 'drudgery' attending every profession and of his own experiences 'as a dogsbody', his work was always stimulating and rewarding. The Mirror Group was rich and generous, encouraging its protégé to travel wherever he had a mind to go. (Occasional references in Crossman's four volumes of diary reveal his horrified surprise at the cost of meals not covered by an expense account; in October 1959 he made a short-lived 'post-*Mirror* resolution to stop taxis and restaurants'.) It is true that his way of life at this time protected him from some of the constraints and difficulties of an ordinary political career, although it is too harsh to say, with some of his closest friends, that Crossman's success as a popular journalist somehow corrupted him, giving him a taste for luxurious living and almost demagogic power. Still, a good many of his colleagues complained, wrongly, that, secure in his parliamentary majority, he shirked the duty of proclaiming Labour's message. Paradoxically, they simultaneously deplored the fact that he enjoyed such an effective outlet for his views.

They disliked, furthermore, the very nature of those views. Crossman was regularly charged with inconsistency, for he was, like Lord Melbourne, 'that rare phenomenon, a genuinely independent personality'. The *Backbench Diaries* illustrate how he would arrive at an opinion through argument with himself and other people and how new or more attractive evidence would lead to a change of mind. Only rarely did Crossman start from his conclusion and job backwards. Generally his opinions were the product of dispute, deliberation (often instantaneous) and a mischievous habit of taking an opposite view. Precedent and consistency were not, unless it suited him, intrinsically good. Such an attitude was bound to be unpopular with devout members of his Party.

It was the more upsetting because Crossman's Party colleagues attached great importance to 'loyalty', particularly at the time covered by the *Backbench Diaries*. In 1945 Labour had been returned to power with its first overall majority and had for a full Parliament enjoyed authority to introduce cherished measures. Now they were obliged to defer to an apparently invulnerable Conservative Government while they themselves wrangled about the proper attitude an Opposition should take, especially where foreign and

defence policy was concerned, raked over the afflictions of their own later
years in power, and tormented themselves with factional quarrels. The
conflicts described in this volume were on broad and general issues: German
rearmament and the European Defence Community; defence expenditure,
the Korean War; inflation; Suez; the hydrogen bomb and the Common
Market; and, in the Labour Party, nationalization and Clause Four; revision
of the Party Constitution and unilateral disarmament. Even small shifts of
position were noted, particularly when they were expressed by a proponent
as conspicuous as Crossman. Only in the development of a pensions plan,
which was not a matter of great controversy within or between the parties,
was Crossman allowed to work away uncriticized.

There were recognized guardians for each strand of opinion — 'the leadership'. the 'old guard', the Bevanites, the Tribune Group, the trade unionists,
the Gaitskellites, the revisionists, the unilateralists and so on — and in this
galaxy each constellation and every star had its appointed place. Not so with
Crossman. His loyalty to persons appeared to be as unpredictable as his
views. Aneurin Bevan, Hugh Gaitskell and Harold Wilson all enjoyed his
attentive support in the period with which this volume deals, not least
because Crossman found the role of kingmaker exciting and the chance to
influence a court irresistible. His colleagues found this unsettling.

They were equally troubled by the extent of his acquaintance. He travelled,
as representative of the *Mirror Group* and the *Statesman*, lecturer at SHAPE,
delegate to conferences, guest speaker welcome all over the world, enjoying
wherever he went enviable access to politicians and officials, generals and
guerrillas, government and opposition, businessmen and academic observers
— for, as Crossman once observed, no-one would refuse to see the columnist
of Britain's largest-circulation newspaper (and, as for those to whom this
introduction meant nothing, they had admired the *New Statesman* all their
lives). At home Crossman did not mix only with fellow-members of the
Labour Party. In regular radio and television discussion programmes he
appeared with Conservative Members and friendships, like that with Robert
Boothby, were not confined to the studio. Though his contemporaries at
Winchester (including Douglas Jay and Hugh Gaitskell) and at Oxford were
not necessarily friends, they formed a large pool of acquaintances on both
sides of the House. Crossman was by no means an isolate nor an ideologue
abhorring any connection with those of different political persuasions. On the
contrary, the unforced, uninterfering companionship of club life rather
appealed to him; as his *Diaries* show, unlike many members of the Commons,
he looked favourably upon this aspect of the House of Lords, which he
saw as an even more comfortable version of his own clubs, the Athenaeum
and the Garrick.

Many of Crossman's colleagues accordingly felt that he was a prey to
dangerous influences. More, they believed he was himself subversive.
Politics, like all professions, has its own codes and secrets and from his first

book[1] to his last lecture[2] and his final television series, a trip around Britain with Sir John Foster, the former Conservative M.P., looking at the February 1974 election campaign, Crossman was preoccupied with understanding and explaining the nature of British parliamentary democracy. Some of his colleagues, long before they learnt that he was keeping a diary, were disconcerted by the thought that their postures and actions should be so regularly analysed and discussed in public.

Crossman was fascinated by political power. He sought to find where and how it was exercised and to describe it. He was a detective and a teacher; four volumes of Diaries record his search, pursued in the Bevanite Group, the N.E.C. and Transport House, the Opposition Front Bench and the Cabinet itself, before, in July 1970, he optimistically returned to the *New Statesman* to gauge how much influence could be wielded from the editor's chair.

For some readers the *Backbench Diaries* will be their first excursion in the company of Crossman and his weekly journal. They will trace, with their loquacious and perceptive guide, the curious path to office—and to *The Diaries of a Cabinet Minister*. Other readers, already familiar with those three volumes, will now find in the *Backbench Diaries* the origin of many of the convictions, doubts, likings and dislikings subsequently displayed by Crossman the Secretary of State. Together, the four volumes of diary offer a remarkable history. They show a character developing and at the same time remaining deeply consistent, a career unfolding surprisingly but coherently.

In 1954 Crossman set out the purpose of the Diaries:

Wednesday, March 24th
My aim was to keep a record of the transient impressions of politics as they are made on one personality in order to note, before they are forgotten, opinions which are proved wrong and judgments which one would rather not have made. Even after a fortnight one tends to telescope events into conformity with one's present interests and so to distort or to improve the path. However, let's have a try at objectivity.

The Diaries are very long. Those covering Crossman's experience as a Minister, from 1964 to 1970, run to some three million words, dictated weekly on to tape and edited to about a third of their original length as *The Diaries of a Cabinet Minister*. The *Backbench Diaries* are as long again, about three million words dictated, with some gaps during periods of illness or disenchantment with politics, between October 1951 and December 1963. They too have been reduced by some two-thirds, to compress the work into

---

[1] *Plato Today* (London: Allen & Unwin, 1937).
[2] *The Role of the Volunteer in the Modern Social Service:* Sydney Ball Memorial Lecture (Oxford: Clarendon Press, 1973).

a single volume. Deciding how to cut this typescript has been one of the most difficult of editorial tasks. Some of the excised material deals with affairs in Crossman's constituency of Coventry East; much of the rest consists of descriptions of his travels. Bridging passages indicate where Crossman went and whom he saw and, as the example of the accounts Crossman would dictate when he returned home, the diary of his visit to the U.S.S.R. in 1958 has been included. The remaining omissions are of complete stories — Labour policy-making on education and municipal ownership, for instance — where the material affords additional rather than exclusive illustrations of Crossman's themes. Small excisions have also been made where passages seemed libellous or in bad taste.

The Editor's Note introducing Volume 3 of *The Diaries of a Cabinet Minister* explained how I came to inherit Crossman's own task of rearranging and revising his original dictated text. As Crossman himself stated in his introduction to Volume 1 much of the special historical value of the Diaries derives from their being 'dictated while the memory was still hot and uncorrupted by "improvements" '. He sought to reassure his readers that the text which he had prepared for publication, though entirely revised, nevertheless remained faithful to his original unrehearsed account. In 1970, when the preparations for publishing the *Diaries* began, Crossman asked me to be his assistant and, in particular, his referee. I was to check the revised draft against the original transcription, to ensure that the content, mood and balance of the original were accurately preserved, before turning to the task of checking facts and providing footnotes, bridging passages and other material. Crossman himself entirely re-dictated the revised text of Volumes 1 and 2. For Volumes 3 and 4, however, the responsibility for selecting, rearranging and often interpreting Crossman's original material fell to me, so that it is especially important that, for this volume as for Volume 3, I should explain the methods I have used and the principles I have followed in dealing with Crossman's material.

Readers of *The Diaries of a Cabinet Minister* will recall that from 1964 to 1970 Crossman used a tape-recording machine for dictating his weekly account of events. He had acquired two of these machines in October 1962, to record and for his secretary to transcribe the discussion at a series of seminars on Cabinet Government, held at Nuffield College, Oxford. Having familiarized himself (though not completely) with this machine, Crossman then used it to record what became the closing sections of the *Backbench Diaries* and, subsequently, *The Diaries of a Cabinet Minister*. This method of recording presented special problems when the time came to edit the transcript.

To begin with, though, I must describe how Crossman recorded the earliest part of the Diaries, from the time that they opened in October 1951 until the acquisition of his machine in October 1962. Interruptions for holidays and illness apart, these diaries, too, were kept weekly, unless political life was sufficiently exciting for Crossman to make more frequent entries or so tedious that he set the diaries on one side. The diaries were dictated to Miss Rose Cohen, Crossman's secretary, who worked at Vincent Square. She would take down Crossman's words in shorthand, type them on foolscap and file them, together with copies of his articles and extracts from his speeches in the House. Only rarely would Crossman look over his account, since he was anxious to avoid the temptation of tinkering with his own prose and wished to set out his opinions of the current week undefiled by the memory of his earlier prognostications.

Two points must be made concerning the way in which this typescript has been edited. First, chronology. In *The Diaries of a Cabinet Minister* Crossman preferred to unravel each weekly chunk of dictation, to make a day by day account, with passages of reflection on the week's events included in the entries for Saturday and Sunday. I followed this method in Volume 3. But while it was appropriate for recording the life of a Minister, attending regular Cabinet, Cabinet Committee and Departmental meetings and fulfilling lists of daily engagements, it was unsuitable for chronicling Crossman's life as a backbencher. Many of his weekly entries for 1951 to 1963 are almost entirely made up of reflections, with actions mentioned more by way of illustration. Weekly entries in the *Cabinet Diaries* were themselves chronologically tangled—stories beginning early in the week were taken to their conclusion some days later, others were begun in the middle with flashbacks filling in their origins and accounts from previous weeks were occasionally repeated—but entries in the *Backbench Diaries* were more complex still. Common sense suggested that I should not attempt to break them down into daily entries, so they have been kept in their original form, with linking passages to provide a change of pace where an entry is exceptionally long.

The second point has to do with style. Crossman had two techniques of composition, as he himself explained in the Introduction to Volume 1 of *The Diaries of a Cabinet Minister* and, at length, in his entries for July 1963 in the *Backbench Diaries*. For a speech he would make a few headings on a piece of paper, glance at them and speak extempore, a practice that helped to make him an entertaining and effective orator but which, first as an Opposition spokesman and then as a Minister, he came to find inappropriate for official explanation of policy. 'Gradually, as the House of Commons came over me,' he wrote in July 1963, 'I began not departing from the manuscript but inserting a sentence here and another there. Everything went pretty well until I wanted a quotation, looked down and found that I had somehow confused the two piles of paper, the ones I had already used and the ones I hadn't ... from that moment I had to *ad lib* the rest of the speech and it became much more my old backbench style ...' Crossman's written material, on the other hand, was painstakingly revised. He would dictate a draft, cursing anyone who interrupted him, and would then redraft it over and over again. (Those who examine the transcripts of the 1964 to 1967 diaries, on which Crossman himself worked, will see his extensive notes, circles, arrows, clarifications and deletions, as he brought order to his original text.) Evidently, then, the typescript prepared by Miss Cohen represented only the first draft of Crossman's prose and some tidying-up was required.

None the less, the original text is remarkably coherent. I have shortened sentences, rearranged paragraphs and altered the order of clauses but there has been little need to correct grammar or punctuation. Where Crossman uses an idiosyncratic construction, I have kept it. Proper names have been checked but Miss Cohen's familiarity with Crossman's doings and associates is reflected in the accuracy with which they were recorded. Names of foreign persons and places presented a special difficulty; I have followed the usage of the relevant volume of the *Annual Register*.

When I came to deal with the entries from October 1962 to December 1963 I found another set of difficulties, familiar from work on Volume 3. It was at this point that Crossman began to use his tape-recording machine, of which he was not yet fully a master. Sometimes material was accidentally erased or overlaid and the order of events became jumbled as the diarist attempted to repair the damage. Dictating to a machine also brings temptations, especially to those whose conversation and argument is as coruscating as Richard Crossman's. In his own preface to Volume 1 of *The Diaries of a Cabinet Minister* he drew attention to the pitfalls. For instance, searching for the right adjective or phrase, he would try a number of alternatives; anxious to press on with the narrative, he would leave tantalizing loose constructions; sometimes he was just tired and, consequently, verbose. When Crossman was at his most relaxed, the material he produced was very much 'a stream of consciousness'.

I was by now accustomed to these stylistic problems and also to the technical problems of editing a tape-recorded diary. The typist who, later, bravely attempted to turn Crossman's spoken words into written prose was not always successful. Some words and phrases were hard to distinguish; even more difficult to decipher were unfamiliar words and expressions. Moreover during the period when he first began to use the machine, Crossman, as Shadow Minister for Science, was mixing in a new world of scientists, industrialists and engineers, with whose names and preoccupations his new secretary, Mrs Jennie Hall, was unfamiliar. Crossman had no opportunity to correct either his own slips of the tongue or later mistranscription of these recordings. Years elapsed before they were transcribed and, even then, Crossman preferred not to examine what he had dictated, believing that his practice of keeping his diaries on tape would afford even greater protection against allegations that he might have tampered with his original text in the light of subsequent events.

As with Volume 3, I used intuition and common sense to unravel this part of the diary. The entire text was unstitched and I then fitted together whole paragraphs, single sentences and phrases from the original account, cutting out superfluous or repetitive passages and supplying omissions. Obvious mistranscriptions were altered. Where Crossman tried out successive words and phrases I pruned what appeared to be his bosh shots. I also completed sentences, disentangled metaphors and corrected the grammar so that his account would read smoothly but would retain the appropriate colloquialisms. I have tried to do all this as inconspicuously as possible, seeking to preserve Crossman's own distinctive manner of writing. If, as he reaches the last section of this volume, the reader notices a slight change of style, I hope that this will reflect no more than the difference between a diary taken down in shorthand and one dictated to a machine. Readers who are interested in close textual comparison will find the full, unedited version of Crossman's Diaries at the University of Warwick.

I have not sought to interpret every ambiguous reference in Crossman's original text. Sometimes his choice of words reflects his own uncertainty and at others he was deliberately vague. The interest and value of the Diaries comes partly from the fact that they show Crossman thinking aloud and I would not wish to lose this. Though I have corrected some factual slips and inaccuracies, I have not tried to make a definitive check of every episode and every meeting which Crossman records. That would take many more years and Crossman was anxious that his Diaries should be published as soon as possible 'so that controversy could take place while memories are still green'. Moreover, a running commentary on Crossman's recollections would require so many additional footnotes that the size of this book would be at least doubled. Crossman and I agreed that annotation should be kept to a minimum. The asterisked notes are his, in the sense that they represent material originally embodied in the text; I am responsible for the other footnotes and the bridging passages. An appendix gives brief biographies of persons who were important to Crossman or who figured largely during the period covered by this volume; where possible, other people are identified in notes at the foot of the page where they are first mentioned, not in the linking passages but in Crossman's text. A list of 'Bevanites' may also be found at the end of the book.

There are drawbacks to the way in which Crossman and I chose to revise and prepare this material for publication. For this volume in particular, published as the last of the series though chronologically the first, the task of cutting the original typescript without distortion, let alone editing it, at times seemed daunting. But our methods have had the overwhelming advantage of permitting the publication of these diaries within memory of the events they recall and, while this book is very long indeed, it does provide a valuable and fascinating account of political affairs during Labour's 13 years of Opposition.

1980   JANET MORGAN

1951

In July 1945 a Labour Government succeeded the wartime coalition and Winston Churchill's brief caretaker Ministry. This was the first time that Labour had come to power with a parliamentary majority over all other parties combined: 392 Labour Members were elected, against 189 Conservatives.[1]

With Clement Attlee as Prime Minister, the Government proceeded to reconstruct the domestic economy on the lines set out in the Labour Party's election manifesto, Let Us Face the Future. *Among the landmarks*[2] *were Acts taking into public ownership the Bank of England (1946), the coal industry (1946), electricity (1947), railways and canals (1948), gas (1948) and the iron and steel industry (1949, with February 1951 as the eventual vesting date). Civil aviation was reorganized in 1946 and 1948 saw the birth of the National Health Service.*

These five years were difficult. There were shortages of manpower, fuel, food and materials; rationing and controls continued; the weather was often exceptionally severe. The Government's energies and the country's resources were strained by the need not only to relieve conditions at home, but also to assist the recovery of a devastated Europe.

In foreign affairs the problems were no easier. Cold war between the West and Soviet Russia intensified, with conflict in Azerbaijan, Greece, Turkey and increasingly, Eastern Europe. Britain's former colonial empire was another area of tension. In 1947 the transfer of British power in India to two new Dominions was followed by much bloodshed. The Egyptian Government became more fervently nationalistic and British troops left the Nile Valley in 1947. British policy in Palestine was vehemently criticized from many quarters, including the ranks of the Labour Party, as terrorism and atrocities continued. In May 1948 the British Mandate ended and the Jewish State of Israel was established. Fighting persisted between Jews and Arabs.

Towards the end of the decade, the German question became pressing. Despite the lifting of the Russian blockade of Berlin in 1948, Germany and Berlin remained divided. Western efforts at reunification met with Soviet obduracy. Another urgent problem was China, where in 1949 the victorious People's Liberation Army took Peking and in the autumn of that year established the Communist regime of the People's Republic of China.

Anglo-American relations had cooled in the immediate post-war period but the recognition that Britain and America faced common problems in international affairs led to a reaffirmation of their close relationship. The turning-point came in 1947, with the offer by the United States of financial aid to help the economic recovery of Europe and to counter the growing challenge of Communism. Twenty-two States were invited to take part in the preparation of

---

[1] The Government were also supported by 12 Liberals, 3 members of the Independent Labour Party, 2 Communists, 2 Irish Nationalists and one member of the Commonwealth Party, and the Conservatives by 9 Ulster Unionists, 2 members of the National Party and 13 National Liberals. There were 14 Independents.

[2] These, and other domestic and foreign events, are discussed in detail in linking passages and footnotes supplementing the main text of this volume.

a plan to assess each country's needs and to co-ordinate resources. Sixteen accepted. The resulting Marshall Plan[1] *was signed in Paris in September 1947.*

Even with American aid, the state of the British economy remained precarious. In September 1949 the pound was devalued from $4·03 to $2·80 and a wage freeze declared. The Government's hope was for a successful export drive. Five weeks later the Prime Minister announced economies in Government expenditure which, it was estimated, would eventually have a disinflationary effect of £250 million a year. There was also to be a saving in defence expenditure of £30 million in a full year. For all except old age pensioners a charge of no more than 1s.[2] *was to be made for each prescription.*

Though these measures fell short of general expectation, by the end of the year, with a dramatic drop in the deficit on the current account in the last quarter, there was a great improvement in the country's gold and dollar reserves. But wage restraint and rising prices were causing increasing frustration and, particularly among the trade unions, criticism of Government economic policy.

It was against this background that in January 1950 Mr Attlee proclaimed the date of the General Election. Polling day was to be February 23rd. The Labour manifesto, Let Us Win Through Together, *included a statement of proposals to nationalize the sugar, cement and chemical industries, the meat distribution service and the cold storage system. The Conservatives (whose persistent overtures to the Liberals were stoutly refused) promised in* This Is The Road *to stop further nationalization, decentralize the coal industry and the railways, denationalize road haulage and repeal the Act of 1949 nationalizing the iron and steel industries.*

The election result was narrow. Redistribution and the abolition of 12 university constituencies in 1948 left 625 seats to be filled, 15 fewer than in the preceding Parliament. Of these, Labour took 315 and the Conservatives 270. Allied with the Conservatives were 10 Ulster Unionists, 9 National Liberals and 8 Conservative Liberals, making an Opposition total of 297.[3] *With this slender majority, Labour struggled on. The condition of the economy improved; some controls were ended and others relaxed. But wage restraint continued and in the autumn, after a rash of strikes throughout the year, the Trade Union Congress repudiated the Government's wages policy.*

During the summer Britain's balance of payments difficulties were eased with the outbreak of the Korean war and the consequent rise in world demand for war materials. At the end of June troops of Communist North Korea invaded the territory of South Korea, whose Government had been elected under United Nations' supervision and which was receiving American economic assistance. The U.S. President, Mr Truman, announced that his country would give full

---

[1] Named after General George Marshall, United States Secretary of State at that time.
[2] 5 new pence. (£1 = 100 new pence.)
[3] The remaining seats were held by 9 Liberals, 2 Irish Nationalists and the Speaker. One seat remained vacant since the Conservative candidate had died just before the election.

naval and military backing to the South Koreans and would simultaneously strengthen support to anti-Communist forces in the Philippines and Indo-China. As a member of the United Nations (though in advance of the U.N. Security Council's call), Britain placed her naval forces in Japanese waters at the disposal of the American command and eventually sent ground and air troops to Korea.

Though the Opposition supported Mr Truman's intervention and the Prime Minister's response, they were far from satisfied with the Government's general conduct of defence and foreign policy. Much of the Conservative criticism was voiced by Mr Churchill. In February, in the middle of the election campaign, he had proposed 'a parley at the summit' between the U.S. President, the Prime Minister and Joseph Stalin, in the light of the President's announcement that American scientists had been instructed to proceed with development of the hydrogen bomb. Labour's Foreign Secretary, Ernest Bevin, called Mr Churchill's suggestion 'a stunt'. In the early summer Mr Churchill swooped once more. The Schuman Plan for the integration of the coal and steel industries of Western Europe was launched in May. In June the Leader of the Opposition told the House of Commons that, if convinced of adequate conditions and safeguards, he was prepared to concede the abrogation of national sovereignty.

But the Government's attitude to European co-operation was lukewarm and, in Conservative eyes, equivocal. The Government announced that, while Britain was ready to take a constructive part in discussions, she could not bind herself in advance to pool production or to accept a supranational authority. Accordingly, when the Six-Power conference on the Plan opened in Paris in late June, Britain only 'kept in touch' with the negotiations.

An important aspect of the question of European co-operation concerned German rearmament. In August Mr Churchill carried a motion in the European Assembly at Strasbourg for a European Army under the authority of a European Minister of Defence. In September he pressed the House of Commons on this matter but, in his own words, found the Prime Minister 'very guarded and very obscure' on the issue of German participation in collective European defence.

But the main thrust of the Opposition attack was on the Government's proposals for rearmament. The Defence White Paper published in March had announced a £21 million increase in expenditure (largely on research and improved equipment, particularly jet fighters) and had admitted a severe drop in Army recruitment. The outbreak of the Korean war provoked the Government into allocating in late July an additional £100 million for defence and in early August it was stated that a further £3,400 million would be spent over the next three years. At the end of that month, large increases in Service pay were announced, together with the extension of conscription for National Service from eighteen months to two years. Further proposals for strengthening the defence forces were made when Parliament was recalled on September 12th. The Government now planned to spend £3,600 million in three years and to establish between six and ten regular divisions, adding one of these to the two already based in Germany, which would themselves be made up to strength. New naval construction, modernization and conversion would start immediately, the jet-fighter force would be increased and production speeded on the new Canberra bomber. The Opposition alleged that each successive stage of rearmament had been belated and inadequate.

Criticism also came from within Labour's own ranks and it was rearmament and its repercussions on other aspects of Government policy that focused Party dissent. Trade union unrest was principally due to the continuation of wage restraint while prices rose, the Government demanded strenuous efforts from industry and, some unionists alleged, large profits were being made from arms production. The constituency Labour parties, more doctrinaire, deplored the Government's dilatoriness in implementing Socialist measures and attacked the moderation of the leadership. At the Party Conference at Margate in early October, Aneurin Bevan, then Attlee's Minister of Health and one of his most forceful critics, again topped the list of Members elected to the National Executive Committee by the Party's constituency section. Two members of the Keep Left Group, Ian Mikardo and Barbara Castle, were elected to the N.E.C. for the first time.

This group had been founded in 1947 by a number of Labour backbenchers, who published in April of that year a pamphlet, Keep Left,[1] criticizing Government policy on two main grounds. They were opposed to what they maintained to be the excessively anti-Russian and pro-American policy the Foreign Secretary was pursuing, and they were deeply convinced of the need for concerted national economic planning under a Minister of Economic Affairs, much swifter demobilization, import savings and the suspension of the convertibility of sterling. By the end of 1950, as constituency Labour parties grew increasingly disenchanted with Mr Attlee's leadership and the policy of his Government, the views of the Keep Left Group attracted wider backbench support. Its founder members were to form the nucleus of the 'Bevanites'.

The new year saw on January 1st the suspension of Marshall Aid to Britain, so much had the country's gold and dollar reserves improved, and in May the Festival of Britain, conceived to mark the centenary of the Great Exhibition of 1851 and to celebrate British art and design, science, industry and technology. According to the official guide, the Festival represented 'one corporate reaffirmation of faith in the Nation's future'.

Meanwhile abroad and at home the Government's troubles persisted. In Egypt the anti-British campaign centred on demands for the release of the sterling balances Egypt held in London. The Egyptian Government continued to block the passage of goods to Israel through the Suez Canal and in early

---

[1] The pamphlet was signed by Richard Crossman, Michael Foot, Ian Mikardo, Geoffrey Bing, Donald Bruce, Harold Davies, Leslie Hale, Fred Lee, Benn Levy, R. W. G. Mackay, J. P. W. Mallalieu, Ernest Millington, Stephen Swingler, George Wigg and Woodrow Wyatt.

October abrogated the 1936 Anglo-Egyptian Treaty and the Condominium Agreements of 1899 concerning the Sudan. British negotiating proposals were rejected.

The Anglo-Persian crisis also grew more heated. Dr Mossadeq, former leader of the National Opposition Group in the Persian Parliament, became Prime Minister in April and a Bill to nationalize the oil industry was immediately passed by both houses unanimously. The Anglo-Iranian Oil Company was dispossessed and by the autumn its remaining British employees had been ordered to leave Persia. Negotiations between Britain and Persia had by this point been broken off and the British Government had announced their intention of bringing the matter before the U.N. Security Council.

Relations between the British and American Governments had been uneasy at the beginning of the year. Mr Attlee had flown to Washington in December 1950, chiefly to explain his Government's attitude to the Peking regime, which Britain had recognized in January 1950, and to express concern at the possibility that atomic weapons might be used in the Far East. Tension between Britain and America worsened in the first month of 1951. General MacArthur, Commander of the U.N. forces in Korea, had swept his troops northwards, towards the Manchurian border, and was edging towards an extension of the war. In April President Truman replaced him by General Ridgway and British anxieties were somewhat relieved.

Korean armistice talks were proposed by Russia in June, immediately after the breakdown of discussions in Paris between the Deputy Foreign Ministers of Russia and the Western Powers. The Western deputies had wished to discuss Communist policy and the heavy armament of Russia and her satellites as the first item on the agenda, while the Russians had sought to discuss German rearmament, American military bases in Europe and the North Atlantic Treaty, signed by America, Britain, France, Denmark, Belgium, the Netherlands and Luxemburg in January 1950 and also agreed between America and Italy. The fundamental and continuing differences between the Soviet Union and the West made the prospect of a thaw in the cold war remote.

In common with the other North Atlantic Powers Britain had agreed in December 1950 to accelerate her arms programme. In January and February detailed statements of the Government's proposals were made by the Prime Minister, the Ministers of Defence, War and Labour and the Chancellor of the Exchequer. The Chancellor, Hugh Gaitskell, explained that on the basis of present costs the Government intended to spend £4,700 million in three years on rearmament, exclusive of stockpiling and capital investment. The cost of defence would rise from £16 per head in 1950/51 to £36 in 1953/54. The country was faced with a deterioration in the terms of trade, which might give an additional burden of £300 million in 1951, and a scarcity of raw materials. There would be a fall in exports of some raw materials, including coal and semi-finished products made of steel and non-ferrous metals and in exports from the engineering industry. This reduction would have to be balanced by increased exports of

*textiles, pottery and other products, at the expense of the domestic consumer.
Rising incomes would not be matched by an increase in the flow of real goods.*

*In his contribution to the debate, Mr Bevan, since January 17th Minister of
Labour, argued that the Soviet Union was a less formidably equipped enemy than
she appeared to be. His criticism of the Opposition, and particularly of Mr
Churchill, for their fears and war-mindedness foreshadowed, however, the
attacks he was to make on his own Government two months later.*

*This came just over a week after Mr Gaitskell delivered his Budget on April
10th. The Chancellor sought to meet the cost of the rearmament programme by
curtailing investment and consumption and limiting the expansion of social
services. He announced only minor increases in taxation: the tax on distributed profits was raised from 30 to 50 per cent, the standard rate of income
tax increased by 6d. in the pound and petrol tax raised by 4½d. a gallon. The
Chancellor also increased the entertainments tax and purchase tax on cars,
wirelesses and domestic gas and electrical equipment. Initial allowances on
industrial and agricultural plant were to be suspended after one year. Industry's
burden was thus increased by £236 million in a full year but tax-free allowances
for married couples and children were increased, together with old age and
supplementary pensions.*

*While Opposition criticism fastened on those of the Budget proposals which
affected productive industry and the businessman, the Government's own side of
the House was thrown into turmoil by the measures which the Chancellor
imposed on the National Health Service. A 50 per cent charge was to be made
for spectacles and dentures and, although as Minister of Health Mr Bevan had
himself introduced the Bill levying a prescription charge, he now described the
Chancellor's proposal for charges as marking 'the beginning of the destruction
of those social services in which Labour has taken a special pride'. On April 21st
Mr Bevan sent his letter of resignation to the Prime Minister, who was being
treated in hospital for a duodenal ulcer. Harold Wilson, President of the Board
of Trade, resigned on April 23rd and John Freeman, Parliamentary Secretary to
the Ministry of Supply, on April 24th.*

*This split in the Labour ranks was emphasized at the beginning of July by the
publication of* One Way Only, *a pamphlet written by Michael Foot and Jennie
Lee (Mr Bevan's wife), the Editors of the left-wing newspaper* Tribune. *Mr
Bevan wrote the introduction to the pamphlet, which demanded that the rearmament programme be reduced and the cost of living stabilized by using the
savings made thereby and by increasing taxation. Though embarrassed by these
backbench rebels, on rearmament the Government were assured of Opposition
support. But Labour was constantly harried by Conservative procedural tactics
in the House and a General Election was widely predicted.*

*By the beginning of August the country was facing a grave balance of pay-
ments crisis, exacerbated by events in Persia. On September 5th the Chancellor
of the Exchequer flew to Washington for negotiations with the American
Treasury. It was known that he was asking for steel and believed that he would*

explain Britain's serious trading position. There was still no hope of peace in Korea and the economic situation continued to worsen. On September 19th Mr Attlee announced that the General Election would take place on October 25th. Meanwhile the views of Mr Bevan and his supporters had been staunchly repudiated in a pamphlet, Our First Duty—Peace, *published by the Labour Party National Executive Committee on August 28th. The President of the T.U.C., meeting at Blackpool at the beginning of September, also rejected the contents of* One Way Only. *But two days after the Prime Minister's announcement of the election date a further* Tribune *pamphlet appeared. In* Going Our Way *all the earlier criticisms were stated once more and it was amid this controversy that the election campaign began.*

Some 82·5 per cent of the electorate voted (compared with 84 per cent in 1950). The Conservatives and allied parties won 321 seats (a net gain of 23) and Labour took 295 seats (a net loss of 20). The Liberals won 6 seats (a net loss of 3), the Irish Nationalists 2 and 1 seat was captured by an Irish Labour candidate. On October 26th Mr Attlee delivered his resignation to the King and Mr Churchill set about forming a Cabinet.[1] It is at this point that the Back-bench Diaries *open.*

Tuesday, October 30th

We had a Group meeting at No. 9 Vincent Square and, to my surprise, twenty-four out of the thirty-two members turned up to crowd out the drawing room. The discussion soon concentrated on one problem: should we regard the pre-election controversy as closed? If so, Nye should stand in the elections for the Parliamentary Committee[2] of twelve, which is to form the Labour Shadow Cabinet. If he stands he will almost certainly be elected, since I heard from George Strauss, via John Freeman, that the other side would regard it as a disaster if Nye didn't serve on the Committee.

Before the meeting, John Freeman and I had come to the conclusion that Nye should serve and I think one or two other members of the Group agreed. But he himself had made up his mind. What was the good of resigning in order to be free to speak if he at once surrenders that freedom by joining the Committee? Had he not promised that the controversy would begin again after the election? Gaitskell and the others are so deeply committed by their actions over the last nine months that they will be fighting the Tories with one hand tied behind their backs. Why should we tie our hands in the same way? Certainly we should try to win over the Parliamentary Party to our point of

[1] For the full Cabinet list see p. 1045.

[2] First elected in 1923 as the Executive Committee of the Parliamentary Labour Party, its name was changed in 1951 to the Parliamentary Committee. It consists of twelve Members of the House of Commons, elected at the beginning of every parliamentary session by Commons Members of the Parliamentary Labour Party. There are also six *ex officio* members: the Party's Leader and Deputy Leader, the Chief Whips of the House of Commons and the House of Lords, the Leader of the Labour Peers and their elected representative. The elected Commons' members of the Parliamentary Committee sit on the Front Bench.

view but this will not be done by agreeing to conditions which make it impossible for us to state it.

Of course, if we all refuse even to be nominated, the Parliamentary Party will regard us as non-co-operative and determined to continue trouble-making, but this is something that we shall have to accept. On the other hand Fenner Brockway[1] and Jennie Lee emphasized the importance of not remaining a small exclusive group, and a long discussion took place on how to enlarge the Group and make it open to all who want to belong, without at the same time losing its cohesion. Nothing was settled and we are due to meet again in a week.

Wednesday, October 31st

The Parliamentary Party met at 11 a.m. Attlee was elected Leader[2] by acclamation and then came the first minor test of power, when it was proposed that the Deputy Leader (i.e. Morrison) should also be elected in the same way. Frank Bowles,[3] on our behalf, suggested that the Deputy Leader should be balloted for, along with the twelve members of the Parliamentary Committee. This was brushed aside and Morrison was proposed. Then Nye was proposed but immediately said that he would not stand, at which there was a considerable cheer of almost friendly relief.

Most of our time was spent in arguing whether we should oppose Shakes Morrison's[4] nomination as Speaker[5] and put up Jim Milner.[6] Milner is

[1] M.P. for East Leyton 1929–31 and Labour M.P. for Eton and Slough 1950–64. He was Secretary of the Independent Labour Party 1923, its Chairman 1931, and its General Secretary 1934–8, before resigning in 1946. He was created a life peer in 1964. His numerous publications include an autobiography, *Towards Tomorrow* (London: Hart-Davis, MacGibbon, 1977).

[2] Since 1922 the Labour Party, when in Opposition, has elected its Leader and Deputy Leader at the beginning of each Session. Most elections have been uncontested, including those of 1951.

[3] Labour M.P. for the Nuneaton division of Warwickshire from 1942 until 1964, when he made way for Frank Cousins. He was Deputy Chairman of Ways and Means 1948–50. Created a life peer in 1964, Lord Bowles was Captain of the Yeomen of the Guard (i.e. Deputy Chief Whip) in the Lords from 1965 until his death in 1970.

[4] Conservative M.P. for Cirencester and Tewkesbury 1929–59. He was Minister of Agriculture 1936, Minister of Food 1939–40, Postmaster-General 1940–3, and Minister of Town and Country Planning 1943–5. Speaker of the House of Commons 1951–9, William Morrison was created Viscount Dunrossil in 1959 and died in 1961. (The previous Tory Speaker was D. Clifton-Brown, who held office 1943–51.)

[5] The Speaker presides over the proceedings of the House of Commons and gives rulings on its procedure. Since the tenure of Shaw Lefevre (1839–57), the Speaker has acted as an impartial servant of the House. He is elected by the House of Commons at the beginning of a Parliament, or after a former Speaker's death or resignation, and in the twentieth century it has been customary to re-elect him for as long as he wishes to continue. On election, the Speaker forswears political connections and ceases to be a member of his party. However, he remains a Member of the House and, should he wish to keep his office, he must stand at the following General Election.

[6] James Milner (1889–1967), Labour M.P. for South-East Leeds 1929–51. He was Chairman of Ways and Means and Deputy Speaker August 1945–October 1951. Created 1st Baron Milner of Leeds in 1951, he was a Deputy Speaker in the House of Lords.

certainly unpopular in the Party and I doubt whether many people really thought he would be a better Speaker than Morrison. On the other hand Labour has never had a Speaker and we had continued with a Tory Speaker since 1945.[1] Moreover, Milner had told his fellow Members from Leeds that he was prepared to be nominated and many of our stalwart right-wingers seemed to feel that it would show weakness to let him be passed over without a protest. On the vote, 108 were for proposing Milner and 86 against, with a large number of abstentions.[2] Then came one of those queer spasms of second thought, when Hartley Shawcross[3] suggested that Attlee should tell Churchill that we would put Milner forward if Shakes Morrison were the Tory candidate, but that we would not put him forward if Sir Charles MacAndrew[4] were their candidate. This beautiful escape got 115 votes to 106.

One minor incident. Towards the beginning, Nye had proposed that we should not oppose Morrison but should acquiesce under protest. Immediately Manny Shinwell got up to denounce such weakness. So we are going to have the old rivalry as to who is the left-wing leader between Nye and Manny, all over again.

The proceedings in the Chamber in the evening were untidy and inauspicious. Sir Hugh O'Neill,[5] moving Morrison, made an incredibly tactless speech, which created turmoil. Milner was proposed competently from our side and then Churchill intervened to reveal every detail of the private negotiations.[6] He couldn't remember the constituencies of any of the Members he had to refer to, but he is so deaf that he can't be prompted. One has to remember that he has only been Prime Minister in a wartime Parliament

[1] From April 1921 to June 1928 the Speakership had been held by a former Coalition Liberal and from 1928 to 1965 by a former Conservative. Douglas Clifton Brown (1879–1958), who was created Viscount Ruffside in 1951, was Unionist M.P. for Hexham, Northumberland, December 1918–November 1923 and 1924–51. He was Speaker from March 1943 to November 1st, 1951, and was succeeded by William Morrison, who held the office until October 21st, 1959.

[2] In the House Major James Milner was proposed by Samuel Viant, Labour M.P. for Willesden West 1923–31 and 1935–59. Morrison was elected by 318 votes to 251.

[3] Labour M.P. for St Helens 1945–58 and Attorney-General 1945–51, during which time he was the Chief U.K. prosecutor at the Nuremberg trials. He was President of the Board of Trade 1951 and a member of the Permanent Court of Arbitration at The Hague 1950–67. Created a life peer in 1959, Lord Shawcross is Chancellor of the University of Sussex. Since 1969 he has been Chairman of the Panel on Take-Overs and Mergers and, since 1974, of London and Continental Bankers. He was Chairman of the Press Council 1974–8.

[4] Charles MacAndrew (1888–1979), Conservative M.P. for the Kilmarnock division of Ayrshire and Bute 1924–9, for the Partick division of Glasgow 1931–5 and for Bute 1935–59. He was Deputy Chairman of Ways and Means March 1950–October 1951 and Chairman of Ways and Means November 1951–October 1959. Knighted in 1935, he was created 1st Baron MacAndrew in 1959.

[5] Hugh O'Neill (b. 1883), Unionist M.P. for Mid-Antrim 1915–21, and for Antrim and North Antrim 1922–52. He was Chairman of the 1922 Committee 1935–9 and Parliamentary Under-Secretary of State for India and Burma 1939–40. He was created 1st Baron Rathcavan in 1953.

[6] Between the Prime Minister, the Leader of the Opposition and the two Chief Whips.

without a real Opposition. How will he fare in our very different conditions today?

My first impression of the morale of the Parliamentary Party is that everybody is so enormously relieved at having got back that they are in the highest spirits. On the Tory side, I got a slight sidelight yesterday when I ran into Bob Boothby, drinking with John Junor[1] of the *Daily Express.* Boothby has not been given a job, despite his loyalty to Churchill. He and Junor both described Lyttelton's[2] anger at being fobbed off with the Colonies, and Boothby said, 'Rab Butler Chancellor! Why, that's Gaitskell all over again, but from Cambridge.' With David Eccles[3] excluded, at least from Cabinet office, and Brendan Bracken sulking,[4] the real free enterprisers and deflationists seem to have been kept out and there is a good deal in the view that the general make-up of the Churchill Cabinet[5] means that it will be only very slightly to the right of the most recent Attlee Cabinet. Just as Attlee was running what was virtually a coalition policy on a Party basis so Churchill may well do the same. In which case none of the drastic remedies propounded by *The Economist*, the *Sunday Times* and all the economic pundits will be attempted.

[1] Assistant Editor of the *Daily Express* 1951–2 and Deputy Editor of the *Evening Standard* 1953–4, he has been Editor of the *Sunday Express* since 1954 and its Chairman since 1968. Since 1960 he has also been a Director of Beaverbrook Newspapers. He was knighted in 1980.

[2] Oliver Lyttelton was Conservative M.P. for the Aldershot division of Hampshire from 1940 until 1954 when he was created 1st Viscount Chandos. President of the Board of Trade 1940–1, he was a member of the War Cabinet 1941, Minister of State in the Middle East 1941–2, Minister of Production 1942–5, President of the Board of Trade 1945 and Secretary of State for the Colonies 1951–4. He died in 1972.

[3] Conservative M.P. for Chippenham 1943–62. He was Minister of Works 1951–4, Minister of Education 1954–7 and October 1959–July 1962, President of the Board of Trade 1957–9 and Paymaster General, with responsibility for the Arts, 1970–3. He was made a Baron in 1962 and a Viscount in 1964, and was Chairman of the Board of Trustees of the British Museum 1968–70 and Chairman of the British Library Board 1973–8. Eccles was made Minister of Works, without a seat in the Cabinet. Bracken declined office, 'on grounds of health'.

[4] Conservative M.P. for North Paddington 1929–45, for Bournemouth November 1945–50 and for East Bournemouth and Christchurch 1950–1. He was Parliamentary Private Secretary to Churchill 1940–1 at the Admiralty and No. 10, Minister of Information 1941–5 and First Lord of the Admiralty 1945. Of Irish origins, deliberately obscured and mystified to his contemporaries, after an exotic early career Bracken entered politics when he worked for Churchill in the Leicester by-election of 1923. A successful publisher, he was Director of Eyre & Spottiswoode from 1925 until his death in 1958, and he managed a string of financial papers, including the *Financial News*, the *Banker*, *The Economist*, *Investors' Chronicle* and the *Financial Times*. Created a Viscount in 1952, he never sat in the Lords. See Andrew Boyle's *Poor Dear Brendan: The Quest for Brendan Bracken* (London: Hutchinson, 1974) and Charles Edward Lysaght's *Brendan Bracken* (Harmondsworth: Penguin, 1979).

[5] Mr Churchill's Cabinet had sixteen members (see p. 1045). The Prime Minister himself took the Ministry of Defence. Co-ordinating Ministers ('overlords') were appointed, all except for Mr Churchill being Members of the House of Lords.

Tuesday, November 6th

At the Parliamentary Party meeting this morning Attlee opened the discussion on the King's Speech,[1] like a schoolmasterly bird snapping up the morsels. What is really significant is the cheerfulness and morale of the Party, compared with its state of semi-disintegration just before the election. What a difference it makes not to be scared of losing your seat! They are even almost friendly to the Bevanites, out of sheer general sense of well-being. Personally I am inclined to regard this sort of optimism as extremely complacent. We are in Opposition, without any idea of a constructive Socialist policy, and it may be a great deal more difficult to unseat the Conservatives than many of my colleagues imagine. It will certainly be much more difficult to work out a Socialist programme and we shall have to discuss on the Executive of the Fabian Society[2] what reorganization of itself the society should do, since nothing much will come out of Transport House[3] Research Department with regard to the Parliamentary Party.

At 2 p.m. we had a Keep Left meeting, at which, thank heavens, we came to a sensible decision about our continued existence. The Group obviously suspected and resented the proposal to establish an Executive Committee since this would simply mean narrowing the active group to only half the membership and leaving the others merely as listeners outside. But we are going to slowly expand the Group and simultaneously organize good outside speakers to address open meetings in the House. The first will be Tommy Balogh.

I went straight from the Group to hear Attlee, snappy and witty, in the first speech of the King's Speech debate. Winston followed in what, on re-reading, I am sure will be shown to be a very revealing speech. It began with a long passage regretting the even balance of parties, half appealing for national unity and half wryly admitting that Oppositions must oppose (no wonder, considering what he did in Opposition). I am convinced that his plans have been completely upset by the narrow majority.

[1] At the formal opening of a Session, the Sovereign announces to Parliament the sessional programme of Government Bills and policies. However, some proposals will subsequently be dropped or deferred and others added. The Speech from the Throne is delivered in the House of Lords with Commons Members in attendance and is repeated in the Commons by the Speaker. On this occasion, since the King was recovering from a serious operation, the Speech was read in the Lords by the Lord Chancellor.

[2] Founded in 1883 to promote 'the reconstitution of society so as to ensure the general welfare and happiness' and so named after the Roman General Fabius Cunctator (the Delayer), who had defeated Hannibal by means of the 'gradual' tactics to which the society adhered. Strengthened by the addition to its membership of George Bernard Shaw in May 1884 and Sidney Webb in May 1885, the objects and methods of the society became more definite. Every member was obliged to sign an explicit declaration of Socialist principles. In *Fabian Essays*, published by the society in 1889, 'dogmatic Marxism' was specifically rejected. The society was one of the sources by which the early Labour Party was nourished. It continues to publish reports, tracts and essays. Crossman joined the society in 1934 and was a member of its Executive Committee from 1950 to 1957 and from 1959 to 1963.

[3] Transport House was, until 1979, the headquarters of the Transport and General Workers' Union and of the Labour Party.

Right at the end he had a carefully worked out peroration, in his old wartime style, with a supreme peace appeal. He completely failed to carry the House with him, because it isn't a wartime House. But I take his peace appeal very seriously indeed. The election has had a real result on both parties. It has made them realize that the people of this country really do want peace and I fancy Winston and Eden have a better chance than Attlee and Morrison. The latter had to lean over backwards in being pro-American for fear of being accused of appeasing Communism. Winston and Eden have to lean over backwards trying to get peace with Stalin,[1] in order to rebut the charge of warmongering. But how far is the Old Man really prepared to go? The key issue is German unity and his mission is not to Moscow but to Washington. Is he prepared to persuade Truman[2] to give up the rearmament of Western Germany (and that really means knocking to pieces the existing plans of Atlantic defence) for an agreement with the Kremlin about a unified, disarmed Germany on the Austrian model? It is just possible that the Americans, who are beginning to realize what rearmament will mean as it really gets going, actually want Winston to pull them into giving up the full extent of rearmament. If this is so, he has a superb opportunity, which would leave him in power for years. On the other hand, if he makes his 'supreme effort' and fails, we shall be very near the ultimatum stage of diplomacy and war will be much more imminent.

The pressure of rearmament, shortages of raw materials and rapidly worsening terms of trade led the new Chancellor of the Exchequer, R. A. Butler, to add to the warning given by his predecessor. By November prices and wage rates were markedly rising and there was a heavy outflow of the country's gold and dollar reserves. Mr Butler described this as 'a general balance of payments crisis and not, as in 1949, a problem predominantly of trade between the sterling area and the dollar area'. In October alone the dollar deficit had been $320 million.

To check this drain, on November 7th the Chancellor declared measures to save £350 million a year, of which £130 million was to come from the re-imposition of quotas on European imports, mainly unrationed foods. Stockpiling of goods was to be slowed down and the tourist allowances for overseas travel halved to £50 a head. Home demand on the steel, engineering and building industries was too heavy and the Government intended to limit the undertaking of new building, even when already sanctioned. On November 8th the Minister of Fuel and Power, Geoffrey Lloyd, announced reductions in the amount of coal which householders might purchase during the following three months.

In his speech on November 7th the Chancellor stated that Government

[1] Joseph N. Djugashvili Stalin (1879–1953), General Secretary of the Central Committee of the Communist Party. He became Chairman of the Council of Ministers and dictator of the U.S.S.R. after Lenin's death in January 1924.

[2] A Democrat, Harry Truman (1884–1972) was President of the United States 1945–52, first taking office on the death of Franklin Roosevelt.

expenditure would be cut. From January 1st, 1952, for the period of rearmament, an excess profits tax would be levied. These measures were supported by changes in monetary policy. Bank rate was raised from 2 to 2·5 per cent and a new rate of 2 per cent was introduced at which the Bank of England would, when necessary, lend to the market against Treasury bills. To restore flexibility to the short-term market, the discount rate for Treasury bills was rendered more elastic. Interest rates allowed on bank deposit accounts were raised from 0·5 to 0·75 per cent; local authorities were to pay to the Public Works Loan Board higher interest rates, raised from 3 to 3·75 per cent, and the long-term borrowing rate from the Agricultural Mortgage Corporation, already increased from 4 to 4·5 per cent in May, was now raised to 5 per cent.

The Chancellor hoped that these immediate steps would demonstrate the Government's intention to keep sterling strong, without resort to severe deflation. The economic situation would also be discussed with members of the Commonwealth (in January) and Britain's partners in NATO and the O.E.E.C.

Wednesday, November 7th

I listened to Butler's speech on the economic crisis; I was sitting next to Dick Stokes[1] and, as Butler announced each item of his economic policy, I checked with Stokes and found it was precisely what the previous Cabinet had decided on. This didn't include the ½ per cent increase in the bank rate but, anyway, in Stokes's opinion, this was so small as not to constitute a real difference in policy. In fact we merely heard the Treasury brief, recited by a different voice. Most of the Labour benches were jeering and laughing throughout the speech in a pretty irrelevant way. The significant thing is that we really have an undercover coalition between the last Labour Cabinet and Butler's section of the Tory Party. By the next Budget, Butler may well introduce really drastic cuts in Government expenditure, and if Gaitskell had been in power and determined to maintain the defence programme, I think he could not have avoided doing the same.

I can form no estimate yet of what the Conservative reaction is, either in the House or in the country, but I don't think many people really believe that Butler's policy is due to appalling discoveries he made after he reached the Treasury.[2] Nor is it right to assume that, because the short-term policy is the same as Gaitskell's, Butler will succeed in the long term in holding his Party back from a deflationary line.

Monday, November 12th

I spent the whole day working for the *New Statesman* and then, rather

---

[1] Labour M.P. for Ipswich 1938–57. He was Minister of Works 1950–1, Lord Privy Seal March–October 1951, and also Minister for Materials July–October 1951. He died in 1957.

[2] Though the Chancellor referred in his speech to the 'ugly situation' bequeathed to the incoming Government, he acknowledged that the previous Chancellor had warned of the worsening position.

gloomily, I went to the House and sat down to dinner with Hugh Dalton. The discussion naturally gravitated to planning for the next phase of Socialism. Whatever his other failings, Dalton remains a first-rate talker, which means not anecdotes but relevant discussion of the subject. He obviously wants now to get into the discussions of the Fabian Society as a patron of the bright young men, which he has always been.

When James Griffiths's[1] name was announced, we went in to hear the winding-up speeches of the day's debate on steel.[2] Everyone was enjoying themselves, in a state of pandemonium and counter-pandemonium, a rip-roaring, gorgeous parliamentary row on great issues, which fortunately we all know by heart, since steel has been debated scores of times and there is nothing new to be said. In a debate this makes for certain success. Actually, the last word had been said in the first speech, by George Strauss, when he announced that, if returned to power, Labour would reverse the de-nationalization of steel and would make sure that no further compensation was paid as a result of the Tory denationalization. This will make de-nationalization extremely difficult, since who is going to provide the money in a free market, under such risk?

I quite wrongly assumed (because everyone had told one the obvious, which is so often untrue) that, once we had got into Opposition, all the left-wingers would have the time of their lives. Actually, the reverse is the case. Once you get into Opposition all the routineers of the Party can make the routine anti-Tory speeches, hammering and thumping away to the plaudits of the crowd, with a delicious sense of release from responsibility. Steel is a secondary issue and what really matters now, of course, is the economic crisis resulting from rearmament. But that is the one issue that is not being debated, because neither Mr Gaitskell nor Mr Butler admit that the economic crisis is caused by rearmament. And if a left-winger were to make a speech along those lines, he would cause acute resentment in the Labour Party by inter-rupting the routine party political controversy with a discordant note which would not be straight anti-Tory.

It looks as though the most interesting work now will actually be in places

---

[1] James Griffiths (1890–1975), Labour M.P. for Llanelly 1936–70. He was Minister for National Insurance 1945–50, Secretary of State for the Colonies 1950–1 and Secretary of State for Wales 1964–6. His autobiography, *Pages from Memory* (London: Dent), was published in 1969.

[2] The iron and steel industries were nationalized by a Labour Government, which passed the Iron and Steel Act 1949, establishing the Iron and Steel Corporation. The vesting date of the Act was February 15th, 1951. A Conservative Government denationalized the industry, by the Iron and Steel Act 1953, setting up the Iron and Steel Board. The industry was renationalized by a Labour Government, with the Iron and Steel Act 1967, effective from July 28th, 1967. The 1947 Transport Act established a British Transport Commission, nationalizing railways, canals and other forms of transport. Road haulage was administered by one of six Executive Boards. It was denationalized by the Transport Act 1953 (see below p. 221). The debate was on an Amendment to the King's Speech, proposed by George Strauss, regretting the Government's proposals for the iron and steel and road haulage industries. The Amendment was defeated by 320 votes to 281.

like the Fabian Society,[1] where the real argument about Socialist policy will take place – or will it? As Hugh Dalton pointed out at dinner, it takes at least three years to get a new idea accepted and before an idea is accepted it's no good inserting it in the Party programme. Unless we are out for four years at least we shall merely be refurbishing old or out-worn ideas – unless, of course, events suddenly transform the whole controversy.

Tuesday, November 13th
The results of the election to the Executive[2] of the Parliamentary Labour Party were announced today. Nothing very surprising. All frontbenchers, with the exception of James Callaghan, who had made a couple of vigorous speeches in this Parliament, and also Glenvil Hall[3] and Tony Greenwood, the chairman and vice-chairman of the Liaison Committee[4] in the previous Parliament. The only frontbenchers who stood and were not elected were George Strauss and John Strachey, and Strauss could certainly have got on if the voting had taken place after his speech on steel this week. We are an extremely decorous, conservative Party when it comes to balloting.

The fact that no Bevanite stood was mentioned to me in the Smoking Room by James Callaghan. 'A pity you are so conscientiously standing aside from the Party,' he observed, to which I replied, 'Well, having just elected you as one of our leaders and humbly shown ourselves conscious of our unworthiness, I feel it's a bit hard to be accused of "standing aside". If we had stood and got on, you'd have accused us of ambition. But, then, you always have it both ways.'

I spent most of the day struggling with the contributions to *New Fabian Essays*.[5] Roy Jenkins and Crosland were very upset at the final draft of my own essay. I see their point. Having written first a right-wing draft, then a

[1] On November 15th Crossman submitted to the Home Research Committee of the Fabian Society a note on the task of Opposition policy-making. He suggested that responsibility for long-term thinking about the 'second stage of Socialism' would fall to the society, rather than to Transport House. Five or six working parties should be established, to examine critically the events of the past six years and to formulate new policies. Crossman's tentative scheme was for groups on: fiscal policy; the nationalized industries; social services; local government; parliamentary and Cabinet government; and colonial policy. A special study might assess the relationship between full employment and inflation. Each working party would have five or six members, including one 'experienced ex-Minister', one or two backbenchers and two or three non-parliamentary members of the society.

[2] I.e. the Parliamentary Committee. Crossman is using its old name.

[3] Glenvil William Hall (1887–1962), Labour M.P. for Portsmouth Central 1929–33, and for Colne Valley 1939–62. He was Financial Secretary to the Treasury 1945–50, and Chairman of the Parliamentary Party 1950 and 1951.

[4] When the Labour Party is in office the Parliamentary Party sets up a small Liaison Committee of three elected backbench Members, the Leader of the House, the Government Chief Whip and an elected backbench Labour peer. The Liaison Committee was intended to link the Cabinet and the P.L.P.

[5] *New Fabian Essays* (London: Turnstile Press, 1952), edited by Richard Crossman, with a preface by Clement Attlee. As well as Crossman, the contributors were Anthony Crosland, Roy Jenkins, Margaret Cole, Austen Albu, Ian Mikardo, Denis Healey and John Strachey.

left-wing draft, then a right-wing draft, and having finally synthesized everything just to the left, they must feel that, with another toss, the coin might
have turned up their way. One of the difficulties of politics is that politicians
are shocked by those who are really prepared to let their thinking reach any
conclusion. Political thinking consists in deciding on the conclusion first and
and then finding good arguments for it. An open mind is considered
irresponsible – and perhaps it really is.

George Wigg is starting work as a West Midlands Whip, and has achieved
one small improvement. In the last Parliament, when we were the Government, we backbenchers were very often able to suit our convenience by
getting a Tory to pair.[1] The new rule is to be that we are never to pair to suit
the convenience of a Government backbencher. So we shall be able to go
away and they will not. All pairing is to be done strictly through the Whips'
Office.

Wednesday, November 14th
I had John Junor to lunch today, just promoted from 'Crossbencher'[2] to
Assistant Editor in charge of politics on the *Daily Express*. He is obviously
right in saying that the main Tory object must be to disprove the Labour
propaganda about Tories being warmongers and opponents of the Welfare
State. This means, of course, that the Tories in their turn have got to give up
all their propaganda about Socialism being the cause of shortages and
controls. But, on balance, if they can do it, they win. He offered me a monthly
column in the *Daily Express* (in addition, of course, to the *Sunday Pic*). I
told him it was no go. He told me that he thought Beaverbrook[3] had
advised Churchill against giving Bob Boothby a job. Dishonour among
thieves.

*In the spring of 1951 Russia had invited Western Foreign Ministers to discuss a
German treaty, linking this question with the issue of West German rearmament, to which the Russians were deeply opposed. France, under American
pressure, had by now agreed to that rearmament 'in principle'. As noted above*

---

[1] Pairing is the arrangement by which Members of opposing parties agree to be absent
from the House at the same time, thus cancelling out each other's votes. As a rule pairing is
arranged by the Whips. Members nevertheless depart from this practice and sometimes
arrange 'unofficial' pairs.

[2] A weekly column of political comment and gossip was, and still is, published in the
Sunday Express under the pseudonym 'Crossbencher' (indicating a point of view independent of party). Lord Beaverbrook himself occasionally contributed to the column, which
has had many authors. John Junor was succeeded by Henry Fieldhouse, who wrote the
column until 1951.

[3] William Maxwell Aitken (1879–1964), the newspaper proprietor (notably of the *Daily*
and *Sunday Express*), was created 1st Baron Beaverbrook in 1917. He was Unionist M.P.
for Ashton-under-Lyne 1910–16, and was Chancellor of the Duchy of Lancaster and
Minister of Information 1918, Minister for Aircraft Production 1940–1, Minister of State
1941, Minister of Supply 1941–2 and Lord Privy Seal September 1943–July 1945. From
1947 to 1953 he was Chancellor of the University of New Brunswick.

(p. 25) conflicts over the agenda of the proposed conference led to the break-down of discussions in June.

The newly elected Conservative Government sought to emphasize the relationship between foreign policy and economic recovery and their intention to put the British point of view firmly before the American Government, even though, as Mr Churchill stated in his speech at the Guildhall on November 9th, America 'had risen to the leadership of the world'. Shortly afterwards it was announced that the Prime Minister would visit Washington at the end of the year.

Meanwhile the Foreign Secretary, Anthony Eden, explained to the House of Commons his view that the main hope for improved international relations lay in patient efforts to resolve limited and practical problems. The achievement of an Austrian peace treaty was one of these — no progress on outstanding points had been made since 1949 and the country was still occupied. Since September 1951 the Soviet and Communist press had vociferously alleged that Austrian foreign policy was inclined towards the 'American war bloc' and that western Austria was rearming.

Early in November Mr Eden joined his American and French counterparts in submitting disarmament proposals to the U.N. Assembly in Paris. (The Russian representative countered with alternative proposals for a Five-Power Pact.) But there was disappointment for those, especially in the American Administration, who had hoped that the new British Government would take a different attitude from their Labour predecessors towards the question of European federation. Britain made it clear, in a meeting at Strasbourg on November 20th, that her Commonwealth connection prevented her from entering a European federation and that she was unwilling to join either the Schuman Plan for a coal and steel community or a European Army. Negotiations for a European Defence Community continued between France, Germany, Italy, Belgium, the Netherlands, and Luxemburg, with General Eisenhower giving strong support.

Two days later, on November 22nd, the British, French and American Foreign Ministers met in Paris and agreed with the Federal German Chancellor on the heads of agreement for the future status of the Federal Republic. Mr Eden asserted in the House of Commons that this agreement did not signify that the West had abandoned all hope of eventual German unity.

Monday, November 19th

Eden opened the Foreign Affairs debate[1] with an extremely adroit per-formance — not the appalling tour of the horizon to which Ernest Bevin and Herbert Morrison subjected us, but a well-composed, well-delivered speech on a few outstanding topics. Herbert Morrison responded for an hour and five minutes. I doubt whether even the best ghost-writer could do anything with

[1] There was, according to custom, no vote at the end of the adjournment debate on foreign affairs, which lasted for two days, November 19th and 20th, 1951.

Herbert on foreign affairs. He manages to flatten out and vulgarize any good points and to give the impression that he has no grip and no seriousness. The only backbench speech which mattered came from Michael Foot, who challenged the whole concept of negotiation from strength and certainly got the ear of a large section of the Labour Party. Noel-Baker[1] spoke beautifully but kept forgetting that he wasn't on the Government side and speaking about what *we* are doing. I sat through the debate, failed to get in, and got a sort of assurance from the Speaker that I would be called on Tuesday.

Tuesday, November 20th

At the Party Meeting this morning[2] there were the first very quiet signs of backbench impatience with the determination of the old gang to keep all control in their hands. There were also clear signs that the old gang are determined to do so. The proposed specialist Party committees[3] were quite sensibly criticized from many points of view, after which Attlee announced that he would try them out. It was then suggested that the Party should meet on Thursday evenings, after the announcement of the next week's business on Thursday afternoons,[4] in order to discuss tactics. We were told that this was never done before the war. We pointed out that the Conservatives had been doing it for five years. We were told that it was very wrong to empty the House. We pointed out that the House is always empty from five to seven. I think that I could have got a vote against Attlee but Stanley Evans[5] for the West Midlands Group conciliated and asked for reconsideration after the Recess in February.

This afternoon the foreign affairs debate was resumed by Anthony Nutting,[6] the new Parliamentary Secretary, who made a first-class speech.

[1] Labour M.P. for Coventry 1929–31, for Derby 1936–50 and for Derby South 1950–70, Philip Noel-Baker was Minister of State at the Foreign Office 1945–6, Secretary of State for Air 1946–7 and for Commonwealth Relations 1947–50, and Minister of Fuel and Power 1950–1. A notable worker for disarmament, he was a Fellow (and now an Honorary Fellow) of King's College, Cambridge. He was awarded the Nobel Peace Prize in 1959 and was created a life peer in 1977.

[2] At which Clement Attlee took the chair. Until 1964 the Leader acted as chairman at P.L.P. meetings when the Party was in Opposition. From 1970 the P.L.P. elected a separate chairman.

[3] In December 1951 the N.E.C. approved the setting up of a number of sub-committees, 'subsidiary to the Policy sub-Committee', charged with the task of considering future policy. Four were established: on Privately Owned Industry; Socially Owned Industry; Agriculture, Food and Rural Life; and Social Services. In May 1952 the N.E.C. agreed to a recommendation from the Policy and Publicity Sub-Committee that a further sub-committee be appointed to consider Financial and Economic Policy.

[4] The 'business statement' delivered to the Commons by the Leader of the House.

[5] Labour M.P. for Wednesbury 1945–56 and Parliamentary Secretary at the Ministry of Food March–April 1950. He resigned his seat in 1956, and died in 1970.

[6] Conservative M.P. for the Melton division of Leicestershire from 1945 until his resignation in 1956. He was Parliamentary Under-Secretary of State for Foreign Affairs 1951–4, then Minister 1954–6. His parliamentary career ended with Suez. He is the author of *No End of a Lesson: The Story of Suez* (London: Constable, 1967), a biography of *Nasser* (London: Constable, 1972) and various works on Arab and African history and politics.

I suppose it seemed so good simply because, under the Labour Government, no one who knew anything about the subject was ever permitted to go to the Foreign Office. Dick Stokes responded for the Opposition, sensible and nice, but once again, like so many ex-Ministers, unable to cease to be an ex-Minister, telling us what he did until the little change-over. This really is continuity of foreign policy with a vengeance.

I was tipped off at five o'clock that I was to be called next on our side and was surprised to find that I wasn't. After forty-five minutes I went down towards the Speaker and Harry McGhee[1] said to me 'You needn't worry. You won't be called. The new loudspeaker over the Speaker's Chair is so sensitive that I heard Herbert Morrison telling the Deputy Speaker who to put in.' Actually this was an exaggeration, for the Deputy Speaker did say 'One has to have all points of view represented' and, sure enough, a Whip and a safe backbencher[2] were called. Then by luck there came a Conservative maiden speaker[3] who was a journalist, and it was suddenly felt that a journalist on our side should make the polite remark.[4] This is how one gets in! I started with a virtually empty House but it filled up fairly well. It's an extraordinary feeling. I spoke from my favourite place, the corner seat three rows up, just below the gangway. Opposite you are your opponents, the Government, but then the Government spills over to include our Front Bench and the rows behind,[5] so that one quarter only of the quadrilateral is Labour Opposition. You feel this as you speak, with Mayhew[6], Woodrow Wyatt and the rest much more hostile than the Conservatives opposite.

Eden came in and listened for thirty-six minutes, not approving but interested, while the brigadiers behind him fumed at the Bolshie and the Mayhews groaned. Eden spent thirty seconds replying to Herbert and half his time replying to Michael [Foot] and myself about Germany, to which Nutting had devoted nearly all his time. Eden was extraordinarily persuasive but completely negative. As we were going out of the Chamber he came aside with me and said, as far as I can remember, 'Well, you certainly got me about Haifa.[7] It was a fair point. But, you know, it just won't do, what you say

[1] Labour M.P. for Penistone, West Riding 1935–59. He was P.P.S. to Richard Stokes 1950–1. He died in 1959.

[2] The Whip was A. Edward Davies (M.P. for Stoke-on-Trent North); the 'safe backbencher' was Malcolm McCorquodale (M.P. for Epsom).

[3] F. M. Bennett, Conservative M.P. for Reading North 1951–5 and for Torquay, and later Torbay, since December 1955. He was Diplomatic Correspondent of the *Birmingham Post*. He was knighted in 1964.

[4] Congratulating a 'maiden speaker' on his first speech to the House.

[5] Crossman is referring to the conservatism of the Labour Front Bench.

[6] Christopher Mayhew, Labour M.P. for South Norfolk 1945–50 and for Woolwich East June 1951–July 1974. From July to October 1974 he sat as a Liberal, contesting Bath unsuccessfully for that Party in the second 1974 election. He was P.P.S. to the Lord President of the Council 1945–6, Parliamentary Under-Secretary for Foreign Affairs 1946–50 and Minister of Defence (Royal Navy) from 1964 until his resignation in 1966.

[7] In his speech Crossman had asked why the Foreign Secretary had not 'seen to it that tankers are streaming through the Canal, and into Haifa Bay', when he had 'upbraided

about Germany. I'd have liked it too. But I am committed now up to the neck. And, even if I wanted to, I couldn't breathe a word about an Austrian solution.' Then, after I had said something, he went on, 'But I assure you that, if I saw the faintest glimmering of hope on the Russian side, I would still go back to it. You put the case very well indeed but too much water has flowed under the bridge.' Then he added, 'That's why the European Army is so desperately important. I must prevent their trying to bring the Germans into NATO. That would be really dangerous.' I said that it might be a *casus belli*. He didn't say yes but he certainly didn't say no, and simply added, 'That's why the European Army is very important. If the Germans are thoroughly mixed up with the French, the Russians won't be so provoked.'

My impression of this conversation is that, now he is in the Foreign Office, Eden feels that the situation is much worse than he realized before, in the sense that we are infinitely more deeply committed to the full American policy of integrating Germany westwards and avoiding anything, such as proposals for German unification, which could upset it. I suspect he thinks this extremely dangerous but unavoidable.

In this two-day debate, the big parliamentary fact was that the controversy was entirely between the Tory Front Bench and the Bevanites. The vast majority of the Labour Party sincerely applauded Eden and agreed with him but a lot of them listened to us. I think this was because we were putting up what seemed to them a Socialist case against the Tories. This should slowly gain us as much support in the Parliamentary Party as we have in the country outside.

But I have a horrible feeling that our opposition is too late, that the last Labour Government committed Britain too deeply and that objectively there is no way back. Germany will be rearmed, we shall take large-scale dollar aid to sustain the arms programme and the war crisis will be on us in the next three years. And, of course, it may possibly be true that, if we had had our way, the Russians would not have agreed. Gaitskellites are more fanatically convinced about the rearmament of Germany than Eden, because he sees its dangers and they don't. Eddie Shackleton told me that after my speech he dined with Herbert and failed to make any dint in his simple-minded belief that all that matters is rearmament and getting the Germans on our side against Russia.

A draft Peace Treaty with Japan, prepared by the American Government, was discussed in the early months of 1951 with representatives of the British,

---

previous Governments' for acquiescing in the Egyptian blockade of the Canal. Crossman also demanded to know how the Foreign Secretary hoped to achieve German unification. The 'Austrian solution' was a 'German central Government with occupation forces on both sides' and Crossman objected that Russian agreement would never be secured if such a German Government were armed.

Australian and New Zealand Governments. Though Australia and New Zealand, in particular, feared a revival of Japanese militarism, the Americans emphasized that it would be unwise and unrealistic to impose on the Japanese provisions limiting their right to rearm. Accordingly the draft treaty recognized Japan's right to 'self-defence' and to voluntary participation in collective security arrangements. Japan would accept the obligations of the U.N. Charter. Japanese assets in enemy and neutral countries were to be sequestered, to provide a fund of some £5 million to be distributed by the Red Cross among former prisoners of war.

The draft treaty was submitted to Russia in March. Meanwhile in April the American President announced plans for a Pacific Security Pact between the U.S.A., Australia and New Zealand and, though Mr Morrison regretted that Britain had been excluded from the scheme, he warmly commended it. In May and June the Soviet Union stated its objections to the draft Japanese Treaty and proposed a conference of Foreign Ministers, including a Chinese representative (unacceptable to the Americans) to resolve the issue. The Soviet proposals were rejected but the U.S.S.R. nevertheless accepted the invitation to the Peace Conference at San Francisco on September 4th. Britain and the United States together proposed draft procedural rules and these, adopted by 48 votes to 3, prevented Soviet efforts to delay or amend the treaty. It was signed on September 8th.

Before signing, Mr Morrison stated that Britain deplored the absence of China from the conference but declared that it would have been dangerous to await the settlement of the Chinese problem before concluding the Japanese Treaty. In One Way Only *the* Keep Left *Group objected strongly to the signature of the treaty not only in defiance of the Soviet Union, but also in the absence of China and India.*

Monday, November 26th

I got to the House just in time for our Group meeting to discuss our attitude in the debate on the Japanese Peace Treaty. Nye was exclusively concerned with the constitutional question of whether the leadership of the P.L.P. in Opposition had the right to take a vote in the Party Meeting on what we should do on the floor of the House. He argued that, with Standing Orders suspended,[1] they had not, and I think that he deliberately arranged it so that the substantial question of whether the Group should oppose the treaty could only be put one minute before we went along the corridor to the big Party Meeting.

At this meeting, with barely 100 people present, Attlee once again behaved

[1] The Labour Party's Standing Orders impose a code of conduct on Party Members, reinforced by a variety of sanctions of increasing severity: a written reprimand from the Chief Whip, suspension from P.L.P. meetings, withdrawal of the whip and, ultimately, expulsion from the national Party. At one of the first P.L.P. meetings of the new Parliament of 1945, Herbert Morrison proposed, in the expectation of 'good behaviour', that Standing Orders be suspended. They were reimposed in March 1952.

like a prissy little schoolmaster. I think that every speech was against the treaty; at twenty-past one he suddenly snapped in a low voice, 'Time to take a vote.' This caused protest but the vote yielded the result of 73 to 14.

To my surprise, Nye contributed to the discussion a rather grandiloquent speech on the subject of America's master plan for disintegrating the British Empire. Pray God this is not the theme of Nye's new book,[1] since it bears no relationship to the policy of *One Way Only*.

This evening I moved along to the House of Lords with Zita for the Fabian annual dinner, where Attlee made an excellent after-dinner speech. This is what he excels at. He seems young, cheerful and friendly on such occasions. If only he were. The best incident of the dinner was its beginning. There were ninety Fabians there and half a dozen M.P.s, the guests obviously overawed by the august surroundings, and, as we filed to table, we all remained standing behind our chairs for a minute. 'Grace or no grace?', John Parker[2] audibly whispered to Attlee. A ghastly pause and then peals of laughter as we sat down without.

Straight from the dinner we went to the Chamber for the vote[3] on the Japanese Peace Treaty. Our little No lobby was rather empty, until I saw Leslie Lever[4] rolling into it, the crude, illiterate, shrewd, inane boss of the Manchester Labour Party. Nye came through a bit sheepishly, the leader led by the followers. (Every paper next morning described how Aneurin Bevan led his men into the No lobby.)

Zita and I went home with Nye, Jennie and Michael Foot for a drink in Nye's really lovely sitting room at Cliveden Place.[5] Nye's theme was that we must capture the constituency parties and so put a squeeze on the Parliamentary Party. If Members knew that they would not be renominated because they were anti-Bevanite, things would move. This is a typical Nye concept, which seems to me impracticable and, if the mere idea of it gets out, insanely dangerous. But I think that it was really partly motivated by his reluctance either to vote tonight or to make any major speech during the last two months. He is an extraordinary mixture of withdrawnness and boldness and he is always advising Ian Mikardo against rushing into action. Tonight, for instance, he dismissed with scorn what we had done in asking for a meeting

[1] For several years Bevan had been preparing chapters of the book that was to be published in April 1952 as *In Place of Fear* (London: Heinemann). It was finished in the autumn of 1951.

[2] Labour M.P. for Romford 1935–45, for Dagenham 1945–74 and for the Barking division of Dagenham since 1974. After the 1979 General Election he became Father of the House. He was General Secretary of the Fabian Society 1939–45, and the society's Vice-Chairman 1946–50 and Chairman 1950–3.

[3] The vote on the Second Reading was 382 in favour and 33 against.

[4] A solicitor and Labour M.P. for Manchester, Ardwick, 1950–70. He was knighted in 1970 and raised to the peerage in 1975. He died in 1977.

[5] A description of Aneurin Bevan and Jennie Lee's house at No. 23 Cliveden Place may be found in Michael Foot's *Aneurin Bevan* (London: Davis-Poynter, 1973), vol. II, pp. 190–1.

for tomorrow morning on dollars for defence,[1] arguing that it is a sheer waste of time to have a discussion in the Party Meeting. From what he said, you would have concluded that he was an uncompromising protagonist of an all-out fight for power, that he hated the idea of conciliation or uniting the Party on a common programme. This is partly true, since he cannot stand the idea of uniting with Morrison and Gaitskell. Yet, on the other hand, when it comes to the point, he jibs at each fighting action when you propose it. When Tom Driberg came in later to tell us that at least eighty people had abstained, Nye showed no interest and went back to his idea of capturing constituency parties.

Monday, December 3rd
After a Fabian day school on Saturday we were off to stay with Nicholas Davenport at Hinton Manor, near Faringdon. We got there at five past nine and found Hugh and Mrs Dalton,[2] as well as Giles Playfair[3] and Ben Nicolson.[4] On Sunday afternoon we went for a walk by the river and Hugh Dalton deliberately lagged behind to talk politics. He started by asking me what the Bevanites were going to do on the Defence Estimates,[5] saying that his mind was open but that it was awkward for a party to vote against defence. This, however, was merely preliminary. The conversation was steered round to Herbert Morrison. Did I think that he would be a disastrous successor to Attlee? When I gave the obvious answer, Hugh then asked me whether I thought Aneurin would succeed, to which I said no. Was it not therefore in the common interest to train up a rival to Herbert Morrison, acceptable to both Gaitskell and Bevan, and wouldn't James Griffiths be just the man?

The idea is really pretty sensible. In any foreseeable future, Aneurin could never be elected Leader by the Parliamentary Party and Herbert Morrison, followed by someone of the same sort, will automatically get it, unless the Bevanites are prepared to collaborate with others in preventing it. James Griffiths, whom I saw at the *New Statesman* weekly lunch last week and who seemed to have matured remarkably as Colonial Secretary, is a real possibility.

[1] The Mutual Security Act, signed by President Truman in October 1951, provided Europe with a total of $7,483·4 million of economic and military assistance (for the first time brought together in a single measure). Some Europeans, among them the Bevanites, were uneasy about the implications of accepting aid on such a scale. For a full discussion of these matters, see Peter Calvocoressi, *Survey of International Affairs 1951* (London: R.I.I.A. and Oxford University Press, 1954).

[2] Ruth Fox, Labour M.P. for Bishop Auckland 1929, who married Dalton in 1922. She died in 1971.

[3] Author, broadcaster and Professor of Drama. His recent works include *Crime in Our Century* (London: Sidgwick & Jackson, 1977).

[4] Elder son of the diplomat, politician and diarist Sir Harold Nicolson. An art historian, his works include *Treasures of the Foundling Hospital* (London: Oxford University Press, 1972) and, with Christopher Wright, *Georges de la Tour* (London: Phaidon, 1974). He was Deputy Surveyor of the King's Pictures from 1939–47. He died in 1978.

[5] These were to be presented to Parliament on February 25th 1952. See pp. 84ff.

Nye, I gather from John Strachey, has a low opinion of him but even Nye might prefer Griffiths to the prospect of Morrison followed by Gaitskell. Gaitskell would prefer Griffiths to Morrison and the whole Party would like a *tertium quid.* No doubt this is mainly a personal idea of Dalton's but the overture is a little more than that. John Freeman, with whom I talked it over today, agrees that it is worth our trying to see whether Nye is in reasonable enough mood to accept something which could hold the Party together, though it might make the Bevanite opposition less exhilarating to those who like conspiracies and explosions.

After dinner on Sunday Ben Nicolson, the son of Harold Nicolson[1] and an artist, told an interesting story about the ten days he spent at Windsor Castle as Deputy Keeper of the King's Pictures. On four of those days parlour games were played after dinner and the Queen chose her favourite game. The master of ceremonies took all the male guests outside and provided them with brass pokers, shovels, etc. After ten minutes' practice they were then made to parade as a squad, with the shovels and pokers on their shoulders, in slow goose step down the long drawing room past the King, the Queen and the Princesses,[2] who found it exquisite fun seeing Sir Stafford Cripps, Lord Ismay[3] and Anthony Eden doing 'Eyes right'. Nicolson said that he hadn't seen anything like Stafford Cripps, who had been forced at two hours' notice to spend a weekend at Windsor and who humbly obeyed the Royal command but suffered the full humiliation which Royalty seemed determined to extract from its Commoner guests.

The other game that the Queen likes is called 'It'. One person is selected as 'It' and all the lights are then put out in the drawing room. Everybody creeps about under the grand piano, etc., and 'It' must then find somebody in the dark and touch them and the person who is touched becomes 'It', and so the game proceeds *ad nauseam*, since there is no point and no end until one of the Royal Family suddenly switches on the lights. Nicolson said that his most embarrassing moment was when he placed his hand on a great expanse of pale flesh. When the lights were switched on, he said, it was a remarkable sight to see distinguished persons and Cabinet Ministers crouching under

[1] A diplomat, author and politician, Sir Harold Nicolson (1886–1968) was National Labour M.P. for West Leicestershire 1945–55 and Parliamentary Secretary at the Ministry of Information 1940–1. His numerous works include the delicate early satirical portraits *Some People* (London: Constable, 1934), *Diplomacy* (Oxford University Press, 1939) and other writings on diplomatic history, the official biography of *George V* (London: Constable, 1952) and the three-volume *Diaries and Letters* (London: Collins, 1966, 1967, 1968). An account of the Nicolson family appears in his younger son Nigel's *Portrait of a Marriage* (London: Weidenfeld & Nicolson, 1973).

[2] King George VI, his Queen (the present Queen Mother), the present Queen, Elizabeth II, and H.R.H. the Princess Margaret.

[3] After a distinguished army career, Lionel Hastings Ismay (1887–1965) was Chief of Staff to Churchill as Minister of Defence 1940–5 and to the late Earl Mountbatten of Burma, the last Viceroy of India, in 1947. He was Secretary of State for Commonwealth Relations 1951–2 and Secretary-General of NATO 1952–7. His *Memoirs of General the Lord Ismay* (London: Heinemann) were published in 1960. He was created a peer in 1947.

grand pianos. This is the only occasion, however, when Royalty can really relax and I suppose the parlour games are introduced for this express purpose.

Today I attended the first meeting of the Parliamentary Defence and Services group,[1] mainly because we had John Strachey to a *New Statesman* lunch and he told me he was being put up as chairman. A bevy of ex-Ministers was there — Shinwell, Henderson,[2] Woodrow Wyatt, Michael Stewart[3] and John Strachey. After a lot of havering about sub-committees, the subject of next Thursday's defence debate was mentioned, and immediately Shinwell pompously offered to sketch in the situation. To my amazement, he poured out a mass of facts and figures, among them the following:

The Western Union[4] plan of two years ago was for sixty divisions and 4,000 aircraft by the end of 1954. Ever since this, the only talk had been about the gap between reality and the plan. By the end of 1951, for instance, there would be not more than twenty divisions in all in Western Europe, though the aircraft situation would be rather better. By the end of 1951 the table of promise and fulfilment stands as follows:

	Promise	Fulfilment
America	6	4
France	10	5
Belgium	$1\frac{1}{2}$	virtually 0
Britain	4	4

The French had promised to provide ten divisions by the end of 1951, fifteen by the end of 1952 and twenty by the end of 1953.

Shinwell also added that we now had eleven active divisions overseas, more than at any time in our history. He and George Wigg argued that the sending out of the Third Division to Egypt had virtually exhausted our reserves so

[1] Both the Conservative and Labour Parties have backbench groups, meeting regularly to discuss particular subjects.

[2] The son of the Labour leader Arthur Henderson, William Watson Henderson, having served as Labour M.P. for Enfield 1929–31 and 1923–4, was created 1st Baron Henderson in 1945. He was a Lord in Waiting 1945–8 and Parliamentary Under-Secretary of State at the Foreign Office 1948–51.

[3] Labour M.P. for Fulham East 1945–55, for Fulham 1955–74 and for the Hammersmith division of Fulham 1974–9. A Whip in 1946–7, he was Under-Secretary of State for War 1947–51 and Parliamentary Secretary of State at the Ministry of Supply in 1951. In the 1964–70 Labour Government he served as Secretary of State for Education and Science 1964–5, Foreign Secretary 1965–6, First Secretary at the Department of Economic Affairs 1966–7 and as Foreign Secretary again 1968–70. He was created a life peer in 1979.

[4] The five Powers of the Western Union, a term coined in 1948 by Ernest Bevin, were Britain, France, Belgium, the Netherlands and Luxemburg. Throughout 1949 regular meetings were held to discuss co-operation in economic and defence policies; by the end of that year the Western Union had been enlarged and developed into the Council of Europe. Defence planning now took place within the framework of NATO, established in April 1949, and in the context of discussions about a European Army.

that, if something were to go wrong in Malaya,[1] there would be no barrel left to scrape.

But the extraordinary thing about Shinwell was that he said that he agreed that we were gravely overburdened with rearmament, that he regarded the defence of Western Europe next year as completely hopeless, despite Eisenhower's statement last week,[2] and that the whole idea of a European Army was sheer moonshine.

I thought that the other ex-Ministers looked a little embarrassed, since in all these points Shinwell is disowning his own Labour Government's policy and confirming everything which the Bevanites said about the unfair burden which Britain has assumed. However, when he had finished he swept out of the room leaving us to a discussion on what should be his own attitude in replying to Churchill on Thursday, particularly with regard to the European Army. Ex-Ministers now have plenty of time to talk and backbenchers suddenly discover, listening, that on a subject like Germany the ex-Ministers know just as little and are just as divided as ordinary backbenchers. However, after a good deal of scrapping, we agreed that Strachey should raise the issue at the P.L.P. meeting tomorrow, where last week's debate on dollars for defence is to be resumed.

Tuesday, December 4th

After our usual weekly Bevanite meeting upstairs, I caught Nye for a moment and told him briefly of my conversation with Dalton at Nicholas Davenport's. He dismissed the whole idea quite summarily, with the comment that Jim Griffiths would be the stooge of Gaitskell and Morrison in a week. Though John Freeman had not dismissed the idea so summarily, I found later that Ian Mikardo's view coincides with Nye's. However, I don't think that this is the end of it.

At four o'clock, just when Dalton was beginning the housing debate,[3] 150 of us assembled in Committee Room 14 to listen to Dr Adenauer,[4] the

---

[1] Communist terrorists had assassinated the High Commissioner, Sir Henry Gurney, on October 6th. A British general, Sir Rob Lockhart, had been given full executive authority, under the High Commissioner, for conducting the campaign against 'bandit operations'. His direction included the police and the Home Guard. The newly appointed Colonial Secretary, Oliver Lyttelton, had visited Malaya and announced that the British would not lay aside their mission there until terrorism had been conquered and there was a reliable prospect of stable self-government by all Malaya's communities.

[2] In a speech to the NATO Council in Rome on November 26th General Eisenhower had declared that Europe 'must achieve the impossible'. He had called for some 34 European divisions on the Continent by 1952, in addition to 6 American divisions. This would require an increase of 14 European divisions, an expectation whose fulfilment seemed unlikely.

[3] The Opposition censure motion on the Government's housing policy was defeated by 296 votes to 274.

[4] Konrad Adenauer (1876–1967), the leading West German politician in the post-war period. Mayor of Cologne in 1945, Adenauer founded the German Christian Democrat Party, was elected to the Bundestag in 1949 and held office as Chancellor of the German Federal Republic from 1949 until 1963. The invitation to Dr Adenauer had been arranged during the term of the previous Labour Government. He arrived on December 3rd.

first German Head of State to visit London since Doctor Brüning[1] in 1932. When he hadn't turned up by four minutes past four, there was a good deal of stamping, and Waldron Smithers,[2] sitting beside me and presumably squiffy already, started shouting. Meanwhile a retinue of black-suited Germans marched in and sat on a line of chairs behind the speakers on the platform. At six minutes past four in came Adenauer, looking like one of those marble bishops on an up-ended tombstone, and with him an unknown character in white bands and with odd black eyebrows, which must have stuck out a quarter of an inch. The latter was the new Lord Chancellor, Simonds,[3] who proceeded to make a fulsome and boring speech about German democracy, with every second sentence translated. Adenauer's speech was quite clever. Twice he referred to the insularity of Britain as the basis of our freedom and, in describing the components of a European Army, he ostentatiously left the British out. It was as though he were saying, 'I'm not one of those awkward Europeans who want to drag the British into Western Union. I'll manage the French without you.' As Adenauer had entered, Arthur Woodburn[4] had got up and so did ten or eleven other Members. The rest of us remained firmly seated and I was relieved to feel that, for most of the Tories there, the situation was extremely unpleasant. There was no warmth in their reception.

Later I went across to Claridge's for a reception in Adenauer's honour, but in between the two shows I slipped into the Chamber to hear Aneurin Bevan. He made quite a good speech to very full Labour benches and received a big hand, partly from Bevanites but largely from ordinary backbenchers, who had seemed alarmed and uneasy at his absence, wondering what was up. Somehow they all felt better and safer, hearing him attacking Tory housing policy, although that policy is largely a continuation of ours.

The fact is that Bevanism and the Bevanites seem much more important, well-organized and machiavellian to the rest of the Labour Party, and indeed to the U.S.A., than they do to us who are in the Group and who know that we are not organized, that Aneurin can never be persuaded to have any consistent or coherent strategy and that we have not even got to the beginning of a coherent, constructive policy. What we have, and it is very important, is a group of M.P.s who meet regularly, who know and like each other and who

[1] Chancellor of Germany 1931–2. A member of the Catholic Centre Party, he was replaced after the second presidential ballot in April 1932 by Fritz von Papen. He died in 1970.

[2] Sir Waldron Smithers (1880–1954), Conservative M.P. for Orpington 1945–54.

[3] Viscount Simonds (1881–1971), Lord Chancellor 1951–4. He was not a professional politician, and, although he was without judicial experience in the Court of Appeal, he was made Lord of Appeal in Ordinary in 1944. He was created an hereditary Baron in 1952 and elevated to a viscountcy in 1954, when he resigned on the reconstruction of the Administration. He retired in 1962.

[4] Arthur Woodburn (1890–1978), Labour M.P. for Clackmannan 1939–70. He was Parliamentary Secretary at the Ministry of Supply 1945–7 and Secretary of State for Scotland 1947–50.

have come to represent 'real Socialism' to a large number of constituency members. This produces an extraordinary bitterness among those who support the Gaitskell line. When I went into the Smoking Room today, just before lunch, I was absolutely bombarded by Christopher Mayhew, Woodrow Wyatt and James Callaghan. The immediate cause was the parliamentary report in last week's *New Statesman*[1] and for forty minutes I had to hear how insignificant and unimportant the *New Statesman* was, along with Bevanism. They have convinced themselves that we are demagogues who are deliberately exploiting the simple-mindedness of the rank and file for our own ends. It is a hard judgment, since, when Nye resigned and we stood by him, it looked a pretty desperate cause. Now we are a bandwagon and they are jealous because they are so far committed that they can't get on it.

Thursday, December 6th

I got back to the House for the defence debate, which was preceded by over an hour of knockabout incidentals after Question Time, during which Churchill, waiting to speak, had to go out twice to relieve himself. Churchill's speech was quite remarkably conciliatory and non-controversial, with several admissions that he found our defence preparations far better than he expected, including atomic development, which he had severely criticized in Opposition. The only dramatic moment was when he stated that Aneurin Bevan had 'happened to be right'[2] and gave him 'a mention in despatches', while doubting these motives and suggesting that it might have been by accident. Nye immediately pressed him strongly to explain whether this meant a slowing-down of the whole three-year plan and, under pressure Churchill seemed to imply that the lag this year implied that much.[3]

I stayed on in the Chamber to hear Woodrow Wyatt make a gallant defence of the £4,700 million and then an extremely intelligent and reasoned case of British participation in the European Army. It is an extraordinary thing that while, in Washington, Paris and Strasbourg (where the Council of Europe is sitting) the whole world is up in arms and incensed by Mr Churchill's cool writing-off of British participation in the European Army which he himself proposed at Strasbourg last year, here in Britain all this alarum has not caused a ripple.

[1] In the issue of December 1st the column by 'Our Parliamentary Correspondent' had stated that 'ex-Ministers, along with a few acolytes like Christopher Mayhew and Woodrow Wyatt, seem to be playing patball across the table with Mr Churchill and his colleagues. Far too obviously, they reserve their energy for flushing their colleagues below the gangway'.

[2] Mr Churchill's words were: 'I was giving the rt. hon. Gentleman an honourable mention for having, it appears by accident, perhaps not from the best of motives, happened to be right' [*H.C. Debates*, vol. 494, col. 2602].

[3] The Prime Minister told the House, as Minister of Defence, that the Government would not 'succeed in spending the £1,250 million this year' (out of the £4,700 million allocated for the three-year programme). Bevan had prophesied throughout 1951 that the Government would be unable to fulfil the rearmament commitments which had provoked his own resignation. His argument had been repeated in *Going Our Way*.

Replying to Churchill, Attlee was not able to berate him for going back on his leadership of the European Movement,[1] for the simple reason that Labour has been wholly isolationist itself. So the major issue which should have been debated today went by default, apart from Wyatt's speech.

After this I found Michael and Jill Foot drinking with Randolph Churchill[2] and Christopher Soames[3] and, having pulled them out and got hold of Jennie and Nye, we went off to the Ivy for dinner and afterwards back to Nye's house, to celebrate the conversion of Churchill to Bevanism and the conclusion of Nye's book. Late at night, Nye began reading aloud from Havelock Ellis's[4] *Introduction* to a book by a Uruguayan called Rodo,[5] giving a Latin-American angle on the U.S.A. Nye may sometimes be pretentious and superficial but it's a relief to talk to a politician who really gets excited by ideas.

In our absence, Churchill got up, after Shinwell had wound up for the Opposition, to give him a tremendous bouquet for his record as Minister of Defence. So this 'Session' has ended[6] in an atmosphere of extreme conciliation between the two Front Benches. It is quite clear that the Conservatives feel that they must win at least the tacit support of the Labour Movement, in order to stay in power as long as they want, and that Churchill is anxious to get at least Labour consent to the disinflation which Butler is now beginning

[1] In December 1947 the International Committee of the Movements for European Unity was founded; it included the United Europe Movement, of which Mr Churchill was Chairman. A 'Congress of Europe', convened in The Hague in May 1948, was addressed by Mr Churchill. In October of that year the International Committee was given the title 'The European Movement'. Membership would be open to all organizations working for European unity, despite their existing differences of attitude.

[2] Randolph Churchill, journalist and author, the son of Winston Churchill. He was Conservative M.P. for Preston 1940–5. He embarked on a major biography of his father, *Winston Churchill* (London: Heinemann), of which the first two volumes (1966, 1967) were published before his death in 1968. The remaining volumes are being written by Martin Gilbert.

[3] Conservative M.P. for Bedford 1950–66. He was P.P.S. to the Prime Minister, Churchill, whose daughter Mary he had married in 1947. After junior posts in the Air Ministry and Admiralty, he became Secretary of State for War 1958–60 and Minister of Agriculture, Fisheries and Food 1960–4. He was Ambassador to France 1968–72 and Vice-President of the European Commission from 1973 until January 1977. In 1978 he was created a life peer. Since 1979 he has been Lord President of the Council and Leader of the House of Lords. He was Governor of Rhodesia 1979–80. In 1980 he became a Companion of Honour.

[4] Havelock Ellis (1858–1939), a pioneer in the scientific study of sex, notably in his seven-volume *Studies in the Psychology of Sex* (Philadelphia: F. A. Davis, 1910). He was also a literary critic and was cited, for example, in Virginia Woolf's *Essays*.

[5] The Uruguayan philosopher José Enrique Rodo (1872–1917), of whom Foot writes: 'Next to Marx, and in a few respects superseding Marx, Rodo had the most powerful effect on his [Bevan's] intellectual outlook.' A translation of Rodo's *The Motives of Proteus* appeared in English, with an introduction by Havelock Ellis, in 1929. Bevan often read aloud from the work and its preface, frequently confronting American visitors with Ellis's summary of Rodo's impeachment of North American civilization.

[6] On November 6th the Prime Minister had announced that the House would adjourn from early December to early February, to afford Ministers the opportunity to study details of administration and future policy. Parliament duly adjourned on December 7th, reassembling on January 29th, 1952.

by a series of highly orthodox financial measures, starting with the raising of the bank rate by $\frac{1}{2}$ per cent and of the rate of interest for local government loans. Already there is an enormous amount of concealed unemployment, with millions of people working on short time,[1] and it looks as though, sooner or later, this must, at least locally, turn into real unemployment, as disinflation gets under way.

Monday, December 10th
I had rather an unsatisfactory weekend, including a visit on Saturday morning in streaming rain to a godforsaken Essex village for a rather dreary Labour Party day school, which ended unexpectedly early, getting me back to London at 6.15. I looked in the evening paper and came to the conclusion that I could either go to the Folies Bergère[2] or *Billy Budd*.[3] In some indecision I entered the underground but, as it was 6.40 when I got to Holborn and I was already ten minutes late for the Folies Bergère, I got out at Covent Garden, on the remote chance of a ticket for the second night of *Billy Budd*. Five minutes before the performance started, I got the centre seat in the Grand Tier. I thought that the opera was terrific, a real music drama, in the sense that you did not distinguish between the music, the words, the plot and the scenery, because the whole thing carried you along, as an immensely stirring story and problem. Maybe it's political bias, but I found the subject oddly topical. Billy Budd is really pure, brave and loyal, but this is the war against the French Revolution and he comes on board shouting 'Rights of Man!' and, moreover, he is deeply moved by the merciless treatment of the lower deck by the upper deck. Benjamin Britten[4] is a Socialist and I am not sure that this opera isn't all about loyalty and the cold war. At least, the critics who find the story episodic and the tragedy not tragic are the music and literary critics, who have not taken the subject seriously.

From December 12th to December 14th Crossman was in Paris, for a seminar at SHAPE, prompted by General Eisenhower and funded by the Ministry of Defence. Twelve Conservative and 12 Labour Members crossed by the Dunkirk night ferry, which, because of a series of accidents, had only one sleeping car. 'The crisis', wrote Crossman, '... was solved by George Wigg's proposal that the

[1] In December the number of registered unemployed had risen to 350,000, compared with 188,000 in June. Short-time working was certainly increasing. The demands of the rearmament programme none the less meant that there was a manpower shortage of 'extreme stringency', with employment exchanges registering 313,000 unfilled vacancies in mid-December.

[2] Appearing twice nightly at the Hippodrome, 'London home of the Paris Folies Bergère Revues'. The programme was 'Our 1951 Show: Encore des Folies' but, as the first performance began at 6.15, Crossman would have been later than he thought.

[3] As part of the Festival of Britain the Arts Council had commissioned *Billy Budd* from Benjamin Britten for the Covent Garden Opera Company.

[4] Composer, conductor, pianist and co-founder of the Aldeburgh Festival, and a seminal figure in twentieth-century British music. He was made a life peer in 1977; he died in the same year.

*names should be drawn from a hat. Otherwise hours would have been con-
sumed in working out the precedence of junior ex-Ministers, members of the
Parliamentary Committee, etc.'*

*Among those who addressed the visitors were Field-Marshal Montgomery
and General Eisenhower. At lunch, Eisenhower talked to Crossman, who
reported:*

Among the points he made were:

  (i) *'I have told the Germans "Nuts!" You are wrong if you think you can
blackmail me and get me to rearm on your terms.'*

 (ii) *'Of course Britain must decide for herself whether it is in her interests to
enter a United States of Europe. Maybe ultimately your choice is either to
become the forty-ninth State or to join the U.S.E. but it is a thing for you
to think out for yourselves.'*

*Crossman added: 'He also made it clear that, in the last resort, Western
Europe can be defended without a German contribution ... [He] was shifty, but
said "no" when I put it to him that, if the Germans were rearmed, American
land troops might be withdrawn from Western Europe.'*

*Crossman also spent a morning with Guy Mollet and lunched with Maurice
Schuman.*

Monday, December 17th

We spent the weekend at Buscot, entertained by Gavin Faringdon,[1] at our
Bevanite conference. By the time we began on Saturday morning at eleven,
some nineteen members of the Group had turned up, but in fact the discussions were in the hands of a very few people. Harold Wilson, Tommy
Balogh and Dudley Seers[2] (the latter are two Oxford economists) naturally
dominated the purely economic argument, with a great deal of tension
between Balogh and Wilson, since the former holds the latter responsible for
the bonfire of controls. Dick Acland[3] and Barbara Castle, in their different
ways, are capable of saying something intelligent on any subject and Leslie
Hale[4] and Fenner Brockway, back from a week of talking to colonial representatives at the U.N. in Paris,[5] have their own special subject. Desmond

[1] Gavin Faringdon, the 2nd Lord Faringdon, succeeded his grandfather in 1934. He was
Treasurer of the National Council for Civil Liberties 1940–5, an executive member of the
Fabian Society 1942–66, and a member of the Parliamentary Committee of the Labour
Party 1957–60. His house, Buscot Park, was used for discussion in relaxed surroundings.

[2] Research officer at Oxford University, where he was later Lecturer in Economic
Statistics 1946–53 and 1954–5. He was Director-General of Economic Planning at the
Ministry of Overseas Development 1964–7, and held numerous development consultancy
posts. For the five years 1967–72 he was Director of the Institute of Development Studies
at the University of Sussex, and thereafter a Fellow.

[3] Sir Richard Acland was M.P. for the Barnstaple division of Devon 1935–45 and Labour
M.P. for Gravesend 1947–55. He was a Senior Lecturer at St Luke's College, Exeter, 1959–
1974.

[4] Labour M.P. for Oldham 1945–50 and for West Oldham 1950–68. He was created a
life peer in 1972.

[5] The Sixth Assembly of the United Nations met in Paris from November 6th to
December 21st.

Donnelly and Tom Williams[1] put in their questions and doubts from time to time and so did Harold Davies.[2] Ian Mikardo was in the chair, but Nye, naturally enough, dominated the proceedings and I suppose that I acted as an intellectual foil.

The conference started rather badly with a paper by Harold Wilson on the immediate financial situation, which led to another sterile argument about whether the £3,600 million arms programme accepted in September 1950 would have been tolerable.[3] The personal problems of the resigned Ministers certainly make difficulties for an objective assessment of the effect of the arms programme on our economy, and there was also a strong reluctance on the part of Nye to accept the thesis, on which Wilson and Balogh agreed, that merely cutting the arms programme would not remove our main difficulty, the dollar gap. What it would do would be to prevent those difficulties being aggravated next year, when our arms programme will begin to have a serious effect on our exports.

The chief interest was to watch the way Nye's personality affected his reactions. I don't think that he really much wanted the conference. (Michael Foot hadn't turned up.) Indeed, Nye had remarked to me that we had been meeting regularly all through the Session and we needed a period of lying fallow. But in fact the Group has no coherent analysis or policy whatsoever and this is partly owing to Nye's reluctance to face some of the unpleasant facts about the long-term crisis which Balogh emphasizes. Nye has a tendency to regard as defeatist anybody who states these facts. Yet under the pressure of discussion he reacts extremely well and suddenly, on Saturday evening, after trying at dinner to get out of having an evening discussion, he got interested when we forced one on him. He began to consider seriously the practical ways of facing these long-term problems. Even here, however, after putting forward two or three good practical suggestions, he slipped into believing that a powerful debating point is a solution to a problem. 'Let us show how American capitalism is entirely responsible for our difficulties,' he said. 'Let us put this to the American trade union movement.' I didn't think that he noticed that, in saying this, he had turned completely round, accepting Tommy Balogh's diagnosis of the situation but with a less defeatist intonation.

The Group, indeed, was a bit scared of facing facts for fear of finding the problems insoluble. Of course, it may well be that the problems *are* insoluble — this is a type of philosophic fatalism which I find acceptable enough but which Nye, as a sensible politician, instinctively rejects, as does Barbara Castle. A certain amount of utopianism is really essential. The question is whether you can control it and keep it within reasonable bounds.

[1] Tom Williams (1888–1967) was the miners' leader and Labour M.P. for the Don Valley 1922–59. He was Minister of Agriculture 1945–51 and was made a life peer in 1961.

[2] Labour M.P. for the Leek division of Staffordshire 1945–70. He was created a life peer in 1970.

[3] See the Introduction, pp. 23–4.

It looks as though, as a result of this conference, we shall not find much difficulty in producing a new Group pamphlet in the spring, formulating a restatement of Socialist philosophy and policy in terms of Britain's new position in the world.[1] This will probably include a demand for a wide extension of public ownership, including the nationalization of oil and chemicals as essential if we are to have sufficient power over the private sector to be really able to plan. But, there was absolutely no answer to Tommy Balogh's awkward question: Why should we expect Labour Ministers, who failed to cope with their Departments and to control the first batch of nationalized industries, to fare any better with the second batch? Here again, I think, Nye instinctively feels that detailed discussion about recruitment of civil servants, organization of statistical departments, etc., is somehow not politics, which is concerned with achieving Power, with a very big and vague P.

The Group is really extraordinarily heterogeneous. What a mysterious thing 'the Left' is. Why is this person Left and that person Right? What binds the Group together? In our case, there is the old Keep Left Group, which did work out a certain homogeneity, with superimposed on it Nye Bevan and Harold Wilson, who have virtually nothing in common, and a number of their personal supporters, such as Will Griffiths[2] and Hugh Delargy,[3] who, as far as I can see, have no coherent political attitude. However, I suppose most Cabinets look much the same.

After lunch on Sunday I said to Nye that the next practical decision would be on the Arms Estimates.[4] What attitude should the Group take? His reply was typical. 'Oh, I dare say the best thing would be to leave each person to decide for himself.' This is a piece of self-deception on a par with his tenacious assertion that the next pamphlet, when it is published, will just be an ordinary *Tribune* pamphlet, whereas it is clear that the Group will be held responsible for it whether it is called an ordinary *Tribune* pamphlet or no. So far from being a great strategist and organizer of cabals, Nye is an individualist who, however, is an extraordinarily pleasant member of a group. But the last thing he does is to lead it. He dominates its discussions simply because he is fertile in ideas, but leadership and organization are things he instinctively shrinks away from.

Harold Wilson was as neat and competent as ever. Whenever an idea is put forward, he remembers without fail an occasion on which he did it or set up a committee on it when he was at the Board of Trade.[5] His complacency must be unique, but he has a good mind, is an excellent member of a group

[1] But see p. 62.
[2] Labour M.P. for Manchester Moss Side 1945–60 and for Manchester Exchange from 1950 until his death in 1973.
[3] Labour M.P. for Manchester Platting 1945–50 and for Thurrock 1950–76. He was a junior Whip 1950–1.
[4] To be presented to Parliament on February 25th, 1952.
[5] From September 1947 to April 1951.

and is likeable into the bargain. Dick Acland made his usual appeal for a Christian acceptance of an inevitable lowering of the standard of living, which he cannot deny that he relishes. He is one of the people who never changes his mind but whose obstinate conservatism of thought is extremely valuable. One needs somebody to say these things regularly and, though Dick must suffer a good many disappointments, he is a good ingredient.

I think Nye really enjoyed the snooker as much as anything.

We broke off after lunch on Sunday and in the evening Michael Foot and Jill had a mixed party for film people and politicians. I watched Ursula Jeans captivating Nye for an hour and then trying to persuade him to dance, pursuing him even to the gents, but he held out and suddenly Roger Livesey, her husband,[1] discovered that she had left the party with injured pride. Hugh Delargy sang Irish revolutionary songs, Ian Mikardo and his daughter[2] did all their slightly embarrassing Fabian jokes, Jill made me dance and I learnt the hokey-cokey. Michael, looking very boyish, supplied us all with too much to drink. In fact, it was a highly successful party, which Zita and I agreed that we wouldn't repeat.

Wednesday, December 19th
Phil Zec[3] came to lunch yesterday and told me the whole inside story of the resignation of Bartholomew[4] from the chairmanship of the *Daily Mirror* combine.[5] Phil had obviously spent the whole of last week on this affair and was utterly emotionally exhausted by it. About a week ago, Cecil King (a nephew of Northcliffe and a great big, beefy, rather silly fellow, who lives in Chelsea, is a Wykehamist but is otherwise insignificant) rang up Zec to say that he and three other members of the board had decided to ask for Bartholomew's resignation. There are seven members of the board, of whom one, Cooke,[6] was in Australia. Zec was flabbergasted and said, 'You can't do

---

[1] The actors Roger Livesey (1906–76) and his wife Ursula Jeans (1906–73) were at this time at the height of their successful film and stage careers.

[2] Ian Mikardo's daughters were Ruth and Judy; this was probably Ruth.

[3] Phil Zec, whilst a Director of the *Daily Mirror*, was also Editor of the *Sunday Pictorial* from December 1949 to 1951. Later, after a brief spell as cartoonist for the *Daily Herald*, he became editorial consultant to the European Movement. He has been for many years a Director of the *Jewish Chronicle*.

[4] Harry Guy Bartholomew, a former office boy and junior reporter on the *Daily Mail*, moved to the *Daily Mirror* as a reporter and became Editorial Director before the Second World War. He was a Director of Daily Mirror Newspapers Ltd, with editorial control of the *Daily Mirror* and by the end of the Second World War had become Chairman of Daily Mirror Newspapers, a post he held until his retirement at the end of 1951. He died in May 1962.

[5] See Hugh Cudlipp, *Walking on the Water* (London: Bodley Head, 1976), pp. 193–4, for an account of this episode. The *Daily Mirror* Group included the *Sunday Pictorial*, newspapers in West Africa, a daily paper in Melbourne and six Australian radio stations, and a Canadian paper mill.

[6] James Cooke, who joined the *Mirror* Group in 1922, becoming a Director of the *Daily Mirror* and *Sunday Pictorial* Companies Ltd in 1947 and Financial Director of the *Mirror* Group in 1962.

things just like that. Come and have lunch.' A few minutes later, Bartholomew rang Zec to tell him what had happened and Zec arranged to see him after lunch.

At lunch King explained that, along with Bolam,[1] the present Editor, a stooge who is solely the creation of Bartholomew, he had come to the conclusion some weeks ago that Bartholomew was in his dotage and must be got rid of. Zec's difficulty is that six months ago he told Bartholomew that he ought to resign, since the old man was drinking too much and getting more and more incoherent and unreliable. Moreover, it was clear that nothing could be done once it was clear that the votes were 4 against 3, with one of the three away. So, when Zec saw Bart that afternoon, he advised him that there was nothing to do but to clear out. Bart asked how that could be possible and slowly realized that Bolam had given the casting vote against him. At this he broke down, after which they both drank a bottle of whisky together. For the next four days Zec was chiefly engaged in trying to get Bartholomew to write the four necessary letters of resignation. He kept on crying and saying, 'How could Bolam do it to me?' One of the difficulties was that, although Bart joined the *Daily Mirror* at the age of fourteen and had built it from absolutely nothing to where it is today, he has never taken a penny out of the firm and has no shares, so that resignation meant complete penury. Zec spent a great deal of time arranging for a pension of £6,000 a year and trying to get a cash payment out of all the various subsidiary companies, totalling £20,000.

All this was told to me in confidence and I had some difficulty in writing a paragraph for the 'London Diary' in the *Statesman*.[2] But when I lunched today with John Junor, Political Editor of the *Daily Express*, I was regaled with a pretty accurate and detailed version, including the actual voting. Junor said to me that, on Beaverbrook's instructions, he had been once again on to the story that Lord Ellerman[3] owns a controlling block of the shares and might have had something to do with it. Personally I don't believe that he does own a controlling block and indeed the whole moral of this story is the extraordinary irresponsibility of a board of directors who are not in any way responsible to anyone, even the investors. This board of directors consisted of Bart, Cecil King, Zec, Bolam and a few complete nonentities from the advertising side, etc., of the firm. As a result, a palace revolution could take place at any time when four votes could be collected against the chairman.

Naturally, Zec is interested in his personal position. Cecil King has lavished

[1] Sylvester Bolam. An economics graduate, he joined the *Daily Mirror* as a sub-editor in the mid-1930s and, apart from a few months as a sub-editor on the *News Chronicle*, remained with the *Mirror* throughout his subsequent career. He was Editor and later a Director from 1948 until his retirement in January 1953. He died in April 1953.

[2] See the *New Statesman and Nation* of December 22nd, 1951, for Crossman's piece, in which he confessed that he could not 'help feeling glad that "Bart" has resigned before old age had seriously impaired his powers and tarnished his reputation'.

[3] Crossman seems to be referring to Sir John Ellerman, Director of Ellerman Lines Ltd, the shipping company.

compliments upon him as the only original mind in the whole combine, which is true enough. But since King has had to rely on Bolam's vote to carry out the *coup d'état* Bolam will be quite powerful, at least for a few months. Of course, if King were really diabolical, he would quite soon sack Bolam (who would not get another job in Fleet Street after his performance as Judas Iscariot) and appoint Hugh Cudlipp. Cudlipp once told me that he was King's appointee to the *Sunday Pictorial* and that, when he was offered the job, Bart, whose man Hugh was, was furious at his accepting it and regarded it as a personal insult.[1] Then, ironically, Bart sacked Cudlipp for spiking a message which King filed from Nigeria during the coal-mine riots in 1949.[2] It was the only journalistic enterprise of King's life and, when the story came in, Hugh said, 'Another bloody message from Cecil. Spike it.' King knew this but pleaded for Cudlipp, unavailingly.

Zec told me that Cudlipp had been offered the editorship of the *Melbourne Argus* and the control of the six Australian wireless stations but had turned it down because Eileen Ascroft,[3] his wife, won't leave London. On the other hand, it is clear from Junor that Hugh is really doing nothing on the *Sunday Express* and his appointment to take John Gordon's[4] place has given Gordon a new lease of life. What Junor would like, as he told me, is for Cudlipp to go to the *Mirror* and for himself to be Editor of the *Sunday Express*. Once again Junor repeated his belief that the ideal thing would be to have a really hot-stuff 'Crossbencher' column at the bottom of the feature page and Crossman's column along the side, and I was given yet another assurance that My Lord Beaverbrook is just longing for this arrangement.

Zec's final comment on leaving me, was, 'Well, I'd always told you politics was a dirty game but I take it all back now that I've seen what happens in Fleet Street.' As for my own position, all one can say at present is that, when Zec mentioned to the new Chairman his wish to send me to America, King replied, 'Of course.' But Zec wants to go a bit further and I suggested that he should say to King that I had been tempted to ask King to my Christmas party but was embarrassed by his promotion, in order to find out if King would accept.

Hugh Dalton asked himself to dinner and we gave him a very good one. He was in tremendous form and very full of himself as the result of his broadcast last Saturday, in which he delivered a ferocious broadside against German rearmament, while very cleverly and carefully keeping within the

---

[1] It was at Phil Zec's suggestion that Hugh Cudlipp was brought back to edit the *Sunday Pictorial* in 1951.

[2] In November 1949 workers at the Government colliery at Enugu, who had been 'going slow', attacked police who were removing explosives from the mine. Eighteen of the rioters were killed when the police opened fire.

[3] Eileen Ascroft, Hugh Cudlipp's second wife, married him in 1945. She died in 1962.

[4] A journalist on the *Daily Express* who became Editor of the *Sunday Express* in 1928, serving in that capacity until his death in 1974, although latterly as Editor-in-Chief. He was a Director of Beaverbrook Newspapers Ltd 1931–69.

Party line by reminding listeners of the four conditions[1] which Attlee listed last February for the Labour Government's agreement to a German contribution. Dalton was obviously enormously titillated by the thought that Shinwell or Morrison would try to rebuke him and I suspect he was rather disappointed that they had not yet done so. I congratulated him on his shrewd timing, just on the eve of the Christmas holiday, when no special meeting of the Parliamentary Committee can be called. This broadcast has its importance in the internal Party dissension, since it very definitely swings the Party further towards the Left. But Dalton repeated to me his views about the need for Jim Griffiths to succeed Attlee, though he added that the little man still has plenty of life in him.

[1] These were: that the rearmament of NATO countries must precede that of Germany; that the 'building up of forces in the democratic states should precede the creation of German forces'; that German units should be integrated in the defence forces in such a way that the re-emergence of 'a German military menace' would be precluded; and that 'there must be agreement with the Germans themselves'.

1952

On the last day of 1951 the Prime Minister and the Foreign Secretary, with an entourage of Ministers and officials, sailed in the Queen Mary *for New York. Crossman, for the* Mirror *Group and the* New Statesman and Nation, *travelled by air (with a Mr and Mrs Bevan, who 'turned out to be two English interior decorators who had set up shop in Houston, Texas').*

Mr Churchill and his party landed in New York on January 5th. The purpose of their visit was to establish a new mood in the Anglo-American alliance. On January 9th an official statement gave the outcome of the Prime Minister's discussions with the President. It declared that the two countries shared 'complete identity of aims', in the Middle East, 'broad harmony of view' in the Far East, despite differences of policy towards China, and that in the event of war the use of the American bases in Britain would be a matter for joint discussion. The American Government, it was said, agreed with the British decision to remain outside the European Defence Community, while collaborating with it as closely as possible.

This last point was developed by Mr Eden in a speech delivered at Columbia University, New York, on January 11th. He emphasized the contribution which Britain had made to the solidarity and rearmament of Western Europe but explained that 'joining the European Federation is something that we know in our bones we cannot do'. The Foreign Secretary also took up the reference to policy in the Far East, declaring that Communist intervention in South-East Asia would be as menacing as the force which the U.N. had met in Korea. United Nations' resistance should be equally determined.

Mr Churchill made a brief visit to Canada on January 11th and in his speech at Ottawa expressed confidence in the North Atlantic Treaty Organization. On his return to Washington, he delivered an address to the Congress on January 15th (Cmd 8468). His speech vindicated Britain on a number of points where Americans had been openly critical. Britain's post-war financial and economic performance was explained and defended. Where European unity was concerned, the Prime Minister stated that what mattered was not 'the form of the fusion' but the strength of the armoury that resulted. On Korea, he promised that, if any truce were made and subsequently broken, the joint response of Britain and the U.S.A. would be 'prompt, resolute and effective'.

In an unexpected passage, the Prime Minister referred to the Egyptian crisis (see below, p. 64), saying that the British would be enormously aided in their task 'as servants and guardians of the commerce of the world' if even token forces of Britain's partners were stationed in the Suez Canal Zone. This suggestion was received with displeasure. On January 18th, however, one firm agreement was announced. The United States undertook to send Britain one million tons of steel. In return Britain would divert to America part of the Canadian aluminium already ordered for Britain, together with an increased supply of Malayan tin.

Crossman's American visit lasted until January 14th. On January 3rd he lunched with Oliver Franks, the British Ambassador, and reported that 'he had literally no idea whatsoever what hand Churchill would play, since he had received no instructions ... Apparently the Cabinet had been so engaged with domestic cuts that Churchill and Eden had only begun to consider their tactics [for] Washington on the Queen Mary*'.*

Crossman's other interviews included meetings with Mr Justice Frankfurter of the Supreme Court, Colonel Byroade – head of the German Section in the State Department – Dean Acheson and Robert Taft. Crossman gives an account of a meeting with John Foster Dulles, with whom he discussed the signing of the Japanese Peace Treaty. 'Mr Dulles', wrote Crossman,

> is an ecclesiastical type of man, with a lugubrious, pallid face, heavy black eyebrows and a twitch in his right eye behind his heavy glasses. Like Lord Halifax,[1] he can lie as only a Christian can lie. But Halifax was really attractive and Dulles is not. I must say, the more I think of it, the more I enjoy the thought of Dulles and Morrison foxing each other. But I think on the argument as a whole Dulles has the best of it and Morrison must have been deceiving himself.

Monday, January 21st

We were due to have a meeting of the sub-committee which had been set up to draft the synopsis of the Bevanite policy pamphlet agreed on at the Buscot Park conference. I arrived at the Commons at three o'clock to find Mikardo alone. Harold Wilson came in a few minutes later. Then we learnt that Nye had telephoned to say that he didn't want to come to the House and would we go over to Cliveden Place. I suspected that something was up. Mikardo had another appointment at 3.30, so Harold and I went across. We were alone in the sitting room for three or four minutes until Nye came in, without a tie, looking very well and a little uneasy. He began in rather a lame way to say that he was in considerable doubt about the whole idea of a pamphlet. Harold and I almost simultaneously intervened to say (we hadn't discussed this on the way over) that each of us, during the Recess, had come to the same conclusion. Nye said that the National Executive had set up a host of sub-committees, the Fabians were at work, our members were working on all these committees, so what would another policy statement do? It might also sharpen differences.

At this point we all sat down and Harold Wilson, from the comfort of an armchair, said, 'Well, now we've agreed about the pamphlet, I want to put forward an idea that may shock you – namely, that I should go back on to

[1] Edward Wood, the future Earl of Halifax (1881–1959) was British Viceroy of India 1925–9 and served as Lord Privy Seal 1935–7, Lord President of the Council 1937–8, Foreign Secretary 1938–40 and Ambassador to the United States 1941–6. He was created Baron Irwin in 1925, succeeded his father as Viscount Halifax in 1934 and was made Earl of Halifax in 1944. In the late 1930s Halifax had visited Hitler, Göring and Mussolini and had urged the Polish Foreign Minister, Beck, to negotiate (i.e. yield) upon Hitler's demand to annex Danzig.

the Front Bench.'[1] Nye observed that Harold Wilson couldn't go back on the Front Bench unless he himself did. I don't really know what Nye thought of the idea. He didn't commit himself against it, yet I have a hunch that he was feeling his way, just like Harold.

I then intervened to say that, if either of them went back to the Front Bench at this particular moment, it would be utterly disastrous, since a major war crisis was brewing. 'The Americans are moving straight towards war,' observed Nye. I then gave a report on the situation in Washington and concluded that we couldn't yet be sure that Attlee, Gaitskell and Morrison would go all out against Churchill and Eden and boldly declare that the British people would not be behind them in spreading the war from Korea to China proper. To go back on the Front Bench before we were sure of that was sheer madness.

We discussed the American situation at great length. Jennie was rather good on this, as she has some understanding of the U.S.A. Or is it, as Harold Wilson observed as he drove me home afterwards, that American public opinion at this moment happens to be behaving according to her preconception? Anyhow, Nye was extraordinarily good at picking up and understanding the situation and it was clear at the end of an hour that any thought of returning to the Front Bench had been put aside by both. Nye had also agreed to make sure that the matter is discussed in full length at the N.E.C. on Wednesday and after that to have a talk with me about whether he should not make a speech giving a lead, instead of letting Dalton jump the gun, as he did before Christmas on German rearmament![2]

My impression is that Nye is a somewhat reluctant Bevanite. In the course of the afternoon, he managed to explain to me that he had not shown his book either to Michael or to myself because (this is a typical piece of Aneurin tact) both of us are professional writers, who couldn't help borrowing the ideas. I replied lightly that I hoped the ideas wouldn't be copyright after publication but I realized that this unwitting shaft had gone home. However, it is obvious that Nye attaches the very greatest importance to his book, which is to be published in March,[3] and I can see that a policy statement by the Group, coming out just before or just afterwards and proving him wrong, might be embarrassing. He is an extremely personal politician.

Nye again dismissed the idea that James Griffiths might be a good compromise Leader and he twice expressed the view that it would be difficult ever to be a colleague of Gaitskell now that he had proved himself a liar. I think Nye is almost exclusively concerned to be Leader of the Party rather than to formulate left-wing policy. On the other hand, he was extraordinarily receptive about China, a subject on which he had obviously thought very little till we came this afternoon.

[1] From which he had resigned in April 1951.
[2] See above, p. 57.
[3] *In Place of Fear* (London: Heinemann) was eventually published in April.

In early January 1952 the Egyptian crisis came to a head. It was precipitated by the activities of the Wafd organization, of which Nahhas Pasha, Prime Minister of Egypt, was the leader. The Wafd were fervent nationalists, who had success-fully agitated against the British administration of Egypt (which was not technically part of the British Empire) in the years preceding the First World War. An Anglo-Egyptian Treaty was negotiated in 1936 by Nahhas Pasha (Prime Minister at that time too) and the British Government, confining British troops to a strip of land on each side of the Suez Canal, separated by a desert belt from the Nile Valley.

Nahhas Pasha denounced this treaty in October 1951, demanding that all British troops should leave Egyptian territory and claiming Egyptian sovereignty over the Sudan, an Anglo-Egyptian Condominium largely governed and administered by the British and believed by them to be almost ready for self-government. Britain rejected Nahhas Pasha's assertions, maintaining that, unless superseded by a new joint agreement, the 1936 treaty had five further years to run.

Guided by the Wafd, the poverty-stricken Egyptian population directed their discontent against British imperialism. Armed bands of so-called auxiliary police were moved into the Canal Zone by the Egyptian Government and, despite warnings from the British Government, sabotage and terrorism in-creased. On January 12th an armed skirmish took place at Tel-El-Kebir, thirty miles west of Ismailia, the central city in the zone. The British garrison was reinforced and artillery was used. In a battle at Ismailia on January 25th the British captured the police headquarters and forty-one Egyptians were killed. Some 790, mostly 'auxiliaries', surrendered.

On the following day a fierce riot broke out in Cairo. Ten British citizens were killed; buildings owned by British institutions were attacked. It appeared that much of the rioting had been organized in advance and that the police and, indeed, the Government were actively involved. King Farouk dismissed Nahhas Pasha, replacing him by Aly Maher Pasha, a lawyer and former Wafd member. The new Prime Minister stated that he intended to maintain order and punish those responsible for the riots but in subsequent weeks it became clear that he was not prepared to defy the Wafd. In March Aly Maher Pasha was in turn dismissed and his successor, Hilaly Pasha, dissolved the Egyptian Parliament.

When the House of Commons reassembled on January 29th, the Foreign Secretary made a Statement on the Egyptian crisis. He declared that the Government's aim was 'to reach agreement on arrangements for the adequate defence of the Canal Zone which would meet legitimate Egyptian aspirations'. The Government was accused of sacrificing the goodwill of the Egyptian people to a legalistic interpretation of the 1936 treaty. Nevertheless, the disorder in the Canal Zone gradually subsided and by April negotiations opened between the British and Egyptian Governments on the defence of the Canal Zone and the status of the Sudan.

These events were of great importance to Crossman, fascinated as he was by problems of foreign policy and, in particular, the Middle East. They also breathed new life into the Bevanite Group.

Monday, January 28th

I dined with Tommy Balogh at the Reform Club before going up to the Castles in Highgate to the Bevanite meeting, which was fascinating. Harold Wilson explained that Nye, he and I had agreed that it would be tactically unwise to launch a policy pamphlet just now, as it would stress our sectarian character. Nye added that there were so many other committees at work, on which our members were engaged. The only vocal opposition came from Ian Mikardo, who stressed that we had discovered such important new philosophical principles at Buscot that it would be wicked to deprive the Movement of them. Despite some uneasiness, the decision was accepted.

Then came two harebrained papers from Mikardo and Brockway, once again urging that the Group should have some sort of relationship with the left-wing French Socialists who run the Socialist movement for the United States of Europe. This was slapped down by Jennie and then by Aneurin, who produced a superb argument that anyone who attended a meeting in France would either have to be paid for by the Group or would have to have enough money of his own, which would introduce the class distinctions we are trying to avoid. Nye made a final appeal that we should not separate ourselves off from the Party in any way. By this time I think most people present felt that Nye didn't want to be a Bevanite at all.

We then started discussing the foreign policy situation, especially Korea, on which there was general agreement. I mentioned the importance of Egypt and, to my astonishment, Aneurin took this up with enormous emphasis, stating that we must advocate a complete evacuation at a very early date. I remember a conversation one Friday in December in the Smoking Room, when, in the presence of George Wigg and several others, Nye had smacked me down for talking about evacuation and had argued that we should take a strong line. But at Buscot he had obviously argued with profit and I think he saw Tony Wedgwood Benn yesterday. Anyhow, tonight his line was almost embarrassingly like mine—namely, that we couldn't restrain the Americans from blitzing China if we committed minor blitzes in Egypt. He launched the most ferocious attack on the right-wingers of the Party, who, he said, would certainly fail to take a proper Socialist policy. It was the Group's duty to fight the right-wing ... In the course of an hour Nye had come full circle back from an attack on sectarianism to an appeal for Group action. Partly, no doubt, this was tactical instinct. Earlier in the meeting he had deflated the Group too much and he felt the need to revive it. But shrewd people like Barbara were really very curious as to what exactly was up. Ian Mikardo was very angry indeed.

In April 1951 President Truman had recalled General MacArthur from Korea

3

where, according to the President, he had prosecuted policy involving 'a very grave risk of starting a general war'. General MacArthur was at first rapturously welcomed by the American public and, indeed, by a joint Session of the Congress. But detailed questioning by the Senate Armed Services and Foreign Relations Committees, meeting together throughout the early summer, exposed the costs of the general's proposed strategy.

Meanwhile in May and June a second Communist offensive failed and on June 23rd Mr Malik, the Soviet Representative at the United Nations, stated his 'belief' that discussions for a ceasefire should begin. On June 29th General Ridgway, General MacArthur's successor, broadcast an invitation to discuss terms to the North Korean Commander-in-Chief. On July 1st the invitation was accepted and on July 10th negotiations began at Kaesong.

But, even by January 1952, there was no evident settlement. The British public was reminded of the economic effects of the war by the Chancellor's Statement of January 29th, in which he announced the second instalment of the programme of austerity introduced in the autumn of 1951. Import restrictions were placed on clothing, furniture and supplies of certain foodstuffs. Home deliveries of plant, machinery, vehicles for civil use and other consumer goods (bicycles, radios, refrigerators, etc.) were drastically cut. The foreign travel allowance was reduced from £100 to £25 and a charge proposed of 1s. for Health Service prescriptions and up to £1 for dental treatment. (The Bill implementing these Health Service charges was to exclude persons under twenty-one from liability for dental costs.)

The Opposition alleged that 'long-standing and external causes' had undermined the country's economic stability. The Bevanite Group in particular were deeply suspicious of Government policy. In defence and foreign affairs they believed that Britain was being brought much closer to the Americans, who were at this time embarking on 'a world-wide anti-Communist crusade' (Michael Foot, Aneurin Bevan [London: Davis-Poynter, 1973], vol. 2, p. 361). Urged by the Bevanites, the Shadow Cabinet decided that in the defence debate on February 5th and 6th the Prime Minister would be pressed to explain his remarks in Washington.[1]

Thursday, January 31st

One or two people said to me afterwards, in the Smoking Room, that the Party Meeting this morning may well have been historic. I doubt whether it was as important as all that, but it was remarkable and completely confounded the predictions of some of the gloomier members of the Group last Monday.

It began with what was substantially a good statement by Attlee, showing dissatisfaction with Churchill's explanation about his talks with Truman and a willingness to accept Dalton's broadcast on German rearmament as the new Party line. Geoffrey Bing followed, not very effectively, and I was then

[1] See above, p. 61.

called and had to start putting the Bevanite case. On China, where I stressed the danger I had learnt of in Washington and the need for Labour to speak for Britain, I received a good deal of support, but I was soon aware of a certain restiveness when I turned to Egypt and made the case that we could not restrain American aggressiveness in China while we were blowing Egyptian policemen to pieces with twenty-pounder guns. I then advocated stating a date by which our troops would be withdrawn and got some confused protest from Mr Shinwell, saying that he had already done so.

Woodrow Wyatt followed, critical of Bing, but, to my surprise, supporting my proposal to get out of Egypt. He was followed by Lord Stansgate[1] in a rich, emotional, pro-Egyptian speech, which received a big round of applause, and John Strachey, who did very well, rubbing in our line on China. Then came George Wigg, full of military expertise about Egypt, and then Aneurin Bevan, on the crest of the wave, saying that a debate was not sufficient: we had to rouse the country. Once again, the Executive rapidly stated that it fully agreed with the backbenchers and promised either to vote against the motion or to move a censure motion if no satisfactory explanations were offered next Tuesday. So we shall meet again next Wednesday morning, in the middle of the debate, to decide on policy.

Several people feel that this is the end of bipartisan foreign policy but Manny Shinwell's long, laborious and largely mythological winding-up speech in defence of himself shows that there is a great deal of latent resistance. On the other hand, there is no doubt that the P.L.P. has swung. This was made completely clear in the afternoon debate in the Chamber,[2] when, after quite a nice speech by Attlee, Nye spoke to packed and wildly enthusiastic Labour benches. Actually it was by no means one of his best-constructed speeches but his argument that there could be no risk of war if stockpiles were being reduced this year was completely unanswered by Churchill (as Minister of Defence) and Nye's attack on the Tories for cutting the Health Service had an enormous demagogic appeal. In fact, Nye was extraordinarily conciliatory to Gaitskell, as well as on the rearmament issue, and this is a real bid for power.

We had a drink afterwards in the Smoking Room. Attlee and Morrison had gone out half way through Nye's speech and now Attlee, who was drinking at

---

[1] William Wedgwood Benn (1877–1960) was Liberal M.P. for the St George's division of Stepney 1906–18 and for Leith 1918–27, when he resigned and joined the Labour Party. He then sat as Labour M.P. for North Aberdeen 1928–9 and for the Gorton division of Manchester 1937–42. He was Secretary of State for India 1929 and Secretary of State for Air 1945–6, and in 1942 he became a peer. From 1947 to 1957 he served as President of the Inter-Parliamentary Union.

[2] On January 29th the Chancellor announced the second stage of his measures to hold the downward trend in Britain's gold and dollar reserves (see p. 66). A two-day debate began the following day. The passage in Mr Bevan's speech to which Crossman refers ran: 'We cannot add together the feared imminence of war and the running down of British stocks' [H.C. Debates, vol. 495, col. 403]. The Chancellor's motion was carried by 309 votes to 278.

the next table, didn't come over to congratulate him but walked out without a word. Not that this means very much with the little man, who is shy to the point of incivility. The whole House buzzed the whole evening with Nye's speech and not even the morning press could fail to make it the major event.

As Zita and I were just going to bed tonight, Eddie Shackleton came in, saying that Herbert Morrison was outside and wanted to have a private talk. So we brought him in and plied him with brandy. He began by saying that he hoped that we shouldn't push him too hard on Egypt, since during the election he and Shinwell had been pretty far committed to a strong policy. We began to talk generally about foreign affairs and Herbert kept on saying to Eddie, 'Make a note of that for my speech.'

He then told me that he was, on the suggestion of some university people at Oxford, writing a book on his experiences as Lord President of the Council,[1] both in terms of Cabinet Government and control of Parliament, and added, 'Don't pinch my idea.' All this irritated Zita a great deal. But he seemed genuinely pleased to have a nice, friendly talk and at the end he said, 'I can't help liking you even if I disapprove of you,' to which I replied, 'Well, that's exactly the way I feel about you, Herbert.' Afterwards Eddie told me that, before Herbert drove away in his tiny car, he asked whether he shouldn't invite me to join in preparing his speech for next Wednesday. Eddie had said that he didn't think that it would be quite the right thing.

This has been a very remarkable week inside the Parliamentary Labour Party. I fancy that most of the Members came back from their constituencies having been mercilessly badgered by their local parties as to why they had been so flat and shown so little fight before the Recess. They were therefore enormously receptive to any fighting lead. Moreover, the coincidence that Butler's announcement of the cuts came in the same week as the revelation that Churchill might have sold us down the river in Washington swung the whole Party to the left, since it seems to confirm the left-wing diagnosis of the domestic and international situation and the Left's opposition to a coalition under the table with the Tories. The fact is, of course, that the Party is moving left and that the leadership is running fast to try and catch up with it. Attlee seems to be the only one who has the art of staying in the Centre of the Party, wherever it is at the moment.

The Prime Minister had already replied on January 30th to criticism of his speech to Congress. Mr Churchill declared that (to describe the action Britain would take in the event of a Korean truce being made and broken) he preferred the words 'prompt, resolute and effective' to 'tardy, timid and fatuous'. In any case, his words did not represent new decisions. Nevertheless the Opposition asked for a general debate on foreign affairs.

[1] *Government and Parliament* was published by Oxford University Press in 1954. It owed much to the encouragement and help of D. N. (later Sir Norman) Chester, Warden of Nuffield College, Oxford from 1954 to 1978.

The debate was opened by the Foreign Secretary and much of his speech was devoted to a review of European affairs. On Korea he stated his belief that the American Government and public desired peace in the Far East as much as the British did, and that indeed the Americans were making heavier sacrifices. He criticized those who cast suspicion on American motives, particularly Mr Crossman (whose article 'The War Against China' in the January 26th issue of the New Statesman and Nation *had been widely judged as anti-American).*

The motion, announced by the Opposition, was tabled on the second day of the debate. It read:

> *That this House takes note of the Foreign Secretary's statement, welcomes his adherence to the policy followed by the previous Administration of his (late) Majesty with regard to the Korean conflict and the relations between Great Britain and China, but regrets the Prime Minister's failure to give adequate expression to this policy in the course of his recent visit to the United States of America.*

Tuesday, February 5th
After a morning at the *Statesman* I went down to the Bevanite Group, where we had a long discussion on tactics for the foreign affairs debate. There was the usual pessimism about the Party but I suggested that we should not oppose a motion criticizing Churchill personally, though a general vote against the adjournment would be preferable.

I knew that I had no chance to speak in the debate, which makes one feel much more comfortable. It began with Attlee's protest against Churchill for not speaking first. Eden was a bit ill at ease and obviously irritated when Churchill kept on talking to Buchan-Hepburn,[1] just behind him, while he was trying to speak. Eden's speech was extraordinarily bromidic and glossily optimistic, reaching a climax in an assertion that he had found no trace in America of any desire to extend the war. I challenged him, quoting the statement last week by the Secretary of the Navy, Mr Kimball,[2] that, if the truce were not achieved, the Navy would take the war to the enemy. Eden at first denied knowledge, then, under pressure, said that he couldn't be responsible for the American Administration[3] and then, in irritation, accused me of anti-Americanism. By answering back, I got more cheers than I have ever had in my life from our own side and a bigger press than if I had made a serious speech.

[1] Patrick Buchan-Hepburn, Conservative M.P. for the Toxteth division of Liverpool 1931–50 and for Beckenham 1950–7, when he was raised to the peerage as Lord Hailes. He was a Whip 1939–45, Deputy Chief Whip 1945–8 and Chief Whip 1948–55. He died in 1974.

[2] A businessman and a supporter of the Democratic Party, Dan Kimball was a friend of President Truman, who appointed him Secretary of the Navy 1951. He continued to hold this office until January 1953, shortly after President Eisenhower's election.

[3] 'The hon. Member knows quite well that American ideas of Cabinet responsibility, their whole system, are different from our own' [*H.C. Debates*, vol. 495, col. 834].

Actually the incident was not unimportant. I had had the luck, without realizing it, to press Eden on his weakest point. The only excuse for Churchill's Congress speech would have been if there had been no danger of America's spreading the war of her own accord and if, therefore, it had been safe for Britain to give her *carte blanche* to do whatever she thought best with regard to China. My exposure, by quoting a member of the American Cabinet, that this was not true, punctured Eden's very uneasy defence of Churchill and I am sure that he vented upon me the irritation he felt at the situation Churchill had placed him in. Attlee followed with an unusually violent speech, accusing Churchill of representing us as a minor ally of the U.S.A. in an American war and John Freeman made a quiet and excellent speech, in which he put our Bevanite policy on Egypt extremely well.

Wednesday, February 6th
We had a Party Meeting at 10.30, to discuss tactics for the second day of the debate. Attlee began by reading the terms of an extremely adroitly worded motion, which the Political Committee had drafted and put down last night, censuring Churchill for his failure to continue the Labour policy towards China. Tony Wedgwood Benn voiced ferocious criticism of this sell-out and, while Bevan was preparing to speak, Sydney Silverman[1] got up to say that we would have to accept the motion but that he wanted to spend just two minutes explaining why bipartisan foreign policy must always be wrong. At this point Attlee slipped out. Eight minutes later Sydney was still explaining why bipartisan foreign policy was wrong, when Attlee returned, looking as though he had had a stroke, and said 'The King is dead;[2] he was always very nice to me.' As Chuter Ede[3] said to me, it takes a king's death to stop Sydney Silverman when he is in full flow.

Before going up to the *Statesman* to write, I went into the Smoking Room and found John Strachey, Nye Bevan, etc., all terribly disappointed that the King's death had postponed this afternoon's debate, in which Morrison would have moved the motion, Churchill would have replied and Nye Bevan would have lashed in. If that debate had happened in the atmosphere that had been created, it would have been a most furious row and ended any sort of bipartisan foreign policy. No doubt we shall revive the issue, but, in the

[1] Labour M.P. for Nelson and Colne 1935–68. He was a member of the N.E.C. from 1966 until his death in 1968. For many years he championed the abolition of the death penalty.

[2] King George VI had been in poor health for some time but on the day before his death he had been shooting at Sandringham. From there it was announced at 10.45 on the morning of February 6th that the King had 'passed peacefully away in his sleep'. The cause of death was later stated to have been coronary thrombosis.

[3] Chuter Ede (1882–1965) was Labour M.P. for Mitcham March–November 1923 and for South Shields 1929–31 and 1935–64, when he was created a life peer. He was Parliamentary Secretary at the Ministry of Education 1939–45, Home Secretary 1945–51 and Leader of the House of Commons March–October 1951.

flood of sentimentality which Royal deaths and innocent young couples coming to the Throne create,[1] we may have to bide our time.

I went to the *Statesman* to find a very delicate discussion going on as to whether the front page should have a black band round it or not. Kingsley finally decided on no black band but, to mark the occasion, to set the front page in one size larger type. Sagittarius's[2] suggestion that we should head our leading article 'The Virgin Queen' was turned down and so was her proposal to point out that Providence had seen to it that Wally Simpson[3] should be responsible for Queen Elizabeth II coming to the Throne.

At 2.30 the House assembled. Prayers, for some reason, were dispensed with on this occasion[4] and, even more remarkable, Aneurin Bevan decided to sit on the Front Bench. After the brief ceremony we all stood as the Leaders filed out behind the Speaker's Chair. It was noted that, on the Labour side, the order was: Attlee, Morrison, Bevan. I sat in the Smoking Room and Wavell Wakefield,[5] ex-Rugby Football star, came up to Nye and me and asked whether this Saturday's International should be cancelled. He wanted to get the feel of those in close touch with public opinion. I suggested that, since the League soccer matches were being played, the International should go on but that the crowd should sing 'Abide With Me'. Wakefield was obviously deeply relieved.[6] The Cup Tie replays are going on today and, as George Wigg remarked, they will have record crowds, since no employer would dare to reprimand a worker who stayed at home out of shock at the King's death. This all sounds very ribald but I must confess that no one I have met genuinely feels anything about this, except for Clem Attlee. This is natural enough, since only Prime Ministers can really have any personal acquaintance with the King.

[1] A week earlier Princess Elizabeth and her husband had begun a tour planned to take them to Kenya, Ceylon, Australia and New Zealand. When the news of the King's death reached them in Kenya they immediately turned back to Britain. The Queen's accession was proclaimed on February 8th, the day after her return.

[2] Mrs Hugh Miller, wife of the actor, wrote verse weekly for the *New Statesman and Nation* as Sagittarius from 1930 until 1950, when she resigned. She also wrote as Mercutio on the *Manchester Guardian* and, under various other pseudonyms, in *Tribune*, *Time and Tide* and the *Daily Herald*.

[3] Mrs Wallis Simpson, later the Duchess of Windsor. King Edward VIII's determination to marry her led to his abdication.

[4] Each day's sitting of Parliament begins with prayers, read in the House of Lords by one of the Bishops and in the House of Commons by the Speaker's Chaplain (specially appointed and usually drawn from St Margaret's, Westminster).

[5] Wavell Wakefield, later Lord Wakefield of Kendal, was National Conservative M.P. for Swindon 1935–45 and Labour M.P. for St Marylebone 1945–63, when he was raised to the peerage. From 1952 to 1955 he was Chairman of the Parliamentary and Scientific Committee. He had captained Cambridge, Middlesex, the R.A.F., Harlequins and England at Rugby Football.

[6] The King's death caused the Rugby match between England and Ireland to be postponed until March 29th. Association Football matches were not postponed but the players wore black armbands.

Monday, February 11th
The King's death really has swamped politics. The hard-boiled reaction of the Commons was extremely esoteric and, directly you got outside, you certainly realized that the newspapers were not sentimentalizing when they decribed the nation's feeling of personal loss. Kingsley told me this morning, as we walked down the Strand, that Dorothy Woodman[1] had been deeply moved, 'Though', he hastily added, 'it naturally didn't affect her in any way.'

What has really astonished me is not British public reaction but the sight of the *New York Times* last Thursday morning, which devoted over half the paper to the news and whose editorial could really have been composed in London by an Englishman. It is also pretty remarkable that India should be in mourning and I found it possible to write a *Sunday Pictorial* column which was truthful, yet suitable for the occasion. Actually the whole *Sunday Pictorial* staff, like all other Fleet Street staff, was mechanically extracting the last drop of sentiment and news value from the story, in a highly professional way.

After spending this morning at the *Statesman*, I lunched at the House in order to attend at two o'clock, when Churchill moved the three resolutions of sympathy with the Royal Family, in a far simpler and, to me, more effective speech than his florid broadcast. For once Attlee spoke at greater length. I think that the fact is that Clem has been more moved by the death of the King than by anything in the last four years. After Clem Davies[2] had given us a dose of his Nonconformist lugubriousness, Walter Elliot[3] rose to speak impromptu for the backbenches. I had noticed a message being passed up to him two minutes before. Afterwards, in the Smoking Room, he showed me this gem from his Chief Whip, which ran, roughly: 'I don't know what other Privy Councillors are likely to do. It might be a nice idea if you spoke for the backbenchers – not, of course, if you don't want to but it would be nice if you would. No need.' So in the Tory Party too Chief Whips have the habit of ensuring that, if anything goes wrong, the other chap gets the blame. Elliot did it admirably.

[1] Kingsley Martin's 'wifely companion' (in C. H. Rolph's phrase) for over thirty years. She was secretary to Philip Snowden, and from 1927 to 1947 secretary of the Union of Democratic Control. The Crossmans had been wartime lodgers in her and Kingsley Martin's house at 14 Buckingham Street. A balanced assessment of her role at the *New Statesman and Nation* appears in Chapter 10 of C. H. Rolph's *Kingsley* (London: Gollancz, 1973). She completed her major work on Far Eastern politics, *Himalayan Frontiers* (London: Cresset Press, Barrie & Rockliff, 1969), just before her death in 1970.

[2] Clement Davies (1884–1962) was Liberal M.P. for Montgomeryshire 1929–62 and Leader of the Liberal Party 1945–56.

[3] Sir Walter Elliot (1888–1958) was Unionist M.P. for Lanark 1918–23, for the Kelvingrove division of Glasgow 1923–45, for the Scottish Universities 1946–50 and again for Kelvingrove 1950–8. He held numerous Government offices, notably as Minister of Agriculture, Fisheries and Food 1932–6 (a period remarkable for the foundation of the Milk Marketing Board), Secretary of State for Scotland 1936–8 and Minister of Health 1938–40. He was Rector of Glasgow University 1947–50 and was knighted in 1952. His widow, Kay, sits in the Lords as Baroness Elliot of Harwood.

At 3.25 we all gathered in the Chamber and proceeded behind the Speaker in full rig into Westminster Hall, where we lined the right-hand side, facing the catafalque[1] while the Peers lined the left-hand side. It was extremely cold, dark and dank, but it was a fine sight as the boys of the Chapel Royal and the Archbishop came down the steps from the south end and then the Heralds, Pursuivants, etc., proceeded slowly down to the main door. After a twenty-minute delay there was a bang, the doors opened and the coffin was carried in by eight Grenadiers and heaved on to the catafalque, with only the crown on top. After the coffin came the most extraordinary sight, the Queens and Princesses, looking more like eight Moslem women,[2] clothed in dead black, swathed and double-swathed with veils so thick that they couldn't read the order of service through them. I was standing exactly opposite the Queen and couldn't see their faces, so the newspaper photographs next day must have been completely fudged. It was a short, quite simple service, fortunately for the aged Peers and Commoners, who would otherwise have caught pneumonia.

Late in the evening Eddie Shackleton came home and took Zita to see the lying-in-state. They were the last people in and there was no one else there. It must have looked magnificent.

Tuesday, February 12th
A great dispute is now proceeding about the Labour Members who are supposed to be marching in the procession. George Wigg's idea was to conscript twenty-six of us, young and vigorous, the sort of people who don't wear top hats. However, his plan was foiled when others got wind of it and the first three applicants at the Whip's Office were Maurice Orbach,[3] Maurice Edelman[4] and Barnett Janner,[5] all Jews with top hats and jolly well determined to wear them. Then in came Tom Driberg, who sidled up to George

---

[1] On Monday February 11th the King's body was transferred from Sandringham Church to Westminster Hall, where it lay in state for the next three days.

[2] The Archbishop mentioned was Archbishop Fisher of Canterbury (later Lord Fisher of Lambeth). The 'eight Moslem women' were, in fact, seven. The procession formed in the following way:

Her Majesty The Queen
(Elizabeth II)

H.M. Queen Mary	H.M. The Queen Mother
H.R.H. Princess Margaret	H.R.H. The Duke of Edinburgh
H.R.H. The Duchess of Gloucester	H.R.H. The Duke of Gloucester
H.R.H. The Duchess of Kent	H.R.H. The Princess Royal

[3] Labour M.P. for Willesden East 1945–59 and for Stockport South from 1964 until his death in 1979.

[4] Labour M.P. for Coventry West 1945–50, North 1950–74 and North-West 1974 until his death in 1975. A prolific popular novelist.

[5] Liberal M.P. for the Whitechapel and St George's division of Stepney 1931–5 and Labour M.P. for West Leicester 1945–50 and for North-West Leicester 1950–70. He was President of the Board of Deputies of British Jews 1955–64. Knighted in 1961, he was created a life peer in 1970.

Wigg and said that he'd heard Dick Crossman was going.[1] Could George Wigg get Dick's name off the list, since Tom wanted to write about it in *Reynolds News* and not see the story also in the *Sunday Pic*? But there is still great confusion. Everything was tentative on Saturday, when the Earl Marshal[2] rang up and said that he must have twenty-six Labour names, so all our names went in and we are due to march from Westminster to Paddington, entrain and march from Windsor Station to St George's Chapel.[3] So I have had to equip myself with a coat and hat from Moss Bros[4] and with a pair of new black shoes.

Wednesday, February 13th

As I came back from the House today, I watched the queue winding like a snake in the little garden on the other side of the Embankment.[5] Roughly speaking, this afternoon, it was five women to one man. I don't know whether the proportion is different in the evenings. My impression is that a good deal of irritation has been caused by the Earl Marshal's announcement yesterday, bidding the public to go into mourning. The press release told us that we need not indulge in undue expense and patted the majority on the backs for having done it already.

Thursday, February 14th

I lunched today at the House. There was only one empty place and that happened to be at the table where Douglas Jay, Hugh Gaitskell and Roy Jenkins were sitting. When I asked if they minded my joining them, Hugh Gaitskell said, very severely, that they were discussing pure economics. I said that would be fine and I could learn something, whereupon Hugh, who is really very courteous, said that I probably could. I found that they had met together to discuss the frontbench policy with regard to the Budget.[6] Douglas Jay was urging that we should press for much bigger import cuts, especially

---

[1] As it turned out, Crossman did not march in the procession. Several of his contemporaries recall that there was certainly difficulty about 'the wearing of hats'; some sources maintain that Crossman refused to wear one, while others say that Moss Bros found him impossible to fit.

[2] The hereditary office of Earl Marshal is held by the Dukes of Norfolk, of whom this was the 16th (1908–75).

[3] The State Funeral took place on Friday, February 15th. At 9.30 that morning a bearer party of the Brigade of Guards placed the coffin on a gun carriage, drawn by naval ratings to Paddington Station. The coffin was transported by train to St George's Chapel, Windsor.

[4] A shop, founded in 1860, which both sells and hires clothing and equipment.

[5] During the three days of the lying-in-state, some 300,000 mourners passed through Westminster Hall to pay their last respects to the King. The doors opened at eight o'clock each morning and were closed only long after midnight, not at 10 p.m. as had originally been planned.

[6] To be presented by the Chancellor on March 11th.

on goods from Europe. He has always opposed the whole E.P.U.[1] idea of liberalizing European trade. Gaitskell reminded me that Douglas doesn't like Europeans anyway, ever since his tooth ached in Vienna during his honeymoon and he left his wife there to return to England to get it stopped.[2]

To my surprise, they also agreed that the Party should press for an increase in the basic rate of old age pensions.[3] I mentioned my reading Titmuss's[4] inaugural lecture,[5] where he remarked that the purchasing power of unemployment and sickness benefit is now less than when they were first introduced. Gaitskell seemed surprised, as though it was a new idea that sickness benefit was low. But James Griffiths and Edith Summerskill, who came across, confirmed this, and so it was added to the list. Gaitskell, however, was very emphatic that we should not take the line that cuts in Government expenditure would have no effect on our external trade position.

Towards the end of lunch, the conversation turned to the interrupted censure motion on Churchill[6] and Gaitskell said to me that it was very unfair to blame the American Government for unfortunate remarks made by irresponsible people. This was clearly a reference to my row with Eden last week. I mentioned Dulles, who yesterday made a new speech demanding war against China,[7] and Gaitskell replied, rather crossly, 'Oh, I knew that you'd

---

[1] The European Payments Union was established in September 1950 as an organ of the Organization for European Economic Co-operation. Its operation was made retrospective as from July 1950 and it was originally intended to remain in force until June 1952, when the Marshall Plan was due to end. The Union in effect supplemented the monetary reserve of participating countries, which could use the credit so provided in their dealings with one another. In 1950 O.E.E.C. countries undertook to remove quantitative restrictions on certain imports from one another, but in November 1951 Britain had largely revoked her agreement.

[2] In 1933. Douglas Jay was to remain profoundly opposed to Britain's joining the European Community. See Crossman's *The Diaries of a Cabinet Minister*, vols I, II and III.

[3] The current basic rate of retirement pensions, unemployed and sickness insurance was 32s. 6d a week for a single person and 54s. a week for a married couple.

[4] A writer and lecturer, Richard Titmuss pioneered the study of social administration as Professor of that subject at the London School of Economics from 1950 until his death in 1973. His advice to the Labour Party laid the foundations of their social security proposals and their attempt to achieve an integrated social policy. Key works were his *Problems of Social Policy* (London: Longmans, 1950), *Income Distribution and Social Change* (London: Allen & Unwin, 1962) and *The Gift Relationship* (London: Allen & Unwin, 1970). He was Deputy Chairman of the Supplementary Benefits Commission 1968–73.

[5] 'Social Administration in a Changing Society', delivered on May 10th, 1951.

[6] See above, pp. 69–70.

[7] In January 1951 President Truman, a Democrat, had appointed John Foster Dulles, the Adviser to the State Department and a Republican, to negotiate the Japanese Peace Treaty. After the Senate's ratification of both that treaty and the Pacific Security Treaty between the U.S.A., Australia and New Zealand in March 1952, Mr Dulles resigned his post in order to devote himself to Republican politics during the months before the Party convention to nominate a presidential candidate. In a speech made in mid-February, while he was still at the State Department, Mr Dulles repeated that America intended to destroy Chinese Communism with the aid of Chiang Kai-Shek.

mention Dulles! But you mustn't blame Acheson[1] for that.' I said that, after all, Dulles is in the State Department and negotiated the Japanese Treaty, to which Gaitskell replied that there are only four men in America who really speak for the Government and it is unfair to suggest that the others do. I said, 'But in that sense of the word "Government", there is no Government in America at all and it's equally misleading for you to suggest that there is.[2] In certain ways Dulles means just as much as Acheson in terms of America's external behaviour.' From Gaitskell's expression I knew that he was feeling, 'There's Dick being clever again, with his superficial generalizations.' I am sure Gaitskell is a very good economist but politically he is just determined to believe that there is a 'good America', which he can side with.

Wednesday, February 20th
This evening I did the first of my B.B.C. 'Serious Arguments'[3] with Bob Boothby. Donald McLachlan[4] was in the chair. Afterwards Bob took us to dinner at White's, a magnificent dinner in a really beautiful old dining room, unchanged since the club's foundation 200 years ago. There were eight or nine Tory M.P.s dining there but, unlike Bevan, I wasn't kicked out.[5]

Bob was unusually informative about the Conservative Party. First he told us that at a recent meeting the Party had voted 95 to 5 in favour of ending the B.B.C. monopoly and that it looks quite likely that something will really be done.[6] No doubt the increased agitation is due to the high-handed B.B.C.

[1] U.S. Assistant Secretary of State 1941-5, Under-Secretary of State 1945-7 and Secretary of State 1949-January 1953. Dean Acheson pursued a policy of collective security against Communist imperialism. He wrote an autobiography, *Present at the Creation* (New York: Norton, 1969).

[2] Ironically, Crossman was taking up the Foreign Secretary's rejoinder (see above, p. 69 and n.) that American government lacked the principle of collective responsibility.

[3] A programme founded in 1952, to interest Members of Parliament in the B.B.C. External Service. A chairman (often a Liberal) and two M.P.s discussed the week's topical questions. The programme's first producer was Donald Baverstock, who was succeeded in 1954 by Robert Finnegan. The programme lapsed in 1965 but was revived in 1968 as 'People and Politics'.

[4] Author and journalist. A member of the editorial staff of *The Times* 1933-6, he taught at Winchester and was Editor of the *Times Educational Supplement* 1938-40, Assistant Editor of *The Economist* 1947-54, Deputy Editor of the *Daily Telegraph* 1954-60 and Editor of the *Sunday Telegraph* 1961-6. He died in 1971.

[5] On Wednesday, January 24th, 1951, Mr Bevan, then Minister of Labour, had been the guest of Marshal of the R.A.F. Sir John Slessor, Chief of Air Staff, and was allegedly assaulted on the steps of the club while leaving. On January 27th the Hon. John Fox-Strangways resigned his membership after a complaint concerning his part in the incident. A celebrated cartoon by Osbert Lancaster shows a clergyman reproving 'Bishop Font-water', who is engaged in kicking the Reverend Hewlett Johnson (the 'Red Dean' of Canterbury) down the steps of the Athenaeum, which now possesses the original drawing.

[6] In January 1947 the B.B.C.'s Charter and Licence had been extended for five years, on the understanding that within that time an inquiry would be made into its affairs and into the future shape of sound and television broadcasting. A committee, chaired by Lord Beveridge, was established in June 1949 and its report was published in January 1951. The recommendations included a reaffirmation that broadcasting should be undertaken by a public authority and the declaration that to charter more than one Corporation was impracticable.

One committee member, however, wrote a minority report, advocating independent

performance during the King's funeral.[1] If there had been a rival, the B.B.C. couldn't have closed the service down in the way it did. Secondly, Bob told us that at a Party Meeting yesterday, the National Health Service Bill[2] was argued for by Crookshank,[3] after which backbencher after backbencher got up, really understanding the subject and expressing consternation at the harm being done to the Health Service. Bob said that it's quite a new thing to have a Tory Party with thirty or forty Members who really know about such things and really care about them. It looks as though the Bill will have to be withdrawn and modified to meet Tory objections. 'When the Old Man dies,' Bob said, 'and Butler and Eden reconstitute the Party, you won't know the difference from the Labour Party.' I wonder. After all, there are a few businessmen who pay for it.

Next, Bob says that, generally speaking, the morale of the Party has never been lower or more bewildered. 'Our boys really believe their election promises and thought they could abolish controls. So they are bewildered. And now the small, articulate group of progressive Tories – Macleod,[4] Maudling,[5] Angus Maude,[6] etc. – are equally bewildered by the attacks on

---

competition, including that from commercial broadcasting (thought of at this time in terms of 'sponsored programmes'). The author of that dissenting report was Selwyn Lloyd, a Conservative M.P. (who in October 1951 became a Minister of State at the Foreign Office). A number of other Members of his Party were also known to favour the ending of the B.B.C.'s monopoly and, in some cases, the immediate introduction of sponsored broadcasts.

The B.B.C.'s Charter was due for renewal on June 30th, 1952 and the Government were preparing a preliminary White Paper. For a discussion of the speculation current at this time, see Asa Briggs, *The History of Broadcasting in the United Kingdom: Vol. 4, Sound and Vision* (London: Oxford University Press, 1979).

[1] During the ten days of national mourning following the King's death the B.B.C. had broadcast only one solemn programme.

[2] This was the measure giving effect to the proposals for Health Service charges presented by the Chancellor on January 29th (see above, p. 66 and n.).

[3] Captain Harry Crookshank, Unionist M.P. for Gainsborough 1924–56. He was Leader of the House of Commons 1951–5, during which time he was Minister of Health 1951–2 and Lord Privy Seal 1952–5. He was raised to the peerage in 1956 as the 1st Viscount Crookshank. He died in 1960.

[4] Iain Macleod, Conservative M.P. for Enfield West from 1950 until his sudden death in July 1970. He was Head of Home Affairs at the Conservative Research Department 1948–1950, Minister of Health 1952–5, Minister of Labour and National Service 1955–9, Secretary of State for the Colonies 1959–61, Chancellor of the Duchy of Lancaster and Leader of the House of Commons 1961–3 and Chancellor of the Exchequer 1970. His widow sits in the House of Lords as Baroness Macleod of Borve. See Nigel Fisher's biography, *Iain Macleod* (London: Deutsch, 1973).

[5] Reginald Maudling, Conservative M.P. for Barnet 1950–79. He was Parliamentary Secretary at the Ministry of Civil Aviation 1952, Economic Secretary of the Treasury 1952–5, Minister of Supply 1955–7, Paymaster-General 1957–9, President of the Board of Trade 1959–61, Secretary of State for the Colonies 1961–2, Chancellor of the Exchequer 1962–4 and Home Secretary from 1970 to 1972, when he resigned after a business associate was tried on a charge of corruption. He died in 1979. His *Memoirs* (London: Sidgwick & Jackson) were published in 1978.

[6] Conservative M.P. for Stratford-upon-Avon since August 1963. An author and journalist, he was Chairman of Conservative Party Research Department from 1975 to 1979 and has been Paymaster-General since 1979. He is co-author with Roy Lewis of *The English Middle Classes* (London: Phoenix House, 1949).

the Welfare State. We are doomed,' he said. But then one must remember that Bob is embittered by not having a job. Last, he said that, after his first survey of the three Services, Churchill had found the Army and Navy unsatisfactory but the Air Force a scandal. In particular, Fighter Command and the whole defences of this country are in as bad a state as they were in the 1930s. Seven out of ten of the Air Council are Bomber boys and only three Fighter.

On January 26th representatives of the six countries concerned (France, Belgium, the Federal Republic of Germany, Italy, Luxemburg and the Netherlands) met in Paris and agreed on the main principles of the proposed European Defence Community. These, with the protocol defining E.D.C./NATO relations were to be put before a meeting of the NATO Council, to be held in Lisbon at the end of February. But, only a few days before, new obstacles appeared.

On February 8th the West German Bundestag voted in favour of continued negotiations for German participation in the E.D.C., but on certain conditions. These were that: a settlement was to be reached on the status of the Saar; the Federal Republic of Germany was to become a member of NATO; war criminals were to be released; all restrictions on German industry were to be removed; there was to be equal treatment in the sharing of defence costs; and that the occupation regime was to end and Germany to have full sovereignty.

When the French National Assembly discussed the E.D.C., Monsieur Schuman's case for German inclusion was opposed. On February 19th a compromise resolution was accepted by 40 votes. It called for: a more equitable sharing of the burden of expense; British and American guarantees against violation of the treaty; an undertaking that French forces would never be smaller than those of any other member; a promise that no German units should be recruited until the treaty had been ratified; and an undertaking that no country with territorial claims would be admitted to NATO.

On February 29th the French Government was defeated. It had held office for only forty days and was succeeded by a Conservative administration, in coalition with members of the Right, Radical and Gaullist parties, the U.S.D.R. and the Catholic M.R.P. The Socialists went into Opposition.

The NATO Council duly met in Portugal and on February 22nd the report and protocols concerning the E.D.C. were approved. The draft treaty establishing the E.D.C. was eventually initialled in Paris on May 9th and on May 29th the six countries signed the treaty and related protocols. Britain, not herself a member of the E.D.C., signed other protocols, setting out the reciprocal assistance which E.D.C. and NATO members would afford one another. Crossman's attack on the treaty may be found in 'The Lessons of Lisbon', New Statesman and Nation, *March 1st, 1952.*

Thursday, February 21st
At six o'clock I went to an emergency meeting of the foreign affairs group of

the Labour Party on the rearmament of Germany. It began with a half-hour speech by Dalton, in which he tried, at the beginning, to be moderate and to unite the Party merely in favour of postponing, but then he put up an overwhelming case against any form of German rearmament, which showed his cloven hoof too clearly.

He was followed by Shinwell, in a twenty-nine-minute speech of such puerile dishonesty that he swung everybody back to our side. His main line was that the French were no good and so we must have the Germans. And he suddenly came down in favour of our entering the European Army, which he was fiercely opposing four or five weeks ago. Denis Healey, on his first appearance, started very well but then gave too long and too machiavellian a lecture. He came down against the European Army, for postponement of a German Army, for strengthening NATO and dealing with the Germans within NATO rather than within a European Community.

I followed Healey briefly, in roughly the same effect, and then Herbert Morrison made a characteristic utterance. We must look all round the subject. Some people here seem to show a hatred of Germans which, as good, international Socialists, we should not feel. After all, people disliked us too and all nations were difficult and we couldn't allow the Germans to stand about with their hands in their pockets while our boys fought for them. We should go into the European Army or something else. And so on, and so on, flattening down and bromiding the whole subject until you could howl, as Dalton, Denis Healey and I did together over dinner and two bottles of burgundy, Dalton in tremendous good humour and Denis discussing existentialism, his main interest. The conversation went on in the Smoking Room till eleven o'clock, when I strolled home with Dalton.

In the morning's *Daily Herald* Attlee had denied the story, first published in the *Guardian* and then in greater detail in the *Herald Tribune* and the *Statesman*, that King George VI had expressed a preference in 1945 for Bevin as Foreign Secretary instead of Dalton.[1] I asked Dalton whether he had talked to Attlee about this denial. 'Yes,' he said, 'I asked the little man and the little man said, "No, there is absolutely nothing in it whatsoever." Moreover,' Dalton added, 'the little man's motive for making the change, as he did over lunch, was quite different. He thought that, if he left Morrison and Bevin on the home side, they would quarrel, whereas Dalton would get on with anyone.' A much more authoritative story is that Bridges,[2] the head of the Civil Service, said on behalf of the Foreign Office, that Dalton was no go. I put this to Dalton and he said it was quite untrue. Bridges had said that Ernie wouldn't understand the figures at the Treasury.

[1] Dalton himself discusses this incident at length – but does not mention Lord Bridges. See *High Tide and After: Memoirs 1945–60* (London: Muller, 1962), pp. 10–14.

[2] Edward, 1st Baron Bridges, son of the Poet Laureate, Robert Bridges. A Fellow of All Souls' College, Oxford, 1920–7, and 1954–68, he was Secretary to the Cabinet 1938–46 and Permanent Secretary to the Treasury 1945–56. He died in 1969.

Monday, February 25th

When we got to our *New Statesman* lunch, John Roberts,[1] the Manager, revealed that this was Kingsley's twenty-first birthday as Editor, and copies of the first number he produced were circulated. It certainly reminded one what he has done for the paper. He is a genius and it is partly the fact that he refused to have a politician's idea of a policy and cares more about the colour of the paper than its conceptual form. Shifts of emphasis and policy contradictions, which I find unbearable, don't worry him, fortunately. As Michael Foot said to me today, Kingsley's great quality is that he will instinctively support any left-wing view which isn't getting a fair hearing or which is unpopular. And that kind of liberalism is, after all, the basic philosophy of a successful weekly. You can see in the *Tribune* what happens when you try to run a weekly merely as the expression of current policy.

Down at the House, the Party is still in the throes of its controversy about German rearmament and the foreign affairs group resumed its discussion this evening. The general feeling was that we should both postpone German rearmament and enter the European Army and it was difficult to persuade even Dalton that to come out with a declaration of this sort would cause complete confusion in Europe, where it is clearly understood that the present plans for a European Army are designed precisely to accelerate German rearmament.

Tuesday, February 26th

The Party Meeting started at eleven o'clock and once again, cutting across the foreign affairs group, the subject was German rearmament. Attlee made a supremely skilful statement, plumb in the middle between the contending views, but just a little to our side. Then at half-past one we had a Bevanite Group meeting at which Michael Foot raised the issue of whether we should not vote against the Defence White Paper, which is due for debate on Wednesday next week.[2] It would be tempting for the Bevanites to put down a reasoned Amendment this week but we couldn't come to a firm decision today because Nye was not there. A small drafting committee consisting of myself, Stephen Swingler[3] and Harold Wilson, was told to draft a reasoned Amendment and submit it to a special meeting on Thursday morning.

Meanwhile Tommy Balogh informed us that, on his calculations, the arms programme this year has been cut by 15 per cent. Since you cannot cut such items as Army pay, this cut has fallen much more heavily on the production side. Tommy reckons this has now been cut back well below the

---

[1] John Roberts, who died in 1967, joined the *New Statesman and Nation* management staff in 1914. He became Manager in 1920 and was Managing Director 1947–57.

[2] The debate on the Statement on Defence 1952 (Cmd 8475) was to be held on March 5th.

[3] Labour M.P. for Stafford 1945–50 and for Newcastle-under-Lyme from 1951 until his death in February 1969. He was Joint Parliamentary Secretary at the Ministry of Transport 1964–7, Minister of Transport 1967–8 and Minister of State at the Department of Health and Social Security 1968–9.

original £3,600 million, compared with the £4,700 million of January. So at first sight the Bevanites have already got their way in slashing back the arms programme to its original level. But this is misleading, because, of course, the whole programme was enormously enlarged and if you spend less on a larger programme you get much less than if you spend the same amount on a smaller programme.

This afternoon came the renewed censure debate. Very reluctantly, on Eddie's pressure, I had provided some quotations for Herbert Morrison, who was due to open for the Opposition. He made a sixty-five-minute speech — cumbrous, ill at ease and with that curious impression of frivolity which made him such a disaster as Foreign Secretary. Churchill began his reply with a very artful reference to the fact that the Labour Government had begun constructing an atom bomb without informing Parliament. He indicated clearly enough that this could not have been due to fear of Conservative opposition. This led up to Churchill's famous disclosure[1] that in May 1951 Mr Morrison himself had entered into a secret commitment that, under special circumstances, America might have to bomb across the Yalu River.

This bomb exploded neatly on the gangway which divides the Labour Front Bench and its supporters from the Bevanites. You could almost hear those above the gangway whistling 'Jesus, he's caught us out', and those below whistling 'Jesus, so our suspicions were right'. Instinctively, Aneurin Bevan, who has always had a strong interest in getting hold of Cabinet papers ever since his resignation, leapt to the attack on Churchill and demanded that the papers should be laid. This showed great political wisdom. There was Nye, battling for a colleague in the wrong, while the Front Bench sat stunned and white. But the atmosphere for Nye's own speech had been ruined and he had to shorten and distort it.

Anyway, Churchill's bomb had worked its effect of creating the impression that Attlee and Morrison had been sheerly disingenuous in staging the debate. Morrison was horribly hoisted on his own petard. The left of the Party disliked this personal censure[2] on Churchill and had demanded a straight No vote on foreign affairs. It was Morrison who had pushed the motion through. Moreover, the terms of the motion, commending the Conservative Party for faithfully continuing Labour policy in Korea and merely reprimanding Churchill for falsely representing it in Washington, were, as Churchill proved, perfectly correct. After all, Churchill's disclosure merely confirmed it. Then why did the disclosure work? Simply because Morrison and Attlee,

[1] The Prime Minister revealed that, before discussions on a Korean truce began, the recent Labour Government had themselves agreed to 'prompt, resolute and effective' action in support of their American ally. Mr Churchill alleged that, unknown to Labour Party Members and the country, the Government had undertaken to associate Britain with retaliatory action 'not confined to Korea', should the Communist forces launch heavy air attacks from Chinese bases. Challenged to lay papers before the House, Mr Churchill replied to Mr Bevan that he had 'not quoted a document but stated a fact'. The motion was defeated by 318 votes to 285.

[2] See above, p. 69.

who Churchill had very slyly ensured should speak before him, had not frankly admitted what they had done.

Moreover, in order to achieve this brilliant personal defence, Churchill really did have to disclose to the Americans that he was right back on the Labour line of opposition to spreading the war. Substantially this was a great achievement for the Labour Opposition and makes the practical blunder of Morrison and Attlee so much the worse. It correspondingly strengthens Nye's position, since he had resigned from the Cabinet a month before the secret commitment was made.

Late this evening Morrison asked me to talk to him and, going down the passage, he said, 'Well, I hope the *New Statesman* says that Herbert Morrison in his speech gallantly tried to put forward its arguments.' This I thought pretty mean and typical. I said that the urgent problem was what the Party was going to do on the Defence White Paper and I hoped that it would put down a reasoned Amendment and vote against it. Morrison replied, rather incoherently but quickly, 'You can't get me to line up behind Aneurin Bevan.' I said, 'Then how can you oppose cuts in the Education Estimates and the food subsidies if you vote for these huge Defence Estimates?' But I could see that Morrison wasn't considering the matter in terms of policy at all but purely in terms of personalities. Also, I don't think that he was fully aware of the desperate catastrophe he had personally suffered in the debate.

Wednesday, February 27th
This catastrophe was clear enough in this morning's papers. I really don't see how Morrison can recover from this. But so far Attlee, with his usual providential skill, seems to have avoided sharing the responsibility which is certainly his. Fortunately for him he had made his own speech before the King died.

Thursday, February 28th
We had a special meeting of the Bevanite Group this morning to discuss our tactics on the defence debate next Wednesday. Harold Wilson and I put forward a long, composite draft resolution and draft letter to Attlee,[1] which we had composed with Aneurin, and I was deputed to see that it was delivered this evening. I got a formal reply from Attlee, saying that the matter would be considered at the Party Meeting next Tuesday morning.

The Defence Estimates published on February 25th proposed an increase of £245 million above the current year's spending. This was in addition to £85 million of aid from the United States. Even so, shortages of capacity and materials meant that defence expenditure would rise more slowly than the previous Labour Government and its Conservative successors had planned. In a sense, therefore, the Shadow Cabinet could be said to have approved the

[1] See p. 88 and n.

Estimates in advance; the formula they adopted for the debate on March 5th illustrated their dilemma.

At the Party Meeting on the previous day, the Bevanites argued that the original £4,700 million defence programme could not be pursued in the conditions of 1952. A resolution on these lines was rejected, together with any compromise proposal. Indeed, the Shadow Cabinet recommended that the Opposition accept the Government motion approving the Defence White Paper but proposed a rider declaring their own lack of confidence in the ability of Ministers to carry out the programme. Labour backbenchers were confused, dismayed and, in the case of the Bevanites, angry. Attlee, Morrison and William Whiteley (the Chief Whip) issued a specific instruction that Party members should abstain from the Government's motion approving the Estimates and should support the Opposition Amendment.

Tuesday, March 4th

The Party met at eleven o'clock and the main item was what the Party should do in the defence debate. Attlee read aloud our resolution and then his own, which censured Churchill's administration of defence but accepted the defence White Paper. I spoke first, in an absolutely icy atmosphere, and sat down in total silence, after suggesting that just as the tactical manoeuvre of foreign affairs had ended in disaster[1] so this palpable tactical manoeuvre would end similarly. I also added that Attlee's announcement that the Party would support increased old age pensions and social security benefits would seem palpably dishonest if we simultaneously demanded increased arms. Harold Wilson also spoke on our side and then came Woodrow Wyatt, John Strachey and four other right-wingers, with a long Shinwell oration at the end. They refused to let Nye speak and the vote showed 4 to 1 against us but only 3 to 1 in favour of the official Amendment, which should have made them realize the Party was uneasy.

At half-past one we had our own Bevanite meeting. Harold Wilson and I wanted to table a drastically cut down and very simple Amendment that, in view of the trade crisis, we could not afford £1,400 million on arms. This is what John Edwards,[2] after the [last Group] meeting, had asked for. Nye said that this would be running away from what we proposed at the Party Meeting and urged us to table that, unchanged. But then all our trade union members, one after the other, advised us not to table an Amendment, since this would be in defiance of a Party decision. Nye very quickly realized that we could not afford to override their caution and we agreed, first, to table no Amendment; second, to abstain from voting for the official Amendment; and, third,

---

[1] See above, pp. 69 ff. and pp. 81 ff.

[2] (Lewis) John Edwards was Labour M.P. for Blackburn 1945–50 and for Brighouse and Spenborough 1950–9. He was General Secretary of the Post Office Engineering Union 1938–47, P.P.S. to Stafford Cripps 1945–7, Parliamentary Secretary to the Ministry of Health 1947–9 and to the Board of Trade 1949–50 and Economic Secretary to the Treasury 1950–1. He died in 1959.

to force a division on the Government resolution. It was also agreed that I should be the main speaker and that Carmichael[1] should also speak to bring in the Scottish vote.

This evening Zita dined with me and then she went off to Central Hall where Kingsley had organized a mass meeting for his Peace with China campaign,[2] with Stansgate in the chair and Kenneth Younger[3] and Barbara Castle speaking as Labour Party Members. Apparently, whenever they suggested that we should resist aggression in Korea, they were howled down by individual members of the audience, saying, 'Don't bring politics in; we came here for a peace meeting.' I heard afterwards that in introducing Kingsley at the beginning, Stansgate had said, 'In view of the change of monarch, I introduce Mr Queensley Martin', and Kingsley had leant across to Kenneth and said, 'Of course, it's not a funny joke but they all seem to enjoy it.' I always thought the Peace with China thing was a Communist front show, which is why I have never done anything with it.

Wednesday, March 5th

I managed to avoid going to the *Statesman*, to give time for preparing my speech today. This time I made much fuller notes, including a verbatim draft of the beginning and a peroration. I was too excited to eat. I went into the Chamber at three o'clock to secure my place on the third row back below the gangway, while the Group met at the same time to make final arrangements about the voting.[4] Rose[5] told me that, at the Group, Nye said that Carmichael would certainly speak but he wasn't so sure about me. Thank heavens I didn't know it.

Churchill began with a very, very artful speech, congratulating the Labour Government on its military zeal, but showing that it had overdone it and that he had had to cut their programme. Shinwell, who had nothing prepared, made a reply of such indescribable vulgarity that the most ardent right-

[1] James Carmichael, I.L.P. M.P. for the Bridgeton division of Glasgow 1946–7 and Labour M.P. for the same constituency 1947–61. He died in 1966.

[2] The growth and decline of Kingsley Martin's enthusiasm for China is described in C. H. Rolph's *Kingsley* (London: Gollancz, 1973).

[3] Labour M.P. for Grimsby 1945–59. He was Parliamentary Under-Secretary at the Home Office 1947–50 and Minister of State 1950–1. Director of the Royal Institute of International Affairs (Chatham House) 1959–71, he died in 1976.

[4] The Bevanites disregarded the Shadow Cabinet's instructions, abstaining from voting on the Opposition Amendment. This was defeated by 314 votes to 219, a majority of ninety-five instead of the customary twenty or so. On the Government motion approving the Estimates, the Bevanites refused to abstain with other Labour Members and fifty-seven dissidents voted against the resolution. The White Paper was thus approved by 313 votes to 55 (plus 2 tellers); the Labour Party split was undeniable.

[5] Saul Rose, Lecturer in International Relations at the University of Aberdeen. He succeeded Denis Healey in 1952 as Secretary of the International Department of the Labour Party. In 1955 he left that post to begin research at St Antony's College, Oxford, and since 1963 he has been Tutor in Politics and Bursar at New College, Oxford. His works include two studies of South Asian politics, the more recent being *Politics in Southern Asia* (London: Macmillan, 1963).

wingers were dismayed. His only complaint was that Churchill hadn't given him enough bouquets. I thought I should be called as the first Labour back-bencher, but up jumped Group-Captain Wilcock[1] to make a long, reactionary oration, and I discovered from the Deputy Speaker that arrangements had been made for the following six speeches. So I went out and got a cup of tea and saw Nye, who promised to rush off. I think he must have done because, directly the Speaker himself came back to the Chair, I was called. This was at 6.16, just in time for the provincial press. Meanwhile Kenneth Younger had very kindly got Zita into the Speaker's Gallery, but Jennie had taken her out for a Pimm's No. 1[2] when they heard I wasn't speaking.

It was an occasion all right because, when my name went up, there was a general move into the Chamber. The House of Commons is very good at sensing occasions. Things were made much easier by Churchill's coming back for the whole speech, so that I could direct it against the Tories and, within an hour of its conclusion, it was fairly clear from the comments in the downstairs bar that it had worked — that is, the Party had heard the first reasoned case for opposing the Churchill Defence Estimates, not for ideological or emotional reasons but for overwhelming economic reasons. When you are a success it makes you realize how little a success you are usually. Nye couldn't have been more generous, which should not be taken for granted, because few politicians are generous enough to accept that somebody else can stage an occasion.

What with having a drink and revising my speech for Hansard,[3] I got back to the Chamber only just in time to see Attlee move the official Amendment. He started by commending three Tory speeches and George Wigg's. At one moment I was tempted to get up on a point of order and ask whether Attlee was moving a vote of censure or supporting Mr Churchill. There was no censure at all and, the longer he spoke, the more it was clear that the Amendment had been mere tactics. The only effective thing he did was to sit down ten minutes early, a secret weapon which put off poor Nigel Birch,[4] who therefore finished all he had to say by 9.50.[5] But Birch did get in one extremely

[1] Group-Captain Clifford Wilcock was Labour M.P. for Derby 1945–50 and for Derby North from 1950 until his death in 1962.

[2] Pimm's No. 1 Cup, a ready-made cocktail, based on gin, to which may be added lemonade, ginger beer, and so on.

[3] The report of each day's Lords and Commons proceedings is colloquially known as Hansard. A Member may make small corrections to the transcript of his remarks only if, in the Editor's opinion, they do not substantially alter the meaning of what has been said in the House.

[4] Conservative M.P. for Flintshire 1945–50 and for West Flint 1950–70, when he became a life peer, taking the title Lord Rhyl. He was Parliamentary Under-Secretary at the Air Ministry 1951–2, Parliamentary Secretary at the Ministry of Defence 1952–4, Minister of Works 1954–5, Secretary of State for Air 1955–7 and Economic Secretary to the Treasury 1957–8, when he resigned with Peter Thorneycroft and Enoch Powell (see p. 653).

[5] Commons Standing Orders close the main business of the day (with some exceptions) at 10 p.m., or 4 p.m. on Fridays. (Since 1980 at 2.30 p.m.) The final speaker in a debate accordingly aims to finish his remarks at 10 p.m. precisely, immediately before the vote is taken.

good crack at Nye Bevan for doping the horse and so ensuring that it lost the race.

In the debate on the King's Speech to the new Session, opened on November 12th, 1946, the Labour Government was challenged by a large group of its own backbenchers. Those who criticized Mr Bevin's foreign policy for being too anti-Russian joined with those alleging that it was too pro-American, an Amendment was tabled calling for a 'democratic and constructive Socialist alternative to an otherwise inevitable conflict between American capitalism and Soviet Communism'. The motion was supported by fifty-five signatures.

At a Party Meeting on November 13th the Prime Minister rebuked these Members and, supported by a motion carried by three-quarters of those present, asked that the resolution be withdrawn. On November 18th, however, Mr Crossman moved the Amendment, demanding that the Cabinet disclose whether a tacit Anglo-American understanding in fact existed. Mr Bevin was absent and the Prime Minister answered, reminding Mr Crossman that the Foreign Secretary had repeatedly denied the existence of such an exclusive alliance and that the Soviet Government was unwilling to collaborate in similar co-operation with Britain.

Mr Crossman withdrew his Amendment but a decision was none the less pressed by two Independent Labour Party Members. Though the Amendment was defeated by 353 votes to 0, 100 or so Labour backbenchers abstained from supporting their leader, and the 'rebels' were censured at a Party Meeting ten days later.

The ostentatious abstention of the Bevanites in the division was the first of its kind since the debate on the King's Speech in November 1946. It may have told against us a little but on that occasion, too, I was the chief speaker. These things are remembered in the Party. I had hoped we would get nearer 100 abstentions than the 60 odd that we got but, on the other hand, our vote of 57 against the White Paper was 12 higher than my highest anticipation. On the other hand, many of those who voted for us upstairs, in secret – John Edwards, Arthur Blenkinsop,[1] Wilf Paling[2] – voted with the Government.

It was a distinctly unpleasant atmosphere, since we ostentatiously abstained on the official Amendment, whereas the rest of the Party ostentatiously abstained when we voted against the Tories. Nothing could have been designed to make the division sharper and what made it worse was that the vast majority of the Party were convinced by our arguments, contemptuous of the behaviour of Attlee and Shinwell and therefore all the more vindictive towards us for putting them in this terrible position.

[1] Labour M.P. for Newcastle-upon-Tyne East 1945–59 and for South Shields 1964–79. He was Parliamentary Secretary at the Ministry of Health 1949–51.

[2] Wilfred Paling (1887–1971), a colliery check weighman, was Labour M.P. for Doncaster 1922–31, for Wentworth 1933–50 and for Dearne Valley 1950–9. He was Parliamentary Secretary to the Ministry of Pensions 1941–5 and to the Minister of Pensions 1945–7, and Postmaster-General 1947–50.

Thursday, March 6th

This morning's papers made the most of the split. Actually it hasn't all that much significance, since, after all, the three Ministers who resigned in '51,[1] could not have been expected to change their minds over the last twelve months, any more than those who had not resigned could have been expected to do so. On this issue, a clash was unavoidable. On the other hand, when the Budget comes,[2] it may well be that we shall all get together on opposing the Butler cuts, though, even here, I am quite sure the Tories are going to use to the very full the argument that Attlee cannot oppose the cuts and support defence. Once again there will be resentment from those who have put themselves in this ridiculous position against those of us who have not.

Monday, March 10th

Looking back on what has happened since I last wrote in this diary, one realizes how confused and muddled politics are. When the Group met last Tuesday (the day before the defence debate), there was a good deal of anxiety that, if we merely abstained and voted against, the press would hardly notice our action and we should not register our point of view.[3] By Thursday afternoon it was clear that we had been noticed all right and that the Labour Party was in the middle of its biggest political crisis since 1931.[4] What had happened of course, was that a crisis had in fact been created by the press treatment of the voting as a major Bevanite revolt, a deliberate test of strength and an assault on the Labour leadership and, in particular, by the vicious *Daily Herald* leading article against the Bevanites.

What really made this split was the fact that the events of Tuesday morning's Party Meeting were thoroughly leaked to the press, with the full details of an annihilating rout of the Bevanites. So, when the Bevanite vote on the floor came out far higher than the vote at the so-called secret meeting upstairs and the press blew it all up, Attlee was forced to look for disciplinary action.

In the late afternoon[5] I went down to the House. As I was leaving, at a quarter to eight, I passed in the Central Lobby Jim Callaghan, who had been our chief speaker on the Naval Estimates, then proceeding. 'Had a good knock-down struggle against the Tories, I expect?' I said to him. Guilelessly, I think, he replied, 'No, as a matter of fact, Jim Thomas[6] could find nothing

---

[1] See above, Introduction, p. 26.

[2] This was due to be published on March 11th. See below, p. 94.

[3] See above, p. 83.

[4] When Ramsay MacDonald, failing to secure Labour Party support for cuts in Government expenditure, formed a National Government in coalition with Conservative and Liberal Members, splitting the Labour Party.

[5] I.e. Thursday, March 6th.

[6] James Thomas, Conservative M.P. for Hereford 1931–56. He served as P.P.S. to J. H. Thomas and Anthony Eden in the 1930s and then as a Lord Commissioner of the Treasury 1940–3, Financial Secretary to the Admiralty 1943–5, and as First Lord of the Admiralty 1951–6. He was raised to the peerage in 1955, taking the title of Viscount Cilcennin. He died in 1960.

to criticize in what I had done.' Then he pulled himself together and said, 'You know, it's very difficult to have friendly relations in this situation.' 'What situation?' 'Well, after the appalling things you've done, working in that way as a conspiratorial group.' 'Jim,' I said, 'you were for two years a member of the Keep Left Group and chiefly responsible for conspiring to reduce the term of military service from eighteen months to twelve.'[1] Jim has some charm. 'Look here,' he said, 'I seem to be talking to you friendlily after all. But what else could we do after your ultimatum?' 'What ultimatum?' 'This letter you sent to the Parliamentary Committee.' 'My dear James,' I said, 'that was a letter which suggested that the whole Party could now unite in opposing the Churchill Defence Estimates, since the situation had entirely changed. Don't you remember the text?' Though he very obviously didn't, he remarked, 'Well, I'm afraid we took it as an ultimatum.' 'We sent it to Attlee on Thursday afternoon. Why didn't one of you take the trouble to see one of us in the five days after that?' 'Oh, the Parliamentary Committee first saw the letter on Monday afternoon and, since it was an ultimatum, we thought there would have to be a showdown.'

As a matter of interest, this was the text of the letter:[2]

Dear Clem,

The undersigned are anxious lest the most important debate on German rearmament, which is to be continued at next Tuesday's Party Meeting, may prevent consideration of the Party's attitude to the Defence White Paper. We believe that it is vital for the Party to move a reasoned Amendment to the White Paper, if it is to be able effectively to sustain its campaign against the cuts in the social services and the standard of living. Such an Amendment we feel should not be a mere tactical manoeuvre such as that moved by the Tories last year,[3] but should make a reasoned case on which continuous and consistent opposition can be mobilized against the Budget.

Moreover, as you recently reminded the Party, you yourself, when you announced the revised rearmament plan in January 1951,[4] were careful to list the limiting conditions for the fulfilment of that programme within three years and you made it clear that, if these conditions were not fulfilled,

[1] In March 1947 the Labour Government proposed the Second Reading of a Bill to introduce 'National Service', in order to build up a trained reserve in support of the then seriously depleted regular forces. Provision was made for exemption or deferment, on grounds of hardship or conscientious objection; otherwise, men between eighteen and twenty-six were to be liable for eighteen months' full-time service and five and a half years with the reserves. Crossman moved an Amendment to reduce service to one year. The Bill was supported by the Conservative Opposition but not by the Liberals and in the division on April 1st it secured 386 votes to 85. Of the objectors, 72 were Labour Members. Two days later the Government announced their decision to cut the term of service to a year, 'as a result of the debate and after consultation with the Chiefs of Staff'.

[2] See p. 82. The text of the letter is included in Crossman's original dictated diary. No date is given and the signatories are not listed.

[3] On February 15th, 1951, the Opposition had moved their lack of confidence in the Government's competence. The motion was defeated by 308 votes to 287.

[4] See the Introduction, p. 25.

the programme would have to be spread over a longer period. We feel that your warning has been amply confirmed by events during the last twelve months, not only in Britain but in France and other countries, and we attach for your consideration a draft of a reasoned Amendment, which would enable the Party to clarify its position in the new situation.

We have, of course, sent a copy of this letter, according to normal routine, to Carol Johnson,[1] but, in view of the importance of the subject, we felt it right to approach you personally on it, so that, if you thought fit, it could be considered not only by the Parliamentary Committee, but also at next Tuesday's Party Meeting or, if necessary, at a specially summoned Party Meeting.

On Friday I caught the 3.15 to Chesterfield, where I was to address a meeting in the constituency of George Benson,[2] a respected, elderly Member of extreme caution and Lib-Lab views. I found the meeting was at Staveley, an adjoining town, and discovered there a Press Association reporter who, rather mysteriously, had been sent down from London on an earlier train. I had a word with him beforehand to ask him why the P.A. hadn't used their local man. He said he had no idea.

It was a full hall and a friendly audience, but dead silent. I spoke for fifty minutes, outlining, first, the precise developments in Parliament, with our letter to Attlee, the Party Meeting, etc., etc., and then dealing with the substance of the dispute. I got a tremendous ovation from an audience which had gradually warmed up. Then Benson rose and said, 'You've just listened to one of the most brilliant speeches you are ever likely to hear. I've heard it three times in the last two days and, of course, he's made it better each time by leaving out the bits which didn't go down. All I'd like to say to you is that it didn't persuade four-fifths of the Parliamentary Labour Party.' (Dead silence.) 'We are determined that rearmament should go on.' (Deader silence.)

Then we all had drinks at a pub and suddenly I found that Benson had disappeared. I went back to the hotel and had a drink with the press man, who told me he'd filed 1,200 words. This surprised me, until, ten minutes later, I was rung up by the *Daily Express* to ask whether I had said that Aneurin Bevan was 'not *seething* with ambition to overthrow Attlee' or 'not *seeking* with ambition to overthrow Attlee'. Then the P.A. man was rung to tell him he'd scored a scoop, with double banner headlines in the *Express* and the *Mail*. I said to him, 'What the hell have you done? Have I committed a blob?' 'No,' he said, 'I gave them the full details of your negotiations.' And so it was when I bought the papers on the station on Saturday morning. Simply because this was the first Bevanite speech before the weekend, the

---

[1] Carol Johnson, Secretary of the Parliamentary Labour Party 1943–50, was Labour M.P. for Lewisham South 1959–74.

[2] George Benson (1889–1973) was Labour M.P. for Chesterfield 1929–31 and 1935–64. He was knighted in 1958.

P.A. had presumably selected me and decided to give the speech in full. Certainly no speech of mine has ever before been covered so thoroughly and thank heavens that a completely impromptu fifty-minute speech from notes contained nothing embarrassing.

Zita met me at Luton Station or, rather, forced her way through the throng of Arsenal supporters arriving for the Cup Tie[1] and we drove back through exquisite Chiltern spring weather to Radnage to do a little hedging.[2]

Yesterday Tommy Balogh and Dudley Seers motored over to see me. To tell the truth, I was extremely worried and depressed, since I really hate political crises and was very nervous about what Aneurin would say that evening. But Tommy assured me that Nye and Jennie had both said to him last week that on no account would they permit themselves to be expelled from the Party. However, I don't really trust Tommy on such things and was not unduly surprised to find, on the way up to London this morning, that the lead story was Nye's speech, headlined, 'I Refuse to Recant or Give Any Assurance'.[3]

At the *Statesman* I found both Kingsley and Aylmer Vallance[4] away with flu. John Freeman agreed with me that Nye should really not have committed us to such an extreme position before we had discussed it. So I rang up Michael Foot and the three of us lunched together. Over the weekend I had come to the conclusion that we should be prepared to give almost any assurance demanded of us by the Party Meeting but to give it under protest, explaining that we were willing to agree in advance to vote against our convictions only in order not to split the Party or, rather, in order to prevent the leadership expelling the Socialist militants and so getting their way. I had come to the conclusion that their main object was to split the Bevanites into the inner clique who could be ousted along with Aneurin, and the majority, who would toe the line. Such a split would make the Left wholly impotent. I spent the morning at the *Statesman* trying to draft such a letter.

At lunch we found Michael Foot assuming that we would all have to be expelled. We spent lunch plugging my line, reaching the point where Michael's journalistic zeal was stirred by my suggestion that this letter, when published, would find a place in the history of British pamphleteering. At last he agreed to ring Nye, who had just got back from South Wales, and we all went over to see him at his house.

Such discussions are very difficult to describe, even two hours afterwards, without a subjective interpretation. Michael remained silent throughout and

[1] Arsenal played Luton in the sixth round of the Football Association Cup on March 8th.

[2] Where in the late 1940s Crossman and his second wife had moved to a country cottage, Town End Farm. Crossman's expertly 'laid' hedges may still be seen there, thirty years later.

[3] In a weekend speech in his constituency Bevan said, 'if you think what you did was right, you cannot promise not to do what you think right again'. See Michael Foot, *Aneurin Bevan* (London: Davis-Poynter, 1973), vol. 2, pp. 364–5.

[4] A journalist and author, he was Financial Editor of the *New Statesman and Nation* 1937–9 and Assistant Editor after the war until his death in 1955.

John gave me virtually no assistance. So it became a dialogue. Nye seemed, at the beginning, to assume that we were going to be expelled and I made him spell out what this meant. Yes, we should be most unlikely to get the decision reversed at this year's Conference.[1] Yes, it would mean setting up a separate Socialist Party organization. Yes, it would mean fights in every constituency.

DICK: And where would our money come from?
NYE: Oh, one shouldn't worry, and Trades Councils would help us. And then we could split the Unions and get the dock-workers' section of the T. & G. on our side.[2]

I said, I'm afraid rather coldly, that I thought this was optimistic, where-upon Nye retorted, 'But this all comes of trying to look ahead so far.' I said, 'But you've really got to face the consequences of your actions. And anyway, how many of the fifty-seven would follow you? Twenty? I doubt it.'

NYE: Well, that sort of realism is sheer defeatism and if you start with that sort of mood we shall be licked before we begin.
DICK: Maybe, but what I resent, and I am not the only one, is that you should have committed us in your speech last night to refuse to sign any assurance and to contemplate leaving the Party.
NYE: I didn't commit anyone. I was speaking for myself.
DICK: Now you can't get away with that. I haven't got suicide mania and I don't intend to get expelled, which is just what they want to do to us.

After a lot more sparring, I said to him, 'Now, let me tell you what I would do and explain my tactic of giving the assurance and protesting.' At this point Nye suddenly said, 'But this is just what my whole speech was about yester-day. I made it clear that, if we had to accept the majority decision, they would have to publish the results of Party Meetings.'
From this point the conversation suddenly became constructive and we began to work out the following line. First, any assurance to carry out majority decisions could not be permitted to remove a Member's right of abstention because of conscientious conviction. This right would justify our action last Wednesday in abstaining from voting for the Labour Amendment. Secondly, an assurance that we should carry out all majority decisions could, however, involve us in voting against the Tories when the majority wanted to abstain. In this event we should have to reserve the right, while abstaining with the majority, to explain to our constituents that this abstention was a decision taken upstairs,[3] against our advice.
We all agreed that the great thing this evening would be to keep the Group together and then to keep the fifty-seven together, by turning their attention

[1] The Labour Party's annual Conference was to be held at Morecambe, from September 29th to October 3rd. See below, pp. 147–53.
[2] Transport and General Workers' Union.
[3] I.e. in the Party Meeting.

to winning the decision at the Party Meeting tomorrow and by telling them that they must postpone any decision on 'what to do if ... ' until the 'if' ceases to be hypothetical. Nye revealed that Wilf Fienburgh[1] was suggesting new elections to the Parliamentary Committee in order to include the Bevanites. We ended by affirming that we should not let ourselves be tricked into procedural disputes and away from the main debate on the real issues, on which we had been doing so well on the floor of the House.

I am not sure who persuaded whom. Certainly Nye scored me off at one point, when I was sketching a draft letter of reply, which included the sentence, 'We consider it wrong for a Member to vote against his convictions but we are willing to do this, under orders, in order to prevent a greater wrong.' 'How will that sort of casuistry go down with our Nonconformists?' he said. And he was quite right. I had seen the issue in the form of giving a promise and getting out of it. He had seen the issue in the form of defiantly refusing to give a promise, in the hope of bluffing them into not enforcing it. Between the two there is a golden mean, which I think we may have reached in our discussions. But, for the life of me, I still don't know whether Nye contemplates being expelled or not. I think he probably feels that in order not to be expelled, he has to contemplate being expelled, whereas I think that, in order not to be expelled, one has to avoid giving the other people a chance to expel one.

At the Group meeting in the evening, the atmosphere was a little strained and Nye was very careful to concentrate discussion on what should be the line tomorrow. There was no direct reference to his statement in his constituency on Sunday night but Barbara Castle and Harold Wilson made it fairly clear that they wanted caution and so did the Group, when it asked for John Freeman to speak first and when it suggested that I should also speak. Indeed, the suggestion that Nye should speak came rather late. I think he was very quick to observe this.

Tuesday, March 11th
The Party Meeting was pretty accurately reported in the press. It began with a rather sentimental appeal by Bob Mellish,[2] the Catholic docker, for unity, restraint and respect for majority decisions. This was followed by an equally sentimental appeal on behalf of the fifty-seven by Manuel,[3] one of our

[1] Wilfred Fienburgh worked in the Labour Party Research Department 1947–51 and was Secretary of the Labour Party Policy Committee. He was Labour M.P. for North Islington from 1951 until his death in 1958, and was the author of a posthumously published novel about an M.P., *No Love for Johnnie* (London: Hutchinson, 1959).
[2] Labour M.P. for the Rotherhithe division of Bermondsey 1946–50 and for Bermondsey since February 1950. He was later to work closely with Crossman as Joint Parliamentary Secretary at the Ministry of Housing 1964–7, from which he went on to become Minister of Public Building and Works in 1969 and Labour Chief Whip, a post he held in both Government and Opposition from 1969 to 1976.
[3] Labour M.P. for Ayrshire and Bute 1950–5 and 1964–70.

Scottish working-class Members. Then came a terrible speech by A. J. Irvine[1] (who had apparently been so good at the meeting of the fifty-seven last night, after I had to go off to do a broadcast, but who just couldn't get away with quoting Burke[2] at length), and a violent attack by Percy Daines, West Ham Co-op[3] on all nefarious groups.

Nye started by raising the temperature with a series of rather wild knock-about attacks. I fancy his purpose was to push Attlee off his perch and get him down on a level.[4] If that was the tactic, it succeeded, since the two got into a slanging match. Then, when the Meeting was nearly breaking up in disorder, Nye suddenly switched to quite a different line, accepting the neces-sity for Standing Orders, reading out the letter we had written to Attlee a week before the defence debate,[5] showing there was no plot and arguing that there was a deliberate attempt to throw out the minority. This caused more bad blood but, unpleasant and unpopular as it was, it did somehow get across the point that Attlee was at least as much to blame.

At this point George Strauss and John Strachey moved the mediating amendment, which deleted any censure of the fifty-seven, removed the demand for an unqualified assurance from each of them and merely recom-mended that the Party should work out and adopt Standing Orders to prevent undisciplined revolts. John Freeman then spoke quietly, saying we could not vote against this but asking for an extension of the definition of conscience. Quite unexpectedly, Tom O'Brien,[6] after expressing undying loyalty to Attlee, made a devastating attack on the ineptness of the leadership in the foreign affairs and defence debates. He said that he had been led to expect a Roman holiday with the press but his impression was that there were more martyrs than lions about and that any attempt to expel the fifty-seven would mean that the whole Party had decided to commit political suicide. Tom made it clear that the trade unions thought that a split would lead to the disruption of the unions and also that the union leaders thought the Labour Party leadership was using its disciplinary powers extremely ineffectively.

After this there was some pressure that Attlee should accept the com-promise amendment[7] but he refused to do so and, in a very poor speech, demanded that his own motion be carried. It was defeated by 2 to 1. If

[1] A barrister and Labour M.P. for the Edge Hill division of Liverpool from September 1947 until his death in 1979. He was knighted in 1967.

[2] Edmund Burke (1729–97), the Irish philosopher and statesman.

[3] In fact, Labour/Co-operative M.P. for *East* Ham North from 1951 until his death in March 1957.

[4] Mr Attlee moved a resolution condemning the fifty-seven and calling for the reimposi-tion of the Party's Standing Orders, suspended in 1945. He called for a signed pledge from all Party Members that they would abide by majority decisions of the Party Meeting.

[5] See pp. 88–9.

[6] Labour M.P. for Nottingham West 1945–50, North-West 1950–5, and West 1955–9. He was on the General Council of the T.U.C. 1940–70 and its President in 1952 and 1953 and was General Secretary of the National Association of Theatrical and Kiné Employees from 1932 until his death in 1970. He was knighted in 1956.

[7] The mediatory Amendment was carried by 162 votes to 73.

Attlee had accepted the amendment, no one would have won. But, by court-
ing a sensational defeat from the floor in order to get a vote of censure, he
did confirm the suspicion that the splitters, if there were any, were on the
Right. Among those whom I saw voting for extreme measures were Tony
Crosland, Douglas Jay, Patrick Gordon Walker,[1] Woodrow Wyatt and Roy
Jenkins, as well as the whole Parliamentary Committee.

We certainly felt that it was a triumph and celebrated it in the Smoking
Room with Tom O'Brien. The fact is that, without Bevin to advise him, Attlee
has completely misjudged the attitude of the unions, which realistically
assess the strength of Bevanism in the rank and file. In this meeting Attlee's
support was almost exclusively middle-class.

*Crossman does not go on to describe the other major event on March 11th, the
presentation of the Budget. The Chancellor's theme was 'solvency, security and
incentive'. Food subsidies were cut from £410 to £250 million; to meet consumers' increased costs, changes were made in taxation, pensions and allowances. Earned income allowances were raised for single and married persons
and for children and rates of taxation were reduced on income immediately
above the exempted levels.*

*Altogether some 2 million wage-earners were removed from taxable cate-
gories. Family allowances were raised from 5s. to 8s. a week, war pensions
increased and measures were promised for improved old age and military long-
service pensions. These increases came to £80 million in a full year and remissions
in tax to £228 million.*

*This total exceeded by some £150 million the sum saved from food subsidies.
Offsetting revenue was to be produced by an excess profits levy (chargeable at
30 per cent net on profits above the average for 1947–9). Petrol duty was raised
by 7½d. a gallon, car tax and entertainment tax were increased. There was to be
complex reform of purchase tax (coupled with the abolition of the wartime
'utility goods' system). Bank rate increased from 2·5 to 4 per cent.*

*Crossman's comment (in a diary entry for March 13th) was only: 'Has
Butler misjudged the number of income-tax-conscious earners, as against food-
price-conscious women? That is the question.' But his own preoccupations were
with the Party's internal wrangling.*

Wednesday, March 19th

The Standing Orders Party Meeting was a dreary shambles, with the first

[1] Labour M.P. for Smethwick 1945–64 and for Leyton from 1966 to 1974, when he
became a life peer, taking the title of Lord Gordon-Walker. He had been Herbert
Morrison's P.P.S. in 1946, and had served as Parliamentary Under-Secretary of State at
the Commonwealth Relations Office 1947–50 and as Secretary of State 1950–1. In October
1964 he became Foreign Secretary but was obliged to relinquish that office in January 1965,
when he failed to win a by-election at Leyton. In 1967 he became Minister without Portfolio and from 1967 to 1968 he served as Secretary of State for Education and Science. He
was a Member of the European Parliament 1975–6. His major work, *The Cabinet*
(London: Cape), was published in 1970.

hour and a half spent on a point of procedure. Last week the moderate resolution had been in favour of newly drafted Standing Orders. Attlee's first action was to ask for a formal vote revoking the suspension of Standing Orders in 1945. Within a minute or two it dawned on us that to revoke the suspension of the old Standing Orders was to bring them into force at once and, later, Morrison revealed the tactic by saying that this would hurry up the Party's decision on the new Standing Orders. What the platform had calculated was that the Bevanites might spin out the discussion on the new Orders for weeks, whereas we would have no purpose in doing so if the old Orders were already in force. It was a quarter to twelve before a vote was forced and carried by 103 to 66 in favour of the platform. They really are to be congratulated on a very smart trick, which we had not foreseen and for which I do not blame them.

We passed to a Second Reading discussion of the new draft, in which Charlie Pannell,[1] an obstreperous, vulgar A.E.U. Member, got on his hind legs. Usually he goes down very badly but this time he spoke on the conscience clause and quoted, with tremendous effect, Arthur Henderson's remark in 1931[2] that, though he could tolerate conscientious objection, he could not tolerate it when it was organized with the Whips on. Pannell went on to lambast secret groups, to tremendous cheers, whereat Walter Padley,[3] General Secretary of USDAW, called Pannell a liar because he had not been whipped into the lobby with us.[4] However, Pannell did get his point across and indicated that a week's very intensive lobbying had been done to make the majority of the Party feel they were voting against a secret group.

In the Smoking Room afterwards, Geoffrey Bing said to me that we might disband the Bevanites. This surprised me and I said, 'If you do that, after this morning's meeting, every newspaper will headline our complete surrender.' Whatever the disadvantages of having a Group, you can't stop having one just at the moment when you are ordered to do so and, if we did, our constituency supporters would be appalled. One of the great difficulties of politics is to harmonize what is required to get on with your Parliamentary colleagues and what is required for the rank and file in the constituencies. They are two such completely separate worlds.

Before dinner I had a small incident with Nye. We were in the Smoking

[1] Labour M.P. for West Leeds from 1949 until 1974, when he became a life peer. He was Minister of Public Building and Works 1964–6. He died in 1980.

[2] Arthur Henderson (1863–1935), Labour M.P. for the Barnard Castle division of Durham 1903–18, for Widnes 1919–22, for Newcastle 1923, for Burnley 1924–31 and for Clay Cross from 1933 until his death. He was Chairman of the Parliamentary Labour Party 1908–10 and 1914–17, Minister without Portfolio in the War Cabinet 1916–18, Home Secretary 1924 and Foreign Secretary 1929–31. There appears to be no public record of this remark. It was probably made in private conversation or at a private meeting.

[3] President of the Union of Shop, Distributive and Allied Workers 1948–64 and Labour M.P. for Ogmore division of Mid-Glamorgan 1950–79. He was Minister of State for Foreign Affairs 1964–7.

[4] In the division on March 6th Charles Pannell did not vote with the fifty-seven.

Room with Harold Wilson, Ian Mikardo and others, and Nye was complaining to me that his throat and chest were so bad that he doubted whether he could get to Wallsend this weekend. He is to address a monster demonstration and all the tickets have already been sold. Then he turned to me and said, 'Can you take my place?', which, for him, is a very generous act. I saw Harold Wilson looking rather bleak.

Thursday, March 20th

Phil Zec came round for a drink to tell me that, on his own suggestion, he was ceasing to be Editor of the *Pic* and Hugh Cudlipp was coming back from the *Express*. It is just two years since Cudlipp was sacked from the *Pic* for spiking a story sent by Cecil King, now the Chairman of the Directors, from Nigeria, where he happened to be during the riots.[1] Cudlipp received £11,000, under his contract, for being sacked and now he comes back. Phil Zec gets promoted without being sacked, so he receives no tax-free £11,000. These are the finances of Fleet Street.

It is very difficult to judge the politics of the *Mirror* Group but there is very little doubt that Zec did not want to be Editor of the *Sunday Pic* very much and certainly he didn't want to become a permanent Editor. So it looks as though he really did arrange the whole thing and is not merely being kicked upstairs.

What will Cudlipp be like after two years on the *Sunday Express*? Actually he interfered far less with my column than Zec has done but that was because Cudlipp took it less seriously and also because he doesn't happen to be a serious-minded Socialist.

From March 21st to March 25th Crossman was in Berlin, delivering a lecture to a group of politicians and journalists and investigating conditions there. (His New Statesman and Nation *article is to be found in the issue of March 29th.)*

Negotiations were under way in Bonn, over the transformation of Western Germany from an occupied territory into an independent ally, and in Paris, on the form of the European Defence Community. On March 10th the Russian Government addressed a Note to the Western Powers, proposing a German peace treaty. In effect, the Note offered Germany unification and the right to limited national forces, on condition that she did not become a member of the Western defence system.

On March 25th, after consultation with Dr Adenauer, the Western Powers replied. They objected to the proposal that the future united Germany should be precluded from belonging to the Western defence system, and in any case, they insisted that free elections were an indispensable requirement for the establishment of any all-German Government with which a treaty could be negotiated. The reply suggested that the conditions for holding such elections

[1] See p. 56.

should be investigated by the U.N. Commission established for exactly that purpose in December 1951.

Tuesday, March 25th

I left Berlin at a quarter to nine this morning, getting home just before two o'clock, to find Bertie Russell[1] had arrived to be taken for a walk by Zita. I rapidly dictated an article for the *Statesman* on Berlin, finishing just in time to get to a joint meeting of the defence and foreign affairs groups. This meeting opened with a rambling speech by Shinwell and then there came quite a sensible discussion, centring on the Russian proposal for a Four-Power conference to consider an independent, armed Germany.

This meeting showed the extraordinary situation prevailing in the Parliamentary Labour Party. Seventy people were there and seventy people, in a general debate, without any preliminary preparation, cannot achieve a policy decision. The Russian Note was delivered eighteen days ago. In the sixteen days between its delivery and the publication of the Western Powers' reply, no one, either at Transport House or in Westminster, was competent to work out the Labour Party's reaction or to put forward our suggestions as to what the Three-Power reply should be. Now that a very negative Three-Power reply has been given, we are in no position to give a Socialist reaction to it.

The fact is that the whole P.L.P. and, in particular, its leadership has been geared since 1940 to Government in which Cabinet Ministers take decisions after consulting civil servants. Now that we are in Opposition there are no civil servants to consult and, now that decisions have to be taken by the whole P.L.P., we simply are not organized to take any decisions at all. As a result, no policy decisions are taken. I talked to Hector McNeil[2] and one or two others about whether we could not try to get the Foreign Affairs Committee in shape by having a small steering committee, which should meet at least twice a week before foreign affairs questions came up and which should prepare papers and at least formulations of the problem to be presented to the committee. Hector and Dalton are mildly sympathetic but all say that Clem Attlee is not prepared to do anything. The situation with regard to foreign policy applies to every other form of policy. There is no machinery for making the Labour Opposition a real fighting Opposition, with a policy. Nor does there seem to be any machinery for organizing parliamentary tactics. This evening, for instance, I learnt that the Lancashire M.P.s are to stage an all-night sitting tomorrow as a protest against unemployment in the

[1] Bertrand Russell (1872–1976), the philosopher and campaigner for unilateral disarmament. He succeeded his brother as Earl Russell in 1931. In 1949 he was awarded the Order of Merit and he received the Nobel Prize for Literature in 1950. His numerous writings include *Principia Mathematica* (with A. N. Whitehead, Oxford University Press, 1910), *History of Western Philosophy* (London: Allen & Unwin, 1946), and a three-volume autobiography (London: Allen & Unwin, 1967–9).

[2] Labour M.P. for Greenock 1941–55 and P.P.S. to Philip Noel-Baker 1942–5. He served at the Foreign Office as Parliamentary Under-Secretary 1945–6 and as Minister of State 1946–50, and was Secretary of State for Scotland 1950–1. He died in 1955.

textile industries.[1] This happened because the Parliamentary Committee could not accept the resolution that the M.P.s drafted and then the M.P.s turned down the Parliamentary Committee's own resolution.

Meanwhile I had picked up news of the Party Meeting this morning, at which the new Standing Orders were agreed, but with a considerably improved conscience clause. Nye was not there and I gather the whole thing went through fairly all right. I share John Freeman's view that the precise form of Standing Orders is not a matter of vital importance, since the majority always has the right to expel us and the real issue is whether they will use that right and whether we shall provide them with sufficient provocation to use it.

Thursday, March 27th
The whole of this week has been curiously flat. The controversy over the sensational Bevanite split has all petered out, as all controversies do, and what is clearer than ever is that the parliamentary Opposition is almost entirely leaderless and without drive or energy.

Monday, April 7th
At the Fabian dinner tonight Nye made a typical and extremely brilliant speech, in which he gave the philosophical case against any form of Socialist blueprints or programmes. One can plan and predict the normal social pattern but political leadership is a catalyst, which creates new patterns, and, therefore, the left-wing party which clings to programmes will not take the opportunity of change. It's a good excuse for not planning anything ahead and I dare say Aneurin would make quite a good job of dealing empirically with an emergency if he got the chance. Anyway, he said it so nicely that two bishops who were present fell in love with him.

Thursday, April 10th
Finding Herbert Morrison sitting lonely in the dining room today, I sat down with him and found him almost relieved to have some company. He straightaway said to me that the Tory backbenchers were playing the same disruptive role in Parliament as the Bevanites.[2] This only confirms my view

[1] In February 1952 unemployment had risen to 1·9 per cent of the working population and the increase fell mainly in the Lancashire textile industry. The slump in textiles was debated on March 26th, when Opposition Members demanded the modification or abolition of the purchase-tax provisions as applied to textiles. On April 7th, in the debate on the Finance Bill, this application was made again, supported this time by Conservative Members from the constituencies affected. The Chancellor rejected the proposal but announced the authorization of £20–£25 million of Government orders, as a form of 'practical assistance'.

[2] During the preceding fortnight Labour backbenchers had used procedural tactics to harass the Government during the Committee Stages of the annual Army Act and of the National Health Service Bill. Conservative backbenchers had been pressing the Government to abolish or amend purchase tax on textiles and to speed up the denationalization of the steel and transport industries. For George Wigg's efforts to harass the Conservatives with procedural 'Wiggery-Pokery', see Wigg, *George Wigg* (London: Michael Joseph, 1972) p. 161 ff.

that the two Front Benches were quite ready to collaborate or, at least, to pull their punches. But the impetus of partisanship during this week has made this impossible. The practical skill of Bing and the parliamentary leadership of Bevan and those of us round him have pulled the Labour Party into an all-out Opposition, resented by the Front Bench but which the constituency parties undoubtedly approve of. Equally, the Tory backbenchers have now forced their Front Bench to commit themselves to a policy of dismantling Socialism, which can only lead us into a head-on party collision, lasting over months.

I have no doubt that a vast number of sensible, independent people will regret this. But it seems to me that you must either have an honest to God coalition or else you must have hard-hitting party politics. Since there was no chance whatsoever of a genuine coalition, it was far better to break up the under-the-counter coalition and this is just what has happened this week.

This morning at half-past ten we had a special meeting of the Bevanite Group. As we seemed to have been up every night till two or three in the morning and many of our provincial Members wanted to get home, it was natural but disappointing that only ten people turned up. But they happened to include all the inner group. Nye, who has not been attending the Group meetings for two or three weeks, did what I expected. He indicated that he thought the Group should cease to be exclusive and a long discussion followed on how to retain cohesion and leadership for Bevanism and yet to avoid the obloquy of being a secret cabal inside the Parliamentary Party.

Nye has never liked the cliquiness of a closely knit group, such as Ian Mikardo delights in organizing. Moreover, as Nye always resents any ideas of seriously thinking out policy, he instinctively rejects the *raison d'être* of the Group, which is precisely to think out policy. On the other hand, he wants support and I think he was very genuinely trying this morning to face the difficulty that, if we break up the Group or invite just anybody to join it, we destroy something valuable but that, if we continue as we are, we are bound to remain small and resented.

The conclusion was that we should propose to a full meeting after the Recess that, in our view, we should let it be known that anybody who is like-minded with us will be welcome at 1.30 each Tuesday. When Nye saw that certain members were really keen on retaining the Group, he managed to convince himself that this tactical device would destroy our unpopularity in the Parliamentary Party but that, after five or six weeks, we would be meeting just the same as ever, with roughly the same numbers. In an impossible situation this was probably the best solution, since we shall now get what he always wanted, the small, informal inner clique really doing the policy thinking, in so far as Nye wants any policy thinking to take place.

There is no doubt that the row over the defence debate was a great setback for us but that since then things have been moving our way very fast inside the Parliamentary Party and in the constituencies, not because of ourselves —

indeed, a good deal in spite of our personalities – but because of the political vacuum of the present leadership.

This afternoon I had my last Thursday meeting with Zec, whose mind is now full of promotions and other schemes. Hugh Cudlipp will be back at work on Tuesday. After doing a broadcast tomorrow evening, I shall get three days' holiday, my first full weekend since February 15th. I had a day and half on March 8th and 9th but that was the weekend when we all thought that we were going to be expelled and it wasn't much holiday. I don't think I have been so tired for many, many months and what makes you tired isn't work, because I have, on the whole, done less for some time, but nervous distraction.

Friday, April 25th
Easter was perfect and I spent the three days mowing the lawn, coming back on Tuesday for the *New Statesman*. On Wednesday Hugh Cudlipp lunched with me at the House and straightaway started by saying that the paper had been deplorably edited, is overstaffed and that everything would be changed, including shifting my column to p. 2.[1] He would be glad to have me working for him but all this Bevanism must stop. It had been a crime to hand the paper over to Mr Morrison for five years after 1945 and the same mistake was not now going to be made with Mr Bevan. Hugh had talked all of this over with Cecil King. I said that, if Hugh wanted a nice Front Bench type of writer, he should get Maurice Edelman and that, if he had a Bevanite writing, this was sometimes bound to come out in the column. To this Hugh replied that I should know perfectly well what he meant. It was a friendly but not completely cordial lunch. I gather that Hugh has turned the office upside-down and issued a whole series of sensational memoranda, which contain a good many insults to Phil Zec. But I dare say that it will all settle down in three or four weeks.

From April 17th to April 23rd Crossman was in Bonn with a Labour Party delegation to a conference with German and French Socialists. He also had private discussions, including two with Chancellor Adenauer. Crossman's account is to be found in the articles in the New Statesman and Nation *for May 3rd, 1952, pp. 514 and 516–17. Just before his departure for Germany he suffered an acute stomach upset, which was subsequently diagnosed as duodenitis.*

Tuesday, April 29th
For the last two days I have been trying to put across the ideas I learnt in Germany. Kingsley has let me do a signed leader on it and yesterday I spent one and a half hours with Hugh Dalton, who had just returned from leading

---

[1] Crossman's column generally appeared on p. 2 of the *Sunday Pictorial* but was occasionally moved to the front page when the Editor considered it particularly dramatic.

the Labour delegation to Bonn to discuss German rearmament with the French and German Socialists.[1] I then cross-referenced Hugh Dalton's account with Barbara Castle, who had also attended. Barbara says it's terrible being led by Hugh, since everybody despises him. The only thing is, he doesn't know it. All the same, he is no fool. Apparently the British and the Germans had immediately found themselves in agreement on the short-term issues. Both parties want to demand a Four-Power conference to consider the feasibility of genuinely free all-German elections. In order to prevent the Russians spinning the conference out unduly, the British and Germans think a time limit should be set. But, while this conference is going on, they hold that the signature and the ratification of the E.D.C. and the Contractual Agreement should be postponed. Apparently the French were very worried, since they are terrified of the Russian proposals for an independent Germany and regard E.D.C. as a lesser evil. Of course, there is no doubt that German national aspirations will grow with strength. What the French do not realize is that they will grow into violent forms if the Western powers seek to prevent the unification of Germany when there is any possibility of it. And that is just what railroading through E.D.C. without testing the Russian proposals, will actually mean. The National Executive is to hear Hugh Dalton's report tomorrow morning and the Parliamentary Party is to discuss the subject next Tuesday.

This afternoon Nye, who had just read my paper on Bonn[2] but who did not attend the Group meeting at half-past one, spent half an hour walking round the Terrace with me. He was still mainly concerned with the National Health Service.[3] Last week, at the Party Meeting, George Thomas[4] had asked that our spokesman on the Third Reading of the Bill should give an assurance that we would restore the cuts if we returned to power and the Parliamentary Committee had been unwilling to do this. This morning, Tuesday, after a meeting of the Parliamentary Party, Attlee made a highly equivocal statement, which no one could really understand. Bevan reminded Attlee that the Labour Government's charges for teeth and spectacles had been limited, by an Amendment conceded to the Party, to the three years of rearmament and that they were to lapse in 1954. Bevan asked why, if these charges were to

[1] A second Russian Note had been delivered on April 9th. It refused to admit the U.N. Investigatory Commission, maintaining that the issue concerned only the four occupying Powers. The Note reaffirmed the demand for Germany's exclusion from any grouping of Powers 'directed against any peace-loving State' and repeated Russian insistence that the eastern frontier of Germany was fixed, at Potsdam in 1945, on the Oder–Neisse line. The Note proposed a Four-Power conference to discuss the question of free all-German elections.

[2] Crossman also prepared a formal report of his visit.

[3] The National Health Service Bill received its Third Reading on May 1st, 1952.

[4] Labour M.P. for Central Cardiff 1945–50 and for West Cardiff since 1950. He was Joint Parliamentary Under-Secretary of State at the Home Office 1964–6, Minister of State at the Welsh Office 1966–7, and at the Commonwealth Office 1967–8, Secretary of State for Wales 1968–70, Chairman of Ways and Means 1974–6 and since 1976 has been Speaker of the House of Commons.

lapse in 1954, there was any difficulty in promising that the Tory charges would lapse at the same time. To this Attlee replied that this was what he had always meant. Of course, this makes utter nonsense of Gaitskell's pretence that the charges were necessitated by rearmament. Since the first lot were imposed last year, the rearmament programme has been extended from three years to four and will therefore reach its climax in 1955, one year after we promised to stop the charges. All this Nye described to me at great length.

We then briefly discussed who should stand for the National Executive this year. I said that neither Michael Foot nor I were keen to, though our names would be useful. Nye agreed that it would be a great mistake for us to get on, as journalists, and it looks as though he is unwilling to have a whole Bevanite slate run. In fact, he is in one of his cautious moods.

Thursday, May 1st

This has been a German week. The foreign affairs group met at six o'clock last night to continue its discussion of German rearmament. As the meeting began, the communiqué came through on the tape announcing the result of the meeting of the National Executive that morning. The Executive issued the following declaration:

> Steps should be taken without further delay by Her Majesty's Government, in association with the Governments of the United States and France, to hold a Four-Power conference with the Soviet Government, limited in the first instance to discussing the possibility of free elections throughout Germany and the means by which such freedom can be assured to the German people.
>
> The National Executive Committee declares that, in order to satisfy the fourth condition[1] laid down on behalf of the Labour Party by Mr Attlee — namely, that before any German rearmament is undertaken there must be agreement with the German people — fresh elections should be held in Western Germany before any commitment is undertaken by the Adenauer Government for a German contribution to the European Defence Community.
>
> The National Executive Committee expresses the hope that in the interests of Western European defence the United States will soon furnish to the French Army the arms and equipment already promised. Only if this is done can there be any possibility of satisfying the first condition in the Attlee declaration, namely, that the rearmament of members of the North Atlantic Treaty Organization must precede that of Germany.

This was a really clever piece of Daltonian politics.[2] Apparently he made

[1] See above, p. 57.

[2] This statement was publicly interpreted as signifying that the Labour leadership had no confidence in Dr Adenauer's Government and, in effect, supported West Germany's Social Democrat Opposition party.

his report on Bonn in such a persuasive form that the whole Executive almost automatically agreed, with the exception of Herbert Morrison, Jim Griffiths and Edith Summerskill. In fact, the vote was 20 to 3 and even then the three were only concerned that the matter should not be decided until the Parliamentary Party had discussed it.

This news was ticked out on the tape while Noel-Baker was making a most moving address to us on the need for integrating Western Germany into E.D.C. By an extraordinary irony, it is the Left of the Party which now supports the National Executive and the right-wingers are an indignant minority, who know perfectly well that they must abide by the decision of the Executive, come what may.

Today I lunched at the American Embassy with David Linebaugh[1] and the head of the English Desk in Washington.[2] They were really disturbed by the National Executive's communiqué, which they thought terribly destructive and rightly described as a complete reversal of Labour policy. There is no doubt that, just before the election, when Gaitskell and Morrison were in Ottawa and New York, they had completely accepted the American view that the Contractual Agreement and the E.D.C. must be put through, whatever the Russians did or said. No one can deny that the present Executive communiqué goes back on that policy, even if it does so by clinging to the four Attlee conditions. Last September the Labour Government certainly took the view that the four conditions were being perfectly fulfilled by integrating Germany into E.D.C. Now it not only demands a Four-Power conference but states that, even if the conference fails, German rearmament shall not be carried through till after a German election. As I made clear in my *New Statesman* article last week, this would mean killing E.D.C. altogether, since after this summer, as the German elections[3] approach, it is most unlikely that any German politician would dare to defend the present terms of E.D.C. and the Contractual Agreement. This whole question shows that it is worthwhile occasionally producing an *aide-mémoire*[4] for Hugh Dalton. But it will cause most frightful reactions and already, this evening, Shinwell and Morrison blew off their heads in the meeting of the Parliamentary Committee.

Meanwhile, as a touch of comedy, this afternoon Churchill announced the British delegation for Strasbourg.[5] The Labour team is headed by Alf

[1] John David Linebaugh, an American diplomat who served in the State Department from 1944 to 1971. His service included two London postings: November 1947–August 1949 and August 1950–August 1953.

[2] Robert Coe. His career in the State Department, from 1928 to 1952, included two London postings: April 1941–December 1945 and April 1946–May 1947. From April 1951 until his retirement in May 1952 he served with the Department in Washington.

[3] The German General Election was to be held on September 6th, 1953. See below, p. 266.

[4] Possibly the formal report of Crossman's visit to Bonn.

[5] Eighteen delegates, from the Conservative, Labour and Liberal Parties, were to attend the Consultative Assembly of the Council of Europe, meeting at Strasbourg on May 26th.

Robens, Patrick Gordon Walker, George Brown, George Darling,[1] Alice Bacon[2] and W. D. Ross.[3] I pointed out at the Party Meeting this evening that only one of the delegation's members, Patrick Gordon Walker, is sufficiently interested in foreign affairs to be a member of the foreign affairs group. There was a very awkward silence, since everyone knew that this was true and that this was the last piece of Mr Morrison's patronage as ex-Foreign Secretary.

Tuesday, May 6th

We went on Friday to Coventry for May Day, Zita by car and I by train, but my duodenum, which has been troubling me ever since Bonn, blew up on Friday night and I retired to Radnage and went to bed for the weekend, including Monday, only to be told today, when I went to Manor House Hospital,[4] that they would like me in as soon as possible. I was really quite relieved at the news, since a fortnight off during the Committee Stage of the Finance Bill is a great relief for somebody with a permanent stomach-ache and I can hope to get some reading and writing done.

Moreover, I had really completed what I wanted to do this morning, when the Parliamentary Party discussed Germany. This was a wildly funny meeting, which began with Attlee making a statement defending the Executive communiqué, and contriving to box the compass by arguing that it would strengthen the E.D.C. Then we had a number of really irritated and indignant right-wingers threatening to defy Standing Orders if it came to a vote in the House. I had the pleasure of starting my speech by assuring Fred Bellenger[5] and Freda Corbet[6] that, if they were a rebellious minority, I would defend them from my new position as a loyal supporter of the majority ruling. John Strachey managed to come out in favour of the National Executive statement, having been a leading advocate of our entering E.D.C. until a fortnight ago, and Philip Noel-Baker, who had opposed the National Executive at the Defence Committee, was put up to defend it this morning. Of course, part of the row is due to the press reaction, which has pointed out too clearly the shift in Labour policy on Germany which all this implies.

[1] Labour M.P. for Hillsborough 1950–74 and Minister of State at the Board of Trade 1964–8. He was created a life peer in 1974, taking the title of Lord Darling of Hillsborough.
[2] Labour M.P. for Leeds North-East 1945–55 and for Leeds South-East 1955–70. Chairman of the Labour Party 1950 and of the Labour Party Conference 1951, she was Minister of State at the Home Office 1964–7 and of Education and Science 1967–70. She was created a life peeress in 1970.
[3] William Ross, Labour M.P. for the Kilmarnock division of Ayrshire 1946–79. He was Secretary of State for Scotland 1964–70 and 1974–6 and was created a life peer in Mr Callaghan's 1979 Resignation Honours list.
[4] An independent hospital, to which trade unions and workingmen's clubs subscribed, situated in North London.
[5] Labour M.P. for Bassetlaw 1935–68. He was Financial Secretary to the War Office 1945–6 and Secretary of State for War 1946–7. He died in 1968.
[6] Freda Corbet (Mrs Ian Campbell) was Labour M.P. for North-West Camberwell (later the Peckham division of Camberwell) 1945–74.

The Allies' reply was delivered in Moscow on May 13th. It stated that they would prefer the U.N. Commission to establish whether impartial all-German elections were possible but that they would consider alternative suggestions. In their opinion, there was no purpose in discussing an all-German peace treaty until there existed a German Government to sign it and before it was known whether Russia would permit free elections in her zone of Germany. Meanwhile the Western Allies would continue their efforts to establish a European Defence Community, including the German Federal Republic.

Tuesday, May 20th

For nearly a fortnight I have been in Manor House Hospital, having my appendix out. Apparently I have been suffering from appendicitis ever since I flew to Germany on Thursday, April 17th, and I was really very exhausted when I got to the hospital. I took with me an enormous load of books and, as usual, read very few of them, apart from *The History of The Times*[1] dealing with the years from 1912 to 1939. What struck me was the enormous power of the press in politics before 1918 and its steady decline since then. Northcliffe[2] could really make and unmake Cabinet Ministers. He could get Lord Haldane[3] sacked simply by attacking him, whereas today, if Lord Beaverbrook or Lord Kelmsley[4] launch a campaign against a Cabinet Minister, the effect is usually to strengthen his position. Of course, the main influence of *The*

---

[1] *The History of The Times:* vol. 1: '*The Thunderer' in the Making 1785–1841*; vol. 2: *The Tradition Established; 1841–1884*; vol. 3: *The Twentieth Century Test: 1884–1912*; vol. 4: *The 150th Anniversary and Beyond:* Part 1: *1912–1920*; Part 2: *1921–1948* (London: *The Times*, 1935–52).

[2] A journalist and newspaper proprietor, Alfred Harmsworth (1865–1922) acquired his own publishing business in 1887, bought up the *Evening News* in 1894, and founded the *Daily Mail* in 1896 and the *Daily Mirror* in 1903, when he became a baronet. In 1905 he was raised to the peerage as Baron Northcliffe and in 1908 became chief proprietor of *The Times*. Northcliffe's papers were much involved in various campaigns relating to the First World War, which he claimed he had correctly predicted in the *Daily Mail*. He successfully pressed for both the foundation of a Ministry of Munitions and the removal of Haldane. In 1917 he was made a Viscount by Lloyd George, whose coalition of December 1916 he had welcomed. Northcliffe declined the post of Secretary of State for Air but served as Director of Propaganda in Enemy Countries from February to November 1918. After this he broke with Lloyd George, who denounced him in violent terms in the House of Commons in April 1919.

[3] Richard Haldane (1856–1928), a barrister, became a Q.C. in 1890 and served as Liberal M.P. for East Lothian from 1885 until 1911, when he was raised to the peerage as Viscount Haldane. He served in the Liberal Cabinet as Secretary of State for War from 1905 to 1912, in which year he undertook a Cabinet mission to Germany in an attempt to defuse the crisis in Anglo-German relations. Although he spoke fluent German, his mission failed. On his return he became Lord Chancellor, leading the House of Lords while the Marquis of Crewe was in India. In 1915 a violent agitation in the press accused Haldane of pro-German sympathies and, when Asquith re-formed his Government in May of that year, Haldane was not reappointed in the new coalition. Out of office his Liberal sympathies fell away and in the nine months of the first Labour Government in 1924 he again became Lord Chancellor. He continued to lead the Labour peers in the Lords until his death.

[4] James Gomer Berry (1883–1968) was Chairman of Kelmsley Newspapers Ltd and Editor in Chief of the *Sunday Times* 1937–59. He was created 1st Baron Kelmsley in 1936, and 1st Viscount in 1945.

Times in its day was in foreign affairs, where its leading articles were really studied as semi-official statements of British policy. But even here I cannot believe that it is taken nearly so seriously today as it was even as late as 1938, when just before Munich Dawson[1] proposed the secession of the Sudeten areas.

Part of the reason is, of course, the rise to power of the Labour Party, which tends to write off all newspapers as capitalist. A Labour Cabinet, for that reason, is not nearly as open to newspaper influence as a Conservative Cabinet. But the basic reason for the change is the extension of the franchise in 1918[2] and the coming into being of a real thing called democratic public opinion, whereas, in the old days, political decisions really were taken by an oligarchy and a newspaper proprietor merely operated as a member of an oligarchy with a particularly loud voice. The last volume of the *History* is very scornful of Geoffrey Dawson for constantly considering public opinion. But, of course, that was not where he failed. Where he failed was in identifying the Athenaeum[3] with public opinion and assuming that you couldn't get the British people to face the responsibilities of rearmament. But the fact is that today the function of the press has entirely changed. Today if you want to influence politics through the press you don't do it by running campaigns against certain politicians or for certain causes. Your aim is to educate or to stimulate opinion to bring the pressure on the politicians.

While I was in hospital I was visited by John Freeman, Michael Foot, Ned Russell,[4] David Linebaugh and Ian Mikardo and telephoned by Eddie Shackleton and George Wigg. The debate on Germany[5] seems to have fizzled out in a somewhat inexplicable way. I heard astonishingly varying accounts of what had happened and of who had spoken well at the Party Meeting and on the floor of the House. There is no doubt that Attlee got

[1] Geoffrey Dawson (1874–1944) was Editor of *The Times* 1912–19 and 1923–41.

[2] The Representation of the People Act 1918 reduced the voter's residence qualification from twelve months to six and enfranchised some categories of men who had not previously had the vote. Women over thirty also became entitled to vote.

[3] A club, founded in 1824.

[4] London Correspondent of the *New York Herald Tribune*.

[5] In the foreign affairs debate on May 14th the Foreign Secretary declared that Labour's statement would delay the efforts to establish European unity and thus cause them to fail. Mr Attlee, however, succeeded in supporting Mr Eden and to some extent disowning his Party's National Executive Committee.

On May 26th the Foreign Ministers of West Germany and the three Allied Powers signed the Contract ending the Federal Republic's status as an occupied country. The following day the treaty to establish the European Defence Community was signed in Paris by representatives of the Governments of France, Italy, West Germany and the Benelux countries. The British and American Governments joined the French Government in a tripartite declaration of mutual action in the event of any hostilities threatening the Community.

The treaties were, however, not yet ratified and this was unlikely to happen before the autumn, since neither the French nor the West German Governments were strongly supported by public opinion or by their Opposition parties. Meanwhile on May 25th a third Russian Note was delivered; this was followed by interference with communications between West Berlin and West Germany.

away with it by satisfying everybody at the Party Meeting that he was backing the National Executive resolution and then, on the floor of the House, satisfying Mr Eden that he wasn't. Really, of course, this was a terrible defeat for the Left. The fact is that, on this occasion, the Bevanites were outwitted and out-manoeuvred and the National Executive resolution, which we hailed as a triumph, was immunized by Attlee. The Party avoided making up its mind or taking a new line. That was a defeat for us.

Behind the scenes, in the Group, everything is vague. The membership has been widely extended but, on the other hand, Nye seems determined to prevent any further policy statements or pamphlets being produced before the Party Conference. As short-run politics, this is wise. The unions are taking their line on the stale old rearmament issue and to inject new ideas into the controversy now would merely disturb things. Nye is therefore quite right, from his point of view, to let things take their course, since he is now assured of such a substantial minority at the Conference that before it starts the Executive will almost certainly compromise with him and so give him a justification for re-entering the Parliamentary Committee and thus closing the Bevanite controversy. There is an interesting leader in today's *Times* which seems to be composed by two hands, since the last paragraph contradicts the rest.[1] However, the writers are correct enough in stating that, though Aneurin is losing ground, Bevanism is not and, if we choose to continue as a Left opposition and to develop a constructive policy, we could very deeply influence the Party. The trouble is that Nye has a profound scepticism about policies and programmes, which will not be lessened when *New Fabian Essays*[2] is published next Friday and it is seen how bankrupt most of the writers are.

The other big event during my illness was the staggering defeat of the Tories in the municipal elections:[3] nine seats won at Oxford, for instance, and in my own East Coventry we won two seats in Lower Stoke, thus making every ward in the constituency 100 per cent Labour. The full breakdown of the Coventry gains shows that they were due much more to an increase in the Labour vote than to the slight decrease in the Tory vote. This, of course, lessened their value, since only 52 per cent voted.[4] But the Government's self-confidence has certainly been shaken by this, as well as by the reception

[1] It is from MR BEVAN and not from MR ATTLEE or MR MORRISON that the members of the Party (confused and wondering) are receiving positive guidance. There is good reason for believing that MR BEVAN's personal position is weaker than it was three months ago, but the influence of his ideas on questions other than rearmament is noticeably growing [*The Times*, May 29th, 1952].

[2] See above, p. 31.

[3] Triennial county council elections took place between April 3rd and April 9th. Labour won a large number of seats and obtained a majority of 55 places on the London County Council. In the municipal borough elections on May 8th the Labour Party once more made considerable gains throughout the country, capturing 614 seats. The Conservatives won 420 seats.

[4] The turnout in Coventry was 52·7 per cent of the registered electorate; this was typical of the country as a whole.

of the White Paper on Transport,[1] which proposes to auction off the road haulage plant of the Transport Commission and to give the railways a square deal by imposing a levy on road haulage. The reaction to these proposals has been almost uniformly bad in the press and Quintin Hogg denounced them in the House of Lords last week. No doubt Churchill is committed up to the hilt to the road hauliers but I fancy there will be a large number of Tories who will be really unhappy about this proposal and about the failure of the Government to have a real policy.

The one chance the Government had was to make a dash for freedom and to permit unemployment to go up rapidly enough to act as an effective instrument of wage restraint, so that the deflation should really work. But they were scared of introducing unemployment, so that the Budget let off the wages spiral and Butler is now having to ask for wage restraint, in contradiction to every Tory policy. We are drifting into the worst economic crisis since the war and nobody really pretends that nationalization or denationalization are any help whatsoever in such a situation.

Monday, June 16th

Politics is very much in the doldrums. For fourteen days, while I was away, the Parliamentary Party churned over the Finance Bill Committee Stage and got heartily sick of it.[2] There is an extraordinary sense of lassitude in the Commons, with the Tories thoroughly dispirited by Churchill's leadership and not many Labour Members worrying about anything, since they all feel safe in getting back next time. What an extraordinary effect one's personal security has on a politician.

On Thursday night, Eddie Shackleton offered me a lift home in Herbert Morrison's car and Herbert came in for a quick drink and stayed for an hour and a half, drinking liqueur Irish whiskey while we all drank milk. He was in tremendously good form. Indeed, you could hardy recognize the little man, with his shoulders squared and his chin in the air, compared to the hang-down figure of Herbert the ex-Foreign Secretary. The explanation, of course, is that he is now back in his element attacking the Tories on transport, and this week on sponsored television programmes,[3] where, apparently,

---

[1] The White Paper on Transport (Cmd 8538) was debated on May 21st. It proposed: that long-distance haulage be returned to private enterprise; the eventual abolition of the distinction between long- and short-distance road haulage; the 'regionalizing' of railway management but not finance; and a £4 million levy on all goods vehicles on the roads, to help compensate for the loss to the railways.

[2] The Report Stage of the Finance Bill ended on the morning of June 19th; the Third Reading was carried without division on June 26th.

[3] On May 15th the White Paper (Cmd 8550) was published on the future of the B.B.C. The Government proposed to renew the Charter for ten years and to continue the public service monopoly of sound broadcasting. Arrangements were to be made for a measure of Scottish, Welsh and Northern Irish control over regional programmes.

The White Paper announced that appointment of the B.B.C. Governors was to be transferred from the Prime Minister to a committee, consisting of the Prime Minister, the Leader of the Opposition, the Lord Chief Justice and the Lord President of the Court of

although I didn't hear it, he made an absolutely first-rate speech. I do not feel as passionately as most of the Party against the principle of sponsoring though I regard the Government's proposals as outrageous, since they really come to a plan for introducing the Canadian and Australian dual system into this country. The one thing we all know is that, if you have Government radio and sponsored radio side by side, the bad currency drives out the good.

What I would have liked to have seen was permission for the B.B.C., under strict limitation, to develop through sponsored programmes the period from five o'clock in the afternoon to seven o'clock, where they cannot now afford to give a television service. Indeed, I think the Government will have done itself great damage by this proposal, since it is really a surrender to a small advertising pressure group of not more than thirty Members on its back-benches. On a free vote, a majority of Tory M.P.s and an overwhelming majority of Tory peers would have voted to retain the B.B.C. monopoly and would not even have agreed to my modest proposal. In the *Observer* on Sunday there was a tremendous attack by Lord Reith[1] on Mr Churchill's immorality in capsizing to a pressure group. This attack, I think, is all the stronger because many Tories were really deeply shocked by the Government's playing about with rail fares a few weeks ago,[2] just before the municipal elections, for purely political reasons. I suppose there is a large number of people who voted Tory simply in order to keep politics out of administration and have good government. This jockeying with fares was just the sort of thing that they attributed to Herbert Morrison, the astute

---

Session, with the Speaker of the House of Commons as chairman. On June 19th the Prime Minister stated that this proposal had been dropped.

But another controversial recommendation remained. Independent and competitive television services were to be permitted – but first Parliament would have the opportunity of considering the conditions under which such a system might operate. An account of the debate in both Houses is to be found in Asa Briggs, *The History of Broadcasting in the United Kingdom*: vol. 4: *Sound and Vision* (London: Oxford University Press, 1979). The author also describes how Gresham's law of currency came to be so frequently cited and explores the evidence for the belief that Conservative supporters of 'sponsored' television were linked with commercial advertising interests.

[1] John Reith (1889–1971), creator of British broadcasting. He was the first General Manager (1922) of the B.B.C. and later (1927) its first Director-General, until he left in 1938. He was elected as National M.P. for Southampton in 1940 and was created a life peer in the same year. He served as Minister of Information (Chamberlain's appointment) 1940–1 and as Minister of Works and Building (later Works and Planning) 1941–2. He was Chairman of the New Towns Committee 1945–7, of the National Film Finance Corporation 1948–51, of the Commonwealth Telecommunications Board 1946–50 and of the Colonial Development Corporation 1950–9. An edition of his *Diaries*, by C. H. Stuart, appeared in 1975 (London: Collins).

[2] In February 1952 the British Transport Commission had announced substantial fare increases for road and rail transport in the London area, to come into effect on March 1st, and for passenger railway travel, to be introduced on May 1st. The Government had stated in March that it lacked the power to interfere with the Commission's rulings, but on April 15th, during the Easter recess, the Minister of Transport had directed the Commission to postpone the second set of increases. On June 16th the Government eventually announced revised and reduced increases, with an annual loss of some £2 million in revenue to the Transport Commission.

party politician, and they are horrified when they find a Conservative Government perpetrating it.

On Friday Hugh Cudlipp came to lunch and made a good observation about this. 'The Parties have got sponsoring all wrong,' he observed. 'The staunchest Tory supporters are all against it but a large number of people who vote Labour would really like sponsored variety programmes.' I am sure that this is true in Coventry, where most of my supporters would love sponsored programmes. Apart from this, Hugh Cudlipp was extremely friendly. Ever since Phil Zec was suddenly kicked upstairs and Cudlipp came back, the *Pic* has been in a complete commotion, with Cudlipp changing everything round and trying out every sort of sensationalism, including a lurid series of articles on homosexuality. I didn't know how long my life would last under the new regime but on Friday Hugh said to me, almost in passing, 'With the column so very well established and everybody who matters reading it, I think you can afford to be a little more personal. Moreover, the one thing that I have learnt by being on the *Sunday Express* is that personalization is the secret of readability. So let's have more about Churchill and Attlee and less about Conservative and Labour.'

I think at the beginning Hugh was ready to get rid of me, on the grounds that Cecil King, the new Chairman, didn't like the *Sunday Pic* sold out to Bevanism. But the two of them went for a week's tour, studying circulation, and they are probably smart enough to realize that the circulation they are stealing from *Reynolds News* might slip back again without a regular Socialist column.

Today we had a *New Statesman* lunch, with the Editor as guest on his return from the States. Kingsley is in tremendous form and at the moment he regards us all as wonderful. He had some really remarkable stories about the witch-hunt in America[1] and the sort of questionnaires a man has to fill up, including whether his wife's mother was a Communist and whether there had been 'any unfortunate incidents in his life'. But Kingsley has also been knocked over by a couple of leading articles in the *Washington Post* attacking him for a completely inane paragraph in the 'Critic's Diary', which he wrote just before he left, stating that he had now come to the conclusion that there was *prima facie* evidence for the Communist charge that the Americans had dropped microbes in Korea.[2] I tried to persuade Kingsley that a couple of

[1] In America the Senate Judiciary Committee and its Sub-Committee, the State Department Loyalty Board and the Subversive Activities Control Board continued their investigation of alleged Communist sympathizers and 'subversives'. Prosecutions were frequently brought to the courts; the Supreme Court and its State counterparts were obliged to rule on the constitutionality of various laws against 'subversion'. Such 'witch-hunts' were led by Senator Joseph R. McCarthy, Republican Senator for Wisconsin 1946–57 and Chairman of the Senate Investigating Sub-Committee.

[2] The paragraph appeared in the issue of the *New Statesman and Nation* for April 12th, 1952, where Kingsley Martin declared ' ... now I am convinced only that there is a case for investigation ... ' In the issue of June 28th, 1952, he describes American objections to his earlier statement and the accusations that he had displayed 'the degradation of a fellow-travelling mind'. See also below, p. 139.

leading articles were the least he could have expected after such a paragraph but he really is the most sensitive man I know to attacks in the press. This is not uncommon among journalists, who expect to attack everybody else but to get off scot-free themselves. As a politician, one has to get used to it.

Tuesday, June 17th
We had a good meeting of the Group today, with a lot of new members, including Ellis Smith,[1] taking a very full part in the discussion. This was on a very important and thorough paper by Dudley Seers, estimating the effect of rearmament on the economy and forming the basis for an analysis of the crisis into which we seem to be drifting. Ellis Smith pressed that this paper should be followed by another, with practical proposals for action, since the Movement should not be caught completely unprepared if the crisis should break this autumn. As usual on these occasions, it was found that Harold Wilson had nearly completed a tremendous work on this subject and he is preparing a summary of his proposals for presentation in a fortnight's time.

After the meeting I had a word with him and Michael and the obvious tactic seems to be that a *Tribune* pamphlet by Wilson on a *Plan For The Crisis* should be launched in August, which would provide both a Group policy and useful advertising for him for the elections to the National Executive at Conference. I discussed whether Michael and/or I should stand and clearly Harold Wilson was very relieved when I said that, if either of us did, the result would most probably be not to get six Bevanites on but to knock one off.

In the Smoking Room afterwards, Boothby came in when I was talking to Dick Acland. Dick had just said that he thought the Tories might well imitate Attlee's example last year and go to the country this October on the ground that they needed a mandate and a larger majority to face the economic difficulties during the winter. I said no, they hadn't been long enough in office to want that and then I turned to Bob and asked him. 'Go to the country? Not on your life,' he said. 'After all, they know that they'll be swept away in the election and won't return in their lifetimes. The Old Man's quite happy where he is and isn't unduly concerned about anything except London fares.'* When I mentioned 1 million unemployed, Boothby said, 'You are ridiculously optimistic. There will be far more than that before the winter is out.'

There had been a small Cabinet shuffle on May 7th. Mr Crookshank, Leader of the House and Minister of Health, exchanged the latter office for that of

---

[1] Labour M.P. for Stoke-on-Trent 1935–50 and for Stoke-on-Trent South 1950–66. He was Parliamentary Secretary to the Board of Trade 1945–6 and General President of the United Pattern Makers' Association 1946–50, 1952 and 1958–64. He died in 1969.

* The new proposals for fares were announced yesterday in a completely unintelligible statement from the Ministry of Transport, which only shows that very slight reductions have been made at the cost of £2 million extra to the Transport Commission, which will then have to increase fares in order to cover it.

Lord Privy Seal. Iain Macleod became Minister of Health. Mr Lennox-Boyd moved to the Ministry of Transport and Civil Aviation, replacing Mr Maclay, who resigned for health reasons. Mr Hopkinson took Mr Lennox-Boyd's place as Minister of State for Colonial Affairs.

Monday, June 23rd

The Smoking Room conversation is now all about the possibility that Churchill will give part of the responsibility for the home front to Eden. I asked Boothby what he thought of it and he said, 'Not on your life. Eden is doing very well in foreign affairs. Why should he take the responsibility for the disasters on the home front?' But many newspapers continue to prophesy it and this weekend we had a pontifical leading article in *The Economist*, tactfully suggesting that Churchill should give way and let Eden assist Mr Butler. I must say I liked the idea of Mr Butler accepting Mr Eden's assistance.

On the other hand, John Freeman, who recently talked to Eden, told me that he got the impression that Eden would like to groom himself for the premiership by getting some contact with home affairs. Certainly, to judge from the weekend press, the myth of Churchill is completely dissipated, even in Tory circles. But the worse the press, the more obstinate I guess Churchill will be and I still feel sure that he will hold on till after the Coronation and delight in frustrating the competing plans of Eden and Butler for shoving him out. He really hates the Conservatives.

The Panmunjom negotiations on an armistice in the Korean war had proceeded for a full year, while Communist resistance increased, reinforced by supplies of Russian equipment and Chinese manpower. On May 7th the Foreign Secretary described the current state of the talks to the House of Commons. The week before, the U.N. negotiators had presented proposals covering three outstanding areas of disagreement, declaring these 'the limit of possible concession'. Agreement was obtained on two of these issues, since the Communists abandoned their demand that Russia should be one of the neutral States appointed to supervise the application of armistice terms and the U.N. team conceded that the armistice should not refer to the right of either side to reconstruct its airfields.

On the third point — the repatriation of prisoners — disagreement persisted. Mr Eden told the House that the general picture was 'very grave', since Communist forces had been reinforced and re-equipped during the lull in the fighting. The U.N. forces, however, now held a strongly defended line across the Korean peninsula. That same day, April 28th, the Minister of Defence, Field-Marshal Lord Alexander, announced his forthcoming visit to Tokyo and Korea, as a guest of General Mark Clark, the successor to General Ridgway as Commander-in-Chief of U.N. forces in the Far East.

Mr Eden had explained to the House that, of the 132,000 prisoners in U.N. hands, 63,700 were unwilling to be repatriated. The Communists insisted on the exchange of these men for the very small number of prisoners they held them-

selves. Mr Attlee fully supported Mr Eden's opposition to forcible repatriation. Many of the prisoners held by the U.N. were housed in an enormous camp on Koje Island, off the South Korean peninsula, and in early June it was discovered that the entire camp had been terrorized by a Communist gang who had kidnapped the American general commanding its garrison. Prisoners had been murdered by the ring-leaders. A detachment of Commonwealth troops was sent to Koje, order was restored and the camp reorganized. On June 11th Mr Eden described these events to the House.

In the statement he referred to the political situation in South Korea. The President of the Republic, Syngman Rhee, had anticipated the end of his statutory term of office by arresting leading Opposition politicians in the Assembly (which elected the President). Mr Rhee ignored British and American protests; on June 11th the Foreign Secretary told the Commons that the first requirement was the return to constitutional government in South Korea by the lifting of martial law and the release of arrested members of the Assembly. A White Paper would be issued as soon as possible after Lord Alexander's return. On behalf of the Opposition, Mr Morrison gave Mr Eden his full support.

On June 23rd U.S. air forces bombed power plants in North Korea, one of them close to the Yalu River, on the Manchurian frontier. On the following day there were questions in the Commons at this apparent departure from current policy. Mr Attlee opened a debate on June 25th and, in reply, Mr Eden stated that, regrettably, there had been no prior consultation with the British Government. He declared, however, that the bombings merely extended present military policy and that the power plants were legitimate and necessary·targets.

There were two fundamental questions. First, did the Communists in fact wish for an armistice or were they set on spinning out negotiations? Second, what should be the form of consultation between the American and the British Governments, particularly since some fifteen or so other Governments were involved in the U.S. action in Korea? These problems were discussed in late June at meetings between the British Government and Mr Acheson, the U.S. Secretary of State, who was visiting Europe for that purpose.

Wednesday, June 25th

In the last moments of yesterday's Party Meeting, Fenner Brockway raised the bombing of the Yalu hydro-electric plants, of which we had had the first news on the tape on Monday. Attlee's reaction was fascinating. He behaved exactly like Chamberlain.[1] One must not jump to conclusions.

[1] Neville Chamberlain (1869–1940), the second son of Joseph Chamberlain and himself Unionist M.P. for the Ladywood division of Birmingham December 1918–May 1929, and for the Edgbaston division from 1929 until his death. In 1911 he became a Birmingham City councillor and Chairman of the Town Planning Committee, in 1914 an Alderman and in 1915 Lord Mayor. He was Director-General of National Service 1916–17, Postmaster-General 1922–3, Paymaster-General 1923, Minister of Health 1923, 1924–9 and August–November 1931, Chancellor of the Exchequer 1923–4 and 1931–7 and Prime Minister from 1937 until May 1940, when hostility to his policy of 'appeasing' Hitler caused him to resign. For the remaining months of his life he served as Lord President of the Council.

After all, it was an objective in Korea. One could only ask questions. In three minutes he had the whole Party storming against him and demanding that the adjournment of the House should be moved, a demand to which he quickly capitulated. But it is typical that it was Nye and Sydney Silverman who had taken the trouble to put down Private Notice Questions, while no member of the Parliamentary Committee had taken action.

After the Party Meeting we had the Group, where we decided on another concerted action on the floor of the House. This went very well and, to do him justice, Attlee did quite a good job. But after nearly half an hour the Speaker refused the adjournment. However, from the point of view of the world press and the public, the half-hour asking for the adjournment was as good as a three-hour debate, as can be seen from this morning's press. Moreover in the evening the Parliamentary Committee decided that, having failed to get the adjournment, it would change the cost of living debate today and have a Yalu debate instead. This duly occurred. Attlee made a very workmanlike speech. Eden's reply was skilful but I was amazed to learn afterwards that a large number of Labour Members had been so moved by it that it was impossible to vote against it. Actually all he did was to spend twenty minutes proving what we all knew: that these were military objectives within Korea; two minutes saying that he had not been consulted; and one minute saying that, despite this, he gave America full support.

This should have given Nye a tremendous chance, as he followed Eden. But for the first time in my experience he had something very like a parliamentary flop. This was due to two things. In the first place, he gave a wide, speculative speech, with all his views about how to make peace with the Chinese and deal with Formosa. The whole Party was waiting for the lightning rapier attack on Eden, which never came. He should have torn Eden's speech to pieces and shown that the really significant thing was the timing of the attack. Granted they were military targets, why had they been left untouched for two years and why had the attack been made at the most delicate point in the armistice negotiations? Was this not another case of the generals trying their own diplomatic methods and thus destroying the work of the civilian authorities? Sydney Silverman made some of those points later but it was too late.

The other reason for Nye's failure was small but important. Half-way through his speech, when he was not being particularly interesting, Freda Corbet's *sotto voce* comments became audible and he turned round and snapped, 'What are you babbling about?' It was such bad taste that he lost the attention of the House and never regained it.

I got back to the House in time to hear Selwyn Lloyd, the Minister just back from Korea, trying to taunt the Labour Party into voting against. He could safely do so, since Shinwell had announced that the Party would postpone judgment till next Tuesday. Then in the Smoking Room Geoffrey de

Freitas[1] told me that Eden's speech was the only one he had ever heard which had really changed his mind. I felt for the first time that it might really have been quite a good thing if I had made the speech instead of Nye. But I doubt whether Nye thought it too.

Monday, June 30th
At the Report Back [to my constituency] on Sunday I had the usual complaints that the Bevanites weren't doing enough. One of the difficulties of the constituencies is that, unless you are having a parliamentary crisis once a week, they think the Bevanites are doing nothing and, if you have one once a week, they think you are splitting the Party.

On July 1st Lord Alexander spoke in the House of Lords about his recent Korean visit. He stated that the U.N. Command had declared that it would be appropriate for a deputy chief of staff, drawn from Commonwealth countries, to be appointed to General Clark's headquarters. On the bombing of the power plants, Lord Alexander said that it was only after the British visit was over that General Clark himself had learnt that this long-standing plan was to be put into operation.

In the House of Commons on the same day a Labour vote of censure was moved. In mild terms, it

regretted the failure of Her Majesty's Government to secure effective consultation prior to recent developments including consultation on the timing of certain recent air operations; and considered that improved arrangements should now be made to enable such consultation to take place between the Governments principally concerned on issues of United Nations policy in the Far East.

In reply, the Prime Minister quoted with Mr Acheson's permission an 'off-the-record' speech in which the Secretary of State had observed that the American Government had been mistaken in its failure to inform the British Government of the intended attack. The motion of censure was defeated by 300 votes to 270 but during the debate the Bevanites expressed their disapproval not just of the failure of liaison between the two Governments, but also of the bombing policy itself. The mildness of the motion was vehemently criticized but this time the Bevanites voted with the Labour leadership.

Wednesday, July 2nd
Yesterday morning we had the Party Meeting on Korea. It's worth recording

[1] Labour M.P. for Central Nottingham 1945–50, for Lincoln 1950–1 and for Kettering 1964–79. He was P.P.S. to Attlee 1945–6, Under-Secretary of State for Air 1946–50, and Under-Secretary of State at the Home Office 1950–1, and was also British High Commissioner for Ghana 1961–3 and President of the Assembly of the Council of Europe 1966–9. He was knighted in 1961.

the background. In the course of last Wednesday's debate on Korea, the Parliamentary Committee met to decide whether we should vote or not. The decision was 8 to 5 against voting. The five were Dalton, Callaghan, Chuter Ede, Greenwood and Shinwell. After this the Whips were sent round to tell people that there wasn't going to be a vote and, in order to reassure those who wanted the vote, it was stated that we were to have another debate this week, with a vote of censure formally moved.

At the normal Thursday business meeting Attlee got up with a rather dirty bit of paper and said that they had roughed out a resolution. He then mumbled it. It was long and wordy and, when it had been repeated rather louder, we discovered that it merely protested against lack of consultation but did not censure the Government for giving full support to the Yalu raid. There was then a lengthy debate, in which we urged that it was not sufficient to protest against lack of consultation, while Reggie Paget[1] and Charlie Hobson[2] put the case against. It was obvious that the majority at the meeting wanted a tougher resolution but Attlee argued against condemning the raid because information was insufficient. Under pressure, he then said that he wouldn't mind including the *timing* of the raid, whereupon everybody assumed that this meant that we should condemn lack of consultation *and* the timing. On Friday the resolution was redrafted and, although Shinwell's and Kenneth Younger's names were attached to it, neither of them actually saw it, nor, we gathered later, was it ever at any stage submitted to the Parliamentary Committee. In its final form the resolution merely condemned the lack of consultation on various matters, including the timing of the raid. By Monday afternoon it was quite clear that a great many people were very angry at what they thought was a gross violation by Attlee of a pledge to the Party.

We had a special emergency Bevanite Group, at which the proposal to put an amendment down on the Order Paper was immediately opposed by Nye, and it was decided to table a motion in the Party Meeting, regretting the failure of the resolution tabled by the Parliamentary Committee to reflect the assurance given by the Leader the previous Thursday. I think we realized this would be taken as a vote of censure but we really didn't see what other course we could take. We have agreed to abide by Standing Orders, which means accepting any decision of the Party. But what are we to do when a decision of the Party is sidestepped by the Leader?

Yesterday morning Nye moved our resolution, in very moderate language. Fenner Brockway followed and rather unfortunately got himself immersed in

---

[1] Reginald Paget, Labour M.P. for Northampton 1945–74. He was created a life peer in 1975, taking the title Lord Paget of Northampton.

[2] Charles Hobson, a power station engineer, was Labour M.P. for Wembley North 1945–50, and for Keighley 1950–9. He was Assistant Postmaster-General 1947–51, and became a life peer (Lord Hobson) in 1963. He served as a Lord in Waiting from 1964 until his death in 1966.

a long discussion about Nehru,[1] which immediately enabled our speakers to broaden the theme from what had happened on Thursday to a general discussion on Korea, in which the Bevanites, the *New Statesman* and the *Tribune* were all attacked for being anti-American. But, to our surprise, Arthur Blenkinsop, who I am sure was called as an anti-Bevanite, got up and said that the decision of the Party Meeting had been traduced and he was supported in this by John Strachey. Indeed, no one except Attlee, as far as I can remember, tried to pretend that the resolution was in conformity with the Party Meeting and most of those who spoke against our motion argued in favour of the bombing of the Yalu plants (for instance, Stanley Evans,[2] and, to my great surprise, Seymour Cocks).[3]

It was a sweltering day but the debate reached a very high level and we were considerably assisted by Christopher Mayhew and Woodrow Wyatt, who led the attack on the Bevanites with arguments and in a tone which alienated the old Labour Members. Herbert Morrison wound up for the platform with a very maladroit speech. He, in fact, had been in favour of the bombing and against a vote of censure, even in Attlee's moderate form, and he did not take much trouble to disguise this. What also lost him support was his extraordinary argument that we must consider the electoral consequences of censuring Eden's full support for the Americans. Herbert was just going to put the vote when Nye claimed the right of reply and made a really brilliant four-minute speech. First of all, he said that we had not wanted to make this a vote of censure on Attlee. (By the way, Herbert had ended by saying this was the vote of censure and that those who voted for it would be impugning the honesty and good faith of the Leader. For that very reason, Morrison added, even though the Bevanites would like to withdraw, he would demand a vote.) Nye went on to say, and this was his brilliance, that those who voted for the platform would be voting in favour of bombing the Yalu plants. 'You may do that here,' he said, 'but I know very well that next weekend you will all be saying in your constituencies that you wanted to protest against it.' Indeed, Nye talked as though the vast majority of the Party would oppose the vote of censure, although they knew that it was justified on two counts: first, that the Party decision had not been held out by Attlee; and, secondly, that the failure to censure the Government for supporting the bombing would make nonsense of us in the debate.

When the vote was taken, the result was 52 for the motion of censure and a 101 against. How many abstained? Optimists claimed that there were 60 but I very much doubt if there were 210 people in Room 14 and my own guess is

---

[1] Jawaharlal Nehru (1889–1964), the first Prime Minister of the Indian Union 1947–64. Leader of the younger generation of Indian nationalists, Nehru was the supporter and successor of Gandhi.

[2] Labour M.P. for Wednesbury 1945–56 and Parliamentary Secretary at the Ministry of Food February–April 1950. He died in 1970.

[3] Frederick Seymour Cocks (1882–1963), Labour M.P. for the Broxtowe division of Nottinghamshire 1929–53.

that between 20 and 30 people abstained. I noticed on the floor Arthur Greenwood[1] and Kenneth Robinson[2] abstaining, while on the platform Tony Greenwood ostentatiously abstained. Among others outside the Group who voted for us were Brothers Paling, Arthur Blenkinsop and Michael Stewart. John Strachey spoke strongly for us and voted for the platform. Dalton and Callaghan, who had not been consulted at any stage in the drafting, had ostentatiously stayed away from the meeting. Though this was not a triumph for us, it was a tremendous defeat for Morrison, who must have completely misjudged the sense of the meeting to force a vote of confidence in such conditions. I am sure there was no one in the room who did not agree that the substance of our motion was the facts and I would guess that there are not more than thirty members of the Party who support Gaitskell and Morrison in their 100 per cent American line.

We had some discussion at the Group about who should speak for us. Nye couldn't because he had spoken last week and I felt it was a mistake that it should be assumed that he and I were the only two who could. It was decided that two names should be put to the Speaker, mine and Michael Foot's. When this was done the Speaker said, 'Oh, we'd better have Foot, since Crossman always speaks.' Actually I have spoken twice in this Parliament, a good deal less often than Mike.

The debate on the floor started in a three-quarters full, tepid House, with a most dreary report by Selwyn Lloyd on his and Alexander's[3] visit to Korea. Then came Noel-Baker. His speech was very curious, starting with a long introduction on the history of Korea, which seemed bound to lead up to a justification of the bombing. But there came a sudden switch, a lengthy condemnation of the bombing and a plea for consultation. It was palpably not a speech for a vote of censure and I fancy the condemnation of the bombing had been spatchcocked in after the morning's meeting. Churchill, who followed, was in quite good form. Though he could have made more of the divisions in the Labour Party and the ridiculousness of the motion, he

[1] A civil servant in the Ministry of Reconstruction, he was Labour M.P. for Nelson and Colne 1922–31 and for Wakefield 1932–54. He was Parliamentary Secretary at the Ministry of Health 1924, Minister of Health 1929–31, Deputy Leader of the Labour Party 1935 and Minister without Portfolio in the War Cabinet 1940–2. From 1945 to 1947 he was Lord Privy Seal, serving as Paymaster-General 1946–7. He was Deputy Leader of the Labour Party 1942, Treasurer 1943 and Chairman of the National Executive Committee 1952. From 1920 to 1943 he was Secretary of the Labour Party Research Department.

[2] Labour M.P. for St Pancras North 1949–70. A junior Whip from 1950 to 1954, he became Minister of Health in 1964, serving until 1968, when he became Minister for Planning and Land in the Ministry of Housing and Local Government. From 1970 to 1974 he worked for the British Steel Corporation. He was Chairman of the London Transport Executive 1975–7 and of the English National Opera 1972–7. Since 1977 he has been Chairman of the Arts Council of Great Britain.

[3] Earl Alexander of Tunis, who was made a Viscount in 1946, after G.O.C. posts in Burma, the Middle East, North Africa and Italy. He was Supreme Allied Commander, Mediterranean Theatre, 1944–5, Governor-General of Canada 1946–52 and became Churchill's Minister of Defence 1952–4. He was elevated to the rank of Earl in 1952. He died in 1969.

said quite enough to make our Front Bench look idiotic. After all, the one thing they had selected for censure was the machinery of consultation they themselves had established.

Michael got up immediately after Churchill and did extremely well, holding Churchill in his seat for thirty-seven minutes. Most of our Front Bench walked out and the Labour side was rigidly divided into the cheering back-benches below the back gangway and the half-empty, silent benches above it. The only tactical mistake in Michael's speech was to build up so much the American change of policy that today's announcement that the armistice negotiations have taken a favourable turn could be misinterpreted as disproving our contentions. I had tried to warn Michael about this, since we had got inside information from Lloyd in the Foreign Office and from Krishna Menon[1] that the repatriation issue was on the verge of settlement, thanks to Indian mediation.[2] But it is difficult to persuade either Aneurin or Michael to sacrifice an emotional success in a debate for the sake of a long-term calculation of the consequences.

Barbara Castle also did quite well and against us were Woodrow Wyatt and Denis Healey, who were stormily cheered by the Tories. Indeed, in this debate, more than in any of the preceding big debates, the division on the Labour side was quite grotesquely obvious to anyone looking down from the Gallery. It really does look like two parties. But this is a superficial judgment. In fact, it's a big Party with two minds and with two small, determined groups fighting to see which of these two minds should prevail. On the one side, Morrison and Gaitskell, with Denis Healey, Chris Mayhew, Woodrow Wyatt as their intellectuals, and on the other the Bevanites. But the vast majority are middle-of-the-wayers, with George Strauss, John Strachey, Callaghan and Dalton, saying 'A plague on both your houses'. And, if the truth be told, on this issue of Korea and Anglo-American relations, there are not nearly such sharp divisions as many people would like to believe.

I had a drink with Dalton after the debate. He was obviously not displeased by the discomfiture of Attlee and Morrison. Like James Callaghan, in fact, who yesterday said to me, 'I hope your majority at the Party Meeting

[1] Vengalil Krishman Krishna Menon, a close friend of Nehru, was Secretary (1927–47) and then President of the India League, and was the Indian High Commissioner from 1947 to 1952. Earlier he had practised at the British Bar and had been Labour Councillor for St Pancras 1934–47. He was the first Editor of Pelican Books. From 1953 to 1957 he was a member of the Council of States in the Indian Parliament and was a member of the Lok Sabha 1957–67 and from 1969 until his death in 1974. He held various posts in the Indian Cabinet from 1956 to 1962, latterly as Minister of Defence. He resigned this post after the Chinese invasion of 1962, and he left the Indian National Congress in 1966.

[2] In the period before the Christmas adjournment of the United Nations the Indian delegate, Mr Krishna Menon, presented a compromise resolution on the question of the repatriation of Korean prisoners of war. It obtained overwhelming support from the Assembly but was rejected by the Soviet delegate. Despite a personal appeal to the Chinese Communist Government by the President of the Assembly, Mr Lester Pearson of Canada, the resolution was also rejected by Chou En-lai, the Chinese Premier and Foreign Minister.

is big enough to strengthen the forces of good on the Parliamentary Committee.' What a time-server he is.

Wednesday, July 23rd

There has been a long gap in this diary, owing to an irruption of private life,
which, strictly speaking, has no place here, although this is a pure intellectual
abstraction, as I now well know.

On Wednesday, July 2nd, I finally went to see Dr Harris about a mild
attack of phlebitis, which I had tried to take care of but which was just rising
above my knee. He ordered me to cancel all engagements for four or five days
and to keep my leg up. This meant cancelling going to Hamish Hamilton's
twenty-first birthday party, which, for Zita, was the event of the summer, as
well as a visit to Heinz Koeppler[1] at Wilton Park, which she was looking
forward to. On Wednesday evening, when I came home with the news, she
was unusually down in the mouth and depressed. But she cheered up when
John and Bridget Bardsley[2] arrived for her with a wonderful packet of old
clothes and shoes for her Lambeth children.[3] We went off to dine in the
House. Zita was in tremendous form. Indeed, for a long time she hadn't
been so cheerful and uninhibited with all the M.P.s we met that night. We
only went to bed at midnight, the second late night running.

On Thursday morning she complained that she hadn't slept much and while
I was having my bath she did come in and say rather vaguely that she was
going to give up Lambeth because it was too much for her and to say once
again how disappointed she was about cancelling the weekend. I said that in
that case we could perfectly well go to Wilton Park. She said no. For her, she
was very out of sorts and what she practically never was – a little unreasonable or a twentieth as unreasonable as I usually am. Then she settled me down
in the sitting room, with my leg up, and rushed out to shop. She came back
loaded, looked in, rather breathless and harassed and said that she must
rush off to Lambeth.

The next thing I heard was forty minutes later, when the school doctor
telephoned to say that she was in a coma. They had heard a noise from the
room where she was working and rushed in to find her saying that she had a
terrible pain in the top of her head. Then she had been sick and gradually
became deeply unconscious. The school doctor was obviously in a panic and
asked me to come over. I said that they were to bring her straight home. I
thought they would bring her in the car but finally an ambulance came, with

---

[1] Born in Germany, Heinz Koeppler was a history don at Oxford 1937–9 and in 1940
joined the Political Intelligence Department of the Foreign Office. From 1946 to 1977 he
was Warden of Wilton Park, Sussex, a discussion centre for members of the Atlantic Community, and was Warden of the European Discussion Centre in 1972–7. He was knighted
in 1977.

[2] Crossman's sister and her husband.

[3] As well as working in North Kensington as a voluntary helper with the Family Planning
Association, Mrs Crossman took a great interest in a school in Lambeth.

the school doctor who, when our dear Dr Harris turned up, was unable to give him any coherent account. But Dr Harris immediately diagnosed a burst artery and rang up Dr Meadows who happened to be at the Westminster Hospital. Harris asked me whether I would be prepared to get Meadows round, although it would mean paying him. I said, of course, yes. He came in forty minutes, confirmed the diagnosis and immediately found Zita a place in the Casualty Ward. I think at that time Meadows knew that the case was hopeless and he did his best to warn me, though he only said that 50 per cent of such cases failed to recover. I telephoned Christopher, and he warned Venice,[1] who immediately wanted to come. They arrived on Friday morning.

Very early on Friday I rang up the night staff, who told me that Zita was miraculously better and had even tried to speak to them. Venice and Christopher turned up during the morning, while I struggled with the *Sunday Pic*, and in the afternoon we went round to the hospital again. Zita was much better, or rather, in a much less deep coma, and almost smiled when I sat by her. We all felt very much more cheerful. Then Barbara and Ted Castle[2] came in to tea in sympathy. Nye Bevan, Jennie and Michael had all come in on the previous evening and Nye had rung up the King's physician[3], who had confirmed the diagnosis, and had heard the late-night news that Zita was improving.

So everything looked cheerful on Friday afternoon but that evening the night sister told me that the coma was deeper and on Saturday afternoon Dr Meadows rang me up to give me a very strong hint. On Saturday evening I was in the hospital with the local vicar, a very fine man, with whom I had a furious argument about immortality over the cups of tea the hospital served without cessation. Later on, Venice came and nearly collapsed. But meanwhile George Wigg had rallied round and on Sunday morning he sent Venice and Christopher back to Radnage and ordered Gilbert[4] up from Brighton where I had let him go for the weekend. From then on George took complete charge of everything, in the way that only he possibly can.

Really it was hopeless on Saturday and I knew that it was hopeless all Saturday night and Sunday morning. It was a very beautiful summer day and I spent it partly sitting with Zita and partly on the terrace outside the Casualty

[1] Christopher Barry, a journalist and B.B.C. producer, was then working at Ealing Film Studios. He was the son of Sir Gerald Barry the Editor of the *Saturday Review* 1924–30 and of the *News Chronicle* 1933–47 and Director-General of the Festival of Britain 1948–51. Christopher Barry married Venice Baker, Crossman's stepdaughter, in June 1954.

[2] A journalist who became Assistant Editor of the *Daily Mirror* in 1943, and then of *Picture Post* in 1944. He was Editor of *Picture Post* from 1951 until 1952. He married Barbara Betts in 1944. He served as a G.L.C. Alderman from 1964 until 1970 and was a Member of the European Parliament 1975–9. He became a life peer in 1974. He died in 1979.

[3] The King's physicians in 1952 were Sir John Weir, Sir Horace Evans and Sir Daniel Davies.

[4] Gilbert Baker was Crossman's stepson. At this time he was working for the *Lagos Daily Times*, part of the *Mirror* Group. He later moved to Standard Motors in Coventry.

Ward, overlooking Horseferry Road, where there is a nice tree in the garden. Those last two hours, before she died at 11.15, were curiously not bad. I thought mostly about Radnage and how the trees look in autumn and decided that was where she should be buried and that the vicar should come and help do it, provided that he knew quite clearly that he was burying an agnostic and that I was one too.

The two memories that I have of those three days, are, first, the warmth of friendship from all sorts of unexpected people, and, secondly, the odious problems of the Health Service. I was a bit puzzled why, about every six hours in the hospital, I was asked whether Zita should go to a private ward. Indeed, on the Friday I was sent up to see the almoner, who told me that Zita could have a bed in a room for three weeks for fourteen guineas a week and that Dr Meadows would cost seventy-five guineas for the first five weeks, since this might be a very long process. Meadows's assistant, to whom I mentioned it, said I wasn't to worry, since Zita couldn't possibly be moved. But the sister in the ward was clearly shocked that Zita was not a private patient and I was asked four times about this in the next two days.

When I mentioned it to Harris on Sunday, after Zita had died, he said to me that, of course, she had only been got into the Westminster because he had said to Meadows that, if he could get her into the Casualty Ward, I would agree to her being a private patient. I said, 'But why couldn't she have got in as a National Health patient?' And he said, 'I haven't got one of my patients into the Westminster, ever. I get them into the lesser hospitals.' And I said, 'You mean that she would have been left to die here if Meadows hadn't had the impression that she was going to be a private patient?' And Harris said, 'Yes. Unless we could have got her into some small hospital.' So much for the theory that we have removed the money element from sickness. It wasn't the fault of anybody in the hospital. It's just the system of having, within one building, the public wards and the private wards. How can you blame the specialist? If I stand on my rights and she goes public, he gets nothing. If I can be blackmailed into sending her privately, he gets a large fee. It's an impossible situation.

On the Friday morning I discovered, not to my surprise, that I was bleeding and assumed, rightly, that my old duodenal ulcer had been activated. It bled furiously all Friday, Saturday and Sunday, but without any pain whatsoever. When Harris saw me on Sunday he said that the real thing to do would be to get me into a hospital for a few days, as though that was totally impossible. However, there is Manor House and by 6.30 I was there and remained there until Friday, the 18th. It was only possible because George Wigg took complete control of the funeral arrangements, of Gilbert, of Mia, of Rose, of everybody, but it was a merciful deliverance.[1]

The funeral was on Thursday the 10th, at Radnage. There had been some

[1] Mia was a German girl working *au pair*; Rose Cohen worked with Crossman during the war and from 1935 to 1962 was his secretary.

difficulties beforehand because, when Nye and Jennie came to see me, I told them that we'd put it out of London and I didn't expect them to go. Then they heard that Barbara and Ted were going and thought that they had been slighted, so I had to explain to Jennie that when public schoolboys really want somebody to go to a funeral they put it in the form, 'Oh, for heaven's sake, you needn't bother'. Actually it worked out beautifully, with just the people coming who really minded. Very adventurously, the padre had determined that we should start with 'To Be a Pilgrim', which would have been a fiasco had not Nye led the singing. There had also been a bit of a problem about where the grave would be. The correct thing would have been to put her in the far corner, with Lord Addison,[1] and it was only after some pressure that she was allowed to be with ordinary people – that is, by Mr White and Mr Alf, which gave Mrs D. a real ecstasy of pleasure.[2]

When I got down before lunch on Thursday I found Mrs D. washing up and she put her arms around me and said, 'We were so afraid that you would keep her in London and now she is going to be with my Alf.' George and Christopher and Gilbert organized, Mia picked cherries ferociously and Mia and Rose and Mrs D., for different reasons, all refused to go to church. Kingsley and John Roberts and Ernest Willison[3] came from the *New Statesman*, Harold Davies and Maurice Orbach (Zionist) from the Group, and there were Nye and Jennie and Elizabeth[4] and Frank[5] and Eddie [Shackleton],

[1] Christopher Addison (1869–1951), the 1st Viscount Addison, held a number of chairs in medicine and anatomy and was Liberal M.P. for the Hoxton division of Shoreditch 1910–22, and Labour M.P. for Swindon 1929–31 and 1934–5. He held various junior offices from 1914 to 1921 (Minister of Munitions 1916–17, in charge of Reconstruction 1917) and in 1929–31. He was made a peer in 1945 and was Secretary of State for Commonwealth Relations 1945–7, Paymaster-General 1948–9, Lord Privy Seal 1947–51 and Lord President of the Council in 1951. During both the Attlee Governments he served as Leader of the House of Lords.

[2] Mr White was the brother of the Misses Lizzie and Annie White, who kept bees and lived in half of Charity Cottages; in the other half lived Mrs D., so called because she was married to Dennis Nuthall. She was also known by her first name, Ethel, or as Mrs Alf, after her first husband Alf Ashby, who had died some years before. An excellent cook, Mrs D. was celebrated for 'Mrs Alf's pud', a filling apple crumble, and for her fish pie.

[3] Advertising Director of the *New Statesman and Nation* from 1926 and Business Manager from 1947 until his death in October 1954. Some account of his work appears in Chapter 14 of C. H. Rolph's *Kingsley* (London: Gollancz, 1973).

[4] Elizabeth Harman married Frank Pakenham in 1931. She was successively Labour candidate for Cheltenham, King's Norton and Oxford. Like her husband, she is a prolific author. Notable among her many works are *Victoria R.I.* (London: Weidenfeld & Nicolson, 1964) and a two-volume biography of *Wellington* (London: Weidenfeld & Nicolson, 1969, 1972).

[5] A Student in Politics at Christ Church, Oxford, 1934–46 and 1952–64, Frank Pakenham was Personal Assistant to Sir William Beveridge 1941–4. He was created Baron Pakenham in 1945, and he was Parliamentary Under-Secretary of State at the War Office 1946–7, Chancellor of the Duchy of Lancaster 1947–8, Minister of Civil Aviation 1948–51 and First Lord of the Admiralty in 1951. In 1961 he succeeded his brother, to become the 7th Earl of Longford. In Harold Wilson's first Cabinet he combined Leadership of the Lords with the posts of Lord Privy Seal 1964–5, and Secretary of State for the Colonies 1965–6. He has been Chairman of the publishing house Sidgwick & Jackson since 1970.

of course – and then there were Carol and Bridget[1] and John[2] and Elsa[3] from my family and Mary Nicholson[4] (I think that she was the most upset person there) and Helga,[5] and John Baker[6] and Liena and Tommy and Pen [Balogh] and, of course, George and Carrie [Hodgkinson].

After tea the party gradually thinned out till the most intimate were left, including George and Carrie, and Mia picking cherries ferociously,[7] and Mrs D. washing up in a smashing mood. I think Eddie was quite right when he said that it was possible to enjoy it – which isn't usual at funerals but has something to do with her and Radnage, which belonged to her so much that I am wondering whether I can go back there more than only occasionally.

Life in Manor House, with a hospital regimen, slackly administered by nurses and doctors who really seemed to be friends, was probably the ideal thing for me. I was able to work through things with Rose and, as well as my articles, we slowly began to answer the letters which came, despite requests for no letters, and to thank for the flowers, which the Matron of the Westminster told me had overflowed from the Casualty Ward into the other wards and even into the passages.

There was a stream of visitors, marshalled by George, I suspect, out of fear that, if I was alone for an hour, I would commit suicide. So, from five in the morning, when I woke up, until eleven at night, when the last doctor and night nurse left me, I was busily engaged, high up on my bed. Of course, it's very easy to be serene and tranquil in the regimen of a hospital and I soon realized that the proposal to keep me there for three weeks was self-indulgence, so I got them to release me on the first day that it was medically possible to do so.

Curiously enough I really did quite a lot of politics in hospital, since having a death in the family removes political inhibitions. I don't mean so much that R. A. Butler wrote me a sweet letter but that Herbert Morrison and Patrick Gordon Walker came in to pay their condolences and within five minutes were discussing the Party conflict. And Hugh Gaitskell was just round the corner, ready to come in if I gave the word to Dora,[8] who sat with me for two hours and, of course, there was Hugh Dalton to bring one

[1] Carol was the wife of Crossman's elder brother, Geoffrey, and Bridget Bardsley was Crossman's sister.

[2] John Bardsley, the husband of Crossman's sister Bridget.

[3] Elsa was Crossman's other sister.

[4] Mary Nicholson was the wife of Max Nicholson, Secretary in the Office of the Lord President of the Council 1945–52 and Director-General of the Nature Conservancy 1952–66. The marriage was dissolved in 1964.

[5] Helga Connolly, Crossman's literary agent (see p. 141).

[6] John Baker, a Fellow of New College, Oxford, was Reader in Cytology at Oxford University from 1955 to 1967 and is now Emeritus Reader. He married Inezita Davis in 1923 and in 1939 Mrs Helen (Liena) Savage. His works include Race (London: Oxford University Press, 1974).

[7] There were eighty cherry trees at Town End Farm, where Zita Crossman had also looked after chickens, bees and two geese (one of which was called Polonius).

[8] Mrs Dora Creditor married Hugh Gaitskell in 1937. She became a life peer in 1963.

the point of view of a man who stood with a cloven hoof in each camp and an unkind word for all – though that's not fair, because to his own young men, including me, he's really affectionate.

When Herbert Morrison came up to see me, we discussed the new book on trade unions[1] and I remarked how far superior the Labour Party was to the Transport and General Workers, because it permitted a real minority on the National Executive and in the Parliamentary Party. To this Herbert replied, without undue emphasis but firmly, 'You know, Dick, we shan't be able to tolerate much longer the sort of organized opposition that you are running. It simply won't do.' So I said, 'Well, if a minority isn't allowed to organize, then what you get is the dictatorship of the Executive or, respectively, the Parliamentary Committee. Opposition is the lifeblood of democracy.' To which Herbert said, 'Yes, in Parliament but not inside a Party.'

I discussed this with Patrick Gordon Walker and of course it's true that, in the long run, no party can tolerate rival, organized factions fighting for power. Our excuse is that what we have is an emergency organization, set up to remedy the particular defect of leadership and policy. On no account must we suggest that we approve in principle of the Group, as part of the constitution of the Party or as a good thing in itself. We must always think of it ourselves as *ad hoc*, something which we are prepared to wind up if we can rectify the balance of power inside the Parliamentary Committee.

While I was in hospital I discussed informally with Eddie Shackleton, Gordon Walker, Dalton and Aneurin what the reaction would be if, say, Aneurin, Harold Wilson, John Freeman and I stood for the Parliamentary Committee next October, on the clear understanding that, if we were elected, the Group would be disbanded. I think that Gordon Walker and Morrison were extremely surprised by this idea that we shouldn't try to have it both ways, and I pointed out to them that, whatever defects Nye may have, he was always meticulous on this point when in the Cabinet. He never, as a Cabinet Minister, intrigued with outside groups. Indeed, the trouble I always found was that, whereas Morrison, Shinwell, Dalton were busy organizing claques, Nye was like a bear in his corner. I don't think that if Nye were on the Parliamentary Committee he would conceive of reporting back to an organized group outside it.

But all this is a long way off. First we must see what happens in the elections to the National Executive, where I haven't yet decided whether to stand or not. What I would really like to do is not to stand for the National Executive and to be elected to the Parliamentary Committee. A strong Left representation on the Parliamentary Committee, with a middle group led by Dalton, should be strong enough to hammer out a really decent policy day by day

---

[1] See *New Statesman and Nation*, July 12th, 1952, for a review of Joseph Goldstein's book *The Government of British Trade Unions: A Study of Apathy and the Democratic Process in the Transport and General Workers' Union* (London: Allen & Unwin, 1952).

and, after all, when Labour next comes to power, Nye and Gaitskell will have to be in the same Cabinet, so they may as well get used to serving on the same Parliamentary Committee. The only alternative is for us all to stay off the Parliamentary Committee and continue these conflicts inside the Parliamentary Party, in which we have been doing well. Objectively, this would have great advantages, since we know that we can do well with our organized group, whereas, in the case of the Parliamentary Committee, we can't be sure that the right people would be elected, and far less that they would get their way.

Coming back to the House last Monday I found people much less bad-tempered and evil-thinking of each other than I had expected. Of course, the fact is that the Government is doing so catastrophically badly that no one on our side can feel depressed or in danger of defeat and it is only when defeat hovers that real hatred begins.

At Monday's *New Statesman* lunch we had Harold Wilson, who fascinated me. When we got down to the questions I have just been discussing, he said that Nye had completely the right idea. What he was going to do after we had won the next election was to go to Attlee and demand that the Treasury should be deprived of the control of economic planning.[1] John Freeman and I protested that this meant absolutely nothing. With the best will in the world, how could Attlee reply to that demand? Then we gradually began to realize that what Mr Morrison was really getting at was that Mr Gaitskell, who could hardly be refused the chancellorship, should be subordinated to a new Minister of Economic Planning, Mr Harold Wilson.

This is the last time that I shall refer in the diary to Zita's death. We got some very nice letters, a lovely cable of reconciliation from Arthur,[2] a really nice letter from Rab Butler and, of course, the nicest letters from Mrs D. and Timothy.[3] It was nice with what extraordinary unanimity people felt that it was somehow unheard of that it should be Zita who had died. A few, no doubt, had regarded her as my wife, in the background, but I think that the great majority of the people that met her knew that Zita was an odd character in her own right and had a vitality completely of her own. Politicians are normally terribly hard-boiled, but I must say that on this occasion, in coming to see one, in telephoning, in writing, in sending flowers, they really did behave as comrades—apart from Mr Attlee, who sent no letter, nor a flower. But I must say that he did speak to me in the lobby quite sincerely, as though he were sorry. So it really may be shyness in him. But now it's over and a really nice number of people seem really glad to see one back and are anxious to invite one to stay with them.

---

[1] See below, p. 1006.

[2] Arthur Koestler and Crossman had quarrelled over what seemed to Crossman Koestler's ambivalent attitude to Socialism and Zionism and to Koestler Crossman's inability to conduct a searching intellectual argument into these matters.

[3] Timothy was the youngest of Mrs Ashby's three children by her marriage to Mr Alf.

Thursday, July 24th

We had a rough Party Meeting. It was supposed to be on the economic situation, with a big statement by Gaitskell, but Nye, with great skill, brashed in by asking whether we should have a resolution approving or disapproving of Churchill's cuts in the defence programme. Then the fat was in the fire and Gaitskell made a defence which so irritated me that I forfeited in two minutes all the Party's sorrow at my bereavement by a polite reminder to Mr Gaitskell that he and Mr Jay had been wrong on every issue for eighteen months and that the poor boobs like ourselves had happened to be right. Couldn't he, just for once, suggest a cut in armaments before Mr Churchill and Lord Swinton,[1] rather than tagging along afterwards?

My speech was a great deal more polite than Nye's and, as John Strachey remarked to me afterwards, for that reason all the more infuriating. Nye is probably quite right. The rudeness of which he is rightly accused makes no difference. What people mind is not rudeness but the knowledge that they are in the wrong and that we are too clever by half.

Monday, July 28th

I came back from the country last night to dine with Nye and found Benn Levy[2] and the Mallalieus. We had a really lovely evening and, after they had all gone, I stayed for an hour to talk politics. The name of Geoffrey Bing came up and I rather tentatively said that I thought that he might be a Communist. Jennie said that she was certain that he was and Nye said that he was certainly very close to them and that he didn't really accept our Bevanite position, any more than Tom Driberg did or many of our pacifists. Indeed, we agreed that there were very few members of the Bevanite Group who really accepted the Bevanite position. Nye, on the other hand, was very careful not to say a word against Harold Wilson, though he made it clear that, in his view, John Freeman had forfeited much influence by staying away from Parliament so much. I felt I had gained a great deal more of Nye's confidence in the last two or three months.

John Strachey told me that in the division lobby last week he had asked Attlee whether he hoped to be Prime Minister again. Attlee had replied, 'Oh

[1] Philip Cunliffe-Lister (1884–1972) was Unionist M.P. for the Hendon division of Middlesex from 1918 to 1935, when he was created Viscount Swinton. (In 1955 he was advanced in the peerage to become the Earl of Swinton.) After junior office at the Board of Trade he was its President in 1922–3, 1924–9 and in 1931. He was Secretary of State for the Colonies 1931–5 and for Air 1935–8. From 1942 to 1944 he was Cabinet Minister Resident in West Africa and he was Minister for Civil Aviation 1944–5. From 1951 he was Salisbury's Deputy Leader in the Lords, serving first as Chancellor of the Duchy of Lancaster (1951–2). From 1952 to 1955 he was Secretary of State for Commonwealth Relations.

[2] A dramatist who was Labour M.P. for the Eton and Slough division of Buckinghamshire from 1945 to 1950, and who worked for the Arts Council from 1953 to 1961. He began his working life as a publisher—becoming Managing Director of Jarrolds in 1923—but switched to the stage. He wrote the dialogue for Hitchcock's first British 'talkie', *Blackmail*, and was married to the American actress Constance Cummings. He died in 1973.

yes, and the election should come in October 1953.' John said, 'Will Vi agree?' And Attlee had replied, 'Oh yes, she will accept it, though she is very fond of Cherry Cottage.' The little man has an imperturbable unimaginativeness which is breathtaking but it is important to note that he has no idea whatsoever of resigning.

On July 31st and August 1st the House debated the Government motion to ratify the Treaty with the European Defence Community and the Contract governing the future status of Germany. Despite the role that the previous Labour Government had played in initiating the negotiations resulting in these agreements, the left-wing succeeded in pressing for an Opposition Amendment, rejecting the Government's present proposal 'as inopportune, particularly at a time when attempts are still being made by the Western Powers to discuss the German problem with the Union of Soviet Socialist Republics, and [reaffirming] the conditions first laid down in the House by the present Leader of the Opposition on 12th February, 1951'.

Neither Mr Attlee nor Mr Morrison (the former Foreign Secretary) spoke for the Amendment, leaving Mr Shinwell and Mr Dalton to do so. The Amendment was defeated by 294 votes to 260. The Opposition did not heed the Foreign Secretary's plea to support the Government resolution, which was passed by 293 votes to 253, with Labour abstentions raising the Government majority to 40.

Friday, August 1st
This has been an exciting, exhilarating, depressing week. The House adjourns with each of the two parties more disconsolate about its own leadership than ever before. It was Bob Boothby who said to me this afternoon that it was only the conflicts on the Labour side which had prevented a complete collapse among Government supporters. Certainly the bitterness has reached a new intensity. But let me record the events as they came.

On Tuesday morning we had the big Party Meeting on Germany. I had hoped that it would be a formality after the decision reached by an overwhelming majority at the previous Party Meeting[1] and the understanding obtained between Dalton and Aneurin. This understanding had been reinforced on Monday by George Wigg, who had put similar pressure on Shinwell and, as a result, the meeting of the Parliamentary Committee on Monday evening had been short and harmonious. As Dalton himself told me, the Committee had quickly accepted a two-paragraph Amendment drafted by him and then added a third paragraph, quoting from the Foreign Ministers' Washington communiqué, just to make quite sure that Herbert Morrison's position was secure. Thus, in exchange for great concessions on the Amendment, Dalton secured without any difficulty an agreement to vote against the substantive motion in favour of ratification. This was widely known on Monday evening and surprised us, since we had presumed that the Committee

[1] Reported by Crossman on May 1st. See above, pp. 102–3.

1 Clement Attlee (*seated, left*) and Ernest Bevin (*standing, second left*) at the Potsdam Conference, 1945

2 Attlee with Service Chiefs in Berlin during the air-lift, 1949

3 John Strachey (*left*) and Kingsley Martin, March 1950

4 Harold Wilson, as President of the Board of Trade, accompanies the King and Queen at the British Industries Fair, Earls Court, May 1950

would not agree and that the Party would be asked to decide the issue for the Committee.

However, at the Meeting Attlee got up and explained that a decision had been taken to table the Amendment and to vote against the substantive motion. He then read the Amendment aloud very fast. Some of us asked him to go slow so that we could take it down and consider it, to which he testily replied that he wasn't used to having Amendments taken down. I had a row with him. It was the only word I got in. Immediately he finished, the right-wing attack started with a passionate speech by Chris Mayhew, stating that the Parliamentary Committee's decision was a triumph for Crossman and *New Statesmanship* and for secret groups inside the Party. Mayhew was reinforced by dear old Reg Paget, who actually suggested that this was destroying Ernest Bevin's policy.

The debate went on all the morning. There seemed to be little question that the Amendment would be carried and John Strachey supported our voting against the substantive motion, with good casuistry. Little Tomney,[1] one of the most ferocious anti-Bevanites, got up and asked why he should be forced to vote against his conscience, which aroused a good deal of laughter, since last February[2] he had taken the lead in demanding the ex-pulsion of the Bevanites for voting against the Churchill Estimates, even when there were no Standing Orders. The whole irony of the Party Meeting, indeed, was that the right-wingers, who had forced the Standing Orders on the Party four months ago, were already hoist on their own petard. Their design had to be to make us vote for German rearmament and now Standing Orders and the will of the Party were going to make them vote against it. The bitterness was very great indeed. But finally the Parliamentary Commit-tee's proposal to vote against the substantive motion was carried by 140 to 27.

This left us very little to discuss at the Group Meeting at half-past one. Here Michael Foot announced that, at the end of September, *Tribune* is to become a weekly in newspaper form at 4*d*.[3] I only hope that they have the journalistic skill to do the job properly. But the new *Tribune* may get the Group out of a serious difficulty. If, as we have all agreed, three or four of us are to stand for the Parliamentary Committee, it will really be impossible for the Bevanite Group to go on as at present. Four members of the Parlia-mentary Committee could not possibly report back to a Group outside without violating the principle of collective responsibility.

However, we might perhaps change the character of the Group into an organization concerned with *Tribune* affairs generally and stop it being a strict group in its present form. During the last ten days I have been discussing this idea with Aneurin and Harold Wilson. Harold Wilson is in complete

[1] Frank Tomney, Labour M.P. for Hammersmith North 1950–79.
[2] In fact it was in March. See above, pp. 92 ff.
[3] *Tribune* was and is published weekly, except for the years 1950–2 when it appeared fortnightly. (*Tribune* pamphlets were produced in the intervening weeks.) In 1952 the price dropped from 6*d*. to 4*d*.

agreement. One is never sure about Aneurin but he has always been concerned for constitutional proprieties and when he was in the Cabinet he kept no contact whatsoever with us in the Keep Left Group nor with anyone else. Moreover, it would be a definite advantage if the brains trusts[1] could now be overtly called *Tribune* brains trusts, so that the collections could be used for *Tribune* and we could get away from the word 'Bevanite'.

Everyone at the Group was very pleased because at the Party Meeting Nye had made a mellow speech, in which, instead of calling Christopher Mayhew a pimp, as he called George Brown last week, he had laughed at him and got the whole of the rest of the Party laughing at him. I said this to Aneurin over a drink and he replied, characteristically, 'Anyone can be good-tempered at the Party Meeting when he is speaking for the majority. But no one in a minority has ever succeeded in keeping his temper.' This is a profound truth, which the right-wingers are now discovering.

On June 12th the Chancellor had announced that the drain on the reserves had eased. The losses of £334 million in the last quarter of 1951 and £227 million in the first quarter of 1952 had fallen to less than £10 million between the end of March and mid-June. Critics pointed out, however, that during this period £37 million had been received from the United States as the first instalment of the rearmament subsidy. Mr Bevan also observed that there had been a reduction in goods held in reserve.

In reply to questions about defence and export priorities, the Prime Minister stated on July 16th that a two-day debate on economic affairs would be held before the end of the Session. He promised measures 'grave and far-reaching, affecting every branch of our national life, both domestic and defensive'. The public feared unpleasant remedies, not least because the Budget proposals had been framed in the expectation of a slump. This had not in fact occurred. Unemployment, for instance, was falling even in the textile industries. Meanwhile, in a speech at Exeter on July 12th, the Chancellor had said that, if wage increases could be restrained, the country could hope for stable or falling prices for just over half of goods and services purchased—for all, that is, but food prices.

The two-day debate was to take place on July 29th and 30th. It proved to be an anti-climax.

At three o'clock I had to see Brigadier Head,[2] the War Minister, about a

---

[1] The *Tribune* brains trusts were organized by the paper's office and the more left-wing constituency Labour parties. An audience would put questions to a small panel of well-known Labour Party members and M.P.s.

[2] Antony Head was Conservative M.P. for the Carshalton division of Surrey from 1945 to 1960. A brigadier in the Guards, he was Secretary of State for War 1951–6 and Minister of Defence 1956–7. Created a peer (Viscount Head) in 1960, he was the first U.K. High Commissioner in Nigeria 1960–3, and in Malaysia 1963–6. Since 1975 he has been President of the Royal National Institute for the Blind.

constituency problem. Afterwards he and I went into the House to hear Butler open the economic debate. This had been precipitated by Churchill's Statement, in answer to Questions, that far-reaching measures were being prepared by the Government to meet the crisis.[1] It had already been suspected that this unprepared supplementary answer was a piece of verbiage but it was the kind of verbiage which sets things rolling. It caused a two-day debate and it compelled Butler to make a grave Statement on the crisis and on the measures to meet it.

Unfortunately there were no new measures and poor Butler was made to look an utter fool, standing there reading platitudes. The only new policies were a cut in defence and the decision to sell equipment for dollars and on these he had to say that the P.M. would speak next day. Gaitskell, in his first quarter of an hour, did a brilliant job, twitting Churchill for having lost the chance of £100 million by his talk about our standing on a trap-door,[2] but after that the debate petered out, while we waited for the Prime Minister on Wednesday. Harold Wilson spoke very competently but somehow his speech did not seem to cut any ice. It's difficult to say why but he does not carry much weight in the Party nor in the House, despite the fact that he is a man of first-rate ability.

I spent Wednesday morning at the *Statesman* and did a note on Egypt[3] and the front page on Churchill and Butler, writing it on the assumption that Nye would make an attack on Churchill which followed up my speech in the defence debate.[4] However, it was not to be; the afternoon debate started with Churchill and it soon became clear that he was not going to reveal any figures about the cut in defence or, indeed, anything further than what Butler had said. It was a sad speech, since the Old Man was clearly quite unable to answer any questions on his brief. At one point Gaitskell asked him whether

[1] See above, p. 130.

[2] The Prime Minister had said in a statement to the Press Association on June 11th, 'What I wonder is whether they have realized the treacherous trap-door on which it all stands? It is an alert that **I** am sounding, yet it is more than an alert—it is an alarm.'

[3] See the issue of August 2nd. Earlier in the year the Egyptian Parliament had approved a Bill providing compensation for loss of life and damage resulting from the Cairo riots in January (see p. 64). On March 1st Aly Maher resigned and was succeeded as Prime Minister by Ahmed Nagib al Hilaly. On March 24th Parliament, with its preponderant majority of Wafd members, was dissolved and martial law extended. Elections were postponed. The Wafd continued to plot against the Government. On June 28th Hilaly resigned, to be succeeded by Hussein Sirry Pasha, who set about cutting Government expenditure in an attempt to deal with Egypt's growing economic problems.

Meanwhile preparations for a coup were being made by a group of officers led by General Mohammed Neguib. Towards the end of July, King Farouk appointed his brother-in-law as Minister of War and secured the dismissal from the Army of General Neguib and twelve other officers. Sirry Pasha resigned and Neguib accelerated his plans. On July 23rd he marched a battalion into Cairo, meeting only token resistance, and on July 26th he proclaimed himself Commander-in-Chief. Aly Maher was reappointed as Prime Minister and on July 26th King Farouk met his request, 'on behalf of the people', to resign and leave Egypt by 6 p.m. That evening the Council of Ministers proclaimed Prince Ahmed Fuad, then only six months old, the second King of Egypt and the Sudan

[4] See above, p. 85.

the import cuts to which he referred were those imposed in the Budget or were new ones and he clearly didn't know the answers.

Shortly after Churchill, Nye rose in a good House. I was a few minutes late and, directly I got in, could feel things had gone wrong. He was in the middle of a personal attack on Gaitskell, which was being listened to with enormous relief by the Tories and with icy silence by our own benches. Then Nye said, 'I now turn my attack on the Prime Minister,' and Churchill did one of his perfect parliamentary turns by looking up like a cherub and remarking, 'At least I am here to hear it,' thus pointing to the absence from the Labour Front Bench of Attlee and Morrison. But, to everybody's amazement, the second half of Nye's speech turned out to be a charming, fresh disquisition on the reorganization of Ministries in Whitehall.[1] In the Smoking Room afterwards I think that we all made it clear to Nye that it hadn't gone perfectly. I said to him, 'I suppose a really brilliant debater gets so brilliant that he can't face doing the obvious thing. The obvious thing for you to do was to attack Churchill for not revealing the figures of the arms cut.' 'Ah,' said Nye, with as much charm as Churchill, 'there is such a temptation to be unpredictable.' Many members of the Group were talking to me in the passages in great perturbation, since they felt that Nye had let them down and had not spoken for them but for his personal whims.

On Thursday I was due to speak in the first day of the German debate. I spent the morning preparing it between telephone calls. The case has been chewed over so often and all the arguments are so drab that I was determined to do three things: first, to continue attacking Mr Eden, who is susceptible to attack, since he both likes me and does not like being attacked by me; secondly, to avoid attacking our own side; and, thirdly, to give the full terribly difficult reasoning about Germany. This meant a very complicated speech.

I got into my place just before half-past three and we were waiting for Eden to begin the debate when Attlee rose to make a personal statement.[2] This proved to be the severest kind of rebuke to Aneurin Bevan for constitutional impropriety in revealing Cabinet secrets in his speech the previous day. And Nye was not there! The Tories were jubilant and I must say those of us sitting on the fourth bench back must have looked fairly perturbed. I had a

[1] On May 6th the Prime Minister had been asked about the role of the 'overlords', the super-departmental co-ordinating Ministers who were members of the House of Lords and thus screened from direct responsibility to the Commons. Mr Bevan now pleaded for: the appointment of a Minister for British Economic Expansion; real amalgamation of the Ministries of Civil Aviation and Transport; the division of the functions of the Ministry of Pensions into those that could be handled by the Ministry of Health and those appropriate to the Ministry of Labour; the amalgamation of the Ministry of National Insurance with the Ministry of Labour; the moving of steel policy from the Ministry of Supply to the Ministry of Fuel and Power; the allocation of Works to the Ministry of Housing and Local Government and the end of Treasury dominance over appointments in the Civil Service.

[2] Mr Attlee declared that, during the second day of the debate on the economy, Mr Bevan had purported to describe proceedings in the Cabinet of which he had been a member, thus breaking the 'well established rule' of Cabinet confidentiality.

horrible feeling that Attlee had told Nye but that he'd had too good a lunch and come in a minute or two late. Ellis Smith very courageously got up and asked whether Attlee had given Nye prior notice. Attlee said 'Yes,' and there were howls of joy from the Tories when, at this precise moment, Nye came pushing along the bench and sat down. While we were hurriedly explaining what had happened, three notes waiting for him outside were passed along. I quickly hid them and one, dirty and insignificant, proved to be that from Attlee. Nye immediately rose to state that he had not received any previous intimation and some of the damage was retrieved.

So the German debate started, with an extremely adroit speech by Eden, elaborately showing that every one of his actions, including ratification, flowed directly out of the policy of the Labour Government. Manny followed him and I could see that George [Wigg] had briefed him admirably. No one else in the world is so dishonest that he could make such a convincing speech, when he had just turned a somersault, as Shinwell. It really sounded spiffing. Herbert Morrison sat silent. Then came thirty-five minutes from John Hynd,[1] the chairman of the foreign affairs group, who exploded every argument against ratification and wound up by saying that he was going to support the Labour Opposition!

I followed a Tory maiden speech and succeeded in holding Eden for forty minutes, part of the time quite angry and uncomfortable. (I had asked him three rather awkward questions during his speech[2] but he is so weak that he can never prevent himself giving way to me. One should give way to silly people, but not to clever ones.) It wasn't nearly such a clear, logical case as I had on the Defence Estimates, and the speech got a little too long. But I think that it was powerful and Manny and I did succeed in putting the Tories on the defensive and showing that there was a powerful case against immediate ratification.

I had been sitting there from half-past three to seven (when I started my speech) and after the Tory who followed me I went out to feed my ulcer, only to hear that Mr Mayhew demanded my return, since he was going to attack me. Perhaps wrongly, I looked after the ulcer and a ferocious attack was delivered on me, to Tory cheers, which was specially commended by Eden on Friday. Paget also spoke. In fact, the loyalists, who on this occasion were rebels, were given a pretty good running. Paget's speech was quite first-rate. Indeed, it could have been the keynote speech of the Republican Convention in Chicago. This German issue really has winnowed out the Labour Party and shown the fissures in it.

On Friday I tried to start the *Sunday Pic* but I couldn't resist going to hear Nye's personal statement at eleven o'clock. Actually we started with Black

[1] A railway clerk, later Labour M.P. for the Attercliffe division of Sheffield from 1944 to 1970. He was Chancellor of the Duchy of Lancaster and Minister for Germany and Austria 1945–7, and Minister of Pensions 1947. He died in 1971.

[2] Crossman asked whether sufficient effort had been made to reply constructively to the Russian suggestion in March 1952 for Four-Power talks.

Rod[1] and Lords' approval for fifty-four Bills and with no less than four ministerial Statements, while Nye waited. I begged him not to put in too many precedents. He was superb, starting with a long passage exculpating the messengers from any negligence. The more he exculpated the messengers, the more he inculpated the unfortunate Mr Attlee, whose idea of giving him previous notice was to leave an insignificant letter, not marked 'urgent', with the messengers in the Central Lobby, at a quarter to one. Apparently it never occurred to Attlee to telephone to Nye. Then Nye went on to the constitutional issue.[2] It is unwise to challenge him on such matters, since he is not only an expert but an expert who cares and he showed quite conclusively that collective responsibility breaks down at the moment of resignation and a resigning Minister then always has the right to reveal Cabinet secrets which led up to his resignation. It was a completely deadly performance and the middle-of-the-roaders in the Party were shattered by it, while all the Tories I talked to regarded it quite genuinely as a magnificent defence of an important constitutional principle. Bob Boothby, who had said to me the day before that Nye's speech in the economic debate was the first that he had ever delivered in twenty years which had helped the Tory Party, was ecstatic. So Nye had foot-faulted. Attlee had then served a double fault and thus enabled Nye to serve a whizzer and win the sessional game.

Afterwards I walked down the corridor with Eirene White,[3] a decent middle-of-the-roader on the National Executive, who was nearly in tears, and in the Tea Room afterwards I had a cup of coffee with Michael Stewart, a middle-of-the-roader, and Arthur Bottomley,[4] one of the twenty-seven who

[1] Sir Brian Horrocks. After a distinguished Army career, Horrocks became Gentleman Usher of the Black Rod in the House of Lords in 1949 and served in that office until 1963. A popular broadcaster, his works include *A Full Life* (new edition, London: Leo Cooper, 1974) and *Corps Commander* (London: Sidgwick & Jackson, 1977). The Gentleman Usher of the Black Rod, appointed by the Crown, is present when the House of Lords sits and acts as the messenger of the Sovereign whenever the attendance of the Commons is required. He also acts as the Secretary to the Lord Great Chamberlain and is thus responsible for other ceremonial duties and arrangements. He may be ordered by the House to take action in cases of disorder or disturbance of proceedings and is responsible for the admission of strangers to the Chamber and the precincts of the House and for giving effect to any orders and rules made in this respect.

[2] A view of the constitutional arguments was given in the 'London Diary' of the *New Statesman and Nation* of August 16th, 1952. It was probably Crossman's own.

[3] Labour M.P. for East Flint 1950–70. She was Parliamentary Secretary at the Colonial Office 1964–6, Minister of State for Foreign Affairs 1966–7 and at the Welsh Office 1967–70. She became a life peer in 1970. From 1972 until 1976 she was Deputy Chairman of the Metrication Board, and she has been a member of the Royal Commission for Environmental Pollution and of the British Waterways Board since 1974 and Chairman of the Land Authority for Wales since 1975. Since 1979 she has been Chairman of the House of Lords European Communities Committee.

[4] Labour M.P. for Chatham 1945–50, for Rochester and Chatham 1950–9, for Middlesbrough East 1962–74 and since 1974 for the Middlesbrough division of Teesside. He was Parliamentary Under-Secretary of State for the Dominions 1946–7, Secretary for Overseas Trade 1947–51, Secretary of State for Commonwealth Affairs 1964–6 and Minister of Overseas Development 1966–7.

had voted against us in the party Meeting.[1] Arthur tried the trick of saying, 'A plague on both your houses'. Michael was cleverer than that. Both were astonished when I said that we were going to stand for the Parliamentary Committee in October and would not, if elected, associate with the Group. I believe if that were got over to the Parliamentary Party a tremendous amount of the present friction could be resolved. But the right-wingers think so evil of us that they can't believe that we would play the game and of course it is true we are now so powerful that our terms for compromise are rising steadily.

I got the *Sunday Pic* done between half-past twelve and two o'clock and rushed back to hear Dalton and Eden winding up the debate. Dalton was unusually quiet and restrained — indeed, so restrained that he hardly held attention. Eden, in a virtually unprepared speech, was at his very best and concluded brilliantly. He could understand the Labour Party's moving the Amendment in order to unify its ranks but surely the responsible front-benchers could not vote against the substantive motion? Surely they must show more responsibility. He turned the knife in the wound until I nearly howled in sympathy with the unfortunate majority, who had let themselves be dragged so far down the primrose path and for whom the substantive vote meant ratting on their obligations.[2] How much better it would have been if thirty or forty had been allowed to abstain. But it was not us who introduced Standing Orders.

Friday, August 8th
George Wigg came to dinner on Wednesday and brought with him a letter from the Director of Education for Burton-on-Trent,[3] asking me whether I would permit my name to be put forward to take A. D. Lindsay's place as Principal of Stoke University College.[4] This had been put to me some weeks

---

[1] See above, p. 129.

[2] The Amendment was defeated by 194 votes to 260. The treaties were approved by 293 votes to 253.

[3] The Director of Education of Burton-on-Trent in 1952 was A. H. Blake.

[4] A. D. Lindsay (1879–1952). A Fellow of Balliol College, Oxford, and Professor of Moral Philosophy at the University of Glasgow 1922–4, he was Master of Balliol College 1924–49, serving as Vice-Chancellor of Oxford University 1935–8. In October 1938 he fought a by-election in the Oxford seat as an anti-appeasement (Independent Progressive) candidate, campaigning against the National Conservative candidate, Quintin Hogg. In 1945 he became a peer, taking the title Lord Lindsay of Birker, and from 1949 until his death he was Principal of the University College of North Staffordshire.

Under the guidance of R. H. Tawney and, later, of Lindsay, the adult education movement had flourished in North Staffordshire since the years immediately before the First World War. At the end of the Second World War Stoke-on-Trent City Council established a committee, chaired by Lindsay, to plan the University College of North Staffordshire. The first students were admitted in 1950 and in 1962 it was freed from the sponsorship of the Universities of Oxford, Manchester and Birmingham and renamed the University of Keele. Lord Lindsay of Birker had died on March 18th. Professor Francis Vick became Acting Principal, until Sir John Lennard-Jones took up the post.

ago by Bob Stross,[1] who is on its Council. At that time I said that I wouldn't mind being considered, because I thought that Zita had had too much of politics and might like to live in a lovely house in a park and have more domestic life. However, she wasn't very enthusiastic. Indeed, rather to my surprise, her reaction was that in that case I wouldn't be Foreign Secretary and that anyway there would be too much entertaining for her. Partly, I think, she said no because of ambition for me but mainly because she never believed that I would go. However, now the letter has come one has to think it over. It's the only job in the whole of education which is open to a strong political Socialist and it would be succeeding A. D. Lindsay, i.e. it's very nice to be asked.

When Phil Zec motored me down to Radnage yesterday (he was going down there to look at the cottage and see if it would do for him), I told him about the idea and then remembered that we had discussed this one night when Zita and I had gone to dinner with them. Old Zec's very enthusiastic about my doing it, partly because he himself accepts every new job that he is offered and partly, I suspect, because he thinks that I may not really get on in politics. Kingsley, to whom I mentioned it, thought that it was a fine idea, then rang me up the next morning to say that he hoped that I didn't regard this as showing that he was anxious to get rid of me from the *Statesman*. He's a Freudian case.

However, to go backwards. On Wednesday night I discussed it with George Wigg and told him that anyway, after Zita's death, I couldn't face going down there alone. George was non-committal and said, 'Well, it's all right staying in politics so long as you're not disappointed if you are not a member of the next Labour Cabinet.' And when I asked him what he meant, he explained that his guess was that Nye would go into the next Labour Cabinet and have me left out. If I didn't feel hurt about this, or bitter, I should stay in politics. If I couldn't stand that sort of disappointment, I should go down to Stoke. This seemed to me extremely good advice. Of course one would be annoyed but I think my immediate reaction would be, 'What fools they are.' I am now without doubt the most prominent backbencher, apart from Nye, and can exert very great influence from outside. Indeed, I think it's true that I have had far more influence from outside than if I had been a junior Minister or a Minister of State for five years in the last Labour Government.

Thursday, August 14th
Dining with the Jays on Monday, I got into a rather sterile but revealing argument. Douglas Jay regards himself as a middle-of-the-road man but he

---

[1] Barnett Stross, Labour M.P. for the Hanley division of Stoke-on-Trent 1945–50 and for Stoke-on-Trent Central 1950–66. A doctor in Stoke since 1926, and medical adviser to miners and pottery unions, he was Parliamentary Secretary at the Ministry of Health 1964–5. He was knighted in 1964.

talks to me with pained surprise about the undemocratic character of the 'party within the party' and said what a pity it was that Nye was not on the Parliamentary Committee. Actually Douglas Jay was too canny to stand for election in 1945 (or rather, Coventry West turned him down in favour of Maurice Edelman by 40 votes to 1). Douglas remained the chief economic adviser to Attlee until he was given a safe by-election in 1947, and then, after a year, he went straight into the Government. Like Christopher Mayhew, Hugh Gaitskell and a good many others, Douglas has had no experience of the backbenches and has grown accustomed to being a part of the Government or official Opposition machine, with plenty of room for self-expression. To him it seems real wickedness that other people should set themselves up to challenge the policies he has worked out.

I tried to explain that what we needed was to rectify the drift to the right by getting a reasonable balance of power on the Parliamentary Committee; say, three or four Bevanites out of twelve. He kept saying, 'We ought to have Nye Bevan back,' and couldn't see that Nye will never consent to be one against eleven again and that anyway the strength of Bevanism in the Party justifies much fuller representation.

Douglas's eldest boy[1] is now at Winchester and his second boy at Dragon's.[2] Though he purports to detest his children, he spent nearly all dinner fussing about whether his eldest boy had strained his heart by bicycling back from Victoria, or had perhaps got a little overheated, and the rest of the time was spent in discussing cricket, at which the boy excels. I have never seen a more doting father, except, of course, that he leaves every practical detail of looking after the four children to the unfortunate Peggy, who very affectionately walked me back to Hampstead Station. Peggy's view has always been that, if it were not for Douglas, she would be my wife. I'm not sure it's true but I think she'd have been much better preserved if she had been.

Wednesday, September 24th

I have now been back from my Italian holiday for ten days and my first impression is that inside the Labour Party there has been a sudden cooling of the temperature. While I was away the whole Bevanite controversy died

---

[1] The elder son was Peter Jay, who went from Winchester to Christ Church, Oxford. In 1961 he joined the Treasury, becoming Private Secretary to the Joint Permanent Secretary in 1964. He left the Civil Service in 1967 and from that year until 1977 was Economic Editor of *The Times* and from 1969 to 1977 Associate Editor of *The Times* Business News. From 1972 to 1977 he also introduced 'Weekend World' and from 1975 to 1976 'The Jay Interview' (both I.T.V. series). He was chairman of the Working Party on Children and Young Persons in Custody, established in 1975 and reporting in 1979. In 1977 he became Ambassador to the United States but resigned that post in 1979, on the defeat of the Government of James Callaghan, whose daughter, Margaret, he had married in 1961. The second son was Martin, who became Manager of various companies in the G.E.C. group.
[2] The Dragon School, Oxford, a preparatory school.

down completely[1] and the Margate conference of the T.U.C.,[2] which turned into the usual Communist/anti-Communist do, did not revive any interest, because Bevanism was noticeable by its absence.

Aneurin Bevan has been away in Scotland, where he caught his first salmon in the River Dee and got so excited that he knocked his knee as a result and has been lame ever since. There have been mildly friendly references in the press to salmon-fishing as a sport of millionaires but no one has revealed the deadly secret that the bait Nye used was a prawn.[3] Typically enough, he has done absolutely nothing political throughout August and September. Nor has there been any meeting of the Bevanite Group nor any attempt to think out strategy or tactics for the Conference. Once again we are going to it as an army of innocents. This should not do us any harm in the actual voting for the National Executive, since most of the constituencies live about four months behind events and will have mandated their delegates while the controversy was still lively. But I must say that I have rather gloomy pre-monitions about what will happen in the actual debates.

On Monday night I was due to have my long-postponed dinner with the Gaitskells. At the last moment it was changed, because Virginia and Aidan Crawley,[4] up from the country, were staying with the Gaitskells and wanted us all to meet Virginia's father, a hard-bitten Southern Democrat from Virginia, who earns a great living as a psychiatrist in New York. Hugh and Dora came for an hour and a half to chat and drink at Vincent Square before-hand and I found Hugh very agreeable and modest in private life. But at dinner, where conversation was mainly about Britain and Europe, Britain

---

[1] In early August Crossman had predicted that 'the official line' at the forthcoming Party Conference at Morecambe would be based on the anti-Bevanite attacks now appearing in the press. In the *News Chronicle* on August 6th, A. J. Cummings had described the Group as 'a conspiratorial campaign'; Michael Foot had replied in the same newspaper on the following day. On August 11th the *Daily Herald* gave prominent treatment to speeches against Bevanism made by George Brown and Aidan Crawley; Michael Foot again replied and John Freeman wrote an (unsigned) article in the *New Statesman and Nation* of August 16th.

[2] The T.U.C. met at Margate from September 1st to September 5th, with Arthur Deakin as President. On September 4th the delegates approved by a majority of over 6 million votes a statement by the General Council warning of the consequences of substantial wage increases. Although some of the delegates voting in favour of the statement belonged to unions which were in fact pressing considerable wage claims, the Prime Minister told his constituents on September 6th that at Margate 'wise statesmanship' had been shown.

[3] The story is correct. Salmon do not care for prawns in their water and will take them not to eat but because they loathe them. In certain conditions of water, all salmon will take is a prawn and this explains Bevan's success. Fly-fishers of the Scottish rivers would have disapproved.

[4] Aidan Crawley, a prisoner of war 1941–5, became Labour M.P. for Buckingham, serving as Parliamentary Under-Secretary of State for Air 1950–1. He resigned from the Labour Party in 1957 and was Conservative M.P. for West Derbyshire 1962–7. He was Editor in Chief of I.T.N. 1955–6, a producer of documentary programmes for the B.B.C. 1956–60, Chairman of London Weekend Television 1967–71 and President of L.W.T. 1971–3. In 1945 he married Virginia Cowles, daughter of Edward Spencer Cowles. A writer and journalist, her works include a number of detailed accounts of Europe before the First World War.

and the Middle East, etc., I observed that, whenever the conversation reached a certain point, Gaitskell's lips would purse as though he were saying, 'It must end here.' At one point Hugh was defending the Labour Government policy towards Europe with the argument that we had constantly to take precautions against the danger of America's withdrawing from Europe. At this point Virginia's father asked him what on earth he was talking about. Who had ever told him that America would withdraw from Europe? And Virginia, Aidan and I all chimed in. Hugh pursed his lips very tight and I could feel an obstinacy which I don't think was there two years ago, whenever an idea was broached which contradicted his idea of Labour policy.

Motoring to the dinner, I told him that Desmond Donnelly had just got back from Peking and had travelled in the plane from Prague with Joseph Needham,[1] the Cambridge scientist who had just been in China with a group of hand-picked Communist scientists and had issued a report on germ warfare.[2] Joe Needham, I said, though of course a Communist, is also a serious-minded scientist and the fact that he has signed this report and was permitted to interview the four American airmen makes me think that we cannot dismiss it like that. I felt a wave of icy disapproval, as though Gaitskell were saying to himself, 'Yes, this is entirely irresponsible and on the wrong side.' However the dinner was very good and, apart from Hugh's primness, the conversation was lively. I'm sure it's worth keeping up social relations.

Friday, September 26th
I was very anxious to see Hugh Cudlipp before I wrote my piece on

---

[1] Joseph Needham, a distinguished biochemist and Sinologist. He was a Fellow of Gonville and Caius College, Cambridge, 1924–66 and Master 1966–76. Since 1976 he has been Director of the East Asian History of Science Library at Cambridge. His *Science and Civilization in China* (Oxford University Press, 1954–) has so far run to twenty volumes.

[2] In 1951 charges had been made that the American Air Force was waging bacteriological warfare. These accusations were raised more vehemently in early 1952 and General Chou En-lai supported the protest of the North Korean Foreign Minister by alleging that American aircraft had dropped insects, rodents, shellfish and chicken feathers impregnated with plague and disease germs on Chinese as well as Korean territory.

On February 27th the United Nations Command Headquarters denied these allegations. A proposed investigation by the International Red Cross was rejected by the North Korean and Chinese generals but a so-called International Scientific Commission was permitted to visit Peking, Manchuria and North Korea from June 23rd to August 6th. Their report found in favour of the Communist charges. (*Report of the International Scientific Commission for the Investigation of Facts Concerning Bacteriological Warfare in Korea and China*, Peking, 1952.)

Professor Needham had met four American airmen, Chinese prisoners of war, who had allegedly confessed to germ warfare. In Crossman's own words in a diary entry for October 6th, 1952, Professor Needham 'had taken part in a public meeting in a school hall which took the place of an interrogation'. Crossman, with his experience of political warfare and interrogation of prisoners, was unimpressed by Needham's evidence. He reported that Needham admitted that he 'went as a scientist, not as a lawyer'.

Morecambe this week,[1] more particularly because he is off to Australia for six months at the beginning of October.[2] Finally, after a lot of to-ing and fro-ing, he asked me to have supper with him on Wednesday at the Bagatelle at half-past ten. I found him there with Eileen [Ascroft] and Rex North[3] in a crowded, small room, with an appallingly noisy West African band. Rex North's wife was the one cabaret turn. Shouting through the band, we talked until two in the morning.

Cudlipp started by telling me that he had been reading all of Aneurin Bevan's speeches and was going to launch an attack on him on the front page on Sunday.[4] We sparred for an hour or two and at about one o'clock (I think that Hugh had been drinking since about seven) he said that he probably wouldn't do a story on Aneurin Bevan and would leave me to do Morecambe in the column. He continued to repeat his line that I twiddled Phil Zec around my little finger but he was Editor, and he, Cudlipp, wasn't going to tolerate a Herbert Morrison or a Bevan and that the *Mirror* Group should be really independent. However, at another point he observed that it was the job of the *Mirror* Group, if they believed in Socialism, to launch their own constructive Socialist programme. Hugh is totally and absolutely incoherent but, curiously enough, he enjoys my company a great deal and is, I think, deeply mystified why I have got myself mixed up with that terrible man Bevan. I am sure Eileen keeps his hatred well fanned.

I managed to get away at about half-past two in the morning. Fleet Street is a very extraordinary place. What is it that makes men like Hugh Cudlipp become the responsible (!) Editors of enormous circulation newspapers? What is it that makes people like myself write in them? Finally, what are the ethics of my going on writing the column when the paper has denounced Nye, as it will have done on Sunday?*

We certainly had, socially, a highly successful evening but, on the other

[1] Crossman's *Sunday Pictorial* column, on p. 2 of the September 28th issue, reminded readers that the forthcoming Conference was the first since 1939 to be held with the Labour Party in Opposition. On the agenda was 'a mass of resolutions, any one of which may cause a violent explosion'. Moreover, the Bevanites, who the previous year had secured four out of seven of the National Executive places elected by the constituency votes, were this time attempting to capture six seats. Although success would none the less leave them outnumbered on the N.E.C. where there were also twelve trade union representatives and eight others, Bevanite gains would effectively demonstrate the strength of constituency party feeling against the political conservatism of the Party's Front Bench and trade union leadership.

[2] He was off to Australia to investigate why the *Melbourne Argus*, owned by the *Mirror* group, was losing circulation and money. The newspaper was eventually sold.

[3] A reporter and War Correspondent with the *Sunday Pictorial* and from the end of the Second World War until 1960 a weekly columnist on the *Sunday Pictorial* and *Daily Mirror*. He died in June 1969. His wife, Lind Joyce, was an actress and singer who worked with the 'Tommy Handley Show'.

* To judge from the *Mirror* this morning, Cudlipp has after all decided to launch an attack.[4]

[4] But in the *Daily Mirror* for the week prior to September 26th, 1952, there is no obvious hint of the forthcoming attack on Aneurin Bevan.

hand, for all I know, Hugh may want to get rid of me in ten days' time. But I fancy that he probably won't. And, since he will be off to Australia the week after next, I may as well cling to my corner of the paper.

The evening was a bit difficult because Rex North's wife was indescribably awful and Cudlipp kept saying so to me. And when the poor girl, who had a bad cold as well, came to have her supper with us, nobody said anything about her turn. Whenever I feel really depressed about the stinkingness of politics, I take a dive into Fleet Street and see what stinkingness really is.

On Thursday Eddie Shackleton came to tea and told me that in August, when the anti-Bevanite attacks were launched by George Brown, Dick Stokes and Gordon Walker, Eddie had strongly advised Herbert Morrison not to intervene and had in fact redrafted one or two speeches. From Eddie's account, Herbert is quite anxious about his own position and, though he thinks it would probably do me no good, he would apparently not be averse to seeing me on the Executive.

In the evening I had John and Mima Freeman to dinner. John brought round a copy of the *Statesman* and couldn't resist reading passages from it. He is totally absorbed in it now. He really is a strangely secretive person. At Overton's fish restaurant in Victoria where we dined, I noticed Hugh Carleton Greene[1] and his wife, sitting with a man that I didn't know. As they were leaving, Hugh came up to talk to me and mentioned that his guest was Graham Greene.[2] I asked John whether he knew him and he said yes but it had never occurred to him to mention it or to greet him, though he had been talking to him over the telephone.

This evening Hugh Cudlipp rang up and began to explain to me, rather laboriously, that he was going to launch his attack on Nye.[3] He asked me whether I would like to hear it and I said no. Then he said, 'Couldn't I read you the toughest passages?' I said that I would have to consider my position. The conversation was very repetitive but I think that it was four times that

[1] Hugh Greene joined the B.B.C. in 1940 as Head of the German Service. He was Director of News and Current Affairs 1958–9, Director-General 1960–9 and a Governor 1969–71. In 1969 he became Chairman of the publishing house The Bodley Head and in 1971 Chairman of the brewers Greene, King & Sons Ltd. During the war he and Crossman worked together on propaganda methods and psychological warfare. He had married Elaine Shaplen in 1951. The marriage was dissolved in 1969. His first wife was Helga Greene (later Connolly), Crossman's literary agent.

[2] The novelist, playwright, essayist and critic. A member of the staff of *The Times* 1926–30 and Literary Editor of the *Spectator* 1934–41, Graham Greene worked in the Foreign Office 1941–4 and was a Director of the publishing houses Eyre & Spottiswoode 1944–8 and The Bodley Head 1958–68. His many publications include *Brighton Rock* (London: Heinemann, 1938), *The Heart of the Matter* (London: Heinemann, 1948), *The End of the Affair* (London: Heinemann, 1951), *The Quiet American* (London: Heinemann, 1955), *The Comedians* (London: Bodley Head, 1966) and *The Human Factor* (London: Bodley Head, 1978). He is the brother of Hugh Carleton Greene.

[3] On September 28th the headline in the *Sunday Pictorial* was 'END THE BEVAN MYTH'. The front page and p. 7 were devoted to an attack on Bevan's 'vanity, arrogance, spleen'. The only Bevanite mentioned by name was Michael Foot, described as one of the 'bewildered disciples'.

Hugh emphasized that he did not want to lose his brilliant columnist and he saw nothing difficult in the paper's taking a line which differed from the column. Curiously enough, I had the feeling that Hugh was apologizing to me for doing something he felt an inner compulsion to do but which he hoped would not involve any difficulties with me. 'I'm telling you because I wanted to be fair to you,' he said, 'and to give you fair warning. I'm speaking to you as a friend. Surely, I have the right, as Editor, to attack Bevan if I feel it is necessary to do so. But that shouldn't interrupt our relationship or prevent your going on writing. Nothing is further from my thoughts.' He then read me one or two passages, in which he attacked the Bevanites as followers of a Messiah or men who were pushing Bevan for their own advantage, and he told me that he had taken out the reference to me by name. Like a fool, I didn't tell him to put it back, since, in fact, from my point of view an attack on Nye which leaves me clear is far more embarrassing than an attack on myself as well.

The whole conversation was an extraordinary tangle. I can't help feeling that Hugh feels that he must assert himself as Editor in the political field and that the best way of doing so is to reverse Phil Zec's policy, which Hugh was convinced was Bevanite, or rather, run by his columnist. Hugh wants to show that he has some political ideas as well and I hope he feels better after his orgasm.

I left Hugh, not quite certain what I should do, and told him that I would talk to him next Friday, when I get back from Conference.

When I got on to the train at Euston, I found Tom O'Brien, the Secretary of his union, and Geoffrey Bing in the first-class restaurant car and we travelled down together. Tom O'Brien, who is next year's T.U.C. Chairman and an Irish rogue of the highest quality, entertained us to the biggest meal that I have ever had in a restaurant car. It lasted from five o'clock till a quarter to eleven and included endless rounds of drinks, two bottles of white wine, two bottles of red wine and then liqueurs—as well as all the courses the Railway had to offer. 'Some of my delegates', Tom said after dinner, 'have the insolence to challenge me on my expense account!' As far as I could see from the bill, the dinner cost £14.[1]

It was driving rain on the illuminated promenade and when I opened the door of my hotel it nearly blasted all the residents, quietly studying television in the dark. The landlady was extremely hospitable and offered me a meal at half past eleven but I went round to the Grosvenor, where the Executive were staying. The first man that I ran into was Hugh Dalton, looking rather grey and anxious, who took Desmond Donnelly and me up to his room for a drink. The waiter said to us, 'Is that the Dr Dalton who was a friend of Rupert Brooke?'[2] And when he produced drinks I asked him if he had been

---

[1] The equivalent of about £70 at 1979 prices.

[2] The poet and author. While serving as a Sub-Lieutenant in the Royal Navy in the First World War he fell ill with sunstroke in April 1915 and subsequently died from blood-poisoning, at the age of twenty-eight.

listening to the recent Third Programme[1] on Rupert Brooke which had
mentioned Dalton. 'No,' the waiter said, 'it comes in Edward Marsh's
biography.'[2] Dalton then told how he had thirty or forty of Brooke's most
interesting letters, which had been written to him. 'The finest letter writer
I ever knew,' said Dalton. 'Up to Horace Walpole's[3] standard?' asked the
waiter.

This evening the general impression in the Grosvenor was that everybody
on the Executive was scared of what the Conference might do and that Right
and Left were seeking to preserve unity and respectability but were terrified
that some individual delegates from the floor would cause Arthur Deakin to
blow off and then the whole thing would catch alight.

Saturday, September 27th
I woke up to a morning of sunshine, rainclouds and a superb view across
the mud to the mountains of the Lake District. There is nothing whatsoever
to be said for Morecambe except this view, which appeared at thirty-hour
intervals for a minute or two throughout the week. It's a minor Blackpool,
dumped down on mud flats, with a four-mile-long promenade, with the
Grosvenor at one end, the Winter Gardens in the middle and the other big
hotel[4] at the other end, so that life was spent in going from one to the other
in a blustering, driving wind. By the end of the Conference everybody had
streaming colds, as well as heartache.

The delegates concerned with composite resolutions[5] had been summoned
to the town hall at half-past two. Having exercised myself in the morning by
walking five miles up and down the front, I arrived on time at the extreme far
end of Morecambe, to find a jostling crowd and, to my surprise, Jennie Lee
who happened to turn up. Also Tom Driberg, who shouldn't have been there
since he is a member of the Executive, but was acting as a substitute for his
constituency delegate, whose train was late. There was also Desmond
Donnelly. We were all concerned with the sixty-eight resolutions on foreign
policy and some sixty of us filed into the council chamber, where we were

[1] Sound broadcasting was at this time divided into three programmes: the Home Service
and the Light and Third programmes.
[2] Edward Marsh (1872–1953), Private Secretary to, among others, Asquith and
Churchill, was a patron of the arts, especially the Georgian poets, much of whose work he
published in *Georgian Poetry* between 1912 and 1921. He was knighted in 1937. His
memoir of the poet Rupert Brooke was published in London by Secker in 1918. A
biography of Marsh was written by Christopher Hassall: *Edward Marsh: Patron of the Arts*
(London: Longman, 1959).
[3] Horace Walpole (1717–97), the 4th Earl of Orford. A novelist, writer, connoisseur and
author of *Memoirs of the Reign of King George III* (London, 1845), his own *Letters* have
been edited definitively by W. S. Lewis, and were published by Yale University Press
between 1937 and 1965.
[4] The Midland Hotel, which housed those N.E.C. members for whom there was no room
at the Grosvenor.
[5] 'Compositing' is the process by which motions for debate, submitted by trade unions
and constituency parties, are amalgamated and grouped.

faced with Jim Hawarth, the Chairman of the Conference Arrangements Committee, and Jim Griffiths, holding a watching brief for the Executive. I had long thought that these compositing conferences are absolutely vital and had written a rather snarky piece on the front of the *New Statesman*,[1] warning delegates that the Conference Arrangements Committee had been captured by the right-wingers and regularly organized the composites so that silly fellow-traveller resolutions could easily be voted down.

I observed from the start that Mr Hawarth was not very friendly to me. He began by saying that, with so many resolutions, it was necessary to get them down to three or four, and he was ready to give his suggestions. I then asked whether before he did this we could discuss the way in which the resolutions would be taken. Would the composites be debated and voted on separately or taken one after the other, followed by a general debate, and then voted *en bloc*, as happened at the T.U.C. at Margate? Hawarth said that we had no right to discuss this, whereupon a babel arose from the floor and I realized that the delegates were on my side. Just behind me was sitting a severe young German-Jewish-looking man,[2] who immediately leapt up and said, 'I've been working at these resolutions and I think that we can divide them into three groups: first, Korea, second, Germany, third, Socialist foreign policy in general.' And he then read aloud his three groups. Hawarth hurriedly observed that this was all very well but that the delegates would not be likely to agree, whereupon I said, 'Shall we see?' And before you knew what, three groups had been established. The German group was under the chairmanship of Desmond Donnelly, the Korea group under Tom Driberg, while Jennie Lee and I, along with the young German-Jew, who turned out to be a certain Jack Mendelsohn from Sheffield, ran the most difficult group on Socialist foreign policy.

After two and a quarter hours we had each produced composite resolutions, in which we had defeated the fellow travellers and produced something which was passably Bevanite, presented them to Mr Hawarth and Mr Griffiths and had them accepted, along with two amendments moved by pacifists and fellow travellers, which we were delighted to accept on the order paper so that we would have the extreme Left distinguished from ourselves. I'm quite sure that Griffiths and Hawarth thought that this was a superb piece of Bevanist organization. Actually it was almost luck that any of us happened to be there and none of us had seen Mr Mendelsohn before and he had taken the leading role.

My only awkward thing was that in my group was the representative of Coventry Borough, a stocky young revolutionary[3] who kept on saying, 'I insist that Coventry Borough's words be used,' till he was howled down.

[1] See *New Statesman and Nation*, September 27th, 1952, for Crossman's article on 'The Opportunity of Morecambe'.

[2] John Jakob Mendelson (habitually misspelt by Crossman). See p. 223.

[3] Eddie Hunter, a shop steward at the Standard Motor Works, who later moved for a time to local government.

Then came the ticklish question of which constituencies' names to append to the composites. This determines who speaks. It was naturally proposed that either Jennie or I should propose. We turned this down and put Mendelsohn up. Then it was proposed that I should second and I realized that, if I agreed, Coventry Borough would pass a vote of censure on me. So I had to solemnly propose Coventry Borough and have him voted down, after which he went to see his fellow Coventrians and said he had stood down for me. In the middle of this hubbub, George and Carrie Hodgkinson walked in and looked very pleased, until Jim Griffiths spotted them and thought they completed the conspiracy.

Comparing notes afterwards at the Grosvenor, we found that all the compositing had been done far better than usual. In the Rearmament section, the USDAW resolution had been left untouched and Wilfred Fienburgh had produced a tremendous composite on domestic policy, for which he was immediately accused of being a Bevanite.

I had dinner with Tom Driberg and his wife at the Grand, having promised to go out with her afterwards round the pubs, since he had business to do. However, meanwhile Jennie and I had been mandated to see the chairman of the Conference[1] about our proposal to have the composite resolutions debated and voted separately. We had got this unanimously approved by the sixty-eight, over the dead body of Mr Hawarth, who finally agreed to be spiritually absent from the room while we discussed it. Just before dinner I heard that the chairman would see me at nine o'clock, so I found that I would have to leave Ena Driberg. I also discovered that Tom Driberg's business was a singularly dreary young man from Preston, who is one of his loves. We finally had our meeting with the chairman at nine o'clock and he listened very attentively to our plea but I knew that he would turn it down. All the talk this evening was about the composite resolutions and the satisfactory way things were going, to prevent any split or row.

Sunday, September 28th

I spent the morning on a long walk with Carrie along the shore to Heysham, while George was at the agents' conference. Since there is nothing else to do at Morecambe on a Sunday morning except be on the promenade it was difficult at first to move along. But after a couple of miles the crowds thinned out and it was quite a nice piece of seashore until we rounded a corner and found the docks. On the way back, through Heysham village, we found hundreds of little booths selling nettle wine for 3*d.*; it tasted rather like home-brewed ginger beer.

At half-past one a car called to take me over to Fleetwood, an hour's drive, where I was to address a Labour Party meeting with Jim Figgins,[2] the General Secretary of the N.U.R. We picked up Figgins, who looks like a

[1] I.e. Harold Earnshaw, a Party organizer and a prominent member of the I.L.P.
[2] James Figgins, General Secretary of the N.U.R. 1948–53.

retired Anglo-Indian country gentleman farmer and who had a very heavy cold which he duly gave to me, and reached Fleetwood in drenching rain, to find to our amazement some 500 people assembled in the hall. Figgins was announced as speaking on denationalization and he spoke on it for a few minutes, after which he entered into a panegyric on the Soviet Union, which was warmly cheered by the audience, which then warmly cheered my Bevanite speech on the dangers of American and Russian imperialism. Then a very nice old age pensioner got up and asked whether I thought it was fair that his rubber heels cost 4s. 6d., so we were in a real Labour Party meeting, which was completed by a high tea with the Conservative Mayor in a butterfly collar.

I dined at the Grosvenor with Desmond Donnelly and Mendelsohn, who had come in with a crowd of foreign policy delegates. We saw Dalton, who was to introduce the foreign policy debate, and discussed the resolutions with him. One small mistake had been made, since the German resolution included the word 'neutralization', and was therefore bound to be rejected. Dalton agreed not to attack it as Communist propaganda but to agree with it, apart from this one word, and ask for it to be remitted. This would avoid a vote. All this showed how pally everybody was today.

But meanwhile, upstairs, the stormiest meetings of the National Executive were taking place on and off between five and eleven o'clock, all devoted to the subject of the allocation of platform speakers. Apparently Morgan Phillips produced a roneo-ed scheme, which showed Nye Bevan as speaking on two minor resolutions on unemployment and housing and every other member of the Executive who could open his mouth as speaking on other subjects, including Mr Attlee to do the two big speeches on defence and domestic policy and Herbert Morrison to do another big speech on home policy and two other minor ones. Alice Bacon was to make three speeches, Edith Summerskill four, but, by some curious coincidence, Barbara Castle, Ian Mikardo and Tom Driberg were omitted. Thunder and lightning. What should the Bevanites do? Should Nye refuse to speak at all? And, while all this was being discussed, the great Sunday evening demonstration was due to begin, with Mr Attlee, Mr Webber[1] and Mrs Alice Horan[2] as the sole speakers.

At the last moment even Morgan Phillips realized (due to the fact that no contestant for the National Executive could speak for fear of winning votes) that this scheme was rather anodyne and he proposed an overflow meeting, with Barbara Castle and Bessie Braddock.[3] The Bevanites smelt a trap. Barbara was certain to get in, so didn't need any votes, but Bessie Braddock

---

[1] William Webber, a railway clerk in Swansea, and a member of the N.E.C. 1949–53. He was General Secretary of the Transport Salaried Staffs Association 1953–62 and was knighted in 1968.

[2] National Women's Officer of the N.U.G.M.W. and a member of the N.E.C. until 1958. She died in 1971.

[3] Labour M.P. for the Exchange division of Liverpool from 1945 until her death in 1970.

would get some. Meanwhile Aneurin had changed his mind and had agreed to speak on unemployment but not on housing. So the demonstration started, while the Executive went on and suddenly Ian Mikardo was offered housing and accepted, with the result that I had to stay up to two o'clock in the morning with Barbara Castle in tears, since she had refused to speak at the overflow demonstration and here she was excluded and Ted Castle saying that this was intolerable. What prima donnas we are, including the Bevanites.

In between all this, I had gone into the residents' lounge upstairs. As you enter, you see, to the left, a sofa, with Mrs Attlee and Mrs Shinwell and their circle grouped round them, and, to the right, a sofa, with Jennie Lee and her circle grouped round her, all talking in low whispers. This scheme remained constant throughout the week. Between the blocs sat Jim Hawarth and Crane[1] of the Conference Arrangements Committee, looking very fierce. Crane said that he had read the *New Statesman* all his life and this week it had told a lie. And, true enough, it had. The Conference Arrangements Committee is nothing to do with the Executive, being elected by Conference itself and doing its job of organizing the resolutions and composites strictly independently. Indeed, it is very proud of its independence and regards itself as a watchdog of the Conference. Hence the fury of Mr Hawarth and Mr Crane at our front page. A long talk convinced me that they were honest men, who had been injured.

What has happened in past years is that Communists and fellow travellers have been active enough in the compositing committees to push their resolutions forward. Since the job of the committee is on the whole to choose the most controversial resolution, i.e. that which differs most sharply from the view of the Executive, it is easy for the fellow travellers to get their way, unless there are others present deliberately determined to defeat them. Even so, every composite resolution is bound to be a terrible mess and the real swindle has been the way in which the Executive members, who answer debates, have attacked composite motions on account of some vague fellow traveller wording, instead of trying to find the best in them. What it comes to is that practically any composite you draft is bound to be so unsatisfactory that it can be torn to pieces by the Executive if it wants to do it. But the procedure, which I had criticized, seems to be perfectly all right.

Monday, September 29th
I got to the Conference in time to hear the chairman read out the obituary notice, which included Cripps and Tomlinson.[2] At this point the chairman turned to Attlee and asked him whether he wanted to say anything. Attlee

[1] Harry Crane, N.U.G.M.W. District Officer and Secretary. He succeeded James Hawarth as Chairman of the Labour Party Conference Arrangements Committee in 1954, serving until 1965. He was knighted in 1966.
[2] George Tomlinson (1890–1952), Labour M.P. for the Farnworth division of Lancashire, was Parliamentary Secretary at the Ministry of Labour 1941–5 and Minister of Works 1945–7 and of Education 1947–51.

doodled ánd shook his head. It was the first indication of the astonishing lack of leadership which he displayed throughout. To let these two names go by without a word was really astounding. A warm speech about them both could have been used to pull the Conference together.

The only other significant thing this morning occurred when I was having a cup of coffee with Carrie at a quarter past eleven. Apparently it was announced inside the hall that ballot papers were now being issued, at which practically the whole hall was emptied and a football scrum poured to the room outside where we were sitting. Normally at Conference the Executive has to appeal every hour during the afternoon to delegates to take up their voting papers. This year there was no need. They all knew what they had come for.

After a rather dull and unanimous afternoon debate on the denationalization of road transport, a violent resolution was moved, suggesting we should take away all the profits of denationalized industries when we renationalized them. When a hand vote was called, the resolution was carried overwhelmingly and then, on the [trade union] block vote, it was only $2\frac{1}{2}$ to $1\frac{1}{2}$, since the A.E.U. and the N.U.R. got in a muddle and abstained. A few minutes later we had another strange resolution, calling for an all-out attack on the Tory Government and pledging Labour Party support to the trade unions if they took industrial action to maintain working-class living standards. Apparently this resolution came from a group of Birmingham Trotskyites, who were sitting just behind me. Anyway, after it had been moved, it was denounced by Deakin and Lawther[1] in the most ferocious language and both of them took the occasion to say that they controlled the money and the Labour Party would not have any if it passed this. Arthur added that, even if the Labour Party did mandate the National Council of Labour along these lines, the miners would take no account of the mandate.

This produced the first real feel of the Conference, especially when Lawther added that the delegates were just the people to shout for industrial action and squeal when it happened. As every delegate I met was an ardent trade unionist who had come there to denounce the trade union leaders, the whole floor rose to boo. It was quite different from the feel of pre-war Conferences, since this rank and file are uninhibited trade unionists, who do not take trade union leaders lying down, as Members of Parliament do. After that I was pretty certain that Harold Wilson and I would both be elected.

I dropped in to a Fabian tea to hear Hugh Dalton, sounding very old and very flat as he discussed new ideas, and went on to a magnificent press reception. There I found Sydney Jacobson[2] from the *Sunday Pic*, who had been sent up to report on the effect of Hugh Cudlipp's Sunday article. I

[1] William Lawther (1889–1976), Labour M.P. for Barnard Castle 1929–31 and President of the National Union of Mineworkers 1939–54. He was knighted in 1949.

[2] A journalist on *Picture Post* 1945–50, he was Political Editor of the *Daily Mirror* 1952–62 and Editor of the *Daily Herald* 1962–4. Editorial Director of the *Mirror* Group 1963–75, he became a life peer in 1975.

should have mentioned that this article, for which posters had been put out all over Morecambe, had produced the expected effect. Herbert Morrison, whom I met yesterday morning and who took me for a long walk, during which we were photographed together,* said to me, 'You were clever enough to persuade the Editor to do that.' I replied, 'I am decent enough not to spread the rumour that you did it.' In fact the article enormously assisted the Bevanites and the only person it really damaged was me, since a great number of left-wing delegates were, I think, shocked at the idea that I was writing for such a paper.

I got back to the Grosvenor, where it was not known whether the votes were being counted or not and where rumours were circulating that we had gained one place. Already by this evening the atmosphere had changed. There was much less hope of managing a satisfactory Conference and much more obvious alarm among the right-wingers at the mood of the rank and file.

When the N.E.C. election results were announced, Conference learnt that six Bevanite candidates had been successful. Mr Bevan won nearly 1 million votes, over 85 per cent of the constituency poll, heading the list. Crossman came seventh, 40,000 votes ahead of Herbert Morrison, who was displaced, together with Hugh Dalton. The only non-Bevanite to be elected was, in the words of the New Statesman *of October 4th, the 'rather unhappy Jim Griffiths ... elected, as we all know, because he is acceptable to everyone'.*

Tuesday, September 30th

The debate on domestic affairs was opened by Attlee with what must have been the flattest speech ever delivered by a Leader. I don't think he could have taken any trouble whatsoever about it. Meanwhile I learned that, in order to avoid the press getting the sensational vote, only the trade union vote and the women's section had been counted last night, while the constituency vote was to be counted this morning. At about eleven o'clock it was announced to an Executive which did not know it. I think Hugh Dalton had certainly faced the worst. Indeed, this morning he told me, before the Conference began, that he would have retired this year if it would not have meant being accused of running away from defeat — and I think he really meant it. Morrison sat there self-controlled. Jim Griffiths, the only one who succeeded, was almost in tears with embarrassment.

Down below on the floor the exultation was tremendous and nobody paid much attention to the debate, in which Fienburgh moved his composite for a five-year plan[1] and was roundly accused of Bevanism. Harold Wilson and I

* He said, 'Will you lose votes?' and I said, 'Will you?' But that photograph didn't appear.
[1] Wilfred Fienburgh was the chief speaker on a motion based on *Facing the Facts*, Labour's policy document published in the summer of 1952. It called for the Executive to elaborate a five-year programme of policy, including the listing of 'key and major industries to be taken into public ownership', and a programme for 'more speedy diminishing of existing inequality of wealth', for increasing 'democracy in the workplace', for radical educational reform and for the extension of the social services.

spent a lot of time being photographed by what seemed about twenty cameras simultaneously and I went to lunch across the way at the one good hotel, the Midland, with Malcolm Muggeridge[1] and the Labour Correspondent[2] of the *Daily Telegraph.*

I had noticed that the *Telegraph* had the finest information on our Parliamentary Party meetings and had wondered who the Labour Correspondent was. To my amazement, I found that it was one of my best friends in the lobby, who I thought, however, was the correspondent for some minor Midland papers and to whom I had talked a great deal! I asked him why the papers get much more information about Labour than about Tory Party meetings. He replied, 'To begin with, the Tories are sensible enough to hold their meetings at six o'clock on Thursday evenings. It takes you roughly three hours to put together a coherent story from the bits and pieces you get and ten o'clock is far too late for most papers for a parliamentary story. Labour meetings take place in the morning and there is plenty of time to get information.' He added that usually one doesn't get a straight story and that his tips always come in the first instance from Tories, who tell him what they have heard in the Smoking Room or at the bar; it's on the basis of that information that he proceeds to tap his Labour friends. 'But really,' he said, 'both Bevanites and anti-Bevanites have been giving me information to correct the false information of the other side. This makes life easy.' He also added that there just aren't such good stories about the Tory Party, because there aren't clear policy issues in a Tory meeting and also because names don't matter. You never hear which Tories said what, except for Churchill or the top leaders. You only hear what views were expressed. Hugh Massingham[3] was also at lunch and he and Malcolm were very agreeable to me.

After lunch the debate proceeded. Gaitskell got a good hearing for a rather dull speech and Herbert received an ovation for what I thought was a really impressive performance. Indeed, he really did achieve victory out of defeat. Afterwards I rushed back to my hotel to write my story for the *Statesman* and in the first draft, completely misjudging the applause, I described this as a policy decision without personal feelings, saying there was no desire for scalps. I hadn't noticed that the applause was, as in fact it was, rigorously divided with people waiting to see which side people were on so that they would know whether to cheer or to boo. Anyhow, the bitterness increased steadily during the afternoon, particularly after another outburst by Arthur Deakin.

[1] A writer, he was Deputy Editor of the *Daily Telegraph* 1950–2 and Editor of *Punch* 1953–7. He has published a two-volume autobiography, *Chronicles of Wasted Time* (London: Collins, 1972, 1973).

[2] Hugh Chevans.

[3] The son of H. W. Massingham, Editor of the *Nation* 1907–23 and himself a novelist and journalist. He was the *Observer*'s Political Columnist from the end of the Second World War until 1961, when he moved to the *Sunday Telegraph,* where he remained until his death in December 1971.

When I went to the Gaumont for the Mayor's reception I soon slipped out, since life was really impossible, with really nice people telling you how unfair the demagogy was. Delegates were divided into two classes: those who found Nye's speech on Monday night a superb performance, full of profound thought, and dismissed Herbert's speech as mere showmanship, and those who denounced the empty demagogy of Nye and praised the statesmanlike profundity of Herbert. I doubt whether there were more than a dozen people there who felt as I did – genuinely of the opinion that both men and both types of speech are absolutely vital for the Party.

Wednesday, October 1st
I woke up early and prepared a five-minute speech, very carefully designed not to say the wrong thing. Hugh Dalton did quite well in moving the foreign affairs debate and everything was very dull and lifeless until I got up to second the resolution on Socialist principles.* As I walked up to the rostrum I thought that I had better start with a sentence or two before I got going, and I did, with results well known![2] It was a very odd sensation, being applauded one moment and booed by practically everybody the next. At the beginning I really didn't understand what had happened and then, curiously enough, I wasn't very upset but just thought that I had better wait until it stopped.

Thank God I didn't try to argue with the Conference but delivered the speech I had meant to give, which was fortunately O.K. and received a reasonable amount of applause at the end. But the consternation of the left-wing and the exultation of my opponents were both extreme. Hugh Dalton was convulsed with laughter on the platform and I am told that Attlee gave the only smile of the whole Conference. Bessie Braddock got into a physical fight with John Baird[3] and Jennie Lee with Wilfred Fienburgh, and when I got back to my place I felt a bit low.

At this point Geoffrey Bing behaved like an angel of mercy and said, 'Come out and have a drink.' So he took me to a pub, where I gave the drinks and he discussed what to do to repair the damage. Indeed, the whole Group couldn't have been nicer. Literally nobody blamed one, which was really very nice, and everybody was busy thinking who should put things right. Jennie this evening did her bit at the *Tribune* meeting (I gather rather clumsily) and so did Nye,

* This resolution, which is infinitely more Bevanite than the USDAW resolution on rearmament[1] and includes a determination to resist American pressure, to expand East-West trade, etc., was, by the way, accepted by the Executive.
[1] The USDAW resolution, moved on October 2nd, demanded a review and a reduction of arms expenditure. It was defeated on a card vote but only by a 3:2 majority and had already been defeated a month earlier at the Trade Union Congress.
[2] In Crossman's own account (*Sunday Pictorial*, October 5th, 1952) he started his speech 'with a mild joke. I suggested that, now I was suspended between the platform and the floor, I would have to be less controversial.' But 'the Conference wanted scalps, not parliamentary humour, and the booing nearly blew me off the rostrum!'
[3] A dental surgeon, he was Labour M.P. for Wolverhampton East 1945–50 and for Wolverhampton North-East 1950–64. He died in March 1965.

who, of course, was completely unperturbed and no doubt mildly enjoyed it. What one learnt, of course, is the intense suspicion with which I am viewed by my own supporters, a suspicion only equalled by the hatred of the other side. The one person who shouldn't try, even in a joke, to be fair, is the politician suspected of trimming.

In the afternoon, though, I was cheered when that swine Ernest Popplewell[1] began his speech by saying that far the most interesting speech of the Conference so far was that of Dick Crossman, who was already revealing a marked shift of policy. This really helped me a great deal, since it was so absurd that it was received in embarrassed silence by the Right. One of the troubles of such scenes is that all day one tends to view the Conference from one's own personal point of view. However, fortunately I had to rush back at lunch-time and spend three-quarters of an hour on the telephone dictating an article to the *Statesman* and by the time I got back Arthur Deakin's declaration of a counter-offensive[2] had produced a new and even larger sensation, which squeezed me into a not too damaging insignificance in the papers.

I had to go straight back from the afternoon session to the Grosvenor, where we had the first meeting of the new N.E.C. I had been warned what it would be like but it did rather take my breath away. The table is three sides of a square and at the bottom of one end sit six little Bevanites, with nineteen members of the Executive and about ten of the staff all ranged around against them. When we got in, Nye glanced at the agenda and saw that the next vice-chairman was down for discussion. As he, Edith Summerskill and Wilfrid Burke[3] all came on in the same year, they had equal rights to the job and an election had to take place. Nye said, 'Shall I stand for it?', to which there was a hurried whisper that he agreed months ago that he wouldn't. 'Well,' he said, 'Who shall we have?' And I found that our organization wasn't big enough to have decided in advance. However, we got in our votes for Burke against Summerskill.[4] The only other item was the selection of two extra members to go to Milan for a meeting in October. Immediately Margaret Herbison[5] and Sam Watson were suggested. There was absolutely no pretence of discussing the merits or the qualifications. Nye whispered to me,

[1] Labour M.P. for Newcastle-upon-Tyne West from 1945 to 1966, when he became a life peer. He was a Whip 1947–51 and in Opposition, serving as Deputy Chief Whip, 1955–9. He died in 1977.

[2] Mr Deakin, speaking as 'fraternal delegate' from the T.U.C., attacked Mr Bevan and Bevanism.

[3] Labour M.P. for Burnley 1935–59. He was Assistant Postmaster-General 1945–7 and Chairman of the N.E.C. 1953–4. He died in 1968.

[4] The 1952/53 Party Chairman was Arthur Greenwood, with Wilfrid Burke as Vice-Chairman. Edith Summerskill became Vice-Chairman for 1953/54 and thus Chairman in 1954/1955.

[5] Labour M.P. for North Lanark 1945–70, she was Joint Parliamentary Under-Secretary at the Scottish Office 1950–1, Minister of Pensions and National Insurance 1964–6 and of Social Security 1966–7.

'I've never been to one of those,' so we put him up and our five little hands went up, while Attlee abstained. That was the end of the N.E.C.

Thursday, October 2nd
I woke up to read through the papers and found that, on the whole, the press reports of my particular incident were a good deal less damaging than the incident itself, since it must have been very puzzling to the reader as to what on earth the row was about. Also, typically enough, I got a telegram, signed 'East Coventry', which I am sure came from Reg Carr,[1] congratulating me on the speech.

Since the afternoon was a private session, I decided to catch the Flying Scot back from Lancaster at five o'clock. A rather unpleasant-looking Welshman got into the carriage and sat down and said, 'I'm Nye Bevan's brother-in-law.' Apparently he lives in Maida Vale. He made one interesting observation, which was that, as he left the Conference hall today, a delegate had said to him, 'I wonder whether Dick Crossman and Nye Bevan will be able to work together for the next twelve months.' Apparently they have no idea that we have been working together for the last twelve months but I am sure one of the things which the other side will do is to do as much splitting as they possibly can. One thing Morecambe proved is the tremendous co-herence of our Group – not thanks to any official organization, but owing to the personal relations that we have established, which enable us to write our weekly articles without consulting each other and, in a surprising way to trust each other. There are, of course, terrible tensions between Barbara and Nye because Nye can't stand her and there is a certain absence of human relationship with Harold Wilson but nobody really suspects anybody else of doing them down and everybody is pretty faithful in carrying out the very few obligations we impose on each other. I suppose the answer is that we all hang together and we certainly do.

Friday, October 3rd
I had expected the farewell dinner to Hugh Cudlipp, given by Cecil King, Chairman of the Directors of the *Daily Mirror* Group, to be a jolly affair. Actually it was the stuffiest formality. Hugh, his wife and I were the only journalists there and the rest were managing directors, executives, etc. Cecil King is so shy that he only conducts conversation in a whisper, which his guests all follow. Moreover, he was too shy to propose the toast to Hugh, far less to make a speech, and ended the dinner at ten o'clock by passing a message across to one of the directors, saying that he would like them to break it up because his wife was waiting at home. As we were going out he took me aside and asked me if I had recovered and then said very earnestly that he hoped that I wouldn't let myself get run down again, since they could ill do without me.

[1] A teacher and at this time Secretary of the Coventry East Labour Party.

Hugh and Eileen, I think, were suffering from a hangover but they brought me home in their car and came in for a drink. Hugh said that he was continuing the attack on Bevan on his front page this week[1] and I asked him to tell me really why he was doing it. 'Somebody has got to knock him off his pedestal,' Hugh said, 'and as no one else can, I am having a bash.' That, no doubt, is part of the story. But King is certainly violently anti-Bevanite and I suspect that the real purpose of the manoeuvre is indirectly to loosen the *Daily Mirror* and the *Sunday Pic* from their Labour Party loyalties generally and altogether to make them more like a *Daily Express* of the Left, i.e. a paper which is broadly against the enemies of the Left but utterly irresponsible in its attack. It will be interesting to see whether this improves circulation. Just as Hugh was going I said to him that I would like to go to Egypt this winter. 'First-rate idea,' he said. 'Let's make it firm tonight and I'll make the arrangements before I go.'

Monday, October 6th

I found that Nye and Jennie had been calling me up. They couldn't have me to dinner since Jennie's very old father[2] is now dying, but I went in afterwards and we stayed talking to one o'clock in the morning and were joined part way through by Tommy Balogh and Pen, back from Paris. Jennie had a terrible cold but Nye is in tremendous form, though I must say that his cultural bogusness took my breath away when he calmly asserted to me that it was Matthew Arnold[3] who had destroyed the natural sense of humour of eighteenth-century Britain. This, by the way, was to explain why the Labour Party had been unable to appreciate my humour in that ill-fated Conference speech.[4] But what a relief it is to have a leading politician who is willing to propound airy-fairy theories about Matthew Arnold and the British sense of humour when he should be discussing practical politics.

We were all of us, of course, first concerned with Hugh Gaitskell's speech[5] last night. Against my expectations, Gaitskell, in a speech issued to the press beforehand, has denounced the 'mob rule' of the Conference, described the successful candidates as 'frustrated journalists' and generally declared war on Bevanism. My own view is that this was about the worst step that he could have taken and Nye shrewdly observed that it will enormously reduce the chance of Herbert Morrison replacing Attlee, since the middle-of-the-roaders

[1] The *Sunday Pictorial* headline on October 5th, 1952, was 'THE BEVAN MENACE'.

[2] James Lee, a former Fifeshire miner.

[3] Matthew Arnold (1822–88), Victorian poet and critic, whose works condemned 'provinciality and philistinism'. He published *Essays on Criticism* (London: Macmillan) in 1865, while Professor of Poetry at Oxford 1857–67. His *Culture and Anarchy* (London: Smith & Elder, 1869) calls for 'sweetness and light' in lives of high purpose and moral seriousness.

[4] See above, p. 151.

[5] On October 5th Mr Gaitskell had delivered a speech at Stalybridge. The *New Statesman and Nation*'s front-page reply, in the issue of October 11th, was written (anonymously) by John Freeman.

in the Parliamentary Party will once again be alienated by the obvious prejudice and spleen of Gaitskell's reaction and so begin to realize what would happen if middle-man Attlee were removed.

A really important thing I learnt from the evening is that Nye is now prepared to sit down and work out a complete left-wing Socialist programme. When I said that I thought it would be rather dangerous to put this to the whole Group of fifty, he said, 'Of course we couldn't. It must be just those of us who matter.' That's a great deal easier said than done, since our colleagues will want to feel that action is being taken. Moreover, I think that it is Nye's tactic to try to get this programme across inside the N.E.C. I was pleased that our minds had been working along parallel lines, since I had just been writing a *New Statesman* leader,[1] arguing that the resolutions accepted from the floor by the platform gave a framework for a new and more militant Socialist policy and were in fact an instruction to the new N.E.C. to work one out. Nye agreed that our trade union colleagues and Morgan Phillips might well feel bound to accept proposals which kept within this framework.

It was really a tremendously friendly evening, with Jennie being a quite matronly hostess, making pot after pot of tea which got mixed up with brandy and every now and then slipping out to see after her mother and father.

Friday, October 10th
I don't think that there is any doubt that Hugh Gaitskell's speech on Sunday was a real catastrophe from his point of view. Eddie Shackleton rang me up yesterday and, after a good deal of prodding, did reveal that Herbert Morrison had not seen the speech beforehand and had expressed some embarrassment at being rescued in this particular way by his friends. Meanwhile, last Tuesday, Mr Attlee made it known to the *Manchester Guardian* that he is not dreaming of resigning and John Freeman and I spent a great deal of time this week trying to ensure that the *New Statesman* line was correct.

Monday, October 13th
I enjoyed my weekend in South Wales. On Sunday evening we had a meeting in Chepstow. By then we had read in the papers Attlee's speech about Bevanism and John Strachey's. Attlee had finally come out, had announced that he was continuing to lead the Party and attacked the Left like selfish footballers. He had described the 'party within the party' as 'intolerable'.[2] John Strachey had come out with a stirring attack on the orthodox right-wingers, who were challenging the Party democracy. I'm longing to see John

---

[1] See *New Statesman and Nation*, October 11th, 1952, pp. 408–9.
[2] In a statement on Saturday, October 11th, Mr Attlee limited his remarks to disapproval of 'sectionalism', censuring 'a party within a party'. Mr Strachey observed that leaders (i.e. Mr Gaitskell) who used phrases like 'mob rule' risked becoming heroes of the Conservatives. Mr Driberg wrote for *Reynolds News*.

Strachey's face when he discovers that what he thought was well in the middle of the road had been made by Attlee a rebellious speech. Poor Tom Driberg was also in trouble this Sunday, since his whole column was called 'Stet Clem', congratulating Attlee on refusing to commit himself to either side in the dispute. For once Crossman showed his wisdom. I knew Attlee was going to speak this weekend, and I kept off the subject.

At the *Statesman* today we discussed Attlee's speech at length. After lunch I rang up Jennie, who told me, slightly embarrassingly, that Nye was composing his article for *Tribune*, announcing the dissolution of the Group. However she seemed quite eager that I should come in this evening while he is writing it—but I fancy some other members of the Group will have to be consulted too. My own feeling is that Attlee had to make a very definite statement that he was not to be thrown out of the leadership by Gaitskell and the trade union leaders. The statement is very hostile to us but, on the other hand, it threatens no sanctions whatsoever and my own inclination would be to do nothing about it for two or three weeks, in order to see what the mood of the Parliamentary Party is.[1] Of course, the difficulty is that we've been ordered to disband an organization which doesn't exist. If we don't disband the non-existent organization, we are in trouble and yet we can't do it, except by not having our regular weekly meetings or by throwing them open to the public, in which case we shall meet as a clique and things will go on precisely as before, except that we don't officially meet. Probably this is the best way out.

Tuesday, October 14th
Last night I was due to dine at Hampton Court with Curly Mallalieu and his wife. Mallalieu picked me up and took me to see Hugh Massingham and his wife, who were also dining, and we all went out to Hampton Court, where the Mallalieus have a superb old house, which they have furnished very nicely but I should think is far beyond their means.

The conversation started with Mallalieu affirming that the only test of good journalism is circulation and that Hugh and I were priggish to suggest that there could be such a thing as good journalism which wasn't merely successful. It's very odd how the *Tribune* group (and this applies to Michael as well as Curly) run down journalism as a profession and support Nye in his continual attacks on the press. But of course this constant anti-journalist bias may account for their type of journalism. Hugh Massingham said to me at one moment, 'You know, we are queerly old-fashioned as writers We really do care about getting the truth and we spend hours worrying about phrases to be sure we are fair and that we've got it just right, whereas they bash away for the cause.'

At dinner Mallalieu (he's an odd chap) then launched into a series of solemn admonitions to me, which were mainly about the fact that he felt with his paws and so understood the Movement, whereas I was an intellectual and

[1] Mr Attlee also bided his time.

didn't understand the man in the street, which made me untrustworthy – or, rather, untrusted. I did finally say that I had spent four years writing for a 5-million circulation paper but we then agreed that maybe Curly had something. Hugh observed that he really detested politics because it was so intellectually dishonest – or, alternatively, because the politicians really believe the nonsense they talk. He then turned to me and said, 'Your difficulty is that you see through it all the time and people feel that you do.'

At this point the telephone rang and it was Aneurin, rather impatiently asking when I was going to arrive. I didn't want to break up the dinner, so I got a hired car, which drove me back the fourteen miles for what I thought was the remarkably small sum of 28s.[1] I found that Michael, Harold Wilson and Ian Mikardo had already arrived and we immediately sat down to discuss for three and a half hours what Nye should write.

He at once suggested that he should announce that some of us were standing for the Parliamentary Committee[2] and that, since people suspected the worst of the secret group, it should be thrown open, so that everybody could attend and see for themselves the ridiculousness of the stories which have been told about it. Largely, I think, because we wanted to get our minds clear, both Ian and I resisted at first. Ian asked why, after a great victory, we should suddenly capitulate and he made the alternative suggestion that we should let the matter be put to the Party Meeting and oppose abolition of groups but accept the decision of the majority if it was forced upon us. There was also a long discussion about whether we should disband the Group or throw it open as a *Tribune* meeting. I kept on putting an oar in, saying that I didn't much mind what the tactics were as long as, in fact, a coherent Group continued to exist, planning policy. Jennie put in, 'Of course they will pass a resolution and all that it means is that we shall have become a conspiracy, like the right-wing.'

Finally Nye got very angry with me. 'To continue the Group now is to perpetuate schism,' he said. 'If you were to continue the Group in these conditions and I were the Leader, I would have you expelled. The Group is intolerable.' I then asked, 'Then why hasn't it been intolerable for the last six months?' 'Well of course it's been intolerable,' he said. 'We've got away with it. And we needed it then. We don't need it now. That's the point of Morecambe. We're in a strong enough position not to need protection and if we go on with it we shall alienate the people we are trying to win in the Parliamentary Party and we shall lose the support of nearly half the constituencies within twelve months because they will be able to pillory us as a sectarian conspiracy.' It was a good discussion because, though the decision was the same as what Nye originally proposed, everybody understood far

[1] £1·40.

[2] Mr Bevan's article in *Tribune*, October 17th, 1952, explained his own intention and that of some of his colleagues to stand for election to the Parliamentary Committee at the beginning of the forthcoming Session.

better at the end what the tactics behind it were and so we were able, I think, to work out a much better way of putting it over.[1]

I spent this morning drafting the *New Statesman* article[2] and, after giving Tommy Balogh lunch, went over to Nye's at two o'clock, avoiding the photographer on the way in. Nye liked the draft, except for one point, where I described him as responding to Mr Attlee's speech. 'No, it must be my own initiative,' he said, 'and Attlee's speech must be described as making the reconciliation more difficult and not easier.' It was a good change and I made it before taking the article over to the *Statesman*.

Kingsley's reaction was interesting. 'Won't this be just the same,' he said. 'as when you were booed at Conference?[3] Won't they think that you've climbed down and capitulated just after your electoral victory? Isn't this a surrender?' And again we began to go through the whole argument which we had last night between Nye and Ian Mikardo. I fear it means that, however we present it, this will be the feeling of a great many people when they hear the news. On the other hand, I have just been in the Smoking Room, talking to John Strachey and George Strauss and tentatively trying the idea out. 'But the right-wingers won't be content with that,' said John. 'It will be regarded as intolerable provocation to continue the Group at all.' On the other hand, both of them are obviously furious with Gaitskell and also with the *Daily Herald*, which plastered across its front page this morning a speech by Lincoln Evans[4] of the Steelworkers, proclaiming that there is an unbridgeable gulf between Morrison's policy and that of Bevan, and backing Morrison. Of course such statements are intensely embarrassing to Mr Attlee and Morrison, who take the line that there is no difference on policy and the whole thing is due to personal animosities on the Left.

Wednesday, October 15th
The atmosphere of the House yesterday, on the first day after the Recess, was worse than I have ever known it. It wasn't tense but there were such hostilities in the air that you sweated before you got hot. It isn't merely that the Bevanites are hated. The anti-Bevanites are all hating each other and blaming each other for our success. Throughout the evening I went on making inquiries about how the Party would react to our decision to throw the Group open, with much the same result as before. I dined with Michael Foot and tried to explain to him what was wrong with *Tribune* and that they really must put some information on their front page and let people feel that the *Tribune* was telling them what is going on in politics. I think for the first time he under-

---

[1] It was announced on Thursday, October 16th, that the Bevanites' weekly meetings were open to any and every Labour Member of Parliament.

[2] Crossman's article, 'Mr Bevan Takes the Initiative', appeared in the *New Statesman and Nation* on October 18th, 1952.

[3] See p. 151.

[4] Lincoln Evans (1889–1970), General Secretary of the Iron and Steel Trades Confederation 1946–53.

stood what I was saying but I couldn't help him with it unless I went and actually wrote it for him, which no doubt is what he'd like me to do.

In the Smoking Room the Bevanites were back in their usual corner, busy discussing the party within a party. 'The Smoking Room within the Smoking Room,' as Tom Driberg remarked, looking at us.

I walked home to find Eddie had arrived and we had a long talk. Apparently Herbert Morrison is still as embittered as ever against Attlee and there is no doubt he would like us to believe that he would like to work with Nye. I suspect he probably would since, if the two could get together, Herbert would become Prime Minister. But why should we do it? Terrible as that little ball-bearing is, he is less dangerous to us than Herbert Morrison with Hugh Gaitskell at his right-hand side.

Eddie told me that he thought the Party would not accept our proposal and I told him that I didn't really mind and, if they chose to disperse the Group by force, after it had thrown itself open to all the Party, they would merely look silly. It was also pretty clear from what Eddie said that the right-wing would like to have Aneurin Bevan and Harold Wilson on the Executive but they have now got themselves into a pother since, if they let their people vote for Harold Wilson and Aneurin Bevan in order to ensure that they are inside the trap, then Bevan and Wilson might top the poll and that would give the wrong impression. So much for the people who don't believe in organization.

When I got to the *Statesman* this morning, Kingsley said to me that the leader would have to be changed because he didn't want a reference to *Tribune*. This is one of his extraordinary kinks. It was quite impossible to write the leader about Aneurin Bevan's statement without mentioning the *Tribune* but Kingsley is so jealous of the *Tribune* or else so snobbishly unwilling to be connected with it that he would do anything to prevent the word occurring in the first line. I spent an hour trying to get it out of the first line and managed to demote it to the fifth.[1] John told me that the first thing that Kingsley had said to him when he came in was that we must get the *Tribune* out of the leader. I said to Kingsley, 'It doesn't very much matter but, if you don't refer to *Tribune*, Nye and Jennie will think that you have done it deliberately and that will make personal relations rather difficult.' 'They can't do that,' he said, 'considering all that I've done to help them.' 'Well, they will,' I said. Then I realized that this is one of those kinks which you can't do anything about. In this respect he is just mean.

We had the Group meeting at half-past one. It was a delicate operation, because by then both the *Tribune* and the *New Statesman* articles were in print and the Group was committed to the policy which it was called upon to decide. Harold Wilson and Nye operated with considerable skill, although they took a fantastic risk in never revealing any of this to the Group and banking on its coming to the right decision. There was a point, after about

[1] In the event the reference appeared only in line 13.

an hour, when one or two people took the line which Ian had taken on Monday — namely, that we should stand and fight — and I thought it might go wrong. Personally, I had a distinctly uncomfortable feeling about diddling forty colleagues in this way and I said so to Harold Wilson on the way out. He was baffled, which shows what good politicians he and Nye are.

I must say that the whole of this atmosphere has made me profoundly depressed. If one feels like this on the first day of the Session, what will one feel next July? I began to think that Stoke University would be an attractive hide-out, where one could do some good.[1] Just at the moment my stock in the Parliamentary Party is zero. One is hated for having got on to the Executive and they are all delighted at what happened at Morecambe.[2] Most of them dimly know that I am one of the brains which worked out the Bevanite tactics, quite apart from my writing what Hugh Gaitskell described in the *Daily Herald* as 'abuse and vituperation'.

After the meeting we all went into the Smoking Room and it was only after he'd finished that I realized that Eden had been making a very important Statement on Germany.[3] It hadn't occurred to any of us to attend, because so far it hasn't registered with us that anything is going on outside the Labour Party. As a matter of fact, I haven't entered the Chamber this Session.

Monday, October 20th
I had a great struggle with the *Sunday Pic* on Friday, since Harold Barkworth[4] laid it down that I must be strictly objective. After lunch Hugh Massingham looked in and, after him, Barbara and Ted Castle, all talking endlessly, endlessly, endlessly about the Party crisis. Just to make sure that Aneurin wouldn't go off the deep end this weekend at Wallsend, I rang him up to tell him the line of my article. When he heard it, he said, 'Isn't that too tough? I should recommend the suave, *New Statesman* approach this weekend,' which is rather annoying, since, if he'd let the *New Statesman* approach be the method of making our offer, instead of his own prickly olive branch in the *Tribune*, the offer would have been three times more attractive. However, I gathered from his secretary that he hadn't slept all the night before, after he'd heard the news that Attlee was going to deliver an ultimatum at the Party Meeting next Thursday, calling for the disbandment of the Group.

[1] See above, p. 135.
[2] See above, p. 151.
[3] On the case of Herr Alfried Krupp, son of Gustav Krupp, arraigned as a war criminal by the International War Crimes Tribunal at Nuremberg but found unfit to plead. Herr Alfried Krupp had succeeded his father as head of the Krupp coal and steel complex. In the Statement the Foreign Secretary announced that, although Germany would be responsible for paying compensation for the breaking-up of the complex, Herr Krupp would not be allowed to use the proceeds to buy his way back into the coal and steel industry or to otherwise acquire a controlling interest.
[4] Editor of the *Sunday Despatch* and later a Deputy Editor of the *Sunday Express* until his retirement.

5 Herbert Morrison has his palm read by Mrs Vaughan Williams at Festival
of Britain celebrations, 1951

6 Preparing to go underground to introduce the new Coventry East M.P. to
some of his mining constituents

7 Crossman correcting copy for the *New Statesman & Nation*

8 Relaxing on the terrace of the House of Commons

9 Richard Crossman marries Anne McDougall, 1954. Seen here with George Wigg (*left*) and George Hodgkinson

I spent the weekend of Zita's birthday at Radnage, where Phil and Betty Zec have settled in marvellously. On Saturday evening we went to dinner with Cassandra[1] and had a first-rate discussion. On Sunday evening, again, Ellis Birk,[2] the solicitor to the *Daily Mirror*, independently made the same point: 'How can you associate with your fellow Bevanites? How can you be taken seriously when the alternative Labour leadership consists of Tom Driberg and Barbara Castle?' There is no doubt about it that to many people in the newspaper world this question of the Bevanite personalities is a very important one. When I point out that apart from three ex-Ministers the rest of us are people who couldn't be famous because we were unworthy of office, they accept it intellectually but it doesn't really click. The fact is that we are an unimpressive collection and, when we are coupled with Aneurin, we do become, to the general public, highly suspect, especially under a day in/day out press campaign.

I walked to the House today with John Strachey, as detached as usual, but he told me that he was going to seek to move an amendment at next Thursday's Party Meeting and that he was very bitter about the damage done to the Party by Gaitskell, etc. The House remains absolutely dead, with the Tories looking on at Labour feuding, and I soon went off home, where George Wigg rang up, just back from a holiday to Montreal and back by merchant ship. Independently, he seems to have assessed the situation pretty well and was mainly delighted that we should have discovered the villainy of Hugh Gaitskell five years after he had himself done so. He has never forgiven Hugh for ousting Manny from the Ministry of Fuel and Power[3] and George's aim will be to get Gaitskell discredited and, I should guess, to work in the long run for an understanding between Herbert and Nye.

Tuesday, October 21st
This morning I rushed down from the *New Statesman* to the Bevanite Group meeting at half-past one, the first thrown open to the Party. Four non-members turned up — the egregious Lord Strabolgi[4] and Emrys Hughes,[5]

---

[1] William Connor, columnist (as Cassandra) of the *Daily Mirror* from 1935 until his death in 1967.

[2] Lawyer to the *Mirror* Group. He was the husband of Alma Birk. See p. 746 and n.

[3] In October 1947 Hugh Gaitskell became Minister of Fuel and Power, which was made a non-Cabinet post. Emanuel Shinwell moved to the War Office as Secretary of State.

[4] Joseph Strabolgi (1886–1953). A naval officer, he was Liberal M.P. for Hull Centre 1919–26 and Labour M.P. for the same constituency 1926–31. In 1934, on the death of his father, he succeeded to the title and moved to the House of Lords, where he was Opposition Chief Whip 1938–42.

[5] A schoolteacher, he had earlier been Editor of *Forward* and was Labour M.P. for Ayrshire South from 1946 until his death in 1969. He was a backbencher with a rather iconoclastic reputation, which was strengthened by his publications, which included *Keir Hardie* (London: Lincolns-Prager, 1950), *Winston Churchill in War and Peace* (Glasgow: Unity Publishing Co., 1950) and *Macmillan — Portrait of a Politician* (London: Allen & Unwin, 1962). He married Keir Hardie's daughter, Nan, in 1924: she died in 1947.

6

whom one might describe as vagrant left-wingers, Norman Smith,[1] the Social Credit crank from the extreme Right and an extremely dim trade unionist called McKay,[2] who represents Wallsend, where Nye was speaking at the weekend. The meeting started with the announcement that twenty-two constituency parties had asked for brains trusts and we spent half an hour manning the trusts, with occasional invocations by Harold Wilson, the chairman, that our new members should join in, which they didn't. Indeed, if we wanted to be overheard at work we were not very successful. Outside there was the usual gang of lobby correspondents waiting to report events. Tommy Balogh then gave a really excellent analysis of the balance of payments[3] and the meeting broke up.

Just before we went out I had a word with Nye. Ian Mikardo came across and said that some of our rank-and-file members were disturbed that there was to be no meeting of the Group to discuss the tactics for next Thursday and they felt that they were being left out in the cold. So, after some discussion it was decided that Nye would have a beer and sandwiches party on Wednesday night, after the House adjourns. Nye then said, 'Of course, these meetings will go on, whatever happens on Thursday. We must keep them on and, if we are challenged, state that they are not a Group but are open to everybody to attend.' He also emphasized that, if the resolution[4] is passed, he will not stand for the Parliamentary Committee. Tommy Balogh questioned the wisdom of this and so, I fancy, would have one or two of the others who were standing by. But it is very difficult to see why we should permit two prisoners to sit on the Front Bench if the other side want to continue the war. The wisest thing would be to wait until after Thursday before any decision is taken.

Thursday, October 23rd

I spent yesterday evening with Patricia Llewelyn-Davies and John Hynd at the High Wycombe by-election.[5] I stayed the night with Patricia and her

---

[1] Labour and Co-operative M.P. for Nottingham South 1945–55. A journalist by profession, he was on the editorial staff of the *Daily Herald* 1919–30, and then worked for *Reynolds News*, *Illustrated* and *John Bull*. He accompanied Ramsay MacDonald on his visits to the U.S.A. and Canada in 1929. He was strongly interested in the monetary reform movement. He died in 1962.

[2] John McKay, a former miner's official, was Labour M.P. for Wallsend from 1945 until his death in 1964.

[3] In the third quarter of 1952 imports totalled £792 million and exports £575 million (of which £328 million was in metals and engineering products). In June there were 295,000 registered unemployed (1·3 per cent of the working population), the same total as in December 1951. In both August and September the Retail Price Index dropped by one point (to 137 and 136 respectively, with 1947 as the base year).

[4] Calling for the 'immediate abandonment of all group organizations within the Party other than those officially recognized'.

[5] W. W. Astor, the Conservative Member for High Wycombe, had succeeded to his father's peerage. The by-election on November 4th returned the Conservative candidate, John Hall, with a majority of 2,100.

husband Richard. Patricia says that he hates all the politicians she consorts with but I think we may see more of each other.[1] It drenched with rain all night and I slept very badly, entirely, I suspect, because of the Party Meeting, but we drove up through the Chilterns this morning in perfect October sunshine. Ten minutes before the Meeting I just got a seat and decided to take a full note, so that I could put into this diary the record of one entire Party Meeting as it actually occurred.

Attlee was received with a minimum of cheering and started by saying that the vote would be taken at a quarter to one. It is our job to turn the Government out as soon as possible. The Government is doing badly and the only strength it has is our own Labour divisions. We must face the possibility of a post-Coronation election and be ready for it.[2] He then spent some time describing the effect of divisions on British political parties and stressed that the danger becomes acute when policy differences are accentuated by personal differences — for instance, in 1935, when Lansbury and Cripps differed from the official line.[3] 'In the 1945 Cabinet I included people who disagreed with me. In any party one is bound to have people who dislike each other. One has got to get on with them. And, frankly, the last year has been the unhappiest year I have had in my seventeen years of leadership.'

He repeated that there were no serious differences of policy and that attempts to talk about a Right and Left of the Party were misleading. *Let's Face the Future*[4] was a left-wing policy. He had hoped, after the election, that the Parliamentary Party would work together and it would have done if there had not been a Bevanite Group. 'You can argue a lot about groups but they're like the elephant. I may not be able to define one but I know one when I see one. Groups are all right for special purposes but what I disapprove is

[1] They did. See *The Diaries of a Cabinet Minister*, especially vol. I.

[2] The Coronation was to be in June 1953.

[3] George Lansbury (1859–1940), a much-loved and respected Leader of the Labour Party, was early in his life associated with the Christian Socialists, and then with H. M. Hyndman's Social Democratic Federation. He became Labour M.P. for Bow and Bromley in 1910 and served until 1912, when he resigned to fight the seat in the subsequent by-election on the specific issue of rights for women (of which he was a firm supporter). A pacifist during the First World War, he was closely associated with the *Daily Herald*, which he edited for a time. He was elected again as M.P. for Bow and Bromley in 1922, a seat which he held until his death. He was First Commissioner of Works in the Labour Government of 1929–31. On its fall in 1931, he was elected Leader of the Opposition. He served until his resignation in 1935. A devout Anglican as well as a pacifist, he published a volume of reminiscences, *Looking Backwards and Forwards* (London: Blackie, 1935), and other works, including *My Quest for Peace* (London: Michael Joseph, 1938).

At the Labour Party Conference in October 1935, Hugh Dalton moved on behalf of the N.E.C. a motion recommending that the League of Nations use sanctions in the dispute between Italy and Abyssinia. George Lansbury, who had earlier stated that in no circumstances could he support the use of armed force either by the League or by any individual member, resigned the Party leadership at a special P.L.P. meeting following the Conference. Stafford Cripps resigned from the Executive; he had declared that, without power, Labour should not join in the responsibility for a 'capitalist and imperialist war, which sanctions might entail'.

[4] *Let Us Face the Future* was the title of the Party manifesto in 1945.

an omnicompetent Group like the I.L.P.[1] used to be. This Group has, in fact, operated under separate leadership and the writings of a number of Socialist journalists have been in support of an organized Group. The proposal to throw the Group open to other members of the Party is not good enough, since it would merely create a rival Party Meeting.' He then stressed that formal resolutions were useless without a spirit of conciliation to give them reality. 'The enthusiastic Socialist,' he said, 'has a fire in himself which burns up the straw of selfishness and ambition. Let the Party abandon all such organizations and the spirit which inspires them.' This was received with moderate applause.

Desmond Donnelly tried hard but made an unsuccessful speech. He started by saying that Nye had saved the soul of the Party by resigning, which was greeted with hoots of raucous laughter. He regained attention by stressing that, if we are going to get together, each side must concede sincerity to the other and he illustrated this by saying that both Morrison and Bevan had behaved admirably since the election. Turning to the motion, Donnelly said that the disbandment of groups would make us ridiculous in the eyes of the public and that nothing would be settled by the motion. The second part, which demanded that we should stop abusing each other, is the operative part, he said. It is a change of mood which matters. The trouble was that he hadn't managed to say anything when he sat down, in dead silence.

Ellis Smith urged in quite an effective speech that the motion should be withdrawn. The motion superimposed further Standing Orders on those drafted last February.[2] 'They are an insult to the Party, considering the loyalty it has shown since 1945.' Turning to the argument that official groups were sufficient, he pointed out that they had been completely ineffective and then said rather darkly that trade union Members, in particular, had been discouraged and had resented the exclusive way that certain non-trade union Members dominated the Government.

Bob Mellish, from Bermondsey, made rather a good right-wing speech. He is a nice, sincere man and he described a visit to Dover as an example of the fact that the constituencies without Labour M.P.s are solidly Bevanite because they believe the Bevanite Group has some cure for all our ills. Indeed, the burden of his complaint was that the constituency parties believe that deep division exists between Right and Left and that this is why the Bevanite Group must be disbanded.

---

[1] The Independent Labour Party, established in 1893 and in 1900 one of the founding bodies of the Labour Representation Committee. Even after the revision of the Labour Party constitution in 1918, the I.L.P. held its own Conferences, sponsored its own parliamentary candidates and promoted its own policies. In 1929 and 1930 dissension grew between the Labour leadership and I.L.P. Members and in 1932 it was disaffiliated by the Labour Party Conference. After the death in 1946 of James Maxton, the I.L.P. Leader, its Members gradually rejoined the Labour Party. At the 1951 election there had been only three I.L.P. candidates, all of whom lost their deposits.

[2] In fact, March. See above, pp. 93 ff.

Paget made probably the best speech of the day. All this feuding, he said, should stop but you can't stop it by legislation. Previous speakers had referred to the social segregation in the House of Commons. There is a very simple way of stopping this — by stopping it. There is a vast fund of friendship in the Parliamentary Party, which is being frustrated in the present situation. He attacked the journalists, stressed that you can't have two personalities and, if the needs of journalism are in contradiction for Party loyalty, the choice may have to be made between them. He turned to Attlee and agreed that we ought to attack the Tories. 'But that attack must be effective,' he said, 'and it has been very ineffective in the last twelve months.' The trouble about Reg's speech was that, excellent as it was, it managed to evade the issue of whether to vote for or against the motion.

Tom Proctor[1] spoke next. On the day of Aneurin Bevan's resignation Proctor had literally saved the meeting from a free fight by the unconscious idiocy of his speech, in which he started to tell us what happened in the train between Cardiff and Chepstow and then got into a tangle as to whether the train went to Chepstow or the Severn Tunnel. The meeting today was not so tense and we didn't need Proctor quite as badly. Funnily enough, some of the things that he said were very good but when he says them nobody believes him. He started by saying that democracy is being used to destroy democracy. When Nye became Minister of Labour Tom had written to him congratulating him because he was a Bevan fan. Now he disagreed with Nye. That's what happens in politics. 'I get fun out of life,' he said, 'because I have a sense of humour.' This sent the Party into convulsions of laughter, since it is his unconscious humour which it enjoys. He begged Nye to drop his invective and said that statesmanship means forgiveness but you shouldn't forgive a man in such a way that he thinks he was very smart.

Then came Nye's own speech. He started by saying that we ought to be honest with each other. It's no use saying that there haven't been policy differences. There have been, ever since 1950, and the rearmament problem was superimposed on these policy differences. However, these policy differences have been resolved by the decisions moved from the .floor at Morecambe, which have created the basis for unity. Nye then went into an elaborate attack on the *Daily Herald* for promoting disunity during the last three weeks and he got a roar of anger when he said that it had made an organized attack on the unity of the Parliamentary Labour Party.

He then turned to the resolution which attacked the Bevanite Group. Why is the attack being made now? If it was justified, why wasn't it made before? The reason is what happened at Morecambe. He got on to rather dubious ground by stressing the need for groups, while stating that it is grossly improper to organize factions in order to change policy at Party Meetings. However, he got away with this, only to fall into a trap when he talked about

[1] Labour M.P. for Eccles 1945–64 and P.P.S. to the Secretary of State for the Colonies 1945–51. He died in 1967.

the XYZ Club[1] holding a dinner, whereas poor members of the Party couldn't afford this sort of conspiracy. As most people regard the Bevanites as Smoking Room men, who have money,[2] this didn't go down.

With a quick recovery, Nye got back to the second part of the motion, censuring personal attacks, and got a friendly laugh when he said that no one would benefit more than he if this was enforced. But this attempt to disband groups was introducing odium in a wanton attempt to mislead the Party, just at a time when the Parliamentary Committee was due to disband. The right course was to hand this resolution over to the new Parliamentary Committee, when it had been elected. This part of his argument was extremely good. He argued that any decision today would be prejudicial to unity. If the motion is passed by a big majority, the newspapers will use that majority to poison relations still further. If the majority is small, then the authority of the official leadership will be weakened. Remitting the resolution to a new Committee, elected in a better spirit, was the statesmanlike course.

Ernest Popplewell, one of the more odious Whips, immediately got up to ask whether Nye meant he hoped to have more Bevanites on the Committee. This went down very badly but he got cheers by demanding that there should be no appeasement of the Bevanites and repeating, 'There is no room for different groups.'

George Thomas, the teetotal N.U.T. Welshman from Cardiff, then made a weak middle-of-the-road speech, in which he managed to convulse the Party by emotionally stating that we must 'gulf the bridge' between the two sides. He made quite an effective appeal to Nye, stating that it wouldn't be a big sacrifice to stop the outside meetings now they are open. Nye was big enough to have his face slapped.

Arthur Greenwood then made a rather moving middle-of-the-road speech, which failed, however, to be middle-of-the-road because it didn't draw a conclusion from the argument that the issue should be postponed. He started by saying that internal dissension is fatal. He remarked that every speaker so far had pleaded for unity and urged someone else to behave better. 'That is a relatively easy thing to do,' he said. But this resolution wouldn't settle anything and he thought the significance of the debate was that the two sides had to re-express their views but with considerably less bitterness than before. 'We've got a very long way to go yet,' he said, 'to achieve unity.' He would welcome an agreed solution but it should not be an ambiguous solution. He then referred to the N.E.C. meeting on Tuesday, to which the results of this Party Meeting would be reported, and repeated that one should not adopt measures which won't work.

---

[1] A group of Gaitskell's friends, described by Crossman in the *New Statesman and Nation* on October 18th, 1952, as a 'select dining club'.

[2] Unlike 'Tea Room men', who allegedly had not. See below, pp. 209–10, for a description.

There were still about thirty speakers trying to get in when Herbert Morrison wound up the debate. His theme was that we couldn't afford to leave the Party or the Labour electors confused – and they had been confused by the existence of the Bevanite Group. The Parliamentary Committee had been asked by Nye why it hadn't imposed the ban earlier. 'Have a heart,' said Herbert Morrison, among laughs. 'After all, we got into trouble in February[1] and the Strachey ideas voted us down.' It was untrue to suggest that this motion was being moved as a result of Morecambe. It was dealing with a situation which had been going on long before Morecambe. You might not agree with every word that Gaitskell said. 'Considering what Gaitskell had to put up with in a year, he couldn't blame him if he didn't choose his words quite right.' This produced an enormous round of applause for Gaitskell and, indeed, was the only reference to Gaitskell's Stalybridge speech[2] in the whole debate, since Aneurin, quite rightly, hadn't launched a personal attack on him. But it meant that Gaitskell got away pretty lightly and will feel himself reinforced by what happened.

Morrison then made even clearer Attlee's view that, if there is to be any discussion, it must be in official groups. He stressed again that it was no good arguing about the Bevanite Group. It was unfair to invest it with a left-wing aura, which deceived the constituencies, or to popularize it with brains trusts, which put a partisan point of view. 'The Bevanite Group has had a function, the same function as the I.L.P., and it creates the assumption that only some Members of Parliament are good Socialists. I resent that,' said Herbert Morrison, to loud applause. 'I played a role second to no one in forging the policy of *Let's Face the Future*, a real Socialist policy.' He then read out a passage from Aneurin's *Tribune* article,[3] in which Aneurin claimed that 'We' would continue our work of political education. 'Who are "We"?' Herbert asked, 'and why have they the right to claim special privileges?' He, Morrison, remembered the first meeting that he attended of the N.E.C., which he got on to almost by accident. He went there with his mind clearly made up on who was Left, Right and Centre, but after a few meetings he discovered that these tabs didn't fit people as they actually behave on the N.E.C. 'The explosive revolutionaries outside were very different inside,' he said, again to a roar of applause. The Bevanite Group confused the rank and file and it was rough luck on the rank and file that they should be deluded in that way. 'Chuck it, Nye,' he said, 'and when we get away from here let's think very seriously about the situation and how to right it.'

When Morrison sat down, Attlee leapt up and moved the motion. I had been consulting John [Freeman] and Barbara and John got up to ask whether he could move an amendment for postponing consideration till the new Parliamentary Committee was selected. At this point Attlee's little face grew

[1] See above, pp. 93 ff.
[2] See above, p. 154.
[3] In the issue of October 17th, 1952.

black and he said, 'Those in favour of taking the vote straightaway?' A few hands went up. Attlee said, 'Agreed. Those in favour of the resolution?' And forced the vote, without even permitting consideration of whether there should be a vote on postponement. This was pretty smart tactics, especially when you remember that Strachey and Strauss, who had been trying to catch Attlee's eye throughout the meeting, were not called.[1] He was determined this time that the moderates should not be permitted to bitch his vote of confidence. The result was 188 for and 51 against.[2] I should reckon that there were not more than ten to twelve abstentions. There is really no doubt that, if John's motion had been called, we would have got well over 100 in favour of it and the issue would have been blurred.

My first impression of this meeting is that it could have been a lot worse. It's not merely that everybody made speeches about unity and friendship. More important, everybody realized that the motion couldn't settle very much and that much more will depend on the constitution of the new Committee. What was also interesting was the admission, in speech after speech from the Right, that the constituencies are Bevanite, though of course the excuse is made that our Bevanite organization has deluded them. It can't be denied that we have really produced a tremendous shock. On the other hand, it also can't be denied that, if we had been wanting to capture power or shift power, we have completely failed. The official leadership has reasserted its grip. Since we were not intent on capturing power, this may possibly be a good thing, provided they don't think that they have won and can do what they like. They've certainly had the fright of their lives.

Monday, October 27th

On Friday I went down to Colchester to a constituency meeting with the candidate, Roy Thomas,[3] a Manchester agent who was making his first appearance. I don't think I have ever known such a dead meeting. They listened to the Chairman on Bevanism and Roy Thomas on Labour and the Asiatics in the deadest silence, though they gave Thomas a nice applause at the end. I did my piece on Bevanism, which, for once, I had written out in advance and made what was, for me, a resounding speech, which pretty well got the audience, and we had some friendly questions.

Ena Driberg had come over to meet me and, when I was going to get my bag the agent and Thomas, looking very grim, said they wished I hadn't spoken on Bevanism at Thomas's first meeting. When I said that, after all, the chairman had introduced the subject, I realized I was in the middle of a fratricidal local party strife.

---

[1] They had moved the mediating amendment in March 1952. See above, pp. 93 ff.
[2] There were 292 Members of the P.L.P.
[3] A schoolteacher who was elected to East Ham Borough Council in 1952, he stood unsuccessfully as the Labour and Co-operative candidate for Colchester at the 1955 General Election.

That same lunch-time had been the annual Colchester Oyster Feast[1] to which Tom Driberg had come and eaten three dozen oysters with Chablis. He had risen from a bed of flu and, by the time I reached him at 9.55 in the pub, it was difficult to know which he was suffering from more, the flu, the oysters or the whisky. He was driven home stertorous and put to bed. I didn't see him again till Saturday evening. Bradwell Manor, where he lives, is a Tudor house with magnificent Robert Adam[2] additions, including a little room on the roof where Gainsborough[3] painted. Tom has done it all up exquisitely and the only difficulty is that he can't pay the bills. The result is that you live in great splendour but they can't afford hot bathwater. For the first two nights I was a second-class guest and was not even offered a glass of sherry. Economy, I suppose. By Sunday evening Tom had relented and broached a bottle of non-vintage claret. To do him justice, I think it was non-vintage because he had a bad cold and his palate was affected.

I must say that I got the impression from Colchester and Maldon that Attlee's counter-attack had been extremely successful. For the twelve months up to Morecambe, Bevanism, since it was not banned by Attlee, was considered quite all right and the Party was having the best of both worlds, with a dynamic Left, free to be dynamic, and the Right not permitted to crab the Left. Now this whole atmosphere has changed. The really resolute Bevanites in the constituencies think the disbandment of the Group in Parliament is tit-for-tat and are anxious lest the Bevanites will betray them by not fighting. The right-wingers have now raised their heads and said, 'So it was a conspiracy after all.' And the middle-of-the-roaders are unhappy. In fact, I suspect the whole life of the Party has been suddenly removed, except in solid Bevanite areas. But I must say, in Colchester and Maldon the atmosphere is damp and disconsolate.

Sunday was an absolutely perfect October day and I managed to get out of the house before anybody noticed for a long walk first down to St Peter's Chapel, a Saxon church built in A.D. 600 from the stones of the gateway of a Roman castle on the North Sea.[4] There I ran into a strange Christian community, which had put down two Nissen huts; they gave me a cup of coffee. From there I walked north and east along the wall which runs across the marshes up into the Blackwater Estuary, a nice seven-mile walk in bright sunshine. Even the wind was sunny. I got back to find Tom out of bed and

---

[1] Believed to have originated in a Corporation lunch in celebration of St Denis's Day, itself dating from 1319. The first recorded mention of the Oyster Feast is in the Municipal Chamberlain's accounts for 1667. The Feast was originally held on October 9th but the change of calendar in 1752 moved it to October 20th. From 1845 distinguished guests were invited to the Feast by the Mayor and Corporation. A limited number of townspeople, chosen by ballot, now attends.

[2] The architect Robert Adam (1728–92), the most celebrated of the four Adam brothers.

[3] The painter Thomas Gainsborough (1727–88).

[4] St Peter's Chapel at Bradwell-on-Sea, believed to be the chapel built by Bishop Cedd in A.D. 654 during his conversion of the East Saxons to Christianity.

excited because Libby Holman,[1] the American torch singer, had sent him some steak. In celebration of this we had lunch in the dining room, instead of in the living room, but the steak turned out, in some curious way, to have no blood in it. Tom was furious because it had been served in state.

In the evening Tom relaxed a little playing canasta with Ena, the only time when they don't bicker, while I went to sleep reading about Hitler.[2] On the whole this was the most successful weekend I have had, since my host and hostess made no demands upon me. Ena is a very nice Leeds Jewess, enormously friendly, but without any sort of intellectual or aesthetic sensitivity. The poor woman is asked to be the wife of Tom Driberg, a homosexual, with an exquisite taste in Adam furniture! The result is that not only can Tom not stand conversation with her, but it irritates him beyond endurance when one chats with her at all. Yet the only point of a guest is to give Ena some company.

I must say the difference between Coventry and Maldon, as constituencies, is remarkable. Maldon is sixty miles long, with no railway service which works, and Tom does at least two to three engagements in every weekend, with an average of 90–100 miles' motoring. On the other hand, there is no doubt that any other candidate would lose the seat. There is a Labour Party but it's a Driberg seat and he has the pleasure, though he denies it, of being a great local figure.

This morning I compared notes with John Freeman, who had been down in the Rhondda and told me that there he had received immense applause when he said that the Bevanites are faced with the dilemma of loyalty to the Party leadership or loyalty to those who voted for them at Morecambe.

We discussed what tactics the Bevanites should pursue. Before my weekend I had been absolutely clear that at all costs Nye should stand for the Parliamentary Committee. John had come back from South Wales convinced that he shouldn't, since this would mean completely destroying Bevanism as a left-wing force. It really is a choice of evils. If we agree, as we must, to disband the Group and Nye goes on to the Committee, there will be no sign of Bevanism whatsoever, since, however loudly we talked on the backbenches, we are nothing without Nye as a mouthpiece. In that case the right-wing will feel completely confident that it can do what it likes and three of us will certainly lose our places on the Executive next year. On the other hand, if Nye doesn't stand and we go on the backbenches, we really must face a year of extreme unpleasantness in the Party and possibly lose the next Election.

[1] A singer, who has been described as 'the personification of the torch singer of the 1920s and 1930s', she appeared in various Broadway shows, particularly during the latter decade She died in 1971.

[2] Probably Alan Bullock's *Hitler: A Study in Tyranny* (London: Odhams, 1952). Crossman's review of this book – and of J. L. Talmon's *The Origins of Totalitarian Democracy* (London: Secker & Warburg, 1952) – appeared in the *New Statesman* of November 15th, 1952, under the title 'The Devil Can Move Mountains'.

On the other hand, to go round in circles again, this may be worth it in order to ensure that we do get an adequate Socialist programme.

One other thing John and I discussed is the oddity that, quite suddenly, my column in the *Sunday Pic* has become the special object of detestation in the Party, mainly, I think, because the mass of our trade union Members don't worry to read the *Tribune* or the *Statesman* but do regularly read the *Pic*. They were infuriated by my article ten days ago and also by the feeling that somehow this is written by somebody far cleverer than the *Tribune* boys. I wonder whether there will come a time when they will try to force the issue that a member of the National Executive must either be a journalist or a member of the National Executive.[1] A letter I have had from Hugh Gaitskell, in reply to mine saying he was unfair in attacking me, indicates that this is the line that they may take.

I caught the half-past five train to Brighton, on the way to a brains trust at Wilton Park, and found myself sitting opposite Lord Hinchingbrooke.[2] He has made two or three rather courageous speeches against military containment and German rearmament and is under threat of discipline from his constituency party. Curiously enough, he succeeded Lord Cranborne,[3] who was threatened with discipline by the same party in 1938 for opposing appeasement! We discussed the Bevanite situation and Hinchingbrooke told me that he didn't know what the Conservative Party would do if 'omnicompetent groups' were expelled. It would mean the end of the Tory Reform Group and, indeed, of the 1922 Committee,[4] which corresponds to our Parliamentary Party Meeting but originated in fact in a meeting of rebellious backbench M.P.s.

[1] See below, pp. 204 ff.

[2] Victor Montagu, Conservative M.P. for South Dorset 1941–57, Independent Conservative M.P. for the same constituency for a period in 1957, and Conservative M.P. again from 1958 to 1962. An opponent of Britain's joining the European Economic Community, he is President of the Anti-Common Market League, and has been Chairman of the Conservative Trident Group since 1973. His publications include the uncatalogued pamphlet *The Conservative Dilemma*, published 1970. Victor Montagu enjoyed the courtesy title of Lord (i.e. Baron) Hinchingbrooke as heir to his father, the 9th Earl of Sandwich. He succeeded to the earldom on his father's death in 1962 but on July 24th, 1964, disclaimed his title for life under the provisions of the Peerage Act 1963.

[3] Viscount Cranborne (the courtesy title of the eldest son and heir of the 4th Marquess of Salisbury) was called to the House of Lords, during his father's lifetime, in his father's barony of Cecil, and was introduced on January 22nd, 1941. He continued to be known colloquially as Cranborne until he succeeded to the marquisate on his father's death in 1947.

He was himself Paymaster-General 1940, Secretary of State for the Dominions 1940–2, Secretary of State for the Colonies and Leader of the House of Lords February–November 1942, Lord Privy Seal November 1942–September 1943 and Secretary of State for the Dominions September 1943–July 1945. He was again Leader of the House of Lords 1951–7, during which time he was also Lord Privy Seal 1951–2, Secretary of State for Commonwealth Relations March–December 1952 and Lord President of the Council from December 1952 until his resignation over the Cyprus issue in March 1957. From June to December 1953 he was also Acting Foreign Secretary. He died in 1972.

[4] The organization of Conservative backbench M.P.s. The Committee took its name from the meeting which overthrew the premiership of Lloyd George in 1922.

After the meeting William Clark,[1] the Diplomatic Correspondent of the *Observer*, motored Hinchingbrooke and myself back in streaming rain. I managed to drive Clark into admitting that he was willing to see a Western European Federation completely dominated by Germany, when, at this precise moment, in Tooting, the rod connecting the car's gears broke and we stopped dead in the middle of the street. However, we got a taxi, which cost 10s. and, as I gave 5s. and I noticed that Hinchingbrooke also gave 5s., Mr Clark of the *Observer* made a nice profit.

Tuesday, October 28th

I don't think there has been a time, since I was in Parliament, when I have been more depressed or more sheerly tired by a political crisis than I was today. Ever since Morecambe no one in Parliament has discussed anything else or felt anything else and the result is a sense of dreary emotional exhaustion, which is difficult to describe. When I got to the *Statesman* this morning Kingsley was ready with delicate allusions to the way we were letting Bevanism interfere with the paper. But as he himself disappeared for the whole of the morning to arrange something or other about his visit to Kenya none of us took him very seriously. Even when he's there, his secretary[2] comes in with some form which it takes many questions of us for him to fill in. I've never known a man who can concentrate less on the job.

John and I were due to lunch with Kingsley in order to meet Radhakrishnan,[3] the Indian Ambassador in Moscow, who was to tell us about his long and fascinating conversations with Stalin. There was a Group meeting at half-past one and an N.E.C. at half-past two and, although Kingsley said the lunch was so important that I must cancel both meetings, he finally agreed that only John should stay. I gather the only interesting thing which Radhakrishnan said was the following: In one conversation with Stalin, Radhakrishnan mentioned Marxism and Stalin suddenly brought down his fist with

[1] William Donaldson Clark, a former lecturer at the University of Chicago, worked for the British Ministry of Information in Chicago 1941–4, when he became Press Attaché in Washington. Having worked for the *Encyclopaedia Britannica* 1946–9, he became, in 1950, Diplomatic Correspondent of the *Observer*. Apart from a period as Public Relations Adviser to the Prime Minister, Sir Anthony Eden, in 1955–6, he worked for the *Observer* until 1960. He was Director of the Overseas Development Institute 1960–8, Director of Information and Public Affairs at the World Bank 1968–73, and of External Affairs Direction 1973–4. He was Vice-President of the World Bank 1974–80 and since 1980 has been President of the International Institute for Environment and Development. His publications include *Less than Kin: A Study of Anglo-American Relations* (London: Hamish Hamilton, 1957), *No. 10* (London: Heinemann, 1966) and *Special Relationship* (London: Heinemann, 1968).

[2] No doubt one of the 'succession of outstanding secretaries and research assistants', described in the chapter 'All Sorts of Interesting Women … ', in C. H. Rolph's *Kingsley* (London: Gollancz, 1973).

[3] Sir Sarvepalli Radhakrishnan (1888–1967), a philosopher, was Leader of the Indian Delegation to UNESCO 1944–6, Chairman of the Executive Board of UNESCO 1947 and President 1952. He was Ambassador to the U.S.S.R. 1949–51, Vice-President of the Republic of India 1952–62 and President of India 1962–7.

a bang on the table. 'Don't talk to me of Marxism,' he said. 'Marxism isn't a dogma but a guide to action.'

Apparently in the same conversation Stalin had indicated fairly clearly that he was jolly well going to hold on to the satellite countries and he wasn't going to tolerate Tito[1] so long as the Americans were difficult. But he had argued that, after all, he was holding countries adjacent to Russia, whereas the American bases were thousands of miles away from America. R.K. emphasized repeatedly that Stalin had made clear that he did want to reach a *modus vivendi* with the West and that his one preoccupation was to keep out of war. R.K. added that, in his view, Stalin was in complete control of the situation in Russia and that there was no chance of this line being reversed.

While this lunch was going on I rushed down to the Group, where the only item on the agenda was disbandment. It was very quickly decided that we must accept the Parliamentary Party's decision without haggling about it, although in the next Session[2] we should have to concert ways and means of continuing to keep contact and possibly even ask for official sanction for continued open meetings. Once this was agreed, the next question was how the announcement should be made and Aneurin made it clear that he wanted it made on Thursday morning in the *Tribune*. It was urged, reasonably enough, that, as the whole press was waiting outside for our decision, we couldn't wait till Thursday, even if it would help the *Tribune*. A somewhat peevish discussion took place about newspaper deadlines. Nye wanted a meeting to approve the statement postponed till Wednesday, and I said that this would be too late for the *New Statesman*.

This is the only meeting where I have known Nye well below form and really rather unconvincing. He announced that he was due to leave that evening and would be unable to see anything we wrote. Nevertheless it was decided to draft a statement at a small sub-committee at half-past four and to have it discussed and approved at a Group meeting at half-past nine. But Nye and Mike got their way that we should then wait for thirty-six hours and publish the statement on Thursday morning. Really the *Tribune* is getting to be a confounded nuisance.

Right at the end of the meeting Nye raised the issue of whether to stand for the Parliamentary Committee or not, and announced rather curtly that his plan was that people should only stand on condition that he challenged Morrison for the deputy leadership. This, he thought, would prevent us from looking as though we had submitted to the ultimatum. At this point it was twenty-five minutes past two and as the N.E.C. was at half-past two nothing more could be said, but I urged that the Group should discuss this at half-past nine and that Harold Wilson should tell Nye of its views.

[1] Marshal Josip Broz Tito. Made Secretary-General of the Yugoslav Communist Party in 1937, he led the people's uprising during the Second World War. He was created a Marshal in 1943 and became President of the Government in 1945 and President of the Yugoslav Republic in 1953. He died in 1980.

[2] The 1952/53 Session began on November 4th, 1952.

We then moved along the passage from Room 8 to Room 5, where the N.E.C. was foregathering. One got the impression that this Executive is not spoiling for a row and this was confirmed when we came to the item 'Report of Resolution from Parliamentary Labour Party'. This referred, of course, to the resolution banning the Bevanite Group. Morgan Phillips said in a muffled voice, 'I suppose I will have to read it aloud, though everybody knows it.' He read it very fast, said 'No comment?' and moved to the next business.

The only quarrel we had was a ridiculous row about the allocation of the members of the Committee to the various sub-committees, raised, naturally enough, by Barbara Castle. Apparently everybody had got their first choice except Barbara and Sam Watson, who both wanted to be on the Policy Committee and had been excluded. Barbara wanted herself and Sam added to this, giving the committee eighteen members. After an awful bicker, Morgan Phillips said, 'Well, if you don't like my sorting out your list of preferences, shall we have a ballot next time?' There was a cold shudder at this point and we passed to the next business.

When we came to endorse a list of forty new candidates, Jim Griffiths pointed out that only six of them were manual workers and demanded that the office should make a breakdown of M.P.s and candidates to see the proportion of manual and non-manual workers. Nye supported this and then said it was all our own fault because we don't pay M.P.s enough and working-class people couldn't afford to be candidates, far less M.P.s. Somebody very sensibly pointed out that probably most of these professional workers were the sons and daughters of Labour workers, who had sent their children to secondary schools. However we accepted Jim Griffiths's proposals.

Straight from the meeting I had to go downstairs to the drafting committee of the Bevanites, which was presented with a four-page draft statement by Michael Foot. With the help of Tom Driberg, I managed to shape it back to the points I had made in my speech at Colchester. After a meeting at Morley College to talk about the future of Socialism and dinner at the Reform Club with Tommy Balogh I rushed back again to the House at half-past nine for the Group meeting. We took one and a half hours to discuss the draft statement and improved it a great deal in the process, to everyone's surprise. After this we did have a half-hour's discussion of Nye's proposal about the Parliamentary Committee. Everyone who spoke supported it, except Ellis Smith, A. J. Irvine, John Freeman and myself. But I think the Group knew that, in a choice of evils so evenly balanced, it was futile to be dogmatic and the general conclusion was that, whatever Nye decided, the Group would back him either way and was glad that it didn't have the responsibility of making such an awkward decision.

On November 4th General Eisenhower was elected President of the United States. In a landslide victory he carried 39 States, with 442 votes in the electoral college, to Governor Stevenson's 9 States, with 89 electoral votes. This was the first Republican presidential victory for twenty-four years but the Party secured only a bare majority in the simultaneous congressional elections. In the Senate the Republicans now had 49 seats to the Democrats' 47 and, in the House of Representatives, 221 seats to 214. Norman MacKenzie's unsigned article, 'They Liked Ike', appeared in the New Statesman and Nation *of November 8th, 1952.*

Wednesday, November 5th

After a three-hour meeting of the Fabian Executive Committee at County Hall last night and afterwards an Israeli party with Gavin Faringdon, I went to dine at the Reform with Tommy Balogh. He was in great distress about Nye Bevan, who, he fears, will not work out a serious policy, and he was anxious that I should get hold of Nye for a meeting next Wednesday. When I got home Nye rang me up and I fixed him for dinner on that evening. He was extremely friendly and anxious to ask for all sorts of advice but mostly, I think, he wanted me to say that he was right to stand against Herbert for the deputy leadership, which I did. Then he asked me what I thought about the American election and I said that I hoped for Stevenson[1] but was pretty certain that Eisenhower would in fact win. Nye pooh-poohed this, since he said the presidential election was a genuine popular plebiscite and therefore Stevenson must win. He thought it monstrous of me to suggest that sometimes a democracy can vote wrong.

At the *Statesman* this morning poor Norman MacKenzie[2] was in a terrible state, since he had proved scientifically that Stevenson was bound to win. While John tried to edit the paper, Norman wrote a poor article which I couldn't improve, and I was busy writing a front page on the Queen's Speech. This meant missing the Party Meeting, where fortunately nothing happened, as I heard from Nye and Curly Mallalieu when I got to lunch at two o'clock. Nye rather gallantly told the story of our telephone conversation last night.

As for our own election, I had based the whole leader on a 'no change' result at High Wycombe[3] and I was relieved to find on the tape at the House of Commons the 2,000 majority I had guessed. Nye, of course, was delighted by this result, which in his view was a perfect demonstration that Attlee's order to disband the Bevanites had not won votes. This, at least, was more

---

[1] Adlai Stevenson, a lawyer, who had worked for the American New Deal administration in Washington, D.C., was elected as Democratic Governor of Illinois in 1948. As Democratic candidate for the presidency of the United States, he was defeated in both the 1952 and the 1956 elections. He was American Ambassador to the United Nations from 1961 until his death in 1965.

[2] A journalist, writer and university lecturer, he joined the staff of the *New Statesman* in 1942, eventually becoming Assistant Editor. He was a Lecturer at the University of Sussex 1962–5 and became Director of its Centre for Educational Technology in 1966. His publications include *Socialism: A Short History* (London: Hutchinson, 1949) and (with his wife Jeanne) *The Time Traveller: A Life of H. G. Wells* (London: Weidenfeld & Nicolson, 1973) and *The First Fabians* (London: Weidenfeld & Nicolson, 1977).

[3] See above, p. 162.

sensible than John Hynd, who, an hour later, proved to me that the Bevanites had lost High Wycombe and then added that he was quite certain, first, that we shouldn't agree a Party policy and, second, that, as a result, the Tories were bound to win the next election, owing to the Bevanites.

The atmosphere in the House of Commons was extremely *piano*. It's a strange fact that four years ago the Tories were very downcast by Truman's victory, since they were enthusiastic Deweyites.[1] But this year I fancy that all of them wanted Stevenson to win and they had been really alarmed by the Eisenhower campaign. A great many people seemed to have wanted Stevenson so much that they expected him to win and only confirmed pessimists like Tommy Balogh and me could regard the result with equanimity. At least it shows that those who accused us of being anti-American for saying that McCarthy[2] and MacArthur[3] represented important forces in the U.S.A. were pretty silly and, as a matter of fact, I am willing to wait and see whether Ike uses the honeymoon period to liberate himself from his self-imposed captivity. He might still do it. At least it's one's duty to say so.

I dropped into the Chamber for the first time since July, to hear Dr Dalton starting the second day of the debate on the Address. Opposite him sat Peter Thorneycroft and the patball went on and on and on. It's as though one hadn't left off last July—the same sort of professional debating, two heavy-weights in a clinch because neither wants to knock the other out. One begins to see what the effect of disbanding the Bevanite Group will be. I don't think I've missed much by not being in the Chamber and at tea-time Nye said to me that he saw no point in making a speech before Christmas.

Just to end a perfect afternoon, Sydney Jacobson rushed round to tell me that a cable had come from Hugh Cudlipp in Australia, ordering the *Pic* to continue the attack on Nye Bevan once again on the front page. Could I think of a way of doing this which would cause the minimum harm? I did and

---

[1] In the 1948 American Presidential election the Republican candidate was Thomas Dewey and the Democratic nominee was the incumbent President, Mr Truman. Though Mr Dewey was widely expected to win, in the election on November 2nd Mr Truman secured an overwhelming victory, with 24,104,836 popular votes (303 votes in the electoral college) against Dewey's 21,969,500 votes (189 in the electoral college). (Of the other candidates, the only one with a significant number of votes was Governor Strom Thurmond of South Carolina, with 169,312 popular votes and 39 in the electoral college.) The Democratic Party also assumed control of the Senate and the House of Representatives. Dewey, a lawyer, became Republican Governor of New York State in 1942 and served in that office until 1955. He was also the unsuccessful Republican candidate in the American presidential election of 1944. He died in 1971.

[2] Republican Senator from Wisconsin from 1946 until his death in May 1957. He was Chairman of the notorious Senate Investigating Sub-Committee.

[3] General Douglas MacArthur (1880–1964), U.S. Commander for the Far East in 1941, Commander of all Allied Forces in the South-West Pacific in 1942, and Supreme Commander in Japan in 1945. He was Commander of the United Nations forces during the Korean war from 1950 until relieved of his command in 1951. His controversial attitudes during the Korean war and his subsequent demotion endeared him to many on the American Right, who saw him as a rival to Eisenhower in the Republican primary race preceding the 1952 election.

also said to Sydney that he should remind Hugh Cudlipp that he was sending me to Egypt this Christmas and it would be more newsy if he also sent me to Ike's inauguration.[1]

As I walked back there was a gorgeous bonfire in the street outside the Westminster Hospital and the November 5th bangers[2] were going in Vincent Square. Now I must get ready for Baloghs and Bevans at dinner and I shall fail to attend Kenneth Younger's party to celebrate Stevenson's victory.

Friday, November 7th
Last Wednesday I had Nye and Jennie and Tommy and Pen to dinner, with the object of discussing the draft directive. The National Executive had decided that the Policy Committee should prepare this to form the framework of the policy statement, so it was obviously necessary that we should clear our own minds on the same subject.

It was an extremely enjoyable evening. After talking about Kingsley Martin and the *New Statesman*, we had a long discussion about Eisenhower's election, with Nye arguing that it would make virtually no difference to American foreign policy because the Democratic regime had always been compelled to carry out Republican policy in the end, however reluctantly. Eisenhower, on the other hand, would be much less afraid of being accused of appeasement. Indeed, he might have to appease the liberals, so the net result would be roughly the same.

Partly, I think, Nye was once again stimulating Tommy and me by opposing us. If he was, he certainly succeeded and we managed to cover the whole area of American policy and to show him that even a slight difference in emphasis or quality could be decisive — in France, for instance, in making the French Assembly repudiate the E.D.C. Equally, pressure from the China lobby might lead Eisenhower to find himself extending the war in Korea. But Nye did in the end agree that the danger of a mismanaged American economy was certainly graver under Eisenhower. I then said, 'You know, if Stevenson had been elected, it would very nearly have proved Gaitskell right.' As might have been expected, this really did annoy Nye, to whom such an idea is inconceivable.

However I think that Nye knows that Eisenhower's election has strengthened the case of those of us who have been arguing that not dollar exports but a cut in dollar imports, in substitution for non-dollar imports, should be the basis of our policy. From this we moved to Nye's main interest, food policy, where he outlined the case for nationalizing the landlords, i.e. all the agricultural land except that farmed by owner-occupiers. He was emphatic that further nationalization would have to be justified in terms of our five-year plan — for instance, Imperial Chemicals should be nationalized to ensure proper planning of artificial fertilizer, etc. He then turned to the

[1] On January 20th, 1953.
[2] Fireworks, celebrating Guy Fawkes Night.

export trade and suggested that we might nationalize the motor-car industry owing to its failure to rationalize the number of models.

Towards the end of the evening I mentioned military commitments and the term of military service[1] and suggested that, even though Shinwell had proposed a reduction in the term of military service, we should not leave it out of the Party programme for that reason, since there were solid grounds for cutting military commitments and the term of service. Nye indignantly denied this, on the ground that, if women found a reduction of the term of service in the programme, this would divert their attention from the central issue. 'We can't give the impression of being pacifists,' he said, 'and, even though we may reduce the term of service under the next Labour Government, we must not fight the next election on that issue.' Jennie and Pen protested feebly on behalf of the women but they were swept away.

Monday, November 10th

The debate on the Queen's Speech is still going on and today and tomorrow are to be devoted to the Labour motion of censure.[2] I looked into the Chamber today and it was obvious that this was yet another bogus motion of censure, with no force behind it. All the Bevanites have been abstaining politely from speaking, to maintain Party amity, with the result that there is a complete flop in the atmosphere.

Wednesday, November 12th

Yesterday I went into the House for the end of the debate, and heard Crook-shank do a brilliant knockabout performance, which really made the Opposition look pretty silly, since he was perfectly right in pointing out that the vote of censure wasn't seriously intended and that the only proper Amendment to the Queen's Speech would be to state that this House has no confidence in Her Majesty's Opposition.[3] The fact is that morale in the Commons is appalling because the Labour Party has nothing to fight on and everybody is beginning to feel the after-effects of disbanding the Bevanites. However, we had the good news from the Party Meeting that the vote for the deputy leadership had been 194 for Morrison and 82 for Bevan. We would have been 84 if Brockway and Hale had been back from Kenya. Nye got all the votes

[1] In December 1948 the term of National Service was extended to eighteen months, in a Bill enacting the Government's original proposal of March 1947 (see above, p. 88). In September 1950 the term was increased to two years.

[2] It is usual for the Opposition Amendment to the Motion presenting the Address to the Sovereign to express lack of confidence in Her Majesty's Government. On this occasion the Opposition regretted the absence of 'positive and effective proposals for dealing with the serious economic position of the country' and declared that 'this House has no confidence in Your Majesty's present advisers whose policies threaten a return to the social conditions of the inter-war years'.

[3] The Opposition Amendment was defeated by 313 votes to 279 and the main question was carried without division.

we hoped and 15 more than we expected. I ended the evening at Nicholas Davenport's, where I talked too much.

This week Weizmann[1] died and I took on writing the obituary for the *Statesman*.[2] I found it extraordinarily difficult. There is so much more to say than one can possibly say. He is the only great man I ever knew well and I am not likely to know another. Indeed, judged by present prospects, what I did about Palestine was probably the biggest job I shall ever do in politics and the biggest thing in it for me, looking back, were the many, many hours I spent with Weizmann. One can't help regretting that it's over, from a selfish point of view. Life's worth living when there is a cause like that to fight for, where you have no inhibitions of any kind and you feel you are absolutely right.

Friday, November 14th
Yesterday morning, on Barbara's initiative, she and I went round Transport House to see how the officials are actually housed. It's an astonishing sight — a couple of back rooms on the top floor and rooms scattered about on each of the others, until you get down to the second floor, where the finance and administrative department are very comfortably housed. *Fact*, the new Labour Party publication,[3] is edited in a small room at the top, which also accommodates all the layout artists and propaganda people. The Local Government department is jammed in at one corner of a tiny room, along with another office, another bureau and so on. When we had finished our visit, I was told that we were the first members of the N.E.C. who had ever asked to be taken round.

I had Morgan Phillips to lunch with Barbara. He told me that Attlee's famous speech denouncing the Bevanite conspiracy[4] had been shown to him just before the meeting and he had told Attlee that it was very unwise. Attlee had said, 'Should I withdraw it?' and Morgan had said, 'No, it's gone out to the press already.'

We discussed the situation with regard to broadcasting. At present, as

---

[1] Chaim Weizmann (1874–1952), a biochemist, who had been a Lecturer at the University of Manchester, was Director of Admiralty Laboratories 1916–19. A strongly committed Zionist, he was President of the World Zionist Organization and the Jewish Agency for Palestine 1921–31 and 1935–46. He became the first President of Israel in 1948 and served in that capacity until his death in 1952.

[2] Published in the issue of November 15th, 1952. In 1945 Crossman had been a member of the Anglo-American Joint Committee of Inquiry, set up to examine the position of Jews in Europe and the problems of Palestine. When the committee reported in 1948, Crossman supported the recommendation that a Jewish State be established in Israel; he never forgave Attlee and Bevin for their lack of enthusiasm for this plan and their disavowal of the 1917 Balfour Declaration. See Crossman's *Palestine Mission* (London: Hamish Hamilton, 1946) and *A Nation Reborn* (London: Hamish Hamilton, 1960). At the end of his life, Crossman was engaged on a biography of Weizmann, 'the greatest Jew of his generation', and his admiration never wavered. (See *The Diaries of a Cabinet Minister*, vol. III, p. 702.)

[3] *Fact* was a monthly publication, appearing continuously between 1949 and 1956.

[4] See above, pp. 163 ff.

Frank Gillard[1] of the Western Region told me again last week, there is a secret informal arrangement with someone unknown that there should be four anti-Bevanites for one Bevanite on the air. I suggested to Morgan that, now the Bevanite Group had disbanded, it was only logical to remove the ban on broadcasting. Morgan said that he had nothing to do with it and I suspect that it comes from the Chief Whip and Herbert. Anyhow, Morgan promised to write to the Director-General.[2] My own position is that, quite suddenly, I have been deluged with B.B.C. requests again and I am due to do a ticklish Home Service discussion on party loyalty on December 4th.

I also asked Morgan about the International Sub., and he gave me an astonishing description of its haphazard method of dealing with foreign policy. Whether the Executive makes a decision or not seems to be entirely up to any individual who happens to read the capacious minutes. So I am reading the minutes very carefully.

At the Party Meeting at half-past six last night there wasn't going to be much business and I slipped off to speak on Bevanism to a reactionary club in London. I therefore missed an extraordinary scene when, right at the end of the Meeting, Attlee muttered that they had decided to introduce a new system for voting for the Parliamentary Committee, in view of the fact that there were fifty-four candidates.[3] No one is to be elected on the first ballot unless he gets a clear majority and, in the second ballot, the number of candidates is to be twice the number of seats available. This, apparently, is an old method used in the trade unions to defeat the Communists. Some of our people are very much up in arms but the newspaper treatment of this obvious trick will merely weaken the right-wingers still further. Tommy Balogh tells me that Nye's reaction has been to say, 'We can't actually oppose a method used in the trade unions.' He is quite shrewd on this sort of thing.

Tuesday, November 18th
At the B.B.C. this morning we had our recording of the party loyalty discussion for December 4th. G. M. Young,[4] who has just published a life of

[1] Francis Gillard, a former teacher, joined the B.B.C. in 1941. He was Head of B.B.C. West Regional Programmes 1945–55, Controller B.B.C. West 1956–63, Director of Sound Broadcasting 1963–8, and Managing Director of Radio at the B.B.C. from 1969 until his retirement in 1970.

[2] Sir William Haley retired on September 30th, 1952, to be succeeded by Sir Ian Jacob, a soldier who had reached the rank of lieutenant-general. Sir Ian was Controller of European Services in the B.B.C. in 1946, Director of Overseas Services 1947–52 and Director-General 1952–60.

[3] The election for the Parliamentary Committee was to be on November 19th (first ballot) and November 27th (second ballot); there were in fact fifty-one candidates for the twelve places. Another new rule was that, to prevent organized 'plumping', each voter was to cast his full twelve votes.

[4] George Malcolm Young (1882–1959), the historian and biographer. Elected a Fellow of All Souls' College, Oxford in 1905, he was a tutor at St John's College, Oxford, 1906–8. He was a civil servant 1908–20. His publications include *Gibbon* (London: Hart-Davis, 1932), *Victorian England* (Oxford University Press, 1936), *Today and Yesterday* (London: Hart-Davis, 1948) and *Stanley Baldwin* (London: Hart-Davis, 1952), an 'official' biography

Baldwin,[1] was in the chair, and the other members were Christopher Hollis[2] for the Conservatives, a dreary ex-President of the Liberal Party,[3] and William Pickles,[4] representing, I suppose, the right-wing of the Labour Party, though he is actually a lecturer at L.S.E. We all worked out beautifully that we shouldn't do too much about Bevanism and we should discuss party loyalty and splits historically. But dear me, before five minutes were up there was a fierce controversy across the table between Pickles and me and I shall be very curious to see how the B.B.C. girls edit the script to make it nice and academic.

At lunch today with John and Mrs Gunther,[5] she told me a nice story about Eisenhower. When they were visiting him near Paris he had shown her his pictures and she had disingenuously asked, 'Have you ever tried an abstraction?' To which he had replied, 'Tried an abstraction? Why, I think that sort of vicious art ought to be banned!' John Gunther rapidly apologized for his wife and tried to find some good in Eisenhower.

Wednesday, November 19th
I missed the Party Meeting because I had to work at the *Statesman* and get things finished before Kingsley arrived back from Kenya. When I got down to the House I found Aneurin and others sitting in the Smoking Room discussing the ballot.[6] Quite clearly, some careful organization had been done,

which won him not only the James Tait Black Memorial Prize but also the disfavour of Baldwin's family, since it presented the former Prime Minister in a far from sympathetic light.

[1] Stanley Baldwin (1867–1947), Conservative M.P. for Bewdley 1908–37. He was joint Financial Secretary to the Treasury 1917–21, President of the Board of Trade 1921–2, Chancellor of the Exchequer 1922–3, Leader of the Conservative Party 1923–37, Prime Minister 1923–4 and 1924–9, Lord President of the Council 1931–5, Lord Privy Seal 1932–3, and Prime Minister again 1935–7, when he resigned and was made an Earl, taking the title Earl Baldwin of Bewdley. There are several biographies of him, in addition to that by G. M. Young. These include K. Middlemas and J. Barnes, *Baldwin* (London: Weidenfeld & Nicolson, 1969) and H. M. Hyde, *Baldwin* (London: Hart-Davis-McGibbon, 1973).

[2] A teacher at Stonyhurst College 1925–35 and Conservative M.P. for Devizes 1945–55. A former member of staff of the *Tablet*, he is Chairman of the publishing house, Hollis & Carter. His own writings include *Glastonbury and England* (London: Sheed & Ward, 1927) and *The Rise and Fall of the Ex-Socialist Government* (London: Hollis & Carter, 1947).

[3] George Elliott Dodds, Editor and Director of the *Huddersfield Examiner* and an ex-President of the Liberal Party Organization. The programme was called 'Taking Stock'.

[4] A former B.B.C. Producer and Reader in Political Science at the London School of Economics, a member of the Fabian Society and a consistently firm opponent of Britain's membership of the E.E.C. His publications include *The French Constitution of October 4th, 1958* (London: Stevens, 1959) and *Not With Europe* (London: Fabian Society, 1967). He died in 1979.

[5] John Gunther, a journalist and writer, worked initially for the *Chicago Daily News* and then from the mid-1930s wrote a series of books on contemporary-politics, including *Inside Russia Today* (London: Hamish Hamilton, 1958) and *Inside Europe Today* (London: Hamish Hamilton, 1961). In 1927, Gunther had married Frances Fineman but in 1944 the marriage was dissolved. In 1948 he married Jane Perry Vandercook. He died in 1970.

[6] James Griffiths obtained the most votes — 194 — and Bevan came twelfth with 108. Anthony Greenwood came fourteenth, with 93 votes. Harold Wilson had 91 and Geoffrey Bing 71. Mark Hewitson in fact had 7 votes and John Dugdale 6. Crossman did not stand.

since, of the twelve previous members of the Committee, eleven were among the first twelve on the ballot, and Tony Greenwood had been rejected for having shown some sympathy for the Bevanites. Nye had just scraped into twelfth place, with Harold Wilson and Geoffrey Bing some way behind. The wooden spoon had been equally shared between John Dugdale[1] and Mark Hewitson.[2] Considering that Mark Hewitson is a member of the N.E.C. and a leading trade unionist, the fact that he got six votes is remarkable. Dalton assured me that he had given him one for his loyalty on Germany.

I think Nye was really much more depressed about the ballot than I had expected. Apparently, at the Meeting he had tried to withdraw from the second ballot and Attlee had suddenly ruled that withdrawals were illegal. In my view, this ruthless reassertion by the Right of their determination to keep things as they are will do us a great deal of good in the country, particularly since Attlee changed the rules after the ballot had been announced. Geoffrey Bing was furious with the Party for giving Frank Soskice[3] 111 votes while he only got 71. He felt that he deserved better of it for all his good works. In fact, he obviously wanted to be on the Committee.

At the end of the day there was no doubt that the net effect of this vote, as published in the press, had been to depress and demoralize the Party still further. Here is the Parliamentary Party voting for all the old guard who were voted down at Morecambe and voting down the Bevanites systematically. No doubt the victory gave some people pleasure but it didn't make them feel any better.

In the afternoon I had three hours of the Organization Sub-committee, where once again there was a mass of papers and where Arthur Greenwood is such an incredibly bad chairman that the thing goes drooling on and on and on. Well, I am learning.

On November 19th Oliver Lyttelton, the Colonial Secretary, reported to the House of Commons that the situation in Kenya had greatly improved. Increasingly, terrorists were surrendering to the authorities. Mr Lyttelton warmly praised the administration of the High Commissioner, Sir Gerald Templer, who had been frequently criticized for his policy of applying communal punishment to villages harbouring terrorists.

[1] A former diplomat who was married to a grand-daughter of George Lansbury, he was Labour M.P. for West Bromwich from 1941 until his death in 1963. He was Attlee's Private Secretary 1931–9, Parliamentary and Financial Secretary to the Admiralty 1945–50 and Minister of State for Colonial Affairs 1950–1.

[2] Captain Mark Hewitson, an official of the General and Municipal Workers' Union, was Labour M.P. for Hull Central 1945–55 and for Hull West 1955–64. He was President of the Public and Civil Service International 1937–40 and of the General Factory Workers International 1945–50. A past member of the Labour Party National Executive Committee, he retired as National Industrial Officer of the G.M.W.U. in 1964. He died in 1973.

[3] A barrister and Labour M.P. for Birkenhead East 1945–50, for the Neepsend division of Sheffield 1950–5 and for Newport 1956–66. Knighted in 1945, he was Solicitor General 1945–51, Home Secretary 1964–5, and Lord Privy Seal 1965–6, when he was made a life peer, taking the title of Lord Stow Hill. He died in 1978.

However, at Kirawara on November 23rd twenty policemen had been attacked by 2,000 members of the Kikuyu tribe, armed with long knives. As a last resort, the police used firearms and several of the rioters were killed. On November 25th the Colonial Secretary announced the Government's 'distasteful but necessary' decision to impose communal punishment (including the removal of livestock) on certain areas. After the Minister's statement, the Opposition obtained from the Speaker an adjournment of the House for discussion of this matter of urgent public importance. The former Colonial Secretary, James Griffiths, expressed concern at the Government's policy as likely to stir the anger of the whole Kikuyu tribe. He asked that an all-party delegation of M.P.s should visit the area and inquire into the Kirawara incident.

Mr Lyttelton declared that the facts of the matter were plain, that the Government must be seen to support the police and that he was hurrying on the establishment of the Royal Commission to look at the whole state of affairs in Kenya and the remedies for it. (It had already been announced on November 1st that Sir Hugh Dow would be chairman of this inquiry but the remaining members had not yet all been chosen.) Mr Griffiths withdrew his suggestion.

Wednesday, November 26th

Yesterday we had arranged that the six Bevanite members of the National Executive should dine together to discuss this morning's N.E.C. meeting. Actually we never got to discussing it, partly because the waiters were going in and out all the time and partly because the whole thing was disturbed by events up in the Chamber, where, instead of the first of a two-day Second Reading of the steel denationalization Bill, there was an adjournment motion to discuss the deterioration of the situation in Kenya. While we were dining we learnt that Jim Griffiths had decided not to press the matter to a vote and when he withdrew all the backbenchers sat there silent. If there had been a Bevanite Group they wouldn't have been silent, so one sees why the Right likes disbanding us.

The fact is, as we agreed at dinner, that since it was disbanded the Group has rapidly disintegrated. We didn't even achieve a full Group vote for all the people who stood for the Executive and the absence of a weekly discussion means that the members have no longer thought things out or achieved a common mind. How are we to deal with this? We decided, first, to appoint six scoutmasters, who shall each have six or seven members of the Group to contact and who shall work to a steering committee composed of the six members of the N.E.C. and the editorial board of the *Tribune* – Jennie, Michael and Curly. Secondly, after Christmas we are going to have weekly Tuesday lunches in Vincent Square for this inner group. Third, we are going to have a farewell Christmas party at Nye's house for all the Group, to discuss how the Group as a whole shall act, and we are going to have a beginning-of-term party at Vincent's Square for another Group get-together.

The discussion at dinner then went on to Labour Party policy. We've just got the Transport House draft of the basic priority framework, which is not half bad, since it at least sets everything against the problem of the dollar gap and the economic crisis. Nye, Tommy and Harold Wilson then discussed what industries we should nationalize and it was agreed that we should press for heavy chemicals, heavy engineering, rented land and aircraft production. Then somehow we got on to education, where, as usual, there was a frightful argument about public schools and privileged education.

Curiously enough, at midnight there seemed to be some thirty Bevanites about the place and virtually no one else. Everyone assumed that there had been a secret Bevanite Group meeting. There had, but only of the six of us. Then suddenly the division bell rang. There was George Wigg, who had staged a count and, as the Tories failed to muster, the debate on the Steel Bill collapsed. This escapade produced an extraordinary constitutional situation, since the Second Reading of the Steel Bill would have to start all over again, as George Wigg explained to me at length as he motored me home.[1] We got into a long argument about whether such tactics were good or bad. Not having taken part in it, I thought this one was schoolboyish. That is the normal situation. When you do a thing of this sort, you think it wonderful. When you are out of it, you think it is silly. But there is no doubt that the morale of the people there had been enormously improved.

This morning we had the N.E.C. for three hours and everything went fairly well with no ructions at all. Partly, perhaps, this was because there was no important business, but partly because, when the Bevanites talked, they talked sense and didn't always vote together.

I brought Barbara and Harold Wilson back to lunch and told them about dear Dr Dalton who dined with me in the House yesterday and told me how, when he was sitting on the Front Bench, he had been shown the piece of paper with the list of candidates[2] to be backed by all right-minded persons. So they disband the Bevanite Group and then organize a vote against it. At the end of dinner Nye came in and sat down at the end of our table. Dalton began to harangue him, telling him not to let himself be put into ridiculous postures by members of the Group. Nye quietly replied that he did not feel his present attitude ridiculous. Surely that epithet should be applied to the posture of the right-wingers in rigging elections? This is indeed true. The whole manner in which this ballot has been handled has, I think,

[1] At 7 p.m. on November 25th the Second Reading of the Steel Bill was interrupted for the debate on Kenya. When it was resumed at 10 p.m. the Opposition demanded that the House be counted and, since there were fewer than the forty Members required for a quorum, debate was broken off. It was not the case that the Bill would have to 'start all over again'. Indeed, next day the Leader of the House announced that, to recover this lost time, the Government intended to devote November 27th both to completing the Second Reading of the Steel Bill and to the business already set down for that day, thus subjecting Members to an all-night sitting.

[2] In the second ballot for the Parliamentary Committee Aneurin Bevan came sixth and last in the list of those elected to the six places unfilled on the first ballot. Anthony Greenwood, who came eighth, and Harold Wilson, ninth, were not elected.

done the right-wing an enormous amount of harm and, as things turned out, they could have got without trickery the result they wanted: that is, Nye alone on the Committee, with eleven opponents.

Monday, December 1st
At our *New Statesman* lunch today we had Douglas Jay, who has just done a very ambitious Fabian lecture on an economic plan for the next ten years.[1] He works out that we must increase our engineering production by 40 per cent in order to bridge the dollar gap, and indicates the need to extend public ownership in heavy engineering and chemicals. Last Saturday Harold Wilson had given me a long list of industries which he thought were ready for nationalization, including heavy engineering, chemicals and aircraft. When Douglas was asked today what he thought of Wilson, he replied, to my great surprise, that he agreed entirely.

It's fairly clear that, on the strict economic level, there is literally no difference between the Left and the Right of the Party. On the other hand, when I asked Douglas about East–West trade, the weight of our overseas military commitments, etc., he replied that, in order to be strictly impartial, he had disregarded these factors. That's where the trouble really lies. But, from the point of view of a united Party policy it's cheering to know that Jay and Wilson have no disagreement. We are publishing next week an article by Jay on his plan.[2] Meanwhile, this week, we are publishing G. D. H. Cole's[3] attack on Bevan,[4] which John and I refused to publish in Kingsley's absence.

Tuesday, December 2nd
After working at the *Statesman* this morning, John and I went to the House for lunch and sat ourselves with Hugh Gaitskell and John Strachey. I was anxious to talk to Hugh after Douglas Jay's conversation and all that Hugh said confirmed my impression that there should be no serious difficulty in

[1] Douglas Jay gave a Fabian lecture at Livingstone Hall, Westminster, on November 25th, 1952. He argued that the sterling countries, while co-operating in the world campaign against the dollar gap, ought first to make a concerted attack on their own dollar deficit. They should seek to establish a gold reserve equal to perhaps five times the current figure before taking steps towards convertibility or dismantling discriminatory import controls. There should be a steady export drive in such industries as coal, steel, engineering (including aircraft, vehicles and shipbuilding) and chemicals. Domestic food production should be raised by about 40 per cent in the next ten years. The inevitable corollary of concentration on a bigger programme of investment in productive equipment would be not a halt in advances in social services, but 'that we could not have lower taxes on the rich or further luxuries'.
[2] 'The Price of Survival', *New Statesman and Nation*, December 13th, 1952.
[3] George Douglas Howard Cole (1889–1959), a Fellow of Magdalen College, Oxford, and University Reader in Economics 1925–44 and a Fellow of All Souls' College, Oxford, 1944–57. He was Chichele Professor of Social and Political Theory at the University of Oxford 1944–57 and Research Fellow at Nuffield College, Oxford, 1957 and Fellow there until his death in 1959. He was President of the Fabian Society 1952–9 and, a prolific writer, was a considerable intellectual influence on the Labour Party.
[4] 'After the Shouting', *New Statesman and Nation*, December 6th, 1952.

reaching an agreement on a Labour Party programme. Since both sides agree on the central importance of the dollar gap, it is possible to agree on Socialist planning for the next five years. The real disagreements are not about economic policy but about relations with America, military commitments, etc.

Wednesday, December 3rd
Mysteriously, and with quite astonishing rapidity, the mood of the Parliamentary Party has changed. The Bevanite and anti-Bevanite feuding has melted away and, as I wrote for the *New Statesman*[1] front page this morning, everyone is rather shamefacedly aware that both sides are on the same side after all. How has all this happened? And when did it happen? I suspect it began at the Parliamentary Party Meeting yesterday morning, when Nye sat with the Shadow Cabinet on the platform for the first time and somehow it was obvious that he belonged there.

The same is true in the Chamber. One underestimated beforehand the astonishing effect of his mere presence on the Front Bench. This afternoon he asked two or three minor questions of Mr Churchill, received with ironical cheers by the Tories and therefore with overwhelming cheers from our side. The fact is, it didn't seem wrong and he didn't seem to feel uncomfortable and so suddenly everyone has begun to feel that it's over; again repeating my article, it's like a patient with a high temperature which suddenly, overnight, falls to sub-normal.

Of course, this couldn't have happened if there had been real fundamental issues of policy dividing the two sides. The fact that Douglas Jay and Harold Wilson really want the same economic policy and that between Nye and Hugh Gaitskell there are really only differences of emphasis, temperament and will as regards domestic policy—well, it's a fact that one has been repeating to oneself but one tended to underestimate its importance.

I suppose what it really is is that the old guard got the revenge out of their system by disbanding the Group and organizing the Shadow Cabinet elections. But it's also true that we'd really reached a deadlock. They couldn't do as their extremists want and expel us or kill Bevanism but, equally, we knew quite well that we couldn't shift the old guard from their complete control of the Parliamentary Party and of the big trade unions. Each side had sufficient power in its own sphere to prevent the other winning but not sufficient to win itself. Then, when you grant the enormous desire of the Labour Movement for unity and therefore the enormous fear in any contestant of being blamed for disunity, you get at least a partial explanation of how the Parliamentary Party can snap within forty-eight hours out of a split mind into an almost sentimental solidarity.

But there is something deeper. From Nye's point of view the really important issues are domestic. He only took to the foreign policy issues rather reluctantly, after he resigned. Yet in foreign policy there are really basic

[1] 'Back on the Front Bench', *New Statesman and Nation*, December 6th, 1952.

issues dividing us – the size of our military commitments, our attitude to America and to Western Europe. Here are great issues of policy where the only reason why we are not more divided is the fact that the leadership does not really think them out. Removing confusion on domestic affairs disclosed that there was no serious cleavage but, if one ever dared to remove confusion on foreign affairs, one would discover that there is much more cleavage than is now realized. But really only Tommy and I and one or two others have done enough thinking about foreign affairs to feel these issues are of first-rate importance. And anyway they aren't issues which would be included in a Party programme or which would come to a head until the next Labour Foreign Secretary is in charge. What is likely to happen now is a period of agreement in fighting the Tories, which will be punctuated from time to time by left-wing bursts of indignation about Mau-Mau or bombing the Yalu River or some other foreign policy incident. But, when these bursts come, the issue won't be clearly defined and the Left will probably be so sentimental that the right-wing realists will have a good deal to be said for them.

Of course, this leaves people like me stranded. A fellow's occupation's gone and I think that Harold Wilson feels it too. He said this afternoon, 'Well, I'm going to get on with my book.'[1] Discussing things with Tommy, I decided that we would weigh in after Christmas on the Defence and Services Estimates, not worrying about a Bevanite Group but working within the official Party Committee with George Wigg and John Strachey. If we do this, there is really no reason why we should not formulate the Party's attitude to defence problems and, by doing so, influence its foreign policy far more than if we had a Bevanite/anti-Bevanite controversy, in which whatever the Bevanites say must be opposed by the others.

In the Chamber this afternoon Churchill was asked a question about the Supreme Commander in the Mediterranean.[2] There was a wild row about his accusation of unpatriotic motives, which extended into the beginning of the Committee Stage of the Transport Bill. How the Labour Party enjoyed booing the Old Man. What a relief it was that Attlee and Morrison and Bevan were all on the attack. To fight the Tories, even on insignificant parliamentary issues, is what our people really like to do and what they really can't abide is thrashing out Socialist policy among themselves. It is this solidarity which keeps the Party invincible against splits and almost impregnable to clear thinking.

[1] *War on Want* (1952) and *War on World Poverty* (1953), written for the Association for World Peace and published in London by Gollancz.

[2] In May 1952 the Prime Minister had told the House of Commons that staff talks were proceeding urgently on the question of the appointment of a Supreme Commander in the Mediterranean and the distribution of commands among the Allies. Mr Shinwell and Mr Attlee now pressed him to state the reasons for the delay in implementing 'the proper organization of defence' in that area. On March 14th, 1953, the new NATO command, 'Allied Forces, Mediterranean', came into being. It was based on Malta and Admiral Lord Mountbatten was its first Commander-in-Chief.

Monday, December 15th

Last weekend we had our long-prepared N.E.C. conference. We began it with a dinner at Vincent Square for the six Bevanites. That was a very great success, partly because of Mia. Tom Driberg has never had a great liking or respect for me but when he saw the delicious array of cheeses and the Nymphenburg dinner service,[1] he expressed a startled delight, which was slightly back-handed. However, after that he relapsed into a bronchial gloom, which increased as we discussed exports, nationalization, etc. These are things which he cannot think of without nausea and, after an hour or so, he interrupted to plead for an ethical approach to the problem. His is really an aesthetic kind of Socialism, which has nothing to do with planning or nationalization or housing but with getting justice for coloured peoples and, though I don't understand quite how, trying to get a Christian social ethic in this country.

We had Tommy Balogh and Dudley Seers there and we went through our plan of campaign against the three and a quarter pounds of background information, statistics, etc., provided by David Ginsburg[2] and the Research Department of Transport House.* We were mostly planning with Tommy and Dudley how to put over the case for the various schemes that we wanted. Nye had three ideas: first, to achieve wage stability during a period of belt-tightening capital investment by putting all pensions and social security payments and National Savings on a sliding scale, regulated according to the rise and fall of the cost of living. Secondly, the nationalization of rented land as a contribution to increased food production. Thirdly, the nationalization of chemicals, heavy engineering, aircraft and machine tools, to enable the Government to expand these industries rapidly for export needs. Nye sort of made his speech to us and we went through it and criticized it. My own feeling was that his land proposals were the thinnest and the phoniest.

The dinner broke up at about one o'clock in the morning and at half-past nine on Saturday morning I set off through a nice, crisp, frosty day to walk across St James's Park to Brown's Hotel, in whose decorous atmosphere we were meeting. When Arthur Greenwood called the Executive to order and asked for an opening speech, there was a considerable pause. Then Jim Griffiths started off with a quite sensible suggestion for a five-year plan to make us viable. There was another pause and Nye Bevan said his piece for

---

[1] A celebrated hardpaste porcelain, made in a factory founded in 1753 and removed to the Nymphenburg Palace in Bavaria in 1761. Crossman's first wife, Erika, had a complete breakfast, dinner and tea set of Nymphenburg china, a modern copy of an old flowered pattern, created for her by a former husband. Half the china remained at Radnage when the Zecs bought Town End Farm.

[2] Senior Research Officer for the Government Social Survey 1946–52 and Secretary of the Labour Party Research Department 1952–9, he has been Labour M.P. for Dewsbury since 1959.

* Actually David had done an extremely good job and his basic papers led the conference inevitably to working out a five-year plan to achieve sterling area and U.K. viability. On whatever point the conference lighted, there were always facts and figures available, though I was the only person who gained, since I had the sense to sit with David at the conference.

about twenty minutes, in the middle of which Attlee walked in. When Nye got to agriculture, Attlee started asking him some questions and for a long time we drifted on to details until we were brought back to the background necessities and the sterling area problem, on which Harold Wilson and I contributed.

By this time it was clear that, apart from the six Bevanites, no one would contribute a single positive, constructive idea. It was also clear that Jim Griffiths's and Margaret Herbison's brief from Herbert Morrison was to intervene after we had made a constructive suggestion and suggest that it should be referred to one of the sub-committees. This must have occurred twenty or thirty times during the conference and the object was clear. On these sub-committees are sitting Morrison, Dalton, Gaitskell, etc. The whole struggle at the conference, therefore, was whether our ideas should merely be referred to the sub-committees or whether they should be referred with a recommendation by the Executive. We soon found that we were either asking for a tentative conclusion or for a reference for consideration.

At the lunch interval we all went upstairs to find an enormous lot of free drink and a gigantic lunch. Rather tactlessly, four of us Bevanites sat together but this was mainly because Tom Driberg was feeling ill and Barbara Castle put me beside him to have no conversation. However, we talked a good deal over burgundy and very good food, after which we went back to the conference, where Attlee, Tom and Barbara were all asleep, to my calculation, for a good forty-five minutes while the meeting slipped into a desultory discussion on nationalizing chemicals. Attlee suddenly woke up and said that he had never heard a *prima facie* case for nationalizing chemicals. Could he hear it? This was really marvellous, since he has sat on the Executive since 1935 and the *prima facie* case has been argued *ad nauseam*, particularly in the 1950/51 preparations for the Party programme. However at this point Mark Hewitson intervened with quite a good statement from the point of view of the chemical workers and after twenty minutes or so Attlee seemed satisfied. We all protested that what we were discussing was not the *prima facie* case for nationalization but whether nationalization would be relevant to our five-year plan for viability.

It was on this basis that the whole of the rest of the conference proceeded. We got agreement in principle to nationalizing chemicals, water went fairly easily and then we got on to a long discussion on minerals, which we finally agreed to refer for consideration. Gradually Nye took over the chairmanship and bulldozed the conference, until, thirty-five minutes before closing time, he suddenly said that he thought we'd all had enough and we stopped.

The Bevanites went off to Barbara Castle's for dinner, where we had a most terrific evening with Nye in his most benevolent form. We spent nearly all the time discussing our friends. John Freeman's name came up and Nye showed his acuteness by observing, 'Throughout the whole of the resignation he behaved with the utmost rectitude. John Freeman is somebody for whom form is all-important, because underneath there is some perversion or repression which he has to conceal. He is the extremest of us all and always has been. Indeed, he is a nihilist and ultimately a defeatist and that's why he isn't interested in Parliament.' And then, turning to me, Nye said, 'Of course, that's why he's gone to the *New Statesman* but he'll never be a first-rate journalist because he'll never have his whole heart in any article he writes.'

After dinner we got on to the subject of history, where Nye tried to prove that, apart from economic and architectural facts, there was no objectivity. No one could be objective about the motives of politicians. I asked him when he ceased to be objective about his own motives for resignation and he observed, 'I never was, because nobody can ever know why he resigns. Not really. It's all a fiction.' As he drove me home in the car, we were discussing the opportunities which come in politics when he suddenly observed, 'Nobody can be great for long. You only get one moment in your life for greatness and it passes.' He was referring to Churchill but I think he was half thinking about himself.

Sunday morning was another crisp day and I walked again across the Park and up St James's Street to resume the discussion on agriculture. Once again Attlee came in late. The discussion was really extremely desultory since it became clearer and clearer that Nye's solution wasn't really one but no one had anything else to say. Nye was at his best, or his worst, trying to conceal the fact that to nationalize only rented land would leave the owner/occupier without incentive. He boldly asserted that owner/occupiers all worked hard and then blandly denied that the aim of nationalizing the land-lords was to increase rents. We really got into a frightful tangle. Surprisingly, the nationalization of aircraft was agreed with almost no opposition and most of the debate centred on engineering. Here, the longer the discussion went on, the stronger the case appeared for nationalization, in terms of our directive: namely, the five-year plan for viability. I watched Nye gradually understanding the case after I had put it quite clearly but not very interest-ingly. He suddenly saw the point and produced a brilliant argument, proving that, if we declare that engineering output is to be expanded by 40 per cent, it will be impossible to make this more than a mere phrase unless we have publicly owned plants, which we can expand ourselves. You can't force private enterprise to increase its plant in the way that you want it to increase.

Harold Wilson in his highly competent way was extremely persuasive throughout this and every now and then, when we were nearing agreement on some tentative conclusion, Ian Mikardo would biff in to say something so Bevánite that the agreement disappeared. Griffiths, Harry Douglass,[1] etc., wanted merely to refer the problem of engineering. Nye wanted to accept in

[1] A member of the Labour Party National Executive Committee 1948–53, he was General Secretary of the Iron and Steel Trades Confederation 1953–67 and a member of the General Council of the T.U.C. for the same period. He was made a life peer in 1967. He died in 1977.

principle the nationalization of the relevant sectors of the industry and to refer merely the technique by which this should be done. Stanley Brennan of the Woodworkers, a new Member, intervened, saying that the Confederation of Shipbuilding and Engineering Workers had been considering this for two years. I recollected that the A.E.U., etc., are far more pro-nationalization than we are, and accepted Brennan's recommendation that it should be referred to the Confederation. Nye made a terrific row, threatening to put his proposal to a vote, and quite suddenly it was agreed to merge his proposal and Brennan's, and there we were. What strange things conferences are. I must say, Nye's strategy throughout was masterly, and the Bevanite team backed him pretty well, since we are obviously not mere stooges and talk quite good and quite different sense from each other.

1953

From December 17th, 1952, to January 8th, 1953, Crossman visited the Middle East, for the Sunday Pictorial. *He stayed first in Israel, meeting among others President Ben Gurion, with whom he discussed the British presence in Suez. According to Crossman, in Ben Gurion's view ' ... Churchill wants to hand over to the U.S.A. and ... only a token American force would be required'. He added that ' ... Neguib was no Ataturk and is losing his dynamic since he has lost interest in land reform.' 'With these social conditions,' he added, 'Egypt can never have an effective Army.'*

On December 27th Crossman passed through the Mandelbaum Gate into the Arab part of Jerusalem. He inspected refugee camps in Palestine and toured the Jordan Valley, looking at hydro-electricity and irrigation projects. One conversation was with Glubb Pasha, who 'reminded me of a little country solicitor. [He] must have the gentlest telephone voice in the whole world'.

Crossman flew to Egypt on New Year's Day. Though he was discouraged from seeing 'any of the Wafdists or the Old Guard' he succeeded in spending many hours with Colonel Sadat, 'a Nubian with gleaming white teeth'. Sadat introduced Crossman to Abdel Nasser and, on his last day, General Neguib, 'much older and more crouched than his photos and much less articulate in his English, in which he has some difficulty in saying what he means'.

Other important talks included those with the former Prime Minister, Hussein Sirry Pasha, staff of the British, Indian and American Embassies and with members of the British and Egyptian Armies.

Crossman's reports in the Sunday Pictorial, *January 11th, 1953, and the* New Statesman and Nation, *January 17th and 24th, 1953, emphasize his conclusion that the British should evacuate the Canal Zone as soon as possible.*

Tuesday, January 20th

The lateness of the plane from Cairo meant that I missed the National Executive meeting at half-past ten on Thursday morning, but I could read every detail of it in the *Daily Express* next day and Ian Mikardo confirmed what had happened. Before the meeting the T.U.C. had decided to turn down the N.E.C.'s proposal for any form of working parties to consider whether there was a case for extending public ownership to the four industries we had selected.[1] Attlee and [James] Griffiths were both away, as well as Barbara, Harold and I, but it would have made no difference whatsoever to the formal proceedings, which I gathered were enlivened by anti-Nye speeches from Lincoln Evans, Arthur Deakin and Will Lawther, a spirited reply by Nye and an unexpected intervention by Edith Summerskill, who no doubt felt herself free to attack Nye, since she hadn't been at Brown's Hotel. Three weeks' absence makes one see this Executive row with rather more detachment. The fact is, we have been engineered into precisely the position we wouldn't want.

So far as the public knows, the sole issue under discussion in the Labour

[1] The water, chemicals, aircraft and engineering industries. See above, pp. 188–9

Party is how much more nationalization there should be and there is apparently no new constructive idea for discussion. However, for the next day or two I was far too busy writing about Egypt for the *Sunday Pic* and the *Statesman* to concentrate much on the N.E.C.

I had Nye and Tommy to lunch last Thursday. Jennie has been ill and Nye also hasn't been very bright. I couldn't find that he had done any more thinking, or was indeed prepared to do any more thinking, about anything and it was only on my suggestion that we are resuming meetings. These will take the form of Tuesday lunches at my house for the six Executive members and the directors of *Tribune*. I think Nye is rather worried by the disintegration of the Bevanites but it's somehow a superficial worry, which doesn't afflict his soul.

Thursday, January 29th

The Bevanite row has suddenly been blown up again in full force. It was quite unexpected, at least to us Bevanites. On Tuesday I had the six members of the Executive and the four members of the *Tribune* board to lunch, in an effort to get us together. I had persuaded Nye to do this last week, but since then he has decided to go to India and he didn't turn up on Tuesday, much to our annoyance, because he was too busy. We decided to hold the lunches regularly and then went through the agenda for the National Executive on Wednesday morning. We only found two controversial items – one, the banning of the Anglo-Polish, Anglo-Bulgarian, etc., Friendship Associations[1] and the other a local Liverpool Labour Party scandal.

At the Executive on Wednesday morning both these subjects were disposed of quite amicably in rather a dreary meeting and I was just preparing to go out to lunch at the American Embassy when Morgan Phillips suddenly said that a message had been received from the General Council of the T.U.C., which was meeting six floors below. He read out the message, which was a protest against a short note in the *Tribune* attacking Lincoln Evans for accepting a knighthood from a Government pledged to denationalize steel.[2] The General Council requested the National Executive to do something about it. Suddenly the whole atmosphere changed and Nye, with his usual tactical acuteness, launched a tremendous attack on Will Lawther, Arthur Deakin, Tom Williamson[3] and Lincoln Evans. All of them, he said, had attacked him personally and all of them had made speeches and written

---

[1] There were, and are, many such groups, with M.P.s and peers among their members. Those Crossman mentions were suspected of 'fellow travelling' with Communism.

[2] See *Tribune*, January 16th, 1952. Mr Evans's knighthood had been announced in the New Year Honours list.

[3] Labour M.P. for the Brigg division of Lincoln and Rutland 1945–8. He was General Secretary of the National Union of General and Municipal Workers 1946–61, a member of the T.U.C. General Council 1947–62 and Chairman of the T.U.C. 1956–7. He was a Director of the *Daily Herald* 1953–62, Chairman of the British Productivity Council 1953–4, a member of the Iron and Steel Board 1960–7 and a member of the Independent Television Authority 1961–4. Knighted in 1956, he became a life peer in 1962.

articles attacking the Morecambe decisions. The *Tribune* was only replying to an attack. How could it be singled out for rebuke?

There was a dreary, bad-tempered debate, at the end of which the motion was passed, with only the six Bevanites voting against. At this point Harry Douglass said, 'The next logical thing to do is to examine the *Tribune* brains trusts and see if they are a party within a party.' This seemed to take Jim Griffiths and Attlee by surprise but they raised no objections, whereupon Edith Summerskill burst out that they had been far too weak far too long in dealing with the danger. Stronger measures were required. Tom Driberg asked her what she meant by stronger measures and she spat out, 'I mean expelling those who are suspect of fellow travelling.' This was said with her eyes fixed on Ian, who I think is the most hated of all the Bevanites. My impression is that Harry Douglass and Edith Summerskill were anticipating an action which had been planned some weeks ahead. The debate made me so angry that I finally said that Edith and Harry were at least logical. First suppress the left-wing press, then forbid us all to speak and you will get the sort of monolithic Party which some people want. The motion was carried by 7 votes to 5. Nye and I went across to the House to have lunch, with our entrails acid with anger. These meetings do really turn your stomach.

Late this evening I picked up a little more information. I had been out to address a Jewish meeting in North London and got back at a quarter past ten to find Nye and Tom O'Brien in the Smoking Room. The others slipped off one by one, leaving Michael and me with Tom O'Brien, who told us the following things. First, at the General Council meeting this morning, Tewson[1] had drafted the original letter, which was far stronger. According to O'Brien, it included a statement to the effect that the General Council would have to reconsider its whole collaboration with the Labour Party unless the National Executive dealt with the *Tribune* and such things. Tom claimed that he and others had watered it down to prevent it sounding like an open ultimatum.

Secondly, Tom described the scene when he had been had on the mat by Attlee, the Chief Whip and Morrison, after his intervention in the Party Meeting last February,[2] when we were all nearly expelled for voting against the Defence Estimates. On this occasion Attlee had told Tom that his speech had swayed the meeting and prevented him from teaching the fifty-seven a lesson by expelling their leaders. Last, Tom also told a strange story of Ernest Bevin's talking to him about Cripps and Morrison. 'Why do I support the little man (Attlee)? Because I detest that whited sepulchre, Cripps, and Morrison, who's nothing better than a policeman's nark.'

[1] Vincent Tewson, Secretary of the Organization Department of the T.U.C. 1925–31, Assistant General Secretary 1931–41 and General Secretary 1946–60. He was knighted in 1960.
[2] In fact, March. See above, pp. 93–4.

If Tom was talking the truth, the relations between the Big Four[1] of the General Council and the National Executive are really bad. The Big Four are out to expel the Bevanites and, according to O'Brien, they don't understand the difficulties of doing so. Meanwhile the chances of a decent policy statement seem to be rapidly fading. I discussed with Nye the possibility that we now start preparing our own statement, to issue when we resign in protest against the official one, say, next June or July.[2] This would give us time to campaign before Conference and get re-elected.

Wednesday, February 4th

Yesterday we had the second of our new lunches in Vincent Square. Nye turned up, on the eve of his departure for five weeks to India, and we had a first-rate discussion of tactics. Nye is convinced that the T.U.C. were planning a real coup against the Bevanites in April but that the timing got a bit wrong, largely owing to Harry Douglass last Wednesday.* Nye then put forward the idea that I had put to him last week that it is quite possible we shall have to resign when the Party policy is near completion and is quite obviously a phoney. In that case we must put our own policy to the Movement. This was agreed by everybody there but it was also felt that meanwhile we must really be active in the sub-committees, and do our very best.

On Monday night, by the way, I gave a little dinner party for the Swiss Minister and Lindt,[3] who have been very good friends of mine. To entertain them I got the Castles and Eddie Shackleton. I really gave them a wonderful dinner but at half-past nine we got to discussing Formosa. Barbara suddenly said that she wanted to look up one or two things in the Library. Nothing could restrain her, so she popped off without saying goodbye. If she wants to know why she is unpopular, I could tell her. As Nye put it to Desmond Donnelly the other day, 'There are only two sorts of good politicians, the dedicated and those who don't care a damn for office. The dedicated are very dangerous people. Those who don't care a damn for office are people like Dick.' Barbara cares for office.

Thursday, February 5th

Last night I went to dinner with Alec Spearman,[4] with whom I regularly pair.

[1] The Big Four were Lincoln Evans (Iron and Steel Trades Confederation), William Lawther (National Union of Mineworkers), Arthur Deakin (Transport and General Workers' Union) and Tom Williamson (National Government and Municipal Workers' Union). The last three had been the leaders of an 'Expel Bevan' movement, originating, according to Michael Foot's *Aneurin Bevan* (London: Davis-Poynter, 1973), vol. 2, pp. 352–4, in a compact made on October 2nd at the St Nicholas Hotel, Scarborough, during the post-Election Party Conference in 1951.

[2] See below, p. 244 ff. and p. 257.

* On Thursday, January 29th, Will Lawther gave an interview to the *Daily Telegraph*, in which he denounced the Bevanites as no better than Hitler.

[3] The Swiss Minister was M. Henri de Torrenté and August Lindt was the First Secretary.

[4] Alexander Spearman, Conservative M.P. for Scarborough and Whitby 1941–66. He was Parliamentary Private Secretary to the President of the Board of Trade, Peter Thorneycroft, 1951–2 and was knighted in 1956.

We had superb food and drink and a really old-time conversation, with Bob Boothby, John Strachey and Tony Crosland. Bob is convinced that Butler is on the up-grade and that the heir-apparent,[1] Eden, is scared that he will miss it after all. The Conservatives have not yet got over their surprise at the fact that they look like being in power for a good long time and apparently Butler and Eden were appalled when Churchill announced in New York that his best work was still ahead of him.[2] They had both absolutely assumed he was going to retire after the Coronation.

Most of the conversation, however, was about the future of the Labour Party and Socialism, with Bob, as usual, talking like a Socialist but finally admitting that the reason he was a Conservative was that he was a Cavalier, while all the real Socialists were Cromwellians. The man who made the running in the conversation was Kent,[3] the Assistant Editor of *The Economist*, an ex-Communist of the Denis Healey type, who advanced the case that the intellectual thesis and antithesis of political debate were represented by *The Economist* and the *New Statesman*. Both had purely abstract positions but they represented the poles in which politics had to proceed. When I asked him why *The Economist* was so unfair to the Bevanites, he replied that Bevanism was the only force in British politics worth taking seriously, apart from Conservatism, and *The Economist* was determined to fight it. I told him *The Economist* was of great assistance in building us up in this way.

It was one of the jolliest evenings I have ever spent.

On April 23rd, 1952, the Sudanese Legislative Assembly had approved a statute of self-government and on May 8th this was submitted to the British and Egyptian Governments. The Foreign Secretary announced on October 22nd Britain's assent to the Statute's implementation. The Egyptian monarchy had, however, insisted on recognition of its rule over the whole Nile Valley but, after the revolution in the summer of 1952, there was a change of policy. The new Government of General Neguib recognized the right of eventual self-determination for the Sudanese and agreed to accord them sovereign status in the interim. For the time being, the British and Egyptian Governments were to take responsibility for the Sudan's external policy.

In a Note of November 2nd, 1952, General Neguib began negotiations with the British Government and by the beginning of February 1952 outstanding difficulties had been smoothed over. On February 12th the Foreign Secretary stated the terms of the agreement to the House of Commons and simultaneous announcements were made in Cairo and Khartoum. It was expressly recognized that the Sudanese had a right to the exercise of self-determination at the appropriate time and with necessary safeguards. In order to promote a free and

---

[1] I.e. to the Prime Minister.
[2] In January 1952.
[3] Tom Kent worked in the Home Affairs Department of *The Economist*. In the mid-1950s he left to edit a newspaper in Canada.

neutral climate, there was to be a transitional period (not exceeding three years) of full self-government; this was to begin after the election of a Sudanese Parliament.

According to the statement, the Egyptian Government had accepted a draft Statute, composed by a Sudanese Commission under a British chairman, setting out the terms of self-government. This gave the Governor-General special responsibility to ensure equitable treatment for all parts of the Sudan, reassuring those who feared that the withdrawal of British protection would worsen the comparative poor and underdeveloped condition of the Southern provinces.

It had been agreed that, when self-determination came, the Sudan might choose between full independence or some sort of Egyptian Union. She might become a member of the Commonwealth, though Britain would in any case cease to administer Sudanese affairs.

For the Opposition, Herbert Morrison welcomed the Foreign Secretary's Statement as a development of the former Labour Government's policy. But on both sides of the House backbenchers dissented. On the Conservative benches, some M.P.s thought Britain's 'withdrawal' premature; some Labour Members alleged that Sudanese independence should be hurried on. Among these was Crossman, who had in January prepared a paper for the N.E.C. on Suez and the Sudan. This drew attention to the military and economic costs of maintaining a British presence in Suez and argued that there was no political or strategic case for retaining it.

Friday, February 13th

On Monday afternoon the joint foreign affairs and defence groups met for the third time on the Sudan and Suez. On this occasion we were presented by John Strachey and John Hynd, the two chairmen, with four draft conclusions. As about a third of those present had been absent from the previous two meetings, we went over everything all over again, with Hugh Gaitskell obstinately arguing that we should not accept the principle of withdrawal from the Canal. To my amazement, Manny Shinwell, who had come for the first time, after starting with a bewilderingly confused speech, suddenly came out with four points, which were a great improvement on the four in the draft. But at this point John Strachey said that he thought that it would be a great mistake to take a vote. I asked whether the two committees should in future spend seven hours on mutual education without reaching any decision but this was thought bad form and we broke up.

I walked out with Hugh Gaitskell, who said that really it was quite impossible for the Opposition to discuss the tactics of diplomacy when they hadn't access to Cabinet papers. I said that, in my view, there were no Cabinet papers required to form a judgment on this issue.[1] To this he said, 'Oh, you are quite wrong. You have no idea of what an amount of information one

[1] That the British withdraw from the Suez Base.

gets from the telegrams.' I replied, 'But in this case we know exactly what the telegrams from Cairo are advising and it is something that you disagree with.' He said, 'Ambassadors are always prejudiced in favour of their countries.' So I said, 'Whose advice would you get in the Cabinet?' And he said, 'The Chiefs of Staff,' to which I replied that one doesn't normally consult the Chiefs of Staff on strictly diplomatic and political issues. This finally annoyed him and he said, 'Anyway, I don't see why the Labour Party should be swayed by the advice of one M.P. who has been to Cairo for a week.' He revealed precisely why he had attended the meeting. What he disliked was my putting in a paper which could easily have swung the two committees into action. He had succeeded in preventing this, most successfully.

Sitting in such committees has some value, as it gives one an idea of how these men behave in Cabinet. Hugh Gaitskell is competent and immensely obstinate; Manny Shinwell is confused but suddenly comes out with something rather good. I have no doubt that, if we had taken a vote, Hugh would never have had twenty-five supporters out of fifty.

On Tuesday we had a Bevanite lunch here. Nye had gone to India and we decided to go ahead with framing a complete programme, which should both guide us in the work of the committees and be ready in the event that we cannot accept the majority programme. This decision was a good deal easier to make in Nye's absence – not that he wouldn't agree in principle but because we should never get the programme done.

On Thursday I went into the Chamber to hear Eden announce the Anglo-Egyptian agreement on the Sudan. The news that it had been signed had leaked out last night. I had been giving dinner to the Swedish Labour Attaché[1] and couldn't make out why the lobbies were literally buzzing with Tory Groups murmuring to each other. Apparently these are the facts. Last night Selwyn Lloyd tried to persuade the Tory Foreign Policy and Commonwealth committees of the desirability of the agreement. He had failed. On Wednesday night, after Cabinet, Eden was rushed over and managed to persuade the imperialists, headed by Julian Amery[2] and Dodds-Parker,[3] to hold their hand. The buzz in the lobbies was the aftermath of their meeting upstairs. I also learnt that last week, when their Far Eastern Committee met

[1] There was no Labour Attaché at the Swedish Embassy until 1959. Crossman is probably referring to Vilgot Hammarling, the Press Officer, who was reputed to be most amiable and approachable.

[2] Conservative M.P. for Preston North 1950–66 and for Brighton Pavilion since 1969, Julian Amery was Parliamentary Under-Secretary of State and Financial Secretary at the War Office 1957–8, Parliamentary Under-Secretary of State at the Colonial Office 1960–2, Minister of Aviation 1962–4, Minister of Public Building and Works 1970, and Minister for Housing and Construction, Department of the Environment, 1970–4. His publications include *Sons of the Eagle* (London: Macmillan, 1948), *The Life of Joseph Chamberlain*, vols IV–VI (London: Macmillan, 1951 *et seq.*), and *Joseph Chamberlain and the Tariff Reform Campaign* (London: Macmillan, 1969).

[3] Arthur Douglas Dodds-Parker, Conservative M.P. for Banbury 1945–59 and for Cheltenham 1964–74. He was Joint Parliamentary Secretary for Foreign Affairs 1953–4 and 1955–7 and was knighted in 1973.

to discuss Eden's protest at the deneutralization of Formosa,[1] Eden didn't get one supporter from the committee.

When Eden made the announcement, the Tories gave him a little cheer. Dodds-Parker welcomed the agreement. Only Assheton[2] and Waterhouse[3] registered disapproval. Afterwards I asked Dodds-Parker, who was at school with me, and he told me that the agreement was inevitable. However, an hour later he was telling George Wigg, whom he knows well as a fellow soldier, that it was the day of deepest humiliation in his life. It was inevitable only because Britain had ceased to have the imperial spirit.

Thursday, February 19th

On Tuesday and Wednesday we had the International Sub. and the Organization Sub. of the National Executive. Both were wearisome days for me. Everything was sweetness and light at the International Sub. Afterwards I had a drink with Sam Watson and remarked to a Bevanite later on, 'Really, the Party has taken a turn for the better. The Committees are really trying to deal with policy on its merits.' Then, on Wednesday, came the reversal. After talking to the United Services Institution on psychological warfare and having all the generals and air-marshals finding me so sensible, I went to the Organization Sub., where the investigation of the *Tribune* brains trusts was the main item on the agenda. We sat there for three and a quarter hours in the most appallingly dreary atmosphere of subdued bickering. It was clear from the start that the trade unionists were determined to ban the brains trusts, come what may. For thirty-five minutes we remained silent while they bumbled round the subject, since it was extremely difficult to find any formula to justify banning. Poor old Alice Horan, to everybody's embarrassment, proposed a motion that the *Tribune* brains trusts be integrated into the propaganda of Transport House. When asked what she meant, she replied that the Executive should have a constructive, not a negative policy but her

---

[1] On June 27th, 1950, President Truman had ordered the U.S. Seventh Fleet to 'neutralize' Formosa, the headquarters of Chiang Kai-shek, thus shielding Communist China against possible raids. President Eisenhower told a joint Session of Congress on February 2nd, 1953, that this instruction had been rescinded. The British Government, informed in advance, expressed their concern and on February 3rd the Foreign Secretary said so again in a Commons Statement. On that day the U.S. Secretary of State, Foster Dulles, and the Mutual Security Administrator, Harold Stassen, arrived in London and discussed the matter with Mr Eden. In a debate on February 5th, Mr Eden reassured the Commons that the Government were convinced that no aggressive intentions underlay the American decision. He and R. A. Butler would visit Washington in March for conversations with the new American Administration.

[2] Ralph Assheton, National Unionist M.P. for Rushcliffe 1934–45, for the City of London 1945–50 and for Blackburn West 1950–5. He was Chairman of the Conservative Party Organization 1944–6, Chairman of the Public Accounts Committee 1948–50 and Chairman of the Select Committee on Nationalized Industries 1951–3. In 1955 he was created 1st Baron Clitheroe.

[3] Captain Charles Waterhouse, Conservative M.P. for Leicester South 1924–45 and for Leicester South-East 1950–7. He was Chairman of the Public Accounts Committee 1951, and of the Estimates Committee 1953. He died in 1975.

closest supporters had to point out that the Executive's intention was not to stimulate *Tribune* brains trusts but to suppress them.

Then Jock Tiffin[1] said that he had the most damning piece of evidence, a letter from *Tribune* to a constituency. He read it aloud. 'Dear Comrade, You want to get the Tory Government out? Of course you do. You want a full Socialist policy? Of course you do.' Here Jock Tiffin paused dramatically. 'Barbara Niven[2] (i.e. the woman who appeals for contributions to the *Daily Worker*) couldn't have done better!'

At this point the division bell rang and we didn't hear the rest of the letter. I intervened to say that we had been instructed to investigate the *Tribune* brains trusts and no investigation had taken place. Shouldn't the Committee send a questionnaire to all constituencies where brains trusts had taken place and should it not study the press cuttings, to see if they had been used for Bevanite propaganda? If they had, the Tory press would certainly have quoted it. To this Len Williams,[3] the National Organizer, at once said, 'Oh, that's not our case. No one pretends that anything wrong has been said there.' And Bill Webber said, 'It is not what's said there that matters. It's the fact that they are organized.' Finally, a resolution banning them was passed, after which in some depression I gave dinner to Helga Greene.

I discussed this at great length at lunch today with Michael Foot and Mallalieu. Their feeling is that this is an issue on which we should fight. If the National Executive passes the recommendation, the six members should resign. I rather dispute this, since it seems to me a bad issue to resign on, especially during Nye's absence in India. My own view is that we should accept the ban and that *Tribune* should merely tell local constituencies that, if they want Bevanite speakers, they should write to any one of the fifty-seven. I'm quite certain that the result would be that instead of doing brains trusts in a few constituencies we should practically blanket the whole country with political meetings.

Thursday, February 26th

On Tuesday we had our usual Bevanite lunch and discussed tactics for Wednesday morning, when the Executive was to meet and the banning of the *Tribune* brains trusts was the main item on the agenda. It was agreed that, if

[1] Arthur Ernest Tiffin, Assistant Secretary of the Transport and General Workers' Union 1948–55 and General Secretary for a short time until his death in 1955. In that year, he was also, briefly, a member of the General Council of the T.U.C.

[2] A writer and propagandist for Communist causes, she was nominally responsible for the appeal for contributions to Communist Party funds which appeared in the *Daily Worker* during this period.

[3] Leonard Williams, a tutor organizer for the National Council of Labour Colleges 1926–36, joined the staff of the Labour Party Head Office in 1942. He was Assistant National Agent 1946–51, National Agent 1951–9, Deputy General Secretary 1959–62 and General Secretary of the Labour Party 1962–8. He was knighted in 1968 and was Governor-General of Mauritius from then until his death in 1972.

we could, we should try to get postponement for a month but should fight hard on the principle.

The Executive started punctually at ten o'clock on Wednesday morning and went on without a break until a quarter past two. Really, we are a most remarkable collection of people. At length we came to the *Tribune* but, before we could get on to the subject, Alice Bacon said she had a most serious thing to discuss — the leak from the Organization Sub. to the press. This leak could only have come from one of five people and four of them were Bevanites. It was pretty clear that we hadn't taken much trouble to avoid people's knowing of the ban and the fact that the ban was in the press had created a hostile wave against it. Harry Douglass, of the Steelworkers, emphasized that this was most unfair, since no ban had ever been intended — a first indication that they had changed their minds. However, we had a long argument about the leak and finally it was decided to call Mr Mallalieu[1] and interrogate him on how he had got the information.

Then we came to the *pièce de résistance*. Attlee immediately made a very sensible speech. First, he said, it is meaningless to suggest that the organization of brains trusts does not conform with the spirit and intention of the Parliamentary Party, since the Parliamentary Party is not concerned with brains trusts. Secondly, an independent Socialist weekly must be able to collect money by public meetings. After all, that's what George Lansbury's weekly[2] had done and, in the old days, the *Daily Herald*. Thirdly, the Committee didn't seem to have investigated the charges against the *Tribune* and this should now be done. He proposed, therefore, a reference back to the Committee.

At this point somebody remarked that this meant a defeat for the Organization Sub. and Jim Griffiths sprang in and said he saw the point. In a long rigmarole, he proposed postponing the matter for a month, to enable the Bevanites to consider what answer they would make to the proposal that the brains trusts should stop at the end of their published programme of meetings.

Then we had the usual rows, with Edith Summerskill interrupting Griffiths and accusing him of shilly-shallying and delay. Strong measures, she said, were necessary. I had a row with Attlee because, in the course of his remarks, he had thrown in that the Committee should investigate the activities of journalist members of the Executive. I asked what on earth this had got to do with brains trusts and whether *he* would be investigated for his writings in the press. Apart from Edith, the meeting was curiously good-tempered but utterly futile. Every half-hour or so somebody would say, 'But you know, we are killing the Party by this sort of idiotic behaviour,' and the chairman would try to find something to vote about. Attlee withdrew his proposal in favour of Jim's but clearly Jim's was absolute nonsense. Harry Douglass

[1] J. P. W. Mallalieu wrote for *Tribune*.
[2] The *Weekly Herald*.

stuck to his resolution. It was, I think, carried by 14 votes to 9, with Attlee and Jim defeated by the trade union bloc, which includes, of course, Alice Bacon and Edith, who were elected on a trade union vote.

By this time everybody was utterly exhausted. Nevertheless, we went on to consider two further matters. First, we had Barbara Castle's complaint against the *Daily Herald* for writing a leading article, on the day after the Executive had demanded fraternal politeness, which attacked the Bevanites for malignant bile, stupidity, etc. Secondly, Ian Mikardo raised the issue of Sir William Lawther's observations on the same morning in the *Daily Telegraph*.[1] It was then that the strange thing happened. Attlee had already popped off but, as we discussed these two cases, Arthur Greenwood suddenly woke up and said that, when he'd opened the *Herald* and read it, he was just plain disgusted and a good many trade unionists said 'Hear, hear.'

Then somebody said, 'Then why shouldn't Arthur be instructed to say to the Editor what he has just said here?' This was carried by acclaim. Much the same happened on the Lawther point. After Ian Mikardo had spoken, I added that, if the T.U.C. could spend two and a quarter hours discussing a personal insult to one of its members in a Socialist weekly and then communicate with the N.E.C., asking for a rebuke, the N.E.C. must surely communicate with the T.U.C. when six of its members are much more grossly libelled. To my amazement, Harry Douglass said, 'Dick's quite logical,' and again this was carried by acclaim, and we all went off, hungry but good-humoured, with Alice Horan saying to me, 'You're still a friend of mine.'

I'm fairly sure that none of this would have happened if Nye had been present. It would be easy to say thank heavens he wasn't. But then, if he had been present, he would have been a catalyst, creating an entirely different chemical mixture, which might have been far better, as well as far worse. I fancy the trade unionists who were present are straight enough people to feel they had no alternative but to carry out the directive we had issued last month and rebuke those who violated it. Did some of them realize that this was extremely clever? I doubt it. Yet next day the press reports made it clear enough that this was the first real gag on the *Tribune*. Now, if the *Tribune* is rude, the six of us on the Executive will be in a very difficult position. I think it's a good thing but, when we had a secret Group meeting at Jennie's house last night and I warned the Group that we should have to be damn careful with what we said and wrote, they were not exactly enthusiastic.

At this meeting it was reported that, in Morgan Phillips's press conference, he had definitely stated that brains trusts were not banned, something which no member of the Executive knew after the meeting, since the resolution was ambiguous. We decided, therefore, that the brains trusts should be continued but, for the present at least, Executive members should not attend them. I expect the public impression of this ghastly N.E.C. meeting will be one of amused boredom at the N.E.C. hitting out, right left and centre in a

[1] On January 29th, 1953. See above, p. 196.

family quarrel which has long since ceased to have anything to do with policy.

Tommy Balogh and I had a long talk on Tuesday about the appalling absence of Bevanite policy. We simply had the slogans of eighteen months ago. Tommy pressed me to see what I could do about getting some of the experts, like Harold Wilson, at least to work out a policy for the present nationalized industries and the private sector. As a precaution, I had David Ginsburg to lunch today and discovered that at their first meeting, with Nye's and Harold's approval the Policy Committee closed down as unnecessary the sub-committees on nationalized industries and the private sector. I asked Harold why and he said, 'Well, the Nationalized Industries Committee has completed the work on the private sector and is unnecessary.' So I said, 'Have we got a policy for remedying the appalling situation in the nationalized industries and the private sector?' After a great deal of pressure, he admitted he hadn't the faintest idea what we should do about them. The fact is that Nye and Harold are not interested in rethinking policy at all.

Here is a little postscript. I ran into Attlee in the corridor this afternoon and, on the spur of the moment, said, 'I was a little puzzled by your reference to journalists on the Executive. What exactly did you mean?' 'I consider that writing every week in the sensational press puts them in a very difficult position.' 'I suppose I have a higher opinion of the press than you have.' 'I have no opinion of the press.' 'But why is it more difficult to write a Sunday column than to make a weekend speech compatible with one's responsibility?' 'Because the speech is made on Labour platforms and most of you write in the non-Labour press.' 'But do you think the newspapers give us a directive and limit our freedom?' 'They always prefer reporting bad things to good things and want to create trouble and that's why you always choose to say the most troublesome things.' We had been walking very fast, since he had been trying to escape me. At this point he reached the door of his room and disappeared with a bang.

Tuesday, March 3rd

I found Kingsley in a ferment yesterday morning. He had spent the whole weekend worrying because last Wednesday I had asked him to sign the leading article about the banning of the *Tribune* brains trusts,[1] so that it should not be attributed to me. The trouble really is that John Freeman wrote the whole article and Kingsley is rather aggrieved at the praise he has received for it! However, he had it out on me by pointing out that this was making his position on the *Statesman* impossible, that the whole paper could not be run in order to suit my convenience, that it was getting too much involved in Bevanism and that I was keeping too many balls in the air. I said it was quite simple. If he felt all this, I was willing to leave the paper; at this he nearly fell backwards.

[1] 'The Issue of *Tribune*', *New Statesman and Nation*, February 28th, 1953.

Friday, March 6th

All in all, the defence debate[1] has gone fairly well. Of course it was over-shadowed by the announcement of Stalin's death.[2] The first announcement that he was ill came on Tuesday and from then to Thursday the communiqués about the effect of haemorrhage in the brain sounded horribly familiar.[3] Some of the papers tried to make out that he had been dead for weeks and that these were spoof communiqués but I knew enough about this particular disease to recognize that the description was accurate. The papers have had columns and columns of speculation and analysis and I think nearly everybody in the country has been thinking about it.

Eisenhower's first reaction to the illness was to send a message to the oppressed Russian people and to express no sympathy, whereas Churchill and Eden did the correct thing. This stimulated Hugh Cudlipp to devote the whole front page of the *Mirror* to a leading article headed 'Crocodile Tears', which was simply Cassandra's column congratulating Eisenhower on saying what every decent person felt. Apparently Cassandra himself didn't want to see his column put on the front page but Hugh Cudlipp had said, 'We've had a good anti-American welt. This will put us in right with the Americans and then we can attack them again in a week.'

My main interest has been to stop people speculating about Russia and, instead, to recognize that this provides an opportunity for an initiative from here. But this is a very remote hope. With Eisenhower pledged to a tough policy and the new men in the Kremlin desperately anxious and therefore having to be tough, the chances are that the death of Stalin will merely harden the blocs.

Monday, March 9th

The weekend was lovely spring weather and I spent Saturday and Sunday morning hedging at Radnage and making final arrangements to hand over to Phil and Betty Zec. Then I caught the 2.49 for Wolverhampton to attend the West Midlands Rally. At the hotel I found Patricia Llewelyn-Davies, Philip Noel-Baker's ex-secretary and one of the Wolverhampton candidates,

[1] The Defence White Paper published on February 19th estimated defence expenditure for 1953/54 at £1,636 million, some £123 million (9 per cent) above spending in 1952/53. Two-thirds of the increase was required by the Air Ministry. The Government proposed to extend the National Service scheme for five years. The debate on the White Paper was held on March 5th. Emanuel Shinwell, who had been campaigning for a reduction of the period of compulsory service from two years to one (see above, p. 178), threatened to rebel against his own Front Bench. Mr Attlee avoided this by moving an Amendment asking for annual review of the period of National Service; Mr Churchill stated that he did not object. The Government motion to approve the White Paper (Cmd 8768) was carried by 295 votes to 254.

[2] It was announced on March 6th that Marshal Stalin had died at 9.50 p.m. the previous evening from the effects of a cerebral haemorrhage resulting from hypertonia and arteriosclerosis. In the reorganization of the Government, Party and Soviet bodies which followed, Mr Malenkov became Chairman of the Council of Ministers.

[3] See above, pp. 120 ff.

stewing with fear of her ten-minute speech. We walked across to the Town Hall at seven o'clock to find the big hall full of hearty Labour supporters, brought in by buses from all over the Midlands and enthusiastically community-singing. There was also a three-quarters-full overflow meeting in a secondary hall. The speakers gathered in a tiny anteroom. Pat was introduced to Mrs Attlee, who said she had never met her. Actually Patricia has met her eight or nine times and lunched with her at Chequers.[1] Pat remarked that this was the worst time for any Labour speaker. 'I know a much worse time,' said Mrs Attlee tartly. 'It's much worse to listen to dull speeches.'

Fortunately, the speeches were so arranged that Jennie Lee and I were always in one hall when Clem was in the other. I started off in the big hall, while the audience was still shuffling in. Rallies used to be very easy things to address but now they demand a great deal of diplomatic finesse. As a Bevanite, you must impress the delegates with the feeling that you are not letting them down, yet you mustn't utter a syllable which can lead you to being accused of disloyalty. I got out of this difficulty by telling them that the policy statement would be published in May and that somebody had said to me that this should end the controversy in the Party. I had replied, 'Not if you know the Labour Party. When the Executive has stopped arguing, then it's the turn of the Party to argue.' And I called for the fiercest argument the Party had ever known to take place in every constituency and every ward as they analysed the policy document line by line and tried to make it better. This went down extremely well. Everybody knew what I meant.

I listened to Jennie, who really is a superb orator. She was talking about the cost of living, and, in the course of fifty minutes, only showed that it had gone up under the Tories. But what a speech, describing in detail everything on the table of a miner in Cannock, with that intimate working-class familiarity, half way between laughing and crying, and with, every quarter of an hour, a side-reference to what university people like Dick Crossman wouldn't understand or to her constituents not coming from Dick Crossman's public schools. Jennie, I think, is the most class-conscious person I have ever known. Pat told us that Attlee had given his usual boring little chat in both halls. There really was no doubt that these 2,800 people were still overwhelmingly Bevanite.

Jennie, Pat and I all went back for supper at the hotel, a fascinating evening, since Pat is a friend of Kenneth Younger's and was trying to plead with Jennie that Kenneth should be allowed to be a Bevanite. Jennie thereupon said, 'But Nye will never forgive Kenneth for that terrible evening in a little Soho restaurant when you all investigated him as though you were F.B.I. agents.' Apparently she was referring to a dinner party just before Nye resigned, which Kenneth had laid on with Patricia in order to discuss what should be done. Jennie's imagination had got the better of her, since there

[1] A house in Buckinghamshire given to the nation in 1917 by Lord Lee of Fareham and used since 1961 as a country retreat for Prime Ministers.

had been no investigation and Nye had enjoyed very good food and drink — so much so that they had all been invited to his home afterwards, where they stayed up till three in the morning.

The fact is that Nye and Jennie have to have a good reason for disliking Kenneth. He and John Freeman tried to persuade Nye to resign in February[1] when the defence bill was up to £4,700 million and Nye refused to do so. When he finally did resign, on teeth and spectacles, Kenneth, at the Foreign Office, felt that he couldn't go out on this issue and Nye has had his knife in Kenneth ever since. Poor little Patricia, who is a passionate Bevanite, was terribly upset to discover that she was included with the others and I had to console her for an hour and a half after Jennie had gone to bed.

I spent the evening dining with Michael Foot and talking to Tom O'Brien, now chairman of the T.U.C. I asked Tom why it was that, whereas people like Dalton and Attlee and Noel-Baker are all quite accepted by the trade union leaders, although they are intellectuals, our generation — Michael Foot, Dick Crossman, etc. — are all bitterly resented on the Executive as thrusting outsiders. 'Oh,' said Tom O'Brien, 'it's quite different with them. They've been in the Movement all their lives.' I pointed out that I had, too. Indeed, all the Bevanites have got very good records. Tom said, 'Well, I can't help it. That's what they feel about you.' I suggested that, as Chairman of the T.U.C., he might conceivably have a few dinner parties, where we would be allowed to meet each other. He vaguely thought this would be a good idea.

It's an odd fact that there is absolutely no social contact between the trade union leaders and the Parliamentary Party. As O'Brien pointed out, their only knowledge of Parliament and politics is the gossip they pick up in the Tea Room from the trade union M.P.s. This is what a Tea Room boy does, says Tom O'Brien. He breakfasts in his Bloomsbury hotel and arrives in time for the Tea Room to open at eleven and serve morning coffee. Then he reads the papers, which are provided there free, till one o'clock, when the Tea Room serves the one and ninepenny lunch. After lunch he does his constituency correspondence in the Library, goes into the House to hear a part of Question Time and, if there is a big debate, the first two speeches. Then he has high tea in the Tea Room at six o'clock, staying there until the policeman shouts, 'Who goes home?'[2] It sounds ridiculous but it is a literal description of the average day in the life of a trade union Member of Parliament.

Thursday, March 12th
I dined last night with Dave Linebaugh and found Denis Healey and his wife

[1] Bevan resigned on April 21st, 1951. See the Introduction, pp. 25–6.
[2] In the eighteenth century Members of Parliament would go home in groups, with an escort, as protection against the ruffians in the streets. Since that time a policeman has cried 'Who goes home?' at the end of each day's proceedings.

there. For once we spent five hours discussing not politics but philosophy and God. Denis Healey is really a very interesting character. He feels himself to be a completely free man, tied to no one and able to make up his own mind on each issue as it arises. He is a very true ex-Communist, 'Beyond good and evil',[1] and, when I hear him arguing and constantly deliberately misconstruing people's words, I realize how irritating I myself must be in argument. Dave Linebaugh rang me up this morning to apologize for Denis. It was very sweet of him but he needn't have worried.

Monday, March 23rd

Nye got back from India last Monday and came to our Tuesday lunch at Vincent Square. It's high time he did get back, since the Bevanites have been languishing without him. In his absence, we have had the defence and Services Estimates debates.[2] I made one speech in the defence debate but in the others our position went by default. In Nye's absence, no one else seems to have the dynamic to do anything and there is a slight tendency to drift apart.

I spent most of last Wednesday in the Social Services Sub-Committee of the N.E.C., for some four hours' disjointed, desultory discussion of the National Health Service and housing. It is really shocking how little serious thought is being given to this programme and how totally dependent the members of the Executive are on the papers and the thinking provided by the office in Transport House. After this I rushed off to Dean Street to talk to the Central London Fabians on party loyalty and the parliamentary system. I thought this would be a small, private group but I found a packed public meeting, to which I made a fairly bright speech on the nature of Cabinet government, the fact that Cabinet government requires a monolithic party and the fact that, in these circumstances, the most important aspect of democratic discussion is a debate inside the party. Getting quite interested, I gave some rather graphic illustrations and at one point said that, in my experience, love was not a motive which got anything done. The only time anybody was influenced by what you said was when they were afraid of you.

I also explained that since, *de facto*, three people in a Cabinet – the Prime Minister and his closest friends – decide everything, it is not irrelevant for a democrat to think it a matter of grave importance whether Morrison or Bevan is the Deputy Leader. During the discussion I noticed that one of the paid staff of the Parliamentary Party was walking out. I met him next day and asked him what he thought of the meeting; he said he was very shocked indeed. I asked him what had shocked him and he said, 'Of course, *in toto* what you said was a really brilliant description of what goes on. But should

[1] A reference to the most mature of Friedrich Nietzsche's books, *Jenseit Gut und Böse* (1886), in which he envisages a time when modern man might enact his life 'beyond good and evil'.

[2] The Army Estimates were discussed on March 9th, the Air Estimates on the 12th and the Naval Estimates on the 16th.

one really tell people outside? I was shocked by the way you described it and the fact that it's true didn't really improve matters.'

Since 1951 discussions had been held on the future of the territories of Nyasaland, Northern and Southern Rhodesia. A conference met in London in January, 1953, which African representatives refused to attend, and in February two White Papers (Cmds 8753 and 8754) were published.

They set out a scheme for federation of the three territories, closely based on a draft plan published in June 1952. Federation, it was argued, would safeguard the interests of the African majority against exploitation by the White minority. The powers reserved to the Federal Government and Parliament were extended and no measure to change the distribution of power between the Federal and Territorial Governments was to be introduced during the first ten years of federation without agreement by the three territorial legislatures. In April the scheme was to be put before the Parliaments of Northern Rhodesia and Nyasaland and in Southern Rhodesia it was to be submitted to a referendum.

Meanwhile the Opposition asked for a debate in the House of Commons. Doubts about the scheme had been strengthened by African opposition but, in reply, it was said that the benefits of federation had not been made fully clear to the native population, for fear of antagonizing the White voters in Southern Rhodesia.

In the debate on March 24th the Opposition proposed an Amendment disapproving of the scheme. This did not satisfy a number of Labour Members, who abstained from voting. The Government motion was carried by 304 votes to 260.

On Thursday evening at half-past six we had our routine Party Meeting and Attlee announced that the debate on Central African federation would take place this Tuesday on a three-line whip. He then added in a mutter that, naturally, those with conscientious scruples would be permitted to abstain. For a couple of minutes people didn't quite understand. Then somebody got up and asked whether Central African federation was an issue like temperance and conscription. Attlee said that obviously one couldn't lay down the law on conscience and that those who had conscientious scruples would naturally abstain. People began to realize that he was quietly driving a coach and four through the Standing Orders which had been drawn up last March,[1] after weeks of discussion, as a result of the revolt of the fifty-seven. Jennie Lee nimbly got up and congratulated Attlee on this tolerance of minorities, tactfully suggesting that it was not only right-wing consciences but also left-wing consciences which should be respected. The fact is that Patrick Gordon Walker, Stanley Evans, Coldrick[2] of the Co-op, Charlie Hobson of the

[1] See above, pp. 94 ff.
[2] William Coldrick, who died in 1975, was Labour and Co-operative M.P. for Bristol North 1945–50 and for Bristol North-East 1950–9. He was Chairman of the Co-operative Party 1946–56.

A.E.U. and a number of other notorious loyalists of the extreme Right have been appeased by Attlee. Nye told me afterwards that the original proposal in the Parliamentary Committee was to have a two-line whip so as to enable them to abstain without being noticed. Nye had opposed this, since Central Africa is a major issue. But certainly a large-scale abstention on a three-line whip provides an enormously important precedent for the left-wing.

After the meeting we went down to our corner in the Smoking Room and discussed it at length. Nye suggested that he, Jennie, Michael and I should go and see Jill Foot, who is in hospital after an operation. We had a very gay evening with her and then we all went off to the Étoile for a terrific dinner, for which Nye was determined to pay and did. The others would naturally have gone off on their own and it was sheer niceness of them to take me with them. I enjoyed it enormously but it's astonishing when, at half-past ten, Nye's eyes start closing with sleepiness. Before he went to India he woke up at noon and felt his best at two o'clock in the morning.

Tuesday, March 24th

At our Bevanite lunch we had reports on the various sub-committees of the N.E.C. and a fierce dispute developed. Apparently the sub-committees have agreed to recommend the acquisition of controlling interests in chemicals, aircraft and certain engineering firms and to confine outright nationalization to water. Nye asserted that this was quite useless. Harold Wilson seemed to argue that one might be able to get 'controlling interest' interpreted as 100 per cent ownership.

The difficulty was that Ian Mikardo and Harold Wilson, in Nye's absence, had agreed on these sub-committees but only Ian stood up for his position. He argued that this was good enough. It looked as though Nye was mainly anxious about what the Party should say, since this would be interpreted in the press as a great concession to the right-wing. I suggested that we might try to draft the positive proposals we should like to see incorporated in the programme. This was reluctantly and hurriedly assented to when everybody was rushing off to the House.

This was the day set for the big debate on Central African federation. I got in to hear only a few minutes of it but it was clear that Stanley Evans had made a very good speech in favour of federation and against the Party line, and that, as a major attack on the Government, the debate hadn't gone too well. I stood at the Bar of the House when Hopkinson[1] was winding up for the Tories, among a hubbub of conversation in a House only three-quarters full. Actually the news had broken that Queen Mary had just died.[2] Since I

---

[1] Henry Hopkinson, Conservative M.P. for the Taunton division of Somerset 1950–6. He was Secretary of Overseas Trade 1951–2 and Member for Colonial Affairs 1952–5. In 1956 he became a peer, taking the title of 1st Baron Colyton.

[2] Queen Mary had been frail for some time. She died at Marlborough House on March 24th, at the age of eighty-five.

don't like scenes, I went home before Churchill made his announcement that
the House would adjourn tomorrow.

Wednesday, March 25th
The adjournment did not stop the National Executive meeting (indeed, we
nearly forgot to pass condolences to the Queen) but Attlee was away because
he assumed we would cancel it. The meeting passed off without any incident,
except the usual discussion about leaks right at the beginning. Then at five
minutes to eleven, Jock Tiffin of the Transport Workers' ominously stated
that he had an emergency proposal to make. He said very solemnly that he
proposed that we should have coffee at eleven. This has been a long-standing
grudge on the N.E.C. We meet on the top floor in the Council Chamber of
the Transport and General Workers' and next to it there is a little canteen,
but for twenty years no coffee has been provided except to members of the
Transport Workers'. Apparently Tiffin had succeeded in making arrangements to remedy this defect. The roars of laughter at this anti-climax showed
how anxious people were to avoid the row which we feared he might be
precipitating.

In the afternoon the House met for the funeral speeches on Queen Mary.
Churchill rather pleased me by mentioning Windsor first of the Royal Dukes
but Attlee stole the show with what sounded like a completely impromptu
speech.

Monday, March 30th
The big gossip today has been the Shawcross story. The Sunday before last,
the *Sunday Express* advertised that next week it would begin a serial on the
life story of Hartley Shawcross, under the title 'Man or Superman', by
Woodrow Wyatt, M.P. There had been a good many jokes about this last
week and then, yesterday, there appeared an extraordinary communiqué
from the Attorney General, stating that Hartley had assured him that he
hadn't given his consent and that such articles would not redound to his
credit.[1] The *Sunday Express* printed this and announced that it had decided
not to publish.

This interested me a good deal. If Hartley had really not given his consent,
there was no conceivable reason why they shouldn't be published. Moreover,
it was very unlike the *Sunday Express* to forego a feature of this sort once it
had been announced. I spent a great deal of time putting the story together
from talks with Woodrow Wyatt, Harold Keeble,[2] who is now Assistant
Editor of the *Sunday Express*, and Hugh Dalton, whom Woodrow Wyatt,

[1] Sir Hartley Shawcross had returned to private practice and it was said by some that the
articles would be a form of advertisement, forbidden by the legal profession. The *Sunday
Pictorial* continued to publish its own series. See the *New Statesman and Nation*, April 4th
and April 18th, 1953.
[2] Literary and Features Editor of the *Daily Express* and an Assistant Editor until he
moved to the *Daily Mail*, as an Editorial Consultant, in the early 1970s.

pledged to secrecy, had selected as his confidant. Apparently the idea originated with Harold Keeble, a success boy himself, who contacted Woodrow Wyatt. Wyatt naturally consulted Shawcross and has a considerable dossier of letters from Shawcross making suggestions for the series and a final letter offering to indemnify Woodrow for any loss incurred when the series was suppressed.

Harold Keeble was away ill when somebody changed the proposed title to 'Man or Superman'. It was this title which caught the attention of Sir Walter Monckton,[1] who has never much liked Hartley's behaviour, who raised the matter at the Bar Council, of which Hartley is Chairman. Hartley got cold feet, went to the *Sunday Express* and begged them not to publish, stating that he was a sick man and his doctor had warned him that he might die if he had any shocks. The *Sunday Express* were going to publish until Max Aitken[2] was rung up by Churchill, who pleaded that the decorum of the Bar should be observed. Of course, the unsolved problem is: why should Churchill want to save Hartley from the predicament he had placed himself in? That's anybody's guess.

This evening I went to see a C.B.S. show, illustrating their weekly television news programme, edited by Ed Murrow,[3] which goes on at three o'clock on Sunday afternoons. It is really superb. As the lights went up, I heard Nye behind me saying, 'Infantile, the whole thing is completely infantile.' The conclusion from this is that Nye does not think he was a great success on a television show he himself did last week. He is like Churchill in this way. They are both babies when their own fame is concerned.

On the way home I saw Westminster Hall still open and thought I would look in on Queen Mary's lying-in-state. It was just midnight but there was only a very thin trickle of people going through. Indeed, this lying-in-state has been a popular flop and at no time has there been a long queue. People say it's because she was so old when she died but I don't think this is true. You really can't have the preparations for a Coronation going on and at the same time enjoy a good funeral. The papers have been in a terrible fix and, for the London public, the gigantic stands now being erected and growing larger and larger make it impossible to have a really good go for Queen Mary.

[1] Conservative M.P. for Bristol West 1951–7, he was Minister of Labour and National Service 1951–5, Minister of Defence 1955–6 and Paymaster-General 1956–7. He became a Viscount in 1957. He died in 1965.

[2] The son of Lord Beaverbrook, Sir Max Aitken was Conservative M.P. for Holborn 1945–50. He was Chairman of Beaverbrook Newspapers Ltd 1964–77 and has been President of the company since 1977. He succeeded to the title upon his father's death in 1964, but disclaimed it under the terms of the Peerage Act 1963.

[3] The journalist and broadcaster. He joined the Columbia Broadcasting System as a reporter in 1935 and was sent to London in 1937 as Head of its European Bureau. His broadcasts from London during the Second World War established his reputation as one of America's foremost (and most respected) broadcasters. As head of C.B.S. News after the war, he started 'Hear It Now', which became 'See It Now' in 1951; it was this programme which was credited with hastening the downfall of Senator Joseph McCarthy. Ed Murrow died in 1965.

Monday, April 6th

On Thursday I caught the five past eleven sleeper from Euston to Whitehaven in Cumberland. The arrangement was for Tommy Balogh to meet me at Workington, a little industrial town fifteen miles beyond Whitehaven. We reached Whitehaven two hours late, at ten o'clock in the morning, and I was there told that on Good Friday the train didn't go to Workington, as it usually does. When I protested that I had a through ticket, they said they would send the train on for me. So I went in my special train to Workington, only to find that Tommy, having discovered the train didn't connect, had gone to Whitehaven!

It was cold but I had tremendous luck for two four-hour afternoon walks on Friday and Saturday, with the mountain-tops snow covered and brilliant blue sky. On the second afternoon Sir Andrew Cohen and the African Queen[1] accompanied us. As soon as he arrived on Thursday evening, Sir Andrew had studied the map and announced his determination to climb four peaks on Friday. Though he is only forty-one, we had looked a little dubious, having glanced at his shape, and finally persuaded him, on his first day out, to join us in climbing Mellbreak, a steep hill, 1,700 feet high, near by.

We set out with Tirril [Balogh], aged ten, and Stephen, aged six, and Pen Balogh wickedly took them straight up a precipitous side of shale. Poor old Crossman took one look and saw that a path led far away to the right and then gently across the shale to half way up. Having reached this point, I had the pleasure of seeing the Governor of Uganda, with an enormous rucksack which he had been determined to take, slipping and slithering 300 feet below me, though he had been half a mile ahead. I've never seen anybody angrier, especially as the children careered up the hill.

We had a wonderful view from the top and then, while they went, exhausted, home, I climbed over two more cols just to show the African Governor. He had rather a thin time during the weekend. We couldn't help calling him the Governor and I couldn't help asking him those simple Socratic questions which are not asked. After one evening of this he said to Pen Balogh that he felt he had been given a horse-pill and, when I left on Sunday morning for Blackpool, he was in bed with a bad cold.

I spent Monday dawdling down to London in the train and discovering with pleasure that the *Sunday Pic* had devoted itself to the life story of Sir Hartley Shawcross. Good old Hugh Cudlipp! John Junor had told me at lunch last Wednesday that Beaverbrook was due back from Jamaica on Friday and Hugh, who has just returned to the *Mirror* group from the *Sunday Express*, must have greatly enjoyed giving John Gordon a lesson in free speech.

[1] A diplomat who was British Governor of Uganda 1952–7, Permanent British Representative on the U.N. Trusteeship Council 1957–61 and Director-General of the Department of Technical Co-operation 1961–4. He married Helen Donington, the 'African Queen', in 1949.

On March 29th the Chinese and North Korean commanders accepted the U.N. proposal, made in February, for the exchange of sick and wounded prisoners. They also proposed the immediate reopening of the armistice negotiations suspended in autumn 1952. On March 30th Chou En-lai declared that, given goodwill on both sides, the exchange of sick and wounded could be followed by smooth resolution of the whole question of prisoners of war. He agreed that those Communist prisoners who refused repatriation might be handed over to 'a neutral state', 'thus ensuring that the question of their repatriation will be justly settled and will not obstruct the realization of an armistice'. Repatriation of prisoners was now the only outstanding issue of difference between the parties to the war.

In the House of Commons on April 1st Mr Churchill cautiously welcomed this development.

Wednesday, April 8th
In all this chronicle I have left out the biggest thing. Ever since Kingsley told me, at a dinner party last Monday, we have been discussing the news of the Chinese proposals for ending the Korean war. These were followed on Friday by a much greater sensation when Moscow stated that the doctors charged with murder had been released and their interrogating officers arrested.[1] There is now really no doubt that the line has switched from hard to soft on the foreign as well as on the domestic front and already the American stock market is reacting.

This morning Kingsley was full of parallels with the period when Litvinov was at Geneva,[2] preaching collective security. I said to Kingsley that I didn't see why we should compare this switch to that period, any more than we should compare it to the Stalin–Hitler pact. This shocked Kingsley, who said he didn't want that sort of thing mentioned this week. But of course it's true. The Kremlin can go collective-security-minded to get on with the West when it wants to and it can go very different-minded when it wants to get on with the Nazis. And it can have a third, different sort of mind when it wants to

[1] On January 13th Tass announced the arrest of a number of 'terrorist doctors', several of them Jews. They were alleged to have tried to hasten the deaths of several Soviet leaders, in two cases successfully. Three were described as British Intelligence agents and some were said to be working under instruction from 'an international Jewish bourgeois-nationalist organization set up by American Intelligence'. On April 14th their complete exoneration was announced. The charges were said to be false, the documentary evidence without foundation and the 'confessions' to have been obtained illegally. The officials concerned were arrested. This episode was preceded on March 27th by a large-scale amnesty declared by the Praesidium of the Supreme Soviet and by Russian acceptance in early April of Dag Hammarskjöld of Sweden as the new U.N. Secretary-General.

[2] Maxim Litvinov (1876–1952). Prominent in the Russian Communist Party machine, he was Foreign Commissar 1930–9 and Ambassador to the U.S.A. 1941–3. As a result of his efforts the Soviet Union became a member of the League of Nations in 1934. While Commissar for Foreign Affairs, Litvinov pressed at Geneva for a permanent body to work towards complete and universal disarmament.

get on with nobody. But one is no better than the other and all are motivated in the same way.

On the other hand, what this does do is to destroy the whole basis of British and American policy since the outbreak of the Korean war. Whatever the motive of the Kremlin may be, if there is a Korean armistice and if the Kremlin suggests Four-Power talks on Germany, it will be almost impossible to hold NATO together and to avoid an American recession which, though its effects might be slight in America, would be sufficient to put all the European economies into a tail-spin.

The only wonder is that the Russians haven't thought of this sooner. My own guess is that they did but that Stalin's illness had the same sort of paralysing effect on their policy that Bevin's illness had on Labour policy over here.[1] He was just well enough to stay in charge and prevent any of his underlings feeling that they could take decisions. Of course that's guesswork but it seems to me more likely than many other guesses which are now being made. Anyway, it will be very interesting to fly to Bonn tomorrow for four days and find out what the feeling in Germany is.

From April 9th to 12th Crossman was in West Germany, for the annual Anglo-German conference at Königswinter. Attlee stayed behind, with appendicitis, and Bevan led the British party, which included Nicholas Kaldor the economist, whom Crossman met for the first time. 'German Diary', in the New Statesman and Nation, *March 18th, 1953, gives Crossman's impressions of the visit.*

Saturday, April 18th
Back in London, we had the Budget on Tuesday and ever since. I've really nothing to add to the *Sunday Pic.* We had a Bevanite party in my house on the Tuesday evening, where we decided that each fortnight one of us should give a midday cocktail party and that Desmond will have a little lunch for a few friends on Thursdays, to discuss the business of the House. My view of the prospects of the Bevanites is very dim. The rank-and-filers desperately miss the Group but there is no doubt that. Nye now feels that its use is over. In the House this week he and Harold Wilson and Hugh Gaitskell, as the cartoonists soon spotted, were a happy trinity. I can't see how we are going to win all our six seats at Margate next October but I suppose one shouldn't be upset if the Group gradually liquidates itself, having achieved its purposes.

Then, on Thursday evening, the news on the tape of Eisenhower's speech[2]

[1] In July 1946 Ernest Bevin collapsed on the eve of the Peace Conference in Paris. A heavy man, he suffered from heart trouble and breathing difficulties. Though his condition worsened, he continued to serve as Foreign Secretary until March 1951. In April he died. Morrison and Cripps were also in poor health during this post-war period.

[2] On April 16th President Eisenhower appealed to the Soviet Union's new leaders, in his first speech since Stalin's death. The President stated that the most convincing signs of peaceful intent which Russia could make would be not rhetoric but specific acts, such as the conclusion of a Korean armistice and an Austrian peace treaty. On April 20th, in the House of Commons, the Prime Minister welcomed the President's speech but advised patience.

eclipsed the Budget.[1] I was away but Desmond tells me that Nye came into the Smoking Room, saying it was superb, until Michael, who had read the full text in the *Herald Tribune*, disillusioned him. Apparently Morrison had seen a copy and rushed to the Parliamentary Committee, saying it was a masterpiece. I rang Nye yesterday morning and found that he had, on consideration, seen that it was not a peace offer but a peace demand. This morning I found in the papers that Churchill had greeted it as a masterpiece,[2] expressing our foreign policy. If Labour has any guts, there ought to be a row about this, since on the subject of Communist China and Formosa it is a major shift of British policy to say that Eisenhower is expressing our views.

Wednesday, April 22nd

A *Daily Express* Austin picked me up punctually at four o'clock last Saturday afternoon to take me to Beaverbrook's. The chauffeur had been with Dick Plummer[3] for six years and had nothing but good to say about him. Beaverbrook's house is at Leatherhead, in a wonderful park, with a south view into a woody valley. Walking up the drive before sunset, B. told me that it had been built to die in by one of Chamberlain's[4] partners in the screw factory but that he had lived for forty-nine years. For once, its comfort is up to expectations. B. took me personally to my room and showed me the private bathroom down a flight of five steps. The bath was specially constructed for

---

[1] The Chancellor declared his intention of stimulating production and providing incentives. The Budget speech on April 14th proposed a reduction in income tax of 6*d*. at all rates, with additions to some allowances, and a general reduction of one-quarter in purchase tax, with complete exemption for pianos, taxicabs and radio batteries. Industry was given tax allowances on new plant and machinery and from January 1st, 1954, the excess profits levy was to disappear. There was to be no entertainments tax on cricket or any amateur sport. Privately owned 'chattels' were to be accepted in payment of estate duty, if kept in houses already owned by the Government or themselves given in place of payment. Authors were to be permitted to spread their royalties, for tax purposes, over two years. The cost of all the tax reductions was estimated at £169 million for the current year, leaving a balance of revenue over expenditure of some £109 million. The Budget debate lasted for three days.

[2] The Prime Minister welcomed the President's 'bold and inspiring initiative', adding that 'Her Majesty's Government, and probably all the countries of the free world, will be glad to associate themselves with his sincere expression of those ideals and aims to which we all subscribe' [*H. C. Debates*, vol. 514, cols 649–51].

[3] Sir Leslie Plummer, a powerful figure in London Labour Party circles. He was Labour M.P. for Deptford from 1951 until his death in 1963.

[4] Joseph Chamberlain (1836–1914), Lord Mayor of Birmingham in 1875, was Liberal M.P. for Birmingham 1876–85 and Liberal Unionist M.P. for Birmingham West from 1885 until his death in 1914. He was President of the Board of Trade 1880–5. In 1886, he broke away from the Liberals and formed the Unionist Party (so-called because of its belief in continuing the union with Ireland), which became allied with the Conservatives. He was Secretary of State for the Colonies 1895–1903, when he resigned to concentrate on his campaign for Tariff Reform. There is a recent biography of him by J. Enoch Powell (London: Thames & Hudson, 1978). Joseph Chamberlain and his brother-in-law, J. S. Nettlefold, founded a successful screw-manufacturing business in Birmingham in the 1860s.

Lord Castlerosse,[1] he said. It was big enough to prevent the water splashing out.

The evening was pretty well ruined by the presence of Sir James and Lady Dunn,[2] the biggest steel magnates of Canada, she a bejewelled stick and he a first-class bore, especially when drinking. The only other people there were John Junor, Political Editor of the *Daily Express*, who came for dinner, and Lady Judith (?) Campbell, Beaverbrook's grand-daughter by the Duke of Argyll.[3] Since the Duke and Duchess have both married three or four times, Beaverbrook seems to look after this very nice, plump, dark girl, who at dinner suddenly revealed to me that she had studied logical positivism at Manchester for a year, and whom I liked a great deal.

I had been sold to B. as a bright columnist and personality but I'm not sure he very much liked the product when he saw it. We sat on the south terrace in a lovely sunset, drinking, while he tried me out. After some desultory conversation he said, 'Next week will be critical in Parliament. Reputations will be made or marred. There is Dalton and Bevan on Monday in the last day of the Budget and there is that young Minister of Transport[4] to show his paces on Tuesday. Will you be taking part?' I said I only spoke really on defence and foreign affairs and he was obviously deeply shocked. 'It's no good specializing,' he said. 'One's got to put oneself forward whenever there is a chance.'

I found him far gentler and more charming than I expected. He doesn't bark as much as the people who imitate his voice and often he sits quiet in a straight-up chair with one leg folded across the other, quizzing. Then he jumps up and walks across the room, or telephones the *Daily Express* or sends for drinks. He can't stay still for long. He had just said, during our talk before dinner, 'You write a very lively column in the *Pic* and you'll be getting on the front page', when Sir James Dunn interrupted us. The same thing happened after dinner, which, by the way, was exquisitely cooked, with great

[1] A protégé and close friend of Lord Beaverbrook, Lord Castlerosse wrote the 'Londoner's Log' on the *Sunday Express* from 1926 until 1940, when he returned to Ireland. He succeeded to the earldom of Kenmore in 1941, but died two years later. There is a biography of him by G. Malcolm Thomson, *Lord Castlerosse: His Life and Times* (London: Weidenfeld & Nicolson, 1973).

[2] Sir James Dunn (1875–1956), the barrister and K.C. who became Chairman and President of the Algoma Steel Corporation Ltd, Ontario, Canada.

[3] Lady Judith Campbell, daughter of the 11th Duke of Argyll and his first wife, the Hon. Janet Gladys Aitken (who was the daughter of Lord Beaverbrook); she was reputed to be Beaverbrook's favourite grand-daughter. The 11th Duke of Argyll (1903–73) succeeded to the title in 1949. He had married the Hon. Janet Aitken in 1927 and the marriage was dissolved in 1934. From 1935 until the dissolution of their marriage in 1951, his second wife was Mrs Louise Vanneck. The Duke married for the third time in 1951 and this marriage to Margaret Whigham was dissolved in 1963, when he married his fourth and last wife, Mrs Mathilda Mortimer.

[4] Mr Alan Lennox-Boyd, in the Commons discussion of the Lords Amendments to the Transport Bill. See below, pp. 221–2.

magnums of champagne poured out by B. himself, interspersed with vintage claret.

After dinner we were compulsorily taken to the private cinema to see a rather boring film. After twenty minutes of it he took John Junor and me out for a drink and *the* talk. Once again we got on to the subject of columns and B. said to me, 'You're in the wrong stable. There'll be big changes on the *Pic* now Hugh's[1] back and they'll get more pornographic. My own are the only papers which aren't pornographic and it's a hard job fighting them in a straight, clean paper.' At this point Sir James Dunn entered again and finally, at one o'clock, we went to bed. I had to catch the 9.45 to King's Cross and was told to go and see His Lordship at eight o'clock in the morning. I found him in a sort of hospital bed in the middle of the floor, with all the papers round him, and he asked me to come and see him again. But I don't think we shall.

At the *New Statesman* morning conference on Monday, I mentioned that I'd seen Beaverbrook. Kingsley was all agog. I then told him that at dinner Beaverbrook asked me something about Kingsley and I had replied, 'Well, you know him very well. You often see him,' and he had said, 'I've only seen him once in my life.' (This is quite untrue.) Kingsley was absolutely stunned by this and it hurt his vanity more than anything I could possibly have said and, as John Freeman pointed out, wrecked our work on the paper for three days. Apparently Beaverbrook had tried to win Kingsley for an anti-Bevin move. B. told me at length how detestable Bevin was and how he had fought him in the War Cabinet.

By the way, Beaverbrook also told me one quite interesting fact about current politics. 'Churchill is often stupidly chivalrous,' he said. 'He was intending at Glasgow yesterday (i.e. Friday) to say that there was definitely not going to be an autumn election. He was going to do it merely because he was so angry at the Socialists calling Butler's Budget, which he thinks wonderful, an election Budget. But then somebody got hold of Churchill and some qualifications were drafted into a denial so as to leave room for manoeuvre. He was the same with the Mountbattens.[2] When Lady Mountbatten got round Stafford Cripps and got him to promote a special Bill so

[1] Hugh Cudlipp. See above, pp. 96 ff.

[2] Louis Mountbatten (1900–79) was the youngest son of the 1st Marquess of Milford Haven and Admiral of the Fleet, Prince Louis Battenburg, who in 1917 took the title of Lord Louis Mountbatten. His early career was in the Navy and he became Chief of Combined Operations 1942–3 and Acting Admiral 1943–6. He was Supreme Allied Commander South-East Asia 1943–6, Viceroy of India March–August 1947 and Governor-General of India August 1947–June 1948, Fourth Sea Lord 1950–2, Commander-in-Chief Allied Forces, Mediterranean, 1953–4, First Sea Lord 1955–9 and Chief of the U.K. Defence Staff 1959–65. He became a Viscount in 1946 and was created 1st Earl Mountbatten of Burma in 1947. In 1979 he was assassinated while on holiday in the Republic of Ireland.

He married Edwina Ashley (1901–60) in 1922. She became Superintendent-in-Chief of the St John Ambulance Brigade in July 1942 and proved extremely effective in organizing relief and welfare work in South-East Asia. She inherited a considerable fortune from her grandfather, Sir Ernest Cassel.

that she could use her family fortune,[1] I fought it in the *Daily Express*. But Churchill wouldn't fight and, when I complained, he said to me, 'Well, if they give jobs to the boys I'll give nuts to the girls.' (Kingsley tells me that this is a fantastic caricature of the truth, since in fact Stafford's Bill was withdrawn. The matter was arranged in the Budget and the anti-Mountbatten campaign had been launched long before.)

Monday was the last day of the Budget debate. I didn't hear much of it. However, after dining with Dick and Naomi Mitchison I went in to hear Nye Bevan and Butler. Nye had taken tremendous trouble with his speech and had been briefed at length by Tommy Balogh. The theme was to be the bankruptcy of Tory economic policy, since mere reliefs in taxation for the entrepreneur do not encourage him to save or, at least, they discourage him from investing in the necessary heavy equipment. Large-scale capital investment to reorganize our industries is only possible with Government control and extensions of public ownership. It was a very good theme and of course it was a good speech. But something went wrong. Nye never got to his climax and had to tack on his peroration rather disjointedly. Butler made a knockabout reply, which surprised some people who don't regard him as a politician. I think he definitely won on points.

On Tuesday, in the Chamber, the Commons were considering the Lords Amendments to the Transport Bill.[2] These had not fallen under the Tory guillotine and they have given the Labour Party a chance of a last-minute

---

[1] In the 1948/49 parliamentary Session, Countess Mountbatten lodged a Petition in the House of Lords for an Act to remove the constraint statutorily imposed upon the enjoyment by married women of interest from certain categories of trust. One trust so affected was that by which much of the Cassel fortune had been bequeathed to Edwina Ashley. The Petition was certified and sent for consideration as a Personal Bill. With Counsel appearing, the Bill was considered in the Lords Committee, which included no less than three Law Lords, skilled in equity drafting. As redrafted, the Bill was reported from the committee and passed all its Lords stages. In the Commons, however, it became apparent from Early Day Motions and other intimations of disquiet that many Labour backbenchers objected to the Bill on the grounds that, if the amendment it proposed to the general law (on behalf of an already very rich woman) was justifiable, it should not be confined only to those who could afford the expensive process of a Personal Bill. Since it was not customary for the Commons to reject Personal Bills once they had passed the quasi-judicial process of the Lords, the Government were in a dilemma. A Second Reading of the Mountbatten Estate Bill was twice deferred in the Commons. Finally on July 5th, 1949, the Government introduced a Public Bill in the Lords—the Married Women (Removal of Restraint) Bill. Lady Mountbatten withdrew her Personal Bill. On December 16th, 1949, the Government's Bill received the Royal Assent.

[2] Seventy Government Amendments had been inserted in the Lords Stages of the Bill. When the measure returned to the Commons the Government introduced a guillotine motion, to shorten the debate and permit the Amendments to be voted on *en bloc*. But seven of the Amendments concerned matters of finance, on which the House of Lords was not entitled to pronounce, and the Opposition tabled a motion of censure, debated on May 5th. Meanwhile on April 22nd Herbert Morrison, acting as Leader of the Opposition during Attlee's illness, repudiated the pairing arrangements made for that and subsequent nights. He justified his action on the ground that the Government had suddenly changed the planned timetable, a course which some said had been forced by Opposition procedural tactics.

demonstration against the denationalization of transport. I've no doubt the demonstration is right. If you tell the industrial worker that he mustn't use industrial action to stop a Bill, you must then carry your obstruction of the Bill in Parliament far enough to demonstrate that you are trying to do his job for him. On the other hand, I must say that all-night sittings are dreary. It's difficult to recapture the rapture of our all-night sittings on Dalton's first Budget.[1] Of course, we were physically younger then but, oh dear, we were mentally younger too and enthusiastic. Now the Party is very old. It staunchly went through the motions and Leslie Hale made a fifty-minute speech on nothing at all and there were points of order during a division, with hats being passed along,[2] and I felt the whole thing was so unutterably tedious, boring, futile, that I began to sympathize with John Freeman in deciding not to stand again.

I had forgotten that we had had an N.E.C. this morning but it suddenly occurred to me when I went to the party given by Tom Driberg and his publishers for his new book, a scissors-and-paste pot-boiling job.[3] It was a wonderful party, with Tom Farr,[4] the leading boxer; the latest American star from the Palladium, a left-winger; Fred Mullaley;[5] Christiansen of the *Express*,[6] actors, actresses, M.P.s, Society, everybody there — after which John and Mima and I and Dick Plummer and his wife[7] had fish and chips in the cafeteria.

Then I sat down to write the *New Statesman* front page on the Eisenhower

---

[1] In October 1946. (A supplementary Budget to cover the remainder of the financial year 1945/46 was also introduced in October 1945.) See Dalton, *High Tide and After* (London: Muller, 1962), pp. 24–31.

[2] Formerly, when it was customary to wear hats, Members would remove them while addressing the House. But a Member wishing to raise a point of order during a division would remain 'seated and covered'; even today a collapsible opera hat is kept for that purpose by the Serjeant at Arms's chair. The practice is generally believed to reflect the fact that it is easier for the Speaker to recognize a Member remaining seated and covered at a time when a large number of Members are standing up and moving about the Chamber. In fact, as John Hatsell (1768–1820, a Clerk of the House) explained, during a division the Speaker must decide 'peremptorily', without debate, whether to accept a point of order during a division; older and experienced Members may show their support for whatever he should decide by 'sitting on their seats, and speaking with their hats on, to avoid even the appearance of a debate'.

[3] *The Best of Both Worlds* (London: Phoenix House, 1953) was Driberg's diary for the 1951–2 period, written up to include some of his journalistic pieces.

[4] Tommy Farr was British heavyweight boxing champion in 1937.

[5] Fred Mullaley, a journalist and press publicity agent cited as co-respondent in the divorce of John Lewis, formerly Labour M.P. for Bolton West. Mullaley was later defendant in a libel case successfully brought by Lewis in 1952. The case caused some stir, as it involved several prominent politicians, including Harold Wilson. Among his several novels is *Deadly Payoff* (London: W. H. Allen, 1978).

[6] Arthur Christiansen joined the *Sunday Express* as News Editor in 1926 and was Assistant Editor 1928–33. He was Editor of the *Daily Express* 1933–57 and Editorial Director of Beaverbrook Newspapers 1957–9. He published an autobiography, *Headlines All my Life* (London: Heinemann, 1961). He died in 1963.

[7] Beatrice Lapsker married Leslie Plummer in 1923. She was made a life peer in 1965 and died in 1972.

declaration.[1] I finished at half-past midnight, discussed it with John and got the Chief Whip's permission to go to bed between one and two o'clock in the morning. I wouldn't have dreamt of doing this two years ago. Now I do it and hope my colleagues haven't noticed. I had thought, when Zita died, that I should go more into public life and I suppose I have, but with a good deal more detachment and with a feeling that, even if one does write every week in the *Sunday Pic* and the *New Statesman*, one isn't leading a very useful life. But then what is a useful life? What one really means, by saying that one isn't leading it, is that one's personality isn't fully engaged or committed.

Tuesday, April 28th
On Thursday evening the unfortunate Jack Mendelsohn, the chief Bevanite in Sheffield, came up to see me at half-past ten, when I was confident that business on the Transport Bill would be over. He had to sit and wait in the Visitors' Gallery,[2] while the debate drooled on until about half-past one in the morning. We were too sleepy to talk until breakfast on Friday, when I was harassed by the thought of having to finish the *Sunday Pic* column by half-past two.

Mendelsohn reported on morale in Sheffield and the surrounding area and expressed doubts whether I should get re-elected,[3] especially if Morrison stood. He thought it could just be done. He is also extremely worried lest we should agree to a programme which will lose us the support of the constituencies. I gave him a list of subjects on which resolutions should be drafted in good time for Conference and then got on with the *Sunday Pic*. At half-past two Nye Bevan and the others turned up to discuss tactics for the Executive weekend. I had been desperately trying to read the volume of typescript provided by Transport House. Tom Driberg emphasized the need for politeness from Nye Bevan, to which Nye replied that it was essential to stage a first-rate row on the Friday evening in order to clear the air.

At four o'clock we duly assembled in the top storey of Transport House,[4] the M.P.s stertorous and somnolent with tiredness and the trade unionists stertorous and somnolent as usual. Arthur Greenwood proposed that we should go through the hundreds of pages of draft policy documents, page by page. Our proposal for a Second Reading debate was turned down. I then suggested that we take the summary of proposals in conjunction with the analysis of the situation in the first section. I thereby achieved a debate on the analysis, which *was* really a sort of Second Reading debate. It was a loosely written document, which might have been a memorandum for *The Economist*. Apparently the research workers at Transport House think *The Economist* is

[1] 'The President's Two Lieutenants' [Mr Dulles and Mr Churchill], *New Statesman and Nation*, April 25th, 1953.
[2] More properly, the Strangers' Gallery.
[3] To the N.E.C.
[4] To discuss the policy document. See above, p. 212.

objective and the *New Statesman* partisan, whereas of course *The Economist* is partisan but in a different direction.

We very soon found that the procedure was that any objection of ours was met with a ready agreement to incorporate it in the redraft. This avoided votes and created an atmosphere of unanimity without letting one know what was really going to happen. We had reached a page on democratic planning, which made no reference to public ownership, as I pointed out, when Nye suddenly intervened, almost irrelevantly, to say, 'In that case I refuse to co-operate.' At this, Edith Summerskill woke up, leant across the table with her finger out and shouted, 'Let's put that on the record! We've got it! He refuses to co-operate! They all refuse to co-operate! There's no point in our sitting any further.' And there wasn't.

We adjourned fairly soon afterwards and Nye got into an extremely cordial conversation with Bill Webber and Jock Tiffin, the ablest of our trade unionists. I had intended to go to bed early but Nye asked me to go home for a drink and when we had settled down I asked him what he had said to the trade unionists. 'Oh,' he said, 'I told them that I knew they'd much prefer to know where we stood. So I told them the conditions I was standing for (chemicals and land nationalization) and that, if I didn't get them, we should not resign from the Executive but stay on it and refuse to speak at Conference. In this way everybody would know what the issues were which we would stand for, while at the same time our opponents would not have the convenience of having got rid of us.' He concluded, 'I can assure you we shall have a sunny atmosphere tomorrow. They much prefer it this way. It's no good Tom Driberg being reasonable. They know it's an issue of power.'

It was by now about half-past eight and Nye suggested we went to dinner. Since he had given me an enormous meal a fortnight ago, I took him and Jennie to the Ivy. Just when we were settling down, Michael Foot and Jill came in for a snack, so my dinner party and its cast were somewhat enlarged. We had an extremely good meal and then Nye told me that I must come back and have coffee afterwards. This included a bottle of brandy, which we drank until two o'clock in the morning, when I said I really must go to bed in preparation for next day's conference.

I woke up feeling fine, strolled across St James's Park on an exquisite spring day and arrived at the Charing Cross Hotel about ten minutes late. Nye came in some ten minutes later. He told me that, after he had taken me home last night, he had had another couple of hours chatting and drinking with Jennie and that it had been so nice.

He was right on one thing. Nothing could have been more remarkable than the improved relationships after his shock tactics. He ploughed ahead through the sections devoted to coal, steel and engineering, to a curious little debate on aircraft nationalization, in which the Bevanites fragmented. The working party had produced a report recommending effective control of some firms and a controlling interest in other firms and they explained that outright nationalization would alarm the industry and might lose us the twelve designers on which it depends. Nye and I pointed out that, if this were so, the objection applied equally to the compromise proposals of the working party, which created the worst of both worlds. Anyway, as Nye pointed out, aircraft nationalization would be extremely unpopular. So he and I voted that we should merely state that any firm which failed to expand to the requirements of national interest could be taken over and the other four voted for the working party scheme. This produced an even better atmosphere for lunch.

After lunch Tom Driberg quite solemnly moved an emergency resolution protesting against the food and, when challenged, pointed out in detail what was wrong with each course, to the bewilderment of colleagues who thought they had eaten and drunk very well. At this point, just when we were beginning the discussion of land nationalization, Clem Attlee entered the room to a mild cheer* and sat down The majority proposals were against land nationalization and for nothing more than the continued operation of the 1947 Act,[1] including extremely severe penalties for farmers who failed to fulfil requirements. Nye made the best speech I have ever heard him make, starting by saying that this policy would not get us a single extra turnip. Land nationalization was the only way of canalizing capital investment into the land. The State would pay off the landlords with the rent received for twenty-five years, after which their claims would lapse. Moreover, as each tenancy lapsed, the State would be able to adjust the rents to requirements and so complete the process over seven years. The whole exposition was extremely convincing.

Then, to everybody's surprise, Clem Attlee chipped in, strongly supporting Nye. He met the objection that it would be difficult to find managers with the remark that the estate agents now working for the landlords would work for the State. The debate went on for some time, with our side taking the offensive and challenging the others to show how output could be increased without nationalization. After long delays and attempts by us to postpone the issue for second thoughts on Sunday morning, a vote was decided upon. At this point we found that Clem Attlee had disappeared. The vote, on a compromise offered by Harold Wilson, was defeated by 9 to 13 and then, for nationalization, by 7 to 14, with Mark Hewitson on our side. Nye again showed how serious he felt this was and indicated we might have to break on it.

* He had just had an operation for appendicitis.
[1] The 1947 Planning Act reduced the number of planning authorities and simplified the process of seeking permission to develop land in town and country. Machinery was established to control development. The new authorities were to make complete surveys of their areas and industrial undertakings were to obtain Board of Trade certificates before they might build; advertisements were to be controlled. Planning authorities were to have the power to designate land for compulsory purchase and arrangements would be made for giving grants, based on need, to local authorities. (See *The Diaries of a Cabinet Minister*, vol. I, for Crossman's own part in the subsequent history of these matters.)
8

It had been decided that we should all go to Barbara's for dinner and that I should go with Nye. When we got outside, he started driving me to his home and I said he had to go to Barbara's. 'Oh,' he said, 'I'm not feeling well and I can't possibly face it. I'll go home to Jennie.' As I had hoped, Jennie sent him up with me to Barbara's dinner, where we discussed tactics. Nye proposed that the first thing we should do on Sunday morning was for him to make the announcement that, in view of what had happened, we were putting forward an alternative programme of our own. I thought this was a bit bridge-burning and said we would be wiser to put forward large-scale amendments. At this point, though, the meeting broke up and at midnight Nye drove me home.

Sunday was another beautiful day for a walk across the Park but, when I got to the Charing Cross Hotel to hear Nye's pronouncement, Wilson whispered to me that Nye was at home with food poisoning. Actually it wasn't too bad a thing, as without fireworks we really achieved quite a lot, particularly when we came to the issue of controls on the private sector. By questioning, I discovered that this subject had never been discussed by a sub-committee and that the Transport House office had merely prepared a draft recommending the restoration of controls eliminated by the Tories. The full absurdity of this is only clear when you remember that the proposal is that we should have an enormous expansion of agriculture and engineering under a mixed economy, with 80 per cent free enterprise. Throughout, the issue of control of the private sector must be of central importance. But Harold Wilson is never at his strongest on the subject of controls, of which he made a bonfire when he was President of the Board of Trade.

However, I pressed very hard, using a variant of the argument Nye had used on land nationalization. Then someone suddenly remembered that in the 1950 programme we had had a section on competitive public enterprise and the private sector and it was agreed to insert all this, as it might roughly meet the bill. This is a curious way of doing things and I pointed out that we should, in that case, have to rewrite the whole section on engineering, which we had passed on Saturday and which solemnly stated that we would not upset private enterprise in engineering. This was straightaway agreed to but I still have no idea what will come out of the agreement.

Harold Wilson and I had both had the same thought overnight and agreed it would be unwise to announce an alternative programme. On the other hand, we would say that we were going to submit extensive amendments. It became more and more difficult to say this in the course of the afternoon, when we were discussing taxation and the social services. Our demand for a capital gains tax was immediately granted. Barbara's demand that we should pledge ourselves in some part to restore the food subsidies was immediately granted. All our proposals on the Health Service were immediately granted and an education report from me got through untouched. So we really had very little complaint on the afternoon's work. Then, to cap it, Morgan Phillips asked us to send in amendments!

The reason for this tactic became clear yesterday morning, when I read the papers. Phillips had given a press conference, emphasizing that full unanimity had been reached on everything but land nationalization and that Labour's wonderful new plan was well-nigh completed. This puts us in a very awkward fix, since, if we break now, when the Executive meets to consider the final draft on May 19th, it will be argued that we are going back on previous decisions. I wanted to issue a statement to the press but Nye, who had recovered from food poisoning in time for the transport debate, in which he is interested, sharply rebuked me for contemplating such a wild step, which would put us in the wrong with the rest of the Executive.

In the Chamber yesterday the guillotine[1] on the Transport Bill was debated. This is now quite an important constitutional issue. The Lords had redrafted such large parts of the Bill that the decision to vote against all the remaining clauses without discussion really means granting the Lords the right to legislate on a major issue without the Commons. I don't believe that this occurred to anybody when the row started and it's a good example of how constitutional issues arise almost by accident. I went in every now and then to see how things were going and once again I marvelled at the parliamentary character of men like Morrison and Callaghan. They live for this sort of thing, in which I can only take the mildest of interest and admire the passion that they manage to feel. But then, they are parliamentarians in the sense that they like Parliament for its own sake, whereas I am only interested in it from the point of view of getting something done.

At our usual Tuesday lunch today we had a full attendance. There was a post-mortem on the Executive weekend and we allocated the writing of the various sections of our version of the programme. Most of us wanted to leave out the social services but Barbara would have none of this, so we shall be writing a whole programme. In the middle of the morning David Ginsburg rang up to ask me if I would write the official draft of the education section. So that completes it. For once, Nye is taking some responsibility. Instead of having an endless drafting committee, all of us are sending our drafts direct to him and he is doing the one on land himself. Outside it's still a lovely spring.

From April 29th to May 2nd Crossman was in Munich, making various broadcasts and addresses, including a May Day speech at an S.P.D. rally. See 'Radio City — Munich' *in the* New Statesman and Nation, *May 9th, 1953.*

Wednesday, May 6th
At the Tuesday lunch yesterday we again discussed our draft amendments. Last time Nye had agreed to edit. This time he was appalled at the prospect and said, 'Well, I've other things to do, you know.' What these other things

---

[1] The Allocation of Time Order for discussion of the Lords' Amendments to the Transport Bill was carried by 307 votes to 275.

are I'm not sure but the conclusion was that Michael, Ian and I will, as usual, do the work and that, if we edit, Nye might be able to manage to draft the section on land nationalization. He is determined that we should not present these amendments before we get the official draft and that they should be presented as a whole by himself. It's fairly clear that he has made up his mind that we shall not resign and that, in some way or other, our draft shall be leaked. How that should be done is the sort of thing that Nye thinks you leave to the gods or to Mikardo, Foot and Crossman.

Wednesday, May 13th

I spent a lovely, quietest weekend at King's College, Cambridge. Richard Kahn[1] is Keynes's[2] successor as Bursar and he and his friends seem to be carrying on the true Bloomsbury tradition, with its stress on quiet personal relationships. He took immense trouble to organize my weekend and to make me feel at ease. The nicest part of it was a long Sunday walk with him and Joan Robinson,[3] the economist. Apparently they walk every Sunday and sometimes the Kaldor children and other children come on horseback or bicycles to the lunch place. It all reminded me of Virginia Woolf's *To the Lighthouse*.[4] How roughly Cambridge guests must feel they are treated in Oxford, where life is public affairs, not private affairs.

At King's High Table[5] I sat next to the Provost[6] and got on with him very well till I asked him if he had read Dalton's memoirs,[7] which came out last

[1] A temporary civil servant in various Government Departments 1939–46, he was a Fellow of King's College, Cambridge, and Professor of Economics at Cambridge 1951–72. He became a life peer in 1965.

[2] John Maynard Keynes (1863–1946), the writer and economist. He was a Lecturer in Economics at Cambridge 1908–1915, when he joined the Treasury, remaining there until 1919. His book *The Economic Consequences of the Peace* (London: Macmillan, 1919), in which he expressed the conviction that it was possible to cure unemployment, immediately launched him into the centre of economic and political controversy, and in *A Treatise on Money* (London: Macmillan, 1930) and the *General Theory of Employment, Interest and Money* (London: Macmillan, 1936) he investigated the nature of saving and investment and their relation to rising and falling prices. He returned to the Treasury in 1940 and was made a baron in 1942. In 1944 he played a leading part in the Bretton Woods Conference, from which emerged the International Monetary Fund. His collected writings, published by Macmillan and Cambridge University Press, appear under the general editorship of Lord Kahn. Twenty-three volumes have so far appeared.

[3] A Fellow of Girton College, Cambridge, and a prolific author, she succeeded her husband, Austin Robinson, as Professor of Economics at Cambridge 1965–71. Her publications include *The Economics of Imperfect Competition* (London: Macmillan, 1933), *The Cultural Revolution in China* (Harmondsworth: Penguin, 1969) and *Freedom and Necessity* (London: Allen & Unwin, 1970).

[4] The author Virginia Woolf (1882–1941), whose novel describes a world of academics, children, regular meals and the countryside. *To the Lighthouse* (London: Hogarth Press) was published in 1927.

[5] At Oxford and Cambridge colleges the Fellows and their guests dine at a table raised above the main body of the hall.

[6] Sir John Tresidder Sheppard (1881–1968). He was Provost of King's College, Cambridge, 1933–54. His book *Greek Tragedy* was published in 1920 by Cambridge University Press in the series Cambridge Manuals.

[7] *Call Back Yesterday* (London: Muller, 1953).

weekend. The Provost is a gentle old Greek scholar, a fuddy-duddy, but Dalton was too much for him. He told me how terrible he was. Having told me, he felt so embarrassed that we couldn't speak again. It must, of course, be rather offensive for these delicate, ethical aesthetics to have Dalton writing about himself, Rupert Brooke and the Cambridge way of life.

It was exquisite, early summer weather for strolling along the Backs[1] and in the Trinity Fellows' garden, full of flowering trees, or for sitting on Nicky Kaldor's lawn just behind, while the children played with hoops, or for walking over the flat country and through the bluebell woods. The Kahn–Kaldor–Robinson set are all keen Socialists but somehow they are detached from practical politics. On the other hand, they curiously succeed in giving one the impression that they care about what one's doing, and mind, which is a nice consoling pillow on which to lay one's head.

On May 11th the Prime Minister made a lengthy Statement on foreign affairs, of which he had taken daily charge since the Foreign Secretary's serious illness in the early spring. Sir Winston (it had been announced on April 25th that he had accepted the Garter) reminded the House of the recent course of events in Korea, the U.S.S.R. and Egypt.

In Korea the resumption of armistice negotiations on April 6th led to the submission by the U.N. representatives of a nine-point plan for the exchange of sick and wounded prisoners of war. The early release of six British civilian internees was followed by a Communist promise to deliver the first group of sick and wounded into U.N. hands on April 20th. But difficulties over procedure arose once more and on May 7th the Communist negotiators abandoned their recent demand that prisoners unwilling to be repatriated should be transferred to a neutral overseas country. Instead, they determined that such prisoners should remain in Korea, in the custody of a commission of five neutral nations, including India. The period of custody should be reduced from six to four months. The U.N. side accepted this proposal and both parties began work on its details.

In Egypt the settlement of the future of the Sudan was succeeded by consideration of the defence of the Suez Canal Zone. On April 27th talks began between a British delegation, led by the British Ambassador to Egypt, and the Egyptian Government. But on May 6th they were adjourned since, according to General Nasser, the Egyptian representatives refused further discussion of details until agreement had been reached on the fundamental issue of national sovereignty and rights in the Canal Zone. On May 10th General Neguib made a violently anti-British speech, in part, it was suggested, to impress the U.S. Secretary of State, then visiting that part of the world.

On May 11th the Prime Minister alluded to this speech, replying that, if attacked, the British troops in the Canal Zone would be able to defend themselves. He spoke of the apparent changes that were occurring in the Soviet leaders

[1] Where the lawns run down to the river's edge.

attitudes to the West and suggested that a small private conference 'at the highest level', not 'overhung by a ponderous agenda', might be productive. He also offered the idea of a defence pact, including Germany and Russia, with the participants each guaranteeing one another against attack.

On the second day of the debate the Minister of State, Mr Selwyn Lloyd, gave details of some thirty attacks on British troops and installations which, since April 1st, had occurred with growing frequency in the Canal Zone. Mr Lloyd went on to explain Egyptian claims with regard to the maintenance and management of the Suez base. The Government intended to resist these demands.

Monday and Tuesday saw the big Foreign Affairs debate. Churchill certainly made a remarkable speech, though my first reaction was to see its demagogy and not its statesmanship. Michael Foot, who had the same reaction, spoke on Monday afternoon, with the result that he sounded querulous and didn't cut much ice. Of course, objectively, the speech *is* demagogy. It indicates that Britain will now take an independent peace initiative and yet I feel in my bones that it won't come to much because there is really no basis for that. But Attlee was certainly right in taking Churchill at his face value and giving him our support.

On Monday afternoon I saw Attlee in the lobby and had a bright idea. I asked him whether I could go into his room and talk to him about Egypt, since I was really upset by Churchill's outrageous, Omdurman, contemptuous references to Neguib.[1] I suggested that Attlee should cautiously rebuke Churchill and might say a word in favour of the new regime in Egypt. Apart from telling me that the Egyptians are pretty awful people, Attlee said nothing. But when he got up to speak on Tuesday, he did extremely courageously on Egypt. Indeed his whole speech was absolutely astonishing. He rebuked those who wanted to bring Germany into NATO, stated frankly that Ho Chi Minh[2] was leading the nationalist movement in Indo-China[3] and remarked that he wondered sometimes whether Senator McCarthy[4] or

[1] Mohammed Neguib, an Egyptian army officer who became prominent in the overthrow of King Farouk in 1952. Supported by Nasser's free officers, he became President of the new republic in 1953 but was himself ousted by Nasser in 1954.

[2] Ho Chi Minh (1890–1969). Later President of North Vietnam. He had returned to Indo-China in 1944 to lead the Viet Minh Army.

[3] In March 1949 Vietnam had been given independence within the French Union and the country became formally independent in December that year. But fighting had continued between French troops and the insurgents of the Communist Viet Minh, led by Ho Chi Minh; by May 1953 the Viet Minh had invaded the State of Laos in Indo-China. The United States now bore 40 per cent of the cost of the war and the French had promised more and more devolution of power to the States of Laos, Vietnam and Cambodia.

[4] In late March Senator McCarthy had attacked America's allies for sending strategic goods to China, announcing that he had personally negotiated an agreement with the owners of 242 Greek ships that they would not trade with Communist-controlled parts of Asia. Mr Harold Stassen, the Mutual Security Administrator, accused the Senator of undermining the Government's own efforts to prevent trade with China but Mr Foster Dulles, the Secretary of State, declared that Senator McCarthy's activities had been 'in the national interest'.

Eisenhower were running America. Six weeks ago, if I had said any of these things in the House of Commons, the entire Labour Front Bench would have regarded it as left-wing extremism. Now the whole of politics has swung to the left and what was anti-Americanism is now normal Front Bench practice.

It all shows what an astonishing power Churchill still has. This movement for an independent British initiative has been underground for years and the Labour Opposition had played it down. For weeks the Foreign Affairs Committee has been pressing that Labour should come out in favour of such an initiative; we were told it was premature. The moment Churchill speaks, it becomes respectable. No less than eight Bevanites got in over the two days. Jennie was the first called on our side after Attlee, who received a real ovation. She began extremely well but the trouble about quite unprepared, spontaneous speeches is that they peter out. Also, she will talk in the House with a barking tone — as though it were a public meeting.

I spoke after Walter Elliot and did all right. The fact is, what matters in the House of Commons is not argument or charm but power. The speech must carry weight and it's usually difficult to define what weight is. Altogether it was a very important two days and the National Executive are very lucky that they had drafted their foreign policy document before this major shift occurred.[1] But then the shift may not last very long, since, if nothing comes of Churchill's proposals for high-level talks or if the talks peter out, the cold war atmosphere will close down again.

Meanwhile we've been struggling along on the Executive policy draft. At the Tuesday lunch the five big amendments were presented and it was clear that Ian Mikardo's and Harold Wilson's just weren't written in a possible way. Curly Mallalieu and Nye are to redraft and edit the whole lot. I've just had a glance at the new official draft, which is a great deal more tautly written and put together, but which is still portentously dull. The salient proposals do not stick out above the general level. Unfortunately this is just what we found in our own draft.

Tuesday, May 19th

As I went through the inner lobby in the House of Commons yesterday, just before dinner, I was handed a document which I discovered to be a complete redraft of the policy statement. Nye had handed our, or rather his, amendments in on Friday and apparently David Ginsburg, under Jim Griffiths's direction, spent the weekend trying to meet our objections and incorporate parts of our draft. We all went to Nye's house late last night to discuss things and decided to table our amendments and vote on them. I noticed that Nye was in one of his cautious moods and kept on asking whether we should put

[1] A discussion pamphlet, *Problems of Foreign Policy*, was published in April 1952. A second document, *Labour's Foreign Policy*, appeared in June 1952, for submission to the annual Conference at Morecambe in the autumn.

things to the vote. 'Of course, I'm only asking for information, just to clear our minds,' he said. But I guessed that his mind was moving into one of his spasms of compromise.

When we met at Transport House at ten o'clock today, it was soon clear that we were in for a dreary, bickering, chaotic morning. Most of the trade unionists had received Nye's amendments yesterday and hadn't got the new redraft from Transport House until this morning. The result was that they had had no time to read anything. Moreover, they must have been rather shaken by the fact that the original draft we discussed at the Charing Cross meeting had now been completely redrafted twice over. Early on in the bicker Attlee said that he thought there was a lot to be said for Nye's style in the first nine pages. (Nobody had got any further than the first nine pages of Nye and the first twenty pages of their draft. These contained the two statements of the challenge we are facing.) Attlee added that he approved of Nye's style in general but he found some parts of it rather biased, to which Nye replied, 'Well, if you want to be provocative you've got to be a bit biased. The trouble about the office draft is that it's so neutral that it's deadly dull.' In fact, I think everybody knew quite well what we all repeated *ad nauseam* – that nobody in the Movement would conceivably read the long economic essay of which the office draft consists. On the other hand, they were most unwilling to admit that the Bevanites had written a document they liked.

So the talk went on and on, with Arthur Greenwood in the chair completely failing to direct the meeting. About every twenty minutes Edith Summerskill would say, 'I propose that we now take the office draft page by page,' and she said it louder and louder and more and more violently, though it was quite obvious that it wasn't any good taking it page by page, since nobody had looked at it. Jim Griffiths made a long speech in favour of the office draft, claiming that it showed the relevance of our public ownership proposals to the crisis. Nye and I hadn't much difficulty in saying that Nye's draft dealt with this much more closely, shortly and readably. There was the usual scene, when Nye refused to co-operate and Edith wanted it all down on the record.

Then Nye suddenly got sweet as a cooing dove and said that there weren't really any differences between us, since he wasn't going to press his amendment about land, owing to the fact that the Executive had already decided. So why not have a little drafting committee to do the whole work and present it to the Executive again on Thursday? This proposal was then discussed for an hour and a half, with Tom Driberg wanting the drafting committee to draft and Jim Griffiths saying that of course it should only look at a draft prepared by the office. It was clear that our opponents' major objective was to prevent us from drafting anything, for fear that they would see nothing wrong with it. I had a nightmare fear that one of us might be on this drafting committee, but fortunately the whole idea fell away because Edith Summerskill and Alice Bacon feared that we would get on to the committee and do something devilish there. It was finally agreed that the poor office should produce a complete new draft by Thursday afternoon. I was sorry for Ginsburg. He must have worked the whole of the weekend and the draft he produced for today was dismissed without anybody having read it at all.

At lunch afterwards Nye seemed quite pleased with his tactics, which were no doubt partly influenced by the fact that we knew in advance that the formula relating to the nationalization of the chemical industry was one on which we could agree. For that reason the only big issue on which there is disagreement is land nationalization. Everything else is a question of presentation, colour and emphasis. But, of course, in such a document presentation, colour and emphasis is much more than 60 per cent of the total, since the average reader or delegate judges a document by its feel and not by its precise proposals. No doubt they will incorporate in their fourth draft a good deal of what we wrote but I fear that it will still be flat and unedifying.

On Monday night, Nye had said several times that, though he would speak about *his* amendments, he would make it clear that he had consulted his friends. This morning he quite forgot to do so and, as the day went on, he began to express more and more strong feelings about his draft and the hours he had spent composing it! On the way home to lunch I said to him, 'I think you almost believe you wrote it, Nye.' He said, 'Well, I could have written it all.' I said, 'But in that case the style would have been a bit different. Anyone with a glimmer of intelligence can see that the land section was written by you and the first section by me.' 'Yes,' he said, 'but they haven't a glimmer of intelligence.' And that's quite true. I am now convinced that they all think Nye got down and wrote 10,000 words. How little they know him.

Tuesday, May 26th
Last Wednesday evening, at the House, I was sitting talking to Nye when the fourth redraft of the policy statement was circulated. This time they had gone a bit further and spatchcocked two-thirds of our material into theirs, at the same time reintroducing a huge section on the dollar crisis,[1] I suppose under pressure from Gaitskell. We agreed to meet on Thursday evening, after Ian had conscientiously compared our draft with theirs, to concoct some amendments.

On Thursday morning I went down to Coventry for mayor-making. The three o'clock train brought me back just in time to go through our amendments with Nye and Ian, who had done an excellent job.

The Executive meeting started at half-past seven and came to an abrupt end at ten o'clock, when a division was called.[2] The meeting really consisted

[1] In fact Britain's position *vis-à-vis* the dollar area was improving. Figures for the first six months of 1953 (January to June) were to show an increase of $521 million to $2,367 million in the United Kingdom's gold and dollar reserves. However, sterling liabilities for that period came to £4,173 million.
[2] The Government had a majority of 181 to 159 votes on the Second Reading of the Valuation for Rating Bill.

of our moving a series of amendments to insert our draft unaltered and of their being voted down by 14 to 6. Ian says, and I believe him, that he has never heard Nye or me as rude as we were then. I spent a good deal of time pointing out the flatulence of their draft, which was full of such phrases as 'The Labour Party is ready to see the State take action', or 'In the long run municipal ownership is the solution', or 'The desirability of a Capital Gains Tax will be considered at the appropriate time'. Nobody else had come with any amendments of any sort. At one point, Bill Webber spotted that ours were typed out and denounced us as a secret group, who had met beforehand. The idea that one should read through the draft to try to improve it is positively subversive and anyway, as Nye pointed out, the voting seemed to show that there was another group of fourteen present.

Attlee sat dumb throughout. When the division bell rang, I found myself walking along the corridor with him and observed that it was a very bad document. 'The worst we've ever produced,' he replied. I then said there was a good deal of author's vanity about Morgan and he should have got some-body in to write it. 'Yes, it always has to be translated from the Welsh,' said Attlee. 'We should have had Francis Williams[1] to do it for us. But still, it's a good deal better than the last draft but one.' Attlee's an extraordinary man. Though he thought it terrible, he had voted solidly for it throughout and not intervened.

One of the reasons why the trade unionists present were a little cowed, was, no doubt, the announcement in the House that Lincoln Evans, Secretary of the Steelworkers, and the Secretaries of the Patternmakers and the Blast-furnacemen,[2] had accepted jobs on the new denationalized Steel Board.[3] I think everybody on the Executive knew that there would be a blow-up about this and I soon discovered that a great many trade union leaders had been approached for the jobs and that the A.E.U. had turned the offer down. However, it was not till our Tuesday lunch today that John Freeman said he had been staying with George Strauss and, when John had blown up about this, George had said, 'You're quite wrong. It was their duty to take the job.' By this time Beard had been forced to withdraw by his own Executive, led by Ellis Smith, and Strauss observed, 'This will spoil our whole case against the Tories. We objected to their not collaborating on our Board.[4] Now that objection goes if we don't collaborate on theirs.' Though John isn't certain, it

---

[1] Editor of the *Daily Herald* 1936–40, he was Controller of News and Censorship at the Ministry of Information 1941–5 and Adviser on Public Relations to the Prime Minister 1945–7. He became a life peer in 1962, taking the title of Lord Francis-Williams and died in 1970. He helped Attlee with his memoir *A Prime Minister Remembers* (London: Heine-mann, 1961).

[2] Wilfred Beard was General Secretary of the United Patternmakers' Association 1941–66. He was a member of the T.U.C. General Council from 1947 until his death in 1967 and President of the Confederation of Shipbuilding and Engineering Unions 1958–9. The Secretary of the Blastfurnacemen was J. O. O'Hagan.

[3] The Iron and Steel Act received the Royal Assent on May 14th, 1953.

[4] In 1951.

seems pretty sure that at least George Strauss, who has been working with the trade unions throughout the opposition to the Steel Bill, must have suggested that the political side of the Movement would welcome collaboration. Of course, there is a case for it. But if Strauss really thought that, it was necessary to say so for months and to prepare the Movement for it, instead of making speeches denouncing the Board as a fiction and a phoney.

This is another instance of the astonishing remoteness of the leadership from the rank and file, in this case even the rank and file in the House of Commons. They just think certain things should be done, which profoundly shock the rest of us, but they think it privately and don't trouble to educate the Movement to their point of view. Of course, it was known for years that Lincoln Evans was anti-Socialist but the terrible row when *Tribune* protested against his knighthood and the General Council protested on his behalf to the National Executive[1] looks a bit silly in the light of these events. Much more serious than his defection was the Tory success in getting two members of the General Council to join the Board part-time and thereby getting T.U.C. blessing. Beard having retired, Andrew Naesmith[2] has taken his job, but this is not very significant, since the old boy is due to resign his secretaryship of his union this year.

Wednesday, May 27th

Everything has been entirely eclipsed by the Coronation, which is gradually gathering strength. On our way back from Radnage, Phil [Zec] and I motored down the Mall at midnight. It has the only really beautiful decorations in London. Everything else seems to me tawdry and a bit cheap. A rather nice American who dined with me last night told me the smallest Italian town could do better and that's a fact. Most businesses aren't prepared to spend the money.

But today's banquet[3] for the Queen in Westminster Hall really was quite an affair. The top table ran along the platform where Charles I was tried,[4] and behind it were magnificent banks of flowers. We also had the trumpeters

[1] See above, p. 196. This time Sir Lincoln Evans was attacked in *Tribune* and the *Daily Worker* for accepting appointment to the Steel Board at an annual salary of £5,000; he replied on May 29th, pointing out that both the T.U.C. and the Labour Party had agreed to the principle of trade union representation on the Board. On June 24th, after some three hours of acrimonious discussion, the T.U.C. accepted by 20 votes to 6 a resolution rejecting as unfounded the assertion that for responsible trade unions to serve on the Board was incompatible with T.U.C. policy.

[2] Andrew Naesmith (1888–1961) was a Director of the Bank of England 1949–57 and a part-time member of the Iron and Steel Board 1953–60. He was knighted in 1953. He was a Vice-President of the British Cotton-Growing Association until his death in 1961.

[3] The Commonwealth Parliamentary Association gave a lunch in Westminster Hall, in honour of the Queen, whose father had attended a similar banquet sixteen years earlier. Sir Winston proposed a toast, before 750 representatives from fifty-five Commonwealth Parliaments.

[4] In January 1649, King Charles I was tried in Westminster Hall, condemned to death, and executed in front of Whitehall.

playing fanfares but this was offset to some extent when the high table entered in single file along the platform and stood there, in a delightfully democratic and discomfited queue, waiting for the Queen. I was right down by the doors at the west end, where I had been tactfully put at a press table with *The Times*, the *Observer* and the B.B.C., but also with a Tory rebel, Air Commodore Harvey, who told me a great deal about the 1922 Committee.[1] It's really extremely remarkable that, by keeping their meeting an informal back-benchers' meeting, the Tories avoid charges of a split when they have a blow-up.

The food was cold and not very good—rather fat New Zealand lamb cutlets and Empire wines. The speeches were commendably brief and I've never heard Churchill speak better. Despite the solemnity of the occasion, he made a light-hearted parliamentary oration, starting with a reference to Oliver Cromwell. At one point he referred to the Americans and said that we had to be very careful these days when we talked about the American Constitution,[2] and then added, 'I will therefore content myself with the observation that no constitution was written in better English.' Everybody was convulsed with laughter and, though it's sheer imagination, one could have thought one heard the Queen laughing through the microphone. Attlee, I am told, was first appalled and then delighted by this very chivalrous support in the middle of a speech which was supposed to be thanking the Queen.

Afterwards the Queen came down past us and stood just beside us while we sang 'God Save The Queen'. She had togged herself up in a singularly sober outfit and looked, close to, a rather dull, ordinary girl. Then Churchill strolled down and three or four of us shook him by the hand and congratulated him on his speech, whereupon, as usual, he nearly burst into tears with joy. Then came David Eccles, Minister of Works, in charge of the show, whose bookmaker's pants had shocked everybody. He told me that the Queen enormously enjoyed the Coronation rehearsals, which means she will probably be very good at being crowned. This really was a very great occasion, with representatives of fifty Parliaments and the whole top table consisting of Speakers and Prime Ministers. It must be the first occasion on which every member of the Cabinet except the Prime Minister was thrown off the top table.

[1] Conservative M.P. for Harrow East 1950–8, Ian Harvey was Secretary of the 1922 Committee 1955–7 and Joint Parliamentary Secretary at the Foreign Office 1957–8. An account of the circumstances of his resignation appears in *To Fall Like Lucifer* (London: Sidgwick & Jackson, 1971).

[2] Sixty-four Senators had joined in sponsoring a constitutional Amendment and in April it was debated in Committee. The Amendment sought to invalidate any treaty infringing American constitutional rights, to forbid control by any international body of matters essentially within American domestic jurisdiction and to require legislation to give effect to any treaty as domestic law. The U.S. Administration vigorously opposed this proposal, which was not brought to a vote but none the less remained a matter of controversy throughout the year.

Thursday, June 4th

Last Thursday I took Pen Balogh to *The Apple Cart*.[1] Strictly, she should have taken me, since this was a result of a bet we had at Loweswater last Easter. I had bet Pen a free cinema ticket that I would get Sir Andrew Cohen to climb more than 1,500 feet and she had bet me a theatre ticket that I wouldn't get him above 2,000.[2] Actually he hit 1,750, so we went to *The Apple Cart*.

I had read in the morning papers that all the theatres had been emptied because the public found the Coronation streets more interesting, but the Haymarket was crammed full with a very smart audience and we only happened to pick up stalls which had been returned at the moment we got to the box office. Noël Coward[3] played the King. The critics had been very hard on him, on the ground, I presumed, that by definition Noël Coward can't play King Magnus. Actually I thought he was superb, whereas Margaret Leighton[4] couldn't manage the part of Orintha. After all, it is a bit difficult to act a charade in which G.B.S.[5] was guying Mrs Patrick Campbell,[6] and the whole incident is extremely silly. The rest of the play was wonderfully topical, especially the last act, where the U.S.A. offers to return to the Empire and the King at once recognizes this as a dastardly American conspiracy to turn Britain into the forty-ninth State.

On Monday morning I worked at the *Statesman* and then had to walk the whole way back along the Strand and through St James's Park, because the traffic was held up by the crowds. Already there were plenty of people lying about on the pavement and Coronation fever was beginning to mount, despite sharp showers which had set in. I caught the 5.40 train to High Wycombe, leaving the house ready for Gilbert, who had taken my Coronation tickets for himself and his girlfriend, Lucy Rothenstein.[7] I stayed the night

---

[1] *The Apple Cart* was described by G. B. Shaw as 'A Political Extravaganza'. Its plot seems calculated to appeal to Crossman. An English king, Robert, refuses to conform to the constitutional convention of being ruled by ministerial advice. A political crisis follows, in which both monarch and civil servants triumph at the expense of Ministers, as the more permanent nature of their office ensures that both are 'more experienced in the problems with which government has to deal'.

[2] See above, pp. 215 ff.

[3] A successful playwright, composer, director, actor, singer and dancer, Noël Coward was also an occasional novelist, short-story writer, autobiographer and a writer of light verse. He was knighted in 1969. He died in 1973.

[4] An actress, who made her professional stage début in 1938 at the Birmingham Repertory Theatre. She played a wide variety of roles, from Shakespeare to light comedy. She died in 1976.

[5] George Bernard Shaw (1856–1950), the Fabian, critic, playwright, novelist and essayist. He achieved greatest fame as a dramatist, and was awarded the Nobel Prize for Literature in 1925.

[6] Mrs Patrick Campbell (née Beatrice Stella Tanner) (1865–1940) was one of the best-known actresses of her time. She worked extensively with G. B. Shaw, who created the role of Eliza Doolittle in *Pygmalion* for her.

[7] Daughter of Sir John Rothenstein, Director of the Tate Gallery 1938–64, and his wife, Elizabeth.

with Venice and Christopher[1] and we woke up on Tuesday to rainstorms and wonderful grey weather. I must admit I felt it was about what the people who were lying on the pavement deserved for being so silly. In 1937, when Zita and I went to Hyde Park Corner for the Coronation, we stood about all night to see what it was like, but in fact we could perfectly well have walked in at midday. Apparently it was exactly the same this year.

Anyway, at Stokenchurch it was blowing grey rain when Venice and Christopher went down to High Wycombe to take part in the competition for dressed-up cars in the procession. They dropped me off at Town End Farm, where I spent a very pleasant morning watching the television by myself, with a lovely lunch provided by Mrs D., whom I found in her own house with twelve people round the television set. In between live the Rosses,[2] with another television set. So Radnage could view all right.

There is no doubt about the immense technical skill of the television performance. I had expected to read a book but in fact I sat looking at the whole service in the Abbey, though I got a bit tired of the procession later on. Comparing notes with those M.P.s who chose to go into the Abbey or to sit outside on the stands by the House of Commons, one finds that everyone is certain they had the best of it, since, curiously enough, everybody felt it was a wonderful show, wherever they were and whatever they were doing. But I don't think that there can be any doubt that those who stayed at home viewing saw more, though, of course, they lost the colour and the sense of the crowds. My own feeling is that the ceremony was completely out of gear with modern democracy but this is apparently shared by a minimal number of people, since those who are against it are against it in principle and those who are for it are completely uncritical.

After lunch I strolled up to the Pavilion, on Mrs D.'s advice, where Radnage Coronation celebrations were taking place in a howling gale, but without rain. A cricket match was going on between men most of whom were dressed as women and women most of whom were dressed as men. There were also hundreds of bottles of beer waiting to be drunk and everybody was getting a free tea, which I also shared, with unlimited ham sandwiches, ginger pop, cakes, etc., all being served by a most solicitous committee. I took part in the third sitting and there were two more to come. On the way up to the Pavilion I passed Mr Bennell,[3] whom I often see at the pub, and asked him if he had been viewing the Coronation. 'It's something I don't take part in in any way,' he said. But he was going up to the tea all right. I asked the Mrs D. family what they had seen on the television and as far as I could tell, they had seen nothing at all. But they had all thought it wonderful. At High Wycombe, Venice and Christopher told me that despite the rain they had

---

[1] At Cherry Cottage.
[2] Mr and Mrs James Watt Ross. Mr Ross was the joint owner and Joint Managing Director of Tarpen Ltd, manufacturers of hedge clippers and similar machinery.
[3] George Bennell, a local character.

had a procession with over eighty floats and decorated cars, with thousands of people watching.

I walked back from the Pavilion to Stokenchurch through two heavy squalls and got soaked in the corn, which in this lovely lush June is now knee-high. After Venice and Christopher had given me supper, they went off to the Coronation Ball at High Wycombe and I took the train to London. There was a delay of forty minutes on the Tube at Marylebone and when we reached Piccadilly I decided to walk the rest of the way home, down Regent Street, across the Mall and the Park and through St James's Park station. To my surprise, the crowds at Piccadilly Circus were quite thin. There were quite a number standing on the Duke of York Steps, but the Mall was just comfortably full of people walking quietly about and the Park was empty.

As I went along I could see the Coronation fireworks going up into the sky above the buildings on the South Bank (£14,000 worth were let off in an hour). I could only see the rockets as they began to explode and then float downwards. They looked very nice, particularly from Victoria Street, where you cross into Strutton Ground. What struck me was that everybody was very peaceful and orderly, particularly in Birdcage Walk, where they were streaming away from Buckingham Palace to the fireworks. I had only been home two minutes when Mia and John came in. They had been to a cinema, since they are anti-Coronation. But we stood outside on the roof garden and watched some more fireworks before we all sat down to sandwiches and hot chocolate, after which we slept soundly. That was my Coronation and a very nice one too.

On Wednesday I went off to a farewell lunch with David Linebaugh, who told me about his dismissal from the State Department. In April he had received a letter saying he had been dismissed with thirty days' notice and was to return to America immediately – this after eight years' service, in which he had been transferred from temporary to permanent staff. He told me that the European Division of the State Department appealed on his behalf and the result was that he was given two months' notice instead of one. Eighteen other people in the Embassy here have been dismissed. David thinks it is entirely owing to the cut in the appropriation going to politics but I have my doubts. He agreed rather wryly that now he didn't feel that the *Statesman* was quite as biased in its handling of American affairs as he used to do.

This morning I went to the *Statesman* to try to plan how the paper should handle the policy statement when it comes out on the 17th. I talked it over with John and then we got Kingsley to ask us to lunch at his club. We hope now that he has thought of it all himself! John says Kingsley is getting more and more difficult. Fortunately I am not in the office enough to know.

Thursday, June 11th

I had hoped to spend the weekend at Radnage but Phil's mother had a heart attack so I decided to impose myself on Tommy Balogh, with whom I was anyway to spend Friday night, as I was speaking to the Oxford Labour Club. Gilbert met me at the station and we had rather a sedate sherry party, which happened to be in my old rooms in New College, and then a very sedate dinner at the Union. The young men are extremely nice but they seem to expect other people to do the sparking.

I found that Tommy and Pen were due to motor to Cambridge early on Saturday. Obstinately, they took me with them, without warning anybody in Cambridge except Richard Kahn, who was told to put me up. As Richard pointed out to me directly I met him (he is a rather wily Apostle), this was an attempt by Tommy to show that I was really his protégé in Cambridge. These economists live in a world of fascinating personal relations.

Tommy and I went out to Harry Walston's[1] mansion at Newton for lunch, which was embarrassing, since we arrived half an hour late and uninvited. Walston is the son of Waldstein, who married an American millionairess and built what must be one of the last country houses, in 1907, in pseudo-Jacobean.[2] Walston's wife, an American, is the heroine of Graham Greene's *The End of the Affair*. No one dares to ask Walston what he feels about this novel, which is all the more embarrassing since Mrs Walston talks all the time about Graham Greene. During the afternoon, while the others played croquet, she rather ostentatiously immersed herself in reading a translation of St Thomas Aquinas,[3] which is being produced by her house guest, a Dominican, Father Gilby. Looking up, she said to me, 'Strange how "the heart of the matter" has become a cliché since Graham's novel.' I said it was a cliché long before – and then I knew she didn't like me.

On Sunday we did a lovely nine-mile walk over the rolling Roman road in grey weather, with a magnificent view, and then I came back to London to give Elsa[4] dinner, since she was staying with me before leaving for her bus tour of Germany. I took her for a long walk round the illuminations, which are still crowded. You can walk fairly easily – indeed, more easily than usual, because you walk in the road and stop the cars, which is fun.

[1] Henry Walston started his career as a Research Fellow in Bacteriology at Harvard in 1934–5. He was Director of Agriculture in the British Zone of Germany in 1946 and Agricultural Adviser to the Foreign Office for Germany in 1947, and in 1948 became a counsellor to the Duchy of Lancaster, a position he held until 1954. He unsuccessfully contested several rural parliamentary seats, first as a Liberal and then as a Labour candidate, before being made a life peer in 1961. He was Parliamentary Under-Secretary of State at the Foreign Office 1964–7 and at the Board of Trade 1967, and was Chairman of the Institute of Race Relations 1968–71 and a member of the European Parliament 1975–7. His occupation as a farmer is reflected in his numerous writings, which are mostly connected with farming and politics, most recently, *Dealing with Hunger* (London: Bodley Head, 1976). He married Catherine Crompton in 1935; she died in 1976.

[2] The original house at Newton was Victorian. It was enlarged in 1908–9 and all that remains visible is the modern section, in the Georgian style.

[3] The sixty volumes of the *Summa Theologica* of St Thomas Aquinas (published in the United States by McGraw-Hill and in Britain by Blackfriars Press and Eyre & Spottiswoode) were edited by P. K. Neagher and Thomas Gilby, who himself translated vols 1, 5, 8, 16, 18, 28, 32–7, 43–4, and 59.

[4] Crossman's sister.

At the *New Statesman* on Monday most of the conversation was about what Malik[1] [might have] said to Churchill last week when he called on him. I had suggested in the *Sunday Pic* that Churchill was willing to have Anglo-Russian conversations if Eisenhower got difficult. Now came the rumour that Churchill had asked Malenkov[2] to London after Bermuda[3] and that Malik had accepted. This was Ritchie Calder's[4] version. I checked it in the afternoon with Bob Boothby, now Sir Robert,[5] who didn't know, but merely told me the Conservative gossip. 'The old boy', he said, 'is a rogue elephant. He hasn't called a Cabinet for a week and he certainly hasn't told the Cabinet what Malik told him and he probably hasn't told the Foreign Office.' This is personal diplomacy and anything may happen.

On Tuesday afternoon, at the Egyptian Embassy, I met Frank Roberts.[6] On the Russian subject, he said, 'If you throw several rocks into a pool, it takes a long time for the ripples to reach the edge. By the time these ripples reach the edge, Churchill will be dead and we shall have to carry the responsibility.' I must say that, on this point, I wholly sympathize with

---

[1] Jakov Alexandrovich Malik. A member of the U.S.S.R. Foreign Service, he was Ambassador to Japan 1943–5, U.S.S.R. Deputy Foreign Minister 1946–53, and latterly U.S.S.R. Representative to the U.N. (1968–76). He became Ambassador to the U.K. in 1953 and served until 1960, when he again became Deputy Foreign Minister. He died in 1980.

[2] Georgi Maksimilianovich Malenkov rose through the Russian party apparatus, to become Deputy Chairman of the Soviet Council of Ministers briefly in 1946. On Stalin's death he became Chairman but was demoted again to Deputy in February 1955. In July 1957 he was removed from the Praesidium and appointed chief of a power station (Ust-Kamenogorsk) in East Kazakhstan, where he served until his retirement in 1973.

[3] In the House of Commons on May 21st the Prime Minister announced a meeting between himself, President Eisenhower and the French Prime Minister, to discuss common problems. It would take place at Bermuda, a British colony and American base, some time after June 15th, for by then Sir Winston would have the views of Commonwealth Prime Ministers, conferring after the Coronation. Mr Attlee asked whether the Prime Minister contemplated subsequent and similar talks with Russian leaders. Sir Winston replied that it was his main hope that the Bermuda discussions might be such a definite step forward.

[4] (Peter) Ritchie Calder, author and journalist, worked for the *Dundee Courier* 1922, D. C. Thomson Press 1924–5, the *Daily News* 1926–30, the *Daily Chronicle* 1930, the *Daily Herald* 1930–41 and, as Science Editor of the *News Chronicle* 1945–56. He worked in the Foreign Office 1941–5 and returned to journalism after the war as a member of the editorial staff of the *New Statesman* 1945–58. He was Montague Burton Professor of International Relations at the University of Edinburgh 1961–7, Chairman of the Metrication Board 1969–72 and a Senior Fellow at the Center for the Study of Democratic Institutions at Santa Barbara, California, 1972–5. He has been Visiting Professor at Heriot-Watt University since 1973. In 1966 he became a life peer, taking the title of Lord Ritchie-Calder. He has published numerous books and articles on scientific and international affairs.

[5] In the Coronation Honours list, published on June 1st.

[6] Frank Roberts was British Minister to Moscow 1945–7, Principal Private Secretary to the Secretary of State for Foreign Affairs 1947–9, Deputy High Commissioner in India 1949–51 and Deputy Under-Secretary of State at the Foreign Office 1951–4. He was Ambassador to Yugoslavia 1954–7, U.K. Permanent Representative of the North Atlantic Council 1957–60, Ambassador to the U.S.S.R. 1960–2 and to the Federal Republic of Germany 1963–8. He has been President of the British Atlantic Committee since 1968 and of the European Atlantic Group since 1973 and Vice-President of the Atlantic Treaty Association since 1973. He was knighted in 1953.

Churchill. It must be enormous fun to do something for a change and watch
the Foreign Office speechless with objection.

I also went to the Speaker's annual tea party, as dreary as usual, and made
even more trying by the Labour wives – Peggy Jay, Mrs Callaghan, etc. – all
talking about their lovely young Queen. They make me more republican than
I am and Peggy finally said, 'I can't stand seeing you again during this happy
summer. We must meet in the autumn.' However, an hour later there she
was at the Egyptian cocktail party and repentantly asked me to dinner.
Fortunately I refused and her good resolutions were thereby preserved.

*Since 1948 the Christian Democrats had been the governing party in Italy but
from late 1951 parties of the extreme Left and extreme Right had been gaining
electoral support. Elections for the Chamber of Deputies were due to take place
in 1953 and for the Senate in 1954; in preparation the Christian Democrats had
formed an electoral alliance with the three lay Democratic parties: Social
Democratic, Liberal and Republican.*

*The Government also sponsored a new electoral law for elections to the
Chamber of Deputies. It took the form of a compromise between the majority
system and the proportional system (the latter continuing to apply to Senate
elections), awarding additional seats to that party or alliance obtaining more
than half the total votes. This bonus would increase such a successful party's
representation to two-thirds of the entire Lower House and was generally
judged to be designed to favour the Christian Democrats. Debate on the
proposed law was bitter; in the Senate so much so that the House was dissolved. The law was finally passed and on June 7th elections were held for both
Houses.*

*During the campaign, Pietro Nenni, leader of the Italian Socialist Party,
outlined a 'vague but appealing' Socialist Alternative and, with the understanding
of Togliatti, leader of the Italian Communists, carefully distanced himself from
that Party, indicating that the P.S.I. would contemplate a coalition Government
with the Christian Democrats. Nenni's strategy was assisted by Sir Winston
Churchill's speech on May 11th, which provided the Italian left-wing with
useful material for their attacks on the Christian Democrats' cold war attitudes
to the Communists.*

*In the election the Christian Democrats polled 8·5 per cent fewer votes than
in 1948 and their allies suffered severe losses. Their combined total of 49·85 per
cent just disqualified the alliance from obtaining the bonus of seats. The Communists and Nenni's Socialists increased their votes, which taken together came
to 35·4 per cent of the total (compared with 31 per cent in 1948). The extreme
right-wing parties increased their vote by nearly 8 per cent. In the Senate the
Christian Democrats obtained just over half the total votes, 50·2 per cent.*

*With a majority of only sixteen seats over the combined Opposition parties,
the Centre alliance was unable to form an exclusive Christian Democrat
Government. In late August Parliament finally accepted a Ministry led by a*

Prime Minister of that party, including two 'non-party experts'. This was widely believed to be only a temporary arrangement.

On Wednesday I had to dinner sweet Senator Hamon[1] of the M.R.P., full of excitement about the Italian elections. They have also stirred Aneurin, who was out there at Whitsuntide and has persuaded himself that it was he who made Nenni[2] run independently from the Communists. It's an interesting piece of self-analysis to observe how glad we are at the Nenni victory and how carefully we didn't sign the Nenni telegram.[3] The fact is that the loosening-up of the political situation is having an extraordinary effect on the emotions of Socialists. The death of Stalin, I suppose, has given us an excuse for thinking better, or hoping better, of Russia. Of course we all intellectually hold our breath but as persons we are different. The thawing-out of the cold war thaws us out too and we get back to more summery fashions of feeling.

From June 12th to 15th Crossman was in Italy, 'the first time the Statesman *will have paid, and not the* Sunday Pic'. *He saw, among others, Fanfani, Gronchi, Nenni and Togliatti (leaving his spectacles in Nenni's office and recovering them in Togliatti's villa); his reports may be found in the* New Statesman and Nation *of June 20th and 27th, 1953.*

Thursday, June 18th
I flew home from Italy on Tuesday morning, got to bed by eight o'clock, slept till ten and spent the remainder of the morning writing my first article on the Italian elections. After the *New Statesman* lunch, I went home and finished the article before going into the House, where the Finance Bill Committee Stage was drooling on. I soon met Nye and gave him greetings

[1] Leo Hamon, Senator for the Seine in the Fourth Republic in France from 1946 until 1958, representing initially the M.R.P. (Mouvement Républicain Populaire) and then the I.O.M. (Indépendants d'Outre Mer). He had a reputation for being both 'intransigent and isolated' within his own Party. He is also a writer of some note on the French political scene. In 1954 he left the M.R.P. to join the Partie de la Jeune République. He was Professor of Law at Dijon (1959), Orléans (1966) and Paris (1968).

[2] Pietro Nenni, the Italian journalist and Socialist politician. Imprisoned (with Mussolini) in 1911 for participating in riots against the Italo-Turkish war, he joined the Italian Socialists in 1920 and became editor of *Avanti*. Nenni was soon forced into exile in France by Mussolini. He made great efforts after the overthrow of Fascism to reorganize the P.S.I., keeping it divorced from the P.C.I. Secretary-General of the P.S.I. 1944–63, after serving in Parri's and De Gasperi's Cabinets in 1945–6, he became Minister of Foreign Affairs 1946–7, a post he held again in 1968–9. He was Deputy Prime Minister 1963–8.

[3] Signed by thirty-eight Labour Members (later known as the 'Nenni-goats') and sent to Signor Nenni at the time of the Italian General Election in April 1948. Signor Nenni, the leader of the Italian Socialist Party, had brought the Party into alliance with the Communists, causing a break with Signor Saragat, who had formed the breakaway Socialist Workers' Party in January 1947. The N.E.C. not only sympathized with Signor Saragat, but had only recently condemned a Communist coup in Czechoslovakia. The signatories were reproved and twenty-one of them gave assurances that they had not 'acted persistently as a group'.

from Dino Gentili,[1] Nenni and so on and found him enormously interested and helpful. He has a wonderful instinct for Italian politics which are the sort of romantic, personal politics he completely understands.

Immediately Nye warmed up and began outlining what Nenni must do to establish his position. He must not concentrate on foreign affairs. He must have a concrete social and economic programme. He must make links with the Centre. Whereas Togliatti[2] wanted the Socialists to be a funnel through which workers were brought into Communism, Nenni must funnel them out of the Communist Party and the way to do so is to have the concrete social programme which the Communists can't and won't have. Nye was also very emphatic that I should not report all these unofficial talks to Morgan Phillips if we really wanted to help Nenni. Obviously Nye wants to do it himself and I think he probably can.

On Wednesday morning the papers were full of the Labour Party policy.[3] It's too early yet to judge but these first press reports and leading articles were not too bad and this morning, after I had taken a party of Coventry school-children up Big Ben for a wonderful view of London, we had a Bevanite meeting at midday. I was very curious to know what Nye's line would be and once again it surprised me. After one or two of the members had expressed a sense of disappointment and let-down at the appalling document, Nye said, 'But we must claim to have captured it. If we admit we've been defeated, it will be hopeless.'

Of course, Nye has always been in two minds whether we should resign in protest against an outrageous document or stay on the Executive and claim a triumph. There are no half measures with Nye and this morning it was a triumph, which was a little hard on John Freeman, who had described it as a defeat in an article which was fully in accord with Nye's views in the last three months.[4]

However, I think that in this calculation Nye is probably much more right than wrong. Certainly it makes the speeches of Bevanite members of the Executive a good deal easier to give. The line must be to state categorically that the Party has decided to nationalize chemicals and to take the blurred passages and make them precise in our direction. Meanwhile, Group members who are not on the Executive can say, 'Good, but not good

[1] An Italian Communist and an old friend of Crossman's. Exiled at the time of Mussolini, he returned after the war to found Cogis, an export company with extensive East European and, later, Chinese business.

[2] Having joined the P.C.I. on its formation in 1921, Palmiro Togliatti edited *Il Comunista* in Rome from 1923 until his exile by Mussolini. He took over the P.C.I. secretaryship from Gramsci in 1926, a post which he held until his death in 1964. Exiled in Moscow, he became secretary of the Comintern in 1935 as well as being deeply engaged in organizing the International Brigade during the Spanish Civil War. He returned to Italy in February 1944, bringing the P.C.I. to the position of the second largest political party in Italy. His approach was constitutional rather than revolutionary and his instincts were to toe the Moscow line.

[3] The policy document *Challenge to Britain*.

[4] See '*Challenge to Britain*', *New Statesman and Nation*, June 20th, 1953.

enough', and go on to list the further measures required and so encourage the constituencies to move the amendments at the Conference.

It had seemed that, in May, there might be some improvement in conditions in the Soviet zone of Germany. In that month the Soviet Control Commission was dissolved and a High Commissioner appointed. Open persecution of the Church was abandoned; rations of fats, sugar and meat, withdrawn on May 1st from all but workers and children under fifteen, were restored. On June 11th it was decreed that some businesses and farms would be returned to their former owners, confiscated ration cards given back to certain categories of people, property restored to refugees, cuts in social insurance benefits dropped and certain non-essential foods sold at their earlier prices. The Ministry of Justice would review all arrests, criminal cases and sentences and there was to be a moratorium on tax arrears.

But the flow of refugees to West Berlin and the Federal Republic continued to increase. Between January and May 184,796 sought asylum. On May 28th workers had been ordered to produce more for the same wage. A strike began on June 16th and a demonstration the following day became a rising. The Berliners fought Soviet tanks and they were joined by the Vopos, or 'people's police'. Communist buildings were burnt and the Red Flag torn from the top of the Brandenburg Gate. In the afternoon of June 17th the Soviet Commander proclaimed a state of emergency and, after summary trials, demonstrators were hanged or shot. Officially 21 civilians and 4 Vopos were killed, and 187 civilians and 191 Vopos wounded. The true figures were alleged to be 569 dead and 1,071 wounded. The Communists blamed the rising on 'Fascist agents and Western provocateurs'.

In Korea, meanwhile, on June 8th an agreement was signed at Panmunjom on the fate of nearly 50,000 prisoners of war who were unwilling to be repatriated to their Communist homelands. It seemed that the only outstanding question concerned the military demarcation on which the armistice would be based. President Rhee now declared that the armistice terms were unacceptable to South Korea and that his country would continue to fight for reconquest of the whole of Korea.

As a sign of protest, President Rhee ordered the release of 25,000 North Korean prisoners of war. On June 19th it was announced that, the day before, these 25,000 had escaped, with the connivance of their South Korean guards, an incident which the Chinese Communists could allege was caused by 'imperialist treachery'.

Of course, the big news this morning was from Korea and Berlin. In East Berlin a riot, which seemed to have arisen spontaneously among building operatives, mercilessly exploited, was obviously then whipped up by people coming in from the Western Zone, where the Russian controls had just been relaxed. This riot may have very serious consequences. If easing off the cold war leads to this sort of thing, can Malenkov afford to do so? Will he have to turn the screw once again?

The other news is from Korea, where Syngman Rhee[1] has successfully released 45,000 North Korean prisoners, just after we have signed an agreement that they should be handed over to the Six-Power commission.[2] Woodrow Wyatt has put down a Private Notice Question and I suggested we should press for an adjournment debate. Nye was much against this and seemed chiefly upset that the Communists had launched an offensive. He was so outraged that he obviously didn't feel inclined to make much of a stink about Syngman Rhee.

For some time Nye has been brooding on the Chinese Communists and I think he is soon going to say that we must demand guarantees of them and not back them as though they were angels. This is probably a wise precaution. All the same, I think Nye will realize by tomorrow that the Syngman Rhee matter is really serious and may undermine the armistice altogether. Typically enough, Nye suddenly became a realistic politician. 'We have to consider the Korean troops. The United Nations will be defeated if they refuse to fight, as they might if we take over the camps or depose Syngman Rhee.' This is all quite sensible but it is not in line with Nye's usual tendencies, nor with the feelings of the Group.

Monday, June 22nd

On Friday, after I had done the *Sunday Pic*, Harold Wilson came to tea and we drove down to Chelmsford, in rain as usual, to do a *Tribune* brains trust. Ever since the ban,[3] members of the Executive had tactfully not been on brains trusts but we felt that a long enough time had now elapsed, so Harold, Tom [Driberg] and I went down, with Hugh Delargy as chairman and Bernard Floud,[4] the candidate, to make up the team. The policy statement was much in our mind on the way down and we discussed at length how we should deal with it. Actually, out of 150 questions, not one referred to it, which only shows how long it takes for something to get into the public mind.

Harold Wilson motored me back in nice time to catch the 11.50 from Euston to Kilmarnock, where I spent the weekend as the guest of Emrys

[1] Syngman Rhee (1875–1965), a Korean who became President of a Provisional Government in 1919 (Korea had been annexed by Japan in 1910). In 1948 a Government was formed under him which claimed to represent all Korea but Rhee proved unacceptable to the Communists. This was one of the facts leading to the outbreak of the Korean war.
[2] In fact, 25,000 prisoners. It was a Five-Power commission.
[3] See above, pp. 162 ff.
[4] Bernard Floud, who died in 1967, served in the Second World War as a civil servant, latterly in the Ministry of Information. He worked in the Board of Trade from 1945 to 1951, becoming an Assistant Secretary. From 1951 onwards he was occupied as a farmer, serving from 1952 to 1955 as a Labour councillor on Ongar R.D.C. An Executive Director of Granada T.V., he stood unsuccessfully for Parliament in 1955 and 1959, but became Labour M.P. for Acton in 1964.

Hughes and Mattie. Emrys was married to Keir Hardie's[1] daughter and he lives in Keir Hardie's house at Cumnock, where the annual Keir Hardie celebration is quite a civic event, with speeches from a stone platform erected on the main playing fields. However, before this I had demanded to do a day school, something almost unknown, apparently, in Ayrshire. I was duly taken to Ayr Burghs, where fifty-four people collected to hear me. For sheer stolidity Scottish audiences take a lot of beating.

Afterwards I had tea and a long talk with the two agents and some of the younger boys about the apathy in the Party, which they put down to a sense of security among the miners. Indeed, the apathy there is exactly the same as in England and, wherever you go, you find precisely the same phenomenon. Members are perfectly easy to get but there is no life or vitality. Of course, as I tried to say in my speech, this is partly owing to the Labour Government's success in removing the necessity which drove people into the solidarity of the Labour Movement. If you give people a bourgeois sense of security, the type of working-class Movement we had forty years ago will no longer appeal to them. The younger people don't feel the same significance in the slogans; on the other hand, the older people won't give up the slogans or the organization. All this is true but the whole situation is made vastly worse by the complete absence of leadership in Parliament. For months we have not had an important speech outlining Labour Party policy from Attlee or Morrison and it will be interesting to see if in this respect the policy statement makes any difference.

Jennie Lee arrived by air at Prestwick and after the day school Mattie drove us home. On the way the sun came out for a gleam and we decided to visit Dunure Castle, a wonderful English fortress on the coast. In Dunure town itself lives a Labour Party supporter, Mrs McCrindle, with a gorgeous rock garden facing over the sea. We went in to see her and found her with her aged mother from Arran Island, just across the water. Immediately we entered, the old lady looked at Jennie, who was wearing a beautiful scarf of red, white and blue, and said, 'So you've given in to the Coronation colours.' After which poor Jennie and I were subjected to a left-wing barrage of the most gruelling kind from these formidable ladies.

I don't mind this sort of thing but Jennie took it very badly, with the result that it got worse and worse until I took her for a walk around the Castle. It gives me a small malicious pleasure that our great working-class leaders, who always accuse me of being cut off from the working class, should be accused of the same thing in their own Scotland. Jennie was deeply nettled by that afternoon. The trouble is that she is rather snobbish and nose-in-the-air. Of course, puckish Emrys Hughes and Mattie were delighted, since they regard Nye and Jennie as utterly cut off from reality.

[1] James Keir Hardie (1856–1915), Labour M.P. for South West Ham 1892–5 and for Merthyr Tydfil from 1900 until his death in 1915. He was Chairman of the Independent Labour Party from 1892 until his death and was Leader of the Labour Party in the House of Commons 1906–8.

I was rather scared about the demonstration, since I don't like open-air speaking or competing with a formidable person like Jennie Lee. However, at two o'clock we went to the centre of the town in order to process behind the silver band, the banner of Keir Hardie, etc., in a nice, warm, light rain. The procession picked up quite a number of people and I suppose for the demo itself we had 3,000 or 4,000. I talked a little about the apathy in the Party and then got on to Syngman Rhee, who was the news that morning. I got a great deal of response. Jennie concentrated on the price of an orange, one of her favourite subjects, and there is little doubt that, even in Cumnock, people are more interested in Syngman Rhee than in oranges, despite all Jennie's wonderful powers of oratory. Afterwards at tea Jennie said, as usual, 'Dick did extremely well, in spite of trying to have a serious argument in an open-air speech.' She says that whenever we have a big public meeting. My own hunch is that in the modern world she would do well to try a serious argument. I was relieved when Emrys told me privately that he had no doubt that, though they liked Jennie, they got much more out of what I said.

John Freeman told me a similar story this morning. He spent the weekend at Abingdon, where Ted Castle is fighting a by-election.[1] John spoke in five small places and canvassed in Didcot. Ted apparently hopes to turn a 5,000 minority into a victory. John thinks Ted will do well to prevent the majority being increased, since the apathy is terrible. After a Sunday evening meeting, in which John and Michael Foot had both spoken, John heard in the dark outside somebody saying, 'Michael Foot hits them but it was the ginger-headed one who made you think.'

Wednesday, June 24th

I have had some fairly violent spasms of boredom in the House but the last fortnight's spasm has been the most violent of all. Apart from Question Time, which has been dominated by Churchill and foreign affairs,[2] there has hardly been a spark of interest in the Chamber. In the country, partly as the result of the Coronation and partly owing to the feeling that political parties don't seem to be in touch with the enormous changes of the outside world, Party activity has reached a new low level. The effect on one personally is extremely unpleasant. We sit about all hours in the Smoking Room in our cliques and coteries, dining for the most part at separate tables, and feel that nothing matters.

Yesterday evening I had Gilbert to dinner with George Wigg and, after I had put him in the Chamber, I met Hugh Dalton and John Freeman. The

[1] Sir Ralph Glyn, Conservative Member for Abingdon, had become a peer in the Coronation Honours and a by-election was accordingly held on June 30th, 1953.

[2] The Foreign Secretary, Mr Eden, had been flown to America for a third operation; Sir Winston Churchill continued to carry his responsibilities until, at the end of June, his doctor ordered a month's rest. Lord Salisbury was appointed Acting Foreign Secretary, while the Minister of State, Mr Butler, represented the Foreign Office in the Commons. The Bermuda Conference, originally postponed because of a Government crisis in France, was now put off indefinitely.

Parliamentary Committee had just been meeting to discuss the method of voting for the election of the Front Bench.[1] Last year Attlee introduced two principles: first, no plumping; and then, in the middle of the election, a second ballot, in order to ensure that the Left didn't get a chance. The Committee had been instructed by the Party to decide what methods should be employed on the next occasion. I gather the meeting was most unpleasant. According to Dalton, only Nye Bevan and Shinwell voted for permitting free elections.

Then came the decision whether to continue with two ballots or merely one, with plumping forbidden. Gaitskell and Callaghan supported the double vote, i.e. the double rigging of the election, but they were just voted down. Even Dalton didn't pretend that the forbidding of plumping was not designed to prevent the Bevanites getting one or two members on. His argument was that groups were disagreeable and that everybody should want to use all their votes.

Of course, this isn't really a very important issue. By getting themselves elected to the Front Bench and permitting only Nye to join them, the right-wing do themselves no good, since when they are there they are ineffective and only confirm the impression that the Labour Party really doesn't want to get back to power. But it was irritating to spend two hours discussing this sort of issue.

Thursday, June 25th

A special meeting of the Parliamentary Party had been called to hear Harold Wilson's report on his Moscow visit.[2] When I went in, I found fifty people there. Harold did his speech extremely well, though it was not new to me, since he had sent me his unofficial record. Actually, of course, Harold had two interviews with Mikoyan[3] and an hour with Molotov[4] and, apart from

[1] See above, pp. 179 ff. and n. and pp. 182 ff. and n.

[2] At this moment of thaw in the cold war, Harold Wilson had been to Moscow to explore the renewal of connections made when he had been President of the Board of Trade.

[3] Active in Georgia during the Russian revolution, Anastas Mikoyan had a career in the C.P.S.U., becoming in 1935 a member of the Politburo. From 1938 until 1946 he was People's Commissar of Foreign Trade, in 1946 Deputy Chairman of the U.S.S.R. Council of Ministers and from 1946 to 1949 Minister of Foreign Trade. Vice-Chairman of the Council of Ministers 1955–64, it was he who led the attack on Stalin at the 1956 Party Congress. He was a Member of the Central Committee 1952–66 and a Member of the Praesidium of the Supreme Soviet from 1965 until his death. For a short period, 1964–5, he served as President.

[4] Originally surnamed Skryabin, Vyacheslav Mikhailovich Molotov (1890–1979) took a leading part in the Russian Revolution. He became a member of the Politburo and then Second Secretary of the Communist Party under Stalin. From 1930 to 1941 he was one of the leading politicians in Russia, supervising the first two Five-Year Plans and taking over the Foreign Office in 1939 in time to negotiate the pact with Germany on the eve of the Second World War. As Foreign Minister until 1949 and again from 1953 to 1956 he was noted as the spokesman of a negative and inflexible policy, for his loyalty to Stalin, and, after the latter's death, to his principles. The wind of change in Communist policy in 1956 led to Molotov's disgrace the following year and his relegation to the post of Ambassador to the Mongolian Republic. In 1960 a limited restoration of favour came with his appointment as Russian Representative to the International Atomic Energy Agency.

that, spent his time in Moscow talking to embassies and Western journalists, who, he told us, had no sources of information. But he did a magnificent job of blowing out his information so that he could tell us everything that was happening in Russia. The technique is to start by saying, 'Of course, I only have 2 per cent of the information necessary to form a judgment but most of the pundits in Washington have only 1 per cent,' and then to go on to give judgments on everything. As a journalist, I wouldn't have the face to do it but Harold did it with the very greatest skill and, as his line was one I agreed with, I was pleased. All his little jokes went down well and Attlee congratulated him on a magnificent inside report. Never shall I be able to give such a good inside report, even with 5 per cent of the information.

Tuesday, June 30th

At the weekend I found Phil Zec in bed with a slipped disc, so I had to do the mowing of the lawn. Meanwhile in came Cassandra and Sydney Jacobson from a day in Abingdon, where they had been listening to Nye Bevan addressing a poorly attended open-air rally. Two reasons for the poor attendance were the perfect weather and the televising of the Test Match.[1] However, to my amazement, Cassandra remarked that he thought that Ted Castle had a good chance. I discovered he had done nothing but talk for a moment to Ted and the Conservative and listen to Nye, who had completely magicked him.

However, on Monday I myself went down for the eve-of-poll meeting with Hugh Gaitskell and James Callaghan. The car, an expensive Triumph, was owned and driven by Hugh Gaitskell's apparently American secretary. When we got there we found there were nine speakers; I had been pushed off into the villages. This was sheer good fortune, since in Abingdon or Wallingford I would have been one of five speakers, whereas I had two nice village meetings all to myself. When I got to the first one at seven o'clock on a perfect evening, I found a chestnut tree with a bench round it, on which four ladies were sitting, with a tiny village clustering round. By 7.25, when Ted arrived, we must have got some seventy or eighty people standing round and listening. Our collection was 25s. 3½d.,[2] a tremendous achievement for a village.

We motored back with Hugh, getting to London at a quarter to one. Conversation was pleasant and not too edgy. At one point they were telling me how wonderful Spithead*[3] was and James Callaghan remarked how

[1] There were five matches between the Australian and English cricket teams; all were televised. This was the first Test series since 1923 in which England won the Ashes on home ground.

[2] £1·26½ new pence.

* When I got back from Italy on June 18th all the talk in the House had been of the Spithead Review. Most of the Members had been down there for the jaunt; the expense of the entertainment for visitors was £40,000, but I didn't feel I missed very much, except free drinks.

[3] At Spithead on June 15th, from the Royal yacht *Surprise*, the Queen had reviewed the Fleet, represented by more than 200 ships and over 300 aircraft of the Fleet Air Arm. The Soviet battleship *Sverdlov* had been among the guests at the ceremony. In the evening, at a signal from the Queen, the Fleet was illuminated.

pleasant it was to spend a day with one's colleagues on holiday. I replied that my idea of a holiday was *not* to see my colleagues and James said, 'But they're such good friends.' I said, 'Well, I've been wondering whether a single one of them would be my friend if I wasn't in politics,' at which Hugh Gaitskell suddenly said, 'Well, you can't avoid having me as a friend, Dick, because I've known you all my life.' I knew that this was a very serious remark and that it meant a tremendous lot. Hugh Gaitskell and his crew have always felt that all the Bevanites are unregenerable except me and that it's only the ghastly mishandling of Attlee or Bevin or somebody else which prevented my being on their side. Of course, it's also true that, if my influence on the *Sunday Pic* and the *New Statesman* were swung over, unpopular though I am, it would make a considerable difference.

I talked this over with John Freeman today on the way back from the office to our Tuesday lunch. He is feeling particularly bitter with Nye, who he thinks has lost interest in the Left. John feels very strongly that the Bevanite movement will fade away this summer unless we have an issue to fight on and with which to rally the constituencies, and he is quite right in saying that, if this fading happens, I shall be one of the sufferers and Ian Mikardo probably the other.

Owing to the Abingdon by-election, we had a very small lunch, with only Nye and Jennie, Harold and Michael, John and myself. We discussed how to get the six names in the minds of constituency delegates and decided to have a series of articles by us in the *Tribune*. I think John Freeman is probably right when he feels that Bevanism, as a movement, is over, though, to be fair, we've had these moods before. But the fact is, we contributed less than we should to constructive criticism of the policy statement and there is some justification for the Gaitskell view that, if Bevanism really were a constructive Left, they would object to it less. However, this won't deter them from doing all they can to remove me from the Executive. If it happens, I shall at least have the advantage of being able to write a good deal more easily.

Thursday, July 2nd

Before lunch yesterday I went into the Smoking Room, where everyone was waiting for the result of the Abingdon by-election.[1] It came through just after one o'clock – Conservative majority up by 1,000. The exact percentages show that the Liberals, who hadn't fought last time, got 7 per cent, thus reducing the Tory vote by 2 per cent and the Labour by 5 per cent. The result is undoubtedly disappointing. Our experts will argue that those Liberals who voted this time would nearly all have voted Labour, but even so it's instructive that a first-rate campaign, which seemed to have roused the villages, should have ended in this way.

[1] The election was won by the Conservative candidate, Airey Neave, with 22,986 votes. Edward Castle (Labour) came second, with 17,126 votes. At the General Election in October 1951 the Conservative majority had been 4,883. It now increased to 5,860. The Liberal candidate, George Allen, obtained 3,060 votes (7·9 per cent of the poll).

Later that afternoon I went down to the Edgbaston by-election.[1] I found Arthur Blenkinsop on the train and we carefully divided up what we should say. This was somewhat unnecessary, since when we got there we found that there were three meetings in various schools, one with seventy, one with forty and one with sixty members of an apathetic audience. Meanwhile, the Tories were having packed-out meetings with lines of cars outside. The Labour candidate was a pleasant, middle-aged councillor with an inaudible voice. Of course, this is a Tory stronghold and Reg Underhill[2] may be right when he says that the Edgbaston result will be better than Abingdon because there will be such a low poll that the Tory majority may be reduced.

Speaking on such occasions is very difficult, since one knows that, under the Butler regime, people feel they are doing quite well and to promise them death round the corner may be a correct prognosis but is not an election winner. The only flicker of interest one could raise was on the peace issue. But even there, only Bevanites can say that they have been urging Churchill to do this and can throw doubts on whether the Tory Party will carry out the policy now that he is indisposed.

I talked to Harold Nash[3] and Reg Underhill. Nash said he thought the leadership was letting the Party down but the fact is, we are in the doldrums and that's that. Blenkinsop and I were quartered at an hotel, where we had dinner after the meeting at 10s. 6d. a head and were charged 38s. 6d. for bed and breakfast.[4] This is how the by-election fund is spent.

Monday, July 6th
Today we had Sir Frank Roberts to lunch at the *New Statesman*. He is extremely pally with us now. He started the discussion on things in Russia and told us one fascinating item. At the fourteen banquets which he had attended when he was in Moscow, there were only two Russians who never spoke to a foreigner — indeed, the table was arranged with these two together, whereas every other Russian was placed between two foreigners. These two men were Beria[5] and Malenkov.

[1] Sir Peter Bennett, Conservative Member for the Edgbaston division of Birmingham, had become a peer in the Coronation Honours and a by-election was held on July 2nd, 1953. The election was won by Miss Edith Pitt, Conservative, with 20,142 votes. The Labour candidate, F. B. Watson, obtained 9,635 votes. The Conservative majority fell, in a low poll, by 2,597.

[2] Reginald Underhill joined the staff of Labour Party Head Office in 1933. After various junior posts, he became Regional Organizer in the West Midlands 1948, Assistant National Agent 1960 and National Agent 1972–9. He was created a life peer in Mr Callaghan's 1979 Resignation Honours list.

[3] A Birmingham Labour Party Secretary in the 1950s.

[4] 52·5 new pence; £1·92 new pence.

[5] Laurenti Beria, the Supervisor of Soviet internal security under Stalin. He joined the Communist Party in 1917 as a revolutionary in Azerbaijan and Georgia and became head of the Security Police (OGPU) in 1924. From 1934 he was a member of the Party's Central Committee, and he went to Moscow in 1938 as head of the Commissariat for Internal Affairs (N.K.V.D.). In February 1941 he became Deputy Prime Minister, and controlled internal security and armaments production. He became a Marshal in 1945 and a member

As far as is known, no Englishman has ever spoken to Malenkov. Chip Bohlen,[1] who is now American Ambassador in Moscow, is one of the very few Westerners who has spoken to Beria. The conversation took place at Potsdam in 1945, when Beria turned up for a day, nobody knows why. The subject was democracy. Bohlen was saying how difficult it was to sell a certain idea to the Americans and added, 'After all, we are a democracy.' 'We are a democracy, too,' said Beria, putting his arm round Bohlen's shoulder, 'but it is my job to see that they think right.'

Roberts added that Beria is immensely popular in Russia[2] because he is known as the man who stopped the great purge of 1938 by himself going to Stalin and telling him it was out of control. This is important to remember now that Beria is head of the N.K.V.D.

Roberts raised the question of how long government by committee[3] could go on and said there wasn't a known instance. I replied that Venice had been run in this way for some hundreds of years and he said yes, but that was an exception and that in Eastern countries, particularly in Russia, they can't get on without a Little Father. Roberts also takes the liberalizing movement seriously and we agreed that the latest news of the New Look in Hungary, Roumania and Bulgaria is in line with developments in Eastern Germany.[4] What is being done in all these countries is what Tito did in Yugoslavia. Indeed, it is the Counter-Reformation, run by the Pope. Roberts was emphatic that it would be quite fatal to seek to exploit Russian weakness in order to overthrow the regime. What we should aim at is to make it easier for the Russians to liberalize.

I then told him Bob Boothby's version of the reason for Churchill's illness, a brain-storm at the end of a Cabinet meeting,[5] when some of his colleagues

---

of the Politburo in 1946. One of four Deputy Prime Ministers on Stalin's death in March 1953, in July he was arrested and in December executed (see p. 255 n.).

[1] Charles Eustace (Chip) Bohlen. A career in the American Diplomatic Service (Prague, 1929; Moscow, 1933; Tokyo, 1940; Moscow, First Secretary 1942; Paris, Minister 1949) led to his appointment as Ambassador to the U.S.S.R. in 1952, to the Philippines 1957–9 and to France 1962–8. He retired in 1969 and died in 1974.

[2] But see, below p. 255.

[3] During Stalin's illness.

[4] On June 30th the recomposition of the Hungarian Politburo had been announced. On July 3rd Mr Imre Nagy, the new President, declared a change of course, with more emphasis on consumer goods than on heavy industrialization, and the enforcement of laws to protect the freedom, individual rights and security of citizens. In Roumania there was acknowledgment that industrialization had been at the expense of agriculture. Western correspondents visiting the World Festival of Youth in Bucharest reported a fair degree of freedom to move about and inquire into conditions. In Bulgaria there was a similar shift in emphasis to consumer goods and agriculture, though drastic amendments to the Penal Code introduced in February were not revoked.

[5] On pp. 218–19 of his book *The Other Half: A Self-Portrait* (London: Murray, 1977), Kenneth Clark gives an account of the dinner party at No. 10 Downing Street, at which the Prime Minister collapsed with a stroke. According to Lord Clark, the account given by Churchill's doctor, Lord Moran, in *Winston Churchill, The Struggle for Survival: 1940–65* (London: Constable, 1966), pp. 408–9, is not quite correct. Lord Clark reports Sir Winston as saying, ' "I want the hand of a friend. They put too much on me. Foreign affairs ... ".' At this point, Lord Clark recalls, 'his voice drifted away'.

had attacked him for saying the Russians had shown restraint in East Berlin.[1] Frank said he was pleased that the Foreign Office statement had given me pleasure – he had obviously written it – but maybe an adjective should have been added to the word 'restraint' in order to quieten the House of Commons. He still seemed to believe that high-level talks were possible and would be prepared for at Washington, where he is going for the Foreign Ministers' conference.[2] On the other hand, he was dubious whether the Russians had any intention of reaching any major agreement or whether, indeed, this was the right time to try to do so.

Tuesday, July 14th

It is eight days since I wrote the diary, so I must recapitulate. After a meeting of the parliamentary education group last Wednesday, I took Alice Bacon into the Smoking Room for a drink, where she looked like a spinster in a brothel. The conversation moved from education to Herbert Morrison. It had been announced that the Transport Workers had decided to nominate him for the treasurership of the Party at the Margate Conference this September.[3] I had written a paragraph for 'Critic's Diary',[4] advising Herbert to refuse and, in our Bevanite corner, we had all assumed that this was a very clever manoeuvre. Herbert would refuse magnanimously and so gain more votes when he stood in the constituency section. However, Alice revealed to me that Herbert had already accepted, against the advice of many of his best friends. Last week, indeed, this new contest had been a major item of domestic news. From Wednesday on, unions were committing themselves this way and that and the pro-Greenwood movement was also gathering weight. Morrison would have had a terrible weekend press if his wife hadn't died on Saturday afternoon.[5]

On the whole Morrison's action is likely to be as helpful to us as Lincoln Evans's accepting a place on the Tory Steel Board.[6] On the other hand, I suspect that Herbert is aware of the temporary unpopularity he will get and of the row there will be in Margate, but he just feels that he must get on to the Executive but avoid the annual risk of being thrown off by the constituencies. It is ironical to think that in 1943, when he stood against Arthur Greenwood, Greenwood was Bevin's selection and Herbert as a politician was defeated by the united trade union vote. Now Herbert is standing, with

[1] After the riots on June 17th. See above, p. 245 and n.
[2] The American Secretary of State and the British and French Foreign Ministers met in Washington from July 10th to 14th.
[3] As an *ex officio* member of the N.E.C., the Party Treasurer need not stand for election.
[4] In the 'London Diary' by 'Critic' in the *New Statesman and Nation* of July 11th, 1953, Crossman wrote: 'to contrive defeat for a well-loved veteran – especially when that defeat will be announced on the second day of the Conference of which he is chairman – would bring no credit on Mr Morrison or his backers.'
[5] Margaret Morrison (née Kent) died on July 11th. (On January 6th, 1955, Morrison married Edith Meadowcroft.)
[6] See above, pp. 235 ff.

the big unions behind him, against Greenwood, the darling of the constituencies. I saw Greenwood in the corridor yesterday. He looks desperately
ill and talks with a terrible twang in his nose. He seemed quite game for the
fight but somebody said to me afterwards, 'He looks just like Ernie when he
was dying,' and it's doubtful whether he will last till the Conference.[1]

The most important event this week, however, has been the news, early on
Friday morning, that Beria has fallen from power in Russia.[2] I chose this
subject for the first of a fortnightly series of Hebrew broadcasts and also
started the *Sunday Pic* article by saying it was a waste of time asking what
would happen next; the thing to do was to decide our own policy without
worrying about things inside Russia. I was very pleased to find, over the
weekend, that this had been a very widespread reaction and, apparently, even
in the Washington Conference of Foreign Secretaries, the view had been that
the West must make a peace initiative.

*The communiqué of July 14th from the 'Little Bermuda' in Washington stated
that the British, French and American Governments had decided, 'in consultation with the German Federal Government', to propose a meeting in the
early autumn of the Foreign Ministers of France, Britain, the U.S.A. and the
U.S.S.R. This would discuss the organization of free elections in Germany and
the establishment of a 'free all-German Government', the first step to a solution
of the German problem. The meeting would also consider the conclusion of the
Austrian Treaty. This agenda was disappointing to those who had hoped that
such a Four-Power meeting would move towards unfreezing the cold war.*

*On July 15th the three Western Powers sent Notes to the Soviet Government
to this effect.*

Inspired by this, I went to the meeting of the parliamentary foreign affairs
group. Then on Tuesday morning we had the full Parliamentary Party
meeting to discuss foreign affairs, in preparation for next week's two-day
debate.[3]

I got there punctually at half-past ten to find Attlee and six others in the
room. We started at twenty to eleven with twenty-two people present and I
suppose by midday we had about fifty. Attlee began with his usual miserable
little statement, not giving any lead at all. When he stopped, no one stood up,
so A. J. Irvine began, quite well, followed by the usual incoherence of
Bellenger.

[1] He died on June 9th, 1954, aged seventy-four.
[2] On July 10th it was announced that Mr Beria had been expelled from the Communist
Party and stripped of his Government posts. He was to be tried for treason, 'organizing an
anti-Soviet conspiracy, terrorist acts and active struggle against the working class and the
revolutionary movement'. With six alleged fellow conspirators, formerly members of the
Ministries of the Interior or of State Security, he was tried in secret between December 18th
and 23rd, found guilty on all counts and shot.
[3] On July 21st and 22nd.

I then made the obvious suggestion, listing the things we should do about Korea, the lifting of the embargo in the event of an armistice, and then I pointed out that Attlee had left out the subject of Indo-China, where we should support the French Socialists in demanding a negotiated settlement. On Germany, I sketched the need for a period of neutralization and ended by saying that the malaise of the Party was due to the sense that the Tories had seized the initiative.

Attlee interrupted me once in the middle, to remind me that he had proposed that we should stop the embargo in the event of an armistice in Korea, and I was too polite to say that no one remembered it and that this was half the trouble. A few minutes later, during my speech, Attlee began a long conversation with one of the officials about a Private Notice Question. So I politely sat down while he concluded it and Austen Albu[1] shouted out, 'Get on, you prima donna.' However, I made Attlee apologize and listen.

Denis Healey made an extraordinary speech, which finally ended in supporting me about neutralization. All the other speeches, except for Reggie Paget's attack on Churchill for appeasing the Russians, were by Bevanites. We were all very quiet and correct and butter wouldn't melt in our mouths, until Will Griffiths, a nice optician and Nye Bevan's former P.P.S., got up. Apparently he had carefully prepared this speech but it sounded wonderfully impromptu. He said he had never spoken on foreign affairs before and he would only like to remind people of the last Party Meeting, the one which preceded Churchill's speech of May 11th. On that occasion, Will said, all the great pundits — Denis Healey, Fred Bellenger, Woodrow Wyatt, Christopher Mayhew — had denounced any idea of appeasing the Russians, opposed the notion of high-level talks and demanded intransigent firmness in defence of democracy. 'I don't want to be offensive to the Leader but, if I understand him aright, he takes the view that his job is to interpret the view of the Party. I must say that I am relieved he didn't interpret the view of the last Party Meeting,' said Mr Griffiths. 'Isn't it high time these pundits were made to realize how wrong they have been?'

I think this speech had quite a considerable effect. The pundits, apart from Healey, were silent. The fact is that the whole policy of the right-wing of the Party is in ruins and we probably achieved a little in inclining Attlee to accept some of our views when he speaks next week. But it's anybody's guess what the little man will say, because the Party has no policy and he can say what he likes. Let's hope that he remains in the middle of the road, as he nearly always does, although the road is moving noticeably further and further to the left as Churchill drags it along.

[1] Works manager of Aladdin Industries, Greenford, from 1930 until 1946, and a Deputy Director of the British Institute of Management from February to November 1948, when he resigned, on election as Labour M.P. for Edmonton. He held office as Minister of State at the Department of Economic Affairs from 1965 to 1967. He was an M.P. until 1974 and has been visiting Research Fellow at the University of Sussex since 1975.

Thursday, July 30th

At the Tuesday Group lunch, Nye began to discuss our strategy at the Conference and indicated that, in his view, none of us should be prepared to speak on behalf of the document. This may well be right but it's a considerable switch from his earlier view that we should bless it. At that time Michael was instructed to headline his *Tribune* article 'Good, But It Could Be Better', whereas the *New Statesman* was much more pungent about it. Now Nye seems to be shifting again to a much more belligerent line.

But there was no sign of this belligerence at the National Executive yesterday, where he couldn't have been more sweet and accommodating, the accommodation including disagreeing with me on two not very important points which we had discussed the day before. At this Executive the one really fascinating topic was the announcement by Morgan Phillips that the B.B.C. had written to suggest that the whole of the Conference, mornings and afternoons, be televised,[1] like a Test Match. It was obvious that Morgan's view was that we should refuse this altogether. I at once urged that, in the long run, it would be impossible to stop the televising of annual Conferences and that it would be a fatal mistake for us to attack as though we were afraid of the public looking at us when at work.

Edith Summerskill said this was totally impossible, since there were subversive influences in the Party which would stage hostile demonstrations. One trade unionist after another said that anyway we must at all costs avoid the televising of the voting. What they meant, of course, was the disclosure to the public that, though practically the whole Conference votes one way, by show of hands, the block vote, when it is taken, usually shows 4 million to 2 million. It was immensely funny listening to the trade unionists showing their terror that anyone should see what really goes on.

As usual, Morgan Phillips angled for keeping the matter in his own hands. He said he just wanted to get the general feeling of the meeting before continuing negotiations and, after some half-hour's discussion, said he'd got it, whereupon somebody pointed out that he must have got three feelings, one in favour of television, one completely opposed to television, and one suggesting that, for this year, it might be limited to evening newsreels plus one experimental session directly televised. This bitched Morgan and he had to consent to a special meeting of the Executive in September to consider the policy.

In the afternoon, we began the two-day debate on foreign affairs. Butler, looking ghastly white and tired and every now and then putting his fingers to his brow as though he had an acute headache, read the Foreign Office brief and then tacked on to it a couple of passages of arid peroration on the need for hard work to face our economic problems. This produced a bored

[1] The Party Conferences were not televised in 1953. Instead, Morgan Phillips, from Transport House, and John Hare, from Conservative Central Office, answered questions at two televised press conferences, based on an existing television programme.

9

murmur. From our side of the House, his speech was a terrible come-down but there is no doubt that his rigid adherence to the Washington communiqué pleased nearly all his supporters.

Attlee then got up and made an extremely moderate, competent speech, though very badly phrased. Having been attacked over the weekend by Deakin for weak leadership, he made his usual come-back and got an enormous ovation for his strong denunciation of the smothering of the Churchill peace initiative. Really this finished the debate but, surprisingly, Ian Mikardo made a quite first-rate incursion into foreign affairs and, on the second day, Kenneth Younger attacked Salisbury even more strongly. Even Herbert Morrison wound up with quite a good speech, in which he made the, for him, astonishing statement that he didn't want a united Germany to be allied with either the East or the West. He probably doesn't realize that in doing so he has proclaimed his adherence to German neutrality.

Yesterday was a sweltering, thundery day. The top floor of Transport House was unbearable and so was the Polish Embassy, where I went for the annual party. Afterwards I had a sumptuous dinner with Alec Spearman, who had invited Quintin Hogg, Sir Edwin Plowden,[1] Jo Grimond[2] and Angus Maude, a young P.E.P.[3] Conservative. They assured me that Butler had lost nothing in the Conservative Party by his performance. They are obviously ardent Butlerites, highly dubious whether Churchill will ever return. Just before this dinner I had listened to an amazingly good speech by Bob Boothby, in which he had attacked Lord Salisbury for the sell-out.[4] All the Conservatives at dinner would have liked an autumn Election but seemed convinced that there would not be one owing to the illnesses of Churchill and Eden and to the general uncertainty about the leadership.

One curious incident worth recalling is that last Friday Aylmer Vallance

[1] A temporary civil servant in the Ministry of Economic Warfare from 1939 until 1940, Edwin Plowden served in the Ministry of Aircraft Production from 1940 to 1946, latterly as Chief Executive. He was Chief Planning Officer and Chairman of the Economic Planning Board from 1947 to 1953, when he became Adviser on the Atomic Energy Organization. In 1954 he was appointed first Chairman of the U.K.A.E.A. In 1959 he became a life peer and was made chairman of a committee of inquiry on Treasury control of public expenditure (1959–61). This was followed by Chairmanship of committees on the Organization of Representational Services Overseas (1963–4) and on the Aircraft Industry (1964–5). He was Chairman of Tube Investments Ltd 1963–76 and is now the company's President. Since 1976 he has also been Chairman of the Police Complaints Board.
[2] Joseph Grimond, called to the Bar in 1937, was Director of Personnel for UNRRA from 1945 until 1947 and Secretary of the National Trust for Scotland from 1947 to 1949. He was elected as Liberal M.P. for Orkney and Shetland in 1950 and served as Leader of the Liberal Party 1956–67 and as Acting Leader May–July 1976. In 1979 he published his *Memoirs* (London: Heinemann).
[3] Political and Economic Planning, an independent, non-party research organization, founded in 1931 and supported by subscriptions from industry, commerce and private individuals and by grants from trusts and foundations.
[4] To the other Foreign Ministers at the Washington meeting, in making what Crossman described in 'Through the Looking-Glass', *New Statesman and Nation*, July 25th, 1953, as a 'negative response' to 'the revolutionary changes in Russia and to the Communist proposals for peaceful co-existence'.

was one of the journalists interviewing Selwyn Lloyd on television. By the way, I had primed him with the right questions. At dinner afterwards, according to Vallance, Lord Alexander, the Minister of Defence, had said that he was perfectly right and that the Canal base was hopeless without full Egyptian co-operation. This confirms my view that, in Churchill's absence, there has been another switch of policy and that we shall now negotiate an agreement to withdraw from Suez.

Wednesday, September 9th

At the end of July I was so sick of politics that I even gave up writing this diary. It is always difficult to analyse why in this job one gets these bouts of nausea. Partly, of course, it is the frustration, under these modern narrow majorities, of spending so many hours gossiping in the House of Commons. That drives one to feel that journalism is really a far more useful and enjoyable form of politics than being an M.P. So one turns more and more to journalism, with the result that one speaks less and less and takes less and less interest in the House. That sets up a vicious circle.

It is certainly true in my case that in the last six months I have virtually dropped out of active House of Commons life. Even a year ago I was one of the outstanding backbenchers. But since I never ask a Question because I don't trouble to get there for Question Time and virtually never intervene in a debate except on defence or foreign policy I am losing that position. And, once you are going that way, it is very easy to start convincing yourself that you despise the people who waste their time sitting in the Chamber taking part in the shadow fight. But of course part of the contempt is exasperation that you are not doing it yourself.

Of course, the basic reason is that there hasn't really been a cause to fight for, now that the Bevanite Group has been closed down. Looking back on my eight years in Parliament, I see that I was only active as a member of a group, fighting for a cause – whether it was the group that fought for Palestine or the Keep Left Group or the Bevanite Group when it was active. I find it very difficult to be an M.P. on my own, just fighting for myself and getting my name in the papers, for the simple reason that I am a political journalist on my own, getting my name in the papers anyway.

Anyway this July I really began to sympathize with John Freeman, who has decided not to stand next time. Not that I ever thought of following his example, because, whereas he really dislikes the life of the House, I intensely enjoy it but know that I am wasting my time. And I also know that, having committed oneself to it, one is bound to go on and have a go at becoming a Minister one day.

What are my chances? I should rate them 50:50, though I think many of my friends would put them lower. But the trouble is that I don't really have a tremendous ambition to have office. In practical politics I have nothing like the self-confidence which I have in journalism. I really enjoy writing and, even more, going abroad and bringing off a coup. In all that life I have no sorts of qualms or pangs. But in the bickering on the National Executive and in those nauseating Party Meetings, I really feel a loathing, as well as a pain in the bottom of my stomach.

It would be easy to conclude that one is not born to be a politician. But, curiously enough, Nye, as far as I can see, has much the same feelings of nausea, though, to be fair, he takes the House of Commons as a career much more seriously than I do. But then again, that is because he hasn't got the other outlet in writing. I suppose one consoles oneself with the thought that Winston Churchill spent months away from the House of Commons whenever there was nothing on which really interested him. In the old days before narrow majorities M.P.s could do that and therefore the sense of frustration was that much less.

After my trip in Austria and Germany[1] I got back to London to find a delicious quiet. I intended to write half a dozen reviews which had piled up but actually I've written none of them, because of the *Statesman* and the *Pic*. To start with, the *Pic*. I arrived home on a Friday to find an urgent message to ring the office. Typical, I thought; they are going to make me work on the third week of my holiday. But when I rang the next morning the Editor said that he wanted me to review Hugh Cudlipp's history of the *Mirror* next week.[2] I said that was a lot of trouble and anyway I wanted to start my column. He said that, as for the trouble, he would pay me £100 and I could do the column as well. So I said, 'Send the book round,' and I read it during a gorgeous weekend at Radnage, to find it was racy and in parts really brilliant, the work, as you might expect, of a talented thug.

On Monday I got a message telling me that I was to ring up Hugh Cudlipp, though it must be understood that he did not want in any way to influence the review. I didn't ring up but Hugh rang me on Wednesday and asked me to go round, which I did, with a draft of the review in my pocket. I found that Hugh's idea of non-interference was a queer one and I soon saw he'd better see the script, which included a good long description of him. 'I can't have myself mentioned. It's the book to be reviewed, not the author.' To which I replied that it was against every principle of *Daily Mirror* journalism to leave out personalities.

Hugh then said we'd better let the Chairman adjudicate and up I was wafted to the Chairman's inner sanctum. Cecil King solemnly sat down and read the review and said he had no objections to the passages about Hugh.

[1] Crossman travelled in Austria with his agent, Helga Greene, and her son James and spent a week touring Bohemia and Bavaria and visiting Cologne. See 'Salzburg Diary' in the *New Statesman and Nation*, August 29th, 1953, and 'Electioneering in Western Germany', *New Statesman and Nation*, September 5th, 1953.

[2] Crossman's review of Hugh Cudlipp's *Publish and Be Damned* (London: Andrew Dakers, 1953) appeared in the *Sunday Pictorial* on September 6th, 1953. The reviewer observed, 'Anyone superior enough to enjoy reading a *Times* editorial to the end is warned not to try this book! Its vulgar readability will choke him.'

Then came a passage where I had written that the *Mirror* started as a circulation stunt and got its social conscience in the war. King really got very angry. 'That's just not true,' he said. 'Do you imagine that our advertisers were pleased when we attacked appeasement and supported left-wing causes? Do you imagine we weren't all risking our jobs? We did it because we believed in it. And then the circulation came.'

I said that the book had given me the other impression but I certainly didn't want to write what was untrue. 'Ugh, the book!' King said. 'After all, it's only a publicity stunt.' Wisely or unwisely, I said, 'Now I've got you. I'm asked to review a book on its merits and you suddenly say it's a publicity stunt. You're all schizophrenes here. You really don't know when you're crusading and when you're making money.' I must say King laughed a good deal.

But that wasn't the end of the matter. I took the precaution of going in on Friday to make sure things were right and found that Hugh had subbed the review, though, I must say, not too badly. Then, on Saturday, I had premonitions and rang up, to find that fifteen more lines had been cut, mostly out of the end, while Hugh had sent in further revisions. At this I blew up and said the review wouldn't come out at all. The unfortunate acting editor, ground between the upper and the nether millstones, started revamping the article, under my instructions, over the telephone, when the first edition was due to go out. Actually, the result was a rather stronger last sentence,[1] though not as strong as originally drafted. Throughout, Cudlipp behaved like a mother with her first child. He certainly got an amazing coverage in the press.

I have also been having difficulties with Kingsley. From the first moment I got back, he nobbled me to discuss circulation. I had known for months from John [Freeman] and Aylmer Vallance that circulation had been sagging. The facts are that when the price was raised from 6*d*. to 9*d*. last summer circulation dropped from 85,000 to 74,000 at once and then suffered its normal summer sag. But, instead of having the normal pick-up in the autumn and winter, it continued a slight decline and the certified figure is now 71,000. Moreover, the graph, which is the important thing, shows a slight but definite falling-off. The management is not unduly concerned because, despite this sag, the increased price gave a bigger profit last year than ever before. Also, if Kingsley is right, John Roberts's whole attention is being given to the Ganymed Press. This luxury show is run in conjunction with a printing firm and so far £30,000 of *New Statesman* profits have been sunk in it and are most unlikely to be recovered. This summer there was a great row and the Directors finally gave instructions that no more *New Statesman* profits were to go into Ganymed, which will leave Roberts in a terrible fix

---

[1] 'But if the job of preventing degrading sensationalism must be left to the individual newspapers, the public has the right to demand that they take their responsibilities very seriously indeed.'

to raise the money to carry on. Kingsley's view is that it is all the management's fault that circulation has not been maintained. It's true that, whereas every other similar paper – the *Guardian*, the *Observer*, the *Spectator*, *Time and Tide* and *The Economist* – have all been advertising and running circulation drives, we have been sitting pretty on our left-wing cultural monopoly.

Well, thank God for the circulation drop, because Kingsley's scared and thinks something has got to be done about the paper. And when he's scared, he usually talks to me. The fact is that the paper has been getting increasingly arid. More and more unreadable, wordy material has been published, a large amount of which appears because Kingsley has agreed to take an article on Malaya from some dreary person who has come into the office or because Norman MacKenzie has gone to Roumania and we have to have two absolutely unreadable articles as a result. I have told Kingsley: one, on foreign policy we have a certain status and credit for such things as our anti-McCarthy campaign and what we've done about Palestine, Germany, etc.; two, on his pet topics, Africa and the Far East, we are crashing bores; three, we have no standing whatsoever on economics or, indeed, on any home subject; four, the back of the paper[1] is still as good as ever; five, Kingsley's choice of letters is often utterly barmy if he wants readers to be interested in them.

What I have proposed is: first, he must make someone Home Editor, responsible for seeing the home front gets a fair showing; second, he must also regain the confidence of such Socialist economists as Richard Kahn, Joan Robinson and Tommy Balogh, who will really work for him if they feel there is a chance of a continuous show for their ideas; three, he must let us remove the dull stuff about colonial affairs; four, he must give up the long, unsigned leader on p. 3 or p. 4, which he regards as the centre of the paper. It simply isn't read. We should completely revamp the first four pages in layout, shape and everything else, to make them readable, succinct, lively and reliable. Last, it is intolerable that Douglas Cole should send us in articles which we just have to publish, without ever seeing him.

Yesterday Kingsley came in to say that his doctor had told him he must take an immediate holiday but that he couldn't take one. We've arranged for him to take it but we still don't know if he will. Meanwhile John comes back on Monday and Aylmer, he and I are going to get to work.

Wednesday, September 16th

Last weekend, when I was feeling more than usually depressed by politics, I went down to Coventry. Superficially I could hardly have had a less worthwhile weekend. The Saturday was spent in the Stratford-on-Avon constituency, where Tom Locksley,[2] a young Coventry schoolmaster, is the

---

[1] Where literary and other criticism appeared.
[2] A Welshman, he was for a short time the Secretary of the Labour Group on Coventry City Council.

candidate. We motored vast distances through rural Warwickshire to meetings attended by a score of people and, in one instance, by none. On Sunday morning I visited the Wyken Workingmen's Club and after lunch had a Report Back with an attendance of ten. Yet, curiously enough, this was a rewarding weekend. At each of the Warwickshire villages I met the handful of people who are struggling to build a party, the majority of them being schoolmasters and schoolmistresses, and one got an astonishingly vivid picture of the problems involved. The schoolmasters in particular really are the salt of the earth.

Up at the Wyken Workingmen's Club on Sunday morning with Harry Stanley[1] I found everything beautifully normal. The wage packet is probably higher than ever in the history of the city, with the inevitable result that the transport men are causing trouble. Whenever the motor-car factories are booming, the local authority staffs get upset. Before the war they had the best conditions in Coventry. Now they have almost the worst and the busmen are staging regular Saturday strikes, which are really expressing their protest at the discrepancy between what you get at the Standard Works and what they get.

As usual, the old gaffers came over and talked to me and it's probably true that a Labour candidate in Coventry does more good in just having half a pint in a workingmen's club than addressing a meeting in a school. Our Report Back was also interesting because the Chief Convener of the Standard Works, a right-winger, had just been to Czechoslovakia and come back finding everything perfect over there. When I got back to London I dined with the Foots, since Jill wants to make a film in Coventry. The conclusion of all this is the thing that matters in politics is people.

On Tuesday the lunch was well attended, with Nye quite relaxed after his holiday in Yugoslavia.[2] At half-past three the International Sub. was due to discuss the emergency resolution[3] for Conference. With some effort, I got the Group to consider the draft during lunch and Barbara and I rapidly knocked out two amendments, one on foreign policy and one on defence. Nye took over the foreign policy one almost without reading it and I said that I'd do the defence one. We all agreed that on no account would we enter a lengthy debate. We would just table our resolutions, be defeated and walk out. It didn't happen that way. It never does.

When we got to the meeting, Sam Watson, in the chair, asked, quite correctly, whether the committee wished to take the draft as a whole or discuss it paragraph by paragraph. The Bevanites were silent and it was decided to discuss it paragraph by paragraph. When this had been going on for about a quarter of an hour, Nye woke up, said he expected somebody

---

[1] A shop steward for the National Union of Sheetmetal Workers and a member of Coventry City Council.

[2] For Bevan's association with Yugoslavia and his friendship with Tito, Djilas, etc., see Michael Foot, *Aneurin Bevan* (London: Davis-Poynter, 1973), vol. 2, pp. 347–8.

[3] On the Government's conduct of foreign policy.

else to speak first and then launched into an attack on the whole document. He was obviously deliberately whipping himself up into a fury. It took a very long time but he finally managed it, said the draft was unspeakable and that he couldn't tolerate it and tabled his amendment.

At this point Alice Bacon asked whether it had been previously discussed by certain members of the Committee, since Nye appeared to have copies of it. Nye took umbrage and said it was his own personal draft and that it was intolerable to have these nefarious suggestions made about his integrity. Since Alice Bacon had made this accusation, he would refuse to distribute his copies. However, the copies were after some difficulty distributed and Nye then made a very good speech, defending our short resolution.

The resolution ran:

This Conference expresses the grave alarm of the Labour Party at the failure of the Western Powers to seize the opportunity to break the East/ West deadlock presented by the changes in Russia after Stalin's death. It repudiates the so-called policy of liberation, which seeks to perpetuate the cold war and to use the United Nations to prosecute an ideological war against Communism. It believes that, unless the opportunity for relaxing the tension is courageously seized and unless both sides make concessions in a genuine attempt to secure a settlement, World War III will become inevitable. Conference therefore:

(i) Urges that the British Government should renew its demand for a round-table conference on Korea, including India, as the only way to prevent the Peace Conference ending in failure.

(ii) Protests against the latest American decision to prolong the war in Indo-China, instead of seeking peace by negotiation.

(iii) Gives its full support to the German Social Democrats in their gallant battle against resurgent German nationalism and against the ratification of the E.D.C. and the contractual agreements before a genuine effort has been made to secure the peaceful unification of Germany.

(iv) Urges that Britain should take the lead in removing the obstacles to East/West trade in other than war materials.

This was then summarily defeated and the committee resumed discussion of the office resolution, paragraph by paragraph, whereupon Nye said that he would take no further part in the discussion. It then lasted three hours and we all took a great part in it. The fact is, it's quite impossible to let a document of this sort go without trying to improve it. We managed to exclude a sentence pledging us to make federation work in Central Africa, to include a statement pledging us to support a negotiated peace in Indo-China and to drastically modify an outrageous passage on Germany, which pledged us to support a united Germany with absolute sovereignty and no limitations. All these were extremely important amendments and, if we hadn't put them in, we should all have been bound by them as Party policy.

As the meeting went on, it got really better and better tempered, as for once we began to debate the substance of genuine issues. The debate on Germany was extremely tense, since Sam Watson leads those who want to rearm the Germans and understood enough to know what my draft was getting at. However, on this we won by sheer force of argument. The amendment on defence,* which I moved, was the only one which was defeated outright. I told them that it was sheer dishonesty to propose huge increases of capital investment, large expansions of the social services and a contribution to colonial development without warning Conference that this could not be done while defence took 12 per cent of the national product. I think I am right in saying that the argument was listened to in embarrassed silence. They all knew that it was intellectually right. But it made no difference. We were defeated, with only the four of us voting for it.

It was altogether an excellent meeting, after which I rushed to the Lyric Theatre to the first night of T. S. Eliot's *Confidential Clerk*,[1] which Kenneth Younger had invited me to, as it was for Indonesian charity. Until the last act I was placidly interested throughout and found the verse extremely attractive, since it manages to elevate the dialogue above the level of ordinary life while keeping it matter-of-fact. This gives you a queer sense that you are hearing something on two levels, which is precisely what Eliot wanted to achieve. In the middle of the second act one felt that the play was really going to develop some emotional tension and there was a beautiful scene between the young man and the girl. But all this was allowed to dissipate itself in a really ridiculous, farcical plot, which was aridly worked out. The young man, who had had a love affair with the girl, became a priest; she married another young man of no interest at all, after which every dramatic tension had been destroyed. Still, it was a great deal better than Graham Greene's *Living Room*, my last first night.[2] *The Living Room* was extremely successful and unpleasant subversive propaganda. The Eliot play was too arid and up in the air to do any harm.

Friday, October 2nd
Last Saturday I motored down to the Conference[3] with Nye and Jennie on

---

* It read:
In view of the fact that the imminent danger of war, which was the justification for the 1950 rearmament programme, has now been admittedly renewed, and in view of the unfair burden borne by Britain—a burden accentuated by the recent decision of the U.S.A. and France to reduce their arms programmes—this Conference demands that the British defence programme, which is jeopardizing capital investment at home and in the underdeveloped areas, shall now be scaled down to a level compatible with a sound, expanding economy, and that the term of National Service be at once reduced from two years to eighteen months, to be followed by an annual review.

[1] Thomas Stearns Eliot (1888–1965), the poet, playwright and essayist. Eliot's *The Confidential Clerk* was first performed at the Edinburgh Festival that summer. It came to London on September 16th.

[2] At Wyndham's Theatre, on April 16th.

[3] The Labour Party Conference took place at Margate from September 28th to October 2nd.

an exquisite, late September morning. Nye picked me up and took me to Cliveden Place, where we found the Mackies[1] and Desmond Donnelly with another car. Five minutes after Nye, Mrs Mackie and I had set out, it was revealed that Nye had forgotten to tell the other car which way we were going and that they had the picnic, including a pie especially bought for the occasion at Fortnum & Mason. Typically, John Mackie chose the straight, built-up road via Rochester, while we went through the country via Maidstone and spent a couple of hours in Canterbury Cathedral.

I was absolutely dreading the Conference, partly, I suppose, out of anxiety about the elections but mostly because I dislike rows, and Nye spent a good deal of the time saying how futile the sort of life he was having was and that he would never address any more public meetings. He was supposed to attend a compositing meeting but after a pleasant journey we quietly arrived two hours late and retired to Nye's bedroom for drinks, after which we dined alone.

Nye was due to make his big speech at the Sunday demonstration and at dinner Jennie said that he would go upstairs early to prepare it. At half-past one I left him still drinking and he didn't wake up till midday on Sunday. We had to go to the mayoral lunch and then sit in the Executive for four and a half hours, after which Nye left and saw the press, so he had no time to prepare his great speech. On the Saturday night I had prepared him some notes, merely on the history of the failure of the peace offensive. As he rose to speak on Sunday, he impressively drew his notes from his pocket and, since he can't read my writing, I was horrified to see that they were mine.

Nye had decided to make his great declaration on foreign policy, but it was a difficult audience, which had responded very warmly to an extremely clever and poisonous attack on the Left by Edith Summerskill, which included even the argument that in their election the Germans had shown their responsibility and wisdom in eschewing all extremists and voting for Adenauer.[2] Because Nye had not prepared and had only half an hour before Attlee, he lost all sense of shape, spent half his time giving his theories about Russia and never got to his concrete proposals. But it was a nice speech.

Let's go back to the mayoral lunch. While we were having drinks, I saw huddled in a corner Harry Douglass, Herbert Morrison, Percy Knight[3] and

[1] John Mackie, Managing Director of family farming companies in Angus, Essex and Middlesex, was Labour M.P. for Enfield East 1959–74. Joint Parliamentary Secretary to the Ministry of Agriculture 1964–70, since 1976 he has been Chairman of the Forestry Commission. He was the author of a Fabian pamphlet on land nationalization. He married Jeannie Milne in 1934.

[2] In the West German General Election on September 6th Dr Adenauer's Party, the Christian Democratic Union, and the Christian Social Union, gained an absolute majority of 244 members in the Bundestag. The Social Democratic Party won 151 seats and the Free Democratic Party 48. The Communist Party did not win a single constituency seat or the 5 per cent of the poll required to qualify for seats from the national list.

[3] He helped to establish the National Maritime Board in 1917. National Organizer of the National Union of Seamen 1942–55, he was General Secretary from 1955 until his retirement a year later. He became a member of the Labour Party N.E.C. in 1945. He died in 1968.

one or two other right-wingers. I said to Nye, when I noticed Herbert writing, 'Look, they're issuing a communiqué that Herbert is standing down.'[1] This should be a good instance of premonition, since at half-past nine on Sunday night Herbert issued the communiqué to the press. But actually I was wrong, as I learnt later from two long conversations.

The first was next morning, Monday, with Harry Douglass, who was sitting next to me on the platform. 'This must be a bright day for you,' Douglass remarked to me. I said that the effect of Morrison's peace action would probably be to swing votes to the right. 'Oh,' Douglass said, 'I didn't mean your damned election. But it's finished Morrison. When trade union leaders choose an ally to go into battle, they don't expect him to pull out at five minutes to twelve. We'll never trust him again.'

On Tuesday night I spent one and a half hours with a very drunken Will Lawther, who had had much the same sort of reaction, though he told me that he hadn't discussed it with Morrison and only learnt of it from the press. 'But,' said Will, 'I knew the little twister would wriggle out of it. If the political monkeys want to behave in that way, let 'em.' There were some young Socialists present and one of them said to me afterwards, 'Well, I've learnt at last that, in the view of trade union leaders, there are three sorts of people: trade unionists, intellectuals and politicians, and they hate the politicians more than the intellectuals.' In a funny way, there is something in this.

The third man who talked to me was Jock Tiffin, Arthur Deakin's Number Two. He told me that, when the T. & G. delegates had discussed this on Sunday, Arthur Deakin wanted to make open war on Morrison. Tiffin said that it was madness to do so and persuaded the majority to vote against Deakin, whereupon Deakin went off again on Monday to London in a pet and only returned to Conference on Wednesday. As far as I can see, what really happened was that Morrison made the decision on his own, advised chiefly by Sam Watson and without consulting the unions who had backed him, except for Arthur Deakin, who disagreed with him. All this, no doubt, will blow over but I think it does show that, if Morrison had gained the confidence of the big union leaders, he has lost it now. However, after Morrison's decision it was no exaggeration when Fairlie[2] said to me, 'This is a Conference which is over before it starts.' The Morrison withdrawal made it clear that there was to be no right-wing attack on the Left and, since the Left had long before decided not to attack the Right, that was that.

There was never really any question about the mass of the delegates failing to welcome this kind of compromise. But, naturally, over the weekend there was a great deal of talk about our elections. Most of the talk was about me, since it was clear that the Right hoped to get my place, not Mikardo's. Two

[1] I.e. from the election for the treasurership.
[2] Henry Fairlie, Political Correspondent of the *Spectator* in the 1950s. He then moved to the *Sunday Express*, and now writes for the *Sunday Times*.

or three journalists were busy spreading the rumour that Nye had decided to drop me in order to placate Morrison. Ian Mikardo was terribly worried and anxious to take steps. I told him that there were no steps that one could take. This particular election is one of the most unpleasant one can go through, because there is nothing you can do about it. For the whole of Saturday, Sunday and Monday you go about totally inactive, while people make up their minds about your personal merits. In a General Election you can always say, 'Well, it wasn't my fault' or 'They weren't voting for *people*'. But here it's your friends voting solely for people and that makes it very unpleasant.

So it was a great relief when I got to the Conference rather late on Tuesday, at the moment when the scrutineers were reading the list.[1] We've discussed a lot the significance of the vote, in which Harold Wilson went up 50 per cent and I 24 per cent, whereas Driberg and Mikardo went down. It looks as though a whole number of constituencies weighed up people rather more than they did before and Ian suffered for being the most purely *Tribune* character on the list. This is exactly the opposite of what Nye believed. Just as I was leaving him at breakfast on Tuesday morning, he said, 'Oh, it will be all right but we'll make sure next time to associate you closer with *Tribune*.' I fancy the *Sunday Pic* has more electoral value.

On Tuesday *The Times* asked Harold Wilson, Tom [Driberg] and myself to dinner. *The Times* were Donald Tyerman;[2] Fairlie; the young leader-writer on Labour affairs, the excellent Labour Correspondent, Wigham;[3] and the Lobby Correspondent, Mason.[4] They had already given lunch to Herbert and Hugh Gaitskell. Fairlie very indiscreetly told me that the lunch had consisted of a silent conflict between Gaitskell and Morrison, with Morrison talking all the time in terms of how to defeat the Left and Gaitskell very statesmanlike and controlled. When I asked why Morrison had decided to oppose Greenwood, Fairlie told me that Morrison had said that he just wasn't going to be kicked about like a football by those damned con-stituency parties.

What struck me at this dinner was how extraordinarily little these journalists know about the inside of our politics. I'd thought for a long time that they knew it all but were too discreet to publish. But really the fact is

[1] As at Morecambe the year before, the Bevanites again took the six N.E.C. seats for which the constituency parties voted. James Griffiths was again elected. Herbert Morrison lost his seat but it was now understood that an *ex officio* place would be made for him, as Deputy Leader, on the National Executive.

[2] Lecturer at the University of Southampton from 1930 until 1936, when he began a career as a journalist on *The Economist*. In 1944 he moved to *The Times* and from that year until 1955 he was Deputy Editor. From 1956 to 1965 he edited *The Economist*.

[3] Eric Wigham, a journalist. Formerly on the *Manchester Guardian*, in 1944 he moved to *The Times* as Labour Correspondent, a post he held until his retirement in 1969. He published *What's Wrong with the Unions?* (Harmondsworth: Penguin, 1961) and *Strikes and the Government 1893–1974* (London: Macmillan, 1976).

[4] Studley (Max) Mason, Lobby Correspondent of *The Times*. He was Parliamentary Correspondent of that paper from 1938 until September 1957, when he went to the Central Office of Information.

that they have no feeling for the motives which make politicians work. Tyerman was very full of anxiety about rumours he had heard that Kingsley was to be sacked and replaced by John Freeman. I'd very much like to know how these rumours got about.

On Wednesday, before the *Tribune* demonstration, I went to lunch with my Russian Embassy friend,[1] who told me that he regarded as sound the compromise that had been achieved between Right and Left. This is the first political judgment that I have ever heard him make and it interested me, because this is the sort of politics Russians can understand.

The *Tribune* meeting was a really brilliant display. Bryn Roberts[2] chose to launch the most extravagant and fantastic attack on the T.U.C., speaking as a trade union Secretary; Michael made the most brilliant attack on the press; and Nye talked a lot about O'Brien[3] and Churchill, because I had given him a cutting in his bath just before and he hadn't had any other ideas for a speech. Altogether it was a brilliant display of oratory to a pretty big audience – but I felt that it was fireworks without concrete substance.

Thursday was a perfect day, really hot. Ever since Saturday I have had an absolutely drenching cold in the head and was unable to go to bed, though that is the only cure, and I decided to go home on Thursday evening. Meanwhile, on Thursday morning, Attlee made a first-rate statement on foreign policy, keeping rigorously to the brief and not divagating a hair's breadth from his middle position. But he sounded like a Prime Minister and made it sound like a policy. After lunch Arthur Moyle,[4] his P.P.S., told me Attlee had asked what I thought of it and that he had told him that I was pleased. Interesting that Attlee should worry – but I suspect that he suspects that I do most of Nye's foreign policy.

I saw quite a lot of the Coventry delegates, who were all terribly depressed and frustrated and wondering what on earth they were to report back. In

[1] Probably Georgi Mikhailovich Zhivotovski, who was from 1950 to 1956 Second Secretary at the U.S.S.R. Embassy in London. In 1957 he returned to Moscow, to become Deputy Head of the International Organizations Department of the Ministry of Foreign Affairs and from 1959 to 1963 he was Counsellor at the Soviet Embassy in Tokyo.

[2] A member of the T.U.C. since 1947, he was General Secretary of NUPE 1934–62. He published *The Price of Trade Union Leadership* (London: Allen & Unwin, 1961). He died in 1964.

[3] The Chairman of the Trades Union Congress, Tom O'Brien, had made a speech of fraternal greetings to the Conference, in which he had suggested 'a searching and serious examination of where the political protection of the working population concentrated in the unions begins and ends'. In an interview in the *Manchester Guardian*, Mr O'Brien had explained these remarks as signifying that the T.U.C. should consider whether the time had arrived for it to divest itself of political activities, to concentrate on industrial matters. Mr Deakin, invited to address the Conference, demolished Mr O'Brien's speech and was loudly applauded.

[4] Chairman of the National Joint Council for Local Authority Manual Workers in 1936 and 1937, he was a member of the National Joint Council for Local Authority Administrative, Professional, Technical and Clerical Staff from 1936 to 1945. In 1945 he was elected as Labour M.P. for Stourbridge and in 1950 for Oldbury and Halesowen, holding this seat until 1964. He was P.P.S. to Attlee 1945–55 and in 1966 he became a life peer. He died in 1974.

fact, of course, it was a deadly Conference, since the so-called democratic debate on *Challenge to Britain* turned out to be a formal ratification, where one couldn't afford to make any concessions.

The only interesting debate was on education, where Hugh Gaitskell and Arthur Deakin criticized the policy.[1] Hugh Gaitskell pleaded for opening the public schools and Jenny rushed to the mike to annihilate him for such class policy, only to find herself howled down. Partly this was because she had attacked Hugh but partly she had forgotten that nearly all the delegates either were at grammar school or have their children at grammar schools and are not quite so susceptible to the romantic Socialism of the 1920s. Alice Bacon, on the other hand, who did speak extremely placidly, managed to turn down Hugh in two sentences without causing a ripple.

Monday, October 26th
Parliament has now been back for a week[2] and it's possible to form some impression of how things are going. As well as a whole series of external crises,[3] the other big issue has been Nye's standing for the deputy leadership. Directly after Margate the *Sunday Express* started stating that he wasn't standing and soon this became an accepted fact. Because Nye disregards the press he said nothing for three weeks. Then last Tuesday at the lunch it was discovered, as we had all assumed, that there was no doubt that he was standing and there never had been any. That evening the *Daily Mirror* Lobby Correspondent came to ask me a question about Coventry cars and, as he was turning away, said, 'Funny that Bevan isn't standing.' I said, 'Of course he is,' and he nearly fell over backwards with consternation.

This is typical of the British press. I have checked and found that no newspaper reporter ever bothered to ask Nye or any of us whether he was standing. They simply took the rumour from Morrison. Or, to be accurate,

---

[1] *Challenge to Britain* proposed abolition of the grammar schools, educating children together until the statutory school-leaving age of fifteen and then sending those who stayed on to a single category high school. Conference rejected this but carried an amendment reasserting the Party's preference for 'comprehensive' schools within the existing system.

[2] Parliament reassembled on October 20th. Sir Winston and Mr Eden, apparently recovered in health, had both addressed the Conservative Party Conference at Margate in the second week of October and now returned to the Front Bench.

[3] On October 9th the Constitution of British Guiana was suspended and the Governor was given emergency powers. The Colonial Office stated, in a White Paper published on October 20th, that the Prime Minister, Dr Jagan, and fellow Ministers of the People's Progressive Party, had neglected their proper duties and seemed to be encouraging strikes and Communist activity. Dr Jagan came to London but his appeals to the Labour Party were rebuffed.

On October 9th, the British and American Governments issued a statement on the Free Territory of Trieste, where dispute continued between Italy and Yugoslavia. The two Governments announced the withdrawal of Allied Military Government in the area and the relinquishing of the administration of Zone A to the Italian Government. The Yugoslav Government protested, the Italian Government expressed dismay and on October 13th it was stated that the British, French and American Foreign Ministers would confer in London on October 16th.

one paper, Michael Foot's local one in Devonport, did, but his editor didn't print it. The scandal of the press is not its partiality but its sheer idleness in not checking facts.

Friday, October 30th
Nye is deeply disturbed by his lack of success in the election to the deputy leadership[1] and feels that he is in a dead end. Should he go on leading a Group which seems to repel everybody else from supporting him? But if the Group is disbanded, doesn't he lose his position on the Left and wouldn't he be a prisoner once again, as he was in the Cabinet? All this makes him needful of self-confidence and so very self-assertive and volatile.

Thursday, November 12th
Last week I spent two and a half days in Vienna,[2] getting back on Friday [November 6th] in time to do the *Sunday Pic* that evening. While I was away, there had been a meeting of the whole Bevanite Group at Gavin Faringdon's, in which, I gather, very bold words were used by many people, demanding restoration of the Group, and much disgruntlement had been expressed when Nye, at the end, urged caution and slowness. All this was related to me by John Freeman on Monday morning at the *Statesman* but I checked it afterwards.

One other small parliamentary incident is worth recording. On Monday George Wigg came to me and said he had found a way of defeating the Government at last. A Tory was praying against an Order annulling control of cut-glass manufacture and a circular had been sent out, stating that this Prayer would not be taken to a division. George Wigg has an interest in cut glass[3] and the plan was to allow ourselves to be defeated badly on the two or three previous items of business, so as to lull the Tories, and then rush our forces into the House, refuse to let the Tory withdraw and defeat the Prayer.

Throughout Monday and Tuesday George was organizing. Part of the organization was to send a canvassing party to the by-election in Holborn, part was to keep a secret posse in a committee room downstairs and, finally, I was to run a Bevanite Group meeting in my house and keep it there from eight o'clock till eleven. However, the Whips had said that everybody must be there for all the votes, which, of course would have defeated the scheme. I sent out a severe whip, asking people to a party to discuss urgent business, and we had a very good turn-out of thirty people, which just filled my sitting

[1] Bevan received 76 votes and Morrison 181.

[2] As the N.E.C. representative at the Austrian Socialist Party Conference, from Thursday, November 5th to Saturday, November 7th. See 'Red Vienna, 1953' in the *New Statesman and Nation*, November 14th, 1953.

[3] George Wigg was interested in the future of the glass industry in Stourbridge, part of his constituency. See Wigg, *George Wigg* (London: Michael Joseph, 1972), pp. 165–6.

room. We had a first-rate Bevanite discussion, continuing that at Faringdon's the week before. (In between, the results of the elections of the Parliamentary Committee had been announced, showing absolutely no change from last year and Harold Wilson failing by one vote.)

Apparently the course of our discussion at Vincent Square was almost the opposite of that at Buscot the week before, largely because of the presence of the Scottish and working-class members; all of them were horrified at the idea of recreating a Group which was banned by Standing Orders, and we therefore decided on a new tactic. For some months Fenner has been running an unofficial colonial group, which has been penetrating the official colonial and Commonwealth group and really getting things done. We are now setting up a number of other unofficial groups on special subjects, which is really quite different from recreating the Bevanite Group as a whole.

By half-past nine we had about finished our discussion and Ian and I had to explain (it was a bit delicate) that there was another reason why they were there. Members of Parliament do not like being hoodwinked and one or two of them got very anxious about their division records and started putting on their coats – particularly Tom Driberg, who was in America last week and has been censured by the Cheshire and Lancashire group. I had to tell a number of formidable lies. Telephoned by George Wigg that the Transport division would be due in twenty minutes, I said it was over and further added that the Chief Whip had sanctioned being absent from these divisions, which was the precise opposite of the truth. I just held them there until George gave the word that we were to enter singly in driblets between eleven and three minutes past. I must say that I was a little anxious, since we have so often done this and failed and this time, if it failed and our Members discovered that the Chief Whip had not sanctioned their absence, I should literally never be forgiven or trusted. However, we won by four votes[1] and, as George Wigg motored the Chief Whip home, the Chief was congratulating himself on instructing us to stay away from the lobby. Our group had been the key to success, since the canvassers had been brought home for the other votes and the secret gang in the committee room had been spotted by the Tory Whips, who collected enough people to deal with them but not enough to deal with the reserves at No. 9 Vincent Square.

At the Party Meeting, on my suggestion, Attlee specifically absolved from blame all those who were absent and congratulated the Whips, as well as George. We are now going to put down a series of Prayers late at night and have George walk through the lobby each time but not vote, so that all our people can go home. Then, in about four weeks, we will stage another of these things and, even if it's unsuccessful, we shall harass the Tories and keep them up, without apparently doing so. This is one step cleverer than what

[1] A Prayer to annul an Order restricting hire-purchase agreements and credit facilities was defeated at 10.40 p.m. by 194 votes to 152. The Prayer to annul an Order removing controls on the import of cut glass was carried at 11.25 p.m. by 145 votes to 141.

Bob Boothby tried to do two years ago.[1] When George was congratulated at the Party Meeting, it was very charming since, for the first time in his life, he looked really embarrassed when there were cries of 'Speech, speech!' But of course the whole incident shows the incredible incompetence of our own machine. In order to defeat the Tories, one has to deceive not only them but one's colleagues and one's Whips.

I spent the weekend in South Wales. On Saturday afternoon, Sunday morning and afternoon, I took three sessions in a weekend school in James Callaghan's constituency. James had done the first session before I got there. This was extremely interesting. We had forty-seven people present, of an average age of thirty. It was as good a bunch as you'd find anywhere but what struck me most was that, keen as they are, they simply knew nothing about the contents of *Challenge to Britain* or the number of practical proposals we were putting forward about housing, social security, education, nationalization, etc. The school took place in a lovely Y.M.C.A. hostel right over the sea at Barry and, since this is the one thing I really can do, it was a great success, with James Callaghan playing along very skilfully and, in his own way, loyally.

Monday, November 16th
This last weekend I went down to Coventry and on Sunday morning George Hodgkinson and I motored over to Leamington to fetch Nye to do his big meeting at the Opera House. I found him in a good humour but he has a terribly bad cold, the one he caught from me in Margate and has not yet thrown off. We got to the Opera House at eleven to find very few people outside and, when we went in, it was scarcely full. Indeed, the top gallery was empty. It did fill up by the time Nye spoke — or, rather, there were thirty or forty empty seats. George explained this by saying that he had sold 1,000 tickets but that not all the ticket-holders had come. But there is no doubt whatsoever that two years ago there would have been a huge, milling crowd outside. It shows the outstanding increase of apathy to find Nye merely addressing a very good meeting.

The audience was overwhelmingly one of young shop stewards. The meeting began with Maurice Edelman, who, to my astonishment, had expressed a wish to speak on Nye's platform and who paid a tribute to his Socialist leadership, which must have surprised a good many of Maurice's Party workers, since he had viciously attacked Nye when he resigned. I suspect it was the price Maurice was paying for ensuring that he was re-adopted. He made a strongly anti-American speech and was heartily cheered.

[1] In an impromptu speech at Banstead in early March 1951 Mr Boothby had urged fellow Conservative backbenchers to harry Labour Members until they were ground down with exhaustion. Archie Manuel, the Labour Member for Central Ayrshire, sought to raise the speech as a matter of privilege; Mr Boothby replied to 'the general uproar' in a letter to *The Times*, March 20th, 1951. It was Boothby's threat, rather than any action it inspired, that Crossman remembered.

Moreover, Nye referred to Maurice frequently throughout his own speech and cast his aura over him. Since Nye has been telling us that we ought to get rid of anti-Bevanites and see that they are not adopted, I pointed this out to him afterwards. But he is a wonderful man. He really is too nice and generous to carry out the things he tells us to do.

His own speech was a very interesting example of his style. It was Sunday morning at eleven and therefore not a suitable time for fireworks. Moreover, it was, as he well knew, a very left-wing audience. He began as hesitantly as anyone could and for ten minutes it was difficult to believe that he was a famous demagogue. The whole speech was a learned disquisition, with a great many long words, on the nature of Soviet Communism and the wickedness of anti-Communist crusades. I fancy that there were a good many passages where no one in the audience could understand what he was about. At one point he observed, 'Churchill is a highly articulate orator,' and it was clear from one or two interruptions that nobody knew what articulate meant. If I talked in that way I should be considered an intellectual but somehow Nye gets away with it.

His speech actually started with an attack on the press and a statement that we were all insane because we were cut off from information about reality. 'Sanity is the proper relationship between the organism and its environment,' he observed. 'But of course, if the environment is insane, then the only thing is to be insane.' Obviously this idea interested him a great deal and he culminated with the remark that he would dare to say in Coventry that it was in America that more motor-cars and more psychiatrists were produced than in any country in the world. (Of course the press only printed the passage where he said that all the British people were insane. and A. J. Cummings[1] picked this up on Monday. That evening Nye came to me and asked me if I would draft a press release for him. This I thought was a very hopeful advance since, when he made his vermin speech,[2] he had refused to correct it. This time he did, in fact, publish a press release.)

Nye came back to lunch with the Hodgkinsons and then demanded to be taken back to Leamington for a sleep. Meanwhile I did my Report Back and, since once again there were only fifteen people, we decided to cancel the Report Backs, for lack of interest. We spent two hours discussing what was wrong. The inner group of my Party is terribly depressed and some of them were advocating that we Socialists should form our own Party. All of them agree that the Party is dying from the roots up and that it is impossible to maintain ward organization. They also told me that, when Gaitskell came a week or two ago for a day school, the boys in the factory had point-blank

---

[1] A journalist whose career started on the *Daily News* in 1920. From 1932 to 1955 he was Political Editor and principal columnist of the *News Chronicle*. President of the Institute of Journalists in 1952/53, he died in 1957.

[2] In a speech at Manchester on July 4th, 1949, Bevan had said of the Conservative Party, ' ... so far as I am concerned, they are lower than vermin'.

refused to buy tickets, since he 'doesn't belong to us', and of the fifty delegates who were present forty-five were from the trade unions and only five from the Party.

I said that they really ought to go and hear Gaitskell and they agreed theoretically but just said they wouldn't. They all welcomed the unity at Margate but all feel that the Parliamentary Party is only shadow-boxing. 'You can't get the boys in the factories interested in politics if there seems to be no real difference between the two sides,' one of them said to me. One very nice young delegate, who used to be one of my most formidable critics, remarked that even Aneurin Bevan had said nothing constructive that morning. 'Why can't he talk constructively, like Dick?' he observed. 'You always say in the end what we ought to do. Why doesn't Nye?' To some extent this is a perfectly fair criticism. Nye always complains that he is not reported. One of the reasons is that he gives fascinating disquisitions but they don't add up to any precise or constructive proposals for what should be done.

In the evening I went over to Leamington, where we were to hold our second meeting. They had taken the huge, great variety theatre in the gardens in the centre of the city and we found it pretty well filled, with what I thought were over 1,000 but the local papers said were only 800 people. However, they had all paid a bob[1] and it was very good for Leamington. Nye had been put off in the morning by the bright lights on the stage, which prevented him from seeing the audience. The same thing happened in the evening. He is intensely sensitive and said to me, 'How can any actor do anything with these footlights barring you from the crowd?' However, I thought he made an almost perfect Party speech. It's worth describing.

Once again he started stuttering and very quiet. He knew that Leamington is an overwhelmingly Tory seat. He is very fond of Anthony Eden and sorry that he has been ill. He wants to see him get really well and so he recommends a long holiday. Now he wants to apologize to the Labour people present because he is only going to speak to the Tories in the audience. He and Anthony Eden have been in Parliament a long time together. When Nye got into Parliament, he knew how ignorant he was. The Cecils,[2] the Edens, they'd had the education and experience and so in 1931 he was very interested to see what they would do. After all, here was all the skill, knowledge and breeding in the country, with an overwhelming majority, able to do anything it liked. Then Nye describes the failure to tackle unemployment and relates it to steel. Though the country needed more steel, steelworks were closed down in Ebbw Vale. And now he reaches his first climax. Very quietly, he says, 'I want to ask any Tory in the audience who is prepared to defend what they did about steel in the 1930s to get up and say so.' Absolute silence. 'Now, I do ask them not to be bashful. After all, there are more Tories here than

[1] I.e. 1s.
[2] The family name of the Marquess of Salisbury (see p. 171n.).

Labour. Isn't there one?' Long silence. 'But surely there must be one?' Absolute silence. And so he has won.

And he goes on listing mistakes until he gets to the point where nobody dares to challenge his views that denationalization of road transport is a grave offence against patriotism. He deals equally effectively with the positive things done by the Labour Government and he gives you the feeling that only a Labour Government can really serve the needs and interests of the community. Of course, once again there was no constructive thing for a newspaper man to take down but as a piece of Party propaganda it was magnificent.

On the whole this was a disturbing weekend from a political point of view. Both at Coventry and at Leamington Nye got an audience but he had to do all the lifting of it. I would say that there was absolutely no swing so far towards Labour and that, on the whole, the vast majority of the electorate are plain uninterested in party politics of any kind. This matters far less to a Tory Government than it does to a Labour Opposition.

Tuesday, November 24th

I had a pleasant time at the Oxford Union on Thursday. At the Union they hold a very grand dinner in old-fashioned style before the presidential debate. There were lots of beautiful girls in evening dress and the two Proctors[1] were also in attendance, both of them taught by me, which shows how old I am growing. The dinner was so good that we were twenty minutes late for the debate but fortunately at Oxford the presidential debate is confined to the presidential candidates and the two guests. There were two candidates, neither of them Conservative, Lady Listowel[2] and me, so the debate was over by half-past ten.

The motion was, 'That the Western Powers have failed since 1945 effectively to meet and understand the challenge of Communism.'[3] As I was speaking for the motion, I had a relatively easy time. Both the young men were fluent, serious and rather moving but in most Union debates they make a good many references to the guests, some of them very rough. This time (I gather because of what happened two years ago, when I absolutely sloshed a young man who

---

[1] Two senior members of the University, each drawn from a different College, according to a rota. They are appointed for one year to supervise the discipline and morals of the University's undergraduates. On certain nights, the Proctors patrol the streets of Oxford, accompanied by bowler-hatted University officers, known as 'bulldogs'.

[2] Judith de Marffy-Mantuano married the fifth Earl of Listowel in 1933. The marriage was dissolved in 1945. A writer and journalist, she has published a great deal on African affairs.

[3] The four main speakers in the Oxford Union Society's debate on November 19th, 1953, were the candidates for the presidency of the Union Society, Tyrell Burgess (the Treasurer), who proposed the motion, and Peter Tapsell (the Librarian), who opposed it. Crossman spoke for the motion and Lady Listowel against. The motion was passed by 324 votes to 164 and Burgess won the presidency.

attacked me)[1] they had all decided to hold off and be serious. Moreover, Lady Listowel, who looked rather like a Puritan prepared for the burning, in black with a lace collar, was intensely serious and rather dull. So I wasn't at all prepared and I knew quite well that I had to be careful about her.

However, I think I succeeded in making the only Union speech of the evening and, having been very gallant to her at the beginning, brought the house down by one of those impromptu absurdities which go in Oxford. All I had to do was to wag my finger at one point and say, 'Ah, Countess, Countess.' I was in full spate, talking about how the Tories always send a cruiser somewhere at the beginning of a Tory Conference[2] (by the way, I had fervently complained of not being attacked at the beginning and said that I was like an old bull in a bull-ring who hadn't had any darts shot into it), when a young Conservative rose and asked me whether I would acknowledge my debt to Mr Mikardo, who a fortnight ago had made the same joke. This, of course, brought the house down and there were uproarious demands for 'Answer' and 'Withdraw'.

I wish I was as comfortable in the Commons as I am in the Union. I merely scratched my nose and said, 'The important thing for us Bevanites is who gets down to Oxford first.' For some unknown reason this was regarded as a most brilliant reply. So I proceeded to my peroration about the Copernican revolution — the solar system, with the white centre of Europe in the middle and the dark satellites going round it, has been irrefragably broken, etc., etc. — only to be told that Harold Wilson had used this the week before. Since the first joke was one of George Wigg's, which I had told Ian, and I had invented the other, I felt more co-ordination was necessary.

Friday, November 27th
In the Commons another assault[3] is being made on Curly Mallalieu for an article he wrote in *Tribune*, contrasting the public behaviour of M.P.s in their constituencies, when they talk Left, with the way they vote for the Parliamentary Committee. Apparently the right-wing have decided to make another attack on the journalist M.P.s. Mallalieu was sent for by Attlee and Morrison for a long, desultory discussion, in which Attlee on several occasions expressed his hatred of the press and told Mallalieu that he would have to decide whether he was a journalist or an M.P. We are to have a special Party Meeting next Wednesday on the whole Mallalieu issue. What a Party we are!

[1] On April 26th, 1951, the Society debated the motion 'That, in the opinion of this House, the record of Her Majesty's Opposition since 1945 gives no grounds for confidence in their ability to form a foreign policy in the best interests of this country'. The undergraduate speakers were David Wedgwood-Benn and Oleg Kerensky (for the motion) and Alastair Morrison and Patrick Mayhew (against). The visitors were Crossman (for the motion) and Boothby (against). The motion was lost by 224 votes to 205.

[2] Perhaps Crossman was applying the joke to Government policy towards the events in British Guiana.

[3] See above, p. 254.

Just at this time the Tory Party is wracked by revolts. I went and heard a little of the great television debate[1] in the House of Lords and there was a great scene in the Commons when a group of backbenchers threatened to vote against the Army Estimates if the grievances of certain pensioned ex-officers were not rectified. This grievance has been pressed for two years on a non-party basis and apparently Tory M.P.s were tipped off by Lord Alexander to put down Questions last Tuesday, because they would get a nice reply. An hour before, they were told that the reply was negative. Lord Alexander refused to give the reply in the Lords and Winston took it over, creating a flaming row.

On Wednesday I dined with Bob Boothby and John Junor and also had a talk with Hinchingbrooke, to try to discover the root cause of the Tory revolts, which are also causing trouble about Suez[2] and agricultural policy.[3] All three agreed that the basic trouble was Churchill's personal method of conducting government and the appallingly bad liaison with the backbenchers. It also looked as though the Tories had been much more upset than we realized at failing to win the Holborn by-election.[4] They have an uneasy feeling that the country is slowly turning against them. There is not much evidence for this view since in 1947, two years after we were in power, we had lost infinitely more public support than they have in the last two years. But they depend much more on personal leadership and obviously they are all worried whether Eden is fit enough to succeed.

All this should make the Labour Party cock-a-hoop but actually the internal feud, though suppressed, is even more acute. You feel it on every

---

[1] In November the Government's White Paper (Cmd 9005) proposed that, subject to parliamentary approval, a new Corporation should be established to provide a television service transmitting programmes supplied by companies deriving revenue from advertisements. The Corporation was to be supervised by a Government-appointed board. On November 25th and 26th the House of Lords discussed a motion of rejection, tabled by Lord Halifax, whose absence through illness meant that Lord Hailsham opened the debate. On the Government side the division was whipped and the motion for rejecting the proposal was defeated by 157 votes to 87. In the House of Commons on December 15th the White Paper was approved by 302 votes to 280.

[2] On December 15th thirty-six Conservative backbenchers had tabled a motion urging the Government to suspend negotiations for a revision of the Anglo-Egyptian Treaty in view of Egyptian breaches of the recent agreement on the Sudan. In a foreign affairs debate on December 17th, the Prime Minister and the Foreign Secretary did not deny the allegations but firmly refused to adopt the course suggested. See below, p. 281.

[3] On October 28th the Minister of Food had announced the end of price control and rationing of milk products and fats and on November 5th a White Paper on farm prices was published. Farmers would be guaranteed an individual price on each transaction, with a collective guarantee of a standard price to the industry as a whole. Full marketing powers were to be restored to the Milk Marketing Boards, with safeguards, and the rationing and price control of meat and bacon would end in the summer of 1954. Many farmers were still not reassured.

[4] Dr S. W. Jeger, Labour Member for Holborn and St Pancras South, had died on September 24th. In a by-election on November 19th, 1953, the seat was held by his widow, Mrs Lena Jeger, who obtained 15,784 votes. The Conservative candidate, W. T. Donovan, won 13,808 votes. The Labour majority increased by some 200 votes.

issue of foreign and domestic affairs. What does exist is a deep *de facto* understanding between the two Front Benches and a growing feeling that both are fighting the extremists on the Right and the extremists, more important, on the Left.

Wednesday, December 2nd

All these last three days Parliament has been seething with the anti-Mallalieu row. Directly I came in on Monday I found it the gossip of the lobby. Frank McLeavy,[1] the old T. & G. fellow from Leeds, who always leads the demand for expulsion, came up to me in the corridor and began to tell me how terrible Mallalieu's article had been.[2] I said, 'Are you going to expel me as well for being a journalist?' And he said, 'You wouldn't write an article like that, Dick. I like your articles.' I said, 'My dear Frank, the only difference is that I would write exactly the same article but so cleverly that you couldn't catch me out.' 'Yes,' he said, 'that's exactly the difference between you and Mallalieu.'

At lunch yesterday we discussed it, rather futilely, at length. There were some who said that Mallalieu was going to be drummed out of the Party but Nye quite rightly observed that the Front Bench now smells office and will want to close the whole row down. He was proved right this morning. Committee Room 14 was packed when Attlee started with a very severe statement, calling the article mischievous and accusing us of infringing the resolution passed last October against groups and fraternal strife. Then he called on Mallalieu, who spoke for three minutes. He said that he had looked at the article carefully and couldn't possibly withdraw a word and then he just added, 'Freedom, you know, doesn't mean giving freedom to those you agree with but to those you disagree with.' At this point, as we had agreed at lunch yesterday, the Bevanites let out a roar of applause, which had an enormous effect.

Frank McLeavy then rose to move the expulsion of Mallalieu. Attlee nipped up to say that this was out of order, since it wasn't on the agenda. McLeavy, quite nimbly, then said, 'All right, I will move the reference of the incident to the N.E.C.,' to which Attlee said he wasn't sure whether that was in order. This made clear which way the wind was blowing and it blew unmistakably when Arthur Woodburn, sitting right up by the platform, was called next. He breathed sweetness and light. We must attack the Tories, who were now tottering. We must show a love of freedom, even when provoked.

All this was greeted with stormy applause and at the end, when about twenty right-wingers rose to speak, there were shouts of 'Next business'. To the fury of the right-wing, Attlee then took a vote as to whether we should

---

[1] Labour M.P. for Bradford East 1945–66. He became a life peer in 1967. He died in 1977.
[2] See p. 277, above.

pass to the next business. It was carried by 160 to 41. Elaine-Burton[1] was among the forty-one. Then, typically enough, we had another twenty minutes of points of order, since no one was sure what exactly had happened. Attlee seemed to suggest that the Party had accepted his statement but Michael Foot said that in that case it must equally have accepted Mallalieu's statement, since we had merely moved to the next business. The Right saw itself trapped and demanded that a statement should be issued but it never became clear what sort of statement this should be. In a way, I sided with the forty-one. They had all been storming and demanding a row and then funked the row at the last moment. How contemptible.

Thursday, December 3rd

Last night, after a pleasant but rather disappointing dinner with Alec Spearman, at which John Strachey, Toby Low,[2] Quintin Hogg and John Foster[3] were present, as well as Roy Jenkins and myself, I took Roy home for a drink. I started the conversation by saying that I thought it was very depressing that the freedom of speech which we had within the Labour Party in the first five years of the Labour Government should be steadily constricted. Five years ago I was able to slosh Bevin about Palestine and he was able to slosh me and nobody doubted the right of free speech. Roy replied, 'Well, they – I mean we – feel that every speech, every action must now be considered as part of the power fight within the Party. That's why we hate Bevanism. Before it began one could have free speech. Now one can't afford to.' He repeated several times, 'We on the Right feel that every force of demagogy and every emotion is against us. In the constituency parties, which are now Opposition-minded, the Bevanites have it all their own way. I suppose one must wait for the tide to turn, as it slowly did in the 1930s, away from the Opposition-mindedness of 1931 to constructive policies.'

I asked him why he felt it was so terribly important to defeat the Bevanites and he said, 'The electorate is extremely Conservative-minded and we can

---

[1] A teacher in a Leeds school 1924–35, she then worked for the South Wales Council of Social Service and Educational Settlements 1935–7, the National Fitness Council 1938–9 and the John Lewis Partnership 1940–5. From 1945 to 1950 she was a writer, lecturer, broadcaster and public relations consultant. Labour M.P. for Coventry South 1950–9, she became a life peer in 1962.

[2] Called to the Bar in 1939, after distinguished Army service during the war, Toby Low was Conservative M.P. for Blackpool North 1945–62, Parliamentary Secretary at the Ministry of Supply 1951–4 and Minister of State at the Board of Trade 1954–7. He was Deputy Chairman of the Conservative Party Organization 1959–63. Knighted in 1957, he became a peer in 1962, taking the title of 1st Baron Aldington.

[3] Elected a Fellow of All Souls' College, Oxford in 1924, he was Lecturer in Private International Law at the University of Oxford from 1934 to 1939, when he became First Secretary at the British Embassy in Washington. He was Conservative M.P. for Northwich, Cheshire, 1945 to February 1974. From 1951 to 1954 he was Parliamentary Under-Secretary of State at the Commonwealth Relations Office. He became a Q.C. in 1950 and was knighted in 1964.

never win except with the kind of attitude represented by the right-wing leadership.' He also added that, for people like himself and Tony Crosland, the very existence of the Bevanites and their popularity was the major factor in making him loyal to Gaitskell. In the sort of hopeless fight that Gaitskell was waging, one had to stand by him.

What was interesting about the whole talk, which lasted for an hour and a half, was Roy's feeling that they were battling against the tide in the constituencies, that they must hang on for dear life. He also repeatedly emphasized that, just because the Bevanites were so strong, Gaitskell was more and more forced to rely on forces such as Arthur Deakin, which made him even further to the right than he would naturally be.

From December 4th to 8th the Prime Minister and Mr Eden attended the postponed Bermuda Conference with the French Prime Minister, the U.S. President and their Foreign Ministers. Their discussion included consideration of the proposal for a Four-Power Conference.

On November 3rd a Note had been received from the Russian Government replying to the invitation to the Foreign Ministers' conference on the German and Austrian questions. The Russian Note made no direct reference to this proposal but laid down a number of conditions which, the Foreign Secretary told the Commons on November 5th, would undermine British security and make the reunification of Germany impossible.

A second Russian Note was published on November 27th. It accepted the proposal for a Four-Power Conference but stated the Russian intention of putting forward at such a meeting the question of a Five-Power Conference, including China. The Western Powers' reply took up Russia's suggestion that the meeting should be in Berlin and offered January 4th as the date. Dr Adenauer, the West German Chancellor, had seen and approved the document before despatch.

At the conclusion of the Bermuda Conference a communiqué was issued, reasserting in general terms that NATO remained the foundation of Western policy, with the E.D.C. as an integral part of its framework, and that the Western Powers' immediate objective in the Far East was the convening of a Korean political conference.

Friday, December 18th
Yesterday we had the big debate on foreign affairs.[1] It was meant to be on Bermuda and, indeed, Churchill, Attlee and Eden all spoke chiefly on this subject, but the Tory Suez resolution made this topic the only real debating matter for backbenchers.[2] Moreover, Nye had claimed and obtained the

---

[1] The debate was on the motion for the adjournment and there was no division.
[2] See above, p. 278.

right to speak from the Front Bench, since he had been attacked on his article.*

When every other Labour speaker who wanted to intervene had been called, I also got in at the end, made the mistake of sitting down too often for interruptions, and so took thirty-seven minutes, thus excluding Bob Boothby, who had been wanting to talk on E.D.C. Nye afterwards told me that it was the best speech that I had ever made, and he came back to 9 Vincent Square to drink whisky till two o'clock. He expressed the view that Pompeiian art and architecture is some of the finest in the world. I found Pompeii the height of ostentatious vulgarity and so did Tommy Balogh, who was at my house with Pen. However, it was a very nice evening. Nye's speech had been a tremendous *tour de force* and a great success in the Chamber, but in the press next day it was made to look as though he had been pretty roughly handled. As for myself, I really needn't have spoken, from the point of view of the press. Yet the effect in the House was, I think, considerable. We managed to corral the Tory rebels and to ensure that the Labour Party supported the Government in continuing negotiations.

Tommy Balogh was terribly upset that, as the result of all this, events in Paris hardly got a mention.[1] What had happened last Monday was a series of public threats by Dulles that, if the French didn't sign E.D.C. very soon, America would walk out and leave them to deal with Germany alone. On Thursday Churchill supported these American threats and it is, of course, lamentable that the Labour Party should not have registered its protest against these efforts to force through E.D.C. despite the forthcoming Four-Power Conference. But, as I tried to explain to Tommy, in the House of Commons you have to debate what is up for debate. Whereas by debate we could do something about Suez, there was nothing that one could do by making a speech about France, since the Labour Party is not united on this subject.

So we come to the Christmas recess. In the Smoking Room yesterday Bob Boothby said, 'I've never known such a bad Parliament.' And Nye and I

* Nye had written for the first number of a new paper run by Neguib's Liberation Front an article on the Canal Zone. He was attacked in the *Daily Express* and the sensation rumbled on for ten days, with other papers taking it up and denouncing Nye for selling himself and writing anti-British articles in the enemy press. At first Nye seemed rather unconcerned about the whole affair but, as the press campaign went on, he began to get angry, particularly as nobody bothered to ask him for a copy of the piece or to discover that it had been published a month before in the many Indian newspapers for which he is writing a weekly syndicated article.

[1] In a debate on foreign affairs, beginning on November 19th, the principal subject on the National Assembly's agenda was ratification of the E.D.C. Treaty. The coalition Government of M. Joseph Laniel secured a vote of confidence by only 31 votes, the Socialists and Communists voting against and most of the Gaullist group abstaining. In his reply to the debate, M. Laniel reiterated the three conditions for ratification spelt out by previous French Governments (see above, p. 78 and n.), on which little evident progress had yet been made. On December 14th Mr Dulles, speaking in Paris, warned the French that, unless the E.D.C. Treaty was ratified, the Americans would have to undertake 'an agonizing reappraisal' of their policy.

agreed that there has never been a Government which by its incompetence has given an Opposition so many opportunities and that there has never been an Opposition which by its incompetence and division has muffed so many opportunities. But I must add that the left-wing of the Labour Party (or should one still call it Bevanism?) is also collapsing as a force. With nobody standing for anything anywhere, British politics drifts. One is left with the feeling that life will really start when one gets into an aeroplane as a journalist on the way to Africa.

1954

From Monday, December 21st, 1953, to Friday, January 15th, 1954, Crossman was travelling in Africa. In Cairo he and Colonel Sadat spent an evening at the home of Colonel Nasser, where they discussed the future of the Suez base:

> *Nasser said, 'the British don't negotiate under duress. You must either negotiate or put the heat on.' And Salem [one of the junta] added, 'Of course, if they would only occupy Cairo, that would be militarily the best thing for us which could happen.' It was obvious that Nasser was most unwilling to break off negotiations and try the use of force ... [He] emphasized that they could not go on waiting for an agreement. I asked why not, and he replied that both the Moslem Brotherhood and the Communists were serious threats. I pooh-poohed the Communists ...*

In the course of the conversation, the talk turned to Israel and Gaza. Nasser started by observing, 'the idea of throwing the Jews into the sea is propaganda. Israel exists and we must face the fact'. Crossman also spent a morning with Nasser, discussing the present state of the negotiations over the Canal Base, and an afternoon with Hilaly Pasha. He then toured the Zone itself.

On Boxing Day Crossman visited Gaza and on December 27th he called on General Neguib, who had retired to his villa with bronchitis. The following day Crossman travelled to Khartoum, in the Sudan, and on December 29th to Kampala, in Uganda, to stay with Sir Andrew and Lady Cohen at Government House, 'the only lotos land I've been in'. As well as interviewing the Prime Minister and Finance Minister of Buganda, he met John Stonehouse, then helping to run the African co-operative federation. '[He and his wife], an extremely nice girl ... [had] been utterly disillusioned by ... the African co-ops and he has formed a limited liability company to set up a string of retail co-ops but desperately wants capital and Government backing, which he hasn't yet got.' On New Year's Eve Crossman dined with Stonehouse, 'who told me a good deal about the persecution he suffered when he arrived there, on the ground that he was a Bolshevik, but said that life had got a lot easier now.'

On Monday, January 4th, Crossman arrived in Kenya. He called on General Erskine, who described the details of the military operation against the Mau-Mau and from Wednesday, January 6th, to Friday, January 8th, Crossman, 'in a suit of denims', went forward into the forest with the troops, spending the first night in a bamboo shed at a military camp. 'I thought the men didn't want to talk to me, but when I got home I found a letter waiting, telling me all the complaints they hadn't dared to tell me when the C.O. was present.' He also spent some days in the country, returning to Nairobi for an interview with Colonel O'Rourke, head of the Kenya Police.

After a further few days in Entebbe, Crossman returned to London. His accounts of the trip may be found in: 'Report on Mau Mau', New Statesman and Nation, January 23rd, 1954; 'Breakdown of the Suez Talks', New Statesman and Nation, January 30th, 1954; 'What Went Wrong in Uganda', New Statesman and Nation, February 6th, 1954.

Friday, January 15th

I caught the Argonaut in the morning at Entebbe and, after twenty-five hours' flying, tottered into London, dead and dazed, to find that Anne had agreed to get engaged.[1]

On February 8th Crossman went as an observer to the Berlin Four-Power Conference, between the Foreign Ministers of Britain, France, the U.S.A. and the U.S.S.R. The conference had opened on January 25th and was to last until February 18th.

The agenda, proposed by Mr Molotov and accepted by the three Western representatives, was: first, methods of reducing tension in international relations and the convening of a Five-Power Conference, including China; second, the German question and problems of ensuring European security; and, third, the Austrian Treaty. Soviet prevarication made it impossible for the conference to resolve even limited objectives in regard to these matters and it quickly became plain that the new men in the Kremlin took a similar view of Russia's interests in Europe to that of their predecessors.

The most hopeful outcome of the conference was the proposal announced in the final communiqué that a further conference should meet in Geneva on April 26th, 'for the purpose of reaching a peaceful settlement of the Korean question'. It was also agreed that 'the problem of restoring peace in Indo-China' should be discussed. The Geneva conference would be attended by the Four Powers present at Berlin, together with China, North and South Korea and, if they wished, other countries whose armed forces had taken part in the Korean hostilities.

On February 24th the Foreign Secretary opened a two-day Commons debate on the Berlin Conference. He stated that the Soviet arguments and proposals had been motivated by the desire to bring all Germany into the Soviet embrace and to force the United States out of the European Alliance. Mr Eden looked forward to the early establishment of the European Defence Community, for such arrangements, within NATO, were, he declared, the best method of ensuring Western security. Discussions on the form of British association with the E.D.C. were soon to be resumed in Paris.

Herbert Morrison expressed the Opposition's official approval of the Government's policy of German rearmament, although a substantial section of the P.L.P. did not in fact agree. The debate was concluded by the Prime Minister, who was cheered by such dissenting backbenchers for saying that it was possible to build E.D.C. and NATO and at the same time to strive for a working understanding with the Russian people. Sir Winston saw the proposal for a Geneva conference as a hopeful result of the discussions in Berlin.

Crossman himself spent a week in Berlin, meeting among others the Editor of Pravda, *who expressed surprise that the Western representatives had not taken seriously Mr Molotov's plan. This was a referendum throughout Germany, to*

[1] They were married in June 1954.

establish whether her people preferred integration with the West, by means of the E.D.C. and the Bonn Conventions on German sovereignty, or a neutralized Germany excluded from the Western defence system. At a party 'given by the three Western Powers to Mr Molotov in return for the party he gave', Crossman records,

> *Eden came up to me and said: 'We really haven't had any negotiations here until this morning, when we had a secret session on China. For an hour or two we did negotiate, but otherwise we've merely had a confrontation of opposing views. The other night I asked Molotov to dinner and talked to him frankly and directly. "Mr Eden," he said, "no Western statesman has talked to me like that since 1945." And then Mr Molotov added slyly, "It would be nice if you would negotiate with me as the three of you negotiated at Bermuda." ' Just after this Dulles came up and heard me telling Eden about my conversation with the Editor of* Pravda. *'So the ·\ussians thought we would take their plan seriously,' he said. 'That's interesting. Maybe the greatest value of this conference is to make us understand each other better. We are constantly being surprised by them and they by us.' The more I think of this remark of Dulles's, the more it illustrates the remarkable change of temper which this conference displayed.*

Crossman's account of his visit may be found in the Sunday Pictorial *of February 14th, and (unsigned) in the* New Statesman and Nation *of February 20th, 1954.*

Wednesday, March 3rd[1]

Let me now go back to mid-January. It is difficult now to describe how low political morale was when Parliament resumed.[2] There was no debate of any importance for three weeks and not even a Party Meeting. Meanwhile, in the country, public meetings were fading away, as was shown at the beginning of February in four by-elections, where the Government proportion of the vote went up substantially and ours dropped.[3]

[1] From February 21st to March 3rd the Diary was 'broken off for six weeks, partly because when I returned from Africa I was so busy writing articles about it; partly because I got engaged; and partly because politics reached a new low level of boredom and lethargy, from which they suddenly recovered in the last ten days.'

[2] The House resumed on January 19th, 1954, after the adjournment for the Christmas Recess.

[3] On February 3rd a by-election took place in Ilford North, caused by the appointment of Sir Geoffrey Hutchinson (Conservative) as Chairman of the National Assistance Board. T. L. Iremonger held the seat for the Conservatives, with a majority of 8,427 votes over T. W. Richardson (Labour). The Conservative vote rose from 55·5 per cent of the poll to 59·8 per cent.

On February 11th by-elections were held in the Haltemprice division of Hull and in Harwich. In Hull, where the Conservative Member, Sir Richard Law, had been made a peer in the New Year Honours, Patrick Wall retained the seat for the Conservatives, with a majority of 6,133 votes over C. W. Bridges, the Labour candidate. The Conservative vote rose from 58·11 per cent of the poll to 61·76 per cent. In Harwich, where the National Liberal and Conservative Member, Sir J. Stanley Holmes, had been made a peer in the New Year Honours, Julian Ridsdale held the seat for the Conservatives and Liberals with a majority

We couldn't even keep the Bevanite Group together. Nye failed to turn up on Tuesdays, asked for our lunch to be changed to Thursdays and then didn't turn up on two successive Thursdays. As usual, he had excellent excuses but really he was evading pressure from Ian Mikardo to start the Friends of *Tribune* as a cover for reorganizing the groups. Nye reacted against this instinctively, though he wasn't prepared to say so. At this time he was also taking the view that the issue of German rearmament was not of great importance in the new atomic age. Sooner or later there would be German divisions, so why worry much?

It was after and as a result of the Berlin Conference that politics suddenly woke up. All the week of the 15th, I was struggling to shape the *New Statesman* Defence Supplement, due to be published the Friday after the Government White Paper.[1] For this, George Wigg, Michael Stewart and Tommy Balogh had all written memoranda and it wasn't an easy job getting them into shape. Meanwhile, on Tuesday the 16th, we had a meeting of the International Sub. and I suddenly realized what was up, since at this meeting Sam Watson said that, as the Berlin Conference had failed, the Party must reach a decision and the decision must obviously be to back E.D.C.

Nye was away at the Parliamentary Committee, which was discussing the same subject, Tom Driberg was ill and Barbara found it more important to make a speech on food.[2] So Harold Wilson and I battled for an hour and a half, arguing that the Berlin Conference was not the end but the beginning of negotiations and that the Party was pledged not to one further effort but to further efforts. However, we were voted down by 10 to 2 and I went off rather depressed.

On Thursday the 18th we held our Bevanite lunch at last and it was realized that Gaitskell and Morrison were determined to force the German rearmament issue before the two-day debate on foreign affairs, due to start on the 24th. Nye was very gloomy but agreed, somewhat reluctantly, that I should draft a resolution to put before the Party Meeting, which, it had been

---

of 5,997, over the Labour candidate, Miss Shirley Catlin (later Mrs Shirley Williams). The Conservative–Liberal proportion of the vote increased from 58·92 to 59·07 per cent.

On February 18th a by-election took place in Bournemouth West, caused by the resignation through ill-health of Viscount Cranborne (Conservative). J. B. Eden held the seat for the Conservatives, with a majority of 11,689 over H. Brinton (Labour), and the Conservative vote rose from 65·49 per cent of the poll to 69·68.

[1] Cmd 9075, published on February 18th, 1954. The size of the 1954/55 defence budget, at £1,640 million, was almost the same as in 1953/54 but the emphasis was different. The armed forces were to be reduced in number and the R.A.F. was to be increased. Within twelve months a supersonic fighter was to be produced and more than four-fifths of aircraft expenditure was to be on jet-propelled aeroplanes. Within the year three aircraft carriers with angled flight decks were to be completed. A force of atomic bombers would be constructed as soon as possible and delivery of atomic weapons to the forces had already begun. The reduction in American aid meant that the British population would have to provide an extra £1 per head to the defence budget. The four-page article, 'Britain's Defence Budget: The Real Cost' was published as a centre section of the *New Statesman and Nation*, February 27th, 1954.

[2] In a Commons debate on a supplementary estimate to be granted to the Ministry of Food.

announced, would take place on the night of the 23rd. Then I rushed to the House to get a text of the White Paper in order to co-ordinate our defence supplement, which to my great pleasure needed no modification.

Travelling down to London after a weekend in Sheffield with Harold Wilson, we were mildly encouraged by the success of our speeches and I was even more encouraged on Monday afternoon when the foreign affairs group met. John Hynd and I were asked to open the discussion. It then transpired that a large majority of the group were on my side, including such surprising people as Donald Chapman[1] and Frank Beswick.[2] But even then we didn't quite believe.

However, George Wigg and I got down to the job of organization. Already, on the previous Thursday, Nye had agreed with my proposal that Harold Wilson should move our resolution in the Party Meeting. It would have been normal for me to do so, but I've opposed German rearmament for three years and we felt we wanted somebody to move it who would lose us fewer votes. George agreed with this tactic and spent two days getting non-Bevanite speakers, such as Wilfred Fienburgh and Bob Mellish.

Tuesday, February 23rd, was the great day. It started rather gloomily for me with the meeting of the defence and services group to consider the White Paper. As usual, it was absolute chaos, with Woodrow Wyatt representing the Gaitskell line and Manny Shinwell talking himself into circles and nobody deciding anything. In desperation, I promised to let them all have proofs of the *New Statesman* supplement at a postponed meeting on Thursday morning.

We went straight from the defence and services group to the Party Meeting, which was fuller than I've ever known it. There must have been 220 there out of a possible total of about 225. Attlee opened with a strange speech, purporting to support the resolution but actually ending with the remark that there was no need to rush into German rearmament. This strongly confirmed what Tom O'Brien told me, namely that Attlee had been pushed into this by Gaitskell and Morrison, who had assured him that they could carry the Party comfortably into support of E.D.C. as a result of the Berlin deadlock. On the Parliamentary Committee this issue had only been opposed by James Callaghan and Chuter Ede, apart from Nye, since Dalton was away ill.

After Attlee, Harold Wilson spoke with very great skill. It was a quiet, inoffensive speech, without any edge to it, such as I could never possibly deliver. I think it was calculated and, sitting beside Harold, as he had requested me to do, to brief him if things went wrong, I rated him even higher as a politician than I had before.

[1] Labour M.P. for the Northfield division of Birmingham, 1951–70. In 1975 he became a life peer, taking the title of Lord Northfield. In 1973 he became a Visiting Fellow at the Centre for Contemporary European Studies at the University of Sussex, in 1974 Chairman of the Development Commission, and 1975 Chairman of Telford Development Corporation.

[2] Labour and Co-operative M.P. for Uxbridge 1945–59, he was P.P.S. to the Under-Secretary of State for Air 1946–9 and Parliamentary Secretary at the Ministry of Civil Aviation 1950–1. In 1964 he became a life peer and served as Government Chief Whip in the House of Lords 1967–70, Chief Opposition Whip 1970–4 and Deputy Leader of the Lords 1974–5. From 1975 to 1979 he was Chairman of British Aerospace.

Next, Attlee called Fienburgh, obviously assuming he would oppose us, but he made the emotional speech of a young Army officer whose best friends have been killed by Germans. To our great relief, he was followed by Percy Daines and John Hynd, speaking against us but, each in his own way, Percy by his rudeness and Hynd by his boringness, assisting our side.

By this time it was clear enough that a very large part of the meeting was against the motion. Morrison began his summing-up quite well but made the fatal mistake of ending by saying that the Party couldn't let ex-Ministers down and he had committed the Party to E.D.C. in Ottawa and Washington during the last weeks of the second Labour Government.[1]

Our amendment was put first and was defeated by two votes, that is, the votes of Callaghan and Ede. Their resolution was carried by a few more. Harold Wilson then rose on a point of order: 'A fortnight ago the Party Meeting supported my motion on the Japanese trade agreement by 100 votes to 25, but you, Sir, then said that I, as the spokesman for the Party, should take into account the minority view in framing my speech.[2] May I take it that, in speaking for the Party tomorrow, you will take into account our minority view?' Herbert Morrison was extremely good-tempered and said that of course he would. He had, within a matter of seconds, realized that it was no good pretending that we were splitters or a minority and that we had accepted the Party decision.

The six members of the Executive went back to Vincent Square to discuss our tactics for next morning's meeting of the N.E.C., where the International Sub.'s resolution was to be considered. We all assumed we should be the only six opposing, and Tom Driberg said, 'This is a chance for a tremendous row and resignation.' This proposal was brushed aside, as it was already clear that the Party would never forgive our resigning and anyway our position was so strong that we could continue to expound our opposition to German rearmament, whatever the Executive decided.

On Wednesday the 24th the Executive discussion was begun by Tom, whose rudeness consisted of a few mild sentences, which stopped so briefly that none of us was ready to speak. So I filled in the silence by discussing what our delegation should do in Brussels,[3] in view of the even division in the Party. I am told I was didactic. Anyway, I infuriated Attlee, who didn't like being

[1] Where Morrison had attended the North Atlantic Council meeting, in Ottawa, in September 1951.

[2] On February 10th Harold Wilson had opened a debate on a motion regretting the Government's entering into a Japanese trade agreement 'without prior consultation with the industries concerned, and without securing assurances that Japanese exporters will not revert to previous unfair trade practices'. The motion was defeated by 296 votes to 265 but an Amendment to the motion on the agreement, supporting the Government while recommending safeguards, was carried by 297 votes to 258.

[3] At the European Socialist Conference from February 26th to 28th. It ended with the adoption of a resolution supporting the reunification of Germany, the independence of Austria and the establishment of a European security system based on the independence of nations, including those behind the Iron Curtain.

told that the idea was to use the Labour Party to bully the French Socialists into supporting E.D.C. Whereas Herbert Morrison was in thoroughly good humour, Attlee's hand was shaking and he was quivering with emotion, when he brushed aside any thought of postponing the issue and said the Executive must vote at once. 'Even if it splits the Party?' asked someone. 'Well, that's their concern,' Attlee said.

A little later Nye staged a tremendous row, which ended by his shouting, 'We all know how the vote will go, with only the six of us against!' 'How do you know?' asked Jack Cooper[1] and Nye shouted at him (thinking he was alleging that we had had a caucus meeting beforehand), 'Because each of us voted that way last night!' But of course Jack Cooper meant that he was going to vote with us. And a little later, twitching his paper and looking very shame-faced, he said that he had consulted with some of his colleagues in the union, that they could not see any reason why this was being brought forward now and that he would move to defer the whole issue. He was at once supported by Edwin Gooch[2] of the Agricultural Workers and Cooper's motion was only lost by 11 votes to 13, with the Steelworkers, the E.T.U. and one other union (I'm not sure which) on our side.

Then there was a long, rambling discussion on the International Sub.'s resolution, which was far sharper than the resolution of the Parliamentary Party and ended with a specific proposal to support E.D.C. This was impossible because the supporters of German rearmament were not agreed among themselves whether it should be under NATO or E.D.C. and the paragraph was deleted.

This fact that five big unions voted with the six Bevanites was far more significant than the vote in the Party Meeting the day before. They all did so, I suspect, because they didn't dare to face their members and I think they were all irritated by what they felt was the gratuitous difficulty in which Gaitskell and Morrison were putting them by pushing this issue now. They realized that this meant breaking the compact made at Margate[3] and they saw no point in doing it just to please Mr Gaitskell, particularly after the events in the Parliamentary Party the day before.

That afternoon the two-day debate in the Commons began, with an excellent speech by Eden, followed by an astonishing Parliamentary performance by Morrison, who got away with an impudent admission that his

[1] Labour M.P. for Deptford 1950–1, he was P.P.S. to the Secretary of State for Commonwealth Relations during that period. A member of the National Union of General and Municipal Workers from 1928 to 1973, he was the Chairman 1952–61 and General Secretary and Treasurer 1962–73. In 1966 he became a life peer, taking the title of Lord Cooper of Stockton Heath. He was Chairman of the British Productivity Council 1965–6, a member of the Thames Conservancy 1955–74 and of the National Water Council 1973–7.

[2] Edwin Gooch (1889–1964), a former blacksmith and, later, a member of the printing trade, was Chief Sub-Editor for the *Norwich Mercury* group until his election as Labour M.P. for North Norfolk in 1945, a seat he held until his death. He was President of the National Union of Agricultural Workers from 1928 until his death.

[3] See above, pp. 264 ff.

Party was split and that he must express two contradictory points of view.[1] I found it a virtuoso show and was peeved afterwards when Nye refused to admit that Morrison showed any skill at all.

On Thursday morning, the 25th, we had our postponed defence meeting. After a terrible, desultory argument, I got a resolution carried by 7 votes to 4, including three points: first, the global burden was too heavy; secondly, the term of service must be cut; thirdly, the allocation between manpower and production was wrong. This was opposed by Woodrow Wyatt, Manny Shinwell and George Wigg, who suddenly changed sides at the last moment, for reasons which he has never been able to explain to me since.

At the Bevanite lunch I reported this and Nye said we could have no hope of doing much about defence, since the Party was suffering from shock and reaction to its behaviour on Tuesday. As I had been working for five weeks preparing for the defence debate, I was a bit depressed, particularly as this is a concrete issue on which we had a far stronger case than on German rearmament, where we had no positive policy and were only delaying.

However, at half-past six I went to the Party Meeting, where Attlee got up and announced that the Parliamentary Committee had still not made up its mind on the Defence Estimates and asked the Party to give it a free hand. At this John Strachey announced for the defence group, that we had sent in our resolution and asked for a special meeting. Attlee tried to resist but the Party voted for it. Immediately after this, the Parliamentary Committee resumed its session and completely turned round, accepting the substance of our motion, redrafted in rather sharper form by Attlee. The only opponents were Gaitskell and Frank Soskice, with Morrison abstaining. The fact is that, faced with the risk of another defeat at a special meeting, the Parliamentary Committee had ratted on its convictions.

At the Bevanite lunch on Tuesday, March 2nd, there was a full attendance and great elation, with everybody forgetting all that they had said a week before. Nye agreed to say a word to the Speaker on my behalf for the defence debate and did so. Otherwise I would certainly not have got in. The debate began with an appalling speech by Nigel Birch.[2] The unfortunate man had prepared a speech to wind up the debate but then Churchill learnt that Labour was opposing and decided to speak at the end, when he had heard Shinwell. So poor Birch had to make a new speech and was then suddenly told to introduce into it two announcements. He's a good speaker and there-

[1] 'It is by now well known, owing to the extraordinarily efficient intelligence service of the lobby correspondents of this House, that there was and is a division of opinion in the Parliamentary Labour Party.'

[2] The debate on the Defence White Paper on March 2nd was opened by Nigel Birch, Parliamentary Secretary at the Ministry of Defence. The Prime Minister deplored the Opposition's insistence on dividing the House on an Amendment criticizing Government policy on the length of compulsory National Service. The amendment was defeated by 295 votes to 270. Mr Birch announced selective improvements in forces' pay and the extension to certain categories of retired officers and civil servants of a recent 10 per cent increase in Service and Civil Service pensions of no more than £400 a year.

fore hated it even more. Finally, to add insult to injury, when Birch was criticized by Attlee, Churchill got up and said this was very ungenerous to a young man who had been given his first chance to open a great debate!

However, Shinwell was far worse than Birch. We all knew what was going to happen, since Shinwell believes in cutting National Service and maintaining all our commitments. For nearly an hour he was baited by the Tories like a poor old bull that nobody even wants to kill. John Strachey practically read aloud the *New Statesman* supplement, which I had intended to do! What John didn't use, Attlee did, thanks to briefing by George [Wigg]. All this may have improved the speech which I made, since I was left to be rather gayer and more amusing, and it came off all right. So ends one chapter of Labour Party history.

Wednesday, March 10th
Last Friday Hugh Cudlipp came to dinner, which is always something of a strain. He came at a quarter to eight and left at a quarter past twelve. During dinner he assaulted me incessantly for being an irresponsible Bevanite, without any constructive policy on Germany or defence, and reminded me how responsible he and the *Mirror* were in all their decisions and how much he thought of Gaitskell. He also told me that it was high time that I made the big decision to write a daily political column. I said there was no room for it in the *Mirror* and Hugh said, 'Leave that to me. But you really will have to give up being a stupid Bevanite.' So I said I much preferred to stay a Bevanite and on the *Sunday Pic*. We also discussed Nye's six weekly articles, which began last Friday in the *Daily Mirror*. Nye is getting £150 an article, the same, Hugh told me, as he received from the *News of the World*, so he really is in the big money.

Just before I gave Hugh dinner, I'd had a chat with Nye in the Smoking Room. 'What's your subject this week?' I asked, and he produced out of his pocket a little bit of typed paper with some notes about the denationalized steel shares and the attempt to sell off the lorries and premises of the Transport Commission. 'Can you pad that out to 1,000 words?' I said, and he said, 'Why not?' I said, 'Well, of course you can but your obvious subject next Friday is Egypt and Suez, since we've got the Army Estimates and Barbara Castle's motion coming on on Thursday.'[1] 'But that's stale,' he said, 'and why should I be so topical?' I didn't try to press him, except to say that he was writing six articles and I thought he ought to deal with six big subjects.

---

[1] The Army Estimates were debated on March 11th. Backbench Members could take part in a ballot before the Estimates debate and the successful Member could propose a subject for discussion, in the form of an Amendment. Two or three hours would be given to this item, with the main debate being broken off for the purpose at 7 p.m. Mrs Castle had been successful in the ballot and had selected Suez as her subject. Crossman and George Wigg had worked to brief her for the debate. Mrs Castle's motion deplored 'the Government's handling of the Anglo-Egyptian negotiations which has prolonged this uncertainty'. It was defeated by 271 votes to 219.

Today Hugh Cudlipp rang me up to tell me that the article had come in, that it was on Suez and that it was much better than last week's.

Nye is being very coy about these articles. He's in a frightful mental fix. He desperately wants to write them well but he is determined not to become a journalist, like Michael and me, and not to demean himself to Fleet Street levels. Actually he caused fury in the *Daily Mirror*. They built him up for his first article, which would obviously be on German rearmament. Then on Thursday he makes a speech at Stratford on German rearmament and so enabled the *Express* to front-page him, using much more vivid language than he had used in the *Mirror* article, for which he'd been paid £150. Why he thinks it's demeaning to write vividly but not to speak vividly is a problem of psychoanalysis. I really sometimes think that it's a problem for him that he is surrounded by able journalists.

Wednesday, March 24th

All last week the House was completely flat but, since Anne was in Banbury all the week with her father,[1] I spent every evening there, wasting time. Once again we had the problem of Nye's article. In the previous week I had put him off denationalization in favour of Egypt but, sure enough, on Wednesday, when we were dining together, he pulled his draft out of his breast pocket in the way that only an amateur journalist can do and asked me what I thought of it. It was denationalization, done quite competently but curiously flat.

I discussed this with Michael Foot on Thursday night, since Hugh Cudlipp had told me that Nye's article had excited no correspondence whatsoever. Indeed, Hugh quoted a figure of seven letters aroused by the first two articles. Hugh is very ambivalent about the whole thing — pleased that he is featuring Nye as a method of getting *Daily Herald* readers and at the same time pleased that he is proving that Nye is a bad journalist. I asked Michael whether we could do anything and he replied, 'I've known Nye longer than you have. No one will ever make him a good journalist. That's where he differs from Churchill.' From Michael this was a very severe judgment.

In October 1953 the Engineering and Allied Employers' National Federation had rejected the unions' demand for a 15 per cent wage increase, giving as their reason that in the previous year wages had risen by 6·4 per cent but retail prices by only 4·4 per cent, while orders had been declining. In protest the Confederation of Shipbuilding and Engineering Unions called a twenty-four-hour strike on December 2nd. This body was dominated by the Amalgamated Engineering Union, largely Communist-controlled. The National Union of General and Municipal Workers meanwhile announced that its members in

---

[1] Patrick McDougall. Livestock Commissioner for Scotland under the Ministry of Food 1917–20, he bought Prescote Manor and its land in 1920. He was instrumental in founding Midland Marts Ltd in Banbury, of which he was Chairman of the Directors and Managing Director.

shipbuilding and engineering firms would not participate in the stoppage. The one-day strike took place, to be followed by discussions among the thirty-nine constituent unions on further action.

On December 23rd the executives of these thirty-nine organizations decided to recommend strict limitation on piecework and a ban on all overtime from January 18th, 1954. This was the declared policy of the A.E.U., unwelcome to some other constituent unions. On December 31st the Minister of Labour, Sir Walter Monckton, had appointed two Courts of Inquiry, both with Lord Justice Morris in the chair and with the same five members, to report on the engineering and shipbuilding disputes. The unions were asked to postpone their action until the reports appeared.

On February 26th the Courts of Inquiry recommended that engineering and shipbuilding employees should be awarded a minimum advance of 7s. a week and that this should apply to unskilled as well as skilled men. The Courts of Inquiry proposed that 'some authoritative and impartial body' should examine the 'wider problems' arising from the year's batch of wage increases and should express its opinion whether 'even a slight upward thrust in the inflationary spiral would be disastrous' to the present or foreseeable state of the British economy.

On Friday the 19th Sydney Jacobson asked me to lunch to meet Victor Feather,[1] the Assistant Secretary of the T.U.C. Victor turns out to be a bouncing little Yorkshireman, voluble and indiscreet, but carefully indiscreet. On the day before the engineers had announced that they would not accept the 5 per cent wage increase which the court of inquiry had recommended. 'Don't fuss,' said Victor. 'They've got to kick up a bit more nuisance and may-be get 6 or $6\frac{1}{2}$ per cent. But they know they can't have any serious trouble after the one-day token strike last December. What really ruined the men's position then was the number of them who went to the employers afterwards and asked for overtime to make up the loss on the one-day strike.' I expect that this is the general T.U.C. and top-level trade union leader view and it probably has a great deal of truth in it. But, all the same, it's dangerous to assume that there won't be trouble.

Under pressure, Victor also admitted to me that Butler's policy suited the T.U.C. pretty well. 'Of the four Chancellors you've had since the war,' I asked him, 'which was the most awkward?' Without any hesitation, he replied, 'Stafford Cripps. He had a policy, which he forced on us. Of course, Butler has a policy, too, but the decontrol suits trade unions pretty well, since we can revert to our old function.'

He also told one superb story about Attlee. Alfred Robens was Parliamentary Secretary at the Ministry of Fuel and Power at the time of Nye's resignation.[2] One morning he was rung up by St Mary's Hospital. 'This is

---

[1] A member of the T.U.C. staff since 1937, Victor Feather was Assistant Secretary 1947–60 and General Secretary 1969–73. In 1974 he became a life peer. He died in 1976.
[2] On April 24th, 1951.

St Mary's Hospital. The Prime Minister wishes to speak to you.' Then the little barking voice: 'Robens? Is that Robens? This is Attlee. Would Labour suit you?' 'Excuse me, Sir ... ?' 'Minister of Labour? Would that suit you?' 'Yes, Sir. Er, excuse me ... ' At this, the telephone was slammed down and Robens added, 'That was the last conversation I had with the Prime Minister before the Government fell in the following September.'[1]

I went to Banbury last weekend, where I found that Anne's father had been cured by the presence of his daughter and her exquisite cooking. On Sunday she motored me over to Oxford, where I had been invited to attend a Magdalen [College] Feast, to which I greatly looked forward. By some accident, Kingsley Martin and Bob Boothby had also been invited and the Magdalen authorities put us all together at the same table, with Alan Taylor.[2] This was a little boring, since we see each other pretty often.

Magdalen is a curious place. When we entered the Common Room, nobody came forward to greet us and nobody took any trouble about us throughout the evening, which seriously upset Bob Boothby, who revealed himself for the first time to be a real prima donna. He only recovered his form next morning at the Baloghs', where we all had lunch.

There, of course, we discussed the Labour leaks.[3] These leaks, both from the Parliamentary Party and the N.E.C., had really been the main political event of the previous ten days. The fact that the *Daily Express* had a round-by-round description of the N.E.C. didn't cause much bother. What really created the crisis was Hugh Massingham's anecdotes on the following Sunday, including one scathing but quite unimportant item about Jim Griffiths. Jim then wrote to the *Observer* denying this and Herbert Morrison made a speech rebuking Massingham, to which I wrote the *New Statesman* reply. In self-defence against Griffiths and Morrison, Hugh Massingham most unwisely stated that he had confirmed the story from three persons who were present. This gave the Right of the Party the precise kind of procedural issue which it loves. It was in a strong position, because the Massingham stories were not the kind of stories anybody on the Right of the Party would ever tell. Nye and Harold were both very upset when a whole series of N.E.C. papers

[1] In fact, October 1951.

[2] Alan John Percivale Taylor, the historian and journalist. He was Lecturer in International History at the University of Oxford 1953–63, Tutor in Modern History at Magdalen College, Oxford, 1938–63 and a Fellow of that college 1938–76, when he became an Honorary Fellow. A close associate of Beaverbrook, he became Honorary Director of the Beaverbrook Library. His many publications include *The Struggle for Mastery in Europe, 1848–1918* (Oxford University Press, 1954), *The Origins of the Second World War* (London: Hamish Hamilton, 1961), *English History: 1914–1945* (Oxford University Press, 1965) and *Beaverbrook* (London: Hamish Hamilton, 1972).

[3] On Sunday, March 7th, the *Observer* had carried details of the recent discussions on German rearmament within the P.L.P. and the N.E.C. In a speech in his constituency during the following weekend, March 13th/14th, Herbert Morrison had attacked Hugh Massingham, the author of the article. Crossman's support for 'this essential form of public education' is discussed in his piece 'Mr Morrison and the *Observer*', *New Statesman and Nation*, March 20th, 1954.

began to come to us, proving that this was going to be made a major issue. Rightly or wrongly, they suspected Ian Mikardo and on Monday I was detailed by Kingsley to give Massingham lunch. Hugh's a very crafty man and didn't reveal anything to me, except that about the only person of whom he didn't say that he hadn't got it was Ian.

However, my guess is — and this is the view of Leslie Hunter,[1] the *Daily Herald* Correspondent — that neither Massingham nor the *Express* rely on a regular single person who gives them their stuff. Almost every member of the Executive feels entitled to tell somebody or other outside what happened there. Every trade union representative tells his General Secretary. Every member of the Parliamentary Committee discusses it with other members of the Parliamentary Committee. I tell Kingsley and John Freeman and no doubt Michael Foot is also informed. This is all quite reasonable, off-the-record, background briefing. But it can't be very difficult for journalists to pick up one or two stories at second or third hand and then to check them, or bits of them, with members of the Executive.

I wouldn't be the least surprised if this is how Derek Marks[2] and Massingham actually proceed, but that's not the kind of view that the members of the Executive hold. Most of them are convinced that there is a traitor in our midst, who has virtually written the article in question. They forget that in the good old aristocratic days the closest secrets of the Cabinet were discussed every weekend in country houses. Nobody really minds leaking and indiscretions to individuals. What is resented is publication and the trouble about Massingham is that he has published enough to cause a violent reaction.

Anyhow, to get back to the Baloghs' lunch on Sunday. In the course of our discussion of the Labour leaks, Bob Boothby, who had had a very good meal, suddenly said that there had been trouble in the Tory Party as well. Apparently the *Daily Express* had published an account of a meeting of their Agricultural Committee, with the names of each M.P. who had spoken, in the right order. 'When the committee met this week, Butler was due to talk about farm prices and immediately took a high and mighty line and said that, to a committee which talked as loosely as that, he could not say anything. Whereupon each member of the committee was made to rise, raise his right hand and swear an oath of secrecy.' Now, this is the kind of story which it would raise Labour morale no end to reveal. Yet how can I reveal it, since my source is only too obvious?

The whole leaks issue came to a head in the Executive this morning — or

---

[1] A former journalist on the *Daily Herald*, he served as Public Relations Consultant to Herbert Morrison. His book *The Road to Brighton Pier* (London: Barker, 1959) is strongly critical of Bevan and his followers.

[2] Derek Marks was Parliamentary Correspondent at the *Daily Express* 1950. In the late 1950s he moved to the *Evening Standard* as Senior Lobby Correspondent, returning to the *Daily Express* as Editor 1965–71. From 1971 until his death in 1975 he wrote a regular political column for the *Daily Express* and the *Sunday Express* and acted as a special adviser to Sir Max Aitken. He was a Director of Beaverbrook Newspapers Limited 1971–5.

rather, didn't come to a head but petered out, as I expected it would. Morgan Phillips announced that informal legal advisers had stated that a case might lie against the *Observer* for procuring confidential information, though it was doubted whether the *Observer* could be forced to reveal the source. The idea of legal action so excited the Executive that they immediately decided to take Counsel's advice, despite Nye's suggestion that it would be fatal to try to deal with leakages by legal attacks on a newspaper.

Nye pressed for a 'searching investigation', whatever that may mean, but was defeated. Tom Driberg and I voted for taking Counsel's opinion because it seemed to me to do no harm, and I strongly suspect what that opinion will be. After this Harold Wilson moved a motion that the Executive should take a vow of secrecy but he didn't even get a seconder, for the very obvious reason, which no one mentioned, that everyone in the Executive feels bound to leak to someone outside. So a harmless motion was moved, deploring the leaks and reaffirming the confidential nature of the meeting.

At this point another item came up, a complaint by Ian Mikardo about a series of articles by Francis Williams in the *People*, describing in lurid detail a series of Bevanite plots to throw out Attlee which had gone on ever since 1947. The chairman ruled this out of order and there was a terrible row, since it was on the agenda and since the Executive has constantly discussed articles in the *Tribune* making allegations about Executive members. After all, Francis Williams is the official historian of the Labour Party.

However, the chairman remained adamant and tried to get on to the next business, whereupon Nye shouted 'Point of order!' for four minutes on end and, since this didn't work, said that Attlee was a liar. At this Attlee rose to his feet and he said he must reply. So Nye rose to his feet and there was a furious altercation, in the course of which Attlee said that he had only just read the article and it was a complete lie. It really would have been more sensible if Nye had gone to Attlee direct and asked for a denial, which he should certainly give. The Executive was utterly exhausted by all these alarms and excursions.

On March 1st, 1954, the Americans exploded a hydrogen bomb in the Pacific Ocean. It was not the first such test, for the U.S.S.R. as well as the U.S.A. had begun H-bomb experiments the year before. However there were angry and fierce reactions to this latest explosion, provoking debate in the House of Commons and argument over the previous history of Anglo-American agreements on the development and use of atomic energy.

The atomic weapon[1] had been developed by teams of British, American and Canadian scientists, with colleagues who had fled from Nazi-controlled Europe. On July 16th, 1945, the first atom bomb had been tested at Alamagordo in the

---

[1] An A-bomb draws its nuclear energy from fission of heavy elements like enriched uranium and plutonium; an H-bomb derives some of its energy from the fusion of two isotopes of hydrogen: deuterium and tritium.

New Mexican desert and in the first and second week of August 1945 the weapon was used at Hiroshima and Nagasaki in Japan.

Two years before, at a conference in Quebec in August 1943, Winston Churchill and President Roosevelt had discussed the terms by which America would continue to aid the Allies. Privately, the two men agreed that there would be 'full and effective collaboration' in nuclear matters. In September 1944, at a second Quebec Conference, Churchill and Roosevelt again discussed economic and military strategy. Churchill then stayed at Hyde Park, Roosevelt's home, and on the day before his departure, once more raised the question of atomic research. Roosevelt apparently promised that Britain, Canada and America should share information on the industrial application of atomic energy but he is said to have been more reserved about undertaking to exchange secrets concerning military uses of the atomic bomb.

On October 3rd, 1945, after the atomic bomb had been used in Japan, President Truman asked Congress to enact legislation for the control of atomic power. In November Mr Attlee flew to Washington for talks. Meanwhile President Truman had made remarks implying that the U.S.A. did not intend to share the technical information constituting the real secret of the atomic bomb. His country, he said, would hold in its hands 'this new power of destruction as a sacred trust'.

From the meeting between Mr Attlee, President Truman and the Canadian Prime Minister, Mackenzie King, emerged a proposal that the U.N. should establish a commission, under which the exchange of 'fundamental'. scientific information should take place, though 'specialized information' on the bomb itself would not be disclosed until effective safeguards had been devised. In the meantime a number of American scientists continued their campaign for civilian control of nuclear research and by the end of December 1945 they had successfully lobbied the Senate to set up a Special Committee on Atomic Energy, with Senator McMahon as chairman.

On June 6th, 1946, Mr Attlee sent a lengthy telegram to President Truman, reminding him of the substance of previous discussions on this subject and expressing his anxiety that Britain should not be excluded from American discoveries in a field in which British scientists had, after all, been among the forerunners.[1]

But President Truman was evasive, refusing to reply until Congress had expressed its own feelings on the matter. By the end of 1946, Congress had passed substantially unamended a Bill introduced by Senator McMahon. This provided for domestic control of atomic energy by a five-man civilian commission, with considerable freedom for research. The commissioners were appointed by President Truman in November. Meanwhile, in October 1946, Mr Attlee had moved the Second Reading of an Atomic Energy Bill, expressing the Government's determination to play a full part in the attainment of an agreed

[1] The text of this telegram may be found in Francis Williams, *A Prime Minister Remembers* (London: Heinemann, 1961), Chapter 8, 'The Atom Bomb'.

international scheme for controlling atomic energy. Britain and America con-
tinued the separate development of a hydrogen weapon (though there was in
practice considerable co-operation between scientists of both countries).

After the American H-bomb test in March 1954, fourteen backbenchers put
down Questions to the Prime Minister. Members wished to know whether the
Americans regarded the H-bomb as a principal instrument in their 'new
strategy' of vigorously resisting Communist aggression in Indo-China and else-
where. They also wished to know how British acquiescence in American develop-
ment of the weapon fitted in with the cautiously welcoming attitude to the 'new
look' in the Kremlin, outlined by Sir Winston in his speech of May 11th, 1953.

On March 30th the Prime Minister made a Statement in the Commons. He
declared that: 'The experiments which the Americans are now conducting are an
essential part of the defence policy of a friendly Power without whose massive
strength and generous help Europe would be in mortal peril.' He spoke of the
atomic weapon as providing 'the greatest possible deterrent against the out-
break of a Third World War'.

Sir Winston went on to say that British knowledge of the American experi-
ments was 'necessarily limited'. He stated, 'In view of what we have learned by
our own scientific researches, and also in view of the progress of the Soviets in
this sphere, I am sure that consultation is to the advantage of both Great
Britain and the United States.' He looked forward to the development of
'favourable tendencies in this direction now evident in the United States'.[1]

The Opposition pressed for a debate before the Easter Recess. This took place
on April 5th, with Mr Attlee proposing an immediate initiative by Her Majesty's
Government to bring about a meeting between the Prime Minister and the
heads of the American and Soviet Administrations, to consider anew the
problem of the reduction and control of armaments and of devising positive
policies.

Sir Winston offered to accept the motion, provided that the word 'immediate'
did not commit the Government to take action at what they believed to be an
inappropriate moment. But the debate left this non-partisan level when the
Prime Minister accused the post-war Labour Government of letting slip the
agreement with the Americans to share technical information on nuclear
weapons research and development. In the penultimate speech of the debate
Herbert Morrison replied with a statement on Mr Attlee's behalf but Mr Eden
closed the debate by quoting what the Government felt were unjust taunts in the
press and the discussion degenerated into an inter-party quarrel. The motion
was approved without division.

Crossman supported the call for discussion between Britain, the U.S.A. and
the U.S.S.R. on the international control of 'unconventional weapons'. He
condemned any strategy of 'massive retaliation', believing that atomic bombing
must be used only in the very last resort. For his views at this point, see 'Heads
in the Atomic Sand', New Statesman and Nation, *April 3rd, 1954; 'Mr Attlee*

[1] *H. C. Debates*, vol. 525, cols 1840–2.

Speaks for Britain' and the first two paragraphs of 'London Diary' (all unsigned), New Statesman and Nation, *April 10th, 1954.*

Tuesday, April 6th

I find I haven't written the diary for nearly a fortnight, the fortnight of the H-bomb, the fortnight, incidentally, when the whole political situation here was completely transformed, with Labour suddenly holding the initiative.

But let's go back to Thursday, March 25th, the day after the meeting of the National Executive, when the only thing which seemed to matter was leaks and Hugh Massingham. On Thursday morning Sydney Elliott[1] had the gumption to come out with a huge front-page story on the H-bomb explosion in the Pacific.[2] This explosion had actually taken place on March 1st but news of it had only leaked out when a Japanese fishing boat reached port and reported that, though eighty miles outside the danger zone, it had been deluged with radio-active ash. These reports began to seep into the *Manchester Guardian* at the beginning of that week and I remember saying to somebody that it was no good trying to get people interested in the H-bomb. I had written about it often enough but people simply refused to take it seriously. Actually, of course, the American bomb has been manufactured since 1950 and the announcement that the Russians had detonated theirs occurred on August 8th last year. But it's only during these last ten days that this country has become H-bomb-conscious and it all began with Sydney Elliott.

On Friday the 26th I rang up the *Pic* to say that I thought we would have to have a special feature. Colin said that really there was nothing to say that wouldn't already have been said. So I told them I would do a piece on H-bomb policy and summed it up in three points: (i) Britain must obtain full information. (ii) The new look strategy must be revised. (iii) Britain must press for high-level talks. Looking back, this article doesn't seem too bad.[3]

The number of Questions going down on the Order Paper showed that there would be trouble on Tuesday and in fact that day, March 30th, was the beginning of the storm. I got down to the Commons just in time to hear Churchill read aloud, in a very unconvincing voice, the bald Statement which first strongly asserted the great advantage to us of America having an H-bomb and then stated that no further information could be obtained. From the Front Bench, Attlee, Morrison, Philip Noel-Baker and Arthur Henderson all put Supplementaries, which infuriated the twelve backbenchers who had Questions down. Churchill's answer was so obviously unsatisfactory that

---

[1] Managing Editor of *Reynolds News* 1929, Editor of the *Evening Standard* 1943, Political Adviser to the *Daily Mirror* 1945, Managing Director of the *Melbourne Argus* and the *Australian Post* 1949, General Manager of the *Daily Herald* 1952 and Editor of that paper 1953–7.

[2] The *Daily Herald* leader on March 25th, 1954, was headlined: 'CALL OFF THAT BOMB!'

[3] Crossman's *Sunday Pictorial* article, on p. 9 of the issue published on March 28th, 1954, was headlined: 'HORROR BOMBS: A Policy for Survival'.

there was a frightful row when the Speaker stopped Supplementaries. As a result, frantic efforts were made to move the adjournment of the House, which, as always, tailed off into a whimper.

At half-past six that evening we had a meeting of the Defence Committee and to my surprise people like Woodrow Wyatt, George Wigg, John Strachey and myself were all in agreement that we should press for high-level talks, that we should get out of the hysterical denunciation of the American experiments and that we should concentrate on the danger of the use of the bomb under the new strategy. But meanwhile that evening Ellis Smith got 100 signatures to a resolution demanding that the Pacific experiments should cease. George Wigg and I consulted, as we have been doing a great deal in the last five weeks, and decided to use our influence to try to get the Party to concentrate on essentials.

On the evening of Wednesday, March 31st, so Nye told me, the Parliamentary Committee met. Attlee arrived, having made up his mind that this was a great crisis in which he must give a national lead. As always, when Attlee does decide to do something, the Committee agreed and asked him to draft the resolution on Thursday. On Thursday morning, when I was working, George rang me up and suggested I should ring up Attlee and go to see him. So I did ring him up and he said, 'Come round in a taxi.'

I took with me a rather cumbersome draft resolution, including a reference to experiments, but concentrating on high-level talks. Attlee glanced at it and said he wanted something simpler, which went further. Three-Power talks were all that mattered. We then discussed the American new strategy, whose dangers he fully seemed to recognize, and he agreed that a very remarkable article of Acheson's in the *New York Times* last Sunday[1] had said the last word on this futile and dangerous policy. After a quarter of an hour I tried to go but the little man kept me chatting in the friendliest way till one o'clock.

At four o'clock the Defence Committee met again and we reached agreement to tell the Parliamentary Committee that in our view the Front Bench should (a) concentrate exclusively on the dangers of the new strategy and the need for high-level talks, and (b) drop all mention of stopping the Pacific experiments by a British unilateral repudiation of atomic warfare. This message was taken to the Parliamentary Committee, where, again according to Nye, Attlee's resolution was substantially adopted, with the addition of a

---

[1] Dean Acheson's article in the *New York Times* of March 28th, 1954, included the passage: 'Strategic atomic bombing is not our first but our last resort, reserved for the dread occasion when we must meet an all-out attack with the full attendant horrors of atomic war. No responsible, certainly no democratic, government would use it on any lesser occasion.' He concluded: 'This democracy and the coalition it leads are lost if the competition for leadership becomes a competition in promising cheap and mechanical solutions to dangers which can only be met by clear and cool heads, and by the courage which made and preserved this country.'

single sentence about the need for high-level talks to deal positively with the removal of fear.

Immediately after this, the Party met to discuss its policy. Many people seemed to have come expecting a long debate but, having talked to Attlee that morning, I was not very surprised when he got up and made the best speech of his life. I was sitting just below him and saw how his hands shook with emotion. But his voice was collected and he swept the whole Party off its feet. When he sat down and John Strachey and one or two others rose to speak, there were indignant cries of 'Vote, vote', and the resolution was carried by acclaim. Next morning the papers had full verbatim reports of this meeting but, as far as I know, there were no objections to these leaks.

I went down to the House on Monday with the vague idea of speaking if there was a chance, but of course assuming that, after Attlee had made a good speech, Churchill would make an even better one, reaffirming his peace initiative of last May.[1] Attlee began quite well but, as we had all heard the dress rehearsal, the edge of our pleasure at the little man's carefully prepared rhetoric had been blunted.

Then came Churchill's extraordinary performance. He started quietly enough but in a few minutes he was attacking Attlee on the ground that British inability to obtain information from the Americans was due to Attlee's abandonment of the secret Quebec Agreement. Gradually the scene worked up to a fever, with all of us shouting, 'Guttersnipe! Swine! Resign!', with Churchill standing there swaying slightly and trying to plough through his script. There came a terrible moment when Bob Boothby got up from his seat below the gangway, turned his back to Churchill and strode out beyond the Bar, stood there glowering and then disappeared. In the middle of the turmoil I suddenly detached myself from myself and thought how nauseating we were, howling for the old bull's blood. I think we really would have lynched him if we could.

In the lobbies we all discussed why Churchill had done it. I reached my conclusion straightaway, having noticed that he attacked both Michael Foot and myself. It's the *Mirror* and the columnists and the cartoonists who have got under his skin. He has never forgiven us for 'Whose Finger on the Trigger?' in the 1951 election.[2] This analysis was confirmed by Eden at the end, who soon got into trouble by saying that, after all, it was only reasonable, that if the Prime Minister was attacked, he should hit back. He then quoted the *Mirror*.

But, of course, the fascinating part of the debate was that Churchill's attack on Attlee was perfectly justified, only he had got it all wrong and kept

[1] See above, pp. 229–31.
[2] In the 1951 General Election campaign, Herbert Morrison had stated that the Conservatives had a 'nineteenth-century outlook dangerous in a twentieth-century world', a remark more pithily expressed in a *Daily Mirror* headline, 'Whose Finger on the Trigger?', in the issue of October 24th, the eve of the Election.

on talking about the McMahon[1] Act in 1946, when the real surrender took place in the spring of 1948 and, of course, later on, when we granted the Americans atom bases in Norfolk.[2] All this is to be found in the Forrestal Diaries and the Vandenberg Papers.[3]

However, Attlee blandly denied that he had abandoned anything, so I walked into his room and said that we had better face it that Eden, in his winding-up speech, would have plenty of material, of which we should be forewarned. I then asked Attlee, 'Is this secret Quebec Agreement still in force?' and he said, 'Yes, in so far as it ever was.' So I said, 'What about the Vandenberg Papers?' and he had never heard of them. So I went to the Library, found the copy and brought it back and Attlee read it. 'I do remember some conversations about atoms in 1948,' he said, 'but not exactly what was agreed.' By the evening a statement had been prepared for Morrison to read out, which indicated clearly enough that secret negotiations had gone on and that the Quebec Agreement had been modified under American pressure.[4] On the other hand, Eden quite clearly realized that Churchill's attack had misfired and had anyway been terribly unfair.

All that evening the lobbies and the Smoking Room hummed with talk of Churchill's failure. After Eden's speech, I rang up Hugh Cudlipp, who was in bed but immediately leapt up. When I got to his house he took me round to the office in the car and I watched him dealing with the *Mirror* Editor, Jack Nener[5] – Nener may edit but Cudlipp disposes. Then we celebrated at the Press Club until three o'clock in the morning, drinking a great deal more whisky than I care to remember. But Hugh was as elated as I was. If we are the gutter press, we had provoked Churchill to enter the gutter with us and thereby probably ruin himself.

Of course, the fact is that, during these hydrogen ten days, the Labour Party has for the first time in a year shown some political nous. Mr Attlee has behaved like an impeccable patriotic leader, putting country before Party, the only way in which to hold the Party, once you've got the initiative.

[1] Brien McMahon, Democratic Senator from Connecticut 1944–57 and chairman of the Special Committee on Atomic Energy.

[2] At the time of the Soviet blockade of Berlin.

[3] James Forrestal was Administrative Assistant to President Roosevelt, Secretary of State for the Navy 1944–7 and Secretary of Defense September 1947–March 1949. He committed suicide in May 1949. *The Forrestal Diaries* were published in New York (Viking Press) in 1951 and in London (Cassell) in 1952. Arthur Vandenberg (1884–1953) was Republican Senator from Michigan 1928–53. *The Private Papers of Senator Vandenberg* were published in Boston (Houghton Mifflin) in 1952 and in London (Gollancz) in 1953.

[4] 'My rt. hon. Friend [Attlee] had the task of negotiating with the United States Government subsequently on this very uncertain basis of an agreement made between two individuals. The United States Administration was in a difficult position. My rt. hon. Friend does not claim to make any further comment, except to say that during the period of the Labour Government the understanding and co-operation between Great Britain and the United States of America grew steadily greater. He would not have anything said to impair that welcome development' [*H. C. Debates*, vol. 526, col. 139].

[5] He joined the *Daily Mirror* in 1943 as a sub-editor and was Editor of the paper 1953–61.

But, simultaneously, we have been furiously attacking Churchill for his impotence *vis-à-vis* America, and the attacks have been extremely effective, so the Labour Party has been having the best of both worlds, officially impeccably patriotic but unofficially in the *Mirror* and in the *Herald* sloshing Churchill in its mass-circulation papers, as well as in the *Statesman* and the *Tribune*. There is no doubt that it was this that infuriated Churchill and made him feel that he had to get his own back. I suspect he can't have shown this part of his speech to Eden, since, if he had done so, the Foreign Office would have got his facts right for him and then the bomb he was going to explode under Attlee might not have been a dud. But in any event it was crazy of him to try to explode a bomb when he could easily have made an even nobler speech than our noble Clem.

Wednesday, April 21st
This diary seems to go in spasms of fourteen days. I last wrote on the hydrogen bomb fourteen days ago, which demolished Winston and brought Attlee to a giddy eminence. Incidentally, it also produced a remarkable change in the East Edinburgh and Motherwell by-elections.[1] In the last batch in January, the Conservative vote had gone up between 3 and 5 per cent and the Labour vote down by between 1 and 3 per cent, on a series of very low polls, with large abstentions. In East Edinburgh and Motherwell the Conservative vote went down by 3 per cent. In Edinburgh Labour went up by 3 per cent and in Motherwell there was a Communist, who confused the issue. It's true that the Scottish figures haven't swung so violently before but the fact remains that everybody attributed these figures to what happened on April 5th and April 6th. April 6th, of course, was the Budget.

The Chancellor described his proposals as a 'carry-on' budget, reaffirming the Government's basic policies. He stated that it would be unwise at this moment to stimulate purchasing power by tax concessions but promised that 'more radical measures' would be taken later in the year if circumstances so required. There were, however, reductions – ranging from a $\frac{1}{2}$d. to $1\frac{1}{2}$d. – in entertainments duty for cinemas, theatres and sporting events. A concession was also made in the terms governing the repayment of post-war credits; this was to cost an additional £19 million in the first year and an extra £2 million in each sub-

---

[1] John Wheatley, Q.C. (Lord Wheatley, 1970), the Member for East Edinburgh, had been appointed a Senator of the College of Justice in Scotland and a by-election was accordingly held on April 8th. E. G. Willis held the seat for Labour, with a majority of 5,028 votes over the Conservative candidate, William Grant. Labour increased their share of votes cast by 3·57 per cent in a poll of 61·83 per cent of the registered electorate. The by-election in the Motherwell division of Lanarkshire was caused by the death of Alexander Anderson, Labour, who had collapsed and died during a committee meeting at the House of Commons on February 11th. There were three candidates in the by-election, held on April 14th: G. M. Lawson, Labour; Norman Sloan, Liberal Unionist; and John Gollan, Communist. Labour held the seat with a majority of 5,829 votes and their proportion of votes cast fell by less than 1 per cent. Nearly 70 per cent of the electorate went to the polls.

sequent year. The estate duty on certain assets of private businesses was reduced by 45 per cent and — the Budget's most important proposal — existing initial tax allowances on industrial capital expenditure were to be replaced by an investment allowance, under which 10 to 20 per cent of the cost of assets might be set against tax. The Chancellor hoped that, together with the depreciation allowance, this measure would stimulate British industry to spend more on re-equipment.

On the last day of the debate the Opposition appealed to the Chancellor to reconsider his decision not to raise old age pensions. Mr Butler replied that in a few months' time the report of the Phillips Committee on the Aged and the review of the National Insurance Fund would both be available and that pensions revision would be dealt with in that light.

In the course of his Budget statement on April 6th, the Chancellor observed that, 'During the coming year we must see to it that we obtain some definite relief from the defence burden.' This remark was taken up by those M.P.s, including the Bevanites, who had been maintaining that intolerably high defence expenditure was preventing improvements in social services. To backbenchers' dismay, the Opposition leaders did not attempt to use Mr Butler's point to drive a wedge between the Prime Minister and his Chancellor of the Exchequer.

It was on the question of defence and the Anglo-American alliance that backbench dissent was to come to a head. Communist pressure in the seven-year war against French forces in Indo-China now took impressive form in an assault, supported by the Chinese, on the French fortress of Dien Bien Phu. (The post was to fall on May 7th.) In a speech on March 29th the American Secretary of State advocated united action by the Western Powers to warn China of the consequences of continued support for the Indo-Chinese Communist insurgents. On April 11th Mr Dulles came to London to discuss with Mr Eden proposals for a 'united front' against Communist aggression in the Far East. There was widespread anxiety, not confined to the Labour left-wing, that the American Government might be about to press the British and French Governments into dangerous action.

On April 13th Mr Eden made a cautious Statement in the Commons, saying that, with 'other countries principally concerned' in South-East Asia and the Western Pacific, the British and American Governments were ready to examine the possibility of 'establishing a collective defence, within the framework of the United Nations, to assure the peace, security and freedom' of the area.

Mr Attlee did not express disapproval of this Statement and only sought assurance that the Government's purpose was to resist Communist aggrandizement in the area rather than to shore up an 'obsolete colonialism'. This promise the Foreign Secretary gave, but then Mr Bevan intervened to state that Mr Eden's statement would be 'deeply resented by most people in Britain'.

On the following day the Foreign Secretary announced to the Commons the details of the British agreement with the European Defence Community, signed in Paris the day before. The Government, he said, had offered to place a

British armoured division with a European Army corps, where it would stay for
as long as the Supreme Allied Commander in Europe required it. In each NATO
air group would be R.A.F. units, which would be directed by a single integrated
headquarters. Mr Eden stressed that this agreement depended on French
ratification of the E.D.C. Treaty and that Her Majesty's Government had
throughout closely consulted the United States Government.

That same day, April 14th, Mr Bevan resigned from the Labour Party's
Parliamentary Committee, to which he had been elected at the beginning of
the Session, explaining that, already profoundly disagreeing with the Committee
'on their decision to persuade the Labour Party to support the immediate
rearmament of Germany', he was further 'deeply shocked' at the parliamentary
leaders' 'failure to repudiate Mr Eden's acceptance of the American initiative,
which is tantamount to the diplomatic and military encirclement of republican
China ... '

Who would succeed to Mr Bevan's place on the Parliamentary Committee?
Labour Party rules laid down that a vacancy caused by death or resignation
was automatically filled by that Party Member who had secured most votes
among those failing to get a place in the previous annual election. In this case,
the Member who had been thirteenth in the ballot was Harold Wilson, himself
a Bevanite.

I remember, not very distinctly, that we had our usual Bevanite lunch, but
without Nye, and we all agreed that he really would have to do something
about Indo-China. Then the rest of them went off to hear Butler, while I sat
down to work. I was right in my calculation, since it was a 'no change'
Budget, with nothing even for the old age pensioner. Indeed, the only
significant thing about it was Butler's explicit statement that in the coming
year there would have to be cuts in defence.

I went into the House on Wednesday the 7th to hear how Hugh Gaitskell
would deal with it. As usual, he was extremely competent but on the defence
issue he made no attempt to challenge Butler. Indeed, he seemed to express
dismay at the idea that the Chancellor could possibly conceive of cutting
defence for economic reasons, disregarding strategical requirements. This
meant that Hugh lost his main opportunity for attack. If Labour is pledged to
enormous increases of social services, it will require huge, crippling taxation
to bring them in, unless defence is cut. Gaitskell could have taken the new
Party line, which demands cuts in defence and National Service, and shown
how, through such cuts, money could be found for increasing the old age
pension without increasing taxation. He did nothing of the sort and not a
single Labour spokesman, in the dreary debate which went on for the next
four days, tried to do so either. George Wigg and I were naturally furious.
What was the good of doing all our work on switching the Party's defence
policy if the Party's spokesmen in the Budget don't adopt the new line? But,
when George mentioned this to Nye when he was taking him down to a gala

at Dudley, Nye hadn't even noticed it, so little has he now been concerned with defence problems.

However, the Budget soon disappeared from public view, apart from its effect on the old age pensioners, and on Wednesday, after hearing Hugh Gaitskell, I went to a specially convened meeting of the foreign affairs group, where Frank Beswick opened a discussion on Indo-China, which was already replacing the hydrogen bomb as the centre of attention. Beswick summarized quite effectively the threat presented by Dulles's new strategy and the demand he had just made in Washington for so-called 'united action' in Indo-China to stem Communist aggression. Beswick urged that before the Recess the Labour Party should find an opportunity for challenging the Government on whether it was accepting this proposal.

Philip Noel-Baker then made a wonderful speech, in which he stated that he had never seen a clearer case of aggression than Communist action in Indo-China and suggested that the United Nations might well consider instituting sanctions against China. I had a wonderful row and Noel-Baker was in a minority of one on the committee, which agreed immediately to inform the Parliamentary Committee of its decision. This was that Attlee should ask a Private Notice Question on the Monday or Tuesday of the following week and, if the reply was unsatisfactory, move the adjournment of the House to debate Indo-China before the Geneva Conference, which starts on the day before we resume after Easter.

Through Wednesday evening and Thursday, April 8th, the Parliamentary Labour Party was steamed up quite successfully on Indo-China, so that on the Thursday evening we had a very full meeting. Attlee read aloud the extremely dull business for the following week. Then John Hynd, for the foreign affairs group, got up and asked him about Indo-China. Attlee was extremely cagey and said that one must await events. This aroused the gravest suspicions. However, these were largely dissipated in the course of the evening, when the news came out on the tape that Mr Dulles was arriving during the weekend. It seemed intelligible, therefore, that Attlee should wait until after the Dulles meeting to put his questions. So we dispersed for the weekend, which Anne and I spent in the splendour of Buscot Park.

Monday, April 12th, was almost blank because it was the dreary end of the Budget debate and on Tuesday the 13th at our Bevanite lunch, with Nye present, we spent most of the time discussing Indo-China and steaming Nye up to the need for a strong Party line. Since German rearmament was due to come up at the International Sub. at four o'clock, I said that it was important that we should all attend and that, anyway, we should move an emergency motion on Indo-China. Nye, however, said he couldn't get there because he had to be on the Front Bench for the Third Reading of the Rents Bill, which he has been getting through Committee. So he left it to Tom Driberg and me to go to the International. When the lunch was over, I stayed behind to draft a good, powerful resolution.

It read:

The N.E.C. declares that one main object of British policy at the Geneva Conference should be to achieve negotiated settlement which ends the Indo-Chinese war and permits the peoples of this territory to achieve full and genuine independence.

It therefore deprecates all attempts to portray this ghastly civil war, in which both sides are being supported by large-scale foreign intervention, as a crusade against Communism which must be prosecuted until final victory is achieved. Furthermore, it declares its opposition to the commitment of this country, either before or after the Geneva Conference,[1] either to participation in united action on behalf of the Vietnam Government or to support for a policy of 'massive retaliation', which would involve the risk of spreading the war outside the frontiers of Indo-China.

I then strolled round to the House. We had heard that, since Dulles was going to Paris, the communiqué on his talks would be delivered on Thursday and Eden would make only a short interim Statement on the Tuesday. So I didn't make a point of being there. When I got to the Central Lobby, I met somebody who told me that Eden had just announced the proposal to investigate a Far Eastern NATO, and I walked up to the committee room.

Here, at the International Sub. we had a frightful row about German rearmament and I then moved the emergency resolution on Indo-China. I had no notion that, half an hour before, an extraordinary scene had occurred in the Chamber. Eden read aloud his Statement on the Dulles conversations and Attlee made some very mild and non-committal objections in Question form, which seemed to be giving a sort of implicit agreement to the idea of a Far East NATO in principle, provided certain conditions were fulfilled. Immediately, Nye rose, pushed his way along the Table, stood literally on Attlee's toes and denounced the whole idea, lock, stock and barrel, in a way which made him seem to be repudiating Attlee's leadership. Certainly at lunch Nye hadn't indicated that he was going to take this line and I am pretty sure he didn't even know that Indo-China would be up for discussion.

However, there I was at the International Sub., negotiating some sort of compromise on our Bevanite resolution, totally unwitting of what had happened downstairs. The International accepted the first paragraph and, to my great surprise, decided to publish it immediately. I only understood two hours later what they were at and what strange lack of co-ordination there had been that afternoon between Nye downstairs and myself upstairs.

Nye's action caused absolute fury among the Right of the Party, a fury which was shared by a great majority of the middle-of-the-roaders, who have been enormously pleased by Attlee's success on the hydrogen bomb and whose stomachs once again began to melt at the prospect of a Party row. I

[1] Due to open on April 26th, to discuss the questions of Korea and Indo-China.

didn't have any chance of seeing Nye that evening because he was busy on the Rents Bill[1] and, when he wasn't, was having a tremendous row in the Parliamentary Committee.

On Wednesday morning, April 14th, all the papers had front-page stories on the split in the Labour Party. Of course, the lobby correspondents had been fully briefed by the right-wingers and already it was difficult to see how Nye could withdraw. With two reasonable men, the whole thing could have been settled over a cup of tea within two hours of Tuesday's incident. But, then, neither Nye nor Clem is reasonable and both did nothing, as usual. However, I was still unaware that anything sensational was going to happen and I sat for one and a half hours in a long, tedious Org. Sub., from four o'clock until half-past five.

When it was finished, I came downstairs and met Harold Wilson, who had been away all Tuesday at Motherwell. I was just filling him in on what had happened, strolling up and down the Library corridor, when Nye came breezing along and said to me that he had just walked out of the Parliamentary Committee and told the buggers that it was quite likely that he wouldn't be returning to them after the Recess.[2] I asked him what had happened and he said that Attlee had started the meeting by making a statement on Indo-China which he had quite clearly concerted with Eden and which meant accepting the SEATO. 'I just told him that this was impossible,' said Nye, 'and walked out of the room.' 'Are they still there?' I said. 'Well, I suppose so,' he said.

So we had a drink before the Party Meeting, forty minutes later, at half-past six. We all went into Room 14 and everybody had an inkling that something was up. However, they were very baffled when, at half-past six, Nye alone came and sat down on the platform. There were facetious shouts of 'Take the chair', at which Nye looked a bit sheepish. At about 6.40 the rest of the Committee all filed in and Attlee dealt with the business of the week after the Recess. He then made a statement on South-East Asia. According to Nye, this statement was far better than the one he had made in the Parliamentary Committee. It concluded with an extremely sharp criticism of Nye for his conduct, but didn't actually mention his name. At this point Attlee said that he thought the best thing now was that, having heard his statement, we should not debate it. The Party was very astonished and said that it had come to have a debate on Indo-China.

One or two efforts were made to adopt the statement, when Nye suddenly jumped up and said that he had to make a statement. He had been given a warning that he would be attacked by Attlee and he must announce that before the Meeting he had already resigned from the Parliamentary Committee. Of course he hadn't but Attlee had just had enough time, kindly given him by Nye, to concert a tactic in his absence and to force his resigna-

---

[1] The Housing Repairs and Rents Bill was given its Third Reading on April 13th and received the Royal Assent on July 30th.
[2] The House adjourned on April 15th and resumed on April 27th.

tion. Had Nye in his heart really decided to resign? John Strachey told me, when Anne and I and he went to dine with the Spearmans that evening, that in the afternoon Nye had discussed resignation with him. But he certainly hadn't discussed it with Harold or me or Ian.

When the meeting finished, I saw Nye standing outside the Smoking Room and said, 'Well, we'd better get the press statement ready.' Nye said, 'I'm off to the Egyptian Embassy. I've got no time,' at which Harold Wilson, who was there, looked a bit surprised and Ian Mikardo and I almost physically dragged Nye to a committee room downstairs. Once we'd got him there, Nye dictated and Ian copied in longhand and we got really quite a good statement. But all the time Nye was complaining that he'd got to change before going to the Egyptian Embassy. He seemed to have no notion that, if he issued no statement at all, he would be in a hopeless situation. At the Spearmans' we naturally discussed all this at length. In many ways this resignation, in the way it happened, was not unlike his resignation from the Labour Government, where he did and he didn't want to resign and finally his hand was forced by his opponents in the way they wanted.

Next day, Thursday, April 15th, in writing for the *Sunday Pic*[1] before the Easter holiday, I had the job of trying to pick up the pieces. But, before I did so, at eight o'clock in the morning George Wigg had rung me. Our minds had worked along the same lines. We both saw that the crux now was Mr Harold Wilson, who was the first on the list of those standing for the Parliamentary Committee last October who had failed to be elected. Nye's resignation had put Harold in an awkward dilemma. If he automatically said no to Nye's place, he would just look like Nye's poodle. If he accepted, he would look as if he were breaking up the Bevanite Group. Both George and I agreed that the main thing was that over the Easter Recess Harold should not burn any bridges and should leave things open. So I got him on the phone in the morning and the first thing he said to me was, 'As the philosopher Confucius observed, "No annihilation without representation".' I laughed at this for a silly reason. I had started a *Sunday Pic* article with this jejune phrase in the previous week[2] and Harold had commended me on a really brilliant epigram, not knowing, apparently, that it was invented years ago by Arnold Toynbee.[3] Now he was using it back and he was obviously extremely, if coldly, angry. So I told him to come round to see me in the afternoon.

[1] See 'After Bevan's Walk-Out', *Sunday Pictorial*, April 17th, 1954, for Crossman's argument that ' … what is now dismissed as anti-American extremism will be accepted as sober statesmanship'.

[2] It was in fact the beginning of Crossman's article, 'Attlee's Lesson for Churchill', in the *Sunday Pictorial* of April 4th, 1954.

[3] Arnold Toynbee (1889–1975) was Professor of Byzantine and Modern Greek Language, Literature and History at King's College, London, 1919–23 and from 1926 to 1955 Stevenson Professor of International History and Director of Studies at the Royal Institute of International Affairs. He is especially famed for his *Study of History* (Oxford University Press), of which three volumes appeared in 1934, three in 1939, four in 1954 and two in 1961.

He came at half-past three and was impressively efficient. We agreed that it would be fatal for him to accept co-option. But we also agreed that he might well consider, later on, stating his willingness to stand for election if a ballot were decided on. Harold was very emphatic that it would be unbearable if he merely automatically did whatever Nye wanted to do, after not having been consulted. 'I've been accused of being Nye's little boy ever since the resignation.[1] I cannot automatically go to the backbench just because he does. I agree with his policy stand, of course, but not with this tactic and with no consultation.'

I told Harold to go from my house round to Nye's, which he did, and then I rang up Nye myself to discuss what I should write. I did this, having some idea what Nye would say, because I had previously heard from Tom Driberg what Nye had told him. Nye clearly wanted us to attack the right-wing of the Party all along the line. However, I told him that I thought that this would be a grave mistake, since he had got to appear as a constructive statesman and not as an ambitious man reorganizing the Bevanite Group. He agreed that there could be no question of reorganizing the Group but demurred when I said that my line would be that his resignation would be justified, as his last resignation was, by events. 'That won't do,' he said, 'because they may anticipate me and, in order to box me, put forward a reasonable policy.' To which, of course, the answer is, though I didn't give it, that he might have thought of that before!

I didn't worry about arranging to see Nye because I knew that I was to meet him on Tuesday, April 20th, at lunch with the Polish Ambassador.[2] On the way back in Nye's car he turned the conversation to Harold Wilson and rebuked me for giving him wrong advice. Then he drove me to his home, where I found Jennie and Ian Mikardo and, though Ian left quite soon, the rest of us talked for three hours. It was a very friendly conversation—I think genuinely friendly. I told Nye that I thought he had treated Harold abominably and that Harold had a perfect right to regard himself as freed from all responsibility to Nye. Nye said, 'Of course he has got the right but he will kill himself if he agrees to go on the Committee.' I then said that, in my view, it was now far more likely that Harold Wilson would succeed to the premiership than that Nye would. He was just the type of man who would succeed Attlee. To which Nye replied, 'If he's that kind of man, I don't want anything to do with him.' I then said, 'Don't be silly. You've always known that he's that sort of man and the events of the last three days have made no difference to that.' Nye observed that he just wasn't prepared to go through all this nonsense for the sake of political ambition. 'If that's the sort of thing you have to do, I'm not prepared to do it,' he said.

I then said that surely it was in our interest that Clem Attlee should be built up just now, because this reduced the power and influence of Morrison and Gaitskell and pulled the Party towards the left. Nye replied that this was

[1] Harold Wilson had resigned at the same time as Bevan in April 1951.
[2] Eugeniusz Jan Minikiel was the Polish Ambassador in London 1953–60.

entirely wrong. Our job now was to destroy the bogus reputation of Clement
Attlee and we must expect a renewed attempt to expel us from the Party. By
now I know what this means. When Nye talks about renewed attempts to expel
us from the Party, he means that we must do things which might get us expelled.
And when he talked about destroying Clem Attlee's reputation, he revealed
what I had feared: namely, that he was genuinely piqued by Clem's success in
the hydrogen bomb debate.[1] He was also apparently unrepentant about not
consulting anybody because he said that in politics one can't spend all the time
consulting and living in committees. But I have a feeling that, as usual, he was
listening fairly carefully and that next Tuesday, at our lunch, he will realize the
need to heed his friends. Meanwhile, ironically enough, Harold Wilson is off in
Paris at an informal discussion of the economics of East–West trade, organized by the European Movement, with British Labour representatives, including Hugh Gaitskell, Tony Crosland, Roy Jenkins, Uncle Tom Cobbleigh and
all. This afternoon Tommy Balogh was intensely alarmed lest Harold Wilson
will be bought off by this gang. I told him he underestimated Harold, who
knows perfectly well that they would only take him in in order to destroy
him, since they hate him more than all the rest of us put together. I predict
that Harold will play an extremely sophisticated and nicely calculated game.

I can't help feeling that Nye's action has immensely increased Harold's
status in the Party and reduced his own. On the other hand, I can't help
liking him enormously for it. In order to test him, in the course of this
conversation I told him of my recent misbehaviour on the International Sub.
(When Margaret Herbison had told me that if I wanted to bust up the
E.D.C., I ought to resign from the Executive, I had replied that as I was much
more of a nuisance on the Executive I intended to stay there in order to
damage E.D.C. as much as I possibly could.) Nye quite spontaneously
showed shock at such behaviour! 'How could you do that, Dick?' he said.
'It's just like you as an intellectual.' But he did half laugh when I said, 'But
I only did it in private, Nye, and you did it in public. I like the feeling that you
are like me, somebody who is prepared to sit on the backbenches and have
ideas and influence people but not be a serious politician, out for power.
But I thought you weren't an intellectual like me.' And of course he doesn't
know whether he is or he isn't.

*In a private letter to Harold Wilson, written on April 22nd, Crossman gave an
account of the above conversation. He did not repeat the remarks about the
succession to Attlee and the premiership. The letter ran:*

April 22nd, 1954

PERSONAL AND CONFIDENTIAL
   Dear Harold,
        I had a long talk with Nye on Tuesday, and I am resuming this to you
[1] See above, pp. 305–7.

because you will get back from Paris before I get back from Bonn at lunch-time on Monday.

Nye started by saying that I had given you the wrong advice, so I straight-away said that I thought he had treated you outrageously. He was rather off-hand at the beginning in trying to make out that consultation was impossible, and 'one can't work in committees all the time'. I then said to him quite bluntly that I had always imagined that I was the kind of intellectual who wasn't seriously concerned with office and power and could therefore afford to act irresponsibly, and that it seemed to me that he had acted in a way which could be expected of me but not of him. I also said (I think I had better tell you this) that what he had done was to weaken his own position and strengthen yours enormously, if you acted wisely and prudently. I didn't exclude the possibility that you would decide not to stand, even after a ballot, because I said I assumed you would consult with your colleagues before you made up your mind.

The whole conversation was, I think, genuinely friendly, and at the end Nye was a bit sheepish about his performance. What alarmed me was the following interlude:

CROSSMAN: *'Surely you agree that if, at this juncture, strength accrues to Attlee through this stand on the hydrogen bomb, that really weakens the position of Gaitskell and Morrison and so moves the Party to the Left?'* NYE: *'No, you're utterly wrong. We have to expose the futility and weakness of the little man.' And a little later he added, 'I'm sure they're going to try and get us expelled.' This did disturb me a little, because it looked as though he had the death-wish on him! To attack Attlee frontally at this point seems to me absolutely insane, when things are going to go so much our way this summer if only we are cool and prudent.*

One other important item I have got from George Wigg. Apparently there was a precedent during the war for this issue about co-option or ballot. Someone resigned, and it was proposed to co-opt, and then Shinwell protested and a ballot took place.

I had a word with Ian privately, who, of course, is very sore at Nye's failure to consult us but is strongly opposed to the line that you and I are taking, since he thinks it will destroy the Bevanites on the National Executive.

Last point. I enclose a copy of the resolution I have tabled for Wednesday's Executive on Indo-China.[1] Its origin is that, in the International Sub. on Tuesday, the 13th, I moved a resolution, of which the first paragraph was accepted by the International Sub. and the second paragraph postponed, on the understanding that I could move it at the Executive on the 28th. Morgan rang me and asked whether I would, and I can see no reason for not doing so. I also discovered that on that day, i.e. yesterday, no other resolution had been sent in on the subject.

This is just to fill you in. Nye is coming to the Tuesday lunch and I have

[1] See above, p. 311.

asked him very firmly to tell us frankly and openly what he thinks our strategy and our tactics should be. I am pretty sure he will do so. There is not only the question of your decision to discuss, but what he is going to do on the backbenches. The only point of being there is to make a series of big, constructive, left-wing speeches, which will carry the Party along the line. But that does need consultation.

Dick

From April 22nd to 26th Crossman was at the Anglo-German Conference at Königswinter, 'a bit like old cabbage, partly, no doubt because the spice of Bob Boothby and Kingsley was not there and partly because, for the third year running, we discussed German rearmament, E.D.C., etc.'

Wednesday, April 28th

When I got back from Bonn on Monday, April 26th, I rang up Nye and I discovered that he and Harold had been in London over the weekend but not in communication. Nye told me there was nothing to discuss because Harold had made up his mind not to go on the Committee. Since I knew this was not true, I rang up Harold, who immediately came round to see me. I was in a bit of a rush, since I was due to go out with Bob Boothby for dinner and debate.

By now it had been made clear that the idea of a ballot was unconstitutional; Harold had either to be co-opted or to refuse. Apparently he had been lunching with George Wigg and, in the course of tea, he and I decided that the right course was for him to go on the Committee, making a public statement that he agreed with Nye's views 100 per cent but that, after consulting Nye, it was felt that for the sake of Party unity he could not refuse to serve.

I then said to Harold that he should go and tell Nye that very evening, so that he had a chance to think it over before the Group on Tuesday. Harold said he wouldn't go unless I went with him, so across we went to Cliveden Place, where we had a friendly but rather uneasy conversation, during which Nye repeated the need to attack the present leadership, including Attlee, and stated that, if Harold went on the Committee, it would be interpreted as a split. I said, 'That depends, of course, on what you do', and suggested that he should give his blessing. This was obviously a surprise to Nye and he didn't seem displeased and said, 'Well, you draft the letter and we'll discuss it at lunch tomorrow.' So we left and on the way back Harold and I agreed that overnight Jennie would get hold of Nye and he would probably turn the letter down at the next day's lunch.

Next morning I went to the *Statesman* and, to my surprise, when I reported to John [Freeman] on events, I found that over the weekend he had modified his views. When I was doing the leader, John had complained that it looked too sycophantic and said that we had to put in some more criticism of Nye.[1]

[1] 'Mr Bevan and the Labour Leadership', *New Statesman and Nation*, April 24th, 1954, had spoken of 'the streak of wilfulness which makes him such a difficult colleague'. 'But,' it went on, 'Mr Bevan's sudden reactions are nearly always based on a sound instinct.'

But on Sunday John had been addressing the Second Eleven, the group of Bevanite candidates, etc., and they had all been enthusiastic for Nye's resignation. Indeed, there is very little doubt that throughout the constituency parties it has caused a surge of militancy, particularly in view of the threatening situation in Indo-China.

At the Tuesday lunch we managed to talk about everything else for half the time. We knew time was short because there were only twenty-seven Questions and Churchill was to answer a Private Notice Question on Indo-China.[1] However, when we came to the point it was soon only too clear that Harold Wilson and I were in a minority against Nye, Jennie, who remained completely silent, Geoffrey Bing, who led the attack on us, John and Tommy, who were obviously passionately desirous to avoid personal breaks, and Ian Mikardo and Tom Driberg, who were equally emphatic. Nye was very careful in what he said not to repeat his suggestion that we should attack Attlee. Indeed, he said we shouldn't attack the leadership at all but merely take over the lead in the Commons and the attack on the Tories, as we had done before he was on the Committee. He made it clear that, in his view, the present parliamentary leadership was hopeless and that an electoral success would be disastrous until the leadership had been completely changed as the result of a mass movement in the constituencies, which we were to lead from the backbenches, while staying on the N.E.C.

We all went to the House to hear Churchill's Statement, which was extremely good, since he said that Britain had undertaken no political or military commitments in Indo-China and would not consider any until after the Geneva Conference. So Nye had no chance of intervening. We went back to Vincent Square at half-past four, when Harold produced his draft letter. Discussion proceeded till six o'clock, when I was giving a farewell cocktail party for Anne to her fellow members of D.R.U.[2] The tea-time discussion was, I thought, slightly more unpleasant, as each side was expressing its position even more clearly and widening the division. Nye said twice that he didn't care one halfpenny about the Labour Party in its present form and he also mentioned MacDonaldism[3] in close connection with Harold.

Nye said the basic division between himself and me was that I thought we could achieve something by co-operating with the present parliamentary

[1] There were twenty-five Questions and two Private Notice Questions, including one on the Geneva Conference and 'Asian defence measures'.

[2] Anne McDougall worked at the Design Research Unit from 1953 to 1954.

[3] James Ramsay MacDonald (1856–1937), Labour M.P. for Leicester 1906–18, for the Aberavon division of Glamorganshire 1922–9 and for the Seaham division of County Durham 1929–31; he was National Labour M.P. for Seaham 1931–5 and for the Scottish Universities from 1936 until his death. He was Chairman of the P.L.P. and Leader of the Opposition 1922, Prime Minister and Secretary of State for Foreign Affairs January–November 1924, Prime Minister 1929–35 and Lord President of the Council 1935–7. A biography, *Ramsay MacDonald*, was written by David Marquand (London: Cape, 1977). By 'MacDonaldism', Crossman is referring to the decision to form a National Government in 1931. This action split the Labour Party and the greater proportion of MacDonald's followers felt themselves to have been betrayed.

leadership and seeking to persuade them to adopt our views, whereas the right policy was to isolate them completely and let them destroy themselves by their incompetence. That we could only do by rousing the constituencies against them. Of course, this is a view which, when Nye is in a different mood, he can annihilate just as easily, and often has. My impression is that Geoffrey Bing, who talked to him for an hour on the afternoon he resigned, has had a very big influence. Tom Driberg and John Freeman, of course, having both decided to give up Parliament, are, in Tom's language, slightly more objective or, as I would put it, they inevitably disregard the importance of the Parliamentary Party. I tried to explain that it seemed to me that we had to do both operations — leading the constituencies and trying to permeate the Parliamentary Party. If we polarized the Party, we should drive the middle-of-the-roaders to the Right. To this, the reply was that anyway there weren't many middle-of-the-roaders to drive.

By six o'clock it was pretty clear both that Harold wanted to go on the Committee and that the inner Bevanite Group regarded this as a betrayal. But I don't think anyone there, including Nye, really believed that he hadn't made a grave mistake in resigning. Indeed, this was confirmed a couple of hours later in the Smoking Room, when Ian Mikardo, after protesting to me, suddenly revealed that he too thought Nye's tactics had been, in his words, disastrous but that we couldn't afford to show any disunity. Of course, the obvious reply to this is that it is up to the inner group of the Bevanites to defend Harold Wilson's actions, even though they disagree with them, as we defended Nye's, even though we disagreed with that. But when I put this to Tom Driberg, he could hardly follow the argument, he was so puzzled. One of the things we object to most strongly is the blind loyalty of the Right but really the Left of the Party shows that kind of loyalty just as strongly. It only confirms my contention that in British politics loyalty to people and not ideas is universally regarded as the prime quality.

This morning we had the N.E.C., which went off fairly uneventfully. We were due to hear the report on legal action to prevent leakages, the subject which had dominated the Executive five weeks ago. The report just wasn't given. When my motion on Indo-China came up, Morrison and most of the trade unionists advised that no action should be taken at the present moment, since it would embarrass the Government. Attlee spoke strongly in favour of a statement and so did Harold Wilson, who quite reasonably criticized the wording of my motion. Nye then spoke in favour of my motion, particularly the clause dealing with a military pact. After some time, the office drafted a statement, including approval of Nehru's initiative[1] and a vague reference to

[1] India was among those countries which believed that to create defensive associations in the South-East Asian area would increase tension with China and the likelihood of war. The Indian Prime Minister, Mr Nehru, appealed for a ceasefire in Indo-China and he persuaded the four other Asian Prime Ministers (from Pakistan, Burma, Ceylon and Indonesia), meeting at Colombo, to advocate an armistice and direct negotiation, on the eve of the Geneva Conference.

military arrangements, which Nye then moved to leave out, so that the only thing he resigned for has now been removed.

I took Harold home to lunch and by this time his mind had finally been made up. So I helped him to redraft his letter to Carol Johnson, and George Wigg, whose foot had been run over by a trolley at a railway station, came in, too, to help with the press relations. Harold then went to see Attlee, who seemed quite cordial, at least according to Harold, who told me that Attlee's interjections of 'Quite', which were his sole contribution to the conversation, were said rather sweetly. Harold says that he delivered Attlee a strong lecture on the need for a proper balance in the Party and re-emphasized his determination to remain loyal to Nye. Then he came back to Vincent Square, we finalized the letter and that was that.

Now it will be very interesting to see what happens. What Harold and I can hope for is that Harold goes on to the Committee and that in three weeks' time this is regarded as perfectly normal because simultaneously the Bevanite Group continues to meet and Harold remains 100 per cent Bevanite. Whether this happens depends on whether Nye restrains the two or three members of the Group who would already like to denounce Harold for MacDonaldism and whether Jennie advises caution. I have quite a hope that it may go O.K. but anyway Harold is in for a very unpleasant time. In terms of the Group I am in just as deeply as he is because throughout I argued Harold's case and in his present mood Nye has ruled us both out. However, he still seems quite friendly to us.

On April 29th sixty-three Labour Members, defying their Front Bench, supported a proposal to secure parliamentary consent before Britain manufactured a hydrogen bomb. Meanwhile the Foreign Secretary had flown to Paris for talks with the American Secretary of State and the French Foreign Minister before the opening of the Geneva Conference on April 26th. But, two days before the conference began, he suddenly returned to London for an emergency Cabinet meeting, to discuss, it was believed, the worsening position of the French garrison at Dien Bien Phu.

At the start of the conference it was agreed that the chair should be taken by the delegate of Thailand (Prince Wan Waithayakon), Mr Molotov and Mr Eden, in that order. On April 27th the Prime Minister told the Commons that the Government were not prepared to give any undertakings about British military commitment in Indo-China in advance of the outcome of the conference. No new political or military commitments had been entered upon. On April 28th the Chinese delegate, Chou En-lai, demanded an end to all foreign military bases in Asia and the withdrawal of all foreign troops, while on April 29th Mr Eden sent a message to the Colombo Conference, asking the Prime Ministers of Ceylon, India and Pakistan whether they would be ready to take part in a guarantee to assure the future of Indo-China, should acceptable results be reached in Geneva.

In the United States members of the Congress had expressed their fears that American Servicemen should find themselves engaged in Indo-China, in 'another Korea', and there had been an outburst of protest against the remark on April 16th by Vice-President Nixon that 'the Executive has to take the politically unpopular decision'. On April 21st, however, the United States Air Force flew a French battalion to Indo-China and on April 27th the United States Chief of Staff, Admiral Radford, came to Paris and London with proposals for armed intervention. The British refusal to take such action was held to represent a major diplomatic defeat for Mr Dulles.

Then, on April 29th, in an article headlined 'Second Thoughts in U.S. on Indo-China', a Times correspondent reported the 'overwhelming opposition' in the Congress to the United States taking a sole initiative in involvement in the Indo-China war. On Monday, April 26th, it was stated, the President had spoken of 'trying to arrive at some situation that at least we could call a modus vivendi'.

In the meantime informal discussions continued between the Americans and the British Government, though they were at first denied by the Minister of State at the Foreign Office, Selwyn Lloyd.

Monday, May 3rd

A special Party Meeting had been called for eleven o'clock on Thursday, April 29th, immediately after the Recess, to discuss Indo-China. Naturally the atmosphere was largely conditioned by the news of Harold Wilson's acceptance of co-option to the Parliamentary Committee. This had got a tremendous press. On the whole, George [Wigg] and I had done a decent job of work, particularly on the Daily Herald, where from Harold's point of view Sydney Elliott had written a very good editorial. I had also managed to ensure that the Mirror did the story straight and didn't pat Harold on the back for knifing Bevan in the back.[1]

The Party Meeting was extremely full, since everyone was expecting a tremendous row, with Nye stating the case for his resignation. It started with a dry little statement by Attlee on the situation in Indo-China. In The Times that morning there had been a sensational message from Washington, suggesting that the Americans had suddenly given up their policy of united action in Indo-China and that a climb-down was on the way. Attlee mentioned this to show that the immediate war danger had been removed, read aloud the N.E.C. resolution and suggested that there was nothing to vote about but there might be a discussion if the Party wanted. After one or two minor questions, Walter Monslow,[2] who is very close to Nye and strongly

---

[1] The article by 'a Daily Mirror reporter', published on April 29th, quoted Harold Wilson as saying: ' ... what matters in the last resort is the unity and strength of the Party'.
[2] Labour M.P. for Barrow-in-Furness 1945–66 and Parliamentary Secretary at the Ministry of Civil Aviation 1949–50 and at the Ministry of Food 1950–1. He was Organization Secretary of ASLEF. In 1966 he became a life peer, but died that year.

opposed to Harold, suddenly got up and moved the adjournment. This was received with a burst of laughter and the Party trooped out.

In the Smoking Room afterwards, sitting with Nye, I checked and found, as I thought, that Walter had not done this after consultation but spontaneously, quite rightly feeling that anything Nye said at that meeting could only do him harm. It was clear that people like George Brown had come there prepared with speeches on Party unity. Of course, the fact that Nye did have nothing whatsoever to say on the great issue which allegedly had caused him to resign made his own supporters even more baffled. I spent a fairly miserable morning and afternoon, since the inner Bevanite feelings were extremely bitter, and it was not easy, though it was essential, to sit with Nye in the Smoking Room and make small talk conversation.

On Friday morning when I did the *Sunday Pic* it was clear from the newspapers that the United States' climb-down was even more sensational than had been expected. At his press conference President Eisenhower said he was in favour of some sort of understanding with the Communists in Indo-China and we later learnt that Mr Dulles had not been informed of this decision while at Geneva. This has given Eden a terrific negotiating position if he wants to use it, since for the time being the U.S.A has opted out of the Geneva Conference. But it has also put the lid on any theory that there was a great issue for Bevan to resign on.

After lunch today I went into the House to test the atmosphere and found Barbara Castle back from three weeks' rest in Scotland with Naomi Mitchison. Barbara thought Harold had done the wrong thing, though she was sure that Nye's resignation had been a disaster. Her view was that, once Nye said he wouldn't give his blessing, Harold shouldn't have gone on the Committee. I said to her that if she and Michael had been there we might together have persuaded Nye, which I think is true. However, I shall be interested to see what she feels when she has been back a day or two longer.

I had tea with Harold, who told me of his weekend. He had arrived in Manchester on Thursday night to find twenty pressmen waiting for him, to tell him that A. J. Irvine had just written, refusing to speak in Harold's constituency owing to his disloyalty to Nye. Harold, of course, had not received the letter – it had gone to the press and in any case Irvine was only due to speak to a Fabian Society which he had himself expressly said he wanted to address. I had been extremely alarmed when I read this news in Friday's papers, fearing an anti-Harold row at the Liverpool May Day demonstration, which he was addressing on Saturday, or the Manchester demonstration, which he was addressing on Sunday. Fortunately Harold took my advice and made the most left-wing speech of his career, with three slogans: not a man or a gun to Indo-China; Nehru's policy, not Dulles's policy; and anti German rearmament. Harold told me there was no sign of a peep at Liverpool and at Manchester Will Griffiths, Nye's most ardent supporter, had warmly shaken Harold's hand when they met in the demonstration and had spoken on his behalf that same evening. This, I think, is significant of Nye's attitude. However, there is very little doubt that for the moment Harold has not done himself a great deal of good and by these proceedings Nye has done himself an incalculable amount of harm.

Behind the scenes, of course, we are all discussing Nye's motor-car accident, which is due to come before the magistrates on Friday.[1] Apparently six weeks ago, when he was driving back to London alone, he ran into the side of a chara and didn't stop. Unfortunately, Clem Attlee's daughter and her husband[2] were behind him and before the smash they had noticed that he was driving so erratically and weaving on the road so violently that Alison had taken his number. When Alison came up to the chara, which had stopped, she told them that she had taken the number of the car so that, as soon as Nye got home, the police were at his door and he had no time even to show that he had rung them up. In my view, having this accident hanging over his head may have been one of the motives prompting Nye's irrationality about Indo-China. But he is no less irrational now, since I heard this afternoon that he is having Sydney Silverman appearing for him on Friday. Mostly, this afternoon, I have been trying to make sure that the Bevanites all turn up to lunch tomorrow, since in this situation behaving decently is the only way of avoiding the destruction of the Left.

Thursday, May 6th

On Tuesday morning it was still touch and go whether Nye was prepared to come to our lunch. Barbara Castle had been to see him on Monday afternoon but I think it was John Freeman who finally persuaded him to come, partly by touching his heart by offering to drive him down to Beaconsfield on Friday for his appearance before the magistrates. However, everything passed off quite amazingly easily. John and I arrived a few minutes late from the *New Statesman* and found Nye there drinking Bols gin. He really can't refuse conversation and before many minutes were out he was well away, apparently quite happy.

The most interesting incident was when somebody remarked that it looked from the morning papers as though Arthur Greenwood was going to die.[3] At this, Nye had a brilliant idea. 'That gives us our line,' he said. 'Gaitskell will certainly stand for Treasurer and I will stand against him.' 'But you will be defeated,' someone said. 'Of course,' said Nye, 'but in defeating me they will split every trade union and expose Deakin and Tom Williamson by making them prefer an intellectual like Gaitskell to a miner like me.' Somebody else objected that in that case Nye couldn't stand for the constituency section and wouldn't be on the Executive. 'That doesn't matter,' he said. 'The elections for the constituencies have served their purpose already as a

[1] See below, p. 327 n.
[2] Alison Attlee married Richard Davis in 1952.
[3] He died on June 9th.

symbol.' He also repeated that, in his view, the right-wing were now preparing for a real show-down.

In the evening I had a most amusing time at the theatre, where a gala performance was given of the Russian State Dancers, a troupe of girls doing folk dances to the accompaniment of four accordions.[1] I had written to Malik saying that Nenni would be with me and asking whether I could have two extra tickets. However, since Nenni couldn't come, I invited Bob Boothby to come with Anne and me. When we got to the theatre we found we had been put into a most prominent box on the stalls level, where we sat like Royalty, with all the fellow travellers giving us the evil eye and with Harry Pollitt[2] five boxes further away from the stage. I was embarrassed but Bob was determined to sit it out in his glory. In the interval things were made worse when the chief Russian there, Zhivotovski, spent his whole time conversing with us. He asked us whether we were surprised by the developments in America and Bob said yes. Then I said, 'Were you surprised at Churchill's flatly turning down the French request for aid?' And Zhivotovski said, 'Yes, I was,' which made me feel that he was not very well informed, for anyone knowing anything about conditions here could have predicted that as a certainty.

The actual performance made a wonderful impact at the beginning, when the girls glided on to the stage in long red dresses, as smoothly as though they had roller skates. But this was their only superb trick. The dances alternated between roller-skate manoeuvres and pseudo-Cossack jollifications, the latter being better done by men. But the dresses and the individuality of the girls were superb. There was one ghastly piece called 'Soviet Youth', in which the whole company, dressed in short tennis skirts, manoeuvred, singing a corking song and, as Anne remarked to Bob, 'John Betjeman should be here. Here are fifty of his Myfanwys at once.'[3] They really were exactly like it and they gave one a horrific picture of the clean fun which Soviet youth now enjoys.

At dinner afterwards Bob told me that Churchill is now in a new mood. For many months he had refused to discuss his resignation with anybody. Now he discusses it with everybody and changes his mind every forty-eight hours, putting his younger colleagues into complete perturbation. We both agreed, however, that the resignation may have to be postponed owing to the

[1] The Moscow State Dance Company, Beryozhka, visited London in May.

[2] Harry Pollitt (1890–1960) was a founder member of the Communist Party of Great Britain, of which he was Party Secretary from 1919 until his death.

[3] John Betjeman, poet and author, was knighted in 1969 and became Poet Laureate in 1972. He has published many volumes of poetry and works on architecture, including *A Few Late Chrysanthemums* (London: John Murray, 1954), *Summoned By Bells*, a verse autobiography (London: John Murray, 1960), *High and Low* (London: John Murray, 1966), *A Nip in the Air* (London: John Murray, 1974) and *A Pictorial History of English Architecture* (Harmondsworth: Penguin, 1974). In two of John Betjeman's poems, 'Myfanwy' and 'Myfanwy in Oxford', their heroine's progress is charted from a children's party to an Oxford women's college. Her physical attraction is chiefly to be found in her 'hair flowing back with an ostentation' and a certain muscular sinuousness, 'strong and willowy'.

"STRANGE COMRADES THESE DAYS, BROTHER!"

international situation. It looks as though both the French and the Americans are going to blame Britain if Indo-China collapses — and Churchill could hardly resign just at that time.

On Wednesday morning Nye's predictions seemed to be confirmed, when every popular paper had a six-column banner headline, 'MORRISON FLAYS BEVAN'. During the day I managed to elicit the fact that, just after Nye's resignation, Herbert had written an article for *Socialist Commentary*,[1] which is the only Socialist periodical that is anti-Bevanite. Then, when the article was already in the press, Herbert had added at the end some twenty lines of vitriolic personal attack on Nye. He had got Attlee's approval for the idea of the article but apparently Attlee claims never to have read the text. Moreover, Morrison clearly meant to have a sensation, since *Socialist Commentary*, which is not a well-known journal, was distributed in a marked copy to all newspapers and lobby correspondents on Tuesday night.

This immediately caused George Wigg and George Strauss to blow up and write letters to Attlee, pointing out that Herbert had violated the Parliamentary Party resolution which he himself had moved, forbidding attacks on colleagues.[2] Indeed, the general impression in the lobbies was that Herbert had made a great tactical error in presuming that Nye had mortally wounded himself and deciding to give him a personal *coup de grâce*. What Herbert had in fact done is to put himself wrong on procedure, the one issue on which the Right always hopes to defeat the Left.

[1] In the May issue of *Socialist Commentary*, Herbert Morrison accused Aneurin Bevan of losing between thirty and forty Labour seats by his remarks comparing the Conservatives to 'vermin' in the 1950 General Election, of costing Labour office in 1951 by his resignation and of being 'the answer to the Tories' prayer' by his action over Indo-China.

[2] See above, pp. 163 ff.

I spent a long and rather dreary afternoon discussing with endless people the meaning of the Morrison attack. Frank Soskice was perhaps typical of the Right. He found Anne and me sitting in the Central Lobby and came up, apparently to say how do you do, whereupon I engaged him in political conversation. Every three minutes he expostulated that surely my fiancée didn't want to hear such unpleasant conversation, but I told him it was her education and went on prodding him. His line was roughly: 'It's such a terrible pity that we have these dissensions, when what we need is unity and comradeship. As for Herbert, he had been provoked beyond endurance and had to reply. Did you see that terrible cartoon in which I was portrayed dancing with Attlee along with Nazi generals?' I hadn't seen the cartoon, which apparently occurred in *Tribune* but which I have now gathered was printed a week after Morrison had sent his article to press.

However, it's fairly clear that the line is going to be that the left-wing periodicals, with M.P.s writing anonymously, had launched such poisonous attacks on the Right that something had to be done. Frank went on talking about personal rivalries for so long that I got mad and said, 'My dear Frank, there are policy issues involved. You seem to have forgotten that Clement Attlee and Ernest Bevin plotted to destroy the Jews in Palestine and then encouraged the Arabs to murder the lot. I fought them at the time as murderers. I can never trust them again and you can't expect me to forgive them for genocide, even though you were an accomplice then, and now, tomorrow, you will be going to the Israeli Independence Day and drinking their good drink, having forgiven them for the ill we have done them.' I must say, poor Frank Soskice looked a little bleak under this attack and Anne was a bit upset, but I told her that all one can do with people like him is to make them realize that there are policy issues involved and not merely personal rivalries.

Meanwhile, thank heavens, Nye, completely on his own, put out to the press a short statement disowning personal rivalries, which exudes an odour of sanctity that he enormously enjoys. Certainly Herbert has succeeded at one stroke in unifying the Left. In the course of the afternoon I was able to discover, partly from Harold Wilson, that, at the Parliamentary Committee, when the issue was raised, Chuter Ede, Hugh Dalton, James Callaghan and Harold were the four who criticized Herbert. Chuter Ede, when George drove him home late that night, was extremely bitter, saying that the showdown would be a show-up of Herbert Morrison and also telling George that, in his view, it was really an attack by Morrison on Attlee for not being anti-Bevanite enough.

Saturday, May 8th
When I wrote my *Sunday Pic* on Friday,[1] there were only two subjects:

[1] The title of Crossman's piece, published on May 9th, 1954, was 'Why Did Herbert Hit Out?' but the last two of its five paragraphs dealt with the consequences of the fall of Dien Bien Phu on May 7th.

Herbert Morrison's attack on Aneurin and the sensational American climb-down in Indo-China. But, of course, what was worrying me at the time was something quite different: namely, Nye's motor car accident.[1] That afternoon I was due to do 'Any Questions' at Brockenhurst and travelled down with Bob Boothby.[2] We saw the first editions of the evening papers and agreed that Nye would be very lucky, particularly since he had chosen Sydney Silverman to represent him, if he got off with three months' suspension of his licence. At the little pub where we stayed, we put on the six-o'clock news and there, right at the end, was the decision and he had got away with three months. This was really a very great relief and the papers this morning showed that he had done extremely well and that Clem Attlee's son-in-law[3] had behaved with discretion.

I had been expecting a question on the Labour Party row but the producer said that this would be unfair, since I was the only Labour person present. This is very characteristic of the B.B.C., since a fortnight before, with a right-wing Labour person there, they had of course had a question. However, the programme went fairly well. The whole evening, though, was over-shadowed by the news that Dien Bien Phu had fallen and in London today I had to recast my *Sunday Pic*.

Tuesday, May 11th
The only interesting thing which happened today was an interview I had with Hugh Cudlipp. I asked to see him to discover whether he would agree that I should accept an invitation to take Anne to Russia in September and also to ask him if I could, as usual, have some money for my summer holiday, even though it was a honeymoon. The interview started with Hugh telling me that I was a bloody Bevanite and that the column wasn't worth twenty-five guineas a week. So I said that was all right and he could find somebody else and that anyway it was quite untrue that I used the column for pure Bevanite propaganda—I had only written about Bevanism when it really had news value. Hugh then said, 'It's madness for you to be a henchman of that man.

[1] Two summonses were issued, relating to a collision between Aneurin Bevan's car and a coach, at 9.50 p.m. on April 3rd, on the London–Oxford road near the junction with the Amersham road. The case was heard at Beaconsfield Magistrates Court on May 7th with Sydney Silverman acting as Bevan's solicitor. Mr Bevan stated that he had been driving at 45 to 60 miles an hour. The chairman of the Magistrates concluded that Mr Bevan's 'attention must have wandered'. He was fined £25 and disqualified from driving for three months. Costs of £34 6s. 5d. were awarded against him.

[2] A radio 'brains trust', first produced (as it continues to be) by the B.B.C. West Region in October 1948. Each fortnight and, from late 1949, each week, the programme was broadcast from a different part of the country, where four invited guests would answer questions, impromptu, from an audience. On May 7th, 1954, the programme was produced by Michael Bowen and, as well as Crossman and Sir Robert Boothby, the guests were A. G. Street and Sir Graham Savage. In the programme a fortnight before, on April 23rd, the guests had been A. G. Street, George Woodcock, Anthony Greenwood M.P. and—'the right-wing Labour person'—Ted Leather, in fact a Conservative M.P.

[3] Compare p. 323, 'Clem Attlee's daughter'.

If you weren't under his shadow you would be far better known. Why don't you get away from him and be an independent character with an independent column?'

Of course, there's a certain amount of truth in what he says and I admitted straightaway that possibly before Nye resigned in 1951 I was much better known in my own right because I was then leading the Keep Left Group. I asked him whether he would really like me to be a John Strachey, wibble-wobbling in the middle. In politics, whether you like it or not, you have to take sides. I had gone there for a quarter of an hour but only left after an hour and three-quarters, when Hugh had suddenly said that my salary would be increased to thirty-five guineas a week and that I could go to Russia on one condition—that I didn't take Anne or receive a single rouble from the Russians, but agreed that the *Sunday Pictorial* should pay the whole of my expenses. Hugh wasn't going to have his men going on free trips for foreign Governments.

From May 12th to 15th Crossman was in Geneva, with Sir Robert Boothby, observing proceedings at the Geneva Conference. He learnt that: 'there are those in the Pentagon[1] who are determined on creeping intervention, which will bring us by stages to the use of the atom bomb'. This fear was confirmed in a briefing given by Eden to British diplomatic correspondents. Crossman's report may be found in the New Statesman and Nation *of May 22nd, 1954.*

Wednesday, May 19th
I returned to London from Geneva at five o'clock on Saturday afternoon, in time to catch the quarter to seven train to Oxford to speak to a Balliol club of economists, organized by Tommy. I gave them quite a witty analysis of the dangers of collective security, stressing that certain Socialists now seemed to believe that every small war should be turned into a universal war and that Britain should fight in them all. It was the sort of talk which, even six years ago in Oxford, would have been received with pleasure, even by those who disagreed, but on this occasion all the vociferous undergraduates were morally appalled by what they regarded as cynicism and materialism. One suddenly realized how completely different the intellectual atmosphere at universities now is. These chaps all seem to regard a fight against Communism as the first priority. Of course, this may be a false impression, since the Socialists there kept quiet and Tommy tells me that on Monday, on reflection, they said that they had all enjoyed it a great deal.

This week we've been back in Labour Party politics, with the two long-awaited meetings, on Tuesday of the National Executive and on Wednesday of the Parliamentary Party, to deal with the problem of unity. In the Executive meeting we sat silent for one and a quarter hours and listened to seven speeches, starting with a moral rearmament one from Jim Hawarth, who

[1] Headquarters of the American Department of Defense.

really tried to be conciliatory. Then the others got going. Jean Mann,[1] the sour little mamma from Glasgow, said that the Left was infiltrated and dominated by Communists and that the Bevanites were their catspaws. Clem Attlee made a vindictive attack on the periodical which had been poisonously and pharisaically preaching so-called Socialism when there were no policy differences. He said there was a danger of the Party being dominated by middle-class elements, which were unreliable. Edith Summerskill started by saying that she did not blame Nye, who was a lazy man with a temperament. 'Nye, Barbara and Dick — I've nothing against them. They are victims of their temperament. The real danger here, the real organizer of subversion, is that man Mikardo!'

After a good deal more of this, it was clear that our opponents were getting more and more uncomfortable, while we sat and listened, and finally they positively appealed for one of us to say something. Nye remarked that this was a meeting about unity but as usual all the speeches we had heard had dripped venom. There had been a great deal of complaint about the *Tribune* and the *New Statesman* and suggestions that the Bevanites controlled the Labour press, but in fact the whole of the rest of the press had been vindictively and obsessively anti-Bevanite and backing Attlee. What Attlee was really asking was that the whole press, unanimously and without exception, should attack the Bevanites. Jim Hawarth then put forward a resolution and Harold Wilson made a very sensible speech about collective responsibility.

After that I weighed in and said that the others were not facing the real problem. Herbert Morrison was personally far more popular in the Movement, for instance, than I was. Yet he had been knocked off the Executive and I was elected with a huge number of votes. Why? Not because I am personally liked but because the policies Herbert stands for are so revolting to the constituencies that they vote even for me. This would go on, whatever disciplinary measures were taken, while the official leadership failed to lead. At this, Attlee snapped, 'What's your alternative policy?' And I said, 'Well, take German rearmament. I stand by what Morgan Phillips said on behalf of the Executive.[2] That's a clear alternative policy.' 'He merely put forward a suggestion,' said Attlee, catching himself out, since I was able to say that Morgan spoke just as officially as Attlee. So Attlee, who was now really quite rattled, said, 'I didn't ask you about German rearmament. What's your alternative policy in general? You haven't got one.'

Nye then intervened. 'Supposing we did put forward an alternative policy, you'd accuse us of splitting the Party!' I then renewed the attack on the failure of the leadership to attack and Attlee said, 'Give instances.' So I said, 'It

---

[1] Mrs Jean Mann was Labour M.P. for the Coatbridge division of Lanark 1945–50 and for Coatbridge and Airdrie 1950–9. She was a member of the N.E.C. 1953–8. She died in 1964.

[2] See above, pp. 291 ff.

always goes like this. We say something. You denounce it as Bevanite heresy. Churchill does it. You support it. Instance (i): Defence. Instance (ii): High-level talks.' I am told this was the most savage altercation which has been heard for some time.

After this there was a long, long bicker, since the chairman had got a soft-soap resolution ready and we should have got it through if Tom Driberg hadn't said *sotto voce* that it was full of acceptable platitudes. This so infuriated the trade unions that they then voted for the much more stringent resolution of Jim Hawarth. The whole thing went on from ten o'clock until a quarter to two and was about as futile and ineffective as I expected. The only significant facts were, first, that the early speakers openly criticized Attlee's weakness and, secondly, that the burden of their charge is now directed against the periodicals. It's the journalists they really fear.

Since my house is now being redecorated, we had our Bevanite lunch at Bing's to discuss our tactics for today's meeting of the Parliamentary Party. It was decided that we should support any motion for adjournment to cut short the slanging and it was generally expected that, since the Parliamentary Party has already passed one resolution against personal abuse, it could hardly pass another.

The Parliamentary Party meeting this morning started with an extremely conciliatory speech by Attlee, who asked for a cessation of personal abuse but urged that discussion of policy must continue. Once again, as I have so often observed, he learns a great deal and he had picked up all the points on which he had been sloshed yesterday. Attlee rather took the wind out of the sails of George Strauss, whose speech, a veiled attack on Morrison for disobeying Standing Orders, I thought a flop. The meeting petered along, since it was clear that no resolution would be moved and no action would be taken. Nye made an excellent speech along the lines he took yesterday and demonstrated conclusively that, whereas he himself had made no personal attacks on anybody, Herbert had launched a personal attack on him. Nye's most effective point was that, every time that Herbert suggested there were no policy differences in the Party but only personal rivalries, he did terrible harm in the constituencies, which were appalled at the idea that the leadership should bicker personally without any differences but which prospered if it was felt that real issues were being debated.

Throughout the meeting there was a barrage of attacks on the journalists who have a monopoly of the Labour press and on the left-wing for giving the impression that they are the true Socialists and that their right-wing colleagues are not. George Brown added that these journalists are so clever that they never attack anybody personally but only do it by implication. Michael and I were trying to speak but failed to get in, which we didn't much mind, since all we had to do was to show we were ready to defend ourselves. The only person who spoke about journalism was Denis Healey. He really improved our case for us by saying that an article which Nye had called scurrilous that he had published in the *New Republic* was really factual.[1] When challenged to read it, Denis read a passage which said that Nye had done an action which did more harm to the Labour Party than anything since MacDonald joined the National Government in 1931. Even Herbert Morrison, who had combed the files and quoted bits of Ian Mikardo, could not find a genuine personal attack. I got the impression that the right-wing of the Party is really getting desperate at the feeling that their support in the constituencies is slipping ever further and further away and that more and more M.P.s are being accused by their constituency parties of betraying Socialism. This, they feel, is all due to some terrible secret Mikardo organization and to the *New Statesman and Nation* and the *Tribune*.

Wednesday, May 26th

I seem not to have mentioned events in the Chamber for a good long time. This is because we've reached a period of record boredom, with the Committee Stage of a completely non-controversial Finance Bill and the Committee Stage of the Television Bill, which is being taken on the floor of the House and which, even after a guillotine,[2] against which, of course, a day was spent in protest, is to last nine days. Herbert Morrison regards the Television Bill, so Sydney Jacobson informed me the other day, as just the sort of thing which a real democratic Party should fight about. Actually, of course, there are far more Conservative voters who object to commercial television than Labour voters and there is no sign that the Labour Movement as such feels strongly about the fight against the Bill.

As for the Finance Bill, we spent hours on it but everybody says that there is nothing to discuss. Yet such is the peculiar discipline of our Party that I had a wonderful contretemps last night. Tomorrow is mayor-making at Coventry and my old friend John Fennell[3] had as Mayor-elect asked me to be one of the speakers at the lunch. I put in a chit asking for a pair till half-past seven and I got a note from my Regional Whip, Jim Johnson,[4] saying that this was impossible and telling me to see the Chief. Will Whiteley,[5] who is growing older and fuddy-duddier than ever, told me it was quite impossible, since he had forbidden no less than thirty-four Labour Members to attend mayoral functions, and before I could say anything he added, 'And it's no use saying

---

[1] Between January and June 1954 Denis Healey wrote regularly for the American fortnightly magazine *New Republic*. The article to which Crossman refers was 'Aneurin Bevan Does It Again', in the issue of May 3rd, in which the author says that Bevan is 'impossible as a colleague and would be intolerable as a leader'.

[2] The motion on the Allocation of Time for the remainder of the Committee Stage, the Report Stage and Third Reading of the Television Bill was debated on May 11th. Seven days were set aside for completion of the debate. The motion was passed by 293 votes to 276.

[3] A Labour councillor in Coventry in the 1930s.

[4] James Johnson, Labour M.P. for the Rugby division of Warwickshire 1950–9 and for Kingston-upon-Hull since 1964.

[5] William Whiteley, Labour M.P. for Durham 1922–31 and from 1935 until his death in 1956. He was Labour Chief Whip 1942–55.

you'll lose any votes; you won't.' I replied that I had 13,000 votes and wasn't concerned but that it was totally impossible for me to let my old friend John Fennell down. William Whiteley said that made no difference and I said, 'Well, I'm going anyway,' and at this point we passed on through the far end of the division lobby. A quarter of an hour later, Jim Johnson came up to me in the Smoking Room, and, in a hoarse whisper, asked me to step aside. 'I've fixed it with the Chief Whip,' he said. 'You can go but don't tell anybody else.' I said, 'I shall go and tell everybody else.'

The fact is that the Opposition has no strategy. The Tories are willing to take unlimited pairs for both these Committee Stages and they are merely being refused on the ground that we must have a show in the lobbies. But in fact there were seventy people away yesterday and constantly people get sick of it and walk out, with the result that Government majorities go up to fifty or sixty. This is one of the troubles of a Party led by three men over seventy.

Meanwhile, of course, the centre of interest remains Indo-China and, as far as I can see, the Government is behaving extremely well, with Eden continuing his efforts to get an armistice in Geneva and Churchill still obstinately refusing to discuss a South-Eastern NATO, as Dulles would like. The result of all this is that, slowly, they are pulling the Americans back and making them see sense. Simultaneously, of course, the Anglo-Russian rapprochement goes on and the Russian Embassy in London is almost comic in its new conciliatory mood.

On February 16th a Select Committee of M.P.s had recommended an increase from £1,000 to £1,500 in Members' salaries, with the introduction of a non-contributory pension scheme to give £350 a year on retirement (after sixty-five) to Members with ten to fifteen years' service and £500 a year to those with more than fifteen years' service. The salary of £1,000 had first been voted in 1946 but the proposed increment was criticized as being too generous. Critics also alleged that the suggested pension scheme offered security in a profession to which it was inapplicable.

But the Prime Minister told the Commons on April 14th that the Government thought it inappropriate 'in present circumstances' to proceed with the recommendations. This provoked a motion, put by Robert Mellish, a Labour M.P., on May 13th, urging the Government to proceed with the increase. The Chancellor of the Exchequer replied, suggesting a system of allowances and reimbursements for M.P.s, and on May 24th this proposal was debated.

On a free vote, the Chancellor's alternative was rejected by 276 votes to 205 and a resolution to raise salaries to £1,500 was carried by 280 votes to 166. The supporters included thirty Conservative Members, among them Sir Robert Boothby and Mr Walter Elliot. Moreover, Sir Winston was widely believed to favour the increase.

On June 24th, however, the Prime Minister announced that the Government still felt it unfitting at the present time to raise salaries by this amount and he invited the leaders of the other parties to co-operate with the Government in devising a system of expense allowances. Protesting at this disregard of the will of the House, expressed on a free vote, Mr Attlee voiced the Opposition's indignation. Labour M.P.s persuaded him not to enter into negotiations with the Government about an alternative scheme and the Opposition also agreed to refuse 'pairs' to Conservative Members.

On Monday, we had, for once, an interesting debate in the House on Members' salaries. There had been a general discussion of this subject when I was away at Geneva but after this a tremendous lot of intrigue and consultation took place behind the scenes, and finally an 'all-party' motion was put down by seven Labour and seven Conservatives, headed by Boothby, proposing a straight salary increase of £500. The rival Tory motion proposed £500 expenses but the expenses would have to be genuinely approved and vetted by the Fees Office, which is far more severe a test than merely having to be O.K.'d by the income tax authorities. I listened to a good deal of the debate, in which the last word was had by Sir Hartley Shawcross, who made a most professional Poor Man's Lawyer speech. As I was going into the Smoking Room afterwards, Boothby said, 'That cost us thirty votes,' and Walter Monckton replied, 'No, forty.' What had infuriated the Tories was the nauseating moralizing tone in which Hartley said that the House should now, as always, vote on the merits without any regard to pressures outside.

I sat talking to Dalton afterwards and overheard a nice little interlude. Just behind me, near the door, was the group of Keep Right Tories, headed by Captain Waterhouse, whose side had been defeated. Churchill came past and stopped to talk to them. 'A bad day, Sir,' said Captain Waterhouse, and I heard Churchill end his reply with the words, 'Tory democracy cannot tolerate a ragamuffin Parliament. That should be a good enough speech for any Tory platform.' Then Dalton started booming again and, the next time I overheard, Churchill was addressing Waterhouse, who is the leader of the Suez rebels, on Egypt. 'You make it too easy,' he was saying. 'We have troops there which we need elsewhere and we are spending vast sums of money and getting nowhere with them.' Then his eyes beamed and he said, 'If I had my way, I'd set the Israelites on them. Goodnight gentlemen.' And he popped out of the door.

On June 24th the Foreign Secretary reported to the Commons that no real progress had been made at Geneva. The two principles for which Britain and her allies stood were, he said, the authority of the United Nations and genuinely free elections in both North and South Korea. On Indo-China he stated that without the support of the Colombo Powers there would never be real security in South-East Asia and the Government looked forward to progress in negotiations to obtain an acceptable form of treaty or defensive alliance. In reply, Mr Attlee deplored the continued exclusion of China from the United Nations and referred to the chronic instability of French Governments and the conflicting voices with which American policy was expressed.

On the following day, June 25th, the Prime Minister and Mr Eden left London for four days for visits to Washington and Ottawa. Their meetings ended on June 29th with the publication of a six-point declaration, expressing the sentiment that the British and American Governments should generally seek to act in concert.

Thursday, July 8th

We got back on June 27th from our honeymoon to find that remarkably little had occurred during our twenty-four days' absence. Churchill and Eden had flown to Washington for conversations and simultaneously Chou En-lai had been at Delhi.[1] Rebels had invaded Guatemala from Honduras with American encouragement;[2] Bevan had been nominated for the treasurership of the Labour Party; and a tremendous row about Members' pay had flamed up in the Commons.

Here I must resume events. On the Thursday before I got back from Italy, the Prime Minister made an unexpected Statement that the Government had decided not to accept the free vote of the House in favour of a £500 salary increase. Apparently this let loose a spontaneous uprush of indignation from our backbenchers, first on the Floor and then in the Party Meeting. Swept by a storm of emotion, the Meeting agreed to forbid all pairing at once and to instruct the Parliamentary Committee to submit as soon as possible a Standing Order on this subject. The idea apparently was a reprisal on the wealthy Tories who earned their money outside the House and who would be unable to do so if pairing were forbidden.

Directly I entered the House this Monday I felt the atmosphere, which was more poisonous than I have ever known it. Of course there were a number of Labour Members who had doubts of the wisdom of this decision to take' extreme measures against the Government on *this* issue, when we had failed to take them either on the Rents Bills or on the old age pension. But anyone who earns anything outside simply cannot say that sort of thing to our colleagues. They were fighting mad but the fight was seeping out of them.

[1] A member of the Chinese Communist Party since the 1920s, he joined Mao Tse-tung at the start of the Long March in 1931. From 1936 to 1945 he was Communist representative with Chiang Kai-shek's Government in Nanking, Wuhan and Chungking and in 1946 he tried, with General George Marshall, to form a coalition Government. The attempt failed. At the inception of the People's Republic of China in 1949, Chou En-lai became its Prime Minister (and from 1949 to 1958 Foreign Minister), holding this office until his death. On the occasion mentioned here, Chou En-lai broke his return journey to Peking from Geneva for three days of talks with Mr Nehru.

[2] On June 18th the republic was invaded by a so-called army of liberation, led by an exiled officer, Colonel Castillo Armas. At an emergency meeting of the United Nations, the United States maintained that the Colonel's campaign was not an aggressive act but a revolution against the Communist-supported Guatemalan regime. On September 1st, Colonel Castillo assumed office as President and at the end of the year he was still, somewhat shakily, in power.

This became very clear last Thursday, when Attlee said that he had been asked by Butler to discuss matters. At once the Party gave him *carte blanche* to negotiate, which, of course, was exactly the opposite policy from the implacable opposition agreed on a week before.

Today, at a special meeting at eleven o'clock, Attlee announced the result of the negotiations. The Government's final offer was a £2 daily allowance to all Members for each parliamentary day, excluding Fridays, of the Session.[1] However, as this was an expense allowance, it would, of course, be deductible from the expenses already charged to income tax, and, as Gaitskell patiently explained, what it really meant was a gross salary increase, liable to taxation, of £288 a year, if the normal number of days were worked. This means that as the result of Labour's tactics Butler's original proposal of a £500 expenses allowance has been halved. It was a miserable Party Meeting, in which it was clear that, if Butler had offered £1 2s. 6d., they would have taken it and humiliated themselves, and this was pointed out by Bob Mellish, Jimmy Hudson[2] and one or two others. But beggars, who have lost all idealistic motives for being here, cannot be choosers.

The only issue left was whether the no pairing edict should continue. Those keenest for the salary increase were obviously anxious to have the edict stopped straightaway, which would have been politically appalling and would prove that we would only fight to the death for salaries and nothing else. Attlee got out of this by saying that the Parliamentary Committee would make its recommendation on pairing next week, and I'll bet that the recommendation is to resume pairing. But this, I think, will be fought.

Meanwhile, last week, George Wigg, characteristically, had decided to test out the effect of no pairing. We chose yesterday's business, the Report Stage of the Finance Bill. The plan was that thirty-four people should come to a housewarming party at Vincent Square, between half-past six and half-past eight. Meanwhile the Whips should ensure that the rest of the Party was given a virtual three-line whip injunction to be in the House from half-past six to nine o'clock. We could hope that the extra thirty-four votes, thrown in suddenly, could tip the balance. This plan was rendered a little complicated by the fact that Michael, Mik [Ian Mikardo] and I were both redrafting our Bevanite pamphlet on German rearmament[3] and Anne had to receive all the guests, alone for the first time. This she did with great aplomb. In her words, it was perfectly simple. Each guest, after a shamefaced quarter-grin at her, dived towards a group of friends and from then on merely held out his

---

[1] On July 8th the Prime Minister announced that Members were to receive a daily allowance of £2 for every day the House sat, other than Fridays (when attendance was usually sparse). This would come to about £288 in an average year and the introduction of allowances was to be back-dated to May 24th. The Opposition nevertheless persisted in refusing 'pairs'.

[2] James Hudson (1881–1962), Labour M.P. for Huddersfield 1923–31, for Ealing West 1945–50 and for Ealing North 1950–5. He was P.P.S. to Philip Snowden 1924 and 1929–31

[3] *It Need Not Happen* was published on July 23rd, 1954.

hand from behind his back for another glass of beer. Politicians are very easy to entertain!

The thirty-four were duly brought back to the House, drifting in either through St Stephen's entrance or underneath the Lords[1] in an undetectable fashion. The vote was nicely timed for half-past eight and the result was a Tory majority of seventeen.[2] All our thirty-four had acted according to instructions and George is convinced that we had a majority of twenty in the House. Yet some thirty to forty of them disappeared when the vote came, mostly because they had secretly been paired and, when told to turn up, hadn't dared to tell the Whips, while on the other hand, with a very inverted sense of decency, they felt they couldn't break their illegal pairs. This is a fascinating illustration of the ethics of the politician, or, shall we say, of the Labour politician, who feels that a pair given to a Tory, even if given in gross disloyalty to his Party edict, is binding. Even more, when told that he need not pair, which is an enormous convenience since you can be away whenever you like, he doesn't feel quite comfortable unless he can make an improper arrangement with a Tory (which, of course, sustains the Government) to ensure that, if ever he is away, a Tory will be away at the same time. What we proved yesterday is that, given any discipline in the Party, an Opposition can, by the kind of organization we set up, defeat a Government with a small majority whenever it really likes.

The other big issue has, of course, been Nye's future. Apparently, soon after Greenwood died, Nye announced his final decision to stand for the treasurership against Gaitskell. It was done by informally leaking it to the press and without consultation with the Group. By today it is clear that he will be defeated. The miners voted five to two against him at their conference and, an even worse slap in the face, the A.E.U. Executive preferred Gaitskell. This put Nye out. Why has he done it? Anne and I went back to his house a few nights ago after dinner and the only topic of conversation was the eighty-acre farm near Chesham which he has bought and is now stocking with pigs, cows, hens and geese.[3] He will be mortgaged up to the hilt and everything will depend on the bailiff whom John Mackie, Nye's rich farmer friend, is selecting for him. But even so, since he is going to sell his Cliveden Place house, keep only two rooms in London and live Thursday to Monday in the country, his centre of balance is bound to shift. I can't help thinking that psychologically this is a partial retirement or at least a reassurance against failure. It fits with his decision to stand for the treasurership, though he must have

---

[1] I.e. through the Chancellor's Gate at the south end of the Palace and through a series of inner courtyards.

[2] In the division held at 8.32 p.m. the Government had a majority of 17; in two earlier divisions, at 6.19 p.m. and 7.07 p.m., the Government majority had been 59 and 50, and in the last division, at 9.49 p.m., the Government majority was 29.

[3] Asheridge Farm in Buckinghamshire was a Tudor farmhouse with fifty-four acres of land, not eighty as Crossman wrote. (And see below, p. 340.) Bevan bought the farm for £9,000, with the help of a £6,000 mortgage.

known it meant defeat and, incidentally, losing his place on the Executive as well as the Parliamentary Committee.

On July 12th the Prime Minister made a Statement on his recent visit to North America with the Foreign Secretary. He revealed that the expedition had not been made as a result of growing disagreement between Britain and America on policy in Indo-China, but that it originated in a suggestion he had put to President Eisenhower in February. Sir Winston had apparently been disquieted by a speech by the chairman of the Congressional Committee on Atomic Energy and alarmed by the lack of information in Britain on the latest experiments with the hydrogen bomb.

A debate on foreign affairs was opened by Mr Attlee two days later. In the course of this, the Prime Minister announced that the British and American Governments had agreed on granting a measure of sovereignty to West Germany, under the Bonn Conventions, if France failed to ratify the Treaty on the European Defence Community. This meant that Britain and the United States were ready to dissociate the two issues, hitherto interdependent, of German sovereignty and rearmament, by deferring the latter question.

The Prime Minister also referred to the situation in the Suez Canal Zone. Anglo-Egyptian talks had recently been resumed in Cairo and as a result the 'Suez Group' of some forty Conservative M.P.s, led by Captain Waterhouse, had become uneasy. On July 13th Sir Winston had privately met Conservative backbenchers to discuss the subject and a statement was subsequently issued that a group of these backbenchers had 'decided to inform the Government' that they would vote against any treaty made with Egypt involving 'the removing of fighting troops' from the Suez Canal area.

In the foreign affairs debate Sir Winston now stated that the terms of British proposals would not at present be announced but that the defence of the Canal Zone was among subjects he had discussed with the American President during his visit.

Monday, July 19th

Wednesday was the long-awaited foreign affairs debate. To some extent it had been anticipated by Churchill's Statement on the Monday. We had all expected the normal type of Minister's Statement at the end of Questions. What we actually got was a discursive political speech of forty-five minutes, which brought Nye to his feet protesting against this abuse of the ministerial privilege of making Statements at half-past three.[1] But of course the Old Man is a rule to himself. No one quite knew what the Labour Party line would be. When the Foreign Affairs Committee met on Monday, immediately after Churchill's Statement, John Strachey and I urged that the Tory climb-down

---

[1] In the House of Commons, ministerial Statements are made 'after Question Time' (i.e. after 3.30 p.m.) and, in the House of Lords, usually at 'a convenient time after half-past three o'clock'.

on Chinese admission to the U.N. should be attacked by our Front Bench
and that this should be the centre of its case. This was fiercely rebutted by
Reggie Paget and a number of other right-wingers. But when I met Harold
Wilson after the Parliamentary Committee on Monday evening, he told me
that Attlee had taken this precise line and had outlined a speech so critical of
American policy that it had created violent expostulation from Herbert
Morrison and Frank Soskice.

I couldn't be at the Parliamentary Party Meeting on Wednesday morning
but I gather that Attlee repeated the speech there with great effect and that
there were a good many dark whispers on the Right that he was once again
appeasing the Bevanites. It's impossible to diagnose his mind but on reflection
I doubt whether internal Party politics much influence him. It's much more
likely that he was saying out loud what Churchill was thinking in private.
Everybody in high places in Whitehall and Westminster is now really scared
of American policy and the congressional reaction after Churchill and Eden
had left Washington has made people realize that, though Churchill may have
talked Eisenhower round, the situation remains as dangerous as ever.

This made Churchill's and Attlee's speeches on Wednesday particularly
interesting. Attlee spoke precisely to form — neat, clipped, and intensely
critical. Churchill tried to reply to him extempore but he's never good at
extemporizing and made a tactical error in describing Attlee's speech as 'one
long whine of criticism against the United States'.[1] Churchill went on to speak
at length about the dangers of the hydrogen bomb and to plead that nothing
should be said that would widen the gulf.[2] In fact, Government and
Opposition were each playing their role, the Government seeking to prevent
a complete break with the U.S.A. and the Opposition merely using its greater
freedom of action to point out the American behaviour which was the cause
of the strain. Nye had decided beforehand to make a big speech but, after
Attlee had spoken, he turned to me and said, 'There's nothing left for me to
say. Attlee has delighted the whole Party. If I attack him, I shall make us all
unpopular, and if I support him, what's the point?'

After Churchill's speech I said to Nye that there was a chance, since
Churchill, at the end, had announced the Anglo-American plan in the event
of the French not ratifying E.D.C. and added that this meant a postponement
of German rearmament 'which should please you people', looking up at us.
Nye could well have taken this opportunity, while approving Attlee's attitude
on Far Eastern affairs, to make a plea for one more Four-Power conference
to solve the German problem, and he could have added an annihilating
attack on Churchill, in view of the news that, having spent nine months
saying no to the Egyptians, he had suddenly conceded the main point of
difference and spent the whole evening reasoning with his own rebels to try

[1] *H.C. Debates*, vol. 530, col. 491.
[2] 'I should have thought there was very general agreement upon this being the way to
proceed' [*H.C. Debates*, vol. 530, col. 502].

to persuade them to accept a withdrawal. However, Nye wasn't playing and he may well have been right. He has obviously genuinely decided to withdraw from the day-to-day in-fighting. (This week's news that he has bought a farm in the Chilterns has received a relatively friendly press.) Once Nye had decided not to speak, the debate petered out, though Barbara Castle got in and tried to do what I had suggested to Nye. But she just isn't able to handle the German problem with conviction, though she tried very hard.

On July 28th there was a small ministerial reshuffle, following the resignation on July 20th of Sir Thomas Dugdale, the Minister of Agriculture, over the mis-handling of the sale of land previously purchased by the Air Ministry at Crichel Down, in Dorset. Sir Thomas was succeeded by Derick Heathcoat-Amory, whose place at the Scottish Office was taken by Toby Low. At the same time Oliver Lyttelton returned to the City and in his stead Alan Lennox-Boyd became Colonial Secretary. He was himself succeeded by John Boyd-Carpenter, whose post as Financial Secretary to the Treasury was taken by Henry Brooke.

Meanwhile on July 20th armistice terms in the Indo-Chinese conflict were reached at Geneva. Vietnam was to be partitioned roughly along the 17th Parallel, with the Communists taking the northern, wealthier part of the country, including Hanoi. India, Canada and Poland were to be invited to provide commissions to supervise the implementation of these terms.

Within a week of the conclusion of the Geneva Conference Mr Molotov presented Notes to the three Western Governments, inviting them to another conference to discuss Russian proposals for a European security treaty. Mr Eden promised 'careful study' of these suggestions. On the same day as the publication of the Notes, it was announced that a British Skymaster airliner had been shot down off the Hainan coast by two Chinese fighters. The Chinese Government expressed regret at 'a mistake' but the Chinese aviation authorities had, it seemed, none the less given bellicose warnings to aircraft searching for survivors.

Agreement had also been reached on the Egyptian question. The Secretary of State for War had flown to Cairo on July 24th to take part in discussions over Suez. On July 27th representatives of the British and Egyptian Governments initialled a resolution on the evacuation of the Base and on July 28th the Foreign Secretary made a Statement in the House of Commons. British troops were to be withdrawn within twenty months; the agreement was to last for seven years and during this period Egypt would assist British civilian staff in keeping the Base in order; should the Base be attacked by any Arab State or Turkey, British forces would be entitled to reoccupy it.

On July 29th, the last full day of the parliamentary Session, the agreement was debated. Mr Attlee mildly criticized its terms and the Opposition was instructed to abstain from voting. Six Labour M.P.s disobeyed and voted for the agreement, but the opposing vote, 26 Members to 257, was almost wholly composed of Conservative Members of the Suez Group.

Friday, July 30th

While I've been describing Labour's troubles, those on the Government side have been just as great. Here the fact that Churchill is leading the Party and has this week reshuffled the Government in order to go on leading it is causing a serious rot. The Keep Right Group is emerging as an exact counterpart to Bevanism. Just as we claim to be the keepers of the Socialist conscience against those who are betraying it by compromise, so they are keeping the Conservative conscience. Both of us hate Butskellism for equal and opposite reasons – and can one blame the unfortunate Tea Room men who can't make out what is really Conservatism and what is really Socialism, after a Conservative Government signs the treaty with China and Russia against the will of America and evacuates Suez, policies which were considered Bevanite by the right wing of the Labour Party only twelve months ago?

Friday, August 13th

During the last fortnight, the first days of the Recess, I have had to spend a lot of time on private affairs, which do not usually occur in this diary but in this case have a certain political interest. We went to Prescote for the weekend of the August Bank Holiday, convinced that the sale of the farm was a *fait accompli* but on the way down I told Anne that I still thought it was a great pity and she said she thought her father might have been impressed when Tommy Balogh emphasized the economic lunacy of getting out of land. To my surprise, Patrick suddenly said at lunch on Saturday that he wanted to have a serious talk to us and it was obvious that he was having second thoughts at the last moment.

That evening we suggested to him tentatively that we would like to go on living at Prescote and asked why he shouldn't pass the farm over to Anne and keep on managing it. Patrick asked his accountant to come over on Sunday because he told us that, if he was to keep the farm on, it needed £10,000 spent on new buildings and drainage and he didn't think we could undertake such a burden. But his accountant said that with my income I could only afford to take on the farm if it was heavily in debt and that the profit on it would be a considerable embarrassment! Apparently the accountant worked out that a £10,000 debt, funded at £1,100 a year, might well mean no less in my income, since it would merely reduce my taxation. This, of course, is a very crude way of putting it, but Anne's poor father was really shocked at the appalling workings of our tax system.

Since then I have been put on to a firm of solicitors and have been plunged into a discussion of post-nuptial gifts, limited liability companies to manage the farm and my literary earnings and all the rest of the caboodle which people with capital plunge themselves into in order to maintain their living standards. Patrick has definitely decided not to sell and it looks as though Anne and I will become that wicked thing, urban gentleman-farmers, just at the time when Nye has sold his house in Cliveden Place and bought fifty acres in the

Chilterns. He and Jennie started moving on the day after the Recess started and I haven't yet revealed to them that I shall be a kulak, with 360 acres to their fifty! Even worse, I shall have to explain to Coventry who, when they came over, were assured that Anne and I had nothing to do with the farm. Now they will have to be told that we've become county gentry after all!

On Tuesday the Labour Party delegation arrived in Moscow,[1] the red carpet was laid out and for two days the wining and dining went on in a blaze of publicity. Sydney Jacobson told me that Morrison had expressed his violent opposition to the trip and told him he'd spent a day trying to prevent Attlee from doing it. Now, of course, the delegation will come back to Scarborough crowned with the laurels of peaceful co-existence. Whatever report they make, they will objectively be committed to that policy, far more by this trip than by any speeches. My only fear, candidly, is that people like Harry Earnshaw, Sam Watson and Edith Summerskill are such vain jackasses that they will be vastly over-impressed by the Russians. After all, as Cudlipp said to me yesterday, 'We're all vain and which of us could claim that our judgment would not be affected if we'd just spent ten hours with Malenkov and Khrushchev?'[2]

Monday, August 23rd

Anne and I dined with Michael and Jill and Tommy Balogh last Thursday. Apparently Jennie is now living in the farm and has received a postcard from Nye, the first letter she has ever received from him when away on such a mission.

We had William Hayter and his wife Iris[3] to dinner on Friday, with Kingsley Martin. William couldn't have been more frank, telling us everything he knew about the Labour Party delegation's two days in Moscow. If one comes to think of it, it's quite a remarkable fact that a British Ambassador will be so totally indiscreet with two leading left-wing journalists, completely confident that they will not abuse his indiscretion. I made some notes that

[1] In August Mr Attlee, Mr Bevan and some other leading figures in the Labour Party visited China as the guests of the Communist Government, stopping at Moscow on the way. Speeches and articles written on their return did not shrink from criticism of the Chinese Communist regime.

[2] Nikita Sergeyevich Khrushchev joined the Bolsheviks in 1918, after the October Revolution, and began his career in the Communist Party in 1925. By 1949 he had become First Secretary of the Regional and City Party Committees of Moscow and Second Secretary of the Communist Party Central Committee. On the death of Stalin, Khrushchev was thus the only man with a seat on both the Praesidium and the Party Secretariat. He was given the title of Party First Secretary in September 1953 and at the 20th Party Congress in 1956 made a secret speech denouncing the abuses of the Stalinist period. He was ousted by his colleagues in October 1964. A new edition of his memoirs, *Khrushchev Remembers* (Harmondsworth: Penguin), was published in 1977.

[3] William Hayter, a member of the Diplomatic Service since 1930, was Minister in Paris 1949 and Ambassador to the U.S.S.R. 1953–7. From 1957 to 1958 he was Deputy Under-Secretary of State at the Foreign Office. He was knighted in 1953. From 1958 to 1976 he was Warden of New College, Oxford. He married Iris Marie, daughter of Lieutenant-Colonel C. H. Grey (formerly Hoare), in 1938.

evening of what he said and here are the rather disjointed impressions he gave me.

On the day the delegation arrived, the Russians rang him up and asked what was the order of precedence of the members of the delegation for seating arrangements at dinner that evening. An unfortunate Ambassador asked to decide where Earnshaw sits in relation to Franklin[1] and both in relation to Wilfred Burke or Edith Summerskill is entitled to be puzzled. Hayter rather brightly replied that he would like to know *their* order of precedence. To this question there was no reply until some hours later, when they telephoned: Malenkov, Khrushchev, Mikoyan. Hayter added that one should not perhaps give too much significance to Molotov's Number Two, since this was a foreign dinner, but it is significant that Khrushchev, who has no official position apart from being Secretary of the Party, came Number Three, and then Mikoyan. Hayter didn't reveal to me the order of priority he gave to ours.

Late in the evening, after a little prodding, Hayter revealed his chief impression, which was that the quality of our delegation was far below the task they were set. After all, they were up against some very big shots and in Hayter's view most of them gave the impression of floundering completely out of their depth. He told me, for instance, that our best translator in the Embassy had gone into action for Sam Watson, after dinner at the Embassy, in a long conversation with Khrushchev, during which Sam Watson had tried to explain to the Russians the significance of British social democracy. Try as the translator did to improve Sam Watson's incoherent platitudes, he could not make them make much sense. Nothing was got across to Khrushchev and of course no Intelligence questions were put to him. He is in charge of the Agricultural Plan. None of the delegation seemed even to be aware of this fact and, if they had been, would they have been able to ask the right questions?

Hayter's impression was that, at the first dinner, given by the Russians, very little happened beyond pure formalities, since this was a Russian dinner, where you spend the whole time at the table exchanging toasts and leave immediately you leave the table, thus giving no time for conversation. At the Embassy dinner he had expected the same thing to happen and had allowed them to sit at table till eleven o'clock. Then things were dragging so badly that he got up, expecting the Russians to go, but just saying, 'There's whisky in the next room.' At this, they stayed for two hours in informal conversation in small groups, which should have given a superb opportunity. When this happened, Hayter went across to Attlee and said, 'Which of them would you like to talk to?' Attlee, who had seemed pretty tired when he arrived, replied, 'Frankly, none of them,' and sat down on a sofa, whereat Mikoyan immediately came up and sat beside him.

Attlee was very bad-tempered and tart, discussing Marxism spasmodically. When the Russians had gone, he said to Hayter, 'Have you read any of this

[1] H. W. Franklin was a member of the N.U.R.

Marxist stuff?' Hayter said that in the Foreign Office one is given long extracts to study, though he couldn't claim to have read *Das Kapital*.[1] Attlee replied, 'I've read none of it, you know.' To cap these Attleeisms, Hayter added an old story from Yugoslavia. A friend of his had arrived last year at Brioni, where Attlee had been staying. 'Have you got the cricket scores?' asked Attlee. 'Nobody out here seems to know a thing about them.'

After the Embassy dinner it was arranged that Nye should talk to Malenkov and this talk went on for nearly two hours, with a Russian interpreter. Parrott,[2] the British Minister in Moscow, who speaks Russian, moved towards the sofa but Nye pushed him away, saying that he didn't want him there. A typical Nyeism but it means, of course, that, whereas the Kremlin has a full account of the conversation, we shall never on this side know, since Nye is the last man to remember anything but what he himself said in a conversation. Apparently Morgan Phillips came up to them towards the end of the talk but otherwise nobody knows what happened.

Edith Summerskill sat next to Malenkov at the dinner and apparently tried to commit him to agree to a return visit in February. By the way, Nye was overheard saying that he would like to come back to Russia later on a special visit. Apparently one of the aims of the delegation was to commit the Russians to a return visit, which Hayter thought rather crude diplomacy.[3] A little later, when they were standing in groups, Iris Hayter came up to Edith when she was talking to one of the Russians. Edith turned round and said, 'We're discussing foreign policy, which won't interest you.'

During the dinner Malenkov, who has tremendous feline charm, took one of the cut carnations on the table and spent most of the time waving it in front of his nose, appreciating the scent and looking like Ferdinand the cat. Afterwards he sent Iris and her daughter each a bunch of phlox, so Edith wasn't the only lady to get the flowers.

Hayter established that the Russians asked each member of the Labour delegation the same two questions. The first was: What is the difference between Conservative and Labour in Britain, since the Russians can't see the

[1] *Capital: A Critical Analysis of Capitalist Production*, by Karl Marx, edited by Frederick Engels, published in three volumes between 1872 and 1894. The English translation from the German, prepared by Samuel Moore and Edward Aveling, was published in London by Swan Sonnenschein, Lowrey & Co.

[2] Cecil Parrott was Tutor to King Peter of Yugoslavia 1934–9. His career in the Diplomatic Service included postings in Oslo 1939–40, Stockholm 1940–5 and Prague 1945–8. He was Head of the U.N. Political Department 1950–2, Principal Political Adviser to the U.K. Delegation to the U.N. 1951–2, Counsellor to H.M. Embassy, Brussels, 1952–4 and Minister in Moscow 1954–7. He was Director of Research, Librarian and Keeper of the Papers at the Foreign Office 1957–60 and Ambassador to Czechoslovakia 1960–6. He was knighted in 1964. From 1966 to 1971 he was Professor of Russian and Soviet Studies at the University of Lancaster. His publications include *The Good Soldier Svejk,* in its first complete English translation (London: Heinemann, 1973), memoirs *The Serpent and The Nightingale* (London: Faber, 1977) and *The Bad Bohemian Hasek* (London: Bodley Head, 1977).

[3] In July 1955 the Prime Minister was to announce that the Russian leaders had accepted an invitation to come to Britain, a visit which took place in 1956. See below, pp. 476–7 and 486–94.

difference? And the second: Who will win the next Election? Hayter didn't gather that very coherent answers were given to the first question but to the second he learnt that Attlee replied Labour would win and the issue would be the cost of living, that Edith replied Labour would win and that Nye replied the Tories would win.

This doesn't seem to add up to much but I fancy there wasn't much to add up. Hayter told me all the delegation behaved well, in the sense that no one got drunk and they made some very spirited toasts and replies, but he kept on repeating that, faced with these big Russian politicians, our people weren't very impressive. The Russians, for instance, knew Kenneth Younger, Hector McNeil, Ernest Davies[1] and Christopher Mayhew from the Foreign Office and people like myself and Harold Wilson from Hansard and writing but they just couldn't place Earnshaw, Franklin, Summerskill, Watson and Burke and couldn't be impressed by Morgan Phillips as Khrushchev's opposite number. It hadn't occurred to me before that, whereas in Russia the Party Executive is the supreme power, in Britain the Labour Party Executive is not. They had expected a full delegation of Labour's real leadership. They didn't get it.

For Crossman, the most important matter on the agenda for discussion at Conference was the issue of German rearmament. On August 13th the French Council of Ministers had approved the proposal of M. Mendès France, the Prime Minister, for modification of the E.D.C. Treaty initialled two years before by the Prime Ministers of the countries concerned. These changes, designed to make the treaty acceptable to the French Parliament, suspended the supranational defence arrangements and limited the integration of armed forces to those stationed in Germany. The amendments were submitted on August 19th to the Brussels Conference of the six members of the proposed Defence Community (France, Germany, Italy and the three Benelux countries) and were unanimously rejected on August 22nd.

The French Prime Minister immediately flew to Britain, for discussions with Churchill and Mr Eden at Chartwell. M. Mendès France also announced that the vote in the French National Assembly on the amended E.D.C. Treaty would not be treated as one of confidence; on August 30th the Assembly rejected the treaty by 310 votes to 264, with the 99 Communist Members among its opponents.

West Germany was, like the American Government, disappointed and angry.

---

[1] Editor of *Clarion* 1929–32 and Associate Editor of *New Clarion* 1932. From 1940 to 1945 he worked with the B.B.C. He contested Peterborough in the Labour interest in 1935 and was Labour M.P. for the Enfield division of Middlesex 1945–50 and for East Enfield 1950–9. He was P.P.S. to the Minister of State at the Foreign Office 1946–50 and Parliamentary Under-Secretary of State there 1950–1. In 1945–50 and again in 1951–9, he was Chairman of the Transport Group of the P.L.P. and was also joint chairman of the Parliamentary Roads Study Group 1957–9 and a member of the Select Committee on the Nationalized Industries 1952–9. He has published various works on transport and public ownership.

On September 3rd Dr Adenauer amplified his first reaction in a statement to The Times, *saying that the conception of West European unity could not be destroyed by French rejection of this particular scheme and that the only counter to France's action was to grant full sovereignty to the Federal German Republic. 'We are not asking for rearmament as such,' he said, 'but only as a part of our sovereignty.'*

The British Government proposed a Nine-Power conference of the six E.D.C. countries, the U.S.A., Britain and Canada to discuss the form of contribution to German defence and, in preparation, the Foreign Secretary set out on September 11th on a tour of European capitals. By September 15th he seemed to have secured agreement, although the French response was elusively worded. After an interview in London between Mr Eden and Mr Dulles, invitations were issued to a Nine-Power conference, to meet in London on September 28th.

Crossman voiced the fears of the Bevanites and other opponents of E.D.C. in articles in the New Statesman and Nation *of August 28th and September 4th. Those hostile to German rearmament supported M. Mendès France's wish for a Four-Power conference (between France, Britain, West Germany and the U.S.A.), at which negotiations on German rearmament might be discussed in the light of the need to achieve Russian agreement to German unification and free elections. Even E.D.C. was regarded as a 'lesser evil', compared with the prospect of a rearmed sovereign Germany. As Crossman saw it, the 'only way out of the impasse is to stop trying to win Germany over to the West and to go back to the policy of seeking to neutralize Germany.' This view was set out by Crossman in notes written for Bevan and the Group to consider before the International Sub-Committee met on September 21st and the N.E.C. on September 22nd. These notes were dictated on September 2nd and, by the time of the meetings, it was clear that the Labour leadership hoped to secure the support of Conference for a resolution insisting on the importance of a German contribution to European defence.*

The resolution presented to Conference was very long; its final paragraphs ran:

... Conference believes that the breakdown of E.D.C. makes it necessary to work out an alternative policy for application by the Western Powers, and accordingly instructs the National Executive Committee to consult with the other European Socialist parties in an attempt to endeavour to draw up a common policy which will:

1 Recognize that German democracy is entitled to be self-governing and that the occupation of the Federal Republic should be ended;

2 Consider how arrangements can best be made for the German Federal Republic to contribute to collective security in accordance with the principles of the United Nations and in a way which would preclude the emergence again of a German military menace;

3 Consider how further efforts can be made to induce the Soviet Union to permit the reunification of Germany on the basis of free elections.

From September 7th to 21st Crossman was in the United States, covering the latter stages of the presidential election campaign. His accounts can be found in 'The Plight of U.S. Liberalism', New Statesman and Nation, October 16th, 1954; 'The Oppenheimer Story', Part I, New Statesman and Nation, October 23rd, 1954, and Part II, New Statesman and Nation, October 30th, 1954; in the Sunday Pictorial of September 12th and 19th, 1954; and, on his return, 'Crossman Cross-Examined', Sunday Pictorial, September 26th, 1954. Crossman came back in time for the Labour Party Conference, held at Scarborough from September 27th to October 1st.

Friday, October 1st

George Wigg and Anne met me at the airport on Tuesday, September 21st, and motored me straight to Transport House, since this was a solid day of sub-committees in preparation for Conference the following week. I got to the Organization Sub. in time to clock in and then we all came back and had a Bevanite lunch at Vincent Square in preparation for the International Sub. that afternoon. We had already had the Executive's draft resolution on Germany, which at first sight looked a very clever compromise which might deceive a lot of delegates. After some difficulty I did persuade them to try to draft a rival resolution. My own paper had a long one which was obviously unsuitable and Harold Wilson very quickly and effectively drafted the following:

> This Conference cannot agree to the rearmament of Western Germany and its integration in the Atlantic Bloc and calls upon the Government to take the initiative in calling a conference and proposing that Western German rearmament should be halted in return for agreement to create a united Germany on the basis of free elections.

When we got to the International Sub. we all sat round and then Sam Watson moved the resolution and there was silence. Nye said, 'Well, isn't somebody going to speak in favour of it?' Attlee, whose plane had been delayed,[1] wasn't there and Morrison sat mum. It was obvious they were in some difficulty. The resolution was then formally moved and seconded, whereat Nye moved our amendment and a not very interesting discussion took place. It was clear that everybody was sick to death of the subject and nothing much happened until Herbert Morrison made a fifteen-minute speech, which ended by calling us all Gaullists and Communists, in his usual style. I said to Nye, 'If he makes that speech at Conference, we shall win.'

We had the National Executive at ten o'clock on Wednesday, the 22nd, with the usual discussions with the Conference Arrangements Committee. At

---

[1] He was returning from a visit to the Far East and Australia.

the end of these I asked whether it would be in order to move an amendment to the Executive resolution on Germany, although it was an emergency resolution, and was assured by Herbert and by Crane of the Conference Arrangements Committee that it would be in order. Very unwisely, I assumed that they meant what they said.

That evening we had a meeting of the Bevanite Second XI, three of whom had amendments on Germany. We went through the agenda as usual and then there was a long, long discussion about what should be done. Relying on the information I had received, I advised that we should draft an amendment to the Executive resolution, as well as a substantive resolution of our own. It was agreed that this should be finally done on the train going up to Scarborough on Saturday. Both here and in the case of SEATO, our aim would be to see that there was a wild left-wing resolution,[1] then ours in the middle and the Executive on the Right, since we had found that this was the way to get the maximum vote at Conference.

I arrived at King's Cross at nine o'clock on Saturday, the 25th, and found the train packed with delegates. Fortunately I was travelling first class at the Executive's cost and found myself opposite Arthur Skeffington,[2] with Ian and the boys travelling third class beyond, but the train was so packed that no work could be done and all I could do was to glance at the resolution. There was no time at Scarborough because the compositing committee started five minutes after the train arrived and Nye and I anyway had to go to another compositing to deal with rents and legal aid.

The Executive were all staying at the Grand Hotel and on Saturday night I dined alone with Nye and Jennie, who were in charming form. We discussed at some length what Nye should do when he was off the Executive and agreed that the thing was to make occasional and very deliberately planned parliamentary appearances, with big speeches. Nye said to me that Attlee was a dirty little traitor because he was going to play up China and be hostile to Russia. The fact was that the Chinese, objectively viewed, are potentially far more dangerous and aggressive than the Russians at this moment. Nye went on to say that Attlee had been deliberately rude in Moscow and, when he saw Mao Tse-tung,[3] had palpably and obviously sought to split the Chinese off from the Russians by advising them to have an independent policy. I said this was precisely the kind of subject on which Nye should make a speech when Parliament opens. As far as I remember, on that evening we had no discussion whatsoever of any campaign among the trade unions.

---

[1] Which the Bevanites hoped Conference would disavow. As it turned out, the motion condemning SEATO was defeated on the first day of Conference by 3·6 to 2·5 million votes.

[2] Labour M.P. for Hayes and Harlington from 1953 until his death in 1972. He was Joint Parliamentary Secretary at the Ministry of Land and Natural Resources 1964–7 and at the Ministry of Housing and Local Government 1967–70.

[3] The Chinese revolutionary leader who was Chairman of the Central People's Government of the Republic of China 1949–54 and Chairman of the People's Republic of China from its inception until his death in 1976.

Later that evening we learnt what had happened at the compositing. Jim Hawarth, who was in charge, said at once that there could be no amendment to the Executive resolution and then, owing to some confusion, which I've never fully understood, between Norman MacKenzie, Jack Mendelson and others, our resolution became thoroughly unpopular and most of the delegates said they wanted a nice black-and-white decision. At this, Casasola[1] of the Foundry Workers, a Communist-controlled union, leapt into the breach with a nice, straightforward, wholly impracticable resolution, blankly against German rearmament. This became the only resolution on the agenda.

Sunday is always the great day of manoeuvres and intrigues at Conference. It was a lovely, sunny, cold day and Barbara Castle, Ted and I spent the morning walking. Then came the usual mayoral lunch, at which everybody always drinks very slightly too much. Afterwards we all went to the Executive meeting, which lasted for three and a half hours, since as well as the agenda we had no less than forty-eight composite resolutions to look at, deciding the Executive line. This always strikes me as the most terrifically haphazard occasion, since a whole number of quite important Party decisions must be taken *en bloc*, each of them having literally a few minutes' time devoted to them before the Executive votes to accept, reject or remit. At half-past seven we were all so jaded that the meeting was broken off, to be resumed on Tuesday, and Attlee went off for a bite before the usual Demonstration, which I don't think a single Bevanite attended.[2]

Monday opened with Attlee's speech, mostly a report on China, of which chunks were word for word the same as his speech at the Demonstration the day before. It was extremely judicious and weak, with a tremendous write-up of China and a proposal that Chiang Kai-shek[3] should be moved out of Formosa, which I thought wildly irresponsible. Attlee didn't get an ovation either at the beginning or at the end of the speech and it was quite clear that we were all wrong in believing that the homecoming delegation would sweep all before them.

Monday, on the whole, was a very good day. The Right was very dissatisfied with Attlee and disturbed by the size of our votes and all Monday evening a terrific lobbying took place. The Grand Hotel was full of rumours

[1] Roland William Casasola, an ironmoulder and President of the Foundry Workers 1954–8 and of the N.E.C. 1956–8. He was a strong Labour propagandist in Lancashire, where he stood unsuccessfully as a parliamentary candidate in 1935, 1950 and 1951. His speech moving the resolution on German rearmament was described as 'absurdly naïve' in the *New Statesman and Nation* of October 2nd, 1954. He died in 1971.

[2] The Sunday evening rally before Conference proceedings opened on the Monday.

[3] Chiang Kai-shek (1887–1975), the Chinese military and political leader who emerged after Sun Yat Sen's death as leader of the National Government at Nanking in 1928. In the Second World War he led united Chinese forces in the struggle against the Japanese, but relinquished the presidency of the Republic after the Communists' successful resumption of the civil war. In 1949 he took refuge with the remainder of his Army in Formosa (Taiwan), where his Government continued to claim to be the rightful Government of all China.

that the A.E.U. were switching.[1] Actually a number of M.P.s pleaded with the A.E.U. for three hours to switch but the vote was unanimously against them. However, it was finally confirmed, first, that the Textile Workers' vote, which was split up at Brighton and cancelled itself out, had now by a 12 to 10 vote been thrown on the Executive's side. Secondly, the news came through that the Woodworkers had switched and this explained to me why George Brinham,[2] who was sitting on my other side and is their Secretary, was so terribly nervous all the afternoon and remained so throughout the Conference. He will have to answer to his annual conference as to why he did it. It was pretty clear, indeed, by late on Monday night that the Executive would have a majority unless we got 90 per cent of the constituencies, which was almost impossible.

Tuesday morning started with the announcement of the poll,[3] in which the surprise was that Tony Greenwood came No. 3, having jumped from 360,000 to 960,000 in twelve months. He had certainly been given the Bevanite ticket but my own feeling is that he got it on both accounts — because he was Bevanite and because he wasn't purely Bevanite, just as Harold Wilson had, as I expected, shot to the top of the poll. I jumped one place and 15 per cent of votes and Ian did very much better than last year, though he still remained at the bottom.

There was an enormous gap between the elected seven and Jim Callaghan and Harold Davies, who were runners-up, 400,000 behind Ian. Frank Soskice, the new right-wing candidate, got nowhere and all this showed that, for the fourth year running, the constituencies were overwhelmingly on the Left. On the other hand, Hugh Gaitskell's majority of 2,300,000 over Nye was greater than the worst I had feared and showed that he must have got something like 50 per cent of the constituency votes.[4]

After this Attlee opened the German rearmament debate and it was straightaway clear that the nature of the composite resolution would tell terribly against us in the debate, since it was wholly negative and something which no Bevanite could vote for except under acute pressure. On the day before, Barbara and I had tried to brief Casasola, a sweet little man of about fifty-five, who couldn't remember the difference between

---

[1] The Trades Union Congress had held its annual conference at Brighton from September 6th to 10th. At the preparatory meeting of the General Council a resolution to support German rearmament had been supported by 27 votes to 3 but at the conference itself the General Council's motion was accepted by only a small majority, 4 million to 3·6 million votes. It therefore seemed that a similar resolution might well be defeated at the Labour Party Conference, where the union delegates' opposition would be reinforced by that of the constituency parties, which were generally more left-wing. As it was, though the A.E.U. continued to oppose German rearmament, the Woodworkers' Union changed their minds and supported the Executive.

[2] Secretary of the Amalgamated Society of Woodworkers and a member of the N.E.C., Brinham supported Deakin in his moves to expel Bevan from the Party.

[3] For the N.E.C.

[4] In the election for the Party treasurership, vacant after Arthur Greenwood's death, Gaitskell won 4·3 million votes to Bevan's 2 million.

Adenauer and Ollenhauer[1] and who had a long speech in which his main contention was that the Russian method of organizing free elections was better than ours. Our efforts on him worked because he really made quite a fairly good emotional speech and then Parkin,[2] seconding, did quite well.

The debate was on a pretty high standard and I think we can claim that our two years of Bevanite activity have provided an immense educational impetus to the Movement. One can't conceive of that sort of debate on foreign affairs taking place even five years ago. What was significant was that the two old-fashioned pacifist speeches were received decorously but with no interest. Indeed, what was really ironical about the Conference was its interest in and knowledge of foreign and colonial affairs and the fact that there wasn't a single home issue on which there was a spark of interest. I fear I have been really too successful among the Bevanites in getting them to take an interest in international things.

After Morrison had been speaking for a minute or two, Nye and I went out to have a walk, since we just couldn't stick it. I came in at the end and there's no doubt Herbert had done extremely well until, in his last minute or two, he tried to say that the Conference should vote for the Executive because otherwise it would embarrass the Parliamentary Party. At this there was a great deal of shouting and booing and he rapidly dropped the idea. The majority of 250,000 was rather less than most people had thought and showed that, if the Woodworkers hadn't switched, the Executive would have lost.[3] Nye had agreed with me, as we were walking, that it would be better for the Executive to win, particularly in view of the composite.

Anyway, what on earth was to happen if it lost, since Attlee and Morrison could in that case no longer lead the Parliamentary Party without jeers every day from the Tories? There are some victories which are too expensive and this would have been one of them. Indeed, I have no doubt the result was as satisfactory as we could hope for, even though it was immediately built up as a final defeat of the Left.

Once the German debate was over, the Conference virtually collapsed. By Wednesday afternoon it was clear that the only other event was Nye's speech at the *Tribune* meeting. This took place in a ghastly hall with dim lights and an audience fanning out all round into the darkness. Typically enough,

---

[1] Erich Ollenhauer succeeded his colleague and ally Kurt Schumacher as Chairman of the West German Social Democratic Party (S.P.D.) in 1952. An early opponent of German rearmament, he later led the opposition to proposals for the Bundeswehr's nuclear armament. He died in 1969.

[2] Ben Parkin, Labour M.P. for Stroud 1945–50 and for North Paddington from 1953 until his death in 1969. One of the M.P.s invited in 1954 by the People's Institute of Foreign Affairs to visit Prague and Moscow, he went on to China. In 1955 he spoke at a Communist meeting in Brussels against German rearmament. In later years Parkin spoke often on the problems of housing, drug racketeering and prostitution in London.

[3] The motion was defeated by 3,281,000 votes to 2,910,000.

Peggy Duff[1] hadn't arranged the chairs on the platform or tested the microphones, which looked like broken chrysanthemum stems. You pulled them up to your level and they had a brilliant habit of slowly sinking down again in sight of the audience.

When Nye started, I don't know what he had intended to say, but he spent forty minutes in a long attack on the press, prefaced by a statement that he never believed in personal attacks. Then there was a wild sloshing at unnamed, terrible, adding-machine leaders[2] and a tremendous attack on trade union leaders. It was all very incoherent until the last fourteen minutes, when he did some excellent stuff on foreign policy. There was some quick applause, people began to file out and then the 'Red Flag'[3] was sung, not very satisfactorily. I was so disappointed that I went to the Royal Hotel, where I found Patricia Llewelyn-Davies, Tony Greenwood, John Strachey and Hugh Massingham, who had all been present and thought it was absolutely terrible. Hugh and I went aside and he was nearly in tears about Nye, to whom he is devoted, and said that this was a tragic collapse. I felt the same and said so but, as I walked home, I slightly regretted it, since I realized that nothing you say in Conference is private.

Early next morning I rang Harold Wilson, whom I expected to agree with me, but when I met him at breakfast he was in buoyant form and thought

---

[1] A tireless left-wing campaigner, active in the 1950s in the National Campaign for the Abolition of Capital Punishment and the National Committee for the Abolition of Nuclear Weapon Tests. From February 1958 she was full-time Organizing Secretary of the Campaign for Nuclear Disarmament. Her account of these and other struggles appeared in *Left, Left, Left* (London: Allison & Busby, 1971).

[2] In opening the debate on German rearmament, Attlee had asked delegates to discard emotional responses. In an ironic comment Bevan now said,

> I know that the right kind of leader for the Labour Party is a desiccated calculating machine who must not in any way permit himself to be swayed by indignation. If he sees suffering, privation or injustice he must not allow it to move him, for that would be evidence of the lack of proper education or of absence of self-control. He must speak in calm and objective accents and talk about a dying child in the same way as he would about the pieces inside an internal combustion engine.

It was subsequently argued (and still is) that it was Gaitskell whom Bevan was describing as a 'desiccated calculating machine'. Bevan always denied this but, in any case, it seemed that the phrase was apt enough to stick.

[3] A set of verses by James Connell (1852–1929), sung to a melody arranged by E. Anschütz to the tune of 'Der Tannenbaum', and described by George Bernard Shaw as 'the funeral march of a dried eel'. Those who sing this Socialist anthem generally remember only the words of the first stanza (and then not always accurately):

> The People's flag is deepest red,
> It flutters o'er our martyred dead,
> But, ere their limbs grew stiff and cold,
> Their hearts' blood dyed its every fold.
> So raise the scarlet banner high,
> Beneath its shade we'll live and die.
> Though cowards flinch and traitors sneer,
> We'll keep the red flag flying here.

In the original version, the traitors 'jeer'.

that the whole thing was splendid, apart from the fact that the justifications Nye had given for resigning from the Executive (actually, of course, he'd stood and had been defeated)[1] were a little unfortunate, since they made the rest of us look either fools or knaves. Harold may be a simpleton but I can't help suspecting that his buoyant optimism was due to a partly conscious recognition that this speech had given him the leadership. This was reinforced in my mind by his odd remark that now Nye would be busy on the industrial side and we must carry the parliamentary burden. At breakfast I told Geoffrey Bing what I thought, because I knew that it would go straight back to Nye, and then I saw Barbara and Ted who also thought it was perfectly O.K. I went down to Conference to take reactions and found roughly what I expected. Keen Coventry Bevanites like Ted McGarry[2] thought it fine but Sid Stringer[3] and Harold Nash, the boss at Birmingham, were extremely worried that Nye would flake off the support of the moderate Left and ultimately get himself expelled.

Nye breezed up to me in the sunshine and said he'd heard I was distressed. I said yes and suggested that we had a meeting of our members. This duly took place that evening at seven o'clock, in my bedroom. It was catastrophic since nobody would raise any subject until I did and then they all said that they thought it was O.K. and left me to carry the can. In a furious temper I went down to dinner with Anne and after we'd finished we went across to Nye, who was dining with Vicky.[4] I said, 'I'm off tomorrow. Goodbye.' At this, Nye bounced up, embraced me warmly and said, 'Now you can't go like that; you and I must drink this evening,' and Vicky, Nye, Anne, Jennie and I drank until eleven. As he and I walked back together to the Grand Hotel, Nye said, 'You know, I ought to have had that speech written down. Don't you think so?' Just as we were entering the hotel he added, 'Vicky told me what you thought was wrong. I agree with you. Goodbye. You'll feel better from your gremlins tomorrow.'

I had to share a taxi to the station with Hugh Gaitskell and we travelled to York together, whence he was going to Bristol for 'Any Questions?' It's no accident that the B.B.C. had given Hugh Gaitskell 'Any Questions?' on the day after Conference. We couldn't have been friendlier or more guarded. Objectively, my impression is that the Right wrongly think that Nye has

[1] Crossman was referring to Bevan's standing for the treasurership, which would have given him *ex officio* membership of the N.E.C.

[2] A shop steward and, later, Chief Convener at the Leyland Works in Coventry. He was a Coventry City Councillor.

[3] Sidney Stringer, an engineer, who subsequently devoted himself to working with the Co-operative Party Mutual Fund. He became a member of Coventry City Council in 1928 and Chairman of its Policy Committee. In 1931 he became Chairman of Coventry Constituency Labour Party, holding that office for some twenty years.

[4] The cartoonist, born Victor Weisz. 'Vicky' came to Britain from Germany in 1935 and worked on several newspapers in Fleet Street before becoming cartoonist for the *New Statesman and Nation* (from 1954) and the *Evening Standard* (from 1958). His characterizations of Harold Macmillan, as Mac and Supermac, became famous. He died in 1966.

finished himself. Actually, by these rough methods his campaign [for support] in the Mineworkers may well be successful. What I have to do is to try and guard his right, which is no joke.

While the Labour Party was meeting at Scarborough, the Nine-Power Conference took place in London. On September 29th, Mr Eden, who had been elected chairman, announced that Britain would continue to maintain in Europe the four divisions and tactical air force at present assigned to the Supreme Allied Commander, Europe. He stated that the British Government would undertake not to withdraw these forces against the wish of the majority of the Brussels Treaty Powers, but this must be subject to the understanding that it could be abrogated 'by an acute overseas emergency'.

This undertaking was a major concession to the French, sought by them since the Entente Cordiale of 1904 and hitherto refused by successive British Governments. After much effort and plain speaking, the London Conference reached unanimous agreement on October 3rd. Their main decisions were that the German Federal Republic, with the occupation regime removed and sovereignty restored, should enter NATO. Germany and Italy were to join the Brussels Treaty Organization (negotiated and signed in 1948 and now revised as a substitute for the framework of the discarded E.D.C.). An agency was to be established within the Brussels Treaty Organization for the control of its Continental European members' armaments on the mainland of Europe.

Their negotiators could not be certain that these terms would be approved by the French Assembly; it was also necessary to submit the agreement to debate in the House of Commons. Crossman's views can be found in articles in the New Statesman and Nation *of October 9th and 16th, 1954. With Bevan he still hoped, like Mendès France, for another conference with the Soviet Union before rearmament began.*

Tuesday, October 12th

Today the Bevanites came to lunch, though as I half expected, Nye and Jennie sent a message yesterday crying off, on the grounds that they had company on their farm. Meanwhile I had heard that, despite my long talk with Nye at Conference on the Thursday night, he had gone into a deep depression when he got home and accused all his friends of betraying him, launching into the wildest talk. What his present mood is I have no idea. The lunch was very interesting, with Harold Wilson very definitely seeking to take over the lead and launching out into a long account of what he is going to say to Morgan Phillips tomorrow about party broadcasting. This seemed to me mostly concerned with the need to give a party political broadcast to Privy Councillor Harold Wilson. He also said that he was going to complain that the constituency members had not been given a fair crack of the whip in Executive speeches at Scarborough. However, he met with a

12

good deal of friendly criticism. What we decided can be seen from the letter which I have just written to Nye:

October 12th, 1954

My dear Nye,

We were all very sorry that you could not manage to get to the lunch today. Barbara was absent in China, Geoffrey in Africa and you on the farm, but otherwise we had a good turn-out, and in the discussion a whole number of subjects came up on which decisions should be reached if possible at lunch next Tuesday, when we all hope that you and Jennie can make sure of being there.

(1) *Parliamentary Committee*. It was tentatively suggested that the candidates we should back this year are Harold Wilson, Geoffrey Bing, Fenner Brockway, George Wigg and Tony Greenwood.

(2) *German Rearmament*. We thought that, since we should certainly get a majority decision against us on the Executive, we should take no action there before the meeting on October 17th. All our energies should be concentrated on getting the biggest turn-out we could of members of the Parliamentary Party for the debate and the vote on ratification, which we expect to take place fairly soon after the House resumes.

(3) *Trade Unions*. We realized, of course, that your campaign in the trade unions was something we could only discuss next Tuesday. However, one suggestion (which has been made before) came up, which you might care to think over in the meanwhile. Would it be possible to arrange a regular dinner, with a downstairs room booked in the House of Commons, at which a few keen trade unionists, such as Alan Birch[1] and Bryn Roberts should regularly attend and others be invited?

(4) *Friends of Tribune*. Ian and I both feel that the idea of forming a Friends of *Tribune* Association should be revived, and that it might meet regularly at Gavin's house — say, once a fortnight throughout the Session. This would be a way of warming up our backbenchers, who are at present a bit out of touch with the inner Group, and giving them a sense that they are doing something. Ian and I also suggested that one of the jobs of Friends of *Tribune* might be to consider home policy, which we have a bit neglected during the last twelve months.

(5) *Broadcasting and Television*. We decided at the first meeting of the Executive to table a resolution proposing that the control of party political broadcasts and television programmes should be placed under the Policy and Publicity Sub-Committee of the Executive, instead of residing, as it now does, in a committee composed of the officers of the Parliamentary Party and of Transport House, who seem to act in a curiously arbitrary manner.

---

[1] General Secretary of USDAW from 1949 until his death in 1961. He was knighted in that year.

This is enough to show you that the boys were in form and looking forward to next Tuesday.

It will be extremely interesting to see the development of the Left between now and Christmas. I am not unhopeful that in Parliament we may be able to get much more of a Keep Left policy-making organization going than we had when Nye was closely collaborating. I am also fairly sure that Nye himself will not come to Parliament very often and will grow increasingly out of touch with day-to-day topics. On the other hand, he can hardly fail to take part in the big debate on German ratification, both in the Parliamentary Party and on the floor of the House.[1] Everything will depend on how often he sees us. If it is rarely, Jennie's political influence on him will prevail and make him more and more the spokesman of a lunatic fringe. That is one danger. The other danger, of course, is that people like Harold, myself and Barbara will be killed with kindness by the Right. However, I fancy the second danger is less acute than the first.

Parliament reassembled on October 19th, the day after a major Cabinet reshuffle. The Lord Chancellor, Lord Simonds, retired, to be succeeded by Sir David Maxwell-Fyfe. His place as Home Secretary was filled by Major Gwilym Lloyd George, who also took the post of Minister for Welsh Affairs. At his former Department, the Ministry of Food, only a few divisions remained and these were to be amalgamated with the Ministry of Agriculture. Lord Alexander, Minister of Defence, retired and was succeeded by Harold Macmillan, whose former post as Minister of Housing was taken by Duncan Sandys. Selwyn Lloyd became Minister of Supply.

Three days later Mr Eden became a Knight of the Garter. It appeared, however, that Sir Winston was in no hurry to retire from the premiership, although it was generally believed that, when that day came, he would be succeeded by Sir Anthony and that Mr Macmillan would become Foreign Secretary.

Tuesday, October 19th

With Parliament starting we had a Bevanite lunch today with Nye and Jennie there. Harold and I at once suggested that we would have to draft the text of a reasoned Amendment to put to the Party and Nye agreed that we should meet next Thursday, if that were necessary, but the right thing was to play for a delay of the foreign affairs debate. Then we got on to the subject of Ian Mikardo's proposal to form a Friends of *Tribune*, and once again Jennie and Nye were overwhelmingly against such reckless action. It was difficult to recognize in this cautious tactician the man who stormed off the Parliamentary Committee and made his wild knockabout speech at Scarborough. Now Nye was saying that we must do nothing to bring down on

[1] This eventually took place on November 17th and 18th. See below, pp. 365–9.

our heads the wrath of the Executive or rather, to be fair, if it were done, he was putting the responsibility for doing it on the rest of us. Jennie also, who is sometimes more ingenuous, made it clear that after all Parliament and the Executive don't matter now, since everything depends on Nye's trade union campaign, a view which Harold Wilson is unlikely to share.

We went into the House for Question Time and heard Churchill answering for nearly half an hour with Pickwickian good humour and then Eden's Statement on Germany.[1] Gaitskell got up to ask about the financial implications, at which Eden was evasive, and Nye was extremely good, both at pressing Eden and at urging the need for delaying the debate until all these implications had been stated in another White Paper. This is the sort of thing Nye does well.

Afterwards I did a preliminary sniff around the Smoking Room and the Tea Room and found, as one always finds after ten weeks of Recess, that five minutes after Parliament has reassembled it snaps into gear as though it has never been interrupted and the quiet routine and gossip proceed on and on.

There were three major strikes in October — of London busmen, newspaper printing and machine staff and, most serious, of dockers and stevedores. This last dispute began in September, when 8,000 ship repairers struck over the principle of 'last come, first go'. They were joined by more than 1,000 dockers and stevedores, in dispute over the rates for handling meat cargoes. Then, on October 3rd, the 7,000 members of the National Amalgamated Stevedores and Dockers came out in support of a ban on overtime. The employers continued to negotiate with the rival union, the T.G.W.U., to which a majority of dock workers belonged. This union was already in conflict with the N.A.S.D., which it accused of poaching its membership at Hull.

When the employers reached agreement with the T.G.W.U. over the handling of meat cargoes, the N.A.S.D. struck. Mr Deakin condemned the N.A.S.D. but was unable to control his own ranks, of whom 11,000 had joined the strike by mid-October. They were supported by 4,500 lightermen and bargemen and the strike spread to a number of ports, with more than 200 ships eventually lying idle.

On October 15th the Minister of Labour, Sir Walter Monckton, announced the establishment of a committee of inquiry and on October 19th he made a Statement on the grave consequences of prolonging the strike. Its extension, in violation of workers' agreements and obligations, was also condemned by the T.U.C. General Council and a further Statement by Sir Walter, on October

---

[1] The Foreign Secretary gave details of the Nine-Power agreement and stated that the work of the conference would be continued and, the Government hoped, completed at a further conference in Paris. Mr Gaitskell and Mr Bevan questioned him about the cost to the British taxpayer when the Germans, having acquired their own forces, no longer contributed to the maintenance of British troops in Germany. At present they gave some £200 million a year in support.

22nd, was supported by a powerful appeal from his Labour predecessor, Alfred Robens.

The court of inquiry, with as chairman the Master of the Rolls, Sir Raymond Evershed, published an interim report on October 27th. It pronounced the strike unjustified and agreed with the employers that individual dockers were obliged, if each man's circumstances reasonably permitted, to work overtime when that was necessary. Despite the unconciliating tone of the report, the strikers' delegates decided on October 29th to recommend an immediate return to work. After a number of partial outbursts, the dockers began to clear their accumulated import and export cargoes. The dispute to be settled was that of the ship-repairers, who returned to work, after a nine-week strike, in the last days of November.

Meanwhile there had been rapid progress on German rearmament. The Paris Conference followed immediately after the Foreign Secretary's Statement to the Commons on October 19th, and on October 21st the Foreign Ministers of Britain, France, the United States and the Federal German Republic had agreed on the outstanding issues of German sovereignty. A Nine-Power meeting under Sir Anthony Eden's chairmanship decided that the headquarters of the new Western European Union should be in London. On October 22nd the protocol inviting West Germany to join NATO was approved, together with the procedure for ending the occupation regime. The problem of the future of the Saar was settled the next day, when, with Sir Anthony's help, M. Mendès France and Dr Adenauer reached agreement.

The Foreign Secretary made a Statement to the Commons on October 25th. His declaration that Western unity had been 'massively reinforced' was welcomed by Mr Attlee. The next hurdle was to secure ratification of the agreements by the parliaments of the countries concerned, in particular France and West Germany. The Soviet Government, meanwhile, continued to denounce the outcome of the London and Paris meetings.

Wednesday, October 27th

For a whole week the House has been dominated by two factors, the dock strike and the Nine-Power agreement on Germany. As far as I can judge, the Labour Party has come back much better-tempered than before and, amusingly enough, the ban on pairs, peremptorily introduced by a Party Meeting one night in protest against the Tory reversal on M.P.s' salaries, has quietly disappeared with a strange notice from the Whips, reissuing a Party resolution prior to the no pairing episode.[1] However, we seem to be all too good-tempered to worry about these things.

Now for German rearmament. We had a meeting of the foreign affairs group on Monday and of the Defence and Services group yesterday, as well as a Statement by Eden on the Paris agreement on Monday, and today one by Macmillan on the financial consequences for defence. To my surprise,

[1] See above, pp. 333–4.

Eden was received with no applause. He spoke to a very lukewarm House and he was very testy when Hugh Gaitskell jumped in with a question on the costs of our Army in Germany. Nye was not there.

After that the foreign affairs group met and Denis Healey made a good statement of facts, after which we had a long discussion, which made it clear that nobody had changed their positions as a result of Scarborough. The issues soon boiled down to two — the first being a theoretical one: does this Nine-Power treaty in any way prevent the Federal Republic from negotiating with the Russians for a unified Germany when it wants to? If it doesn't, this is an interim arrangement, with very great dangers. This point was well made by Ungoed-Thomas.[1] The second issue is whether Four-Power talks should take place only after ratification. In that case, as I argued, they are bound to fail, since, once the treaty is ratified and Russia is presented with a *fait accompli*, there is no chance of a neutralized, unified Germany. Of course, it's true that we are all beginning to feel that all this is too late and that the Russians must have made up their minds to stay in Eastern Germany. This is very much confirmed by George's report of his talks with Malenkov and Molotov. On this we are fighting a retreating battle, since all one can say is that we at least must make one more try before accepting partition and all that it implies.

I agreed at the end to draft a resolution for next Monday's meeting and have sent in the following:

> It is the view of this committee that the coming into effect of the Nine-Power treaty and the granting of full sovereignty to Western Germany before another Four-Power conference takes place would present the Russians with a *fait accompli*, which would destroy the last chance of reaching agreement with them for unifying Germany under a system of free elections. Our recommendation, therefore, is that, if the Government turns down the Russian proposal for a Four-Power conference and decides to submit the treaty for immediate ratification, the Parliamentary Committee should oppose the Government motion asking for approval of the treaty by means of a reasoned Amendment on the lines of this resolution.

On Tuesday the Defence and Services group considered the military commitment and I started off with quite a good, objective statement of the costs, as I had learnt them from the Foreign Office. Woodrow Wyatt, in his usual ebullient way, challenged these from total ignorance, thereby winning me a great deal of sympathy. I was able to convince the group that it would be impossible to ascertain the full costs, since one couldn't ascertain how much the Germans would charge us, and we also had the danger of creating

[1] Lynn Ungoed-Thomas, Labour M.P. for the Barry and Llandaff division of Glamorgan 1945–February 1950 and for Leicester North-East 1950–62. He was Solicitor-General April–October 1951. From 1962 until his death in 1972 he was a High Court judge (Chancery Division).

a Suez base all over again owing to a Treasury economy campaign which would keep our Regulars over there in poor conditions. Woodrow kept on saying that it really wouldn't cost us anything because anyway we'd have to pay for the troops. This is like saying that, because your uncle has paid for your children's schooling up to the age of fifteen and you always knew that after that you would have to pay your bill yourself, therefore there was no extra bill to pay when fifteen came.

Curiously enough, this afternoon Macmillan got up and made exactly Woodrow Wyatt's mistake, stating that the financial burden would be trivial and that all that mattered was the balance of payments. As Gaitskell had been putting his questions in order to disprove my assertions that the cost would be large, this had its ironical side, since within ten minutes Gaitskell and I were jointly hammering Macmillan. This was his first appearance as Minister of Defence and it really was a disastrous failure, since it was clear that he had been deliberately evasive for fear of admitting a commitment which would terrify the House.[1] All this shows that there is some point in going to groups, since nearly all the group put questions based on the briefing they had been given yesterday.

The other great thing hanging over us has been the dock strike and last Friday Michael Foot launched a blast in the *Tribune*, denouncing Arthur Deakin for betraying the dockers. This produced its inevitable reaction. Yesterday the *News Chronicle* carried a spirited attack on Nye by Percy Cudlipp[2] and, when I met Victor Feather in the lobby yesterday night, he told me that we should expect our usual letter from the General Council to be delivered in the middle of the National Executive meeting. This has now become a ceremonial, rather like Black Rod[3] entering the House of Commons from the House of Lords, and it duly took place without Nye and with Harold Wilson remaining absolutely silent.[4]

It was a ticklish business, since as usual Michael had left himself wide open

[1] Mr Macmillan stated that the additional amount which would fall on the defence budget 'in terms of money … is not large'. But since British expenditure would have to be met in foreign currency, the NATO Council would be invited to review the position if these arrangements put 'too heavy a strain on our external finance'.

[2] Percy Cudlipp was Assistant Editor of the *Evening Standard* in 1931 and Editor in 1933, and he was Editorial Manager of the *Daily Herald* 1938–40 and Editor of that paper 1940–53. From 1954–6 he was a columnist for the *News Chronicle* and he was also a founding member and Editor of the *New Scientist* from 1956 until his death in 1962.

[3] See above, p. 134 and n.

[4] In a speech at Liverpool, Mr Deakin had argued that the dock strike was 'a Communist plot' and had described the Stevedores' Union as 'led by a moronic crowd of irresponsible adventurers'. Before the full text of the speech had been released, *Tribune* had stated that Mr Deakin had shown 'that he did not know what the strike was about and had little interest in finding out'. The unsigned front-page article in the *New Statesman and Nation* of October 23rd, headed 'Another Lesson for Mr Deakin', had blamed the leaders of the T.G.W.U. for provoking the strikes of dockers and busmen. Mr Deakin and Mr Williamson (of the Municipal and General Workers' Union) were reproved for 'dictatorial intolerance of criticism'. The N.E.C. then condemned the *Tribune* article as 'unwarranted, irresponsible and scurrilous'.

to criticism, first by asserting that there were no Communist members of the Stevedores' executive, when there are, and secondly by personally attacking Deakin without any attempt to state the objective facts, which are on his side. Tom Driberg and I tried to plead for the independence of Socialist papers and to rebut Sam Watson's insinuation that, because the article was unsigned, the editorial board had been cowardly. But the rest of the Executive was determined on action. They duly condemned *Tribune* for scurrility, a word introduced by Gaitskell, although I pointed out that whatever else you could call the article it wasn't scurrilous, and they decided to demand an explanation from Jennie, Mallalieu and Michael, who form the editorial board.

In the course of the argument I asked why only the *Tribune* was being attacked, since the *Statesman* had also had a front page criticizing Deakin and I myself had at Oxford personally attacked the oligarchs. There was really no answer to this, except a little interlude when Morrison, after calling me a liar, said that anyway the *New Statesman* was an anti-Labour paper. Attlee warmly concurred. To this I replied, 'Unlike *The Economist*, I suppose,' and Jack Cooper quite naturally said, 'Well, it's a very well balanced paper, you know.' I don't think there is anything these people hate more than Socialist weeklies. They really do feel that *The Times*, the *Guardian* and *The Economist* are fair and impartial, though politically in disagreement, whereas we are vicious enemies of the Labour Party. The nuisance is that Mike's type of journalism and editing does give them some justification for attacking us.

When I met Harold Wilson this afternoon and asked why he had kept silent, he replied that he didn't see why he should intervene on behalf of *Tribune*, which had asked for it. Even Hugh Delargy, one of Nye Bevan's boon companions, took a very similar view. After this week I can't help feeling that Nye's star is falling. He wasn't present when Macmillan was being questioned, even though he said that he is trying to beat Gaitskell for Treasurer. He has given Gaitskell a clear field this week on Germany, which was his main issue at Conference, and, though this *Tribune* row will spark a little enthusiasm among the dedicated Bevanites in the constituencies, it will flake off a lot more of the less dedicated support.

Monday, November 1st
I spent the weekend on the road, not quite as frustrating as usual. On Sunday evening I was due to speak with Harold Wilson at Huyton. We drove out in a dense fog to find a meeting of 130 people. As I entered the door, five enormous dockers stood towering over me, saying, 'What have you written in the *Sunday Pic* about £30 a week for dockers?' Apparently, next door to my column there was a news story saying that, by working overtime to make up for the strike, due to end today, the dockers might earn as much as £30. Both in Huyton and Toxteth, where I had spoken in the afternoon, all the

officials of the Party are dockers. They spoke about Deakin in terms which are almost impossible to reproduce, since they clearly regard him as the greatest single enemy of the people. Yesterday they were full of the idea that they were going to have a mass meeting to tear up their white cards and take out blue cards for the Stevedores. But it hasn't happened yet.

I had a long talk to Harold, whom I hadn't seen since the N.E.C. meeting where the *Tribune* row had blown up and he hadn't opened his mouth. He was extremely critical and made his favourite crack that Bevanism is impossible without Bevan but would be far better without the *Tribune*.

Thursday, November 11th
Last Thursday afternoon had been very complicated for me, owing to Nye's behaviour on *Tribune* and various other things. At the Tuesday lunch on the 2nd, Nye had urged that *Tribune* should publish its great reply that week and I had said it really couldn't be published without all of us having a look, since I gathered it was 10,000 words long. So we agreed to meet last Thursday morning and by Wednesday evening I had a text. The actual demonstration that the *Tribune* was justified in attacking Deakin was superbly done but it was preceded by an astonishing first two pages, denying the right of the Executive to have any control over expressions of opinion in the Party.

At half-past eleven that morning, after waiting half an hour, we had a message that Nye wasn't coming, since there was nothing important to discuss. Jennie came in at midday to find a considerable scene, since both Harold Wilson and I had made it clear that in our view publication of the document as it stood would be tantamount to deliberately seeking expulsion. Michael seemed to have no serious answer to this and I then said, 'What will Nye do?' I was told that he had already said that if they were expelled he would resign. Harold said, 'But then Nye would have completed the process of doing exactly what his opponents want.' Altogether there was quite a scene. They then agreed to work all the afternoon and produce a redraft at half-past six.

I managed to go in at half-past five, hurriedly look through the revised document and recommend the elimination of eight more passages. I then went on to a party, where I found Hugh Massingham, who had already learnt from George [Wigg] that there was some tremendous document being prepared as a reply. I told Hugh a great deal about what was going on and extracted a solemn pledge that he wouldn't write a word about it. Next morning, however, he rang me up to say that, when he got home, he found an urgent message from the *Tribune*, wanting to see him, and that he had just rung Curly Mallalieu, who had urged him to treat the subject in his column. Massingham added that Curly had said that I was behaving splendidly but that Harold Wilson had virtually opted out of the Group. This, of course, induced me to tell Hugh that it wasn't true and to describe the real situation.

As a result he published a really stinking column[1] on Sunday, which was dangerous to us because it might have induced the other side to believe that we wouldn't do anything about expulsions and that therefore they could afford to expel the three.

All this produced a rather tense lunch on Tuesday and it would have been a great deal tenser if I hadn't said that, on the Thursday before, I had persuaded Massingham to say nothing and that he had only written at Mallalieu's request. People gradually came to realize that possibly the only villain was Hugh Massingham. Nye asked me to come to the House with him and characteristically sat down to drink a huge double Armagnac with me. He disclosed that Massingham had warned Mallalieu that, if he wrote about the episode, he would have to give it an anti-Bevanite slant to save his own position. I said to Nye, 'We are hoist on our own Massingham petard this time and we now have some idea how angry other members of the Executive have been when they've been treated in a similar way.' However, by Tuesday, Harold Wilson, who had carefully read the revised draft, had come to the conclusion that it was an impregnable case, and, when Nye urged that Harold should tell Attlee that expulsion would bring about all our resignations, Harold agreed to do so. In fact he did so yesterday afternoon, before going up to the key by-election in West Derby.[2]

All this had, of course, deflected a great deal of energy and attention from the German problem. On several occasions last week Nye said it was a waste of time going to these Party groups and he even suggested not coming to the Party Meetings on Wednesday and Thursday morning this week. However, on Tuesday he was really quite sensible, agreed to come and, if necessary, to speak on the Wednesday. At yesterday's meeting, Attlee announced the Parliamentary Committee's recommended approval of the [Nine-Power] treaty. What had actually happened, as Harold Wilson told me, was that four members – himself, Chuter Ede, Dalton and Callaghan – all wanted a

---

[1] The column, 'A Left Foot and a Heavy Hand', appeared in the *Observer*'s Political Diary on November 7th. It stated that 'what might be described as the *Tribune* group within the Bevanite group' had 'become convinced that some members of the Executive long ago decided on their expulsion and that they will not be judged on the merits of the case or given a fair trial'. The article went on to discuss Michael Foot's 10,000-word 'latter-day version of Milton's *Areopagitica*' and the pruning of this draft by a meeting of Mr Foot's 'friends and admirers'. Mr Massingham was, in his own words, seeking to put 'this rather frivolous dispute in its proper perspective'. He concluded, 'That it should ever have been built up to these apocalyptic dimensions shows what a strange state the Labour Party must be in.'

[2] Of the six by-elections which had already occurred since late October, all had fallen in safe seats, with the vote for each major party dropping by an almost equal proportion and with the result in each case little changed from that at the General Election. On November 18th a by-election was to be held in West Derby, a Liverpool suburb, where the former Conservative Member, Sir David Maxwell-Fyfe, previously Home Secretary and now Lord Chancellor, had been made a peer. This seat was marginal and the Conservatives had held it by only 1,707 votes at the preceding General Election. Since then the constituency had seen a marked increase in the number of council tenants, who were confidently expected to support the Labour cause.

reasoned Amendment but that Alf Robens had joined the majority who were for qualified support. John Strachey, Nye and I all did pretty well, putting the case for a reasoned Amendment.

The debate was interspersed with demands by Charlie Pannell and other right-wingers for a vote to be taken, but Nye, who got up to speak at midday, made that pretty well impossible and, after he had finished, Attlee moved that the debate would be adjourned. Then somebody wanted to put to the vote the issue that the vote should be taken and Attlee refused, whereupon George Brown asked by what right he refused and was told that it was for the Chairman to interpret the will of the Party. This was the first occasion for a long time that I have heard Attlee's leadership challenged from the Right. During the afternoon the right-wing were fuming with anger.

Monday, November 15th

When the Party Meeting resumed on Thursday morning, it did not go nearly so well for us. Towards the end, George Strauss and Tony Greenwood moved an amendment to the effect that the Party should table a reasoned Amendment, asking for talks with the Russians while ratification was going on.* Attlee immediately asked George whether this was an amendment or an addendum, to which George said it was an addendum, which of course destroyed its whole purpose, since there would be no vote on an addendum. Morrison then rose and made hay of this. When the vote was taken the result was 82 for the addendum with 110 against and for ratification 120,[2] with 72 against. I myself thought we came pretty well out of this and it was clear that Nye's speech the day before had restored to him a little of his lost prestige.

But the whole thing had an atmosphere of rather dreary *fait accompli*, and we spent a long time discussing in the Smoking Room what tactics should be followed on the Floor of the House.[3] Emrys Hughes and Sydney Silverman said that, whatever happened, they would call for a division and Nye was emphatic that we must go into the lobby against the motion, while I argued that everything depended on the numbers. If you could get forty-five into the lobby, it would be O.K., but a well-organized, ostentatious abstention would be more effective than a handful in the lobby.

Since then we have received a most remarkable whip for this Thursday. It runs as follows:

* In seconding George, Tony Greenwood made a blob almost as bad as mine at Morecambe.[1] Looking very prim and well dressed, he started by saying, 'I hope the comrades will not misunderstand me when I say that the high level of yesterday's debate has not been carried on today.' 'National Executive!' shouted somebody and the rest of his speech was lost, though it was a reasonable enough plea that, to keep the Party together, a reasoned Amendment was required.

[1] See above, pp. 151–2.

[2] Officially reported as 124.

[3] When on November 17th and 18th the House of Commons debated the Government resolution to ratify the recent London and Paris Agreements.

Debate on Eastern Europe on a Government Motion.
MEMBERS ARE REMINDED OF THE PARTY MEETING DECISION TO SUPPORT THE
NINE POWER TREATY. THE VOTE THEREFORE MUST NOT BE CHALLENGED.
YOUR ATTENDANCE AT 3.30 P.M. AND THROUGHOUT THE SITTING IS ESSENTIAL.

The other strand in last week's business was, of course, the *Tribune* affair.
On Wednesday, just after the debate on Germany, Harold Wilson saw Clem
and briefly told him that he and I had seen the *Tribune* document[1] and
regarded it as a cast-iron case. If there were expulsions, we would be bound to
resign. Attlee, of course, just grunted. Harold then went up to Liverpool to
the West Derby by-election and found himself travelling with Morgan
Phillips. Apparently Morgan received a summary of *Tribune*'s reply on his
arrival in Liverpool and on their way back he told Harold, first, that there
had been no intention of expulsions and that the T.U.C. had been a bit
surprised by the violent reaction of the N.E.C., and, secondly, that he himself
would probably issue an interim statement which would enable the Executive
merely to endorse him on the next occasion if he wanted to drop the business.
This interim statement[2] came out on Sunday and I regard the whole affair
as pretty well cleared up, since the whole press treatment of it, though mean,
does grudgingly admit that it would be intolerable to expel people on this.
The leading articles from today's *Times* and *Guardian* are not untypical.[3]
Both deny there is an issue of principle, when there clearly is one, presumably
because of their loathing of the knowledge that the Bevanites should ever
have an issue of principle on their side. *The Economist*, to its credit, was a
great deal better.[4]

Of course this is a minor victory but unfortunately it is a very minor one
compared to the catastrophic decline in Nye's position as a result of his
absence from the SEATO debate and his general failure to give any leadership
to the Left since the House resumed.[5] Though he spoke well in the Party

[1] I.e. the Editor's reply to the N.E.C.'s reproof.
[2] The General Secretary's reply, circulated to the Press, stated that,

... On the particular issue of the dock strike the Party took its official stand through
Alfred Robens in the House of Commons. This was based on the view that freely
negotiated collective agreements should be honoured by all the parties to these agreements ... *Tribune* chose to take the opposite view ...

[3] *The Times* scorned the view that 'some mighty principle of freedom is at stake in this
back-biting squabble about the comradely rules and ways of a voluntary body ... ' According to the *Manchester Guardian*, 'Every time the Labour party has tried to state the rights
of its minorities on paper it has landed itself in confusion ... Mr Deakin does not need the
officious help of Mr Phillips and the National Executive in swatting every gadfly.'

[4] In the issue of November 13th, *The Economist* supported the right of *Tribune*'s Editors
to state their views: 'If the Executive is really bent on blood-letting, it should not start in
one of the few cases where the Bevanites have a freedom-fighting Foot to stand on.'

[5] The South-East Asia Collective Defence Treaty was signed on September 8th. It was
discussed in Parliament on November 8th but Bevan, who had resigned from the Shadow
Cabinet on this issue, stayed away, leaving Harold Davies and William Warbey to
represent the left-wing opposition.

Meeting, he just isn't leading and doesn't want to, and the Left gets weaker day by day, though, on the other hand, the Right, having won, seems to have no idea what to do with its victory.

On November 13th, four days before the House of Commons was to debate the Nine-Power treaty, the Soviet Government sent Notes proposing a conference of all European countries, to be held in Paris or Moscow on November 29th. The Notes warned of the retaliatory action that the 'peace-loving' countries would be obliged to take if the Western Union agreements were ratified.

Two days later, the Foreign Secretary told the Commons that the only new item in the Russian proposal was the suggested date. He repeated the Government's view that talks with Russia should take place only after the ratification of the agreements. The British reply, in these terms, was delivered to the Russians on November 29th.

Monday, November 22nd
The whole of the last six days have been permeated by the German rearmament debate. We received a whip for the last week, ordering us, under three-line penalty, to turn up on Thursday, although the official Party policy was not to force a vote. This made it clear enough that the Shadow Cabinet feared a vote forced by the pacifists. I saw John Freeman at the *Statesman* and told him that I had had a very simple but possibly effective idea. It would be fatal for the Bevanites to vote against a three-line injunction, since this would enable the N.E.C. to expel Michael, Jennie and Mallalieu next Wednesday. Moreover, Nye would then go into the lobby with some twenty-five or thirty rag-tag-and-bob-tail supporters and the net effect would be to show our decreased power. I would therefore try a new line: to announce that we were abstaining under protest because otherwise we would be expelled. John agreed that this would be a good idea to try out on Nye and Jennie at the Tuesday lunch.

Jennie turned up rather late to say that Nye couldn't get there and then, after some prodding, said that she could only tell us in the greatest secrecy what he felt, since, if a word of it leaked out, he would be ruined. His view, she said with bated breath, is that on balance ('and of course it's a terribly difficult balance') he feels we should not go into the lobby. Sighs of relief from John, Harold and myself but fervent repetition from Jennie that, if it were suspected that this was Nye's advice, he would be ruined. I then put my idea and found it surprisingly favourably received. We were also told that Nye was to speak on Thursday and it was agreed that I should try to get in on Wednesday and try out this line in order to lead up to a great declaration by Nye. Michael was also to try on Wednesday on the same tack.

There followed a discussion of a meeting called that evening by Ian Mikardo, to which all the fifty-seven Bevanites had been invited. We had all agreed the week before that it would be desperately dangerous to call such a meeting but it transpired that Ian had done this after talking to Nye, who no doubt had been approached by a great many frustrated individuals. It was obvious that, given Nye's view, he could not go to the meeting and indeed that the meeting should not be held. However it was agreed that Geoffrey and Ian should go and try to lead it to this conclusion.

After dinner I slipped upstairs to the Bevanite meeting, where I found thirty-three people, including myself, with Leslie Hale in the chair. There was a terribly demoralized atmosphere but it was clear that, apart from Sydney Silverman and Emrys Hughes, everybody had already made up their minds to toe the line and abstain, including Will Warbey[1] and Harold Davies. Will Griffiths, Nye's old P.P.S., put it quite bluntly when he said, 'The eccentrics can afford to force a division because they won't be expelled but if Jennie, Michael and Curly go into the division lobby, they will pick them off and leave the rest.' I've seldom felt more utterly depressed than I was after this meeting. It showed that our Group, if it ever existed, had now totally disintegrated.

Early on Wednesday morning George rang up to tell me that he had secret information that Morrison and Gaitskell were going to propose a second three-line whip, reversing the previous decision. Now the order would be that the Party must abstain from voting either for or against! The reason for this change of front was Morrison's alarm that right-wingers, if forced to vote publicly, would shirk the lobby, so that the abstentionists might outnumber the loyalists and thus give the Bevanites a crowning victory. I then told George my idea, which he thought fitted in very well, since I could announce that we were abstaining under threat of expulsion, knowing that within a few hours the right-wing of the Party would be forced into the same ignominious position. With this rather unfair advantage I sat down to prepare a speech, but the longer I worked at the concluding section on abstention the more impossible I found it. Moreover, half way through the morning Zhivotovski of the Russian Embassy rang up to say he must have lunch with me before the debate. He spent the lunch insisting that Russia did not, as some people say, tacitly accept the Nine-Power treaty and vaguely warning me of the terrible things which would follow if it was ratified.

I went to the House with a speech which was not bad but which had no end. The debate began with Eden in curiously lackadaisical mood, with no kind of enthusiasm or interest in the House. He was followed by Morrison, so jejune that Nye and I couldn't avoid a little private conversation, which a parently infuriated the right-wing, who thought we were barracking the

---

[1] William Warbey, Labour M.P. for Luton 1945–50, Broxtowe 1953–5 and Ashfield 1955–1966. He was Tutor-Organizer at the National Council of Labour Colleges from 1937 to 1940, and Chief English Press Officer to the Norwegian Government in exile from 1941 to 1945. He was Executive Director of the Organization for World Political and Social Studies 1965–80, Secretary of the World Studies Trust 1966–80. From 1968 until his death in 1980 he was Chairman of the Rossetti House Group. His publications include *Vietnam: The Truth* (London: Merlin Press, 1965).

boss. I learnt later that the Tea Room boys decided to come in and barrack me in return.

However, I had a very long time to wait. Sitting there for four hours, it suddenly occurred to me to take a risk. Instead of ending with the stuff about expulsion, why not just mention it, quite quietly, at the beginning, not making too much fuss about it but just giving Nye a little bit of a lead-in for his great speech the next day? However, it didn't work out like that! The moment I said that we had decided to accept the majority ruling,[1] there was an astonishing bay of ribald cheering from the Tea Room, who had crowded in to hear. This enabled me to shout back at them that we were doing it because otherwise we would be expelled, that we were determined to live to fight another day, etc., etc. After that I got back to my speech but it was pretty well deranged and I had to leave a lot of it out, though it was a fair success. Indeed, objectively, I must admit the debate didn't really start till I got up.

When I sat down Nye gave a good loud cheer and then said, 'I wish you hadn't said that at the start.' This depressed me a bit, since I felt it might have been a schemozzle. However, by half-past nine it was clear that for once the trick had worked, since the B.B.C. had decided this incident was the news of the day and therefore the whole country knew of the threat of expulsion. Moreover, one hour later the whip had been delivered into the hands of the right-wing, whose fury was indescribable.*

The Parliamentary Committee had met before I spoke but, though I had told Hugh Gaitskell in the morning that I would discuss German occupation costs, he, Morrison, Attlee, etc., preferred to have dinner during my speech and only Chuter Ede sat in — which, of course, only accentuated the atmosphere. That evening Anne and I had a drink with Jill and Michael down below

[1] 'A word about tomorrow. If some of us whose convictions and principles would take us into the Lobby to vote against this Agreement tomorrow yet do not vote, the reason will not be any change of conviction, but the fact that if one wants to survive in our party to fight another day one has to accept a majority decision, however unpleasant it may be' [*H. C. Debates*, vol. 533, col. 481 ff.].

* It ran:

November 17th, 1954

CONFIDENTIAL

Dear Colleague,

As many Members, feeling uncertain about Thursday, are making inquiries, it is well to remind you of the actual Standing Order

'*1 The privilege of membership of the Parliamentary Labour Party involves the acceptance of the decisions of the Party Meeting. The Party recognizes the right of individual Members to abstain from voting on matters of deeply held personal conscientious conviction.*'

The dividing of the House or voting against a Parliamentary Party decision can only be regarded as a serious breach of Party discipline and Standing Orders and must be dealt with accordingly.

The Parliamentary Committee have considered the situation which would arise if nevertheless, and despite this warning, a vote is challenged: in that event the Committee have come to the conclusion that all Members of the Party should ABSTAIN.

C. R. ATTLEE (Leader)
H. MORRISON (Deputy Leader)
W. WHITELEY (Chief Whip)

and I was enormously pleased when Jill said to Mike, 'You see, dear, Dick's quite right. Your tactic is to keep the rules and then to tell people about the rules you are forced to keep.' I think Mike did see that this was the logical next step after his Miltonian pamphlet in defence of the *Tribune*'s freedom. So I went to bed feeling that, despite Nye's comment, maybe I had been right.

When I read the papers on Thursday morning it was clear that I had been right. The story of the change of front, by which the Party was now ordered not to vote for the treaty, was in the *Telegraph* at full length, linked with my speech. Only the *Daily Herald* and *The Times* tried to conceal the surrender of the Shadow Cabinet. I rang Nye to make sure he knew and found he had no idea, since he has no newspapers in the country. On the other hand, he brushed aside my apology and reassured me by at once saying that we must continue to hold to our line of abstaining, whatever happened, and that the job had been done by me and nothing more was needed from him on this point.

The debate was re-started on Thursday by Gaitskell with a very well reasoned answer to me, which put the Government's case better than Eden. This was followed by a long waffle from Macmillan. Nye rose to a fuller House than there had been in the debate so far and made what I still think a brilliant tactical oration. Though he could not prevent himself from baiting Gaitskell a little bit, he didn't do it too badly. He then launched out into the most moderate and good-humoured exposure of the futility of the treaty. He ended with the even more moderate demand that there should be talks with the Russians *after* ratification, which really took my breath away. I still don't know why he did it, since I don't think he really persuaded many of our right-wingers that he was being anything but crafty. However, it was a wonderful performance, which certainly restored his parliamentary position.

After Nye had finished Reggie Paget launched the same attack on us as he had done at the Party Meeting but he apparently did not know about the whip ordering abstention and accused me of cowardice for abstaining. This enabled me to rise and say he was embarrassing our own Front Bench. Soon afterwards Bob Boothby made what he hoped to be his great oration, since he regards himself as the architect of the Nine-Power treaty, but curiously enough his speech didn't cut much ice. As Nye remarked to me at dinner with Anne that night, 'In this debate what matters is what you represent. Why you counted yesterday was because you were speaking for a powerful group. Bob speaks for nothing but himself and the *News of the World*.'

By now it was clear that the pacifists were going to force a division and the only other remarkable thing in the debate was Sydney Silverman's explanation of this.[1] Attlee's winding-up was pretty ordinary, except right at the end,

---

[1] '... there are large numbers of people in this country who are sincerely and passionately convinced that to ratify these treaties would be a tragic and catastrophic error ... they are entitled to have their representation in the Division Lobby' [*H. C. Debates*, vol. 533, col. 661 ff.].

where he became a bit too clever and outdid Nye by demanding talks before ratification. This enabled Eden, who made a superb wind-up speech, to describe Attlee's speech as 'prudent' and bring the House down. Eden also succeeded in slightly puncturing Nye by telling him, after an interruption, to take my advice, since I at least knew something about the subject.

But the most extraordinary feature of the whole debate was the deliberate refusal of the Tories to break the official Labour leadership, as they could easily have done by challenging them throughout the debate as to how they could conceivably speak in support of the treaty and abstain. That the Tories did not do so makes it clearer than anything else could that they are really more concerned than anything to prop up our leadership against the Left and that our leadership relies on them to do so. The concluding scene was fairly lively when the division was called, and the vote took place with the Labour benches full of people sitting abstaining.[1] I seem to remember vaguely — since on these occasions tempers are so hot that one's memory is fogged — shouting to Patrick Gordon Walker, who had said we were all cowards, 'No, we're not cowards, Patrick, we've merely decided to stay in and fight you!' But I should think that there has seldom been such a sense of frustration and humiliation as was created on that evening.

Friday morning's papers tried their best to cover up the appalling débâcle of the Labour leadership but when I got back to the House this afternoon it was only too clear that everybody appreciated it. The only question was how on earth the Shadow Cabinet is now to get out of the dilemma it created for itself. If it doesn't expel those who violate a special three-line whip,[2] Standing Orders are gone. But will the Parliamentary Party vote for expulsion? I chatted with both Callaghan and Harold Wilson. Callaghan told me that he himself had moved the proposal to abstain and had been surprised how quickly Morrison and Gaitskell supported it. Harold Wilson was, I think, quietly pleased with what had happened, particularly that the Wilson–Crossman tactic had been successfully employed, despite the last-minute efforts of people like Tom Driberg and Ian Mikardo to rush into the martyrdom lobby. But one has to agree, particularly in the light of the West Derby election,[3] where Labour's defeat was the other main news of Friday's papers, that what we think to be our efforts to save the soul of the Party are certainly helping it to disintegrate as fast as possible. All one can say is that, by keeping strictly to the rules and exposing the Party oligarchy, we are taking the only tactic we can, though it doesn't make us any more friends on the Right of the Party.

[1] The vote was 264 in favour of the treaties and 6 against; 6 'pacifists' voted against the Government and 1 Labour Member, John McGovern, voted with them.

[2] I.e. the six pacifists and John McGovern.

[3] J. V. Woollam held the seat for the Conservatives, with a majority of 2,508 over the other candidate, C. R. Fenton (Labour). The Conservative proportion of the vote, on a low poll, rose by 1·55 per cent.

Monday, November 29th

Last Monday evening I was just going to bed when George Wigg rang up to say he must come and report on what the Parliamentary Committee had decided. So he came round to say that expulsion of the six pacifists and of John McGovern[1] had been accepted, with only Wilson, Chuter Ede and Callaghan voting against and Shinwell abstaining. I got a checking report on this meeting from Harold Wilson the next day, though Harold's reports tend to have such long speeches by himself that you get the impression that no one else in the Committee spoke a word.

The Party Meeting, at which all this was to be ratified, took place on Tuesday at five o'clock in the Grand Committee Room, which meant that it was crowded and most people were standing all the time. I got a seat on the corner of a table. The meeting started with a very tart speech by Attlee, who explained how the Parliamentary Committee had kindly decided to ease everybody's conscience by ordering abstention, 'only to receive a characteristic speech of abuse by Mr Crossman'. This produced a howl of irate rage from all around him and I soon discovered that my speech, followed by my *Sunday Pic* article, had made me Public Enemy Number One at least for last week.[2]

In the debate which followed, Emrys Hughes made the main speech for the pacifists. Each of them managed to put across that he was a person with conscientious objections and I certainly realized that, if we had voted with them, the whole atmosphere would have been different, since on this occasion the Party Meeting did know it was excluding seven individuals and not an organized group. But far the most effective speech came from John McGovern, who accused the Parliamentary Committee of gutlessness and said that he was the only person who had the courage of Mr Attlee's convictions in voting for German rearmament.

It was a very queer meeting, since the whole atmosphere was one of reconciliation, yet the vote was a block vote if ever that term has been legitimately used.[3] I've never felt people feeling more depressed and dejected than the Labour Members as they drifted through Westminster Hall. The Bevanites felt uncomfortable at not having voted [in the debate] with the expellees and the right-wing, as one or two people openly remarked in the

[1] John McGovern (1887–1968), Independent Labour M.P. for the Shettleston division of Glasgow from 1930 to 1947, when he joined the Labour Party and then served as Labour M.P. for the same constituency until 1959. He was arrested on two occasions in 1931 and imprisoned in connection with the Free Speech campaign. In 1933 he protested in the House of Lords during the King's Speech against the Government's failure to restore cuts in Unemployment Benefit and to abolish the Means Test. He left Britain in 1962 to settle in Australia.

[2] In his column, 'Black Day for Labour', on November 21st, Crossman pointed 'the moral of this ignominious episode' at the end of the debate on the previous Thursday. He wrote, 'There is a point beyond which you cannot dragoon people with deeply felt convictions.'

[3] The seven were not asked to leave the Party but all were deprived of the whip.

meeting, felt that the minnows and not the big fish had been caught in the net which had been laid. Even Herbert Morrison wasn't at his brightest. He had wound up the debate with a perfectly cynical admission that abstention had been ordered so that Members would not be embarrassed in the voting lobby and with an equally cynical statement that McGovern had had to be expelled 'on balance', which was received with a round of strangely hearty laughter.

By the time we got back across Westminster Hall, the tape was reporting the results of our meeting, interspersed with Churchill's birthday address to his constituents,[1] which included a few not very spiteful remarks on how tolerant the Conservative Party was to him when he was a rebel. Politicians being politicians, we all looked at these remarks and hardly observed his extraordinary statement about the order he gave to Monty in the last days of the war to stack German arms for eventual use by Germans if the Russians moved. But by Thursday morning this had become the main political news of the week, with a thundering leader in *The Times*, in chorus with the *Daily Herald* and the *Daily Mirror*.

Meanwhile we had a meeting of the N.E.C. on Wednesday morning, at which, as we expected, it was decided that the withdrawal of the whip from the seven had come too soon for consideration by the N.E.C. After a desultory debate, the *Tribune* issue was also settled by another offensive letter but nothing more. It was quite obvious that the N.E.C. was determined to avoid expulsions of any sort in view of the forthcoming election.[2]

From Wednesday until the weekend the row over the Churchill clanger continued, as a result of George Wigg's activities. Personally I am not terribly keen on this as an issue for reviving the Labour Party but it immediately occurred to me that the old boy was deliberately laying a time-bomb for Attlee and Morrison. He had disclosed one secret telegram, which would tempt the Labour Party to force a vote of censure. What if he revealed one or two more in the vote of censure and so produced the kind of reprisal he achieved in that terrible debate on the Yalu River bombings, in which he knocked out Herbert Morrison?[3]

Most of Thursday, however, I was concerned with a ridiculous controversy

---

[1] Churchill was to be eighty years old on November 30th. On November 23rd, at a celebration with his constituents at Woodford, he recalled that, at the time of the German surrender in May 1945, he had ordered Field-Marshal Montgomery to preserve the arms yielded by the Germans, as Britain might need German help against the Russians. Revealed in the midst of the controversies over German rearmament, this episode provoked varying reactions. On December 1st, however, Sir Winston apologized to the House of Commons, telling them that his memory had betrayed him at Woodford. Although the telegram to Montgomery entirely represented his views, apparently it had not been despatched, since in the official record there was no trace of its existence.

[2] Of the Parliamentary Committee, at the beginning of the new Session, to start on November 30th.

[3] See above, pp. 84-6.

with Herbert, which I had started in high spirits.[1] I was finally getting so tired of this that on Thursday I rang him up. He spent twenty-five minutes on the telephone telling me he couldn't see me, until I finally said, 'Well, if you publish our correspondence, you will have to publish the last letter, which comes from me and is in my pocket and which says that this is too silly as between Socialists and should be settled by a chat.' 'You're too clever by half,' he said. 'I will see you at four o'clock.'

When I went to his room I found him rather sheepish. 'You know, Herbert,' I said, 'our behaviour to each other in the last three days is what's wrong with the Labour Party. You know perfectly well that I am not dishonest.' 'No,' he said, 'but you're clever and like arguing.' 'But that's not dishonest,' I said. 'Well, it's as bad,' he said, grinning a bit. So then I said, 'You will always have this trouble, because there is no real leadership in the Party,' and began to explain about West Derby.[2] At this, he suddenly interrupted me and said, 'You're the only one of the Bevanites I used to be able to talk to. You used to give me a nice dinner every now and then but I suppose you're afraid of doing that now.' This really took my breath away but I did manage to say, 'Look, it was you who spent twenty-five minutes two hours ago saying you couldn't have a word with me! What's wrong with you, Herbert?' Then I suddenly realized that he had assumed that I was making some devious political overture for a combination to get rid of Attlee. It was a most curious talk and in it was wrapped up most of what is wrong with the Party today. Of course, something else that is wrong is that, if it got out that we had had any talk at all, I should be done irreparable harm.

On Friday I had the bright idea that we might utilize the Churchill incident as a cover for a Bevanite meeting tomorrow at my house by inviting people to celebrate Churchill's birthday by absenting themselves and having a drink. This also seemed a good idea to Geoffrey Bing, who realized how terribly demoralized our people in the House have become. So, having got his consent, I rang up Nye, to get Jennie on the phone. She was in a tremendous fluster, telling me that Nye regarded Barbara's action in publicly

---

[1] In his speech on November 17th, Crossman had stated that Herbert Morrison had

said two completely opposite things while being in one and the same Government. Having passionately opposed German rearmament in April, he turned right round in September and accepted the American ultimatum, and he did exactly what he had denounced as irresponsible five months before.

Herbert Morrison argued in an exchange of letters with Crossman that a statement should be published, making it clear that

while of course Mr Morrison as a member of the Labour Government in 1950 shared in the decision to which I took exception, the speeches which I had in mind were made not by him but by the then Foreign Secretary, Ernest Bevin.

Eventually this statement was published in the press on November 27th.

[2] Crossman had also exchanged several letters with Edith Summerskill, that year's Party Chairman, who had protested about his articles, particularly that in the *Sunday Pictorial* on November 14th, which attributed the defeat in the West Derby by-election to 'the Tories' secret weapon' — apathy in the Labour Party.

cancelling her subscription to the Churchill Fund as sheer demagogy.[1] They would have no part in any anti-Churchill demonstration. After all, didn't I appreciate that Jennie had been on the committee and that Nye was lunching with Churchill next Tuesday? Of course they don't bother to tell us any of this beforehand. What a past master Nye is at rationalizing his own convenience. If Gaitskell had made such a slip, Nye wouldn't call it demagogy to expose it. But here again I think Nye's instinct was sound and that you don't gain anything politically by spiteful things like withdrawing your contribution or refusing to sign a Birthday Book.[2]

Friday, December 3rd
Tuesday was the State Opening of Parliament, combined with Churchill's eightieth birthday celebrations. When I walked round to Westminster Hall for the ceremony, I found that at twenty-five to twelve most seats were already full, and I stood at the door half way up with Archie Manuel, Dick Plummer and so on, in a howling draught. But we saw better than if we had been sitting. The ceremony started rather ridiculously with the V-sign beaten on the drums of the Grenadier Guards, introducing Frank McLeavy and Jennie Lee of the Reception Committee. However, after this bit of highfalutin' nonsense, the show was a pleasant sort of House of Commons affair, which, indeed, would have been more suitable in the Chamber than for that vast building and that vast assemblage. Curiously enough, the motion was very restrained, I suppose because the Tories didn't feel all that enthusiastic about the Old Man staying on, while we for our part didn't feel all that enthusiastic about allowing them to make too much Party capital out of it. Attlee's speech was pleasant, dry and witty. Churchill's reply only had one good sentence, where he talked about roaring for the British lion. He made one allusion to the Sutherland[3] picture, when it was unveiled, which was an augury of trouble to come.[4] I gather the television effect was not very terrific.

After this I walked back home, where I had invited some thirty Bevanites to beer and a sandwich. Eighteen turned up, which wasn't too bad, since a good many of them were giving their wives lunch after the ceremony. In addition to our normal lot we had three rather important recruits — Kenneth

---

[1] A fund in Sir Winston's honour, open to contributors from all over the world, was to be partly used for the endowment of Chartwell, his house in Kent, 'as a museum containing relics and mementoes of my long life'.

[2] Signed by nearly all the Members of the House of Commons and presented to Sir Winston on his birthday.

[3] Graham Sutherland, the painter and designer. He received the Order of Merit in 1960. The first exhibition of his portraiture was given at the National Portrait Gallery in 1977. He died in 1980.

[4] It was a backbench Opposition Member who had suggested that there should be a ceremony to present Sir Winston with his birthday tributes. The portrait, by Graham Sutherland, was described as 'formidable'. It was not displayed again and, a quarter of a century later, it was announced that Lady Churchill had ordered its destruction.

Robinson, one-time Whip, Dick Plummer, one-time groundnuts chief,[1] and George Wigg. We discussed what should be done that evening at the Party Meeting on the Queen's Speech. Most people agreed that the atmosphere of the lunch was a great deal more useful than when only the restricted Group meet, though right towards the end we had the usual problem, with people like Dick Acland and Bill Warbey asking whether we shouldn't go through lists of Members and make up our mind on organization. I replied rather emphatically that nothing had happened except that I had invited them for a sandwich and a glass of beer and that, if anything else had happened, it would be reported to the Chief Whip within twelve hours, so it hadn't.

Afterwards I had a talk with Geoffrey Bing, who was quite pleased and agreed that, since groups are forbidden, the only thing to do is to have such social occasions and, to avoid the charge of re-forming a group, to have no central planning but only a series of *ad hoc* affairs with different people at each. All this sounds fantastically elaborate but the fact is that the ban on group activities really does make it difficult to formulate any serious policy or to behave in a reasonable way. Yet, on the other hand, the ban has got to be accepted and acted on or else we shall be in trouble.

On Wednesday, the serious Debate on the Address began. Manny Shinwell had been selected to open and to probe Sir Winston [on defence]. He spent forty-five minutes in his usual unbearable, shifting, vague, semi-bombastic, repetitive style but on this occasion it was perfect. If a really competent person had delivered a competent, incisive attack on Churchill, the effect would have been disastrous. Manny's blurred, vague, questioning promptings were about the most that the House would take. Moreover, on George Wigg's advice, his theme was a series of questions, suggesting that the [Montgomery] telegram had never existed. These were greeted with hoots of derision by the Tory Party, derision which soon changed to gloomy silence when Churchill rose and admitted that this was so. He must have known on the previous day that he would have to make this apology, which really was rather painful, and he did it fairly well. Indeed, he only came very near to tears in an extraordinary later passage in which he said that he was still determined on the high-level talks and added, *sotto voce*, 'This is the only reason I am still here.' After this everyone was quick to draw the conclusion that, since the talks aren't coming for a long time, Sir Winston intends to be here for a long time.

As for the Labour Party, the right-wing are frozen into a rigid attitude of suspicious fear and hatred of their left-wing colleagues. The more the official leadership loses the support of the general public, the more they lay the blame on wicked journalists and conspirators who are suborning their supporters

---

[1] He had been Chairman of the Overseas Food Corporation until his resignation in May 1950, amid criticism of the administration of an immense enterprise to promote the large-scale cultivation of groundnuts, sorghum and maize in East Africa. In 1949/50 this project had cost £600,000, with no allowance for non-farm overheads, and crops of only £100,000 had been produced. The cry of 'groundnuts scheme' became an Opposition expression of mockery.

from them. Meanwhile little Attlee manipulates and twitters to and fro in the centre. One other little sidelight. Talking to Dick Stokes in the Smoking Room, I said I was amazed to see hé had voted to expel his old friend Sydney Silverman, though no one in the past had voted oftener against the whip than Stokes the rebel. 'Yes, I was a bit ashamed about it,' he said. 'But I've talked it over with my gang and, since I had failed to persuade them to vote for the Edelman amendment,[1] I felt bound to vote for expulsion.' 'Gang?' I said. 'Is that a group decision?' And Dick began to back-pedal as fast as he could but he had given me the first bit of concrete evidence that real right-wing groups do exist and work collectively together.

Thursday, December 9th

I had got back on Monday morning to find Kingsley in a state of high tension because of a paragraph in the *Observer* which suggested that he was intending to resign from the *Statesman*, that it had been recognized that I was too erratic to take over and that John Freeman, despite his left-wing views, was the most likely candidate. When we had read this on Sunday neither Anne nor I noticed anything very remarkable about it, since I am fairly used to this sort of gossip. But Kingsley was all agog and particularly indignant that no one on the *Observer* had rung him up to check the facts. I remarked that no one ever rang the Bevanites to check the facts before they wrote about us but this didn't satisfy Kingsley, who pointed out that he had been personally libelled. I then replied that, if anybody had been libelled, it was not him but John and myself, a view which hadn't occurred to him. The work of the *New Statesman* has completely stopped all this week while this great incident has inflamed Kingsley's mind. One of the funniest things was that Kingsley had been told, very improperly, by Hugh Massingham that the source was Woodrow Wyatt, whereupon Kingsley said, 'We must denounce him.' When I said that after all there were rules about editors and sources which we should observe, Kingsley said that this was an entirely different case, where such rules didn't apply! A silly affair—but it's these little affairs which really bring out the inner personality of each participant. Kingsley cares about himself, John Freeman about the paper and I can't take it seriously.

Throughout 1954 industrial production, employment, the volume of exports and consumers' expenditure had continued to rise. The general level of employment was higher than in previous peacetime conditions. Imports remained at much the same level as in 1953, while exports increased by some 5 per cent. Retail prices had risen by about 3·5 per cent and wage rates by more than 4·5 per cent.

[1] At the Party Meeting which discussed the fate of the rebels in the division on ratification of the Nine-Power treaty, Maurice Edelman had proposed a compromise resolution that the seven should merely be reprimanded and reported to their constituency associations.

*The central gold and dollar reserves rose on balance by $244 million during the
year, despite substantial repayments of special debt.*

Sunday, December 26th

I haven't kept this diary for a fortnight, about the most depressing Parliamentary fortnight in my experience. What has been interesting is that, though Nye has virtually gone into retirement and the official leadership might have been expected to feel easier and more self-confident, it has actually been more ineffective than ever, with the underlying ill-will between the Right and Left in the Party just as strong.

On Monday, December 13th, I attended my first meeting of the N.E.C. Finance Sub., where the agenda was largely the result of suggestions I had made at the Policy Sub., about facing the problems of Socialism in a boom. Gaitskell was in the chair and immediately suggested that we should ask the opinions of four representative economists on the prospects of the boom's continuing. After some consultation with Harold Wilson, Gaitskell named Richard Kahn, Austin Robinson[1] and Sir Donald MacDougall,[2] at whose mention even Harold jibbed. I myself was baffled as to what these eminent gentlemen are to do and, as a division bell rang at that moment, I asked Gaitskell in the lobby. He explained to me that, from his strict economic point of view, the sort of questions I was putting were irrelevant: I was talking about a psychological boom, not an economist's boom. He seemed to feel that I should be content with this reply. When we resumed the committee I pressed him on the possibility that the election of a Labour Government might itself precipitate a slump. He said categorically that, first, this was unlikely and, secondly, that, if it did happen, we would have all the power to

[1] Edmond Austin Gossage Robinson, a Fellow of Sidney Sussex College, Cambridge, since 1931, Professor of Economics at Cambridge 1950–65 and Emeritus Professor there since 1966. He was Secretary of the Royal Economics Society 1949–70 and Joint Editor of the *Economic Journal* 1944–70. The husband of the economist Joan Robinson, Austin Robinson served in an advisory capacity to the Government both during the Second World War and immediately after it. He was also Chairman of the Council of the National Institute of Economic and Social Research from 1949 until 1962. His numerous publications include *The Structure of Competitive Industry* (Cambridge University Press, 1931) and *Economic Consequences of the Size of Nations* (London: Macmillan, 1960). He was knighted in 1975.

[2] A Lecturer in Economics at Leeds University from 1936 to 1939, he worked for the Government as a statistician during the Second World War, before becoming an Official Fellow of Wadham College, Oxford, 1945–50. Economic Director of the O.E.E.C. in Paris 1948–9, he was also a Faculty Fellow of Nuffield College 1947–50, a Professorial Fellow 1951–2, and an Official Fellow from 1952 to 1964. He was also Nuffield Reader in International Economics at Oxford in 1951–2 and served as Chief Adviser at the Prime Minister's Statistical Branch from 1951 to 1953. He was knighted in 1953. A Director of Investing in Success Equities Ltd from 1959 to 1962, he was Economic Director of N.E.D.C. from 1962 to 1964 and Director-General at the new Department of Economic Affairs from 1964 to 1968. In 1969 he became Head of the Government Economic Service and Chief Economic Adviser to the Treasury. His publications include *The World Dollar Problem* (London: Macmillan, 1957), *The Dollar Problem: A Reappraisal* (London: Macmillan, 1960) and the two-volume work, *Studies in Political Economy* (London: Macmillan, 1975).

deal with it. In this committee I couldn't help noticing that, when they get together as economists, Harold Wilson and Gaitskell get on fine.

On Tuesday the 14th, the Literary Department of the *New Statesman* gave a party, which gathered together a really interesting number of people but unfortunately, to save money, offered them cheap champagne and closed the bar at eleven o'clock, when most of them were still arriving. The nicest person I met was Raymond Mortimer.[1] The previous Sunday the *Observer* had published a grovelling apology for its libel on the *N.S. & N.* Raymond sidled up to me and said, 'I do hope you'll be Editor when Kingsley goes, and wasn't it funny that the libellous word "erratic", used about you, was your characteristic which really qualifies you for editorship? A good Editor must be erratic, unlike that dreary John Freeman.' I've been thinking about this a good deal lately and I am now pretty sure that, if I had the chance, I would take the job[2] and that I would have the chance if Kingsley fell down dead — but only, of course, if Kingsley were out of the way!

On Wednesday I went to an enormous and lengthy lunch alone with Hugh Cudlipp and Sydney Jacobson. Sydney had been anxious to run a series of articles in the New Year, outlining a policy for Labour. We all agreed that, if four eminent persons were asked to write articles, the result would be catastrophic. (Hugh spent a lot of time saying he wanted to have a piece called 'The Flop of the Year — Aneurin Bevan'. Sydney and I persuaded Hugh that it is bad journalism to try and sensationalize a flop, so the article duly came out a few days later, headed 'Query of the Year'.) The more we thought about it the more difficult we found it to do anything helpful about Labour policy. At one point Hugh Cudlipp said, 'The *Mirror* might not be able to win you the next election but, if we turn against you, we can certainly lose it for you.' If it isn't lost already, this is certainly true.

On October 12th the French Assembly had approved the signing of the London Agreements by 350 votes to 113 and on December 10th the Foreign Affairs Committee of the Assembly had reported in favour of ratification of all the agreements. Ominously, though, the Article providing for German rearmament received only 16 votes, with 15 members voting against and 11 abstaining. The Assembly itself began the plenary debate on ratification on December 20th and the discussion lasted for eleven days. On December 24th the agreement to restore German sovereignty was accepted (by 393 votes to 180) and so was the Franco-German Saar Agreement (by 361 votes to 147). But on the same day Article 1, providing for German rearmament, was defeated by 280 votes to 259, with 83 abstentions.

Two days after Crossman's diary entry on December 9th, the Assembly

---

[1] A man of letters, and regular reviewer for the *New Statesman and Nation* and *The Times*. His own account of his life appeared under the title *Try Anything Once* (London: Hamish Hamilton, 1976). He died in 1980.
[2] In 1970 he did. See Crossman's *The Diaries of a Cabinet Minister*, vol. III.

agreed to Germany's entry into NATO (by only 289 votes to 251) and the Government accepted an Amendment that none of these agreements was to be applicable unless all were ratified. On December 30th a new Bill was accepted by the Assembly by 287 votes to 260, with 74 abstentions. This incorporated the provisions for German rearmament within a Western European Union and the French Prime Minister made its passage a matter of confidence.

Meanwhile, in the Federal Republic of Germany, the agreement had been given only a First Reading in the Bundestag on December 16th. The Social Democratic Party and the West German Trade Union Federation continued their campaign of opposition to ratification.

On Tuesday evening, December 21st, Nye, who hadn't seen me for ten days, mainly, I think, because Jennie has been ill, came into the Smoking Room and asked me to go out into the lobby. What he really wanted to discuss was the international situation and defence. Things were now so bad that we really must do something in Parliament when we resumed. I did not reply that he had been rebuking me for trying to do anything in Parliament only a few weeks ago, but asked what he thought we should do. He said he had a tentative idea that we should table a resolution – perhaps 1,200 words long – putting out all our views on the international situation. We should collect a lot of signatures and then launch a national campaign, which would inspire the country. I wasn't very forthcoming but I promised to motor over and see him at his farm when I get back from the Middle East.

That night I had John Strachey alone to dinner at home and found him, as usual, extremely pleasant company and very intelligent. But how effective he will be when it comes to the point of fighting the Defence Estimates next March is quite another question, especially as I can't get him and George Wigg to work together at all.

Well, that's the end of this patch of Parliament before the Recess. My own mind has been increasingly dominated by my thoughts about the effect of the H-bomb on our whole strategy and policy. How mad all this German rearmament is in view of the H-bomb and how much I sympathize with the French Assembly, which on Christmas Eve voted against German rearmament. I am more and more convinced that this whole idea of the West's containing Communism is the sheerest nonsense. My observation,[1] describing us as a Byzantium which would be lucky to survive the century of totalitarian man, is much nearer the truth than I like to think.

---

[1] In a draft synopsis for *Fabian International Essays*, edited by T. E. M. McKitterick and Kenneth Younger (London: Hogarth Press, 1957).

1955

From December 26th to January 19th Richard and Anne Crossman were in the Middle East. Several articles were based on impressions gathered during this visit, including 'Nasser's Plan for Peace' and 'A Visit to Cyprus' in the New Statesman and Nation, *January 22nd, and 29th, 1955, and 'Invite Her — She's Our Friend!', 'War Drums in Jericho' and 'It's Just Asking For Trouble' in the* Sunday Pictorial, *January 9th, 16th and 23rd, 1955.*

Parliament reassembled on January 20th; on the following day the Foreign Secretary made a Statement on the fighting in the islands off the Chinese mainland. The Cairo conference of 1943 had agreed that Formosa, a large island occupied by Japan since 1895, should be restored to China. In 1945 the Nationalists took over its administration and in 1948 Chiang Kai-shek established his Government in this refuge, under American naval protection. The Nationalists also retained other islands: the Pescadores near Formosa, and the Tachen, Quemoy and Matsu islands near the Chinese coast. The Communists demanded possession of all these, claiming them as an integral part of China.

In December 1954 President Eisenhower had stated that the American Government would defend Formosa and the Pescadores from Communist attack but his reference to policy for the inshore islands was unclear. By January 1955 there was fighting between the two Chinese Governments in the vicinity of Quemoy and Matsu and the United States Navy and Air Force were assisting the evacuation of the Tachen islands.

In the week following Crossman's return, he heard

inspired reports that Eisenhower was going to give a special message to Congress in order to get Congressional backing — but for what? From what I learnt in September [during Crossman's visit to America] I should have been confident that his aim was gradually to withdraw from Quemoy and the other islands and so to keep Chiang relatively harmless on Formosa.

But by the evening of Monday, January 24th, 'it was clear that the President had once again reached a compromise. Instead of drawing a clear line, across which the Communists should not pass, he had left it completely ambiguous whether America intended to defend Quemoy or no.'

In his Statement on January 25th, Sir Anthony declared that the Government's first concern was to stop the fighting and that he was certain that this was also the American Government's object. 'But,' reported Crossman, 'Attlee brushed all these considerations aside, accused America of intervening in a Chinese civil war and left the implication that his [own] policy is to bring Communist China immediately into the U.N. and give no protection to Chiang on Formosa at all.'

Crossman's view was that this 'would all be fine if it bore any relation to Labour policy in Europe'. His principal immediate concern was to continue, with Bevan, to press the Party leadership to propose Four-Power talks on the question of Germany's future. A further Russian Note had been delivered on December 9th, attacking the Paris Agreement, and on January 15th, 1955, a threatening declaration was issued from Moscow. It condemned the treaties and stated that, by abandoning them, West Germany might still discover opportunities for reunion with the German Democratic Republic. There should be free all-German elections, under the terms of the electoral laws of both German States, and 'all democratic parties and organizations' should be entitled to nominate candidates and put forward electoral lists.

The Federal Government replied on January 16th that peace and unification could be achieved only by the union of free peoples, who would be able to negotiate with the Soviet Union. In a broadcast Dr Adenauer emphasized that, without friends in the West, Germany would be at the mercy of the Russians.

On January 25th the Soviet Government announced officially that it was prepared to end the state of war with Germany and resume normal diplomatic relations with the Federal Republic. The German Government attributed this move to the Russians' wish for diplomatic recognition of the Soviet Zone (which already had an Ambassador in Moscow); the leaders of the S.D.P. in Germany, however, stated that to reject the Soviet overture would be irresponsible. Crossman thought this continuation of the Russian 'peace offensive' to be of great importance, 'as Nye rightly saw'.

Crossman wrote that Attlee and Bevan agreed that 'it would be a good thing to table a motion, not mentioning the Russian proposal but proposing Four-Power talks straightaway'. According to Kenneth Robinson, reported Crossman, there was a majority for this in the Parliamentary Committee 'with, of course, Gaitskell, Morrison and Soskice against'. He went on,

> *Yet, mysteriously, the motion has not been tabled and all we have at present is a similar motion by Sydney Silverman, to which I have added my name, not knowing what was going on. Apparently Attlee was unwilling to risk an open break with Morrison and Gaitskell and has merely proposed a Party Meeting on Germany for the week after next.*

Wednesday, February 2nd

This week Labour politics have woken up. On Monday, the *Daily Herald* front-paged an exclusive interview with Attlee, in which he demanded that Chiang Kai-shek should be removed from Formosa and Formosa removed from the American strategic chain of islands and then neutralized under the United Nations. This was pretty extreme for Mr Attlee but more was to come. Yesterday the Defence and Services group was due to start its annual discussion in preparation for the defence debate[1] and it was announced on the whip that Mr Attlee would attend and take part. I had to go to the L.S.E. to talk to the Labour Club and only got in when he was being questioned, but apparently what he had said was, first, there is no defence whatsoever against the H-bomb and the only thing to do is to outlaw war by world disarmament,

---

[1] The Defence Statement, Cmnd 9391, was to be presented to Parliament on February 17th.

with drastic inroads on sovereignty. Secondly, he said, conventional armies with huge divisions are sheer waste and so is the idea of calling up the reserves and shipping Territorial forces across to Germany after the war starts. Thirdly, the American bases in Britain should be removed, since this is far too vulnerable a spot. Fourthly, on civil defence he showed some mild interest, but not very great, in mobile columns but in nothing else. Some rather remarkable versions of this private talk were headlined today in the *Chronicle* and the *Herald*.

Meanwhile, George Wigg tells me there was consternation in the Tea Room, where it was concluded, both from Attlee's extreme attitude on Formosa and from his line on defence, that he was utterly betraying the Right. John Junor rang me up this morning and observed straightaway, 'Your little man has tipped the pendulum your way. There will be no election now in the near future.' And he added, 'Unlike your Nye, the little man has a wonderful sense of timing.' This is probably true but for the life of me I don't quite understand what he is at. Did he know that his private talk at the defence group would be headlined in the press? Did he realize that his remarks about conventional armies made nonsense of German rearmament?

At yesterday's lunch, Nye expressed the view that Attlee's extremism about Formosa was designed to cover up on German rearmament, i.e. the Party would be so pleased about our China policy that it would not press for Four-Power talks in response to the Russian Note of January 15th, conceding free elections under international control. But I fancy Nye is wrong. Attlee feels that this is the moment to give the Party the lead it has been waiting for over months and to show that he is not a prisoner of the Right. Though Nye may not like to think it, Attlee's activity may be due to the fact that Nye is in semi-retirement. This makes it easier for Attlee to talk Left. But all this is sheer surmise.

In reply to a Parliamentary Question on February 4th the Foreign Secretary spoke of the offshore islands — Formosa and the Pescadores — as 'undoubtedly' belonging to China. He appealed to Peking to halt the fighting and on February 7th deplored the Peking Government's refusal to attend a meeting of the United Nations Security Council to discuss the Formosa issue. Sir Anthony sought to avoid further questions, explaining that to answer them would only increase the difficulties of the matter. The Government was generally believed to be embarrassed by the fact that standing by America brought with it the obligation to support Chiang Kai-shek. Opposition Members continued to demand the inclusion of Communist China in the membership of the U.N.

Several Labour backbenchers also pressed for Four-Power talks on the German question. On January 31st, Sir Anthony told them that none of the recent Russian proposals indicated any change in the Government's policy on this matter. In the U.S.S.R., meanwhile, changes were taking place among the leadership; they were announced on February 8th. Mr Malenkov resigned his post as Chairman of the Council of Ministers, admitting 'guilt and responsibility for the unsatisfactory state of affairs which has arisen in agriculture'. He became Minister of Electric Power Stations. Malenkov's successor was Marshal Nikolai Bulganin. Though 'collective leadership' was maintained, power appeared to be exercised by Khrushchev, with Bulganin and two of the First Deputy Chairmen of the Council of Ministers, Molotov and Vlazar Kaganovich. Since Malenkov had been so closely identified with the 'new look' that followed the death of Stalin, there were fears that his fall might mark a return to former attitudes. Supporters of the London and Paris Agreements hoped that these events might encourage the French and German Parliaments to ratify the treaties.

Tuesday, February 15th

I had Sydney Jacobson and George Wigg to dinner last Thursday and learnt from Sydney that James Callaghan had been asked to do the political column in the new women's *Sunday Mirror*.[1] This paper has been bothering the *Sunday Pic* for weeks, since Colin Valdar[2] has been terrified of its competition and has been making us even scattier than ever. When I met James he was enormously pleased, since this has removed his financial worries. What a difference journalism makes to the outlook of a politician!

On Friday I gave a talk at the Oxford Labour Club and afterwards I went in to see Tommy and Pen Balogh, just back from Australia and terribly depressed because Nye Bevan had made it clear that he couldn't bother to see them on his farm in the country. He certainly treats his friends pretty roughly. Last night I was discussing with Harold Wilson what to do to stir Nye out of his lethargy. Then I went into the Smoking Room and found him sitting there with Michael Foot. 'We've got to do some important business at lunch tomorrow,' he said. 'We've got to go into action. What do you think of this?' He handed me a draft resolution to be tabled in the Commons and a draft article for *Tribune*, all on the subject of high-level talks and German rearmament. They are quite sensible, apart from the fact that, having waited a week, he is going to table them just when the defence White Paper comes out and, if the Party starts quarrelling about Germany, we shall subtract attention from defence, where we really have a chance of moving a vote of censure on the Tories.

The other big event was the news which broke last Tuesday – that

---

[1] The *Women's Mirror* began as a Sunday paper and changed to a Friday paper on June 27th, 1958. In 1960 it was amalgamated with *Woman* magazine and published on a Thursday. James Callaghan wrote a column called 'The Intelligent Woman's Guide to World Affairs'.

[2] A freelance journalist 1936–9 and, successively, Production Editor, Features Editor and Assistant Editor of the *Sunday Pictorial* 1942–6, Features Editor of the *Daily Express* 1946–51, Assistant Editor of the *Daily Express* 1951–3, Editor of the *Sunday Pictorial* 1953–9, Editor of the *Daily Sketch* 1959–62, Director of *Sunday Pictorial* Newspapers Ltd 1957–9 and Director of *Daily Sketch* and *Daily Graphic* Ltd 1959–62. In 1964 he became Consultant Editor and Chairman of the Bouverie Publishing Co.

Malenkov had resigned. Sydney Jacobson gave me the news flash and we made a quick decision that the interpretation of this was that the Russians had scrapped the soft policy for the hard policy, as they did when Litvinov went in 1938. We agreed that Nye should do the big article and I rang him up to tell him the news, which caused him consternation. However, he turned out in two hours the best article he has ever done giving this interpretation. It was well written, though it would have been better if he had referred to the Russians' internal crisis on agriculture, etc.,[1] and not committed himself 100 per cent on hard versus soft. But by and large I am sure he is right and all the news since has confirmed that the immediate significance of this change is the 100 per cent backing which Russia is now giving to China. Now America must know that she cannot reckon on Russia staying out if she gets into war with China about Quemoy. This means, of course, that the chances of war are somewhat increased. Somehow I think the Americans will climb out but it's an extremely tricky situation.

On February 10th Bevan tried, unsuccessfully, to persuade the Party Meeting to support a motion calling for Four-Power talks. He therefore tabled a resolution of his own on February 15th and more than 100 Labour Members signed it. The motion condemned the Government for refusing to take part in discussions with the Soviet Government.

But the issue of German rearmament was now being swallowed by a larger question — whether or not Britain should manufacture the hydrogen bomb. In the defence Statement, published on February 17th, the Government announced their decision to begin production of such a weapon. A fortnight earlier, Mr Attlee had told his Party that Britain required a thermo-nuclear weapon; the Bevanites now had to decide on their own attitude.

Tuesday, February 22nd
Last Tuesday, the 15th, we had an unusually interesting lunch. We discussed Nye's German resolution, which had been redrafted in the light of our criticisms and was really excellent, since it was a condemnation of the Government and only implicitly a reaffirmation of the demand for Four-Power talks, which had been defeated at the Party Meeting. It was agreed that the resolution should be shown to the Chief Whip and tabled that afternoon, obtaining as many signatures as possible. Towards the end of the meeting, I said that

---

[1] In 1954 great efforts had been made to increase agricultural production. There were campaigns to reclaim and plough vast tracts of virgin and waste land, to develop methods of stock breeding and to reorganize the management of collective farms. Though the grain harvest was slightly higher than that of 1953, the crop was nevertheless disappointing, in part because of severe drought in the Ukraine and the Volga regions. In January the Communist Party Central Committee declared targets for 1960 of 164 million tons of grain — two-thirds more than the current figure — of at least twice as much wheat, milk, wool, poultry and so on, and of some five times the 1953 figure of fodder for livestock. Further pressure was put behind the attempts to cultivate virgin and waste land and more than 400 State farms were to be established.

13

there was also the important problem of defence coming up and raised the issue of whether we should oppose British manufacture of the H-bomb. Nye was emphatic that we should not, on the grounds that the British people were not prepared to see themselves denied a modern weapon. Since this was not the *New Statesman* line, I held Nye and Michael afterwards and we had a long discussion on defence policy. Nye was quite good, saying that not the H-bomb but our strategy and foreign policy were the real issues and that anyway the H-bomb made nonsense of German rearmament.

By the evening I heard that 104 people had signed the resolution, thirty more than had voted for Nye in the Party Meeting.[1] All Wednesday the Parliamentary Party simmered with this news and now the Right were jumping mad, claiming that Nye had put down a resolution in defiance of a Party decision.

At the Party Meeting on Thursday evening I found an atmosphere of division, disunity, hatred and all uncharitableness which I have rarely known. Apparently, according to Harold Wilson, the Parliamentary Committee had realized that Nye had found a chink in Standing Orders, since the rules of privilege prevent the Party from forbidding a private Member to table a resolution, and it had instructed Attlee that on no account should a debate take place on this issue. But this didn't deter the anti-Communist crusaders and, though I was a quarter of an hour late, I arrived in time to hear Bessie Braddock fulminating that this was a Communist conspiracy and that the *Daily Worker* was terrorizing M.P.s by printing the names of those who had signed the resolution and instructing constituency parties to question those Members who hadn't.[2] Bessie concluded that, if this sort of thing has to go on, she would have to resign from the Party—a disaster which many of us could meet with equanimity.

George Brown demanded a special Party Meeting on Monday, Tuesday, Wednesday, Thursday morning and finally got it on Thursday evening, though no one quite knew what it would be about. As I was going out to the meeting Stoker Edwards[3] said I was a dirty Communist who had done nothing but dirty Communist propaganda in the *Pictorial*. I said he shouldn't talk like a shit, whereupon he called me a bastard and honours were even.

There is no doubt that Nye's manoeuvre has been extremely effective in exposing the Parliamentary Labour Party to renewed pressure from the constituencies on German rearmament. Moreover, it has brought into line people like John Strachey, Michael Stewart and Fred Lee,[4] who are not

[1] On February 10th.
[2] On February 17th the *Daily Worker* printed the names of the 104 Members who had signed the motion, with the question: Is Your M.P.'s Name Here? If Not, Ask Why Not.
[3] Walter James ('Stoker') Edwards. Formerly a stoker in the Royal Navy, he was Labour M.P. for the St George's division of Whitechapel 1942–50, and for Stepney 1950–64. He was Civil Lord of the Admiralty 1945–51.
[4] Frederick Lee, Labour M.P. for the Hulme division of Manchester 1945–50, and for the Newton division 1950–74. An engineer, he was a member of the National Committee

Bevanites but who must now either admit they were fooled into signing the resolution or find reasons from loyalty for supporting it. A great effort had been made before the Party Meeting to make people take their names off the Order Paper. Ivor Thomas[1] of the Wrekin solemnly announced that he had been tricked into signing in the Library without reading it and he expected many others were in the same plight. On the other hand, Fred Lee, who used to be a Keep Left Member and since then has become very respectable, met me in the Central Lobby and said, 'We've got to make sure we win next Thursday by getting all the 104 present.' I was so surprised that I said, 'Who's we?', and Fred said, 'If the T. & G. think they're going to dictate Parliamentary policy, it's time the A.E.U. told them to get out and that, if the Party is split, we'll be on the Left.' John Strachey, on the other hand, was by no means so cheerful, since he had discovered that Attlee was furious with him for having been the second signatory and the one thing he believes in is friendliness with Clem. However, I think I stiffened his resolution.

Wilfred Fienburgh, another middle-of-the-roader, had a different view. He had voted for Nye in the Party Meeting but not for the resolution, on the ground that it was flouting a Party decision. He agrees that, by persuading Attlee to turn down Nye's resolution in the Party Meeting, Morrison frustrated a genuine move for Party unity, but then he goes on to accuse Nye of being equally bad the other way round. I believe the real basic truth is that the whole storm is anyway due to the indecision which Attlee has suddenly begun to show. After all, he had last November[2] taken the line which Nye reaffirmed in the resolution and he had gone back on that line under pressure from Morrison and Gaitskell. All Attlee had to do was to hold his ground and he could have unified the Party on all foreign policy without any difficulty.

Meanwhile, however, a new subject of controversy has arisen as a result of the defence White Paper, published last Thursday, which reveals the decision to make the H-bomb. If Nye hadn't talked as he did on Tuesday, I think I would probably have come down in favour of opposing this decision but I was extremely impressed by his argument that public opinion was not ripe for that. George and I spent the weekend drafting a formidable *New Statesman* Defence Supplement, which says that the choice now is a sharp one between advocating complete neutrality *à la* Nehru or accepting nuclear strategy. We point out that, under such a strategy, the whole idea of land forces in Europe, armed with nuclear weapons, and of German rearmament,

---

of the Amalgamated Engineering Union 1944–5 and was Minister of Power 1964–6, Secretary of State for the Colonies 1966–7, and Chancellor of the Duchy of Lancaster 1967–9. He became a life peer in 1974, taking the title Lord Lee of Newton.

[1] Labour M.P. for the Wrekin 1945–55. An engine cleaner for the Great Western Railway, he later worked in the N.U.R. Head Office from 1925 to 1945. He served as a Labour member of Battersea Borough Council from 1928 to 1945 (he was Chairman of the Housing Committee 1934–8), and was elected to Parliament in 1945. In 1955 he returned to the N.U.R. and later worked for British Railways.

[2] In the debate on the London and Paris Agreements on November 18th, 1954.

is completely insane.[1] On balance the second is a better Socialist policy for the time being.

Wandering around on Monday, it became fairly clear to me that Ian Mikardo, Geoffrey Bing and Barbara Castle were all appalled by this idea and felt that the Left should choose the manufacture of the H-bomb as their great issue for the next Party Conference. I suppose, if I am objective, I would concede that of all the issues this is the one on which one could maximize a left-wing vote, provided one was not awkward and didn't ask what the implications were. On the other hand, I had always been intellectually as well as emotionally opposed to German rearmament and the Paris Treaty, whereas in this case I felt that Nye was putting forward a responsible view. I certainly wouldn't be comfortable making this a great issue, since it really is a phoney and a deception, but I was only half surprised when today Nye and Jennie failed to turn up at the lunch, although this problem of Germany, the redrafted resolution on Formosa[2] and the issue of what is to be done on Thursday night's meeting all needed urgent discussion.

I had three hours last night with Barbara on this. It was an extremely good discussion but, the longer she talked, the clearer it became that her only real argument was that we must appeal to morality 'by refusing to enter the thermo-nuclear race'. She repeated this eight or nine times in the course of our talk but she was reluctant to admit that we'd been in the race for nine years and even more unwilling to explain how, by simply not manufacturing the bomb while remaining in NATO, protected by the American strategic air force, we should cut a very moral or edifying figure. Yet she is right that the left-wing of the Party will expect us to take this line and I am equally right in saying to her that Nye and I have never had a foreign and defence policy which satisfied the cravings of most of our Bevanite supporters in the country.

Wednesday, February 23rd
The National Executive this morning was all sweetness and light. The Formosa resolution came up early and I moved to substitute for the first sentence the first two sentences of Attlee's *Daily Herald* interview,[3] on the irrefutable ground that they made sense, whereas the draft didn't. No one really disguised that this was quite an important policy issue and, in Mr Attlee's presence and with Mr Attlee's vote, my motion was turned down.

---

[1] A 3½-page supplement, 'The Dilemma of the H-Bomb', appeared in the *New Statesman and Nation* on February 26th, 1955. The authors concluded that Britain's choice must be to accept the H-bomb as a fact, reshaping both her armoury and her policies to take into account the new weapon and making as certain as possible that its unlimited force was used for deterrent and not destructive purposes.

[2] At a meeting of the International Sub-Committee on February 15th, Mr Attlee had proposed a compromise resolution which 'merely asserted as a fact' that the Cairo declaration (of 1943), stating that Formosa should be returned to China, had been made and juxtaposing a resolution of the 1953 Margate Conference, which had proposed neutralization of the island and a plebiscite.

[3] See above, p. 382.

After the meeting, I went up to the *Statesman* and, not having heard from Nye, rang him up in the country. As I knew he would be, he was extremely embarrassed, knowing what was coming. So I told him briefly what was in the *N.S.* Supplement and said I would send him a copy. He spluttered a bit and said that this week all he was doing was to answer a question. (It's a regular feature in the *Tribune* that he should answer a reader's question.) His line would be that, since Britain cannot now be defended, American bombers should be removed from the country. 'But that evades the main issue,' I said. 'Oh, I know I'm not dealing with the main issue,' he replied. So what he is doing is hedging. The ironical thing is that, purely from my own personal point of view in the Party, it would do me a power of good if Nye were to come out against making the H-bomb, disagreeing with me, since I have a very powerful case and would then be seen to be independent of him. Moreover, he would do himself no good, since after all he was a member of the Labour Government which invited the American bombers here. However I'm going to have a real try with him tomorrow.

Despite what Barbara says, I doubt whether this will in fact, over the long run, be a great issue in the Party or in the country. Sydney Jacobson told me that, having devoted the whole of the Friday and Saturday front pages to the H-bomb (Saturday was an extremely toughly written argument in favour of Britain having one), the *Mirror* received a total of ten letters on this issue. Arthur Creech Jones,[1] with whom I lunched today, was probably right when he said, 'They're not interested because they always assumed we'd got it already and that, even if we hadn't, we were bound to make it in a world as crazy as this.' To run a campaign against an accomplished fact is difficult at the best of times.

We had a meeting of the defence group last night to consider motions. That too was interesting. No one opposed a British H-bomb and the difference was between Woodrow Wyatt's minority, urging a narrow motion attacking arms production, and John Strachey, urging a broad motion, emphasizing disarmament and the failure of the Government to adapt our forces to nuclear war, but mentioning arms production, civil defence, recruiting, etc. It was only too obvious that the ex-Labour Ministers would make a very poor showing in a vote of censure on the narrow issue, since they were all horribly on the defensive, though they had a very strong case. The group resolved by 12 votes to 4, with a good many abstentions, to support John Strachey's broad motion. I found, as usual, that Michael Stewart was thinking on the same lines as myself, in this case that the real issue was NATO policy, the whole subject of land forces in Germany, etc. Only Philip Noel-Baker was left defending the Government and urging that we must prepare for a major

---

[1] Labour M.P. for Shipley 1935–50 and for Wakefield 1954–64. He was Parliamentary Private Secretary to Ernest Bevin at the Ministry of Labour and National Service 1940–5, Parliamentary Under-Secretary of State at the Colonial Office 1945–6 and Secretary of State for the Colonies 1946–50. He died in 1964.

nuclear war and for a major conventional war in Europe at the same time. This is what pacifists finally come to in their old age!

The defence White Paper was to be debated on March 1st and 2nd. Total defence expenditure in 1955/56 was estimated at £1,537 million, excluding receipts from American aid. This was some £97 million less than in 1954/55. U.S. aid was estimated at £43 million, compared with £85 million in the previous year. The Opposition Amendment did not censure the Government for their decision to manufacture the H-bomb but merely regretted that the Government had made no adequate proposals for the reorganization of the Armed Services and had 'failed to explain the grave and admitted deficiencies in the weapons with which Her Majesty's forces are at present furnished'.

Monday, February 28th
Since I last wrote, I seem to have remained submerged in the defence problem. On Thursday morning we had the Party Meeting, at which a resolution, not unlike that submitted by John Strachey, was proposed by Attlee. By the time I got to the Meeting, walking through the most appalling sleet, Attlee and John Strachey had already spoken and George Wigg was in full swing, taking the line of our Supplement but breezing it up for the plebs. Then one or two pacifists moved a motion against the H-bomb and Attlee suddenly said, 'We'll take a decision on that,' and before there was any more debate it was defeated. I agree with Kenneth Robinson that about twenty people voted for it but the papers all said that it was only eight. I fancy the opposition is greater in the Parliamentary Party than the Executive imagines. Indeed, Kenneth Robinson told me today that he was organizing an abstention on the Labour Amendment, which would not be a disaster, since there is a vote on the substantive motion to follow and, as this is a vote of censure, the Party will have to vote unanimously against the Government.

It was an extraordinarily flat discussion, in which Attlee made an extremely good reply to the pacifists, with a surprising reference to Cyprus, which seemed to indicate that he read our Supplement.[1] Sure enough, he had, and after the meeting he ran along the passage, put his arm round George Wigg, congratulated him on it and said it was so well thought out. I think we have done quite a job of uniting the Party behind a vote of censure and there is no reason why the anti-H-bomb move should be very embarrassing, provided we don't snarl at each other too much.

In the evening we had another Party Meeting, this time on the Bevan resolution.[2] I have never heard a more cacophonous row. Attlee started off, very tart and severely schoolmasterly, and he was followed by a dim Railway

[1] The Supplement said that in military terms it was 'ludicrous' to spend nearly £40 million on constructing barracks, airfields and hospitals on Cyprus in the wake of withdrawal from Suez. The island was described as 'even more vulnerable than Suez to nuclear attack'.
[2] On Four-Power talks.

Whip called Sparks,[1] Bessie Braddock and Wally Edwards, who made straight McCarthyite speeches, all exclusively on the subject of the Communist campaign against German rearmament, which was terrorizing unfortunate M.P.s like themselves. Nye's speech was the best I have heard him make for two or three years at a Party Meeting. He clearly and conclusively showed that he had supported Attlee's policy[2] and that Morrison had forced Attlee to rat on us and thereby caused disunity. To prove his point, Nye said he gathered that, at the morning meeting, the Party had accepted a resolution from Fred Peart[3] in almost identical terms to his own, only leaving out the sentence on Germany. If he could be guaranteed that this would go down as an official motion with a debate, he would withdraw his own.

At this, there was a gasp of relief from everybody and a number of people went out, thinking there would be no vote. Wilf Fienburgh then got up and said that Nye's motion should be accepted. Even Jim Johnson, our Regional Whip, tried to do the same, but Attlee tartly refused to accept Nye's offer and forced a vote. It came out in figures as 133 to 72. This is the first occasion on which Nye has won a really major tactical victory. The vote is of no importance. What matters is that everybody at that meeting knew that Nye had tried to keep unity in the Party by a concession and that Attlee was being compelled by Morrison and Gaitskell to impose the censure.

However, to make matters a bit better, Attlee did after the vote get up and say that, with the bank rate going up,[4] a fine position on defence and unity on Formosa, the Party should fight the Tories. He added that this was not a vote of censure on the past but only an admonition for the future. To my astonishment, virtually none of this got into the press, which didn't announce another Labour split. Not even Massingham recorded a trace of this on Sunday — mainly, I suspect, because George Wigg was at Dudley!

In Coventry this weekend I found to my surprise that nobody seemed to object very much to my view, mainly because they seemed to feel that it makes no difference whether Britain has an H-bomb or not. At least, that was the point of view which Sid Stringer and George Hodgkinson expressed. Today I found in the *Manchester Guardian* a main editorial dealing with Wigg, myself and Attlee and the heading 'GOING ALONE', an astonishing

[1] Joseph Sparks, a railway clerk for the Great Western Region and from 1934 to 1945 President of the London District Council of the N.U.R. He was Labour M.P. for Acton 1945–59.

[2] Set out on November 18th, 1954.

[3] A schoolmaster, he was Labour M.P. for Workington from 1945 until 1976, when he was made a life peer. He was Parliamentary Private Secretary to the Minister of Agriculture in the post-war Labour Governments and from 1964 to 1968 served as Minister of Agriculture. He succeeded Crossman as Leader of the House of Commons and Lord President of the Council from 1968 to 1970; and served again as Minister of Agriculture from 1974 until his ennoblement in 1976, when he became Leader of the House of Lords, holding that office until May 1979. He is now Leader of the Opposition in the House of Lords.

[4] Bank rate had risen to 3·5 per cent on January 27th and to 4·5 per cent on February 24th.

headline considering we advised staying in NATO! We are accused of misleading Attlee into a kind of British Knowland policy[1] by wanting to make the H-bomb in order to be independent of America. I have no doubt that this is written to warn Mr Attlee that evil communications will corrupt good manners, as indeed they will.

The other item of political news is Butler's emergency measures to deal with inflation.[2] To my amazement, in this morning's *Herald*, Hugh Gaitskell has gone off the deep end, announcing an economic crisis caused by Conservative freedom and saying he doesn't see how the Government will get out of it. This is going out on a limb with a vengeance! If a serious economic crisis really is beginning, we shall gain no extra votes by having gloated over it at the start. If it isn't, Gaitskell's article will be filed for future reference and quoted *ad nauseam*. It's quite interesting to ask what induced him to take an action which one might have thought typical irresponsible Left. The answer, I suppose, is that he wants to break the Butskell[3] story and also to get rapidly into a Left position of having been all the time in favour of controls. In fact, Gaitskell is moving to the Left to save his position on economics, just as Attlee did on Formosa. The fact is that no one can foretell whether Butler's measures will shake the inflation out of the economy and enable him to have a comparatively soft Budget (their obvious intention) or whether they will be ineffective because the terms of trade continue to go against us. In the latter case there will certainly be no Election this year.

Thursday, March 3rd

Last Tuesday, the 1st, we had our usual lunch and Nye rather palpably got Tommy to talk about economics, though the defence debate was due to start that afternoon. Then, right at the end, he said he couldn't possibly vote for the Labour Party's vote of censure. Harold had gone and I was the only one present who was against Nye on this. However, we agreed to meet again yesterday for lunch, before going into the defence debate. There Churchill made his majestic oration about the H-bomb and then Shinwell, despite George's briefing, made an appalling speech, in which he began to suggest that the nuclear deterrent of NATO was something we shouldn't commit ourselves to.[4] (This recalled an incident at the Party Meeting on the 24th. Will Warbey had asked in particular whether we would only use nuclear weapons in retaliation against nuclear weapons. Shinwell had got up and

---

[1] William Knowland, Senator from California 1940–59, the uncompromisingly right-wing Leader of the Republicans in the Senate.

[2] The bank rate increase on February 24th was accompanied by a reimposition of restrictions on hire-purchase trading. The Exchange Equalization Account was authorized to use 'wider discretion' in markets abroad in 'transferable sterling'.

[3] The economic policies of the Chancellor and of Mr Gaitskell were thought to be sufficiently similar to earn the name 'Butskellism', a term invented by the *Economist* in February 1954.

[4] Emanuel Shinwell referred to what he believed to be a NATO decision that nuclear weapons might be used in retaliation even against an attack with 'conventional' arms.

clearly shown that he hadn't read the White Paper by saying nobody suggested we should use them except in retaliation. Then Attlee had given a very evasive answer.)

Shinwell drooled on and on. Then we had two speeches, one by George Pargiter,[1] a straight pacifist speech, and one by Maurice Edelman, saying that for moral reasons he couldn't support the H-bomb. After that the Speaker told me he couldn't have two Coventry M.P.s and I would get in next day.

I spent the evening with Nye, discussing his speech. We agreed that Churchill had given him a tremendous opening, since he proved that, if we wait another four years before we negotiate with the Russians, we shall be weakening our position.[2] At present, according to Churchill, America still has atomic ascendancy but in four years' time it won't. Nye also agreed that it would be impossible for him to vote with the pacifists against the H-bomb and that he would have to support the Labour vote of censure. He popped off with Jennie and, as I expected, when he got back to lunch on Wednesday she had changed his mind again. Only Barbara and Michael were there, Michael trying to be a bridge but obviously willing to vote whichever way Nye went, and Barbara, as I observed in this diary some time ago, fanatically scenting an issue for this year's Conference. I said Nye should attack Churchill and take over the vote of censure, centring it on the need for negotiation, and I argued that there was no reason why, if Nye did that, he should not vote for it. But he left fairly determined to lead a new split. In the House he was met by George Wigg, who showed him his opportunities to question the Government on this issue of nuclear deterrence and swung him back again. We went into the debate together and, as we entered the Chamber, Nye said to me, 'I'm still completely in two minds which I should do.'

In the event, Mr Bevan challenged the Leader of the Opposition on whether the Amendment associated the Labour Party with the statement that Great Britain would use thermo-nuclear weapons in repelling attack with conventional arms. Mr Attlee only replied that he was basing his views on the belief that effective deterrence was the best way of preventing another war.

Mr Bevan then spoke of his suspicion that the American Government was preventing the Prime Minister from having the negotiations with the Soviet Union that he in fact desired and which Sir Winston had accepted in principle on April 5th, 1954. Sir Winston's reply included the first public disclosure that his illness in 1953 had been a paralytic stroke and he explained that in recent months both the British and American Governments had agreed that, until France and Germany had ratified the London and Paris Agreements, there

[1] An engineer, he was Labour M.P. for Spelthorne 1945–50 and for Southall from 1950 until 1966, when he was made a life peer.
[2] The Prime Minister had stated his belief that for three or four years to come the free world would have an overwhelming superiority in hydrogen weapons, 'a breathing space'.

should be no negotiations with the Russians. Mr Bevan concluded his speech,
'If we cannot have a lead from them, let us give a lead ourselves.'

The debate started with an appalling exhibition. Selwyn Lloyd, as Minister of Supply, was replying to the accusations about aircraft production made by Woodrow the night before, and within half an hour he had turned the debate into a vote of censure on the Opposition, with Arthur Henderson, George Strauss and Shinwell bobbing up to defend themselves and ask for approbation for what they had done. This was all the worse since it followed a really very good speech by John Strachey, which had set exactly the right tone and had given Nye the perfect lead to follow. Nye did follow that lead and did a magnificent job exposing Churchill and demanding negotiations. But when he came to the point of questioning the Government on the nuclear deterrent, he put the question to Attlee and made it a point of principle that he couldn't vote with Attlee until Attlee had removed the ambiguity.

To do Nye justice, he did this after saying that he could see no difference, moral or legal, between the hydrogen bomb, the atom bomb or even saturation bombing. After he had finished I tried for a couple of hours, not very enthusiastically, and was told by the Speaker that I would be called next but asked if I would be brief, to leave room for Victor Yates.[1] Then Percy Daines was called and I discovered that the Whip had put him in to keep me out, which showed singularly little understanding of the Bevan–Crossman axis at this moment!

I dined with Barbara and Kenneth Robinson and the other anti-H-bombers, chewing the same old cud over again, and then went in to hear Attlee, who made an acidulated, almost deliberately insignificant speech, as though he was determined not to rally the Party. I was so disgusted that I went out into the Smoking Room, where I found Hugh Delargy, Stephen Swingler and Bob Stross. By a strange coincidence all of us, individually, had come to the decision that we would have to vote with Attlee, despite himself, and not abstain with Nye. For Hugh Delargy this was a very remarkable thing and I was also surprised to find how emphatic Stephen was. We sat there gloomily until the division was called and then found in the lobby A. J. Irvine. Another surprise was John Freeman, who had told me in the morning that he had to vote with Nye but who, I think, had been so disgusted by Nye's personal behaviour to me that he finally came into the lobby with us. So, besides Harold Wilson, John Freeman and myself, Nye has flaked off Stephen Swingler, Bob Stross, Hugh Delargy, A. J. Irvine and Leslie Hale. Quite an expensive loss![2]

[1] Labour M.P. for the Ladywood division of Birmingham from 1945 until his death in 1969.
[2] The Opposition Amendment was defeated by 303 votes to 196, with 57 Labour Members abstaining. The motion to approve the Government's Statement was carried by 353 votes to 303.

I went into the Smoking Room afterwards to find Nye in the usual corner, delighted with the abstention of fifty-seven. I was so depressed that I went out but was detained by Hugh Dalton at the door. I was just checking with him when Nye came across and asked me to go outside. 'I know you're depressed,' he said. 'But don't talk to these dangerous people when you're depressed. Nothing has changed.' 'That depends on you,' I said. 'As things are, something has changed.' 'No, nothing has changed,' he said, 'it will all be as before.' But, looking at this morning's papers, it is only too clear that all is not as before. Labour's vote of censure has collapsed into Labour's split, though only the *Daily Herald* has the names of some Bevanites who voted with Attlee. But that story will dribble through by Sunday, since of course Hugh Massingham was on to it straight away.

Since then I've had the odious experience of being commiserated with by Honour Balfour[1] and Woodrow as though one had done something very courageous, when in fact, as I tried to explain to them, I had no choice in the matter. What is depressing is when you are bound to do something and Nye is bound to do something but doesn't do it. If only Barbara, Kenneth, Tom Driberg and the rest of them had realized that their duty was to register their conscientious abstention, and if only they had advised Nye to go into the lobby with me and Stephen [Swingler] and the rest of us, who are not sentimentalists and have no background justifying this action! George Wigg rang me up and characteristically said that the issue was whether we should resign from politics altogether. I know what he means. The only man who was any good yesterday was Nye Bevan and he took a palpably dishonest decision, whereas the rest of the leadership were nigglers, knaves or cowards. And now we shall have the delicious situation in Coventry where Maurice is one of the fifty-seven and I am with Elaine Burton and the loyalists![2]

Tuesday, March 8th
Ever since that fatal Wednesday evening, Nye's action has hovered over us. I seem to have been talking about nothing else. Political crisis seems to mean chatting on the telephone and doing nothing. Sometimes the chat was optimistic, sometimes it was pessimistic. I suppose this is called the process of forming public opinion.

All through Thursday I was terribly gloomy and on Friday morning I woke

---

[1,2] A Liberal, who contested the Lancashire constituency of Darwen in a famous by-election in 1943 during the political truce of the war years. She stood again in 1945, but then left active politics to pursue a career in political broadcasting and journalism, working for *Picture Post* and later as Chief Editorial Assistant at the London bureau of *Time & Life*.

[2] On March 7th Crossman sent a letter to Edward Davies, his Constituency Secretary, explaining the reasons for his voting with the Labour leadership for their Amendment. Having 'written extremely frankly about the rift which has sundered Harold Wilson, John Freeman and myself from Nye during this debate' and not wishing this to get into the press, Crossman asked Ted Davies to destroy the letter after reading it to the constituency party executive. He kept a copy in his own file.

up to find that Bob Edwards[1] of the *Tribune* had attacked me and George, which made me absolutely furious. I sent off a letter to Mike and wrote a tough piece in the *Sunday Pic*. However, I then learnt that, thanks to George Wigg, Hugh Massingham had decided to devote his whole column to a description of Nye's duplicity to me and I begged him to tone it down, using the argument, which I didn't very much believe at the time, that Hugh would feel awkward if he was held responsible for getting Nye expelled. I remember thinking and saying to John Strachey on Thursday that at last the other side had got the perfect case for framing Nye, since here he had acted individually and completely alone and could be expelled without expelling anybody else. But nobody else seemed to take a very serious view at that time.

On Friday night Anne and I went to Michael and Jill's house for a couple of hours and chewed all this over time after time. Michael made it clear that Nye hadn't known of the decision to attack me in *Tribune* but he couldn't do much to defend Nye's action. Indeed, the more one looked at it, the more fantastic it appeared. Barbara Castle, for instance, rang me on Saturday to say how upset she was that Nye was in her lobby and how much better it would have been had he not embarrassed all those with moral scruples by joining them. I later learnt that she was intensely resentful of Nye's climbing on her and Tony Greenwood's bandwagon and taking it over! So the poor man has lost on the one side Harold Wilson, John Freeman, myself, Hugh Delargy and Stephen Swingler and has got no credit from the other.

We had Venice and Christopher Barry for the weekend and were just settling down for lunch on Saturday when Jennie rang to say how terribly sorry she was to hear about this dastardly attack on me in *Tribune.* I could scarcely believe my ears. Then Nye came on the phone to add his apologies. I'm afraid I said it was too late; I had written my answer in the *Sunday Pic* and I was afraid he wouldn't like it but there were limits to what I would stand.

Yesterday there was nothing but talk, talk, talk in the Commons lobbies. The general mood was created that there would be no action taken because the Parliamentary Committee didn't approve of it. However, George and I went to see Attlee at a quarter past two. Before we went, we saw Harold Wilson, who had just seen Attlee and told us that he had explained to him the danger that, if he let Nye be expelled, the Right would gun for him, etc.,

[1] Robert Edwards, a journalist, was Editor of *Tribune* 1951–4, Deputy Editor of the *Sunday Express* 1957–9, Managing Editor of the *Daily Express* 1959–61, Editor of the *Glasgow Evening Citizen* 1962–3, of the *Daily Express* 1963–5 and of the *Sunday People* 1966–72; he became Editor of the *Sunday Mirror* in 1972. His article in *Tribune*, March 4th, 1954, was headlined 'Dick Crossman's Bombshell'. Crossman's letter to Michael Foot deplored 'this kind of journalistic interchange without consultation', which 'called into question the continuance of our Tuesday lunches'. He enclosed a reply to the *Tribune* article, in the form of a letter describing his consultations with Bevan on the issue of H-bomb manufacture and Bevan's 'strongly expressed view that it would be quite wrong to oppose this'. Crossman's *Sunday Pictorial* column on March 6th had the title and theme 'Bevan — Again His Own Worst Enemy'.

etc. Harold said that Attlee had told him that he had regarded Nye as his successor but that in the last four years he had ruled himself out. Again according to Harold, Attlee had added, 'I can't see a successor. That's the trouble.'

So at a quarter past two George and I trooped in together. I suggested that this policy issue was of the first importance and that we should try to continue the debate on the nuclear deterrent and on the Army Estimates.[1] We then suggested that, on the Wednesday morning, the time for the great debate on Nye, Attlee should propose to take policy first and only deal with personalities afterwards and that he should demand that the Party should give him an immediate vote of confidence on his policy on the H-bomb.

All this seemed to liven up the little man quite a lot and he was really quite agreeable. We didn't, of course, discuss the Nye issue, except that I said that he really should have ended his speech not by raising the ludicrous issue of whether we were committed to the nuclear deterrent but by showing that, since we were committed to it, German rearmament was irrelevant. Attlee cordially agreed, to my surprise, and said, 'If he had done that it wouldn't have mattered a bit.' So, as often happens in politics, George and I went out rather lightheartedly, thinking we had been doing a good job of work, and we talked around the lobbies to John Strachey, Stephen Swingler and the rest of them.

By now everybody knew that there would be no expulsion. Stephen told me that he had been at a brains trust in Birmingham on Sunday with John Baird, Ted Castle, Jennie Lee and Julius Silverman.[2] Jennie had said that the H-bomb was irrelevant; what mattered was policy. Ted Castle had said that the H-bomb was all-important and should be banned. Julius Silverman had said, 'Don't be silly. If you ban the H-bomb you've got to ban all weapons.' John Baird had said you must not only ban all weapons but be neutral. And Stephen had said he was in favour of the H-bomb. So there you had five contradictory policies on a Bevanite platform. The audience had seemed somewhat bewildered but least interested of all in the 'Ban the H-bomb' line.

I myself found much the same thing when by some mischance last night I had to go through the sleet to Epsom, to find twenty-eight shivering Labour Party members waiting in a Co-op hall, bewildered — utterly bewildered — and disheartened by the latest row because they really couldn't understand who was standing for what and why anybody was on any side. I explained about the H-bomb and in particular about the deterrent, spelling it out for them rather brutally, and no one raised a whisper of objection. I'm afraid the real fact is that it is now the dispute itself and not the issues that people are worrying about.

[1] To be debated the next day. The Navy Estimates had been discussed on March 3rd and the Air Estimates debate followed on March 10th.

[2] Sydney Silverman's brother, and himself Labour M.P. for the Erdington division of Birmingham 1945–55, for the Aston division 1955–74, and again for the Erdington division since 1974. He is a barrister by profession.

When I got back from Epsom, George rang me up to say that the Parliamentary Committee had appeared to concede to Nye by tabling a resolution demanding immediate Four-Power talks but that their other decision had remained a close secret.[1] And sure enough, the eleven-o'clock news gave the impression that Nye had won. I smelt a rat and wasn't surprised when Harold rang me up to say they had decided on expulsion. Attlee had acted as chairman (in the afternoon, after he had seen George and me, he had told John Strachey that expulsion would be quite wrong) but had apparently spoken against and then not voted. Tommy was staying with me but, since Harold pledged me to secrecy, I couldn't tell him. The news was to be kept secret so that Nye should receive the letter first. It was then assumed he would tell the press.

This morning the telephone began to ring. I have decided not to speak this afternoon[2] for fear of having another left-wing argument in public, since now the only thing we've got to do is to try and rally the votes in the Parliamentary Party. I'm extremely gloomy about the prospects, even if we persuade Nye to continue to have his cold and stay away until after the weekend. This will be put by Clem to the Party Meeting as a vote of confidence – i.e. as a frank choice whether the Party wants him or Nye as Leader – and there is little doubt what the decision will be. We shall be fighting a losing battle at the Party Meeting and knowing it. We are all more or less discredited. I shall undoubtedly be accused by Michael and Ian of having caused Nye's expulsion by writing in the *Sunday Pic*. Indeed, life looks pretty bleak. What is so maddening is that for ten days I had been trying to persuade Nye merely to stand by what he agreed with me but not to do something which would get him expelled.

Tuesday, March 15th
At last week's Tuesday lunch Jennie was there, but not, of course, Nye, who was in bed. So much has happened since then that all I can remember is that the tremendous row that they were going to have with me about what I had written in the *Pic* about Nye and the letter I had written to Michael and everything else was wiped out by the decision the previous night to withdraw the whip. Now they were mainly concerned to get a clear understanding that we would all resign from the Executive if Nye were expelled, an undertaking which neither Harold nor I were for one moment prepared to give. Having got Nye into this terrible fix, Jennie and Michael, of course, assumed that I would help to get him out, which I would. The other great plan was to get a

---

[1] The Parliamentary Committee decided to table a censure motion, calling on the Government to take immediate steps to arrange a meeting of the Prime Minister with the American and Soviet Heads of Government, with a view to lessening world tension and promoting effective disarmament. The Shadow Cabinet's other decision, not announced until March 9th, was to recommend the P.L.P. to withdraw the whip from Mr Bevan, after his challenge to the Party leaders during the defence debate.

[2] In the debate on the Army Estimates.

round-robin of 130 M.P.s, so powerful that it would stop the expulsion. I advised that we should first try out if the M.P.s were ready. We met again that evening at seven o'clock—that is Jennie, Barbara, Michael and I—to compare experiences. There was no more talk of a round-robin, since it was only too clear that Nye really had blotted his copybook and that, apart from the stalwarts, it was by no means certain how many would vote for him.

On Thursday evening I had to give a dinner at Cecil King's request for him to meet the Elaths.[1] I didn't hear much of what was going on, since King and Elath were at the other end of the table, but I did have a talk with King about the Labour Party crisis, in which he expressed the utmost contempt for Attlee. This was important to me, since I had spent a great deal of Wednesday night discussing Labour politics with Hugh Cudlipp, who had compelled me to pick him up after the vote from a nightclub at Oswald Mosley's[2] house on the riverside in Chelsea. We sat up until two o'clock in the morning, after which we went back to Hugh's home for another drink. He told me that on Tuesday they had in print a leading article strongly advising the Labour Party against expelling Bevan and that, when the news broke, they had had to substitute another one, mildly approving of the expulsion. I kept on asking Hugh why he had to support official Labour against Bevan. I didn't ask him to support Bevan, but why on earth didn't he take what would be a popular view and blame both sides for ruining the Labour Party? I could say this with some effect since I reminded Hugh that, at our last meeting,[3] I had strongly advised him against doing his series of four articles by Labour leaders on a constructive policy for Labour, and had told him they'd be a dead flop. Actually they came out at the height of the Bevan crisis and excluded the paper from treating the news adequately. We had talked on and on and I didn't think I'd got very far but I was glad to find that King was violently anti-Attlee. This morning, Tuesday, sure enough, the *Mirror* has come up with an admirable centre page saying it's Attlee's crisis as well as Bevan's and putting the thing extremely fairly. So there was some point in talking to King and Cudlipp.

On Friday Barbara, Tony and I went off at cock-crow into the Chilterns to see Nye at his farm. We found him sitting up, wonderfully obstreperous, in bed. The interview didn't go too badly. As I expected, when Barbara said he

---

[1] A member of the Political Department of the Jewish Agency for Palestine in Jerusalem from 1934 to 1945, Eliahu Elath was Director of the Political Office of that body in Washington from 1945 to 1948. He was Israeli Ambassador to the U.S.A. 1948–50, and then the Israeli Minister (1950–2) and Ambassador to the U.K. 1952–9. Zehava Zavel married Eliahu Elath in 1931.

[2] M.P. for Harrow (Unionist 1918–22, Independent 1922–4 and Labour 1924) and Labour M.P. for Smethwick 1924–31. He succeeded to his father's baronetcy in 1928. Chancellor of the Duchy of Lancaster 1929–30, he left the Labour Party in 1931 to form the New Party (with, among others, John Strachey). This led to the foundation of the British Union of Fascists in 1932. Some account of his life appears in his autobiography *My Life* (London: Nelson, 1968).

[3] See above, p. 377.

ought to apologize to Attlee in a statement over the weekend, Nye shouted, like a petulant child, 'I won't! I won't!' So I said, 'It's no good asking you to act out of character, Nye, but in that case you mustn't ask Harold Wilson to act out of character. Or me. If each of us is to express his individuality to the full, that's O.K.' If you say that often enough to Nye, it sort of brings him into some order and he did in fact make a fairly good statement over the weekend, saying he had no personal differences with Attlee.

On the other hand, directly we arrived Nye had insisted that all six of us should announce we were going to resign from the Executive if he were expelled. I was able to reply that this was something each of us would make up his own mind about, just as he would make up his own mind what he would do. Anyway, I said, it was futile to announce this beforehand, since we would be calling our own bluff. To my great surprise, when I asked Nye what our strategy should be, he then said we must try to prevent him from being expelled. I said that in that case everything we said and did between now and the Executive meeting, including his speech to the Party Meeting, must be designed to that end and not be written by suicide maniacs. Tony Greenwood, after vaguely backing Barbara on apologizing, remained silent and we drove back to London.

I spent the weekend, by good fortune, in East Anglia, where I addressed the annual dinners of Bury St Edmunds and Harwich Labour parties and had a regional conference at Witham, in Tom Driberg's constituency. At two of the meetings Wilfred Young, the East Anglian Organizer, was in attendance to keep a good look on me. I tried in all cases to give them a fairly objective picture of how the policy differences had arisen after the death of Ernie Bevin and Cripps and the completion of Labour's mission in 1948. I also dealt with the H-bomb, which was obviously worrying them. At Harwich the candidate is Shirley Catlin,[1] the daughter of George Catlin[2] and Vera

[1] Shirley Williams, the daughter of Professor Sir George Catlin and Vera Brittain. In July 1955 she married Professor Bernard Williams; the marriage was dissolved in 1974. She was General Secretary of the Fabian Society from 1960 until 1964, when she was returned as Labour M.P. for Hitchin. From 1974 to 1979 she was Labour M.P. for Hertford and Stevenage. She served as Parliamentary Private Secretary to the Minister of Health 1964–6, Parliamentary Secretary at the Ministry of Labour 1966–7, Minister of State at the Department of Education and Science 1967–9 and at the Home Office 1969–70, and was Opposition spokesman on Social Services from 1970 to 1971, and on Home Affairs 1971–4. On the Labour Party's return to power in 1974 she became Secretary of State for Prices and Consumer Protection, adding to these responsibilities for a short time the post of Paymaster-General in 1976. From April 1976 to May 1979 she was Secretary of State for Education and Science.

[2] Concerned with Atlantic Community policy since 1925, George Catlin was a Professor of Politics at Cornell University 1924–35. This post heralded a distinguished academic career in several institutions, including Yale, Calcutta, McGill and Washington Universities. He stood as a Labour candidate at both the 1931 and 1935 General Elections and was for a time a member of the executive committee of the Fabian Society. In 1925 he married Vera Brittain, the writer. His many publications include *The Atlantic Community* (London: Coram, 1959) and an autobiography, *For God's Sake, Go* (London: Coram Smythe, 1972). He was knighted in 1970 and died in 1979.

Brittain,[1] a wonderful girl, whom I got to know at Oxford. She is also an eager Catholic convert and was introducing on this occasion her fiancé, whom I found to be my successor as Philosophy Tutor at New College.[2] So we had a gorgeous evening of old-fashioned Socialism.

But even in these two constituencies there was nobody in favour of expelling Nye, and everybody was completely bewildered as to what was going on at Westminster. Most of them just wanted the Party to get together and be decently led. Altogether the weekend gave me the impression from this region that the Labour Party would just be knocked groggy by the expulsion. At the Conference it wouldn't, as I imagined, be so much a matter of internecine in-fighting, as of just sheer, disheartening collapse by a rank and file horrified and appalled by what is going on in the stratosphere far above it.

Altogether this last fortnight has been one of the most interesting I've ever had in politics and also the most battering. Looking back now, one can see only too clearly that Nye's action was one of the most insane any man could conceivably have committed. He did himself no good whatsoever, he caused a completely confused split in the Labour Party and, if they hadn't threatened to withdraw the whip, he might have become a Maxton.[3]

I had two little interesting talks in the course of yesterday afternoon. First of all, Leslie Hunter detained me in the lobby to tell me that some people had quite the wrong idea about the attitude of certain members of the Shadow Cabinet. I said — I now see rather stupidly — that I thought we had a good chance of preventing expulsion at the N.E.C. Hunter agreed but went on emphasizing that the members of the Shadow Cabinet were not anxious for expulsion and everything would depend on what Nye said on Wednesday. Then, at dinner, Arthur Moyle came across and I put him the question, 'What will happen after Wednesday?' He replied, 'That will entirely depend on Nye's speech.' Arthur Moyle is the appallingly stupid P.P.S. of Attlee, but is also no fool and an old trade union negotiator. I regarded these as very strong and important tips.

However, when I went up to the *Statesman* this morning to write their

[1] A writer, she lectured widely in Europe, America, and the Commonwealth. Her books include *Testament of Youth* (London: Gollancz, 1933; and in a new edition, with an introduction by her daughter, London: Virago, 1979), *Testament of Friendship* (London: Macmillan, 1940), *On Becoming a Writer* (London: Hutchinson, 1947) and *Radclyffe Hall: A Case of Obscenity?* (London: Femina Press, 1968). She died in 1974.

[2] Bernard Williams, Knightsbridge Professor of Philosophy and Fellow of King's College, Cambridge, 1967–79, and Provost of that College since 1979. A Fellow of All Souls' College, Oxford, 1951–4 and of New College, Oxford, 1954–9, he was a lecturer in Philosophy at University College, London, 1959–64 and Professor of Philosophy at Bedford College, London, 1964–7. His publications include *Problems of Imagination and the Self* (Cambridge University Press, 1966), *Morality* (Cambridge University Press, 1971) and *Descartes* (London: Allen Lane, 1978).

[3] James Maxton (1885–1946). A former teacher, he was Independent Labour M.P. for the Bridgeton division of Glasgow from 1922 until his death. He was Chairman of the I.L.P. 1926–31 and 1934–9. A former editor of *Forward* and a much respected but isolated representative of his Party in the House of Commons, he published *Lenin* (London: Nelson, 1932) and *If I Were Dictator* (London: Methuen, 1935).

leader after the verdict of Guilty,[1] I was rung up by George with some interesting news. He had been told by Sydney Elliott that yesterday Attlee had had a long talk with Leslie Hunter. Leslie is the Lobby Correspondent of the *Herald* and the husband of Margaret Stewart,[2] a bosom friend of Herbert Morrison, and on normal occasions they provide Morrison's chief leaks. Leslie said to Elliott that Attlee had been very disturbed at the way affairs were developing and that, if Nye made an adequate apology on Wednesday, he would immediately move the adjournment of the meeting. Apparently Attlee had also said that he had come to the decision that 50 per cent of the Movement was irrevocably opposed to German rearmament and he was trying to reach an agreed policy.

I now have the job of trying to persuade Nye that there is this chance and to do it apart from the lunch, which is taking place in half an hour! It's just a chance.

Wednesday, March 16th

Yesterday's lunch was most unpleasant. From the start it was clear that Barbara and I were the only two people in the room who really felt it necessary that Nye should at least in some degree admit that he had messed things up in the debate. The lunch took place against the background of the meeting which Barbara, Tony and I had with Nye at the farm last Friday. On Tuesday it was clear that, as usual, Michael, Jennie and Curly Mallalieu were already working on the assumption that expulsion was inevitable and that therefore the great thing to do was to fight back and not to grovel.

Nye said his main point would be that the Party would be hopeless as long as it tried to decide its policy in a secret parliamentary meeting. I said that, if Nye started that way, he'd lose in the first minute. He then went on to outline a most powerful speech, proving himself wholly right on everything and receiving plenty of approving suggestions along this line, till I got furious and said, 'You're being advised by suicide maniacs. The basic thing to realize is that you were wrong last week and everybody knows you were wrong except the people in this room.' To this he replied that he couldn't come and have lunch here if he was treated in this way and, a little later, he added that he thought I was too much affected by personal considerations, to which I asked whether he wasn't affected by them too. It was a most horrible lunch and it didn't make it any better to hear from John Freeman today that both Barbara and Tom Driberg had told him how magnificently I had behaved! Barbara helped me a little, Tom not at all and, as for Harold Wilson, who had carefully arranged to be in Paris during today's Party Meeting, he seemed so blithely to accept the removal of Mr Bevan that I could hardly stand him.

---

[1] 'The Trial of Aneurin Bevan', *New Statesman and Nation*, March 19th, 1955.
[2] She was the Industrial Correspondent of the *News Chronicle* at the time. Subsequently she worked for *The Economist* and the *Observer* and later for various trade union journals.

Later I went into the Smoking Room and found the group in their usual corner. I gave Nye a drink and was given one back and I went on hammering away at three things. First, that he must at least admit that he was not right about the H-bomb (this was George's idea) and say the whole Party was in a bit of a confusion and so was he. Second, he should say that he wasn't going to exploit it emotionally or form a third party. And, third, he should refrain from attacking Gaitskell. However, when I went to bed I felt absolutely hopeless and this morning, when George picked me up to go round to the meeting, I felt no better.

When George and I arrived, we found quite a crowd of photographers and so on. One thing Nye has done is to make the British public interested in politics again. When I got to Room 14, a quarter of an hour early, I just managed to get a seat.

The meeting started with Attlee prosecuting quietly and I thought very effectively because he simply described a series of challenges to his leadership on the floor of the Chamber, which were terribly embarrassing, and then widened out to say that for three years the Party had been a terrible mess and Nye had been chronically disloyal. Nye didn't want to speak then but was made to do so. He looked rather stumpy standing there, and, obviously terribly nervous and chesty, he started straight off with an attack on the left-wing conspirators and with sympathy for poor Clem Attlee in his position. I was appalled but I think it worked because Nye got all his horrible stuff over to begin with and kept his more pleasant stuff for the end, which he doesn't usually do. He managed to build up a picture that he wasn't being judged strictly on his behaviour in Parliament but framed by men who had been determined to get him for years.

When he got to the actual incident, thank God he roughly took our advice and actually did get the sentence out, 'I don't claim that I was right,' as well as saying that we were all in terrible confusion. Then he made a passionate assurance that he would never exploit the H-bomb emotionally in a campaign in the country and he would never make a third party, because he was a member of the Labour Party and would remain so all his life, whatever was done to him.

Afterwards, in the Smoking Room, he told me it was the most difficult speech he had ever had to make. I think, looking at it now, it was probably a tremendous achievement. Curiously enough, it gave me and several other people I have talked to the same impression—that Nye has given up or, rather, that most of him has given up hope of leadership. One of his most effective points was when he said that, if he had been trying to capture the leadership, he'd have been completely daft in doing what he'd done in the last twelve months. He knew how to become a leader. It was the way they did it on the platform, intriguing in committees and behind closed doors. Again, towards the end, he claimed the right to be a rebel, the right to be a Socialist rebel in the Party, in a way which made one feel that it was true that he just wanted to rebel, whereas other people really were intriguing against Attlee for the leadership.

Nye was followed by Fred Lee, an A.E.U. member, who moved his amendment. This started with a vote of confidence in Attlee, went on to censure Nye and then appealed to the Party to get together to defeat the Tories. Attlee ruled it out of order on the ground that it contained two ideas — first, confidence in him and, second, censuring of Nye; and that, if people voted against it, they would be voting against the vote of confidence in him. Silverman then very smartly asked whether the official resolution didn't contain two ideas — censure of Nye and a vote of confidence in the Parliamentary Committee. Had it not been stated in the press that the committee would resign if the resolution were not carried? Attlee hedged and said they might have to consider doing so.

Lee then deleted the part praising Attlee and started by saying that he doubted whether anybody there would fail to agree that Nye had behaved outrageously. To this there was no dissent whatsoever. Lee went on to discuss the effect in the Movement and to speak for the A.E.U. against the big general unions. Maurice Edelman followed him, jumping in to establish kudos and getting a good deal in Coventry but not much in the Party. After that we had a terrible speech from A. J. Irvine on parliamentary democracy. I like A. J. but he is distrusted as an ex-Liberal, ex-President-of-the-Union lawyer and when he started a sentence, 'It is my most passionate political conviction ... ', the end was lost in a gust of uproarious laughter. It's a cruel Party.

Next Tom Fraser,[1] a Scottish-miner, junior-Minister type, delivered what was obviously the routine right-wing attack on Nye, dragging up health charges and God knows what to prove his disloyalty. Nye punctured him completely by asking why, in that case, Tom had so often asked him to speak in his constituency. Tom replied that it was at the request of the constituency party and there was another gust of laughter. Then we heard the famous George Brown, who had been explicitly accused by Nye of intriguing against Attlee in 1947. Rather courageously, Brown didn't deny this but seemed to suggest that backstairs intrigue was more loyal than voting against the majority. He made it quite clear that he was gunning not only for Nye, but for all his associates, the left-wing conspiracy. By now it was clear that the Party had got the impression that there was a right-wing conspiracy and that all the loyalty to Attlee on the Right was synthetic.

Finally, Tom Proctor, who by making such a fool of himself saved the

[1] Thomas Fraser, a miner from 1925 to 1943 and a Miners' Union branch official and Secretary of Lanark Constituency Labour Party 1938–43. He was Labour M.P. for Hamilton 1943–67 and served as Joint Parliamentary Under-Secretary of State at the Scottish Office 1945–51 and Minister of Transport 1964–5. He was a member of the Highlands and Islands Development Board 1967–70, Chairman of the North of Scotland Hydro-electric Board 1967–73, and became Chairman of the Scottish Local Government Staff Commission in 1973.

situation during the meeting after Nye resigned,[1] almost did it again by retailing some futile story about what Nye had said to him in the lobby about his constituency. When challenged, Tom said, 'I always give them a full précis of the Party Meeting,' and this, in view of the accusation about leaks, again produced hilarious laughter. But most of the meeting seemed to consist of memories of what somebody had said to somebody else on the Left, including, of course, Bessie Braddock. Then came what always happens, the unknown speech. Percy Collick,[2] a railway clerk crippled with arthritis, was called, and made a very simple, straightforward speech about Party unity. Nobody knew which side he was coming down on until he said that, when he looked at it conscientiously, he couldn't see how anybody could vote for withdrawal of the whip without making electoral disaster certain.

Attlee wound up in a very short speech, merely repeating the demand to withdraw the whip. Then, just before the vote, Elaine [Burton] leapt to her feet and said she must know something. As comrades had read in the press, she had been approached yesterday from Coventry and was in difficulty because she couldn't give the assurance given by her two Coventry colleagues. Could she be told whether this was a vote of confidence in Attlee? Otherwise she would have no answer. Characteristically, Attlee said, 'Well, if it's necessary, yes.' The vote was taken. For the Lee amendment there were 124 and, against, 138. For withdrawal of the whip 141, against, 112. It was an infinitely better result than I had anticipated but I couldn't discuss it because John and I had to rush up to the *Statesman*.

At half-past three I went back to the House to find the lobbies humming and the Chamber empty, as usual. John Strachey found the result excellent but the Right were looking terribly depressed and disappointed, since they had calculated on a majority of at least 70 for sure. Once again the Whips had let them down. Some people were saying that the Right would be so infuriated by this that they would now go berserk and that it was certain the N.E.C. would now expel. I can see no grounds for jumping to this conclusion and I got Barbara to agree that we now had a strong position on the Executive, provided Harold and Tony would play. We can now say that, since the Parliamentary Party pretty clearly indicated by its vote that it wanted to censure and not to expel Nye, the Executive are perfectly free to keep him on ice and thereby to control *Tribune* for as long as they like. We should point out that we really do want to work together but that if, in these circumstances, Nye were expelled, we should have to make our protest, since it would be a proof that the Right wanted not unity but the liquidation of the Left.

[1] See above, p. 165.

[2] Organizing Secretary of ASLEF from 1934 to 1940 and its Assistant General Secretary 1940–57, he was Labour M.P. for West Birkenhead 1945–50 and for Birkenhead 1950–64. A member of the General Purposes Committee of the T.U.C. 1930–4, he served on the Labour Party N.E.C. in 1944 and was Joint Parliamentary Secretary at the Ministry of Agriculture 1945–7.

I said all this to Nye, adding that in the circumstances, though not a word would be said beforehand, I thought we might all agree not to threaten the Executive with an ultimatum but, at the right moment, to make our position clear. I then rang Michael and did my best with him, explaining this and telling him not to write anything which would make it impossible. Michael was very evasive on the phone, naturally enough, because he and Jennie and Curly think of me as nearly as treasonable as Harold and have said a good deal about this, as I learnt from John Freeman in the House. This is terribly silly of them, since if Nye's closest friends say that other close friends are traitors, it merely convinces people that he is weaker.

However, after this I suddenly decided to go and see Attlee. I put it to him that he should make this proposal at the Executive and that, if he did, it would almost certainly be carried. He non-committally committed himself to approval, put his feet up and leant back in his chair and said, 'Nye had the leadership on a plate. I always wanted him to have it. But you know, he wants to be two things simultaneously, a rebel and an official leader, and you can't be both.' I said I thought Nye's speech indicated that he wanted the leadership a good deal less. Attlee grinned and seemed in extraordinary good humour, considering the fact that he had put the matter as an issue of personal confidence in himself and had very nearly been defeated. I felt very much that he believed me but I took care to emphasize that I was not delivering an ultimatum but merely asking him to think this over and do something about it. In the lobby I met Tom O'Brien, who had written a very amusing letter to *The Times*, really on Nye's side. He told me he had started work on the trade union leaders to try and get them to be sensible.

Altogether this has been a better day than we've had for three weeks, which isn't saying much. These three weeks have convinced me, if I needed convincing, that Nye never will be nor should be a Leader of the Party. Somehow he has got to be eased into a situation where he can blow off without too much harm and the rest of us must try to form a left-wing, as distinct from a Left explosive noise. If the Executive does the right thing, this possibility will have been created.

Monday, March 21st
When I looked at the papers on Thursday morning, I found to my surprise that the splash *Herald* story was a very carefully phrased report that I would lead the opposition on the Executive to Bevan's expulsion. After a glance at the article, I was convinced that George Wigg had given this to the *Herald*, although I remembered that, just before I saw Clem, I had met Leslie Hunter in the lobby. Since Hunter had been our intermediary on the Tuesday, I talked to him quite freely and told him that the vote in the Parliamentary Party now left a good chance for the Executive to decide not to expel and that, if that chance were not taken, our position might well become impossible. Of course, normally Mr Hunter of the *Herald* wouldn't dream of paying any

attention to me because I work on the *Mirror* and it was therefore clear that somebody had put the *Herald* up to it. However, George rang me up, assuming that I had put it in and it was only somewhat later that we got a little information that suggested that Leslie Hunter may have talked to Hugh Gaitskell and Attlee and found them not unfavourable to flying this kite. However, politics being politics, it put me in a slightly embarrassing position with Barbara, Tony Greenwood, etc., none of whom like being told that I am leading them into anything.

I spent most of the morning trying to square Barbara and Tony. Barbara was very anxious to put out a statement to make her position clear and Tony was very anxious not to commit himself. Later that day Harold Wilson rang me up, having returned from Paris, where he had gone coincidentally for one day while the trial of Aneurin Bevan was being staged. Harold seemed self-confident as ever but I did warn him that his absence had not done him any good. Over the weekend he put out a very good statement. Meanwhile, this interminable crisis, with telephoning, talking and nothing doing, has gone on and on.

However, on Saturday morning something new turned up, when the *Daily Express* ran a story that Churchill is due to resign before Easter and that the Election will then take place in June. The newspapers yesterday and today all seemed to have taken this for truth. No doubt Tory papers like the *Telegraph* are this time extremely anxious to try to make what may be a rumour into truth, so as to persuade Sir Winston to resign. I was chiefly interested to know what effect the Bevan crisis would have on the date of the Election. Certainly it will make it easier for those who want to compromise on Wednesday to urge their case in view of an imminent Election, but it is also true that, if we have an Election in June before the Party has time to disintegrate, we could fight with Bevan expelled, with certain advantages. On the one hand, the Tories would not be able to talk about our being split; but on the other hand most people would work hard when faced with a snap Election. If the Tories were wise, therefore, they would let us spin this thing out till October. They, on the other hand, have their own worries. This morning it was announced that Australia has imposed import controls, which will make our adverse balance of trade even worse, and it's possible that a whole summer of electioneering would make sterling unstable. My bet, therefore, is that the Election will take place in June; that, because Attlee doesn't intervene emphatically enough, Nye will be expelled by a small majority on Wednesday and that despite this the Party will go into the Election in relatively good heart.

During the weekend I suggested that George Hodgkinson should bring over Ted McGarry and Ted Davies, my Constituency Chairman and Secretary, for a talk about the situation. I mainly wanted to discuss whether I should resign from the Executive and to my surprise I found them very averse to this, on the ground that resigning is bad anyway. They fully agreed with my suggestion that we should stay on the Executive and fight, immediately releasing a statement after the meeting on Wednesday if Nye is expelled. They mainly wanted to talk to me about Elaine Burton, since the borough party has called a special meeting to protest that they have no confidence in M.P.s who voted for Nye's expulsion. They talked very fiercely about an A.E.U. candidate being put up against her at the next election, but I warned them that if they tried to do this on the ground of her vote against Nye they would come unstuck.

It was a lovely weekend at Prescote and we discovered that since Sunday afternoon the new manager, Mr Pritchett, had managed to prepare the ground and sow seventy-five acres.[1] These were looking magnificent and this has put Prescote ahead of every other farm in Warwickshire this season. Of course, if the weather gets bad again it will mean ruination, but Anne's father was happier than he's been for ten years as we walked round the farm together, seeing it miraculously recover as a result of the new dispensation.

Thursday, March 24th

The Tuesday lunch started with a long discussion of Geoffrey Bing's opinion, which he had drafted on the privilege issue involved in Nye's expulsion. I don't blame Nye for giving enormous importance to his view that expulsion, which would automatically mean his losing his grant from the Mineworkers,[2] would put the Mineworkers' Union and, collaterally, the N.E.C. in breach of [parliamentary] privilege. However, it was agreed at the lunch that it would be fatal if this facet of the affair became public knowledge before the Executive met or should be regarded as Nye's main line of defence. It was therefore agreed that he should go secretly to Attlee and merely tell him that, since the Tories would raise it anyway, he was bound to raise it on Wednesday afternoon if expulsion took place.

At the lunch Nye said, 'But what about the Executive? Will you all threaten to resign if I am expelled?' After two or three minutes he remarked, 'Well, I've said my say and will not say another word,' it being fairly clear that Tom and Ian, who was in Karachi, would threaten to resign, that Harold Wilson and Tony Greenwood would not and that Barbara and I were doubtful. Barbara made an excellent speech, saying why we should not threaten to resign, and added, two minutes later, that she would have to do so. I said that I refused to commit myself and that anyway the best thing might be to stay on and continue one's protest until one was thrown off. Nye made a series of further long speeches, ending with the usual remark that I was in fundamental disagreement with him. It's curious that he always feels that this is a way of settling an argument.

[1] For a description of Dennis Pritchett, Crossman's farm manager, see *The Diaries of a Cabinet Minister*, especially vol. III, p. 45.

[2] A number of Members were sponsored by a trade union. Bevan received a small grant from the N.U.M.

When I went into the House, I found a message that Attlee wanted to see me at six o'clock. I went in to find him changing, before taking the chair at an English-Speaking Union meeting. He sat on the sofa, pulling off one of his socks and looking up expectantly. I observed that he had asked me to see him. He looked surprised and then said, 'Oh yes, it was about the draft N.E.C. statement on the H-bomb. But I think it's too late. It's gone to Transport House.' However, while he changed into a stiff shirt, I stayed on and chatted. He was in extraordinarily cocky humour. I asked whether Nye had seen him about this privilege matter and he said yes. He agreed that Nye had not made it an ultimatum and that it was very serious indeed, since it was a *prima facie* case. 'I shall have to inform the Executive,' he added. 'Strange. You and I can get expelled at any time, Dick. It's only these trade union fellows who can't!' Once again he was non-committal on the line he was going to take but he was so friendly that I felt fairly confident.

That night, thanks to a one-minute telephone conversation I had that morning, Hugh Gaitskell came secretly to a drink at Vincent Square. I had done this on George's advice, to see what chances there were of weaning Hugh from his lunatic advisers. What the interview told me was that there are none. Hugh is just as infatuated, if not more so, than Nye. I started by saying that I thought, from Hugh's point of view, withdrawal of the whip was a grave mistake, since Nye had damaged himself much more in the defence debate than he had damaged the Right. There was now a Left Centre emerging which was not merely Nye's stooge. I said that, from Nye's point of view, it might be better to be expelled but, surely, from the Party's point of view, there was now everything to be said for keeping him on good behaviour.

To this Hugh replied that it was too late for all such compromise. If my policy were carried at the Executive, it would utterly destroy the morale of the Right or, as he preferred to call them, the loyalists in the Party, who had been going through hell in their constituencies owing to the unfortunate accident of boundary changes and redistribution.[1] He also said we must consider money and that many of our big backers were asking why we hadn't acted three years ago.

I said we knew about Gaitskell's meeting at St Ermin's Hotel[2] and he said, 'Oh, that's a pure phoney. We've been having regular meetings on the National Agents Service and last Monday happened to be the last of them. But I don't deny that, in discussing the money, this issue of Bevan has been not unimportant.' I said that Gaitskell should realize that he seemed to be playing

[1] In November 1954 the Boundary Commissioners had published their recommendations for alterations to parliamentary constituency boundaries, to take account of population changes in the preceding six years. With great difficulty, fifty-two Resolutions had been carried through Parliament at the turn of the year.
[2] On Monday, March 21st, when Gaitskell as Party Treasurer had discussed the issue of Bevan's expulsion with Bevan's sworn opponent Arthur Deakin and other trade union leaders.

the role of merely being a stooge for big forces outside. Was that really good for his political reputation? He replied with a long speech about Bevanism. 'Bevanism,' he said, 'is and only is a conspiracy to seize the leadership for Aneurin Bevan. It is a conspiracy because it has three essentials of conspiracy, a leader in Bevan, an organization run by Mikardo and a newspaper run by Foot.' I laughed and said, 'You really believe in this talk about the Bevanite organization of Mikardo?' Gaitskell said, 'Certainly. It's widespread in the constituencies.' I said, 'How can you take the *Tribune* seriously, with a genuine circulation of not more than 18,000?' He said, 'It's read everywhere in the constituencies. It's the single most important factor which our people on the Right complain of.'

I tried to suggest that Bevanism was also a protest against the totally inadequate leadership of Morrison and himself. I said that in my view Nye was only half wanting to be Leader and that certainly there had been no serious conspiracy to replace Attlee with Nye. Gaitskell then repeated his whole speech at length and said, 'It's got to be cleaned up. There are extraordinary parallels between Nye and Adolf Hitler. They are demagogues of exactly the same sort.' I remarked mildly that I thought Nye showed a really genuine interest in parliamentary liberty. 'Oh,' Gaitskell said, 'there are minor differences but what's striking is the resemblance.'

I said that the Left would not be smashed by Nye's expulsion and indeed it would only increase the division. 'Yes,' he said, 'up to the Conference. But no one survives in the wilderness and after that it would soon be forgotten.' I said, 'If there was any real leadership in the Party that might be true, but what about Attlee and Morrison and Shinwell in the defence debate and in every other vote of censure we had? What's really wrong with the Party is the official leadership.'

Gaitskell then criticized Attlee very bitterly and made the good point that, if he had only run the Shadow Cabinet as he ran the Cabinet, things might have been better. But he'd merely been a chairman and not a leader. Hugh was extremely careful, despite one or two prods by me, not to make any reference to Morrison. He concluded that, if Nye were out of the Party, the main Tory propaganda for the next Election campaign would be killed, whereas, if the Executive failed to carry his expulsion, the Tories would assert that Bevan is indispensable and the main master of the Party.

I said, 'The whole thing will last much longer than you imagine, if you have your way.' He said, 'Of course we shall have to do some cleaning-up in the constituencies,' and remarked what a nice time he'd had in Exeter, where the *Socialist Outlook* had been successfully cleaned up. I said, 'But do you really think cleaning up Bevanism is like cleaning up the *Socialist Outlook*? Look at Coventry, where if you don't look out, they will select another candidate instead of Burton.' 'Oh,' he said, 'we may have to clean up Coventry too.' I said, 'What do you mean?' And Gaitskell said, 'We've cleaned up the shop stewards' movement before now.' I said, 'When?' He looked a bit blank and

I said, 'My agent, George Hodgkinson, happens to have been in it since it started in 1916 and you should ask somebody other than Charlie Pannell to brief you on the A.E.U.'

The whole interview was perfectly polite. Gaitskell drank a great deal of whisky and stayed from half-past seven until ten to nine, refusing to have supper because he was engaged elsewhere. We both promised not to tell our closest friends. I think I can now occasionally repeat this exercise. Two impressions are left on me: first, that I am a much better interrogator than he is—that is, he revealed much more to me than I did to him; and, second, that he was extremely uncomfortable and all the way through, whenever his facts were challenged, said, 'Well, that's what our boys think and you can't blame them.' He seems to have consorted exclusively with the small McCarthyite group in the House and with Williamson and Deakin and got himself into an anti-Bevanite hysteria roughly equivalent to that of Nye and the *Tribune*.

The Executive meeting on Wednesday has been so fully reported in the press that I needn't describe it all over again. I entered through a battery of cameras and for once deliberately managed to ensure that Attlee left with Barbara, Tom and me, all being photographed, and five of us piled into Tony Greenwood's tiny Sunbeam Talbot. From the start it was obvious that Gaitskell had organized the prosecution, with Jack Cooper and Percy Knight moving the resolution. Then came the pitiable mediating intervention of Jim Hawarth, the Buchmanite,[1] who said this was his tenth draft. The actual draft resolution violated every point of parliamentary privilege by making Nye agree never to speak against the Shadow Cabinet and so on and so on. It was after this that Attlee weighed in. He did it with great boldness, saying that the Parliamentary Party had given no mandate for expulsion and that the Conference would not carry it, probably, if the N.E.C. had failed to hear Nye and try conciliation.[2] He was immediately supported by Jim Griffiths on exactly the same line.

Under normal circumstances, when these two had spoken the motion would have been immediately dropped and Attlee's advice accepted, but in fact the debate went on for a full three hours. It was clear that Morrison and Gaitskell had decided that the time had come to push the expulsion through against Attlee's lead. This is what gave the meeting its tension. Attlee's point was only carried because Jean Mann said she was in favour of not only doing justice but seeming to do it and because she clearly voted for the compromise on the view that Nye would hang himself by his behaviour before the sub-committee. However, the really important thing from Nye's point of view

[1] The reference is to Frank Buchman, founder of the Moral Rearmament movement which flourished in Oxford in the 1930s.

[2] Attlee suggested that instead of immediate expulsion the N.E.C. should recommend that Bevan appear before a special N.E.C. sub-committee of eight, which would seek assurances from him about his future conduct and would report to the full N.E.C. a week later. James Griffiths seconded this amendment, which was narrowly approved by 14 votes to 13.

was that, after two major insults in public, Attlee had done what was for him a tremendous action in giving Nye one more chance to save the Left of the Party.

Last night I tried at length to put all this to Nye. I found him, not unnaturally, impatient with me. I tried to describe to him Attlee's psychology and feelings and how important it was for Nye to respond. He told me that Attlee had of course had his mind made up by the number of telegrams and pressures he had received. I said this might be true but Attlee felt he had done something himself for Nye and that Nye should respond. Nye then said, 'I shall go to that committee and read aloud a written statement and refuse to answer questions. I won't let myself be cornered by Gaitskell.' I said, 'But if you treat colleagues like that and it's reported to Conference, you'll have proved yourself guilty. And, anyway, I know you will talk, so you may as well prepare for it. Will you at least submit the statement to Attlee beforehand?' 'You talk to me as though I were a child,' Nye said. 'Of course I will. I'll fix it with Attlee.' I said, 'If you'll do that I don't very much mind what you do at the meeting, except that you must remember that Attlee will not be able to control that meeting or prevent people asking you questions.' Nye replied, 'The most important thing for me is to stand by the hundreds and thousands of people in the country who support my stand. I can't betray them just because people like you want to make appeasement in the Parliamentary Party. I'd rather be expelled than that.' He has now got into one of his heroic moods but there's no reason to believe that he may not be quite sensible when it comes to the meeting. Nevertheless, I must admit that, as this goes on and on and on, I get more and more tired of it and feel that Nye and everybody else might be happier if he could only get himself expelled. What a life!

Thursday, March 31st

On Monday I knew that there was not much point in seeing Nye, since he was not very pleased with me anyway and there was a much better chance of Barbara's getting him to make his written statement a good enough assurance to be acceptable. So I spent Monday afternoon and Tuesday morning working for the *N.S. & N.* and got back to the Tuesday lunch at my house, eager to hear Barbara's report of what had happened at the committee of eight that morning. When I got there, a message came from the Commons that Nye and Jennie thought that at this juncture Nye would be unwise to lunch at my house. Michael stayed with them, whereas Curly and Ian turned up together at a quarter to two. It was obvious that there was some state of tension, which gave me the chance of saying that, since the Stalingrad delegation — now visiting Coventry — was lunching with me next Tuesday, there would be no more lunches until after Easter.[1] It will be interesting to see if the lunches are ever resumed after this.

[1] Coventry City Council had been particularly active in international affairs and had sent delegations to many countries. An all-Labour group was sent to Stalingrad, and just before

However, Barbara gave a really brilliant piece of reporting. By sheer mistake she had told Nye to come at half-past ten, not half-past eleven, as he had been instructed, thus preventing the committee from formulating its tactics and enabling him to read his statement out. This statement included a really abject apology to Attlee and unequivocal assurances that Nye would be loyal to his leadership.[1] When I had suggested this at lunch last week, there had been an almost unanimous murmur from everybody else of 'You're trying to make him grovel.' Yet when the statement was read this Tuesday, Mallalieu said it was wonderful, particularly the apology to Attlee. Once this statement was there, it was obvious that expulsion could not be carried through, but apparently some effort was made by Jack Cooper and Hugh Gaitskell to obtain assurances about attacks on trade union leaders. They saw that Nye had very cleverly concentrated everything on Attlee and refused to be drawn outside the parliamentary scene. Apparently he battled with the committee extremely skilfully for two hours—remember last week he swore he wouldn't say a word or answer a question. When he wants to be bland, he certainly can be.

On Wednesday we had the N.E.C. and ploughed through the ordinary business, waiting for Clem Attlee before coming to Mr Bevan. When we at last got down to Mr Bevan, Morgan Phillips read a quite objective report. Then there was about half a minute's silence, till Attlee and Griffiths proposed briefly that we should welcome Mr Bevan's assurances and call for unity in the Party. At once Jack Cooper moved a counter-resolution, which he had typed out. Instead of welcoming the assurances, it noted them, approved the withdrawal of the whip, threatened harsh measures in the future and was generally unpleasant. In the course of the debate, Jim Hawarth, who had been for mediating last week, proposed expulsion, thereby showing how extremely unstable last week's majority against expulsion was. Cooper's harsh resolution was carried by 15 votes to 10, with Attlee and Griffiths voting with us for their soft resolution.[2]

After that we dealt with the H-bomb and the resolution which Attlee had redrafted and into which I had another paragraph inserted. All the same, I

---

the General Election it was announced that £2,000 had been spent on entertaining a return delegation. Crossman attributed some of the disenchantment felt by voters in his constituency to their reactions against the local Labour party, whose headquarters had been christened 'the Kremlin of Coundon Road'.

[1] ' ... The charge is that, in what I have done and also in the way I have done it, I have created difficulties for Mr Attlee and caused him embarrassment in his post as Leader of the Party. This was certainly never my intention. But if my actions or speech could lend themselves to the interpretation that such was my motive, then I am sincerely sorry and I apologize to Mr Attlee for any pain I may have caused him ... '

[2] According to Michael Foot's *Aneurin Bevan* (London: Davis-Poynter, 1973), vol. 2, pp. 479–80, Cooper's amendment was carried against Attlee's motion by 15 votes to 10, with Attlee in the minority. A Wilson amendment to remove part of the Cooper amendment, now the substantive motion, was defeated by 20 votes to 6, with Attlee in the majority. The Cooper motion was then carried, as the N.E.C.'s final decision, with Attlee and Griffiths abstaining.

think it's a grave mistake to publish it in its present form. We should have waited and done a really good job.

I went back to the *Statesman* and wrote their leading article, in addition to a signed article by me on Party discipline,[1] and then went down to the Commons, where Nye found me and George Wigg walking in the corridor. He kept us for an hour. The first part of the talk, which was a little laboured, I thought, was a long explanation of his strategy ever since last year, when he announced his decision to stand for the treasurership in order to launch the battle against the industrial oligarchy and the big unions. Step by step he traced, throughout the year, the foresight and the sureness with which he had planned each battle and fought it to a successful conclusion, only by the *Tribune* principle of No Concessions. 'You, Dick,' he said, 'you get worried about little incidents such as a dispute with me about the hydrogen bomb or a silly *Tribune* article and lose sight of the strategic picture. See things in terms of long-term strategy and not in terms of your weekly column.'

He then suddenly jumped to his real object, which was to say that he was terribly upset by what had been written in the *New Statesman* last week. I racked my brain as to what he could mean. Then he brought it out that, in our last sentence, we had talked about a united Labour Party, with Attlee as Leader, Gaitskell as its financial adviser and, in Nye's words, himself as Jimmy Maxton.[2] 'In moments of crisis, when the knives are out,' he said, 'equivocation is tantamount to treachery. Gaitskell is not a financial expert. Everybody knows that now. And to rehabilitate him in that way was treacherous.'

It was impossible to point out to Nye that, whereas all the things which personally rile me are regarded as trivial incidents, which must be forgotten in the broad strategy, an odd sentence in the *Statesman*, which as a matter of fact had been changed by John Freeman after I had drafted it, is something Nye can legitimately complain of. He went on to say that he often found the *Sunday Pictorial* column too detached and wondered whether it wasn't produced under the pressure of Mr Cudlipp. I tried to explain that, whereas I deferred to him on all questions on politics and statesmanship, there was one thing I did know about, which was writing. This was a form of action in which I was a master and I had come to the conclusion that the best propaganda is indirect propaganda and the best help Nye could get was from an

---

[1] 'Aneurin Bevan Back In The Team' and 'Reflections on Party Loyalty', *New Statesman and Nation*, April 2nd, 1955.

[2] In an article commenting on Attlee's decision to establish a sub-committee of eight to hear Bevan, rather than recommending immediate expulsion, the *New Statesman and Nation* of March 26th, 1955 had stated:

> The vast majority of Labour supporters pin their faith on Mr Attlee as their leader, accept Mr Gaitskell as their financial expert, and look up to Aneurin Bevan as the spokesman and inspirer of their Socialist faith. Mr Attlee has created the atmosphere in which the party can achieve this kind of unity in time for the election.

independent *New Statesman* and from an independent column. I added, 'Certainly we've given more help to you in the last three years than *Tribune*, which has done terrible damage very often.' This statement literally took Nye's breath away and he explained to me how the valiant fight of *Tribune* had been his greatest assistance, whereas the *New Statesman* was not read by trade unionists. He went back to the point about equivocation, etc., but Jennie interrupted him and we went off and had a drink together. I think I shall write him a long and interesting letter.

Crossman did write to Bevan, pointing out the 'immensely refreshing' way in which Bevan's mind worked in 'a totally different way' from his own:

> As you have often remarked, I am an intellectual, which means that, though I have warm personal feelings, my loyalty is primarily to ideas and to chasing ideas in argument, which is the only way I can think. This is why I was so angry with you when I thought you had been intellectually *equivocal with regard to the H-bomb*. You, on the other hand, are far less sensitive to intellectual equivocation, but much more sensitive to anything you regard as equivocation in action!

Crossman went on to declare that he believed Bevan's strategy in the last four months had taken him further from effective power:

> Perhaps the main difference between us, which makes you a great politician and me a pretty good writer, is that I am sometimes sceptical about my own strategy as well as about yours, whereas you are only sceptical of mine. But I don't see why that difference of temperament should prevent collaboration, provided that we both keep to the rule you once told me years ago — that it's no good trying to change a person from what he is.

Crossman emphasized that, though there would be occasions when they would disagree publicly as well as privately, these need not be harmful 'if we continue to believe in each other's integrity'.

In the last week of March a newspaper strike began, unprecedented in its length. (There had been a ten-day strike during the 1926 General Strike and a one-day stoppage in the autumn of 1954.) The strike affected all London weekday and Sunday papers, with their Manchester and Glasgow editions. Local newspapers (including the Manchester Guardian*) were not affected and the weekly reviews also continued to appear.*

The Newspaper Proprietors' Association had offered a wage increase to all unions in the London newspaper printing industry. This had been refused by the A.E.U. and the E.T.U., which organized the maintenance engineers and electricians. They contended that their wages had fallen behind pre-war levels and refused the employers' offer of arbitration. Instead of increases of 14s. 6d. for night workers and 12s. for day workers, the unions demanded increases of £2 18s. 6d.

One major item of news thus not covered by the national daily papers was the end of Sir Winston's premiership. On April 4th he and Lady Churchill had entertained the Queen and the Duke of Edinburgh to dinner at No. 10 Downing Street and on the afternoon of the next day Sir Winston tendered his resignation. Sir Anthony Eden accepted office as Prime Minister on April 6th.

The following day there was a small ministerial reshuffle. Harold Macmillan took Sir Anthony's place as Foreign Secretary and his former post as Minister of Defence went to Selwyn Lloyd. Reginald Maudling succeeded Mr Lloyd as Minister of Supply. Edward Boyle followed Mr Maudling as Economic Secretary to the Treasury. Other new appointments were the Earl of Home as Minister at the Commonwealth Relations Office and Charles Hill as Postmaster-General. The fact that the changes were so few strengthened the widespread belief that a General Election was imminent.

Thursday, April 7th

At Bob Boothby's last Friday night,[1] I heard a fascinating discussion between him and Walter Elliot about Anthony Eden, Butler and Macmillan, who we now knew were due to take over from Churchill on Tuesday. 'A triangle, not a triumvirate,' said Walter Elliot. 'Anthony has no friends except his smooth young men in the Foreign Office, whereas Butler has acquired a regular following and Macmillan is also more popular than Eden. Anthony will be inclined to work closer with Salisbury in the aristocratic Mayfair tradition. He is a diplomat but Prime Ministers have to give orders.' Bob said that what had brought matters to a head was Churchill's conduct of the Commonwealth Conference,[2] which had been mercilessly caricatured by Menzies[3] at so many dinner parties, but they all felt it was time for a change. When I got into the House on Monday, Churchill's impending retirement was the sole subject of discussion. That evening Dalton came home with me and I had a long talk. He brought the news that the date of the election had not been decided, since Salisbury was urging Eden to play himself in.

On Tuesday afternoon, in the Smoking Room, Attlee came along to our corner and discussed the speech he was to make for Eden's takeover. 'I made the speech eighteen years ago,'[4] he said, 'when Chamberlain took over from Baldwin.' And he showed us a terrible joke he had composed, giving Russian names and turning it into a Malenkov incident, at which we dutifully laughed.

[1] After a broadcast of 'In The News', with Boothby, Elliot and Dalton.

[2] Held in London from January 31st to February 8th.

[3] Robert Menzies practised as a barrister in Australia until 1928, when he became a Member of the Victoria State Parliament. In 1934 he was elected as Member of the House of Representatives for Kooyand, a seat he held for the Party until his retirement in 1966. He was Attorney-General 1934–9, Prime Minister 1939–41, Leader of the Opposition 1943–9 and Prime Minister from 1949 to 1966. In 1951 he became a Companion of Honour and was knighted in 1963. He was Warden of the Cinque Ports from 1965 until his death in 1978. His memoirs, *Afternoon Light* and *Measure of the Years* (London: Cassell), were published in 1967 and 1970 respectively.

[4] On May 3rd, 1937: *H. C. Debates*, vol. 324, cols 682–3.

Nye drifted in and sat down, too, and we were all quite pally together, while Attlee described the exact route which had been planned for his General Election tour with Vi. Harold Wilson said, 'I hope you will come to Huyton,' and Attlee said, 'Oh yes, it's on my list for the fourth day, coming down the West side,' which shows a remarkably accurate memory. After Attlee had gone, Nye said to me that he had been asked to speak in Coventry but felt he shouldn't come because of Elaine Burton. I suggested he should come on from Wolverhampton, as he did last time, but added that I couldn't really claim Coventry as a must, since we were quite safe there. 'I have to go and do John Baird and Jennie,' he said. 'I'm not sure I can come to Coventry. Wouldn't it be better politically for me to tell those who have invited me why?' I suppose rather stupidly I agreed and then realized afterwards that I had probably hurt his feelings. Still, as he made no reference to the letter I had written him, that was that, and we parted cordially but not intimately.

On Wednesday I went in to hear the actual takeover by Eden, which, after an admirable speech by Attlee, consisted of anti-climax piled on anti-climax. All the same, it somehow was a great occasion, with a great yawning gap, and Eden being charmingly modest, thereby making the gap seem even larger. We dined with Alec Spearman and met a member of the Conservative Central Committee, who told us that the Election decision had not yet been taken. But, since the council election results[1] got worse and worse, I can't believe that it won't be fairly soon.

On April 15th, while Parliament was in Recess, the Prime Minister broadcast the announcement that the General Election would take place on May 26th. Two days earlier the court of inquiry into the newspaper workers' claim had declared the unions' demands unrealistic and the employers' offer reasonable. Meanwhile the employers had served a fortnight's notice on some 22,000 of their other employees, and when this matured the printers' unions sought the T.U.C.'s assistance and a formula was eventually devised to allow the men to return to work on the basis of accepting the existing offer, with the initiation of new talks in eight weeks' time. On April 21st the London daily papers reappeared.

Two days earlier the Chancellor presented his Budget. Mr Butler announced a surplus for the previous year of £282 million, about half of which would be devoted to remissions in taxation. The standard rate of income tax was reduced by 6d. to 8s. 6d. with 3d. reduction of the lower rate. A single person's allowance of untaxed income was raised by £20 to £140 and a married person's allowance by £30 to £240. Child allowance increased by £15 to £100. The limit of relief for small investment incomes was raised by £50 to £300. These proposals wholly relieved some 2,400,000 taxpayers of income tax.

[1] In county council elections held between March 31st and April 6th, Labour lost control of five counties. In the London County Council elections the Conservatives gained 15 seats, although Labour retained a substantial majority.

14

The Chancellor stated that, in view of the inflationary danger, he had not felt justified in making general reductions in indirect taxation. As a special measure to assist the ailing Lancashire cotton industry, however, there was a reduction from 50 to 25 per cent in purchase tax on piece-goods, sheets, towels, other non-woollen textiles and plastic sheeting.

Tuesday, April 19th

I lunched with Sydney Jacobson, who told me the newspaper strike was to finish this evening. He also told me that Cecil King had wanted the *Mirror* group in this Election to adopt the slogan, 'We are pro-Labour but not this time,' meaning, of course, that the Labour Party was so divided and poorly led that the *Mirror*, its strong supporter, could not conscientiously recommend it as a Government. This would have been the most harmful thing possible. Sydney told me that he and Hugh Cudlipp had managed to over-persuade King and that Hugh is in tremendous good form. They have decided, however, to hold their hand and give their support only in the last week, since at present the people are too apathetic.

After that I went into the House to hear Butler's Budget speech, which was a tame but competent performance. In the Smoking Room I found Nye had blown in for half an hour. However, as far as I can find out, over Easter he hasn't seen Ian Mikardo, Barbara Castle, Harold Wilson or anybody, and there has been no effort whatsoever to have a concerted Bevanite view of the Election Manifesto[1] or of anything else. But I have a feeling that the snap Election has already put some ginger into the Labour Party. If we can get a decent Manifesto and Attlee beginning and ending the television and radio campaign, we stand a chance of doing quite well. We shall soon discover who on the Executive wants to lose the Election and who wants to win it.

Tuesday, April 26th

While I was talking to Bob Boothby and Hugh Fraser[2] in the Smoking Room today, Nye came in and took me outside to ask what was in the Manifesto.[3] I briefly told him and then pressed him to come to a meeting of shop stewards in Birmingham, which Harold Nash would hold specially for him. Nye

[1] Both Labour's *Forward With Labour* and the Conservative's *United For Peace and Progress* were published on April 29th.

[2] Conservative M.P. for Stone from 1945 to 1950, and for Stafford and Stone since 1950. He married the Hon. Antonia Pakenham in 1956. He was Parliamentary Private Secretary to the Secretary of State for the Colonies 1951–4, Parliamentary Under-Secretary of State and Financial Secretary at the War Office 1958–60, Parliamentary Under-Secretary of State for the Colonies 1960–2 and Secretary of State for Air 1962–4.

[3] It emphasized the need for international agreement to halt the H-bomb tests, for high-level talks and for German reunification. The manifesto promised a review of the period of National Service, the abolition of the 11+ examination, the promotion of comprehensive schools and a number of economic benefits—fixed guaranteed farm prices, free N.H.S. teeth and spectacles, higher pensions, speedier repayment of post-war credits and the reimposition 'where necessary' of price controls on essential goods.

explained at length how he is booked up. He is going to spend most of the time travelling. He was perfectly amiable, and, as always when Elections come, quite conventionally loyal to the Party. Barbara and Ian Mikardo are still convinced that 'Ban the H-bomb' is enough to win the Election on and they got some evidence for this view from an analysis which the *Daily Herald* made today of a questionnaire they had printed asking people what they were most worried about. Out of forty-eight items, the H-bomb and the cost of living easily came first, but I still think that, on peace, the H-bomb and all that it is unlikely that we shall make much impact in trying to overbid the Tories. We are far more likely to do well on practical bread-and-butter issues.

Tuesday, May 3rd
On Friday morning I went along to the press conference for the Tory Manifesto, which costs 6*d*., is 10,000 words long and says nothing. There is no doubt we've done a far more workmanlike job of drafting. At the Tory conference there were three people on the platform — Eden, with Butler and Woolton[1] flanking him. Woolton remained completely silent throughout the meeting. Eden was at ease in foreign affairs but Butler took over from him on any detail of home affairs.

My impression from the press is that everybody is a bit surprised at how specific and workmanlike the Labour Manifesto is. Certainly at the Caxton Hall meeting this morning it went over quite well, though I had one slight embarrassment at the beginning. In the *Observer* on Sunday Mr Massingham had somewhat maliciously revealed the fact that Morgan Phillips's first draft had been turned down and the second prepared by Tom Driberg and myself. When I was standing in the anteroom with the other members of the Executive, Attlee pushed his way across and said to me, with Morgan standing two yards away, 'Congratulations, the Manifesto's a first-rate bit of work.'

All this sounds terribly trivial but there's no doubt that, during the last four weeks, some strange changes have taken place inside the Labour Party. I would be prepared to bet that, if we win the Election, Attlee will offer me and other left-wingers jobs in his Cabinet. Indeed, it is now common discussion in the Party. I lunched with Elath today, who told me he had overheard three right-wingers discussing last week what would happen if we won. They were all saying this and one of them (I suspect it was Sam Watson) observed that it was not inconceivable that they would have to put Crossman at the Foreign Office in order to avoid trouble on the Left, since he was far the cleverest of them and the most reliable. But the other two said he would go to Education, so as to keep the schoolmistresses out of the job!

[1] Frederick Woolton (1883–1964). Senior Managing Director of the John Lewis Partnership, he was knighted in 1935 and created Baron Woolton of Liverpool in 1939, when he also became Director-General of Equipment and Stores at the Ministry of Supply. He was Minister of Food 1940–3, Minister of Reconstruction 1943–5, Lord President of the Council 1945 and 1951–2, and Chancellor of the Duchy of Lancaster 1952–5. He was Chairman of the Conservative and Unionist Central Office 1945–55.

Eliahu added that he had found a strange change in the Labour hierarchy, which he knows extremely well, all dating from the notorious H-bomb debate. Apparently the right-wing was astonished when Harold Wilson, John and I all went into a different lobby from Nye and stood up for ourselves. What has really happened, I think, has been a kind of dissolution of all existing groups in the Party. Nye is still perfectly charming to me but there have been, of course, no kind of Bevanite confabs during the drafting of the Manifesto nor any kind of policy discussion between us. This means that Nye is now virtually limited to the *Tribune*.

Meanwhile Gaitskell and his friends do seem to have learnt something from their failure to expel Nye. Their particular anti-Bevanite clique has become weakened, so that the Party is much more centred round Attlee and Griffiths than ever before. I would be fairly confident that, if we won, Attlee would use all the powers he possesses to produce a Government of all the talents. If we lose, however, and particularly if we lose badly, we are in for a most frightful period of recrimination. Six weeks ago it would have sounded absurd to talk about winning, but George Wigg was right in his prediction that the announcement of the Election would be a catalyst in the local parties.

In the House I have found an astonishing change of feeling, partly owing to the constituencies and partly owing to the Manifesto, which few people seem to realize is merely *Challenge to Britain*, properly written. A third element was undoubtedly the Gallup Poll,[1] which last Thursday showed that the mere announcement of the Election had given Labour a slight edge on the Tories. I fancy the Tories are beginning to wonder whether they did the right thing. A summer Election is an enormous advantage to us and we have never lost one. The most important factor is that the last hour of polling is in daylight and this will bring a number of elderly Labour voters to the poll, who on a dark winter night don't venture out. Moreover, a municipal campaign will run over into our parliamentary campaign. A Labour triumph in the municipals, if we achieve it, will bring us a long way towards victory in the parliamentary contest. The Tories have this difficulty. Their best way to win is to have a quiet Election and a low poll. On the other hand, if they see us doing well on a programme which has some pretty solid and attractive promises for working people, they may feel the need for some stunts and scares at the last moment. Yet these stunts and scares would undoubtedly increase the total poll. My guess, as of today, however, is that we shall get a plurality of the votes but that the Tories will have a small majority.

On May 12th landslide Conservative gains were announced in the borough council elections. The Conservatives regained about three-fifths of the seats lost in 1952, when these municipalities were last contested. This was a net gain of 311 seats for the Conservatives, 24 for the Independents and 8 for the Liberals,

---

[1] In fact, the Gallup Poll for April 1955, published in the *News Chronicle*, gave the Conservatives 41 per cent to Labour's 40 per cent.

while the Labour Party suffered a net loss of 341 seats. Crossman's next entry, for May 31st, covers his part in the municipal and the General Election campaign. In the afternoon of May 26th, polling day in the General Election, Crossman was worried about the Coventry results and his anxiety deepened at the count, especially since 'we stayed looking at television for an hour and a half, which showed about a 2½ per cent swing' [to the Conservatives]. When the results were announced, Crossman's majority had dropped, like that of Maurice Edelman, by some 6,000 votes and Elaine Burton was also 4,000 down, 'about as bad as I had anticipated at my gloomiest moments but worse than anything I would ever put on paper'.

The number of Conservative seats increased from 319 at the dissolution on May 6th to 345 (including 10 Ulster Unionists). The number of Labour Members fell from 293 to 277. Liberal strength remained the same, with 6 seats, and there were two Sinn Fein Members.

Redistribution had increased the number of seats from 625 to 630; of these the Conservatives now had a majority of 59 over the rest of the House (taking into account W. S. Morrison's re-election as Speaker). The total poll had fallen from the 82·6 per cent of the registered electorate voting in 1951 to 76·8 per cent. The Conservative Party lost 0·5 million voters, Labour 1·5 million; the election result was judged a Labour failure rather than a Conservative success. The decline in the Labour vote was greatest in safe Labour seats and it was interesting that losses were more or less similar whether seats were fought by Bevanites or non-Bevanites.

Monday, June 6th

For the last week I have been picking up threads in London, most of which are not there. The Labour Party is an extraordinary organization. After an Election there is no gathering to a central point — only a few knots of conversation between odd individuals. The National Executive is having only two sub-committees before its June meeting, the Shadow Cabinet is only meeting this afternoon and meanwhile I would bet that everybody has just been sitting at their homes. Of course, all this has been intensified by the railway strike,[1] which began at midnight last Saturday week and which has pretty effectively prevented movement, except for somebody like Barbara Castle, who sportingly bicycled to Fordingbridge for a holiday weekend.

I've been chiefly interested in trying to ensure that, when the Parliamentary Party meets, we don't start off where we were before the Election. I did my piece in the *Pic*[2] the Sunday before last and it was followed by three quite

[1] This arose out of a dispute over differential payments between the two railway unions, ASLEF and the N.U.R. The strike began at midnight on May 28th. Though a minority of N.U.R. footplate men remained at work and some trains ran, the position was sufficiently serious for a state of emergency to be proclaimed on May 31st. The strike was eventually called off on June 14th. Meanwhile another dock strike had begun on May 24th and this lasted until July 4th.

[2] 'Now — Let's Come Back FIGHTING', *Sunday Pictorial*, June 26th, 1955.

good articles in the *Mirror* by Sydney Jacobson, the first on an ageing leadership, the second on Bevanism and recriminations and the third on lousy organization. Sydney did his best but couldn't prevent the first being headed 'ATTLEE MUST GO', since the main point that Cecil King feels is that Attlee is a little wet. But the attack was mild and even Hugh Cudlipp's attack on Nye was also relatively moderate in tone.

However, the day after the last of the articles appeared, Desmond Donnelly turned up. On his way from Pembroke he had passed by Dalton's cottage at Aldbourne and he brought with him the news that Dalton was writing a letter to Attlee along lines he had talked over with me just before the Election. He would announce that he would not stand for the Shadow Cabinet, suggesting that those over sixty-five should make way for the young men and that he hoped Attlee would respond.[1] Desmond told me that Dalton's letter would appear in Saturday's press but he carried with him a manuscript press release by Dalton, whose purpose was unspecified. I immediately saw an advantage for the *Mirror* if I could get hold of it and I managed to persuade Desmond to bring it round to me on Thursday morning. I then rang Dalton, who told me that Desmond was a perfect leak and that this had been given to Desmond to leak with. So I saw it got into Friday's *Mirror* as an exclusive advance, but when the letter was published on Saturday there was not the expected reply from Attlee. Moreover, in the *Telegraph*, characteristically, Mr William Whiteley had expressed surprise at Dalton's behaving in this way, remarking that he had always been unanimously elected Chief Whip and it was up to the Party to get rid of him. On Sunday Shinwell produced a rather similar piece in the *Pic* but George tells me that Manny has privately agreed to go and so has Chuter Ede.

All this seemed to me fairly all right, since an anti-age campaign is less harmful than a Left/Right bicker. In the course of the week I had talks with Tony Greenwood, Barbara Castle and Kenneth Robinson. The main thing which they all wanted to know was whether Nye was standing for the Parliamentary Committee or challenging Morrison for Deputy Leader. I couldn't tell them because I hadn't been in contact with Nye since the beginning of the Election but I had Michael Foot and Jill to dinner on Wednesday to find out.[2]

When I asked Michael about this, he said that Nye would have no alternative but to stand against Morrison, since, if he suddenly stopped standing, people would ask why. I then pointed out that he had not stood last October after the Scarborough Conference. This seemed to surprise Michael a great deal and he remarked that the fight must go on and that it was absurd to talk of unity in the Party until we had overthrown the right-wing leadership of

---

[1] Nine of the fifteen members of the Parliamentary Committee were over sixty-five and, of these, four were over seventy. Mr Dalton nevertheless expressed his hope that Mr Attlee, aged seventy-two, would continue to lead the Party.

[2] Michael Foot had lost his seat at Devonport to Miss Joan Vickers, Conservative, who had a majority of 100 votes.

the trade unions. Michael was also appalled at the idea that we should have a standstill on policy controversy in the Parliamentary Party, apparently not having read Nye's contribution to *Tribune*! I didn't really get very far with him. Nor, apparently, did Tony Greenwood, who saw Michael at lunch last week at Maurice Edelman's, where Nye talked a great deal about the fight being on and dismissed Tony's proposal that Jim Griffiths should be induced to stand against Morrison, since Jim might defeat him. I must say I rather agree with Nye that that's pretty futile and the obvious course this year would be to have Attlee and Morrison both unopposed and to concentrate on trying to get a change of Chief Whip, in the first place and, in the second place, on getting a rejuvenated Shadow Cabinet.

Today I discussed all this with Harold Wilson at lunch. The idea of getting rid of the Chief Whip seemed novel to him and he said that he would raise it at the Parliamentary Committee's meeting at five o'clock. He also agreed that he must raise the issue of the railway strike, since this will be the first topic on which the new Parliamentary Party will have to show its mettle. He liked the idea I put to him that he should urge the Shadow Cabinet to co-ordinate its policy at once with the T.U.C., in time for a debate.

On the issue of Nye and, generally, what the Left in the Party should do, Harold was unusually forthcoming. He thought it was silly of Nye to stand for the deputy leadership but added that he would probably do so and that it wouldn't do much harm. Harold was convinced that Attlee would try to hang on so as to prevent Morrison from becoming Leader but that then Gaitskell was bound to take over and everything would depend on who was the Deputy Leader to Gaitskell. I said it might well be Harold and he didn't dissent. I added that Gaitskell detested him and rather liked me and that this was because Harold was a real rival whereas I was not. Harold then said that he was not a real rival to Gaitskell, but that Gaitskell realized that if ever he made a mess of things Harold was there to step into his shoes as a *tertium gaudens*. When I told Harold that Barbara and some others were thinking of standing for the Shadow Cabinet, he didn't show any great enthusiasm but was tactful enough not to dissent. We agreed that I should invite Sam Watson to lunch before the Executive meets in order to try out the ground and, if that were successful, we might do the same with Jack Cooper and/or Jim Hawarth.

Harold has also obviously been very impressed by the unpopularity of nationalization, though he himself thinks there is a case for nationalizing chemicals. He was against the resumption of our Tuesday lunches on the ground that they didn't serve any real purpose now, but tentatively suggested I should resume them with a changing personnel. I said I would wait and see how things were going. We finally agreed that, after the cocktail party I am giving on Wednesday, I should try to get Harold, Nye, Jennie, Ian and Barbara to go out to dinner.[1]

[1] On June 8th.

This afternoon, I heard a rumour from Ian, which he seems to have got from Nye and Jennie, that the proposal would be made tomorrow to carry on with our present officers and Shadow Cabinet until October. From Ian's tone of voice, I gathered that Nye likes the idea. It is, of course, an absolutely shocking proposal, since nothing could dispirit the Party in the country more than a failure to shift things at the moment when shifting is easiest, which is when a new Parliament meets and before the Parliamentary Party settles down. But I expect, from Nye's point of view, it simply means avoiding an awkward decision.

Altogether I rather dread meeting my parliamentary colleagues again. There will be a dozen new faces and only nine absentees and the difficulty of getting anything very new and vigorous out of us all will be immense.

Tuesday, June 7th
The last twenty-four hours are worth recording in some detail. Anne and I had just decided to have dinner and go out to see a new American film when Tommy Balogh turned up, asking for supper. He had asked himself over to see Nye, who had apparently ranted at him for an hour about the terribleness of middle-class intellectuals and, though no names were mentioned, Tommy got the impression that Nye felt that the only thing which had been wrong in the last few years was that his proletarian instincts had been thwarted by too much contact with a clique of middle-class intellectuals.

Just as we were preparing to go to the cinema, Hugh Dalton rang, saying he wanted to have a drink and tell me the result of the Parliamentary Committee's meeting that afternoon. He came booming in, much elated, and described at the greatest length and at the top of his voice how he had baited the old 'uns. 'Can you honestly say, any one of you,' pointing his finger at each round the table, 'can you honestly say that you are as fit and quick-witted today as you were when you were invited to join the Cabinet in those wonderful days of 1945? And can you honestly say that in five years' time you will be fit and able to do a better job than any of the younger members of the Party?'

Chuter Ede and others had apparently expressed their fury that Dalton had come out with all this publicly in his letter to Attlee. Each of them said that of course they had made up their minds privately to resign but didn't like to be forced by Dalton. Pressed on the subject of the Chief Whip by George Wigg, who by then had turned up as well, Dalton was somewhat evasive but continued to regale us with repetitions of his sallies about old age and his hope that such excellent young men as Anthony Greenwood and Arthur Bottomley would replace them. Questioned whether he really thought Anthony and Arthur Bottomley would be much more vigorous fighters than the old 'uns, Hugh replied that Anthony Greenwood stood by him on German rearmament and Arthur Bottomley had fought a gallant fight in a marginal constituency. Anyway, the thing was to have a shake-up and he, Dalton, had started it.

We discussed the possibility of the Parliamentary Committee's becoming a real Shadow Cabinet, with members with functions and a small Secretariat, but Dalton's mind was entirely on his great personal coup in embarrassing all his fellow veterans. He rolled off across Vincent Square with George at midnight, leaving Anne and me to wash up an appalling amount of dirty glasses.

Early this morning George rang up to say Dalton had double-crossed us by not revealing that Attlee had made a sensational statement to the Shadow Cabinet — that he had decided to resign in October. I didn't take this very seriously, despite some hints in the *Daily Telegraph*, which is usually very well informed, and we went off together to the Party Meeting for the election of officers.

At this meeting, Attlee carried out the agreement reached at the Shadow Cabinet. Apparently Morrison had proposed that, since the Session would only last until the end of July, and new officers and Shadow Cabinet members would have to be elected in October, the best thing was to carry on with the present officers and Shadow Cabinet. This had been pulverized by Dalton on the quite correct ground that the public would hardly be impressed by a Labour Party which suspended its own Standing Orders and, after a sensational defeat, kept its old leadership unchanged for four months. It has therefore been agreed that the normal cumbrous machinery of election should be put in motion. This is what Attlee read aloud today from a bit of paper. Since those who stand for Leader or Deputy Leader must be given the chance to stand for the Shadow Cabinet as well, election has to take place in two stages and therefore take a minimum of three weeks. So we shall be nearly through the Session before we have our new officials.

Not having spoken to Nye for weeks, I went down to the Smoking Room and suggested to him that, after my party tomorrow, he might like to dine alone with Harold, Barbara and Ian. He looked very embarrassed and said, 'I think we shall have to enlarge our contacts.' So I dropped the suggestion and began to go out, when he moved across with me and sat down at a table along with Ian, where we were later joined by Barbara. At once the discussion came on to the decision whether Nye should stand against Morrison for the deputy leadership. He said there wasn't any alternative. I then said I didn't see any point in getting defeated, as he probably would, by a worse vote than last time, and he said that, if he didn't stand now, he would have no case for standing in October, and that anyway the fight must go on. Ian supported him, Barbara mildly supported me and I then said what was vital was that, when he had been defeated, Nye should stand for the Parliamentary Committee. This he agreed to rather reluctantly and we left it at that.

Mentioning to Harold Wilson that Nye didn't want to have a private talk with us, I also reported George Wigg's rumour about the Shadow Cabinet. Harold at once completely confirmed it. Under the closest pledge of secrecy, Attlee has apparently said that he had made up his mind to resign in October and had remarked, 'In order to get the Indians and the Pakistanis to the point of accepting independence, we had to put a time limit, which forced them to put their house in order.[1] I am putting a time limit on the Labour Party by going next October.' There had apparently been some discussion about the *Mirror* campaign and surrendering to it but Attlee had been quite firm.

From three o'clock to six o'clock, there was one of those extraordinary Lobby/Smoking Room/Tea Room moving conversations which make politics. Nye had dismissed my first hint to him about Attlee as absurd, but at four o'clock, when I was talking to Harold about my impasse with Nye and Jennie and his unwillingness to discuss anything, he came and sat down with us and said, 'The reason why I can't have dinner with you is that it would offend Geoffrey Bing and Michael Foot, who would feel left out.' So I suggested we should all take a private room and have a complete Bevanite dinner tomorrow evening to discuss the strategy and in particular Nye's own position. I then, together with Harold, confirmed to him the story about Attlee, at which point John Strachey came in and said he'd just been to see Attlee, who didn't give any impression that he'd made any definite pledge and said he was at the disposal of the Party. And, sure enough, the little man has apparently issued a statement for the *Daily Herald* which does not in any way commit him to resign. But of course he has done this after the rumour has leaked to the lobby correspondents of what happened at the Shadow Cabinet.

Meanwhile, however, Nye suddenly seized on Attlee's resignation in October and said the whole situation had been transformed. This meant that he should not stand against Morrison this time but go on the Parliamentary Committee, reserving himself for the great struggle in October. 'The only possible salvation for the Party,' he said, 'would be for Morrison to be Leader and me to be Deputy Leader. If Morrison and Gaitskell are elected, the Party won't split; it will disintegrate and never recover.' John Strachey reinforced Nye in this view and we both pointed out that the one chance of winning the 100-odd floating votes in the centre of the Parliamentary Party would be if Nye were elected to a new, rejuvenated Shadow Cabinet, where he played along with the team throughout the summer. He seemed suddenly aware that the Parliamentary Party, which he has always dismissed as irrelevant, really does matter. I think he has begun to realize that, if Attlee resigns and he is not made Deputy Leader in October, his fate is virtually sealed.

During these hours my mood has varied from extreme depression during the morning meeting to the kind of elation one gets when one imagines one is actually doing something. After Nye had told me that the strategy was fixed, I said to him, 'In that case we don't need the dinner tomorrow.' 'No,' he said, obviously greatly relieved, 'no, there's nothing to discuss.' But will he still hold to his view after seeing Attlee's statement in the *Herald*? I think

[1] In 1947.

he probably will, since I suspect that the Attlee resignation was only an excuse for reshaping his view from that formed by Bing and Foot to one in line with Harold Wilson and myself.

I found Nye—and even more Jennie—extremely distracted and what I suspect they feel is that his fate is likely to be sealed in the next months. But in this, as often, he is wrong. In my view, if Attlee resigns, there is no chance whatsoever of avoiding the election of either Morrison and Gaitskell or the election of Gaitskell as Leader and someone, say Harold Wilson, as Deputy Leader. I simply don't see the Parliamentary Party ever giving Nye a majority. But the main thing is to make him try to win some support by being sensible.

Thursday, June 9th
The party I had here yesterday, which was intended to be entirely social, settled down quite unexpectedly to be one of the most interesting political discussions I have listened to for months. It went on till half-past nine, when Ian and I went into the House to be sworn in but found the Speaker had gone away. What occasioned all this was the arrival of Harold Wilson from the Shadow Cabinet, with the news that, instead of the short Session we had been expecting, the Government plans to run the Session unbroken until October 1956. All the calculations about nominations for the leadership and so on and about Attlee's retirement had been based on the assumption of a short Session, which would have meant two elections in the Parliamentary Labour Party, one in July and the other in October.

It was on this assumption that Nye had agreed not to stand for the deputy leadership. It was also on this assumption that many right-wingers were content to see Attlee re-elected without opposition, hoping that he would resign in October and give way to Morrison and Gaitskell. This, indeed, had also been the plan of the Chief Whip when he called all the Whips together a couple of days ago and told them that he and Attlee would be resigning together at the end of July. This statement had caused George Wigg to organize one of his campaigns. George got himself nominated to oppose Whiteley, having arranged that Bowden[1] would only stand if Whiteley were opposed by somebody else. His plan was to withdraw his nomination and leave Bowden to oppose Whiteley. All this apparently succeeded and Harold Wilson told us that the Chief Whip had stated that, since he would not be elected unanimously, he had decided to withdraw voluntarily. Thus the

[1] Herbert Bowden, Labour M.P. for Leicester South 1945–50 and Leicester South-West 1950–67. He was Parliamentary Private Secretary to the Postmaster-General 1947–9, Assistant Government Whip 1949–50, a Lord Commissioner of the Treasury 1950–1, Deputy Chief Opposition Whip 1951–5, and Chief Opposition Whip 1955–64. He was Lord President of the Council and Leader of the House of Commons 1964–6 and Secretary of State for Commonwealth Affairs 1966–7. Created a life peer (with the title of Lord Aylestone) in 1967, he served as Chairman of the I.T.A. (subsequently the I.B.A.) from 1967 to 1975.

Shadow Cabinet has already changed to the extent of Dalton, Shinwell, Chuter Ede, the Chief Whip and Soskice.

The other item of news which shifted everything was the possibility, which before the party I had discussed with George and Kenneth Robinson, that this time Jim Griffiths would stand against Morrison. This again had been discussed on the assumption of a short Session. It became clear, as the party went on, that there was so much confusion that people wanted to sit down and talk. So they did, soon dividing themselves up into the following groups. First, the staunch Bevanites, such as Harold Davies, John Baird, Fenner Brockway, Bob Stross and Stephen Swingler, who just thought there could be no question about it that Nye should challenge Morrison, whatever happened and whoever else stood. As far as I could judge, their view is not merely that Nye is the only possible Left candidate but also that he has some chance in the end of being elected.

The second group were the Griffithsites — Kenneth Robinson, Tony Greenwood, Leslie Plummer and George Wigg — who came in late and left early, but who said his piece and was supported by Maurice Edelman. One or two of them may believe that Jim Griffiths is a man of substance, with views coinciding with theirs, but most seemed to hold the view that, if he were put up, he might defeat Morrison, which would cause fissures and weakening in the Right. Thus his election would be a pure tactical manoeuvre against Morrison, which is why it had the strong support of Hugh Dalton.

Thirdly, there was a much smaller group, including Ungoed-Thomas, who turned out to be the great acquisition at this particular meeting, Harold Wilson and myself. Ungoed-Thomas straightaway argued that to put up Jim Griffiths was a fraud and that it would in fact be playing into Gaitskell's hands to do so, since, even if Griffiths did defeat Morrison, there was no chance of his ever becoming Prime Minister and in due course Gaitskell would replace him as Deputy Leader and so finally as Leader. Ungoed-Thomas argued that it was better to have Morrison as Leader after Attlee, since he is weak and old, than it was to have Gaitskell, who is young and strong, and he didn't want to see the issue confused by a man of straw being put up to represent those who dislike the Gaitskell/Morrison combination. On the other hand, he did not want Nye to stand either, since this would merely antagonize people in the Party, resurrect Bevanite recriminations and possibly militate against the chances of getting some left-wingers on to the Parliamentary Committee.[1]

Harold Wilson followed a closely similar line, stressing the need for Nye, if he was to have any chance, to prove to the Parliamentary Party that he could muck in with the Parliamentary leadership. What really mattered, therefore, said Harold, was that Nye should not only stand for the Parlia-

---

[1] There were fifty-four candidates for the twelve places on the Parliamentary Committee. Crossman had reluctantly let his name go forward, 'to ensure a sufficient number of left-wingers'.

mentary Committee but should stick it on the Committee for the whole of this long Session. If he did this and if the Left did well in the course of the year, things might change. But, whether the tactic was successful or not, it was the only practicable one.

The discussion really was very good, with each person spontaneously stating his view. The most revealing point came towards the end, when Jennie said she would like to state her view, which was that Nye should stand for the deputy leadership and not for the Parliamentary Committee. 'There are differences of function,' she said. 'I like to see people like Harold on the Parliamentary Committee while Nye keeps himself free outside.' This was said right at the end and I came in for the first time to say I thought this was absolutely fatal, since no Leader has ever been elected from the backbenches or without proof that he is capable of working in a team. Ungoed-Thomas resumed his position, supporting mine.

It was by now so late that we found no food at the House, as well as no Speaker, so Nye and Jennie and Anne and I went out to dinner, since Nye was unable to return to his farm and we had to put him up for the night. He was quite relaxed and easy. Right towards the end, before bed, when he was alone with me, I said he really must spend the next fourteen months playing in with the team if he was ever to have a chance of being Leader. 'I'm not sure I really want to be under these conditions,' he said, 'I'm not a proletarian or an intellectual. I am an aristocrat, with a real distaste for that kind of politics.' 'Well,' I said, 'aristocrats are no good in the Labour Party. If you want to be taken seriously, you had better stick on the Parliamentary Committee and not get off it, as you did last time.' But the truth is that Nye is three-quarters finished now and three-quarters knows it. His furious determination to oppose Morrison if Jim Griffiths stands, as well as his sudden statement to me this morning that, if Griffiths doesn't stand, he will withdraw his nomination, shows how much personal pique counts in his thought now and how much Jennie's escapism is carrying him back to his farm, which he discussed with me at great length for an hour, showing real enthusiasm.

Monday, June 13th

At about half-past ten on Thursday morning Nye went off to the House of Commons. The last thing he said to me was, 'We do agree, don't we, that, unless Jim Griffiths stands, I don't stand? It's only if Jim stands that I must challenge Herbert.' This was the first time he had said anything of the sort but I thought it was an improvement and said, 'Yes, but anyway, in my view you shouldn't stand.' To this Nye said it was impossible not to take up the challenge. However, I think he'd been shaken the night before. When he was having his nightcap, Hugh Dalton rang me up and asked how things had gone. I told him that Nye had decided to oppose Herbert, whereupon Hugh shouted down the telephone that, if that bugger behaved in that way, he wouldn't even vote for him in the Parliamentary Committee. He said a great many other things about Nye, all of which were perfectly audible to him, as he was standing just beside me with his elbow on the mantelpiece. What finally convinced me that Nye had heard every word was that when I put the telephone down he said, 'Of course, I couldn't hear what Dalton said.' On Thursday morning Lynn Ungoed-Thomas had also rung me up to say much the same thing and so had George Wigg, both while Nye was talking to me in my bedroom. I think all these independent people expressing their violent views may have shaken him a bit, to judge by what happened afterwards.

The Party Meeting that morning started with a most ungracious statement by Willy Whiteley, who attacked the press cliques and everybody else before saying that he had faced the *fait accompli* and was refusing to face a ballot on re-election. There came a whole series of little thank-you speeches to Willy Whiteley, in which Nye, somewhat surprisingly, joined. Attlee rose to make his position clear. He said that, under great pressure, he had decided not to resign in October but, now there was a long Session, to stay on and resign at the end of that Session, i.e. October next year. At this, Nye immediately sprang up and implored Clem not to give a date, since this would mean intrigues and press campaigns throughout the year. Then, to everybody's amazement, Nye added, 'In order to make my own position clear, I want to say that I shall not compete for any office in the Party,' by which he clearly meant that he would not stand for the deputy leadership. This produced a tremendous round of cheering, not least amongst those most ardent Bevanites, who, all the previous evening, had been supporting Nye, saying that he would have to stand against Herbert. I was probably the only person there, except for Jennie Lee, who knew the full contradiction of his statement.

After this there was a perfunctory discussion of the Queen's Speech, before we all streamed out to discuss Nye's statement for the rest of the day and to read it at length in Friday's papers. Nye was a little sheepish afterwards and very anxious to talk to me, but, for the first time in our relationship, I avoided a conversation, since I saw no good purpose in it! He gained an enormous lot of kudos by what he did, though I doubt whether he is aware how much he has tied himself up by this statement. If he now gets on the Parliamentary Committee, as he will, it will be quite impossible for him to resign again without becoming a Maxton. Nye has, in fact, ended his bid for the Parliamentary leadership for fourteen months and, in my private view, however well he behaves, there is very little chance of his becoming either Leader or Deputy Leader when Attlee chooses to resign and to take Morrison with him. This is really the end of a very interesting chapter. If things had gone differently last week and the Left/Right recriminations and struggles had been resumed, it would have brought the Labour Party into the state of the Liberal Party in the 1920s. What we managed to do was to prevent this happening. On this occasion (compared with the episode of the H-bomb) Nye havered and hovered and then, while on his feet, fell off them but on the right side of the fence.

Meanwhile the debate on the Queen's Speech has been going on simultaneously with the railway strike and in an atmosphere of complete flatness. In fact, this debate in the new Commons is exactly like the General Election. There is simply no challenge to the Government and no issue, as far as I can see, on which the Labour Party is fighting. Personally, I think it is no bad thing that things should be completely flat just for the present, while the leadership reconstitutes itself and the elections to the Shadow Cabinet take place. Nor can anybody blame the Party for not intervening in the strike nor taking sides in it. It just is a Party without policy and without leadership but on the whole that is a better state of affairs than its being a Party without policy but rent by personal rivalry for the leadership.

Wednesday, June 22nd
At the Executive meeting this morning we had a report on the Election by Morgan Phillips, who was obviously scared of a tremendous row, since the press had predicted his dismissal. However, once again this had been anticipated and Harold, after consulting me and Gaitskell, had lobbied for a special committee to study organization and report to Conference. This was not a direct attack on Morgan Phillips but was opposed by Edith [Summerskill] and Alice Bacon. With great skill Harold got it agreed, with Gaitskell's support, and got himself on it, along with three weaklings – Jack Cooper, Peggy Herbison and one other.[1] Herbert Morrison ended our inquest with a most dreary pontification about policy, which bored everyone. If Nye had been present, he would have launched a terrific policy attack on Herbert and the fat would have been in the fire. As it was, we got through and got our way without rows, though I failed to get Ian put on the committee, which is a pity.

Harold came back to lunch with John Freeman and we discussed informal groups. Both of them are strongly against the Tuesday lunches or a Keep Left Group. We began to feel towards the idea of doing six *New Statesman* supplements from October to March, outlining plans on such subjects as transport, pensions, housing, inflation. The supplements would be anonymous and the result of group work by M.P.s, who would be given very good dinners at the cost of the *New Statesman*. The groups' drafts might possibly be submitted to a larger permanent group. I rather like this idea, which could then issue in a *New Statesman* pamphlet.

We are also having some success with the campaign for trying to make the Parliamentary Committee something approximating to a Shadow Cabinet, with a staff and with specialist committees working to it. Altogether, since the Election I think we've had a major victory behind the scenes. We've avoided relapsing into recriminations, and, once the new Shadow Cabinet is

[1] The 'one other' was Arthur Skeffington (see p. 347).

elected, we shall have steered the Party through a period in which it might have disintegrated. I think there has been a real melting of the anti-Bevanite and Bevanite blocks, which were really preventing free discussion, and that there have been regroupings on the Left and the Right. For the first time for months, though on very little evidence, I am a great deal more cheerful about the prospects of the Party. I am also looking forward to a year in which writing and formulating ideas will not only be essential but will be much more likely to occur.

Tuesday, June 28th

The elections for the Shadow Cabinet were announced last Thursday evening.[1] Since Anne was ill, I missed the Party Meeting at half-past six but George Wigg met me in the Central Lobby and told me I had done fairly well. He was obviously terribly upset and finally revealed that his vote was twenty-three. He told me, as he so often does, that this had finally tipped the balance and he would now earn his own living, since there was no gratitude in politics.

I went into the Smoking Room and in the corner with the gang found Nye and Jennie, whom I hadn't seen for several days. Jennie was terribly downcast and assured me it was because John Rankin[2] had only got thirty-one votes. But really, of course, it was because Harold's vote had gone up and was twenty ahead of Nye, who at this rate stands small chance of the leadership. I was ahead of Barbara and Ian. Most people were either agreeably or disagreeably surprised at the size of my vote.

We analysed this complex ballot for a long time. It's fairly clear that the vast majority of the Parliamentary Party still voted either Left or Right — or, shall we say, started from the Right and moved to the Centre, or started from the Left and moved to the Centre. But at least the McCarthyite hatchetmen, such as Charlie Hobson, had only scored seventeen, and even Stanley Evans, despite every effort, was ten below me. I concluded it was a fairly good result and so, naturally, did Harold Wilson, who was in bubbling form.

I discussed with Harold at length the tactic for next week. We agreed that he should make an effort to get across at the Shadow Cabinet the idea of having Shadow Ministers and of a Shadow Secretariat, as well as of linking the Shadow Ministers with the Party's specialist committees. The meeting of the Shadow Cabinet took place yesterday and immediately Gaitskell said he had two propositions to make. First, he proposed functionalization, i.e. allocating jobs to members, and he suggested that the Leader should do this. Secondly, he proposed a skeleton Shadow Cabinet Secretariat. 'May I explain,' he added, 'that these proposals are not derived from Dick Cross-

---

[1] Those seven Labour Members who stood for re-election were successful. They were joined by Aneurin Bevan and Dick Stokes and three others, by the three Party officers (Attlee, Morrison and Herbert Bowden) and by three members of the House of Lords.

[2] Labour M.P. for the Tradeston division of Glasgow 1945–55 and for the Govan division of Glasgow from 1955 until his death in 1973.

man's article in the *New Statesman*.[1] I had thought of them before, but I must add that I thought the article was extremely good.'

Apparently Attlee steered the thing along quite nicely and they agreed to functionalization and a room for a Shadow Secretariat. They decided to let the relationship of this with the specialist committees be discussed tomorrow morning, at the Party Meeting.

Altogether I am still fairly cheerful about the present mood of the Party. I was relieved that Nye disappeared to Paris this weekend (none of us knows what he is doing), since this enabled the first Shadow Cabinet meeting to go without a hitch, as we had intended. Of course, our danger in all this is that the left-wing in the country will not keep up with what is happening and may therefore disavow us or turn against us as traitors. But my feeling at present is that at Conference next October the delegates will want Party unity and, if we can provide some results in the form of the beginning of a practical offensive against the Government this July, we may be able to hold the position and get the Party's discussion of policy on to less sterile lines than the Bevanite controversy was before the Election.

Thursday, June 30th
Hugh Cudlipp came to lunch yesterday and immediately asked me what I thought of Fienburgh. I always find it's best to tell Hugh the exact truth, so I told him that in my view he is an outstandingly good journalist. I described how he had been asked to do a profile of Eden for the *New Statesman* and had brought in something totally inadequate. I had then briefed him for ten minutes, talking very fast and pouring out ideas. Two hours later he had come back with every one of those ideas incorporated in a first-rate piece.[2] That, I said, was a very unusual characteristic.

Fienburgh is worth having on one's staff, as long as you realize that he is an able, professional young man with a career to make, no principles and few ideas of his own. Hugh said he agreed entirely, now that he had seen him three times, and then revealed that he had been considering Fienburgh for his big new political column in the *Mirror*, which he has been discussing with me on and off for two years. Hugh's idea is to make the man who writes it the Walter Lippmann[3] of British journalism. So I said, 'Well, what about Denis Healey? Now he really has ideas. He's brilliantly clever.' But Hugh dismissed him on the ground that he can't write and turned back to me,

[1] The faults of existing arrangements and a design for an effective 'Opposition Cabinet' were set out by Crossman in 'Shadow Cabinet or Caucus', *New Statesman and Nation*, June 25th, 1955.

[2] Probably 'Success Through Indecision', *New Statesman and Nation*, February 19th, 1955.

[3] Walter Lippmann (1889–1974), author and journalist, was an Associate Editor of *The New Republic* in the 1930s and Editor of *New York World* and in the 1950s and 1960s an influential columnist, whose articles on political affairs were widely syndicated, with the *New York Herald Tribune* and the *Washington Post*. In the late 1960s he left Washington to live in New York, making thereafter only occasional contributions to *Newsweek*.

making it clear that he had not intended to discuss this. We then warmed to the subject. I said that, since the Election, my mind had changed but that this would mean giving up the *New Statesman* altogether.

Hugh then said, 'Yes, you'd have to have a room in the *Mirror* and work very closely with Sydney Jacobson,' and he began to expand the scheme further and further, finally saying it would mean a five-year contract, a whole-time devilling researcher and a secretary, to which I said I had one. I asked whether we hadn't better wait until the Chairman and Sydney returned from America, to which Hugh replied, 'No, we could decide this ourselves today. I've nothing to fear from Cecil.' It all reminded me of the times seven years ago when Hugh hired me, in very similar circumstances, after I had given him a very good meal. He is an astonishingly pertinacious man with his ideas. I have no doubt he will put this up to King as a serious proposal.

This morning I asked George Wigg what he thought about it. To my surprise he advised accepting but added the very sensible proviso that I should not get myself too closely integrated into the *Mirror* and that I should get a lawyer to vet the contract. The contract should give me complete independence, a top-hat pension and sufficient compensation to live on happily ever afterwards. I think there is something in what George says. I shall refuse a room in the *Mirror* if they offer it and merely have a desk in Sydney's room and work at home. It would probably mean, if I did it, giving up the National Executive, which I should quite like to do. But Hugh Cudlipp was quite clear how he envisaged it. 'If you take this job,' he said, 'you can have half an hour's talk with the Prime Minister whenever you want,' and he's probably right.

Friday, July 15th

I have not written in this diary for a fortnight and when I look back at the last entry I find that it is concerned with the sole topic that has been in my mind, for ever since that lunch with Hugh I have been negotiating or discussing Hugh Cudlipp's offer. First of all, I put it to John Freeman at lunch and he, after consideration, said that, rather than lose me he would like to see Kingsley resign and me take his place, in which case he would serve under me. I think John meant it perfectly sincerely but I never seriously considered the possibility of Kingsley's resigning in order to make way for me, particularly after V. S. Pritchett[1] had asked himself to stay at Vincent Square for a night and I had had a morning's talk with him. V. S. Pritchett is a Director of the *N.S.* and a very cautious little man. He confirmed what I had always thought—that Kingsley both likes me and is passionately jealous of

[1] Author, critic and visiting professor at various American universities, he was a Director of the *New Statesman and Nation*. His publications include *George Meredith and English Comedy* (London: Chatto & Windus, 1970), *Balzac* (London: Chatto & Windus, 1973) and *The Camberwell Beauty and Other Stories* (London: Chatto & Windus, 1974). He was knighted in 1975.

me — and he dismissed as a pure absurdity the idea that Kingsley would ever resign or retire. V. S. also seemed to be in the clique which is anti-Freeman/MacKenzie/Vallance and, though he would probably like to see me as Editor, he has been told so often by Kingsley that I want to be a Cabinet Minister and am unsuitable that he has never taken the idea very seriously.

Most of the people I have talked to have been surprisingly in favour of my going to the *Mirror*, including particularly Harold Wilson and John Strachey, who see this as a tremendous opportunity to influence the *Mirror* in the right direction and, incidentally, as a job which I can really do. On the other hand, Hugh Dalton and Tommy Balogh both agree (about the only thing they really do agree about) that it is somehow degrading to work for the *Mirror*. They were deeply shocked at the idea of my leaving the *Statesman*. Rather impressed by this, I informed Hugh that I could not possibly make up my mind until Kingsley had come back and until he had been given a fortnight in which to offer me an alternative whole-time job on the *Statesman* and to consult the Board. Hugh was very peeved by this and said that he was not used to auctions. He asked whether he was next going to have a triangular offer from Lord Beaverbrook. However, he went on to offer me £3,000 a year and £1,000 expenses, for a four-year contract.

All this was happening whilst Kingsley was away in Helsinki and Moscow. The day before yesterday he came in unexpectedly and John Freeman told him of the problem, whereupon he rang me up and I asked him to lunch. I sat Kingsley down over coffee and he then expressed surprise that I should conceive of leaving the *Statesman*, since he had offered me a weekly column and, as he put it, wasn't my public really the educated public and wouldn't I degrade myself on the *Mirror*? I said I had been degrading myself for eight years on the *Pic* and that anyway he couldn't possibly give me a whole page in the *Statesman* each week to comment quite differently on the subjects of the editorials, since that would make the paper ridiculous. What I wanted was to reshape the paper as an *Economist* of the left — not, of course, imitating *The Economist* but keeping the second half of the paper intact and giving the first half the weight it requires before it is taken seriously. That would mean getting rid of Norman MacKenzie, pensioning off Aylmer Vallance, stopping publishing very dull articles on India or articles merely put in so as not to hurt somebody's feelings.

Kingsley took it all quite well and asked me whether I thought this could be done while he was Editor or whether I should become Editor. I replied that I would be absurd to deny that I thought I could edit the paper if he fell down dead tomorrow but it was equally absurd for me to ask him to resign when he was in such good health. As to whether it could be done under his editorship, I wasn't sure, since I thought he rather wanted the paper to tick along nicely and would resent its being so serious. Kingsley then said that money was no problem at all and, when I expressed some surprise, asked me how much I would require. So, without thinking it over, I said £3,000 and

£10 a week in expenses. 'Oh, that goes without saying,' he said. 'No problem there.' We then spent a long time discussing the sort of way I should like to do the paper, in which it was only too clear that he would resist at every point but that, on the other hand, he could not deny the reforms were right. We really had a very nice discussion and both liked each other. He went off to the paper in tremendous form, saying it could all be worked out.

However, this morning Kingsley rang up at half-past eight and said, 'I've thought it over, Dick. It's quite definite that there's no room for the three of us on the paper, so I must tell you straightaway that I can't accept your proposition.' At this I said mildly that I hadn't made any proposition and I thought he had made one to me, but I quite understood if he had thought better of it. Was his decision final? At this he gasped a little and I said, 'Well, it's a waste of time to go on discussing it if you really have made up your mind.' So he said, 'Yes, I have.' We then agreed that I should go at the end of my holiday in mid-September, after having seen the others through their holidays in August, and that I would not be barred from writing reviews.

In the afternoon I rang up John, who was amazed to hear that Kingsley had finalized the thing, since all he had said to John was that there wasn't any point in meeting to discuss it next Monday, since he had made up his mind. But, characteristically, Kingsley did not tell John that he had not only made up his mind but had also agreed that I should inform Cudlipp that his decision was final. I have written a careful letter to Kingsley this afternoon, since I am very much interested, in the not so very long run, in returning to the *New Statesman* if, as I think a real possibility, I were offered the editorship in the next five years. The explanation of Kingsley's change of mind is clear enough. Either in bed with Dorothy or sleepless alone, he suddenly realized to his horror that, if he had me back as Deputy Editor at £3,000 a year, I should be in the office all the time, editing, and he wouldn't last more than two or three years. I don't in the least blame him but it has certainly strengthened my position with the *New Statesman* Board to have been willing to accept any offer of whole-time work they could make me and to have been told by Kingsley that there was no offer to be made.

I'm afraid this very egocentric concentration on my own future has made me take relatively little interest in politics. Not that there has been very much. The Opposition has continued to be almost lethargic, while slowly a new Shadow Cabinet was constituted by Attlee, with Shadow Ministers and Shadow Parliamentary Secretaries. I was with Anne at the Royal Garden Party yesterday but at the Party Meeting at half-past six somebody mentioned that the *Star* had got a leak about most of the appointments, whereupon the whole list was read aloud, showing Nye as Shadow Minister of Labour and Alf Robens as Shadow Foreign Secretary. So now we are right back before Nye's resignation in 1951. The whole Bevanite Group has disintegrated and Nye has become once again a lone wolf, this time as a member of a Shadow Cabinet in which everybody has been given Shadow jobs as a substitute for the real thing. I only hope they won't feel that, having done this, they have achieved anything. Though I suggested moving away from caucus rule to a stronger Parliamentary Committee, I never dreamt that they would envisage setting themselves up so pretentiously as a full-scale Shadow Government, looking very much like the Labour Government in its worst, last phase in 1950.

The fact is that the results of the Election are already proving far more profound and pervasive than anybody expected. Not only is the Labour Party ideologically disintegrated by the fact that Keynesian welfare capitalism is proving, for the time being, quite an adequate substitute for Socialism. Each of us, individually, is being changed. During the last three weeks, when I have come home to dinner and then just dropped into the House to vote, I have begun to realize how ordinary politicians, for generations, have regarded politics—not as a mission or vocation, but as a rather pleasant public service, which one takes on in addition to one's main interests and one's private life but without permitting it to tyrannize over the others. Each of us in our own way is becoming a private person again, whereas, ever since I can remember in my adult life, I have been first a public person, in the sense that I have never dreamt that politics should not be given first place —or rather, if I failed to give it to politics, I had a bad conscience. I don't think there is any doubt that one reason for my going to join the *Mirror* is because of this loosening of the sense that one was fulfilling oneself in service to the Labour Movement.

Others are behaving in the same way but in different environments. Ian is now immersing himself in his business, Nye is out on his farm or drinking and merely playing his part as a politician in the Shadow Cabinet. 'Things fall apart, the centre cannot hold.' And, ironically enough, all this happens to the Labour Party because people in Britain are more prosperous and more contented and because peace is breaking out all over the world. We suddenly feel that our mission to save people from cataclysm and disaster has come unstuck. We are missionaries without a mission, or missionaries more and more dubious about the mission. And what I cannot deny is the enormous enjoyment of being a private citizen with a private life and a farm in the country and books to read which one doesn't review and all the things which, I suppose, most people take for granted but which I haven't taken for granted because I was far more of a political Puritan than I ever realized.

All reports from America show just as miraculous a change of atmosphere as in Moscow. The world is really turning away from war to co-existence, without the mediation of a Socialist Britain, which we have so often said was essential to prevent world war between the U.S.A. and the U.S.S.R. How can I fail to have a different view of what is worth doing? I cannot help feeling enormously excited by this chance on the *Mirror*. It sounds absurd but in one sense it is the biggest chance in the world for a columnist. I shall be freer without the *Statesman*, I shall have the largest public in the world and it will be my fault if I have nothing worth saying, week in, week out, for the next four years. This is a time, in fact, when it's better to have a vehicle for thinking and teaching than to work in a political party.

After an exchange of Notes between the British, French and American Governments and the Soviet Union, the Four-Power meeting was arranged, to open in Geneva on July 18th. Proceedings were amiable but there were no dramatic results.

The problems of German reunification were referred to a further meeting of Foreign Ministers, to be held in Geneva in October. On July 21st President Eisenhower proposed that America and Russia should exchange all blueprints of their military establishments and should provide facilities for mutual aerial inspection. This suggestion was subsequently rejected by the Russians. The Heads of Government also discussed contacts between East and West, or what President Eisenhower called the removal of 'curtains'.

Crossman stayed in Geneva from July 16th to 21st. 'What was clear to me,' he observed,

> was that there was a distinct difference of tone between the State Department and Dulles on the one side and the White House gang on the other, the State Department always taking the gloomy view of a breakdown and the White House being much more optimistic. And one very soon knew somehow or other that Ike was making a tremendous effort against his expert advisers to break through the Russian guard and establish good relations with them.

Crossman's reports on the conference may be found in the New Statesman and Nation *of July 16th and 23rd, and the* Sunday Pictorial *of July 10th and 17th, 1955.*

On Wednesday July 20th, Crossman took the train to Paris, where he lectured on the Thursday at the NATO Staff College. He dined with Paul Johnson,[1] the New Statesman and Nation *Correspondent, 'who told me that on the previous Saturday John Freeman had offered him a full-time job on the* Statesman. *To my surprise, this cool young man added that he thought John Freeman would be useless as an Editor!'*

On his return to London Crossman found a letter from Kingsley Martin, to whom he had written on July 15th, confirming the 'extremely hard decision to leave the paper'. Crossman's next, brief diary entry, written on August 3rd, looked forward to joining the Mirror, *with its 'extraordinary spontaneity' and 'irresponsible* joie de vivre'. *In a letter to John Roberts, the* New Statesman and Nation *Manager, Crossman wrote:*

> For some months now I have realized that any ministerial ambitions I may
> have had – and they were less than some people imagine – are unlikely to be

[1] Paul Johnson was Editor of the *New Statesman* 1965–70. His publications include *The Offshore Islanders* (London: Weidenfeld & Nicolson, 1972) and *A History of Christianity* (London: Weidenfeld & Nicolson, 1976).

*realized and that my future lies in the realm of ideas and public opinion ...
This* Mirror *column is a real challenge ... to anybody who believes in
democracy and adult education. On the other hand, there are great risks of
the column being a flop. It was the risks involved which attracted me. Here
was a chance of either succeeding or failing in something for which I would
be personally responsible.*

Crossman spent the early part of August in transferring himself to the
Mirror, with the help of his new solicitor, 'George's friend Mr Goodman,[1] a
vast orang-utang of a man'. Crossman wrote to Hugh Cudlipp asking various
questions about holidays, sick leave, the independence of the column and his
desire 'to ensure that the Daily Mirror does not kill me or dry me up within a
short time by over-production'. (To this last point Cudlipp replied, 'our present
contributors are looking remarkably well, and if your Mr Goodman is as
rosy-cheeked as they are he also has nothing to worry about.') Crossman's
comment on Cudlipp's reply was:

The picture of the Daily Mirror *as a kind of tribe of comrades whom one
joins without the vaguest suspicion that anybody might do anybody else an
injury is fantastic but not fantastic when you are talking to Hugh, who keeps
on saying to me in an injured tone of voice, 'Can you remember any time
when I have ever changed a word of your column or denied you a holiday or
refused you money?'*

The most important news of August, in Crossman's view, was a report in
the Daily Mirror on August 19th that, while on holiday at Cherry Cottage,
Attlee had suffered an attack of cerebral thrombosis. 'Cecil King is merciless
to his opponents,' wrote Crossman. 'Every other paper reported that Attlee is
now getting better from a slight indisposition.'

After some lecturing at summer schools, Richard and Anne Crossman spent
their holiday in Italy, mostly in Tuscany. From September 12th to 14th Crossman attended the Congress for Cultural Freedom in Milan, where he saw
'quite a lot' of Hugh Gaitskell, who, Crossman wrote, 'couldn't have been more
polite ... In fact he was doing all he could to be collaborative'.

On his return to London, Crossman was immediately caught up in the
preliminary manoeuvrings before the opening of the Malta Conference. Dom
Mintoff, the Labour Prime Minister of Malta, had come to London at the end
of June and Crossman learnt from Tommy Balogh and Dudley Seers, now

---

[1] Arnold Goodman, a solicitor, and Senior Partner in Goodman, Derrick & Co. He
became a life peer in 1965. A director of the *Observer* since 1976, he was Chairman of the
Arts Council of Great Britain 1965–72, Chairman of the *Observer* Trust 1967–76, of the
Newspaper Publishers' Association 1970–5, of the Industrial Reorganization Corporation
1969–71 and of British Lion Films Ltd 1965–72; since 1973 he has been Chairman of
Charter Film Productions. He was also Chairman of the National Building Agency 1973–8
and of the Housing Corporation 1973–7, and became Chairman of the Theatres Trust in
1976 and, in the same year, of the Theatre Investment Fund. In 1977 he was appointed
Chairman of Motability. He has been Master of University College, Oxford, since 1976.

Mintoff's 'chief advisers', that he had come to seek union with the United Kingdom on 'an Ulster basis'; that is, with Maltese Members in the House of Commons. Attlee and Eden discussed the matter several times and on July 6th the Prime Minister made a Statement that the Government proposed to convene an all-party Round Table Conference, to meet in the summer Recess and discuss the constitutional, economic and financial issues involved. Crossman was a member of this conference and he dined with Mintoff and Balogh on Monday 19th, the evening of the first day of the conference: 'The atmosphere was curiously like my first relationship with the Jews in the Palestine Commission. Naturally enough, politicians are terrified of people who say they want to make up their minds independently and won't take their advice.'

Crossman's other preoccupation was with his new column, which first appeared on September 20th.

Friday, September 23rd

We flew home from Milan on Wednesday, the 14th, and on Thursday I clocked in to see Sydney and Hugh about the column. While waiting for Hugh, I went into the *Sunday Pic* and found Reg Payne[1] in charge. He told me, I think quite sincerely, that he was very sorry to see me go, since it made the paper even more flibberty-gibberty. We discussed Fienburgh's column, which is extremely competently written but, as I had expected, a bit thin. Then we went down to Hugh's room and for the rest of the afternoon he was trying to give me confidence that everything would be O.K. and I would be all right. Eileen picked Hugh up in the Jaguar and they dropped me at Vincent Square, where I began serious newspaper reading to fill in four weeks' total ignorance.

We came back to London early on Sunday and I did my first big piece for the *Mirror* on Adenauer in Moscow.[2] I had wanted to do Attlee but Sydney was against it. I didn't listen to the wireless as I should have done and so missed the Burgess and Maclean story, which I only saw early on Monday morning.[3] I completely redid the column, leading with Burgess and Maclean, only to be somewhat disconcerted on Tuesday to find that the whole front page of the paper had led it, too.

The following Tuesday, I did my second column quite successfully. In the afternoon, after a meeting of the International Sub., I brought Harold

---

[1] Editor of the *Sunday Pictorial* and, later, of the *Sunday Mirror*.

[2] Crossman had gone to Moscow on September 8th, in response to an invitation issued on June 7th.

[3] Guy Burgess and Donald Maclean, two former Foreign Office officials, had left the country on May 25th, 1951, and fled behind the Iron Curtain. In September 1955 the publication of the Report of an Australian Royal Commission, investigating Soviet activities in that country, revived interest in this episode. The disclosures of a former Soviet agent, Vladimir Petrov, provided new information about Burgess and Maclean and suggested laxness in the Foreign Office attitude to its personnel and in its procedures for examining allegations about them. On September 23rd a Foreign Office White Paper appeared; it was with this forthcoming document that Crossman's column dealt.

Wilson and Barbara home for a drink. Barbara told me she had seen Attlee, who said he was willing to stay on for twelve months. With Barbara one is never sure whether Attlee hadn't merely grunted at intervals while she told him what to think. I tested her view by myself talking to Attlee during a tea-time interval of our meeting on Malta. He certainly has not committed himself to staying on the whole twelve months but merely to staying on if the Party insists, which is slightly different.

After Barbara had gone, Harold Wilson stayed, obviously bursting with information. After a little palaver, he rushed out to his car and brought in his 'Report on Party Organization'. This is a really sensational document, since it provides detailed evidence from the centre, the regions and the constituencies for all the complaints about organization which all of us, individually, have made. It is, in fact, an annihilating destruction of Morgan Phillips and, to a lesser extent, of Len Williams.

Harold told me that Herbert Morrison was in favour of publication and that he himself is determined to run organization now by getting himself made chairman of a committee of four. Harold has been very adroit in retaining the 100 per cent support of Jack Cooper of the Municipal and General, Peggy Herbison and Arthur Skeffington, a Morrison stooge, so no one can accuse Harold's sub. of being left-wing or cliquey.

I told Harold that Nye was very puzzled at his not seeing him. Harold replied cheerfully that his wife had hardly seen him in the last two months. He has done no less than 145 meetings up and down the country taking evidence.

This morning I cautiously mentioned this to Sydney as background. Sydney was embarrassed. He brought himself to tell me that he had a copy of the Report lying on his table and that he wanted to release it next Monday in the *Mirror* if this would not embarrass me too much. I told him I had better get this row with my colleagues over early, since I would always be blamed about such things and in this case would not like myself to be suspected, now that I knew that Sydney had got hold of a copy before I had spoken to him.

Nye came to lunch with me yesterday and wasn't very impressed by what I told him about Harold, because of course he has never bothered about organization and dislikes thinking Harold can really do a job.

Tuesday, September 27th
Yesterday I had Attlee to lunch between the sessions of our Malta conference. As soon as we got into our sitting room and I had given him a drink, he said he hadn't been able to hear a word of what the boring speaker had said all morning and had spent the time reading the Wilson Report. I had been staggered on opening my *Daily Mirror* that morning to read a most masterly and comprehensive survey of this. On Sunday night Sydney had warned me that they were going to publish it and I had taken the precaution of ringing

up Harold to tip him off. Harold was cool and told me he knew all about the leaks. I said I presumed it would be better that only I and Harold knew that a copy of the Report had been lying on Jacobson's table for the last few days. Harold said it would be better. I then said I had rung him since I would certainly be accused of leaking, though I could easily rebut the charge and had taken the most careful precautions against saying anything to the *Mirror*. The thought had crossed my mind that I had been planted with this but I'm sure that's untrue and that Harold had simply not thought of my position.

However, to go back to Attlee, he had not read the *Mirror* and merely said, 'Absolutely first-rate! Superb job!' When I said I thought the Report should be published, Attlee said, 'Of course! It would do the Party the world of good. Put new spirit into them. Why, in my constituency there was nobody under seventy in the committee rooms and they were doing the same old routine they had done for the last thirty years. Won't do at all!'

I then said that the Report seemed to me to be a tacit criticism of Morgan Phillips. 'We haven't had a Secretary we can trust,' said Attlee, 'since Arthur Henderson. I've never taken much interest in organization myself but it's important and I'm glad that Harold has taken over.'

I discussed with Attlee Eisenhower's coronary thrombosis[1] and he said, 'When I saw Ike I advised him against becoming President. I said to him, "All the Generals who have been President have been disasters except the one who died six weeks after he was elected,"[2] but he didn't take my advice. Now Harry Truman was a different type. Real courage and understood politics.' 'Were you friendly,' I asked Attlee, 'when you flew over that time to stop the atom bomb being thrown?' 'Why, yes,' he said, 'we agreed entirely.'

I think Truman might give a somewhat different account of Attlee's stay in the White House, though Clem added one amusing item: 'It was while I was there,' he said, 'that Margaret and Truman wrote the letter to the journalist who criticized her.[3] What a splendid thing to do! Of course, he asked my advice that night and I told him not to worry about criticism but he dashed off the letter, calling the journalist an S.O.B. That's the spirit!' It seemed to me that Attlee was almost envying Truman for doing and being all the things he isn't.

[1] The President suffered a heart attack on September 24th. He was pronounced fit to travel on November 11th and left Denver, Colorado, where he had been taken ill, for his Gettysburg farm.

[2] William Henry Harrison (1773–1841), Commander of the North-West in the War of 1812–14, was in 1840 elected ninth President of the United States by an overwhelming majority. He died at Washington a month after his inauguration on April 4th.

[3] On December 5th, 1950, the day after Attlee's arrival in Washington, Margaret Truman, the President's daughter and a concert singer (1947–54), gave the last of a series of recitals. Paul Hume, Music Critic of the *Washington Post*, wrote a savage review of her singing. The President sent a letter to Hume, describing him as sounding like 'a frustrated man that never made a success, an eight-ulcer man on a four-ulcer job and all four ulcers working'. Truman's assistants thought the letter unfortunate, especially when the *Post* published it. According to Margaret Truman (*Harry S. Truman*, Hamish Hamilton, 1973, pp. 502–3), 80 per cent of the letters received from the public supported 'Dad's defense'.

In the course of the lunch I asked him an important question, which I had been brooding over, about Burgess and Maclean. This has suddenly blown up as a major political issue, thanks to Petrov's[1] revelations in the *People* the previous week. The White Paper caused every single newspaper to denounce the Government for covering up and I wanted to know how Attlee stood. I told him my suggestion for a Lynskey Tribunal[2] and he grunted approval. 'If I'd been at the Foreign Office,' he said, 'I'd have been more brutal when that sort of thing was discovered. I am more brutal than people imagine.' I then asked him the 64-dollar question. 'Was the matter ever brought to your attention as Prime Minister before Maclean disappeared?' 'Certainly not,' he said. 'I knew nothing whatsoever.'[3]

He had asked for this lunch to discuss defence but eventually all he did was to say that he agreed with my article and that we should go for small professional forces and for getting rid of National Service altogether.[4] He added that he had been told that he was going to deal with the thing at Margate.[5]

Thursday, September 29th
Tuesday's dinner party was a rather sad affair. I had originally arranged just to have the Executive members to discuss Wednesday's important meeting. Then Barbara suggested that Nye would be aggrieved if he were not invited, so I mentioned it to him on Monday morning and, to my surprise,

[1] Vladimir Mikhailovich Petrov, the former chief of Soviet Intelligence in Australia, and his wife Evdokia Alexeevna, also an Intelligence officer, applied for asylum in Australia in 1954. Petrov had defected, fearing punishment as a supposed adherent of the Beria faction. Mrs Petrov, while being forcibly escorted back to the U.S.S.R., was freed by Australian police when the aeroplane stopped at Darwin and, in consequence, the U.S.S.R. broke off diplomatic relations with Australia. The Petrovs testified before an Australian Royal Commission investigating Soviet espionage and later they published *Empire of Fear* (London: Deutsch, 1956).

[2] A tribunal may be appointed by the Sovereign or a Secretary of State upon a resolution of both Houses of Parliament on a matter of urgent public importance. Such a body has all the powers of the High Court regarding the examination of witnesses and production of documents. In 1948 a tribunal chaired by Mr Justice Lynskey had investigated allegations of bribery of Ministers or other public servants in connection with the grant of licences, etc. Its report was published as Cmd 7616. Sir George Lynskey was called to the Bar in 1920. He became a K.C. in 1930 and from 1937 to 1944 was a Judge of Salford Hundred Court of Record. He was knighted in 1944 and in that year became a Judge of the High Court of Justice, King's Bench Division.

[3] The status of the security services is deliberately unclear. The head of the Security Service (M.I.5) is directly responsible to the Home Secretary, and the head of the Intelligence Service (M.I.6) to the Foreign Secretary. The heads of both M.I.5 and M.I.6 have the right of direct access to the Prime Minister. It was on this last point that Crossman fastened, as he was to do again in 1963, when the third agent, Kim Philby, defected.

[4] 'The New Case Against Conscription', *New Statesman and Nation*, August 13th, 1955. Crossman argued that in the nuclear age universal military service had become outdated. Only civil defence, with the entire adult population trained for ambulance and rescue work, was now relevant.

[5] Where the Labour Party Conference was meeting from October 10th to 14th.

he said he would like to come. So there were six of us – Nye, Barbara, Ian, Tom Driberg, Harold Wilson and myself.

When Nye arrived, Harold immediately began to tell us about the organization committee and his plans for a committee of four with himself as chairman, which would assure his control of the whole machine. I had heard all this before, first when he came to this house and then twice on the telephone. The others were obviously a bit shocked by the exhibition of personal power politics, though, as the evening went on, they became more and more impressed as to what he had actually achieved in the Report.

Nye obviously felt a bit out of it until after dinner, when Barbara protested that 'Harold is destroying the democracy of Org. Sub.' I said this was pure nonsense, since there wasn't any democracy on the Executive. To everybody's surprise, Nye, after humming and hawing, said that he agreed with me and that Harold was right to try to make the Executive an efficient power machine and that meant really establishing ministerial responsibilities. Nye added – rather farsightedly, as it proved – that one shouldn't reckon that when one has created the machine one would necessarily run it, but at least one would know where responsibility lay and be able to attack it.

We then discussed the Report in some detail and towards the end Harold said, 'We must discuss Conference and what sort of speech Nye should make.' Barbara said he should speak on automation, a nice safe subject, and then Harold proposed (he had mentioned it to me before) that the parliamentary report, referring to the withdrawal of the whip, should be referred back and that Nye should intervene on this occasion, i.e. on the Monday. Barbara and Ian both had my reaction when Harold first said this to me. He would be hated for reviving the old feud, they said, and heavily voted down. At this Nye said, 'But I'm going to be voted down anyway in the election for Treasurer, and, if you let this pass, where do I stand?' I suspect that Nye's and Harold's motives for both agreeing that Harold should speak on this issue were somewhat different but I couldn't help agreeing that it was the only issue he could speak on and, if he made the right sort of conciliatory speech, putting feuds aside, etc., it might come off.

Nye finally got going and pounded out a long speech about the Labour Party being hopeless, dominated by four trade union leaders, etc. He ended by turning to Barbara and saying, 'And what you will have to seriously consider, Barbara, is whether this Labour Party is worth working for at all.' After this he went. I think all of us felt that somehow an epoch had ended. It was not simply that Nye was out of it through not knowing about the Executive or being more interested in pigs. It was a feeling that somehow a wave of history on which he had risen seemed to be falling, that he was still as brilliant as ever but didn't count so much. There was also a sense that he himself was bored with the evening and would have preferred to have had a dinner without politics.

Yesterday was the great Executive day, when we had to fix everything for

Conference and then deal with Harold's Report. Every now and then during the dinner party on Tuesday, Harold would whisper to me something about the *Daily Mirror* leak, how he would deal with it and, if necessary, state that the Committee knew about it and that I wasn't concerned.

In the course of all this, I more or less gathered from him (my memory isn't accurate and I probably got some of this from Sydney) that what had actually happened had been that the *Daily Mirror* had collected quite a number of leaks about the Committee and patched them together for a sensational story of what the Committee had done, under the headline that it had destroyed Morgan Phillips. It was the old, old trick and Harold fell for it. He begged them not to publish, to which they replied that of course they wouldn't publish an incorrect version if he could just give them the correct one.

We were all discussing what was going to happen but we had to wait throughout the whole morning while we got through the ordinary business. One not unimportant thing was that we had to fix the business for Tuesday morning at Conference, which will be televised,[1] and after some discussion it was decided to have the H-bomb, but there was doubt whether we should have National Service as well, since we hadn't a clear policy. Attlee looked up and said that we should have a debate on national defence, including the H-bomb and National Service, as one subject. This was very smart, since he is speaking on the H-bomb and will now introduce the whole issue of defence, along the lines he had discussed with me.

After lunch we all returned to the meeting and I was expecting and rather hoping that we should start with a tremendous demand to discover the source of the leak. This would have given me an opportunity to explain my precise position under my contract on the *Mirror*. By pure luck, my position was strengthened by the fact that I had a cast-iron alibi, since I had only returned to London at half-past seven on Sunday and my copy of the Report had only been opened by Rose [Cohen] on Monday morning. But I realized that the Report could have turned up on Friday and been opened, in which case I would have had no way of proving that I had not passed it on.

However, all these personal anxieties were unnecessary, since, by a strange sort of common consent, nobody asked where the leak had come from and during the whole discussion there were only one or two snide references to being pressured by the *Mirror*. At first I was puzzled as to why it was all going so lamely. I knew that what Harold had wanted was a decision to publish the Report and let him present it to Conference without the Executive approving each resolution, apart from the single resolution establishing the great Committee of Four. But after a very few minutes it was clear that the Executive was not willing to concede this and Harold had to retreat and withdraw the demand.

On the whole, the Committee did extremely well, since only one inaccuracy

[1] As an experiment, one day of the Conference was to be televised.

was proved by Morgan Phillips and Len Williams, and, on the crucial issue of the division of powers between the General Secretary and the National Agent, a little adroit questioning by Harold and Jack Cooper got the two of them at loggerheads, calling on members of the staff to substantiate their allegations against each other. But, as the meeting went on, it became clear that, though the Report would be a terrible blow for Morgan Phillips, it would not provide Harold with the victory he had anticipated.

As soon as I got home and thought it over, I saw what had happened, though this was partially assisted by a chat with George Brinham of the Woodworkers, as we went down in the lift. George was one of the five who voted against publication and he remarked to me that he didn't like having a revolver put to his head. The fact is that the *Daily Mirror* leak had pressured the Executive into publication and, by the afternoon session, it had somehow got into their hands that Harold had organized the leak in order to put a revolver to their heads. Well, under the threat they caved in but they weren't going to give Harold his chairmanship as well.

Friday, October 7th

Yesterday morning I went down to Bournemouth to get a glimpse of the Tory Conference[1] and found George Brown on the train, going down for Independent Television. In the evening we had a tremendous dinner on the *Mirror*, with Cassandra [William Connor], Vicky, Sydney, Wilf [Fienburgh] and George Brown. It proved to be one of the most interesting evenings I'd had for years, since George Brown, warmed with wine, really revealed his trade union philosophy, which culminates in the argument that 'It's our Party, not yours'. When challenged by Bill as to why it belonged to George Brown and not to Dick Crossman, he said, 'Well, just think what each of us was doing before the war. I was working for the Party. And what was he doing? Writing!' The word 'Writing' was said with such exquisite loathing that Cassandra intervened, 'When he hears the word "writing", he reaches for his revolver.' 'That's not far from it,' said George Brown. 'That's how we feel about these intellectuals. If they want to come in and serve us, well and good. The trouble is, they are so active that there's a danger of their controlling the Party and we can't have that sort of nonsense!'

Brown's view is that it would be fatal for Attlee to continue in the leadership and that Morrison should take his place. When we asked why gaga Morrison was better than gaga Attlee, the reply was that under Morrison's leadership the trade unions would be able to reassert their authority and smash the intellectuals. Both Wilf and I pointed out that this was somewhat of a delusion, since Morrison, as Leader, would play the middle way like

---

[1] That year the Conservative Party Conference preceded the Labour Conference. It opened at Bournemouth on October 6th and on the first day the Chancellor of the Exchequer addressed the delegates, announcing that when Parliament reassembled further measnres would be taken to curb inflation.

Attlee. Cassandra asked why on earth the Labour Party would look any better with Morrison than with Attlee and why Brown didn't want Gaitskell. Brown said he was no longer sure that Gaitskell was reliable. He was showing dangerous tendencies to move towards the Left in order to get the leadership. Every time poor Wilf tried to intervene with a reasonable remark, he was smacked down as being just as bad as Crossman. 'At least I know where I am with Crossman, but people like you, Wilf, are the people who destroy the Party by wobbling.' As the evening wore on, Bill Connor's eyes grew bigger and bigger. In fact, I think he began to understand for the first time what the feelings of the Bevanites were and why they behaved as they did.

I enormously enjoyed this brief trip to Bournemouth, simply because it's great fun going to somebody else's Conference, where you haven't the uneasy feeling that some disaster is going to happen to you or to your friends, and partly because it was nice being with Bill Connor, Sydney and Vicky. It's extraordinary how much room the *Mirror* takes up in the minds of politicians and how seriously it is regarded. Butler, at one point in his speech, said that he would carry his policy through, despite whatever the *Mirror* said, and added that he wasn't afraid of Vicky! It was his only reference to the press and, though it was a joke there was just an element of seriousness in it. There is no doubt that the Tories regard the *Mirror* as one of their most formidable opponents and that, at the Tory Conference at least, being on the *Mirror* gang gives you much more kudos than being on the *Statesman*.

Saturday, October 15th
Conference proper began on Monday in an atmosphere of such utter and complete boredom as I cannot describe. The debate on general policy was a Tory's dream, with left-wingers talking the emptiest nonsense and a reply from Jim Griffiths which pulled out every fifty-year-old stop. And said nothing. The platform thought Jim's reply very fine. Indeed, Mrs Attlee and another lady bent forward to me and said how wonderful Jim was. I replied that I thought he had a great way with Conference. 'No, he's got such a human touch,' they said, and when I said, 'He's very skilful with Conference,' I knew that I had scored a black mark. But despite the applause he got, I discovered that even I had been wrong. He had not gone down in Conference, which was sickened by the hypocrisy and the same old stuff. This was one of the reasons, no doubt, why, when the National Executive election results were announced on Tuesday, I found myself well above him, since he had dropped 100,000 votes. I was immensely depressed by Monday's proceedings.

The National Executive results were announced before Tuesday's debate on defence started. I had wondered if my attachment to the *Daily Mirror*, just at the moment of the leak, would have damaged me. But I fancy the whole-page ads in *Tribune* did me more good and I went up to fourth place. Geoffrey Bing was chucked off the Conference Arrangements Committee by a T. & G. official and Nye was crushingly defeated by Gaitskell, as I expected.[1]

In the afternoon we had the private session on Harold's Report. I had heard rumours and tipped him off that it was to start with fireworks by Bill Webber, head of the T.S.S.A. and two years ago one of the most vitriolic anti-Bevanites on the N.E.C. Sure enough, Bill was called and, instead of discussing organization, launched a vicious attack on Harold's integrity, suggested that the left-wing was using the report to conceal the fact that dissensions had caused our defeat and in general bitched the debate. Obviously this was done in cahoots with Morgan and Edith Summerskill, the Conference chairman, and it made it inevitable that, after an hour and a half, Nye should get to the microphone.

In the course of twelve minutes I do not recall Nye mentioning the Report. He merely replied to Webber on the subject of his expulsion, on the hypocrisy of the debates, on the trade union oligarchy and on anything else which came into his head. It was a brilliant and spontaneous *tour de force* and as Nye returned to his seat he was nearly mobbed by the delegates. The Conference divided into sullen, silent trade unionist and ecstatic constituency representatives. Poor Harold's Report and all his work had long since been forgotten. The dreadful thing was that people who were completely without vitality on the previous day when trying to discuss general policy were really happy and at home again, fighting each other in the old, dreary feud.

I walked home, feeling gloomy, to find Barbara, who said that she thought it was very good and that, after he'd blown off steam, Nye would be in a mood for co-operation. To this I replied by asking who would co-operate with him. She gave me a look as though I had betrayed the cause. However, when people like Barbara read the papers on Wednesday, they were not quite so cheerful.

Anne arrived on Tuesday and we went out to dinner with Manny, George Wigg and Hugh Massingham — far the nicest two hours we had. Manny is completely rejuvenated, looks about fifty and was in such sparkling form that I could understand for the first time why people liked him. On the whole he sided with Nye, in the sense of justifying his behaviour, adding the proviso that after this Nye would have to behave with perfect moderation in the open *Tribune* meeting on Wednesday night. He also seemed to accept Morrison's succeeding Attlee as a *fait accompli*. The evening was mainly just nice and good fun.

I was extremely scared about my own debate on Thursday.[2] Since my débâcle at Morecambe three years ago, I have only spoken for two minutes at Conference, and such incidents leave a trauma. So I prepared the speech with enormous care on Wednesday evening and went through it all again on

[1] In the contest for the Party treasurership Gaitskell received 5,475,000 votes to Bevan's 1,225,000, increasing his majority of 1954 by more than 2 million.

[2] Crossman was to reply for the Executive in the debate on national insurance, in which he had been deeply interested since late 1954 (see *New Statesman and Nation*, December 4th, 1954).

Thursday morning, making elaborate and careful notes of each paragraph. However, for the first time for a very long time, I had real luck. Our debate came on earlier than expected and it was excellent, with Nye, Sir Alfred Roberts, Head of the T.U.C. Social Services Committee,[1] and Arthur Blenkinsop clearly putting the three conflicting points of view which I had outlined in my notes as the three points I had to explain. Moreover, what Sir Alfred said enabled me to reveal our disagreements with the T.U.C. and what Arthur Blenkinsop said enabled me to deal with graduated benefits, which are an unpopular concept.

When I got up to reply, there was not a single clap, mainly, I think, because they couldn't see who was replying but also because they weren't interested and wondered why on earth I was doing it. Apparently I cannot have looked at my notes because I was congratulated warmly on speaking without them and asked how I could deal with such a complex subject without preparation! By the time we got back to the Grand Hotel, I knew that I had had a real political success, having been congratulated by Hugh Gaitskell, Sam Watson, Clem Attlee, Maggie Stewart and, not least, by Sydney Jacobson and Bill Connor, who were absolutely astounded at what had happened and didn't trouble to disguise it. Strange what a difference a quarter of an hour can make in one's life! After that I was a potential Minister! It only shows on what very flimsy evidence people base their estimates of one's capacity.

I have not been able to describe the strange alternations of mood or the pervasive atmosphere of manoeuvres about the leadership in which little Mr Attlee kept perking in and out, cheerful and chirpy and completely unperturbed. My only feeling is that quite a considerable shift of power and change of constellation took place within the leadership. We had our first meeting of the new Executive on Thursday afternoon and there the division which had begun to arise on the Wilson Report became clear. It is a division between a Young Guard, who want efficiency, and an Old Guard, afraid that efficiency means giving the Young Guard power. There is no doubt whatsoever that Jack Cooper is now ready to work with Harold Wilson and myself, that Gaitskell is ready to work with us and it is probable that the new T. & G. member, who replaces Tiffin, will do the same.[2] In fact, a new Centre of the Party is forming, which is trying to create a policy and leadership neither subservient to the unions on the one side nor appeasing Bevan on the other. There is no doubt, however, that, if Herbert succeeds Clem in the near future, he will fight this new Centre for all he can.

---

[1] General Secretary of the National Association of Card, Blowing and Ring Room Operatives 1935–62, Chairman of the Social Services Committee of the T.U.C. 1947–57, a Member of the Nationalized Industries Advisory Committee 1963, a member of the Cotton Board from 1948 and a Director of the Bank of England from 1956 until his death in 1963. He was knighted in 1955.

[2] This was Frank Cousins.

From October 16th to 23rd Crossman was in Malta, with other members of the Round Table Conference. The all-party committee was to report in mid-December, with only two dissenters, that Mr Mintoff's proposals were 'practicable and reasonable' but that, before proceeding further, a plebiscite would have to be held to assess popular opinion in the island itself.

He returned to London in time to hear the debate on the Budget, introduced on October 26th. The Chancellor's theme was that consumers' expenditure remained too high. Current purchase tax rates were to be raised by one-fifth, some household goods previously exempt would now be subject to this tax and the 'D' scheme, giving tax relief on some articles of clothing, furniture and bedding, would be abolished. The rate of tax on distributed profits was increased from 22·5 to 27·5 per cent. Charges for telephone calls and rentals were to be raised. The increased yield from taxation changes was estimated at £112·5 million in a full year.

The volume of Government lending to local authorities was to be reduced and the Exchequer housing subsidy to be abolished as soon as possible, and meanwhile to be cut, except where it applied to slum clearance and rehousing in overpopulated areas. Hospital boards were to be requested to undertake only urgent projects and work on the new Colonial Office building was stopped.

The Opposition tabled a censure motion, accusing the Government of 'incompetence and neglect in their economic and financial policy'. This was to be debated after the conclusion of the three days devoted to discussion on the Budget.

Friday, October 28th

I don't know what I expected on Tuesday when I went into the House on the day of the resumed Session. The atmosphere was very flat and very normal and the only thing which I could notice was that I personally was still living in the reflected glory of my speech at Margate, combined, of course, with writing a column in the *Mirror* in which every Labour M.P. feels he might one day appear. In fact I am, at the moment, respectable and even slightly important.

On Wednesday I went into the House for the Budget. I had known that Butler would have a rough time but he stood there like St Sebastian, waiting for the stones [*sic*] and reading stubbornly on through a dull script. Attlee immediately responded with an extremely bright and lively speech. I don't think that even then I appreciated how violent the reaction would be in the next morning's press. On the one side, Butler was assailed by *The Times* and the *Telegraph* for cowardly softness but, on the other, the popular press all flayed him for flaying the housewife. I think the key factor which set off the excitement was the sense of swindle and deception created by the contrast between this autumn Budget and his April Budget.

Yesterday morning, while I was trying to do the *Mirror* column, we had a Party Meeting. I went in to hear Gaitskell, who said quite briefly that the line was obvious and then sat down. At this, Percy Daines got up and said he didn't want any of this public school shadow-boxing and theorizing but a straight personal attack on the Chancellor as a swindler. Gaitskell is certainly receptive to suggestions. If you look carefully at the speech he then made in the House, you can see how, after this meeting, he must have spatchcocked into it the extra personal insults to Butler. These made the headlines and in fact made his speech. No doubt he saw at last the opportunity to destroy once and for all the figure of 'Mr Butskell' — a demolition essential if he is to become the Leader of the Labour Party.

Friday, November 4th

Monday was the day of the Labour Party's vote of censure. There is always a certain risk for an Opposition in trying to repeat a parliamentary triumph and to raise the steam on Monday which was raised so spontaneously on the previous Wednesday. This risk was, of course, greatly increased by the selection of Herbert Morrison to begin the debate.

I went in to hear him and agreed with Nye, who came to Vincent Square that evening, in feeling sympathy with the old boy for the treatment he got. The Tea Room was utterly heartless. They were really just like the spectators in a bullring, booing a matador who is past his years.

However, there is no doubt whatsoever that Morrison's speech knocked him out. George Brown said to me last night that Morrison now wouldn't get twenty votes in competition with Gaitskell.[1] Morrison's flop, of course, enabled Butler to stage a tremendous come-back and a devastating personal attack on Gaitskell. I think I have described in this diary how Gaitskell spatchcocked into his speech his more vitriolic assaults on Butler. In terms of his general position in the country Gaitskell has done extremely well. Inside politics, however, I think he has damaged himself. On our side he has done so by showing that he is inclined to weakly give way to pressure, against his own instincts and judgment. On the Tory side he is thought to have behaved like a cad in referring to Butler's personal problems when he knows Butler's wife died six months ago.[2] The effect, of course, of all this was to make the Tories solid behind Butler on Monday.

Of course, the only news which mattered to the public on Monday evening was Princess Margaret's announcement that she is not going to marry.[3]

---

[1] In an eventual contest for the leadership.

[2] Sydney, daughter of Samuel Courtauld, married R. A. Butler in 1926. She died in 1954. In 1959 he married Mollie, widow of Augustine Courtauld, brother of Sydney.

[3] On October 31st H.R.H. Princess Margaret had issued a statement from Clarendon House, where she lived with the Queen Mother, saying that she had decided not to marry Group Captain Peter Townsend. The statement continued,

I have been aware that, subject to renouncing my rights of succession, it might have been possible for me to contract a civil marriage. But, mindful of the Church's teaching that Christian marriage is indissoluble, and conscious of my duty to the Commonwealth, I have resolved to put these considerations before any others.

Ungoed-Thomas rang me up late on Tuesday, to ask whether I had read her communiqué carefully and to point out to me the extraordinary constitutional problems which arise from it. Princess Margaret has stated a view about the succession which is probably bad law, a view of the Church's attitude to divorce which may be the Archbishop of Canterbury's[1] but certainly doesn't cover the whole Church, and she has somehow identified the interest of the Commonwealth with the maintenance of the Archbishop's view of divorce. All this has been done without the Queen's consulting either her British Ministers or her Commonwealth Ministers.

The explanation is that Eden and three other members of his Cabinet, who are divorced, were desperately anxious not to proffer any advice during this crisis, and, if they had been obliged to proffer it, they could not possibly have supported the Archbishop. I spent a lot of Wednesday morning discussing whether we should put all this in the *Mirror* and persuading Kingsley to write a rather good beginning to his 'Critic's Diary'. I thought I might deal with it myself but on Thursday the papers were full of the Archbishop giving his views on television and I felt it was the wrong moment for me to intervene.

Wednesday, November 16th

Last Monday, while we were waiting for a division, I had a long talk to Nye, the first serious talk about the future I have had since the hydrogen bomb row last spring. Of course, we see each other a tremendous lot and he couldn't be nicer. Since he went out to his farm in the Chilterns and began breeding pigs on fifty acres, his health, both physical and mental, has improved. This is partly, no doubt, because Jennie is also happier out there. Nye berated me soundly for the line I have been taking that it would be a disaster if Morrison were to succeed Attlee – a line, by the way, which leads logically to accepting Gaitskell as our next Leader, though I never say so. 'You can't force the Party to accept Gaitskell,' Nye said, 'and I must warn you that, if he is Leader, I might not be able to collaborate.' 'But what's the alternative?' I said. 'Well, there are times when no decision is best,' he said. 'The right thing to do now is to wait. After all, something may turn up.' He added, as an afterthought, 'Gaitskell might be more acceptable in nine months' time than now.'

The whole conversation was conducted in a perfectly rational way between friends. Right at the end, I said, 'But you've got to understand that many of us know all the drawbacks of Gaitskell but accept him as inevitable because

Group Captain Peter Townsend had joined the R.A.F. in 1943, becoming a Wing-Commander in 1941. He was Equerry to King George VI in 1944 and in 1950 was appointed Deputy Master of H.M. Household. At the King's death in 1952, he became Equerry to Queen Elizabeth II, serving until 1953. As Air Attaché in Brussels from 1953 to 1956, his name was associated with that of Princess Margaret in 1955, but a match with a divorcé and a commoner was considered unsuitable for the Princess. Some account of his life appears in an autobiography, *Time and Chance* (London: Collins, 1978).

[1] Geoffrey Fisher (1887–1972), Headmaster of Repton 1914–32, Bishop of Chester 1932–9 and of London 1939–45, was appointed Archbishop of Canterbury in 1945. He retired in 1961 and was made a life peer, taking the title of Lord Fisher of Lambeth.

you've ruled yourself out.' I added, 'This is the first serious conversation you and I have had since last spring.'

At this point the division bell rang, with my knowing and Nye not knowing that next morning he would find another article in the *Daily Mirror* along the same lines. But the fact that he doesn't feel violently was proved by his willingness to have another long and most friendly drink and talk today. My impression is that, once the change has taken place, he will accept it. After all, he is on the Front Bench, collaborating happily under Attlee, for whom he has a supreme contempt. When I was discussing this with Hugh Dalton last night, I said, 'A Leader or Deputy Leader of the Labour Party is always pretty contemptible. Why shouldn't Nye convince himself that he is too big a man for these jobs?' Dalton roared and said, 'You're quite right. That's the kind of job for which I've never felt any jealousy of the man who occupies it. Ernie Bevin, I and others aren't going to be little Attlees. Why can't Nye feel the same?' And it's true that he may.

Friday, December 2nd

Throughout the past fortnight the vague speculation about Attlee's future continued and in this morning's press there is another rumour that he is being pressed to make up his mind before Christmas. I have seen him a good deal recently, during our discussions on Maltese representation, but I have no idea what is going on in that inscrutable little head. I should guess that, during November, Hugh Gaitskell lost a little ground, mainly because our trade union M.P.s and some of the trade union leaders outside Parliament are getting scared of the bright young men taking over the machine. They have seen a close collaboration between Gaitskell and Wilson, which, on the protracted debates on the Finance Bill, produced the first effective fighting Opposition we've known for a long time. This enormously heartened the Members of Parliament. One can always discover how well an all-night sitting has gone by going away early, as I had to because I was writing the *Mirror* next morning, and coming back. As I entered the House on the day after, someone came up to me and said, 'You missed a wonderful thing last night,' and expressed real sympathy with me. When things go badly, you are called a swine for being absent. Moreover Gaitskell and Wilson had the shrewdness, after one successful all-night sitting, to ensure that the dose was not repeated, with the inevitable anti-climax. But this parliamentary success has certainly scared some people.

Meanwhile, Nye has addressed the trade union group on wages policy, with phenomenal success. There is a strange new alignment growing up in the Party. On one side are the Socialist intellectuals, who want to prepare blue-prints on the municipalization of rented houses, National Superannuation, etc., and on the other side are the trade unionists, who are suspicious of this kind of Socialist planning. More and more the trade unionists feel that Nye belongs to them and will be able to express their views for them. After this particular meeting, I met Charlie Pannell, the egregious A.E.U. Member for Leeds, who said to me, 'As we sat there I looked around and felt this was a real, old-fashioned trade union branch and that we might each have had our beer mugs on the table and that Nye belonged to us.' Actually this is a much more realistic and much healthier division of the Party, since it represents the traditional conflict between the trade union, working-class Members and the Socialist minority, whereas the Bevanite/anti-Bevanite division split people in quite artificial ways.

However, all this has had its effect on Hugh Gaitskell's position and it might possibly be true that, if things went on like this for another year, Nye's backing in the Parliamentary Party would steadily increase. Even so, however, I don't think he would get a majority of the votes. On the other hand, I continue to feel extremely uneasy about having as Leader a man who has to try so hard in order to drag himself anywhere near the centre of the Party. When Hugh Gaitskell expresses a Socialist sentiment, he sounds artificial and demagogic but I suppose he will settle down and we know that nothing whatsoever is going to happen in terms of new policy or drive under a stop-gap leadership.

At the National Executive on November 23rd we had the expected row about the Organization Sub-Committee. The week before there had been an unseemly intrigue and Alice Bacon and Harold Wilson had tied for the chairmanship. Moreover, a full and detailed report of the proceedings had been published in the *Telegraph* and the *Mirror*. Harold tried to have a ballot taken with the members of the Organization Committee present at the N.E.C., Alice Bacon made a long speech about the insinuations in the papers that there had been any intrigue against Harold, and the atmosphere was extremely uneasy. Harold lost on his claim and the Committee is to meet again but I fancy that, after the repercussions in the constituencies, it will elect Harold to the job.

One little thing. On Tuesday, in the House, John Strachey came up to me and asked whether I would be the Party spokesman on War Office matters, since Michael Stewart is now doing Education. My first instinct was to say no out of hand but I said I wouldn't mind John's investigating whether this was a firm offer. 'It will involve you, of course, in sitting on the Front Bench every Tuesday,' he said, 'and in leading for the Party on the Army Estimates.' (We've scrapped the old defence group and now it's only the inner group which is working.) If a firm offer comes, I shall talk to George Wigg about it. From my own personal point of view it would suit me quite well to be forced to sit in the House, to ask questions and make a Front Bench speech once a year. I shouldn't dream of doing it with George's active hostility, particularly as I derive 99 per cent of my Army information from him. However, such incidents are personal turning points. I have a feeling that, once I was established as a Front Bench speaker, even on a single thing like the War Office, I should be likely to stay there. If the leadership changed over the

Christmas Recess, there would be no objection, apart from George, since Nye will be doing the same for the Ministry of Labour. Moreover, if I do not soon do something of this sort, I shall cease to take any active part in the House of Commons and merely become a journalist. Would I prefer that? I really don't know. But I'm always in favour of letting things be decided for one.

Clement Attlee, who had led the Labour Party for twenty years, announced his retirement on December 7th. He accepted an earldom. On December 14th Gaitskell was elected as his successor, with 157 votes to Bevan's 70 and Morrison's 40. Mr Morrison thereupon resigned the post of Deputy Leader, which remained vacant until after the Christmas Recess.

Friday, December 16th

The whole of the last ten days seems to have been absorbed in the selection of Attlee's successor — and not unnaturally, for in a modern political party machine the position of the Leader is of critical importance. So far from personalities mattering less in politics, they matter more and more, in the sense that the one or two people who get the key positions thereby achieve a chance of imposing their personalities on affairs.

From my point of view, the story starts on the evening of Tuesday, 6th, when I had arranged, by coincidence, to discuss with Herbert Morrison a paper on the reconstruction of the Party Publicity Department and the first propaganda directive. I came into the House of Commons to find the lobbies humming with rumours that Clem Attlee had finally made up his mind to announce his retirement next day. From half-past six until a quarter to eight I sat with Morrison discussing publicity and throughout this time he was being telephoned, first by Maggie Stewart, then by Trevor Evans[1] and by most of the other press correspondents. 'Yes, there will be three candidates,' he replied to one. 'No, I have no intention of standing down,' to another. It must have been trying for him to have me there throughout and certainly from that hour and a half I learnt how carefully and systematically he has cultivated the press. At one point he looked up and said to me, 'I feel like Princess Margaret,' and, a little later, 'It's a bit hard that I should be the only person Attlee hasn't consulted in any way.' Then, in answer to an unspoken interrogation, 'Yes, I think he's going tomorrow but he hasn't mentioned it to me. A rum fellow — and I could tell you a lot more about that if I wanted to.'

[1] A journalist, whose career started with the *Glamorgan Free Press* in 1922. He joined the *Daily Dispatch* in 1924, went to the *Daily Mail* in 1928 and in 1930, as Industrial Correspondent, moved to the *Daily Express*. He retired in 1967 and became an industrial consultant to Beaverbrook Newspapers Ltd, of which he was also a Director 1954–69. He became a member of the Press Council in 1964. He was knighted in 1967.

I must record, to Morrison's credit, that throughout this interview he was extremely good-humoured, indeed, almost buoyant. I still don't know whether he was trying to win my support or was merely being decent but what shocked me was how old and slow he had become. It took him a quarter of an hour to sign three or four letters, before we could start discussing our work. Then, on the proposals to reconstruct the Department, he accepted everything I said and, after discussing the draft directive for forty minutes, he observed about what was naturally a strictly confidential document for office circulation, 'But surely, Dick, this sentence would look a bit funny when we publish it.' I said this was not for publication and he said, 'Oh, I thought we were discussing a pamphlet.' The fact is that he's suffering from hardening of the brain. In public he tends to forget the first half of a sentence when he has already articulated the second, and Dimple,[1] as his new wife is known, may have stimulated his hormones but the stimulation has certainly not reached to the synapses of his brain.

On the next morning, Wednesday the 7th, I walked across to the House to hear Attlee make his resignation speech at a Party Meeting, summoned for eleven o'clock. As eleven struck, I was crossing the Central Lobby, and thence I went up the stairs and along the corridor to Number 14 Committee Room. As I reached the last door, the cheers which followed the conclusion of Attlee's speech had just begun! Who is going to believe that the man who was Leader for twenty years would finish his speech in under one minute?

I got there in time to hear practically every septuagenarian in the Party making a speech, followed in due course by Alice Bacon, speaking on behalf of the Women's Advisory Council, the Women's Joint Consultative Board and God knows what, and Tony Wedgwood Benn as the youngest M.P. Attlee thanked the meeting in three sentences, got up and walked out. And that was that.

Herbert Morrison took the chair and arrangements were made for nominations. Then he asked for scrutineers to be elected and a fascinating ballot took place, full of politics, in which Kenneth Robinson, our pleasant Bevanite ex-Whip, scored fifty-seven left-wing votes. George Wigg, who was sitting beside me, said very audibly, 'So they're even against having one scrutineer who can read and write and add up without using his fingers.'

In the morning it was not quite certain whether Bevan would stand as well as Morrison and Gaitskell but I knew by evening that he was certain to do so. On Thursday afternoon, I went into the House at tea-time and met Barbara Castle, just back from a trip to Kenya for the *Daily Mirror*. She told me that round the lobbies was the rumour that I had said I was determined to vote for Gaitskell. By this time I had made up my mind that there was no problem. On the first ballot, with three candidates, it was essential that the

[1] Edith Meadowcroft, a businesswoman who had retired in 1953, became Herbert Morrison's second wife in 1955.

Left should poll its full strength. Then, if Gaitskell did not get a clear majority and he and Morrison were left in the running, I would either vote for Gaitskell or tear up my ballot paper. I was therefore a bit peeved when Barbara told me this and I knew at once that George Wigg was already at work!

Late the night before, I had spent a couple of hours at home discussing the future with Wigg. He and Manny Shinwell are fanatically anti-Gaitskell, because they believe that Gaitskell conspired with Stafford Cripps after the fuel crisis in 1947. At that time Gaitskell was Parliamentary Secretary in the Ministry of Fuel and Power and Shinwell was Minister. Thanks to George's astonishing efforts at lobbying, Manny did not lose his job as a result of the disastrous episode, in which I have no doubt he was very largely to blame, but received a great ovation and was kept on. However, a month or two later he was moved to the War Office and Gaitskell took his place. Hence the vendetta.

George's view was that Gaitskell had been flirting with the Left since he failed to expel Bevan last February. But George believes that the moment Gaitskell obtains the leadership he will revert to type and become the stooge of the big trade unions. 'I will stop at nothing,' George said to me, 'to prevent this disaster occurring.' And, sure enough, from that moment George has been busy working up working-class sentiment against a Winchester intellectual. In the course of doing so, he has convinced himself that as a fellow Wykehamist I am bound to support Gaitskell and that the only issue now is the conflict between the class-conscious workers and the Old School Tie. Therefore, when Barbara told me her rumour, I knew at once where it came from.

Barbara and I had been having tea in the Smoking Room and, as I went out, I ran into Nye and impetuously said, 'I hear there is a ridiculous rumour that I am going to vote for Gaitskell against you. This is completely untrue and I'd like you to know it.' I was a little bit baffled that, though Nye smiled, he looked a bit embarrassed but said nothing whatsoever and walked down the lobby. Half an hour later, I ran into young Tom Williams,[1] an earnest Co-operative candidate who was the hero of a Hammersmith by-election and has since been an earnest Bevanite. 'Have you seen the tape?' said Tom. 'My name's on it, or rather, they're confusing me with old Tom Williams.' I had no idea what he was talking about but finally elicited the fact that ten elderly Labour M.P.s, including Dick Stokes, Manny Shinwell, Tom Williams[2] and

[1] (William) Thomas Williams, Q.C., Labour M.P. for Hammersmith South 1949–55, for Baron's Court 1955–9 and for Warrington since 1961. He was Parliamentary Private Secretary to the Minister of Pensions 1950–51 and to the Minister of Health 1951, and Attorney General 1955–67. A Baptist minister, he was called to the Bar in 1951. Since 1976 he has been President of the World Council of the Inter-Parliamentary Union. He was knighted in that year.

[2] (1888–1967) Labour M.P. for the Don Valley 1922–61, he was Parliamentary Secretary, Ministry of Agriculture 1940–5 and Minister of Agriculture 1945–51. In 1961 he became a life peer.

Charlie Key,[1] had apparently proposed that Herbert should be permitted to become Leader without a contest. They had put this proposition to Nye, who had immediately agreed and released it to the press, while Gaitskell was sitting on the Front Bench conducting the last stages of the Finance Bill.

I was just off to a debate against Enoch Powell[2] in the L.S.E. and I didn't return to the Commons that evening, but by the morning of Friday the 9th all the papers had the story of this brilliant manoeuvre. I read them and was as wild as Tom and rang up Barbara and found that she was as wild as I was. For Nye to form a tactical alliance with Morrison, even before the first ballot was over! I rang up Hugh Cudlipp and said I wanted to do a special Saturday column and I did it.[3] Reflecting on it now, I can see why, when I read the article over to Ted Castle, he said, 'I agree with every word but I wouldn't have the courage to publish it.' I can also see why Denis Healey said to me later, 'Of course, I agree with it but it didn't do you any good.' There are some things in Labour politics which people do not like having printed. At the time, I was quite interested to know whether a column published in Saturday's *Mirror* would be read by anybody, since that is chiefly a sports edition. Now I know. If you publish anything important, everybody knows about it, though a negligible number will actually have read what you have said.

This is not the first time I have made myself unpopular and on this occasion there was a further reason for it, which I only fully realized as the week went on. I am regarded as somebody who is much more personally and intimately acquainted with Gaitskell than I really am, and, as every paper has been publishing accounts of our being at school together, this was really felt to be an Old School Tie collaboration. Moreover, in a sense it is. I do know Gaitskell better than most people and realize how wrong people get him. He is not a cold man but a person of competence with an enormous lot of rather

---

[1] Charles Key, Labour M.P. for the Bow and Bromley division of Poplar 1940–50 and for Poplar from 1950 until his death in 1964. He was Parliamentary Secretary at the Ministry of Health 1945–7 and to the Minister of Works 1947–50.

[2] Conservative M.P. for Wolverhampton South-West from 1950 to February 1974, when he left the Conservative Party. He returned to Parliament in October 1974 as United Ulster Unionist Coalition M.P. for South Down. A former Professor of Greek Literature, he was Parliamentary Secretary at the Ministry of Housing and Local Government 1955–7, Financial Secretary to the Treasury 1957–8 and Minister of Health 1960–3. His many publications include *A Lexicon to Herodotus* (Cambridge University Press, 1938), *The House of Lords in the Middle Ages*, with Keith Wallis (London: Weidenfeld & Nicolson, 1968), and *Joseph Chamberlain* (London: Thames & Hudson, 1977).

[3] Crossman's column condemned the manoeuvre, which

> obviously put Mr Gaitskell in an extremely embarrassing position ... He is far too deeply committed to consider Mr Bevan's offer. So the contest goes on ... Like many other left-wingers, I, myself, would have preferred Mr Bevan to have the leadership – and it was his for the asking until he threw it away ... I cannot support Mr Morrison because I do not believe that the Labour Party, in its present state of health, is strong enough to stand two or three more years of disintegration at the bottom and infighting at the top.

vague emotions, which lead him often to burst into tears. He is a man not at all sure of himself outside his special subject, a man who felt himself a hero and a St Sebastian when he stood up to Nye and, most serious of all, someone who takes a moralizing and reactionary attitude, which is in my opinion almost instinctively wrong on every subject outside economics. But he is also an extremely honest and sensible man, with the kind of mind that will take advice, and who might become a very good Leader.

All this week, until the vote was announced at seven o'clock on Wednesday evening, the curious atmosphere in the Commons continued. By my article I had committed myself pretty clearly to supporting Gaitskell against Morrison and so, now, against Bevan, but most Labour M.P.s were canny and, until somebody pointed it out, I was too stupid to realize that they were not revealing their votes because they wanted to be on whichever band-wagon succeeded. Actually, when the result was announced I was down in Torquay for the by-election.[1] It was a poor little, sweet little by-election in a Tory boarding-house constituency, with no Labour organization, but when I told a meeting at Paignton what had happened, there was a spontaneous round of cheers. This means that every Labour person now feels we have a Leader and can say who the next Prime Minister will be and that they all feel this makes a difference.

I had gone to Torquay straight from N.E.C. It had been a curiously quiet meeting, apart from an odd incident when Alice Bacon complained inanely of something she did not like in the *New Statesman*. At this, Herbert Morrison suddenly woke up and said, 'Moreover, I resent the interference of the press in the election of our Leader and, what's worse, one member of the N.E.C. is writing for the capitalist press for pay.' This remark fell like a stone into a pool, since the whole front page of the *Sunday Express* had been devoted to an exclusive interview with Mr Morrison.

On Thursday, the 15th, I went into the House and found that Nye was already busy trying to find out if he stood a chance of being elected Deputy Leader. Arthur Bottomley, a right-wing trade unionist, told me that he him-self had been approached by Nye, despite the fact that only a fortnight ago Nye had been talking of walking out of the Party if Gaitskell were elected. As I was going out with Anne to her birthday dinner, I ran into Gaitskell, who was affability itself — too affable for my liking.

[1] Caused by the death of Charles Williams, Conservative M.P. for Tavistock 1918–22 and for Torquay from 1924 until his death on October 28th, 1955. In the by-election, held on December 15th, F. M. Bennett retained the seat for the Conservatives with a majority of 10,581 votes over W. Hamling (Labour). The Conservative vote fell by 9·5 per cent and the Labour vote by 0·1 per cent.

1956

At the end of the year the Prime Minister announced extensive Cabinet changes, expected for some time but delayed until after the autumn Budget. Mr Butler left the Treasury, to become Lord Privy Seal and Leader of the House of Commons. He was succeeded by Harold Macmillan. Selwyn Lloyd became Foreign Secretary and his place as Minister of Defence was taken by Sir Walter Monckton. The Ministry of Labour went to Iain Macleod and the new Chancellor of the Duchy of Lancaster was the Earl of Selkirk. Patrick Buchan-Hepburn became Minister of Works. Nigel Birch went to the Ministry for Air, Aubrey Jones to Fuel and Power, Robin Turton to Health and John Boyd-Carpenter to Pensions and National Insurance. Harold Watkinson became Minister of Transport and Civil Aviation. Several backbenchers were given junior posts. In the New Year there were rumours of Sir Anthony Eden's retirement and on January 7th he published a denial.

On the Labour side there continued to be bitter exchanges over the election of Hugh Gaitskell to the leadership. An article appeared in Tribune *on December 16th by 'John Marullus' (a tribune in Shakespeare's* Julius Caesar*, and here the pseudonym of Michael Foot). It referred to a campaign to get rid of Attlee and described 'the loudest bagpipe in the squeaking train' as the* Daily Mirror*, supported by its columnist, Richard Crossman. Not* Tribune*, so often accused, but the* Mirror *had been engaged in a conspiracy to undermine the Party leadership and 'Hugh Gaitskell had long been the* Mirror*'s candidate for the post'.*

That same day Crossman wrote tersely to Michael Foot, enclosing a letter to be printed in Tribune*. This appeared on December 30th. It looked back at* Daily Mirror *pieces written on the last day of the Margate Conference and on November 15th, in which Crossman hoped that both Attlee and Morrison would resign together, as soon as possible.*

It also surveyed the article on December 10th describing as a damaging manoeuvre Bevan's offer to withdraw in Morrison's favour. Crossman now stated that he had always declared his views openly and that he stood by them. In the same issue of Tribune *Ian Mikardo published an open letter to Crossman, examining his 'horrifying'* Daily Mirror *column of December 10th, and saying, 'it is by writing so incredible an explanation of your attitude towards Bevan that you have given the impression that you never intended to support his candidature anyway and welcomed any excuse as a rationalization of your intention.' Mikardo referred to the charge that Crossman was 'too ambitious, too clever by half and glaringly inconsistent'. Since Mikardo had often defended Crossman against his detractors, he wrote, he claimed the right to reprove him openly and publicly.*

Crossman, meanwhile, wished to turn away from discussions of personalities to policy-making for 1956. He wrote to Gaitskell just before Christmas and on Boxing Day received the following reply:

My dear Dick,
Thank you for your very nice letter which I did indeed appreciate. Nobody in

their senses could possibly accuse you of jumping on to bandwagons. On the contrary I could make out something of a case against you for jumping off *rather than* on *at some moments during the last 10 years! But seriously, Dora and I are very happy not to have this thing between us and you and hope that in this respect anyhow the future will be smoother than the past.*

You are, of course, an excellent 'ideas man'. But in apparently confining yourself to this I think you underrate your ['range' crossed out] *potential range. I hope this doesn't sound too patronising. God knows we want the ideas — particularly just at this moment — though they've got to pass both administrative and political tests to be of use — and I know you'll play a big part in providing them. But we also need more skilled but straightforward on-the-Party line, anti-Government debating in the House — as opportunity offers and not only in foreign affairs. I hope you'll give that consideration too. I should like to talk about this and lots of other things. There's so much to be planned and done. If you're not rushing off to Tierra del Fuego or somewhere equally far, let's meet soon.*

Yours ever,
Hugh

On the same day, December 26th, Crossman set off for the Middle East, travelling in Egypt, Jordan, Israel and Cyprus until January 14th. All these places were in a state of tension. In Cyprus anti-British demonstrations had led to a declaration of a state of emergency on November 26th. In a Commons debate on December 5th the Foreign Secretary had stressed that, since Cyprus was strategically important to Western defence against Communist aggression, the problem of Cypriot self-determination was not simply a matter of colonial policy. This view was repeated by the Colonial Secretary in answer to Parliamentary Questions on December 21st. He reminded the House that 'it was more an international than a colonial problem' and added that, 'were it not for the fact that Turkish interests were involved, a way out of this difficulty could have been found long ago'.

Earlier in the year Greece and Turkey had both rejected proposals devised by Mr Macmillan for Cypriot self-government, Turkey because they provided inadequate protection for the Turkish minority on the island and Greece because they contained no promise of self-determination, which might allow the Greek Cypriot majority to secure union with Greece. On September 25th Field-Marshal Sir John Harding, Chief of the Imperial General Staff, had been appointed Governor and Commander-in-Chief in Cyprus. Crossman's account of the 'impossibility' of Sir John's task, in the face of London's 'chronic dithering', appeared in the Daily Mirror *on January 13th, 1956.*

The conclusion of the Anglo-Egyptian Agreement of October 1954 had persuaded the Egyptian Military Government to consider improving relations with Turkey, and the Turkish Prime Minister was expected to visit Cairo in January 1955. However, he first chose to visit Baghdad, where agreement was

reached with the Iraqi Government to move towards a mutual defence arrange-
ment – the Baghdad Pact. Egypt failed to rouse a special meeting of Arab Prime
Ministers, assembling in January, to restrain the Iraqi Government, which Egypt
believed was challenging her own pre-eminence in the League.

On February 27th Iraq signed a five-year pact with Turkey and on March
30th Britain entered the pact and also signed a new Anglo-Iraqi Agreement. On
September 23rd Pakistan joined the pact. On October 23rd Persian adherence
was approved by her legislative assembly. It also appeared that the Lebanese
Government found the Pact attractive but, although the Lebanese and Turkish
Presidents exchanged visits in April and June, the Lebanon maintained that her
only aim was to reconcile the two antagonistic blocs in the Àrab League.

In November the Turkish President visited Jordan and in early December
Jordan asked Britain what new arrangements the British Government were
prepared to offer in return for Jordan's joining the Pact. (An annual subsidy of
£7·5 million was paid to the London account of the Jordan Army, the 'Arab
Legion'.) Jordan nevertheless asserted that membership of the Pact would be
without prejudice to her obligation to the Arab League.

Meanwhile there was considerable tension between Egyptian and Israeli
armed forces on the Palestine/Sinai border and Israel was also involved in
clashes with Syria. The Soviet Union vigorously opposed the Baghdad Pact
among the 'Northern Tier' of States. On September 27th the Egyptian Govern-
ment announced that it had signed an agreement with Czechoslovakia by which
Egypt would secure arms. The Western Foreign Ministers, then meeting in
Washington, expressed 'grave concern' and instructed their representatives to
protest to Colonel Nasser.

On October 10th it was announced in Cairo that the Soviet Union was to
assist Egypt and other Arab countries in various development projects, including
the supply of technicians and materials for building the Aswan High Dam. The
Soviet Union also restored diplomatic relations with Saudi Arabia and offered
arms to that country and to Syria.

The first consignment of Soviet war material for Egypt arrived on October
20th and, on that day too, Egypt and Syria signed a five-year military alliance.
A week later Saudi Arabia joined them, making Syria an initial loan of $10
million. In Geneva the Four-Power conference of Foreign Ministers opened on
October 27th and the first weekend, October 28th/29th, was largely occupied
with discussions about the Middle East. Mr Macmillan protested to Mr
Molotov about Russian support for the Czechoslovak arms deal with Egypt; in
exchange, Mr Molotov attacked the Baghdad Pact, whose inaugural conference
Mr Macmillan was to attend when the Geneva meeting ended on November 16th.

In London, meanwhile, at the annual Lord Mayor's Banquet on November
9th, the Prime Minister had devoted much of his speech to events in the Middle
East. Heavy fighting had begun between Egypt, which claimed territory awarded
by the United Nations in November 1947, and Israel, which held to frontiers
secured by military action in 1948–9. There was a large-scale raid by Israel into

Syrian territory on the night of December 11th; British attempts to bring Jordan into the Baghdad Pact were increasingly frustrated.

The British Foreign Secretary attended the first meeting of the Baghdad Pact signatories, in Baghdad on November 21st and 22nd. Emphasis was put on planning for large-scale economic development and it was announced that an American official would maintain permanent connections with the economic committee. But, while the United States approved of the Pact, she was not prepared to join it, sensitive as she was to Israel's concerns (and to her domestic Jewish vote). In an attempt to soothe the Middle East crisis, America offered dollar aid and Mr Dulles warned his countrymen that military and economic assistance would need to continue 'at about the present level'. On December 18th America and Britain undertook in their turn to make grants to Egypt to assist the construction of the Aswan High Dam.

By the end of 1955 it seemed that a full-scale Arab–Israeli conflict could not be averted. The Arab States were united in nothing more than hostility towards Israel and the prospects for the Middle East could not have been worse.

This was the background to Crossman's visit at the turn of the year. His own accounts can be found in 'Egypt Would be Mad to Attack Israel', Daily Mirror, *December 30th, 1955; 'Don't Make Jordan Another Cyprus', January 3rd, 1956; 'Arm Israel Now — To Keep the Peace', January 7th, 1956; an account of an interview with the Israeli Prime Minister, Ben-Gurion, in the* Daily Mirror, *of January 10th, 1956; and his summary of the whole tour, in the* Daily Mirror *of January 18th, 1956.*

He returned to 'a nice, rainy, English day' on Saturday, January 14th, and, 'fairly exhausted', spent Sunday at home in London before getting down to work on the Monday.

Thursday, January 19th

On Monday afternoon I found myself back in politics. Hugh Gaitskell came home with me for a cup of tea after a meeting of the Home Policy Sub. He told me that he hoped that, for the rest of the Session, foreign affairs could be handled by a small, informal committee, consisting of Alf Robens, Kenneth Younger, Denis Healey and myself. 'I am not going to make any important changes in the Shadow Cabinet,' he said, 'for one reason: because I have not the power to make them. This is a matter for the officials of the Party and at present we have not got a Deputy Leader. This little committee will therefore be rather difficult to arrange and must be kept strictly private.' I said I thought this would be quite impossible and added, 'Of course, if you make John Hynd a fifth member there will be no difficulty because then all you will be doing will be asking the two Front Bench spokesmen to consult with the chairman and the two vice-chairmen of the foreign affairs group.' This solution delighted Hugh and I confirmed it with Alf Robens today at lunch.

We then turned to another subject. I had got back to find that my Fabian

Lecture[1] had already been put into galley proof and a copy sent to Hugh Gaitskell, as well as Harold Wilson, Austen Albu and Margaret Cole,[2] who were reading it for the Society. The readers were all enthusiastic but Hugh Gaitskell told me that he was extremely alarmed at a whole number of things in it and that it would be most injudicious to have it published at all. 'There's not only a very dangerous passage about the trade unions,' he said, 'which would cause a flaming row, since you know how sensitive they are. There is also that piece about Ministers and the Civil Service, which I think is utterly wrong.'

I said that he might think it wrong but I thought there was something in it. To this he replied, 'But you know, from now on we've all got to behave responsibly, Dick, to prepare ourselves and present ourselves as members of the next Labour Government.' 'I told you,' I said, 'that I was not joining any bandwagon.' 'Now,' he said, 'don't be silly. Your great fault is not getting on to bandwagons but jumping off them and you make a positive habit of it. You really can't afford it this time.' 'Well,' I said, 'I'm not sure I want to be a Minister. I'm quite happy as an ideas man and we really do need some ideas.' 'Yes,' Hugh said, 'but we need a strong Party too and you know quite well that, if we are to take you seriously as a politician, you've got to behave responsibly in future. So I do ask you to make sure that the pamphlet isn't published.' I said I would consult with the Fabian Society and that was that.

However, next day I found that it was quite impossible to postpone publication, so I spent a very large part of this week going through the text with a toothcomb to try to ensure that it should not cause too much alarm and despondency. I think Hugh has got a point. The last thing we need at the moment is that I should publish a pamphlet which could be headlined as a left-wing attack on the trade union oligarchy and set the row off all over again. It seems fairly clear from Hugh's talk that he is terribly nervous of the trade unionists and uncertain of himself.

Crossman's diary entry for January 25th dealt largely with an account of the previous day's Commons debate on British arms shipments to Egypt, a debate demanded by Mr Gaitskell at the beginning of the year. On January 19th a White Paper had been published in which the Government regretted that surplus arms had found their way 'through third parties' to Egypt but indicating that the

[1] *The New Despotism* was published in the first week of February 1956.

[2] Margaret Postgate, a former schoolteacher, was Assistant Secretary in the Labour Party Research Department when she married G. D. H. Cole (*q.v.*) in 1918. She became a lecturer for university tutorial classes in the University of London in 1925, serving until 1949, and from 1941 to 1944 working also at the University of Cambridge in a similar post. She was Honorary Secretary of the New Fabian Research Bureau 1935–9 and Secretary of the Fabian Society 1939–53, its Chairman in 1955 and its President from 1963. Her many publications include *Women of Today* (London: Nelson, 1938), *Beatrice Webb — a Memoir* (London: Longmans, 1945), *The Story of Fabian Socialism* (London: Heinemann, 1961) and a *Life of G. D. H. Cole* (London: Macmillan, 1971). She died in 1980.

quantity had been small, the quality poor and that they had been balanced by a similar amount reaching Israel.

In the debate itself, Mr Gaitskell enlarged the discussion with what Crossman judged as an 'adroit' attack on the Government's Middle East policy. Crossman's own speech was attacked by the Foreign Secretary as delighting all Britain's enemies. On Egypt Crossman stressed that, though Britain could give economic assistance, 'the ground defence of the area must be left to the peoples themselves, for they have been under our rule for so long that they resent our presence'. He concluded:

> *Of course, it will be a risk to do this and to let them grow up, but it is an even greater risk to humiliate ourselves by hanging on to a façade of military strength which is no genuine military strength and merely antagonizes the Arabs, makes the Jews distrustful and increases the contempt which is felt out there when the British name is mentioned. It is a terrible thing to admit. I beg the Government to do the same thing as we did in India. Then, they will get the same results.*

Immediately after the debate the Prime Minister and the Foreign Secretary sailed for America, for talks in Washington and Ottawa on the crisis in the Middle East. President Eisenhower had now completed his convalescence and he returned to Washington in mid-January. In the previous week he had received a personal letter from Marshal Bulganin, offering a twenty-year treaty of friendship. The President sent an immediate rejection, before the arrival of Mr Eden, who found the American reply 'admirable', but the U.S. response nevertheless left open the possibility of further exchanges.

Crossman himself flew to America on January 26th, spending eight days covering the beginning of the conference for the Daily Mirror. *There was one particularly amusing incident on January 28th:*

> *I left for dinner with young David Butler, the psephologist,[1] who is doing a year at Washington with the rank of Counsellor. Angus Maude, who was also there, was sitting opposite me. Suddenly I saw him, while sitting bolt upright, topple slowly over on to the floor in a blackout. He'd only been in America for a week and I suspect he didn't realize the strength of American drinks and the care one must take before dinner. That was the last I saw of him. For once in my life I found myself less incompetent than anybody else. There he lay on the floor, with the others looking at the body and David saying 'What's to be done?' Remembering vaguely what comes in books, I took off his tie, opened the window and he recovered.*

---

[1] A Student 1949–51, Research Fellow 1951–4 and Fellow since 1954 of Nuffield College, Oxford. He served as Personal Assistant to the British Ambassador in Washington 1955–6. His books include a standard study on *The Electoral System in Britain 1918–51* (Oxford University Press, 1953), a series of studies of the *General Elections of 1951–74* (London: Macmillan, 1952–75) and *Political Change in Britain* (London: Macmillan, 1969).

Crossman's diary entry for February 3rd was on Eden's press conference,

which he conducted as though he was answering Parliamentary Questions. Of course from this point of view it was child's play, since there were no Supplementaries. Moreover, in Parliament the questioner is on an equality with the Minister and half the House is on his side, whereas, in an American press conference, the journalists are invited guests and are deferential. A good many Americans remarked to me that Eden's parliamentary technique was smooth but unsatisfactory. The real art of an American press conference is the calculated indiscretion, the giving of just a little extra beyond the communiqué, but Eden was brilliantly successful in giving nothing.

... My impression is that Eden genuinely felt the conference had been a great success and this was quite natural, because his own public appearances had been personal successes and he and Selwyn Lloyd had gone to Washington with no very clear idea of what they wanted to get out of the Americans in serious negotiations. It must be extremely difficult for an Englishman who arrives in the stratosphere to get any truthful idea of the impression he is really creating down below.

Crossman's view of the Washington meeting can be found in the Daily Mirror *of January 31st and February 3rd, 1956.*

Thursday, February 9th

I got back on Sunday morning to find that a thaw had succeeded the freeze-up and that Anne had had to stay in London, since the pipes had burst at Vincent Square. So we motored straight back there and spent a quiet day. As I grow older, this seems to be more essential than ever after air trips. If one tries to start working as soon as one gets back, it's all right for the first day but one grows more tired throughout the week.

Nothing whatsoever seems to have happened in my absence — except, of course, that on Saturday Nye Bevan had gone to Manchester and made a most characteristic speech.[1] While I was in Washington, the election of the Deputy Leader had taken place and, though James Griffiths had won with 141 votes, Nye had done astonishingly well with 111. Now Nye chose to burst out, saying that he didn't want to be Leader of a Party which wasn't Socialist, complaining that he was asked to play tiddlywinks when he wanted to play Rugby Football and making a long and rather confused harangue about the evils of the Party caucus and secret meetings upstairs.

I had read this speech in the papers at London Airport on Sunday morning and felt a slight personal annoyance, since my pamphlet on the New Despotism was due out on Monday and I knew that Nye would succeed in killing any interest the press might have had. Anyway, I had been trying to deal with the same subject in a rational, non-divisive way and here Nye was not stealing my thunder but thundering while I was cooing sweetly. However, it

[1] On February 4th.

doesn't really much matter, since any hopes I have are always long-term hopes.

What is important is that, throughout this week the Labour backbenchers have for the first time refused to take one of Nye's outbursts very seriously. The stock joke in the lobbies — it's still going on because stock jokes last longer in the House than anywhere else — is to say to anyone who passes, 'Do you play tiddlywinks or Rugby?' Gaitskell immediately made it clear that he would take no action, particularly in the week when the Parliamentary Labour Party is celebrating its Jubilee, for which Nye is due to speak at a big public rally. Nevertheless in the constituency parties, to judge from Coventry, Nye's speech will have had a considerable effect in confirming the suspicion of the rank and file militants that the new leadership is no good and that it's not worth doing much work for the Party. This is a bit hard on the constituencies where by-elections are now taking place and where people are inclined to resent being told that their canvassing is tiddlywinks.[1]

I have also returned to find George Wigg in a rather mysterious mood, more than usually convinced that the Party is going to utter ruin and more than usually violent about Gaitskell, the *Daily Mirror* and everything else. Perhaps the explanation was given me yesterday by John Strachey, who whispered the rumour that George and Manny are trying to persuade Nye to resign from the Front Bench and join them and Herbert Morrison as a real working-class group on the backbenches. George has been heard to say that, if they got together, nobody would listen to what those intellectuals on the Front Bench were bleating when the great men thundered from the rear.

This would certainly be an interesting development. Will Nye really agree to join Herbert and Shinwell and become the last-ditch backwoodsman of Labour's House of Lords? On the other hand, one is bound to be anxious about whether people like Gaitskell and Robens and Wilson can take over the political leadership and hold the Movement, even if they are supported by the big trade union leaders. Harold said to me the other night, 'You see, for the next twenty years I shall be dealing with the Treasury either as Chancellor or Shadow Chancellor, so I've been making a special study of financial problems and I can assure you that my first Budget will be the most

---

[1] On February 9th there were by-elections in Leeds North-East, where Osbert Peake had been raised to the peerage as Viscount Ingleby, and in Blaydon, where William Whiteley had died on November 3rd, 1955. In Leeds the Conservative candidate, Keith Joseph, had a majority of 5,869 votes over H. M. Waterman (Labour) and in Blaydon the Labour candidate, Robert Woof, had a 10,714 majority over John Reay-Smith (Conservative). On February 14th there were three further by-elections. At Hereford, where J. P. L. Thomas had been raised to the peerage as Viscount Cilcennin, David Gibson-Watt (Conservative) had a majority of 2,150 over Frank Owen (Liberal). At Gainsborough in Lincolnshire, where Harry Crookshank had been raised to the peerage as Lord Crookshank, Marcus Kimball (Conservative) had a majority of 1,006 over Harry Walston (Labour). At Taunton, where Henry Hopkinson had been raised to the peerage as Lord Colyton, Edward Du Cann (Conservative) had a majority of 657 votes over R. Pestell (Labour). Though these last three Conservative seats were held for the Party, in each case the majority was reduced.

controversial since Lloyd George's in 1910.'[1] I asked Harold whether it wouldn't be a good idea just to share his views with a few people and have them discussed. Wasn't the time ripe for a house party somewhere or a weekend? 'Ah,' he said, 'Hugh's mind is working that way. He wants to form a small, informal group, including myself, Alf Robens ... ' and he mentioned two or three other names and then, as he always does, added that of the person he was speaking to.

Wednesday, February 15th

Last weekend was the Jubilee of the Parliamentary Labour Party and some preparations had been made for staging celebrations. The only really piquant show was at Merthyr Tydfil, where Nye Bevan and Jim Griffiths were on the same platform, with fellow-travelling S. O. Davies[2] in the chair. Apparently Nye ran rings round him and made a great appeal for no gag in the Party but the edge had been slightly taken off by Leslie Hunter who, in Saturday's *Herald*, reported that Nye had accepted from Gaitskell the Shadow Ministry for the Colonies.

I found myself at Wolverhampton. I've never felt a flatter audience or less lift. The speeches were interspersed, on National Executive instructions, with Labour songs, sung by five ugly women, one man six-foot high and another about three foot high, in shirt-sleeves, described as the Clarion Choir. Afterwards, the chairman whispered to me, 'I wonder what the audience would think if they knew this is the local Communist Party. They are the only people we could get to sing Labour songs.' The fact is, the Party has grown so

[1] David Lloyd George (1863–1945), a solicitor by profession, was Liberal M.P. for Caernarvon 1890–1931 and Independent Liberal M.P. for the same constituency 1931–45. He was President of the Board of Trade 1905–8, Chancellor of the Exchequer 1908–15, Minister of Munitions 1915–16, Secretary of State for War 1916 and Prime Minister 1916–22. His publications include six volumes of *War Memoirs* (London: Nicholson & Watson, 1933–6) and the two-volume *Truth About the Peace Treaty* (London: Gollancz, 1938).

Lloyd George's 1909 Budget had included a 20 per cent tax on 'unearned increment' (increase in land value for which an owner was not responsible) when land was sold or passed to an heir; a tax of *2d.* in the pound on the value of undeveloped land; a 10 per cent tax on the enhanced value of terminated leases; a 5 per cent tax on mine royalties, the proceeds of which would be used to establish a miners' welfare fund to improve conditions in mines and pitheads; a higher and more steeply graduated income tax, with special heavier rates on 'unearned' income; a new supertax on large incomes; an increase of one-third in inheritance taxes; a sharply raised tax on alcohol licences and a larger tax on spirits. The 1909 Budget was intended to cope with 'unprecedented financial strain', exacerbated by the cost to the Exchequer of newly introduced old age pensions and the construction of Dreadnought warships. The projected Government deficit was £16 million; the Chancellor also promised to 'wage implacable warfare against poverty and squalidness'. The Budget was rejected by the House of Lords and a General Election was held in January 1910 and the Liberals were returned. The Budget was reintroduced in April that year and, after the death of King Edward VII in May 1910, a second Budget was introduced in August. Continued difficulties with the House of Lords provoked a second General Election in December 1910.

[2] Stephen Owen Davies (1886–1972) was Labour M.P. for Merthyr Tydfil 1934–70 and Independent Labour M.P. for the same constituency from 1970 until his death. A former miner, he was Vice-President of the South Wales Miners' Federation 1924–33 and representative of the Welsh miners in the Miners' Federation of Great Britain 1924–34.

respectable, so dull, so middle-aged that it's difficult to see how it can be speedily revitalized. However, what the public probably wants at the moment is this kind of respectability as an alternative to Macmillan.

Wednesday, February 22nd
Last week Hugh Gaitskell published his Shadow Cabinet reshuffle, which shows Harold Wilson as Shadow Chancellor and Nye Bevan promoted to Shadow Colonial Secretary. Nye had asked for Shadow Foreign Secretary, had been turned down and then accepted this job. What will he do now? My own view is that, if he does the Colonies well, there is every reason to believe that he will become Shadow Foreign Secretary next October, since there is literally no one else. Alf Robens, though a pleasant fellow, is only too obviously not up to it every time he tries to make an appearance. Kenneth Younger is a good Number Two and Denis Healey and I, the only two possibilities, are not real possibilities, except, again, as Number Twos.

In his diary entry for March 2nd (largely concerned with constituency difficulties) Crossman mentioned that day's news from Jordan of Glubb Pasha's dismissal from his command of the Arab Legion. Glubb had served the Jordanian King's family for more than twenty years. It was widely believed that the King had been pressed by members of the Arab League, who had become increasingly frustrated by their British commander's refusal to allow hostilities against Israel (from which more than one-third of Jordan's population were Arab refugees). 'Incited by George Wigg', wrote Crossman, 'I broke a ten-year tradition and put down a Question which, if it isn't ruled out by the Speaker, will mean my attendance on Monday afternoon.'
The Question was asked on March 5th and a debate arranged for March 7th.

Thursday, March 8th
Since I last wrote, I seem to have been almost entirely engaged on the parliamentary consequences of Glubb's dismissal.[1] When I went into the House on Friday morning to put my Private Notice Question down, I went out behind the Speaker's chair and down to Hugh Gaitskell's room to tell him that I had done so and that I would, of course, transfer the Question to him or Alf Robens if the Front Bench wanted to deal with it. Hugh had only just seen the news in the evening paper and was rather canny. I told him that I had discussed with the Clerk at the Table the possibility of moving the adjournment and that I had found that there was some difficulty in this,

[1] Lieutenant-General Sir John Bagot Glubb (Glubb Pasha), a soldier during the First World War, resigned his commission in 1926 to become Administrative Inspector for the Iraqi Government. He commanded the Arab Legion in Transjordan in 1939 and was Chief of General Staff, the Arab Legion, in Amman from 1939 until his dismissal in 1956. His publications include *A Soldier with the Arabs* (London: Hodder & Stoughton, 1957) and *The Empire of the Arabs* (London: Hodder & Stoughton, 1963). He was knighted in 1956.

since Glubb is not a British officer and his dismissal had nothing to do with the British Government. Under Standing Order 9 the Adjournment can only be moved if the matter is novel, urgent and a direct ministerial responsibility. Certainly events in Jordan were novel and urgent but the question of ministerial responsibility remained in doubt. Hugh asked me what line I would take. I pointed out that this was the most recent of the disastrous consequences of the Baghdad Pact policy. 'But there's nothing wrong with the Baghdad Pact as such,' Hugh said. 'Don't go too far. Anyway, I'm sure it's better for you to do it than for Alf or me.'

By Monday morning, however, the whole thing had developed into a parliamentary crisis and I was distracted from writing my *Daily Mirror* column by the exigencies of my Private Notice Question. First, Alf Robens rang up to say that he'd been telephoning the Prime Minister on Saturday, only to discover that he had been anticipated by a Private Member. Since I had put down my Question to the Foreign Secretary, could I drop it so that he could ask one of the Prime Minister? I pointed out that this would be bad parliamentary tactics. In the absence of Selwyn Lloyd, Nutting would reply but the Prime Minister was able to have the Question transferred to himself. If he did that, I could ask the Question. If he didn't, we could slosh him for not taking responsibility. That pretty well finished Alf and at that moment Hugh Gaitskell rang to say he wanted to see me at eleven o'clock.

I found Jim Griffiths and Kenneth Younger there and Alf came in towards the end of a longish interview, which was quite revealing. I said that, from a British point of view, the important thing was immediate action. Otherwise the whole situation would continue to crumble and the risk of incidents on the Israeli frontier and also the risks to our own people in Jordan would therefore increase. Kenneth Younger said that, in view of the nationalist fever, he thought the Government would be right to do nothing at all but Hugh rather took my view. It was agreed that we should move the adjournment of the House if some formula could be found, while I kept my Question.

We then discussed the whole situation at some length but didn't get very far. I was extremely nervous about my Private Notice Question and took a great deal of trouble to draft my Supplementary. It all took place in a very full House but I think we gained by being non-partisan and showing a concern for our people in Jordan. On the other hand, most of the Parliamentary Party were chiefly curious why Robens had not asked the Question and they drew quite false deductions.

Meanwhile, however, on the threat of the adjournment, the Government had agreed to give a day for debate on Wednesday. I spent a lot of Tuesday morning, along with Kenneth Younger, discussing Jordan with Hugh Gaitskell. Hugh started very sensibly by outlining to us the sort of things he intended to say. This mostly centred around the danger to Israel and the need to reinforce the Tripartite Declaration[1] and to provide Israel with arms. Hugh was also quite sound on the obsolescence of Glubb's paternalism and the importance of our dissociating ourselves in the debate from the position of the Suez rebels, who would demand the reimposition by force of the British Protectorate.

I said that Hugh really couldn't leave out the problem of the Baghdad Pact. Equally he could not fail to mention Egypt and our attitude to it or, indeed, the general subject of the Anglo-American conflict in the Middle East, arising out of the futile feuds of the oil companies. He was obviously very uneasy about the Baghdad Pact until I explained that one must distinguish between the strategy of the Northern Tier, which was sound enough, and the whole British policy of taking over the Turkish–Iraq alliance and transferring the centre of balance from Ankara to Baghdad, thereby arousing the rivalry of Nasser.[2]

By a strange accident, John Hynd, the Chairman of the foreign affairs group, had gone off on a long-standing engagement to visit Jordan, and Denis Healey, my co-vice chairman, had gone to America. On Tuesday, for the first time in my life, I was in charge of the foreign affairs group. On Wedgwood Benn's suggestion, I decided to take a risk and switch the subject of the meeting to Jordan, in view of the debate next day. I also arranged to have the steering committee meet half an hour before, so that I could get some agreement about policy with Robens and Younger. All this worked quite well.

After an hour and a half I tried to stop the meeting and go home to dinner, whereat Percy Daines said, 'So we're going to end in futility once again. Aren't we going to send any advice to the Parliamentary Committee?' At this, I said I would try to sum up the meeting and did so in eight points, which, to my complete amazement, were received with enthusiastic unanimity as the views of the group. We recommended that we should be extremely responsible, attacking Eden more in sorrow than in anger, though exposing the futility of the Washington talks; make it clear that we were ready to see the troops in Cyprus used unilaterally, either for the defence of our own people in Jordan or for the defence of the Israeli frontier; be extremely careful to keep within the framework of UNO and, for this purpose, raise the issue in the Security Council as a threatened breach of the peace; send some quality arms to Israel; declare that Jordan, if she willed, had the right to become a neutral ally of Egypt but in that case would forfeit all British subsidies and compel us to withdraw all our troops; make clear that, if

[1] Made in May 1950 by the British, French and American Governments, when they had stated that, if either Israel or the Arab States were preparing to abrogate frontiers or armistice agreements, the three Powers would 'immediately take action, both within and without the United Nations, to prevent such violation'.

[2] General Gamal Abdel Nasser (1881–1970), an Army officer, led the revolution of March 23rd, 1952, which brought about the abdication of King Farouk and the establishment of an Egyptian Republic. He became Prime Minister and Military Governor of Egypt in 1954 and President in 1956. He remained President until his death in 1970, and also served again as Prime Minister 1967–70.

Jordan remained our ally, the size of the Arab Legion must anyway be scaled down and priority given to economic aid; expose the Government's blundering in trying and failing to bring the Arabs inside the Baghdad Pact; demand action to achieve Anglo-American agreement on oil and a policy for channelling oil profits into the Middle East; and, finally, as part of a final settlement, demand Four-Power talks with the Russians within the framework of UNO.

Throughout the evening I found myself being approached by all sorts of people about the miraculous success of the meeting and the surprising quality of my chairmanship. Immediately afterwards I had gone down to Hugh's room to report all this to the Parliamentary Committee, then in session. But I heard such a row going on that I retired to dinner and decided to approach Hugh after the ten o'clock division. I found him looking dead tired and dejected. 'I've had a terrible meeting', he said, 'with those paranoiacs. Arabists, Jews, neutralists, they were all at each other and at odds with each other. What on earth are we going to say during the debate?' I then reported to him unanimity in the foreign affairs group and gave him the eight points, which he seemed really pleased to have. Then we checked the policy through once again.

Partly, perhaps, as a result of this, the speech with which Hugh followed Nutting in the big debate yesterday was his greatest success to date. The members of the foreign affairs group duly noted that all their eight points were not only in his speech but were important parts of his speech. When I went into the Tea Room, I ran into Hugh. He was being congratulated, really warm-heartedly, by everybody and he came up and thanked me for what I had done. In fact, this wasn't a bad bit of teamwork and the debate was a considerable achievement.

Rightly, I think, I had decided not to try to speak, since I had spoken in the last Middle East debate. In fact, this time not very much happened. Alf Robens made a rather laborious, ham-handed effort at the end and then we all waited for Eden. He made the fatal mistake of a pernickety attack on Alf, particularly for inconsistency on the Baghdad Pact, which put the House against him. What Eden should have done, seeing that he had nothing to say, was to deal with Alf in half a minute, pay tribute to the remarkable quality of Gaitskell's speech and answer it. As it was, he was barracked mercilessly at the beginning and once again at the end, when he mentioned that Moscow had described the Baghdad Pact as the Colonial Pact and asked whether Hugh Gaitskell's reference to the end of semi-colonial status was an echo of Moscow. This kind of party polemics by a Prime Minister on a great occasion has an utterly disastrous effect on the House and this vote of censure was the first on foreign affairs since 1945 which I felt had been really substantiated.[1]

I went home, not having spoken but feeling really pleased, an almost

[1] The motion of censure on the Government's foreign policy in the Middle East was defeated by 312 votes to 252.

unique concatenation, which was confirmed this morning when Woodrow rang up to ask us to a party. He told me that he had rung up Hugh to congratulate him and heard nothing else but of my helpfulness.[1]

One other small incident. In the course of Wednesday evening, I went into the Smoking Room and found George Brown in our corner, with Nye and Barbara on the other sofa talking to each other. After some time, Nye looked across at me and said to Barbara, 'Follow Dick Crossman's precept and never permit intellectual excitement to divert you from following your personal self-interest.' After a moment he said, 'What do you think of that, Dick?' I thought for a moment and said, 'I was just reflecting, Nye, to which of us in this corner that was most apposite.' I had seen Nye come in during Hugh's ovation and go out before it had ended. He was obviously terribly put out and I think probably knew that I had been working with and for Hugh, as on previous occasions I had worked with and for Nye and would do today if it were possible.

In late February the 20th Communist Party Congress was held in Moscow. In a speech delivered to a closed session on February 25th, Mr Khrushchev denounced Stalin, who was described as an autocratic ruler, a tyrant personally responsible for the pre-war purges and post-war liquidations. The present rulers were dissociated from Stalin's policies and from 'the cult of personality'. The details of Khrushchev's speech gradually became known and it was against this background that preparations were made for the visit he and Marshal Bulganin were to pay to Britain in the spring. In his Daily Mirror *column of February 24th Crossman had recommended Gaitskell to meet the Russian leaders 'with a completely open mind ... It would be folly to rule out the possibility that the Russians had learned from Stalin's failures and now sincerely mean what they say'.*

Tuesday, March 13th

Last Friday Zhivotovski rang up, saying he wanted to see me urgently. The preparations are now being made for the reception of Bulge and Crush in the middle of April. I asked Zhivotovski what B.[2] and K. are expecting of the Labour Party while they are here. Do they hope to have serious talks? He

[1] After the debate, Gaitskell wrote to Crossman:

My dear Dick,
I feel I must write you a line to thank you for all the help you gave me for yesterday's debate. It was quite invaluable—both the discussions and the report of the Foreign Affairs Group. I am looking forward to coming to lunch on Tuesday—though I shall be a little late. Don't of course wait for me.

Yrs,
Hugh

[2] Marshal Nikolai Bulganin. He was a member of the Communist Party from 1917, of the Politburo 1948–52 and of the Praesidium of the Central Committee of the Communist Party 1952–8. He was First Deputy Chairman of the U.S.S.R. Council of Ministers 1949–55 and Chairman 1955–8. In 1958 he became Chairman of the State Bank, but some months later was moved to the post of Chairman of the Stavropol Economic Region, where he remained until his retirement in 1962. He became a Marshal of the U.S.S.R. in 1947.

said he hopes to have something serious at the dinner we are giving them, which I rather pooh-poohed and then, after my prodding, he said yes, they would seriously like to discuss politics with us as much as with the Government. As Hugh, Alf, Kenneth and Peter Ericsson[1] were all due to lunch today, I said I would discuss it with them.

This was the first of our foreign affairs lunches. Hugh led off and, turning to me, said, 'In view of what you have written in the *Mirror*, I want to define my position on the Russian visit. There can be no question of formal talks with the Russians, because that would set a precedent for the Opposition's having the right and we don't want to see the Conservatives doing that. But I've seen Eden and he has asked me and the Deputy Leader to come down to Chequers for an informal talk.' Somebody else suggested that we might have some talks after the dinner but Hugh agreed that this was no good.

I said that I thought he was being unduly cautious and that anyway the Movement would be disappointed if there were ten days of talks between the Government and the Russians and nothing to announce about us except a lunch at Chequers, in which the talks had taken place in the presence of the Prime Minister. Wasn't there a very real subject of exclusive discussion for us on the relation of Western Socialists with Communists? Hugh said he thought that Eden might allow him and the Russians to talk alone and then Alf supported me about the Party. Hugh then said, 'But I've got to go to Russia some time and I am quite willing to have serious talks there.' I jumped at this and said that would be a far better arrangement, since I accepted the point about the precedent for the Tories when they are in Opposition.

However, Alf and Peter and I all pressed Hugh whether one other Labour contact could not be made. It was finally agreed that this could be done if Malik would invite us to the Russian Embassy to have talks. Hugh thought this would be O.K. and added that he wouldn't have objected to a small private lunch but there wasn't time on the schedule. I agreed to transmit all this to Zhivotovski and I don't think we've done badly, since I have no doubt that Malik will arrange for a talk at the Embassy and our people should be satisfied by an announcement, during their visit, that there will be a Labour delegation to Moscow. I thought it was quite an interesting example of Gaitskell's kind of leadership. He was obviously very negative and had fixed it all with Eden but he is prepared to modify things. He is equally obviously an inveterate *Daily Mirror* reader, since he remarked to me, 'That's the second time you've said this.'

After lunch I suggested this meeting should be weekly and Hugh was very keen. The only person who wasn't was Kenneth, who wondered whether we'd have enough to talk about. He's a queer man, who has a passion for not wasting time, but I've been wondering how he uses all his time. Hugh was keen that one of us should specialize on disarmament but I managed to get out

---

[1] Peter Ericsson succeeded Saul Rose as Secretary of the International Department of Transport House, where he remained until the late 1950s.

of it as I really can't face studying documents on a subject I don't believe in. I suggested Denis Healey, which Hugh turned down, and then John Strachey, whom he accepted, with the reservation that he might not be accurate.

Hugh was emphatic about the tremendous chance we have in the Cyprus censure debate on Wednesday and is obviously going to watch Nye carefully on this occasion. He remarked that Nye was really pleased to get the Colonial job, which I certainly don't believe, since I know that Nye asked for Foreign Affairs and was rejected. Hugh was also very curious about Nye's present mood and asked whether I saw him. Otherwise, everything went off reasonably well, though Anne voiced the suspicion afterwards that Kenneth Younger would like to see Alf Robens briefed as little as possible during the course of this year.

Wednesday, March 21st

The Cyprus debate was really a very stylish parliamentary occasion and everybody agreed that Nye's performance was first-class, though Anne, who was in the Gallery, had the uneasy feeling that he didn't know much about colonial affairs, and next day the *Daily Worker* launched a tremendous attack on the not unreasonable ground that his attitude could not have been more right-wing.[1] There was no doubt that this was a successful appearance. As a left-winger, Nye was inhibited from even the vaguest suggestion of condoning terrorism. He certainly gave the appearance of playing tiddlywinks for our side and not Rugby Football for himself. But what he also did was really to neutralize the debate, which did not produce the trouncing of the Government we had expected after the debate on Glubb Pasha. Somehow, no one on the Labour side seemed seized with the tragedy of the situation or passionately concerned with the Cypriots, and the fact that the Americans had let us down gave the Government a psychological let-out.

A great subject this week has been the changes in Russia and the arrival of Mr Malenkov as a kind of John the Baptist for Bulganin and Khrushchev's visit in a month's time. I saw Zhivotovski last Thursday morning and he carefully wrote down my message from Gaitskell and took it to Malik.

On Monday evening, Malenkov came to dinner with the National Executive at the St Ermin's Hotel. He was accompanied by Malik and three officials. One thick-set official was standing next to me at the drinks with, on the other side of him, Romanov, the fair-haired Press Attaché at the Embassy.[2] I asked Romanov what role the official played in Soviet electricity,

[1] The motion of censure on the Government's handling of the Cyprus issue was defeated by 317 votes to 252.

[2] Aleksander Iosisovich Romanov, Soviet Attaché in London 1948–53, and Second and later First Secretary at the Soviet Embassy in London 1955–8. He was Deputy Head in the Second European Department (dealing with Britain and the Old Commonwealth) at the Ministry of Foreign Affairs, Moscow, 1958–60 and Counsellor and later Minister at the Soviet Embassy in London 1960–4. He was Ambassador to Nigeria 1964–70, returned to the Ministry of Foreign Affairs in Moscow 1970–3 and from 1973 to 1979 was Ambassador to the Netherlands.

since Malenkov was heading an electrical delegation. I understood Romanov to say that this man was an administrator, who had studied law at the university, and that he was now acting as Malenkov's private secretary. This made me think he was worth sitting by, so I carefully arranged myself between Romanov and him, with Barbara beyond him and Nye one further on.

For an hour during dinner, I plied the man with questions on electricity, on Germany (he told me he had been in Berlin in 1945), and so on. Absolutely nothing happened. He had no comments to make and, even more peculiar, Romanov kept saying that he would himself answer the questions. Barbara finally said, 'You're not handling him right. Let me ask him an interesting question.' She proceeded to say, 'There are complaints that the security arrangements during Malenkov's visit are too complicated. Is that the fault of the British or the Russians?' To this, my friend gave the reply, 'No, I am Malenkov's private secretary,' and then added, 'the British are responsible for the security.' I then said, 'Are there no Russian security officers round Malenkov when he visits Battersea power station?' I asked this, having seen a photograph which showed several of them there. To this question I got the reply, 'I am Malenkov's private secretary,' and it suddenly dawned on me that he was the security officer and really knew nothing about anything. I hope this gave Barbara a good lesson. She is too earnest a left-winger, however, to laugh as much as I did.

It had been agreed that there should be no set speeches. At the end of dinner Edwin Gooch gave a toast to the Soviet Union and Malenkov replied by giving a toast to working-class unity, which we all drank in a slightly embarrassed way. (He speaks no English, by the way, and everything was translated by an interpreter.) Then he submitted himself to questions. The dinner had been extremely good, with a lot of drink, and the questions did not flow, they exploded from all round the table, with four or five people often shouting simultaneously.

They started from Edith Summerskill, who regards herself as a Malenkov expert, having received a bouquet from him during her Moscow visit.[1] She asked him, very coyly, about the Khrushchev speech. It so happened that, over the weekend, the news had been released of Khrushchev's denunciation of Stalin in a secret session of the Communist Congress. Malenkov replied that it was quite true that the cult of personality had been attacked by Khrushchev and this was an error which was now being put right.

There followed about an hour of questions on this subject, during which Malenkov gave absolutely nothing away, told no anecdote, revealed no new fact, but somehow managed to appear candid, gracious and, above all, really eager that we should understand and appreciate the tremendous change which had taken place from personal dictatorship to collective rule. Nye asked a very complicated question about the juridical basis for collective rule, to which Malenkov replied that no juridical basis was necessary to

[1] See above, p. 343.

permit criticism in modern Russia. He then went on to deny that there had
been any serious demonstrations in Tiflis, as had been announced in the
press and said that, if there had been any demonstrations, they were the kind
of demonstrations which would receive no sensational treatment if they took
place in Britain.[1]

Malenkov was pressed from various positions about the nature of collective rule and the rights of minorities. Here again, he gave nothing away.
There were no problems because people were unanimous in wanting the end
of personal dictatorship and accepting collective rule. When asked what
evidence there was that he and his colleagues were any more acceptable than
Stalin, he replied that it was quite clear they were and emphasized that, in his
view, the important change we should make was to stress our points of
agreement rather than our differences. Working-class unity, he said, was the
great thing which would now have to be rebuilt.

Malenkov was then asked about the Popular Front and he, like Romanov,
with whom I had been discussing this at dinner, grew rhetorical and
emphatic about the need for working-class unity. I thought he put on an
amazing performance. First of all, he abounded in an extraordinary self-
confidence. There he was, alone for the first time in a not unfriendly yet
deeply hostile environment, and whenever he chose he dominated us. Yet
throughout he gave the earnest impression of wanting to reach a genuine
understanding with us. He wasn't even nettled when he was told that the
Labour Party represents the workers in Britain and that the British Communists are a nuisance and he shouldn't go on supporting them.

Right at the end, when we had been told by Romanov and the others that
Malenkov was getting up at six next morning and it was now half-past
eleven, he said he wanted to turn the tables and ask us questions. By this
time Hugh Gaitskell had come in and put him a shrewd question about the
priority for heavy against consumer goods. Malenkov, of course, knew that
we knew that he'd been sacked on the ostensible ground of preferring consumer goods.[2] He replied that on this subject the Politburo was unanimous.
There are no differences between them. Then he proceeded to ask us what we
would do about disarmament, to which Hugh gave a formal reply and
Barbara added a little more, and that was that. In fact, it was the only part
of the talk about Russia which was exciting.

When I got outside, I found Morgan Phillips surrounded by a swarm of
journalists. I was bursting to tell somebody and in about two minutes I told
'em what my impression had been. If I'd gone home, I'd have told Anne. It
didn't occur to me what I'd done until I woke up at three o'clock in the
morning. I feared that this would be a front-page story and there'd be all the
problems of a leak. It was a front-page story but there was no problem of a

---

[1] It had been reported that at Tiflis in Georgia there had been some 100 casualties in
demonstrations by students loyal to Stalin, himself a Georgian.
[2] On February 8th, 1955. See above, p. 384.

Attlee, Dr Edith Summer-
skill and Aneurin Bevan
set off on a trip to Moscow
and Peking, August 1954

Attlee, Crossman, Tom
Driberg and Barbara Castle
leave Transport House
after a meeting to consider
whether to expel Bevan
from the Party, March 1955

12 Crossman, Edith Summerskill and Morgan Phillips at the Party Conference in 1955

13 Nye Bevan and Jennie Lee at the Labour Party Conference in Blackpool,

leak because the whole thing was attributed to me and a bit to Sydney Silverman. I must say my heart sank rather as I went through the papers, because I very much dislike not being security-minded and I particularly disliked it on this occasion because my lips had been unsealed by too good a dinner. So, in the course of the morning, I rang up Morgan, who seemed to think it was a very satisfactory press we'd had and said he'd talk to me at lunch.

There I found a rather chilly atmosphere from Barbara, who thought I had been tough to the Russians, and Edith, who felt I had scooped her on Malenkov. Rather gloomily, I decided with Morgan to write a letter of apology to Malenkov, dictated it to Rose and went into the Chamber for the debate. Suddenly I saw Harold Wilson standing behind the Speaker's chair and had an idea. I pulled him out and told him I was upset. 'Yes, I can understand,' he said. 'I've had one or two slip-ups like that on security. But I shouldn't worry. Hugh's delighted.' 'Well,' I said, 'this is a very grave lapse and I ought to apologize because otherwise the Russians may refuse to talk to us in future.' 'Oh, don't send them a letter,' Harold said. 'That will put you in their power and they may ask you to publish it. Have a word with Hugh, anyway.' Ten minutes later I ran into Harold and Hugh in the lobby. 'What are you worrying about?' said Hugh. 'I thought it was very successful and what you said was just right. Mind you, if you had said anything wrong, like discussing the Popular Front or revealing anything – of course, there was nothing to reveal – you'd have been in trouble. Don't worry, my dear boy, don't worry.' And he swept on.

This morning, at the Executive, when it was announced that K. and B. would be dining with us on April 23rd, Edith launched her attack. 'No leaks, I hope,' she said, looking me straight in the eye. 'Remember, Dick, you let us all down by what you did.' I said something about being sorry and having seen Morgan and asked him to express regret. There was a hum of indignation, chiefly from the women, until Hugh said, rather gruffly, 'I don't know why we're wasting our time on something so trivial.' Here's an object lesson in Labour politics. If you're brought up as I am, you worry about principles and violations of rules. If you're a real Labour politician, you only worry about unsuccessful violations of rules and apparently this was a great success – or rather, I got away with it. Of course, if there had been a Bevanite row on, we should never have heard the end of it.

After the debate [on the Consolidated Fund Bill], I walked into the Smoking Room and found George Brown and Curly Mallalieu. We had a fascinating talk. Curly is still a personal Bevanite but he is a strangely lost soul in the Commons. When I sat down, he was saying to George that he was now a constituency M.P. on the one hand and a journalist on the other and he didn't attend Party meetings for fear of being accused of leaks. In order to write well, one had to be detached and not know too much of a background one couldn't write about. Anyway, he detested the feeling of his colleagues

16

suspecting him. I said this was sheer nonsense. I'd done it for ten years and, anyway, you couldn't write well without knowing the background and you couldn't know your job on the *Statesman* without telling Kingsley so much that he could print nothing you didn't want.

Then we got on to a long discussion of the future Labour leadership. George, who was a T. & G. official, maintained that he has been trying to go back to the T. & G. and will yet do so in a year. This is rather like my saying I will go back to Oxford and Curly obviously didn't believe it. After all, George is one of the coming forces, since he's far the ablest young trade unionist in the House and is very close to Gaitskell. George asserted that Alf is one up on him. George can't get higher than Minister of Defence, whereas Alf is certain to be Foreign Secretary. I disputed this and Curly said I should be Foreign Secretary. But George and I both agreed that, though I undoubtedly deserve to be Foreign Secretary, I just would never be, for the same reason as Dalton. One has to have a trade unionist and that's why Alf would get it. I said that I knew Gaitskell didn't want Alf and George said, 'Whether he wants him or not, he will have him, and your task, my dear Dick, is to work away on him and turn him into the next Foreign Secretary, whatever his capacities.' I said that Nye was the obvious choice and George at once agreed. 'That', he said, 'was the advice I gave to Hugh. But Nye will never make it because he won't do his homework. You'll see,' George said, 'he just won't make it — not because we won't have him, we will — but because he's not prepared to work.'

The whole conversation was an interesting sidelight on the new situation inside the Labour Party. I think a new, young leadership is actually taking over and the old men are actually moving to the sidelines. Even six weeks ago, I had an uneasy query whether Hugh and Co. could really take over from the generation of Dalton, Griffiths, Shinwell, Stokes, etc. Now I have little doubt that they can and that they are actually doing so, just at the moment when the Tory leadership is showing every sign of disintegration.

Friday, April 6th

I haven't written for some time, partly because nothing much has happened — or rather, such gigantic things have been happening in the outside world that one could not put them in this diary. However, let's record the laying of the Coventry Cathedral foundation stone on Friday, March 23rd.

The wireless news said it was going to be raining but it turned out to be perfect — hard, brilliant sunshine, with a bitterly cold wind. On the whole it was a nice ceremony because Maurice and Tilly Edelman,[1] Anne and I were sitting among the Councillors and had a fine time chatting. We had been a little aggrieved that the wives of M.P.s had been excluded from presentation to the Queen but we were delighted to find that the Coventry Corporation

---

[1] Matilda Yates married Maurice Edelman in 1933.

had treated the visiting M.P.s from Warwickshire, including a junior Minister, Mr Profumo,[1] even worse by not even asking them to lunch.

The ceremony was all televised and beforehand we were given careful loudspeaker instructions that, though it was sacred ground and a church service, we could wave our programmes in the air and applaud as the Queen entered. The result was about the most half-hearted applause I have ever heard. As far as I could judge, very few people in the city had bothered to turn out, apart from the masses of schoolchildren in the Precinct. Of course, this was partly because it was a Friday and nobody's going to miss work when there's short time on.

The only amusing thing happened between the ceremony and the lunch in St Mary's Hall. In the Council House lavatories are in short supply. The Queen went into the Lord Mayor's Parlour and his little lavvy behind, whereas the gentlemen were pushed into Committee Room 3, half way along the passage, with instructions, if they wanted to go to the lavatory, to turn right out of the door, go thirty yards along the passage and find it. What they had forgotten was that all the Council employees would come out of their offices and line the passage. So each time the Prime Minister or the Duke of Edinburgh[2] or the Lord-Lieutenant[3] went in and pulled the plug, there was a resounding cheer. 'What a place!' said the Prime Minister, as he came back, looking like a rather raddled *ingénu* actor. 'You sit there waiting for a cheer as you pull the plug!' The Duke of Edinburgh was also out of sorts because he hadn't got a comb, until Maurice gingerly produced a two-penny one.

The Duke is a great deal rougher-looking than I had expected, with a slightly wild look in his eye. Although the Prime Minister was in the room, the Duke spent his time talking to Maurice and me, especially on the subject of Crush and Bulge. 'They've arranged that we should have them to tea,' he said. 'I don't know what the hell we shall give them. I think it's bloody silly. But they think we should give them too much importance if we had them to lunch.' This remark seemed delightfully natural to Maurice, who is not a political prig, like me. Considering the Prime Minister had said to me a few minutes before what a wonderful fellow the Duke was, how alert and on top of every political subject, I couldn't help feeling it was illuminating that he should have criticized the P.M. to me, a Member of the Opposition. For, after all, when he said to me, 'They've made us have them to tea' and called

[1] John Profumo, Conservative M.P. for Kettering 1940–5 and for Stratford-on-Avon from 1950 until his resignation in 1963. (See below, pp. 988 ff.) He was Joint Parliamentary Secretary at the Ministry of Transport and Civil Aviation 1952–7, Parliamentary Under-Secretary of State for the Colonies 1957–8, Parliamentary Under-Secretary of State for Foreign Affairs 1958–9, Minister of State for Foreign Affairs 1959–60 and Secretary of State for War 1960–3.

[2] Prince Philip, Duke of Edinburgh.

[3] John Verney, the 20th Baron Willoughby de Broke. After a career in the Army and in the Auxiliary Air Force, he served on various bodies connected with National Hunt Racing, including the National Hunt Committee, the Jockey Club and Racecourse Technical Services Ltd. He was Lord-Lieutenant of Warwickshire 1939–68.

it bloody silly, he was criticizing no one except the Prime Minister. We may have trouble with this young man.

From what I could see of the Queen, she really is a very dull little thing, who cares nothing except about horses. We heard at the time that she had only come to Coventry on condition that not more than ten people were presented to her and that she didn't have to make any speech whatsoever. After the lunch she was presented with a £350 model Jaguar for Charles and a lovely ribbon doll for Anne,[1] by the Lord Mayor,[2] who made a nice little speech. However, a bargain is a bargain, and when he'd finished she got up and left the room without a single word of thanks. With that sort of wife, how tame for the Duke to have to play the part of a Prince Consort. But if he criticizes a Tory Prime Minister like that to the Opposition, what will he do to us?

Parliament and politics are extraordinarily quiescent. But why? For heaven knows, the world is a very exciting place. The Khrushchev speech, announcing the end of the Stalin cult, is still reverberating round the world, while Mr Malenkov inspects two power stations a day, beams at the workers, pats the children on the head and generally does a magnificent job of publicity. Meanwhile, the whole Western position in the Middle East continues to fall to pieces and in every other part of the world the end of the cold war disintegrates the Western alliance.

The only place where things look like settling down is on the economic front here at home. Only three weeks ago, we were all in a tizzy about the motor-car industry and the incipient crisis, but now the Macmillan disinflationary measures[3] seem to be having a quiet, steady effect and the Government may well get through, at least until the autumn, and without too much trouble. If it does, as Hugh Gaitskell remarked to me yesterday, Conservative free enterprise will have scored a considerable victory (though no one will notice it) by showing that a controlled inflation can take place without physical controls or planning.

But let's get back to Malenkov. I had heard that Hugh Gaitskell had had a little talk with him. I rang up Hugh yesterday and was asked to come round to the House to read his note of the meeting. Actually, Hugh had been invited to the Russian Embassy and on two successive days had had talks, with only Mrs Malenkov[4] and Mrs Gaitskell, Gromyko[5] and Malik present, lasting

---

[1] H.R.H. Prince Charles and H.R.H. Princess Anne.

[2] The Lord Mayor of Coventry at that time was T. H. Dewis.

[3] Announced on February 17th and designed to dampen continuing inflation. They included further limits on hire purchase, cuts in subsidies on bread and milk, suspension of the capital investment allowance for firms, further cuts of £50 million in the State industries programme and of more than £20 million in Government Departments' capital spending, and restriction in local authority projects.

[4] Born Elena Khrushcheva.

[5] Andrei A. Gromyko. A scholar, he became Chief of the American Division of the Russian National Council of Foreign Affairs in 1939 and served as a Counsellor at the Soviet Embassy in Washington 1939–43. He was Ambassador to the United States of

some five hours. On this occasion, Malenkov had done nearly all the questioning and Hugh had given him some very tough answers about how British politics works, how irritating the British Communist Party is and how idiotic the Russians are only to have contact with fellow travellers and Communists. Hugh had mentioned as an example the proposed conference on disarmament in Moscow,[1] to which no one but obvious fellow travellers had been invited. 'But surely,' said Malenkov, 'no Labour Party member would go to such a conference without your consent?' This question indicates that the Russians really do misunderstand and regard every left-winger who goes to them as an undercover agent for Gaitskell! Hugh said that the only kind of conference he would agree to would be on the Königswinter basis and organized through Christopher Mayhew's Anglo-Soviet association.

Hugh discussed the Middle East with Malenkov at some length and emphasized the importance of the Tripartite Declaration for assuring Israel's frontiers. He was astonished when Malenkov cordially agreed with this. 'That is sensational,' said Dora, 'do you really mean it?' At this, Gromyko demurred to some extent but Malenkov said that this was just what he thought. Russia, too, was determined to prevent Israel being overrun and to maintain her frontiers. Hugh's impression confirms William Hayter's – that Malenkov was the original proponent of the soft line at home and the soft line abroad. Actually, he may well have opposed the sale of arms to Egypt.

Last week Joe Alsop[2] came to lunch and met Alf Robens and Kenneth Younger. I had forgotten that Joe is a domestic creature, who loves his house, and by inviting him to eat at home with me and be entertained by Anne, I had tamed him. He was charm and courtesy itself and is the kind of guest who notices everything, including your dining-room table and your lampshades. He is on the way to the Middle East and one thing he said in passing struck me. 'Of course,' he said, 'we have a Chamberlain regime in Washington. Ike is just as provincial, just as well-intentioned as Neville Chamberlain, just as blind and contemptuous of experts who mention facts he doesn't agree with.' Joe repeated a good deal of what he had said to me in Washington at the end of last year, about the possibility of losing Malaya and the Middle East and the doubts about what we would then do. But he is so obsessed by military balance of power that he fails to see the tremendous

---

America and Minister to Cuba 1943–6, Soviet Representative on the U.N. Security Council 1946–8, Deputy Foreign Minister 1946–9, First Deputy Minister of Foreign Affairs 1949–52, Soviet Ambassador in London 1952–3, Deputy Foreign Minister 1953–4 and First Deputy Foreign Minister 1954–7. Since 1957 he has been Minister of Foreign Affairs.

[1] In talks in London Mr Gromyko had proposed the reduction of conventional arms to agreed levels under international control, an agreement to be reached independently of any pact on banning nuclear weapons. He had also suggested the creation of a zone of limited disarmament in central Europe, policed by both sides.

[2] Joseph Wright Alsop, a journalist. His career started in 1932 with the New York *Herald Tribune*. From 1945 to 1958 he was, with his brother Stewart, co-author of a column, 'Matters of Fact', syndicated by the New York *Herald Tribune*. Since 1964 he has written a column syndicated by the *Los Angeles Times*.

opportunities for diplomacy which are there today, if we would only forget for a few months about armaments, which anyway the Russians are apparently now willing to slash.

Crossman set off for the annual Königswinter Conference on April 12th, together with his wife, Anne, and after a short visit to West and East Berlin they arrived in Poland on April 18th. There they saw for themselves the first signs of the revolt against Stalinism. On April 20th Crossman gave a lecture to the Polish Institute of International Affairs in Warsaw, which, in the words of Zycie Warszawy, *was 'devoted to the problem of a better mutual acquaintance'. A* Daily Mirror *column on Germany appeared in the issue of April 17th and reports on Poland on April 20th and 24th. He also wrote an article on 'The New Revolution In Poland' for the* New Statesman and Nation *of May 5th, 1956.*

Meanwhile, on April 18th Marshal Bulganin and Mr Khrushchev arrived at Portsmouth in the Soviet Cruiser Ordjonikidze *and made their way by train to London, where they were met by the Prime Minister. A series of secret talks with the Prime Minister, the Foreign Secretary and others began on April 19th. There was no agenda for these discussions and, as agreed, they were reported only in the form of communiqués. The talks were described on April 20th as frank, useful and cordial.*

At the weekend the Russian leaders stayed at Chequers, visiting Oxford on the way. Here there were demonstrations by the undergraduates (which the visitors wrongly believed to have been officially inspired). But the most eventful part of their stay was the dinner arranged by the Labour Party N.E.C. on Monday, April 23rd. At this, Mr Khrushchev was asked about Social Democratic victims of Soviet Government oppression and this so angered him that he harangued his hosts, provoking spirited interruptions from George Brown. (On his return to Russia, Marshal Bulganin referred to this jarring episode; it had evidently struck the visitors forcibly.)

Crossman's own accounts of the visit may be found in the Daily Mirror *of April 27th and May 1st. He does not include with his papers a transcript of the speeches at the N.E.C. dinner but he does attach an interesting note of a conversation between Khrushchev and Harold Stassen, the Foreign Policy Adviser to President Eisenhower.*

Tuesday, May 8th
Anne and I returned from Poland on Monday, April 23rd. When we got to Brussels, we found that Summer Time had changed the schedule and just missed the B.E.A. plane for London. However, I rooted round and found a Pan-American from Frankfurt to New York that was stopping in Brussels and London. It was a President Super-stratocruiser and we crossed in forty-one minutes, with Martinis served to light radio music. We were loaded with gramophone records, carpets and books but we got them through the

Customs and I arrived at the House of Commons at seven o'clock, to find The Dinner was to begin at twenty to eight.

In the Smoking Room I found Nye and we had a drink. At about a quarter past seven we went downstairs to find most of the other members of the Executive already busily drinking. K. & B. arrived about twenty to eight and began busily shaking hands. Meanwhile Peter Ericsson had mentioned to me that the Russians wanted to have a few questions placed beforehand and would I ask the first — about the liberalization policy, remarking that I had just got back that day from Warsaw? Another would be asked by Alf about disarmament and Peter mentioned that another would come from Sam Watson about the Social Democrats imprisoned in Eastern Europe.

I found myself sitting between a Russian diplomat, whose name I've forgotten, and the inventor[1] of the new Russian jet airliner, a dear old boy who could speak even less French than myself or the Chief Whip, who sat beyond him. My own Russian, between me and Kenneth, was enigmatic. I am not going to record what happened at the dinner because I shall insert the full transcript of the actual speeches.[2] My own memory, for what it is worth, does not include any idea that anything had gone wrong at the central table during the dinner, but then I could not possibly have known, sitting where I was.[3] Everything seemed O.K. when Bulganin sat down at a quarter past ten and James Callaghan shouted 'Khrushchev!' I joined in, since I knew we only had ten minutes left and it seemed polite and he looked quite jovial. My own first reaction was concerned much more with Khrushchev than with his interrupters. I suppose, because I've been concerned about Germany, I was really appalled by his open threat to repeat the Stalin–Hitler[4] Pact and titillated by his cynicism about controlled disarmament. My other feeling was that we were in for the hell of a mess, since nothing could prevent the press knowing about it.

At the end of the dinner I got hold of Gaitskell and said, 'You must hold a press conference,' to which he replied, to my surprise, that one had been fixed already. I said, 'You must spill the whole story and get the whole evening in proportion. Otherwise we shall be in trouble.' I myself, if my memory serves right, was much surprised by Gaitskell's reference to the Jews and the Social Democrats in his reply to Khrushchev and not the least surprised when Khrushchev thought Gaitskell was accusing him of anti-semitism. I suppose this was because I had just come back from Warsaw and I realized that the Socialists were being released in droves and the Russians

[1] Sergey Vladimirovich Ilyushin, a soldier and pilot, graduated from the Zhukovsky Air Force Engineering Academy in Moscow in 1926. His aircraft designs included the Il-2 Stormovik armoured attack aircraft, the Il-12 twin-engined passenger aircraft, the Il-18 Moskva four-engined turboprop transport aircraft and the Il-62 turbojet passenger aircraft. He eventually became a lieutenant-general in the Soviet Red Army engineering technical service and a professor at his former academy.

[2] He did not.

[3] Crossman is referring to the altercation between Mr. Khrushchev and George Brown.

[4] The Russo-German Non-Aggression Pact, signed in August 1939.

were obviously aggrieved at our failure to recognize the changes they had begun.

On Tuesday morning, when I had a glance at the press, I realized that we were in for trouble in the Party. The trouble, of course, was that nothing was reported about the tone or content of Khrushchev's speech and the net impression was that the only thing which had happened was a tactless demand about the Social Democrats, whereas in fact this demand was made long after the main trouble had got under way. George [Wigg] rang me up in one of his frenetic furies, regarding this as a breaking-point and trying to swing me into line for sending an immediate apology to the Russian Embassy.

Ericsson came to lunch and I found out from him what a mess there had been about the Social Democrats. The American trade unions had sent to the Russian Embassy a protest list, which was totally different from ours and included a lot of old Mensheviks and 1918 cases, whereas ours was concerned with Socialists for the most part arrested after 1947. Khrushchev's violent reference to Mensheviks and enemies of the people showed that he assumed our list was the American list and that we were acting for the Americans. Ericsson obviously felt the whole thing had been mismanaged and that the right way to deal with this issue was through private pressure behind the scenes.

When I got to the House, I found Gaitskell wanted to see me. He immediately said, 'We must get the Sunday press right. Can you help? We must get them to publish the purport of Khrushchev's paranoiac speech.' I said, 'You can't deal with the press until you've decided what you're trying to achieve. Hadn't we better face the fact that the constituency parties will be up in arms against the Executive?' 'I think the net effect of this will be to increase our popularity in the country,' Gaitskell replied. 'After all, you agree Khrushchev was paranoiac.' I said that might be the effect in the country but we also had to deal with the effect in the Party and I warned him that most of the Parliamentary Party would be up in arms as well, a fact I had discovered by five minutes in the Tea Room.

I also said that I thought George Brown had behaved outrageously during Khrushchev's speech. I laughingly added that Nye Bevan, in attempting to pour oil on troubled waters, had actually fanned the flames. On this occasion Nye would have to be on the same side as Brown and Gaitskell and this was a considerable advantage in dealing with the Party. I then said I thought the really vital first move, before we discussed the press, was to get the Russians to have a private meeting with Hugh and a few others in order to clear up the mess. 'There can be no question of an apology,' said Gaitskell. I replied that there was no need to apologize, since I was pretty sure we had the whip hand of the Russians on one point. Both they and we had verbatim records made of the speeches and I was sure that they would not like them published. Having cleared up misunderstanding about the dinner, Gaitskell should raise this issue and ask Khrushchev if what he had said to us was his last word, since, if that was so, we should like to publish it. Gaitskell didn't like this idea at all.

That evening the Russians held a party at Claridges, a sardine-packed affair. I was standing talking to Kingsley and he said, 'Where's Khrushchev?' At this moment something like a human torpedo was pushed through the crowd and I said to Kingsley, 'He's just under your chin,' and there he was. I had a word with Malik, along with George Wigg, and said I regretted that the really serious issue between us had not been discussed. Malik replied, obviously in great distress, 'We used to complain about the Americans at the United Nations always raising irrelevant propaganda issues. You people have been no better.'

On Wednesday morning, April 25th, we had the Executive, and it was soon clear that we would have to discuss the dinner Actually Barbara raised the matter on the extraordinary ground that it had all leaked to the press and there should never have been a press conference. After this Edith Summerskill weighed in, attacking George Brown, whereupon Jack Cooper, who had sat next to me at the dinner, supported her and said George's behaviour was intolerable. The only person who said a word for George was Alice Bacon. I was amazed to hear the Executive in such unanimous mood. Edith Summerskill then proposed a delegation to apologize to the Russians. I countered with my proposal, which was broadly accepted. Harold Wilson suggested that the Chairman should rebuke George Brown and this was only not carried because Hugh said it was parliamentary business and a matter for the Shadow Cabinet of the Party. As I expected, within a few hours it was known that the Russians had agreed to have a meeting on Thursday morning, despite their packed schedule. On Wednesday afternoon the Shadow Cabinet met and I was told that George Brown had sort of apologized. It all looked as though the matter would be settled fairly amicably. I was still enormously under the impression of the brutal frankness and self-confidence of Khrushchev's speech but I was by now aware that the whole affair had been a gift to the Tories and had also unloosed all the fissiparous elements in our Party. When the Tories are in trouble, they bunch together and cogger up. When we get into trouble, we start blaming each other and rushing to the press to tell them all the terrible things that somebody else has done.

However, on Thursday morning, when I was writing my column, I read the *Tribune* and found that Nye had stood fairly firm by Gaitskell, while Brown was criticized. In view of the competition for the treasurership, this kind of slightly dirty politics was, I suppose, inevitable, and at least Nye was supporting Gaitskell. I rang up Gaitskell to find out what had happened at the meeting with the Russians and he gave me a fairly detailed account. It had started once again with a row, but, as I had told him, that quietened down when the subject of publication was raised. However, on the advice of the Parliamentary Committee, Hugh had not pressed this home and the end was merely a handshake, which I felt might be temporary.

On Thursday evening I had to go and do a meeting for Peter Shore[1] in Harlow, which meant that I missed the Parliamentary Party Meeting. On Friday George telephoned me to say that Hugh Gaitskell had done extremely well and the whole Manny Shinwell revolt had been quelled.[2] But everything blew up again when Hugh went on television on Friday evening, virtually defending George Brown and violently attacking the Russians. That meant that the usual weekend speeches were nothing but recriminations. However, I didn't worry about them, since I was having a lovely weekend at Prescote with Mike and Connie Bessie,[3] who were excellent company.

Throughout this K. & B. affair I had been brooding and ruminating on what I saw in Poland. The more I reflect on it, the more convinced I am that something epoch-making has begun in the Communist states. The French Revolution ended in Bonapartism; the Russian Revolution seems to have got through its Bonapartist stage and to be reverting to a more democratic liberal tradition. This was confirmed to me today by Oscar Lange,[4] the Polish academic, who turned up from India and Egypt. In his curiously laborious style, he made his sociological analysis of what has happened since the death of Beria, emphasizing that what I saw in Poland had started long before and that the Khrushchev speech on Stalin had only been important because it gave people the feeling that the change was final. Before then, everybody was looking over their shoulders and failing to speak out, he said, for fear that the new policy could suddenly be reversed, with a return to Stalinite despotism.

Oscar's theory is that throughout Eastern Europe and Russia the working class which made the revolution of 1918 had been virtually destroyed and a new industrial working class had developed, composed of conformist petit-bourgeois and peasant elements, without any revolutionary fervour. This made the Stalinite period easier, since the revolutionary situation has only been retained by the intelligentsia, which, however, has been increased

[1] Labour M.P. for Stepney 1964–74 and for Tower Hamlets, Stepney and Poplar since 1974. He joined the Labour Party in 1948 and was Head of the Research Department 1953–64, and on his election to the House of Commons became P.P.S. to the Prime Minister, serving in that capacity 1965–6. He was Joint Parliamentary Secretary at the Ministry of Technology 1966–7, and at the Department of Economic Affairs 1967; Secretary of State for Economic Affairs 1967–9; Minister without Portfolio 1969–70; Secretary of State for Trade 1974–6; and Secretary of State for the Environment 1976–9.

[2] Shinwell was one of those Labour members anxious to improve relations with the new leaders in the Soviet Union.

[3] Crossman's American publisher and his first wife.

[4] An economist, he was a Lecturer in Economics at the University of Cracow and in the 1930s held fellowships at universities in the United States and Britain. In 1937 he was Lecturer in Economics at Stanford University and Professor of Economics and Statistics at the University of Chicago 1938–45. He was Polish Ambassador to the U.S.A. and Polish Delegate to the U.N. Security Council 1945–8. He was an adviser on economic planning in Poland, India, Ceylon, Iraq and the United Arab Republic during the 1940s and 1950s and was Professor of Political Economy at the University of Warsaw 1956 and Chairman of the Economic Council, attached to the Polish Council of Ministers, 1957–62. He was also Chairman of the U.N. Economic Commission for Europe. He died in 1965.

enormously by education and which is carrying the new movement forward in Russia. 'What form does this movement take?' I asked him. 'It is pragmatic,' he said. 'The Russian new intelligentsia is not concerned, like the Polish, with the independence of the judiciary, etc. Its main concern is to get hold of Western techniques and technology. Its complaint is that under Stalin we became antiquated and out of date and we have been deliberately deceived about the technological development of the West. It is contact with the West they want, to bring them up to date.'

By an accident, last week's *N.S. & N.*, which contained my article on Poland, also contained a long article by Cole,[1] which said, in rather abstract terms, pretty well what I had been thinking. I simply can't get people here to understand that a Communist dictatorship can actually liberalize itself and re-establish a degree of freedom, which demands a revision of our attitude to it. However, I have arranged for Alf Robens to go to Prague and Warsaw and I hope that Kenneth Younger will go to Budapest, since the more people who report on the changes the better.

I find on reflection that I'm a bit schizophrenic about K. & B. I share Hugh's horror at the tough, brutal pragmatism of Khrushchev, who is obviously the master. I share his feeling that the Russians don't care two hoots what we think or do, because they are sure they can get away with whatever they want, and this is very alarming. On the other hand, I do have the feeling that what they want is pacific, and can no longer be condemned by a Western Socialist as pure totalitarianism.

Last Wednesday, May 2nd, I had a brief talk with Walter Lippmann, who is on his annual European Grand Tour. One of our difficulties has been to discover what really went on at the talks with Eden. George Wigg's report is that the Russians were just as tough to Eden as they were to us. All we know for certain is what Callaghan overheard when he sat in on K.'s three-hour talk with Stassen[2] at Claridge's, a note of which I attach.[3] Lippmann told me that K. had told Eden that he objected to the Baghdad Pact as a threat to Russia's soft underbelly and that Eden had assured K. that there was no intention of building H-bomb bases along the Northern Tier. Kingsley got hold of a story from the Foreign Office that, early in the conversation, K. had brusquely told Eden that of course he recognized that we had colonial interests, but nothing was going to stop his denouncing colonialism, whereat Eden had made clear to K. that we should regard it as an act of war if the Russians took our Middle Eastern oil.

[1] In his article 'Socialists and Communism', published in the *New Statesman and Nation* of May 5th, G. D. H. Cole said that it was 'sheer nonsense to say that there is *nothing* in common' between them.

[2] An American lawyer and politician, Harold Stassen was a candidate for the Republican nomination for the presidency in 1948 and 1952. He served as President Eisenhower's Special Assistant for Disarmament 1955–8, acting at the same time as the Deputy U.S. Representative on the U.N. Disarmament Commission.

[3] See p. 492.

Crossman's papers include the following report:

Note on Conversation on April 24th, 1956

Present: Mr Khrushchev
         Mr Gromyko
         Mr Malik
         Mr Stassen
         Sir William Hayter
         Mr James Callaghan

The conversation was mainly about disarmament and was conducted between Mr Khrushchev and Mr Stassen. Mr Khrushchev said that inspection and control were not at all valuable. Anyone could conceal what he was doing, especially in a country as big as the U.S.S.R. He thought that there was no need to have any fly-over arrangements. He did not think that the Americans wanted disarmament. He was not sure that American public opinion was ready for it. Otherwise he could not understand why the Russian proposals, which incorporated some of the original proposals made by the West, had not been taken up. 'We seem to be getting on,' he said, 'and then you, and Moch[1] *and Nutting get together and everything gets muddled up.'*

Mr Khrushchev believed strongly that we ought to reduce the number of men under arms:

> *Perhaps there is no need to reach formal agreement and sign documents. Supposing we take a unilateral decision and disarm a million men, would there be no response from your side to such a gesture? We want to do it but we are not ready to have controllers in our bedrooms. We would be glad for you to send some friends to watch us wave goodbye to the demobilized soldiers.*

Mr Khrushchev also said in passing, and the point was not taken up, that the U.S.S.R. intends to withdraw troops from Germany, but it was not clear whether it would be all the troops or some of the troops. He added that the Germans should be allowed to work out their own solution.

This does not include Stassen's side of the conversation, but I ought to make it clear, that, at this point, he interposed that without inspection and control the generals on either side would feel very dubious about whether an agreement

[1] Jules Moch, an engineer, was Director of Services for the Industrial and Agricultural Restoration of Germany 1918–20 and was a Member of the French National Assembly 1928–40, 1946–58 and 1962–7. During the Second World War he supported General de Gaulle, and his post-war political career included service as a member of the Algerian Consultative Assembly 1946–58, as Minister of Public Works and Transport, Minister for Economic Affairs and Reconstruction, Minister of the Interior 1947–50, Minister of Defence 1950–1 and Minister of the Interior again in 1958. He was a member of the French Delegation to the U.N. 1947–60 and his country's Permanent Representative at the U.N. Disarmament Commission 1951–61.

was being carried out, and they would raise doubts. Mr Khrushchev said they would not be allowed to do so in the Soviet Union. In Russia, generals are the servants of the Government; 'if they protested, we should dismiss them'. Two or three times after Mr Khrushchev had made his suggestion, he urged Mr Stassen to think it over. He said he would like to see Mr Eisenhower. He did not want to see him in order to insult him, but to talk over with him some of these problems. Perhaps Mr Stassen could come to Moscow. It might be inconvenient for him to come and see Mr Khrushchev but would he not like to look up his old friend Mr Bohlen? That would give them a chance of continuing the conversation.

On more general topics, Mr Khrushchev said that Eisenhower had captivated him at Geneva, but he did not understand Mr Dulles nor his attitudes. Surely the Americans did not want to rule the world. In any case, 'We are not ignorant savages any more. You cannot frighten us as you could have done thirty years ago.' In reply to Mr Stassen's opinion that both Mr Eisenhower and Mr Dulles wanted peace, Mr Khrushchev said that he was sure Mr Eisenhower did but Mr Dulles always seems to inflame opinion. 'Whereas', he said, 'Gromyko would not have said that, but he is a diplomat; I am just an amateur.'

'Do the Americans want better relations with Russia? Last September, a visiting American came to my holiday resort to see me and I agreed to buy a lot of grain from him. No doubt he was going to make a substantial profit out of the deal. I did not mind that. But the Americans would not give us visas to send four or five of our people to look at the grain, so eventually I said we could do without it.'

Mr Khrushchev wondered whether the state of American opinion was such that it was impossible for the American Government to do anything to improve relations. Several times he used phrases such as: 'We must wait for better times'; 'We must wait for better weather'. He said he did not mind people using the word Communist about him as a term of reproach. He was proud of it. 'You are right to defend your system, although we think it weaker than ours.'

There was discussion about the meaning of the word 'co-existence', which ended very obscurely.

Mr Stassen also analysed in a very acute way the differences between the press and the parties in the U.S.A. and the U.S.S.R. Mr Khrushchev said that he could understand that and, no doubt, it had an effect upon our thinking. He said that he felt sorry for Gromyko: 'He is our sacrifice for peace.'

The conversation was divided about half in half between Mr Stassen and Mr Khrushchev. It lasted for two hours. Mr Stassen put the point of view of the U.S.A. with very great eloquence and argumentative force, but it seemed to me that at times, especially in relation to disarmament, he was on the defensive. The conversation was very amicable all the way through. Mr Stassen promised to report what had been said to Mr Eisenhower. He said that he would be agreeable to talking to Mr Khrushchev again in London if Prime Minister Eden had no objection.

The party broke up with Mr Khrushchev saying that: 'Politicians are worse than drunkards; they sleep after drink but we go on talking.'

My own reaction is that Khrushchev means business on disarmament and he is only searching round for the best way to try and ease the present arms burden on the U.S.S.R.

On the whole, relations between the Soviet leaders and their British hosts had been polite and friendly, but no particular results emerged from the visit. On April 26th a long and empty agreed communiqué had been issued and on the next and last day of their visit the Soviet leaders gave a press conference to some 450 journalists in the Central Hall, Westminster. This took the form of a lengthy, prepared statement by Marshal Bulganin but, when the conventions were explained, Mr Khrushchev agreed to answer questions, which he then handled adroitly. The same evening, after the guests' departure for home, the Prime Minister had broadcast his impressions of the visit, describing it as 'certainly worth while'. Though the results did not constitute 'a revolutionary agreement', they could be 'a beginning of a beginning'. No progress had been made on some issues, Germany for example, but both sides were anxious for a resolution of the Middle East conflict. On trade the Russians were eager for some £200 million, annually, of British goods, compared with the £23 million for the previous year. At least two-thirds of this shopping list was for articles which would not be excluded for strategic reasons.

Friday, May 18th
On Tuesday, Bob Boothby, Julian Amery and I gave a farewell dinner to Zhivotovski, who had known us all very well. As this diary shows, I had seen a good deal of him before the famous dinner for K. & B. After the dinner I met him at the Czech Embassy and he said, 'Why didn't you see that I was on the invitation list! I could have tipped off Khrushchev not to take George Brown seriously.' They had already told Zhivotovski he was going back to Moscow fairly soon, but the dinner certainly turned his return into a kind of rebuke. I made a rather silly joke about the dinner. 'All we public school boys', I said, 'behaved perfectly. It was only your proletarian working-class, Zhivotovski, who misbehaved.'

The Chancellor of the Exchequer introduced his Budget on April 17th. It proposed a number of measures to encourage private savings, including the issue of new savings certificates and defence bonds with improved rates of interest, and of 'premium bonds' carrying no interest but with tax-free prizes of up to £1,000, for which there would be a three-monthly draw. The first £15 of interest on savings and bank deposits was to be free of interest.

The rate of tax on distributed profits was raised by 2·5 per cent to 30 per cent and on undistributed profits by 0·5 per cent to 3 per cent. Tobacco duty increased by 3s. in the pound and the remainder of the bread subsidy was abolished. Family allowances were raised by 2s. a week for third and subsequent children and an extension was made in the qualifying age for children still at school or apprenticed. A tax-relief scheme was introduced for retirement provisions made by the self-employed; stamp duty was removed on up to £5,000 of the cost of house purchase. These changes meant that some £20 million of taxation was removed but £28 million was taken back in new taxation.

It was announced that for the next two years the capital expenditure of the nationalized industries would be met by the Exchequer, to a maximum of £700 million, but there would be an immediate examination of Government expenditure, to find savings of at least £100 million.

Opposition to the Chancellor's proposals focused on the premium bond scheme, which Harold Wilson described in the Budget debate as a 'squalid raffle'. On the whole, however, the passage of the Finance Bill embodying the Budget proposals was a quiet affair; the Opposition leadership were, like the Government, anxious to stem inflation.

On June 26th the Chancellor reported to the Commons on his search for £100 million savings in Government expenditure. Of the £76 million which he had so far attained, £26 million was on domestic spending and the remainder on defence costs. His statement was severely criticized, since the domestic economies were allegedly 'very small beer'. The annual defence White Paper, published on February 17th, had already announced that during the next few years Britain would rely on smaller forces equipped with deadlier weapons. Estimates for the War Office and the Air Ministry were lower, while those of the Ministry of Supply increased. Of the £15 million savings which the Chancellor now promised, three-quarters seemed to depend on the running-down of stocks. Three days later, on June 29th, the Minister of Defence, Sir Walter Monckton, announced that the German Government had agreed to pay £34 million (for the year ending in May 1957) towards the cost of British troops stationed there. Since the full cost was estimated at £64 million and the British Government had asked for £50 million, Sir Walter's statement was coolly received.

The Labour Party, meanwhile, had published the first two of the series of pamphlets commissioned from study groups the previous October. Personal Freedom: Labour's Policy for the Individual and Society *appeared on June 17th, in Crossman's words 'a fairly harmless, wordy document, which, however, neglects the main issue of freedom in the trade unions'. A week later* Homes of the Future *was published, unaffected, Crossman felt, by the*

great many hours I had spent trying to make the study group realize that compromise sentences which square committees cannot be subjected to public scrutiny for months on end without their weakness being exposed ... the net result is a document which really leaves the next Labour Government all the important decisions.

Other papers were still being prepared. Crossman led the group which drafted the foreign affairs pamphlet and he was closely involved in the preparation of the defence document.

Friday, June 22nd

I seem to have spent the whole of the last ten days sitting on Party policy committees or drafting documents. It has been quite an interesting experience and has made me reflect on the whole problem of formulating new policy in a party organized like the Labour Party. The Labour Party has an absolute passion for splitting itself by taking votes in committee and on draft amendments moved and counter-moved by different groups. This, of course, is our whole Party tradition and the strange thing is that, directly we get into Government, Labour Cabinets abandon it altogether and try to concert policy with a minimum of voting, by taking the sense of the meeting.

It is this practice I have been trying to build up in the foreign affairs group. We had quite a success in doing so last Tuesday, when the special consideration of SEATO took place on a paper by Harold Davies. Harold wanted SEATO abolished and a regional pact, including China, substituted. Christopher Mayhew and the others on the right wanted SEATO retained. But the discussion was very reasonable and I finally suggested that Harold, Chris and Tony Benn be asked to form a committee of three, to see if agreement could be reached. 'I hope you don't want to blur the irreconcilable difference,' said Bill Warbey, and I said, 'Not blur, just see if it really exists.' Jennie Lee looked very angry, too, but the rest of the committee concurred and it took the three of them just an hour and a half to draft an agreed paper for presentation next Tuesday.

When the committee was over a nice old pacifist, George Craddock,[1] came up and said, 'I hope you're not going to deny me my right to put my own point of view by voting. What's the good of the committee if you do that?' I replied that it was my main object to prevent George Craddock voting at the foreign affairs group. 'Even if we do take votes of the people who happen to be present that day, what does it actually matter to the Parliamentary Committee or the Parliamentary Party?' I asked him. 'Isn't it better to try and work as a body, seeking to reach maximum agreement? If votes have to be taken, they should be taken in the right place, which is the Parliamentary Party, with everybody present.' I've never seen a man more nonplussed. 'Nobody ever talked to me like that,' he said. 'It sounds quite a good idea.'

The other subject was defence. Here we had a far more complex procedural problem. The meeting ended in complete deadlock but the following morning I redrafted a complete paper on National Service and made a really good job of it, producing quite a logical case for a decision to end conscription within a limited period and simultaneously to reduce the global weight of defence.

---

[1] Labour M.P. for South Bradford December 1949–70. He died in 1974.

All this has been rendered much easier by the fact that the Government is obviously concerned to do the same. One of the difficulties of this particular committee, which is fairly common in the Labour Party, is that you never have the same people on two successive occasions, so that the draft sways to and fro according to who is present.

When we met again there were divisions every twenty minutes or so and I thought there was no chance of agreement. But suddenly everybody was most agreeable and after two hours we had a complete draft.

Under pressure from Manny and Nye, who have ceased to believe in NATO, we had watered down all the NATO parts and inserted a proposal to cut back the global defence budget to 6 per cent of the national income. At this point it was a very bold left-wing paper and I was not surprised when next day, Friday, Hugh Gaitskell was anxious to see me. He had seen the draft and was appalled, particularly at the global cut. We had quite a discussion before I realized that we were back in the Bevanite controversy. I pointed out to him that a firm commitment to end the call-up by the end of 1958 was far more risky than a commitment to reduce the defence budget to 6 per cent of the national income by 1958. To this he replied, 'But do be serious. This is politics. I can agree to the abolition of conscription but you can't make me a fool by making me agree to a global cut in the defence budget.' In a desultory fashion this week negotiations are now going on about what was a unanimously agreed draft last Thursday. I shall be amused to see what comes of it.

This question of drafting policy documents is really fascinating. Once again everything depends on the draft presented. Once it is there, it becomes a document, which is amended and counter-amended and one tends to take for granted that the draft itself is substantially correct. Meanwhile the world proceeds onwards and, while you spend week after week drafting, the policy gets out of date.

This whole experience has put me in two minds about the Labour Party. Certainly, from one point of view, the atmosphere at the Centre, both on the N.E.C. and in the Parliamentary Party, is improving. There is a great Centre body of opinion which wants us to have policies, take decisions and get on with things. The division is now between this great Centre and the people on the extreme Right and extreme Left. To some extent, I suppose I can claim that, in doing all this drafting and sitting on all these committees, I have in fact helped to create a kind of Centre policy which makes this Centre possible.

What I have discovered in so doing is that the psychology of Nye, Jennie, and to some extent of Kingsley in the *New Statesman*, makes them instinctively feel that there is something wrong if this is the way the Party is divided. They feel happy when there is a right-wing policy and a left-wing attacking it and they always assume that any Centre policy you produce must in fact be right-wing, in the sense that they must find a position from which to attack it as reactionary. In the case of foreign policy, for instance, Nye, Jennie and the *Tribune* are obviously determined to label my document a sell-out and produce a rival left-wing policy. But, because the document is in fact rather a good left-of-Centre document, they have been forced to define their left-wing policy in very extreme terms.

I met Nye this week in the Smoking Room and he said to me, 'You've produced a terrible document, just the same as Tory policy. What the Party should do is to denounce all these cold war treaties and advocate an alliance with Russia.' As Jennie had put in a paper to the foreign affairs group along these lines, I was not surprised. 'But if you were Foreign Secretary today,' I said, 'would you actually instruct the Foreign Office to repudiate NATO, MEDO[1] and SEATO?'

'Don't be silly,' Nye said, 'we've got four years and this sort of responsibility is what is fatal to the Party.'

Even if the argument about four years were justifiable, I don't think Nye's right in terms of public opinion. If Labour today were to demand the repudiation of NATO (I'm not so sure about MEDO and SEATO), it would not win enormous support in the country, and Nye wouldn't dream of advocating our doing so if I had not managed to produce an official, orthodox policy sufficiently far to the Left to drive him even further. I had Kingsley to lunch this week and he too said, or half said, that I had sold out by failing to repudiate cold war treaties, but of course he collapsed in two minutes when I put the question to him. He made the same kind of argument as Nye, namely that when you are in Opposition you should not be quite so literal.

The other item I might record is a dinner Stephen Spender[2] gave on Sunday to let me meet Wystan Auden,[3] whom I haven't seen since Oxford. Stephen is always on tenterhooks, as I found when I had him to dinner at the House of Commons the other day. He is now Editor of *Encounter* and so subsidized with American dollars and full of suppressed conscience. Wystan Auden was as pleasant as ever and started by saying that he was due to preach in St Giles, Edinburgh, so I spent an hour trying to find out about his religious beliefs, since he said very firmly that he was now a convinced Christian. Stephen listened in agony, since the more Wystan talked – and he talked very volubly – the more he revealed that he is now a comfortable, unreflective pundit, with extremely conventional, washy views. His inaugural

---

[1] The Middle East Defence Organization.

[2] The poet, a friend of Crossman and with whom Crossman had contributed to *Oxford Poetry* (O.U.P.) in 1947. His greatest lyric writing was done early in his life, of which an account appears in *World Within World* (London: Hamish Hamilton, 1951) and *The Thirties and After* (London: Fontana, 1978). His *Collected Poems* were published by Faber (London, 1965).

[3] The English poet, playwright and critic, W. H. Auden. His *Collected Poems* were published in an edition by Edward Mendelson (London: Faber & Faber, 1976). He, too, was a friend of Crossman and a contributor to the volume *Oxford Poetry*. He died in 1973.

lecture as Professor of Poetry at Oxford,[1] published in the *Sunday Times* that morning, had made me suspect this. After that evening I was certain. America has done him a power of good in the sense that it's given him assurance and confidence and let him be a pundit and at the end I couldn't help saying to him that he's the only ex-Englishman I know who has become a thoroughly balanced American. I'd dearly like to know what he and Stephen said about me when we'd left the restaurant. How have I changed since Wystan saw me last? I strongly suspect — less than he has. But, then, he has probably improved.

During the first half of 1956 the Middle East crisis grew worse. In Cyprus terrorism increased and it was suggested that broadcasts by Athens radio, which the Greek Government found itself unable to control, were inciting political crime. On March 5th the British Government began jamming such broadcasts, a policy which had never before been adopted, even in wartime. No political solution was in sight. At the end of January the Governor had given Archbishop Makarios, thought at this time to be a moderate leader reluctantly linked with the EOKA movement, proposals offering self-government as soon as order was restored, and self-determination (that is, the choice of reunion with Greece, at some future time). Negotiations failed. In early March the archbishop and three of his principal associates were deported to the Seychelles, after stores of bombs, grenades and ammunition had been discovered in his palace. Motions of censure were introduced on March 14th and May 14th; demands for British withdrawal were answered by the arguments that enosis (union with Greece) would be resisted by Cypriot Turks, reinforced by their countrymen on the mainland, and that Britain needed to retain Cyprus as a base for the defence of her oil interests in South-West Asia.

The Maltese Government, meanwhile, had been hoping for closer relations with Britain. The referendum to ascertain whether the Maltese wanted unity 'on an Ulster basis' was to be held on February 11th and 12th. On February 5th the Archbishop of Malta, the Most Reverend Michael Gonzi, who opposed the Maltese Government's policy, asked for the referendum to be postponed and, when refused, advised Catholics to boycott it. Though the proposal was supported by 74 per cent of those who voted, there was a large number of spoilt ballot papers and a very large number of abstentions. The plan was approved by only 57 per cent of those who usually voted at elections and by a mere 45 per cent of the registered electorate. In a Commons debate on March 26th the Colonial Secretary and Mr Bevan agreed to proceed with the plan, but two days later the Prime Minister announced that the Government had decided to introduce a Bill giving effect to many of the Round Table's recommendations but

---

[1] Auden's inaugural lecture was later reprinted as 'Writing' in *The Dyer's Hand* (London: Faber & Faber, 1958). Crossman does scant justice to the elaborate religious position evolved by Auden in the American years, especially his critical appreciation of Kierkegaard.

excluding those relating to Maltese representation at Westminster. Such clauses would be brought into operation only if the Maltese people had approved them at a General Election.

The most intractable problems concerned Israel and Egypt. In January the U.N. Security Council unanimously condemned Israel for an attack, in reprisal, on Syrian posts north-east of the Sea of Galilee. In the same month the Secretary-General, Dag Hammarskjöld, visited the Middle East and during his tour made proposals about the demilitarized area on the Israeli–Egyptian frontier at Mitzana (Auja–Hafir). These were accepted by Israel and, later, by Egypt.

But General Glubb's dismissal from the command of the Jordan Arab Legion on March 2nd was followed by increased raids on Israeli territory by Egyptian fedayeen *(irregulars) from Jordan, the Gaza Strip and Sinai. During March Israel protested to the Security Council that eighty raids had been made since the beginning of the year. On April 5th Israel launched a major reprisal against Gaza, with 140 Egyptian casualties. The Secretary-General thereupon returned to the Middle East, to try to persuade all parties to accept a ceasefire and to comply strictly with the terms of the 1949 Armistice Agreement.*

At first his efforts seemed successful. On April 18th he announced an unconditional ceasefire between Israel and Egypt and, later, similar undertakings between Israel and other Arab states. Nevertheless, Israel reserved the right to act in self-defence. But, within a few days of the agreement with Egypt, hostilities began anew. In May the Egyptians arrested a Greek ship seeking to pass through the Suez Canal for Eilat, the Israeli port on the Gulf of Aqaba. The U.N. Security Council meanwhile held long debates over the Secretary-General's report and eventually passed a resolution that he should continue his peace-keeping efforts. On Soviet insistence, however, a clause calling for peaceful settlement of the problems by negotiation was taken out of the resolution.

The Secretary-General's task would have been eased if Britain, France and the United States had managed to agree on a policy for implementing the Tripartite Declaration of 1950, intended to preserve a balance of arms between Israel and the Arab States and to resist aggression by either side. After the Prime Minister's visit to Washington in February, apparently unfruitful talks were held at the State Department with the British and French Ambassadors. In April France supplied Israel with twelve Mystère-IV jet fighters, while the Soviet Union continued to supply arms to the Arabs. On June 13th the last British troops left the Suez Canal base; it was feared that this would be the prelude to further trouble.

Monday, June 25th
For weeks the National Executive has been asking to see the Foreign Secretary about Israel. First he was ill, then he was busy, so that the particular crisis over the fighting in the Gaza Strip had long since disappeared

when today we finally filed into his room behind the Speaker's chair. The delegation had agreed to meet at four o'clock to prepare what it had to say. Characteristically, it was found that Gaitskell and Griffiths were too busy to come and we were left with no ex-Minister and nothing but Peggy Herbison, Alice Bacon, Tony Greenwood and myself. So, against the grain, they had to ask me to speak, since no one else knew it.

It was an illuminating experience. Poor Selwyn Lloyd, who two years ago was a pleasant, coming young man, looked harassed and bedraggled. Apparently he has had some domestic disaster, with his wife in a car smash, and anyway he's only an office-boy to Eden. I began by explaining to him that we had been deeply shocked by the British behaviour during the Security Council debate on the Hammarskjöld[1] mission, which had done an astonishingly good job in pacifying the armistice frontiers. Then, during the debate, the British had agreed, under Arab pressure, to withdraw the words 'a mutually acceptable statement', a concession which had been the last straw in Israel and caused the resignation of Sharett,[2] whose Western policy had been bankrupted by our behaviour.

I was in full swing when Selwyn interrupted me. 'Is this on or off the record?' he said. 'Because I would like to tell you we did this under Russian pressure. It is our view that this affair should be handled now not on a tripartite but on a quadripartite basis and the Russians insisted the words should go out.' I said I was glad that the Government was now taking the advice given it by the Labour Party in the last Middle Eastern debate. Then we had been pooh-poohed for suggesting a four-power approach. 'Not four-power talks,' Selwyn Lloyd said, 'but quadripartite action in the Security Council.' 'That is precisely what Robens advocated,' I said. 'Does that mean that we regard the Tripartite Declaration as a dead letter? The last time we heard from the Government it was the mainstay of their policy.'

Selwyn Lloyd re-emphasized that, 'though one had to be loyal to one's allies,' Britain believed in cautiously trying to get the Russians in. 'In that case, what about a United Nations embargo on arms to the Middle East?' 'We discussed that with K. & B.', said Selwyn Lloyd, 'with relation to the Middle East but finally it was only put into the communiqué in general terms. Yes, it's worth exploring, though the trouble is that we should observe it and they wouldn't.'

He then said that Nasser is now a megalomaniac, who is determined to

---

[1] Dag Hammarskjöld, a Swedish politician, was Secretary-General of the United Nations from 1953 until his death in 1961. A posthumously published collection of his meditations was translated by W. H. Auden and published under the title *Markings* (London: Faber & Faber, 1964).

[2] Moshe Sharett, Foreign Secretary of Israel 1948–53, Prime Minister 1953–5 and Foreign Secretary again in Ben-Gurion's coalition Administration of 1955. Immediately before the Israeli occupation of Sinai in 1955, Ben-Gurion dismissed Sharett as insufficiently 'activist'. He died in 1965.

eliminate Israel altogether, and everything must be done to counter his plans. Lloyd made this observation a few days after General Robertson[1] had attended the Cairo celebrations for the last British troops leaving the Canal Zone and an appearance had been made of patching up terms with Nasser. I don't know how seriously Lloyd meant this, since a few minutes later he was arguing that it wasn't necessary to give Israel any more arms, since the Egyptians really hadn't got a great interest in the area and anyway the arms they got from the Russians were lousy. 'Why didn't the press report the fact', he said, 'that the great procession in Cairo was a flop and only a small proportion of the tanks got off from the starting base?' I might have replied, but didn't, that it could have been reported a great deal more easily if the British Attaché in Cairo had told the newspapers, which he presumably hadn't.

We then asked him about the £10 million subsidy to Jordan. 'It's still being paid,' he said, 'pending a renegotiation of the treaty.' 'Is the preservation of Jordan as an independent State an interest of H.M.G.?' I asked. He replied rather sweetly, 'The trouble about you is, you ask such pertinent questions! If it broke up, who would get it? A bit to Iraq, a bit to Syria, a bit to Egypt? One can't be sure.'

The general impression he gave of talking completely frankly and the sense he imparted of being as small and insignificant as the delegation enormously pleased Peggy Herbison and Alice Bacon, who thought him so much better than Macmillan. What silly women they are! When Macmillan saw us and behaved like an Edwardian diplomat, he was just skilfully putting us off. This poor little fellow was rattled and harassed, like a man in the water who has just got his head above the surface but is swallowing a gulp every now and then. I went away convinced that there is absolutely no settled Western policy in the area.

Tuesday, July 3rd

On Monday, June 25th, I was asked to a big dinner at the German Embassy and at the party I was accosted by a rather sinister, slender young man with dark glasses, who had been present during our deputation to Selwyn Lloyd. In my ignorance I thought he was a leading Foreign Office official, all the more when he asked me how the Foreign Secretary had gone down and what I thought of him. 'We discussed it afterwards,' he said, 'and the Foreign Secretary was quite cheerful because he said you'd nodded your head several times and that was a good sign. Of course I told him the truth—you were nodding your head merely to egg him on to make more and more indis-

[1] General Sir Brian Robertson, Chief Administrative Officer in Italy from 1943 to 1945 and A.D.C. General to King George VI 1949–52 and to Queen Elizabeth II in 1952. He was Commander in Chief, Middle East Land Forces, 1950–3 and Chairman of the British Transport Commission 1953–61. He succeeded to the baronetcy in 1933 and in 1961 was raised to the peerage as Lord Robertson of Oakridge. He died in 1974.

cretions.' Gradually it occurred to me that I was talking to Lord Lambton, a Tory backbencher who is Selwyn's P.P.S.![1]

Monday, July 16th

I have the impression that the Fabians' publication of Gaitskell's pamphlet on nationalization,[2] and the work we have done on *Equality*[3] and foreign policy and defence are having an effect on the public. They are making people think that the Labour Party is a party to be taken seriously, that it is thinking, that it is beginning to get a policy and that there can be such a thing as a second stage of Socialism. Moreover, there is no doubt that in the formulation of this second stage Gaitskell and his friends are playing the major role, since no one else has anything positive to propose. Such ex-Bevanites as Mikardo and Barbara Castle have contributed nothing whatsoever on the Executive and the *Tribune* is milk and water. It does a tiny bit of quiet snarling but, ironically enough, it is increasing its circulation the more respectable it becomes and the more it looks like a conventional Socialist weekly, without any of the publicity it used to have at the time of the Bevanite controversy.

The Tonbridge result has been succeeded by another excellent result at Newport, where Frank Soskice got in.[4] Very slowly, but I think steadily, the pendulum is swinging away from the Government to Labour, as the new leadership with a new policy slowly emerges. What is Nye's part in all this? No one knows. He did not bother to turn up at the Party Meeting when either foreign policy or defence were discussed. I suspect that all his emotions are centred on his battle with George Brown for the treasurership. Nye still somehow feels that, if he is elected Treasurer, this will mean a shift in the balance of power in the Party. But of course it will mean no such thing. Whichever wins will win by a negligible majority and, once Nye is back on the Executive, as I hope he will be, very little will be altered.

[1] Antony Lambton (known under the courtesy title of Viscount Lambton before his father's death in 1970, at which time he disclaimed the peerages to which he succeeded as Earl of Durham) was Conservative M.P. for the Berwick-upon-Tweed division of Northumberland 1951–73. He was P.P.S. to the Foreign Secretary 1955–7 and Parliamentary Under-Secretary of State at the Ministry of Defence from June 1970 until his resignation in May 1973.

[2] *Socialism and Nationalization* concluded that the traditional arguments for nationalization were weakened but not destroyed.

[3] The third of the Labour Party policy statements to appear.

[4] Gerald Williams, Conservative M.P. for Tonbridge, had resigned because of illness and a by-election was held on June 7th. Richard Hornby held the seat for the Conservatives by a majority of 1,602 over the Labour candidate, Robert Fagg, but the Conservative majority fell by 8,594.

On July 6th there was a by-election at Newport, where Peter Freeman, the Labour Member, had died on May 19th. The seat was held for Labour by Sir Frank Soskice, whose former constituency at Neepsend had been abolished in the previous redistribution of seats. Sir Frank had a majority of 8,485 votes over the Conservative candidate, Donald Box, an increase of 4,125 votes. Labour was especially pleased with the results, since this time a Welsh Nationalist candidate took nearly 2,000 votes.

Richard and Anne Crossman spent the month of August in Canada, where a conference on The New Canada was being held at Lake Couchiching, Ontario, in the early part of the month. The conference was organized by the Canadian Institute of Public Affairs and the Canadian Broadcasting Corporation. Uncharacteristically, Crossman kept neither a diary nor jottings, although he sent two columns to the Mirror, *published on August 13th and 23rd.*

While he was away a serious crisis arose in the Middle East. In mid-May President Nasser had recognized Communist China, without warning to other Powers. It was believed that he feared a U.N. embargo on arms sales to the Middle East and saw China, not a U.N. member, as an alternative channel through which the Soviet Union could continue to support the Egyptian re-armament programme. The American Government was angered, as the Egyptian Ambassador to the United States reported to President Nasser. In a reaffirmation of her neutralism, Egypt withdrew various amendments to the aides-mémoires *concerning financial aid for the High Dam and announced her immediate and unreserved acceptance of American funds. President Nasser also flew to Belgrade, to meet President Tito and Mr Nehru, demonstrating his wish for 'peaceful coexistence'.*

But on July 19th the American Government withdrew their offer of aid for the dam, giving as reasons the instability of the Egyptian economy and the lack of agreement with those States south of Egypt which bordered the Nile. On the next day Britain also withdrew her offer, on the grounds that the Egyptian economy was unsound, and the third participant in the loan, the International Bank for Reconstruction and Development, was obliged to follow suit. President Nasser, newly returned from Belgrade, expressed bitter criticism, of the United States in particular, at a speech made on July 24th at the opening of the Suez–Cairo oil pipeline at Mosorod. He promised plans to finance the dam without Western help; these were announced two days later, in a two and a half hour speech at Alexandria. The President vigorously denounced the Western Powers and, as his climax, declared the nationalization of the Suez Canal Company. He read out a law transferring to the State the company and all its assets and commitments; out of these revenues the dam would be financed. Shareholders were to be compensated. The funds of the company in Egypt and abroad had already been frozen and an independent board, responsible to the Ministry of Commerce, would run the Canal in future. All employees, Egyptian and foreign, were retained and they were to continue their work on pain of heavy fines and imprisonment. The President's announcement was fervently greeted by the Egyptian people, who had a month earlier overwhelmingly approved the draft of the new Constitution and the election of Nasser as President (he was, however, the only nominee). His domestic standing was triumphant.

The Suez Canal Company had hitherto been only formally an Egyptian joint stock company. Its headquarters were in Paris and, of its 32 directors, 16 were French, 9 British and but 5 Egyptian. Freedom of navigation through the Canal was internationally important, particularly in view of the rapidly growing demand for Middle Eastern oil. Though the nationalization of the Canal was not wholly unexpected, Egypt had affirmed (as recently as June 4th) that this would occur, legally and by negotiation, in 1968, when the existing 1868 Convention would expire. It was argued in the Western press, however, that Egypt's act must have been premeditated and that, since her act needed more than a week's planning, the withdrawal of support for the dam must have been not tne cause but the occasion for the seizure.

Western reaction was immediate and hostile. Egypt's act was condemned as an illegal and unwarranted breach of vital international commitments. On July 27th Britain and France presented Notes of protest, which Egypt refused to accept, and in the House of Commons the Prime Minister stated that the Government were consulting other Governments concerned. Mr Gaitskell supported Sir Anthony's Statement and asked whether the matter would be referred to the Security Council. This, he was told, was one of the subjects of consultation.

Britain and France next brought under exchange control all Egypt's foreign trade operations and, on July 29th, their Foreign Ministers met Mr Robert Murphy, the American Under-Secretary of State, in London. On July 30th the Prime Minister told the Commons that arms exports to Egypt had ceased and intimated that the Government would not hesitate to use force against Egypt. The next day the Admiralty and the War Office announced the undertaking of precautionary measures, 'with the object of strengthening our position in the eastern Mediterranean and our general ability to deal with any situation that may arise'. The Prime Minister postponed his summer holiday and Mr Dulles flew to London.

President Nasser assured the West that Egypt's international commitments would in no way be affected by the nationalization of the Canal. Such statements did not still the prevailing alarm; Eden, who had been Foreign Secretary from 1935 until his resignation in 1938, took deeply to heart the general warnings that Nasser was a dictator who would not be deterred by 'appeasement'.

On August 2nd the American, British and French Foreign Ministers, meeting in London, announced their decision to call an international conference on August 16th. This would seek to establish an international company or agency to preserve the freedom and security of passage through the Canal and to ensure that dues remained stable and fair and profits undiverted. Meanwhile the Queen issued a Proclamation, giving the Government wide powers and calling out reservists. That same day the House of Commons debated the matter. The Leader of the Opposition stated that, though the act of nationalization was not itself wrong, it had to be considered in the light of President Nasser's frequent declarations that he intended to create an Arab Empire from the Atlantic to the Persian Gulf. An increase in the President's prestige would be matched by a diminution in British influence in the Middle East. Mr Gaitskell welcomed the proposed conference but warned that, though he did not object to the military *precautions, the Government must avoid the possibility of Britain's being branded an aggressor by the United Nations.*

The following day, August 3rd, the American attitude became clearer, when Mr Dulles broadcast a message that 'moral forces [would be] bound to prevail' in persuading Egypt as a member of the forthcoming conference to accept some form of international control of the waterway. On August 8th, in another broadcast, the Prime Minister pointed to 'Colonel Nasser's record' as a reason for distrusting his promises not to interfere with shipping. Sir Anthony emphasized the importance of the Canal route, by which came half the oil used by Britain, Western Europe and Scandinavia.

Twenty-four nations were invited to the conference, of whom twenty-two, including India and the U.S.S.R., attended. Egypt and Greece were the absentees. Three days before the meeting began, Mr Gaitskell was commissioned by the Shadow Cabinet to seek assurances from the Prime Minister that Parliament would be recalled immediately the conference finished. The Leader of the Opposition was also instructed to ask the Prime Minister to make plain that recent military measures had been 'merely precautionary', intended solely for deterrence against possible aggression and not as preparations for armed intervention outside and inconsistent with our obligations under the U.N. Charter. Mr Gaitskell met Sir Anthony and declared that the interview was satisfactory.

On August 16th the London Conference assembled and the Canal users' discussion centred on two alternative plans. The 'Menon plan' would leave the Egyptian Government in control of the Canal, establishing a purely advisory international body. Mr Krishna Menon, the Indian representative, defended Egypt's right to nationalize the waterway but not the way in which the act had been committed. His plan, he said, was put forward because he did not think any other would secure Egyptian acceptance.

The other scheme was the 'Dulles plan', for the creation of an international Suez Canal Board, associated with the U.N. Egypt would be a board member and would hand over to the board all 'rights and facilities appropriate to [the Canal's] functioning'.

When the conference ended on August 23rd, the Dulles plan was supported by eighteen of the twenty-two nations which had attended, and they set up a committee, chaired by the Australian Prime Minister, Mr Robert Menzies, to approach President Nasser with these proposals. (The other committee members were representatives of Ethiopia, Persia, Sweden and the United States.) Mr Menzies was to emphasize two fundamental aspects of the Eighteen-Power proposals: that the Canal's operation should be insulated from any one nation's politics; and that the operation, maintenance and development of the Canal should fall to a body established by international convention. Egypt's ownership would be recognized and, while all future financial burdens of the Canal would be borne by the controlling body, Egypt would alone receive all profits from it.

Meanwhile the Shadow Cabinet pressed for the recall of Parliament but the Prime Minister stated on August 31st that the date could not be fixed until the result of the Menzies mission was known. President Nasser did not agree to receive Mr Menzies until September 3rd and on September 6th the Government announced a special meeting of both Houses, on September 12th and 13th, to debate the Suez question. By the time this Statement was issued, it had become plain that the Cairo mission had failed.

It was at this moment that, on his return from Canada, Crossman resumed his diary.

Wednesday, September 5th

We dived out of a black cloud on to London Airport about nine o'clock on Saturday evening, which was one o'clock in the afternoon by Vancouver time. We had heard about the rain, but oh dear, it was depressing to breathe the sodden air as we drove into London. We rang up Patrick [McDougall], who described the gales and rain throughout August but told us that all the oats had been got in, thirty-seven acres, leaving the wheat still to be cut. But it wasn't only the weather which felt depressing. When we met him in Vancouver, Bob Mackenzie,[1] the Canadian L.S.E./B.B.C. commentator, had observed, 'What a relief to be in a country without a dollar crisis, where everybody knows that things will go on expanding and developing for the next fifty years.' I thought it a good remark at the time but, coming into London that evening, it hit me in the stomach — the sense of restriction, yes, even of decline, of an old country always teetering on the edge of a crisis, trying to keep up appearances, with no confident vision of the future in front of it. It's always a bit dreary coming back from a holiday and having to pick up the strings but this time it felt more than usually depressing.

I spent Sunday reading a week's newspapers, as well as the Sundays and having long telephone talks with Barbara Castle, Sydney Jacobson and Hugh Massingham. All the talk, of course, was about the Suez crisis and I suddenly realized what in Canada I had never believed — that the Government's bluff was not all bluff. Hugh Massingham, who had written an interesting article in the *Observer*, is convinced that Eden and Macmillan really want a war — not that they would attack Nasser but that, if an incident occurred which would justify them, their plans are all exactly prepared for a *coup*, which they are convinced would clean the whole thing up in a few days. It is the belief that this is their mood which has set off most of the Left press in supporting the line which had been taken from the first by the *Manchester Guardian*.[2] So

---

[1] A Canadian political scientist, who has taught at the London School of Economics since 1949. In 1964 he became Professor of Sociology. He has published a seminal study, *British Political Parties* (London: Macmillan, 1955).

[2] The Government's policy was severely criticized by most of the national press, including the *Manchester Guardian*, the *Observer*, the *Spectator* and *The Economist*. The *Daily Telegraph* and the *Sunday Times* and most of the popular press supported the Government; *The Times* was, some said, dispassionate or, according to others, hesitant.

much for Hugh Massingham and Sydney, who confirmed it from other sources available to Hugh Cudlipp and Cecil King.

Barbara's story was, of course, about the internals of the Labour Party. According to her, Hugh Gaitskell had let the whole Movement down by supporting Eden and getting the cheers of the Suez rebels in the debate at the beginning of August. But Barbara added that Nye had been just as bad and had written an article in the *Tribune* which had caused a storm among his supporters and forced him to veer round week by week into a more anti-war line.

Actually, as far as I can see, the line which Nye and Hugh Gaitskell took was not too bad in the circumstances, since I can remember the gust of public anger when Nasser grabbed the Canal. And anyway, Nasser really did grab it in an intolerable way and, if he got away with that grab, might well launch the war against Israel. Really everybody has had second thoughts as a result of the vast scale of the Anglo-French mobilization and the realization that Macmillan, who always was an Edwardian Tory, now thinks he has a chance, while Eden has swallowed the bait. I don't think the Party leadership has done too badly so far.

I spent all Monday writing, first, a column for the *Mirror*, and then an article for the *New Statesman*.[1] Just when I was through, Hugh Cudlipp rang up to say he'd had a brilliant idea for the front page, which he was going to turn sideways into a broadsheet, quoting all the people who were asking what the Government's intentions really were and whether they were war-mongers and liars. As I suspected and Anne feared, Hugh then asked us out to dinner with Eileen. This started at nine in the Belle Meunière with cham-pagne cocktails and ended at No. 9 Vincent Square with Canadian rye and Hugh telephoning the final detailed instructions for the layout.[2] Anne observed that Hugh's genius is that, each time he does a newspaper stunt, it's as though it's the very first he's ever done and he's as excited as a child and as skilled as a craftsman of fifty. Hugh's main theme was that the Labour Party must be prepared for an Election this year and for the possibility of office. I didn't take it very seriously on Monday but by now I am half con-vinced, having visited the T.U.C. at Brighton.[3]

Before I went down there yesterday evening, Hugh Gaitskell came in to see me, a little aggrieved with my *Mirror* piece, which had slipped in the sentence that the Shadow Cabinet had had a rush of blood to the head. He spent forty minutes explaining this was not so and defending his and Nye's position, until

[1] 'Suez: The Lesson for Socialists', *New Statesman and Nation*, September 8th.

[2] The *Mirror* article, on September 4th, reported that military plans had already been agreed by the British and French Governments and that the Cabinet had already accepted the advice of the Chiefs of Staff that Egypt could be quickly knocked out by the expedi-tionary force now assembling in the Mediterranean. Since the Prime Minister 'manoeuvred himself into a situation where anything less than an abject Egyptian surrender' would be a defeat for the Government, everything now depended on the Opposition. Mr Gaitskell should denounce this 'vulgar nineteenth-century jingoism'.

[3] Where the annual conference was being held.

I told him I didn't really need any justification and wanted to know what he thought was the present position. Hugh is not nearly so scared of the Government attacking Nasser as others are because he believes it's sheer lunacy. But I still think there's a chance of their doing it, though, if they do, I believe that Eisenhower would call the Security Council together and collaborate with the Russians in stopping it. We discussed it round and round until I caught my train.

At this morning's big debate on wage restraint there came what everybody had been waiting for, the speech of Frank Cousins, the new General Secretary of the T. & G.[1] We saw Cousins for about six months when he was a member of our National Executive after Arthur Deakin died and Jock Tiffin took over. It was only when Jock Tiffin died suddenly that Cousins quite unexpectedly got the job. He seemed to be a very nice, vigorous man, who was obviously going to intervene on every kind of issue but wasn't terribly well-informed. His speech on this occasion was a very curious performance, intellectually weak but with a real sense of drama and power. The really significant thing about it was that it was not detached or neutral but 100 per cent political. It was, in fact, a political speech, which denounced the Government and made it quite clear that Cousins was not prepared to collaborate in any form of wage restraint except with a Labour Government with full control or, as he added in a brief reply at the end which I didn't hear, with a Tory Government which had accepted a 100 per cent Labour policy, which, of course, is an absurdity.[2]

Harold Wilson had turned up and was listening to the debate, and at drinks before lunch in our hotel, he and I both congratulated Cousins. He said, 'Isn't it about time that we trade union leaders starting helping the Labour Party throw this Government out?' Hugh Cudlipp, Sydney, Harold and I got down to business. Hugh was in tremendous form. 'Front page stuff,' he said. 'Trade Unions declare War on Tory Government. You write it, Sydney, and I'll go back with Dick on the 3.25.' Then we got down to discussing Suez, on which Hugh and Cecil King had received some apparently real inside information (one of their sources was certainly Walter Monckton) on the seriousness of the Government's desire to have a war with Nasser. Harold Wilson suggested that, since Charlie Geddes,[3] who is moving the Suez resolution from the platform tomorrow, was one of the people on the General Council who wanted to support the Government, Frank Cousins should be encouraged to go to the rostrum and support the Opposition line in the name of the trade union movement. This would make the attack on the Government

[1] General Secretary of the Transport and General Workers' Union 1956–69, except for the period of his office as Minister of Technology October 1964–July 1966. He was Labour M.P. for Nuneaton 1965–6.

[2] The Congress carried by acclaim a resolution rejecting an appeal for wage restraint which the Chancellor had made at a press conference on August 29th.

[3] General Secretary of the Union of Post Office Workers and a Member of the T.U.C. General Council. He retired in 1957 and was created a life peer in 1958.

cover both the home and the foreign front and produce another front-page story for Mr Cudlipp. Harold said Hugh ought to ring up Hugh Gaitskell to see if it was all right and Hugh and I just caught the 3.25.

During our conversation on the journey back to London, Hugh was enjoying his politics. He spent the time advising me that it would be insane to be in the next Labour Government. 'Your job is to be the great ideas man of the Left,' he said. 'You'd be quite a good Minister but they wouldn't make you Foreign Secretary and quite right too, because an ideas man doesn't administer or is wasted on it. Let them offer it to you but keep your own position.'

When I got back I rang up Hugh Gaitskell, who had immediately seen that in any suggestion that he had asked Cousins to intervene in the debate tomorrow lay the danger of losing half his friends on the General Council.[1] We had a long talk about Cousins and I emphasized the importance of striking while the iron is hot and while there is all this goodwill towards the Labour Party. I stressed the importance of getting going as soon as possible talks in which Mr Cousins, who is a pretty rough customer and pretty dangerous, begins to ask himself at what price he would be prepared to have wage restraint and a Labour Government. It's all very well, and it's fun for us, if the trade unions have a free-for-all instead of collaborating with the Tory Government. But we've got to make sure they collaborate with us when we get in. Hugh liked all this, though I think he's really very alarmed at the new trade union dynamism, which may really get this country into a ghastly depression.

In a final exchange of letters with Mr Menzies, President Nasser rejected as 'provocative' the Eighteen-Power plan for the creation of an international body to administer the operation of the Canal. The proposals were, he said, a hostile infringement of Egyptian sovereignty; Egypt was willing to negotiate a settlement only in conformity with the U.N. Charter. In London, the British and French Prime Ministers met to discuss the next steps and it was announced that they were in complete agreement.

Meanwhile the accumulation of forces continued. British reservists were called up, ships were requisitioned as transport and forces assembled at Malta and on Cyprus, where French troops had been permitted to assemble.

On the day before Parliament met, September 11th, three-quarters of the non-Egyptian personnel working on the Canal resigned and on September 13th they were allowed to leave the country. Instead of the usual 215 trained pilots, seventy men, almost all Egyptian and nearly half lacking experience or training, handled the continuing Canal traffic.

When the debate opened in the Commons, the Prime Minister announced that the Government had agreed with France and the United States to establish

---

[1] The Congress unanimously adopted a resolution warning the Government against the use of force without United Nations approval.

immediately a provisional 'Suez Canal Users' Association', to which other countries would be invited to belong. This body would employ pilots, co-ordinate traffic, exercise Canal users' rights and collect dues. Egypt would be asked to co-operate; if she did not, Sir Anthony declared, the British Government and others concerned would be 'free to take such further steps as might be required'. The Government were 'not prepared to embark on a policy of abject appeasement'. The eighteen nations supporting the Dulles plan would be invited to another London conference the following week.

Mr Gaitskell called the Prime Minister's speech provocative and certain to be rejected. On the second day of the debate the Opposition moved a vote of censure, calling for the urgent reference of the dispute to the United Nations Security Council. In the House of Lords debate there were pleas for parlia-mentary unity but, although there was regret at the Opposition's intention to divide the House, speakers in the Lords also deplored the Prime Minister's handling of the whole affair. On September 13th the motion of censure was defeated by 319 votes to 248, the Liberals supporting the Government.

Meanwhile America's attitude veered ambiguously. In Washington it was revealed that, while Mr Dulles had proposed the scheme for a Users' Associa-tion, he was shocked by the strong terms of Sir Anthony's announcement. On September 13th Mr Dulles emphasized that no United States ships would 'shoot their way through' the Canal, implying, rather, that the Association might be merely a body to organize the by-passing of the waterway.

Friday, September 14th

This has been a Suez week and if I had kept this diary day by day it would have been a truer account of the astonishing ups and downs of emotion, anticipation and excitement which have occurred in these five days. We heard before the weekend that Parliament was to be recalled, and spent Saturday and Sunday at Prescote watching the rain fall steadily on our corn, while it sprouted, standing, into green shoots.

On Monday, thanks to a bright idea from Sydney, I did a very nice piece for the *Mirror*,[1] predicting what the real issue of the debate would be. I anticipated that Eden would refer the affair to the Security Council but only give an assurance that force would not be used while the matter was under consideration by U.N. Labour's stand would be that we must accept U.N. as final arbiter and not use force without its consent. It wasn't very difficult to make this prediction, since I've been seeing quite a lot of Hugh Gaitskell. He was very much aware that we must not become the pro-Nasser party and that the United Nations line, as the Gallup Poll had shown, was the one which would get the widest electoral support.

[1] Crossman's article set out two questions and answers: Can Eden Unite the Country? *Yes.* Has America Let Us Down? *No.* He stressed the belief of Eisenhower and Dulles that 'a war against the whole Arab world … would be disastrous to the whole Western Alliance'. They had therefore vetoed any warlike solution, 'unless Nasser himself starts trouble, which most unlikely'.

On Tuesday, the Shadow Cabinet met and agreed to take this line. Meanwhile Anne and I were attending the wedding of Maurice Edelman's daughter.[1] Maurice had had one of his fits of intellectual independence and had written a terrific letter to *The Times*,[2] praising the eighteen-nation plan for internationalization and accusing the frozen Left of a reactionary support for a nationalism which would balkanize the Middle East. I pointed out to him that the Middle East had been balkanized by Britain and France's dividing it up and maintaining ramshackle dynasties, but I did not make much impression. I didn't think much of this until Maurice said, over a glass of champagne, 'If only I could speak as well as I can write, I would make a real impression in politics.' I replied, 'You can speak as well as you can write but the trouble is that what you say doesn't matter unless you represent something or have some votes behind you.' I didn't add, 'Unless you've got something to say,' because, after all, he had.

We motored back to London through torrential rain to a meeting of the Suez Emergency Committee, those twenty-four Labour M.P.s who had signed a letter of protest in mid-August and felt very pleased with themselves. I found Barbara Castle there and, as old professional groupers, we didn't think much of this meeting. It consisted of Sydney Silverman and Konni Zilliacus[3] discussing Clause 51 and Clause 43 of the U.N. Charter in an extremely profound way. For some reason they were all convinced that Gaitskell would fail to lead the Party in the right direction, so I just told them what he was going to say.

Blow me if next morning, when the Party gathered, he didn't say it. Of course he started by repeating the long apologia for his own behaviour which he had given me the week before. I was a bit bored, but afterwards I realized that it was quite effective because 90 per cent of those present were having to shift their position without noticing it, just in the same way as he had, and he was making it easy for them. There was rather a desultory discussion afterwards, in which Maurice made his little contribution and Stanley Evans suggested that we should do a deal with the Jews by offering them an enlargement of their territory if they'd fight Egypt. This was too much for most of the people there. Reggie Paget, who had been one of the chief advocates of force in early August, now said that, since force had failed, the only thing to do was to appease Nasser 100 per cent and also to get out of Cyprus and give it to the Turks, since what was the good of having a base if one didn't use it? This is the kind of mad logic which makes Reggie an excellent entertainment at a Party Meeting.

[1] Sonia Edelman, who married Philip Abrams (son of Mark Abrams, see below, p. 517 n.)
[2] Published on August 11th and stating, 'The parallel with Hitler's occupation of the Rhineland is almost exact'.
[3] Konni Zilliacus, M.P. for Gateshead 1945–50, first as a member of the Labour Party and then, after his expulsion in May 1949 for persistent opposition to the Government's foreign policy, as an Independent. He was readmitted to the Labour Party in 1952 and was Labour M.P. for the Gorton division of Manchester from 1955 until his death in 1967.

14 A demonstration in Trafalgar Square against Eden's Suez policy,
November 1956

15 Crossman with Morgan Phillips in Venice, February 1957

16 Jim Callaghan and Barbara Castle travelling to the Party Conference in Scarborough, 1958

17 Sir Tom O'Brien (*left*) and Frank Cousins (*right*) leaving T.U.C. headquarters, 1959

18 Harold Macmillan and Hugh Gaitskell share the platform in 1959 at a conference on productivity with Sir Miles Thomas as chairman

I had had no time really to think about a speech when I went in at half-past two to hear the debate. Moreover, I knew I was doing an overseas broadcast that night and that was that. However, I thought I'd stake a claim sometime in the debate. Eden's speech was quite effective and completely took our breath away because, instead of referring the matter to the Security Council, he announced the plan for a Canal Users' Association, which had been kept a close secret, and claimed that America had decided to join it. I was quite sorry for Hugh, since this knocked his prepared speech sideways. He did extremely well to pull himself together and fit in some off-the-cuff comments. I was not a very good appreciator, since this wasn't the first time I had had to hear his recitation of the events of August. His speech was very variously judged. Mallalieu thought it was the noblest speech he'd ever heard. Barbara and I thought he'd said all the right things, thank God, but he was rather like an opera singer who is supposed to reach a high note and then just fails to do so.

I went out and had a good long tea and, as I came back, a Tory speech was just finishing. I thought I might as well stand up in the crowd of thirty people who leapt to catch the Speaker's eye. Actually, to be perfectly honest, in the five minutes while I was sitting there, I had a vague feeling it would be awkward if I was called and so I wrote down five headings on a card I found in my pocket. Then blow me if the Speaker didn't call me and off I went. I soon discovered the Tory rebels were listening with fascination to a psychological warrior's analysis of the Government's psychological war.

I think the thing which fascinated them was my assumption – correct, as it is now made clear – that this was a psychological war, in which the military preparations were propaganda – or rather, in which the Government had never faced the question whether it was pure propaganda or whether, in the last resort, they would use it, though certain members of the Government had no doubt decided to do so. Although my speech went on about ten minutes too long, it was all right.[1] In the lobby afterwards three Tory backbenchers, whose names I don't know, came up and, each in his own way, said, 'Of course we really agree with you. Don't imagine we're all members of the Suez Group.'

Bob Boothby wound up for the Government, from below the gangway, in a speech which answered me very gratifyingly. Poor Bob had climbed on the bandwagon in mid-August with a trenchant *Times*[2] letter supporting a strong policy of do or die, and he had been thrown from the rich man's table this crumb of summing up for Eden. Unfortunately, by the end of the week the bandwagon had turned into a sinking ship.

My feeling, at the end of the first day of the debate, was that we had fairly

---

[1] He spoke for thirty-five minutes.
[2] In fact published on September 11th and supporting the proposed Suez Authority as 'a classic example of the new form of international organization ... whereby ownership is separated from control and a degree of sovereignty is yielded for the collective benefit'.

17

well shaken the Government but that honours were about even. But there were two interesting incidents. As I was moving to the Smoking Room after my speech, I ran into Selwyn Lloyd. 'As naughty as usual!' he said to me (for some reason Foreign Secretaries always behave to me in this way, because this is what their young men tell them about me as an ex-Foreign Office man). And Selwyn added, 'What let us down, of course, Dick, was the press.' I looked a bit surprised because I thought he meant the *Daily Mirror* and he said, 'You've no idea. You've only got to move a soldier or a ship and they blow it up into an armada. If I could tell you how little we have out there, you'd realize how crazy is this idea that we're going to war.' 'But that's just what I've said,' I replied. 'Yes, I know you did,' he replied. 'That was so naughty of you.'

After Bob Boothby had wound up I was walking out behind the Speaker's chair when Eden ran into me. He took me aside and said, 'I want to ask you one question which I wouldn't ask everybody.' (Another piece of odious, Foreign Office camaraderie.) 'If you'd been Prime Minister, would you have referred it to the Security Council?' I said, 'Yes, to get world opinion on one's side, though I wouldn't have had any great anticipation that you'd get an automatic solution. I'd get world opinion on my side and then I'd use the occasion for serious negotiations.' 'Ah,' Eden said, 'serious negotiations – that's just what we want. That's the whole purpose of the Users' Association.'

I looked very surprised and said, 'But I thought you were going to shoot your way through if Egypt resisted.' 'Oh no,' Eden said. 'We're going to get negotiations out of it.' 'Do you really think you can negotiate a settlement with Nasser?' I asked, since, after all, this had been one of the great issues of the debate – whether Nasser was a Hitler whom one couldn't negotiate with. 'Oh yes,' Eden replied. 'Of course, he'll get worse terms as a result of negotiating on the Users' Association than he would have got from the Eighteen-Nation plan but I think there's a good chance of a peaceful settlement.'

When I got to Oxford Street, to do my overseas broadcast, Bob Boothby, who had had to be briefed for his speech, completed the story. The Users' Association was a Dulles plan, which Dulles had insisted the British and French should take on as the price of further American co-operation. Dulles thought it could start new negotiations. 'Well,' I said, 'then Eden will come unstuck tomorrow because Dulles won't let him give the appearance that he's taking part in an Anglo-French provocation. Why on earth did Eden say that, if the Egyptians didn't accept the Users' Association, he might take grave measures?' Bob then said, 'Well, whatever you do, we mustn't discuss that tonight because Eden sent a special message down that Dulles might be upset if we did.' I must say I thought at the time that Dulles was much more likely to be upset by Sir Anthony than he could possibly be by some damn little broadcast on the British Overseas Service by a few backbench M.P.s.

So next morning I rang up Alf [Robens], who, of course, was still convinced that the Users' Association was heading us straight for war but who
was persuaded to ask Eden about this in his speech. I wrote a rather
ingenious piece,[1] saying all this about Dulles, for Friday's paper, before going
in to hear the second day of the debate. It began with a sad effort by Alf, after
a singularly offensive and tactless performance by Selwyn Lloyd, who
managed to indicate that the United Nations was no damn good and the
Labour Party was objecting for purely spiteful reasons. Then came a remarkable intervention by the ex-Attorney General, Heald,[2] who followed Lord
McNair[3] in the House of Lords in saying that it was inconceivable for the
British Government to go to war to support the Eighteen-Nation plan
without reference to the Security Council. Hugh immediately challenged
Selwyn Lloyd to accept this view, which had clearly paralysed the Tory Party.

One hour later the news came through on the tape that Dulles was fulfilling predictions by telling his news conference that he would not dream of
shooting his way through and that, if there were trouble, American ships
would go round the Cape. This was Dulles's snub to Eden and, thank
heavens, when Hugh came to the final speech, he really waded in, pressing and
pressing Eden whether he would shoot his way through, as he had suggested
on the day before, and finally among scenes of wild excitement, extracting
what we all thought was a clear negative but what next morning appeared to
be an ambiguous statement.[4]

However, the debate had been won by the Opposition, in the sense that
Eden had been boxed, cribbed and confined. I hear from Alec Spearman
today that the real turning point was the meeting of the Tory Foreign
Affairs Committee, where over half the speakers were pro-United Nations
and the whole mood of the Party had changed. It was this, combined with
Dulles, combined with the Labour Party, which forced Eden to his
ambiguous climb-down.

[1] In 'Dulles Drops a Bombshell on Tories', *Daily Mirror*, September 14th, Crossman
declared that, as a method of getting ships safely through the Canal, the Users' Association was 'an unworkable monstrosity'. Moreover, President Nasser was almost certain to
refuse it. Thus, concluded Crossman, Mr Dulles's purpose was 'purely diplomatic' – to kill
the Eighteen-Nation plan and 'shift the argument on to this new issue'.
[2] Sir Lionel Heald, Conservative M.P. for Chertsey 1950–70 and Attorney General
1951–4.
[3] Sir Arnold McNair (1885–1971), a distinguished lawyer in Cambridge, was raised to the
peerage in 1955. He was President of the International Court of Justice 1952–5, Chairman
of the Burnham Committee 1955–8 and President of the European Court of Human
Rights 1959–65. Crossman had met him earlier in 1945 when Arnold McNair was Chairman of the Palestine Jewish Education Commission.
[4] MR GAITSKELL: Is [the Prime Minister] prepared to say on behalf of Her Majesty's
Government that they will not shoot their way through the Canal?
THE PRIME MINISTER: I said that we were in complete agreement with the United States
Government about what to do ... I repeat that the first action was to ask the Egyptian
Government ... We propose to ask for that co-operation ... if they do not give it, they are,
in our view, in default under the 1868 Convention, but if they are so in default, we should
take them to the Security Council ... [*H. C. Debates*, vol. 558, col. 297 ff.].

There was an extraordinary sense of exultation in the Labour lobbies. You could feel the Party at last feeling that it had done a good job, that they were all together, that the Government was on the run. As one might expect, today the Smoking Room was full of surmises about the immediate dissolution of the Tory Party. There won't be an immediate dissolution but there will be some terrific recriminations, as I have gathered from Hugh Fraser and Julian Amery, two Tory rebels who always flatter me by thinking my analysis wonderful and my conclusions fantastic.

On September 19th representatives of the eighteen nations which had supported the Dulles plan earlier in the month met again for the second London Conference on the Suez question. Mr Dulles set out the scheme for a Canal Users' Association and his remarks suggested that it was indeed intended as a political gambit for reopening negotiations with Egypt, rather than the more vigorous body which Sir Anthony Eden had first implied. As now proposed, the Association would have no specific function and very few powers. Moreover, its members would be allowed to decide for themselves whether they would pay dues to Egypt. France withheld her support from the Association and several members of the conference urged that the question be referred to the U.N. On September 23rd the British and French Governments announced that they had decided to do this at once and to ask for a meeting of the Security Council on September 26th. It appeared that this was a British decision, unwelcome to France.

Meanwhile the Egyptian Government had continued to operate the Canal, efficiently and without discrimination against any nation's shipping. Until September 16th only the team of largely Egyptian pilots was used; after that they were assisted by others from the U.S.S.R., Yugoslavia, the United States and elsewhere. Egypt was supported by the Arab States and countries of the Soviet bloc and the Afro-Asian group. Some of these nations nevertheless pressed President Nasser to take part in a compromise settlement and, using Mr Menon as an emissary, the Indian Prime Minister, Mr Pandit Nehru, urged acceptance of the 'Menon plan'. The Kings of Iraq and Saudi Arabia, anxious about oil revenue, met for discussions, so that President Nasser was obliged to go to Riyadh to reassure his Arabian allies. It was thus that the Egyptian Foreign Minister, Dr Mahmoud Fawzi, flew to New York for the Security Council's discussion. He was joined by Wing-Commander Aly Sabry, the President's chef de cabinet.

Two resolutions were put before the Security Council, one sponsored by Britain and France and the other by Egypt. When the Council met on September 26th, it was agreed to confine the discussion to procedural matters, since several Foreign Ministers were expected to attend the substantive debate the following week. The Council unanimously voted to place the Anglo-French resolution on the agenda but the United States refused to support a British and French attempt to exclude the Egyptian resolution. The American representative, Mr

Henry Cabot Lodge, did, however, agree that the Anglo-French resolution should take precedence.

Friday, September 28th

This has been a betwixt and between fortnight, after the recall debate on Suez and before the bout of party Conferences. It had been planned that five of us should go across to Paris for private talks with Ollenhauer and Mollet.[1] Then Parliament was recalled on the day the talks were due and they were postponed to the weekend. Next the Parliamentary Committee met and thought talks were inappropriate. Originally the subject was to have been Germany and the NATO contribution but I rather agree with the Parliamentary Committee that, with Mollet and Eden in an *entente cordiale*, the talks would have been awkward. The new alignment, in fact, is very peculiar. The Labour Party finds itself broadly in accord with Mr John Foster Dulles and the Conservatives have a real sense of *entente cordiale* with the Socialist Monsieur Mollet.

Meanwhile the Suez crisis drags on and on. Thank heavens I was away for five weeks of it during August and didn't have to write about it then, because I am sick to death of writing about it now. And yet there's nothing else to write about because it's a fascinating crisis. Talking to Mark Abrams[2] at Maurice Edelman's daughter's wedding, I learnt that, in his experience as a pollster, there has never been a subject on which there is more genuine bewilderment and divided don't-knowism. The fact is that everybody is divided about this. There are many more Labour people than we sometimes like to think who feel they would like to have a go at Nasser and who, when faced with the prospect of Britain's ceasing to be a great Power, are emotionally repelled. But there are also any number of Tories who are deeply shocked by the idea of an Anglo-French attempt to impose internationalization by military sanctions.

The country is divided broadly on party lines but also across party lines. The number of Socialists who are really Little Englanders, in the sense that they are prepared to see us in the same sort of status as West Germany, is still pretty small. Radicalism—the kind of Radicalism which made Byron[3] fight for the Greeks and Lloyd George pro-Boer—is now relatively rare and predominantly middle-class. That is why Nye's instincts in this crisis have really been much more pro-Government than pro-Nasser.

[1] After the French General Election on January 2nd, the Socialist Secretary-General, Guy Mollet, succeeded in forming a Government by an overwhelming majority in the Assembly. Mayor of Arras in 1945 and a Member of the National Assembly from 1945 until his death in 1975, Mollet was Secretary General of the French Socialist Party 1946–68. He was Prime Minister January 1956–May 1957 and a Minister of State in de Gaulle's emergency Government 1958. From 1959 to 1968 he led the Socialist Party in Opposition.
[2] A pollster, who was Managing Director and later Chairman of Research Services Ltd 1946–70. He was Director of the Survey Research Unit of the Social Science Research Council 1970–6 and from 1969 to 1979 was a member of the Metrication Board.
[3] George Gordon, 6th Lord Byron (1788–1824), the Romantic poet. He died at Missolonghi during the Greek War of Independence.

In the last fortnight I have attended two public meetings organized by the Suez Emergency Committee—one at Croydon and one in Coventry. The atmosphere at both was very much the same. People weren't there to demonstrate but to try to understand what on earth was going on and to sort out their own minds. At the Croydon meeting I was speaking with Zilliacus. In view of the packed mass meeting they had had at the Caxton Hall when there was a real fear of war, the committee had expected full houses, but by the second week of September the war fear had gone. I found at Croydon, in a hall to hold 800, some 300 people, a good sprinkling of them non-political United Nations Association, Liberals and even Conservatives.

Zilliacus had tried to insist that he should speak after me. I knew perfectly well that he wanted to do this in order to give the meeting a rousing wind-up, such as he thought I couldn't do. However, he turned up a quarter of an hour late instead of meeting me on the train, so I wasn't obliging and, within a few minutes of starting off, he found that this wasn't a great left-wing demonstration. He was heckled by quite a number of people, including some young men, at the front, who called themselves United Empire Loyalists. These are the people who present Eden with a coal scuttle or grab his microphone and shout that he has betrayed the Empire. Their technique is embarrassing because their interruptions are single words, like 'Murderer!', 'Thug!' or 'Traitor!', ejaculated with no reference to what you are saying.

I came on after the interval. I rather liked the look of the two young Empire Loyalists at the front and, when one of them interrupted my description of Nasser, I had a bright idea, broke off and said that it had suddenly struck me that the exact description of Nasser was a United Egyptian Empire Loyalist and that his views were just like those of the young men in front of me, pure and undefiled. To my amazement, the young men were delighted and gratified and from then on the meeting went with a swing, turning into a W.E.A. lecture.

As I came down the platform to catch the train back, a young man said, 'Fancy meeting you, Mr Crossman,' and it was one of my United Empire Loyalists, who travelled up with me. His parents had been killed in the blitz and he'd spent years in the Marines and merchant ships, since cooking was his only skill. We had an interesting talk and I asked him why he was a United Empire Loyalist. 'Oh, I'm not,' he replied. 'But they pay me to go to meetings and I like getting round and listening to speakers. I particularly liked what you said.' So back he went to his single room in Bloomsbury.

All these events make me think that, since I've been back, Hugh Gaitskell's leadership has been quite good. He has seen the dangers of getting ourselves tagged as simply a pro-Nasser, anti-British Party. He has made great efforts to get the Left and Right of the Party working together, with some success, and his own speeches really have been very good. I went in to see him on the Sunday evening after the debate because he was due to make a speech next day to the Foreign Press Association. We discussed at some length what he should say, but we talked rather vaguely. I merely emphasized that he should challengingly state not what was wrong with the Government but what we would have done had we been in Government. What Hugh produced next day was really first-rate and was brilliantly displayed by Sydney on the *Mirror* front page. Hugh had got it all written up in the morning and it was an excellent job of drafting. He had apparently answered the questions well, too.

People are still discussing exactly how Britain got into this jam. I was asked to lunch this week by Chancellor,[1] the head of Reuter's, who also had Francis Williams, Kingsley and Nye there. What has made men like Chancellor so angry is the memory of the off-the-record briefings which the Government gave at the early stages to proprietors and editors, and at which they clearly and emphatically encouraged the press to threaten war against Nasser. A man like Chancellor is quite shocked that Eden should now lie and say that no such briefings were ever given nor suggestions made. The fact is that every proprietor and editor knows as a matter of fact that these briefings were given for at least ten days. Chancellor, on the other hand, seems to me ridiculously pro-Nasser, just because he met him once in March and found him very attractive. Nye was his usual, rather withdrawn self. He certainly doesn't feel at home in this Suez crisis and is just as statesmanlike as Hugh Gaitskell.

The substantive U.N. debates on the Suez crisis were to take place on October 5th and 13th. Meanwhile, on October 1st the Suez Canal Users' Association, with certain committees, was formally established at a meeting in London of the eighteen countries' representatives, with Selwyn Lloyd presiding. The following day, however, Mr Dulles told a press conference in the United States that there was 'some difference in the approaches to the Suez Canal problem', and referred to the 'somewhat independent role' played by America in 'the so-called problems of colonialism'. Though Mr Dulles later modified his remarks, this apparent American retreat caused great anger in Europe, aggravated the next day by a report that the U.S. might organize a consortium of business firms, including American oil and shipping companies, to operate and develop the Canal, in a separate arrangement with President Nasser.

Though such a scheme did not materialize, the Security Council debates themselves produced little result. After a public session on October 5th, the U.N. Secretary-General brought together the Foreign Ministers of Britain, France and Egypt for private negotiation. Here six principles for a settlement emerged. They were: free and open transit through the Canal, without discrimination; recognition of Egyptian 'sovereignty'; 'insulation' of the Canal from politics; agreement between Egypt and the users on the matter of tolls; allotment of a fair proportion of dues for Canal development; and settlement of disputes by

---

[1] Christopher Chancellor joined Reuter's in 1930 and worked in the Far East 1931–4, rising to the position of General Manager 1944–59. He was knighted in 1951. He was later Chairman of Odhams Press 1960–1 and of the Bowater Paper Corporation Ltd 1962–9.

arbitration. The six principles were presented to the Security Council as part of an Anglo-French proposal and were unanimously approved. But the second part of the proposal, providing for a Users' Association, was rejected by the U.S.S.R. and Yugoslavia, the Russian vote being a veto. The British and French Governments now maintained that Egypt should present detailed bases for a settlement, while Egypt held that this was contained in the six principles. The Russian veto on October 13th relieved the Security Council of the obligation to take any further steps.

Meanwhile relations between Middle East countries had grown steadily worse. At the end of September a party of archaeologists, visiting ruins south of Jerusalem, had been fired upon, with fatal casualties, from Jordanian lines. The next day Israeli forces had attacked and destroyed a Jordanian police station. When the Mixed Armistice Commission failed to find Jordan responsible for the first shooting, Israel announced that she would no longer take part in the Commission. On October 10th America and Britain jointly approved the admission of Iraqi troops into Jordan, where parliamentary elections were about to take place, in order to maintain authority and prevent an Egyptian or Syrian coup. This provoked loud opposition from Israel, who regarded the move as a threat. On October 12th Britain warned Israel that any attack on Jordan would oblige Britain to come to King Hussein's aid, under the terms of the Anglo-Jordan Treaty. Four days later Mr Dulles reasserted American's determination to support any victim of aggression in the Middle East.

It nevertheless seemed that America's attitude to the Middle Eastern question remained ambiguous. After the failure of the negotiations in New York, Britain asked for American aid in launching the Users' Association, with scant success. American officials stressed that their Government had always intended that 'a fair share' of the tolls collected by SCUA should be paid to Egypt and American ships were still paying dues to the Egyptian Canal Authority. It was generally thought that American eyes were not on the problems of Britain and France but on the presidential election which was to take place at the beginning of November.

Crossman, for his part, omits to mention the Suez crisis in his diary entry for the remainder of October. His own preoccupation was the party Conferences — of the Labour Party, meeting at Blackpool from October 1st to 5th, and the Conservatives, at Llandudno from October 11th to 13th.

Friday, October 26th
Every year I get an increasing phobia of the Labour Party Conference. Why? Partly, no doubt, it is suppressed anxiety about one's place on the National Executive. I always say to myself that I would like to be off it. But, as Conference draws near, one is always increasingly aware of a tremendous atmosphere which surrounds the constituency elections. All over the country, wards or parties are solemnly meeting and balloting to mandate their delegates. But that is only one half of the problem. The other half is that

probably something over a third of the delegates are unmandated and therefore open to influence during the first weekend before the ballot closes at half-past four on the Monday. So everyone on the constituency side is edgy.

People like Barbara and Tony Greenwood electioneer the whole year through. This year, for instance, they sent a telegram to President Bulganin, asking him to ensure that the Bolshoi should arrive,[1] which must have got them twenty extra votes.

Sure enough they topped the poll. I was sitting with Barbara and Ted at the table, since Anne was not there, and on the Tuesday morning Barbara said to me, quite solemnly, 'I do feel hurt. The whole of yesterday Harold Wilson failed to come and congratulate me on heading the poll.' As Barbara was Number One this year and Harold had sunk to third place, I replied by asking whether she had condoled with him on sinking to Number Three! She didn't think this funny and said, 'Of course I realize that Tony will get ahead of me next year. One can hardly stay Number One.' I think it wouldn't be exaggerating to say that I am not quite as keen as Barbara about my place in the Executive but it would be self-deception to deny that I am quite keen and that, unlike Barbara, who expresses all her worry and does something about it, I manage to pretend to myself that I don't mind, do nothing whatsoever to improve my position, do a great many things to make myself extremely unpopular and then feel vaguely anxious that all this may have the expected effect.

This year there was no doubt whatsoever that by openly breaking with Nye Harold Wilson and I had done ourselves no good. Harold had gone further and antagonized all the agents,[2] but, on the other hand, had not had an open quarrel with Nye, as I had done. To make matters worse, this year Anne and I decided that she should spend the week with her father. In a way I didn't want Anne to come, because I hate the atmosphere of Conference and I expect I disliked the idea of her being there if I was knocked off the Executive. On the other hand, Conference is extremely dreary without her, since, if you haven't your wife to talk to and have meals with, you've got to do even more politicizing in order not to be alone, the one state of affairs which no member of the Executive can tolerate for one moment, for fear that his being alone means that nobody wants to see him!

---

[1] The Bolshoi Theatre Ballet Company were to dance at Covent Garden in October but the visit was very nearly cancelled after Russian protests at the arrest, on August 29th, of Mrs Nina Ponomareva, the Russian Olympic champion discus thrower. She had been competing with the Russian team at an athletics match in London and was now charged with stealing five hats from a department store. After vanishing for some days, Mrs Ponomareva appeared at Marlborough Street Police Court on October 12th, where she was found guilty but was discharged on payment of 3 guineas costs. Meanwhile on September 28th it was announced that the Bolshoi Company would fulfil their engagement. They arrived on October 3rd. Of their performances, *Romeo and Juliet* and *Giselle* were particularly praised and audiences and critics were especially enraptured by the dancing of Galina Ulanova.

[2] By his report on Party organization.

On Saturday evening the Coventry delegates turned up to have a drink with me at our Executive hotel. As usual, they were all shop stewards, all illiterate, all self-assertive and every one of them, I must admit, succeeding in busting through during the week, getting to the rostrum and making quite a good splash. While we were talking, Frank Cousins came along and they forced me to introduce them to him so that they could air with him some local grievance, which he much resented discussing in my presence.

At this moment Nye came up. In two minutes he and Cousins were having an argument about the T.U.C.'s attitude to public ownership, in the presence not only of us Coventry people but of several journalists as well. Since this was the first occasion on which the two men had met, the incident produced quite a little sensation and I told Sydney about it on Sunday morning. He straightaway put a paragraph in the *Mirror*, not knowing that on Sunday afternoon the two men had carefully happened to meet again and have a perfectly amicable conversation in the presence of Vicky, both obviously feeling that they didn't want to commit themselves to hostility to each other.

Indeed, it became perfectly clear at this Conference that there were three men concerned — Gaitskell, Cousins, and Bevan — and throughout the proceedings every word each man said was weighed in relation to those of the other two. My impression is that Cousins did a very artful job of endearing himself to the Conference as being a keen and loyal Socialist, without in any way committing himself in the Gaitskell–Bevan feud, except in so far as he automatically, of course, accepts the Leader *qua* Leader. Indeed, Cousins spent a good deal of his time trying to undo the impression that at Brighton he had militantly declared war on the Government and trying to make himself respectable. I saw quite a lot of Cousins when he was six months on our Executive during Tiffin's period as General Secretary and formed the impression that he's a much more naïve, gawky and vain man than most people think. Of course he knows his job in the trade union world and is supremely self-confident there, but on the political side he is extremely inexperienced and, quite unexpectedly, in a position of vast authority. Nothing he did at Blackpool changed that impression. He certainly has the ability to make the kind of speech the Conference wants to hear without committing himself to any policy, which I suppose one can say is the first essential quality of Labour leadership, and a quality I certainly don't possess.

But of course the real interest was in the treasurership. Morgan Phillips told me that, as far as he could add it up, George Brown was going to win by a small majority and if Nye got in he would have to have over 90 per cent of the constituencies and even then couldn't win by more than 50,000 or 60,000. It was already clear on Sunday that there was virtually nobody left who wanted George Brown to win. Sam Watson made no bones about it. He would have liked to see Nye returned unopposed and that's why the Miners had nominated him. Jack Cooper told me the same thing of the Municipal and General Workers. The fact is, George Brown had jumped the gun by getting his constituency party to adopt him and then forcing the two big unions to back him because his name had been published. Now, when it came to the point and everybody realized that the Conference would split wide open at the *Tribune* meeting on Wednesday night if Nye was not elected, everybody, whatever their motives, wanted the old boy back on the Executive.

On Monday night, when I was going to bed, I found Sam Watson and Tom O'Brien sitting up at the bar and had a long talk with them. At such times people are pessimistic and I remember Sam telling me that he was afraid two disasters would happen: Nye wouldn't be elected and Harold and I would be defeated. 'If that happens,' he said, 'the trade unions will change the Constitution back, making all members of the Executive elected by the whole Conference.' I don't think I have ever felt more strongly than on that Monday the power (to be precise, the negative power) which Nye exerts. Here was one man who, it was felt, could wreck the Conference if the vote went wrong.

I'm sure this explains the explosion of noise which greeted the announcement that Nye had been elected by a larger majority than anyone thought possible. It was ecstasy from most of the constituencies and real relief from everybody else, including most of his enemies. Characteristically enough, he then gave a series of press conferences, radio conferences and television conferences, in which he left it open whether he would contest the leadership, although he knew perfectly well that he wouldn't. This had the effect, ironically enough, of killing the *Tribune* meeting on Wednesday night. If he had kept his declaration of intention for that evening, the meeting would have been the high point of the Conference. As it was, his perfectly sedate behaviour at that meeting and expression of good intentions came as a complete anti-climax after his press interviews the day before.

I've given the impression that Nye and Cousins were what mattered, whereas in fact Hugh Gaitskell did at least as well as either of them. Indeed, the more I reflect on the Conference, the more remarkable his achievement was. He'd had a reception at the Sunday demonstration which would have emptied my stomach with sheer disappointment and, when he rose on the Monday morning to answer the Suez debate, there was again no rise whatsoever in the audience. Moreover, he had to spend his first quarter of an hour deliberately damping down the rank and file's sentimental desire to see the issue in terms of being either pro-Nasser or pro-Jewish.[1] It's a real test, for a new, untried, suspect Leader to have to start by rebuking and educating the Party.

I thought Hugh did extraordinarily well, reinforcing it on Wednesday morning with a very skilful reply to the debate on equality. This had been opened by Harold Wilson, an opening which had an element of humour.

[1] Mr Gaitskell warned the Party against doing exactly as the Conservatives hoped by making Labour appear unpatriotically pro-Nasser. He urged delegates to concentrate on the case that to intervene with force would be disastrous.

Poor man, he had been appalled by the drop in his vote for the Executive and had jumped to the assumption that, if he opened the equality debate, he would be regarded as having become Gaitskellian and having abandoned public ownership. I've never heard anything worse than his opening passage, in which he tried to play down the whole concept of equality and establish himself as an earnest adherent of nationalization. Then, almost by accident, he came on to the subject of tax evasion and got a resounding cheer, since the audience could bite on something concrete where they could hurt the wealthier classes in this country. When Harold stepped down, he was amazed, after a second-class speech, to receive a standing ovation. Why? I think I know exactly why. The Conference was making it clear that, if he was Number Three on the Executive, that didn't mean they weren't supporting him. They were supporting everybody in this Conference – Gaitskell, Cousins, Wilson, anybody who was any good whatsoever – because this was a Unity Conference.

PEACEFUL CO-EXISTENCE

In retrospect, I don't think I've ever enjoyed a Labour Party Conference less than this one. But that was mainly because, by some perversity, I refused to go to any of the socials and refused to enjoy myself because Anne wasn't there, although I had deliberately ensured that she wasn't.

Llandudno started the following Wednesday and I decided to motor up with Anne in the lovely autumn weather. It's a beautiful little seaside resort, like a greater Lyme Regis, with a Georgian front set between two big headlands. Many people had been predicting that the Government was in for trouble, but I had sensed from the start and said in the *Mirror* that there would be no serious trouble. It was obvious that the Tories couldn't afford it this year and, after Labour's unity at Blackpool, any chance of a serious rebellion totally subsided. My pleasure in the Conference was reduced by the fact that I woke up on Thursday morning with pneumonia, though I didn't know until a week later that I had it. All I felt was that the whole of my right side and chest was contracted and pressured.

What I really learnt from going to the two Conferences was something very important. That is, the different kind of extreme emotions in each. What the Conservative Conference wanted, if you had asked its general will, was to make war on Nasser, restore the cat, smash the trade unions and relieve the middle class of taxation. How odious, you say. But now turn to the Labour Party. Here there is an equal and opposite extremism of emotion. Here the delegates were much more inclined to be pro-Nasser than pro-British and to be fantastically pacifist. The Labour Conference is temperamentally anti-British, anti-war, for giving everything away and for taking everything away from anybody who has anything. This, I must say, is an odious frame of mind. The only question is not which is more odious than the other, but to which kind of pressure it is better for Government leaders to be subjected. Any Tory who adopts a tough policy will be appeasing his Conference. Any Socialist who adopts a tough policy will be doing so in defiance of his Conference. The pressure on the two party leaderships could not be more different. Each has to remember that the pressure of his Conference is wholly unrepresentative of public opinion and that, if he concedes to it too far, he will certainly lose the next Election.

The end of the autumn saw intense and angry debate, within and between the political parties and in the country at large, over the Government's foreign policy. Argument focused on action in the Middle East but the crisis there must be seen in the light of events elsewhere, particularly in Eastern Europe and the United States.

The repercussions of Mr Khrushchev's denunciation of Stalin in February were noticeable throughout Eastern Europe and most quickly of all in Poland. During and after his visit to Warsaw, Crossman had enthusiastically welcomed the changes there; these continued throughout the summer and autumn. After the death in March of the First Secretary of the Polish United Workers' Party (P.Z.P.R.), Boleslaw Bierut, Ministers and senior officials of his regime were dismissed, transferred and in some cases arrested. In early April Wladislaw Gomulka, First Secretary of the Party from 1945 until his replacement in 1948 by Mr Bierut, was released from the confinement that had followed his expulsion from the Party in 1949. An Amnesty Bill was published later in the month.

It was in this more liberal climate that a deputation of workers from Poznan went to Warsaw in late June to ask for a wage increase and revised contracts. On June 27th they returned, unsatisfied, and a peaceful demonstration the following day soon turned into a riot. Some 300 people were arrested and there were many Western witnesses to the struggles, since the Poznan Trade Fair was taking place. Meanwhile unrest was reported from other industrial areas in Poland.

Significantly, the Government not only announced on July 6th that most of the workers' demands would be met, but the Prosecutor-General also reassured the public that trials of those arrested in the riots would be conducted by the ordinary provincial and district courts, with the prosecution attempting to distinguish between demonstrators with 'largely justified demands' and 'adventurers, criminal elements and agents provocateurs*'. Moreover, in his address to a plenary meeting of the Central Committee of the P.Z.P.R. on July 18th the First Secretary, Edward Ochab, blamed the workers' grievances on 'the callousness and bureaucratic attitude' of the central and local authorities, who had neglected to compensate for the national fall in real wages in the early part of the decade. At this meeting there was also much talk of constitutional reform and economic development.*

The meeting was still in progress when a Soviet delegation led by Marshal Bulganin and Marshal Zhukov arrived in Warsaw to celebrate Poland's National Day, July 22nd. At a public meeting Marshal Bulganin delivered his very different interpretation of the Poznan riots, which were, he suspected, 'provoked by hostile agents', furnishing 'evidence that international reaction has not yet discarded the mad plans for the restoration of capitalism in Socialist countries'. While the Soviet leaders toured the countryside, the plenary meeting resolved, after merely deferential allusion to Marshal Bulganin's view, to modify Poland's Five-Year Plan, allowing for important economic and social changes, including an increase of at least one-third in workers' earnings. The Soviet leaders' departure was followed by the announcement of Mr Gomulka's 're-habilitation' and on August 5th the restoration of his Party membership. Two of Mr Gomulka's supporters were simultaneously rehabilitated and were appointed to the posts of Deputy Minister of Justice and Commander-in-Chief of all internal security forces.

Reconciliation was everywhere encouraged. In late August a national pilgrimage to the shrine of Our Lady of Czestochowa attracted 1½ million pilgrims from all over Poland. A new session of the Assembly, in early September, was told by the Prime Minister that the Government intended to make this body more influential. There would be a reduction in the number of Government decrees and greater opportunity to consider and amend them and to press the Government at Question Time. A commission was established to reform the electoral law, in time for elections promised for December 16th.

In late September and early October trials began in the Poznan provincial and district courts of those arrested during the riots. By late October all indictments had been revised and all those not charged with murder or robbery had been released. Those few who were sentenced were lightly treated and on November 6th the prosecution abandoned all proceedings against defendants still awaiting trial. Meanwhile, on October 9th, the last of the Stalinist Ministers, Hilary Minc, resigned his office as chief industrial and economic planner.

On October 15th the Politburo met to prepare the next plenary session of the P.Z.P.R. Central Committee, beginning on October 19th. Mr Gomulka took part in the Politburo's proceedings and on the opening day of the plenary session he was readmitted, with three close associates, to the Central Committee itself. Later the same day there unexpectedly arrived in Warsaw an important deputation from the Central Committee of the Communist Party of the Soviet Union, consisting of Khrushchev, Vlazar Kaganovich, Mikoyan and Molotov.

The visitors left on the following day and the plenary session resumed. The composition of the Politburo and Secretariat, announced on October 21st, represented a success for the Polish rather than the Russian or pro-Soviet groups, and the proceedings of the meeting, published for the first time, showed the significance of the victory of Mr Ochab, Mr Gomulka and their supporters. The Soviet leaders had expressed their 'deep disquiet' at the turn of events in Poland and the Polish leaders had sought to explain the 'irrevocable character' of 'the process of democratization'. The visitors had insisted that their supporter, the Minister of Defence, Marshal Konstantin Rossokowski, be included in the Politburo. They were unsuccessful. On October 19th it had become evident that columns of tanks were approaching the capital and Soviet troops moving on Poland's western frontier and within the country. The Central Committee did not believe Marshal Rossokowski's statement that these troop movements were part of normal military manoeuvres and, with support from the internal security forces and from demonstrators in the Warsaw streets, a possible intervention by the Marshal was forestalled.

On October 20th Mr Gomulka had addressed the plenary session, setting out the principles of a wide programme of reform and declaring that, within the framework of mutual support which Socialist states should enjoy, there should be 'complete independence and freedom', and sovereign and independent rule of every country. A Government Bill was introduced to reform the workers' councils, restrictions on newsprint supplies were removed and on October 28th, the feast of the Kingship of Christ, the Primate of Poland, Cardinal Stefan Wyszynski, was released after three years of imprisonment. A commission was set up to examine Church/State relations; religious freedoms were restored.

In sixteen out of nineteen provinces, pro-Soviet members of the Executive and the Secretariat were dismissed and similar changes were continued in the central government. On October 24th the forthcoming elections were postponed from mid-December to January 20th, 1957, but the electoral law now approved permitted the number of candidates nominated to exceed, by a maximum of two-thirds, the number of seats available. In Gomulka's words, the people would be allowed 'to elect, not only to vote'. The Western Powers watched these changes with amazement and admiration, waiting to see what the Soviet Union's reaction would be. For, though the thaw came most swiftly in Poland, it was not confined to that country. Neighbouring regimes were also beginning to assert their independence from the Soviet grip.

Hungary was one of these. In the early part of the year 'de-Stalinization' was dutiful and modest. There were some posthumous rehabilitations, a number of political prisoners were released and greater freedom to criticize the bureaucracy was allowed to writers and the press. However, some sixty 'intellectuals' were censured for stepping beyond the bounds of freedom; in other respects Government policy was little changed. The Budget emphasized the development of heavy industry and the continued collectivization of agriculture, and the second Five-Year Plan, published in draft in late April, followed the same outline, with priority given to the working of local raw materials and sources of power, including Hungary's recently discovered deposits of uranium, of which most was going to Russia.

Protest began in the summer. The Yugoslav press reported a stormy meeting of the Petöfi Circle, a group of leading intellectuals formed secretly two years before, at which attacks were made on the Hungarian leadership, in particular on the First Secretary of the Hungarian Workers' Party, Mátyás Rákosi. He was summoned, with his colleague Mr Ernö Gerö, to Moscow and on their return Mr Rákosi resigned, giving age and ill-health as the reason but admitting also that he had indulged in the 'cult of personality' and had 'violated Socialist legality'.

Other changes were made in the Government, the Politburo and the Party Secretariat and, when Parliament was recalled on July 30th, legislation was promised—and in some cases enacted—to reform the legal and penal systems and to introduce changes in economic policy. But these concessions were hollow. Though some of the new office-holders, appointed with the agreement of Marshal Tito of Yugoslavia, had Social Democratic or nationalist sympathies, others were hardline pro-Soviet supporters, especially Mr Gerö, who succeeded Mr Rákosi. Mr Gerö stated that on matters of principle there would be no wavering and that no concessions would be made to the group represented by Mr Imre Nagy, the former First Secretary who had set Hungary on a new course in 1953 but who had been brought down in 1955.

Economic disasters increased public resentment. Poor planning and bad weather led to a disastrous harvest, coal stocks were run down, an important oil-field was found to be waterlogged, there were shortages of food, hard currency and raw materials. For much of this misfortune Russia was blamed, for she was still importing Hungarian food and uranium and now offered little assistance. In early September the Hungarian Trades Union Congress demanded fundamental reforms in the relationship between workers and the State, while the peasants sabotaged deliveries of agricultural products and the Writers' Congress elected as its officers determined critics of the regime.

At the end of September a series of meetings began between members of the Hungarian Government, the Soviet leadership and President Tito. In their aftermath, more posthumous rehabilitations were celebrated, Mr Nagy was readmitted to the Workers' Party and a mutual non-intervention pact was concluded in Belgrade by Mr Gerö and President Tito. While these two leaders were meeting in Yugoslavia, an immense demonstration was organized in Budapest by the students of Hungary. Their delegates prepared and published a list of sixteen demands, a programme for the 'new Hungary'. These included: a new provisional Government under Mr Nagy; free elections; independent courts of justice; religious freedom; the neutralization of Hungary and denunciation of the Warsaw Treaty; the promotion of Hungarian nationalism and Hungarian management of the uranium mines; the end of collectivization; and complete solidarity with the Polish national movement.

This programme, and another drafted by the Writers' Union, was widely distributed on the night of October 22nd, and the following day huge crowds demonstrated in sympathy with it. Mr Nagy was acclaimed by a crowd in Parliament Square, another group demolished Stalin's huge statue, while others besieged the radio station, demanding that the reform programme be broadcast. Here, however, they were denounced as 'Fascists' by Mr Gerö and were pressed back by the State Security Guard, one of whose officers shot and killed a student delegate. Workmen and soldiers were called to disperse the demonstrators but, instead, joined in with them, distributing arms.

Early on the morning of October 24th it was announced that Mr Nagy had been appointed Minister President and some 'nationalist' Communists included in the Party Committee and Secretariat and the Politburo. However, not only was Mr Gerö's position as First Secretary explicitly reaffirmed and strengthened, but the Deputy Minister President, Mr Andras Hegedüs, a Soviet supporter, was also confirmed in office. It was he who later admitted summoning the Soviet tanks which now appeared in Budapest. In consequence, the demonstrators refused to give up their arms and when, on October 25th, State Security men and Soviet tanks fired on a large crowd in Parliament Square, vigorous fighting broke out in the capital. The revolt spread to towns and villages and within a few days Revolutionary Committees were almost everywhere in charge. It appeared that, outside Budapest, Soviet troops did not intervene.

Delegates in the bigger towns now presented the Government with uncoordinated but similar lists of demands. Gradually the Government submitted. Already, on October 24th, Mr Gerö had been replaced by Mr János Kádár, formerly imprisoned for his Titoist and nationalist sympathies. The next day Mr Nagy had promised domestic reform and the negotiation of Hungary's relationship with the Soviet Union. By October 30th an inner Cabinet had been formed, with representatives of the National Communists, Social Democrats, Smallholders and National Peasants. The last three of these political parties began to reorganize under new leaders; the Catholic People's Party and a Catholic Alliance Party were soon established. Cardinal Jozsef

Mindszenty returned from imprisonment to Buda; political prisoners were released.

On October 31st Soviet troops left Budapest and on the next day Mr Nagy formed a coalition Government. He then cabled to the United Nations — and told the Soviet Government — the message that Hungary now withdrew from the Warsaw Treaty and asked for recognition as a neutral state, under the joint protection of the Great Powers. But now the Soviet leaders acted. On October 30th they had apparently ordered troops to enter north-eastern Hungary, reinforcing other units which had left the country only to refuel their stocks of oil. The Hungarian Government protested to the United Nations and to the Soviet Government, which gave only evasive replies. Troop movements continued and by November 2nd Soviet forces were approaching the country's main military and industrial areas. Support for the Hungarians was shown in Poland, where on the night of November 2nd the P.Z.P.R. issued a statement of solidarity.

But, at the moment when it received the Hungarians' appeal, the United Nations was preoccupied with events in the Middle East. On October 27th Israel had mobilized her forces, calling up her quarter of a million reservists, and two days later she had invaded Sinai. At first Israeli troops appeared to be advancing on the Suez Canal but Israel announced that her objectives were, in fact, the elimination of Egyptian outposts and commando bases in the Sinai desert, the end of the Egyptian occupation of the Gaza strip, the destruction of Egyptian batteries preventing access to Eilat through the Gulf of Aqaba and, last, the negotiation of a peace treaty with Egypt. Israel had immediately attained the first three of these goals, taking control of the greater part of the Sinai Peninsula, occupying Gaza, Rafa, El Arish, taking prisoner the Egyptian garrisons at Sharm-el-Sheikh and on the island of Tiran and capturing some £30 million of equipment, including a large quantity of Russian arms.

On October 30th the French Prime Minister, M. Mollet, and the Foreign Minister, Christian Pineau, flew to London and that afternoon Sir Anthony Eden told the House of Commons of the decision which the two Governments had taken. Britain and France had asked the Egyptian and Israeli Governments for an immediate ceasefire and to withdraw their forces to a distance of ten miles from the Suez Canal. Egypt had been asked to agree that Anglo-French forces should move temporarily into crucial positions at Port Said, Ismailia and Suez. If, after twelve hours, either or both of the combatants had not undertaken to comply with these demands, British and French forces would intervene 'to secure compliance'.

Mr Gaitskell pressed the Prime Minister to pledge that further military action would be deferred until the Security Council had come to a decision or Parliament had discussed the crisis; Sir Anthony Eden stressed the urgency of the matter and regretted that such an undertaking could not be given. The Prime Minister stated that neither the United Nations Charter nor the British, French and American Tripartite Declaration of 1950 contradicted a Government's right to take essential steps to protect its citizens' lives and vital international rights.

On the same day, October 30th, the Security Council met. Britain and France vetoed an American resolution calling on Israel to withdraw beyond her frontiers and on all U.N. members to refrain from threatening or using force in the area. This was the first veto which Britain had used in Security Council proceedings. Israel accepted the Anglo-French ultimatum. Egypt rejected it and President Nasser began to withdraw from Sinai the forces he had started to send over the Canal. On October 31st an air force based in Cyprus began, under British and French command, to bomb military targets in Egypt. Within a few hours President Eisenhower had condemned the attack and British representatives in Washington were informed of his 'severe displeasure' at the failure to inform, let alone consult, the American Government in advance of the publication of the Anglo-French ultimatum. Indeed, a senior American official, believed by some to be Mr Dulles himself, alleged that there had been prior 'connivance' between Britain, France and Israel. This rumour was to gather strength.

The next day, October 31st, the Prime Minister reiterated in the Commons the case he had made the day before and also stated that, in view of Egypt's provocation, his Government could not support the American resolution before the Security Council, which condemned Israeli aggression. Mr Gaitskell led the attack on the Government and promised a strongly worded vote of censure on the following day.

When business began on November 1st, the Speaker was obliged to suspend the sitting for half an hour, so turbulent was the House. Proceedings resumed with Mr Griffiths moving the censure motion. This deplored the Government's action as a violation of the U.N. Charter, thereby affronting the convictions of a large section of the British people, dividing the Commonwealth, straining the Atlantic Alliance and damaging the foundations of international order. In his reply the Prime Minister described the British and French policy as essentially a police action to stabilize the position in the area. No one would be better pleased than the Government, he said, if the U.N. were then willing to take over the task of peace-keeping. In the vote, on party lines, the Government secured a majority of 69.

That same day President Eisenhower broadcast to the American people, five days before the presidential election. Emphasizing that criticism of Britain and France in no way 'minimizes our friendship for them', he stated that American policy was based on the United Nations and that the United States would not become directly involved in the crisis. America had accordingly moved the ceasefire resolution in the U.N. and had reminded the combatants that American-supplied arms were not to be used in the hostilities. The Americans were, in fact, in an embarrassing position. Not only had President Eisenhower his own electorate to think of, but it was also awkward for the United States to find herself siding in the Security Council with the Soviet Union against Britain. America exerted every pressure on Britain and France to end hostilities and, meanwhile, in the American press accusations of British 'trickery and deceit' continued.

On November 1st the U.N. Assembly held an emergency meeting to consider the British and French military action and in the early hours of November 2nd its members called on Britain, France and Israel to cease fire immediately. There was a majority of 64 votes for this resolution, with 5 members (Britain, France, Israel, Australia and New Zealand) voting against it. On that morning, too, it was learnt that Israeli forces had won a decisive victory over Egyptian troops in the Sinai Peninsula. British and French bombers had also destroyed most of the Russian-supplied Egyptian Air Force, which had remained on the ground.

That Friday had been the last day of the 1955/56 parliamentary Session but, in view of the urgency of events, it was agreed that Parliament should sit on the Saturday and Monday. Mr Gaitskell warned the Government that the Opposition expected the Prime Minister to announce that the Government accepted unequivocally the resolution of the U.N. General Assembly. On November 2nd Crossman gave his view of 'Eden's gamble' in his Daily Mirror *column. That same day he returned to the House of Commons after his illness.*

Friday, November 2nd
Since I got ill at the Conservative Party Conference, I have had the detached feeling of watching things from home, or, I suppose, the normal feeling of the average citizen who doesn't participate in politics. It so happens that the things I have been watching have been unusually large-scale. The first week-end, after I got back from Llandudno, it was clear that things were moving in Poland, with Gomulka[1] due to come back, while there were rumours all the week of what was going on in Warsaw. By the following Sunday, when I was in hospital, the crisis had broken, with Khrushchev arriving, etc. By the next week Poland had been eclipsed by Hungary and the revolution there.

By the beginning of this week things looked extraordinarily hopeful. The whole of world public opinion had been marshalled on the side of independence for the satellite states and it looked as though the Russians could not resist the demand that their troops should be entirely withdrawn and Eastern Europe permitted, if it wished, to be neutral. True, one had the gravest doubts whether, in places like Hungary or Poland, Western parliamentary democracy was really practicable. Would it not merely mean the rise of a violent right-wing Fascist Party, since there is no 85 per cent agreed basis, such as we have in this country and without which our system doesn't work? And of course it was true that, just as the Poles had got beyond Tito in their liberalization and

[1] Wladislaw ('Jan') Gomulka, one of the leaders of the Polish Resistance 1939–45 who after the Liberation became Deputy Premier but, disliked by Stalinists for 'nationalist' and 'independent' policies, was forced to resign in 1949. After the Poznan riots of 1956 he was elected First Secretary of the Communist Polish Workers' Party and dominated the Government of Poland until serious strikes in 1970 brought about his resignation and suspension from the Party leadership.

the Hungarians had jumped beyond the Poles, so each of these jumps endangered the situation by undermining Communist control far too rapidly. Nevertheless, one couldn't help feeling enormously stirred and elated by what was happening. It was too good to be true that one was living through 1848 all over again. And yet there it is, that was just what one was doing.

And then came this extraordinary week, which started with the rumbles of the Jordan elections, a louder rumble of Israeli mobilization, the crash of the Israeli attack on the Negev and then the thunder-clap of the Anglo-French ultimatum. One has been listening to the radio, bulletin after bulletin, as one used to in the war. I've been doing it mostly from bed while, half a mile away, in the House of Commons, the Party turmoil at least was proceeding. I say 'the Party turmoil at least' because, when one is in bed and detached, one becomes far more critical of the scenes, schemozzles, uproars, alarums and excursions of the Commons. One jumps over them to picture oneself with armies in the Negev or at Ismailia or at Cairo airport. In a way I've been far closer to things in the Middle East than I have to Westminster, until I went in there last night to vote.

I had had John and Celia Strachey[1] to dinner and got in just in time to see Nye get up and make the last Labour speech on our vote of censure. I should guess his speech was most unlike the tone of the debate — reflective, philosophical, starting from the H-bomb stalemate and then working up to an attack on Eden for believing in lynch law. It was, I think, a very fine and (though it's a cliché) statesmanlike performance, his first statesmanlike performance since his speech on defence in February 1951.[2] It is characteristic that Nye had the daring and impudence to allude to the views he expressed in that defence speech — and to get away with it. The Labour benches, of course, were so warmed up to cries of 'warmonger!', 'murderer!', etc., and to moral appeals to save the United Nations, that Nye's reflective style was hardly to their taste.

Then I listened to Butler and here I learnt something quite new. The fact is that the Government's case is so terribly unconvincing, so ingeniously disingenuous, such a palpable tissue of prevarications that I began to realize why the House had turned into a bear-garden — because it's almost impossible to listen to this nonsense and stay still. Nor can you really believe that it's possible that a British Government could commit aggression in this way.

I agree with Kenneth Younger, with whom I talked it over this morning and who, on this sort of thing, is pretty objective. He doesn't think this was a long-laid, devilish plan. He thinks we were hooked into this by the French, half-prepared and without really thinking over its full implications. He told me one little interesting confirmation. When the Shadow Cabinet received

---

[1] From 1925 Celia Simpson had worked on the *Spectator*, where she met Strachey, who was then writing a column for the paper. After living with him for about a year, she married him in 1933. A committed Socialist, she visited the U.S.S.R. in 1928.

[2] See the Introduction, p. 25.

the draft of Eden's first Statement, there was an ambiguity in it as to whether we should put our troops into Egypt even if the Egyptians agreed. Dick Stokes said, 'Let's go along the lobby and find out from the Prime Minister.' He himself went along and asked Eden, who said, 'I'm not sure. I'll check with the Foreign Secretary.'

This really does seem to indicate that, when they started this thing, they hadn't worked out its implications, though I suspect that they somehow assumed that, a week before the American presidential election, an American President who is a candidate would not be able to affront the Jews and that therefore the General Assembly wouldn't meet in time to prevent the *fait accompli*. I'm sure the whole essence of the thing was the belief in the *fait accompli* — that somehow, within forty-eight hours of starting the operation, Nasser would have disappeared and everything would be O.K. It is now over three days since the twelve-hour ultimatum and nothing has happened except Anglo-French bombing of Egyptian aerodromes while the Israeli Army annihilates the Egyptians in the Negev and in the Gaza Strip.

Yesterday was a great chance for the Tory Party. If twenty or thirty of them had abstained, they would have made it possible for the Government to shift its view. But, with 100 per cent Party discipline, they put Eden in an even greater fix. Now Parliament is to sit permanently all through the weekend, waiting to see what Eden will do in face of the General Assembly's overwhelming vote, instructing us to stop fighting. If he accepts the instruction, he is personally finished and so too, I think, is his Government. But, if he goes on, he smashes the United Nations altogether. Already by far the most ominous news is that the Russians, who forty-eight hours ago seemed ready to withdraw from Hungary, are now reinforcing and settling in. They may well be saying to themselves that world public opinion no longer demands of them what it was demanding five days ago, in view of the British and French performance at Suez.

All these are reflections frustrated and from the sidelines. Not, of course, that it would have made the vaguest difference my being there, since there were always a dozen people to say the obvious right thing. The Labour Party could hardly go wrong this week. Yet one feels a bit frustrated and when I went back last night I felt slightly claustrophobic, taking part in three divisions surrounded by people whose stench was stronger than usual because I've stopped smoking. This has its advantages when one is drinking sherry but its disadvantages are equally apparent when one passes through the lobby with one's colleagues. It's a very nice, sobering experience, since, of course, nine-tenths of them haven't noticed your absence and, of those who have, the majority feel only a pang of the kind of professional sympathy a politician must feel for anybody in public.

While the Western Powers were preoccupied with the Anglo-French action in Egypt, the Soviet Union moved swiftly in Hungary. By the night of November

3rd Soviet troops had enclosed the most important military and industrial centres in the country and, some hours before dawn on November 4th, they attacked, simultaneously. By eight o'clock that morning Soviet tanks were before the Parliament in Pest, where the Government had assembled. Mr Nagy sought refuge in the Yugoslav Legation and Cardinal Mindszenty in the American Legation.

Though Mr Gerö and other leading Stalinist Communists had left Hungary, there were those, surprisingly including Mr Kádár, who had evidently known of the Soviet Union's plans. Almost as soon as the attack began, a broadcast from a Soviet-controlled radio station announced the formation of a 'revolutionary peasant-worker Government' and, within an hour, Mr Kádár announced its composition. He himself took the post of Minister-President; his colleagues were all Communists. Mr Kádár condemned the 'reactionary forces', which had destroyed the original intention of the revolution, and explained that Soviet troops had been called in to assist the restoration of peace and order and prevent the return of landowners and capitalists. When this was achieved, he would begin negotiations on troop withdrawal with the Soviet Union and other members of the Warsaw Treaty (which, implicitly, Hungary no longer repudiated). Though Mr Kádár stressed his dissociation from the regime of 'the Rákosi–Gerö clique' and promised various internal reforms, he did not offer coalition government or free elections.

Throughout the country there was vigorous fighting between Hungarian freedom fighters, most of whom were very young, and Soviet troops, many of them ruthless, equipped with bombing capacity and heavy artillery. Workers and miners supported their countrymen with a total general strike. The strikers followed the instructions of the Central Workers' Council of Budapest and the population refused to recognize any authority but that of the various Committees established after the revolt at the end of October. Gradually, however, the invaders broke Hungarian resistance, deporting eastwards people known or assumed to have taken part in the fighting. In fear and despair, a torrent of refugees crossed the unguarded frontier to Austria.

The United Nations Security Council was reconvened on the night of November 3rd, to consider an American resolution calling on Russia to introduce no additional armed forces into Hungary and to withdraw without delay all those already there. The Soviet Union used its 79th veto to oppose the resolution. The question was immediately transferred to the General Assembly and on the evening of November 4th a U.S. resolution was there adopted, calling on the U.S.S.R. to immediately withdraw all its forces from Hungary. Voting was 50 to 8, with 15 abstentions. The next day Mr Kádár's Government had replaced that of Mr Nagy; no official news now came from Hungary.

At this moment the U.N. was obliged to return its attention to events in the Middle East. The resolution passed by the General Assembly early on November 2nd had called for a ceasefire and the withdrawal of attacking forces. On the following day, Saturday, November 3rd, the Prime Minister reported in the *emergency Commons debate on the terms of the Anglo-French reply. This stated that Britain and France would willingly stop military action on condition (i) that Egypt and Israel both accepted a United Nations peace-keeping force; (ii) that the U.N. decided to establish and maintain such a force until the attainment of an Arab/Israeli peace settlement and until satisfactory arrangements had been agreed for the Suez Canal; and (iii) that in the meantime, until such a force was constituted, both combatants forthwith accepted limited detachments of Anglo-French troops, to be stationed between them.*

In his reply, the Leader of the Opposition demanded the Prime Minister's resignation, declaring that he had defied the General Assembly. At three o'clock the sitting ended, with the House in uproar at the Foreign Secretary's Statement that troops were about to land in Egypt. That night the Prime Minister broadcast to the nation, defending the Government's first and principal objective to separate the armies and stop the fighting, a task which fell to Britain and France until the U.N. arrived to assume it. On the same day it was announced that on October 31st Anthony Nutting had resigned his post of Minister of State at the Foreign Office.[1] Edward Boyle, Economic Secretary to the Treasury, also resigned his office.

On November 4th, at 2 a.m. local time, the General Assembly accepted by 57 votes, with none opposing but 19 abstaining (including Britain, France, Israel and Egypt and the Communist countries, excluding Yugoslavia), a Canadian resolution requesting the Secretary-General to submit within forty-eight hours a plan to establish, with the consent of the nations concerned, an Emergency International United Nations Force 'to secure and supervise the cessation of hostilities'. A time-limit of twelve hours was also set for a reply to the previous ceasefire resolution of November 2nd. By now Egypt had blocked the Canal by sinking ships in it.

That evening the Leader of the Opposition broadcast his reply to the Prime Minister's address the night before. He declared that the Government's purpose was not, as Mr Eden had stated, to separate the combatants but to occupy the Canal, and he appealed to Conservatives to secure Sir Anthony's resignation. Mr Gaitskell pledged that the Opposition 'would undertake to support a new Prime Minister in halting the invasion of Egypt; in ordering a ceasefire; and in complying with the decisions and recommendations of the United Nations'.

When, on Monday, November 5th, the House of Commons met again, the Prime Minister announced at six o'clock that at dawn British and French airborne forces had been dropped in the neighbourhood of Port Said. He also stated that the allied paratroop commander was by now discussing surrender terms with the Governor of Port Said. Meanwhile the Soviet Government sent a series of Notes to the Security Council, to President Eisenhower and the Prime Ministers of Britain, France and Israel. That to President Eisenhower invited

---

[1] He later published his account of the episode in *No End of a Lesson: The Story of Suez* (London: Constable, 1967). For Crossman's reaction to these revelations, see *The Diaries of a Cabinet Minister*, vol. III.

the American Government to co-operate with the U.S.S.R. in the Mediterranean until the United Nations should act to dampen aggression in the Middle East. The Note to the British Government threatened Russian intervention. The American Government immediately announced that it would oppose any attempt of Russian or other military forces to enter the Middle East.

The next day, Tuesday, November 6th, was the first day of the new parliamentary Session. After the customary speeches by the mover and seconder of the Address in reply to the Queen's Speech, the Leader of the Opposition spoke solely on the Suez crisis, appealing for an end to the division within the Commonwealth and the Western Alliance and at home. At six o'clock the Prime Minister entered the House. By this time the Secretary-General of the United Nations had reported to the Assembly, on November 5th, on the powers and duties of a U.N. Emergency Force which would be subject to the Assembly. The UNEF would be, in Mr Hammarskjöld's view, a para-military holding force, not an army but more than an observer corps. It would have no power to operate in any country without that country's permission. On that condition the force would enter Egypt to establish a ceasefire and secure compliance with the other terms of the U.N. resolution of November 2nd, in particular, the requirement that invading forces be withdrawn and free navigation restored in the Canal. The United States offered to contribute air and sea transport and supplies for the Emergency Force, which, by the Assembly's decision, excluded any units from the Great Powers.

On the same day, November 5th, Mr Hammarskjöld had negotiated the ceasefire with Britain and France. Now, in the Commons the Prime Minister announced that at midnight British forces would cease fire, unless they were attacked. This action was being taken pending confirmation that the Egyptian and Israeli Governments had accepted an unconditional ceasefire and that the international force would be competent to secure and supervise the attainment of the objectives set out in the Assembly's resolution of November 2nd. The British Government had emphasized, in the message to the Secretary-General, that the clearing of obstructions in the Canal, not a military operation, was a matter of great urgency and that the Franco-British force was equipped to set about this task immediately. There would be no forward movement of British troops from existing positions. The Prime Minister also read to the Commons the reply he had sent to the Russian Note, vigorously asserting that the Anglo-French action had limited the area of the Middle East conflict.

November 6th was also the day of the American presidential election. In a landslide victory President Eisenhower was re-elected, with 58 per cent of the popular vote to the 42 per cent of his Democratic rival, Adlai Stevenson. (In the electoral college, Eisenhower secured 457 votes to Stevenson's 74.) In the Senate, however, Republicans and Democrats took 4 seats each, so that the Democrats retained their two-seat majority (49 to 47); in the House of Representatives the Democrats gained 2 seats overall, giving them 234 seats to 201. Richard Nixon became Vice-President.

The news of the Anglo-French ceasefire was announced in America on polling day; it was warmly welcomed. Indeed, the Americans had put great pressure on London and Paris to end the attack. They were assisted by the weak position of sterling and the fall in the United Kingdom reserve, which eventually obliged the Chancellor of the Exchequer to apply for a waiver of interest payment due at the end of the year on the American and Canadian post-war lines of credit and to seek a dollar loan from the International Monetary Fund, using the Treasury's holding of U.S. securities as backing.

After efforts by President Eisenhower and a message from Marshal Bulganin, Israel announced that she would withdraw her forces from Sinai when the U.N. international force arrived in the Suez Canal area. President Nasser accepted the landing of the force but refused to agree to a Canadian contingent. The force itself was, however, commanded by a Canadian, General Burns. Now, as Crossman warned in the Mirror *on November 6th, the general view was that 'the real test will begin when the military operations end'.*

Wednesday, November 7th
I had better record some more impressions before they are all flattened out by rational improvements and self-justifications. Even now it is quite impossible to remember accurately what my own feelings were before Eden's announcement last night of a ceasefire. However, one must do one's best.

On Saturday the House met from noon to three o'clock, once again expecting that at last the news would come that the landings in Egypt had begun. Already the daily air communiqués about the pounding of Egyptian aerodromes are beginning to get on people's nerves. Designed, no doubt, to reduce casualties and carried out with every possible precaution, somehow this air offensive was morally unbearable and increased the feeling of phoniness about the whole operation.

Saturday's Commons was another bear-garden, with the Prime Minister and the Foreign Secretary trying to justify the Anglo-French decision that the attack on Egypt would go on, despite the resolution of the Assembly; with the Opposition making endless points of order; and with the nightmare of Hungary adding to the bitterness on both sides.

Partly, no doubt, because I was convalescing, I felt claustrophobia after sitting there an hour, tore up the notes I had made for a speech about Israel and went and had lunch with Eric Fletcher,[1] who had just come back from America, convinced that the Americans would back us if we pulled it off and that they were not really too disturbed about our behaviour. Then I went in to hear the concluding exchanges, which consisted of boos and catcalls for Selwyn Lloyd. Afterwards Anne and I motored down to Prescote, where we listened to the Prime Minister making his broadcast to the nation.

It was one of the most plangent appeals I have ever heard to the soapy

[1] Labour M.P. for Islington East 1945–70. He was Minister without Portfolio 1964–6 and Deputy Speaker of the House of Commons 1966–8. He became a life peer in 1970.

floating voter and the liberal conscience. For some reason, the broadcasting and television experts have now reached the conclusion that the British public cannot stand anyone who sounds decisive and strong but like the nice intimate chat from someone who shares all their feelings of distress. Eden's performance was remarkable, because, after all, what he was supposed to be doing was reasserting British and French power and our imperial strength, but clearly it was assumed that this reassertion was not to the taste of the public, who needed persuading.

Motoring up on Sunday night, we heard Hugh Gaitskell's reply, which was delivered in almost exactly the same plangent tone but which, of course, contained a good deal better argumentation. It ended, surprisingly and rather dramatically, with an appeal to Tories to throw Eden out and an assurance that Labour would support a Prime Minister who stopped the war, etc., etc. Anne thought the broadcast very effective and so did Rose, but I must say I was rather nauseated by its tone. I at once commented to Anne that, if any Tory M.P. had ever dreamt of abstaining in the vote on Monday, Hugh's appeal would have finally dissuaded him. Anne replied that Hugh wasn't talking to the Tory M.P.s but giving the non-political floating voter the feeling that Labour was above party and thinking in terms of the nation.

By Monday morning it seemed to be clearer than ever that Britain was now irrevocably committed to going into Suez. My view, in August and September, that there was no chance whatsoever of our acting if our bluff was called, had been proved completely wrong, but I was convinced that now I could at least be sure that, having started to go in, we would go right in and do the job. That made me feel certain that the Tory Party would rally solidly to Eden and gamble on his success and I did my column along this theme. I had tried to get Gaitskell in the morning but he said, 'Come in at half-past two.'

When I went in to see him, I remarked that, if he had left a chink of a chance for any Tory to abstain, I had closed that chink in the column. He looked very distressed and said, 'But I think we've got to persuade the Tories. Some of them are almost ready to do so and I was trying to help.' Chatting later on in the Smoking Room with Kenneth Younger, I found to my surprise that he shared Hugh's view that it was, first, desirable, and, second, possible, for the Labour Opposition to organize — or at least to stimulate — a Tory revolt. As an old psychological warfare addict, I know better. One can't actually make people desert if one is their enemy — unless, of course, they are crooks or psychopaths — and the more you encourage them to do so, the more you stiffen their morale.

Monday afternoon was the adjournment debate and once again we were off to the catcalls and booing, with a series of Government statements. Gaitskell pleaded, even at this late hour, to accept the ceasefire and pressed the Government very hard on why they had abstained from voting at the Assembly for the proposal for an international police force. Selwyn Lloyd made it clear that the Government adhered to all its conditions for accepting a ceasefire, which included our saying what kind of police force was necessary, and he seemed to imply that British and French contingents should be there, although this would obviously mean that there would be Russian contingents too. Nothing could have been firmer on Monday than Selwyn Lloyd's commitment to continue operations.

There was some quite effective Labour questioning, started by Wedgy Benn and continued by Nye, on the leaflets and broadcasts of the Supreme Commander, which had obviously been prepared for the August operation against Nasser and were being used in the new operation, in which we were supposed not to be attacking Nasser but only to be putting a force between the Israeli and the Egyptian combatants.

Then, to get the Foreign Secretary out of his difficulty, Eden announced the flash news that Port Said had surrendered. This sparked an astonishing Tory demonstration. Its importance was that it showed the desperate anxiety both of the Cabinet and of the Tory backbenchers for quick success in Egypt. Clearly the pressure of public opinion in Britain of a split Commonwealth, of America and, last but by no means least, of what the Russians were doing in Hungary, was having its effect inside the Cabinet. But I certainly didn't meet anybody on Monday night who even conceived that it was possible that within twenty-four hours Eden would concede to Gaitskell's demand for a ceasefire. Yet so it was.

On Tuesday morning I went into the Party Meeting to discuss our attitudes after the Queen's Speech. It was a great relief to hear Percy Daines get up from the floor and demand that we should behave with dignity so as to win the independent voter. At once, and quite rightly, Denis Healey stressed the importance of Hungary, where the Russian suppression of the revolution is still proceeding with terrible ruthlessness. He suggested that the whole of Gaitskell's theme should be that, in view of the unity which the West required to meet this terrible event, the Government should desist from its aggression in Suez.

Of course, this argument had been greatly strengthened overnight by Russian actions. At the Security Council the Russians had moved a revolution demanding sanctions against Britain and France within three days unless they ceased fire. Persia had voted for this resolution and even Belgium had only abstained. Meanwhile Bulganin had written a letter to Eden and Mollet, threatening them, in the crudest terms, with rocket attack, and generally stating that Russia would feel free to join in the Middle Eastern war if we went on.

I lunched with Bill Connor and Sydney. (Hugh Cudlipp, by the way, has been away in Australia for the last four weeks and only arrives back tomorrow.) None of us had any premonition of what was going to happen in the afternoon and mostly we discussed how it was possible for a man like Eden to give himself enough backbone to be an aggressor and carry out this war. We also discussed the strength of the Tory opposition, which might, we thought, number as many as thirty people who were seriously alarmed. I told Sydney and Bill I had had some talk with Walter Elliot and Bob Boothby, both of whom were convinced that the only way out for the Government was, by accepting an international police force, to replace the British and French after we had landed. I asked Walter and Bob whether they thought Eden would be prepared to see our troops totally withdrawn and they both said yes, they were convinced that was the only way out. To my surprise, when I asked Hugh Fraser, one of the leading members of the Suez Group, he agreed. 'I'm a member of the Cairo group,' he said, 'not the Suez Group. I always thought it was fatal just to reoccupy Suez. We had to knock Nasser out and, if we don't, most of what you predict will come true.' All this seemed to us, at lunch-time yesterday, to be something which might happen in two or three weeks' time.

The first inkling we got that something was on was when Gaitskell got up (by the way, this was supposed to be the debate on the Queen's Speech but, for the first time in history, it never got mentioned!). He made it clear he was having to speak in the absence of the Prime Minister and the Foreign Secretary, who were busy on international negotiations. This made it impossible for Eden to speak first. Gaitskell proceeded to make by far the best speech of his life, the first in which he showed something near statesmanship. The first half was an extremely dignified reasoned argument that there was really no case for going on a day more with the attack on the Egyptians. Then he switched to the Hungarian disaster and the need for Britain to have clean hands. He ended with a tremendous demand that the West should reunite in the crisis and that the Government should recognize the need to end the split in the country by ending the attack on Egypt.

After that Butler rose and, in his last two sentences, gave a hint. The Queen's Speech, printed some days before, had not mentioned the United Nations. Butler emphasized that the Prime Minister's Statement would please all of us who believed in the United Nations and responded to Gaitskell's appeal. In the Smoking Room the rumour was round that Eden would announce a ceasefire. Bob Boothby was saying that, in that case, Eden would have to go. I refused to believe the rumour but it was obvious that the unfortunate Tories were in a state of mental turmoil. Yesterday they had cheered a premature and, as it turned out, false flash that Port Said had surrendered. What were they to cheer today—a surrender by the British? So we all filed in and, at six o'clock, Eden made the announcement. It got tremendous Labour cheers. Then the Tories rallied and cheered him afterwards.

As we left the Chamber, I think the general Labour view was that this was the greatest climb-down in history and that Eden couldn't survive. This certainly was Boothby's view, too. When I got home, I rang up Alec Spearman, who, I knew, had always been one of the main opponents of the attack on Egypt. I said that, in my view, the Tory Party required Eden desperately in order to turn this into a great victory for Tory policy. Alec told me that he thought Gaitskell's broadcast had had exactly the opposite effect to that required and that he thought it was in the national interest that Eden should go. However, he was obviously unwilling to talk and rang off. Two minutes later he rang back to say, 'Country before Party, Dick. I beg you to stop the "Eden must go" campaign, since this will make it impossible to get rid of him.'

Anne and I then went to the Pakenham silver wedding party, where I met Quintin Hogg, First Lord of the Admiralty and very tired. Poor Quintin! He didn't need very much pressure from me to elicit that he was appalled by the surrender, as he termed it. Let me be fair. I think I put everything in his mouth to enable him to say that he didn't disagree. How, I asked, could one start a thing and turn back half-way? 'Well, we Service Ministers are small figures. We have to carry out the instructions without very much notice and we weren't once consulted throughout the day.' He confirmed, however, with Bob Boothby, that there had been a four-hour Cabinet with violent disagreements, in which Eden had fought to the last for continuing the attack and had been overruled by a majority. It was clear that Quintin felt this was utter surrender and disaster and so did Hugh Fraser, who was also there and just unable to speak because he thought it so terrible.

This morning's papers show that the popular Tory press has taken the view I regarded as likely and turned this into a great victory for Eden, the United Nations and everything under the sun. The *Daily Telegraph* is utterly ambiguous, with some menacing phrases about the need for toughness now. *The Times* is rather ominous and the Left, of course, heralds a tremendous victory. Kingsley tells me that the ovation that Hugh got in the Albert Hall last night was like nothing he had ever seen—cheering for over five minutes from 5,000 people. So it looks as though we shall have a competition about whose victory it is—unless the Tories, after their inquest, really decide they can't afford to have Eden any longer, in view of what he has done. After all, the net effect of this half-in/half-out is surely utterly disastrous, even though we manage to persuade ourselves in Britain that it isn't.

By the way, Eisenhower was re-elected with a landslide yesterday, though nobody noticed it.

Friday, November 9th
I suspect, though I cannot clearly recollect, that the atmosphere today is entirely different from what it was on Wednesday, when I last wrote in this diary. Now it seems to me that everything is overshadowed by the horrid feeling that the Anglo-French invasion of Suez may correspond to the Austrian attack on Serbia in 1914, or alternatively (if one tries to see the best and not the worst of it), that by leaping in despite all the dangers Eden and Mollet just saved Egypt from the Russian grip. Whichever way you like to

put it, the underlying fact is the same. We are now back, right back in a cold war, with the new men in the Kremlin using all Stalin's ruthlessness and savagery to repress the Hungarian rising and prepared, apparently, to take the kind of risks Stalin used to take in order to throw us out of the Middle East. Last week the Bolshoi ballet company disappeared from London, along with peaceful co-existence. This week it is quietly announced that the reciprocal Sadler's Wells visit to Moscow has been cancelled and nobody shows the least surprise. This week, on the anniversary of the October Revolution, all of us instinctively avoided going to the Embassy, except for a handful, including Sydney and Julius Silverman.

One could begin to feel this change of atmosphere in the debates this week in the Commons. The orgasm of the Anglo-French invasion was over – or rather, to be obscene, we were half-in/half-out, an astonishing situation, with a very few troops landed at Port Said and up as far as Kantara. Now we are asking, not 'Will it succeed or fail?', but 'Now that it has been stopped half-way, what will happen next and why was it stopped?'

The stories about a Cabinet crisis seem fairly well substantiated. Bob Boothby, Walter Elliot, and Alec Spearman all played leading roles behind the scenes, so that I was not totally uninformed. Coming home last night to supper I saw Edward Boyle[1] and gave him a lift in my taxi, saying I was a bit surprised that he, on the periphery, should have felt like resigning. 'One is never sure,' he said, 'but what tipped the balance was my feeling that every fragment of information which comes out will make the whole thing look more indecent. It will look the worse the more we know.' I said what a pity it was that some twenty or thirty Tories hadn't abstained on the first vote of confidence last week, since that would have really made the Government's position easier. Boyle looked surprised but said, 'You're right', and then added, 'The trouble, is, we weren't organized. But now Alec Spearman's got the group well organized and in hand.' So Alec Spearman's house, like my house, has become the headquarters of a conspiracy. It is, of course, a law and order group as against the Suez rebels, and each group is conducting a savage inquest from its extreme and opposite position.

Yet I personally cannot help feeling that the whole basis of argument should be moving away from the rather abstract debate on the rights and wrongs of the ultimatum and the last seven days. That ultimatum is now a past event in a much larger situation, the return to cold war, in which, of course, all the major decisions must be taken by America and Russia. Are we moving into a real world war crisis? Possibly. There are rumours of American

---

[1] Conservative M.P. for the Handsworth division of Birmingham from 1950 to 1970, when he became a life peer. Sir Edward was Parliamentary Secretary to the Ministry of Supply 1954–April 1955, Economic Secretary to the Treasury 1955–6, Parliamentary Secretary to the Ministry of Education 1957–9, Financial Secretary to the Treasury 1959–62, Minister of Education 1962–4 and Minister of State at the Department of Education and Science April–October 1964. In 1970 he became Vice-Chancellor of the University of Leeds and in 1971 Chairman of the Top Salaries Review Body.

partial mobilization, of Russian planes in Syria and of repairs to Egyptian airfields.

Meanwhile, in Europe, there are virtually no NATO ground forces, since the British and French have pulled theirs out for the Middle East, and the Russians have their own appalling problems in Eastern Europe, where I notice that Tito has once again got alarmed and started criticizing the Russians for their behaviour in Hungary.[1] In Poland, I heard that a B.B.C. man coming back from Poland yesterday said that every Pole was wearing Hungarian colours, that they were draped on the streets and that people were contributing to flag days for Hungary, but that the Government was remaining extremely cautious. The fact is that the Warsaw Pact has collapsed as badly as the NATO pact, both for very different reasons. Equally, everything in the Middle East has collapsed. I read that our officers attached to the Jordan Army are all being brought home because it is not safe for them and there were rumours over the week not only of Russian planes being flown to Syria, but of Persia giving Russia leave to move troops through.

The only cheerful news was that Ben-Gurion,[2] after a megalomanic speech on Wednesday, reversed himself in twenty-four hours after receiving a severe note from Eisenhower. I think one of the reasons why I have felt sad and depressed throughout this Middle Eastern crisis and not wholeheartedly engaged in the Labour Party's assault on the Government is because of a sad sense of divided loyalties. I couldn't really name Israel an aggressor or call for sanctions against her and I'm not the kind of moralist who can believe that an action such as Eden and Mollet planned would not be justified by entire success. I just knew it wouldn't succeed; I just knew the Israeli would find themselves landed; and I just feared that the most awful consequences would occur as a result of the first British independent initiatives.

And now what I suppose I'm going to find myself arguing is that we must never act without the approval of America. In my present mood I'm inclined to think that this would be damn good advice, since in the last four months American policy has been far more responsible and sensible, despite its appalling deficiencies, than the neurotic pseudo-Great Power policy of Britain, which I'm very much afraid a Labour Government would also ape.

In Eastern Europe resistance continued against the reimposition of Soviet control. In Hungary the Central Workers' Council of Budapest negotiated on behalf of the workers with Mr Kádár, refusing to call off the general strike until

---

[1] On November 4th, just before the Soviet attack, Marshal Tito had addressed a letter to both Mr Nagy and Mr Kádár, appealing to all Hungarians not to 'lose faith in Socialism'. While the Yugoslavs had warmly sympathized with the liberalizing trend in Poland, it seemed that President Tito now took to heart the strictures of those, especially in the Soviet Union, who denounced the 'Titoists' for their invention of 'differing roads to Socialism'.

[2] David Ben-Gurion (1886–1973). For sixty years he was one of the leaders of the Zionist Movement. He was the first Prime Minister of Israel 1948–53 and held that office again from 1955 to 1963.

Mr Nagy had been reinstated and all previously promised reforms had been enacted. Mr Kádár was bound by instructions from Moscow to retain Soviet troops until 'order was restored' and to preserve Hungary's membership of the Warsaw Treaty; he nevertheless stated that the domestic reforms demanded by the Council were for the most part acceptable. On this basis, on November 17th the Council recommended the end of the strike, but many workers refused to return to their employment until Soviet troops were withdrawn. A fresh crisis arose on November 22nd, when Mr Nagy sought to leave the Yugoslav Legation under a promise of safe conduct. He was kidnapped and abducted to an unspecified destination. The guerrilla war continued.

The Yugoslav reaction to Hungary's crisis had meanwhile provoked angry criticism in Pravda *and other Soviet organs. On November 11th Marshal Tito had delivered an address (published four days later) to workers in Pula, condoning Soviet intervention in Hungary as 'the lesser evil' to the liquidation of the Communist regime but calling for radical change in the Soviet and Communist systems. He had proclaimed that the Soviet leadership was 'divided' and threatened by Stalinism. Protests against the Yugoslav attitude were to come from all other East European parties, except the Hungarian and Polish.*

The Poles, for their part, appeared to have had mixed success in standing out against the Soviet Union. On November 14th Mr Gomulka and Mr Jozef Cyrankiewicz, the Prime Minister, went to Moscow for discussions with the Soviet leaders. On November 18th a declaration was published, stressing the 'similarity of views' of the two countries on Egypt and Germany and on Hungary, and declaring Poland's continuing association with the Soviet Union's foreign policy. The declaration went on to reaffirm the Polish–Soviet alliance, on the basis of 'full equality of rights, respect for territorial integrity, State independence and sovereignty, and non-interference in internal affairs'. In addition, the Soviet Union waived outstanding Polish debt, which had for a decade been repaid in coal, and promised deliveries of grain, on credit, and a long-term credit of some 700 million roubles for goods to be imported — arrangements which increased Poland's economic dependence on the U.S.S.R.

The last part of the declaration stated the terms on which Soviet military units would continue to be 'temporarily stationed' in Poland. This should 'in no way infringe upon the sovereignty of the Polish State, or lead to their intervention in the domestic affairs of the Polish People's Republic.'

Meanwhile the Kádár Government in Hungary sought a meeting in Rome of its representatives and the U.N. Secretary-General, to discuss whether U.N. observers might visit Hungary and whether the U.N. might provide relief for its people. Mr Hammarskjöld rejected this suggestion, repeating his wish to visit Budapest itself 'in view of the value of a broader personal contact' with the authorities there. On November 19th the Assembly passed by 55 votes to 10, with 14 abstentions, a resolution condemning the continued Russian repression and by 57 votes a further resolution urging Hungary to allow the Secretary-General to visit the country and report to the Assembly.

18

By this time there had been further developments in the Middle East. After President Nasser's agreement on November 12th to accept the Emergency Force in Egypt, an advance guard of officers had arrived in Port Said. Contingents of the Emergency Force began to come in by air and Israeli troops were quickly withdrawn from the greater part of the Sinai Peninsula but not from the Gaza Strip. On November 16th and 17th the Secretary-General visited Cairo, where the Egyptian Government asked him for U.N. help in clearing the Canal of the forty-seven wrecks and obstructions which had been sunk there. British salvage teams were already at work; they were now to assist a U.N. team under the charge of the American General Raymond Wheeler.

Nevertheless the British and French Governments were still not prepared to withdraw their troops until they considered that the international force was competent to discharge the tasks assigned to it by the U.N., including the clearing of the Canal. The Opposition continued to press the Government in Parliament and in a debate on November 8th an Amendment was moved calling for a Commonwealth Prime Ministers' conference. This debate covered the whole of the Government's policy of Middle Eastern intervention. The Amendment was defeated by 320 votes to 262. It was followed on November 12th by a further debate on a motion deploring the economic effects of the Government's Middle East action. The Chancellor stated that, apart from an additional £35–50 million military expenditure, he saw no reason why the Budget forecasts should not be realized. Mr Butler closed the debate with a strenuous defence of the Government's policy.

On November 19th it was announced that the Prime Minister was suffering from 'severe overstrain' and on November 21st he left the country for three weeks' rest in Jamaica. Mr Butler was to act on his behalf. On November 20th the Government announced that petrol rationing would be introduced on December 17th; ordinary motorists were to be allowed sufficient fuel to drive some 200 miles a month. On the day of this announcement, Crossman reported in the Mirror that the American Government had refused financial aid to Britain to pay for the 'extra dollar oil' needed until the reopening of the Canal and that President Eisenhower had forbidden American oil companies to put into action an emergency plan, previously agreed with Western Europe. Crossman resumed his diary on the following day.

Wednesday, November 21st
I see that it is now ten days since I last wrote in this diary — ten dragging, crawling days of singularly gloomy English autumn weather, with everybody having colds and semi-flu, and the news, both from Hungary and from Suez, as dreary and dragging as the weather. I suppose, if one wanted to give these ten days in the Middle East a title, one would describe them as 'From Cease-fire to Withdrawal'.

For Hungary there is no adequate description. The popular revolt has dragged on day after day after the correspondents said it was bound to stop and, as a result, there is now an open breach between Tito and the Kremlin, as well as between Warsaw and Moscow. I know that I ought to feel passionately about the Hungarian affair, but, mainly because I went to Warsaw and am enormously elated by the Poles' success in avoiding violence, I haven't felt much about Hungary. Anyway, we can't as a country do very much there.

For once it's not an exaggeration to say that nearly all my thought and my feeling have been hanging round this Suez crisis. Among my Labour colleagues in the Commons, the mood of raucous, anti-Government derision and shouting has, thank God, subsided ever since the ceasefire and the slow recognition that the British people is divided and unhappy and is by no means enthusiastically backing a Labour crusade for 'Law not War'.

On Tuesday, the 13th, came the last day of the Queen's Speech debate, once again devoted to foreign affairs. I had prepared a nice speech, largely as a result of talking to Hugh Cudlipp. He had been in Australia for the five weeks of the crisis and got back that weekend. On Tuesday he came to lunch alone with Anne and me. Just before he arrived, Anne had told me that our charlady, Mrs Meek, had retailed the following incident. In our newsagent's she had heard a lady observe, 'Please cancel my *Daily Mirror*,' to which the newsagent had replied, 'What, another cancellation!' After the lady had left, he told Mrs Meek that there had been a shower of cancellations by *Mirror* readers, indignant at our unfair, unpatriotic attacks on poor Sir Anthony.

Hugh doesn't much like criticism but we have a nice new jug for making dry Martinis and after he'd drunk his second I told him the story. He replied, 'It's funny you're telling me this because this morning I've been going through the reports from our circulation agents all over the country and I can tell you that never in the history of the paper have we run a campaign which has aroused such passionate antagonism amongst our readers. Of course, our circulation men know that their reports won't affect in the least what I say in the paper, but I must say this is a remarkable phenomenon.'

I then said I'd been a bit worried at the way in which Gaitskell and Cecil King had just rushed headlong into calling a war, in which Britain was engaged, an act of aggression and slambanging 100 per cent directly against it, when in fact it was obvious, first, that a very large number of people would feel that we should all get together in a crisis and, secondly, that anyway the bulk of the British people would judge the Government not by morality but by success or failure. We had a fine time discussing what would have happened if Hugh had not been in Australia and I hadn't been in bed. Of course, there's nothing easier than hindsight by absentees about politics and political journalism, and I don't think either Hugh or I believed we could have made all that difference. What I think we could have done was to warn Gaitskell and King against certain very obvious excesses which they could have avoided.

Hugh told me that in his absence King had had a wonderful time leading his grand crusade against Eden. I responded by telling Hugh the extraordinary story of how the other Hugh[1] had told me he was genuinely convinced that, by asking Tory M.P.s to throw Eden out, he was encouraging revolt in the Tory Party. I think it's fair to comment that the Labour Opposition was in danger of countering 'My country right or wrong' with 'United Nations right or wrong,' and really the second slogan has no more justification than the first, besides expressing an idea repugnant to most normal people.

One could see this during the last ten days, as the so-called international police force gradually began to dribble into Egypt. In the *Mirror* I described it as a smokescreen, under cover of which the British and French could withdraw and as a symbol of the United Nations' determination to make peace between Jew and Arab. But there are a lot of Socialists who want to 'put teeth into UNO' by equipping it with a vast Army, which can order us all about, and who would like to see this police force as the first experiment in creating such an Army. I agree with Nye Bevan, who wrote a good article in *Tribune* last week, that this is a great misconception for a Socialist. Anyway, whether we like it or not, a British Labour Government could not create any such force and there's no prospect whatsoever of either America or Russia permitting one to be created. So it's a pity to delude ourselves that, when we come to power, we can get out of our problems by adopting a 'United Nations' policy, which will in some mysterious way prevent our having to have a national policy.

It would be untruthful to say that these were the thoughts coursing through my brain as I sat in the House last Tuesday waiting to make my little speech. I had tried to get in on the previous Thursday, when I was told by the Speaker, who has a strange sense of humour, that he had paired me with Bob Boothby. This was outrageous for poor Bob, who wanted to say why he was abstaining — or rather, even more complicated, wanted to speak in order not to abstain,[2] having criticized the Government sufficiently. After twenty-seven years in the House, he was excluded. But for that reason he was certain to get in on Tuesday. I thought I was, too, and sat solidly through the debate. I was glad I didn't miss it. It started with a rather routine speech by Lennox-Boyd, after which Alf Robens made a remarkable recovery and a reasoned speech, raising the issue of collusion between Britain, France and Israel.

Then the main interest shifted to the Tories, since we had speeches from Hugh Fraser, Julian Amery and Bob, all attacking the Government from the extreme-Right position and urging that the situation could only be saved if, instead of remaining half-in half-out of Port Said, we bodily occupied the whole Zone, overthrew Colonel Nasser, etc., etc. They were very stirring speeches but I found them absolutely lunatic because it seemed to me that, even if these objectives could have been achieved a week ago, none of them could possibly be achieved in view of Eisenhower and Hammarskjöld's attitude, which had been steadily hardening into insistence that Britain and

---

[1] I.e. Gaitskell.
[2] There was, however, no division at the end of the debate on November 13th.

France withdraw from Egypt before any oil comes to Western Europe and before the blockade of the Suez Canal starts being removed. What was the good now of pleading for a tougher policy and nostalgically remarking how effective Israeli action had been?

Bob Boothby spoke for twenty-five minutes and sat down at fourteen minutes to nine, just after I had received a message from the Front Bench that Mr Noel-Baker would like to start at five minutes to nine, as he had a great speech to make. So I had nine minutes for my carefully prepared speech and probably, from the point of view of the House, made a much better speech than I would have done otherwise. There were a lot of people there and I said quite a lot in a very short time and proved that I was back from my illness. I went to bed quite satisfied, as M.P.s always do when they've spoken reasonably well, even though the speech is printed nowhere.

On Wednesday morning, the 14th, we had a Party Meeting and I gather that, after I had gone out at midday, the Party had a short discussion on the Middle East, in view of the sensational figures published that morning by the Gallup Poll, showing a tremendous swing to support of the Government's policy, to confidence in the Prime Minister and even to voting Tory in an Election. Hugh Gaitskell said very heroically that, despite this swing, we must go on, a view which he very genuinely feels. When I met him and Dora in the lobby one evening and congratulated him, he said to me, 'And what's so wonderful, Dick, is that we are morally in the right.' However, two days later the Tories had the gilt taken off Dr Gallup's gingerbread by a by-election at Chester,[1] which showed a 5 per cent swing to Labour (about the same as before Suez last July), as against a 5 per cent swing to the Government shown in the Gallup Poll, taken six days before.

That week there was a great deal of talk in the Party, which has its fashions in expression, about how the lumpenproletariat and the lumpenbourgeoisie had swung to the Government. It was not a bad way of expressing a truth, whose antithesis is that the Establishment and the liberal conscience had swung against Eden. I saw the reverse on Wednesday evening when John Strachey took me to the Political Economy Club's dinner at the Reform. This collection of bankers, professors of economics and pundits meets four times a year to dine, drink good claret and listen to a pundit expounding. On this occasion, it was James Meade[2] on European Free Trade.

But what interested me was the chat beforehand with, among others, Lord

---

[1] Caused by the appointment of Basil Neild, Q.C. (Conservative), as Recorder of Manchester. In the by-election on November 15th John Temple held the seat for the Conservatives, with a majority of 6,348 over Lewis Carter-Jones (Labour). The Conservative proportion of the poll fell by 5 per cent, while the Labour vote rose by 4.6 per cent.

[2] An economist with experience in Geneva and Whitehall, he was Professor of Commerce at the London School of Economics 1947–57 and Professor of Political Economy in the University of Cambridge 1957–68. He was a Fellow of Christ's College, Cambridge, 1957–74. His many publications include the four-volume *Principles of Political Economy* (London: Allen & Unwin, 1965, 1968, 1972, 1976).

Brand,[1] Professor Robbins[2] and a Sir Jeremy Raisman,[3] now a banker and at one time Financial Secretary of India. Nobody I talked to had a word to say for the Government's policy, which they all felt was reckless because it separated us from the Americans, without whom we could not survive. All the news which came through last week has shown that the rumours are true about high officials in the Foreign Office not being brought in on the decision and *The Times* reports that none of our Ambassadors in the Middle East was consulted and that the Commander-in-Chief only heard by wireless when the ceasefire was decided on in London. It is this kind of conduct – a man, with his intimate colleagues, taking a snap decision without consulting the Establishment – which appals Whitehall. Of course, I rather like politicians to take that sort of decision, just as I like them to go it alone, and therefore it's all the more disastrous that, when they do, they come a cropper and the Establishment says, 'Look what happens.'

We took Dora Gaitskell down by car to the Coventry annual bazaar on Friday and heard a splendid lot of gossip. Dora's line is that she doesn't influence Hugh about politics in any way, though she has very strong views of her own. She certainly does, particularly about people, whose failings, whether real or imaginary, she sees with great clarity. One amusing little incident about Hugh was worth recording. Dora told me he was due to go to Winchester to address a school. The night before, the new Headmaster had rung Hugh up and said that of course nothing controversial could be said. 'I suppose Hugh cancelled the visit,' I replied to Dora. 'I rather wish he had,' she said, 'but he agreed.' So off he went to an off-the-record, non-controversial talk to the school, of which fairly detailed reports, of course, occurred in all the Tory papers, making him look a fool. What a silly thing to do! And almost equally silly has been his hurried departure this week to Paris to a meeting of NATO Parliamentarians, quite unworthy of his status. I wish he wouldn't do this sort of thing, since it makes him look so inexperienced, which he is.

Last Tuesday afternoon we had the first meeting of the International Sub. When I had seen him the day before, Nye had tentatively agreed that he

---

[1] A Fellow of All Souls' College, Oxford, and from 1902 to 1909 a member of Lord Milner's 'kindergarten', Robert Brand (1878–1963) returned from South Africa to a successful career in the City and in public finance. He was a Director of Lazard Brothers, Head of the British Food Mission to Washington 1941–4 and H. M. Treasury's representative there 1944–6. With J. M. Keynes, he was responsible for negotiating American Loans, Lend-Lease and loans from the International Monetary Fund. He was raised to the peerage in 1946.

[2] After junior posts at the London School of Economics and New College, Oxford, Lionel Robbins was Professor of Economics at the London School of Economics 1929–61. In 1959 he became a life peer. His *Autobiography of an Economist* was published in 1971 (London: Macmillan).

[3] A member of the Indian Civil Service who rose to become Secretary of the Finance Department (1938–9). He was Finance Member of the Government of India 1939–45, and after his retirement was Chairman of the Fiscal Commissions for Rhodesia and Nyasaland 1952, for Nigeria 1957–8 and for East Africa 1960–1. He died in 1978.

would stand for the chairmanship against Sam Watson, if the people who were there at four o'clock seemed to give him a chance. At half-past three I got a telephone message that Nye couldn't come, so I knew that his character hadn't changed. He just had cold feet and anyway thought it wasn't worth the trouble.

The most interesting thing in the meeting was a long discussion of a proposal I made to publish a pamphlet on the need for a Committee of Inquiry into the charge of collusion between the British, French and Israeli Governments in the attack on Egypt. At once Sam Watson, Alice Horan and George Brinham, three of the trade unionists present, said that this was an academic issue and what was needed was a simple, factual pamphlet to bring our own supporters back from their fervent belief that the Government is right. In Sam's case, of course, this is simple, because he is 100 per cent pro-Israel and thinks that only the Communists want an inquiry. But these trade union leaders are really incredible in the opinions they form about public opinion. It is true enough that many Labour voters are pro-Government but these are not the kind of people who read our pamphlets. Our own Party members are 100 per cent anti-Government on this—indeed, too much so, and the proof of that came when Stanley Evans was forced to resign by the unanimous decision of the Wednesbury Executive.[1]

Indeed, the party machines on both sides can seldom have been as hysterically loyal to the party line. Alec Spearman was summoned to Scarborough, although he hadn't abstained and had only spoken critically of Government policy. There was virtually nobody who thought he was right in his very moderate estimates about Suez and it was only by two votes that it was decided not to move a motion demanding immediate resignation from the seat. Edward Boyle, who is immensely popular, had a similar experience in Birmingham and Nigel Nicolson[2] got it even more roughly in Bournemouth. But in Nigel's case I'm not surprised, since he's been chopping and changing for weeks. Discussing this with Angus Maude today, I heard him remark, 'My Executive has never criticized me in any way for my position on capital punishment. The reason, of course, is that I've been O.K. on Suez all the way through. When I asked for a vote of confidence for opposing the Government on Suez, I got it by 36 to 2.'

So there we have the two phalanxes, loyal for the reasons party machines are loyal—the Conservatives out of a sense of growing anxiety, which will soon be desperation and which forces them to cling together, and the Labour Party because it smells office, and, to do it credit, because it is happy to be

---

[1] It was announced on November 20th that he had resigned his membership of the Labour Party and his seat in the House of Commons.

[2] The son of Harold Nicolson (see above, p. 44). He was Conservative M.P. for Bournemouth East and Christchurch 1952–September 1959. Since 1947 he has been a Director of the publishing house Weidenfeld & Nicolson. His recent works include an edition of the *Letters of Virginia Woolf* (three volumes to date: London: Hogarth Press, 1975–6, 1978) and a biography of *Mary Curzon* (London: Weidenfeld & Nicolson, 1978).

crusading on a clear, simple issue, which, as it seems to most of our members, portrays the eternal conflict between the immoral, power-political, machiavellian Tory and the peace-loving, high-minded Socialist.

All this lengthy excursus is here to prove that a pamphlet of ours must be on collusion, because it is on the moral issue which this Government can be attacked. Prove to the British people that Eden pretended to move in for the purpose of stopping a war when in fact he had connived at starting the war as a pretext for moving in – prove that, and you really will shatter people's faith in any Government. Of course, we shall never be able to prove it, but I think we should be able to muster sufficient facts to make a *prima facie* case which justifies a Committee of Inquiry.

The other event this week was the announcement at midnight on Monday of the P.M.'s illness. Why was it announced then? Everybody is asking. Maybe the official version is the correct one – because the doctor was called in then and finally told Eden to take a rest. I accept this as the explanation, but when we went into the House yesterday there was no doubt whatsoever that Tory morale was very low indeed. What proved this was the way that Tories rushed up to one with remarks about a new Prime Minister, asking what was on. None of them took the story at its face-value and most of them were listening to wild, informed gossip of Bob Boothby's. He, having abstained and been nearly thrown out by his Executive, is making the best of it.

I went today to the lobby correspondents' lunch, which Eden was due to address. Macmillan and Butler were both guests and it was quite interesting that, rather than either of these two, Gwilym Lloyd George,[1] the Home Secretary, took the P.M.'s place. Talking to Francis Boyd[2] and Dick Scott[3] of the *Guardian*, I learnt, as Sydney Jacobson later confirmed, that there's no hard evidence whatsoever for any of these sensational stories about the Government's cracking up or the British troops being out within forty-eight hours. They are all really symptoms of alarm in the Tory Party. They may be true but the first information we shall have will come from Selwyn Lloyd, who flies back from the United Nations tomorrow and will have to state the Government's policy on withdrawal. In my view, the Government has no alternative to accepting whatever terms Hammarskjöld lays down.

---

[1] The son of David Lloyd George and himself Liberal M.P. for Pembrokeshire 1922–4 and 1929–50 and Liberal and Conservative M.P. for Newcastle-upon-Tyne North 1951–7. He was Parliamentary Secretary at the Board of Trade 1931 and 1939–41 and at the Ministry of Food 1941–2, Minister of Fuel and Power 1942–5, Minister of Food 1951–4 and Home Secretary and Minister for Welsh Affairs from 1954 until 1957, when he was created 1st Viscount Tenby. He died in 1967.

[2] (John) Francis Boyd, a reporter on the *Leeds Mercury* 1928–34 and on the *Manchester Guardian* 1934–7, was Parliamentary Correspondent for the *Manchester Guardian* (later the *Guardian*) 1937–9, Political Correspondent 1945–72 and Political Editor 1972–5. He was knighted in 1976.

[3] Richard Scott was Diplomatic Correspondent of the *Manchester Guardian* (later the *Guardian*) 1963–71 and its Paris Correspondent from 1971 until his retirement in May 1974.

At this time and in subsequent years, charges of 'collusion' between Britain, France and Israel were officially denied. Selwyn Lloyd's memoirs, Suez 1956: A Personal Account, *published posthumously in 1978 (London: Cape), describes on pp. 180–8 three meetings between various Ministers and officials of the three countries. The first was a discussion at Sèvres on October 22nd, 1956, at which Lloyd met the Israeli party, including Ben-Gurion, Moshe Dayan and Shimon Peres. The Foreign Secretary learnt that*

> *Ben-Gurion wanted an agreement between Britain, France and Israel that we should all three attack Egypt. In particular, he wanted an undertaking from us that we would eliminate the Egyptian Air Force before Israeli ground troops moved forward ... British prior air action was a* sine qua non *... He did not tell me, nor did I know, of the extent to which the French and the Israelis had already made joint plans.*

The second meeting Lloyd described was a conversation on the next day, October 23rd, between himself, Eden and M. Pineau, who had flown to London, perhaps because 'he was afraid that I would give too negative a report of the Sèvres talks'. Here it was decided that there should be another meeting at Sèvres the following day. Lloyd himself was occupied with business in the Commons but he wrote a letter to Pineau that same evening, making it clear 'that we had not asked Israel to take action. We had merely stated what would be our reactions if certain things happened.'

The third meeting, on October 24th, was attended by Patrick Dean, a Deputy Under-Secretary at the Foreign Office, and Donald Logan, one of Lloyd's Private Secretaries. The Prime Minister saw Dean before his departure and, according to Lloyd, 'gave him instructions that the discussions were to be about actions which might be taken in certain contingencies, and that British forces would in no circumstances act unless there was a clear military threat to the Canal.' At the third Sèvres meeting, Lloyd reports, the Israelis

> *refused to give details of their operational plans, except that they proposed to capture the Straits of Tiran, and the date of 29th October was mentioned as the earliest possible for them. The terms of the appeal which would be made to Israel and Egypt to stop hostilities were discussed.*

Lloyd continues:

> *After a time quite unexpectedly a document was produced ... There had been no earlier mention of committing anything to paper and no reason to regard the document as anything other than a record of the discussion on which the three delegations would report. As that, Dean signed it.*

Lord Selwyn-Lloyd also described the meetings of the 'Egypt Committee' of the Cabinet and of the full Cabinet at which British policy was discussed. In the words of his Epilogue, he tried to set out 'as correctly as I can, after months and months of the reading of records and books, what I believe happened and why. I have written for the record, because my account has been missing from the record.' Official documents covering the Suez episode were declared closed to the public for a particularly long period of time; Lloyd's book, and works cited in its text, nevertheless throw some light on these events.

Crossman was known to be anxious for a full-scale inquiry into the Suez episode and when, with Anne Crossman, he left London for a fortnight's holiday in Israel, many of his associates believed that he had gone to investigate what part Israel might have played in 'collusion' with Britain and France. In fact, he spent most of his holiday, from December 2nd to 16th, resting in the sun and seeking to dispel the last traces of his illness. He wrote, ' ... after I had spent ten days investigating collusion by the Sea of Galilee, even the greatest sceptic in the world became convinced.'

None the less, in various conversations Crossman found evidence to strengthen but not confirm his suspicions that Britain, France and Israel had discussed and concerted their policy in advance of the Israeli attack. His diary does not, however, record whether he talked about this with Ben-Gurion, whom he saw at the end of the visit. After this conversation, Crossman concluded:

Ben-Gurion, in the course of an hour and a half, couldn't have been nicer or gentler. There wasn't one word of recrimination about the Labour Party and only a long series of questions about how on earth Eden could possibly have stopped half-way. That was a subject where he genuinely wanted elucidation. He was baffled, disappointed, sad. Yet for his own people he shared in the relaxation.

While Crossman was away, the decision was made to withdraw the British and French forces in the Port Said area. The Foreign Secretary made this announcement on December 3rd, to bitter questions from the Conservative Members of the 'Suez Group'. The next day the Chancellor reported to the House on the economic situation. In November there had been a fall of $279 million in the gold and dollar reserves, slightly larger than the rise which had accumulated during the first half of the year. Mr Macmillan announced an increase in the tax on petrol and fuel oil from 2s. 6d. to 3s. 6d. a gallon, bringing the cost of petrol to motorists from 5s. 6½d. to 6s. 5d. a gallon. The Government was to ask the United States to waive the interest about to fall due on loans negotiated at the end of the Second World War.

On December 5th and 6th the Commons debated the Government's policy during the Suez episode. The Foreign Secretary opened the debate and Mr Bevan moved an Opposition Amendment which, while condemning past actions, was moderate in its call for restoration of Commonwealth unity, renewal of con-fidence between Britain and her allies and a strengthening of United Nations authority. Captain Waterhouse and other M.P.s of the Suez Group voted with the Government on the rejection of the Amendment but not on the main motion. The Amendment was rejected by a majority of 67 for the Government and the main motion accepted with a majority of 52. The Conservative rebels therefore numbered fifteen.

Meanwhile wrangles continued about the composition and methods of the salvage force that was to clear the Canal. On December 22nd the last British troops left Port Said; on the last day of the year the U.N. salvage force began its work. It was thought that by early March 1957 the Canal would be sufficiently clear to take ships of less than 10,000 tons and that clearance would be complete by May.

The Prime Minister returned from Jamaica on December 14th. On December 20th, in answer to Opposition questions, he emphatically denied all charges of collusion, saying that the British Government had no foreknowledge of Israel's attack on Egypt and had in fact been assured by Israel that her mobilization was purely defensive. Crossman continued to ask, in the words of his Mirror *column on November 23rd, 'Who is* Really *in Charge at No. 10?'*

Tuesday, December 18th

We touched down at London Airport at half-past eleven on Sunday night, half an hour early, after a very remarkable December flight including a cloudless, full-moon crossing of the Alps just after new snow and an equally cloudless view of London at night. I found to my relief, but not to my surprise, that really nothing had happened in the fortnight I'd been away — nothing private and nothing public. There had been a two-day debate, in which Nye had made a very brilliant speech. In cold print, it was competent but not brilliant. I gather that what had impressed people was his charm and good humour and general tone. Petrol rationing had been introduced just at the moment of our arrival, the sun had not shone and altogether Westminster had gone on groaning and wheezing, with the Prime Minister flying back from Jamaica on Friday. There can rarely have been a fortnight of Parliament in Session when so little had happened. So it's not surprising that, when I walked into the House of Commons yesterday afternoon, the wheels seemed to be turning rather monotonously and I soon felt not that pang of the guilty absentee, but the sense of superiority of somebody who is well and happy after ten days in the sun, whereas these other poor fools have been going on with their colds and milling over the same old ground.

I got into the Chamber in time to hear Sir Anthony answer his first Question. The press today all report that he had a chilly reception but I must admit that I did agree when I met Beverley Baxter[1] afterwards that the reception had been just about right, with the Opposition silent and the Tories careful not to be too enthusiastic, for fear of producing an Opposition demonstration. But what is the real view of Eden and the Government? To judge from Bob and Beverley and Hugh Fraser, the only three Tories I talked

---

[1] Conservative M.P. for Wood Green 1935–45 and 1945–50 and for Southgate 1950–64. He was knighted in 1954. A Canadian, he was Editor-in-Chief of the *Daily Express* 1929–33. He died in 1964.

to, anger and desperation are giving place to a curious frivolity. 'Just been seeing Elath this morning,' said Hugh Fraser. 'The only man in this crisis I really admire.' How strange that the right-wing Tories should now be viciously anti-American and sincerely pro-semitic! While I was talking to Bob and Beverley, Quintin Hogg came up, just back from Port Said where, as First Lord, he had been inspecting the salvage operations. He was full of his exploits in being rude to General Wheeler,[1] the American whom the U.N. has put in charge of salvage. Quintin Hogg's attitude was what interested me. As a member of the Government, he made no attempt to conceal his contempt for the Government's policy and his complete lack of any sense of responsibility for that policy. It is this kind of disloyalty which really threatens the authority of a Government and which makes one feel that something will have to be done.

Later in the evening, I heard Nye being questioned by Mallalieu on his view. Mallalieu was expressing the average backbencher's rather silly judgment that Eden is off his nut and that the whole Government must collapse tomorrow. Nye said that he thought the Tories needed a scapegoat, that in due course Eden would be made that scapegoat and that, when that happened, a Leader would be found. Mallalieu kept on pressing Nye and trying to prove that one couldn't name the new Leader, to which Nye replied, rather sensibly, that parties need a catharsis and that the Leader is found, whether we can now name him or not. Nye agreed, however, that if Eden were not got rid of during the Recess, the Conservative Party would begin to decline very rapidly and the catharsis would have to be increasingly violent.

Nye has made himself chairman of the foreign affairs group. John Hynd has been elected vice-chairman and Tony Benn, Denis Healey and myself members of the steering committee. We had a meeting yesterday to decide the policy line in the Hungary debate on Wednesday. Afterwards Nye sat with me for a long time, having a very friendly drink. I told him something of my experiences in Israel and remarked that one of Ben-Gurion's friends had said that Gaitskell would have made an admirable funeral oration over the dead body of Israel if Israel had not attacked Nasser and permitted itself to be destroyed. 'That's not fair to Gaitskell,' said Nye. 'After all, he did, as you know, write to Ben-Gurion withdrawing that Supplementary Question, accusing Israel of aggression.' This confirmed what I had felt, namely that the Gaitskell–Bevan axis is now pretty firm and is certainly strong enough to survive the extraordinary press campaign which is suggesting that Gaitskell is a nauseating creature and that Bevan is the only man fit to lead the Labour Party. This is perhaps the only thing which has happened while I've been

---

[1] General Raymond Wheeler (1885–1974). An American Army Officer, he was Deputy Supreme Allied Commander, South-East Asia 1944 and Commanding General India/ Burma 1945. He was also an engineer and served in the Indus Basin during the dispute between India and Pakistan 1952–60. His special U.N. assignments included the supervision of the clearance of the Suez Canal 1956–7 and of the operations in the Belgian Congo 1960 and 1963.

away and, curiously enough, it actually, of course, compels Nye to be loyal to Hugh.

Wednesday, December 19th

I lunched today at the House with Elath to tell him all the gossip and found him in tremendous form. While we were talking, Tufton Beamish[1] came over to welcome him. I told Elath that yesterday Hugh Fraser had told me he was the only man worth talking to. 'Strange new friends,' I said. At this moment a Tory called Kerby[2] stepped across and spoke to Elath in Russian. Kerby was the translator for Khrushchev and Bulganin. 'Kerby must have a Russian mother,' Elath said, 'and she must be a Russian Jewess, because [? though] he never told me. Do you know what he told me? He said that Eden's fate was sealed at the 1922 Committee last night but they can't agree on his successor, so he will be allowed to lead them to defeat in the Election and then they will get rid of him.' This, I guess, is a pretty shrewd comment. Since Eden has been back it's pretty clear he isn't going to regain ascendancy. But, on the other hand, the Suez rebels will not take Butler and the Tory progressives will not take Macmillan. There's a terrible sense of collapse and decrepitude. But all the same, it's interesting that Kerby should have said all this to Elath.

[1] Conservative M.P. for the Lewes division of East Sussex 1945–February 1974. He was vice-chairman of the 1922 Committee 1958–74 and chairman of the Conservative Foreign Affairs Committee 1960–4. He was knighted in 1961 and in 1974 became a life peer, taking the title of Lord Chelwood. He was a noted supporter of European federation.

[2] Henry Kerby, Conservative M.P. for the Arundel and Shoreham division of West Sussex from 1954 until his death in 1971. He was a fluent Russian speaker.

1957

Friday, January 4th

For once, not writing has been justified by lack of events. The Session petered out very suitably with a drifting, unsatisfactory debate on collusion, which occurred quite unexpectedly and unintentionally on the motion for the Adjournment. On a Question from Kenneth Younger, the Prime Minister said he would like to say much more about this charge. That, of course, created a row and then, on the adjournment motion which followed, Gaitskell argued that we must hear more and so a three-hour debate took place. It was a pretty unsatisfactory affair and ended not with a bang but with the most protracted whimper by George Wigg that I've ever heard. His speech went on and on and on until any drama the debate had was completely squeezed out and the House settled down to debate the economic situation. Having duly done my column for Friday and learnt that, owing to petrol rationing, which is reducing the size of the *Daily Mirror*, I need do no column until the week after Christmas, we departed by train for Prescote and a quiet week, with some unexpected snow and ice.

On January 9th it was announced from Buckingham Palace that Sir Anthony Eden had submitted his resignation from the premiership. A bulletin signed by four doctors was also published, referring to their anxiety about the health of the former Prime Minister, who had undergone serious abdominal operations in 1953 and, since then, several attacks of fever. On January 11th Sir Anthony announced the resignation of his parliamentary seat; he also declined an earldom, customarily offered to retiring Prime Ministers.

It was widely expected that Sir Anthony's successor would be the Deputy Prime Minister, Mr Butler. After consultation with Conservative elder statesmen, including Sir Winston Churchill and Lord Salisbury, the Queen sent for Mr Macmillan. His appointment was announced on January 10th. This choice led Crossman, as he wrote in the Mirror *on January 11th, to expect a General Election fairly soon. Parliament and the electorate now waited to see what the marks of Mr Macmillan's Government would be.*

In America, too, a new Administration had taken office. Though President Eisenhower had been triumphantly re-elected the previous November, he now faced a Democratic majority in both Houses of Congress. His approach to the problem this presented was expected to emerge in the three regular presidential messages to Congress, customarily delivered in January — on the State of the Union, the Budget and the Economic Report. But, before any of these addresses were given, the President appeared before Congress on January 5th to give a major speech on the principles of his foreign policy — the 'Eisenhower doctrine'.

This was the result of the evident crumbling of British and French authority and prestige in the Middle East and of Western fears that the vacuum would be filled by Russian influence, bolstered with arms and technical advice. American behaviour during the latter months of the Suez crisis, including her strict reliance on the United Nations, might have led other Powers, particularly the Soviet

Union, to conclude that the United States was withdrawing into a non-interventionist, neutralist mood. The new doctrine, assiduously leaked before the President's speech, was designed to dispel such opinion.

In his address the President asked Congress for authorization to enable him, first, to employ the U.S. armed forces 'to secure and protect the territorial integrity and political independence of any [Middle East] nation or group of nations requesting such aid against overt armed aggression from any nation controlled by international Communism'. His second main request was for authority to 'use for the purpose of this resolution, without regard to the provisions of any other law or regulation, a sum not exceeding $200 million from any appropriation now available for carrying out the provisions of the Mutual Security Act of 1954 as amended'.

There was mixed domestic reaction to these proposals but eventually Democratic opposition focused on the argument that the doctrine offered no solution to the major existing problems of the Middle East. The Foreign Affairs Committee of the House of Representatives asked Mr Dulles, testifying before it, what American policy would be if the Communists took over a country by subversion, rather than open aggression. They were told that the United States would not 'invade any country to overthrow its Government, however it gets there', a reply taken to expose a basic weakness in the policy. Nevertheless, on January 24th the House Foreign Affairs Committee approved the doctrine by 24 votes to 2 and on January 30th the whole House approved it by 355 votes to 61.

In the Senate, however, the Administration had a much more difficult time. After six days of testimony before joint sessions of the Senate Armed Services and Foreign Relations Committees, Mr Dulles conceded, first, that Congress should receive fifteen days' advance notice of a proposal to spend any of the $200 million economic and military aid; and, second, that emergency powers for the handling of these funds would expire on June 30th, at the end of the fiscal year. After making extensive verbal changes in the President's original proposals, amendments which put the responsibility for determining the need for assistance squarely on the President himself, the Senate approved the doctrine, by 72 votes to 19, on March 5th. The Senate's revisions were debated in the House two days later and accepted by 350 votes to 6. On March 9th President Eisenhower signed the resolution authorizing his doctrine and announced that he would send the former Republican chairman of the House Foreign Affairs Committee, James P. Richards, as an Ambassador to the Middle East countries to explain its purposes and report on ways of carrying them out.

Elsewhere the President's announcement had been coolly received. In the Soviet Union Mr Khrushchev had predicted that the doctrine would end on 'the garbage heap of history'. In the Middle East only Lebanon was enthusiastic: Syria was hostile and other States disdainful. On January 19th the leaders of Egypt, Syria, Saudi Arabia and Jordan, meeting in Cairo, announced their

agreement to oppose any foreign Powers trying to fill the Middle East vacuum.
If there were such a need, it would be filled by a united Arab nationalist policy.
They would never allow their countries to become a sphere of influence for any
foreign Power.

Crossman was deeply interested in these developments. His other concern,
however, was purely domestic. On July 3rd he had the first meeting, attended by
Professor Richard Titmuss, of his working party on National Superannuation.
This was to be one of his principal preoccupations in 1957.

Friday, January 11th

This week I've been working away at the latest draft of our *Half Pay on
Retirement* and I got the good news from Gerry Reynolds[1] that Dale,[2] the
T.U.C. social services man, has submitted to his sub-committee a completely
fair and neutral report on our recommendations. This means that the T.U.C.
will not be prejudiced against us. It has been quite a job going through
Titmuss's draft page by page and trying to make it intelligible to the layman
without destroying its practical significance. With a thing as complicated as
this, one is never sure that, in simplifying it and making it clear, one isn't
inadvertently glossing over a genuine difficulty or a problem which they have
been trying to tackle, whether successfully or not.

However, I am getting more and more convinced that this is a practical
scheme. I was much tickled to receive a letter from Harold Wilson today,
which confirms this view. He had submitted a section of our report to Gordon
Walker, who is now one of our Shadow Exchequer team, and, in his comment,
Gordon Walker had written that the whole plan was fascinating and had gone
on to say it would be interesting to be the Minister introducing it![3] I suspect
a good many other people will think this when the scheme gets at all known.
My rivals for the job will not be limited to Edith Summerskill, Hilary
Marquand[4] and Peggy Herbison.

Of course, this week's news has been Eden's sudden resignation, the crisis
which succeeded it from seven o'clock on Wednesday night till midday on
Thursday and Macmillan's appointment. From our particular Opposition
angle, the main fact to notice is that Gaitskell was at Harvard, Morgan
Phillips was in Vienna, Nye Bevan, as usual, was with his pigs, having

[1] Gerald Reynolds, Labour M.P. for Islington North from 1958 until his death in 1969.
He was Parliamentary Under-Secretary of State for Defence 1964–5 and Minister of
State for Defence 1965–9.

[2] Clunie Rutherford ('Dick') Dale joined the T.U.C. in 1939 as head of the Social
Insurance and Industrial Welfare Department, serving until his retirement in 1971.

[3] The 'Minister introducing [the scheme]' was to be Crossman himself, in 1970. See *The
Diaries of a Cabinet Minister*, vol. III.

[4] A professor of economics and industrial relations, Marquand was returned as Labour
M.P. for East Cardiff 1945–50 and for the East division of Middlesbrough 1950–61. He
was Secretary for Overseas Trade 1945–7, Paymaster-General 1947–8, Minister of
Pensions 1948–51 and Minister of Health January–October 1951, and was Director of the
International Institute for Labour Studies at Geneva 1961–5 and Deputy Chairman of the
Prices and Incomes Board 1965–8. He died in 1972.

successfully warded off an attack by his parish council on their stench, and Crossman was in Paris lecturing to the NATO Staff College. The one thing Eden has shown a faculty for is secret-keeping. The secret of his resignation was as well kept as the secret of the Suez venture. But already it is fairly clear that his decision to resign was genuinely taken on medical grounds and Hugh Massingham told me last night that he has sound evidence for believing not only that Eden was rapidly becoming incapable of business, but that his medical advisers had given him the gravest report, which indicates that the plastic tube inserted during his operation is wearing away.

This would not prove, however, that Eden was not deposed by a cabal. Yet the curious thing is that all the behaviour up to Thursday seems to indicate that his successor had not been decided on before his resignation was announced and that a genuine crisis took place during that evening and morning, in the course of which Butler was pushed aside and Macmillan substituted for him. Since Winston is gaga, it looks as though Salisbury played the decisive role. I think it is highly significant that *The Times* this morning has a leader which, characteristically, starts by saying one shouldn't speculate or even think about the exact advice proffered to Her Majesty and then proceeds within a few sentences to think very accurately about it and to indicate that her decision was taken only after the most representative advice had been given, which made Macmillan's selection a virtual certainty.

I tried to talk to Bob Boothby but found he was in Monte Carlo, poor man. He no doubt thought this was his last chance for a job and there he is gambling in the South of France. Alec Spearman was in Scarborough and also in blissful ignorance. Indeed, this whole operation has been conducted from the top by a very few people with great speed and skill, so that Butler was outflanked and compelled to surrender almost as quickly as the Egyptians at Sinai.

Labour's reaction was a formal call for a General Election from Gaitskell at Harvard. It's always difficult to make a quick newspaper comment but I think mine was roughly right. A Macmillan Government, must in my view, be a nostalgic Tory Government compared to a Butler Administration. On the other hand, one must observe whether, in selecting the Cabinet, Macmillan takes trouble to bring the Butlerites right in and give them more than their share. If he does this, I must modify my view that Macmillan will prove as phoney an imperialist as Eden and that a crisis will hit him which will make him come unstuck.

The more I think about Suez, the more schizophrenic I become, particularly since my journey to Israel. I think the whole action was utterly disastrous and that it was crazy to do it without consulting the Americans and, even more, to do it on a false pretext. Having said all this, I am still left with the uneasy feeling that I don't want to find myself on the side of inaction against action in an Arab world where our inertia and inability to act has been perhaps our greatest crime. Indeed, perhaps the worst thing about Eden was that his grotesque, ill-conceived, muddled action has effectively discredited all kinds of action by ourselves except a token compliance with the Assembly of the United Nations.

Some of these thoughts became a great deal clearer to me during the discussion period after my lecture at the NATO Staff College in Paris on Wednesday. When you analyse the situation from the narrow, professional point of view of a psychological warrior, you do achieve a useful clarity, particularly on such aspects as Eden's pretext. It is, I think, true that the Suez venture proved that a Western democracy cannot start a war on a pretext, with its Government's real motives concealed, because the result is to spread such confusion that the war cannot be carried on. If Eden had either tried to seize the Canal quite overtly or, alternatively, to overtly come to Israel's assistance as the victim of aggression, which she was, he would have had more chance of completing the operation.

On the other hand, both these actions would have been wrong, the first because a direct attack on the Canal would have been a pure act of aggression, in violation of the Charter, which, once we had referred the affair to U.N., would certainly have involved us in sanctions against ourselves. The second suggestion – overt support for Israel as a victim of aggression – has a lot more to be said for it in terms of British and American public opinion, if it had been prepared for in the previous two months. But it has the fatal objection that, if we had overtly assisted Israel against Egypt, Nuri Said[1] would have fallen in Iraq and we might have lost control of Kuwait as well. Thus one is driven back to the conclusion that there was no action to be undertaken and that all we could do was to patch up an agreement, leaving Nasser in control, and pay more and more danegeld.

That is my conclusion, which I express in the formula that I approve of the Eisenhower doctrine if it means keeping out of the Middle East and treating Arabs like adult Latin Americans, who don't want to be improved or democratized and who must be allowed to have what regimes they like, including neutrality. It is, I think, the policy least unlikely to fail, but the trouble is that it is such an unedifying, dreary, self-interested policy that the British and American people can hardly accept it. I recall a remark of Margaret Mead's[2] when, a few months ago at Patricia Llewelyn-Davies's, she was telling me about the Aramco Company in Saudi Arabia. Dame Margaret was explaining how the Company's servants were forbidden not merely ever to curse an Arab, but ever to try to improve one. 'You know,' she said, 'Americans are idealistic and if you tell them that their job is to get

---

[1] Nuri-es-Said (1886–1958), a leading Iraqi politician, the chief architect of the Baghdad Pact. He was Foreign Minister in a number of short-lived Cabinets 1932–6 and was Prime Minister 1930–2, 1938–40, 1941–4, 1949–52, 1953–7 and from March to May 1958, when he was killed by the mob in the Baghdad rising which also removed King Feisal II and his uncle.

[2] The distinguished American anthropologist, whose *Coming of Age in Samoa* (London: Cape, 1929) pioneered a generation of fieldwork. She died in 1978. She was not a Dame.

the oil and to leave the Arabs stewing in their own juice, they just can't take it.' This, I think, is our trouble in the Middle East as a whole.

Tuesday, January 15th
On Friday I was amazed to hear that the Shadow Cabinet had had a long meeting and issued a communiqué on the constitutional crisis arising from the Queen's decision to summon Macmillan. It's true enough that by resigning before his successor had been determined Eden created a constitutional vacuum, which had to be filled by the Queen's summoning another Tory, theoretically at her own discretion. From what we now know, as a result of Randolph Churchill's *Evening Standard* article and other information, she was fairly fully guided. Immediately after Eden's resignation, a kind of Gallup Poll of the Cabinet was taken, so that, when she took the advice of Churchill, Salisbury and Eden, they were unanimous in saying that the general will of the Tory Party was for Macmillan. One Tory, a newcomer called Iremonger,[1] wrote a letter of protest to *The Times*, but today there were two replies in the *Telegraph* from Tories who said that, before they went off on their Christmas Recess, they sent precautionary letters to the Chief Whip,[2] backing Macmillan!

Whatever the constitutional rights or wrongs, I have very little doubt that, in nominating Macmillan, the Queen not only carries out the wishes of the Establishment but also the general will of the Parliamentary Tory Party. On the other hand, as Nye said to me today, it's probably true that, if the Tory Parliamentary Party had been summoned to vote (as the Labour Party would be in similar circumstances) and had had to vote between Butler, the Deputy Leader, and Macmillan, they might well have selected the Deputy Leader.

All this was discussed by *The Times* in a remarkable leading article,[3] which, as I have learnt with careful talks from Callaghan and Harold Wilson, had been read by Nye before he breezed into the Shadow Cabinet on Friday. With Hugh Gaitskell away, they had expected a quick, easy meeting but Nye was full of the constitutional crisis. Callaghan tells me that Nye first of all said that this should form the subject of our first debate when the Commons resumes. Actually this was ruled out by the Royal Prerogative and there was

[1] Tom Iremonger, Conservative M.P. for Ilford North February 1954–February 1974 and for Redbridge and Ilford North February–September 1974. He was P.P.S. to Sir Fitzroy Maclean as Under-Secretary of State for War 1954–7.
[2] In January 1957 the Conservative Chief Whip was Edward Heath.
[3] Published on January 11th. In a B.B.C. programme broadcast that evening, representatives of each of the three parties were interviewed on the implications of the change of leadership. In Mr Gaitskell's absence abroad the Deputy Leader of the Opposition, Mr Griffiths, said that the Conservatives had 'placed the Crown in a very difficult and embarrassing position', suggesting that, when Parliament reassembled, the Opposition might pursue the matter with a vote of censure. A report of discussions in the Shadow Cabinet, earlier that day, alluded to the difficult situation in which the Queen had found herself, 'one that might involve the Crown in party politics'.

really nothing to debate unless we were to allege that the Queen had made a bad choice. If the Tories choose to have their Leader selected by the Queen, that's their own affair. But Nye's influence was enough to produce this remarkable communiqué, which in my view had only the effect of stopping a real big row inside the Establishment about the method of selection. Once the Labour Party had intervened, everybody felt it was disloyal to continue the controversy.

On Sunday night when we were coming back to London by train from Prescote, we found Mr Ormsby-Gore[1] in the restaurant car. Anne and I had met him at Königswinter last summer and he is a nice young man. He came and had a drink with us after dinner and I said to him, 'Well, are you all right in the reshuffle?'[2] We were talking at about nine o'clock and he knew that I didn't know that the names of the new Cabinet had been given to the press for publication in Monday morning's papers.

Ormsby-Gore almost at once told me that Selwyn Lloyd was still Foreign Secretary and that he was O.K., and so was Commander Noble,[3] at which I expressed some surprise. 'Why has Selwyn stayed?' I asked Ormsby-Gore. 'Oh, he was always absolutely loyal to Harold in recent troubles,' he replied. That interested me a good deal, on reflection, as a reason for Selwyn's staying. I said I had thought there was a chance of Lord Salisbury's taking over and Ormsby-Gore replied, 'No, Bobbety is completely emphatic that it would be totally unsuitable for anybody in the House of Lords to be Foreign Secretary today. He's ruled himself out.'

I made some reference to Eden, to which Ormsby-Gore said, 'You know, by a strange accident, my wife and I were spending our first night at Sandringham as guests of the Queen when Eden turned up unexpectedly to announce his resignation. We all had dinner together.' 'Had Eden told the Queen before dinner?' I asked. 'Yes,' he said, 'he had about forty minutes with her but he made no sign to me that he had said he was resigning. But of course I had a pretty strong impression that he was, though he didn't formally tell me. And afterwards he opened up on the Middle East.' 'How could he have done it,' I said, 'and risk a break with the U.S.A.?' 'It was a terrible shock when it came,' Ormsby-Gore replied. 'He was confident that America couldn't

---

[1] David Ormsby-Gore, Conservative M.P. for the Oswestry division of Shropshire 1950–61. He was P.P.S. to the Minister of State for Foreign Affairs 1951, Parliamentary Under-Secretary of State for Foreign Affairs 1956–7 and Minister of State 1957–61. He was knighted in 1961 and served as Ambassador to Washington 1961–5, during which time he succeeded his father, in 1964, as the 5th Baron Harlech. He was Deputy Leader of the Opposition in the House of Lords 1966–7.

[2] He had been an Under-Secretary of State at the Foreign Office and now became a Minister of State in the same Department.

[3] Commander Allen Noble, Conservative M.P. for Chelsea 1945–59. He was Parliamentary and Financial Secretary of the Admiralty 1951–5, Parliamentary Under-Secretary of State for Commonwealth Relations 1955–6 and Minister of State for Foreign Affairs 1956–9. He led the U.K. delegation to the U.N. General Assembly 1957–8 and was knighted in 1959. He had succeeded Anthony Nutting as Minister of State at the Foreign Office on November 9th, 1956, and remained there until January 16th, 1959

oppose outright something Britain and France had done, especially when it was in conjunction with Israel.' 'That was exactly what infuriated Ike,' I said, 'especially that implication about the Jewish vote.' 'You're right,' said Ormsby-Gore. 'It's easy to see now but I'm sure Eden didn't anticipate outright American opposition. He thought Ike would give us time and also prevent the United Nations being organized so 100 per cent against us.'

We then discussed the whole affair. At one point I said that the only really convincing argument Selwyn Lloyd ever put forward was that, if the Anglo-French intervention had not occurred, Jordan and Syria would have been bound to march against Israel. At this Ormsby-Gore's face lighted with a genuine pleasure. 'Oh, I'm delighted you say that,' he said. 'That was the point I got Selwyn Lloyd to insert in his speech. He said he didn't think it was at all important.' 'How can that be?' I said. 'That seems to be the only good defence the Government had.' 'Well, their minds were fixed on quite different things from that, I assure you,' he replied.

On January 13th the Prime Minister published his appointments to the new Cabinet. Selwyn Lloyd remained Foreign Secretary and R. A. Butler Leader of the House, taking on in addition the office of Home Secretary, on Major Lloyd George's retirement to the House of Lords. Peter Thorneycroft succeeded Mr Macmillan at the Treasury, his former place at the Board of Trade being taken by Sir David Eccles. Duncan Sandys became Minister of Defence, succeeding Anthony Head, who left the Government, and Henry Brooke became Minister of Housing in Mr Sandys's stead.

Sir Percy Mills, a leading industrialist who had assisted Mr Macmillan with his housing drive, was brought into Parliament with a peerage and became Minister of Power, in charge of nuclear development. Lord Salisbury retained his position as Leader of the House of Lords; Lord Kilmuir remained the Lord Chancellor. Alan Lennox-Boyd remained Colonial Secretary, Derick Heathcoat Amory Minister of Agriculture and Iain Macleod Minister of Labour.

The list of junior ministerial appointments was announced on January 18th.

Sir Edward Boyle, who had resigned in protest against the Government's Suez policy, became Parliamentary Secretary at the Ministry of Education (whose Minister, Viscount Hailsham, was in the Lords), while Julian Amery, who had abstained in the vote on withdrawal from Suez, was given a place at the War Office.

On Monday I had to do my piece about the Cabinet changes and realized that, despite Ormsby-Gore's extreme caution, he had inadvertently let me into the secret that Noble and he were staying at the Foreign Office, although only full Cabinet appointments had so far been announced. This shows how difficult it is to be discreet if an Old Etonian meets an Old Wykehamist in the restaurant car of the 7.30 from Banbury. Anne thought he was absolutely charming and he was. Would you believe it? He was reading a beautiful calf-bound edition of Disraeli's *Lothair*, which he found rather overwritten.[1]

Today we had a meeting of the International Sub., which I reached a quarter of an hour late. What was interesting was that, despite Sam Watson's being in the chair, the balance of power in the International has shifted and Nye, on the whole, can get his way in most things, if he wants to and if somebody is there to brief him that a thing is on the agenda. Of course, today he arrived not knowing there was anything on. So it was just like old times, with me as his ghost.

Nye said that he wanted to raise the whole issue of the P.S.I. and the importance of the British Party's intervening to try to achieve the reunification of the Italian Socialists.[2] He gathered that the Socialist International was sending Morgan Phillips as its observer to the P.S.I. Conference this February but he, Nye, felt that more was needed and that the Labour Party should send an observer. (In an awe-inspiringly loud whisper he shouted to me that he wanted to be sent!) There was then a babel, out of which came Sam Watson's voice saying we couldn't possibly discuss this, since we had received no invitation. I pointed out that we all knew that an invitation would be forthcoming on the slightest tip and I asked whether it wouldn't therefore be more candid for us to discuss whether we would recommend the acceptance of an invitation if one arrived. This was regarded as a horrifying proposal, particularly if it should be minuted. So we reached the unminuted conclusion that we were in favour of this. Everybody knew that it meant that I would cable my friends and get an invitation in time for next Wednesday's Executive.

As we went back to Vincent Square for tea with Barbara, Nye denounced Morgan for getting himself invited to all these conferences and complained bitterly that he wasn't invited. But we assured him that for any conference he wanted to attend he would be selected, a pacifying remark which really irritated him because he knew it was true and that he had no more ground for complaint.

Over tea Nye dilated with me on the constitutional issue raised by Macmillan's appointment. When I said we shouldn't put our oar in he indignantly repudiated me. Then, two minutes later, he added that the Establishment had dried up the correspondence in *The Times* and the *Telegraph*. 'There was to be a spate of letters on this, if they hadn't stopped it.' Nye quite failed to see that this proved my point. The correspondence had dried up because the Labour Party had taken the issue over and made it partisan.

[1] Benjamin Disraeli (1804–81) led the Conservatives in the Commons for most of the mid-Victorian period. He rose 'to the top of the greasy pole' and served as Prime Minister 1868 and 1874–80. He became 1st Earl of Beaconsfield in 1878. He wrote a number of novels, including *Coningsby* (London: Colburn, 1844), *Sybil, or The Two Nations* (London: Colburn, 1845) and *Lothair* (London: Longmans, 1870).

[2] The Congress of the Italian Socialist Party, led by Signor Nenni, was to take place in Venice from February 6th to 10th. It was widely thought that, in view of the Soviet Union's action in Hungary, which had caused turmoil in the Italian Communist Party, the Congress might favour breaking with Communism and reunification with the more right-wing Democratic Socialist Party, led by Signor Giuseppe Saragat.

Friday, January 25th

On Sunday Hugh Gaitskell rang up to say he'd like to see me on Monday. He agreed to come to lunch, so I got Sydney along too. Hugh arrived in bouncing form, a little plumper than I have known him and warm with the ovations he'd received in America from coast to coast. It's easy to laugh at this but already two or three people have told me that he did have a spectacular success in the universities he visited. Unfortunately, he'd been forced to break off when his lecture engagements were over and his week in Washington was about to begin.

Hugh spent rather a long time telling us about the American success and about his meetings with Greta Garbo,[1] but it was nice to see him so happy and so apparently unaware that, while his American reputation was soaring, his English reputation was sagging, in comparison with Nye's. I asked Hugh about the Shadow Cabinet's extraordinary meeting, at which the Conservative methods of selecting their Leader were the main object of discussion.[2] He brushed this aside as an obvious error and said he'd issue the kind of statement he thought should be issued after the Shadow Cabinet meeting that afternoon. I thought he seemed rather ambitious but I was wrong. After the meeting the statement was issued roughly as he'd drafted it, so he'd had his way.

Of course the other subject we discussed was Israel and post-Suez.[3] I happened to have done a column saying that Israel was right and I showed it to Hugh. He agreed with every word and added a very sensible sentence, saying that Israel should agree to United Nations forces on her side of the frontier. I vaguely alluded to the contradiction between Hugh's broad support for the Eisenhower doctrine and Nye's heavy attacks on it and he remarked very amicably that they wouldn't very often be so far apart when such big things happen. Altogether he was in confident form, but, even more than before, I got the feeling that there's a streak of naïveté about him and a rather naïve self-importance and enjoyment of the exterior aspects of success. What an outrageously pompous remark to make! We all have that. Yet there's something in it because, though we all have it, it strikes one more strongly in Hugh.

[1] A Swede, born 1905 as Greta Louisa Gustafsson, she starred in many films, including *Mata Hari* 1931, *Grand Hotel* 1932, *Anna Karenina* 1935 and *Ninotchka* 1939.

[2] At a meeting on January 21st the Shadow Cabinet had confined itself to defining the procedure which the Labour Party would follow in circumstances where the Leader, as Prime Minister, resigned. It decided that, before accepting the Sovereign's commission to form a Government, the politician concerned would submit himself to election as Leader of the Party.

[3] Israeli forces continued to occupy the Gaza Strip and the Sharm-el-Sheikh area of the Gulf of Aqaba. In a two-day debate in the United Nations (January 17th–19th) the Israeli Foreign Minister, Mrs Golda Meir, stressed that her Government sought U.N. guarantees against the renewal of Egyptian attacks and the reimposition of the Egyptian blockade in the Gulf and the Straits of Tiran. President Nasser meanwhile declared that, until Israeli troops withdrew, he would not permit British and French ships to pass through the Suez Canal. Crossman's article was published in the *Mirror* on January 22nd.

That afternoon we had a final meeting of our working party on *Half Pay on Retirement*. I agreed to draft the first half of the conclusions. We all ended in tremendous form, before Anne and I went off to see the Polish dancers.[1] That working party really has got a sense of excitement and achievement. The paper is now in the hands of the members of Home Policy, who will discuss it on Tuesday afternoon. I am having the working party to lunch beforehand.

At Wednesday morning's Executive the letter from the Italian Socialist Party duly arrived and Hugh Gaitskell proposed that Nye should go to represent the Party, an amicable arrangement between him and Nye. Morgan tried to scotch this by having Peggy Herbison nominated by Jim Griffiths. Nye seemed quite glad when I said I would like to come too.

Friday, February 1st
The big thing in my life this week was the meeting of the Home Policy Committee on Tuesday afternoon to discuss *H.P.R.* [*Half Pay on Retirement*]. I preceded it with a buffet lunch for Titmuss, Harold Wilson, Hilary Marquand, Jay and Gerry Reynolds, where we decided roughly what each would say at the Committee. This all broke down because Jay and Marquand both had to be on the bench in the Commons and I therefore had to do rather more talking than I expected. Then, too, Titmuss was extremely brief. Moreover, Nye was out of the room for the first hour and Gaitskell for the first hour and a half, so it was a typical Home Policy meeting, with Jim Griffiths in the chair saying very carefully that this was a second reading discussion, that we shouldn't commit ourselves to anything, that we should go to the T.U.C. with an open mind and that afterwards we should have a working party with them. If this advice had been accepted, the whole of seven months' work would have been wasted.

Fortunately, however, the three trade union members of the Committee who were present — Davies of the Steelworkers,[2] Padley of USDAW and Harry Nicholas of the T. & G.[3] — were all fascinated and I had the luck to emphasize in my first speech how *H.P.R.* would produce transferability from job to job. We had no serious criticism but only a number of questions, which proved we had a pretty detailed plan and knew what we were talking about.

Hugh came in towards the end and asked about the financing of it, to

[1] The Warsaw State Dance Company, Nazowsze, opened a visit to London at the Stoll Theatre on January 21st.

[2] David ('Dai') Davies, Assistant General Secretary of the Iron and Steel Trades Confederation 1953–66 and its General Secretary 1967–75. He was Vice-Chairman of the Dock Labour Board 1966–8 and in 1976 became the first Chairman of the Welsh Development Agency. He was knighted in 1973.

[3] Herbert ('Harry') Nicholas became Assistant General Secretary of the T.G.W.U. in 1956 and served in that capacity until 1958. A member of the N.E.C. 1956–64 and from 1967, he was Treasurer of the Labour Party 1960–4 and General Secretary 1968–72. He was knighted in 1970.

which Douglas Jay gave a very good answer. Then I said we must have a decision on whether new entrants would be compelled to join our scheme. Jim tried to evade this and Hugh Gaitskell had just gone out when Nye, who hadn't read the paper, had an instinct that this was the real point and violently backed Titmuss, who, of course, wants compulsion. Nye was singularly brilliant at getting to the point and spotting what was the Left position, to the horror of David Ginsburg. In order to thwart Nye, Jim Griffiths said we'd better take a vote, whereupon there was a unanimous vote for Titmuss, with all the trade unionists on his side on the ground that one can't work without compulsion.

This, of course, is not the end of the matter. I shall have to try to find some formulas which won't put all the banks and insurance companies against us in the next Election. It shouldn't be difficult to do, since, after all, the progressive employer will be able to let us take over his pension scheme and save him the overheads which are giving the unprogressive employer an unfair edge. It is only the unprogressive employer who will be compelled to have pensions for the first time. I was very elated and took the boys down for a drink. There I met Arthur Horner,[1] who said we should negotiate the take-over of their scheme so that they would be able to concentrate on fringe benefits.

Today I had Hugh Massingham here, wanting to be briefed on the scheme, and every time I talked about it he got more fascinated. 'But it changes everything,' he said. 'It solves so many things I thought were insoluble.' 'Well, then, don't mention my name,' I said, 'and don't have any gossip.' 'But there are going to be no names,' Hugh said. 'This is an idea I want to put over' – the first time I've ever heard him believe in anything.

On Thursday I went down to the kick-off of Lewisham by-election[2] and found myself in my usual pleasant and helpful trouble with the Empire Loyalists. The candidate is a sleek young lawyer, an old friend of Kenneth Younger's, typically middle-class, but I expect quite suitable. He talked far too much about Suez, however, whereas this election should be decided on rents and the cost of living, as nobody, at least in that audience, wanted to look back and discuss the merits of Suez. We've settled down again in the most amazing way. Though the whole foundations of the country have been shifted by the earthquake, we are inclined to deny it ever occurred.

From February 6th to 10th Crossman was in Italy, at the Congress of the Italian Socialist Party. As expected, the Congress voted almost unanimously in favour of reunification with the P.S.D.I. but in the voting for the P.S.I. Central

---

[1] General Secretary of the National Union of Mineworkers 1946–59. He died in 1968.

[2] The Conservative Member for North Lewisham, Sir Austin Hudson, had died on November 29th, 1956. In the by-election on February 14th, Niall MacDermot took the seat for Labour with a majority of 1,110 votes over the Conservative candidate, Norman Farmer. There was a 70·8 per cent turn-out and the Labour proportion of the poll rose by 3·5 per cent, the Conservative share dropping by 7·5 per cent.

Committee only some 30 per cent of members wholeheartedly supported Signor Nenni in this policy. Opposition came largely from old Party officials, who feared not only a rupture in working-class unity but also the introduction into the Party hierarchy of new, younger men, which the change in policy would bring. Signor Nenni made it clear that in his view the next move lay with the P.S.D.I. and Signor Saragat, who had become increasingly uncomfortable in supporting the ever more precarious Government coalition.

Thursday, February 14th

My four days in Italy were enormously enjoyable and gay. I enjoyed them more than anything for a very long time, but whether the British intervention was successful or not is a very different question. I had discussed with Nye some time ago whether I shouldn't go out and join him when he was observing the Nenni-ite Conference at Venice for the Labour Party. It was known that Morgan Phillips would also be there for the International and Dino Gentili duly made all arrangements. Then I heard that Nye had decided to start out on Monday via Paris, since he wanted to spend a few of the francs he had earned from articles in *L'Express*. On Tuesday he was proceeding from Paris to Milan by air on his own and thence with Dino to Venice. Only after this expedition did I learn that Morgan had been unable to go on Tuesday because of a vital meeting with the trade union leaders. At this meeting Frank Cousins asked where the Treasurer was, which was slightly awkward, since the Treasurer was gallivanting in Paris, and, after all, his presence in Venice was less essential than Morgan's.

However, Morgan and I didn't get there in time either. We started out on Wednesday morning in an Italian plane which was due at Milan at lunchtime. When we'd nearly got to Geneva, we were told we were going back to Paris because Milan was closed down by fog, and when we got to Paris, about two o'clock, we were told we would be sent by night train to Milan. This meant we would get to Milan at eight o'clock on Thursday morning and then have a four-hour railway journey to Venice on top of this. It also meant — even more grave — that Morgan, whom I had met at the airport, not knowing he was on the plane, would be my companion for a very long time. I didn't know what to do in Paris and then it suddenly occurred to me to take Morgan for a walk.

So from the airport terminal along the bank of the Seine we went for 100 yards and there was the National Assembly. 'Have you ever seen the inside?' I said to Morgan. He's an extremely silent man on such occasions but, when I admitted that I hadn't, I finally found out that he hadn't. So in we went and asked for the Socialist fraction, whose offices we discovered, though it was just slightly embarrassing to admit that we were only visiting them because our aeroplane had broken down! However, I survived the embarrassment and persuaded them to walk us through the Members' libraries, restaurants, etc., and on to the floor, since the Assembly was recessing for twenty minutes.

One Socialist we met on the floor looked at me and said, 'You two are very brave men to visit us.' This was quite an interesting hint of the relationship of the two parties over Suez. The whole atmosphere is much more like the American House of Representatives than the House of Commons and the only thing distinctively French is the superb suite of reception rooms kept by the President of the Assembly.

This filled in time very nicely until we were embussed for the Gare de Lyon, where we found that we were provided with a free meal but were sharing a second-class sleeper. This meant all night with Morgan. The only incident I remember is when he suddenly came out of his shell and told me that his son had just got a classical scholarship to Downing College, Cambridge. Like a fool, I said, 'Classics, Morgan? Be ashamed of yourself! I'm a Classic and the only thing it has taught me is how to write articles in the *Daily Mirror*. A Classic can really express himself accurately.' 'Do you think I don't know that?' said Morgan. 'Do you think it isn't always a terrible thing that we can't express ourselves like you?' This gave me a hint about Morgan's character. I suspect that he feels hurt and injured and takes offence fifty times a day at things which one has no notion will hurt him. He has the acutest inferiority complex.

However, we duly arrived at Venice Station at midday to find Dino meeting us and wafting us into a motor-launch. It was a beautiful winter day. The fog had just lifted as we crossed the Lagoon and as we went up the Grand Canal it was an elegant, pale Canaletto. Morgan had never been to Venice before but he remained stolidly impassive. I did, next day, drag him to St Mark's Square, but he refused to look—I think partly because he didn't want to be caught out being ignorant about it or showing innocent enthusiasm or saying the wrong thing. He was rather the same about the wonderful food and drink we were offered. He would eat practically none of the food, pushing it aside and saying, 'Can't stick any more of this stuff.' He drank steadily—I think mainly to avoid conversation—with the result that he got tiddly by midday and soaked by dinner-time. Observing that I took with me a briefcase and a small suitcase, he said, 'What's all that luggage for? I travel like this.' And he literally had a tiny briefcase for five days. It's no doubt his proletarian snobbery.

What a contrast Nye was! Bland, ebullient, impeccably dressed in his beautiful new suit, fresh white linen, with his handkerchief falling out of his breast pocket, pretentiously discussing the qualities of Italian wine, pretending to knowledge of Venetian architecture, laying down the law about Italian politics with vitality and charm and occasionally with the wildest irresponsibility! If I had been an Italian watching the two, I would have been rather puzzled about the Labour Party.

Morgan and I had, of course, missed the big day, Wednesday. I managed to follow two sessions with the help of an interpreter and noticed that only Nenni was permitted to take a real anti-Soviet imperialist line. The other speakers were very fellow travellerish. Looking down from the gallery of the cinema where the meeting took place, I asked my interpreter how many of the 700 delegates were working-class. 'Not more than 15 per cent,' he said. 'Why not?' I said. 'Well, the working-class can hardly make speeches,' he said, 'or become delegates.' 'What are these then?' 'Oh, lawyers, professional people — and that applies to trade union leaders, too.' This confirms one of my previous impressions — that Italy is still an eighteenth-century country, with an oligarchy and masses really below the level of political articulation.

I also happened to ask my interpreter how the Executive would be elected. He said that there hadn't been very much democracy in the Party for the previous twenty years; the speeches had all been carefully vetted beforehand and the Executive list read aloud by the platform and voted by a show of hands. 'But this year,' he said, 'we shall have a secret ballot, just as our Conference has been much freer this year, with people preparing their own speeches.'

Certainly there was a genuine sense of individualization between the speakers, though little controversy. Indeed, all that happened in the Conference was that, after Nenni spoke, 110 people put in their names and, as long as possible, made half-hour orations. Lombardi,[1] the ablest right-winger, was very effective when he made the point that until events in Hungary they had sincerely believed that it was possible to have a People's Democracy.

Outside the Conference we spent most of our time listening, first of all to people inside the P.S.I. and then to representatives of the Social Democrats, who were present in great strength. On Thursday afternoon Nye held a press conference with some 120 journalists and announced blandly that the International could only recognize one Party and he would rather that they didn't have to choose between the Nenni-ites and the Saragatites. Saragat,[2] in Rome, immediately took this as a threat and through the press there was quite an interchange of persiflage between him and Nye, with constant telephoning going on. Hugh had told me before I left to make sure that Nye went to Rome and we had soon decided that we should go on Friday. Rather mysteriously, Morgan had already decided to leave Venice on Friday afternoon and see Saragat that night, but he altered his plans. We left at midnight on Friday and saw Saragat at ten on Saturday.

The meeting with Saragat was quite an experience. After the press thunders, as we drew up at the office of the Vice-Premier we expected a flaming row. He has grown a good deal plumper since I saw him last and received us with the greatest chill, partly, no doubt, because he had a very bad cold himself.

---

[1] Ivan Matteo Lombardo, Secretary-General of the Partito Socialista Italiano di Unità Proletario 1946. He was a Member of the National Assembly 1948–53 and Minister of Industry and Commerce 1948–9 and of Foreign Trade 1950–1. At this time (1955–67) he was President of the National Productivity Council (C.N.P.).

[2] Giuseppe Saragat, the founder in 1947 of the Italian Workers' Socialist Party (later the Social Democratic Party). He was Deputy Prime Minister 1947–8 and 1954–9, Foreign Secretary 1963–4 and President of the Italian Republic 1964–71. He was Secretary of his Party 1949–54, 1957–64 and in 1976.

But for the first twenty minutes he said almost nothing and left it to us to talk it out, which Nye did very blandly. Then somehow Saragat suddenly came round, made it clear that he regarded fusion as completely inevitable, that there could be no question merely of joint electoral lists, that he would see that his Executive approved fusion next week and that a Congress was held within three months. After this there must be negotiations on the aims, constitution and programme of the new United Party, then one unity Conference before the elections.[1] This programme was outlined very succinctly and unambiguously.

Saragat said that Nenni had made a good speech, in the sense that he really renounced Communism, though his history of the past was ridiculous and his views on foreign policy very wrong, particularly his pleasure in a neutral belt (this was a dig at Nye, who had approved the same idea). When I asked Saragat, however, he said that foreign policy itself would not prevent reunification.

At this point he suddenly said he would like his three Social Democratic colleagues in the Government to meet us too. They were brought in like First, Second and Third Murderers, and placed on stiff chairs in front of us— Romita,[2] a tiny, tough, little working-class corporal; Vitorelli,[3] sleek, and middle-class; and Rossi,[4] a great big, blond, right-wing anti-Communist. Each of them tried to make his position clear to us but each was petulantly interrupted by Saragat, who made it quite clear that they should behave as marionettes under his orders. After this we agreed a communiqué for the press, who were howling outside, and left for lunch with Sir Ashley Clarke.[5]

At the lunch Nye gave a harangue about how out of touch the British people were, after which we took our leave. Nye spent the next hour telling me what ignoramuses they all were at the Embassy. Nye then went off to see Gronchi,[6] who told him all about the evil conspiracies of Saragat to prevent unification, while I went down with Nye's friend Karol[7] from *L'Express*, to

---

[1] Due to take place in 1958, at the end of the Italian Parliament's five-year term.

[2] Pier Luigi Romita has been a member of the Italian Parliament since 1958 and since 1976 Secretary-General of the Partito Socialista Democratica.

[3] Paolo Vitorelli, head of the International Section of the Italian Socialist Party. He later became a Senator and was for a time Editor of *L'Avanti*.

[4] Paolo Rossi, a lawyer. A member of the Social Democratic Parliamentary Group, he became Professor of Law at the University of Pisa and, subsequently, at the University of Genoa.

[5] He entered the Foreign Office in 1925 and rose to become Ambassador to Italy 1953–62. Now living in Venice, he has been since 1970 the Vice-Chairman of the Venice In Peril Fund. Since 1973 he has been a Director of the Royal Academy of Music. He was knighted in 1952.

[6] Giovanni Gronchi (1887–1978), President of the Christian Democratic Parliamentary Group 1946–8, Speaker of the Chamber of Deputies 1948–55 and President of the Republic of Italy 1955–62.

[7] K. S. Karol, a Pole in exile, who wrote regularly for *L'Express* and through whom Bevan also became a contributor. He was described by Michael Foot (*Aneurin Bevan*, London: Davis-Poynter, 1973, vol. II, p. 417, n.1) as 'a leading Socialist authority on Communist affairs'.

walk round St Peter's and to go to the airport to catch the plane to Paris. There we all spent a pleasant, purely private evening, visiting French strip-tease and afterwards dining late. The striptease was extremely professional and Nye held me spellbound at the end by saying, 'That is perfect dancing without a trace of pornography.' There was certainly very little dancing in what I saw. However, we all had a lovely evening, after which I felt it was time to come home. I took the midday plane to London, feeling that we had done quite a job. There was no doubt whatsoever that Saragat was fiercely opposed to unification but the bandwagon was so big that he had to jump on it. It looked as though the presence of Nye and Morgan might have helped by making it clear that the International could not support a mere fractional Social Democracy when the Nenni-ites had genuinely broken with the Kremlin.

It was along this line that I wrote my piece for the *Mirror* on Monday, only to find that night that the election of the Nenni-ites had gone according to the predictions of Blakeway, the former Consul at Bologna, now in charge of press at the Embassy.[1] He had said that he thought there'd be tremendous resistance from all the officials and all the bureaucrats down below, whose jobs depended on a united front with the Communists. Blakeway had fore-seen the refusal of the Party apparat to let itself be purged passively by Nenni. This gave Saragat a chance to denounce the conversion of the Nenni-ites as insincere. All one can now say for certain is that the chance of striking while the iron is hot and having a rapid unification is almost gone.

On Tuesday night we had a meeting of the foreign affairs group, with Nye in the chair. At the end there were a few minutes to spare and somebody asked for a report on Italy. The net impression in the British press was that Nye had intervened and had a row with Saragat. But Nye gave a most brilliant and amusing account, which made everything look perfect and the group went away delighted.

Of course the other really big event for me was the meeting yesterday between our Labour Party deputation and the T.U.C. Social Services Committee. I had taken the trouble to have Miss Godwin[2] of the Clerical Workers to lunch on Monday and George Woodcock[3] to lunch on Tuesday. George Woodcock amazed my by saying it was a first-rate paper and a first-rate scheme, which ought to be accepted. When I met him, at the House, I told him we might be lunching in the same room as Gaitskell, Morgan and Roberts. 'Oh, Alf can't see me with you,' George said, so we had to rush out and hide ourselves. George didn't know whether Sir Alfred was still adamant but he told me that, once he accepted the principle of differential

[1] John D. Blakeway. He joined the Foreign Service in 1946, rising to become Consul-General at Istanbul in 1975 and serving in that capacity until his retirement in 1978.

[2] Anne Godwin, General Secretary of the Clerical and Administrative Workers' Union from 1956 until 1962, when she became a D.B.E.

[3] Secretary to the T.U.C. Research and Economic Department 1936–47, Assistant General Secretary 1947–60 and General Secretary of the T.U.C. 1960–9. He died in 1979.

19

contributions, everything was in the bag. We should only know that next day. George couldn't have been friendlier or warmer and I think he was genuinely impressed by the paper. That evening Gaitskell told me that his lunch with Roberts had been equally successful and that Roberts seemed quite impressed by the scheme.

So at ten o'clock on Wednesday we assembled in Room 11, or rather, the N.E.C. delegation assembled — our officials, then Gaitskell, Nye, Harold Wilson with Harry Nicholas of the T. & G. and Walter Padley of USDAW, plus Marquand and Jay. We really had nothing to discuss and filled in until half-past ten, when the sixteen-odd T.U.C. filed solemnly in to do battle. We had made careful preparations to arrange the agenda in the way they liked, whereupon Sir Alfred reversed the order. We had also made preparations about which of us should speak on pensions, but Sir Alfred, when we came to it, wanted nobody to speak, so there was my speech wasted, with nothing but questions. However, it all went wonderfully because he started by saying the paper was extremely good, full of clever ideas, which would solve a lot of their problems. Characteristically, his first big question was about our calculation of the Exchequer liability in 1980! There was no question on the differential principle, which seems to have been swallowed. Now the experts among us are to submit ourselves to cross-examination by Sir Alfred and his colleagues. I think we are through the worst — apart from the writing.

Friday, March 29th
Since I last wrote in this diary, I have amassed sufficient material to write a thesis entitled 'Problems of Policy Formulation Inside a Social Democratic Leadership'! I can look back with an ironical amusement at the cheerfulness I felt when we received the broad approval of the T.U.C. Social Services Committee for our draft. That is a hurdle so far behind that I can scarcely remember it. The next stage was a meeting of the Working Party at which my draft was discussed. I had fallen ill with a bout of virus flu, which was a merciful deliverance, since it gave me a chance to write, and in the course of three and a half days I had sketched out the first two chapters of a new, readable, popular version, as well as the general framework of the rest of the draft.

After the working party meeting, I began to realize that we should have no adequately thought-out solution in time for the Home Policy Committee on April 8th. I therefore persuaded Hugh Gaitskell to call a meeting which would be attended by him, Harold Wilson and Patrick Gordon Walker from the Party's financial experts on the one hand, and by a working party drafting committee on the other. As it was, Harold Wilson failed to turn up and Hugh Gaitskell hadn't had time to read the document, though he had been in to see me the night before and I had been able to fill him in on one or two of the issues. But here you get to the difficulty. Gaitskell is now doing so much that he is in a continual flap about urgent little nagging problems which have to be resolved. He cannot sit down and easily discuss with one the basic outline of a thing like National Superannuation. The difficulty about his views, which were very quick-witted and intelligent, is that they were views which Marquand and I held six months ago at an early stage in our investigations but which we had since had to modify.

The evening was rather difficult and I was much relieved that in the face of this pressure Titmuss and Abel-Smith[1] restrained themselves. It was also very difficult that Harold Wilson wasn't there, since I knew we should have to go through the whole business at the proper meeting the next day. Our difficulties were made much worse by Douglas Jay, who throughout repeated his view that anyway we should publish nothing definite. However, I wasn't unduly depressed owing to a lunch which Alec Spearman had arranged for me with six of the highest-powered actuaries in the City. We had lunched in a lovely room at the top of a building overlooking the old Roman wall and Temple of Mithras, on a splendid spring day with gigantic storm clouds, brilliant sunshine and a vast view.

I learnt a tremendous lot from the actuaries. Redington,[2] their leader, said, 'Of course, most of the employers will wind up their own schemes and join yours and then add fringe benefits on top in order to hold their staffs.' This was a thought I myself had had some months ago but I had been told by all our experts that it was a silly idea. Maybe it isn't so silly. But another thing I learnt was the most important. 'By the way, who's going to invest all these savings for you,' asked Redington, 'and how much will they be?' I replied that I hoped we should have between £180 million and £200 million of new savings every year. 'Do you realize how much that is?' he said. 'It's over three times as much as the Pru[3] has to invest and the Pru has as much as all the rest put together. Why, you'll own the country in ten years at that rate!' 'As a Socialist, you know,' I replied, 'I cannot accept that as a final argument against the National Pensions Fund.' 'But you don't expect us to accept it?' he said. 'No,' I said, 'but I expect you, in the national interest, to welcome a Party which makes a genuine attempt to reduce consumption by increasing national savings and using those increased savings for capital investment.'

I repeated this conversation at Hugh's meeting. It was clear that both he and Harold were enormously attracted by the idea of a National Pensions Fund run by Government-appointed trustees, with the right to invest in

[1] Brian Abel-Smith, a Lecturer at the London School of Economics in 1957, who became a Reader in the University of London 1961 and since 1965 has been Professor of Social Administration at the London School of Economics. He worked closely with Crossman, who brought him into the Department of Health and Social Security. He served there as Senior Adviser 1968–70 and 1974–9. His publications include *A History of the Nursing Profession* (London: Heinemann, 1960), *The Hospitals 1800–1948* (London: Heinemann, 1965) and *Value for Money in Health Services* (London: Heinemann, 1976).

[2] Frank Redington, Chief Actuary of the Prudential Assurance Co. Ltd 1950–68 and President of the Institute of Actuaries 1958–60.

[3] The Prudential Assurance Co. Ltd.

equities as well as gilt-edged securities. The reason they like it is the new policy statement on nationalization,[1] which has accepted Hugh's philosophy that the road to further nationalization lies through the buying up of equity shares through great public companies. What a delicious discovery—that, in the course of getting a decent pensions plan, we shall have evolved by far the most efficient and unobjectionable machine for buying up equities! Brian Abel-Smith is a bit alarmed about this. Won't people be afraid, he says, of the charge that the Labour Government is gambling with the savings for their old age pensions? Won't our trustees have to be over-cautious and therefore unsuccessful in their investment policy? Douglas Jay has another objection. Since we have to publish our accounts, he says, won't people see the hundreds of millions in the Fund and ask for increased old age pensions? To this, Hugh and Harold reply that anyway we have a Budget surplus and it is easier to defend not raiding a Pension Fund than it is to defend amassing a huge Budget surplus instead of reducing taxation.

After this meeting with Hugh last Friday I went down to Coventry, where a typical mess-up had occurred, which I really can't bother to write about here, because it merely shows that Coventry is as anarchically, parochially against itself as it always has been. Hugh was addressing a dinner there, and I had agreed to take him back to Prescote for the night. After my own dinner I found him at a dance in the Drill Hall, rocking and rolling with Pearl Hyde.[2] He loves dancing and thank God he does, because I gather the loss on the dance was £250 and the only justification for it is that all our left-wingers will now be in love with our right-wing Leader.

It was a perfect spring morning at Prescote on Saturday and we walked Hugh up over the fields to Upper Prescote, in which he showed no real interest. I had forgotten that he's a passionate gardener with no interest in farming and, once he had seen that our garden was in a scandalous mess, he couldn't help feeling contemptuous. However, I did manage to talk to him a little about the draft. I found him insistent on modifying the paragraphs on inflation-proofing the pension and he was also saying that, in view of Douglas's remarks, the whole thing should be put forward as a working party report and not an Executive policy statement. Of course, in this he was being tacitly supported by the three young men from Transport House. However hard I work on them, I don't convert them. They resent working hard for me and they are an obstacle to any idea.

However, I tried this week to do all the changes Hugh required in the draft, only to find, as one might expect, that Hilary Marquand and Brian Abel-Smith were at once up in arms, saying that the working party wouldn't tolerate it. In desperation, I finally got Harold Wilson and Marquand

[1] *Industry and Society*, published in July 1956 and discussed at that year's Party Conference.
[2] She was elected to Coventry City Council in 1937 and became an Alderman in 1952. She was Coventry's first lady Lord Mayor May 1957–May 1958; she was killed in a road accident in 1963.

together to dinner last night and Harold turned up trumps. To my annoyance, having said he was coming early, he arrived forty-five minutes late, but he melted my heart when he explained that this was because he had been with his secretary,[1] who had just had a nervous breakdown. He had spent twenty minutes on the phone with her husband. All this was really endearing, since afterwards he said, 'Take my mind off her, for God's sake, by discussing pensions.' So I did.

Harold was infinitely quicker and shrewder than Hugh. 'Why does Hugh fuss about those inflation-proof bits?' Harold said. 'There will be no financial liabilities under it for ten years and it's good in itself.' He quickly agreed with me the paragraphs dealing with financial cost, suggested we should have an alternative draft on inflation-proofing and then threw out an idea: 'I suppose you've thought of it before, but why not have the first three chapters as a Party statement, with an Appendix signed by Titmuss, Abel-Smith and Townsend.[2] We shall get all the kudos for their research and they will have to be responsible for all the detailed figures.' Deliverance indeed! But when, this morning, I put this to Transport House, they fought me for an hour. However, in two minutes, at one o'clock, Hugh Gaitskell agreed. Abel-Smith and Townsend are all right, Titmuss has been written to and now we are on the road again, though heaven knows how many more obstacles we shall have.

I am now an obsessed man and, curiously enough, in the Commons this raises my status, since I now need do no work on any other subject. Everyone knows I am cooking this wonderful vote-winner. I hope to God it is.

Wednesday, May 1st

This seems to be becoming a monthly, not a diary—having glanced at my last entry, I can only repeat that I am certainly an obsessed man. 'Heaven knows how many more obstacles we shall have,' I wrote on March 29th. Well, there were quite a number, but I think—repeat think—I can say that after this morning there should be no more major obstacles before publication.

The pensions plan had to go first through the Home Policy Committee on the afternoon of April 8th and then through the National Executive on the morning of Wednesday, the 17th. I had been at Königswinter that weekend and I specially arranged to catch the Rheingold Express at half-past seven on Sunday evening in order to be sure of arriving in time for the committee. Having cleared everything, as I thought, with Hugh and Harold,

[1] Marcia Williams, personal and political secretary to Harold Wilson since October 1956. She was married to George Williams 1955–60. In 1974 she became a life peeress, taking the title of Baroness Falkender. Her account of her work in Government appears in *Inside No. 10* (London: Weidenfeld & Nicolson, 1972).

[2] Peter Townsend, a Research Fellow, and later Lecturer, in Social Administration at the L.S.E. 1957–63 and since that date Professor of Sociology at the University of Essex. His first work, *The Family Life of Old People* (London: Routledge & Kegan Paul) was published in 1957 and in 1979 he published *Poverty in the United Kingdom* (Allen Lane).

I had assumed that we should have a fairly light passage in the Home Policy Committee and that it would be eager members of the Executive who would raise objections. How I misjudged my colleagues! Barbara Castle hadn't had time to read it and anyway was grateful to me for helping her to become the *Pictorial* columnist.[1] So, having asked one or two questions, she went out after half an hour. Tony Greenwood was jealous but, despite very great efforts, had failed to read the scheme through because his mind isn't up to it, as it never has been since he worked hard for a Third at Oxford. Ian Mikardo had read it, knew something about it, made one or two quite good offhand comments and disappeared after an hour. Harry Nicholas and Walter Padley had both been briefed on it by somebody in their Union and were O.K. except for a worry about how much it would cost. That really left Harold Wilson and Hugh Gaitskell.

To my amazement, Hugh began to go through the draft as though he were a drafting committee of one, making all sorts of minor changes, which was silly, and trying to go back on the agreements he had made with me, which was worse than silly. For nearly three hours, from a quarter past four until seven, I fought him, and at the end Brian Abel-Smith said, 'Well, you gave nothing away,' and I don't think I had. I think the trade unionists there – and by midway there must have been sixteen people present – were a bit baffled at this exhibition of intellectual shadow-boxing. They would have been much more baffled had they known that Gaitskell had spent hours with me beforehand on the drafts. There was one moment when Nicholas asked about the cost. Before I could say a word, Harold Wilson jumped in. 'As Shadow Chancellor,' he said, 'I have had to consider that and I can tell you there is a net saving on the scheme for the next twenty years and that's all you need to know.' He proved himself an absolutely loyal ally throughout.

Between the Home Policy and the Executive a good deal of redrafting had to be done, not to mention consultations with the working party, who I got together for a special meeting which kept Hilary Marquand and Douglas Jay in support. Simultaneously I had to keep the peace between Transport House and the L.S.E. experts, who really are like cats and dogs, the L.S.E. being the cats and Transport House being dull dogs at best.

At the National Executive over half those present had not been at the Home Policy or any previous meeting, so I had to explain the scheme to them in principle. Once again it was clear that nobody had bothered to read it and once again I was left with Hugh and Harold as the only people who understood. Once again Harold was 100 per cent a loyal ally. Hugh was fighting a rearguard action for somebody else, who has been advising him to be careful about this extreme scheme. Finally, in a burst of spontaneous indignation, I exclaimed, 'It really isn't tolerable for the Leader to be playing politics in this way with the finances of our scheme!' There was a ripple of extremely natural laughter all around the Executive, because I hadn't quite

[1] Barbara Castle wrote a regular column in 1957.

realized what I'd said after I had said it and yet, on the other hand, I had obviously said the truth. It was agreed that all the redrafting and final drafting and O.K.-ing of the technical sub-committee's appendix, as well as the writing of a new preface, should be left to me, Jim Griffiths and Harold Wilson, and the Executive went on to other business.

Since then, there have been many more alarums and excursions than I would like. I found in the end, after a weekend working on the proofs, that I had some five foolscap pages of amendments, which I had worked out with Abel-Smith and Townsend, whom by now I have got to know very well. Abel-Smith is said to be thirty-eighth in succession to the Throne, while Peter Townsend tells me that he spent his youth going round each summer to the seaside piers, where his mother was a pierrette. Peter has done three years studying old age and poverty in Bethnal Green, while Abel-Smith is the intellectual who works out all the mathematical formulae. The relationship between them and my three Transport House men is fascinating because it is the same relationship as that between the public school intellectuals and the secondary school intellectuals in the Parliamentary Party. Each is intensely suspicious of the other.

Friday, May 3rd
However, when the drafting committee met this Tuesday morning, everything was accepted and agreed. Once again Harold Wilson was in great form. I had rung him the night before and warned him that I would have pages of amendments. He had gone on reading our thing until half-past two in the morning. He helped me through with the amendments but, much more important, he made one or two extremely good suggestions. He has the quickest brain I know and the most fertile with expedients, though I admit the expedients seem rather better at the time than they do two days later. Even so, they are better than anyone else's. It was owing to Harold that we at last realized that our Paragraph 17, on making the scheme inflation-proof, had got the emphasis all wrong by describing our device as an anti-inflation measure when it is really a measure to ensure the pensioner his increasing share in an increasing national cake. By this afternoon the page proofs will be cleared and then it will be too late for anyone to do anything about it.

Looking back at this whole job, I feel I can now write a sociological study of policy-making inside the Labour Party. But then, is this a normal example? Certainly not. Normally what has happened, at least since I've been on the N.E.C., is that the office prepares a draft, which is discussed by people who haven't had much time to read it, and then the draft is redrafted and redrafted in the light of these informal discussions between busy men, with somebody like Hugh Gaitskell in the background, advising the officials on the sort of draft he wants. This has meant that absolutely no original research or new idea is possible, since the officials simply haven't the time or ability to have new ideas and can't be blamed for that.

What is unique about this document of ours is that it is, by political standards, new. Of course, none of the ideas in it are brand-new, since they are borrowed from Sweden or Germany. All the same, there is an attempt to have a new approach to the pensions problem, which is post-Keynesian. On reflection, I see that the really original concept is that of a rapidly expanding economy, in which the pensioner will always be left behind not merely by prices rising owing to inflation, but by wage increases related to real increases of the national income. 'In ten years' time,' Harold Wilson remarked at the N.E.C., 'the National Assistance Board will be instructed to provide television sets to all applicants.' That is the way standards rise. This plan of ours is an attempt to make sure that the old people get their share of the rise automatically and are not merely jerked up out of the slough by political pressure every now and then.

How has so much of this been incorporated in the draft? The answer is perfectly clear to me. We have merely taken the ideas of Titmuss, Abel-Smith and Townsend. They have provided all the dynamic, with genuine assistance from Marquand and a sort of haphazard assistance from Jay, with fairly sturdy opposition from Transport House and with my backing the Titmuss boys because I had a hunch it would work. But it would give quite a false impression to say that we borrowed Titmuss's ideas ready-made. The striking fact, looking back, is how un-ready-made Titmuss's ideas were when he was challenged to cook up a scheme. Suddenly he and Abel-Smith discovered that they hadn't the answers to half a dozen major problems. What has happened, therefore, is that, by making them members of the working party, one has accelerated the development of their thought by about ten years. Without their sitting on this working party, they just wouldn't have had to solve all these problems because, as academics, they haven't got to provide a finished working plan. So for them too this has been a tremendous education, to see the relationship between real politics and their academic study of social services. Right up to the last moment, I was catching Abel-Smith out with unsolved problems in their own working model at the end of our report. And still the scheme is only three-quarters-baked – but then it can't get baked any more without public discussion.

What we can hope to do, in fact, is to have the effect of a Beveridge Report.[1] But can we? The Beveridge Report was an all-party document, or,

---

[1] In June 1941 the Government established a Committee, with the Liberal M.P. Sir William Beveridge as chairman, to study social insurance and allied services. The report of the Committee, Cmd 6404, was published in November 1942, and in September 1944 the Government published a White Paper based on its proposals for a compulsory universal scheme of national insurance, family allowances, sickness, invalidity, unemployment and maternity benefits, grants for industrial training and pensions for widows and the retired. Lord Beveridge himself had a distinguished career in the Civil Service, after which he became Director-General of the L.S.E. 1919–37. He was Master of University College, Oxford, 1937–45 and represented Berwick-upon-Tweed 1944–5. His Report was hailed as the foundation-stone of postwar Labour social policy. A *Life* of Beveridge by José Harris was published by the Oxford University Press in 1977.

rather, was a Beveridge document which, when it was successful, the parties didn't dare to oppose and the Coalition vaguely adopted. Our document will be launched as a Labour Party Socialist document and whether it is implemented will depend quite a lot on the Conservative reaction.

We know that the Ministry of Pensions is hard at work producing a Conservative pensions policy and I learnt at Königswinter from young Kirk,[1] a very nice Tory journalist who replaced Dick Acland at Gravesend, that their Party committee is busy at work. 'We are a year behind you,' he said, 'and we have just reached a point where we've realized it's got to be compulsory.' Brian Abel-Smith hasn't been able to get any positive information from his contact with the officials of the Ministry, except a leak that they may be increasing the pension by 3s. to cover recent rises in the cost of living.[2]

I happened to be at the Cambridge Union on Tuesday, debating with Enoch Powell, and I devoted a good deal of my speech to National Super-annuation. Talking informally afterwards, I found him looking passionately interested and bewildered when I said that our scheme would produce net National Savings. 'Surely it won't?' he said. 'You'll be having to pay the pensions.' 'No,' I said, 'there will be net savings.' 'No, really?' he said. 'Then the contributions will be very high.' 'Yes,' I said, 'our aim is to make people sacrifice present consumption.' I could see that this had taken Powell absolutely by surprise. Apparently the Tories had assumed, as *The Economist* had assumed, that we would make an attempt to bribe the electorate with high benefits and low contributions.

Now what will the Tories do when the scheme is launched? Intrinsically, there is no reason whatsoever why Macmillan shouldn't borrow the scheme virtually complete, except for the fact that it enlarges the domain of State control of finance and poaches on the preserves of the insurance companies. In that case the Tories are bound to denounce it as flagrant Socialism and try to disprove all the assurances we have given that the scheme is financially sound. That will make it infinitely more difficult to get National Super-annuation across than it was to launch National Insurance, which was virtually bipartisan.

Going back to the question I started from, I can claim to have proved it is possible to make the Labour Party adopt a new policy, provided you have people outside Transport House to do all the thinking, provided you do all the writing yourself and that you get your Shadow Chancellor on your side, and—most important of all—provided that nine-tenths of the Executive don't bother to read anything. How the Party outside will react to a new idea I don't venture to think. I suppose the answer is that, if it goes over well, they will like it and, if it goes over badly, we shall get the blame for a disaster.

[1] Peter Kirk, Conservative M.P. for the Gravesend division of Kent 1955–64 and for Saffron Walden from March 1965 until his death in 1977. He was Parliamentary Under-Secretary of State for Defence 1963–4 and 1970–2. From 1973 he led the Conservative delegation to the European Parliament. He was knighted in 1976.

[2] This did not occur.

But that's reasonable enough. So far we've been able to inspire the press to be pretty friendly and I think we shall find that the first press reaction will be cautious until they see how the Government's mind is going.

On February 11th it had been announced that the Prime Minister was to meet President Eisenhower at Bermuda, for an Anglo-American conference. On March 19th the Prime Minister, the Foreign Secretary and their officials had left Britain for the meeting, which began on March 21st and was followed by an Anglo-Canadian conference. It was hoped that the Bermuda discussions would heal the recent differences within the Atlantic alliance, especially since Mr Macmillan and President Eisenhower had been close colleagues in North Africa during the latter part of the Second World War.

The communiqué published at the end of the conference, on March 24th, promised co-ordination of the two countries' foreign policies, but, of the eleven points on which 'agreements and conclusions' were reached, only three gave definite undertakings: the United States Government would 'participate actively' in the work of the military committee of the Baghdad Pact; both Governments would continue nuclear tests; and the U.S. Government would make available certain guided missiles for the use of the British forces. No conclusions were reached on the Suez Canal and the problem of Palestine.

The Prime Minister had returned to domestic difficulties within the Conservative Party, provoked by the Government's latest action in the Cyprus disputes. On March 14th leaflets signed by EOKA leaders had been distributed in Nicosia, offering to suspend all terrorist operations as soon as Archbishop Makarios was released from the Seychelles. On March 20th Mr Lennox-Boyd had told the Commons that the Secretary-General of NATO, Lord Ismay, had offered to assist with conciliation on the Cyprus question and that the Government had decided to accept. After various exchanges between the Government and the Archbishop, whose attitude remained ambiguous, the Archbishop had been released on March 28th. This decision had led to the immediate resignation of Lord Salisbury, whose place as Leader of the House of Lords was taken by the Earl of Home.

The Prime Minister had been expected to show his reaction to this event in a Commons debate on April 1st, when the Bermuda Conference was to be discussed. Opening the debate, Mr Macmillan had first stated that no secret undertaking had been made at Bermuda and then had spent the greater part of his time explaining the need for Britain to carry out a series of nuclear tests in the Pacific. This subject was one on which the Opposition was split, as it had demonstrated after a recent broadcast by George Brown, the Party's defence spokesman, who had supported the tests.

The Government had scored a further success with the Budget, presented by Mr Thorneycroft on April 9th. He had announced more than £130 million of tax relief, including the removal of the extra 1s. of petrol duty imposed the previous November. Surtax payers were to have their two-ninths earned income allowance limit raised from £2,000 to £4,000; the limit was then to be one-ninth up to £10,000. Personal allowances (e.g. for children) other than the single man's allowance were henceforth to count in calculating surtax.

The child allowance was to be raised from £100 to £125 for children over twelve and to £150 for children over seventeen still receiving full-time education or apprenticed. Income tax exemption for single persons over sixty-five was to be raised to £250 and to £400 for married couples, where either was over sixty-five. The income limit up to which the elderly would qualify for such relief was to be raised from £600 to £700.

Purchase tax was to be reduced from 30 to 15 per cent on hardware, kitchen, table and toilet ware, cutlery, some furniture and domestic appliances and various floor coverings. Overseas trade corporations, other than shipping, banking and insurance, were exempted from income tax and profits tax. (This relief amounted to £35 million.) Investment allowances on new ships were raised from 20 to 40 per cent. Entertainment duty was abolished on sport and the live theatre; reductions in duty on cinemas were to be offset by an increase from £3 to £4 in the annual television licence fee. The Opposition had protested that the Budget neglected the poor and did nothing for pensioners. On the last day of the Budget debate, April 15th, they had divided the House; the Government had secured a majority by 317 votes to 252.

Five days before Budget Day the Government's White Paper on defence (Cmnd 124) had been published and on April 16th and 17th it had been discussed in the House of Commons. It had been announced earlier in the year that the Government intended to reduce expenditure and manpower; the changes now set out were intended to completely reshape the Armed Services over the next five years. There was to be no further call-up of National Servicemen after the end of 1960 and by the end of 1962 the forces, wholly Regular, would be cut from the current size of 690,000 men to about 375,000. Defence expenditure that year would be pared by about £78·5 million.

Fighter command was to be substantially reduced and its role limited to defending bomber bases. In due course fighter aircraft were to be replaced by a ground-to-air guided missile system, with V-class bombers being supplemented by ballistic rockets, initially of American manufacture. The supersonic bomber project was to be abandoned. Britain would continue to develop ballistic missiles and nuclear bombs and warheads. The Government had stated that, since Britain could not be adequately protected against nuclear attack, the overriding principle must be to prevent war.

Army manpower would be reduced, largely by curtailing its overseas commitments and establishing a central reserve at home. During the course of the year the British Army of the Rhine was to be cut from 77,000 to 64,000 men, while the number of aircraft in the tactical air force in Germany was to be halved. (It had been announced on March 3rd that the Anglo-German economic committee in Bonn had agreed that Germany's offset payments for the current year would

*now be some £50 million, rather than the maximum of £34 million on which
Germany had earlier fixed.)*

*The Navy's contribution included the scrapping or disposal of many ships in
reserve, including four battleships, and a reduction in NATO support. The nine
cruisers of the active fleet were to be replaced in due course by the three* Tiger
*class cruisers under construction. British naval strength east of Suez was to
remain at about its current level but was henceforth to be based mainly on a
small number of aircraft-carrier groups.*

*The new plan, the Prime Minister had said, would give smaller but more
efficient forces, 'more mobile, better trained, and better equipped'. 'But,' he
had added, 'all this depends upon our readiness to base ourselves on the deterrent
power of nuclear armament.'*

*These were the main events of the first months of the new Government, as
Crossman summed them up at the beginning of May.*

April was politically one of the most interesting months since I entered
Parliament. Looking back now, I realize much more than I did at the time
that in February the Government was on the very edge of disaster. It was
touch and go whether they would throw their hand in and have the kind of
General Election which Attlee had in October 1951. Macmillan hadn't yet
asserted his leadership, there were terrible divisions, feuds and uncertainties
and the Labour Party was doing extremely well. And then, in the course of
April, the whole situation quietly transformed itself.

Curiously enough, I can date the transformation from the moment when,
one Saturday morning, Anne's father said to me at Prescote that Lord
Salisbury had resigned on the issue of Cyprus. We were all flabbergasted.
Was this the final blow to the Macmillan Government? Over the weekend,
it looked just like this and there was poor Macmillan faced with a major
debate on the Bermuda Conference for Monday afternoon. Yet that debate
turned out to be the moment when he consolidated his leadership and stopped
the collapse of the Tory Government. He made his speech without mentioning Salisbury, and he chose to give a learned scientific disquisition on the
H-bomb tests, which inveigled Gaitskell into argument on the one subject
where the Government was united and the Labour Party disunited. It had
been realized in the previous week that the Party was disunited on H-bomb
tests and at the Thursday evening Meeting, which I didn't attend, there was a
great demand made that the Labour Party should come out insisting on the
postponement of the British test. This threatened to start the Bevanite defence
split all over again. Hugh pacified the meeting by saying there should be a
Party Meeting next week to decide the policy and that meanwhile everybody
should exercise discretion over the weekend.

Of course, I didn't know this when, in the kitchen at Prescote, I saw George
Brown's television performance, in which he urged that we must test our own
British H-bomb, so that, if the Russians sent submarines to attack us, we

should be able to nuclearize them, even if the Americans weren't prepared to. The television performance was terribly brash anyway but of course, in view of what had been agreed on the previous Thursday, it was intolerable provocation. Again being wise after the event, I realize now that Gaitskell should have accepted Brown's resignation from his Shadow Defence Ministry on the following Monday. But Gaitskell didn't and there followed the effort to maintain the Party policy on H-bomb tests without a concession to the Left.

Before all that, though, there came the Monday debate. Here was Macmillan, with Salisbury just resigned and yet, so far from being broken or depressed, the Prime Minister was cool, collected, complete master of the House, playing Gaitskell as an angler plays a young, inexperienced trout. That was the beginning of the turn of the tide for the Tories. By a strange accident, Nye left for India at this precise moment and only got back when the transformation had already taken place. But more of that later.

The second stage of the Tory come-back was the Defence White Paper and the defence debate after the Budget. The Budget, by the way, had been a fairly even drawn battle, soon forgotten. But in the Defence White Paper debate Macmillan once again asserted, through Sandys, an obvious ability to make bold decisions and stand by them. The Labour Party entered that two-day debate only too obviously aware that, instead of attacking the Government, it must entirely concentrate on keeping its unity. That was achieved by an odious performance from Mr Brown, quoting Passion Week and 'Father, forgive them' and revelling in our disagreement as the sign of our morality. It was a good enough defensive tactic but it meant that we were no longer attacking a weak Government. On the contrary, there was a strong Government, with a strong defence policy and a weak, indecisive Opposition.

The more I think about the Government's defence policy, the more utterly reckless I think it is. All this should have given the Opposition an enormous opportunity and at least caused a great debate on a great issue. But actually the poor old Labour Party could only debate its own internal moral problems. I think I can claim that the only person who really rattled the Government was me, with interjections about atomic tactical weapons which, for a moment, had Duncan Sandys looking really embarrassed.[1]

The only fly in Macmillan's ointment has been Suez. All last week and all this week it has been prophesied day by day that British ships will go through the Canal on Nasser's outrageous terms. But it hasn't been as easy as some people thought to get an agreement in the Users' Association. There is no doubt that this is something really odious to the Tory mind, since Macmillan

---

[1] On the first day of the debate, Crossman interrupted Duncan Sandys to ask whether the Minister of Defence was suggesting that 'a non-major effort by a Russian satellite, shall we say Germany, could be repelled with atomic tactical weapons without involving us all in a nuclear war' and whether it was now the view of the Government that we should 'rely on atomic tactical weapons to counterbalance Russian conventional weapons'.

was just as deeply committed as Eden and so was Selwyn Lloyd. Of course, you would have thought that the demonstration over the last fortnight of the Eisenhower doctrine, with the American Sixth Fleet backing up what used to be Britain's Protectorate in Jordan, would cause the Tories some anxiety.[1] Macmillan is really dismantling the Empire far more rapidly than Eden. Kenneth Robinson told me that when the Cyprus conciliation committee went to see Macmillan privately he used the extraordinary words that he was 'intent on unravelling another imperial skein'.

Meanwhile, on the Labour side, the discomfiture comes, I think, from the discovery that the Government is not going into an automatic decline and that the Party cannot just automatically take over. I find that I myself have been affected by this mood. Particularly during the last two months, which I have spent mostly thinking about National Superannuation, I have come to assume that we shall win the next Election and that I shall be the Minister in charge of the Bill. I don't suppose that ever in my life up till now I have ever thought in this sort of way—certainly not since 1945. In 1950 and 1951 I not only was convinced that we were going to lose the Election, but was sincerely hoping that we should do so, since it would have been quite disastrous for us to be in power with nothing to do. But now I see a whole number of jobs I want us to do. Much more serious, there is a job I want to do and I have been deeply assuming that, once I have got the Labour Party to adopt this pensions plan, it would become the law of the land. Yet during the last month, although this is quite possible, it has ceased to be more than possible. It is also now quite possible that, if industrial prosperity continues and there is another good Budget next year, the Tories might conceivably win again and National Superannuation be postponed until Crossman was over fifty-five and too old to think it worth while becoming a Minister. And, if I've been thinking about jobs like this, what about my colleagues, who are always job-conscious to a degree I can hardly conceive of? Yes, it's been quite a month for shifting of values.

And during this month, by an extraordinary freak of chance, Aneurin Bevan has been absent and absence has made the heart grow fonder, until he has come back with a quite fantastic reputation. It isn't so much what he has been saying out in India, Pakistan, Persia, Iraq and Israel, though that has

---

[1] On April 25th King Hussein had decreed martial law, in his efforts to stem left-wing agitation. In what appeared to promise the first test of the Eisenhower doctrine, the American President sent part of the U.S. Sixth Fleet from French waters to the Eastern Mediterranean, to protect the 'integrity and independence' of Jordan. On April 29th the U.S. Secretary of the Army announced the readiness of American troops to be parachuted into Jordan and on the same day $10 million of U.S. economic aid was offered to the King. However, the Jordanian Foreign Minister declared that his country would not receive the President's special envoy, Mr Richards, and that the Eisenhower doctrine was not in his Government's mind. On May 2nd Mr Richards broke off his Middle East tour, omitting visits not only to Jordan, but also to Egypt and Syria, and reported on his return to the United States that events in Jordan made it preferable to give economic help there by means other than those set out in the doctrine.

been very good and sensible.[1] It is that he has been absent while Macmillan has staged his recovery and Gaitskell has not been particularly adroit. Immediately on Nye's return he has announced himself more anti-Nasser than any Suez rebel and then, at the first meeting of the Shadow Cabinet, he told me over a drink yesterday in the Smoking Room, he has made two propositions. First, the moment the decision is given to send the British ships through Suez, a vote of censure must be tabled. Secondly, the nuclear dispute must be resolved by a big debate on disarmament. Not very original, you will say, but they are both right decisions. Nye told me that the morale of the Shadow Cabinet was at zero when he came back to find them all wondering what had happened and why Macmillan was doing so well.

I remarked that at Cambridge I had had quite a success by describing Enoch Powell as an unreconstructed Tory, a genuine Macmillanite, unlike the wishy-washy compromisers of the Eden–Butler regime. 'You're right,' Nye said, 'and that's why the only proper alternative to the Macmillan Government is a really Socialist policy.' Of course I couldn't find out, when I asked him, what Nye meant by this, even in relation to nationalization. But there's no doubt whatsoever that his stock has soared, while Gaitskell's continues to decline.

Gaitskell, by the way, went off to spend five days as the guest in Rome of the Italian Social Democrats. He apparently stayed with Rossi, the ultra-reactionary Minister we met the other day, and associated himself with the Rossi fraction against the fraction who want unification. How this will be sorted out I don't know. On his way home, Nye had talked to Dino in Rome and Dino rang me up to tell me the damage Hugh Gaitskell's visit had caused.

Indeed, the actions of Hugh are an almost constant topic of discussion wherever you go. My own view, often expressed, is that he is extremely nice and intellectually honest and that his real deficiency is not what Nye always talks about — that Hugh is instinctively on the right-wing of the Party. That is a deficiency he could get over by adroit tactical manoeuvre and seemed to be getting over very well in his first four months. No, his real deficiency is an inability to leave well alone, to sit in the middle and reserve himself for the moment when his weight is needed — an inability, if you like, to choose the essential issues and leave everything secondary disregarded. Here he really is a genuine don. All of us dons, whenever a paper or some proofs start to come into our hands, get hold of our pencils and start drafting amendments. It is an instinctive reaction to any written document, just as it is an instinctive reaction to plunge into a conversation whenever you feel inclined. But the real leader is withdrawn, in the centre, with a space all round him — is, in a sense, indolent until the moment for intense activity. Hugh has no intuitive sense of timing and no very great self-confidence and his conscientious ability

---

[1] During what was his second visit to India (the first was in 1953), Bevan addressed both Houses of the Parliament, soothing Indian irritation over Britain's Suez policy and recent criticism in the United Nations of Indian policy in Kashmir. On his way home Bevan visited Karachi, Baghdad, Teheran, Istanbul and Tel Aviv.

has not made up so far for these deficiencies. On the other hand, there is no reason to think he is in the faintest danger. He can afford for quite a long time to be quite a bad leader, on one condition – that he does not overwork and get ill through these endless visits and talks he does.

Thursday, May 16th

So, after a lot of preliminary alarums and excursions, we have finally, officially and successfully launched National Superannuation. This morning I looked at the newspapers and was content. But I had better go back and take up where I left off this diary. Since my last entry, we had been making the final arrangements for publication of the great plan. I had privately arranged with *The Times*, the *Guardian*, the B.B.C.'s 'Panorama' and one or two other people who really needed to get things early that they should have the first copies. I knew these would be ready on Friday and would be given them for the weekend, whereas the official day for the press to receive their review copies was to be Tuesday, the 14th, with a press conference on Friday, the 17th, and publication on Sunday, the 19th. Everything seemed to go perfectly smoothly and I took a copy home to show Anne's father. I was very much touched when I found him on Sunday, when he had retired to bed, sitting up very portentously. He made me a speech, saying that this was the most important policy statement since 1945, that he thought that it was a work which required a genius and that, though he had begun to read it without any particular interest, it had held him spellbound as the first policy which seemed to be coping with inflation and the realities of the world.

We went back to London quite happy that Sunday evening, but on Monday morning I found that the *Daily Express* had a huge front-page story with a version of our Plan, obviously based on our document for the Executive. I was lunching with Donald McLachlan in order to soften up the *Daily Telegraph*. When I got to Scott's, very late and harassed because my column was going wrong, McLachlan said, as I was sitting down, 'You needn't worry to tell me anything. We've got your document.' I said, rather artfully, 'You'll find there's an embargoed copy on your desk by the time you get back.' I foresaw that, at any rate. After this we had a rather delicate ten minutes at the beginning of the lunch, but he had a very nice economist called John Applebey[1] with him and we spent the time seriously considering the policy.

So the worst had happened. When I woke up on Tuesday I had an omen and went down to the front door for the papers at quarter past seven. There was the *Daily Telegraph*, with its own pirated version. Of course I could envisage what my colleagues on the Executive would think and what fantastic conclusions they would draw. But after the International Sub. on Tuesday

[1] He joined the *Financial Times* in 1946 as a leader writer, specialising in economic and financial subjects. In 1955 he moved to the *Daily Telegraph*, whose Deputy Editor he became in October 1960. In January 1961 he died of leukaemia.

afternoon, Sam Watson took me downstairs and said, 'You'd better give me a bottle of champagne to celebrate the brilliance and drafting of your pamphlet. I've seen nothing like it.' Nothing would convince him that I hadn't planned the whole leak.

All this was a welcome relief from what I had been having the week before. That week, the Tory press had been full of inspired stories about Chequers, where Macmillan was holding informal talks with those concerned with pensions, including John Boyd-Carpenter, the Minister. The *Express* was running the line that the Government was seeking to forestall the Labour Party. The *Telegraph*, a great deal more cautiously, was outlining the alternatives to be presented informally at Chequers on Sunday.

It was, of course, this Chequers meeting about pensions which made our pamphlet such hot news and which certainly tempted first the *Express* and then the *Telegraph* to put out pirated versions. The net result was that by Tuesday evening, as the *Manchester Guardian* remarked, Labour's Superannuation Plan was famous even though it hadn't yet been published. I don't know how many of my colleagues came up to me last week and said, 'So they've outwitted you after all and the Tories will get a plan out first.' It was no good my explaining to them what I was fairly sure of — that we were at least eight months in advance and that you can't cook up a pensions plan in a week. I don't think these people have any idea of ,the amount of work required to do a serious job of this sort.

However, on Tuesday morning, I knew we were in for trouble and rang up Morgan Phillips who, characteristically, however, didn't get to his office until a quarter to twelve. I also timed Mr Bax[1] for half-past ten, when I persuaded him that we must antedate publication in order to keep the friendly daily newspapers sweet. I got him to agree to Thursday publication. After this the *Daily Mirror* rang him up and told him that the embargo had ceased to exist, while Sir William Haley[2] of *The Times* said that the outrage of the *Daily Telegraph*'s performance would compel *The Times* to publish on Wednesday.[3] Well, we soothed them down, and got them to agree to Thursday publication and a Wednesday press conference, which duly took place yesterday.

I went along with Abel-Smith and entered Morgan's new Mussolini-like[4]

[1] Arthur Bax, Press and Publicity Officer at Transport House from 1946 until 1962, when he moved to the Oxford University Press. He established the Publicity Office for the Borough of Enfield in 1966 and worked there until 1969, when he joined the *Enfield Weekly Herald*.

[2] A journalist who became Director of the Press Association and of Reuter's 1939–43, Editor in Chief of the B.B.C. 1943–4 and Director-General 1944–52. He was Editor of *The Times* 1952–66 and was knighted in 1946.

[3] The first *Times* leader in the issue of May 16th discussed 'Labour's Model', describing it as 'a good opening for what must become a fundamental debate about the development of social security during the next half century. It stands on a much higher plane than previous instalments of Socialist rethinking'.

[4] Crossman was fond of this expression, which he used to describe a room where the furniture was so arranged that the occupant could gaze intimidatingly down the table or desk at those who entered.

room to find them gathered round the table. How my colleagues hate success for anybody else! I had decided to say only a few words but in fact made an amusing and quite good speech, to which I was told journalists are not accustomed, and *The Times* and the *Guardian* used it almost exclusively for their main reports. Apparently it all went all right and this morning we had the satisfaction of running about level with the British H-bomb and altogether knocking the big Suez debate off the front page.[1]

One interesting sidelight was the accident that I happened yesterday to be lunching with Hugh Cudlipp and Sydney Jacobson. I got there half an hour late, after the press conference, and Sydney said, 'You didn't ring me up yesterday did you?' 'No,' I said. 'I didn't want to particularly, because I suspected that you might be breaking the embargo.' 'Well,' he said, 'I had given instructions that I wasn't in any time you called all day,' and Hugh added that it was Sydney who finally decided that the *Mirror* should not break the embargo on the ground that he'd got his copy from me.

We discussed how they were going to put the Plan across. I made some rather obvious remarks about the grinding poverty of old age and how we couldn't tolerate it. Hugh said, 'That can't be mentioned. We're a paper of youth. We can't have pensioners and old people. I've sent all the photographers into Hyde Park to photograph young people whose future is free from fear. That's our slogan.' 'Well,' I said, 'I hope to God that you will mention that they will have to pay a bit for it,' at which Hugh turned to Sydney and said, 'Have we got that in?' But that was only a joke. Of course both of them had mastered every detail of the scheme, as was quite clear this morning. The fact is that this kind of thing is almost impossibly difficult to explain in a popular paper and they've really done a wonderful job.[2]

The other part of our conversation at lunch was devoted to Gaitskell and Bevan. I told them that on Tuesday Hugh had asked to come and have a drink in order to discuss his Suez speech. This was quite unlike him, since for many months he has never asked for my advice on foreign policy. I wasn't surprised, when he came, to find he wanted a pep talk. I told him he had nothing to fear except his own lack of self-confidence and inability to be

[1] On April 24th the Egyptian Government issued a memorandum, reaffirming the terms, first published on March 18th, on which the Canal would be reopened. All dues were to be paid to the Egyptian Suez Canal Authority, which would operate and manage the waterway. On May 9th the Suez Canal Users' Association met and stated that, though these terms fell short of the six principles, member nations should decide for themselves whether to accept, under protest, and resume their use of the Canal. Most member nations took this course and on May 13th the Prime Minister told the Commons that the Government could no longer advise British shipowners to refrain from using the Canal. Strong objection came from eight Conservative M.P.s, who announced their decision to resign the Party whip, and the Opposition tabled a motion of censure. This was debated on May 15th and 16th and, despite the abstention of 14 dissident Conservatives, the Government had an unexpectedly large majority of 49. Petrol rationing ended on May 15th.

[2] In November and December 1968 Hugh Cudlipp was to help Crossman launch a 'popular version' of the White Paper on National Superannuation. See *The Diaries of a Cabinet Minister*, vol. III, pp. 276, 299.

indolent at the centre. If he would only do less work, speak first in a discussion less often and leave it to others. At this last point, Hugh said, 'But there are only two others on this Executive to whom I can leave anything, you and Harold,' and he added: 'I've three sorts of friends—real friends like you, panicky friends who come and report that Nye is trying to overthrow me and, worst of all, so-called candid friends, who try to destroy my self-confidence.'

He admitted that he was feeling tired. I've no doubt I did him really a power of good when I finally said, 'As for your speech, Kenneth Robinson told me the other day that I would never appreciate your qualities because I was ill during the first three days of the Suez crisis, when the Labour Party was led by a man of conviction for the first time for years. All you've got to do, Hugh, is to repeat that, know you are right and go for Macmillan.' This pleased him and he began to tell me some of what he had planned to say about Macmillan. As a matter of fact, in the first day of the debate yesterday he did pretty well and Macmillan was a complete flop. But it's all old cabbage. I don't think anybody outside Parliament really minds about a Suez debate, even though the British ships have now been told to go through the Canal and pay their dues to Colonel Nasser.

Thursday, May 23rd
On Friday I had to go to Newcastle to a meeting in a school so I set off from King's Cross on the two o'clock train, the Heart of Midlothian, on the kind of long train journey I love, reading a new book by Alger Hiss.[1] There I was, as we passed through Yorkshire, having tea in the restaurant car, with lovely sunshine on plenty of spring corn, when who should walk in but Oliver Poole and his wife.[2] Somehow I know Oliver from the days when he was in the House as a Tory backbencher and anyway he's an Old Etonian and anyway, even more, he had greeted my National Superannuation with what I thought was an outrageous press release, headed 'Half Pie in the Sky for Women', implying that the Tories would give married women even more. So we sat together for two hours and he told me really a very great deal.

To begin with, I hadn't realized that he's an insurance broker and well up

---

[1] An American lawyer who accompanied Roosevelt to Yalta and advised the early American delegations to the United Nations. He was a member of the State Department from 1936 until 1946, when he became Executive Director of the Carnegie Endowment for International Peace, a post he held until his resignation in January 1950, when he was convicted of espionage upon the evidence of the journalist Whittaker Chambers. Hiss's own view of the case is described in his book *In the Court of Public Opinion* (New York: Knopf, 1957; London: Calder, 1957) and the episode has been extensively described in a study by Allan Weinstein: *Perjury: The Hiss/Chambers Case* (New York: Knopf, 1978). The *New Statesman and Nation* of June 1st published Crossman's review of Hiss's book.

[2] Conservative M.P. for the Oswestry division of Shropshire 1945–50, he was Chairman of the Conservative Party Organization 1955–7. In 1958 he was created 1st Baron Poole. He married his second wife, the former Mrs Daphne Percy, in 1952. The marriage was dissolved in 1965.

in superannuation. Indeed, he told me that he is of the fifth generation of insurance brokers. According to him, superannuation work for some companies has taken the place of the industrial business they lost as a result of National Insurance being introduced and finally ending such rackets as burial insurance. He had no doubt that a National Superannuation scheme would, at the very least, kill the expansion of such business, on which many companies are depending for the next fifteen years. 'What a curious coincidence,' he observed, 'that Low[1] had the same idea as I did.' Low had published a cartoon on the theme of Pie in the Sky, with the two parties competing with pension schemes. 'Hardly a coincidence,' I said, 'since Low must have had his idea the day before he saw your release.' 'Oh, but I got that ready two days before your press day,' Poole remarked, and then he looked a little embarrassed and remarked, 'Of course, you know we had a copy of your policy document at Chequers and we prepared our release there.'

This confirmed something Hugh Massingham had told me. He had seen Iain Macleod, who had boasted that the Tories have all our stuff at Tory headquarters and that the releases by the *Express* and the *Telegraph* were part of a Tory plot to embarrass us, since the copies were supplied to the papers by Tory headquarters. If this is true, and I'm not by any means sure that it is, then they made an extraordinary miscalculation, since all they did by this plot was to give us unrivalled publicity.

However, Oliver told me he thought it was good publicity for the Cabinet to be thought to be considering something like pensions. He also made it very clear that they wouldn't take over our scheme but would try to put something on the Statute Book which was irreversible and which would prevent us going ahead with our plan. There's something in his view. Theirs seems to be a scheme which relies on the present National Insurance, possibly with Government assistance, to extend coverage of superannuation. Poole didn't make it clear whether this would be voluntary, in which case at least a third of the workers would be left uncovered, or compulsory, in which case our scheme would be simpler.

After all my broadcasts on Friday, over the weekend and on Monday, I found on the whole surprised, pleasurable reaction among my colleagues in Parliament. Several of them expressed surprise at my boldness in saying that one has to pay for anything these days, which they thought a most original idea of propaganda. But the net result was that, at the Party Meeting, where I had to explain the scheme on Tuesday morning, I had, for me, an extraordinarily friendly reception, with old Tom Williams, the old Minister of Agriculture, saying this was the best scheme the Labour Party had ever put forward in his whole memory of the Party history. In reply, another old trade

---

[1] David Low, the political cartoonist and caricaturist. Born in New Zealand, he worked on the *Star* 1919–27, the *Evening Standard* 1927–50, the *Daily Herald* 1950–3 and the *Manchester Guardian* (later the *Guardian*) from 1953 until his death in 1963. He was knighted in 1962.

unionist, Charlie Gibson[1] of the T.U.C., said that he didn't see how £10-a-week-men could be expected to see their contributions go up by half a crown [12·5 new pence] a week without asking for higher wages. But, by and large, I think the Members of Parliament have been staggered by the amount of serious attention the scheme has got in the press and they are fairly ready to think that it's a great success and a credit to the Party.

On Wednesday we had an Executive meeting, which I thought was going to be completely uneventful until Sydney Silverman said he'd been in Italy and raised the whole question of Saragat and Nenni. At this point, Mr Bevan and Mr Gaitskell proceeded to commit themselves in implacably hostile attitudes, Mr Bevan stating that Mr Saragat was a liar and that Nenni was the only figure, apart from Togliatti, who could rally the masses. For this reason, we should come out in a public statement in favour of unification. Hugh said he couldn't accept Nye's version, expressed the view that it would be fatal to make any public statement and said he might write a letter. The situation soon got extremely tense and I thought, ironically, that it would be very funny if we managed to split the Labour Party on the issue of how to unify the Italians!

I've been thinking for some weeks how much better Bevan and Gaitskell are together, but this episode showed that there are still very strong passions underneath. Once again I think the bigger fault is on Hugh's side, since he has made Nye Shadow Foreign Secretary and should let him have his head in these things. And anyway he's invariably wrong. After the behaviour of these two, the morale of the Executive went to pieces and we had the kind of irritable meeting that we used to have months ago, with all sorts of minor matters causing disagreements.

The only other thing I need mention here is the progress of my libel actions.[2] Talking to Morgan Phillips the other day, I was amused to discover that he had never spoken either to Nye or to Mr Goodman about the action and had just been dragged into it, much against his will. No wonder! I told him I was determined it shouldn't go to court and wasn't particularly keen on money.

[1] Charles Gibson (1889–1979), Labour M.P. for the Kennington division of Lambeth 1945–50 and for the Clapham division of Lambeth 1950–9. He worked on the staff of the T.G.W.U.

[2] Crossman was engaged in two disputes, one with Viscount Hailsham over an allegedly defamatory reference in the *Mirror* column on May 21st and the other concerning comment on the visit he had paid to Venice with Bevan and Phillips.

On March 1st an article about the P.S.I. Congress had been published in the *Spectator*. It included the following passage:

And there was the occasional appearance of Messrs Bevan, Morgan Phillips and Richard Crossman who puzzled the Italians by their capacity to fill themselves like tanks with whisky and coffee, while they (because of their livers and also because they are abstemious by nature) were keeping going on mineral water and an occasional coffee. Although the Italians were never sure if the British delegation was sober, they always attributed to them an immense political acumen.

For the conduct of the libel action, see below, pp. 628 ff.

Friday, May 31st

Just after I dictated my last slab of diary, I walked into the House of Commons and was standing reading the tape when a voice said, 'So I'm your opposite number now.' It was Iain Macleod, the Minister of Labour. 'Oh, no,' I said, 'I've finished my job.' 'Well, you did a good job,' he replied, 'and you were quite wrong in the *Daily Mirror*. We accept all the three principles you say we reject — compulsion, transferability and a fund.' I was interested that Macleod had read the *Mirror* so carefully and I said, 'Well, how do you come into it and not John Boyd-Carpenter?' 'Oh, I'm the chairman of the Cabinet Committee,' Macleod said, 'and I can tell you we shall have something on the Statute Book before the Election and it will be based on your principles.' 'What will be the difference?' I said. 'We shall make the compulsory State scheme a long-stop and encourage private superannuation.' Macleod was so haughty, precise and confident that I was inclined to take his remarks without question. But when I compare them with Oliver Poole's, I think Macleod was trying to put over to me the impression that things are far more fixed on this issue in the Tory Party than they actually are.[1]

From June 3rd to 25th Crossman and his wife were on holiday in Bavaria and Austria. During his travels, Crossman reported:

> *I happened to read a nauseating new vulgarized Lucky Jim book called* Room at the Top[2] *and also* Point Counter Point. *When I told him about the intellectual teddy-boys, Hans Habe[3] observed, 'In Germany there is a new teddy-boy style, in which the modern novels are written.' Why is it that* Room at the Top *is a success? It is lower middle-class, anti-working-class, describing the working classes as dirty, smelly people, eating fish and chips and favouring the upper class as people who have tiled bathrooms and beautiful voices. Anyway, there was* Point Counter Point. *The difference was that the basic assumption of the intellectuals of the 1920s described the ruling class as stupid, blind and living an abstract, unreal life, while the working class were pure, alive and basically cultured. I found a fascinating passage in* Point Counter Point, *which, of course, is partly based on D. H.*

[1] On May 29th in a speech at Hornby, the Minister of Pensions and National Insurance, John Boyd-Carpenter, had described Labour's pensions plan as 'an interesting theoretical exercise'. He had continued:

> The working out of a sound method of provision for old age is one of the great problems of our time. I believe it can be done. But it can't be done by playing politics, as Mr Crossman and the Socialist Party are doing — even if they take two or three amiable egg-heads for a ride with them.

[2] A novel by John Braine (London: Eyre & Spottiswoode, 1957). *Lucky Jim*, a novel by Kingsley Amis, was published in London by Gollancz in 1954; Aldous Huxley's *Point Counter Point* was published by Chatto & Windus in 1928.

[3] The novelist, an old friend of Crossman. Under the pseudonym of Janos Benessy he published numerous novels including, in translation, *Agent of the Devil* (London: Harrap, 1958), *A Thousand Shall Fall* (London: Hamish Hamilton, 1969) and an autobiography, *All My Sins* (London: Harrap, 1957).

Lawrence.[1] *But there you can see the difference between the post-war after the First World War and the post-war after the Second. What the intellectuals failed to see in the 1920s and 1930s was that the working class are not more responsible or understanding or pure than the stupid ruling class. Indeed, they share all the bourgeois, abstract illusions and behave as stupidly, directly they get the chance. The new factor of the post-war world is that today it is the middle class who are resentfully class-conscious. But, whereas the 1930 class-consciousness took the form of Marxism, the present class-consciousness takes the form of Lucky Jim.*

Shortly after their return Crossman set off again, this time to East Germany. He spent August 6th and 7th in West Berlin, being briefed for his visit to the Eastern Zone by various members of the S.P.D., including Herr Willy Brandt. On August 8th, 'rather nervously', he crossed into East Berlin. His nervousness was due to the fact that he had already illegally changed £40 into Eastmarks at twice the official rate. Since it was thought inadvisable to have large denomination notes, he had 'a pocket of 50s and then, I should think, eight ounces of 5 Mark and 2 Mark notes, which seemed to be as damning as anything could be, since they filled my bedroom slippers. I never knew what to do with them in East Berlin and brought them back safely!'

During his visit Crossman raised the question of the Social Democratic prisoners but he was able to obtain only the promise of an up-to-date and complete list, to take back to West Berlin. Even this did not materialize. Crossman's reports on the visit appeared in the Daily Mirror on August 13th, 16th and 20th.

At the beginning of September, Crossman attended the Trades Union Congress, held at Blackpool from September 2nd to 6th. On September 3rd the Congress cautiously welcomed the Labour Party's National Superannuation scheme; on September 5th a motion proposed by Mr Cousins, rejecting any form of wage restraint, was agreed with acclamation. The T.U.C. General Council did not offer any collective comment on this resolution and neither rejected nor accepted it. Crossman's reaction may be found in his Daily Mirror article of September 6th.

Crossman had set out for Blackpool with some trepidation. In the Daily Mirror of July 5th he had published an article saying that 'the decline in quality' of trade union candidates adopted by constituencies was gravely affecting the Parliamentary Labour Party. Crossman had declared that, of the ninety-seven sponsored trade union M.P.s at present in Parliament, only four (James Griffiths, Aneurin Bevan, George Brown and Alfred Robens) suggested them-

---

[1] David Herbert Lawrence (1885–1930), the poet, novelist, critic and author of studies of psychoanalysis and travel books. His novels include *The White Peacock* (London: Secker, 1906), *The Rainbow* (London: Secker, 1915), *Women in Love* (London: Secker, 1921), *The Plumed Serpent* (London: Secker, 1926), and *Lady Chatterley's Lover* (first published in an expurgated edition by Secker, 1928; and later, in a complete edition, by Penguin, 1960).

selves for office in a future Labour Administration. On July 9th Crossman had been summoned to discuss his remarks with the chairman and secretary of the trade union group. This episode rankled for many subsequent years.

Crossman was particularly anxious to see how the Congress would handle not only his National Superannuation scheme, but also the N.E.C. document on public ownership. In statements and articles in Tribune, Forward *and elsewhere, various members of the Labour Party, including Gaitskell, Crossman, Wilson and Mikardo, had offered different interpretations of the document* Industry and Society *prepared by a fourteen-member N.E.C. sub-committee. This had been drafted by Peter Shore but, according to Crossman, 'extensively redrafted by the office at Transport House, removing most of its radical trimmings and making it a great deal more reactionary. Apparently this was completely unnoticed when it came before the National Executive.' The document had been published the previous July, for discussion at the Party Conference in the autumn.*

Industry and Society first described how British industry was concentrated in several hundred large private companies, in whose management the shareholders had ceased to play any significant part. A firm commitment was then given to renationalize the iron and steel and road haulage industries and to bring into municipal ownership privately rented houses, but otherwise no pledge of further major nationalization was offered. Indeed, it was suggested that a future Labour Government should extend public ownership by purchasing shares in 600 companies. 'Too pink, too blue, too yellow,' was Jennie Lee's comment on the document; others, including Herbert Morrison, disowned it. In Crossman's words,

> *there was a good deal of indignation, not only among* Tribune *circles but also outside, in the constituencies and, even more important, in the Parliamentary Party, where what you might call the working-class elements had taken the occasion to assume that the Wykehamists were corrupting the Gospel by a too-clever-by-half intellectualism.*

Friday, September 6th

When I got back from Germany, we went down for our last weekend at Prescote before we settled in London to wait for Anne's confinement. It was lovely, lovely weather and the last of the 100 acres of corn was cut and baled at half-past nine on Saturday evening. This year Pritchett's automation was working. The combine has a tank on it so that, instead of the corn being sacked on the combine and the sack tipped off on the field, to be collected in a lorry, the tank merely empties into a tanker lorry, which then drives down to the barn and empties the corn into a hole in the floor. From there it is automatically sucked up, sent down the drier and then sucked back up and into the sack. I spent most of Sunday walking over the fields before we returned to London and I prepared to go to the T.U.C. conference.

I don't know why I decided to go this year. Partly, I think, because, having not travelled much after I got ill last October, I was anxious to do some away columns and reporting; partly also because I wanted to break my nervousness of meeting trade unionists. I spent Monday morning doing a column and then took the five past five from Euston. When I got to Blackpool I was a little nervous and apprehensive as I drove along the front to the Imperial Hotel, where we were, as a Labour Party Executive, last October.

The Congress had started that morning but directly I got into the hotel I felt nice and at home, sitting with Sydney [Jacobson] and Len Jackson[1] and, of course, Tom O'Brien, Dora and Hugh Gaitskell, Uncle Bob Millar, the Editor of *Tribune*,[2] and all. Hugh and Dora were there because Hugh had been invited by Tom Williamson, this year's President, to attend the Jubilee Dinner of the Municipal Workers. By some strange slip-up, this fact hadn't been given to the press and nor had Morgan Phillips done so nor the T.U.C. Result: newspaper sensation, since that day it was known that Jim Campbell[3] of the N.U.R. had tabled an amendment rejecting the nationalization document that had been prepared for our Brighton Conference. Every paper jumped to the conclusion that Hugh was up to some secret confabs, a palpably untrue theory, since who would try a secret confab. at the Imperial Hotel during the Congress?

That first evening I was able to get a pretty good impression on this issue. Whatever the sense of crisis and split in the Labour Party felt down in London, it was not reflected up in Blackpool. Already that evening I had heard a story that Frank Cousins was preparing to ask for certain assurances from Hugh at Brighton, which Hugh would be prepared to give. From the *Tribune* people, among others, I tried to elicit what was wrong with *Industry and Society* and got no very clear reply. Morgan Phillips also, semi-blotto as usual, denied there was any real crisis. Then, about half-past eleven, Hugh and Dora were seen at the end of the room and came rushing across to sit with friends. By this time I had discovered that whatever crime I had committed against trade union M.P.s was not felt as a crime by trade union leaders, who were mostly interested to congratulate me on National Superannuation, where they felt — and quite rightly — that there had been adequate co-ordination between the T.U.C. and the Labour Party and that everything was in apple-pie order.

So I went to bed on Monday evening, at two in the morning, feeling pleasantly cheerful, a mood which lasted and increased throughout the Congress. Actually, Tuesday morning turned out to be quite a personal success for me, since the only big debate was on National Superannuation. It was opened by Sir Alfred Roberts, who spoke for half an hour, giving a

[1] Leonard Jackson, a correspondent for the *Daily Mirror* from 1937 until his death in 1962; latterly the paper's Industrial Correspondent.

[2] A journalist and Business Manager of *Tribune* until 1960. He also wrote a column of advice to consumers, under the name of John Kerr. In 1960 he became Consumer Affairs Editor of the *Daily Express*.

[3] General Secretary of the N.U.R. from 1953 until his death in 1957.

beautifully balanced analysis of the scheme and its difficulties and describing it as 'imaginative but not utopian'. I responded not unamiably to this unexpectedly pleasant atmosphere, in which all the members of the General Council, from Sir Alfred Roberts to even Frank Cousins, seemed to think of me as a Socialist who gets things done and not as an intellectual who despises the working class.

Of course, the main preoccupation of Gaitskell, who left on Tuesday evening, of Harold Wilson, who blew in for a couple of hours on Thursday morning, of Harry Nicholas, Cousins's Number Two on our N.E.C., and of Ray Gunter,[1] also on our N.E.C., was what was to happen on Thursday afternoon, when nationalization was debated. I say 'debated' but that's a misnomer in terms of this year's T.U.C. No doubt the atmosphere is anyway very different from our Party Conference because everybody is in a trade union delegation and most of the delegates, therefore, do not expect to speak or take a line. The Congress is therefore, by nature, apathetic. There are no people jumping up, or trying to get the chairman's eye, and almost everything can be fixed beforehand. This year, I am told, was the worst Congress ever in this respect. There was no real debate. By Thursday it became only too clear that this was due to the determination of the General Council to avoid a row either amongst its own members or with the floor. Of course, I had gained by this attitude. I have no doubt that, in a livelier Congress, the latent hostility of a good many people to our Superannuation scheme would have been brought into the open, with a real debate and a card vote.

At a quarter past four came the long-awaited debate on nationalization. It looked as though it was all going our way. Everything seemed to be over when the resolution was accepted, calling on the T.U.C. to reaffirm its belief in public ownership and continue its study of the industries suitable for nationalization. But then someone came to the rostrum to move a separate resolution, asserting Congress's belief that a major part of the machine tool industry should be nationalized. Tom Williamson explained that this resolution should have been part of the general resolution but that delegates had insisted on its being taken separately. It was therefore moved in a five-minute speech and then accepted suddenly by the platform, on the ground that an investigation into the industry had already taken place and that, broadly, the General Council agreed with the principles. At this point, a delegate from the floor sought to speak against but was ruled out of order. At the time, I really didn't know this was going on because I was assuming remittal, which would have meant nothing, and only realized the truth when I got back to the hotel and Sydney talked to me about it.

During the course of the evening I made inquiries. I finally went to Victor

[1] Labour M.P. for the South-Eastern division of Essex 1945–50, for Doncaster 1950–1 and for Southwark 1959–72. He was Minister of Labour 1964–8 and then Minister of Power for two months until his resignation. A member of the N.E.C. 1955–6, he was President of the Transport Salaried Staffs Association 1956–64. He died in 1977.

Feather, who said, 'It's approved, but only with qualifications.' 'What qualifications?' I asked, and he replied, 'With qualifications! You know what that means.' I'm afraid the blunt fact is that this year there has been no kind of leadership from the General Council because it has had no collective mind on any subject at all. The impression I gathered is that the struggle for power is still going on. Frank Cousins alienated almost everybody last year and this year was trying to get back a few friends, while retaining his militancy. In estimating the T.U.C.'s acceptance of our Superannuation scheme, it would be only wise to remember this atmosphere and the reasons for it. On the other hand, acceptance is acceptance. We shall have a much easier job at Brighton at the end of the month as a result of what happened at Blackpool on National Superannuation, just as we shall have a much more difficult time as the result of what happened on machine tools.

Sydney and I caught the night train to Preston, after a wonderful farewell meal in the Imperial's Gala Room, where we made the *Daily Mirror* pay for our meals rather than eating *à la carte* in the hotel restaurant. It had been for me a wonderful three days, because I still like nothing better than absorbing a new experience. East Germany and the T.U.C. have both been gorgeous new experiences, none the less gorgeous because both were odious. But I felt I was understanding them and in neither case was I too thoroughly disliked.

Friday, September 13th
When I lunched with Hugh Cudlipp and Sydney last Friday, I induced Hugh (to do him justice, against his will) to tell me that he regards my column as stuffy and pontifical. By the end of a very exhausting lunch Hugh had come to the conclusion that I shouldn't write a column at all but that my brilliant snap judgments should be attached late at night to all news stories. As we went away, Sydney said to me, 'Don't worry. Nothing will happen about it and he will forget it by tomorrow.' At Blackpool Sydney was extremely candid about how unpleasant Hugh is getting, how disloyal to his old friends and how impossible to work with. Fortunately I am incapable of changing my spots in this regard. One can only hope that he will recover his pleasure in my snob value. That is, one can hope that if one wants to go on writing on the *Mirror*, which I'm not sure I do.

Tuesday, September 17th
I decided to do a *Mirror* piece on this nationalization controversy and had got it all ready when Hugh Gaitskell came to lunch on Monday before the policy Sub.[1] He was wearing that horrible brown suit which Anne detests

[1] In his *Daily Mirror* piece on September 17th, Crossman wrote:

I wonder if Mr Mikardo has ever considered what would happen if by any mischance the Party conference at Brighton accepted his advice and his wild threats of wholesale nationalisation became official Labour policy. *The only result would be to discredit the Labour Party and stimulate a Liberal revival, which might well save the Tories from defeat* [emphasis in original].

and seemed more amiable and less effective than ever. Why do I go on nagging him in this diary? Partly, I suppose, because, if you were at school with somebody who seemed innocuous and insignificant throughout your school life and who since then has been an ascending backroom boy, it is difficult to believe in his greatness. But I was quite willing to believe that Hugh would be made great or at least made clever and Attlee-like by his office, and of this there is so far no sign. Indeed, I feel he is less competent than when he started because I suspect that he is less self-assured, and that is a thoroughly bad thing.

I showed Hugh the *Mirror* article, which he liked, and we had the usual kind of tittle-tattle, in which he continued to say he wasn't too alarmed about Conference. He continued to share my annoyance with Barbara and Ian Mikardo, making it clear enough that, if they can't stand by a document which, like *Industry and Society*, they have helped to draft on the N.E.C., he wouldn't trust them in a Cabinet.[1]

On July 25th the House of Commons had discussed the state of the economy. Throughout the summer the Chancellor had given repeated warnings of imminent unbridled inflation; wage demands and prices continued to increase. In the debate Mr Thorneycroft announced that, despite the opposition of trade union leaders, the Government was determined to appoint an independent council on prices, incomes and productivity. The four themes of the Government's strategy were, he said: planning investment to match savings, continuing the credit squeeze, relating wages and profits to production, and curbing Government expenditure. Appointments to the Council were announced on August 12th.

During that month and early September there was speculation against the pound as overseas traders grew doubtful of Britain's ability to maintain its exchange value. This was exacerbated by a de facto *devaluation of the French franc on August 10th and by what turned out to be groundless rumours of an impending revaluation of the D-Mark. In the seven weeks preceding the publication of the September figures, the gold and dollar reserve fell by more than one-fifth. Accordingly, on September 19th the Chancellor announced an increase in bank rate from 5 to 7 per cent, the highest rate since 1921. The banks were asked to restrict their advances during the next twelve months and the Capital Issues Committee was instructed to 'take a more restrictive and critical attitude' to applications to borrow. Current civil and defence spending were to be limited, and the Government proposed to keep the total investment expenditure by Government departments, local authorities and nationalized industries 'within the level attained this year'.*

These measures, announced just before the Chancellor left for the annual meeting of the I.M.F. in Washington, stemmed the outflow of gold and dollars.

[1] They had both published critical articles, Mrs Castle in the *Sunday Pictorial* and Ian Mikardo in the *Tribune*.

For the remainder of the year the reserves rose. On September 23rd Mr Gaitskell wrote to the Prime Minister, asking for the early recall of Parliament to debate the financial and economic crisis. Mr Macmillan replied on the following day, stating his belief that immediate debate was unnecessary. It was thus at the Party Conference, in Brighton from September 30th to October 4th, that the Opposition was to deliver its first attack on the Chancellor's measures.

This was not, however, the most prominent item on the Conference agenda. As well as the debate over Industry and Society, *there was certain to be argument over the Party's attitude towards manufacture of the hydrogen bomb, and on this it seemed that there might be a fundamental split. At the time of the debate on the Defence White Paper in mid-April, many Labour backbenchers had wished the Opposition to condemn entirely the production of nuclear weapons, but the Front Bench agreed neither with this nor the proposal that the forthcoming series of British nuclear tests be abandoned — for, if the weapon was being manufactured, tests were essential. The compromise on which the Opposition fixed was to offer an Amendment proposing only the postponement of the British tests while American and Russian agreement was sought for abandoning tests altogether. At that very moment the U.S.S.R. was testing nuclear weapons in Siberia and the U.S. Government was about to begin trials in the Nevada desert.*

On May 16th the Prime Minister told the House of Commons that on the previous day a British test had taken place in the Pacific. This, he stated, emphasized the Government's intention to proceed with the current series of tests, adding that possession of those weapons would place the U.K. in a stronger position to negotiate on their control or abolition. The next day, May 17th, the Minister of Supply, Aubrey Jones, published a Statement saying that the explosion had been in the megaton range (i.e. the equivalent of 1 million or more tons of T.N.T.) and that the 'fallout' from it had been insignificant. There were further tests on May 31st and June 19th.

Though public anxiety was slow to manifest itself, various protest demonstrations were held. One of these, arranged by the H-bomb Campaign Committee, attracted several thousand people to Trafalgar Square, where they were addressed by three N.E.C. members, Barbara Castle, Ian Mikardo and Anthony Greenwood. Unilateral repudiation of the H-bomb was demanded by a large number of constituency Labour parties, 120 of which submitted resolutions on the subject for discussion at Conference.

Clearly the Party leaders would have to settle what line they would take at Conference and here the attitude of Bevan was crucial. As the Party's Front Bench spokesman on foreign affairs, he might be obliged to reply for the N.E.C. in the defence and foreign policy debate, although this task might equally well be given to the Chairman of the International Sub-Committee, Sam Watson. At this point Bevan and Jennie Lee were in the Crimea, for talks with Khrushchev, so that Bevan was absent when the International Sub-Committee first met to discuss what the N.E.C.'s line would be at Conference.

Friday, September 20th

On Tuesday afternoon we had a meeting of the International Sub. As soon as it started Sam Watson, the chairman, said we had to decide whether we were going to have a statement prepared for Brighton on defence and foreign policy. Immediately Hugh Gaitskell jumped in saying we should. I said we should think again, since on the central issue of the H-bomb we were divided, and I presumed we didn't want to finally commit the Party and split it. Hugh was, of course, backed in his demand by Sydney Silverman and Barbara Castle, who pointed out my cynicism in suggesting that we could get away with fewer commitments if Nye wound up![1]

We had quite a long discussion, in the course of which I said that, if the statement recommitted the Party to H-bomb production, I should resign and fight it, since, I added, I don't fight inside the Executive but outside. This made Barbara explode with wrath next door to me, as my article had appeared that morning in the *Mirror*. Sydney Silverman also looked a bit aghast and said he thought the entire committee were agreed that the whole point of the statement would be to pronounce that the Party had not yet made up its mind. I said this was a comic sort of statement and better made by Nye after the debate. But Hugh had committed himself. However it didn't very much matter, since it was agreed that this must all be reconsidered when Nye came back and when a draft had been prepared.[2] This morning Hugh rang me up to ask if I'd seen the draft, which dealt exclusively with disarmament, and I have been working on it.

After the International Sub. Sam Watson came for a drink with me. He agreed how naïve Hugh was to commit himself in this way. 'There is no apex of the Party,' Sam said. 'There is no firm group round Hugh and he hasn't many more months to hold on. Nye will never do anything for him and the Establishment in the trade unions has completely disintegrated.' All this I heartily agree with.

By the time I had written my column this week,[3] I realized that the country might conceivably be interested in a 7 per cent bank rate. It was too late to change what I had written but I rang Harold Wilson, who told me we should know within a week if the gamble of the 7 per cent bank rate had held the flight from the pound, so that Thorneycroft could bring back the necessary

[1] Both favoured unilateral cessation of H-bomb manufacture by Britain. Mrs Castle was angry because Crossman had referred in his *Mirror* piece to her remarks in *Tribune* about *Industry and Society*, which she had helped to draft.

[2] According to Michael Foot's *Aneurin Bevan* (London: Davis-Poynter, 1973), Vol. II, p. 568, the draft 'reflected the compromise of the previous April, offered no concession to the demand for unilateral cessation of the manufacture of the bomb, and in effect excluded the real issue of the British H-bomb altogether'.

[3] The column, published on September 20th, discussed two subjects, the Government's colonial policy and the transfer of Viscount Hailsham from the Ministry of Education to the post of Lord President of the Council and the chairmanship of the Conservative Party.

loan from the I.M.F. in New York.[1] Sigmund Warburg[2] had told Harold at lunch that he thought it was a gamble which would not come off and that we were in for a 1931 crisis, but this time with rising unemployment and rising prices simultaneously. Harold said we would have to put out an interim statement but we had to be careful not to seem to be attacking the pound and not to be committing the Shadow Cabinet too far in advance.

On the whole, my impression is that Harold and Hugh are on these subjects extremely capable and sober. That view was not changed by a wild telephone conversation this morning with George Wigg. 'This is the final proof of their bankruptcy as leaders,' he said. 'They should have announced that this is a proof of the inherent contradictions of capitalism and summoned the Labour Party to the fray.' I think I may have pacified George slightly. The fact is that, if the Labour Opposition were to denounce a gamble, however irresponsible, which has a chance of saving the pound from devaluation, our behaviour would not be appreciated by the electorate.

This afternoon I did my best with the draft on disarmament prepared by Morgan Phillips and got Hugh to agree my revise. After all the fuss and bother at the International, the draft was solely concerned with disarmament and excluded the topic on which I had disagreed. So I won. I also talked to Hugh about the importance of an apex to the Party, à la Sam, and of working in Cousins, to which Hugh now agreed. As Hugh was leaving, I said that Nye was back today and I hoped he would ring him up. 'We're away,' Hugh said, 'but I might ring him up on Sunday evening. What do you want me to talk to him about?' 'Not nationalization,' I said. 'But I think it would be tactful to welcome him back from Russia and show a real interest to hear the message he brings.' This seemed to our Leader quite a novel idea but I think he may actually act upon it. So ends, as I say, a week in which nothing happened and a great deal was said. Of course, the only thing which really happened was that Anne grew larger and even more blooming, if that is possible.

Thursday, September 26th
In the middle of the Home Policy Committee yesterday, Nye Bevan walked in, fresh back from Russia, looking very bright and hearty.[3] My high spirits were somewhat cast down when we arrived at the draft statement on disarmament. I have written previously about Hugh's mistake in asking for such a

---

[1] At the end of October $250 million was drawn from the $500 million line of credit granted by the Export-Import Bank of Washington at the end of 1956. In the last weeks of the year the I.M.F. renewed for a further year the U.K.'s standby credit of $739 million, thereby maintaining existing arrangements until December 22nd, 1958.

[2] The Director of S. G. Warburg & Co. Ltd, London, 1946–69 and President 1970–8. He was knighted in 1966.

[3] Bevan had attended the 5th Congress of the Socialist International, meeting in Vienna from July 2nd to 6th. Their resolution had proposed that the suspension of H-bomb tests should not be made dependent on first obtaining agreement on the remainder of a disarmament programme or on the sort of political settlements upon which the Western Powers were insisting.

statement, despite advice from Sam Watson and myself. Morgan had done a draft and I had done a redraft, in which the issue of the British H-bomb was carefully excluded. At first it looked as though the discussion would all go quite pleasantly yesterday, until Nye made a speech, saying he had just got back from Russia, where Khrushchev had assured him that, if Britain were to stop all H-bomb tests, Russia would follow suit and thus America would be forced to comply. Nye went on to say that, in his personal view, a decision to stop H-bomb tests must logically lead us to a decision to stop the British production of all nuclear weapons. He then mentioned the resolution of the Socialist International on this matter.

We had all been teetering a bit and at this point I heaved a sigh of relief, particularly when Nye read the whole long resolution out very slowly and said he stood by that. Hugh immediately agreed with him and said we might well substitute that for our draft statement. But at this point Sydney Silverman and Barbara Castle began to needle him. The statement covered the International Socialist position but evaded the crucial issue of British unilateral cessation of tests and the British attitude to the production of the bomb. Was Nye evading this? 'No, no,' Nye said. 'We need a footnote to the International resolution.'

At this point Sam Watson asked Nye whether he really meant that, at this forthcoming Party Conference, the Executive should commit the Party to this complete reversal of policy on the British H-bomb. Nye said that he had thought about this matter more than any other political problem in his whole life and had come to the conclusion that this was what he meant; that, if he were to speak for the Executive, this is what he must say; and that, if he could not say it, he must decline to speak. He put it forward not on grounds of military security, such as Ian Mikardo had mentioned, which seemed to him opportunist, but on moral grounds, because the weapons were evil.

The discussion was interrupted by the entry on two occasions of the Conference Arrangements Committee, and it is therefore difficult to describe it. Directly it was clear that Nye wanted a complete break, Hugh said quite briefly that he personally could not possibly agree to this proposal, which had had at this meeting the clear and unambiguous backing of only Barbara, Ian and Sydney Silverman. I said I agreed with Nye's position and had indeed said on the International Sub. that I could not remain on the Executive if we were to reaffirm at Conference the decision to make the H-bomb. Gaitskell put in that we had agreed that this should not be reaffirmed and that the statement on our behalf should make it clear that, on these great issues, the Party had not reached final decisions.

I supported this very strongly and said it was fantastic to expect the Executive, between today and tomorrow, to come to conclusions which override all the decisions on the subject of defence reached by the Parliamentary Party in the last six months. To take one problem only: would Nye in his speech say that, since we had abandoned nuclear weapons, we must insist that the abolition of conscription must be postponed? Otherwise, what sort of defence would we have? And I repeated my suggestion about a joint European repudiation of nuclear weapons, initiated by Britain. By this time, however, it was clear that the main decisions would have to be taken the next day, after consultations behind the scenes, and we passed on to the rest of the business.

There was only one interesting incident, when we discussed *Industry and Society*. Nye weighed in and said that he had remained silent during the whole controversy, though he had been unbearably attacked and provoked. Someone had even written suggesting that he had reached an agreement with Gaitskell about nationalization, although in fact he had not discussed the matter with Gaitskell even for five minutes. Such suggestions and imputations were unbearable and it was grossly improper for members of the Executive to say that the decision was unanimous, since this was a revelation of the secret proceedings of the Executive. If this sort of thing went on, he would be forced to register his protests and disagreements in writing.

All this speech was clearly directed at me,[1] and, talking to Sam Watson, whom I brought home to lunch, I came to the conclusion that it was the most illuminating thing Nye said this morning. No doubt he has come back from Russia, sold by Khrushchev on his role as peacemaker in the nuclear age. But what has really riled Nye is having to sit down under the imputation of agreeing with Gaitskell about nationalization. It is clear from what Nye said that he is not psychologically prepared to work on this basis and I wouldn't be surprised if his behaviour this morning was much more an attempt to get out of responsibility and retire to the country than an attempt to achieve supreme power in the Party, which is the last thing he wants.

Of course, the whole thing is very depressing, since it confirms what Sam Watson said to me last week about there being no apex to our Party at all. There is no coherent group of people running it and the Bevan–Gaitskell co-existence is extremely fragile. Any beliefs which have been growing up inside me during the last six months that we were getting a stable basis for a Labour Government have been pretty well shattered by this morning's experience. What a man Nye is! As we were leaving the room, Sydney Silverman said to me that, when he had discussed nuclear weapons with Nye at the end of July, Nye had smacked him down for wanting them abolished and said that such ideas were entirely obsolete. Yet this morning he looked in the peak of health and was extremely jolly on other subjects. I think the real trouble is that he has had two months alone with Jennie, being fed up with illusions, and what he is doing this afternoon heaven only knows.

---

[1] Crossman's *Mirror* article on September 17th had spoken of the agreement reached by Gaitskell and Bevan on 'a balanced programme of nationalization' and described *Industry and Society* as 'fully supported by Mr Bevan'.

20

Friday, September 27th

Hugh Gaitskell rang me at six last night and asked me to go and have a chat. He told me that Nye Bevan had arrived half an hour late for his talk at three and that the first half-hour had been spent discussing arrangements for Nye's American tour. Then they had begun on a discussion of *Industry and Society* and Nye had reaffirmed that he did not want a shopping list but expressed some mild but not very strong resentment against Harold Wilson and myself. He seemed, however, not in the least inclined for a row. He himself raised the issue of foreign policy and said he was in a great personal difficulty and wanted to feel he had a logical case to argue. This, in fact, was why he felt that, if we were in favour of suspending nuclear tests, we must also be in favour of stopping production of the weapon.

Of course this is true and we've known for nine months that the Labour Party's position was evasive. But Hugh Gaitskell had been forced to adopt it last April in order to keep the Party together and there seems no very good reason why Nye Bevan should not continue to adopt it today. Hugh thinks that the old boy isn't intending to bust up the Party or to get out — or, rather, that he wasn't yesterday afternoon before he got home to talk to Jennie. Nye has asked for the issue to be postponed till Sunday, so that he and Hugh can talk over a draft statement in the meanwhile. This Hugh personally has agreed to and will suggest to the Executive this afternoon.[1]

So we're off to Brighton. I go with yet another ferocious attack on me in the *Tribune* by Ian Mikardo and remembering a very shrewd estimate which George Wigg made to me on the phone this morning: whether I stay on the Executive depends largely on the strength of Gaitskell's position; I've been dubbed Gaitskell's apologist and will be thrown off if the constituency parties dislike him and will stay on if they tolerate him. This, I guess, is a pretty shrewd estimate. I've no relish for this Conference at all, particularly as it takes place during what we hope will be the arrival of our child.

Monday, September 30th

I got to Victoria on Friday to find the whole Pullman carriage packed with the Executive. I deposited my bags in the empty one next door, only to find that Tom Driberg had occupied both seats, so I sat by him and chatted during the journey. I took the occasion to ask Tom what, quite apart from content, was his estimate of me as a journalist. 'Of course,' he said, 'you take a lot more trouble about your *Daily Mirror* than you do about your *New Statesman* articles. The *Mirror* is really polished, whereas some of your longer reviews in the *New Statesman* are sometimes left rather in the rough. I wonder that you can do such a thing in a high-class journal like the *Statesman*.'

Otherwise he only talked to me about two subjects. About every twenty

---

[1] At the meeting Bevan proposed and Gaitskell seconded a motion to defer the matter until the Sunday before Conference. Sydney Silverman proposed an immediate discussion but was defeated by 18 votes to 6.

minutes he would bring in the subject of his chairmanship of the Party next year and the possibility that, at the last moment, somebody would move against it. I said to him, quite sincerely, that I thought there was no conceivable chance of this happening now, since trade union leaders are men of protocol and, if they had wanted to stop him being Chairman, they would have done so when he was elected Vice-Chairman last year.

Interspersed between these bouts of anxiety was a fountain of items about homosexuality, including a long and extremely obscene story about the Anglo-Catholic Rector of a local Brighton church, who had come into the room of a friend, to find him in bed with a boy and, after saying it was a deadly sin, had jumped into bed to join them. I suppose one can conclude that psychologically Tom is anxious lest his homosexuality denies him the chairmanship and he was revealing this in his long conversation with me, a subject which extended not only over the journey in the train but over a forty-minute walk on the front which I took with Harold Wilson. I told Harold about Tom and he replied, 'Oh, but he's quite right. Some of them are going to make an effort before this Conference is out.'[1]

The big Executive meeting took place in a conference room in the Pavilion, which I had last visited when I was convalescing last February with Anne. It was a torn, frayed, dreary, untidy meeting, which dragged on from half-past two until half-past five. The main subject was the allocation of speakers to the main debate, but this gave an occasion for a brief discussion of the H-bomb crisis. The secret had been well kept and not a breath had appeared in the morning press. As Hugh Gaitskell had told me the day before, the decision was that he and Nye should together prepare a paper. Morgan Phillips now announced that it would be shown to the Executive on Tuesday. At this there was a sigh of agony, since Tuesday seemed a bit late and, as Morgan said, the secret would anyway leak. Hugh also looked surprised, revealing that this had been fixed between Morgan and Nye.

Nye immediately gave way and agreed we should discuss it on Sunday afternoon, whereupon somebody else proposed, rather smartly, that Sam Watson, as chairman of the International Sub., should be a fellow member of the Committee, and Nye said, *sotto voce*, 'Two against one.' At this point Edith Summerskill complained that everything was being fixed by these two men and asked whether the views of other members of the Executive should not be considered. Sydney Silverman supported her and there was a half-hour discussion of this before the Executive decided to go on to the next business.

The only other scene was about *Industry and Society*. This produced the occasion for a voluble outburst all round, with Barbara and Ian both accusing me of having interpreted the document quite wrongly and Nye repeating his complaints that he had been accused of agreeing with Gaitskell and that the press had been loaded against the Left. The row was proceeding quite breezily when Ray Gunter burst out with a furious attack on members of the Executive

[1] They did not succeed.

who conducted their row in the public press – particularly, he added, those who, like Dick Crossman, exploit the Party's wounds in the capitalist press and are paid heavily for it.

I suppose we were all feeling terribly ratty as a result of not knowing whether Nye was going to blow up the Party this week. Anyway, I was boiling still when the Executive came to an end and I went up to Ray Gunter to tell him so. 'You needn't think we've forgotten your attack on the union,'[1] he said, 'and you may as well know the honest truth – that most of the fellows say "and what's worse, he does it for pay".' We then had a conversation hardly worthy of the name, since I was so angry I just abused him, with Sam Watson and Harry Nicholas looking on a bit uneasily. I finally got so worked up I said I would clear out, so that I really could write what I thought about the whole lot of them and then they would notice what somebody who writes really can do if he's free to do it. After which I proceeded stormily to the station and took the train to London. I had scarcely got back when Hugh Gaitskell was on the phone, which was nice of him. He merely said, 'Don't do anything hasty,' and when I said they were all bleeding buggers and that he'd been the only one who had stood up for me, he said, 'You mustn't expect much else. But don't blow off.'

I returned to Brighton for the compositing. I had expected an easy time on National Superannuation and we roughly got what we wanted – a blunt negative and a strong positive composite – but it took longer than I expected. At the second compositing meeting there were some sixty constituency parties represented to deal with pensioners and they were positively embarrassing in their willingness to eat out of my hand and gave us a very tame resolution.

I got back on Saturday night and had Sunday morning off before I went down to Brighton again at midday to the big Executive at half-past two. I had lunch at the Bedford Hotel and passed Hugh's table. He showed me the three disarmament composites. 'I gather we're O.K.,' he said. 'Nye wants to accept 1 [No. 23] and 3 [No. 25] and of course we must reject 2 [No. 24].[2] Have a look.' I took a look and said, 'You may have to have two remitted,' at which Hugh turned up his nose. 'Have you seen Nye?' I said. 'No, I haven't had a word with him. I've left it all to Sam.'

So at half-past two we went into the big meeting, at which we were to discuss our attitude to the composites. After the tea interval we got down to the disarmament resolutions, Nos. 23, 24 and 25. No. 23, from Paisley constituency Labour party and the A.E.U., was a perfectly harmless demand for an international disarmament agreement, in line with Party policy; No. 24 was a Harold Davies motion, demanding the renunciation of any British

---

[1] In his *Mirror* article on sponsored M.P.s, published on July 5th, 1957.

[2] No. 24 was proposed by the Norwood constituency Labour party and Leek constituency Labour party, Harold Davies's constituency. No. 25 was proposed by the Bristol North-West and Oxford constituency Labour parties.

nuclear weapons; and No. 25 was an odd little resolution, demanding an immediate British cessation of H-bomb tests. It differed from 23 in asking for unilateral British action as a help to disarmament. It was, however, very ambiguous, since it didn't ask for a suspension but a cessation, and it was a bit puzzling to hear that Nye, having gone late to the compositing, had insisted it should be included, presumably in order to give himself some special point in the big debate. The recommendation was that we should accept 23, reject 24 and accept 25, on the understanding that cessation meant suspension.

At this point the debate started, with Ian and Barbara saying that the thing had been argued out *ad nauseam* and they would merely like formally to move the acceptance of 24. Then Edith Summerskill made a long speech, in which she said she was not emotional on the subject but calm and objective, proceeding then to talk about the poisoning of the atmosphere and climaxing with the statement that, though she was not emotional, she had cancelled her order at the butcher for English meat! This was followed by Jack Cooper, who argued quite sensibly against unilateral repudiation, which maintained existing policy. He was followed by Jean Mann, who was as emotionally pro-nuclear as Edith had been emotionally against, and who started by saying that, if Edith had five sons who were all doctors, she would know there was a division of opinion in the medical world.

I came next and said we weren't likely to resolve our differences on the substance of the matter during this Conference, differences which for months had divided the Parliamentary Party. I thought the best thing for us to do was to adopt the compromise successfully reached in the Parliamentary Party, including toleration of disagreement. I pointed out that the resolution couldn't be accepted unless we were able to state what we would put in its place. You can't repudiate nuclear weapons without stating the alternative defence policy. If we accepted 24, our spokesman must at least be able to say what we should do about American bases in Britain and our membership of NATO, as well as announcing that we were in favour of postponing the abolition of conscription, so as to strengthen our conventional forces. It seemed to me absurd to suggest that we were ready to make any statements on these three subjects. I concluded by urging that in this case, where feelings were so deep, a remittal of 24 would be justified, on the ground that the Party was certainly in duty bound to consider the case for a defence policy which did not rely on nuclear weapons.

At this point Nye spoke and proceeded, without turning a hair, to repudiate everything he had said on Thursday morning, in the guise of answering Edith and Sydney, the chief independent advocates of nuclear renunciation. Nye started by saying that we could not consider nuclear weapons in the abstract. Composite 24, if properly considered, involved the whole of our foreign policy, since the repudiation of nuclear weapons by Britain would affect every relation we had with every other country all over the world. How, for instance, could we do this without consulting the members of the Commonwealth? How could we do it without ending our alliance with America? How could we do it without jeopardizing the Baghdad Pact? (Here he realized he'd gone a bit far and said, 'Of course I'm not denying one might not have to jeopardize it, but only pointing out the facts.')

The passing of this resolution, Nye said, would come as a terrible blow, not least in Moscow, where the Russians regarded us as a moderating influence and would be appalled if we suddenly abdicated. On the other hand, it was perfectly proper to propose the suspension of tests as a contribution to breaking the disarmament deadlock. And, if we proposed the suspension of tests, we would have to be realistic and admit that this might in fact involve holding up the production of nuclear weapons, since, for all we knew, Britain might be unable to produce weapons without further tests. But, if this holding up of production did in fact take place as a result of suspending tests, the motive for it would not be moralistic, like Edith's and Sydney's, but purely practical. Nye concluded with the words, 'Surely it would be a mistake to take all the cards out of the hand of Labour's next Foreign Secretary' — a sentence which followed an emphatic assertion that 24 should not at any cost be remitted but should be rejected out of hand by the Executive.

I think this was the first occasion on which a majority of those present had heard one of Nye's intellectual emotional somersaults. I leant across to Sydney and said, 'You are the only honest man here.' As I said it, Barbara Castle welcomed Nye's speech as a magnificent statement of policy, but asked whether he would not consider letting 24 be remitted as a method of softening up the Conference. Tony Greenwood, one of the great anti-H-bombers, remained absolutely silent. So did Ian Mikardo. Gaitskell said he agreed with every word Nye had said and only wished he could have said it as well, at which there was a murmur of relieved applause. Sydney observed that he didn't know whether Nye had been contradicting Edith or his own speech three days ago. He, Sydney, could not see anything else in this speech but a complete and utter repudiation of everything for which Nye had stood three days before. He, Sydney, was going to stand where he had stood, a remark which I alone cheered.

Afterwards Sam Watson told me that he had taken to Nye a bottle of whisky and ten little bottles, five of tonic and five of soda, and that by the end of the evening Nye wasn't noticing whether it was tonic or soda. They had really talked for two whole evenings and Sam had gradually got Nye round to the mood of the next Foreign Secretary and the representative of the world's mineworkers. As we came out the photographers were photographing and Gaitskell said to me, 'I suppose we oughtn't to look too pleased.' I also suddenly remembered that the sub-committee of three — Gaitskell, Bevan and Watson – had been instructed to draft a policy statement, which had never materialized! So in fact we are adopting the procedure I suggested at the International Sub. a week ago — of having a debate and relying on Nye's impromptu to see us through at the end.

I caught the 6.25 to London feeling cheered and happy and not caring really what happens now at this Conference. Certainly the mood was different this morning when I got to the Ice Rink. Harold Wilson moved the Emergency Resolution on the 7 per cent bank rate not to an enthusiastic Conference, but to what I think is called a responsible (i.e. a rather dull) Conference. But it's far too early yet to see what it's really like.

Friday, October 4th
Conference is now over, so this will not be a true reflection of my moods and feelings during it, but only a considered judgment on what, from Hugh's point of view and from the Party's point of view, has been a monumental success. In the first place, the Bevan–Gaitskell axis, which I have been talking and preaching about for months, is now securely and publicly established and — to mix my metaphors — Nye has burnt so many boats and bridges that he will find it very difficult to get back to Bevanism and the *Tribune*. As Sam Watson remarked to me, 'The apex I talked to you about is slowly beginning to be formed. I've been seeing a platform here able to handle Conference and give the leadership required.'

In the second place, on two really critical issues — nationalization and the H-bomb — the two big leaders, Gaitskell and Bevan, have strengthened their position with the electorate at large by curbing the Party extremists and asserting their authority over them in defiance of their dogma. After all, the two most important emotions of the Labour Party are a doctrinaire faith in nationalization, without knowing what it means, and a doctrinaire faith in pacifism, without facing its consequences. An old, well-established leadership can steer these two emotions into sane channels, provided it is united. A young and divided leadership finds it extremely difficult to stand up to either of them. But at Brighton this year this is just what Gaitskell and Bevan did.

Seen from the inside, it has, of course, been a complete victory for Hugh. After three years he has got his own interpretation of nationalization through without conceding an inch to his opponents[1] and, even more surprising, he has maintained his position on nuclear weapons without conceding an inch more than he conceded in the Parliamentary Party.[2] No wonder he looked pleased and confident when the Mayor gave us dinner in the Prince Regent's dining hall last night. Moreover, every member of the Executive has watched this test of strength between Hugh and Nye and knows from inside the qualities which each man showed — Hugh firm, obstinate, not very adroit but keeping his eyes fixed on his long-term objectives; Nye immensely more powerful personally, practically far more skilful but completely failing to

[1] Conference debated *Industry and Society* on Wednesday, October 2nd. The critical amendment, moved by James Campbell of the N.U.R., was defeated by 5,383,000 votes to 1,442,000.
[2] Resolution 24, proposing unilateral repudiation of nuclear weapons testing, manufacture and use, was defeated by 5,836,000 votes to 781,000.

achieve his long-term objectives because of the pendulum swing of his emotions.

I shan't record here at great length the actual events of the Conference. I was expecting a close shave when the results were announced on Tuesday morning, whereas poor Sydney Silverman had never conceived the possibility that he might be knocked off the Executive. There he sat in the glaring television lights, sweating and nearly in tears. It would, of course, have been even more dramatic if I had had my success in Superannuation after being defeated! But most members of the Executive are curiously unimaginative and remarked what a pity it was that I didn't make the speech first and so get to the top of the poll. Actually I wouldn't have made nearly such a good speech from the top of the poll.

I had stayed down for Monday night without going back to Anne in order to prepare my speech after dinner. But when I went down to the *Daily Mirror* rooms, Bill Connor was in singularly odious form and spent an hour accusing me of being a coward and double-crosser and generally trying to undermine my morale. I got angrier and angrier and he told me that I rebuked him. Of this I have no very clear memory, nor, indeed, of the dinner which I had with Vicky and Jimmy Cameron[1] at English's Restaurant. And I have the vaguest idea that I did sit for some time in the hall of the Bedford, talking to Joe Harsch.[2] What I know for certain is that I woke up at five in the morning, not remembering how I got to bed nor having done any work on my speech, feeling that God would reward me for such gross negligence, though I could remember that I rang up Joe Harsch to make sure that everything I said was off the record. However, nobody seemed to have noticed anything of what I did, and I had duly got my key, taken off my clothes, taken all my money out and done all the proper things. So there I lay in bed, dutifully trying to be asleep until seven o'clock, when I got up, feeling fine, and began to work on my speech.

I had suggested that I should only reply to the debate, partly because I didn't want anybody else speaking on National Superannuation and partly because I thought that the atmosphere would be better if we forwent an Executive opening. Fortunately the composites and the resolutions covered practically all the questions anybody has asked at the dozen conferences I have taken on the subject. So I did the most obvious thing and merely ticked the passages one after the other and answered them. There's no more secret in it than that. If you look at my speech you will find that that is it, with two minutes of pep at the end and three or four minutes of thanks at the beginning.

It was a quarter to nine by the time I was getting to the end of making some notes on very thin paper, which kept on curling. So I went down and

---

[1] James Cameron, a broadcaster and journalist on numerous papers, including the *News Chronicle*, where he was Foreign Correspondent. He was Journalist of the Year in 1965.

[2] A journalist and broadcaster, he was Senior European Correspondent of the American National Broadcasting Corporation 1957–65.

tried to start breakfast, when Peay[1] came up and said he wanted me to give him three cue-in and cue-outs for the television cameras. This was difficult when there was nothing but a few notes, but it made me think hard about the peroration, which was a good idea.

Having to prepare a speech was a very good thing, since I could scarcely worry about the National Executive results. My whole mind was set on worrying about the thin paper curling up and the more I sat on it the more it curled round my behind. I asked Harold for some paper (he was sitting next to me) and out of an immense folder he produced half a dozen different sizes of paper, all fixed together ready for a speech. But by this time the election results were being announced and I found I had scraped on, with a terrific loss of votes. Curiously enough, my result was exactly what everybody had expected: I couldn't possibly be knocked off but I should only scrape through. What the Left had done by its campaign was to substitute Jim Callaghan for Sydney Silverman, which is hardly a strengthening of the Left! I had managed to infuriate everybody by the combination of my remarks about the trade unions and by what was resented as improper intervention in the *Daily Mirror* on the subject of *Industry and Society*. Somehow, I think, even the supporters of the Executive resented my argy-bargying about the document with Barbara and Ian. That is not what respectable people do.

Anyhow I really didn't hear any of the beginning of the debate, since I can't listen much before making a speech. I did note down the names of two or three delegates, only to find in each case that somebody I thought was supporting me was rejecting me and couldn't be used. It was rather a flat but quite competent debate. Throughout it I couldn't raise a spark of interest and kept on wondering whether I could keep going, since I felt so flat and deflated by being on the Executive after all that fuss, and the paper kept curling up all the time, and Harold warned me that, for a tall man, it was almost impossible to see one's papers, since there was no book-rest and there was an electric light right in front of you to stop you looking down.

However, in due course there comes the moment. I had to walk along the whole length of the platform from my seat at one extreme to the rostrum at the other, to quite a friendly round of applause. It was only when I was at the rostrum that I remembered about thanking the Woolwich branch of the T. & G., and then I remembered something Nye had told me ages ago. 'There's only one tip I can give you about speaking,' he said. 'Spend the first few minutes trying to get your audience in good humour. Don't kick them. Don't knife them. Don't prick them for the first two minutes. Jolly them into a good humour with you.' And it occurred to me that the best humour they could be in was if I said I had to tear up my notes in view of the excellence of

[1] Kenneth Peay, a Labour Party agent for a group of constituencies in East Sussex from 1949 to 1952. In 1952 he moved to Transport House, where he held a number of posts, including those of National Youth Officer, Propaganda Officer, and, eventually, Broadcasting (and later Television) Officer. In 1959 he left Transport House to establish his own firm.

the debate and would merely answer it. This would justify any length of speech. And it occurred to me that it would be a good thing after that to do a lot of thanking other people, because then they wouldn't think I am conceited, as they normally do. I'm pretty sure it was these two oratorical tricks which really worked. Anyway, within half a minute, they were silent and listening just like a university lecture audience and, fortunately for me, I saw right in the middle Frank Cousins, who is the ideal W.E.A. three-year tutorial class member — a long, not very intelligent face, which nods when it's got it at last.

So I talked to Frank throughout and then found, as I walked back, that Jim Griffiths was clutching my left hand and Hugh Gaitskell my right hand and that awful Ian was patting me on the back and the long journey back along the platform was quite triumphant. And finally, to my complete astonishment, I was having to get up again to receive the cheers and, owing to my having to shampoo my hair to get rid of dandruff, it couldn't be kept from flopping over my face throughout my speech, which was regarded as highly characteristic.

Anyhow, I was a famous man that day and all along the front people came rushing up to grasp one's hand. It's nice to bask in a beautiful October sunshine in fleeting fame. And, by Jove, Hugh Cudlipp basks too. He was down for the day with Eileen and at cocktails that night his local boy had made good and he'd known it all along. He is genuinely and completely generously pleased when his boys are famous and do well, and he had apparently been taking credit all along the front. Dear Sydney Jacobson, though, was genuinely deeply moved as a Labour Party member and pleased in quite a different way.

But the man who was absolutely overwhelmed was Cassandra, who seemed to think I had revealed some mysterious qualities which he couldn't conceive possible and kept asking me how one did it. Indeed, all of them were a bit puzzled as to why this had been such a great success, because there was nothing witty, clever or revolutionary in the whole speech. But of course there was. To be willing to answer, and, above all, to give the Conference a moral justification for liking a new idea — that was the secret. For the British Labour Party has a fear and suspicion of ideas and the intellectuals who produce them. Just as intellectuals are potential traitors, so the new ideas they put forward are always by nature assumed to be anti-Socialist, until you can show that they are not. What I had done was to convince Conference that a really practical, workable scheme was compatible with the Socialist conscience, and I had done so by conscientiously dealing with all the objections of Socialist C.O.s.

That night came the *Tribune* meeting, to which I went after the Cudlipp party. It was in the newly repainted and exquisitely elegant and beautiful Corn Market, a long Regency ballroom with vast mirrors and a barrel-vault roof in pale grey and pink. It was full of everybody in the Conference under forty — very striking that Nye still appeals to youth. Michael was at his most blaring demagogic. One last gallant bang at *Industry and Society*, at the H-bomb, at the National Executive. I think he knew worse was coming and the moment Nye got up it was clear. Here he violated his own precept, antagonizing his audience from the first sentence by saying it would obviously be improper for him to discuss either *Industry and Society* or the H-bomb, the two subjects they wanted to hear.

Then he made a long, statesmanlike speech and if he goes on like this he will be as statesmanlike as Herbert Morrison, since truisms and platitudes are now curling round his lips in a very serene way. The audience got a bit restive, particularly when he moved to a peroration in which Michael was to go on at the *Tribune* while we are busy elsewhere and there is to be unity at all costs in the Party. It was clear enough from this speech that the *Tribune* and the Bevanites had been put out to grass for the time being, though Nye might possibly want them later on.

I caught the train back to London on Wednesday night and went down on Thursday morning for the big debate on foreign affairs. As a result of this to-ing and fro-ing to Anne, I missed all the social events of the Conference and a good many of the conversational sidelights, since I had very few conversations. The H-bomb debate went pretty well, as one might have expected. Here again, the conflict between sense and emotion couldn't have been sharper. But on this occasion a number of people with responsibility had surrendered to emotion and, because we had no initial spokesman, the only voice for sense before Nye got up was that of John Strachey, which is not particularly persuasive. Everybody else, climaxing in a huge African from Hampstead (he was preceded by a number of hysterical women, who gave me the jim-jams), was trying to save Nye's soul from the Foreign Office and working up the Conference into a welter of nuclear spasms.

As a speech, Nye's performance was far the worst I have ever heard him make. Indeed, he didn't ever succeed in making his speech at all, since he rasped off about the H-bomb straightaway (again violating his own advice), got the audience up against him and then just floundered round and round in circles, trying to say to Conference what he had said to us privately last Sunday but failing to find the words or the arguments. It was a ghastly performance. And yet it was immensely impressive directly they started heckling him, for at this point the old bull turned. I was sitting at the far end and I could see that vast, blue-suited figure and bright red face and the iron grey hair – angry (and he's terrific when he's angry), mortally offended and repudiating with violent indignation the suggestion that he was grooming himself as Foreign Secretary. It was this suggestion which really brought out his best replies.

Before Nye had spoken, there had come the extraordinary speech of Cousins, which was interpreted by the Conference as pledging the T. & G. to vote for abolishing nuclear weapons.[1] After Nye had finished, I turned

---

[1] Frank Cousins asked for time to consult the Transport and General Workers delegation, which outvoted by 16 votes to 14 the line he had just taken.

round to Harry Nicholas and asked what it meant. 'Does it leave you open?' I asked. 'Yes,' Harry said. 'That's the point of it.' This doesn't coincide with the ordinary journalists' story that Frank Cousins and the union were going to vote against the motion, but I believe it's nearer the truth. I believe Frank Cousins was making an odious attempt to get the best of both worlds: i.e. to make a speech which would persuade Nye to change his mind but which, if this failed, could still justify his voting with the Executive. Anyhow, the moment Nye had finished, the appeal was made for an adjournment to reconsider things and I went off to lunch with the Coventry delegates.

How had Nye taken it? I had given him a drink immediately afterwards and told him that he wouldn't want me to say it was one of his best speeches, but it was one of his greatest performances, an odious thing to have to do but a tremendous job—which is true. He was flustered and flurried but when Barbara and Ian attacked him immediately afterwards he did not concede to them in any way. My impression is that his mind is very much made up and he is now ready to be on good terms with Hugh. But one thing which the day's events did change was the status of Mr Frank Cousins, who, up till then, was the wonderful trade union leader but who is now thought by some to have one foot of clay, compared to Mr Carron,[1] who is not an orator but does not perform somersaults in public quite as ineptly.

Of course, the real hero of this Conference was Sam Watson, who went down with Asian flu yesterday and was in bed for the show. But I have no doubt that now the apex will be formed with an inner circle of Labour policy-makers and deciders, built round Hugh and Nye and including myself as well as Harold, and Carron as well as Cousins.

Throughout the time we were at Brighton the sun shone, with piled-up beautiful white clouds over the land and clear blue over the sea. The moon shone over the sea at night and the town looked exquisitely beautiful. But maybe I wouldn't have noticed all this beauty if the election results had been different and my speech worse. Anyhow I could enjoy it very much this time and it was nice getting the attached letter from old Hugh.

The letter from Hugh Cudlipp ran:

My dear Dick,

I think you'll have had the best day of your political life, so far, last Tuesday. I'm awfully glad! Clearly you were in top form and Conference knew it. Now you come in the straight and unchallengeable line for that particular job, and it will be a key job, in the next Cabinet.

If you'd spoken before the N.E. election, you'd have topped the poll. But Mikardo clearly did you harm, as he intended. This, however, is quite transitory, gone already. I'm very glad Jim Callaghan is on, though I wish he'd beaten Mikardo or Driberg, rather than little Sydney.

[1] The President of the Amalgamated Engineering Union 1956–67. He was knighted in 1963 and became a life peer in 1967. He died in 1969.

The broad results of the Conference are quite first class, both for our Party and the General Public. And now no more Gadarenery!

I asked your secretary yesterday about Anne and the Baby. I hope all goes, and will go, well. I go to the country tomorrow till Tuesday, but shall see The Times.

Love to Anne, and a Bugle salute to you!

Hugh.

October 5th, 1957
Birth of PATRICK DANVERS CROSSMAN.

Thursday, October 24th
Since my last entry, the main interest in my life has been fatherhood, which doesn't concern this diary but which possibly may yet affect my character and chances as a politician. However, what matters here is that, during these three weeks, the Gaitskell–Bevan axis has strengthened in all sort of ways. I have no doubt whatsoever that Nye has decided, as irrevocably as he can, to work with Hugh, win the Election and to be Foreign Secretary. He has been to lunch with Hugh and Hugh told me rather coyly last week that he was motoring down to Cholsbury to lunch with Nye. These are really decisive events in the life of these two men, who had never before had a drink with each other, far less a meal, in their lives.

In my political life, the other incident worth noting has been the decision of Mr Boyd-Carpenter to launch a frontal attack on our Superannuation plan. He started it at the Tory Conference by lambasting Titmuss and Abel-Smith as a skiffle group of professors who had got their sums wrong. I replied in a letter to *The Times*,[1] which I posted on October 15th and was amazed to see in the paper next morning. Titmuss and Abel-Smith contributed a long letter to which Boyd-Carpenter had replied in two more speeches, each more offensive than the last. This strongly suggests to me that the Government has made up its mind not to put forward any major long-term reforms of pensions.[2] Since they have done this, it will be to their interest to explode, as far as they can, our long-term proposals, which they might have considered on their merits if they themselves were seeking to improve them.

Discussing this with me yesterday after the Executive, Hugh Gaitskell said we must now be prepared for major assaults. I mentioned I was writing another letter to *The Times* and asked if I should show it to him. 'Oh, for God's sake don't do that,' Hugh said. 'I'm trying to establish a principle now of having one man in charge of each job.' I doubt whether he realized what he was saying or what Edith Summerskill, Douglas Jay, Hilary Marquand

[1] Crossman's letter was published on October 16th and was followed by one from Richard Titmuss, Brian Abel-Smith and Peter Townsend on October 18th and another from Crossman on October 25th.

[2] In the Queen's Speech in November the Conservatives were to announce that the first legislative item of the Session would be a Pensions Bill, but see p. 625 below.

and Peggy Herbison would think if they had overheard his bland assumption that I was the one man in charge of social security.

Altogether these three weeks after Conference have been rosied over by a pleasant afterglow of success, in which the success of having a baby has played an important political part. When I was down at Coventry, after dealing with war pensioners in the Town Hall, I went up to a social at Upper Stoke, the usual dreary kind of affair, in which you enter a long school hall and see a few elderly ladies scattered around the edges of the empty dance floor, sitting chattering in low voices, while a woman plays the piano and the master of ceremonies fails to get anybody dancing.

Usually I try to make a speech from the middle of the floor but on this occasion I was presented with a giant panda, unexpectedly, and found myself speechless and only able to say that this was the first thing I had ever done since I became a candidate twenty years ago of which no one in Coventry had disapproved. There is no doubt that this was the best speech I have ever made.

Undoubtedly the coincidence of Patrick and Super-Anne, which Vicky would have liked to immortalize in the unpublished cartoon he has presented to me, has for the first time given me a sort of respectable political position and, for the time being, eradicated memories of some of my past. In a funny sort of way I suppose I am proceeding as Nye is proceeding, recognizing that, if I don't serve in the next Labour Government, I shall never be a Minister in my life, that I am too old now to remain a young man with adventurous ideas and that I had therefore better settle down to polishing myself for responsibility, even if this means my column becomes far too respectable for Hugh Cudlipp's taste.

This is something I have been thinking about quite a lot recently. I think the only way of counterbalancing the flatness of respectability is to make the column 100 per cent reliable in predicting, or anticipating at least, official Labour attitudes. It must, in fact, be the super-duper official Labour view, précised succinctly a week before Bevan and Gaitskell have thought it out. Will anybody notice? The answer probably is: just enough to get the column a kind of cachet.

Parliament had reassembled on October 29th, to finish the business of the 1956/57 Session; the new Session began on November 5th. During the Recess there had been two by-elections. Richard Stokes, the Labour M.P. for Ipswich, had died on August 3rd, a fortnight after he had been badly injured in a motor accident. A by-election was held on October 24th, and Dingle Foot held the seat for Labour with a majority of 7,737 votes over John Cobbold, Conservative. Miss Manuela Sykes, the Liberal candidate, took 12,587 votes, an increase of nearly 4,000 votes for her Party, which had last contested the seat in 1950. The Labour proportion of the poll fell by 7 per cent, while the Conservative proportion rose by 14 per cent.

Mr Moss Turner-Samuels, Q.C., the Labour M.P. for Gloucester, had died on June 6th and a by-election was held on September 12th. John Diamond held the seat for Labour with a majority of 8,374 over Francis Dashwood, Conservative. The Liberal candidate, Lt Colonel P. H. Lort-Phillips, took 7,393 votes, the highest Liberal vote at Gloucester for twenty-five years. The Labour proportion of the vote rose by 0·4 per cent, while the Conservative proportion fell by 20·5 per cent.

Perhaps the most dramatic event of the autumn was Russia's launching of two earth satellites. The first, Sputnik 1, a sphere 23 inches in diameter and weighing 180 pounds, was launched on October 4th, entering its orbit more than 500 miles from the earth at a speed of 18,000 m.p.h. This carried it round the world in ninety-five minutes. Sputnik 2 was launched on November 3rd. It was sent to a distance of 900 miles from the earth and its circuit took 1 hour 42 minutes. Six times heavier than Sputnik 1, this satellite contained an Eskimo dog, Laika.

Western countries, particularly the U.S.A., were awed and alarmed at the technological and strategic implications of this achievement.

Wednesday, November 6th

Last time I wrote in this diary I described the rosy after-glow of Conference success. What did I expect of the new Session? I wish I had written a week ago and then I might have the truth in this diary. We came back to wind up the last Session in a four-day tag-end, of which two were devoted to a big debate on the economic situation, which was dominated by the Government's rather clumsy efforts to achieve a wages freeze without being accused of actually imposing a wages policy.

My chief impression was that the Recess had altered nothing and that Parliament had resumed at the crawling, lethargic pace at which it left off in July. All the terrific events of the Recess, whether they were the domestic 7 per cent bank rate or the Russian sputnik, or the Tories' by-election defeats, seemed to have changed nothing in the make-up of the Labour Party, which didn't even bother to have a Party Meeting. That much I did observe. What I did not foresee was the effect this would have on me personally. A number of people, headed by Bob Mellish, told me how proud they were of me, which was nice to think of, considering that most of them wouldn't speak to me at the end of last Session.

Meanwhile, in the great wide world, the second Russian sputnik is circling the earth, dog and all, and, from what I can gather, has devastated American morale. The reaction, of course, as Macmillan, back from Washington, probably overemphasized, is a desire to get the Western world together in a frantic effort to catch up with the Russians. I'm not sure that this isn't exactly the wrong reaction from the British point of view. It means, as Nye would put it, increasing polarization, another period of cold war and gigantic arms expenditure, and Western Europe tighter than ever in the Atlantic system.

Perhaps the proper reaction would really be a loosening rather than a tightening, leaving America and Russia to face each other as super-Powers, with Europe more or less independent in between. But of course that would only work if Khrushchev and Co. do not use this fantastic new dominance they have acquired for aggression and expansion. After that evening with Khrushchev, I find it very difficult to believe that he will be both self-sacrificing and self-controlled. He seems to be a boss and a bully, who doesn't believe in world expansion with his brain but will practise it in a quite sincere effort to make Russia safe. I will never forget his contemptuous attitude to us, his couldn't-care-less suggestion that we should join the Russians because, if not, they would swat us off the face of the earth like a dirty old black beetle.

But supposing Khrushchev does believe this? Supposing he has the power? It seems to me futile to believe that the Western world, with its present type of capitalist organization, could discipline itself to a twenty-year arms race. So back we come to the idea that it might be better to opt out of that race, reckoning that the Russians have nothing much to gain by mopping us up and could well be induced to leave us alone. Of course, that's the sort of thing one can write in one's diary, but it isn't the sort of thing which one can publish or even suggest in speeches, since it's still regarded as defeatist and .unrealistic.

By the way, Nye is now on a tour of the States and is keeping very faithfully to his Labour Party brief. I should think he is making a devastating impression, combined with the sputnik, but I should also think that he is not being remarkably adroit and is causing offence everywhere he goes by his queer combination of sophisticated charm and pretentious left-wingism. However, you have to paint with a fairly broad brush in order to get the Americans to notice and I am not prepared to criticize Nye in any way for what he is doing.

Oh dear, how small and unimpressive the Front Bench is when you try to match it against the problems with which it will have to cope! Harold Wilson grows fatter, more complacent and more evasive each time you meet him. George Brown is a slick upstart with a yellow streak. Alf Robens is a nice old thing with a good manner and nothing behind it. Jim Griffiths is gaga and so is Edith Summerskill. Tony Greenwood is a clothes-horse and Dick Mitchison a dear old thing, with the most blundering mind I've ever met. That leaves Gaitskell and Bevan, who are, I think, a pretty good pair if they work together. Anyway, I am more convinced than ever that the only thing one can do is to try to see that they work together, to back both of them as long as that is possible.

Friday, November 15th
This week I've been chiefly concerned with the Government's National Insurance Bill. I had heard from Harold Wilson that, at the Shadow Cabinet,

the suggestion that I should speak on the Second Reading had been strongly opposed by Edith Summerskill, Tony Greenwood and James Callaghan – an interesting trio. Marquand and Jim Griffiths were elected to do the job. Even so, I somehow thought that, when the debate came on Wednesday, it would be a big day, with a sense of crusade on our side, since we've both had our own good ideas for solving the problem and haven't had a Government Bill to oppose which was a real swindle.

Directly we got down to the debate, with Boyd-Carpenter's speech, the House thinned out and I doubt if there were ever more than fifty people there during the whole afternoon and evening – and usually the number was nearer fifteen. Boyd-Carpenter was competent and clever but it's a terribly bad Bill and he was far less cocky than anyone expected. I had been told by Hugh Dalton, who had seen the Speaker, that I should be called fourth, as the second on our side, and I made quite a good speech, which surprised many of our own people, who apparently had no idea that it really was true that the Tory Bill was a swindle.[1] The debate quietly petered along until Jim Griffiths wound up with quite a good speech and, last, Miss Edith Pitt,[2] who I thought was really rather a charmer, scoring me off quite neatly about my figures. You can get away with being a woman, naïve and pert, and she did.

Yesterday the row about the leak[3] went on in the Chamber, while I went down below at the working party, which had at last come to the job of preparing Amendments for the two-day Committee Stage. I suppose I was bad-tempered, but I did find the whole thing inexpressibly amateur and dreary and after two hours I went upstairs to see what was going on. I had just sat down when Jim Griffiths looked round and signalled. When I sat beside him, in the gangway, he whispered that I should be on the Front Bench for the Committee. 'Who says so?' I said. 'Nobody's told me.' 'Well, it was fixed at the Parliamentary Committee last night,' Jim said.

My immediate reactions to such situations are always fatal. I made it quite clear I didn't much want to be on the Committee Stage unless I was invited and that anyway I might be more useful below the gangway. Poor Jim looked very hurt. I didn't think very much more about it until I went to the Party Meeting, where, after the announcement of the elections, the business was discussed. Hugh said that the Committee Stage would be taken

[1] Crossman always called the Conservatives' superannuation proposals 'the Tory swindle'. Under the Conservative scheme, the additional pension was strictly related to the additional contribution, on an actuarial basis, in terms of cash. On any reasonable assumption about inflation, contributors would thus inevitably receive in real terms less from the scheme than they had contributed. The Crossman scheme was dynamic and inflation-proofed; Boyd-Carpenter's was neither.

[2] Conservative M.P. for the Edgbaston division of Birmingham from 1953 until her death in 1966. She was joint Parliamentary Secretary at the Ministry of Pensions and National Insurance 1955–9 and Parliamentary Secretary at the Ministry of Health 1959–62. She became a D.B.E. in 1962.

[3] See below, pp. 626–8.

by Jim, Marquand, Margaret Herbison and Bernard Taylor.[1] At this, Arthur Lewis,[2] who has never said a friendly thing about me before, put me into acute embarrassment by suggesting that my name should be added. Hugh Gaitskell said, 'We don't usually do this but in this case we did ask him and he's too busy.' So I got what I deserved.

Previously we had had the announcement of the elections to the Shadow Cabinet. A large number of people, including George Wigg, hadn't even bothered to vote and only about 100 bothered to turn up to hear the revolutionary election result, which turns out Edith Summerskill and Kenneth Younger and replaces them with Patrick Gordon Walker and Arthur Bottomley. During the week I have discussed with several people the extraordinary state of lethargy and desultoriness in Parliament. Douglas Jay said to me yesterday at tea that it was all because the decent salaries had come too late and everybody had got their main interests outside.[3] There is something to this but not all. I think this parliamentary atmosphere probably in a way reflects the atmosphere outside Parliament. After all, it's not very different when you get down to Coventry for municipal affairs or to a trade union.

Instead of a struggle, what we have now is an Establishment, including the Conservative and Labour hierarchies, in which the masses acquiesce and against which the angry young men foam in a non-political repudiation of politics.[4] The real opposition now is anti-political, not Left or Right, and it is clear to me that even the best party in the world, with a nice sensible programme of action, including three other ideas as good as National Superannuation, would not fundamentally change this situation.

On September 24th, five days after the 2 per cent rise in bank rate, Harold Wilson had written (since the Chancellor was in America) to Enoch Powell, Financial Secretary to the Treasury, stating that it had been indicated that information about the forthcoming increase had leaked before the new rate was published. Mr Wilson asked for an investigation, but on September 26th Mr Powell had replied that 'careful investigation' had disclosed no evidence, either in the operations of the gilt-edged market or elsewhere, to suggest that a leak had occurred. Mr Wilson sent another letter on October 4th, including the

[1] A former coalminer, who served as Labour M.P. for the Mansfield division of Nottinghamshire from 1941 until 1966, when he became a life peer, taking the title of Lord Taylor of Mansfield. He was Parliamentary Secretary to the Ministry of National Insurance 1950–1.

[2] A former official of the National Union of General and Municipal Workers, 1938–48, he was Labour M.P. for the Upton division of West Ham 1945–50, for West Ham North 1950–74 and since 1974 has been M.P. for Newham North-West.

[3] On July 4th the Prime Minister had announced a net rise in the allowances of M.P.s not holding any Crown office. Instead of the existing 'sessional allowance' of £280 a year, Members would now receive an annual expenses allowance of £750.

[4] The archetypal 'angry young men' were John Wain, who wrote *Hurry on Down* (London: Secker & Warburg, 1953); John Osborne, whose play *Look Back in Anger* was produced in 1956 and published the following year (London: Faber); and Colin Wilson, whose critical essay *The Outsider* was published in 1956 (London: Gollancz).

statement that prima facie *evidence had been brought to his attention, 'suggesting that the leak emanated from a political source'. The Prime Minister immediately replied, asking that this evidence be laid before the Lord Chancellor. Private and informal inquiries conducted by the Lord Chancellor led him to conclude that there were no grounds for inviting Parliament to establish a formal inquiry and on October 22nd the Prime Minister so informed Mr Gaitskell.*

On that day Mr Gaitskell, after consulting Elwyn Jones, James Griffiths and Harold Wilson, published a statement that an inquiry by the Lord Chancellor, a member of the Government, was no substitute for an investigation by 'an independent judicial person'. The matter was raised again on November 12th by Sir Leslie Plummer, in a Parliamentary Question to the Chancellor. He asked whether prior information of the intention to raise the bank rate had been given to Oliver Poole, Deputy Chairman of the Conservative Party Organization. The Chancellor denied that any such information had been so confided; Sir Leslie pressed his questions, supported by Mr Wilson, who alluded to Mr Poole's 'vast City interests'.

On Tuesday, prompted by Harold Wilson, Dick Plummer asked a Question about the bank rate leak and, on the Supplementary, mentioned Oliver Poole, the Vice-Chairman of the Tory Party. From that moment the leak became the main political news. On Wednesday Macmillan conceded an inquiry and on Thursday we debated the precise terms of reference.[1] Of course, it's very easy to be narky about a topic of this sort, simply because you don't happen to be concerned with it. Nevertheless, I can't help feeling slightly uncomfortable that this is the only issue which has stirred real fervour so far in this resumed Parliament.

Unfortunately it's a nasty sort of fervour. I haven't met anybody who really believes that anything can possibly be proved against Oliver Poole, although it is noteworthy that we should certainly never have included the Vice-Chairman of the Labour Party as one of the inner group of people to be informed in advance of Government economic policy. Yet, on the other hand, one can hardly blame Harold Wilson for stimulating the Question, since, in view of the rumours circulating in the City, it has been outrageous of Macmillan to deny an inquiry. It's just like him to go on refusing until one of his friends is defamed, at which he immediately concedes it.

Now that the terms of reference are widely drawn and the tribunal will have power to cross-examine the stockbrokers concerned as to the names of the clients who sold after closing time on the famous Wednesday, some interesting information may be obtained. But what was happening this week

[1] On November 13th the Prime Minister announced the establishment of a Tribunal of Inquiry, at the request of the Chancellor and Mr Poole, to enable them to rebut these imputations. On November 14th the names of the Inquiry's members were published. Lord Justice Parker would preside over the Tribunal, assisted by two Q.C.s, Mr Holland and Mr Veale.

was a real Party rumpus, with insinuations from our side and indignant personal repudiations from the other. At bottom, a good many on both sides have been feeling uncomfortable. I talked to Hugh Fraser and Alec Spearman and both of them of course realized that an inquiry should have been conceded weeks ago and great damage has been done to the Prime Minister by his refusal. Equally, on our side most people dislike the feeling that we'd started personal recrimination, since it can go quite a long way.

This has been a very gloomy ten days – gloomy in the weather, with the sky mostly so dark that it seemed almost dusk, gloomy internationally, with the Americans reacting to the sputnik with a blind determination to renew the arms race, and, above all, gloomy in Parliament. It's now quite clear that we've come back and settled down to the same appalling type of ill-tempered lethargy we had in July.

Friday, November 22nd

This has been a mixed bag of a week, ending with our libel action.[1] Monday, Tuesday and Wednesday were the Committee Stage of the National Insurance Bill and, in view of Gaitskell's statement to the Party Meeting, I had to sit on my backbench for as long as possible throughout the proceedings in order to reduce the bad impression. On Tuesday I really did spend the whole day successfully in the House and thanked my lucky stars I wasn't sitting as fourth string on the Front Bench. I found nobody really anxious to have a fight which involved a late night. Of course one tends to be self-centred about the things one is interested in but I wonder if I am being really self-centred about pensions. In the 1930s, when the scales of unemployment assistance were being discussed, they were fought for days and nights on end by the Labour Opposition. This particular Pensions Bill is the most niggardly, mean measure and could have been opposed outright by us without any difficulty whatsoever. The argument that we should have been misunderstood if we had voted against it is fantastic.

It does seem to me rather serious that we should have all got our new salaries last July before the pensioners and that, now we've got them, the Labour Party shows no spark of conscience in denouncing the present pension rates. If we had threatened real opposition on this occasion and threatened to delay the Bill, I believe we should have extracted concessions from the Minister. As it was, however, the Bill went along with not more than twenty or thirty people in the House for the whole of Tuesday and stopped punctually at half-past ten, the usual time.

[1] Bevan and Others *v.* The *Spectator* Ltd, heard in the High Court of Justice, Queen's Bench Division, on Thursday, November 21st, and Friday, November 22nd, before the Lord Chief Justice, Lord Goddard, and a jury. Mr Gilbert Beyfus, Q.C., and Mr J. Montgomerie (instructed by Messrs Goodman, Derrick & Co.) appeared as Counsel for the Plaintiffs. Mr W. A. Fearnley-Whittingstall, Q.C., Mr Colin Duncan and Mr Owen Stable (instructed by Messrs Oswald Hickson, Collier & Co.) appeared as Counsel for the Defendants.

On Wednesday, too, the passage was strictly clockwork and the Third Reading speeches were being made long before ten o'clock. I think I did myself some good with the Party by sitting in and making two or three quite good speeches. No one on the Front Bench tried to be aggressive or really seemed very indignant and, apart from the old professionals, no one was sitting on the Tory backbenches at all and only about twenty on ours.

I think it's the first Bill I've seen right through all its stages, which shows what has been wrong with me since 1945! I am very glad I did it. I certainly made myself a lot more hated by the Front Bench by proving I could be infinitely more effective from below the gangway than if I had taken the place of Bernard Taylor in the front and only been permitted to speak on those Amendments which were rejected first by Jim Griffiths, then by Hilary Marquand and then by Peggy Herbison.

Then, at the end of the week, came our two-day libel action in the High Court. I had to rush out of the House for an hour on Wednesday to a conference in Mr Beyfus's chambers.[1] The Counsel we had chosen, Mr Aldous,[2] had fallen ill and Mr Beyfus had taken over at short notice It had been agreed with Goodman, our solicitor, that we should consult together on the day before the hearing in order to have one last negotiation to achieve a settlement out of court. I knew, of course, that Goodman was determined to fight the action if he could, but realized he couldn't fight it without me. I realized that Morgan Phillips, though he was scared stiff of fighting the action, is weak as water and would do as he was told. I realized, finally, that Nye, dear Nye, is always his old pendulum-swinging self.

On Wednesday everybody was in form. Mr Beyfus started off by discussing at length our procedure in the court, on the bland assumption that we were going to fight. After an hour I forced Goodman to intervene on the subject of negotiation. At this point Nye immediately said he didn't want any money and would be perfectly content with the apology and £500, the amount they had paid into court already. I said I must insist on their printing the apology I had drafted, stating that they had received it from me, paying £500 damages and also paying every penny of the costs. It was agreed that our lawyers should go into court, wait for the other side to make their offer, if they made it, and then, at twenty-nine minutes past ten, make our offer. I was still determined to settle the case if I could but I was also aware that Beyfus and Goodman very much wanted to fight it, since they thought they could win, and win kudos.

I was not surprised, therefore, when I got to Goodman's office at exactly a quarter past ten on Thursday morning, to find him coming out with Nye

[1] Gilbert Beyfus. An unsuccessful Liberal candidate for the Cirencester division of Gloucestershire in December 1910 and Coalition candidate for the Kingswinford division of Staffordshire in 1922, he was called to the Bar in 1908 and was a Bencher of the Inner Temple from 1940. In 1933 he became a King's Counsel. He died in 1960.

[2] Guy Travers Aldous, a Q.C. since 1956, retired from the Bar in 1967. Since 1968 he has been a director of Showerings Ltd.

and Morgan. 'You talk to Dick,' said Nye, rather shamefacedly, and he explained to me that they had decided that they would ask for £1,000, not £500, as minimum terms. And, as we entered the Law Courts and met Beyfus, it was clear that this had been prearranged. As I had agreed that, whatever two decided, a third should support, I had to agree. But I've no doubt whatsoever that our previous offer would have been accepted.

So the case began, with quite a good presentation by Beyfus, after which Nye and I went into the witness box before lunch. Nye, I thought, was extremely good and Fearnley-Whittingstall,[1] who I had been told was one of the bitterest Conservatives and who had been boasting that he was looking forward to cross-examining Mr Bevan and dressing him down, seemed to me to get very little out of him. I fancy I was fairly all right, although I was always a danger to my own side, owing to a streak of voluble candour, which works usually but can of course also undo you if the candour lets a cat out of the bag.

In this case it didn't. Indeed, I am fairly sure that the impression I created – that I was genuinely, sincerely and, as a journalist, professionally determined to try to get Gilmour[2] to print an apology – was a completely decisive element in winning the case. Or, to put it another way, Nye wanted to fight (until he got cold feet at the last moment, a fact he will certainly forget) and get big damages; but the man who won him his big damages was the man who didn't want to fight and genuinely wanted to settle, because what got us damages was our ability to disprove the other side's assertion that we had turned down all their draft apologies.

At the end of the morning we were told that the other side were offering to settle for our terms of £1,000, etc. I at once turned this down, since it was clear to me that, once the case had started and the first evidence about the drinking had been printed, it was essential to get right on and have the Lord Chief Justice's[3] comments, which I knew would be favourable, at the end. For, even after half an hour, it was clear that this astonishing old monster of eighty[4] had made up his mind that we were in the right and that the *Spectator*

[1] William Fearnley-Whittingstall became a K.C. in 1949 and from 1957 until his death in 1959 was Recorder of Leicester.

[2] Ian Gilmour, Conservative M.P. for Norfolk Central November 1962–74 and for Chesham and Amersham since 1974. In 1951 he married Lady Caroline Montagu-Douglas-Scott, the daughter of the Duke of Buccleuch. He was Editor of the *Spectator* 1954–9 (and, as such, responsible for the alleged libel). He was Parliamentary Under-Secretary of State at the Ministry of Defence 1970–1, Minister of State for Defence 1971–January 1974 and Secretary of State for Defence until the February 1974 Election. He was Chairman of the Conservative Research Department 1974–5. In 1979 he became Lord Privy Seal and senior Foreign Office Minister in the House of Commons. His works include *The Body Politic* (London: Hutchinson, 1969) and *Inside Right: A Study of Conservatism* (London: Hutchinson, 1977).

[3] Rayner Goddard (1877–1971) was a Judge of the King's Bench Division of the High Court 1932–8, Lord Justice of Appeal 1938–44 and in 1944 became a Law Lord. From 1946 to 1958 he was Lord Chief Justice of England.

[4] Lord Goddard was to announce his retirement on August 20th, 1958.

had behaved outrageously. He was quite friendly to me when I was standing in the box. Indeed, at one point he said *sotto voce*, 'Do remember you're not in the House of Commons,' not in a rude but in a helpful way, to stop one talking too much; and at another point he commented, when I said I wanted to settle, 'Of course. Dog does not eat dog.'

But Lord Goddard really came into his own after lunch. First we had to endure the cross-examination of Morgan Phillips. At lunch Goodman had said that whether a witness is good or bad depends on his self-confidence and quickness of wit. That is why a man like Fearnley-Whittingstall is so surprised when he is confronted with Nye or me, because the usual witness can be hectored or bullied and made to take the attorney's line, whereas we gave a good deal better than we got. But, directly Morgan got into the box, it was clear he was a sub-normal witness—shifty, fearful, sweating with panic (legitimately, for he'd been dead drunk for most of the conference)—and within ten minutes the cross-examiner was exploiting his inferiority complex and forcing him to admit things he'd never thought of admitting an hour before.

However, Morgan didn't do much harm. Then came the cross-examination of Gilmour. I had rather liked him when I met him at Roy's at that famous dinner, which now forms such an important part of the evidence,[1] and I had liked his wife even better. It became clear very soon that I had guessed right when in my original telephone conversation I had warned him that, in order to satisfy us, he would have to disown Jenny Nicholson.[2] I managed to get this into my evidence and thereby to tip off Beyfus, who had the sense to extract from Gilmour the admission that he couldn't disown the truth of the story completely for fear of an action from Miss Nicholson! Since Gilmour had previously made a complete fool of himself by saying that he'd published the article, seeing nothing libellous in it, this finally finished him with the jury. That concluded the first day.

This morning Gilmour's examination went on. I thought Beyfus rather exceeded himself by calling him a liar[3] for saying in the *Spectator* that no draft apology had been offered by us and defending the statement on the grounds that I had specifically stated that our communications were off the

---

[1] At a dinner at Roy Jenkins's house in the early spring Ian Gilmour and Crossman had discussed 'off the record and without prejudice' the terms of an apology which the *Spectator* might print. The cross-examination included much discussion of the terms under which these private talks and negotiations occurred.

[2] The author of the offending article.

[3] Crossman's papers contain a shorthand-writer's record of the proceedings. The relevant extract reads:

MR GILMOUR: Mr Beyfus, it is not a lie, and I suggest that with your considerable experience of these cases you ought to know full well, this was without prejudice, and the whole basis of 'without prejudice' negotiations is that they should never be published. You have chosen to break those rules, with respect, and I think it very wrong that you should accuse me of lying because I keep them.

record. I would have called this disingenuous, dishonest, dishonourable, and pointed out that, though one certainly can't be blamed for not *mentioning* what is off the record, it's quite a different thing when one says the *opposite* of what happened off the record. Beyfus put it more crudely and, I thought, enabled Gilmour to get a little sympathy. Then we had the speeches of the two leading Q.C.s, both stock speeches, Fearnley-Whittingstall working up all the emotion he could against our insistence on a grovelling apology, and Beyfus replying with some fine fustian about the lies of Gilmour and his scurrilous newspaper. I didn't think either of them very good and thought they both missed some important points.

But, as soon as lunch was over, the Lord Chief Justice changed all that by making the speech on our behalf which I had hoped Beyfus would make. It was a devastating exposure of Gilmour's disingenuousness, incompetence and weakness and it was an instruction to the jury. Looking at the jury, I couldn't believe that they could understand much of what was going on, particularly the question of what was a real and what was a spurious apology, and I don't think they would have given us adequate damages if they hadn't been ordered to in the precisest detail by the Lord Chief.

The only thing which scared us in the summing-up was his advice that the jury should not give extravagant but moderate damages. After all, by this time the size of the damages was all-important. From the morning press accounts of the first day, it was clear enough that, unless we got swingeing damages, we should be turned into a laughing-stock, and the *Daily Mail* had already tried to do this on its front page. Did these twelve jurymen have the same idea of moderate damages as the Lord Chief, or would they think that £500 was moderate?

I also had my own private worry, since Beyfus, who obviously didn't like me and did like Nye, had in his winding-up speech carefully distinguished between Nye and Morgan, with their international reputations, and me, whom he left out altogether as a mere journalist. After that it was possible that the jury would give distinct damages to each person. I was unutterably relieved when the L.C.J. specifically advised them that it would be fair to give each of us the same.

We had twenty minutes waiting outside. Then came the judgment — £2,500 each. And, after a few words outside, we each went our separate ways, escaping from the photographers. When I told Sydney Jacobson the result, he remarked 'If I could get £2,500 tax-free for being called an alcoholic, I would gladly submit myself to the libel!' George Wigg was delighted, especially for the effect it would have on the Labour Party that somebody was fighting at last. I was relieved, though not surprised after today, but I still think the risk we took was appalling. If it hadn't been the Lord Chief Justice but a more moderate Judge, the damages might have been quite small. If Gilmour hadn't been such an appallingly bad witness, the *Spectator* could have sustained its case far better. Finally, if I hadn't preached moderation and genuinely tried to get an apology without damages, there would have been no damages for Nye or Morgan. So altogether you can say it was a very satisfactory result. I'm sure of one thing—that Mr Goodman, whom I regard as a pleasant villain, will sleep easier in his bed tonight now that he's got his verdict, despite the disparate and discordant views of his three clients.[1]

Tuesday, November 26th

Yesterday afternoon at the foreign affairs group Nye was billed to give his impressions of America. Since John Hynd was a little late for the meeting, I found myself elected to the chair, thanks to my libel action, and Nye proceeded to give a most statesmanlike address, decorated with one or two of his most characteristic elegant and empty witticisms. 'The difference between America and France, is that America is a noun without a verb, France a verb without a noun.' It sounds superb until you try to work out which is which and then you can't tell the difference.

Most of Nye's speech was devoted to an account of what he had said to Eisenhower. He remarked first, however, that Eisenhower looked very old, even transparent, even, Nye added, two-dimensional, obviously incapable of sustained work, whereas Foster Dulles is immensely active. Nye made a good point about Dulles's lawyer's mind. 'When Dulles says something,' Nye said, 'he says it in big print and has his eye on the reservations in little print at the bottom of the page, which are not meant to be communicated.' He said that he had told Eisenhower that, in his view, the Russians might now be easier to negotiate with because they were confident and could negotiate from confidence. Eisenhower had remarked that it was worth trying and had convinced Nye, as he convinces everybody else, that he is personally anxious to be known as the general who made peace. There wasn't much added by the questioning, except that it was clear Nye was feeling that there was going to be a vacuum in America for three years and that a British initiative was needed to fill it.

I had gone into this meeting after spending the morning writing a *Mirror* column inspired by the discovery that Hugh Gaitskell is off to India on Friday

---

[1] On April 15th, 1978, the *Spectator* published a profile by Auberon Waugh of Lord Goodman, whose role in the case of Bevan and Others *v.* the *Spectator* was mentioned. Waugh added, 'Fifteen years later, Dick Crossman was happy to boast to a party of journalists in my hearing that he and Bevan had both been as pissed as newts.' This statement provoked a lengthy correspondence in the columns of the *Spectator* and *The Times* and a variety of articles, indignant or amusing, elsewhere. On pp. 536–8 and n. of *Aneurin Bevan*, vol. II (London: Davis-Poynter, 1973) Michael Foot gives an account of what Bevan's friends sometimes referred to as the case of 'the Venetian blind'. Mr Foot reminds the reader of two other allegations that the plaintiffs committed perjury, one appearing in a book by Iain Adamson, *The Old Fox: A Life of Gilbert Beyfus* (London: Muller, 1963), and the other in an article in the *Western Mail*, July 9th, 1963, by the 'Junior Member for Treorchy' apparently the pseudonym of a former Cardiff Conservative M.P., Sir David Llewellyn.

for the rest of the parliamentary Session.[1] Hugh seemed very surprised when I suggested he should return in order to ensure that we had a big debate after the NATO conference and to announce Labour's attitude to it. 'But they're not going to settle anything in NATO,' Hugh said, 'Nye told me. I don't think it's going to be very important.' This, of course, is yet another example of the strange lethargy which now afflicts our Front Bench and, indeed, the whole House of Commons.

This lethargic atmosphere was thick in the place again this afternoon and I found it no consolation whatsoever to have everybody congratulating us on our libel action. It seems to me, the more I reflect on it, to have been the kind of gamble which no one should responsibly have undertaken, even though we did win it in the end. I have a feeling, though I have no evidence for it, that, having immunized Nye, as he probably has, Gaitskell now feels sure enough of his position to consort chiefly with his old congenial clique. I confirmed with Roy Jenkins yesterday that there are meetings most Sunday evenings, at which Tony Crosland, Roy, Patrick and Frank Soskice turn up, and there is also the XYZ Club. Certainly, also, though Hugh has always been saying he wants to have a chat with me, he has only had time to see me once since Conference. But the people who feel strongly about this are trade unionists, like George Brown and Bill Blyton,[2] who growl around the place but are excluded from the secret confabs and who generally give an extra stench to a moribund atmosphere.

I expect that if I ever broke my principles and looked back through this diary[3] I should find at least ten other occasions when I have said I never felt more depressed at the low level politics had reached. Well, this is certainly one of those occasions. Even a first-rate meeting of the working party on social security this morning, at which we managed to sort out – or should I be more truthful and say to find more complications in – the problem of women's pensions, after which I had an excellent lunch with Peter Townsend and Gerald Kaufman,[4] has not removed the dank sense of depression.

[1] On December 16th the NATO Council was meeting in Paris, to discuss future strategy in the light of the development of new weapons and missiles (see below, pp. 638–40). In his *Mirror* article on November 26th Crossman advised Mr Gaitskell to return to London on December 12th, after his visit to India for the Conference of the Commonwealth Parliamentary Association and to the Far East. Crossman declared that the Shadow Cabinet should formulate a 'Socialist answer to the challenge of the sputnik and submit it for discussion, first in the Parliamentary Labour Party and then on the floor of the Commons before Christmas'.

[2] A Durham miner who was Labour M.P. for the Houghton-le-Spring division of County Durham from 1945 until 1964, when he became a life peer.

[3] Only rarely did Crossman reread his diary entries; when, later, he contemplated publishing the diaries, he justified this on the grounds that, unrevised and undoctored, his versions of events would be a true account of his views at the time.

[4] Labour M.P. for the Ardwick division of Manchester since 1970. He was a Political Correspondent of the *Daily Mirror* 1955–64 and of the *New Statesman* 1964–5. He worked closely with Harold Wilson as the Labour Party's Parliamentary Press Liaison Officer 1965–70. He was Parliamentary Under-Secretary of State at the Department of the Environment 1974–5 and for a short time at the Department of Industry where he subsequently served as Minister of State 1975–9.

It really is amazing to look back and remember that it's only seven weeks since those lovely days at Brighton, when the sun and the moon shone, the sea gleamed, white clouds billowed and the Labour Party was wafted on them into an empyrean of unified self-confidence and Socialist exaltation. Now we are right down in the dumps, not because we've been kicked there or defeated but because that crystal-clear autumn atmosphere has been replaced by dankest November, in the political as well as in the physical climate.

From December 2nd to 7th Crossman was in Germany, lecturing for the Deutsch-Englische Gesellschaft, meeting old friends and interviewing politicians. He gave his impressions of popular German reaction to Dr Adenauer's foreign policy in a Mirror *piece published on December 6th. On his return, Crossman found that he had annoyed his colleagues by his previous article, published on December 3rd and headlined 'Labour Must Stop these Milk-and-Water Tactics in Parliament'.*

Tuesday, December 10th
I got back to find life at Westminster even flatter than when I left it. Some slight flurry was caused, apparently, by my last week's article on the subject and I was summoned this morning to attend on Mr Griffiths and the Chief Whip in Gaitskell's rooms. We had an hour's wasted conversation, since they at once admitted that I had the right to write such articles and all they were telling me was that some of my colleagues disliked this one.

Jim tried to make out that I shouldn't have written this piece since I had been invited to sit on the Front Bench and help in fighting the National Insurance Bill. Towards the end, I tried to point out that the important issue was not my popularity but whether what I had described was a true account of the situation. Both of them denied it, not very convincingly.

I saw Nye for a moment yesterday. He is due to go to Bonn on Wednesday and Berlin on Friday and, chiefly for this reason, there is to be no debate in the Commons before the NATO conference starts on Monday. So the Labour Party is losing yet another chance of regaining the initiative. Another tiny but significant symptom is what has happened this afternoon about the International Sub. of the N.E.C. There was to be a most important meeting, to discuss papers on Germany and the Middle East, and Morgan Phillips has cancelled it because so few were due to attend. Gaitskell is in India, Nye, though here, has no doubt said he hasn't time to turn up, and that was that.

Of course, it would be absurd to put all the blame on to the Parliamentary Party or the leadership of the Labour Party. The Labour Party is suffering from the disease which afflicts the whole nation, a sense that Britain no longer counts, combined with a feeling that, as each of us is doing quite well individually, there is really no point in making a commotion. Maybe even the best Opposition in the world could not drag the nation out of its lethargy. But when I've written that down, I know it's untrue. Of course it could be done, and the fascinating question is why, since Brighton, the Labour Party leadership has sagged, now that Bevan and Gaitskell have made it up. Never in my gloomiest forebodings did I have a glimmer that this would be the result of unity.

Wednesday, December 18th
Since I wrote last Tuesday, quite a lot seems to have happened. On Tuesday evening (though I didn't know this at the time and what I am writing is gossip), a meeting of the trade union group took place, at which there was some further complaint about my article in the *Mirror* but, much more important, a ferocious attack by Bill Blyton on the Gaitskell leadership. Apparently there was a tremendous sense of disgruntlement and Blyton said that, if Gaitskell gave all his Hampstead friends jobs and bought off one or two trade unionists like George Brown, the Opposition would be behind him and not in front of him under the next Labour Government.

What happened at this meeting was duly the subject of Hugh Massingham's column in the *Observer*, of the Student of Politics[1] in the *Sunday Times* and of Crossbencher [John Junor] in the *Sunday Express* at the weekend, all of them commenting in their various tones that the trade union Members were getting more and more discontented with Mr Gaitskell's leadership and, in particular, with his habit of consorting in Hampstead with a small, select group. Moreover, the old and stale story of the XYZ Club was hawked out as well. I have, I think, reported in this diary already the rumours about the Hampstead group, meeting Gaitskell on Sundays, who are said to include Frank Soskice, Patrick Gordon Walker, Alf Robens, Roy Jenkins and Tony Crosland.

As seems to be normal for me on these occasions, I was quite unaware of all this thunder and lightning and woke up on Thursday morning to read, in every paper except the *Daily Herald*, the long and substantial account of how I had been once again the subject of discussion for two hours at the Shadow Cabinet, since I had proved unsatisfactory in my interview with the Chief Whip and the Deputy Leader.

This was as surprising to me as when I read in the *Herald* last June that the trade union group was demanding an apology for my article in the *Mirror*. I strongly suspected the same hand was at work in arranging that, while I was bound strictly by the rules of confidentiality, the issue against me should be pre-judged by a carefully organized press campaign. I rang up George Wigg, who, quite rightly, said that the thing to do was to immediately write a letter to Carol Johnson, protesting against this character assassination and insisting that I should make a personal statement at the Party Meeting on Thursday evening.

[1] James Margach, the Political Correspondent of the *Sunday Times*. He published *The Abuse of Power: The War Between Downing Street and the Media* (London: W. H. Allen, 1978) and *The Anatomy of Power* (London: W. H. Allen, 1979). He died in 1979.

This I did, writing the letter by hand and taking it round personally before Carol arrived in his office at ten o'clock in the morning. In due course, I heard from Jim Griffiths that two letters would be ready for me on the messenger board that afternoon, but I didn't get them till quite late, since I was at a big lunch party at the Polish Embassy. Afterwards I got down to the House and picked up some of the gossip.

The common view was that this onslaught on me was a diversion staged by Mr Brown, in view of the Blyton attack on him at the trade union group, and it was hoped to repeat the success he had achieved when I was panned by the trade union group. Harold Wilson told me that at the meeting he alone had supported me, that Mr Callaghan had insisted that I should be forbidden to write on the *Daily Mirror*, that others demanded that I should be reported to the National Executive and that Harold had pointed out that this was purely a matter of parliamentary discipline and that anyway nothing I had written contravened the resolution forbidding fraternal abuse.[1] They might not like what I wrote, but I was entitled to write it.

All this puzzled me, since the letter I received from Carol Johnson informed me that, in the view of the Shadow Cabinet, I had contravened the resolution, but that they were not going to take action on this occasion. At this time, of course, I didn't know that the Shadow Cabinet had decided to report all this to the Parliamentary Party at half-past six that evening and to dispose of the whole matter by a quick adverse resolution against me. So I expected at the meeting to be able to say that I wanted to make a personal statement about the press leak, while the major subject could be discussed at a later meeting.

However, when I got there Jim Griffiths told about eighty or ninety people that he regretted the leak, although he must point out that they also occurred in the National Executive, but that anyway the Shadow Cabinet decision was to rebuke me for the article and take no further action. I then made my statement, relating solely to the press accounts and to the lies told about me, including the accusation of being too busy when I had been invited to lead the attack on the Pensions Bill. I obviously made some impression on them and I was quite pleased with myself, since I didn't realize why I had made it until Bill Blyton got up and said I had been abominably treated. As he was the man who had denounced me at the Miners' Gala and is normally my bitterest enemy, I realized that he and his colleagues were delighted to catch George Brown out in one of his devious devices.

Then up rose George Wigg and made the most extraordinary speech, which included a description of poor innocent Crossman walking quietly through the lobbies and then being furiously assaulted by Mr Brown one week,[2] and next week having his character assassinated. It was an appalling,

---

[1] Of 1952.
[2] On Wednesday, November 6th, Crossman had a violent argument with George Brown about a reference he had made to Brown in the previous day's *Mirror*. According to Crossman.

vulgar speech but it had its effect, since most of the people there learnt for the first time that this wonderful judicial Shadow Cabinet, which was supposed to be reprimanding me for misusing the press, was full of people perfectly prepared to misuse the press anonymously for their own devices.

After this it was positively embarrassing when Fred Peart rose and said it was no good my pretending I was an ordinary backbencher; I was one of the national leaders and it was this which made my comments embarrassing. Why should I put it in the *Mirror*? Why shouldn't I make my comments frankly at the Party Meeting, since he really agreed with them? After this Mr Emanuel Shinwell, who had been primed by George Wigg to make a furious attack on George Brown, sensed the possibility of a great personal success if he sat on the fence. Having congratulated me on my nimble wit in choosing to counter-attack instead of answering the charges, Shinwell then, in a statesmanlike way, remarked that I wasn't the only person who wrote in the press. 'Why, there's an article every day somewhere or other from one of these Shadow this and Shadow that. And anyway, Dick writes for himself and not as a Shadow and has managed to say everything in the course of his life, so why worry? But really he ought to be careful,' etc., etc.

At this point the Meeting accepted the resolution, which no one had read and which I still haven't seen, and ended. George Wigg and I regarded it as a draw, achieved by an effective and rapidly organized counter-offensive. So it was, since nobody there, after listening to Jim Griffiths read the whole *Mirror* article, could deny that every word of it was true, and after the meeting those present realized that the chief charge against me was untrue.

One minor matter of interest was the papers next morning. Those people who had leaked so successfully from the Shadow Cabinet were absolutely watertight after the fright they had got. All the papers had was a tiny official announcement that no further action would be taken. This means, of course, that, outside Parliament, the hostile rumours about me have never been contradicted. But that's a relatively small matter, since, by and large, outside Parliament I suspect that people thought I was quite right to say what I did.

The NATO alliance had been strained by the Anglo-French intervention in Suez; confidence in Britain was further diminished in the first half of 1957 when it was announced in February that she intended to drastically cut her forces in Germany and to halve the strength of the Second Tactical Air Force in Europe. Division between Britain and the Continental members of NATO increased in the spring, when the White Paper on defence demonstrated the Government's intention to emphasize Britain's own nuclear weapon programme and V-bomber

To my amazement I received four large blows across the face, which left me a bit speechless, but I had the sense to stay still. 'Come along, now, we'll go,' I said and put my hand on his arm again, whereupon he hit me again, and the next thing I remember is kneeling on top of him, with George Brown saying, 'I slipped, otherwise I'd have sloshed you.' This was all done in the semi-dusk and I had a vague feeling that somebody scuttled past when we proceeded to Gaitskell's room.

force, with the implication that this justified a reduction in her contribution to NATO's conventional forces.

The British attitude was challenged primarily within the Western Union, whose members successfully urged Britain to slow down the reduction of her troops in Germany. This pressure was strengthened by the known views of the Supreme Allied Commander in Europe, General Lauris Norstad. He had been asked by NATO to undertake a review of NATO's strategy, in the new technological and military circumstances, and, though his report was not published after its completion in August, his principal conclusions were generally known. His belief was that continuing refinements in the precision and deadliness of nuclear weapons made the building-up of conventional forces more rather than less necessary, since it might become essential to defend Europe without recourse to strategic bombing or retaliation by either side. General Norstad therefore concluded that NATO's force should reach 28 divisions by 1962. This required Germany to furnish her full quota of 12 divisions, France to bring back 4 divisions from Algeria and Britain to cease the reduction in her own forces.

It had also become evident that NATO must reconsider her planning for anti-submarine warfare. The Soviet Union was adding to her fleet, now numbering more than 500 submarines, at a rate of eighty a year. NATO exercises in October revealed serious weaknesses in the anti-submarine forces of the NATO navies. Meanwhile, the U.S.S.R. was also developing the Inter-Continental Ballistic Missile, I.C.B.M., with a range of 5,000 miles. At the end of August, Tass had claimed that the Soviet Union had successfully carried out a number of tests. The United States had experienced several failures with trials of their own Atlas missile, though they were to succeed in a limited range test on December 17th.

Britain was developing an Intermediate Range Ballistic Missile, I.R.B.M., with a range of some 2,000 miles, and had successfully tested models at the Woomera range in Australia. In May a meeting of NATO Foreign Ministers had discussed the creation of an 'atomic stockpile' in Europe of both tactical atomic weapons and intermediate range missiles, but no firm decisions had been taken. By now, American official and public opinion was deeply worried by Soviet successes in missile and satellite development.

Since the United States believed that successful nuclear deterrence could only be maintained by securing European bases from which its medium-range missiles could counter those of the Soviet Union, American interest in NATO was renewed. Many of the Continental European members of NATO, led by Dr Adenauer, hitherto a strong supporter of American policy, repudiated this strategy. This group of NATO countries preferred to attempt a new diplomatic approach to the U.S.S.R., leading towards a general disarmament agreement.

It was to discuss these differences that the heads of the fifteen NATO Governments met in Paris from December 16th to 19th. In the previous week Mr Bulganin sent letters to the heads of the Governments of the U.K., U.S.A., France, West Germany, Holland and Belgium. The Note to the British Prime Minister, *published on December 12th, drew Mr Macmillan's attention to Britain's vulnerable position and the folly of her participation in NATO policies. Mr Bulganin set out the Soviet Union's prescriptions for disarmament. Though the Soviet letter was dismissed by the American State Department, its contents gave additional material for preliminary discussion of what the NATO Governments' arguments should be.*

Meanwhile the Parliamentary manoeuvres for the NATO Paris conference were proceeding. Nye Bevan duly disappeared to Germany on Wednesday and I am waiting to hear from Lilo[1] what was the real impression he made. Meanwhile it had been agreed that the debate should take place after NATO on Thursday of this week and, if that was too early, on Friday. To co-ordinate Party policy, a joint meeting of the foreign affairs and defence groups was set up for Tuesday afternoon and a Party Meeting for Thursday morning. Meanwhile the Executive was due to meet on Wednesday.

Tuesday's meeting was fascinating. There must have been forty or fifty people there, with Nye in the chair and George Brown sitting beside him. Nye said that we should start with a statement by Denis Healey. I took a careful note of this statement, since it was clearly concerted between Healey, Brown and Nye. Healey said that three things had been agreed at a foreign affairs group held previously: first, that we must work out an effective political control for the use of nuclear weapons; secondly, that there must be a Western diplomatic initiative towards a European settlement, based not on old presuppositions but on new proposals, including the Gaitskell plan; and, thirdly, that all ideas of NATO's competence being extended beyond the military sphere should be opposed by the Labour Party.

Denis then made some comments on each of the above points. With regard to the first, he remarked, in reference to a resolution tabled by Sydney Silverman, that, if we wished to submit the United States' nuclear weapons to NATO control, we must logically be willing to surrender control of our own nuclear weapons and make sacrifices of sovereignty. However, Denis added that, in his view, we should support the attitude which the Norwegian Prime Minister[2] had adopted that morning in Paris. We should insist that there should be no physical distribution of atomic weapons or rocket missiles until and unless agreement had been reached on how these weapons could be controlled and on the strategic doctrine under which they should be used.

With regard to the second point, Denis said, rightly, that there was very little disagreement in the Party, since we are committed to the Gaitskell plan

[1] Lilo Milchsack, the initiator of the Deutsch–Englische Gesellschaft e.V. (the Königswinter conferences) and its Honorary Secretary since its foundation in 1949. She was awarded a D.C.M.G. in 1972 for her services to Anglo-German understanding.

[2] Einar Gerhardsen. Mayor of Oslo in 1940 and 1945, he was Chairman of the Norwegian Labour Party from 1945 to 1965. He was Prime Minister in the post-war coalition Government June–November 1945, and in the Labour Governments of 1945–51, 1955–63 and 1963–5.

and we are glad to see that George Kennan[1] now supports it. In a reference to the plan of the Polish Foreign Secretary, Rapacki,[2] for a nuclear neutrality zone,[3] Denis said it would be difficult to accept as a matter on its own that there should be no atomic weapons in Europe, but that this should be treated as a basis for negotiation.

Finally, on the third point, Denis observed that this was no longer an important issue, since the British view was supported by the Americans. He added that we should not press for summit talks immediately, since the first job was to persuade Western powers to accept our proposals as a basis for their initiative.

There was then a very long wrangle about the procedure to be adopted now that it was known that the debate must be postponed from Thursday to Friday. Nye was extremely shifty and argued for a quarter of an hour against having a three-line whip. I called a vote and defeated him by 30 votes to 5. After John Hynd had made quite a good point about the necessity for the West German Government to take a big part in negotiations, I took up Denis Healey's statement of what he had called the Norwegian position. I pointed out that this was not the position adopted by Norway and Denmark. They had gone much further and jointly insisted that there could be no question even of an agreement to permit rocket bases in principle until and unless there had been another effort at a negotiated settlement. I suggested, therefore, that our line should be that no further military commitments of any kind whatsoever should be undertaken by Britain until the political initiative had taken place.

George Brown said that he couldn't agree with my position about objecting in principle to military commitments. He thought it would be silly to discuss the rocket bases because they are not yet ready. How provocative to talk about them until we actually have them! This, of course, was a very different position from that which I had adopted: 'Don't talk about the damn things but tacitly agree to have them when they are ready.'

Nye then sought to wind up and did so by apparently opposing me. He

---

[1] As George Eastman Visiting Professor at the University of Oxford 1957–8, he gave the Reith Lectures in 1957. He was U.S. Ambassador to the U.S.S.R. 1952–3 and a Professor at the Institute for Advanced Studies at Princeton University 1956–74. At this time he was giving the six B.B.C. Reith lectures in the 1957 series, on 'Russia, the Atom and the West', and had stated that to arm West Germany or any other European country with nuclear tactical weapons would be to imperil the chances of peace. His numerous publications on Russia and on diplomatic subjects include two volumes of autobiography, *Memoirs 1925–50* and *1950–63* (London: Hutchinson, 1968, 1973).

[2] Adam Rapacki. A Polish politician of a Liberal cast, he was Minister of Higher Education 1950–6 and Foreign Minister April 1956–68. He died in 1970. In 1957 Rapacki had presented to the United Nations the Rapacki Plan, which aimed to prohibit 'the presence and production of all atomic weapons in any part of Central Europe'. Both this and a modified version of the Plan, presented in 1958, were rejected by the West. General Norstad, in particular, was not reassured by the Plan's proposals for ground and aerial inspection of neutral territory and was a strong critic of the scheme.

[3] The plan was for neutralizing Central Europe by a simultaneous withdrawal of American and Soviet troops.

21

started by saying that the I.C.B.M. is no different from a hydrogen bomb or atom bomb. It is just another weapon and therefore logically we cannot oppose it if we do not oppose the others. However, rearmament is creating a stalemate and that is why there must be a political settlement. On the other hand, going round in circles, we cannot deny to NATO technological advance by imposing on NATO a rigidity, whereas the Eastern bloc is fluid. What we can do is to say that the arms race is sterile.

So, Nye said, why all this fuss and emphasis on the need for denying the Americans their right to put missiles in Europe? We allowed our allies to possess the H-bomb, so now we must allow them to possess rocket missiles. But, Nye once again ended, rearmament is a cul-de-sac, and that is why we should put all our emphasis on political initiative, while making it clear that we are not meanwhile in any way halting the technological advance on which the Americans insist. At the end of Nye's speech, Mr Tomney rose and said, 'Well, that satisfies me,' and Mr Zilliacus and Mr Warbey, sitting next to me, nearly blew off their tops.

I then went out to dinner and after the vote went into the Smoking Room. At this point Nye came in and sat down alone, obviously wanting to talk to me. A vote came a little later and we spent forty-five minutes walking up and down the lobby, having the first serious political discussion we have had for many weeks. I began by asking Nye whether he really objected to the position which I, as well as the Norwegians and the Danes, adopted. He said, 'I don't like the way you put things,' and then he added, 'Anyway, there upstairs is a bad place to try and formulate policy.' 'Yes,' I said, 'but you differed from me and seemed to support George Brown.' 'Oh, don't discuss what we said upstairs,' Nye said. 'Let's really discuss the matter.' And he began to repeat his arguments all over again.

At one point I referred to atomic tactical weapons and Nye said, 'Well, why do you oppose them?' 'Oh,' I said, 'we can't go into all that now. Surely we know.' Then I suddenly realized he didn't know the case against them and wanted me to tell him. Finally, under considerable pressure, he admitted, first, that he is opposed to the equipment of any armies in Europe with atomic tactical weapons; secondly, that he is opposed to any preparations being made for rocket bases anywhere in Europe, and under preparations he includes any kind of signed agreement; and, thirdly, when I said, 'But, after all, we agreed last year to rocket bases in England,' he added that he was opposed to having them here too.

Afterwards I took George Wigg home and told him all this. He immediately pointed out that obviously Nye had taken me for this walk because he had found that the view he expressed in the Committee was so unpopular that he had decided to change it. I must say I tend to agree with him. What I witnessed was yet another of Nye's pendulum swings on the H-bomb which we saw at the Brighton Conference. Where he will have swung to by the Party Meeting on Thursday morning and the Commons debate on Friday, heaven only knows. But, as things are going in Paris, he will have to swing far to the left if he is to outbid Macmillan as peacemaker.

This morning we had the Executive and I went there determined to protest against the scandal of the International Sub.'s being cancelled on 10th December. Nye had asked me what was on and I had said, 'Not much,' but I didn't imagine this would mean that he wouldn't bother to turn up. This made it difficult for me to raise the issue since I wanted to attack him to his face, knowing that he had been in the House at half-past three on the 10th but said that he wouldn't turn up at the meeting at four o'clock. However, I made my protest to a very frigid Executive, pointing out that this meant that the Executive had been denied any policy-making role with regard to the NATO Conference.

After this a good many other points of business were taken, till at last one of the trade unionists, Casasola, woke up and asked why the Executive shouldn't pass a resolution. The new member called Boyd[1] chipped in and said that the Party didn't consist of Gaitskell and Bevan and even in their absence the Executive could pass a resolution. He was prepared to submit one, urging immediate Summit talks. I pointed out that we had better have a resolution not committing us to Summit talks and suggested, 'This Executive welcomes the line taken in Paris by the Norwegian and Danish Prime Ministers[2] and joins with them in insisting on renewed negotiations with the Russians in order to break the nuclear deadlock.'

At this point the fat was in the fire and, if my resolution had been put, it could not have been defeated. So Mr Griffiths weighed in. Should we really have a resolution, he asked, in the absence of Gaitskell and Bevan? Was it really wise for the Executive, impromptu, without preparation, to launch itself into this affair, which the Party was debating on Thursday? How could we know what was being decided in Paris? Why, it was these very considerations which persuaded the Shadow Cabinet to have the debate after the NATO Conference.

Tony Greenwood pointed out that the Shadow Cabinet had lost the initiative and that, if the Executive didn't pass a resolution, Macmillan would get in first on Friday. This was supported by Jean Mann and Edith Summerskill but Jim Griffiths managed to insist that the first vote should be on the issue of whether we should have a resolution at all. When this vote was taken we lost by 11 to 10. The ten consisted almost entirely of members of the

---

[1] John Boyd, an engineer, was Assistant Divisional Organizer of the A.U.E.W. 1946–50, Divisional Organizer 1950–3 and a Member of the Executive Committee 1953–75. He was President of the Confederation of Shipbuilding and Engineering Unions 1964 and a Member of the T.U.C. General Council 1967–75 and since 1978. In 1975 he became General Secretary of the Amalgamated Union of Engineering Workers. He was knighted in 1979.

[2] The Danish Prime Minister was Hans Hansen. He was Secretary of the Danish Social Democratic Party 1939–41 and from 1945 until 1953, when he became Party Chairman. Minister of Finance 1945–7, Minister of Trade, Industry and Shipping 1947–50 and Minister of Foreign Affairs 1953–7, he was Prime Minister 1955–7.

Shadow Cabinet—Jim Griffiths, Harold Wilson, Jim Callaghan, Edith Summerskill, plus Sam Watson and one or two others, who saw that it would leak to the press that the Executive had sensationally taken the initiative in the absence of Bevan and Gaitskell.

Meanwhile I gather from George that a great deal of excitement is being worked up on the Left of the backbenches. I am meeting Zilliacus at three o'clock this afternoon to discuss the terms of a resolution for tomorrow morning's Party Meeting. This whole business completely justifies the advice I gave to Hugh. It's strange to remember that a mild article on interdependence which I wrote in the middle of November was denounced by Hugh as a reversion to neutralism; strange to remember that, when I urged Hugh to return for this debate, he told me that nothing was going to happen in Paris; strange to remember that, when we urged them to have the debate before the NATO Conference, Nye preferred to go to Germany.

Of course, the truth is that the leadership has been strategically and tactically utterly deplorable. On the other hand, I shall be under no illusions. Nine-tenths of the Parliamentary Party intensely dislike my criticisms, resent the fact that they are justified and would like to expel me if I go on making them public. Desmond Donnelly, a very dubious and suspect character, brought Megan Lloyd George[1] round to a drink with me last night, full of ideas of a ginger group and a dining club. I listened to this attentively. Meanwhile Fred Peart, Tony Wedgwood Benn, Bob Mellish and others have formed a backbench ginger group, with no foul associations, and, according to Roy Jenkins, I seem to be the only person who hasn't been invited to join it! I await what happens tomorrow with the greatest interest.

Friday, December 20th
Yesterday morning the Party met to discuss defence, knowing that the Shadow Cabinet had discussed it at length the day before and had succumbed to the vote of the foreign affairs group and ordered a three-line whip for Friday. Before the discussion started, Jim Griffiths announced that, since the NATO communiqué was not published, the debate would be resumed at half-past six and the Front Bench would not speak till then. So all we could do in the morning was to try to create an atmosphere in which the Shadow Cabinet would make up its mind in the afternoon.[2]

[1] Lloyd George's younger daughter, Lady Megan Lloyd George was Liberal M.P. for Anglesey 1929–31, Independent Liberal M.P. for the same constituency 1931–43 and Liberal M.P. again 1945–51. From 1957 until her death in 1966 she sat as Labour M.P. for Carmarthen.

[2] The communiqué attempted to reconcile the divisions within NATO but only Britain and Turkey (and eventually Italy) agreed that U.S. missile bases should be established on their territory. The others, including West Germany, refused to give any commitment. The European Prime Ministers urged a new diplomatic initiative towards securing a disarmament agreement. The House of Commons delayed its adjournment for the Christmas recess so that the communiqué could be debated. The Opposition pressed a division and, though the Government obtained a majority, this had dropped to 38 votes.

On the whole it went fairly well, in the sense that Manny Shinwell made the only speech in favour of NATO military measures, that the pacifists and nuclear abolitionists were more restrained than usual, and that the few of us that were speaking from the middle were heard with silence and some attention. Since everybody spoke in favour of voting against the Government and since Nye could hear, from the way the debate was received, that my position was about the furthest to the Right that was acceptable without splitting the Party, the thing went fairly well.[1] It was ended by a really rousing oration from George Wigg in favour of a large conventional Army, which everyone cheered and no one understood. His crack has already been published: 'I don't mind when Nye thinks himself God, but when he assumes the mantle of Napoleon I shake in my shoes.'

After this I went back and wrote the column.[2] When I got to the meeting at half-past six a very characteristic scene occurred. Actually the communiqué had only just been received as the Shadow Cabinet entered the room, but in their wisdom they had decided to vote against the Government and Nye was put up to say a few pontifical words about the line which they would take. He managed to muzz it very nicely, so that no one could tell exactly what he would say and everyone could be satisfied. After this there was an immediate cry of 'Vote! vote!' and the great parliamentary democracy opted itself out of existence in a few minutes.

I went out feeling very depressed. Anne and I went straight on to Barbara's Christmas party. I didn't realize that we had actually scored a triumph, since the mere fact of a vote, i.e. a vote of censure, compelled Nye to make a far more left-wing speech than he would have made in a mere adjournment debate on a Friday. However, I learnt at the party from such people as Dick Plummer, Kenneth Robinson and Lynn Ungoed-Thomas that the Wigg/Crossman line had really been decisive in making people realize that, if we didn't vote against the NATO communiqué, we would be positively committed to the full nuclear policy.

And so we come to this morning's debate, with Selwyn Lloyd making what Nye rightly described as a ritualistic speech—so dreary, so ideologically platitudinous that I can't think he himself believed it. Nye's performance was a great Parliamentary occasion. He began quietly and he wasn't very comfortable and soon lost himself in answering questions about Communism, which destroyed the balance of his speech. As a result, the main constructive passage on the disengagement policy in Europe had to be shortened, although Selwyn Lloyd had given him a most wonderful chance for it by flatly denouncing disengagement altogether. Nevertheless, though it was not a well-balanced speech and though the attacks on rocket bases and H-bombers were

---

[1] The vote was 289 to 251 in favour of the Government's policy.

[2] On the 'half sanity' of the Danish and Norwegian Prime Ministers and the 'half brinkmanship' of the U.S. Secretary of State and the lack of sanity of the British Prime Minister and Foreign Secretary: *Daily Mirror*, December 20th.

extremely demagogic and disingenuous, it did fulfil its main purpose. It regained the initiative for the Labour Party and seemed at last to be speaking for the common man against the Anglo-American cold warriors in Paris.

As I went out, Douglas Jay said to me, 'Nye doesn't seem quite to have kept to the line he took last night!' He hadn't, indeed, but what he had done was to fully satisfy his critics of last Tuesday. I don't know what poor George Brown will do when he winds up. While Nye was speaking I looked up to see Dora Gaitskell in the Speaker's Gallery. Poor girl, she had heard the only effective point of Selwyn Lloyd's, when he quoted the absent Gaitskell at length, rebuking his Party for neutralism! What a fantastic fool Gaitskell is! Coming down from Barbara's party, Megan Lloyd George observed to me, 'You see, one can't conceive the Old Man being absent from a great parliamentary occasion when he was a great Party Leader. It is just incredible that a Party Leader could be away when things of that sort are on. Gaitskell can't be a Leader.' I agree, but then we don't need a Leader in the Labour Party. We need a centre. On Monday I shall compose a letter to Gaitskell about what has been going on.

One last thing. Just as I was leaving for the debate, I got a call from Hugh Cudlipp. 'Your phone was out of order last week,' he said. 'I just want to tell you the column's been better than ever in your life for the last five weeks. Magnificent!' All this means, of course, is that Hugh Cudlipp has recently met some people who have spoken well of the column or, alternatively, it is because there is something in it. I have been making politics with the column without being too unpopular in the right places. However, it's nice to know, and I said to him, 'Thank you for a sweet Christmas present, Uncle Hugh,' and rang off.

Crossman did write to Gaitskell, on December 23rd, welcoming him back and inviting him to bring Dora to dine at Vincent Square on December 29th. 'Only Roy and Jennifer Jenkins will be there.' He continued:

> *About politics I would rather talk to you than write. I presume that, before we meet, you will have heard a great deal of gossip, and some of it will be about me. Since most of this relates to an article I wrote in the* Mirror, *I am sending you a copy of it, so that you can judge for yourself whether I was guilty of any crime worse than writing for publication what people as respectable as Bob Mellish and Denis Howell[1] had been muttering round the lobby.*
>
> *Meanwhile there is only one thing I want to tell you in this letter. If anyone has whispered to you that I have been working against you in your absence, this is the sheerest invention. Ever since Attlee announced his resignation I*

---

[1] Labour M.P. for the All Saints division of Birmingham 1955–September 1959 and for the Small Heath division since 1961. He was Joint Parliamentary Under-Secretary of State at the Department of Education and Science, with special responsibility for sport 1964–9, Minister of State at the Ministry of Housing and Local Government 1969–70 and Minister of State (Sport) at the Department of the Environment 1974–9.

have regarded the acceptance of your leadership by everyone, including Nye, as the sine qua non *of Party revival and I am unlikely to have changed my views now that the Party has been reviving. Indeed, one of the few things which has pleased me during the last two months has been the complete loyalty to you which Nye showed in a very difficult situation, particularly last week. What has disturbed me has been the loss of initiative since Brighton, which I attribute to the following factors, listed in order of their importance: (i) the success of Macmillan in creating a mood of public apathy; (ii) a general demoralization of the nation, caused by the bankruptcy of Western leadership since the sputnik; (iii) our failure as a Party, after working out a workable programme of action, to sell it to the nation, or, indeed, to behave as though we meant it; and (iv) the unimpressive performance of our Front Bench speakers in debate and their even less impressive performance as tacticians behind the scenes, which together have combined to depress and irritate the Parliamentary Party.*

The reports of your success in India have been quite good in the British press and I was not surprised, therefore, when I met Will Henderson in the Army and Navy Stores this morning and he gave me a very glowing account. However, don't expect me not to feel I was right in suggesting that you should have flown home and forgone your Far Eastern trip in order to make the debate last week a really clinching attack.

1958

From December 31st to January 6th Crossman was in Czechoslovakia. He kept a diary of his conversations and travels, which ended with his being bundled into Poland. He wrote:

We had a lot of toasts in Slivovic and Pilsen beer and right at the end, when I was due to go to the railway station to catch the train for Warsaw, I was told, 'By the way, I'm afraid we haven't got a ticket for you after all.' This question of the ticket had dogged me from my first day in Prague. I had tried to buy a railway ticket from Prague to Warsaw in London and had been told this was impossible. In Prague, they said it required me to pay Valuta. I said I had travellers' cheques, which I would change, to which they replied that it wouldn't be normal Kroner but a special rate of Kroner, which required a special permit that I didn't possess. So it was postponed till Ostrava, where we visited the tourist agency in the morning. There were six girls there, doing nothing. 'How much would a ticket to Warsaw cost?' I asked. Impossible to know without ringing Prague. This went on for a long time until I put 350 Crowns down on the desk and said, 'Here is more than enough' (I had already got my sleeping car booked to Warsaw and my ticket to the frontier). 'Let me have the ticket at dinner.'

Now the dinner had come and there was no ticket. 'Unfortunately,' I was told, 'the girls misunderstood what you said and thought you only required a ticket to the frontier.' 'But I have got a sleeping car to Warsaw!' 'I know, but they just misunderstood, so there is no ticket from the frontier. But we are sure the Poles will be very helpful.' This was probably the most characteristic Czech episode in this whole five days. They really couldn't care less what happened when they had delivered me to the train and got me out.

I had had something of the same impression when I had asked to buy some Bohemian glass in Prague and had been fobbed off with the excuse that they were stocktaking and had every sort of difficulty. The Czechs are wonderful at just quietly obstructing the foreigner and I suspect that they are equally effective at obstructing their own Government whenever they feel inclined. In the course of my five days I had argued from morning till night and got nowhere. I had had a thoroughly nice time and the more I saw them the more attracted I was. At first I called them Welsh but of course the real fact is that they behave as the English would behave if they had been oppressed by the Welsh for 500 years. For they are extremists of the middle way, ruthlessly pushing forward along the path they have set themselves, carefully avoiding risks and showing all the time the most attractive kind of amiability, combined with a power to fight dirty which is only equalled by that of the British public schoolboy. The more I saw of them, the more I generally liked being with them, but the reasons why I liked it were, I fear, wholly discreditable to me.

The farewell dinner was drawing to its close when suddenly we realized the train was due and I was rushed to the platform with my packages of glass and with, I reckon, a hundredweight of literature, which had been loaded on to me.

The train was in. I was shoved on board, only to find I was the wrong end of the train. But by then my hosts were going back to have another drink and I was alone with the conductor, without a ticket, in an International Wagons-Lit, where I had no sleeping car. My sleeping car was a Communist sleeping car in the last coach at the end. To do him credit, the conductor did help me at the next station to drag my luggage back to the end, where my sleeping car was to be found, equipped, Communist-like, with a lovely coal stove and every form of fish being cooked in a gorgeous smell of Eastern Europe. (The other sleeping car was empty.)

I got through the Czech frontier without difficulty and at this point, about three hours later, (we had done twenty miles), there was a new sleeping car conductor, charming, polished, addressing me in French. He was a Pole and I explained my plight. 'But there is no difficulty,' he said to me courteously. 'Some time or other the train conductor will see to you. Have a good night.' And I went to sleep in a snowstorm.

On January 7th I woke at half-past four in the morning, when it was still snowing heavily and we were approaching Warsaw. 'You must get up now', the conductor said, 'and get ready. The train conductor has not come because he does not know what to do. He has never had a passenger without a ticket before. So will you wait when we get to Warsaw?' This seemed a gloomy prospect, as we were due to arrive at a quarter to six in a snowstorm at an open platform and I didn't know whether I would be met. I had arranged for the British Embassy to telegraph the time of my arrival and I was fairly confident. However, as the train drew in the conductor arrived and I could see there was going to be a terrible confusion. For, strictly speaking, I didn't exist, since a passenger without a ticket cannot exist in a Communist country. Moreover, I had no Polish money and there was no possibility of cashing travellers' cheques for five hours.

Disconsolately, as we came into Warsaw, I watched everybody else get off and then a perky little woman with peroxided hair rushed up and said, 'Are you Mr Crossman? The British Embassy said you were arriving at twelve o'clock but the Polish Embassy said you might arrive at a quarter to six in the morning. So I am here after all.' Within minutes she had paid the conductor the princely sum of 110 Zloty, under £2, and the crisis was over.

Crossman's report on Czechoslovakia appeared in the Daily Mirror on January 8th. He did not keep a diary of his five days in Poland but his papers include a note of the conversation on January 11th with Dr Adam Rapacki, the Polish Foreign Minister. It was he who had launched the plan, first advanced in the United Nations on October 2nd, 1957, for banning the production or storage of nuclear weapons in Poland, Czechoslovakia and both parts of Germany, and establishing a neutral zone in Central Europe.

The discussion began with a forty-minute explanation of the plan by Dr Rapacki. Crossman concluded, 'I have thought a good deal about this long *introductory speech but still do not understand the point of it. The more he denied that his plan was designed as propaganda, the more Rapacki gave me the impression that its main aim was psychological warfare in Western Germany.' Crossman then spent an hour asking Dr Rapacki questions of detail about the plan itself. In turn, he explained 'the Gaitskell plan', emphasizing that British Socialists wanted the simultaneous banning of nuclear weapons and the reduction of conventional forces. Rapacki agreed with Crossman's interpretation of the official Polish view that 'the task of the four Powers is rather to encourage integration of the two Germanys than to impose a German solution.'*

On February 5th an article appeared in the Polish press Słowo Powszechne, *No. 30, ascribing to Crossman's visit some of the developments announced after a meeting between Dr Rapacki and Mr Gromyko. The Rapacki–Gromyko declaration contained a statement that Poland and the U.S.S.R. were ready to examine the question of the reduction of conventional troops in the territories of the four countries included in the Rapacki plan, within the framework of its execution.*

Crossman's own report of his Polish visit appeared in the Daily Mirror *on January 10th. The three articles which followed, on January 14th, 17th and 21st, all dealt with the resignation of the Chancellor of the Exchequer, Mr Thorneycroft, and of his Treasury colleagues, Enoch Powell and Nigel Birch, frustrated in their wish to press even stricter measures against inflation. The resignations were announced on January 6th, together with the names of those replacing the three former Ministers.*

The new Chancellor was Derick Heathcoat Amory, whose place as Minister of Agriculture was taken by John Hare, the former Secretary of State for War. That office was now filled by Christopher Soames, until then a junior Minister at the Admiralty. Enoch Powell's office as Financial Secretary to the Treasury went to Jocelyn Simon; Nigel Birch, the Economic Secretary, was not immediately replaced, but it was announced that the Paymaster-General, Reginald Maudling, would assist the Chancellor of the Exchequer over the whole range of economic matters, in addition to his duties with the European Free Trade Area.

In his letter to the Prime Minister, Mr Thorneycroft had written, 'I am not prepared to approve estimates for the Government's current expenditure next year at a total higher than the sum that will be spent this year.' It appeared that the difference between the Treasury team and their Cabinet colleagues, described in Mr Macmillan's reply as 'a narrow one', came to some £50 million. On the eve of his departure for a Commonwealth tour the Prime Minister spoke of 'these little local difficulties'.

On January 14th Mr Thorneycroft reaffirmed his view in a speech to his constituents in Newport, Monmouthshire. At the same time he said that he would not 'engage in fractious criticism of my late colleagues'. When Parliament reassembled on January 21st Mr Amory declared to a private meeting of the Conservative backbench finance committee that the Government intended 'to continue unabated the fight against inflation'. On January 23rd the Commons was to discuss a motion in support of the Government's economic and financial policy.

Tuesday, January 21st

Since I got back I have been faced with a mass of Party committees, which has enabled me to see something of my colleagues and study how the Labour Opposition is facing up to the Thorneycroft crisis and preparing itself for what is now assumed to be inevitable power after the next Election.

At the Publicity Committee on Monday, the 13th, we had a characteristic report from Mr Peay, a smooth young man who deals with television. He pointed out that in the world of television it is personalities that count, not policy arguments. Of course, this is just what Gaitskell and Bevan want to hear and I took him up. 'If you knew anything about advertising or psychological warfare,' I said 'you would realize that getting an audience is only the first stage. The second and crucial stage is successfully getting an idea across to the audience. If, in a Labour Party political broadcast, you are merely content to see that your Leader makes a favourable impression, you are doing no better than the *Daily Mirror* does if it wins its audience by non-political news. The real test of the *Mirror* is how much serious politics it can inject. The test of a party political broadcast is how much Socialist propaganda it can get across without upsetting the amiability.'

These remarks were received with black looks but the seed fell on some fertile ground, as I have discovered since in various talks with officials in Transport House. This was particularly so at a lunch I had today, with David Ginsburg and Mark Abrams, who is one of the best of our public opinion pollsters. Mark entirely and strongly supported my point of view and was equally insistent that it was a fatal mistake of Bevan and Gaitskell to imagine that all they now have to do to achieve power is to make amiable appearances on television and avoid committing themselves to anything. This thought has been at the back of my mind all through this week and has influenced my column a good deal. Three times I have successfully dealt with the Thorneycroft crisis and what should be Labour's attitude to it.

I had a talk with Harold Wilson and pointed out that, in my view, this 'promise all' attitude would cut no ice whatsoever and that our proper line was to congratulate Thorneycroft on his courage and then point out that we agree that cuts must be made. Where we differed was in our priorities, i.e. in what we should expand and what we should cut. This, of course, would involve us in explaining in the debate what a Labour Chancellor would do.

Harold talked pleasantly about defending the pound and substituting expansion for restriction, whatever that may mean. I was disconcerted by a talk on Sunday with T. Balogh. 'There is no need to think about cuts,' he said. 'All you need to do is to restore the expansion of the economy and then you will have plenty enough to enable you to pay for increased capital investment, social services, etc., and defence.' 'Defence, too?' I said. 'Why, certainly,' he replied. 'As a result of Tory restrictionism we have lost £2 billion of national production. Put this back and we can afford everything.'

This sounds to me typical economists' nonsense but I made Balogh admit, under pressure, that the conditions for this pipe-dream were, first, at least one year of wage freeze; and, second, no additional public expenditure in the first year of the Labour Government. I pointed out to him that this was nonsense, since, to name one item, we are now pledged to the immediate introduction of a £3 basic old age pension, and I suspect that others will be equally insistent that the National Health charges should be abolished in the first year.

It also seems to be an illusion that one can do more than check wage increases, since the unions will say that they have been artificially held back under the Tories and must be allowed their whack now their own side is in power. Moreover, whether I am right or wrong in that prediction, I am quite certain that the mood of the electorate is one in which it will believe no one who says we can afford everything and follow no one who does not demand severe self-sacrifice.

When I went into the House of Commons, which resumes today, to discover some reactions, the first person I ran into was Thorneycroft. George Wigg and I had just been discussing the astonishing Gallup Poll, which appeared in this morning's *Chronicle*. This showed that, after a momentary fall in Government popularity, the Thorneycroft speech had actually revived the Government's figures, so the net loss was only one point. Moreover, it seems that about twice as many people think Thorneycroft right in the dispute as think him wrong—including a majority of Labour voters. It is clear that the vast majority of people in this country think that a wage-freeze and cuts are necessary to halt inflation. I said something about the figures to Thorneycroft, who seemed exultant and replied, 'Yes, we ought to trust the people more than we do,' and passed on into the outer thaw in Palace Yard.

Inside, I found a wonderful mood of ambiguity among the Labour people I ran into. Those on the Left, of course, were delighted with what I'd written and, for the first time for many months, I sat down and had a long and serious talk with Stephen Swingler, partly about Czechoslovakia, which he knows well, but more about the need for reviving the Keep Left Group and doing some serious thinking.

But obviously everyone else was fighting shy of committing himself, until in the Smoking Room I ran into Nye: 'What on earth do the last sentences of your article mean?' he said. 'This appeal that Gaitskell and I should stop speaking half-truths?[1] What do you want us to say?' 'Well, you might make

---

[1] In the *Daily Mirror* on January 21st, Crossman wrote, '[The Opposition], too, are tempted to suppress unpalatable truths which might upset the floating voter. And too often they engage in vague generalities, which enable them to avoid settling the differences which still divide the Left and Right of the Labour Party.'

up your mind', I said, 'about Cabinet priorities — for instance on defence, or what you would do about rocket bases.' 'If we make statements on all the things you are insisting on,' he replied, 'there will be nothing left for us to do when we get to Downing Street.' He pushed his cup away and walked out in a huff. Of course, the truth is that Cudlipp splashed this column precisely because, while attacking the Government, it also admits that at the moment the Opposition leadership is spineless.

Moreover, as I found in Coventry last weekend, the effect on our own people is terrible. I was down there for a really excellent conference on employment in the machine tool industry. After the meeting had broken up quite amicably, Reg Underhill, the Midlands Organizer, said, in the presence of everybody, 'Those three articles in the *Herald* are first-rate. They tell the leadership what should be done.' He was referring to three feature articles recently published in the *Herald*, culminating in an anonymous attack on the leadership for not putting over the Party policy and getting on with the job. 'You fellows are sitting on your arses in Westminster,' said Reg. 'What do you think the Organizers can do down here when there's not a particle of leadership at the top? It's time Gaitskell and Bevan realized this.'

Tuesday, January 28th
We are lumbering towards what may blow up into the first policy crisis in the Party since the Bevan–Gaitskell axis was formed. What an irony it is, by the way, that more and more people are coming to me and saying how disastrous this axis is, since it has destroyed the vitality of the Party to have both these men now determined to have no genuine discussion of policy at all.

But one discussion they cannot avoid is rocket bases. At the Executive last week, it was reported that the T.U.C. wanted a joint meeting with us on this, whereupon poor Peggy Herbison said, quite mildly, that the Scottish Members would be extremely grateful if a campaign could be launched which would allay Scottish anxiety. Nye then attacked her, saying it was no good having a campaign without a policy, and that anyway it wasn't a Scottish question. Why should the Scotch object to the bases being in Scotland? Did that mean that they wouldn't mind their being in Lincolnshire or South Wales? 'Anyway,' he concluded, 'you people who have been supporting NATO have got to swallow these bases because they are merely a logical extension of our atomic defences and Peggy Herbison has no right, therefore, to bleat about them.' Nye concluded by saying that personally he didn't think they would ever come into existence and that anyway the Party policy was now agreed, namely to accept them on the condition that they were under British control.

This amazing pack of nonsense was too much even for Hugh Gaitskell, who actually supported me when I pointed out that it was absurd to say that you couldn't draw the line somewhere. In my view there was serious doubt about the military utility of rocket bases (Nye interjected: 'This is quite irrelevant') and anyway it was perfectly logical to say, 'This far and no further', and to consider concentration on conventional weapons as a strategy. Hugh supported me and said this was surely the moment for a new political initiative. We agreed to meet the T.U.C. in a fortnight's time and meanwhile we are having a meeting of the parliamentary foreign affairs and defence groups this evening.

Last night I ran into Denis Healey, who has just had a very good press for his pamphlet on a neutralized belt in Europe.[1] 'Will you be starting off the discussion tomorrow?' I asked him. 'Good God, no!' he said. 'I've given up the old man, he's absolutely hopeless. He doesn't understand any of these subjects, but I'm not going to try to help him out of his difficulty.' So I shall be going to the meeting this evening in high expectancy.

One other thing I must record. By accident, we had a party here on the evening of Tuesday, the 21st. That was the day on which I scored my first double page, when the column suddenly spread itself over the front and back pages of the *Mirror*. Hugh Cudlipp rang me up to ask how I liked it, since it came as a complete surprise.[2] 'If you had rung up, we'd have kept it a secret from you,' Hugh said, 'because otherwise you would have been fiddling with it.' I think it's perfectly fair for them to say that I must be prepared to stand by what I write, even if it occurs in capital letters. Actually it looked quite good.

Anyhow, and this is truthful, this was simply a party for those we hadn't had at our party before Christmas (but we didn't ask Hugh Cudlipp). Cecil King stayed for two and a half hours, drank a great deal and talked to everybody, mainly because it was the evening on which the bank rate report had been published and he was furious with it as an outrageous whitewash (a view which got the agreement of Hugh Gaitskell).

From December 2nd to 20th, 1957, the Bank Rate Tribunal had heard witnesses and taken statements, its proceedings conducted by the Attorney General, Sir Reginald Manningham-Buller. Harold Wilson gave evidence on December 19th, stating that at no time had he alleged that there had been an improper or premature leak of information that bank rate was to be increased. He had been concerned, rather, to ensure that a full inquiry be held to allay anxiety in the City and in the press. He agreed that the 'evidence' which had led him to press the Prime Minister for an inpuiry, after his first refusal, had been based in part on what turned out to be groundless rumours.

The Report of the Tribunal, Cmnd 350, was published on January 21st. It concluded, unanimously, that there was 'no justification for allegations that information about the raising of Bank Rate was improperly disclosed to any persons'. The committee also found that in every case in which prior disclosure

---

[1] *A Neutral Belt in Europe?* (Fabian Tract 311) was published by the Fabian International Bureau in January 1958.

[2] Subsequent columns were printed in the usual fashion, until March 18th, when there was another two-page spread.

was made by Ministers of proposed restrictive financial measures 'the informa-
tion disclosed was treated by the recipient as confidential and that no use of such
information was made for the purpose of private gain'.

The proceedings of the Tribunal had drawn attention to the delicate position
of certain members of the Court of Governors of the Bank of England who were
also directors of large private companies. In this particular case, two such
persons, Sir William Keswick and Lord Kindersley, had given evidence; their
companies had in fact made large sales of gilt-edged securities shortly before the
announcement of the rise in bank rate. Both these men emerged honourably
from their cross-examination. The Report of the Tribunal offered no opinion on
this general issue but merely drew attention to its importance.

The Shadow Cabinet greeted the Report with a statement that the evidence
submitted to the Tribunal and its conclusions fully justified the holding of an
investigation. Conservative Members, for their part, received the Report as an
implied rebuke to Mr Wilson and others. In his Mirror *column on January 24th*
Crossman wrote that Labour should accept the Report and that the City of
London should be grateful to Mr Wilson for pressing the Prime Minister to
establish a Tribunal which had so completely scotched the rumours and
vindicated all concerned.

On the following morning [January 22nd] I met Hugh and Harold on the way
up to the N.E.C. meeting. Hugh said to me, 'On reflection, and seeing the
press, you will agree that the idea we voiced at your party of putting backbenchers up to denounce the Report and avoid libel under privilege would be
fatal.' I said I had had exactly the same reaction. Either one rejects the
Report, I said, or one must unreservedly accept it and express pleasure at the
complete vindication of the persons involved. 'That's our view, too,' said
Hugh.

On Thursday morning I wrote a column precisely on these lines and
checked it over with Harold Wilson, who agreed it, with some minor
demurring. That afternoon, however, I was amazed to hear Hugh insisting
that there must be a two-day debate[1] and offering one of Labour's Supply
Days, to give our backbenchers a chance. This, apparently, was the result of
Nye Bevan's pressure in the Shadow Cabinet and also of the insistence of our
lawyers, who wanted a field day, to show how they would have conducted the
cross-examination. But I suspect that it is really the result of a particularly
odious desire to continue the vendetta under the shield of privilege, although
no one who had read the evidence really believes, as far as I can gather, that
there was a leak or that anyone behaved improperly.

The trouble is that people only read the press reports and, combined with
their prejudices, this made them feel there was 'something in it'. Add to this
the very legitimate feeling that the Tribunal has revealed an astonishing
method of deciding on a bank rate rise and an astonishing conflict of loyalty

[1] To be held on February 3rd and 4th.

among Bank of England directors, and you get the kind of state of mind which insists on a two-day debate, although I can't see how it will be of any profit to the Labour Party. What this really shows is the weakness of Hugh and Harold, who should have insisted on one day and shut down their supporters. But I suppose Nye's adherence to the lawyers was too strong for them.

Wednesday, January 29th

I shall describe at some length what happened in the Commons yesterday because the whole thing was characteristic. A meeting had been called for six o'clock of the joint foreign affairs and defence groups to discuss missile bases. I had assumed that this was because the National Executive is due to meet the T.U.C. on the subject in a fortnight. I was wrong. The reason was that efforts had been made to put resolutions on the Order Paper, denouncing the Government for agreeing to American missile bases, and the Members had only been persuaded to forgo this if a meeting were held.

There were some forty-five people present, with Nye in the chair and George Brown on his right. Nye started by outlining what he thought would be the right policy, emphasizing that we had reached agreement before the December debate and that we should do nothing to emphasize our differences. His statement, in his own words, was merely a reaffirmation of what he and George Brown had been saying on this issue in the frequent bouts of question and answer on this subject since Christmas. This was: first, we are in favour of summit talks as soon as possible. Secondly, the main danger of failure of these talks would be if the West were to put forward far too ambitious proposals. Success could only be achieved by trying to get modest agreement on secondary topics.

Thirdly, the Labour Party is opposed to permitting the Americans to construct missile bases in Britain now. Any hurry in building the bases is not justified on military grounds since for some years ahead the bomber can still deliver the deterrents. On political grounds, anyway, the new agreements need to be negotiated, which would ensure that, if missile bases have to be constructed in Britain, they will be under effective British control. On general grounds, the Labour Party opposes the establishment of the bases before a further attempt has been made to end the cold war. Fourthly, the Labour Party accepts the need for a British nuclear deterrent but is opposed to either British or American aeroplanes on patrol being armed with H-bombs. Fifthly the Labour Party urges the cessation of H-bomb tests by international agreement and a unilateral British cessation as a peace initiative.

It would not be true to say that these points were put by Nye as clearly as this in his initial speech, but by the end of the meeting it was clear that they were the policy that George Brown and he had proposed. All Nye's emphasis was on the point that all this had been agreed before Christmas. This, of course, was not the case. Before Christmas it was I who moved in the

Committee that our policy should be no further military commitments, particularly with regard to missile bases, until a further effort to break the East/West deadlock had been made.

Nye had abruptly turned me down on this, so that, as usual, he and George are conceding to pressure slowly. Moreover, from his and George Brown's insistence it was clear that they could not oppose missile bases in principle. In fact their plan is to make a noise in Opposition, knowing pretty well that they will carry on the same policy when in Government. However, this is something of which it is quite impossible to accuse them and it seemed to me clear that the Committee must be content with what they do concede for the time being.

Indeed, the real interest of this meeting was not the policy announcement but an incident which arose because Bill Warbey had submitted a lengthy Warbeyist resolution, which had been stencilled in advance for circulation to the group, as is our normal practice. Suddenly, in the middle of the proceedings, Nye urged the group not to have the resolution circulated, since it would certainly get into the press that we were going to discuss it next time and then the Party's disunity would be emphasized. 'This, after all, is not a policy-making body,' he said. 'Our only function here is exploratory. Policy-making is done by the Parliamentary Party and I urge Warbey to withdraw this resolution, since I do not believe this Committee should pass resolutions or try to make policy.'

Of course, as I myself have admitted in the past, there was a lot in Nye's argument that arguing about resolutions and counting heads and trying to get snap judgments gets you very little distance. But, coming from Nye, who we all know hates committee meetings, this was pretty hard to swallow, and there was a good deal of protest. On the other hand, Bill Warbey's resolution was so silly (it never was read to anybody, by the way, so we never knew officially what we were voting against) and Bill Warbey himself made such a terribly dreary speech that, when Nye insisted that we should vote on whether the motion should be circulated, he won, though not by more than a comfortable majority.

Afterwards I went down to the Smoking Room with Will Griffiths and Curly Mallalieu. Will was blowing up with anger at Nye's performance about the committee, which was exactly the same as Ernest Bevin's eleven years ago. In came Nye and rather reluctantly, as I saw, sat down beside me. I gave him a drink and said he ought to be ashamed of himself, at which he burst back, 'You just like talking for the sake of talking, Dick. We are getting absolutely jaded with these endless committees – committees of the Parliamentary Party, committees of the National Executive. They're killing me and they're just kept going by people like you, who talk for talking's sake. There's only one place worth talking and that's on the floor of the House of Commons, where hings are decided. You're just a talker, whereas I believe in action.'

I said Nye could hardly complain that the foreign affairs group had met too often, since it had only met twice since Parliament came back from holidays. 'And a good thing, too,' he said. 'It's been far better off not meeting.' 'Yes,' I replied, 'but you said you were jaded because of all these committees. I agree you're jaded, but the reasons, my dear Nye, are very different, if you want to discuss them.' 'One of the reasons', he said, 'is your behaviour in the *Mirror*. You in the *Mirror* are one of the causes why the Opposition's attack is failing. You are actually fomenting the trouble by your idiotic demand that we should deliver a knock-out blow against a Government with a majority of seventy.' 'But when have we ever demanded this?' I asked. 'You are doing it all the time,' he said, 'and though you pretend to attack the Government, your real attack is on the Opposition leadership. Look at that article which they put on the front page last week, a sensational smear on Gaitskell and myself, and all the worse because it wasn't precise.'[1]

At this, even Curly Mallalieu protested that he thought this was rather a mild comment to be described as a smear and Will Griffiths whispered to me, 'Desiccated adding machine'. 'Your type of sensational journalism, with its personal smears and attacks,' said Nye, 'is incompatible with your standing as a member of the National Executive. You will soon have to realize that Michael Foot had the dignity to withdraw. It's time you made your decision.' I then said, 'But Nye, since I've known you, you have earned as much by journalism as I do and I really can't see what difference there is between writing in the *News of the World* or the *Daily Mirror*.' 'I don't write smear attacks on my colleagues,' he said. 'Nor do I,' I replied, 'and, whereas your articles would be read by nobody if they weren't signed by you, I am a journalist who is read not merely for the name with which his articles are signed.' 'There are many who dispute that,' he replied sharply. 'What you fail to see, Dick, is that it isn't the leadership of the Parliamentary Party that is wrong but the Party itself. One thing is certain. You can't deliver an effective attack on the Government with half-empty benches behind you.'

'But what incentive are you giving to us to sit on the benches behind you?' I asked him. 'Is it our only function to sit and cheer while you make brilliant speeches? That's the trouble about us today, my dear Nye. There is no function for us behind you.' 'Of course it's true', he said, 'that Parliament has declined since groups and individual backbench activity were forbidden. Nothing effective comes except by individual initiative on the floor of the Commons.' At this point I was two minutes late for Anne's dinner and replied, 'And since individual effort is forbidden by the leadership to which you belong, I have chosen my field for individual initiative in the press.'

It really was a fascinating conversation and, reflecting on it afterwards, I realized, knowing my Nye, that it's a delayed reaction to two incidents. First, he has now heard, no doubt from Sam Watson, that I raised the issue of his absence from the International Sub. at the Executive, when again he was absent, and complained that he should not have meetings cancelled when he

---

[1] On January 21st. See above, p. 655.

was there in the House and could have attended. Secondly, though he doesn't probably read me very often in the *Mirror*, he did look at the front page article last week and I would guess has discussed it with Gaitskell. Hence his remark about its incompatibility with the N.E.C. But, of course, what this generally brings out is the fact that, apart from myself, there is no one at all in the Parliamentary Party who is raising a cheep of comment, let alone criticism of the Gaitskell–Bevan leadership. This makes anything I say or write stick out so prominently that all the fury concentrates on me like a lightning conductor.

The other thing, of course, which struck me is that, if Mr Bevan complains of the number of boring committees he has to sit through when he is in Opposition, what will he feel like as Foreign Secretary, with six committees a day in the Foreign Office? What this again reveals is the really appalling indolence of the man. However, I am very glad the whole thing happened, since it was high time he blew off his top at me and said in my presence what he had been feeling behind my back.

Friday, February 7th
After my extraordinary talk with Nye last week, I was amused to find myself sitting in the Smoking Room with him for an hour for dinner last night. He was charm itself and took the greatest care, in the presence of Mallalieu and Griffiths once again, to treat me as an old and honoured friend. I suspect that after I had left both of them must have told him what a fool he had made of himself. It's certainly true that the story has gone rapidly round the corridors and has not done me any harm.

This week's big public political event was the two-day bank rate leak debate.[1] It ran a good deal better than I had feared. In the morning I rang Harold Wilson to wish him good luck. He certainly has been dreading the occasion and preparing for it with immense perseverance, and he put on a tremendous show. He flogged his way through in what was a brilliant but parliamentary forensic performance. What adroitness he showed in flipping over the weak points and putting in laughs just at the right times, and what sheer guts he showed in battling his way through the entrenched hatred he had engendered among the Tories!

After that, the rest of the first day was an incredibly boring field-day for the lawyers and the second day only woke up with a fantastically funny speech from Leslie Hale, which ended, ironically enough, in a passionate

---

[1] In the debate on February 3rd and 4th Mr Butler proposed a motion welcoming the Tribunal's findings, while Mr Wilson replied with an Amendment regretting 'prior disclosure on September 18th, 1957, by the Chancellor of the Exchequer of secret information about the Government's financial policies to certain selected journalists and to officials of the Conservative Central Office', and calling on the Government to take steps 'to obviate the present conflict between public duties and private responsibilities of part-time directors of the Bank of England'. The Government defeated the Opposition Amendment by 320 votes to 256 and the Government motion was carried by 322 votes to 253.

denunciation of the tribunal as a kind of lynching procedure. It was really quite funny to remember (how new M.P.s did!) that we Labour people had insisted on this method. Yet in the debate most of the really effective speeches were exposing the terrible injustice of the tribunal procedure.

The debate ended in the usual appalling yahooing hullabaloo and I doubt whether it had any effect outside Parliament, except to make people say, 'There are those M.P.s misbehaving again'. However, in this respect I am not at all representative, since nearly all my colleagues were convinced that the whole Report was a whitewash and were furious about it. I don't believe there is any evidence to suggest this. The real truth is that in the technical sense there was no leak and everybody behaved with perfect propriety. On the other hand, the workings of the City as revealed by the Report are more fantastic, cumbersome, priggish, hypocritical than even I believed.

Tuesday, February 18th

Last night I went to a dinner at the Garrick, organized by Desmond Donnelly. The Garrick is a lovely club,[1] mainly for actors and lawyers, and we dined in a beautiful private room, with only Hugh Gaitskell, Megan Lloyd George and Dingle Foot[2] present. I thought it was going to be an awkward meeting but, on the contrary, Gaitskell felt entirely at home — indeed, much more at home than I have ever known him in my house, talking very freely and expansively.

Megan turned the conversation to the recent Rochdale by-election[3] and Hugh at once listed the reasons why those disillusioned with Toryism are not voting Labour. Labour is a high taxation party, Labour is a trade union party, Labour is a nationalization party and Labour is not as sound as the Tories on the foreign issue. When asked what he would do to change this hostility to Labour, he said there was a very limited amount one could do. He himself would play down the nationalization of steel but, after all, we are a trade union party, with these views, and, even with all this hostility, he was confident we should get in. He would be content with a majority of 50 to 100. I said, 'Surely, for a Labour Government, fifty is pretty low,' and he agreed but added, '100 would in certain ways be more convenient than 200.'

Indeed, I very much got the impression that Hugh would not be reluctant to be the Prime Minister of a Government with a relatively small majority, able for this reason to say that there wasn't a popular mandate for going too

[1] Crossman himself became a member on November 4th, 1965.

[2] Michael Foot's eldest brother and Liberal M.P. for Dundee 1935–45 and Labour M.P. for Ipswich 1957–70. He was Parliamentary Secretary at the Ministry of Economic Warfare 1940–5 and Solicitor General 1964–7 and was knighted in 1962. He died in 1978.

[3] Caused by the death on December 16th, 1957, of Lt Colonel Wentworth Schofield (Conservative). In the by-election on February 12th, John McCann captured the seat for Labour, with 22,133 votes, a majority of 4,530. The Liberal candidate, Ludovic Kennedy, came second, with 17,603 votes, and the Conservative candidate, J. E. Parkinson, came bottom, with 9,827 votes. The Labour proportion of the poll dropped by 3·8 per cent and the Conservative proportion by 31·7 per cent.

fast or too far and possibly even to postpone steel nationalization till the second Session. (At one point he actually suggested doing this.) Three times he said, 'Do remember there isn't a country in the world, with the possible exception of New Zealand, where the Labour Party and the Communists together have over half the electorate and therefore we must always remember that if one is to get to power one may have to rely on non-Labour votes.' I said, 'But there isn't a country in the world, Hugh, which has a political system like ours, specifically designed to create two parties, so that Labour can capture half.' He said, 'Well, there's something in that. But I still think my point is crucial.'

I asked him whether he thought that he or Nye should have launched the ferocious onslaught on the Liberals made by Lord Hailsham last Saturday[1] (a very fine speech, I thought, and not only because it roughly took the line of my own article).[2] Hugh said, 'No, we should leave the two anti-Labour parties to quarrel among themselves and indeed, in general, leave the Liberals alone.' I asked him whether he would positively like to see a Liberal revival and he said, 'No,' but not, I thought, very fiercely.

The conversation went round and round on the subject of how to win the uncommitted voter. Megan pressed that the Party should somehow have a general theme and philosophy to bind its parts together and Hugh agreed. I then said we should be wise to tell people frankly of the difficulties which will face us in the first eighteen months and Hugh said we mustn't overestimate the desire for self-sacrifice. This was a totally different situation from that which faced Cripps[3] and the electorate was in no mood to be asked to face up to things. There was a severe limit to that kind of talk, though he admitted, under pressure, that nearer the Election we might warn them that the introduction of our improvements in the Welfare State would have to go *pari passu* with increases in the national income.

We turned to the H-bomb and Hugh said, very sharply, 'The Gallup Poll was much more important than Rochdale.' He didn't accept Massingham's view that the H-bomb had played a great role, since the Poll showed clearly that the British people do not want unilateral disarmament. I said I didn't think the Poll could be taken to indicate any such thing. What it did suggest was the direction in which people were moving and that direction was an ever-increasing distrust of nuclear arms and of the politicians who made speeches about them.

This was one of the few points of the evening where we got edgy, though, when I outlined once again my proposal for a European pact, renouncing

---

[1] In a speech on February 14th to a meeting of the Glasgow Unionist Association, Lord Hailsham (the former Quintin Hogg) had described the Liberal Party as having 'a number of inconsistent policies tailor-made to suit every constituency'.

[2] Crossman's column on February 14th ascribed the Liberal revival to 'Tory bankruptcy and Labour weakness'. The attraction of the Liberals, he said, was that they had no real programme.

[3] In November 1947.

nuclear arms for a period, Hugh did say that he regarded this as a perfectly serious proposition for which there were very strong arguments but which he didn't yet accept. He said that in the big debate[1] he thought he'd concentrate on the Rapacki plan and disengagement. It's obvious that he feels that, whether there is any chance of their coming off or not, these propositions will fill in a useful gap.

Friday, February 21st

Well, the big debate is over. It was preceded by a characteristic joint meeting of the defence and foreign affairs groups on Tuesday night. Nye started the meeting by saying that, as our foreign policy remained unchanged from that agreed before Christmas, there was no need to discuss it. He suggested that George Brown should introduce a discussion on defence policy. There was some muttering but George proceeded to take Paragraph 12 of the defence White Paper and say that it was the most terrible and monstrous thing he had ever read and we must concentrate on denouncing Duncan Sandys for his murderous statement that we would use nuclear weapons.[2]

After this Nye made a long speech, telling us that we were all united and our policy hadn't changed and outlining it quite competently. Then we filed out. The prophet had once again come down from the mountain and once again there was a good deal of sardonic comment in the lobbies, particularly when George Strauss began to point out that what Duncan Sandys had written was official Labour Party policy.

The first day of the debate was misleadingly reported in Thursday's press.[3] True, the Prime Minister made a good bipartisan speech, with its tacit tribute to Mr Attlee and a tardy admission that, so far from destroying the Empire, we had transformed it into a new Commonwealth. Hugh, I thought, made the best speech of his life, in the circumstances. He couldn't possibly have launched into an attack on the P.M., but he did put forward our positive

[1] On foreign affairs, to be held on February 19th and 20th.
[2] Paragraph 12 of Cmnd 363 ran:

The West, on the other hand, relies for its defence primarily upon the deterrent effect of its vast stockpile of nuclear weapons and its capacity to deliver them. The democratic Western nations will never start a war against Russia. But it must be well understood that, if Russia were to launch a major attack on them, even with conventional forces only, they would have to hit back with strategic nuclear weapons. In fact the strategy of NATO is based on the frank recognition that a full-scale Soviet attack could not be repelled without a massive nuclear bombardment of the sources of power in Russia. In that event, the role of the allied defence forces in Europe would be to hold the front for the time needed to allow the effects of the nuclear counter-offensive to make themselves felt.

[3] On February 14th the Prime Minister returned from his Commonwealth tour. Five days later he opened a two-day debate on foreign affairs with the statement that, while he was as anxious as anyone for a summit conference on the lines suggested by the U.S.S.R. at the end of 1957, he insisted on the need for serious preparatory work, to set out an agenda and procedures calculated to achieve results on specific issues. The subject which seemed to him the most promising was disarmament. The Government's foreign policy was approved by 308 votes to 242.

policy extremely well and in some detail, and he made a great impression on the House. It was quite clear to me that, even if I had prepared a speech, it wasn't worth delivering. I went out and gave John Strachey and Dick Mitchison dinner. I was amused to find that John, who has just returned after a heart attack, never spoke a word to Dick Mitchison, so that, whenever I was discussing housing with Dick, John was discussing Celia with Anne, and vice versa. How separate my friends all are!

On Thursday morning, when I was busy writing, Stephen Swingler rang up to say that there was great dissatisfaction because there wasn't to be a vote. He asked if I would stir Nye up. So I rang up Nye and told him to bait Selwyn Lloyd and he said, 'O.K., Dick boy,' and rang off, quite cheerful. I had sat with Nye in the Smoking Room both on Tuesday and Wednesday in a most amicable way, and also with Jennie. Nye had told me that the theme of his speech was going to be that no initiative could possibly come from America, from France, from anywhere except from Britain, and, there, look at Macmillan and Selwyn Lloyd – a good enough theme.

That was how he started, in wonderful, subtle, amusing form, until he went off on to this ghastly, cumbrous, pretentious re-explanation of his Brighton speech. Very soon young John Eden[1] was baying from below the gangway and all around me there began that quiet conversation which shows a speaker has lost the House. Nye regained it by repeating the Party policy quite adequately and then ended with a very pretentious piece about the urbanization of Iraq through oil royalties and without adequate industrialization. It really showed Nye at his very worst. Of course, if he had tried out his ideas on anybody intelligent, we could have knocked some sense into him, but who did he talk to before doing this? I do not know.

I came into the House that evening to find Macmillan making a brilliant winding-up speech, having jumped into the breach at the last moment to replace Noble. Curiously enough, by so doing he had saved Nye's prestige, since this morning all the popular press had the story of Selwyn Lloyd's fiasco, which followed Nye's, and of the fact that Selwyn was so bad that the Premier had to speak.

Going through the lobby I ran into Hugh Gaitskell, who couldn't have been friendlier or happier and we discussed the poor old boy's flop. 'Do you think it will make him rat to the Left?' Hugh said to me. 'Oh no,' I said. 'I don't think so. He's fixed for good.' 'Why does he do these things?' said Hugh, very sadly, but he couldn't conceal his relief, which is natural enough.

The evening was made even more piquant for me by another incident. I learnt from George in the early afternoon that the Shadow Cabinet was still undecided whether to oppose the Defence White Paper in next week's debate.

[1] Conservative M.P. for Bournemouth West since February 1954. Minister of State at the Ministry of Technology 1970, Minister for Industry 1970–2 and Minister of Posts and Telecommunications 1972–4, he was Chairman of the House of Commons Select Committee on European Legislation 1976–9. He succeeded to his father's baronetcy in 1963.

Yet at half-past six, in the Party Meeting, I heard the terms of the most slashing resolution, censuring Duncan Sandys. In the lobby I said to Hugh Gaitskell, 'That's a very nice resolution.' He remarked, 'Yes, when I saw it I said to George Brown, "If you don't take care, you'll find yourself on the same side as Dick and George Wigg." ' Presumably this means that Hugh let George draft the resolution at the last moment, when our Chief Whip had begun to get the feeling in the Party about nuclear weapons and to realize the untenability of the official Front Bench position. I suspect it was a sensitivity to this move which made Nye behave as he did in his speech. Are we to expect that George Brown and John Strachey are going to produce some equally embarrassing performance next week? I really don't know.

The Government's 1958 Defence White Paper (Cmd 363) announcing massive spending on Britain's nuclear deterrent, was discussed in the House of Commons on February 26th and 27th. The debate followed publication of an agreement reached in Washington for the supply of American ballistic missiles to the United Kingdom; the Opposition leadership was split on what the official reaction would be. The 'anti-nuclear' rebels were supported by the Daily Herald, *which in a front-page article on February 26th demanded unilateral cessation of H-bomb manufacture and the rejection of missile bases in Britain. Some sixty-five Labour Members wrote a letter to the* Herald *agreeing with this view.*

Meanwhile Ian Mikardo and other former Bevanites had initiated Victory for Socialism, a movement with the declared policy of 'recreating agitation for the application of the fundamental Socialist principles'. On February 28th Transport House sent 618 letters to secretaries of constituency Labour parties, warning them that the Party's electoral chances would be jeopardized if the Victory for Socialism movement was permitted to establish 'a party within a party' at constituency level.

The 'nuclear disarmers' drew strength from public opinion. In the same month the Campaign for Nuclear Disarmament (C.N.D.) was launched at a meeting in the Central Hall, Westminster. With Bertrand Russell, J. B. Priestley, the playwright John Osborne and Canon John Collins of St Paul's Cathedral among its leaders, it attracted a large and impassioned following.

In the debate itself, the Opposition declined to 'approve a defence policy which relies predominantly upon the threat of thermo-nuclear warfare, insists on the installation of strategic rocket bases in Britain before the projected Summit talks, and fails to provide effectively for Britain's defence requirements'. The Opposition Amendment was defeated by 318 votes to 263; the White Paper was approved by 317 votes to 261.

Friday, February 28th
For some time now I have been running in the *Mirror* a campaign against the British nuclear deterrent, not on pacifist but on strictly political and military grounds. It was obvious at the beginning of this week that this was going to

be the great issue of the defence debate. Already on Tuesday a group of sixty-five Labour M.P.s had written a letter to the *Daily Herald*, going far beyond what Nye had said and insisting that we should forbid the Americans to have missile bases in this country not merely till after the Summit talks, but indefinitely. Thus the Left pacifists have broken loose again. By an accident this coincided with the announcement that Ian Mikardo was organizing a Victory for Socialism re-Bevanite organization.

This was the background to the Executive meeting on Wednesday. It was further complicated by the fact that the *Daily Herald* had come out that morning with a huge front page saying that the Labour Party should commit itself to suspending not merely nuclear tests but the manufacture and use of nuclear bombs, in order to break the deadlock. This, of course, was a surrender to the Left, which infuriated Gaitskell. I rang him up that morning to say that it must be raised at the Executive, since the precedent would be enormously dangerous. If the *Daily Herald* ever got loose, Odhams would soon turn it into a Labour rag, like the *People*.[1] Gaitskell at once agreed and was obviously relieved that on this I was on his side.

The Executive started with a long and rambling discussion of what to do about the *Herald* and also what to do about the joint Labour–T.U.C. policy. Ian Mikardo proposed that we should insert the proposal to suspend the manufacture and use of nuclear bombs. This was turned, down, with only three votes in favour—his own, Tony Greenwood's and one other. Hugh had been extremely anxious in case Nye should rat on him, but he remained solid alongside Hugh, saying that we must stand by the policy agreed with the T.U.C. in all its five points and then put that across to the nation; it was a perfectly satisfactory policy. The only time I spoke was to give a warning that it was not a satisfactory policy but an obvious makeshift compromise to patch over the differences in the Party and it would be an illusion to believe it would be a satisfactory field for a national campaign.

Nye was obviously unwilling to envisage a national campaign. He had caught me in the lobby on Tuesday evening to tell me this. He had had word of the left-wing letter in the *Herald* and said to me, 'We oughtn't to launch a campaign in this winter weather. Moreover, it would be fatal to raise the political temperature in the North while it was still lukewarm in the South.' Indeed, he was spinning words and thinking of anything as an excuse for not having a campaign. I told him I thought it would be difficult to avoid one and that, anyway, whether there was a campaign or not, we would have to say what we thought about the subject and in saying this we couldn't avoid the basic problem of our defence policy, i.e. our attitude to the question of

---

[1] The *Daily Herald* was published by Odhams Ltd and, as an official Labour Party organ, was controlled in its political sections by the T.U.C. In 1957 there had been rumours that the *Herald*, which was losing money, might be merged with the Liberal *News Chronicle*, published by the Cadbury group of companies. Instead, on July 24th, the T.U.C. General Council signed an agreement with Odhams Press, as a result of which, in the *Herald*'s own words, 'Our future as Labour's daily newspaper is assured'.

whether British defence should rely on nuclear weapons. This question was not answered at all in the agreed principles which we had worked out with the T.U.C.

Once again on Wednesday morning this same thing came up. Bevan and Gaitskell managed to persuade the meeting that the policy would be sufficient for our needs, although they conceded to me one point, namely that the International Sub. should be instructed to consider defence as the first item at its next meeting, a somewhat Pyrrhic victory, since the defence debate was starting that day and this meant that the International Sub. would consider the problem eleven months before the next defence debate!

So we came to Victory for Socialism, where the Chairman's Committee recommended circularizing the constituencies, warning them against the campaign on constitutional grounds. Nye at once said that the constitutional grounds were wrong and that we should merely tell people that it was unwise. Tony Greenwood and I said that, since this would produce a great deal of publicity, before any of it took place we should first see Stephen Swingler to see if we could get him to limit the affair to strictly educational activities to which we could take no exception.

At this point Ian Mikardo made a long, disingenuous speech, which made it practically impossible for anybody to believe that Victory for Socialism was purely educational. It was then revealed that all the constituencies had already been circularized, from his office, by Victory for Socialism and that in the press conference it had been announced that a network of branches would be established throughout the country. That put the fat in the fire. At once all the trade unionists there clicked back into the intolerance which had marked their behaviour throughout the whole Bevanite crisis. What Ian had done was to make all discussion infinitely more difficult in the Party. Hugh Gaitskell was as rigid as ever. Nye and I both pleaded hard that at least the circular to the constituencies should stress the lack of wisdom and not the unconstitutional nature of the action. This was finally agreed, but next day's press showed that what I had feared had come true. By the decision to take action and not merely to see Stephen Swingler, we had, so to speak, created the very split in the Party we were seeking to prevent.

By this time it was after two o'clock and I rushed to have a bite in the cafeteria before the defence debate. Afterwards I met Nye in the Smoking Room and we had a contretemps like a French farce. I was furious with Ian for his elephantine behaviour in irritating everybody and I started the conversation by saying, 'How right you were to say of a friend of ours that he has the antennae of an elephant.' Nye heartily agreed and said, 'Yes, throughout the whole meeting he showed himself absolutely impervious, making enemy after enemy.' I only discovered that Nye had been talking about Gaitskell when he added, after five or six minutes, 'And Ian is nearly as bad.' This is the first time for some months that Nye has been willing to talk in such violent terms as this about Gaitskell.

I then said to Nye, 'Will you please now understand the need for having an adequate defence policy? You and Hugh have worked out a foreign policy but left defence to John Strachey and George Brown to do what they like with. This is madness and you will come unstuck with the Party as a result.' Nye didn't like this much, since I know quite well that he has done a sort of deal with George Brown on the basis that they are both working-class chaps and not intellectuals.

So we went into the first day of the defence debate, where, after a skilful and competent speech by Sandys, George Brown had almost as bad a fiasco as Nye in the previous week and for much the same reasons. In trying to challenge the Government on nuclear deterrence, George had got into an absolute tangle and only extricated himself by insisting that the gap between the police incident on the frontier and the major nuclear invasion of Western Europe must be filled by the use of atomic tactical weapons in medium-scale incidents. Thus George was pressing the Government to add to its nuclear armoury. After that George Wigg made a really excellent speech and nothing else really happened in the debate.

I went to dinner and found John Strachey alone. He very bitterly said, 'Well, George put the military arguments well. They're more convincing than the political arguments you people add.' 'What are they?' I said, and he replied, 'I'm not going to reveal my weapons for tomorrow night.' At this point George Brown came and sat down, saying, 'I made such a balls-up that I shall never recover.' I replied, 'No, you made an excellent recovery at the end and did jolly well on guided missiles. How well I know, that, after a clanger, the main thing is for one's own self-esteem to recover during the same speech.' This put him in quite decent form and he proceeded to say, 'You know, I'm not pledged to any particular kind of weapon,' a remark which made Strachey wince. What odious characters these politicians are to each other!

On Thursday I had to do a column before the debate, which is never an easy job. Then I had an hour or so to think out the lines of a speech before going down to hear the discussion, which was resumed with incredible dreariness by de Freitas and Ward.[1] However, it soon brighted up in a knockabout, farcical intervention by Shinwell, which achieved all he wanted. He had told George the night before that he was determined to seize the headlines and really make trouble for the Front Bench and for Gaitskell. He certainly succeeded in making the Front Bench look pretty silly in its inane suggestion that Russia would be more likely to make peace at the Summit if we postponed the American missile bases in Britain. Having delivered his thrust to the Front Bench, Shinwell then sloshed the pacifists and nuclear abolitionists

[1] George Ward, Conservative M.P. for Worcester City 1945–60, Parliamentary Under-Secretary of State at the Air Ministry 1952–5, Parliamentary and Financial Secretary to the Admiralty 1955–7 and Secretary of State for Air 1957. He was created 1st Viscount Ward in 1960.

with equally farcical violence. It really was an astounding performance for a man of seventy-three.

He was followed with an admirable speech by Birch, Thorneycroft's Number Two, who resigned with him. Thorneycroft was sitting beside Birch as he spoke, weightily intervening to emphasize the appalling economic strain of nuclear weapons and asking the Government to reconsider whether the first priority should be given to them. It was, in fact, the Tory correlative to George Wigg's speech on the previous day.

Anne had waited since four o'clock in the Speaker's Gallery, sitting next to Mrs Paget, Mrs Soskice[1] and Celia Strachey. At eight o'clock I got in, to continue this particular line of argument. I did it quite well, in Anne's presence and with the satisfaction that the House filled up while I was speaking and emptied immediately I stopped.

When John Strachey came to reply, he picked a quarrel with the Government on the notorious Paragraph 12 of the White Paper but then proceeded to spend the rest of his time attacking his own side, though we had been scrupulously careful to address our attacks to the Government. Nothing will deter John from his passion as a nuclear warrior and when he sat down our side was saying once again, 'Was that a speech for or against the Government?' It will be interesting to see what the next explosion is, as the result of a debate which mainly showed the Labour Party splintered into fragments.

Last week Elath asked me to see him after the foreign affairs debate but he had to go out early and then off to Paris. I was very puzzled what he wanted to see me about. I went across there this morning and he told me a fascinating story about a lunch he had with Eden, who rang him up out of the blue and asked his Zehava, as well. They motored down to the Wiltshire cottage and found Clarissa[2] cooking the meal. Within a moment of entering the door Eden was on to the subject of 'living through Suez again'. So Zehava, who is bright, said, 'Would you do it again and, if so, what changes would you make?' Eden has his answer pat. 'I miscalculated two things,' he said. 'I underestimated the hostile American reaction and I overestimated the value as a bargaining counter to us of holding Port Said. Because Israel had the whole of Sinai, at the end she was left with a free passage to Eilat – something gained. Port Said was no bargaining position.'

'What about the Russian intervention?' he was asked. 'Was it as strong as the American?' This baffled Eden. 'Of course not,' he said. 'They didn't do anything for the first three days and they only intervened when they felt it was safe to do so, after the Americans. They were not a real peril.' So much for that wonderful Government theory about the threat of Communism in the Middle East and the Russian plot.

---

[1] Reginald Paget's wife, formerly Sybil Gibbons; and Frank Soskice's wife (Lady Soskice), formerly Susan Cloudesley.

[2] Clarissa, only daughter of the late Major John Strange Spencer-Churchill, married in 1952, as his second wife, Anthony Eden, later the 1st Earl of Avon.

A little later, at lunch, Eden said to Elath, 'Of course, I must admit that I wasn't too friendly to your country.' Then he added, 'You see, I was advised by pro-Arabs in the Foreign Office.' Elath said this was too odious for him to stomach and he nearly walked out. Think of saying this on the first occasion when you ask to come and see you the Ambassador of a country which you have systematically tried to destroy! The Elaths have been invited again next week and a visitor in between has been Henriques.[1]

I found the purpose of Elath's request was merely to find out from me what the Labour Party attitude really is and how I estimated the situation. I told him I thought the whole idea of disengagement in the Middle East and of four-Power talks with the Russians had become extremely dangerous to Israel. It was a good policy four years ago but had unfortunately been adopted too late. We agreed that the danger was that, after finding they could do no disengagement in Europe, a Labour Government might be driven to try it in the Middle East, with fatal consequences, since it would merely mean, in this case, withdrawal before the Russians.

In the course of this I did discover the strength of Elath's feeling that Gaitskell and Healey's attachment to disengagement in Europe was misguided and misjudged. I observed that I had believed in disengagement for years — indeed, *up to* the Hungarian affair — whereas Healey began to believe in it *during* the Hungarian affair. 'How right you are,' said Elath. 'It's just like him. He always gets on to a good idea, along with the Foreign Office, after it has been killed. I wish he didn't influence Gaitskell in that way. How sensitive Gaitskell is! One has to be careful in handling him. The other day Malik came to lunch and kept on saying, "Of course, it's no good telling you anything about the Labour Party because you know everything, as you run it from inside." We Israelis are supposed to have a tremendous influence in the Labour Party and of course I threw up my hands, saying, "No," but with the kind of denial which made Malik believe I meant, "Yes." But the fact is Gaitskell knows this and, with his Jewish wife, one has to be careful with him.'

'Nye Bevan is different,' Elath added sadly. 'I arranged to see him a few weeks ago and, after I had waited forty-five minutes in the Central Lobby, Kenneth Younger came through and asked what I was doing. "Waiting for Bevan," I said, and he replied, "Oh, I've just met him sitting in the Smoking Room and he said he was due at a meeting." I know that Bevan hadn't forgotten and I'm not prepared to try to see him again. What a silly fellow he is to treat one as badly as that and as gratuitously.'

Monday, March 10th
Last week seems to have concentrated itself, in my life at least, on the endless

[1] Perhaps Sir Basil Henriques (1890–1961), founder in 1914 of the Oxford and St George's Club (later St George's Jewish Settlement), of which he was Warden until 1947. He was the author of several pamphlets on Judaism. He was knighted in 1955.

argument about nuclear weapons. We now seem to have got into one of those dialectical clinches in this country when there is only one subject of political conversation. Everybody has views and I can't help feeling, when a discussion starts, whether in the Tea Room at Westminster or the Senior Common Room at King's,[1] that I've heard it all before and that the person isn't going to get beyond the conventional gambits.

Last Tuesday I was so angry with John Strachey that I did a column about him, which caused quite a flurry. Anne and I went to a party on Wednesday evening, where I ran into Dora Gaitskell. By then John had been permitted to reply in the *Mirror*, in a letter attacking me for first endorsing nuclear weapons, as a member of the N.E.C., and then going back on my endorsement.[2] 'I'm glad John gave you what you deserve,' said Dora. 'It's about time somebody told you that you can't do that sort of thing. You've been doing it for months. As a member of the Executive, it's outrageous that you should be attacking the leadership all the time.'

Old Cassandra, who was also there, was even more violent, saying that this was a filthy personal vendetta, for which one should never misuse one's column, that it was totally unintelligible to the general public (which may well be true), etc., etc. It was only when we were driving Bill to Marylebone station that I finally found out why all this furore was on. 'Just now, when that filthy Victory for Socialism is resurrecting its head, you are making the same mistake,' he said. 'How can you be disloyal and create disunity at this moment of crisis in the Labour Party? Why can't you stand together now that you know that man Bevan is a crook?'

Bill Connor is quite a sensitive creature and I had evidence later in the week from the Tea Room that he was expressing a mood which I think I noted in this diary last week. The emergence of Victory for Socialism has switched all the trade unionists and right-wingers back into their mood of intolerance of any discussion and into their feeling that one must either be for them or against them. The idea that one could be for the orthodox leadership and for the great deterrent and yet think Strachey's views on atomic tactical weapons insane—this idea seems utterly remote not only to the average reader of the *Mirror*, but also to the vast majority of so-called enlightened public opinion. It is probably true that the speeches which George and I and Nigel Birch made in the debate, and what I wrote in the *Mirror*, were almost universally regarded as in some sense welshing on Britain's responsibilities and appeasing the pacifists.

---

[1] King's College, Cambridge.

[2] Crossman summarized Strachey's winding-up speech in the defence debate, saying that he quite unambiguously believed that Britain should 'Retain the British H-Bomb; Equip our ground and sea forces with nuclear tactical weapons as well; and Use these tactical weapons against a Russian attack in force, even if it were made only with conventional weapons'. The only difference between Mr Strachey and Mr Sandys, said Crossman, was that Strachey would use atomic weapons rather than the H-bomb 'in the first instance'. Mr Strachey's reply appeared on March 5th.

22

Nevertheless, I am quite sure we were right to do as we did. That view was strongly confirmed on Thursday morning, when we had our meeting of the T.U.C. and the N.E.C. to draft our joint *pronunciamento*. The draft prepared by the office was a dreary, semi-literate document, which did, however, accurately express the agreements we had reached at previous meetings. I thought we should have a formal meeting agreeing it, until Frank Cousins, looking at Clause 11 said, 'Why can't we express this positively instead of negatively? Why not write in this clause a declaration that we should never use nuclear weapons unless they are first used against us?' Nye Bevan strongly supported Cousins and I sat back, amused to hear poor Gaitskell as the only man arguing against them. I should think a majority of those present sympathized with Frank and Nye, while the minority who didn't were quite unable to say exactly why they were wrong.

Gaitskell had once again on this occasion made the mistake of coming in at the beginning instead of waiting to see how the debate went. Of course Barbara backed Frank Cousins and Nye straightaway and so did Edith Summerskill. I then asked how we could conceivably make this declaration in Paragraph 11, whereas, in the preceding paragraph, we had stated that a declaration against nuclear war could only be made at a stage when a considerable amount of disarmament had already been agreed between the Powers. We had all agreed that we could only dispense with nuclear weapons when Russia had substantially reduced her conventional weapons, and not before.

Nye then made a powerful speech, saying that he himself would rather see a Russian conventional army occupy Britain than make the world a charnel house by using nuclear weapons first. He said it was totally impossible for any rational man to make up his mind to use nuclear weapons to ward off a conventional attack. Frank Cousins added, 'Of course, Nye is right and, if he isn't right, there is no difference between Tory policy and Labour policy.'

I pointed out that there wasn't on this point and never had been; ever since 1945 we had relied on using nuclear weapons against a conventional attack and that had been the whole Western strategy. 'I hate this defence policy myself,' I said, 'and I have been opposing it all this week in the House, when Strachey and Brown have been advocating it. But you can't suddenly discard a defence policy by merely writing a statement into Clause 11 of this document. Defence policy must be considered as defence policy, on its merits, in a way that this committee has never done.'

After an hour and a half somebody quite sensibly remarked that, anyway, it wasn't worth discussing this proposal, since neither the T.U.C. nor the N.E.C. had any mandate to make such a declaration, and the whole idea would have to be referred back to our separate bodies. At this Nye moved that we should agree the draft declaration and put the new proposal as the agenda for another meeting in the near future. Then we got on fairly rapidly with tidying the document up.

The scene was absolutely fascinating because of the genuine confusion of mind of Frank Cousins, who went on asserting that the T.U.C. had gone to the Prime Minister and told him that it was never prepared to use nuclear weapons first. Moreover, Nye Bevan was a bit of a puzzle, since he had told John Strachey that he warmly applauded his speech, advocating the use of tactical atomic weapons against Berlin, and yet here he was advocating a declaration that we would never use them at all! Of course, the truth was revealed when Nye said, 'I must have something I can say at one of our great public meetings in the national campaign,' to which somebody, rather crudely, replied, 'But you will also have to know the answer to the hecklers after you make that kind of declaration.'

As we went downstairs, Gaitskell thanked me for my intervention. I said, 'Well, you had better tell Dora to recognize your true friends, Hugh, and you had better tell John Strachey and George Brown that on this issue I was the only person willing to stand up and defend them. Why can't they stop being silly fools and trying to commit us to graduated deterrence? If anybody took them seriously or even knew what they were saying, it would split the Party from top to bottom.' Hugh grunted. Nye was just behind us at this point and we stopped talking.

I haven't seen Nye since then but I had a moment of anxiety when Hugh Massingham rang up on Friday to ask me about the great scene that Nye and Frank Cousins raised at Thursday morning's meeting. Hugh had it quite accurately and, for the first time in my life, I lied to him by blandly saying that I hadn't noticed any row, though of course I was aware that Nye was saying this kind of thing in private to his friends. This put Hugh off the scent so satisfactorily that he then copied out everything I said and put it in his column. This was a good thing, since it would only cause difficulties if the press revealed Nye's astonishing behaviour.

On reflection I realized that what Nye did on this occasion was almost exactly the same as what he did just before the Brighton Conference. He's like a great big jelly, which has to be pulled back into shape about once every three months. Not a very good look-out for a future Foreign Secretary. What luck he has that this is the second time on which a story hasn't leaked which would have completely ruined his reputation as a great statesman.

I find my own middle position on tests, abolition, etc., beginning to percolate. Indeed all the evidence of the last ten days convinces me that in the end, before our next annual Conference, Gaitskell and Bevan will have to accept my position as the one way to keep the Party together and to have a constructive programme they can in fact carry out. The only thing which is beginning to alarm me is the thought that once again the sensible policy I have advocated will only be adopted after the point of no return has already been reached and the policy has become impracticable.

Friday, March 14th

The nuclear pot continues to simmer and yesterday the *Daily Mail* published a front-page disclosure about our meeting with the General Council. I was amazed that the leak had taken so long to drip and relieved that it was so inaccurate as to report Nye moving a resolution, which was quite untrue. However, this enabled *The Times* today, on a back page, to publish a completely accurate account of what happened and forced Gaitskell to take some action. He rang me up to say he wanted an evening at Frognal Gardens of informal talk with Nye, Lynn Ungoed-Thomas (Nye's special request), George Brown, John Strachey, Denis Healey and myself. I agreed, only to be told that it would have to be a talk in Gaitskell's room at the House at five o'clock on Monday, before he goes to welcome the Queen Mother at the Guildhall that evening and before Nye flies to Tunis, for a reason nobody knows. Hugh believes that an informal talk will enable us to achieve a common policy and I would like to believe it, since I am convinced that it must be along the lines which George Wigg and I are proposing.

Wednesday, March 19th

Last Sunday we had the Cudlipps to dinner. I had arranged to have Hugh and Pauline Massingham but this was no less than the third occasion on which Hugh Massingham has fallen ill as a result of a Crossman invitation! Consequently, George Wigg took Hugh's place, bringing Pauline with him. Hugh [Cudlipp] and Eileen were back from a month's tour of Canada and America and Hugh had signalled his arrival on the *Mirror* by a sloshing 100 per cent support for the Labour Party's official line against what he called the H-bomb hysterics of the *Daily Herald*. I noted that he had been extremely careful in this only to commit us to our fair share of Western defence and not to make any kind of pronouncement about nuclear weapons. The evening was unusually successful. Both men were agreeably surprised by the other and I watched Eileen being absolutely fascinated by George Wigg's obvious sincerity in wanting to see our troops adequately armed and in opposing the British H-bomb for strict military reasons. He didn't fit into her category of a left-winger, who should be a dirty pacifist and intellectual.

In the course of the evening Hugh Cudlipp revealed that he had been under great stress from what he called 'the Olympian Wykehamist', i.e. Cecil King, to switch the paper's line and go for what he called, 'neutralism and anti-H-bombery'. On the other hand, Hugh is extremely clever and really had briefed himself sufficiently to see that there were at least two sides of the Strachey/Crossman/Wigg controversy. But he said to me, 'You must realize that what is really required is a steadying of public opinion. Quite a negligible number of *Mirror* readers understand what your controversy with Strachey is about. What they have first to be reminded of is the danger of appeasement, and then we can have a rational controversy about the best kind of arms and the proper role for Britain to play.'

However, the really interesting thing this week has been the two hours on Monday evening and two hours this morning in which we have had informal defence talks in Hugh Gaitskell's room. Those present on each occasion were Hugh and Jim Griffiths, Nye Bevan, George Brown and John Strachey and Denis Healey, Lynn Ungoed-Thomas and myself. This is the first time Hugh has ventured on such informal talks on a really important subject and I think on the whole they have been a success, though not at all as I expected. We started by Hugh laying down three topics: first, atomic tactical weapons; secondly, conditions on which Britain must rationally renounce her nuclear weapons; and, thirdly, the desirability of a declaration that we shall never use the H-bomb first.

Monday evening was devoted entirely to tactical weapons. Almost at once it became clear that not only were George Brown, John Strachey and Denis Healey completely prepared and united, but also that Hugh Gaitskell had discussed the subject closely with them. Since Griffiths remained silent throughout, this meant that it really was a confrontation between the four of them and me, with Lynn Ungoed-Thomas as a rather uneasy ally of mine. They had all got Nye completely convinced that the proper sharp division is no longer between conventional and nuclear weapons but between controllable weapons, including conventional and atomic tactical on the one hand, and uncontrollable thermo-nuclear on the other. According to them, there is a whole range or spectrum of new nuclear weapons, from a rifle bullet to a large Hiroshima bomb and John Strachey's theory of graduated deterrence is obviously their accepted doctrine.

I said at one point that it was difficult for us to persuade our European allies that they must be atomized to preserve us and the Russians from thermo-nuclear destruction. Hugh said, 'But it is only rational to limit war as far as we can and prevent the use of thermo-nuclear weapons.' 'Rational,' I said. 'Yes. For us. But what about the Germans and the Poles?' To this Nye replied, 'We've got to get it across to the Russians that, if they attack us, we shall create a belt of destruction behind the Russian armies right across the satellite countries.' This from the man who, only ten days ago, was saying that he would rather see Britain occupied by Russia than use a nuclear weapon! I came to the conclusion that Nye had been squared by an agreement under which, if he will become a supporter of nuclear tactical weapons, the others might agree to a declaration against the use of thermo-nuclear weapons first. This kind of deal seems to me absolutely odious but I suppose it's practical politics.

When we continued this morning, we moved to the second item, conditions of repudiation. Hugh Gaitskell said he supposed that, since we had disposed of tactical weapons already, we would only discuss repudiation of production, not of use. I said that would make nonsense of any plan and was then asked to speak. I said there were two versions, the *Manchester Guardian* proposal that we should sign an agreement with other nations, agreeing to renounce nuclear weapons and submit all our economies to U.N. inspection. This might be called the Universal Plan. The other, which I personally had proposed, was more limited, suggesting that, if summit talks failed, we and our Western European allies in NATO might, for a period, agree to rely solely on conventional weapons and leave the nuclear shield to the Americans.

I was at once bitterly attacked simultaneously by everybody around the table except Lynn and Jim. I say 'attacked' because, although this was supposed to be a discussion, it was clearly turning into a test of the arguments they had already decided to use to defend their prepared positions. Of course, a number of the objections were pertinent and formidable, as I remarked. It is perfectly true that my theory gives us no kind of moral kudos and can only be defended on practicable grounds of policy and expediency. It is also true that it would mean repudiating the decisions reached some time ago by the top authorities in NATO about reliance on nuclear tactical weapons. Most of them poured scorn on the idea that the French and Germans would show any interest. But the chief criticism was that it deprived Britain of her power to defend herself against Russia, in the event of the Americans letting us down, and of our power to influence America and be independent of America if the alliance continued.

At the conclusion there was no doubt in my mind that we were back at the old issue of the status of Great Britain, with Nye, Hugh and George Brown all fanatically united in their determination to keep these islands completely independent both of America and Western Europe, even though this means devoting our resources to maintaining the whole armoury of war, from the thermo-nuclear to the atomic tactical to the conventional. 'The British nuclear weapon makes us feel independent,' said Nye, 'and feeling is something dangerous to underestimate.'

There was also implicit in the discussion the recognition that the kind of policy I proposed would ultimately involve our joining a Western European Union and, in the immediate run, would certainly commit us to quite a large army and possibly to the continuation of conscription. I didn't find any of them in the faintest degree interested or concerned about our police or Commonwealth responsibilities, apart from the problem of facing up to Communism.

What did surprise me was the degree of unity and preparedness, which came out even more strongly in the second session and so confirmed my view that it is all going to lead up to an agreement to announce that we shall never use the H-bomb first. In this Lynn Ungoed-Thomas will concur and then how nice it will be to let it be known discreetly that I objected to that, as well as to the abolition of conscription. But things may not work out this way, since it will not be nearly so easy to sell this idea of graduated deterrence to a larger meeting.

One of the striking features of the discussion was the extraordinary gap about the factual situation and the costs. The others all seemed sincerely convinced that atomic tactical weapons were now already an important part of the Western armoury and that we shall all have all our forces equipped with them in the near future. According to George Wigg and his friends, however, they are still in a very early stage, many of the smaller weapons being at least ten years away and, moreover, they are almost prohibitively expensive. George's friends quote a figure for the Matador, for instance, for which, though the actual vehicle only costs £40,000, the warhead still costs £500,000, and the same sort of sum must be paid for each warhead for each small tactical weapon. So using this kind of armoury will prove quite costly. On the other hand, we find ourselves in the greatest difficulty when we are asked what kind of conventional forces we envisage.

During his visit to the annual Anglo-German Königswinter conference, Crossman interviewed the West German Defence Minister, Franz-Josef Strauss. In the Daily Mirror *on April 2nd there was an account of their conversation, in which Herr Strauss promised that the development of an H-bomb by other European countries, particularly France, might well mean that 'Germany would be sucked in too'. Crossman published a second, longer article in the* New Statesman *of April 12th, excising this 'linguistic misunderstanding' after objections from the West German Defence Ministry.*

Meanwhile on March 31st, after completing an intensive series of nuclear trials, the Soviet Government announced its decision to stop testing atomic and hydrogen weapons and called on the West to do the same. Answering a Parliamentary Question the next day, the Prime Minister refused to follow the Soviet recommendation. He recalled that the Government had for a long time hoped to negotiate a disarmament agreement, including the ending or suspension of tests, with an agreed inspection system. Mr Gaitskell declared that there was a widespread public desire that Britain should make an effective reply to the Russian invitation and should indicate her willingness to suspend tests. Mr Macmillan reminded him that the Soviet Government had hitherto failed to reply to Western proposals for an expert committee on control.

On the same day, however, the Atlantic Powers in effect proposed to the Soviet Government that diplomatic exchanges should start in Moscow in the second half of April, in preparation for a Foreign Ministers' meeting, which would in turn lay the ground for a summit conference. The preparatory talks would not aim for decisions but would clarify the areas where agreement was possible.

Wednesday, April 2nd
We got back from Königswinter on Monday afternoon and found ourselves still in this queer Labour Party nuclear dispute, this time strengthened by the announcement that, after a record series of tests, the Russians had decided on unilateral suspension. On Tuesday I received Hugh Gaitskell's note of the

results of our three secret meetings. I had known, of course, when the third ceased, that the aim was to produce a new statement, satisfying Nye's demand for a pledge never to use the thermo-nuclear weapon first by a reliance on atomic tactical weapons, which would please Mr Strachey. But somehow this plan had come unstuck in the process, largely, I think, because Hugh Gaitskell had been really impressed by George's and my contention that these weapons do not exist except in limited quantities and that, anyway, if they did, Britain could not afford to make them.

Before leaving for Königswinter I had gone in to see Hugh and discussed the situation. I told him I was sorry I had been so bad-tempered during the discussions but one against five was a bit tough. 'I thought I had balanced it evenly,' he said, 'but Nye, to my surprise, was against you and Ungoed-Thomas and with George Brown.' I then thanked Hugh for noting the seriousness of my objection and our talk moved on to the *Daily Mirror*. I told him of my thought that I should not stand for re-election to the Executive because people objected so much to one's writing in it. He said, 'Oh, you're quite right. Nye has been worrying about this for months. It might well be a good thing from your point of view that we should lose you.' I said, 'But one thing would deter me from this step and that would be if I knew my resignation from the N.E.C. and continuing my column would prejudice my position in the next Government.' 'I don't think it would make the faintest difference to my view,' he replied. This interested me a good deal, since it is clear he would like me to go on writing.

However, to return to Tuesday. During the debate in the afternoon, I received Hugh's note of summary[1] and went to see him twice. 'That note satisfied me,' I said, 'since it doesn't commit us to atomic tactical weapons but simply to not renouncing them. I like it.' 'Yes, I've been pretty fair to you,' he said, with quite a twinkle in his eye. It was obvious that he had had quite a time with Mr Bevan and quite an effort to break Mr Brown off from him.

So we came to the famous Party Meeting this morning, which was to be the climax of three meetings of the Defence Committee, not to mention our three secret meetings. It started with Nye saying that, as everything was agreed, he would only speak for a few minutes and then proceeding to speak for forty-five. His task was to expound the N.E.C./T.U.C. statement, which he did at inordinate length. He then subjected us to his own summary of Gaitskell's notes, which he managed to thicken out with every kind of confusion. He also, in the course of his speech, accepted Barbara's and my resolution about German nuclear weapons, expressing resentful surprise that we had thought it necessary to move it, since it seemed to him obviously mad and wicked even to conceive of the idea.

The debate afterwards was appallingly ragged, since nobody quite knew

[1] In a four-page document, Gaitskell had set out the principal conclusions of the three meetings.

what they were debating. The document itself is perfectly harmless, provided you don't read too much into it, and the one thing which came out clearly from the debate was the Party's furious determination to win the next Election by avoiding disunity. By and large it was a drawn battle. Our gain was that the Party is not committed to nuclear tactical weapons in any way, except for the vaguest principle that we might have to use them if sufficient other forces were not there. The whole incident has been extremely interesting, showing the extremely fluid situation behind the scenes in the leadership, the extraordinary lack of information on which policy decisions are based and the influence which two people, George Wigg and myself, can exert if they are bloody-minded and apply the pressure at the right place.

Thursday, April 10th
How much my whole political life seems to gyrate round nuclear weapons! But, then, it probably is the single greatest issue for us and the one on which the Labour Party is inclined to commit itself with an extraordinary combination of irresponsibility and prejudice. Since I last wrote in this diary, three things have happened. In the first place, the nuclear abolitionists staged over Easter an extremely successful march to Aldermaston.[1] They had the good fortune of wonderful weather on Good Friday in Trafalgar Square and the equal good fortune of drenching weather on Easter Saturday to bring them sympathy after a sunny start. They also had television coverage every day of the holiday and this brought them a rousing climax on Easter Monday.

Next day, on Tuesday, John Strachey's famous pamphlet was published with quite a bang in the press, including front-page main story treatment in the *Telegraph*.[2] The indefatigable George Wigg has made a page-by-page comparison of the original proofs with the final text, which shows that it has been slightly, but only slightly, watered down. It still remains an extremely polemical explanation by a nuclear warrior of why he supports the T.U.C./N.E.C. statement. Everything Strachey says is, of course, strictly within the terms of that statement, but I have to admit that after reading it I came to the conclusion that, if his main contention had been correct (namely, that the only logical alternative to pacifism is his own policy), then I would be a pacifist.

This sharp dichotomy between nuclear warrior and nuclear abolitionist is, of course, what Gaitskell, Bevan and Brown want in order to keep the Party steady in its committal to a nuclear strategy. But what the Party would really like and what really makes sense is precisely the kind of half-way house between the extremes of nuclear warriordom and nuclear abolition and it is

[1] During the Easter weekend the Committee of the Campaign for Nuclear Disarmament led a march, some 4,000 strong at the start, from Trafalgar Square to the Atomic Weapons Research Establishment at Aldermaston in Berkshire.

[2] *Scrap All the H-Bombs* (The Labour Party) was published on April 8th. It had a foreword by Hugh Gaitskell.

this half-way house which George and I have been looking for, along with Peter Thorneycroft, Nigel Birch and Antony Head, not to mention the *Manchester Guardian*. All of us, however, are brushed aside as immoralists, wanting to save money by sheltering under the American nuclear shield. The third event was the visit to SHAPE of Bevan, Gaitskell and Brown. I gather that this was originally planned as one of George Brown's regular visitations for briefing, but on this occasion he took Nye and Hugh with him and they received a great deal of publicity.

This morning we had yet another of our joint meetings between the International Sub. of the N.E.C. and the International Sub. of the General Council of the T.U.C., to agree a policy on disengagement. We were meeting in the new Council Chamber in the brand new building in Great Russell Street, high above the Epstein[1] monument, unveiled last week. On the other side there were only six people present, headed by Sir Alfred Roberts and excluding Frank Cousins. On our side there was the usual turn-out—Nye, Hugh, Edith, myself, Barbara, Ray Gunter and Harry Earnshaw.

Directly we got down to business, the question was fired from the other side, 'What did you learn in SHAPE?' In answer, Nye started by reporting that he had found General Norstad[2] 'rather comforting'. The general had seen difficulties in our plan for disengagement but, on another issue, the reliance on the thermo-nuclear weapons, he had reassured Nye that this would not be necessary, since there are, or are to be, a whole number of tactical weapons available, some of which are, or are to be, substantially less destructive than the Hiroshima bomb. Nye then soared off once again into his picture of a whole range or spectrum of weapons, so it was arranged that we would be able to select just the right amount of force with which to repel whatever attack the Russians launched. However, he added that General Norstad is not expecting an all-out Russian attack and that he has sufficient forces on the ground to deal with a local disturbance.

Hugh followed Nye with a rather different version. Unlike him, he admitted that Norstad had most serious military objections to the creation of a completely neutral belt, including Western Germany, but he explained that the general was not so strong in his objection to the thinning out of the forces on both sides and to a pilot experiment in local disarmament. Thus, said Hugh, while we should certainly maintain the neutral belt as our long-term objective, we might regard this pilot experiment as a half-way house, with the assurance that General Norstad would be willing to countenance it.

At this point I came in with strong support for Hugh's approach. 'If we regard this half-way house as the object to be achieved at the summit,' I said, 'then we have to face another problem, which is that, for some time

[1] Sir Jacob Epstein (1880–1959), the British sculptor, knighted in 1954. The sculpture on the T.U.C. headquarters shows a fallen man being raised by a brother.

[2] General Lauris Norstad, Commander-in-Chief U.S. European Command and Supreme Allied Commander 1956–62.

ahead, there will be NATO forces in Germany, of which the German Army will form a large element. In that case I must point out that it is quite absurd to believe that we can deny the Germans the use of atomic tactical weapons while retaining the use for ourselves. Up to the summit, it is possible, say, that we should delay arming the Germans with nuclear weapons, just as we are delaying the erection of missile bases in Britain. But after the summit the problem will be acute.'

At this point Hugh was very nettled and said he much resented the discussion's being spread far beyond the concept of disengagement. Once again, he said, we are asking ourselves how we would deal with hypothetical cases. I said I was sorry, but I had only taken up one or two of the interesting points made by Mr Bevan in his report from SHAPE. I also pointed out the passage in a document Nye had attached, which emphasized that the thinning-out must be accompanied by increased reliance on atomic tactical weapons, a view which I thought was an absurdity.

However, we agreed that this was something to be discussed afterwards. It was soon clear that after Edith, who made her usual portentous speech about strontium-90[1] and added to it her usual assertion that she strongly believed in collective security, there was nobody who didn't think we should accept Hugh Gaitskell's broad presentation.

Only Nye was still nettled at me. 'I think it's most ominous', he said, 'that the German divisions should be forming such a large part of our NATO forces and I was disturbed by Norstad's indication to us that, because the German contribution was growing so much, their influence on our policy was bound to increase. This is something we have to avoid.' I snapped back, 'The simplest way to avoid it is to keep your pledge to have four divisions in Germany up to strength and you can't do that if you give nuclear weapons top priority.' At this Hugh Gaitskell barked again and I duly piped down.

One amusing feature at the meeting was the portentous solemnity with which Nye said that he could not reveal to us all the secrets of the Norstad briefing. All the members of the T.U.C. who were present had already been to SHAPE a few weeks ago and received an identical briefing and, from what Nye said, I could recognize whole slabs of what Norstad had said to me last summer.[2] However, this veil of portentous secrecy will no doubt be useful when it comes to dealing with the Parliamentary Party.

And now one other thing, which may possibly in the long run and in domestic politics prove more important than all this palaver about nuclear weapons. Ten days ago Brian Abel-Smith cooked a really magnificent dinner for the Titmusses, the Townsends and the Crossmans and we then discussed a startling new proposition which the skiffle had hatched. Why not extend the

[1] Strontium-90 is a long-lived radioactive product, abundant in every nuclear fission reaction. The particular biological danger arises because it can replace calcium in human metabolism. The ratio of strontium-90 to calcium was commonly expressed in 'sunshine units'; the reason is now obscure.

[2] When Crossman had lectured at SHAPE.

principle of graded benefits and contributions from old age pensions to sickness and unemployment benefit as well? It is one of those extremely simple ideas which are also extremely brilliant. Ever since the dinner, this scheme has been in embryo, rapidly growing in my mind. I think the skiffle group enjoyed watching me catch hold of a nice policy idea and start making it grow. I have warned Harold Wilson that he must come to our meeting of the sub-committee next Tuesday and I had a word today with Hugh Gaitskell about it as well. I'm not sure we haven't got hold of another winner and, incidentally, made the job of Minister of National Insurance even more worth while.

On April 11th the Soviet Government replied to the suggestion of the three Atlantic Powers for preparatory talks on a summit conference. The U.S.S.R. agreed to begin discussions at ambassadorial level in the following week but proposed that these, and the meeting of Foreign Ministers, should be restricted to considering matters of the time, place and composition of the summit meeting. The American Government immediately replied that this suggestion amounted to rejecting the essential principle that the preliminary exchanges should deal with the possibility of reaching agreement on substantive issues. None the less, on April 16th the British, French and American Governments informed their Soviet counterpart that they were ready for ambassadorial discussions in Moscow.

The previous day, April 15th, had seen the reassembly of Parliament after the Easter Recess. On that afternoon Mr Heathcoat Amory presented his Budget, which was firmly anti-inflationary. There was some simplification and reduction of purchase tax, with the existing seven rates being brought down to four, of which the highest rate would be 60 instead of 90 per cent. The reductions would cost £41 million in a full year. Cinema duty would be cut by more than half. There was to be a reduction of 12s. a gallon in duty on imported heavy wines.

On profits tax there was to be a single rate of 10 per cent, replacing different rates on distributed and undistributed profits. Income tax exemption limits for persons over sixty-five were to be raised from £250 to £275 for single people and from £400 to £440 for married couples. The initial capital expenditure allowance was raised by a quarter to 25 per cent on plant and machinery and to 12·5 per cent on industrial buildings. On estate duty, relief for land passed on death twice within five years was now extended to all property; it was also to be charged only once where two people died simultaneously. Tax relief would amount to £50·5 million in 1958/59 and to about £108 million in a full year.

Opposition criticism concentrated on one proposal — new legislation to make dividend stripping illegal was to be made retrospective to October 26th, 1955. (During the Finance Bill discussions the Government announced that the retrospective provision had been abandoned.)

There was no easing of restrictions on lending or of controls on capital-

raising operations. In March bank rate had been reduced from 7 to 6 per cent
but further reduction, to 5·5 per cent, did not occur until May 22nd.

Wednesday, April 23rd
After the Executive meeting this morning Nye said, 'Come back to the
House,' and I found myself driving in a superb new Rover which he has just
bought. We had a long and very friendly talk. I think I got him, in the first
part, where he was listening carefully, to understand some of the things which
I have included in my new paper on strategy and nuclear weapons.[1] He also
assured me that, whatever he had said yesterday at the International Sub.,
he didn't in any way object to serious consideration by sub-committees of the
details of disengagement.

This was actually a reversal of his behaviour yesterday. We had agreed a
second draft T.U.C./Labour Party statement, this time on disengagement, in
the normal vacuous form. After it, Nye said, 'Since we've agreed it all, why is
there a meeting of the Defence Committee this afternoon on the military
aspects of disengagement?' I replied, 'Because, Nye, some of us want to do
some serious thinking on the subject. Now that you and the top-level people
have agreed it in vague outline, we thought we would like to decide what it
really means, and we knew that if we went into detail you would say, "These
people are concerning themselves with the technical aspects and losing the
broad vision".' This remark had caused a certain wry smile on the International and today Nye couldn't have been more polite or friendly about it.

He told me, in passing, that, when he had discussed disengagement with
Adenauer, he had been told by Adenauer, as an objection to disengagement
and German neutrality, 'But, Mr Bevan, you cannot trust the Germans', a
remark which I regard as a further proof that Germans and Americans are
very similar people, since in no other two nations would a leading statesman
be so disloyal to his own country. Nye also told me that General Norstad
had warned him that, since the Germans would soon be providing more
troops in Europe than the rest of NATO put together, they would have to
have most of the command posts. 'That is the case', I said, 'for keeping four
divisions on the Continent,' and Nye looked rather glum and agreed.
'Gaitskell is getting more elastic now,' he said, and I replied, 'Yes, but you
know I like him because he has some intellectual integrity.' This took Nye
aback. He remained absolutely dumbfounded, until he said, 'I don't trust
him a yard with his figures. That's not what I mean.'

I then said I thought that Harold Wilson had overdone it in the Budget in
pledging us to uphold the value of sterling and Britain's status as banker of
the sterling area. 'Yes,' said Nye, 'far too much, he went far too far.' I then
said, 'But in private Harold assured me that, when we come to power and

---

[1] Which Crossman was preparing as a memorandum for the defence and foreign policy
groups. A version was published in *Encounter*, in July 1958, as 'Our Bomb and Theirs: The
Nuclear Obsession'.

something has to go, that something will be defence.' 'How does he know that?' said Nye. 'I don't think he does,' I said, 'because defence isn't the thing which goes, especially when George Brown is in charge.' 'Certainly that is a problem,' said Nye, 'a very serious one indeed, and Harold is treating it far too lightly.'

Altogether we had an unusually friendly conversation, which ended with the disclosure that Nye's farm is doing even worse than ours and that he will now have to sell fourteen of his Guernseys owing to shortage of grass.

Wednesday, May 21st

The most interesting political talk I have had recently was when Harold Wilson and his wife came to dinner on Sunday. Harold told me, which he hadn't told me before, that, whereas our wives are pacifists really, 'You and I, Dick, are both economic opponents of nuclear weapons.' He repeated his advice that one should retain all positions of strength—stay on the *Mirror*, stay on the Executive, etc., since one needs all the strength one can have when the moment for Cabinet-making comes. He was critical of Hugh, whom he kept on talking about as 'Our Leader' and emphasized that he was now too much under the thumb of Tony Crosland. 'Roy Jenkins', Harold said to me, 'is now absolutely loyal to me and it's true that Hugh has never tried to overrule me, though he takes Crosland's advice regularly.'

Harold seems to be recovering from his nerves about his standing in the City and to be preparing a tremendous organization for this year's Finance Bill. But when he says Roy Jenkins is entirely loyal to him he shakes my faith in anything else he says, since I also talk to Roy and know he is still absolutely Gaitskell's man, though a disappointed Gaitskell's man. Harold's attitude to Nye is equally stand-offish, about the 'poor old boy who has become a softie', and so on and so on.

Even Anne had to admit on this occasion that it's difficult to dislike Harold or not to be somehow impressed not only by his extraordinary competence but by his grasp of politics as they are played. And there's a sort of decency about his attitude. It's that of the ambitious practitioner and not of the self-seeking man. Anyway, he remains a good friend of mine and I now know that both he and Hugh Gaitskell would be willing to see a lot more of me if I wanted to, and that is something I must do after the Recess.

Crossman spent early June in France, where General de Gaulle had assumed power on May 29th; a report of Crossman's conversations in Paris appeared in the Mirror *on June 17th. His diary entries for the remainder of the month deal almost exclusively with the Cyprus question and the Party's reactions to proposals announced by the Government on June 17th. The scheme invited the co-operation of the Greek and Turkish Governments in the running of the island, but the Greek Government declared it entirely unacceptable, while the Turkish Government maintained its preference for partition.*

Otherwise Crossman's main concern was with a Commons debate on pensions, on July 7th, to mark the tenth anniversary of the establishment of the National Insurance scheme. By mid-July, however, his thoughts had returned to the possibility of a General Election and to the strategy of a future Labour Government.

Friday, July 11th

On Wednesday the *News Chronicle* published a Gallup Poll, showing, as anybody who has a feeling for such trends must have expected for some time, that Macmillan's popularity has vastly increased, that Tory voters are drifting back to voting Tory and that the two parties are level, a fact which would give the Tories a small victory.[1]

This morning I rang up Harold Wilson. He said he wanted to talk to me about this next week, adding (he is a great flatterer) that the only thing which had cheered him since the Gallup Poll was my article in this morning's *Mirror*. I also found that Tony Wedgwood Benn had been busily at work on a memorandum on the necessity for a tactical staff to advise the Leader on operations in Parliament. I asked Tony to lunch, after ringing up Mrs Skelly[2] to see if I could talk to Hugh. She replied that he was busy all day but that she would fix an appointment for me after Monday. Just after I had fixed the lunch with Tony, I was rung up to say that Hugh wanted me to lunch. So Tony came round and gave me his memo to pass on to Hugh and then drove me over to the Athenaeum.

Our main topic was the Gallup Poll. I started by discussing Tony's paper and handed it over, at which Hugh said, 'But the real problem isn't the technical problem of tactics in the House but our general methods of communicating with the electorate. Here we are fighting with bows and arrows against the organized army of the Tories. We just don't start.' He then analysed quite sensibly the reasons for Macmillan's recovery, omitting, as I noted, any reference to his television performances. This was natural, since Hugh himself had had the same television opportunities. He also mentioned the enormous effect of the press boom launched on Macmillan's behalf. Hugh entirely agreed with all I'd written this morning and kept repeating, 'We've got to win the next Election. And one thing,' he added slightly sheepishly, 'surely, for purely technical reasons, the Party should be ready to build me up in the way that Macmillan is built up by his people. After all, I am their Leader, at least till after the next Election.' I took the opportunity of saying I thought Nye was fairly O.K., although his morale went down when his chances of soon being Foreign Secretary were reduced. Hugh thought there was no danger of Nye's ratting on him before the next Election.

[1] In the poll published on Wednesday, July 9th, which showed Conservative and Labour running level, with 47·5 per cent of sample voters committed to supporting each party 'if there were to be a General Election tomorrow'.

[2] Mrs Beryl Skelly, Gaitskell's secretary from 1954 until his death, when she became Hugh Cudlipp's secretary until he left I.P.C. in 1974.

He agreed about the necessity of working out a concrete overall policy out of all our policy statements and had obviously received a full report from Dora about our joint speeches to the Leamington Rally. 'Dora said you made a wonderful speech,' he said. 'Indeed, she said it was incredibly frank and brave, considering all the press were there, but she agreed with every word of it. I think you've got to help us by putting over one or two more things, particularly the fact that working-class people are week by week becoming less working-class, less class-conscious and more allergic to such old appeals as trade union solidarity or class loyalty. Anything we say which can be used as being merely class interest loses us votes.'

Hugh said he would like to see three outside experts, say a T.V. man like Bernstein,[1] a press man like Jacobson and one good advertiser, writing an absolutely objective report on what Labour should do to win the next Election. I replied that they would have some difficulty if they didn't know all the limiting factors, like the internal structure of the Party, and if they weren't given an objective appreciation of the situation. Why couldn't this be written by Mark Abrams, myself and one or two others? Hugh wasn't used to the military use of the word 'appreciation' but soon twigged what I was saying and was delighted with the idea that this objective report should be presented to [? by] the three wise men. 'But this will have to hurry up,' I said. 'Oh yes,' said Hugh, 'it will all have to be done before we recess at the end of July.' He agreed that it was now essential that the new integrated policy should be presented by him in a keynote speech to our annual Conference. At the end he asked me to put all my ideas down in a memorandum and seemed really quite pleased ...

... At that moment I was interrupted in dictating by Tony Wedgwood Benn, ringing up to find out what Hugh said. Tony told me he had just been lunching when Douglas Jay had come past and said, 'Of course, we're bound to lose the Election.' 'What are you going to do about it?' Tony had asked and Douglas replied, 'Ten years ago I proposed a concerted propaganda plan and my advice was not taken.' Actually, of course, Douglas, Tony Crosland and Roy Jenkins, Hugh's closest friends, have been the great addicts of the policy of saying nothing and playing safe. However ...

Tuesday, July 15th
Over the weekend Tony Wedgwood Benn rang me in high excitement to say that Hugh Gaitskell had demanded thirty more copies of his paper and that he had decided to do a completely new version, in view of its importance. On Sunday he read me over his draft and I made three or four comments, which he incorporated. On Sunday afternoon he spent two hours with Hugh Gaitskell, going over it. It's all perfectly sensible and so was the Home Policy Committee yesterday, which accepted my proposal that we should have an overall programme statement on the lines of *Let Us Face the Future*, pulling

[1] Sidney Bernstein, Chairman of the Granada Group Ltd. He became a life peer in 1969.

all the documents together. But is being perfectly sensible sufficient to revive the Labour Party and enable it to win? I don't know. I did notice however, with Roy Jenkins last night, that even he, who was one of the great addicts of the theory that we were bound to win, now admits that we are faced with a possibility of defeat.

Tuesday, August 12th
I have left a long space since I last wrote in this diary but it is the vacuum of the first days of the Recess. On the last day of the Session, we had been invited by telephone by Mrs Skelly to dinner at the Gaitskells'. Anne wanted to say no and get down to Prescote before the holiday rush but I told her dinner engagements with the Leader are Royal orders. At one minute past eight we drove up in heavy, pelting rain, to see at least ten people and six cars there already. By nine o'clock it was clear that we were in for a buffet supper with three ambassadors — American, Polish and Yugoslav; three political pairs — (the Healeys, Pagets and ourselves); Hugh Cudlipp, Malcolm Muggeridge and Billy Listowel with his new torch-singer wife.[1] As the evening wore on, each of us confessed to the other that we wouldn't have dreamed of staying in London for the buffet, especially as there wasn't enough to eat and Anne had to have a meal when we got home!

There was a time, about a week ago, when I was due to go to New York to the Summit, before travelling on to Moscow and Peking. Fortunately it was cancelled and I have had time to finish things here and get quietly ready for this Moscow/Peking trip, which alarms me a little by its loneliness.

During the summer continued efforts were made by the Western Powers to embark on talks in preparation for a summit conference. Sudden impetus was given to their attempts in July, with the murder in Iraq of the young King Feisal, his uncle and the Prime Minister Nuri-es-Said. On the following day the Lebanese President asked the U.S. to land Marines in Beirut and on July 17th the King of Jordan appealed for assistance by British troops. On July 19th Mr Khrushchev sent despatches to the British and American Governments, suggesting that their intervention might well provoke a chain reaction leading to nuclear annihilation, and demanding an immediate Summit conference, to be held in Geneva in three days' time. The Prime Minister's reply was delivered on July 22nd. Though Mr Macmillan stated that while he did not share Mr

---

[1] William Hare succeeded his father in 1931, to become the 5th Earl of Listowel. He was a Labour Whip in the House of Lords 1941–4, Parliamentary Under-Secretary of State at the India Office 1944–5, Postmaster-General 1945–7, Secretary of State for India April–August 1947 and for Burma 1947–8, Minister of State for Colonial Affairs 1948–50 and Joint Parliamentary Secretary at the Ministry of Agriculture and Fisheries 1950–1. He was Chairman of Committees in the House of Lords 1965–76. 'Billy' Listowel married his second wife, Stephanie Wise, in 1958. The marriage was dissolved in 1963.

Khrushchev's judgment 'that the world is on the verge of a military catastrophe', he agreed that a meeting would be useful and, taking up a phrase of Mr Khrushchev's referring to the United Nations, suggested that the discussions should take place within the forum of the Security Council. Mr Khrushchev announced his acceptance, proposing that the meeting in New York should open on the following Monday, July 28th.

The American Government, however, disliked Mr Macmillan's suggestion and on July 25th President Eisenhower sent a deliberately discouraging Note to Mr Khrushchev. After angry exchanges between the U.S.S.R. and the U.S.A., Mr Macmillan eventually proposed a special meeting of the Security Council on August 12th. Mr Khrushchev meanwhile paid an unexpected visit to Peking and now ruled out the Security Council as the arena for the summit. This was welcomed by President Eisenhower and regretfully accepted by Mr Macmillan.

Crossman had by now set out on a long tour of Russia and China, departing on August 13th. He was away until September 16th, keeping a full diary during the entire trip. Eight articles appeared in the Daily Mirror *and the* New Statesman *carried two pieces on September 27th, 1958, and January 10th, 1959. The Russian diary is given here; though there is unfortunately insufficient space to reproduce the Chinese diary, a long article based on it, 'Chinese Notebook', may be found in the March 1959 issue of* Encounter.

Wednesday, August 13th

I left London Airport at ten o'clock in the morning in order to catch the midday Sabena D.C.7 to Moscow, and found my fellow travellers were the Canadian, British and Italian shooting teams, proceeding to Moscow for the world shooting championships. This caused a three-hour delay, since we had to wait for the rearrangement of the luggage on the plane, to ensure that the ammunition and the petrol we carried did not clash. The Captain explained to me that every Western plane going into Moscow has to carry all the petrol for the return journey, since the Russians make no high-octane petrol available to us. We had a most beautiful flight, first north over Amsterdam to Copenhagen and then due east over the Baltic to Riga, where we crossed into Russian territory, on a lovely blue day with billowing white clouds.

We reached Moscow at half-past eight, that is, half-past ten Moscow time, and sat in the airport for exactly an hour and a half while our passports were stamped. If I had been kept waiting alone I would have been annoyed, but the shooting teams were also kept for an hour and a half, solely because the officials collected all our passports and then couldn't sort out whom they belonged to.

I went to Moscow by car and booked in at the Hotel National and found that my room was on the second floor, with five gigantic windows facing across to the Kremlin and with the only terrace on that side. It had previously been occupied by Trotsky[1] when he delivered his last speech (which was received with rotten potatoes), by the Dean of Canterbury[2] and by Burgess and Maclean, when their presence was revealed to foreign correspondents. It was a suite of quite astonishing dimensions, with its furniture all taken from museums. At the far end of the sitting room was a mirror fourteen feet high, made of porcelain, with gigantic Cupids and gold fittings. There were five inlaid tables and then folding doors into an equally large bedroom, beyond which there was another anteroom and a bathroom. However, I paid nothing extra for it because, once you have paid your £11 a day, you get whatever they give you. My room really decided me not to move outside Moscow, since it really was lovely to see the Kremlin, particularly at dawn and at sunset, and in Moscow I saw nothing else equal to it.

Thursday, August 14th

I had been assured at the Russian Embassy that my best course was to arrive in Moscow with a tourist visa and then to make my own contacts. But within hours I discovered this is the one thing you cannot do. A tourist in Russia is treated as a tourist; that is, he has laid on for him, if he is a luxury tourist, a permanent guide, all his meals and a motor-car whenever he wants it. With these he can do the tourist sights but that doesn't include seeing collective farms or interviewing anybody. So on my first morning there was a certain misunderstanding. I was allocated a gloomy but quite charming guide, who came up to my sitting room and for whom I listed all of the people I wanted to see. He duly took them down, saying nothing, and I then went to lunch with Patrick Reilly,[3] who was two years my junior at Winchester and New College and who is now the Ambassador, living in a Gothic mansion of incredibly bad taste which, before the Revolution, was owned by one of the most famous exploiting millionaires.

[1] Leib Davidovich Bronstein (1877–1940) (known as Lev Trotsky) was originally a Social Democrat exile from Tsarist Russia. A brilliant orator and journalist, he worked with Lenin for *Iskra* but from 1903 gave his support to the Mensheviks. He returned to Russia in 1905 and, after arrest and deportation to Siberia, escaped into exile but came back to the U.S.S.R. once more in 1917. He led the peace talks in 1917 at Brest-Litovsk and as Commissar for War created the Red Army. Between 1924 and 1927 his theory of 'perpetual revolution' lost ground to Stalin's aim of 'Socialism in one country'. He was banished in 1929 but remained an effective critic of the Soviet Government, by whose agent he was assassinated in Mexico in August 1940.

[2] The Very Reverend Dr Hewlett Johnson (1874–1966). He founded the *Interpreter*, which he edited from 1905 until 1924, when he was appointed by Ramsay MacDonald to the Deanery of his native Manchester. After toying with the ideas of the Social Credit Party, he became a Communist. He was Dean (known as the Red Dean) of Canterbury Cathedral 1931–63. A distinguished preacher and prolific pamphleteer, his tract *The Socialist Sixth of the World* (London: Gollancz, 1939) ran to twenty-two editions in Britain and was translated into twenty-four languages. He was Chairman of the editorial board of the *Daily Worker*.

[3] A diplomat, whose service included postings as British Ambassador in Moscow 1957–60 and in Paris 1965–8. He was knighted in 1957.

Reilly arranged for me to see my friend Zhukov,[1] whom I had met at all the international conferences with the Russians and who is now, broadly, Minister in Charge of Cultural Relations. I saw him that afternoon and gave him my list of requests. I said I wanted to see a State farm and a collective farm, to interview the head of the Moscow Sovnarkhoz,[2] to meet the editorial boards of *Krokodil, Kommunist, Young Komsomol, Pravda* and *Izvestia*, to see the Lenin Library and the University and, in addition, to interview Khrushchev and Furtseva.[3]

After this, Zhukov looked up and said, 'You've made a great mistake. What have you come here as? You are not here as a tourist at all but as a journalist. But your accreditation is that of a tourist.' However, he promised to try and get the matter put straight and meanwhile to try to get me some of my interviews. Actually he did me extremely well and I got practically everything I asked for except the top level, entirely through his favours.

Friday, August 15th

At lunch time I took Miss Ben-Gurion,[4] a distinguished scientist, in Moscow for three days after a Stockholm conference, and Mrs Shomron, the wife of the First Secretary at the Israeli Embassy,[5] to a fashion display at Moscow's one big store, GUM. My two female companions were both infinitely better dressed than any of the models and their shoes stirred up envy. I sat between them, feeling very good, while we looked at those plump ladies displaying sacks and trapezes[6] to the music of a string band.

In the afternoon I went out with my guide to the great Agricultural Exhibition. This is Moscow's greatest sight and is a kind of permanent Royal Show, which made me completely convinced that our own Royal Show should be in permanent buildings in London. It's the biggest park and show I have ever been in, with a pavilion for each of the Republics, as well as

[1] Georgi Alexandrovich Zhukov. After an early career as a journalist with *Pravda*, Zhukov was Chairman of the U.S.S.R. Council of Ministers' Committee for Cultural Relations with Foreign Countries 1957–62. Since 1976 he has been an Alternate Member of the Central Committee of the Communist Party of the Soviet Union.

[2] A central or regional economic board. See below, p. 696.

[3] Yekaterina Alekseevna Furtseva. Head of the Propaganda Department of the Moscow City Soviet in 1939, her career prospered with that of Khrushchev. From 1950 to 1974 she was a Deputy to the U.S.S.R. Supreme Soviet and from 1954 to 1956 First Secretary of the Moscow City Party Committee. In 1955 she became the first woman to appear on the reviewing stand in the May Day parade. She was a member of the Praesidium 1956–61 and Minister of Culture from May 1960 until her death in 1974.

[4] Dr Renana Ben-Gurion (after her marriage in 1956 Mrs Renana Leshem Ben-Gurion), Senior Research Scientist at the Israeli Institute for Biological Research 1956–69 and since 1969 Professor of Molecular Biology at the University of Tel Aviv.

[5] Gideon Shomron and his wife Hanita. Shomron was First Secretary at the Israeli Embassy in Stockholm 1955–8 and in Moscow 1958–60, Consul-General in London 1960–3, Head of the Director-General's office at the Ministry of Foreign Affairs in Jerusalem 1963–5, Director of the President's office 1965–7, and Minister Counsellor in Washington from 1971 to 1974, when he returned once more to the President's office.

[6] Dresses of rectangular and trapezoid shape, launched in the West and fashionable in the late 1950s.

a gigantic pavilion for Industry, for Livestock, for everything in fact. I saw a quite interesting sheep competition, with sheep of every shape and size. This show made me realize what a continent the Soviet Union includes. Next door was an exhibition orchard, which was extremely poor, and I learnt later that one reason for this was the strange tax on fruit trees, introduced by Stalin, which had caused millions of peasants to burn their fruit trees as firewood rather than pay. It was one of Khrushchev's first acts to remit this tax and thereby make it possible for fruit to be grown widely in the Soviet Union.

The Agricultural Exhibition is about five miles out of Moscow and we had sent the car home because I had wanted to travel by Underground. We were returning to Moscow at the rush hour, with two changes. The older type of stations are as fantastically monumental as I had expected, with something of the splendour of a particularly tasteless German Baroque church, with chandeliers, marble plaques, etc., etc. The more modern stations are much more chaste. Here again Stalin's monumentalism has been quietly dropped. Even more extraordinary was the fact that the rush, of which the Russians are so proud, leaves ample breathing space in the carriages and even more so in the subways, which are about three times as wide as those in London. The trains go much more slowly and I think that in total there are fewer than twenty stations on the system. I haven't to this day discovered how the Russians go to work. The Underground isn't particularly full and nor, as far as I could see, were the single-decker buses and trolley-buses. Nor, on the other hand, do the Russians, like the Chinese and the Danes, use bicycles in their capital. I asked several Russians why they didn't bicycle to work and they obviously felt the question was an insult. No civilized person could bicycle. I suspect they walk or live near their factories. The charge on the Underground is half a rouble, wherever you go, and this may also deter people, since there is no season ticket.[1]

Sunday, August 17th

I decided to go to Zakursk with my guide and we motored out in sunshine through lovely birch woods to this fantastic painted monastery where Boris Godunov was buried.[2] It gave me a useful piece for my column but after that I had a most interesting talk with the Inspector of the cemetery behind the church. This church is for theological students and here are the facts he gave me. In Russia today there are 20,000 churches in use and 35,000 priests. Each year there are some 2,000 to 3,000 students in eight seminaries for village priests and two academies for urban priests. So great is the number of applicants that only one in four can be accepted. Before 1917 there were

---

[1] At the official rate of exchange, there were approximately 11 roubles to the pound; in purchasing power, however, the rate was nearer 40 roubles.

[2] Boris Godunov (*c.* 1551–1605), a Russian nobleman of Tartar origins who became Regent and, from 1598 until his death, Tsar of Russia. In legend, in Pushkin's play (1826) and Mussorgsky's opera (1869) he was characterized (it seems, wrongly) as a Russian Macbeth.

more students but most of them entered the Civil Service, so the entry to the Church is as great today as before the Revolution. Anyone who goes to a seminary has to do National Service but anybody who goes to the academy avoids it altogether. My guide, who interpreted, was very scornful. 'They go there because they get paid so well,' he said. But there is no doubt that there is quite a religious revival in Russia.*

I lunched at Zakursk with my guide and our chauffeur and talked about salaries. On his monthly salary, the chauffeur has bought a nice wooden dacha, with twenty trees in the garden, and he runs a motor-car. The poor guide, an intellectual, lives in one room in a suburban industrial city, twenty miles from Moscow, with his mother-in-law, his wife and his child.

One of the things I noticed on this journey was the television masts, which I was later to see wherever I travelled, sometimes thirty or forty sticking out of a roof, indicating the most appalling overcrowding, since there was at least one television set for each room in the house, if not more. That evening, in Red Square, where the loudspeaker blares every night, I heard what I thought was a tremendous political speech and strolled out to find a crowd of some 10,000 people gathered in front of a stage set up in the Square. Here, I thought, at last, I am seeing a member of the Komsomol[1] making a Sunday pep talk to the workers. I was disconcerted when, at the conclusion of his speech, a conjurer started! The speaker was, in fact, the director of a variety troupe, which every Sunday evening plays simple games with members of the crowd, such as musical chairs and blind-man's-bluff. By the time I left there were at least 20,000 people, laughing heartily. Russians have very nice simple tastes.

I dined with Ruge[2] of the Westdeutscher Rundfunk, who has been in Moscow for two years. He gave me a pretty good fill-in and I formed a very high opinion of him. The thaw, he is convinced, has iced up a good deal, especially in literature and journalism. The reason is that no one knows how far you can go in criticizing Communism without challenging the system. This lack of a directive has caused great uneasiness in the Writers' Union. Ruge gave me a most amusing account of how a book gets published, which I was later to confirm in the Union itself. First of all, when you have written a few chapters, you try it out on fellow authors and they tip you off if they think you are going wrong. Then the publishers appoint a reader, who also discusses it. Then it is submitted to the censor and after that it is published and submitted to the critics. The so-called Khrushchev liberalization[3] has left

* I was to find in China that in this respect the two countries could scarcely be more different. Wherever I went throughout China I couldn't find a single temple or church of any kind that was open.

[1] The Communist Party youth organization.

[2] Gerd Ruge, the first regular radio correspondent in Moscow 1956–9. He left Moscow in 1964 and was later Chief Correspondent of *Die Welt* in Peking from 1973 to 1978, when he became Moscow Correspondent of the German television network, A.R.D.

[3] On March 27th Mr Khrushchev became Soviet Premier, retaining his post as First Secretary of the Communist Party. His former colleagues were gradually demoted; he himself was supreme.

this system completely unchanged and at present no one quite knows what one ought to publish.

Ruge's other great point is that there are no ideological Communists left in Russia. This is something I had heard before. If Malenkov had survived, the whole system would have become more centralized, more demonstrably efficient, less unpredictable. Khrushchev is *the* empiricist and the only thing he is popular for is his determination to break the incipient ruling class, or élite. He is anti-élite, as Ernest Bevin was anti-élite, because he is a worker. That is why he had abolished paying secondary schools, opened the universities, broken up the Ministries and reintroduced the career open to the talents.[1]

Monday, August 18th

From Soutou,[2] in the French Embassy, I had a full account of what Mendès France[3] had reported about his China trip. He arrived in Moscow on the 13th after three weeks as the guest of the Foreign Affairs Institute in Peking, where he had been received by the Foreign Minister and Chou En-lai. He was also, incidentally, received by Khrushchev in Moscow. Mendès France's main impression was of the enormous and unexpected industrial advance and of the great skill with which Russian aid had been given to China. In the north he had found the Chinese volunteering all the information about Russian aid, whereas further south they only did so under questioning. The extent of Russian aid had been five times what Mendès France had expected and it had been given much as Marshall Aid had been given to Britain, as distinct from Russian aid to other countries. The Chinese stated their requirements and the Russians fulfilled them, after making suggestions. The extent of the aid had been deliberately suppressed in Russia for domestic reasons.

[1] Earlier in the year Mr Khrushchev had announced that the last two years of secondary education were to be abolished. Pupils were instead to take up full-time employment, finishing their general or vocational education with three or four years of evening study or by correspondence courses, though some might be selected for polytechnic or specialized secondary education. University entrance, hitherto largely available, according to Khrushchev, to children of the intelligentsia, was now to be strictly regulated in accordance with candidates' political reliability, as established by the Komsomol. All courses were to be made more practical.

[2] Jean-Marie Soutou. A French diplomat, he was joint Director of the *cabinet* of Mendès France 1954–5 and Ministre-Conseiller at the French Embassy in the U.S.S.R. 1956–8. He subsequently became France's Permanent Representative to the European Communities in 1975 and Ambassador the following year. In 1976 he became Secretary-General of the Ministry of Foreign Affairs.

[3] Pierre Mendès France, a radical politician who was Finance Minister of the French Provisional Government 1943–4, Minister of National Economy 1944–5 and a Governor of the International Bank for Reconstruction and Development 1946–58. He was Prime Minister and Minister of Foreign Affairs June 1954–February 1955 and Minister without Portfolio January–May 1956. With Bevan, Nenni and Jean-Jacques Servan Schreiber, he was co-author of *Rencontres* (Paris: publisher not given, 1959) and author of *A Modern French Republic* (London: Weidenfeld & Nicolson, 1963).

Mendès France's second main impression was of the *orgeuil*, the arrogance, of the Chinese, which he said was sheerly incredible and sometimes intolerable. They showed it to everyone except the Russians and their general attitude had made him perfectly certain that, if they haven't got an atom bomb already, they will very soon have one.[1] Sometimes their pride is barmy, as when they indignantly repudiated the idea that good weather had anything to do with their record harvest this year. I pressed Soutou to tell me whether anybody had told Mendès France about the Chinese atomic bomb. 'No,' he said, 'no one had said so but Mendès France gained the impression that many statements they made to him were only explicable on the assumption that they have one.'*

I spent Monday morning in Moscow's free market, the huge area, partly enclosed and partly open, where collectives and peasants sell their wares at open prices. As I had been told, I found a great many Georgians selling loofahs and grapes; they had found it worth their while to travel all the way to Moscow and back. I had a long talk with an old man selling yoghurt from the one cow he kept on his private plot and then I found some singularly disgusting cow meat going quite fast. 'What is that?' I asked him. 'This is my old cow,' he said. 'How old?' I asked. 'Very old,' he said. 'But I hope you've got a young heifer to replace her for the milk?' 'Unfortunately the heifer is still six months away from milking,' he said. 'Then why did you kill the cow?' I said. 'Because she would have died otherwise. You see, the meat is very bad.' 'And how long will it take you to get rid of it?' 'I started this morning,' he said, 'and nothing will be left by this evening.' This shows how short meat is in Moscow and the kind of quality you can expect from the State marketing scheme, for the meat in this free market costs more than in the State market and is regarded as a great delicacy.

Tuesday, August 19th

I spent the morning having the first of my formal interviews, with Mr Borisov,[2] who is the Deputy Director of the Moscow Sovnarkhoz. These are the new, decentralized, local organizations for running industry. Borisov was a great big Russian, who looked just like an American business executive. As usual, he first made a speech. His Sovnarkhoz controls 430 big enterprises and consists of a Council with a chairman and five deputies. When they set up the new, decentralized organization, they expected three difficulties: first, a failure of economic co-ordination between the Sovnarkhoz; secondly, a

[1] China was to explode her first nuclear weapon on October 16th, 1964.

* Even after my own visit to China, I still don't quite know what he meant. What I was able to establish is that there is absolutely no moral compunction in China against having an atomic bomb and absolutely no fear of a war in which one is used.

[2] Boris Andrianovich Borisov was the Secretary of the Moscow Gorkon (City Party Committee) in the early 1950s and Deputy Chairman of the Moscow Sovnarkhoz from February 1958 until 1959, when he became Deputy Minister of Foreign Trade. In 1970 he became President of the All-Union Chamber of Trade and Commerce (subsequently, the Chamber of Trade and Industry).

danger of self-sufficiency; and, thirdly, the difficulty of introducing new techniques in separate regions. All these have been satisfactorily solved. Co-ordination had been achieved by regular conferences. Recently a conference had taken place of twelve Sovnarkhoz around Moscow, which had agreed a programme of common action. He then gave me various examples of successes achieved by the new organization.

After he had finished I asked him my first question. 'I gather that the Sovnarkhoz is an example of decentralization. Why not decentralize right down to plant management and let each make their own decisions?' Borisov: 'You misunderstand the whole idea. We are not decentralizing leadership but substituting a horizontal for a vertical form of centralization. Previously, leadership was centralized in each branch of industry by means of a Ministry in Moscow. Now it is centralized regionally. As a result, we have not less supervision but more, and a Sovnarkhoz has much more power than a Ministry. The Sovnarkhoz is the executive body which works out the plan on the basis of the figures provided by Gosplan.'[1]

We had a long discussion arising from this and finally I said, 'But doesn't this reorganization merely mean that you are concentrating all decision in Gosplan? After all, if you have scores of Sovnarkhoz and if every issue which cannot be resolved between them has to go to Gosplan, you will have an appalling bottleneck there.' He gave no real answer to this question.

I then asked him how they prevented a rubber-stamp attitude in plant managers. In his reply he emphasized workers' meetings and remarked, 'After all, workers are always interested in progress.' Crossman: 'Are they? Our workers in Coventry certainly are not. They are interested in getting the highest wage for the smallest amount of work.' Borisov: 'It is not the same here. Here it is our main interest to ensure that production always rises much more than wages. In order to achieve this, we identify the workers with the State by propaganda and education.'

In the afternoon I had an amusing meeting with the editorial board of *Krokodil*, the Russian *Punch*. In asking for this, I had suggested that I might meet them informally, since they were dealing with a humorous paper. My object had been to be invited to somebody's home. But no. I went to the newspaper office, entered the board room and saw six bottles of champagne. This was four o'clock. By six o'clock, when I tottered out, the bottles were all finished. *Krokodil* had taken advantage of the foreigner's presence to have quite a good time and they welcomed me as a successor to Malcolm Muggeridge, with whom they had apparently had another beano. They were extremely pleasant and also extremely careful to say nothing too subversive.

We had quite an interesting talk about *Krokodil*'s correspondence. They receive 100,000 letters a year and have a staff of thirty dealing with every letter, both by reply and by use as material. I asked them, towards the end, what was their single greatest problem. 'To get young people to work,' they

[1] The State planning organization.

replied, and one of them proceeded, 'After all, the period of the Revolution and genuine self-sacrifice is over. In the modern Communist welfare state, young people haven't the incentive to work like their fathers had. They are spoilt and pampered.' I interrupted, 'That is what leading articles in *The Times*, the *Daily Telegraph* and every other Conservative paper write about British youth.' 'Oh, we have our teddy boys, too,' they said and we toasted the identity of youth in all countries.

That evening at Reilly's I heard one good story about Russian planning. A new block of flats was being built and, when the timber came in, it was found to be entirely green. However, in order to fulfil the norms, the wood was installed as a floor. Once this was done, the doors had to be fitted, the paint put on — and everything in the flat was hopeless. When the flat was inspected and these deficiencies were found, somebody said, 'But how was it possible to do such work? This will be a ruin.' 'No,' was the reply, 'The Repair Department has not yet fulfilled its norm for 1958.'

Wednesday, August 20th

By now the weather had broken and it remained foul for the rest of my time. It was cold, either with a low overcast sky or with torrential rain. The thin suits which I had brought for China were shivery things to wear in Moscow in August. My temper was not cheered by a morning of complete frustration. All my arrangements were cancelled and Surkov,[1] the General Secretary of the Writers' Union, insisted, to my inconvenience, that he could only see me at midday exactly. I said I would have to be away by half-past twelve to meet Zhivotovski for lunch. Nevertheless, although I arrived at Surkov's office at ten to twelve, he arrived at twenty past. I saw my chance and, rather frostily, said that he might find time on Monday to deal with two questions: first, to let me know how book publishing was carried on; and, secondly, to discuss Anglo-Soviet friendship relations, in his capacity as Chairman of the Anglo-Soviet Friendship Society. He was forced to agree that the discussion could start at half-past ten and he himself would be present from midday until one o'clock.

I lunched with Zhivotovski, the only one of my Russian friends who dared to ring me up, in a private room at the Praga Restaurant, which is far the best restaurant in Moscow. After a few politenesses and a remark that no one worth meeting was in Moscow, he asked me why Labour wouldn't take the lead in renouncing the production of the H-bomb, as Russia had taken the lead in ending tests. He showed no interest at all in the idea that Britain should stop the spread of the bomb by offering to renounce it if France and Germany did likewise. He was also extremely bitter about Nye's behaviour

---

[1] Alexei Alexandrovich Surkov, a Secretary of the U.S.S.R. Writers' Union since 1949 and First Secretary of that body 1953–9. In May 1960 he was replaced as Secretary of the Soviet Writers' Union by K. A. Fedin, who in the debates at the 3rd Congress endorsed the need for greater freedom to experiment in literary forms.

at the last Conference. At one point he remarked, 'I would return to the Embassy in London if there were a Labour Government, since I really know everybody pretty well. I've always been a strong supporter of Labour but now I am getting sceptical whether there will be any difference.' His whole attitude was as self-confident as it used to be in London but far cruder. Indeed, he seemed strangely out of touch.

I left him at ten to three to go to see housing with Mordvinov,[1] a very eminent architect, who had reconstructed Gorki Street and some other of Stalin's monumental horrors, and his colleague Osterman. Afterwards, Osterman, who is, I suspect, a Riga Jew, took me and Mordvinov home to his house for a drink and a slice of cake. This was the only Russian house I entered and it was in one of the monumental ten-storey Stalin blocks, about three miles off. Owing to the structure of the Stalin archways, there were some curious, awkward-shaped rooms round the curve of the arch and Osterman had taken these and constructed them into a fascinating, extremely modern flat, decorated with modern pictures.

Over tea, Mordvinov gave a long sociological justification of the old monumental style. 'If, in 1945,' he said, 'we had tried to build lovely little Dutch workers' dwellings or British neighbourhood units, with our primitive Russian standards of architecture and building workmanship we should have built slums. At this stage of our development we had to go for the monumental style to elevate ourselves and, incidentally, to give Moscow a skyline, now that we are pulling down all the churches.'

Mordvinov and Osterman then told me all about the row. For some time they had been in a minority, fighting the ten-storey blocks of flats, on the grounds that they are not only ugly and inhuman but more expensive than four-storey buildings, owing to the requirements for steel and lifts. They had been allowed to do the famous Block 3, which I had inspected, and this summer an international conference of architects had backed them with glowing praise.[2] After this, Khrushchev came out, backing the four-storey blocks against the Stalinite monumentalism.

Thursday, August 21st

I spent most of the day visiting the State Farm Bolshevik, which is close to a district called Serpuhov, fifty miles from Moscow on the main road south to the Crimea. There was an appalling lot of traffic, all of it lorries. Here is an interesting contrast with the Western world. Russian traffic is heavier on weekdays than on Sundays, for the very simple reason that there is only

---

[1] Arkadi Grigorevich Mordvinov, a Soviet architect who initiated the so-called 'conveyor belt' system of building apartment houses, which was praised by Molotov at the C.P.S.U. Congress of 1939. He was President of the U.S.S.R. Academy of Architecture from 1949 until 1955, when he was criticized for 'extravagance in design and construction'. There are no records to show who Osterman was.

[2] The theme of the International Union of Architects' Conference, held in Moscow in July, was 'Construction and Reconstruction of Towns 1945-57'.

heavy traffic in Russia and virtually no private motor-cars. We had been given instructions to turn right at Kilometre 112 after Serpuhov. So we went beyond, crossed the River Oka by a wooden bridge, with several sentries all along it, and tried to turn off. But there was no turning till Kilometre 117. Here we turned right, and within a few hundred yards were ploughing through seas of mud until we crawled into a really ghastly scene of rustic squalor, with dilapidated cottages and a few plaster buildings with tattered posters. I sent the guide off to find out where we were and he replied, 'This is the district capital.' This gave me an excellent idea for the second story in the column – which, however, the censor totally deleted! So back we crawled to Serpuhov and soon found State Farm Bolshevik on the near side of the Oka.

After lunch we motored down from a little office to a magnificent strip of flat alluvial ground, ten miles long, running beside the river. All the Central Committee had been brought out to see the farm last week as a model for growing vegetables and for livestock. I discovered, however, that the average potato crop was 17·5 tons per hectare, say 8 per acre, which is far less than Prescote produces. The land was 6,200 hectares of arable soil, with forest and pastures in addition. They had 500 milking cows with a total retinue of 900 animals, 870 hectares of vegetables, 300 of potatoes and a working staff of 1,500. There are 100 men and women working whole-time on the herd. At Prescote we have 50 milking cows and $1\frac{1}{6}$th men to deal with them. They have a herd ten times as large as ours with staff eighty times as big.* I asked what proportion of the budget went in wages and was given the following figures: Gross income 25,000 roubles; wages and salaries 10,000 roubles. We should go bust at Prescote on this basis.

I found the chief mechanic down on the field, showing off some not very impressive machinery. In the course of the afternoon I learnt that the workers on this farm are divided into brigades, each under a brigadier and each working exclusively on its own section of the farm. This, of course, reduces the value of the large unit of organization. 'But why can't you move people from one part of the farm to the other?' I asked, and was told that the whole system of incentive payments would in that case break down. Each section gets what its own field earns and they wouldn't work hard unless they did. Throughout Russia I found an absolute passion for incentive payments and workers would always say to me, 'Why, we should be lazy if we could get the same amount for doing less.'†

At this farm I also made house visits and, in conclusion, insisted on seeing the deputy manager. As I suspected, he had never done farming in his life and was a Communist bureaucrat, imported to control the peasants. The same applied to the chairman of the Young Komsomol, who took me

---

* I was to find later that this proportion of manpower to cows is constant from the Polish frontier to Canton, since, in the State Farm just out of Peking, they also had an average of 10 animals to 1 person without mechanical milking and 16 animals to 1 person with it.

† This was quite different in China.

round. I asked him what the Komsomol did and how much time it spent on Marxist education. 'Oh, it's not for that,' he said. 'We Komsomols work harder than the others.' 'So I suppose you earn more money?' 'Yes,' he said, 'but we do it also for the State.' 'But don't you have courses in Marxism or in Communism?' I asked. 'No,' he said, 'that is far too hard for us. We leave that to the city people.'

Just as we were standing at the river's edge, I looked back to the right and saw the tails of twelve aeroplanes gleaming in the sun, three or four miles away. 'What are those aeroplanes?' I asked. 'Never seen them before,' the chairman said, so I turned to my guide. 'Those are military planes,' I said. 'No, they are not,' he said, 'they are for civil aviation.' 'Twelve planes?' I said. 'For Serpuhov?' And suddenly the guide, who was a sweet, kind man, lashed out. 'You are foolish,' he said. 'If they were military, we wouldn't have let you come within 100 kilometres of this place.'

Friday, August 22nd
I visited the Kolkhoz Gorkyova — again, chiefly vegetable and livestock farming but much nearer to Moscow and serving the city. Here I was taken round by the assistant manager, another Party man with no experience of agriculture. When I went to the stalls, however, I had a long talk with the cowman, who knew his job. 'Previously they had planned us,' said the cowman, 'now we draw up the plan and submit it to the District Council, who do not alter it much.' I had a long argument with them about milkmaids and cows, inspired by a table on the wall, showing the milkmaids in keen rivalry and listing their daily achievements. 'But it's the cows' achievement,' I said, 'not the milkmaids'!' 'But it is all for incentives for earnings,' I was told. Then it was explained to me that the cows were carefully allocated and that each milkmaid had a fair chance and that the difference in earnings in a whole year was small since it was fairly averaged out — in which case, of course, the elaborate incentive system is quite unnecessary!

'Do you use artificial insemination?' I asked the cowman. 'Yes,' he said, 'we have just gone right over to it. It is a modern, progressive idea.' I replied that we had thought so ten years ago and had gone right over to it in Britain, but we found this very unsatisfactory and had returned to a balance between bulls and A.I. The cowman was absolutely enthralled and it then became clear that he had opposed the switch over to A.I., which the manager had supported. There was going to be a hell of a row after I left. It was clear that the whole thing is run in a highly bureaucratic way. 'I suppose you manage the calving,' I said to the cowman. 'Oh no,' he said. 'A commission, with an agronome and a zoologist on it, decide when to bull the heifers and the cows and when the calving actually takes place. The zoologist is responsible, not me.'*

* My visits to the State Farm and the Kolkhoz were to prove extremely useful to me as background when I got to China.

That afternoon I submitted my first story to the censor at the Central Telegraph. This is a fascinating ceremonial. There is a special, very splendid hall at the back of the Telegraph Office, with carpets, tables, typewriters and, behind the counter, three magnificent big-bosomed ladies, sitting doing nothing at all. Copy must be submitted in quadruplicate, with quite a number of official stamps on it, and in due course one copy comes back, marked by the censor. The job of the three Gorgons is to take your copy and pass it through a green baize door to the censor, who remains permanently invisible. It may take anything from two hours to two days before the copy is returned. On the other hand, once it has been censored, it automatically goes off, sometimes without your knowing, so that your home office gets the story in an absolutely unintelligible form before you can warn them.

On this occasion I submitted my copy a day before I telephoned it home, a procedure which is possible for columns but impossible for hot news and which enables me to tidy up the nonsense created by a few minor deletions. I arranged to telephone the *Mirror* from my room at the National and gave the time. The conversation was tape-recorded. If you diverge from the approved text, a voice comes in and cuts you off.*

In July, at Geneva, there had been an Eight-Power conference of experts on the detection of nuclear explosions, attended by representatives from the U.S.A., the U.K., France, Canada, the U.S.S.R., Poland, Czechoslovakia and Rumania. After thirty sessions, the conference ended on August 21st; its report, published on August 30th, concluded that it was technically feasible to establish a world-wide system to detect violations of any agreement to suspend nuclear weapons tests. On August 22nd the British Government issued a statement, welcoming these conclusions, emphasizing the need to resolve the associated practical and political problems and announcing their readiness to begin negotiations on October 31st for an agreement on the suspension of tests under effective control. From the date of the opening of negotiations, the Government would be prepared to refrain from further testing for one year, provided that the U.S.S.R. and all Governments which had tested nuclear weapons did the same; if negotiations proceeded satisfactorily, this mutual restraint would continue for successive annual periods. The U.S.A. issued a similar statement on the same day and subsequently announced that the current American programme of tests would end on October 31st. The British Note stated that the Government were beginning a short series of tests which would be concluded as soon as possible.

---

* In Peking, in contrast, there is absolutely no censorship of outgoing press cables, which on average were to take forty minutes to be received by the *Daily Mirror*. While I am on this point, let me mention another queer contrast. Moscow has no telephone directory, with the result that it's really a great problem to ring up anybody at all. Each person has to keep his own telephone directory on odd bits of paper and can only telephone if he personally knows whose numbers he has down. I thought this was a piece of Communist security till I got to Peking, where there is a perfectly normal telephone directory, received free of charge every year by each subscriber. Don't ask me why there is the difference.

After much diplomatic discussion, in late October the U.S.S.R. declined to suspend tests for one year; none the less the conference opened on October 31st.

That evening I went in to see Reilly, who gave me a copy of the statement on the British decision to end H-bomb tests for twelve months from October 31st. This was quite useful, since on Saturday I was due at the Supreme Soviet at ten o'clock in the morning to meet one or two fellow parliamentarians.

Saturday, August 23rd

For my visit to the Supreme Soviet I noticed that Intourist had provided me with an even higher class of car than usual, a Zis instead of a Zim. It duly took me the 400 yards from my hotel to the gate of the Kremlin. I was then wafted along various passages until I found myself in the presence of Mr Volkov[1] and Mr Gafurov.[2] Volkov is some kind of Minister for Machine Tools and Gafurov is Head of the Institute of Oriental Studies. The third member present was someone whose name I didn't get but who knew English quite well and was on the Supreme Soviet Parliamentary Delegation last year. Here is the course of the conversation:

CROSSMAN: What do you think about our proposal about H-bomb tests?

VOLKOV: Of course we approve of it. But how much better if you had announced an immediate cessation of tests!

CROSSMAN: But in this case we have followed your example and announced the cessation of our tests at the end of a long and successful series.

(Volkov: inaudible disapproval; Crossman changes the subject to the spread of the bomb, explains that his view is that Britain should renounce it on condition that West Germany does the same.)

VOLKOV: But West Germany has nuclear weapons already.

(Crossman: Corrects him at length, explaining that what the West Germans have is a missile with an American-controlled nuclear warhead.)

VOLKOV: We are concerned not with the technical details but with the parliamentary decision.*

(At this point Mr Gafurov intervened violently: 'I was in Germany last year,' he said, 'and both scientists and retired officers assured me that they would never fight against the Soviet Union. When I asked them against whom

---

[1] Perhaps Nikolai Nikolaevich Volkov, Deputy Minister of Machine and Equipment Building 1946–9, Director of the KIM Factory at Kontsevo 1949–53, and from 1953 until his death Director of the Second Moscow Watch Factory. Or it could be that the man Crossman met was Grigori Ivanovich Volkhov, who was at this time Head of the Administration for the Mechanization and Electrification of Agriculture, at the Ministry of Agriculture.

[2] Bobodzhan Dafurovich Gafurov, Director of the Institute of Oriental Studies at the U.S.S.R. Academy of Sciences from 1956 until his death in 1977.

* This was some obscure reference to our function as members of the Inter-Parliamentary Union.

they would use the American nuclear weapons, they replied, "We know whom to use them against." ')

CROSSMAN: I am very interested in this story. Are you telling me that responsible West Germans informed you that they would fight for Russia against America in the event of war?

(This produced considerable furore. The Russians talked for five minutes and then Mr Gafurov said that he had been mistaken in what he had said.)

CROSSMAN: If you object to the Americans providing the West Germans with nuclear weapons, surely the same objection would apply to Russia's providing the Chinese with nuclear weapons?

(This bow, drawn at a venture, scored a bull's eye.)

VOLKOV: I can assure you that we have supplied no nuclear weapons to China. Now that we have declared a ban on testing nuclear weapons, supply would mean giving them inferior weapons, which we are not prepared to do.

CROSSMAN: But suppose we all agree to ban tests. What is the next step?

VOLKOV: The next step would be to first ban the use of nuclear weapons and then to eradicate stocks.

GAFUROV: I would say the main thing is to ban atom weapons absolutely, for it is the atomic bomb, not the rifle, that threatens us today.

CROSSMAN: I do not quite agree. In Iraq we were very nearly confronted with a non-nuclear war between West and East.

VOLKOV: Do you really suggest that the Soviet Union threatens the West? I believe that the Labour Party, which represents the mass of the people, should do more than it does do for peace. I was surprised at the Inter-Parliamentary Union Conference at Rio de Janeiro[1] to hear the views about peace expressed by Mr Herbert Morrison. They were not encouraging.

(At this point Mr Gafurov added: 'It is a sheer crime against humanity to postpone the banning of atomic weapons on the excuse that conventional weapons must also be banned. I regard the Labour Party as very dilatory.')

CROSSMAN: You have no right to tell the Opposition in Britain that it should be more vigorous. Do you not realize that you have suppressed all opposition in Russia and it is sheer impertinence to demand activities in Britain which you suppress in your own country?

GAFUROV: Lenin allowed independent parties. They were only banned in the civil war.

CROSSMAN: Mr Gafurov, all I ask you is: will you allow opposition parties now?

VOLKOV (hurriedly intervening): Such parties are quite unnecessary. In Russia we have real practical criticism. In the West, the criticism of opposition parties makes no difference. See how ineffective the Labour criticism of the Government's intervention in Jordan was. In the West, criticism is for criticism's sake. Here it is the common people, not the Party, that do the criticism and as a result members of the Supreme Soviet are often removed

[1] In July.

from their posts. I ask you, Mr Crossman, do you maintain that NATO helps the peace? I ask you, Mr Crossman, have you in the Labour Party any real difference with the Tories about NATO? I ask you whether Labour really believes that the Soviet Union threatens your security?

At this point I realized we were not getting very far and bade my farewells. After this I had a fascinating visit to Lenin's apartments, which have been preserved, completely unaltered, in the Supreme Soviet building. The rooms were bleak but I found extremely convincing the kitchen, with a fridge full of the actual cups and saucers he used, and a spare bedroom for his sister and his writing-table with his dreary decorations. Nothing of any character or individuality, everything petit-bourgeois.

At five o'clock I sped to the office of the *Komsomol* newspaper, who had agreed to an interview with me. The Editor is Khrushchev's son-in-law.[1] He was absent and his deputy and the Foreign Editor received me.[2] The Deputy Editor was a tall, lean, handsome young man of, say, twenty-eight and the Foreign Editor was plump, rosy, red-haired, English-speaking and thirty-five. We had a fine two hours together, which culminated in our all standing up, shouting at each other simultaneously.

The first and least interesting part of our talk was devoted to a proof by the editors that they print criticism. Of course I knew this. They print the most appalling defamatory letters, denouncing saboteurs, etc. I let them go on for an hour or so and finally I said, 'Of course I know that you print criticism, but how do you ensure that it is not libellous?' To this I received three replies. Reply Number One: 'We have forty correspondents throughout Russia and also readers who contribute. We ask them to check on a criticism of an individual and they do.' Reply Number Two: 'We have a staff of thirty, whole-time, dealing with the letters received.' Reply Number Three: 'We have a special section of the paper criticizing Ministries. Sometimes a column is called "Results of Letters" and sometimes "Results of Unpublished Letters".' They gave me no answer whatsoever, of course, on the problem of libel, because it had never occurred to them.

I then asked what difference the 20th Congress had made to the paper. This is the reply I received: 'It is wrong to think that all criticism started after the Congress. On the other hand, it is fair to admit that many of us preached

---

[1] Alexei Ivanovich Adzhubei was a member of the Editorial Board of *Komsomolskaya Pravda* 1951–7 and Chief Editor 1957–9. From 1959 to 1964 he was Chief Editor of *Izvestia*.

[2] There were two Deputy Editors. One was Yuri Petrovich Voronov, Deputy Chief Editor from 1957 to 1959, when he succeeded Adzhubei as Chief Editor, holding that post until 1966, when he became the Berlin Correspondent of *Pravda*. The other was Boris Vladimirovich Ivanov, also Deputy Chief Editor from 1957 to 1959, when he moved to another newspaper, eventually becoming Deputy Chief Editor of *Sovietskaya Kultura*. Since mid-1958 the Editor of the Foreign Department had been Abram Yefimovich Nepomnyashchy (who sometimes wrote under the name of 'Karl'). He eventually became a member of the editorial board of the Novosty Press Agency, remaining there until his death in a helicopter accident in Czechoslovakia in August 1968.

Stalinism before the Congress, as the result of the cult of personality. The main difference is that, before the 20th Congress, we published far more official material. Now we publish it only in summary and then give our own attitude. But foreigners are always misinterpreting our criticism. For instance, Khrushchev recently attacked a certain song, whereupon the foreign press said that Khrushchev was against jazz in principle. This is sheer nonsense.' The speaker then launched into a long attack on articles which he had found in the Western press. There was one he discovered in a Utah newspaper, which accused Moscow of having second-class hotels. 'Could one', he said, 'conceive of any more foul attack on a friendly nation than this?' I said I could, whereupon he got very angry with me and quoted another article in the *New York Times*, in which someone had said that there were no genuinely free contacts in the Youth Festival two years ago. 'I had to answer this', he said, 'by pointing out that no less than four *New York Times* correspondents had proved this an infamy.' 'But then what have you got to complain of?' I asked. 'After all, if one correspondent in five is unfair, that's not too bad a proportion.'

Sunday, August 24th
We went to Tolstoy's[1] villa along the same road I had gone along to the State Farm Bolshevik. We started off at eight o'clock in the morning with a rather nice American Professor of Sovietology and an American girl who was taking photographs for a New York paper, as well as an interpreter, who had diarrhoea.

When we got to Serpuhov I said, 'Let's get out,' since my guide-book described this as a town with a Kremlin built by Ivan the Terrible.[2] We wandered down towards some churches I had noticed on my previous visit. The first we entered was packed with people and suddenly I noticed two coffins with two little human hands sticking out of the flowers. In front of the coffins was a mass of baked-meats, which made me realize what Hamlet had meant.[3] It was a Mass, combined with a funeral for two old peasants, and it was packed with people. The second church was equally crowded. Then we saw three more, which, however, had been ruined. Next we went on to the Kremlin, from which all the walls had been removed so that there was nothing but a green hill. We had a gorgeous walk for an hour, in a fresh autumn morning, and returned by some terrible slummy lanes to the main street, where we found a restaurant and had a cup of tea.

[1] Leo Tolstoy (1828–1910), the Russian author, whose works include *War and Peace* (1869) and *Anna Karenina* (1875–7). After 1880 he published many works on moral and political themes.
[2] Ivan the Terrible (1530–84), Tsar of Russia from the age of three, as Ivan IV (1533–84). Under his rule Russia increased her territory across the Urals and into Asia.
[3] The reference is to *Hamlet*, Act I, Scene ii, lines 180–1:

> Thrift, thrift, Horatio: the funeral baked-meats
> Did coldly furnish forth the marriage tables.

Thence we proceeded to Tula, which we knew as the town with the first Russian arms factory and also the home of samovars. On entering the town we noticed a huge building, which was probably a prison, since it had barbed wire and turrets with armed guards. Then, as we got to the centre, I saw a really lovely red brick Kremlin with a dome and asked the chauffeur to stop. He accelerated and drove straight on and our interpreter said, 'You have only transit rights in Tula.' 'But supposing I am taken short?' I asked. 'That makes no difference to your transit rights. You are permitted to go to Tolstoy's villa but to stop nowhere on the way.' I had just been getting accustomed to Russia and feeling very humanized when this happened.

Tolstoy's villa was some twenty kilometres beyond and there were plenty of charabancs outside the park. I hadn't brought a mackintosh and, as usual, it had started raining. However, we wandered through the rather dull park to the grave, which is a perfectly simple mound in the middle of a wood, since the Russian Orthodox Church forbade him to be buried in a graveyard and he himself insisted on no ceremonial. Then we were taken round the little country house by a guide who really did know every detail about every photograph and every article of furniture. It was a terrible house, with pitch-pine the only wood used, but I really felt that Tolstoy had lived there.

Monday, August 25th

This was the day I had arranged talks with Surkov, Secretary, of the Writers' Union. He had agreed to give me people to talk to from half-past ten to twelve o'clock, after which he would come himself, but at half-past ten I found him present. For some reason he had decided to talk to me at length and we spoke until half-past one and then again from three o'clock to five. He started off with a long speech, arguing that Russian literature has always had a sense of social responsibility. Tolstoy and Dostoevsky,[1] for instance, were teachers and preachers. This was all the easier, he said, because the Western bourgeois decadence didn't affect Russian literature. At this I boggled a bit. He went on to remind me that Soviet readers today read twenty times as much English literature as English readers. He said that, between 1917 and 1952, 45 billion translations of English books have been sold in Russia, ranging from Chaucer[2] to Graham Greene.

At this point I interrupted. 'I am an author,' I said, 'and you are adding insult to injury. You must be aware that you publish all our works without paying us anything for them. I wouldn't mind this as long as you didn't boast of it. I am not concerned about Chaucer or Graham Greene but about myself.' Consternation — and a long explanation: (a) the Berne copyright

[1] Feyodor Mikhailovich Dostoevsky (1821–81), the Russian novelist, whose works include *Crime and Punishment* (1866), *The Idiot* (1868), *The Possessed* (1872) and *The Brothers Karamazov* (1880).

[2] Geoffrey Chaucer (*c.* 1340–1400). M.P. for Kent, as a member of John of Gaunt's party, 1385; he was described by Dryden as the 'Father of English Poetry'. His works include *The Canterbury Tales* and *Troilus and Criseyde*.

Convention was signed neither by the U.S.S.R. nor by the U.S.A.;[1] (b) the Soviet Union was isolated; but this isolation had changed and it is now in a new position; (c) however, it is only for the Government to decide about copyright. Surkov is only in a consultative capacity on this issue.

As for my objections that British writers would like some royalties, Mr Surkov said that he felt there were spiritual values involved. Crossman replied, 'It is easy for a Russian writer to speak about spiritual values because he does jolly well materially compared to an English writer. Moreover, what is worse is the fact that wealthy writers, such as Graham Greene and J. B. Priestley,[2] can go to the Soviet Union and spend their royalties, whereas hard-up left-wing writers, who earn their Russian royalties in roubles, cannot. How can you victimize your best friends?' Surkov said: 'I do not feel bound to give an answer to this question. The explanation derives from the abnormal political situation. This can only be resolved internationally. But by this I do not exclude bilateral discussion. However,' said Mr Surkov, recovering himself, 'this question of copyright should not exclude other problems.' Crossman then said, 'What other problems would you put on the agenda?'

Surkov replied, 'First, selection of books for translation. Russian writers, in my opinion, are victimized from this point of view. Secondly, stopping publishing translations which are perversions of the text, and without acknowledgment.' (This I heartily agreed with, quoting German examples.) 'Thirdly, action to ensure the quality and faithfulness of translations on both sides. Fourthly, a plea for poets to be translated' (Surkov is a poet). 'Last, ensuring the text of play is not changed in the course of production.' Surkov went on, 'I have another complaint. On my recent visit to England I went to your universities and found that the teaching of Russian literature and history is in the hands of émigrés. This should be changed.' I replied, 'I am surprised at you. I have found that in Moscow the teaching of German history is in the hands of German émigrés of Communist extraction. I suggest we drop this topic. I would like to ask you about the directive for Soviet writers after the 20th Congress.'

Surkov said, 'Many people thought we had changed cars at the 20th Congress. Quite wrong. We threw out some luggage but we are still travelling in the same car. I know that when we say this we are accused of slipping back from the new line of the 20th Congress. This is a misunderstanding. Many outside critics have tried to assert as a fact something which they themselves

[1] First signed in September 1886 and completed in Paris in May 1896 by nine countries, agreeing on effective and uniform protection of the rights of authors over their literary and artistic work. The Convention was frequently revised. The U.S.A. subscribed to the Universal Copyright Convention of September 1955.

[2] John Boynton Priestley, the novelist, essayist and dramatist. His works include *The Good Companions* (London: Heinemann, 1929), *Angel Pavement* (London: Heinemann, 1930) and *The English* (London: Heinemann, 1973). He and his wife, the archaeologist Jacquetta Hawkes, were old friends of Crossman.

wanted to believe about Russia. Certainly, after the 20th Congress there did appear friction in Russia, which criticized everything since the Revolution. These books were a reaction against the too optimistic type of literature which appeared during the period of the cult of personality. This period brought forth a whitewashing tendency, in which everything was far too smooth. An example of the reaction against it is *Dr Zhivago*.'[1]

I had at this time only the vaguest idea of who Dr Zhivago was. Surkov then plunged into an elaborate defence of its banning, from which it was clear that this had been something in which he had been personally interested. 'It has been issued', he said, 'in Italian and will be issued in Britain by Collins. We are refusing to print it here because Pasternak has written a novel showing the 1917 Revolution was a crime against Russia.' I asked, 'Was this charge explicit or implicit?' Surkov said, 'Both. Pasternak said, for instance, that collectivization was a disaster.' I asked, 'Did Pasternak say that in his own right?' Surkov answered, 'Dr Zhivago says this and we can identify him, as Pasternak's own verses are put in the doctor's mouth, and in the last chapters of the book the author speaks openly against the Revolution.' 'Openly?' 'Well, he makes it clear from the horrible characters he draws, who are authors and products of the Revolution, that the Revolution was a disaster.'

I then asked, 'Tell me now, how, normally, is a novel produced in Russia?' Surkov replied, 'The Writers' Union has 4,500 members writing in fifty-five languages. Of these, 1,200 live in Moscow and 350 in Leningrad. In addition, each Republic has its own Writers' Union. There are 350 members in the Georgian Union. Each Republic has its own State publishing house and some have a Writers' Union publishing house as well.'

CROSSMAN: How many chances has an author got?

SURKOV: In the Ukraine there are four publishing houses – State, Youth, Trade Union and Writers' Union. One of the books of Michael Stel'makh[2] was published by the Moscow Writers' Union after being turned down by the four Ukraine publishing houses, but this happens seldom. More often there is simultaneous publication in the Republic and in Moscow.

CROSSMAN: Now tell me about book writing.

SURKOV: It is unusual for the Writers' Union to deal with books before publication but we frequently discuss newly published books.

---

[1] The poet and novelist Boris Pasternak (1890–1960) was forbidden to publish *Dr Zhivago* in the Soviet Union, but at the time of Crossman's visit to the U.S.S.R. it had already been published in Italy and translated into several Western languages. On October 23rd Pasternak was to be awarded the Nobel Prize for Literature and four days later he was expelled from the Soviet Writers' Union. On October 31st he withdrew his acceptance of the award and addressed an open letter to Mr Khrushchev pleading against expulsion from his homeland. After much equivocation by the Party leadership, Pasternak was permitted to make an apology and to remain.

[2] Mikhail Panasovich Stel'makh, a Russian author, whose works in English translation include *Let the Blood of Man Not Flow* (Moscow: 1962).

CROSSMAN: Are there no discussions before publication?

SURKOV: Yes, informal, unofficial discussions. No one is obliged to come to the Union but many writers do come and ask members of the Writers' Union to discuss their manuscripts before they present them to publishers. For instance, I am a poet and in 1952 I wrote a new volume of verse. Shall I show it to the publishers first, I asked myself? If so, since I am the Secretary of the Writers' Union, they will be bound to publish it.' (At this point a publisher of the Writers' Union, who was sitting there, made a derisive noise in his throat.) 'Instead, I had ten copies printed and distributed to ten poets and then I invited seventy people to come and criticize my verses. Their criticism was so strong that I could not publish. So I worked the book over and again I submitted it to a group of authors and again it was completely rewritten before publication.

CROSSMAN: Now I would like to hear the publisher's point of view.

PUBLISHER: My house is peculiar because it is run by the forty-four-strong board of the Writers' Union. However, they cannot control new books. They have to trust the publishing house. The writers on this board are selected by the Praesidium and there are twenty-nine of them.

CROSSMAN: But why can't you trust your readers to condemn Pasternak?

SURKOV: Our feeling for the moral state of our people and the present international tension fully justify the control of publishing policy. We do not feel we are committing a crime when we forbid publishers to print horror comics. In your society the freedom is conceded not to Shakespeare and Graham Greene but to pornography. We see nothing immoral in forbidding it. In the history of the Soviet Union only two novels have been published abroad which have not been published here. Pasternak is a peculiar phenomenon. He is a member of our Union but spiritually he is not a member of our society but a lonely bird.

CROSSMAN: But so was Nietzsche.[1]

SURKOV: Yes, and we would not have published Nietzsche and that would have prevented the rise of Hitlerism. Anyway, Pasternak submitted *Dr Zhivago* to three periodicals and one publishing house, which turned him down. Then a member of the Writers' Union told him how to rewrite his book but he rejected their advice and sent the manuscript to Italy. Then, once again, the publishers here tried to publish it with amendments but he refused. It is not a great loss for him, since a book of his verses will soon be published and he is comfortably off as a result of his translation of Shakespeare.

At this point I had to break off, since it was half-past one and I was already late for my lunch at the Peking Hotel. However, I said, 'Why shouldn't we

[1] Friedrich Wilhelm Nietzsche (1844–1900), the German philosopher who emphasized the role of the will. His thought influenced the Existentialist movement. His works include *Also Sprach Zarathustra* (1883–91) and his autobiography *Ecce Homo* (1888).

all adjourn for lunch to the Peking Hotel?' But Surkov evaded this by saying, 'We will meet again at three o'clock.' I got the very clear impression that the discussion had to take place in that particular room with those particular loudspeakers.

When we met again Surkov was alone with my interpreter. The whole conversation was devoted to the chairmanship of the Anglo-Soviet Friendship Society, lately formed, and its intentions in relation to cultural freedom. Unwisely, he told me what I knew already, that he had been in England as the guest of the Anglo-Soviet Friendship Society, that he had stayed with Emrys Hughes and Naomi Mitchison and that, to use his own words, his visit 'had culminated in a stirring address to 10,000 people at the Empress Hall on the anniversary of the October Revolution'.

At this point I intervened:

CROSSMAN: I do not, of course, ask that I should be invited to address 10,000 Russians in Moscow on Empire Day next year. Such a request would be absurd. But I do ask you, as Secretary of the Writers' Union, whether you feel you are improving Anglo-Soviet relations by doing something whose objective aim is to upset the British social system?

SURKOV: But I said not a word at the Empress Hall against Britain.

CROSSMAN: I am not talking about your subjective views, but about the objective result of your accepting an invitation from a front organization of the British Communist Party. In Russia I am unable to do such a thing because you have liquidated all such organizations, but surely we should have reciprocity in these affairs?

SURKOV: But I said not a single word against Britain.

CROSSMAN: I can assure you that, if I had the chance to address 10,000 anti-Communists in your Stadium, I would be clever enough not to say a word against Russia. All I demand is reciprocity. I do not suggest that we should forbid the Communist Party in Britain. What I suggest is that distinguished Russians like yourself should deny themselves the right to accept the invitations of the British Communist Party.

SURKOV: But when I came, nobody else would invite me.

CROSSMAN: I agree. We should have an opposite number to your Anglo-Soviet Friendship Society, an official Society whose invitations you could accept.

SURKOV: But if we could have that, things would be entirely different.

At this point I realized that he was already assuming I was in some sense negotiating on behalf of the Government. Although he had refused to lunch with me, he was busy telling me that on my return from China I must lunch with him and discuss these matters further. So I broke things off and reported all this to Reilly. I was quite excited by the idea of doing some good but soon discovered that my idea had already been considered and rejected by the

Foreign Office. However I did tentatively agree to stay with Reilly for two nights on my return from China and to give the first night to Surkov and the second night to him, to see how far we could go in discussing this matter. The whole conversation had been extremely tough. Surkov had sweated a great deal during it but had obviously indulged a masochistic pleasure in punishment by the Englishman. I had also indulged my own sadistic desires. So we had had five hours of delightful companionship.

Wednesday, August 27th
This afternoon I had a charming visit to Lenin Library, just behind my hotel. The Deputy Director, Madame Abrikosava, and her assistant, received me. The Library was founded in 1862 and in 1863 began to receive the usual obligatory copies of everything published in Russia. (Forty-three Russian libraries now receive such copies.) By 1917 there were more than 1 million books and annual bound files of newspapers. In 1922 the Library obtained a second obligatory copy and in 1945 a third, plus three further copies for exchange purposes. It now has 20 million books, including newspapers' annual files. Anybody can read there, including children over nine, and about 1,000 people can borrow books, including the members of the Government, Academicians, Lenin Prize writers and a few members of the Writers' Union.

I tried to find out what non-Russian books it collects. The selection is wide — all branches of science, including periodicals, which it exchanges with sixty-eight countries, and all branches of history. In selecting British books, it uses the National Bibliography. The Library has 130,000 readers, who this year paid it 1,800,000 visits. It has twenty-one reading halls and 2,300 seats. It also has microfilms of books but not of newspapers and it is part of an inter-library system which links 4,500 libraries in the Soviet Union. They told me that the country now has 400,000 libraries. Then they took me round and showed me everything I wanted to see. It was one of the nicest visits I have ever made. 'We are short of money,' said the Assistant. 'Our annual budget is only £2,500,000.'

We had now reached the day of my departure for Peking. I packed and Zhivotovski took me out to a final dinner and motored me to the airport, whence the plane was due to leave at midnight. I said, 'You can't wait for ever,' and so he said goodbye. We had been talking about my final round-up article, in which I had said that the centre of the world seemed to have moved to Moscow. 'Goodbye,' he said, 'and good luck. By the time you get back the centre of the world will probably have moved a good deal further East.'

This fortnight in Moscow was frustrating, partly because the weather was foul, partly because I arrived on the wrong sort of passport, partly because the Russians are extremely defensive. On the other hand, Zhukov really did get me a great many visits and appointments in a very short time and I was able to have a number of extremely free and easy conversations with

Russians.* I was also able to see a good deal of the British Embassy and of the Shomrons at the Israeli Embassy, as well as the Indian Embassy. I don't think anybody could really complain too much of what I got through in the time or even of the activities of the Russian censors. Nevertheless, if I remember aright, I was dissatisfied when I left. But then I had no idea of the frustrations that would confront me in Peking.

Crossman returned to London on September 16th. On September 12th the Prime Minister stated that there would be no General Election in the ensuing winter, an announcement that made the Party Conference rather flat. Labour's Conference was at Scarborough, from September 29th to October 3rd.

Wednesday, October 8th
The extraordinary thing is the exhilaration which those five weeks in China caused and which I'm still feeling. Not only did I return physically well, but I have been more interested and excited about life in general. A little of this, no doubt, is because in a sense it was a scoop to be there at all and my articles had been a success. But basically it had been an extraordinarily exciting thing for me to do and now I am determined that next year I shall go to Delhi via Moscow and compare India with Russia and with China.

And now to Conference. The day after I got back, I strolled into Transport House to find Home Policy and Publicity, which in previous years have taken hours, polished off in forty minutes, indicating the atmosphere of the Executive. Then I had Hugh Gaitskell to dinner. He really wanted to hear all about China and seemed to be extraordinarily unworried by the general atmosphere of depression about the Labour leadership and Labour policy which I found on my return. People really had begun· to believe the Tory press statements that Labour had no leaders and no policy and was utterly down and out. I soon began to ´realize that at Conference we should have quite a time raising the morale.

At conference Anne and I spent Sunday morning walking on the beach with Barbara and Ted, which gave the gossip columnists a great deal to write about Barbara's paddling. What a girl she is! This Conference publicity was like blood to a ghost. She throve on it, though sometimes she had slight indigestion.

Most of the time our weather was exquisite – billowing white clouds, blue sky. We made a lovely expedition to Rievaulx Abbey and had splendid walks around the Castle. Having one's wife at Conference has its advantages, since it means one eats with her and speaks to no one else unless spoken to, which isn't often. I wasn't as nervous as usual this year, since I knew I was O.K. on the Executive. At least, I thought I knew, until Jim Callaghan came up to me twice a day and said, 'Of course, we two are shivering on the edge.' When the scores were announced on Tuesday my vote had gone right back again

* At least, compared with Peking.

and the only sensations were the knocking off of Edith Summerskill and the dreadful arrival of Bessie Braddock, as well as Eirene White and Jennie, which should be quite nice. The Conference, having vindictively jeered Edith's defeat, felt so guilty that, when she replied on the Health Service at inordinate length and with outrageous exploitation of its existing state, they gave her a staggering reception.

The story is soon told. Each day the morale got better, starting with a shindy on education on Monday, which could have been reduced by an adequate reply from Alice Bacon but couldn't have been avoided. That was a good low point to start with. On Tuesday morning, in a lively debate, we succeeded in getting the Conference round. This, retrospectively, was quite important tactically. On Wednesday Harold Wilson and Hugh Gaitskell had a nice solid success on economics. On Thursday Nye did quite well on foreign policy and Hugh extremely well. And that was that. Day by day the morale went up as the delegates were agreeably surprised to find their leaders weren't so bad and their policies made sense. Even Hugh Massingham, who came to jeer, had to report the improvement. The only one who obstinately refused to do so was Malcolm Muggeridge, characteristically selected by Kingsley to do the *New Statesman* report[1] and characteristically selected by Cudlipp to choose the winner in a competition, planned by the *Mirror* in conjunction with *Tribune*, for a dynamic Socialist policy.

On the Wednesday I went to a drink with the *Mirror* people and found Hugh Cudlipp and Eileen, who had been in unusually friendly form. On the spur of the moment I told Hugh that he must undertake the organization of the writing of the overall policy pamphlet to end all pamphlets.[2] I did this because he was obviously flirting with the idea of swinging the *Mirror* to the Left. 'As you're bound to lose next time,' he told me, 'let's lose on a fine anti-privilege campaign.' Next day I saw the draft prepared by Peter Shore. It was quite hopeless and I asked for a meeting with Gaitskell, at which, to my relief, I managed to get him to agree to approach Cudlipp. Now, this week, work has been going on towards what should be a real popular pamphlet.

Friday, October 17th
Since I last wrote I seem to have spent half my time on the new simple policy statement[3] and the other half on Superannuation. The policy statement has developed since that evening at Scarborough when I told Hugh Cudlipp that no one but he could do it. Next day I had to persuade Hugh Gaitskell to give the job to the other Hugh, and succeeded, and since then Cudlipp has produced the glossiest layout, with the most brilliant, simple idea. I was swept round to his office on Friday. He and Sydney were both back from the

---

[1] He wrote the 'London Diary' that appeared on October 4th, 11th and 18th.
[2] The need for such a document had been announced in Crossman's *Daily Mirror* on September 26th.
[3] *The Future Labour Offers You* was published on November 25th.

North and it was duly laid out on his standing desk for me to react to. And I reacted just as everybody else has reacted. I put my thumb in the thumb-hole and looked up the place I was interested in.

Is that all there is to it? Of course not. Someone has got to put the words in and one of the requirements of the layout is that we should not change the order of the subjects and that we should write the exact number of words which can fit in. So I've been busy this week working out in conjunction with Hugh Gaitskell a so-called synopsis, which is really a first treatment. What has been necessary is to get the points in order of priority and that to some extent means simplifying them.

Now the synopsis has been finally prepared and roneoed for the Executive next Wednesday. Today, after Hugh Cudlipp and Eileen had left for Russia, I had Percy Clark[1] and Thomas Atkins,[2] the two production men, to lunch at the Athenaeum. Among the bishops and over a glass of Châteauneuf du Pape, Thomas Atkins handed over the envelope to Percy Clark, a strange, sandy-haired Jew with a red beard, whose face lit up with a quiet joy. 'I've never had to handle anything quite as good as this,' he said and the two practitioners got down together to discussing lithograph versus polychrome and so on.

Afterwards I went into Morgan's office to see if by any chance he was there. Of course he was still lunching, but his two secretaries were waiting. They, too, reacted in the way Hugh Cudlipp had anticipated and in the way that Dora Gaitskell, apparently, reacted when Hugh Cudlipp purred up to Hampstead in his Jaguar to show the Gaitskells the layout. As I saw, Cudlipp has been a schoolboy about his work. He had the idea one afternoon, worked most of the night, got the rough layout done in the morning and since then has been ringing me up on and off and making arrangements. Will it be too glossy? Will it be dismissed as a publicity stunt? All I know is that, if this is no good, no one can do any better in selling the Labour Party policy.

Meanwhile, at the Tory Conference, Boyd-Carpenter announced the new pensions White Paper,[3] which duly came out on Tuesday afternoon. It wasn't until I went down to Dudley, where I was speaking on China for George Wigg, that I had time to read it in the train. My first reading exhilarated me. Thank heavens, they have borrowed the whole of our machinery and so made their scheme truly comparable with ours. There can really be a debate about

---

[1] Percy Clark came to work for the Labour Party at Transport House in 1948. He was the Publications Officer in the 1950s and became Deputy Director of Publicity in 1962 and Director of Publicity in 1964.

[2] Thomas Atkins had worked with Odhams Press and was at this time Publicity Officer for International Printers Ltd.

[3] The Government's White Paper, published on October 14th, announced that the basic flat-rate pensions would stay as they were for all contributors, but those earning £9 a week or less (of whom more than half would be women) would pay smaller contributions. Those earning between £9 and £15 a week would, with their employers, pay graduated contributions, in return for wage-related supplementary pensions. Employers who satisfied the Government that their existing occupational pension arrangements met certain standards would be able to contract out of the State scheme.

it. If they had dismissed the whole idea of National Superannuation and refused to switch to graded pensions, Labour's scheme could have been knocked out as 'my eye'. But now we are arguing on roughly equal terms.

Wednesday, October 29th

On Saturday I had a most useful morning in Coventry. I visited half a dozen old members of the Party and then went to see the Secretary of the Section in Binley Ward. He is a queer, lumbering fellow, who said everything was going fine. It was then revealed that he hadn't called a meeting for eleven months and when I asked whether he wanted to be relieved of his office he immediately exploded 'Yes!' Before seeing him I had discovered an ex-Communist (ex since Hungary) who was willing to take it on. But, oh dear, it's against the tide, and I can't help feeling that all the time our Labour support is not melting away (that's the wrong metaphor) but growing squashier and squashier and less and less solid, so that one fine day a sudden landslide could take a whole section of it off us. On the other hand, my constituency know me more. On Coventry platform now, as I walk up it to the train in the morning, everybody greets me. This is partly owing to television, no doubt, but even more owing to Superannuation, which in Coventry has somehow earned me a solid, respectable name. Personally, I shall do quite well next time.

I had arranged with Sydney Jacobson to have his completed text of the policy pamphlet delivered to me care of the station master at Coventry. Last Wednesday, the Executive authorized its production without further check, leaving it extremely vague who should vet the final text and not even nominating the author. We had then handed it over to Sydney, who went into purdah, while I went into the spasms of a most terrible cold. Somehow or other by Friday the first five or six pages had been finished. Now I found the package in the parcels office, where the man at the desk replied, 'All sorts of junk is sent care of the station master and we never bother to inform you, Sir.' This shamed the station master so much that he gave me his private office to work in for an hour while I waited for the train. I continued to work hard at it all the way up, since I had arranged with Hugh Gaitskell and Peter Shore that they were to come to my house on Sunday and sit there until they had finished it. We also had a Transport House secretary laid on.

Peter Shore came in at three o'clock and so did Tom Driberg, who had insisted, against my will, on studying the draft. He's the greatest verbal snob in the world and I knew we were in for trouble. This wasn't rendered any easier by his conviction that the stinking cold he was suffering had been caught from me at the Executive. So I put him grilling over the fire in the drawing room and sent Peter Shore downstairs to the study, with Gaitskell, when he turned up.

I was a bit puzzled by Hugh, who had rung up to ask at what time he should come and had then said he wanted to get away to dine with Roy Jenkins. This cheered me, of course, since I thought he wouldn't spend so long on the draft. After he had read it for an hour he said, 'This shouldn't take me long. I've only got three or four points.' At this point I made the fatal mistake of saying, 'Let's go upstairs and do them with Tom Driberg.' Forty minutes later we were still drooling over the first page, of which practically every sentence had been almost rewritten, including Driberg's semi-colons and Gaitskell's policy haverings, which always recur when he has time to think.

At seven o'clock it was clear there was no dinner with the Jenkins and Anne's excellent dinner, which had been prepared in advance, was hurried on. At half-past ten Gaitskell left, having completed the document as far as Taxation, leaving out all Commonwealth and Foreign Affairs and Defence. 'I must run now,' he said and doubled out of the door, as though scared that he would be held against Dora's will. In his absence I got the thing finished in half an hour, after which Tom left in a gorgeous chauffeured car and I was left alone with a Transport House girl, for whom I finally got a taxi at a quarter to one in the morning, when she had finished typing the whole thing magnificently.

It was a terribly depressing evening, which I am afraid bore hardly on Peter Shore's ideals. One thing Hugh had been most insistent on was the theme of the waste caused by running the economy below capacity. I had put in a figure for how much we would have gained if the Tories had kept productivity rising at the same rate as us. On two previous occasions Hugh had complained that this was unfair and instructed Transport House to work out what the gain would be if production under the Tories had increased at only half the rate. This figure was inserted in the draft. 'That's much too small,' said Hugh, 'don't be ridiculous.' However, it was proved to him that it was the correct figure, whereupon he said, 'All right, then give the figure for the same rate.' Shore looked up and said, 'Surely you told us that this would be unfair?' 'Ah, this is only propaganda,' said Gaitskell.

Another curious incident came when we were giving the pledge to give one per cent to underdeveloped areas. 'You needn't worry about that,' said Hugh. 'Harold Wilson's taken care to leave so many loopholes that we're not bound by it.' This, in Tom Driberg's presence, was not perhaps the most tactful remark for a great leader to make if he doesn't want cynical gossip. Once again I felt an utter depression about Gaitskell as Leader. Month by month he gets softer and more complacent and more hopelessly unaware of his deficiencies. I slaved and sweated all Sunday, and have done so ever since, to get all these drafts finished. Granted it wasn't much more difficult than getting agreement on *Keep Left, Keeping Left, It Need Not Happen* or any other Bevanite pamphlet. I reckon I've been in on every famous pamphlet and master-drafted them, but in this case the whole thing was somehow more complicated and the longer I worked at it the more I had an uneasy feeling that Gaitskell himself doesn't believe in it. After all, this is the policy which he personally has pushed on to the Party and which he at least should believe in with conviction.

Meanwhile the first meeting of the Parliamentary Party since the Recess has come and gone very drearily indeed.[1] We met after the televised Queen's Speech and Hugh made quite a nice little speech, but, though there was nothing wrong, there was nothing new or fresh. I wasn't surprised when Manny Shinwell got up and made one of his terrible pleas for Socialist inspiration. However, I still had hopes when I went into the debate after another desperate lunch rush, clearing the final amendments to the policy draft. But when Hugh started, it was really deadly. Absolutely competently, he went through the measures of the Queen's Speech, making his points about them. There was no sense of novelty or of setting a new framework or starting us off with a bang. The benches behind him were scarcely full. I'm afraid this opportunity has already been missed and this Queen's Speech is going to put us back into the mood of July.

Gaitskell has called a special Party Meeting next week to discuss our responsibilities for selling the policy in the country. What he fails to realize is that this and our reaction to the Queen's Speech are not separate. I am now more and more gloomy about him and Nye and, indeed, about the whole Opposition as an alternative Government. They are not worthy to be called extinct volcanoes. They are just what the Chinese would call paper tigers.

Friday, October 31st
On Wednesday we had our beginning-of-term party. This year we had decided not to ask the routine politicians — John Strachey, Roy Jenkins etc. — but to have mostly young people, plus a few distinguished elders. It worked out surprisingly well, partly because the Kaldors and the Marrises[2] arrived from Cambridge, giving it a certain intellectual sheen, but mainly because the young people liked each other and Cecil King, Hugh Massingham, Sydney Jacobson and Harold Wilson provided a sufficient impression that the Top People were there. Hugh Gaitskell sent a message that he hadn't got time to come. Nye Bevan didn't send word but told me yesterday he was sorry he couldn't manage it. Both were a little silly, since the people I had in my house were precisely the people these two men most urgently require to like and respect them. One of the curious features of the Party is that all the wives there seem to have already had three children by the age of twenty-six or, even better, to be in the process of having a fourth! Nanny[3] was wildly excited, since babies were a central topic, and she held Royal reception at one

[1] Parliament had met on October 23rd to complete the business of the 1957/58 Session. The opening of the new Session on October 28th was televised for the first time.

[2] Robin Marris, an economist, was an Assistant Principal at H.M. Treasury 1947–50, a Fellow of King's College, Cambridge, 1951–76 and University Reader in Economics there 1972–6. Since 1976 he has been Chairman of the Department of Economics at the University of Maryland. His publications include *Economic Arithmetic* (London: Macmillan, 1958), *The Economic Theory of Managerial Capitalism* (London: Macmillan, 1964) and *The Corporate Society* (London: Macmillan, 1974). He married his second wife, Mrs Jane Ayres, in 1954. The marriage was dissolved in 1972.

[3] Miss Barbara Fayers.

end of the room. There is one curious advantage of not starting a family young and that is that it makes you have a contact with much younger people, something denied to my coevals, who are grandparents.

Before going home to my party I was in the House for the second day of the Queen's Speech debate. I went out for an hour and in the Tea Room I was asked, 'When is your speech?' I was quite pleased by the reaction and I said I wasn't speaking since I hadn't been asked to. I had, some days earlier, decided to stand this year for the Shadow Cabinet and I had told George Wigg. On Wednesday morning he told me that I would get only the right-wing vote, since the Left has entirely written me off as part of the Establishment. Yesterday morning George rang me up to tell me not to be too modest, since I should get elected and should at once challenge the leadership. Between our Wednesday and Thursday talks he had been round the Tea Room. The mood of the Tea Room is certainly somewhat dejected by the feeling that there is no change and not much punch in the Front Bench.

This pessimism was slightly reduced yesterday, when Nye Bevan answered Selwyn Lloyd on foreign affairs. I sat in my usual place on the fourth row back and watched Nye straining himself to work up the House, which remained completely phlegmatic, forcing him to ever greater paroxysms. There was nothing wrong with the speech as far as content was concerned but it was flaccid, diffuse, and, from the point of view of the House, unsuccessful.

In the Smoking Room afterwards, Nye asked me if his speech was all right. I told him that exactly the right subjects had been chosen and commiserated with him on the floppiness of the House. He told me he wasn't feeling well and added that he has been suffering for some time from undulant fever, with his temperature constantly going up. Whether this is hypochondria or truth I have no idea, but it was quite obvious he wanted all the moral support he could get and I think on this occasion he earned it.

Last night I found myself speaking to the Military Commentators' Circle on China. There was a strong representation from the French and American Embassies, as well as John Strachey, Reggie Paget and Patrick Blackett,[1] all sitting in the front. I gave a pretty racy lecture, which made them all laugh. Why can I make people laugh at lectures and never at speeches? Afterwards John turned to Patrick Blackett and said, 'He really is the most brilliant lecturer I've ever heard,' and Blackett replied, 'Yes, it's an embarrassment for us professionals to listen to that kind of virtuoso performance.' Of course I realized that John, whom I now know, was only too relieved to praise me for something which is not competitive politically and indeed is almost a disadvantage in a rival for the Cabinet. They were all spellbound by what I had

[1] A physicist who specialized in nuclear and atomic physics and the study of cosmic rays and rock magnetism. He was a Fellow of King's College, Cambridge, 1923–33, Professor of Physics at Birkbeck College, University of London, 1933–7, at the University of Manchester 1937–53 and at Imperial College, University of London, 1953–65, and was President of the Royal Society 1965–70. He became a Companion of Honour 1965, received the Order of Merit in 1967 and in 1969 became a life peer. He died in 1974.

to say and I myself was quite interested to discover how much one had collected, even if one only gave impressions of what one had actually seen. On the way back in the pouring rain I shared a taxi with John and told him I was standing for the Shadow Cabinet. I could hear his face fall, but he said, 'Of course, the *Daily Mirror* is a grave disadvantage.'

Now let me make my prognostications. I would quite definitely not be surprised if this year I were elected in the place of George Brown for part of a rather bigger shift, which might even include Wedgy Benn. There is definitely a sense of dis-ease among the backbenchers and of desire for new leadership. The only doubt is whether enough of them believe I would give it. I should be quite pleased either way. What an enormous relief if I am not on the Parliamentary Committee but scotch the accusation that I shirk responsibility because I earn so much money. On the other hand, what fun to balance not on a dual but on a triple tightrope and carry it off!

I am sorry to admit to myself that I have never felt such a strong sense of personal superiority as I have had this week, looking at Mr Gaitskell or even at poor, soft Nye. Each of them is going squashy and the squashiness of each infects the other. Midweek, Harold Wilson rushed up to me (he is coming to be our main speaker at our twenty-first anniversary celebrations in Coventry tonight) to tell me that the pamphlet was the best political document he had ever read, apart from one or two ghastly concessions to the elector inserted by Hugh Gaitskell, owing to his panic about the Gallup Polls.

'It's time we had one of our serious talks,' Harold said. I at once cancelled arrangements to travel to Coventry with Anne and arranged to go alone with Harold in his car. I am quite sure that the little man, who has remained curiously detached in the last three months, is much more aware than most of the electoral disaster which may well confront us if we cannot have more bite and fight in our leadership over the next six months. And no doubt Harold is sure that, if Gaitskell fails, Bevan won't get it and he will. Of course, this would be after the defeat, but in Harold's mind one can plan as far ahead as that.

As for me, I feel I have spent so much time in the game that it would be just plain silly to pull out now. And if one doesn't pull out, one has got to go in 100 per cent and do what one can to achieve a victory. But what is the objective truth? Are we to believe that the objective situation is such that Labour leaders are bound to go squashy and lose their bite or, alternatively, to be biting and lose their votes? In that case I make no difference. Or can it be possible that at least part of the Party's failure is due to Gaitskell and Bevan, in which case each of us, by our contribution, could make some difference. George Wigg, Hugh Massingham, Alan Taylor and such like have all long assumed the first — and intellectually I can hardly disagree with them. But my decisions are not formed by my intellectual conclusions. On the contrary, they are the result of some strange internal dynamic, which makes me go on trying. This new policy pamphlet must be about the seventh of which I have been the architect, in the sense of the patient appeaser of other people's author's pride. I can never get out of this kind of job, presumably because I really like it. And so why not try to get myself into the Shadow Cabinet this year and pull it together?

Monday, November 10th

Since I last wrote, the final tidying up of the great pamphlet has taken place. Of course the job could have been far better done with more time and it isn't really very distinguished. On the other hand, Harold Wilson, who saw the galleys, was, I think, really genuinely impressed. Now all that we can do is to wait until the campaign is launched on the 25th.

Meanwhile the day has at last been fixed for the great pensions debate, and this time I am to speak. Of course, it would have been nice if I had spoken at the beginning, immediately after Boyd-Carpenter, but Marquand, who is a Rt Hon., insists on doing it and I am to wind up at the end.[1] When this was announced at the Party Meeting last Thursday, I gather there was actually some applause! By some curious accident, polling for the Shadow Cabinet finishes on Wednesday, so I shall be making the last speech before it and, if I do reasonably well, could increase my chances. I came up specially from Prescote on Sunday night to have dinner with Brian Abel-Smith and Peter Townsend. We went through our ideas and I am getting them to collect various pieces of information in preparation for tomorrow.

Friday, November 14th

This has been an up and down week and extremely educative. My first Front Bench appearance went off much as I might have expected. At half-past three, with my notes and documents, I rather shamefacedly slipped into the House from behind the Speaker's chair, only to be wafted up behind the Despatch Box, where I found myself very low down, in a cavern. Boyd-Carpenter spoke very clearly, in the sense that he was deliberately flat. If you are introducing a flat scheme, be flat and try to flatten the debate. After he had been on for more than an hour, Marquand replied with another hour's go, which he did really quite well, scoring some tough points. The House emptied fairly steadily and, according to the *M.G.*,[2] I yawned. After that we had a very characteristic three hours of backbench contributors, one very lively Tory insurance broker,[3] some very dull people on our side and, finally, Reg Prentice.[4]

[1] As a Privy Councillor, Hilary Marquand was entitled to speak first.
[2] *Manchester Guardian.*
[3] Arthur Tiley, Conservative and National Liberal M.P. for Bradford West, 1955–66, and Chairman of Clarkson, Tiley, Hargreaves Ltd, Northern Capital Ltd, and the Northern Housing Association Ltd.
[4] Labour M.P. for East Ham North May 1957–February 1974. He was elected as Labour M.P. for Newham North-East in February 1974 but in October 1977 left the Labour Party and acted as Conservative M.P. for that constituency until May 1979. Since May 1979 he

The trade union group had been meeting during this but they all streamed in when I got up and I had a very full House on both sides. I had made one intervention a little earlier to test the feeling of the Despatch Box and was horrified by the proximity of the microphones and the general sense of crowdedness. I had always felt how naked one is on the backbenches but one feels more crowded on this Front Bench. Moreover, throughout I couldn't really believe I was there and, though I was extremely nervous in one sense, I was quite collected in another and saying to myself, 'Now you ought to be really impressed that you are addressing the greatest assembly in the world, with the Prime Minister sitting in front of you, but you are not, because it doesn't seem very real or very important.'

I sat down for quite a long ovation and once again felt a sense of disappointment that one had got through yet another experience without too much exaltation. Afterwards Harold said to me in the lobby, 'If only you had made that speech a week ago.' Hugh Gaitskell, sitting beside me, purred and said how wonderful it all was. The other members of the Shadow Cabinet were polite, but, not unnaturally, unecstatic. Altogether, it was, in Party terms, quite a success. I was very much aware of old Nye on my right and of trying to persuade him to take an interest in pensions.

Harold Wilson is shrewd and immediately afterwards said to me, 'It's come too late to get you on the Parliamentary Committee.' This is exactly what was proved when the results were announced last night.[1] Less than a third of those who bothered to vote — and twenty-nine didn't — thought me worth giving one of twelve votes to. Yet most of them would say I had done very well in a first try. This is not unreasonable and is something one feels about the National Executive. On the other hand, it is fair but quite unreasonable to observe that the next twelve months are decisive. Next year there will either be a real Labour Cabinet or a convulsion in the Parliamentary Party after a Labour defeat. In that case I am much better off. The main thing is that this year I have proved my willingness to go on. All I need now do is to show no signs whatsoever of irritation with my colleagues and to carry on enjoying life as before and getting the best of both worlds.

Nevertheless, of course, one is riled and annoyed because I would have liked to have spent the next year helping to put some guts into the Party. There's an enormous difference between being a member of the Shadow Cabinet and not being on it. No doubt I greatly overestimate the difference I would make to it, but I find it difficult to see how we can very easily afford to have such an undistinguished and parliamentary dead-mutton type on the

Front Bench. What an irony that just now, when Nye is really soft and has lost all leadership, he should head the poll! And what idiocy that George Brown, who at least is capable and effective at the Despatch Box, has been replaced by poor old, effete, numskull Edith Summerskill as a result of a sympathy vote for her being chucked off the N.E.C. But hush! I must not admit such thoughts even to my own diary.

Thursday, November 27th

I see that the last time I wrote in this diary I was still irritated by the results of the elections to the Shadow Cabinet. That seems a long time ago. I am now used to the fact that not only people like Charlie Pannell but both Hugh Gaitskell and Harold Wilson assured me I did very well at my first try and should be reasonably sure of standing a good chance next year. No doubt this is true, judged by the moment, since I am now on the crest of a wave or in a spasm of sunshine between storms, or whatever else you like to call it. But it is certainly true that what has been happening in the last fortnight makes me feel a good deal less peeved. Actually, I have scored a treble with my role in the policy pamphlet, my book coming out[1] and also once again with good old National Superannuation.

I rushed back from Coventry last Saturday morning to the candidates' and M.P.s' briefing meeting in Church House [in Westminster]. Everybody felt elated and cheered by the feeling that they had a policy, even though they were not permitted to see the document, which was at this time still a secret from members of the Executive. Indeed, it is a fact that, until it appeared this Monday, the Executive, whose policy it was expounding, never saw it, with the exception of Hugh Gaitskell, Harold Wilson and myself. I suspect this was all done on security grounds. If so, all it proved was that you can produce a Labour Party policy document without a leak, on condition it is seen by no member of the Executive or the staff and only by journalists of the *Daily Mirror*! Anyhow, I gather, I came out from this Saturday meeting with flying colours, colours which, however, have been higher in the Commons as a result of publication.

Looking back over this period (which dates, by the way, from the meeting in Hugh Gaitskell's room at Scarborough, when he agreed that Peter Shore's draft policy statement should be scrapped and Hugh Cudlipp approached), I think one can draw one or two lessons about politics. Once again, and even more dramatically, it has been shown what a few people can do if they are given the chance. Quite literally, this policy statement is the product of three men — Hugh Cudlipp, Sydney and myself — working with Hugh Gaitskell, plus all the *Mirror*'s skilled machinery and layout staff. But really the three of us have done it and we have only been able to do it by excluding everybody else.

In this we were not quite successful, since Tom Driberg did work his way

[1] *The Charm of Politics*, a collection of forty-eight essays (London: Hamish Hamilton).

in, an irruption of which the net effect was probably harmful to the product, since Tom's ideas and style did not merge very sweetly and we spent hours trying to wed his text to ours. But, apart from Tom, it was really a three-man show, with each of us performing his proper function and Hugh Gaitskell, to do him credit, making all this possible. True, he was a nuisance. True, he interfered much too much. But then, after all, he is the Leader.

I must add one other thing about Hugh Gaitskell. I now see that it was his simple, passionate faith in this pamphlet and in our capacity to write out the best piece of propaganda ever seen which contributed an essential element to the publicity build-up. If we had had Attlee leading and not believing in it, there would not have been this strange belief spread about that something unique was occurring and there is no doubt that, brilliant as the pamphlet is, it is even more brilliant because for five weeks people have been saying what a brilliant thing was coming.

Secondly, all this — and this again repeats an old theory — was only possible because it came at the right time. Ever since Scarborough people have been waiting for the simple declaration of policy, summing everything up, and almost anything produced now would have been acceptable to the Movement. But this, because it is very good, has made the Movement swallow a great softening of the policy far more easily than it otherwise would have done.

Thirdly, the link with television was something I had quite failed to appreciate at the start. If we had recognized the impact of the television, we would have ordered half a million copies the moment we went to the printers. But, because we are all journalists still, we had failed to foresee this. Fortunately, although it was a bit over-ambitious and amateur, the television launching was on the right lines — not an attempt to make five people agreeable, but an attempt to put over a policy through subordinating five personalities to it.

Fourthly, this is absolutely all right as a presentation of the Labour Party, where policies should come first and personalities second. I was much struck yesterday by the reaction of Emrys Hughes. He thought it was the best thing the Party had ever done and I know why. It did give the impression that we are a serious Party, with a policy, and this was precisely what was needed to stiffen our own rank and file. But of course all this will only be a shot in the arm if it is not consistently and consecutively followed up. There needs to be months of teaching in every ward, with people going through it page by page and almost learning it by heart. There needs to be follow-up speeches every weekend by Members, who also should learn it by heart, quote it and drive it home. There is still very little evidence that the Centre, either in the Shadow Cabinet, or in the Executive, has that kind of drive, and there is every evidence that Nye Bevan has no drive at all.

One last point about the television. I learnt a good deal about this.

Unfortunately, Nye is pre-television. He simply will not take the trouble to master the technique and that means he will never be very successful except in a purely impromptu interview. By spending seven or eight hours on his performance, Gaitskell did put himself across and prove that success in television is, quite literally, a capacity for taking pains. Anyone who is willing to take enough trouble can learn to be reasonably good. Anyone who is not willing to take trouble risks being at worst a flop and at best never being a real success in a set speech.

Tuesday, December 16th
I should perhaps here put a note in about the publication of *The Charm of Politics*. I got two resoundingly successful reviews to start with, from Alan Taylor in the *Guardian* and Robert Blake[1] in the *Sunday Times*; then one from Christopher Hollis came in the *Listener*, friendly but complaining the reviews were stale and brief, and one from someone in the *Telegraph* panning the book as stale journalism.[2] After this the *Times Literary Supplement* last week had a wonderful catty piece, which I now conclude must have been written by my dear old poison-pen pal Rowse[3] of All Souls'. However, this was pleasantly counteracted on Sunday by a review so adulatory from Harold Nicolson that even Gerald Kaufman felt embarrassed. Yesterday I was telephoning outside the Smoking Room when Nigel Nicolson passed me. 'I hope you are pleased with the *Observer* this week,' he said. 'Indeed I am,' I replied, 'and in the circumstances I regarded it as a generous action.' 'Very generous indeed,' he said, turned on his heel and stalked off.

This incident should teach me a lesson about how self-revelatory remarks can be. I had guessed that Harold Nicolson's failure to review the book three weeks ago, when it came out, was somehow connected with a pretty harsh judgment of Nigel Nicolson's own book which I had published in the *Statesman*.[4] Harold Nicolson cares too much about writing to review me badly, I thought, and his simplest way out, in loyalty to his family, is to have the review omitted, which one can always do on grounds of pressure of space. My second guess was that, when I got an extremely good review in the *Sunday Times*, Harold Nicolson read my book, really enjoyed it and then fell over backwards in not favouring his own family. Hence the adulatory review and the references to the healthiness of astringent criticism. I can hear Harold softly telling Nigel that it was good for him to be reviewed by me in

[1] Student and Tutor in Politics at Christ Church, Oxford, from 1947 to 1968, when he became Provost of The Queen's College, Oxford. In 1971 he was made a life peer. His outstanding work is a biography of *Disraeli* (London: Eyre & Spottiswoode, 1966).
[2] The *Daily Telegraph* reviewer was H. D. Ziman. At this time reviews in the *Times Literary Supplement* were anonymous.
[3] Alfred Leslie Rowse, Fellow of All Souls' College, Oxford, 1925–74 and a notable historian of Elizabethan England, of which an outstanding survey is offered by his three-volume history *The Elizabethan Age* (London: Macmillan, 1950, 1955, 1971–2).
[4] Appearing in the issue of October 18th, 1958.

this way. Of course, all this would have been sheer surmise if it hadn't been for that little scene yesterday outside the telephone booth.

Thursday, December 18th

Yesterday morning was Executive, as usual, and at the end of it I had the idea of asking Nye to dinner to have a good talk, taking up a suggestion he had made to me the night before. He duly came at half-past seven and behaved like a lamb. It was an extremely interesting evening. Straightaway he began to discuss the hopelessness of Gaitskell's leadership, his lack of instinct, his tendency to look over his shoulder and to hold up his finger to see which way the wind was blowing. 'He simply isn't a Leader,' Nye said. 'Baldwin, Chamberlain, Attlee were not leaders like Churchill but at least they had an instinct and at least they knew when to stop talking. This man is hopeless from the start.' 'But do people in the Shadow Cabinet feel so?' I asked. 'Oh, Gaitskell's position is impregnable,' said Nye. 'There is no question of his losing the leadership.' Crossman: 'Then do you think we are doomed to defeat?' Bevan: 'No, I think we shall win the Election and the trouble will come very soon afterwards. Gaitskell's an honest man, a man of integrity. Gaitskell's an intelligent man. He's not an intellectual, by the way, like you, but he is an intelligent man who hates ideas, and that's why he always distrusts you and me and consorts with dreary people like Roy Jenkins and Patrick Gordon Walker. They're the ones who are always advising him to hedge and to avoid dangerous debates. They are the ones who will advise him when he is Prime Minister, and there is a crisis, to go National. And of course there's Harold Wilson. He's much more dangerous than Gaitskell because he isn't honest and he isn't a man of principle but a sheer, absolute careerist, out for himself alone.'

I asked, 'But if Gaitskell's like this, why can't you take over the real spiritual leadership and let him be the formal Leader and just advise him and push him?' Bevan: 'Because he isn't a man you can advise. He's too brittle for that. If he disagrees with you, that's that, and you can't influence him. He isn't a man who is impressed or influenced. He is just scared or runs away. Gaitskell's piddling all the time for fear of losing the Election. That's the basic trouble. He thinks of nothing else except the Election and every single principle is sacrificed. It's no good asking me to change that.' Crossman: 'But don't you see a lot of him?' Bevan: 'No, only occasionally from time to time, on business. We have no other relations.' Crossman: 'Then who does see him regularly?' Bevan: 'For a time I thought it was you but I know it isn't. I suppose it's that fellow Gordon Walker mainly, and Crosland — all the wrong advisers. Harold Wilson doesn't, because Hugh doesn't trust Harold any more than I do.'

We then discussed policy a little. 'Of course, the new policy statement is very well done,' Nye said, 'but there's no lift in it, not a particle of lift, and that's all the Party know, though you may not have been told it yourself. It doesn't move them. The only difference between us and the Tories is public ownership and, once you abandon that, you betray Socialism.'

On the whole it was a very friendly, amiable evening. Anne thought he wasn't wholly at ease. On the other hand, he was not so embarrassed that he couldn't talk pretty freely and I think he quite wanted to resume that kind of relation with us. Also he was astonishingly resigned to the whole thing, without fury or anger as he used to be, and I did not myself feel any particular sense of destiny about the Foreign Office or anything else.

I've tried to sum up my own views in a very discreet way in my column for tomorrow.[1] Probably I see it from far too close to judge objectively. But the Labour leadership at present is certainly a depressing spectacle and I see no reason why it should ever get any better.

[1] Headlined 'Labour Must Take Risks to Sharpen Up the Opposition'.

1959

Crossman and his wife spent the New Year in Paris and on January 4th Crossman went on to a fortnight's tour of Algeria with four other British journalists. He then flew to Naples, returning to London on January 18th. His reports were published in the Daily Mirror *on January 7th, 9th, 13th, 16th and 20th.*

Monday, February 2nd

So back to Party chores. I returned from France and Algeria to find the Home Policy Committee chewing over a popular pamphlet on education, with questions and answers on the comprehensive schools, and a document on municipalization, both of which were raising the same old problems we were discussing before Christmas. There is no doubt that on these issues I am now labelled, not unjustly, by the way, as Gaitskell's closest associate and that this has made people like Barbara and Ian Mikardo extremely suspicious. Unfortunately this helps neither Hugh nor me. The fact that I advise him makes him even more suspect to every other member of the Executive and the fact that I am thought to be close to him makes me more suspect to everybody else. There is no more talk now of co-opting me on to the Campaign Committee. For which relief, much thanks, but also, of course, some suppressed resentment.

At the Executive last week it was decided that there could be no written reports from the Campaign Committee, for fear of leaks. All we had was a verbal report from Barbara which, on my protest, will be recorded as a memorandum in one single copy for reference. In fact, the Executive has virtually abdicated its power to the chairmen of committees on the grounds of security. I detest the grounds but in fact this is extremely sensible, since the Executive was an impossible body and the chairmen form a much more effective executive.

Meanwhile the Gallup Poll has revealed that the Tories' popularity is once again in decline but that once again the Labour vote is not proportionately rising.[1] This disappoints me, although I suppose we should have realized that the campaign to sell the glossy is not really getting going until this month and will not affect public opinion polls for six or seven weeks. Nevertheless, public opinion had one of its sudden irrational swings, confidence in Tory victory has slumped, the possibility of Labour victory is now being considered again and the morale of the Parliamentary Party, when we started the Session again, was very much higher.

Last week we had our Second Reading debate on the National Insurance Bill. Again, in terms of the Labour Party in the House, I did very well, but outside the impression was confirmed that M.P.s were arguing about

---

[1] In January 1959 the Gallup Poll registered 37 per cent support for the Conservatives, compared with 40 per cent the previous month. Labour support had risen to only 36·5 per cent, from 36 per cent in December 1958. Liberal support had fallen by 1 per cent and the proportion of 'Don't Knows' had risen by 4 per cent.

trivialities which no one could understand. The truth is that the difference between the Government and ourselves on this issue is not only a difference of principle but a conflict of practice, which will make the difference between happiness and unhappiness for millions of people. Yet how is one to get this across?

One story I want to put in here happened before Christmas but I have confirmed it since. Kenneth Younger has decided not to stand again for Grimsby and he went in to Hugh to tell him the decision. 'What is your majority?' was the first question. When Kenneth said, 'Three thousand,' Hugh said, 'Oh, that's all right,' and then expressed relief that the reason for resigning was adequate and would not cause questions.[1] Finally Hugh said, 'Grimsby, that's a possibility for Tony Crosland,'[2] and Kenneth left the room. I heard this from Tony Wedgwood Benn and checked it with Kenneth this week. 'The whole thing took under two minutes,' Kenneth said to me. 'Neither Hugh nor the Chief Whip seemed in the vaguest degree upset that I should want to go or made any attempt to deny my wisdom in doing so.'

From Kenneth's own point of view, he is quite right. Nye detests Kenneth, almost entirely because Kenneth wanted to resign over the arms programme six months before Nye did and said so. He would never have him as Minister when he could have Denis Healey, and Kenneth will not become Home Secretary because it has been given to Patrick Gordon Walker. Moreover, there is a real job to be done at Chatham House and the opportunity was offered when that clever Monty Woodhouse[3] got himself nominated Conservative candidate for Oxford. Faced with a good opportunity at Chatham House and a bleak prospect in the Labour Party, Kenneth, at the age of forty-nine, was, I think, quite right to move. But his decision does indicate something that is wrong about the feeling of Labour politics today. Another symptom of this is Wilfred Fienburgh's posthumous novel,[4] of which Sydney has been warning me and which is now being serialized.

As for me I cannot prevent each review of my book, monotonously repeated, strengthening my feeling that it is very much more useful my writing about politics than being a mediocre politician. I do happen to feel at the moment that I am capable of investigating well and writing well, but on the other hand I must be in the Cabinet if I am going to write the book I want,

[1] He became Director of the Royal Institute of International Affairs, at Chatham House in St James's Square.

[2] He had represented South Gloucestershire from 1950 to 1955 and in the 1955 General Election stood unsuccessfully for the Test division of Southampton.

[3] The Hon. Christopher Montague Woodhouse. The second son of the 3rd Baron Terrington, he was Conservative M.P. for Oxford 1959–66 and 1970–September 1974. He was Parliamentary Secretary of the Ministry of Aviation 1961–2 and Joint Under-Secretary of State at the Home Office 1962–4 and was Director of the Royal Institute of International Affairs, at Chatham House, from 1955 to 1959. His works on Greek history include *The Philhellenes* (Oxford University Press, 1969) and *The Struggle for Greece 1941–49* (London: Hart-Davis, MacGibbon, 1976).

[4] Wilfred Fienburgh had died after a motor accident. His novel *No Love For Johnnie* was published by Hutchinson.

which is not a repetition of Bagehot[1] (Bagehot was never in Government) but something of my own, even more from inside; and, incidentally, the pensions plan is possible and won't be done by the Tories or by anybody else except me.

Thursday, February 5th

I had better prepare the way for what should bulk very heavily in the next eight weeks, the Committee Stage of the National Insurance Bill. Last week Marquand called a meeting of the working party at four o'clock. At ten-past four I turned up to find a girl alone in the Committee Room. After me came Douglas Houghton;[2] then, at a quarter past, Marquand and Reg Prentice, and we sat down to work on preparing our Amendments for the Committee Stage. In came Barnett Janner and sat down beside me. After twenty-five minutes he said, 'But line 25 on Page 2 doesn't read like that,' and discovered he was in the wrong Committee Room.

I asked whether we couldn't get our usual gang of experts and was told they could submit Amendments if they wished. I asked what our tactics would be and was asked what I meant. I said I presumed that we must decide whether we wanted to hold up the Bill and, if not, at what point we wished the guillotine to fall. Marquand then said we should try to be as helpful as possible in improving the Bill and I said I wasn't as innocent as that. At this point Douglas Houghton intervened. 'You can have your propaganda debates,' he said, 'but you must leave time for us to have serious debates, trying to improve the clauses about contracting out.' I replied, testily, that it was a bit of an illusion to think it would be possible to improve any clause by Amendments in Committee. If the General Council of the T.U.C. wanted improvements, its best chance was to go to the Minister now, behind our backs.

Obviously by Parliamentary standards all this discussion was most unseasonable and untimely. Marquand's chief interest had been to get Dick Mitchison as our lawyer, which, thank God, he failed to do. We've got A. J. Irvine and, on George Wigg's advice, we have made an agreement with him that we should quietly submit all our Amendments to the officials in the Public Bill Office to make sure they are in order. Apparently the official

[1] Walter Bagehot (1826–77). A Victorian essayist and journalist, he was Editor of *The Economist* 1861–77. His classic work *The English Constitution* (1867) was issued in a paperback edition by Fontana (1963), with a notable foreword by Crossman.

[2] Labour M.P. for Sowerby 1949–February 1974. An L.C.C. Alderman 1947–9, he became widely known as a broadcaster on the B.B.C.'s 'Can I Help You?' programme 1941–64. He was Chairman of the Public Accounts Committee from 1963 to 1964, when he became Chancellor of the Duchy of Lancaster, moving in 1966 to become Minister without Portfolio, with special oversight of social security matters. In 1967 he left the Cabinet and replaced Emanuel Shinwell as Chairman of the Parliamentary Labour Party, a post he held until the General Election of June 1970. He served in the same capacity from November 1970 until 1974, when he became a life peer. He was Chairman of the Committee on Financial Aid to Political Parties (Cmnd 6601) 1975–6 and of the Committee on Security of Cabinet Papers 1976.

Opposition is always finding its Amendments out of order because Mitchison drafts and is too vain to submit them. I spent last Saturday morning with Brian Abel-Smith, getting his ideas, and he has submitted a long letter to me. I feel a little uneasy, plunging, for the first time in thirteen years, into a Standing Committee upstairs and wondering how I shall fare in that arid atmosphere.

Monday, February 9th
I spent most of Wednesday evening, when I had to be in the House for divisions, reading *No Love for Johnnie*. This was Wilfred Fienburgh's novel and when he was killed he was negotiating about publication. Since then, I gather, it has been edited for publication by Bob Edwards, once of *Tribune*, now of the *Standard*, and it is running as a serial in the *Standard*. The B.B.C. has bought television rights and I think we can assume it will be filmed as well. However, the really interesting question is the book itself. I was nauseated by it. It's an extremely compelling novel, with a uniquely unpleasant combination of peep-hole sex and career politics. Of course, one can say, as some of Wilfred's friends do, that he was writing about Desmond Donnelly. But there is a strong element in it of the confessional and the autobiographical.

I wrote a little piece about it for Friday and, by a coincidence, Mallalieu reviewed it on the same day in the *Statesman* and Tom Driberg gave it a tremendous write-up in the *Tribune*, expressing his deep regret that he hadn't known the author while he was alive. On Sunday we were sitting having coffee, when suddenly there came a book review programme on I.T.V. and there were Mrs Fienburgh and Tom Driberg discussing my review![1] For some reason the whole subject has got under my skin. I had not only been furious when I read the book, I had also brooded over my review, since it wasn't at all easy, in a few words, to say what one had meant without seeming to be unfair to a dead man. Actually I changed the final text at nine o'clock on Thursday evening, after the first edition of the paper had gone out.

This had one very curious result. I went to Cambridge on Friday to speak to the Labour Club. The Club executive had, the night before, all been at the *Daily Mirror* and had come home carrying the first edition with them. One of them was particularly horrified that I should have said that I was 'relieved' at Fienburgh's death. I was rather relieved to find that, when I was quoted extensively on this television programme, the quotation was all from my final version. Nobody has spotted the discrepancy, which would have put me in a slightly awkward position.

[1] At the end of his *Daily Mirror* column on February 6th, Crossman had asked how, if Fienburgh had lived, he would have enjoyed

> the money and the fame which this nauseating caricature of Labour politics will earn? It is a windfall for the Tories ... If he had survived to see the earnings of his pen coming to look uncommonly like the thirty pieces of silver, he would have bitterly lamented his success.

It's an interesting little incident because, as George Wigg says, the reaction to it is a kind of litmus test of the Labour Party. Of course, people who write that Wilfred will do us no harm do so partly because they want that to be the case. But there is also a curious blindness amongst professional politicians to the effect that books of this kind have on ordinary people outside. I can remember how shocked people in Coventry were at the mixture of sex and politics in Maurice Edelman's novels and, heaven knows, they were harmless enough compared with this. The fact is that the more this book circulates and particularly the more it is filmed and televised, the more appalled Labour people will be that a Labour M.P. should write it.

The other thing which has happened since I last wrote is the delightful confirmation of the utility of the Abel-Smith/Townsend brains trust. I am now pretty sure that Brian's major Amendment will be in order and he and Peter have been busy drafting other Amendments over the weekend. On Friday I went up to the Public Bill Room. After thirteen years in the House, I didn't know where it was. I was directed up in a lift to a room on the left and found a man in an armchair, with his feet up. I addressed him politely, assuming he was the official, but found he was the messenger. He took me into a fine room and there were three of my New College students — the whole Public Bill staff taught by me[1] — and at the far end was a white-haired pundit, Mackenzie,[2] who is five years younger than me and who looked as though he had been sitting there twenty years, waiting for my arrival.

We had an excellent talk, in which he could see no objection to Brian's Amendments. I was glad of the interview, particularly since George Wigg had ticked me off that one of the weaknesses of the Opposition is to draft their Amendments without consulting the Clerks, who will always tell you in advance what advice they will give the chairman of the Committee. Here George was completely substantiated by my experience.

Tuesday, February 17th
I am now well into the Committee Stage of the National Insurance Bill. We started last Thursday morning and, as luck would have it, Marquand went down with flu. So, when the steering committee met on Wednesday night, I found myself in the Chair. About a dozen of the twenty-five-odd Labour Members of the Committee turned up and we had quite a sensible, practical discussion, in which they were all delighted with Brian's Amendments.

---

[1] The staff of the House of Commons Public Bill Office in February 1959 consisted of the following Clerks: Clerk of Public Bills, A. Dent; Clerk of Standing Committees, K. Mackenzie; other Clerks: T. Odling, D. Limon and J. Wilcox. Of these only Odling had in fact been taught at New College by Crossman. But it is not unlikely that Clerks from other Offices in the Department of the Clerk of the House may have been in the room. Certainly other pupils of Crossman's were Clerks in the Commons.

[2] Kenneth Mackenzie, a Commons Clerk who had joined the House in 1930. He was Clerk of Standing Committees 1953–9 and Clerk of Public Bills 1959–73. An author and translator, his most recent publication has been a translation of Dante's *Divine Comedy* (London: Folio Society, 1979).

Marquand, by the way, hadn't bothered to ring me up and, when I rang him, only very reluctantly told me he wasn't coming. I think he would have left me, if he could, to find it out for myself that morning.

We didn't want to come to dynamic pensions, that is, the benefit clause, until next Tuesday, because the skiffle group is still working at the figures. However, this morning Marquand came back from having flu and it was soon clear that he and Boyd-Carpenter had had a walk up and down the passage, where an agreement had been reached that these three Amendments should be disposed of before the morning was over. I asked Marquand why and he said, 'I think the debate's gone on long enough and there's no reason not to give the vote to the Minister.' I said, 'But the steering committee wanted us to postpone the vote on the second group until Thursday morning and I feel we ought to go on.' To this Marquand replied, rather characteristically, 'One gets much more out of debating small, interesting points in the Committee Stage than out of long speeches in which we go on hammering at the big principles.' 'Why?' I asked, and he replied, 'I must explain to you.'

Well, at twenty minutes to one no other Labour speaker got up, so I rose to talk it out, obviously carrying out the wishes of our own people, apart from Marquand. I got quite warmed by the subject and I'm afraid I didn't talk like a proper Committee man but developed my exposure of the swindle with some vigour, forgetting myself at one point and saying, straight across the room, 'Mr Minister,' which apparently is a ghastly floater! Anyhow, Boyd-Carpenter thought it was terrible, was furious at not getting his vote and went out with Marquand in a huff.

Afterwards Edith Pitt, who is his stupid, rather nice Under-Secretary, said to me, 'The trouble is, we are having more Second Reading speeches on the Committee Stage.' That, of course, is Marquand's view but I can put it into other words. The trouble for the Government is that the Opposition is fighting this Bill and using the Committee Stage to rub in what a swindle it is. I would have thought that was the right tactic. When I said so to Gerry Reynolds as we went out, he replied, 'But you see, Marquand is probably thinking of himself as a Minister one day and he will want Boyd-Carpenter to help him with his Bill.'

If this is true, what a fool Marquand is, for the Tories don't help you with Bills unless they want the Bills, and in this case we don't want this Pensions Bill. And if the Minister is compelled to guillotine us and we have a blazing row, we gain and he loses. What is it that makes our Labour frontbenchers feel that, in a Committee Stage, one behaves like a good committee man: that is, one obliges the Government? For I have already seen clearly enough that the Committee Stage has ceased to be such if, by this, you mean a stage when Members cease to be pure party men and sit down together to improve a measure, without pressure from the Whips. It is already clear that Boyd-Carpenter is not going to concede anything to us, whatever we say, and we are not going to persuade him one iota. Therefore this is not strictly a committee but a continuation of a debate in another place and there is no point in being conciliatory or collaborative unless we should lose in public opinion by failing to be so.

All this has been brought home to me because, for a fortnight, I have been re-reading Bagehot in the new edition[1] and I suddenly understood something I had been brooding on for years. Bagehot distinguishes the dignified from the practical element in the Constitution. The monarchy, he says, is dignified and can only advise, warn, etc., whereas the practical part of the Constitution is the Commons and the Cabinet. What has happened since his time is that the House of Commons has become merely one piece of the dignified part. It can only advise and warn, as the monarchy could 100 years ago, whereas the effective power is outside the Commons.

Thus the Committee Stage of a Bill, which 100 years ago really was a Committee Stage, is now only a pretence of that. From the point of view of improving a Bill, you could cut this stage down to one day, and therefore the only possible value an Opposition can get out of it is propaganda value. And, if this is so, everything is a question of propaganda tactics. It is this which makes so ridiculous the respectable attitude of people like Marquand and Douglas Houghton. They are taken in by their own myth and like to pretend that we are doing some good in Committee, whereas in fact we are having to waste our time – unless we can get some propaganda value out of it.

That's a little bit of an exaggeration. It's no doubt quite useful for me to have this opportunity to rethink a number of details and I had the skiffle group here last night with their wives, frantically trying to work out a table to illustrate dynamic pensions and finding all sorts of snags. But this must be relatively unusual. One doesn't always have one's own measure ready, as we have, when debating a Bill. One isn't always able to use the Committee Stage in order to sharpen one's wits and rethink one's own blueprint.

Moreover, it is already clear that, without the skiffle group, we would not have had any of the good Amendments down at all. In that case, let me admit it, the Committee Stage would have been nice and quiet and happy, without these great debates on principles. Everything would have been cosy in the garden and Marquand and Boyd-Carpenter could have had a shadow fight. However, it's not to be. It seems to me that the best propaganda value we can get out of this Committee Stage is to gradually irritate the Minister to a point where he loses his temper, tries to dragoon us, threatens the guillotine and, above all, becomes offensive. For then the newspapers will take notice of the dog-fight. After all, the object of the Government is to get this Bill through with the minimum of public understanding, so that a tiny fraction of the people appreciate the true difference between our scheme and theirs. In this case the more stink there is, the more we gain. The more irritated the

[1] Norman St John-Stevas's *Walter Bagehot* (London: Eyre & Spottiswoode, 1959). Crossman's review appeared in the *New Statesman* on March 21st, 1959.

24

Minister, the more likely he is to commit indiscretions. At least, that is my calculation.

Tuesday, February 24th
The little story of the Pensions Bill proceeds. Yesterday we had a meeting of the steering committee and, although there was nothing on in the House, twelve people turned up, which was pretty good. Once again there was that slight, rather baffling tension, with Marquand always saying we must get on with the Bill because otherwise we might be left with the clauses undiscussed and the Minister guillotining and I and most of the backbenchers saying, 'Why should we worry too much? The clauses we want to debate are the early clauses and anyway we want to leave the Minister in suspense and not give him any kind of assurance that he will get his Bill.'

If I were younger, and therefore more suspicious, I should immediately conclude that there was an understanding between Marquand and the Minister that the Bill should be through before Easter. But I am pretty sure that this is not so. It's simply that Marquand is a tidy ex-Minister, who feels that it is wrong to guillotine and anyway that we are somehow making too strident an opposition on the early clauses.

His difficulty is that he is so uninspiring in the chair that people naturally tend to side against him. He really has no idea of how to lead a team. In the Committee, he sits there on the Front Bench or goes out to do a pee or have a cup of tea. Does he ever go back to chat with the boys and encourage them to speak? Not on your life. At this meeting, he urged that the speeches should be short and sharp today, since it was more effective. I said this was one of the subjects on which one couldn't be too short, since it was extremely compli-cated and I hoped he wouldn't abbreviate himself and weaken our case. He said he thought a series of ten-minute speeches was what we needed. Today he opened the proceedings with a speech of thirty-two minutes, as crashingly boring as ever. After this we had excellent speeches from Reg Prentice and Gerry Reynolds and Douglas Houghton, interspersed with the usual long and skilful empty reply by the Minister, who takes each of our questions and then sedulously avoids it.

At a quarter to one I got up and was most surprised when suddenly the chairman said, 'Order, Order,' and it was one o'clock! I shall have to go on in full spate on Thursday. All I was doing, as usual, was to take the points put by the others in a rather professional, expert way and put them in much simpler language. Somehow, by doing this, one is much more spicy and polemical and amusing and the atmosphere in the room changes. The Tories wake up and the civil servants smile slyly, as one gently chides the Minister — perhaps in his view not so gently. Today I was able to point out with great enjoyment that it was we who were making precise, detailed, expert speeches and all we heard from the Minister in reply were Second Reading speeches on general principles. Surely he and the Tories should play real committee-men's parts by joining with us to improve the Bill in detail? There are half a dozen first-rate Tories with expert knowledge. So far, in four sittings, only one of them has been allowed to speak once, and they are getting exasperated almost beyond endurance.

Thursday, March 19th

Nearly a month since I last wrote in this diary — but there are reasons for the gap. First of all, Anne's father's death and her illness[1] disturbed our private life. Secondly, in politics I have been concentrated more than I thought possible upon the National Insurance Bill Committee Stage. When I last wrote, it was just getting under way. Now we are at it three times a week and last Tuesday we spent not only from half-past ten to one o'clock in the morning but from four o'clock till seven o'clock in the afternoon, slogging away. This has required not only attendance at the meetings of the committee itself and of the steering committee each Monday, but also quite a lot of outside work with the skiffle group, who have been nobly collaborating by preparing tables, drafting Amendments and so on. Without them our opposition would have been amateur indeed. With them I think we have put up a very formidable case and I cannot deny that the person who has put it most formidably, most humorously, most brutally, most mostly, is the author of this diary.

I suppose I could claim to be in my element in the Committee Room, if I hadn't always believed that one of my few wise actions was to refuse, despite my father's pressure, to go to the Bar. But the atmosphere is altogether too congenial and the target is too easy. The fact is that the Minister and his associates, however much they are riled and provoked, dare not answer back for fear of giving an opportunity for a continued debate. So they sit there, making brief, inadequate statements.

What we have gained out of this Committee Stage — and this surprised me in each successive debate on each successive Amendment — is an ever new and ever more outraged comprehension of the utter futility of this Bill, which sets up the most elaborate machinery in order to achieve the most pitiable results in terms of pension. In a way I believed this at the start but there is no doubt that the gruelling compulsion to think about the Bill for ten or twelve hours a week has made me realize much more deeply its shoddiness and inadequacy.

What do the civil servants think, as they sit there hour after hour, flanking the chairman? I fancy they must realize that the Bill is being given some pretty thorough rough handling and that the replies of the Government are not brief merely for reasons of brevity, but because there is no answer to our attack, other than the admission that this is not a Pensions Bill but a financial device for relieving the taxpayer of a burden.

[1] Patrick McDougall had died in late February of complications following an operation on his prostate gland. Anne Crossman had congestion of the lungs which turned into pneumonia.

I have no doubt that my own position in the Parliamentary Party has been enormously strengthened by what is regarded in the lobby as a tremendous job. Last night, when things were going very badly (we had just moved a vote of censure on the Government about unemployment, only to hear that the figures for March were 58,000 down),[1] little men I hardly know came up to me and said, 'I hear you're handling them pretty rough up there in the Committee. It's a wonderful job you're doing for the Party.' Of course, this does make me realize one reason for the resistance to my being elected to the Parliamentary Committee. The rank and file party Member spends a large part of his life upstairs in these Committee Rooms, listening to frontbenchers, hour after hour, arguing the detailed Amendments. Of course a number of backbenchers, including all the trade unionists, were bound to resent the fact that we intellectuals, and particularly the journalists and lawyers, never turn up for this morning work because we are earning a very good living outside. I can see why Dick Mitchison gets such a big vote. It's because he is always there in the mornings, when the work of the Party is really done.

What good does this Committee Stage do? On this I have been ruminating, as I did a 'Books in General'[2] on the collected political works of Bagehot. I have now promised Hamish Hamilton that after Whitsuntide I shall make a start on trying to produce a modern Bagehot in serial parts in *Encounter*,[3] for re-publication later on. I am sure that, if it can be got out, it will not merely be a *succès d'estime* but quite a commercial success. The theme would be that Parliament has joined the monarchy as a dignified, not an effective, element in the Constitution.

On November 27th, 1958, the Soviet Union had delivered a Note declaring that the existing situation in West Berlin could no longer be tolerated and announcing its intention to hand over to the East German authorities the functions it had previously exercised, according to the post-war agreement. The Western Powers had rejected the Soviet arguments in a reply on December 1st, had reasserted their rights and declined to negotiate under threat. They nevertheless offered discussions on the Berlin question and these were taken up in a Soviet Note, dated January 10th, 1959, proposing a peace conference and attaching a draft peace treaty. Its terms appeared to recognize the division of Germany and required the withdrawal of the Federal Republic from Western military alliances, without establishing any alternative security system.

On February 16th the reply to the Soviet Union stated that these terms were unacceptable but suggested a conference of the four Great Powers, with German advisers in attendance, to discuss all the aspects and implications of the German problem. Mr Macmillan now decided to seek personal contact with Mr

---

[1] The motion of censure was defeated by 309 votes to 247.

[2] In the *New Statesman*.

[3] Crossman eventually published two articles in *Encounter* in March and April 1963, basing them on his Introduction to a paperback edition of Walter Bagehot's *The English Constitution*, published by Fontana in the same year.

Khrushchev and, in a long-postponed acceptance of Marshal Bulganin's invitation to the British Prime Minister in 1953, arranged to visit Moscow from February 21st to March 3rd. His conversations with Mr Khrushchev remained private and the joint communiqué issued on March 3rd confirmed that they had not amounted to negotiations and that the two leaders had failed to agree about Berlin and Germany. Immediately after his visit Mr Macmillan called on Britain's European allies; he was in Bonn on March 12th and 13th. From March 19th to 23rd he was in Washington for discussions with President Eisenhower. The Foreign Minister's conference was to take place in Geneva on May 11th.

All this occurred after Königswinter, which this year took place under unusually interesting circumstances. Ever since Dulles fell ill,[1] Macmillan has taken over his journeyings, in my view with conspicuous success. He seems to me to have done well in Moscow and his talks in Bonn coincided with the first day of Königswinter. The real value of these Königswinter conferences is their regularity. Since one sees the same people at the same time of year, one is able to take the temperature successfully. On this occasion all the resistance against negotiation with the Russians and against disengagement was melting away extremely fast. The main German preoccupation was Berlin. Most of the thoughtful people present now suddenly realized that, when Eisenhower assures the Berliners he is prepared to use any weapons, including nuclear weapons, to maintain our position in Berlin, this assurance is either a horrifying bluff or an announcement of the end of the world, and it's far more likely to be the former, since the Russians will so arrange it that we have to make the first act of violence. These were things which I myself had thought and written in the last few weeks but I was pleased to find them confirmed by all the Germans present, who rubbed them into the British, day in, day out.

Remembering his performance at Algiers,[2] I myself believe Macmillan may well have a miraculous success in Washington and really establish a new, flexible Anglo-American line which Eisenhower and de Gaulle have to accept. If he succeeds in doing so, we can expect a successful summit conference, following a Foreign Ministers' conference at which at least the groundwork for a German peace treaty can be laid. All this will continue until the autumn at the very least. If Macmillan fails, the situation will be extremely dangerous, since the Russians will then go ahead unilaterally in Berlin.

But it's worth noticing that it's only if Macmillan fails and the situation looks dangerous that there is much real possibility of the summer Election about which everybody has been talking this week. A summer Election, in fact, would mean that Macmillan was anxious about the autumn and driven

[1] On February 10th Mr Dulles had been admitted to hospital for treatment of a hernia and four days later it was announced that he again had cancer. On April 16th he resigned; on May 24th he died.

[2] A reference to Macmillan's service as Minister Resident at Allied Forces Headquarters in Algiers 1943–5, where he was exceptionally successful at co-operating with the Americans.

to go to the country for fear of the future. If things go well, he will postpone it. At least, that's my analysis.

For a whole variety of reasons, the Labour machine, under the Campaign Committee which meets every Tuesday, has spluttered almost to a full stop. Once again there is no sense of lift or drive outside in the country, while in the Commons Macmillan continues to win success after success over Bevan as well as Gaitskell. I don't think there has been a single occasion on which Gaitskell has got the better of Macmillan and it has been depressing to watch how, in debate after debate, our Front Bench has been out-manoeuvred or, alternatively, has blundered into defeat. Outside, as I have found for myself in the meetings I have done, our people are conscientious and are doing a little more work and things are rather better. But all the evidence shows not only that we are not making progress, but that the doubts about our leadership are increasing instead of decreasing.

While my Committee was on, I walked down to Mrs Skelly's office and asked Gaitskell to come out to lunch, which he did. Once again I put to him the necessity for a psychological warfare directive, which would lay down the strategy on which we could base our tactics in the House and outside. Once again I pointed out to him that, in a world where television is increasingly important, we don't even try to brief or prepare our people who appear on the big programmes, such as 'Panorama' or 'Who Goes Home?'

I asked him, to take one example, whether the Campaign Committee had now come to the conclusion, as I had, that the Don't Knows could only be won for Labour by concentrating on simple bread-and-butter home issues. He said he agreed entirely. I said, 'I don't mean you, but is there a firm decision that the Party strategy should be based on that assumption?' Of course the answer is that there isn't, partly because the Campaign Committee is dominated by people like Barbara Castle, Ian Mikardo and Nye Bevan, who don't believe in a strategy of that kind and who have driven Morgan Phillips so wild that he has now decided to leave Transport House and take to politics. Personally, I don't blame him. But I equally don't blame all the other people in Transport House who have been leaving it to get away from Morgan Phillips! Altogether the whole internal situation of the Labour oligarchy could hardly be more decrepit. The Parliamentary Party is rusty, idle and disconsolate. Transport House is a machine which is gummed up and the whole structure of constituency parties is only barely alive.

Today Hugh made one observation to me which he had got from Mark Abrams. One of our long-term problems, he said, is that the kind of emotions and behaviours which held the Party together in the past were all based on class. Yet, since the war, progress has all been such as to weaken these senses of class loyalty upon which the Labour Party is based. More and more the younger people don't feel class-conscious in that sense of the word, and they are actually repelled by what they feel to be the fusty, old-fashioned, working-class attitudes of the people who run the Labour Party. How can one meet the demands of these young people without seeming to betray all the ideals of the old people? I told Hugh I thought all this tremendously true but irrelevant to the job we had ahead of us, which was quite simply to get people to feel that with a fighting spirit they can win the Election.

Hugh couldn't have been more pleasant with me or more grateful for help. But of course I am as aware as he is that all the people who came across to us (we were in the Visitors' Dining Room) or eyed us from the doorway would be running round saying that Hugh was being nobbled by Dick. I must add that Hugh will denobble himself in the course of the evening in order to keep the peace and that therefore I can't expect very much out of the conversation.

My own feeling at this moment, for what it is worth, is that in a summer Election the Tories would get in with a somewhat reduced majority. The best thing for us would be if they got back with a majority of ten, so that we really were on the edge of victory and were forced to fight. I think this is not impossible, but neither do I exclude the possibility that they could get in with a majority of thirty or forty. Last thing: there is the possibility that we might win by a small majority. In this case we should have a Government which could only carry out one reform, and that would be National Superannuation. Would I have time to get it through before the Government broke up? I very much doubt it. What I can say now with some certainty is that, if a Labour Government comes, I shall be in charge of the Pensions Bill and it will be the only Bill we have ready to get on with straightaway. But what seems to me more likely is another Tory Government—this time much weaker, which might be no bad thing.

Wednesday, March 25th

Last week I happened to have lunch with Nye, as well as having a long chat with Hugh. Both were illuminating but rather depressing. I talked to Hugh at length about the whole strategy and tactics of the Party and the lamentable way in which we were being outmanoeuvred almost every day. He listened extremely sympathetically, as always, grasped what one was saying with great precision and has asked me after Easter to concert some proposals with Tony Wedgwood Benn and the Chief Whip.

Then on Friday I had lunch alone with Nye. He said he was doubtful whether it was worse to win with a small or a very large majority and then voiced a long, long complaint about Gaitskell's lack of intuition and failures of leadership. The great leaders of the working class, he said, are all patricians by nature—Keir Hardie, Bob Smillie[1] and (but he didn't actually say it) himself. The worst of Gaitskell is that he isn't a patrician but a bourgeois. Nye had said this to me only half-seriously three years ago, leaning against my mantelpiece one evening. I was terribly depressed to hear it on Friday, as it meant really nothing.

[1] Robert Smillie (1857–1940), miners' leader and Labour M.P. for Morpeth June 1923–31. He was Chairman of the P.L.P. in 1924 and a member of its Executive Committee 1924–7.

On the whole, it's high time I went off on my holiday, as my mind goes round and round on this dreary party politics. I stick into this diary an article in today's *Daily Mail*[1] by Christopher Hollis, because it does actually sum up my own mood as well. I got back to London this morning to find that, in the one session of the National Insurance Bill Committee which I missed, the Minister had rushed them ahead, finished Clause 4 and got through another clause before I got there! This, I think, has broken the back of our resistance and, as I shall be away for the first two meetings after the Recess, I shall expect to see most of the Committee Stage over before I get back.

From March 26th to April 10th the Crossmans were in Israel, where Richard Crossman gave the three Weizmann Memorial Lectures. On their way back they spent two days in Athens, returning to Britain on April 12th.

Five days earlier, on April 7th, the Chancellor had presented his Budget. In July 1958 the credit squeeze had ended; now the Government were anxious to foster the expansion of the economy. Tax relief amounted to £360 million in a full year, of which two-thirds resulted in a reduction of 9d. on the standard rate of income tax and a 6d. reduction on each of the lower rates. Of the remaining relief, most came from cuts of one-sixth in each of the three higher purchase tax rates. Beer duty was lowered sufficiently to take 2d. off the price of a pint. Improvements were announced in the interest rates and regulations for the repayment of post-war credits.

There was to be a general restoration of investment allowances at a rate of 20 per cent for new plant and machinery, plus 10 per cent initial allowance, replacing the existing initial allowance of 30 per cent. For new industrial buildings a 10 per cent allowance plus 5 per cent initial allowance replaced the current initial allowance of 15 per cent. New mining works were to be supported with a 20 per cent allowance plus an additional 20 per cent initial allowance; for new agricultural and forestry buildings and works the allowance was to be 10 per cent.

Crossman read the Budget's main proposals in the Jerusalem Post *and admitted in his diary,*

My first reaction, I am afraid, was that I had saved about £100 on my new Humber Hawk by postponing delivery until after the Budget. In fact, as far as I can calculate, I shall also get nearly £200 in reduced income tax and there will be something on the farm, owing to the reintroduction of initial allowances. Of course, this sums up what was wrong, and immediately I saw it I felt a certain pang that I was in Israel, whereas I should have been in London, representing the old age pensioners.

[1] Headlined 'Why Are So Many M.P.s Giving Up For Good?', it analysed the reasons why some 113 Members of the current House of Commons did not intend to stand at the next Election. According to the article, 'The years of this Parliament have been doldrum years'.

Thursday, April 16th

The really striking fact about this Budget is that, for the first time for months, Macmillan has made a major psychological and political blunder, completely misjudging the mood and moral sense of the British people. That it was a blunder was confirmed by the violence of Quintin Hogg's speech in the Lords yesterday.[1] But the misjudgment on which it was based was, as usual, shared to a large extent by a large number of Labour M.P.s and members of the Shadow Cabinet. One has only to read the speeches made last Tuesday, where Labour Members were speaking off the cuff, before getting their directive, to see that they were enormously impressed by the Budget concessions and only just mentioned the old age pensioners, the sick and the unemployed.

Rather to my surprise, Harold Wilson, on the next day, got it exactly right at the beginning of his speech, making the excellent point that the prescription charges imposed on the old and chronically sick in a period of economic crisis have not been removed in this year of prosperity. He also rightly pointed to the fact that during last year £200 million of extra tax had been imposed on National Insurance contributors and £200 million remitted from wealthy taxpayers by the Budget. But even Harold talked too exclusively of old age pensioners and seemed insufficiently aware that the problem extended to the unemployed, the sick and the disabled, the submerged fifth of the community, who are on the edge of destitution.

Here at last was a simple, great big Socialist issue, which the British public not only could understand but obviously had understood instinctively in its revulsion from a selfish, egotistical Budget. Here was a vote of censure which should have been moved by our top brass, with the maximum of publicity, as a great occasion, but all that is going to happen is another dreary debate, inaugurated by soft little Marquand, with a drunken brawl at the end when I wind up, breathing into the post-prandial fumes of Tory diners.

Since I've returned, I've had two long, pleasant talks with Nye, in which he has been very anxious to listen to news about the Middle East and to talk about the receding chances of anything very positive being agreed at the Summit. I have also seen something of Harold Wilson and had one good talk with Hugh Gaitskell, who seemed very much aware of the electoral assets in our old age pensions policy. The Party is obviously greatly relieved at the Norfolk by-election victory,[2] relieved also, I fear, by the diminishing prospect of a May Election and altogether settling down once again to a complacent Westminster routine.

[1] In the debate on the economic situation.

[2] Caused by the death in a motor accident on December 9th, 1958, of Sidney Dye (Labour). The by-election in Norfolk South-West was held on March 25th. A. V. Hilton (Labour) had a majority of 1,354 votes over Mrs Elaine Kellett (Conservative). Andrew Fountaine (Independent) received 785 votes and lost his deposit. The Labour proportion of the poll rose by 0·6 per cent, while the Conservative proportion fell by 3·26 per cent. Five days earlier, there was a by-election at Harrow East, caused by the resignation of Ian Harvey (Conservative). Commander Anthony Courtney held the seat for the Conservatives, with a majority of 2,220 over Merlyn Rees (Labour).

Wednesday, May 6th

The most interesting event since I last wrote has been the circumstances surrounding the imminent publication of *The Road to Brighton Pier*.[1] Sydney sent me his copy of the book and then, next day, Janet Newman[2] rang me and asked me to review it for the *Statesman*. This Monday I completed my review and was standing in the Central Lobby when Attlee turned up. 'I've just been reviewing a book about you,' I said. 'Ah yes, I know,' he replied. 'He says I hated Herbert. It's quite untrue. I pitied him and pity is a kind of affection. His trouble was vaulting ambition, which o'erleapt itself.' He turned to leave me and then he turned back: 'Of course, it's a pack of lies,' he said.

Next day I ran into Attlee's old P.P.S., Arthur Moyle, who was given an astonishing write-up by Hunter as a man who knew everything and reported everything to Clem, when all the rest of us know he was a half-wit. Fortunately I didn't say this to Arthur, who proceeded to tell me that Clem had recently announced, I think in a television show, his view that a Leader of the Party's first allegiance is to his P.P.S. and not to his Chief Whip! 'By the way,' said Arthur, 'I reassured Clem about you when he asked me yesterday. I told him you were certain to come down on his side.'

One little end to this story. Ever since a rebuke I administered to Kingsley in the *Mirror*[3] for publishing Paul Johnson's article, 'Shall We Help Mr Gaitskell?', Kingsley has cut me off and refused to speak to me. I ran into him at the Polish Embassy last night and he had some proofs in his hand. He was talking to Alma and Ellis Birk.[4] Alma turned to me and said, 'Kingsley says you've written the finest bit of vituperation he's ever published,' and, true enough, he was in danger – or shall we say in sight – of forgiving me my sins.

From all of which one may conclude that life ticks over. Since I last wrote, of course, the Prime Minister has announced that there will be no May

---

[1] The book, by Leslie Hunter, Lobby Correspondent of the *Daily Herald*, and published in London by Arthur Barker, described the events leading up to Attlee's resignation and, eventually, to the Labour Party's Brighton Conference in 1957. In the *Daily Mirror* on May 1st Crossman spoke of it as 'an "inside" story that paints a false picture'. Crossman's *New Statesman* review 'Et tu, Clem?' appeared on May 9th, 1959.

[2] Mrs Newman (formerly Janet Gates), was Crossman's secretary at the *New Statesman* and subsequently at the Ministry of Housing and Local Government, the Lord President's Office and the Department of Health and Social Security. She returned to the *New Statesman* with Crossman in July 1970.

[3] Published in the *New Statesman* on January 17th. Crossman had discussed the 'astonishing article' in the *Mirror* on January 23rd.

[4] Alma Birk led the Labour group on Finchley Borough Council in 1950 and 1955 and was Labour candidate for the Northwood division of Ruislip in 1950 and for Portsmouth West in 1951 and 1955. Formerly a prison visitor and lecturer, she was Associate Editor of *Nova* 1965–9 and served as Chairman of the Health Education Council 1969–72. In 1967 she became a life peer, holding office as Parliamentary Under-Secretary at the Department of the Environment 1974–6 and as Minister of State in that Department 1976–8. She was Minister of State at the Privy Council Office 1978–9. In 1939 she married Ellis Birk (*q.v.*), the lawyer of the *Mirror* Group.

Election, thereby confirming my published premonitions and my inmost convictions about him. I am pretty sure that the Tories would have won by a sharply reduced majority and that this will be confirmed in this week's local elections.[1]

Meanwhile, Hugh Gaitskell has on two occasions said to me that pensions is the only issue we've got and urged Brian [Abel-Smith] and me to provide detailed figures on our contributions and benefits, with which we can win votes. God, he's an electioneer, and it might easily boomerang, quite apart from the appalling prospect for the Minister of Pensions of being rigidly tied to a particular scheme which might prove to be unworkable.

Thursday, May 14th
Today I went to a most characteristic lunch in a private room at the Café Royal. Present: the two Hughs, Sydney and myself. I got there a few minutes late to find Hugh Gaitskell quaffing a Bloody Mary, while the other Hugh and Sydney were drinking their first huge champagne cocktail. At half-past one we sat down to caviar and vodka, followed by Scotch salmon and claret. H.G. left at half-past two. The ostensible reason for the lunch, which I only fixed up with Sydney yesterday, was a snap idea that the autumn campaigning season should be started by the second glossy, a great anti-Tory gimmick, timed to coincide with a television show on the same theme on September 15th.

Apparently the Campaign Committee met on Tuesday and, realizing that the odds on an autumn Election are now very strong, decided that something should be done in September to prepare for it. Hugh Gaitskell called me aside last night and said, 'I managed to persuade them to accept your idea, so I hope you'll be pleased,' as though Hugh Cudlipp, Sydney and I were just longing to write pamphlets and would be gratified by the fact that, despite their strong objections, Mr Bevan and Miss Bacon had finally agreed that we should be permitted to do the pamphlet if it didn't cost anything.

Apparently, at lunch, H.G. started by telling them that he had a hangover from too much champagne the night before. Oh dear, he behaved so revealingly! We had a long discussion about the state of affairs after the municipals. For the first time, I heard Hugh admit the possibility that it was quite probable we should lose the Election and that there would be a tremendous rumpus inside the Labour Party.

At this point Hugh Cudlipp said, 'You appreciate, of course, that the

---

[1] In the week of May 4th to 9th there were elections for some 430 urban district councils in England and Wales. The Conservatives won 12 of these from Labour. In rural district council elections, held in the same week, Labour made a net gain of 12 seats. In elections for the English and Welsh municipal boroughs, held on May 7th, the Conservatives made a net gain of 181 seats, virtually all at the Labour Party's expense. The Liberals gained 17 seats and Independents 25. Labour lost 233 seats altogether. On the same day polling took place in the London metropolitan boroughs, giving Labour control of 28 boroughs and the Conservatives the control of 9.

Mirror will be absolutely loyal to you right up to the final day of the Election campaign. But, if you lose, we shall turn right round. From that moment on we shall be all out for a genuine radical movement and we shall be tearing to pieces the old men and the old institutions which are holding us back.'

We began to discuss why the Party was disintegrating, why youth was disaffected, and so on and so on. Cudlipp asked whether we couldn't find a young man, say Tony Greenwood or Tony Wedgwood Benn, who could write three articles on what youth really wanted, to which Gaitskell replied, 'Well, I think I'm opening a new secondary school in Birmingham when I get back from Ghana, and I might do it myself.'

Then he put to Cudlipp what he has been putting to me. 'In Sweden,' he said 'the Socialists told me they won two Elections on pensions. But to win you have to be precise, with precise figures.' I interrupted to say that up till now we had attracted the old people by a hard offer of an improved pension but one of the most important elements of our appeal to the working population was that we hadn't promised 9*d*. for 4*d*.[1] but, on the contrary, had made a moral appeal to them to redistribute national wealth in favour of the aged. 'I think in terms of votes you can put aside your moral appeal,' Hugh Gaitskell said to me somewhat cavalierly, and he turned to Cudlipp: 'Now what do you, as an expert, think of the chances of making this the major Election issue?' Even Cudlipp looked a little embarrassed, and said, 'Of course it would suit the *Daily Herald* down to the ground, since most of their readers are over eighty. But I'm afraid we couldn't do it on the *Daily Mirror*.'

After Hugh Gaitskell had left, I'm sorry to say that the trio had a real go together on the wetness and, above all, on the complacency of our Leader, combined with the holy panic he is in about the Election.

I tell this story at some length because it sums up quite a lot of what has been happening in the last ten days. I saw Gaitskell a week ago, when he pressed me again to do this job. Again I pointed out, even if it did win votes, a so-called popular pensions policy would destroy the accumulated savings of the first ten years which had been an essential feature of our scheme, providing a barrier against inflation and a fund for investment. When Gaitskell swept all this aside, I asked whether we ought not to consult Harold Wilson. 'Wilson isn't an economist,' he said rather sharply and, when I looked surprised, he said, 'Talk to an economist like Jenkins or Crosland. You do like him, don't you?'

After some consideration, I asked Wilson to lunch and rehearsed this story to him verbatim. Even he winced a little. Of course he realizes that, if he were Chancellor in a Labour Government, he would need the pensions contributions for the first two or three years, with small benefits, precisely the kind of thing you don't win votes with. So Harold Wilson is a moralist from this point of view, though I rather suspect that, if he were Leader

[1] The promise of Lloyd George's Insurance Act of 1911.

and Hugh were Shadow Chancellor, their views of morality would be reversed.

Yesterday I talked to John Edwards, a singularly narrow, ambitious, Christian careerist, who had never sat on the backbench from 1945 to 1951. Suddenly he poured his heart out to me, sitting in the Smoking Room among the Tories. 'Under the Labour Government I was busy doing something constructive. Since '51 I've had nothing to do, so I've worked away in the Council of Europe and was elected Chairman this year, the first Englishman to get the job.' He was obviously, and not surprisingly, a little full of self-importance, when he added, 'But all I get is envy and hatred from my colleagues here, who expect you to sit here and do nothing, futilely, while everything falls to pieces. People who can't do anything stay here, doing nothing. But people who can do anything are driven to go out and are hated for it.' There's a great deal of truth in this.

Going into the lobby, I met Barbara and told her that last night I had Titmuss and Brian to dinner to work on pensions. 'So you still think we're going to win?' she said, and passed on brightly. Our Chairman, our leader for the year. Like the rest of them, she is already reinsuring against defeat by preparing a case for blaming Hugh Gaitskell and the Right. So, of course, is George Brown, who made a vaguely critical speech about nuclear weapons, which was printed only on the centre page of *The Times*.[1]

This brings me to my last incident. At the International Sub. this week I found a draft statement on strontium-90 and nuclear tests. I insisted on having it read carefully. Nye Bevan suggested it should be submitted to scientists before being put for approval to the Executive. I said I thought we should consider it ourselves and guilelessly suggested that the last paragraph should be made more precise, making it clear whether we were in favour of suspending or stopping tests. I did this because I knew that on the night before, in a television interview, Nye had talked emotionally of stopping all tests, whereas the Party policy, as held by Gaitskell, is merely for suspension.

Within three minutes there was a wonderful row between the two, each saying he couldn't possibly withdraw. I pointed out that if we issued another statement on the tests it would have to fall off the fence on one side or the other — hence their statesmanlike doubt whether the statement was desirable. At once Nye blithely suggested the whole thing should be referred back to our Committee. 'A certain degree of ambiguity', he said, 'is necessary in such cases.' Maybe, but ambiguity of this kind is precisely what the electorate suspects of the Labour Party and constitutes the main reason why it has little confidence in us.

---

[1] At Houghton-le-Spring, County Durham, on May 10th. Until Russian refusal to accept effective control and inspection arrangements had been overcome, he said, there was 'a real limit to the risks that can be taken with our security and defence arrangements'.

Friday, June 5th

At the Executive on Wednesday the issue of nuclear weapons came up once again from the International. In the interval, however, the T.U.C. had written to us, suggesting a meeting to discuss a memorandum from them. The fact is they have been pressured by Frank Cousins and there has also been the Aldermaston March, which this year occurred while we were in Israel. Yesterday, at dinner, Michael Foot told me something of what happened. On the last day, apparently, Frank Cousins joined in the march as a private individual and Reg Willis,[1] this year's Chairman of the T.U.C., was spotted in the crowd in Trafalgar Square in his black hat, pinstripe trousers and carrying his umbrella. Dragged up to speak, he said he hoped the T.U.C. would go twice as far next year and that twice as many trade unionists would take part in next year's march. He added that he had seen Frank Cousins in the crowd. For full measure he ended with an attack on the police for obstructing the demonstration.

It was obvious to anyone, therefore, that there was an underground movement of opinion, which would have to be dealt with. Yet, on Wednesday this week, David Ennals[2] hadn't put the T.U.C.'s letter into the business of the day. When we insisted on seeing it, and Ian Mikardo remarked that it would be a pity if we seemed to be dragging our feet, Hugh Gaitskell replied sharply that, as far as he knew, the T.U.C. was not proposing any change of policy. I replied that anybody who believed that we could have a meeting with the T.U.C. without modifying our policy was a bit unrealistic. At this meeting we learnt that the two issues they wanted to discuss were a more precise definition of our attitude to tests and also, to my surprise, the concept of a non-nuclear club, the very concept I had been urging as the one positive attitude which could unify the Movement.

That afternoon I had a long talk with Nye in the Smoking Room. He told me that he and Frank Cousins saw eye to eye on the matter. When I talked to him about the non-nuclear club, a subject on which Gaitskell is quite open-minded, Nye said it was diplomatically impossible and raised every kind of objection. 'Don't you think it would be a good idea,' I asked him as he went away, 'if some of us were to meet together and discuss things privately before the T.U.C. Conference?'[3] To which he heartily agreed.

By accident, yesterday I had Michael Foot to dinner and, since

[1] Reg Willis was a member of the T.U.C. General Council 1947–64 and Chairman of the T.U.C. 1958/59.

[2] Labour M.P. for Dover 1964–70 and for Norwich since February 1974. He was Secretary of the United Nations Association 1952–7 and Overseas Secretary of the Labour Party 1957–64. From 1966–7 he was Parliamentary Under-Secretary of State for the Army and from 1967–8 at the Home Office. He was Minister of State at the Department of Health and Social Security from 1968–70. From 1970–3 he was Campaign Director of the National Association for Mental Health. On Labour's return to office in 1974, he became Minister of State at the Foreign and Commonwealth Office 1974–6 and Secretary of State for Social Services 1976–9.

[3] To be held in Blackpool, from September 7th to 11th.

Kissinger[1] had rung up, I got him as well. George Wigg came to meet him at drinks beforehand. Michael arrived first and told me that never in his whole life had he felt more depressed about the Party. When I suggested we might recreate an informal group with Nye to discuss nuclear weapons, Michael told me he had no kind of relations with Nye. Only once this year had he seen him. He had been over to the farm just after Aldermaston. He had a pleasant afternoon but only because each side had carefully avoided discussing anything serious at all. In fact, Michael and Nye have had no political contact for over a year. When I asked Michael to come in with us, he said, 'People like you and Barbara and Tony Greenwood had better talk to Nye. I'm no good these days.'

As for Kissinger, who wrote that sensation-making book three years ago,[2] he turned out to be a rather fat, oily, pompous but nice American Jew and so traitorous and anti-American that he even put me in the shade in the horrible things he said about his own country. There was no point, however extreme, in our diagnosis with which he did not agree, whether it was the futility of the nuclear obsession or the stupidity from the British point of view of British nuclear weapons, or the reckless irresponsibility of the Baghdad Pact and the American guarantee of Iran. The only point where he disagreed strongly was on what would happen in America if there were a Munich over Berlin. I had assumed the Americans would take it and try to pretend to themselves that it was really a successful compromise. Kissinger asserted that the Americans are a young, virile people with a tradition of brutality and violence and that a Munich would be followed in two years by an American preventive war.

When I put this to Galbraith[3] at lunch today, he said, 'A brilliant fellow but no judgment. Wrong on everything. Always hysterical. One of that score of eminences who have established their reputation on sensational defeatism. Thank heavens they are all going out of fashion — Nitze,[4] Bowie,[5] Dean Acheson and the rest of them.'

[1] Henry Kissinger. Director of the International Seminar at the University of Harvard 1951–71 and of the Harvard Defense Studies Program 1958–71, he was Assistant to the U.S. President for National Security Affairs 1969–73 and Secretary of State 1973–7. In 1977 he became University Professor of Diplomacy at Georgetown University. His memoirs, *White House Years*, were published in 1979 (Boston: Little, Brown).

[2] *Nuclear Weapons and Foreign Policy* (Council on Foreign Relations) was published in New York by Harper & Row in 1957.

[3] John Kenneth Galbraith, a Professor of Economics at Harvard University 1949–75 and U.S. Ambassador to India 1961–3. His works include *The Great Crash* (Boston: Houghton Mifflin, 1955), *The Affluent Society* (Boston: Houghton Mifflin, 1958) and *The Age of Uncertainty* (London: B.B.C. and Deutsch, 1977).

[4] Paul Nitze. He worked for Dillon, Reed & Co., the investment bankers, 1929–37, serving subsequently as Special Counsel to the War Department 1941–4, Director of the U.S. Strategic Bombing Survey 1944–6, Director of Policy Planning at the Department of State 1950-3, Assistant Secretary of Defense 1961–3 and Secretary of the Navy 1963–7. He was a member of the U.S. delegation at the talks on strategic arms limitation 1969–74.

[5] Robert Bowie, Special Assistant to the Military Governor for Germany 1945–6, Counsel and Special Adviser to the U.S. High Commissioner for Germany 1950–1, Assistant Secretary of State for Policy Planning 1955–7, Counsellor to the State Department 1966–8 and Professor of International Relations at the University of Harvard since 1957.

Galbraith gave me a most interesting description of the new emerging leadership in the Democratic Party. I learnt for the first time that he is the chairman of the Home Policy Committee and one of the top four or five in the Democratic leadership.[1] How subtly success changes a man! When we last spent an evening with him, he was a wonderful, brilliant, potato-in-his-mouth intellectual. Now here he was at Hamish Hamilton's table, a success, a bestseller in every country in the world, telling very long but quite funny stories about life in Russia or Yugoslavia or Poland. But he is still enormously nice and I agree with him, as I happened to be writing this morning before I saw him, that there is an astonishing undertow of change moving American public opinion away from Dulles and Eisenhower. Of course it is this movement in America which makes Hugh Gaitskell's so-called pro-Americanism so strangely out of date.

Wednesday, June 10th
On Friday night I had Abba Eban[2] and Guy Mollet to dinner. Abba, who is now head of the Weizmann Institute, had rung up saying he was in London and had virtually asked himself. Guy Mollet came, I thought, because Morgan Phillips could find no one more important to give him dinner even if the Labour Party paid for it.

Mollet told two good stories about his visit to Russia. At the dinner given in the Kremlin for the French Socialists, Bulganin was speaking and, before he had finished, Khrushchev interrupted and launched into a forty-minute diatribe, much along the lines of his attack on the Labour Party in London. When he had finished, Mollet got up and read aloud his own, very boring, formal reply. Then he stopped and said, 'Now, after the formal speech, I will talk like Khrushchev,' and made a ferocious counter-attack. At the end he said, 'I will now sit down and let Mr Bulganin conclude his speech.'

To begin with, Khrushchev was furious but finally he roared with laughter, put his·arms round Mollet, embraced him and said, 'You're quite a man.' As a result, Mollet was invited to another get-together in the sanctum in the Kremlin. When he came in, he was sat down in a chair and suddenly he saw Khrushchev and Mikoyan sniggering together. The snigger became a broad laugh and eventually Mollet asked why, to which he received the reply, 'My dear man, we suddenly remembered you are sitting in the chair where Beria sat when we shot him.'

Of course my main interest was to discuss the Suez fiasco with Mollet and

[1] Galbraith was at this time chairman of the Committee on Domestic Policy of the Democratic Advisory Council, one of the two main adjuncts (the other was a committee on foreign policy) of the Democratic National Committee. It provided a forum for influential, senior members of the Democratic Party who were not currently holding public office.
[2] Israeli representative at the United Nations in 1948 and 1949–51 and Ambassador to the U.S.A. 1950–9. He was Minister without Portfolio 1959–60, Minister of Education and Culture 1960–3, Deputy Prime Minister 1963–6 and Minister of Foreign Affairs 1966–74. His writings include *An Autobiography* (London: Weidenfeld & Nicolson, 1978).

Eban. On this, Mollet made the following points. First he said, 'I am not prepared to discuss this yet but I can tell you one thing. When the history comes to be written, the man who really double-crossed us was Dulles. It was really generous of people like Selwyn Lloyd and myself to talk of him as we did in his obituaries.' Mollet was particularly incensed about Dulles's double-cross in first backing the idea that the Users' Association should force the Canal and then in climbing down. Mollet also virtually said that Dulles had given the green light for the Suez campaign and then retired to hospital. Secondly, I asked Mollet whether it would not have been better to let the Israelis carry on without any Anglo-French intervention. He replied, 'But their whole campaign was quite impossible without it.' This was strongly applauded by Eban. Mollet said, 'They couldn't have moved without us.'

At this point Mollet made it very clear that the Israeli move and the Suez intervention were a French plan, to which Eden had acceded. 'Once I had brought him round,' he said, 'Eden was absolutely reliable, trustworthy and honourable. He was a splendid comrade. It was the high peak of both our lives, if only we hadn't been let down.' 'But wasn't Eden ill?' I asked. 'Very ill indeed. That's why he allowed it to be stopped when, in another eighteen hours, we would have finished the job and occupied the whole Canal Zone.' 'How, finish the job?' I asked. 'You would then have had to occupy the whole of Egypt.' Mollet answered, very sharply, 'On the contrary, one thing we had completely agreed was that the moment Nasser fell we were going to withdraw. There was no question of our remaining in Egypt or even in the Canal Zone for more than a matter of days.' I asked, 'Did we really then have plans for a Government to replace Nasser?' There was no clear answer, but a suggestion of yes.

On the question of the Gaza Strip, Mollet and Eban, who had been together in Washington on this, were very bitter that Hammarskjöld had permitted the Egyptians to take over the civil administration once again when the Israelis withdrew. They thought he was strongly and unfairly biased against them.

We drove them both to their hotels, leaving Mollet first at the Strand Palace. 'I have never heard him talk so freely,' said Abba, as we took him away. Actually Mollet hadn't said much. He is a much stronger and more forceful character than I had expected but he is a most unpleasant man as well and I didn't feel he had anything whatsoever to do with any Socialist ideas I have ever had. In fact, he is a schoolmaster who worked in the Resistance, joined de Gaulle and still believes in him.

Meanwhile we have been moving a little on Labour's attitude to nuclear weapons. My *Mirror* piece[1] yesterday was based on the T.U.C. memorandum, which we were due to discuss that afternoon in the International Sub. I didn't succeed, before I wrote it, in testing whether either Gaitskell or Bevan could be brought round to positively supporting the non-nuclear club, but it

[1] 'Labour Can Avoid Split'.

seemed quite obviously the only thing. Sure enough, yesterday afternoon Nye, from the chair, made a long, extremely good speech, developing the idea as though he had just thought of it.

He pointed out that we were likely in the near future to see an agreement on nuclear tests. The next step must be an agreement to stop production. There should be a conference on this, which would almost certainly fail for the time being and at this point there would be an acute danger that any chance of world disarmament would be destroyed by the French developing a nuclear weapon, followed rapidly by the Germans and the Chinese. Was there anything Britain could do to prevent the bomb spreading in this way? If there were a Labour Government, it should summon a conference in London of all non-nuclear powers interested in producing nuclear weapons and there raise the issue of the non-nuclear club. We should point out, that, to be effective, it must be all-embracing, and there must be inspection, and that there could be no question of Britain's abandoning production and destroying her stocks unless this were achieved.

On the other hand, it must also be made clear that we were going to stand by our previous principles and do nothing to destroy our alliances. For this reason our decision to join a non-nuclear club and stop production would not mean that we or the other non-nuclear allies of America would insist on the withdrawal of American bases. It would mean that America would be the main producer of nuclear weapons for the Western alliance. But — and at this point Nye became to me for the first time unconvincing — this would not mean a division of labour with America or, even worse, the suggestion that we were sheltering under the American nuclear umbrella. That impression must at all costs be eliminated from anything we said.

Gaitskell followed with a long, rather pedantic speech, the main point being that we should not seem to be departing from our principles. The statement we should make should be very long, should include Berlin and should spell out in considerable detail the precise conditions for membership of the non-nuclear club. By the time Gaitskell had finished, as I pointed out, he had succeeded in tying Nye's hands quite effectively before he entered the conference and, incidentally, in making the non-nuclear club sound extraordinarily unattractive. However, it was clear that everybody agreed with this, with the one exception of Tom Driberg, who said that he personally stood for unilateral disarmament. So we are to go ahead and try to get agreement on this with the T.U.C., as quickly as possible.

I have spent the last two days on the Report and Third Reading on the National Insurance Bill. Hilary Marquand has insisted on being our parliamentary leader on this issue, and why should I dissuade him? I arrived at half-past three on Monday for the Report Stage, having noted that we had had no meeting of the steering committee or of Hilary, myself and the Chief Whip, or of anyone, to plan our strategy, decide our timetable, or even to discover which of our Amendments would be called. It was the most amateur performance I have ever seen. Moreover, virtually nobody had turned up to speak. I soon decided that our policy should be summed up in the slogan 'Plenty of votes and few speeches on the Report Stage; lots of speeches and only one vote on the Third Reading'. This formula proved a delirious success. The Party, which had been expecting a late night, was sent home at five past ten, with six divisions added to its record, and I was solemnly thanked by the Whips for what is apparently a record achievement in helping them — or, should we say, helping the Government?

After that we had our Third Reading yesterday. I went downstairs to talk about nuclear weapons at the International Sub. while Miss Pitt and Marquand performed to an empty House. This was the fourth pensions debate in six months. I had perhaps 150 Labour people and 100 Conservatives to hear me and made an excellent speech. But I was bombinating *in vacuo*, since it just wasn't a parliamentary occasion. There was no sense of tension and, most important, our only frontbenchers present for my reply were Jim Griffiths and Frank Soskice. This illustrates exactly what is wrong with our parliamentary leadership.[1]

Thursday, June 18th

The famous meeting of the International Sub. began this morning. It was deeply depressing. We started with a not unsensible general discussion on the situation, in which Sam Watson, from the chair, suddenly intervened that we were discussing a thoroughly defeatist document and that he hoped a Labour Foreign Secretary would never regard himself as bound by anything which a T.U.C. or Labour Party Conference might say. There was then the usual to-do.

At this meeting we stuck on nuclear tests. The draft referred to the truce now existing, the terrible damage to future babies and so on, but this passage concluded with no recommendation. Innocently, I pointed out that we should surely put in one sentence saying a Labour Government, even if other powers broke the truce, would continue it, as an example. Gaitskell snapped back, 'We're not bound to that. That wasn't what we agreed a year ago.'

After that we wasted one hour, during the course of which I proposed seven draft sentences. My seventh ran: 'For this reason the Labour Government, even if other powers broke the truce, would refrain from tests, as its contribution towards the achievement of an international agreement.' Gaitskell said he couldn't accept this unless the word 'suspend' was introduced instead of 'refrain'. Suspension was Party policy. He knows, of course, that Nye had said 'stop', and he must have known I had used the word 'refrain' in order to square both of them. But he was making no concessions.

Finally Nye blew up. 'My dear Hugh,' he said quietly, 'if you believe I am going to cross every *t* and dot every *i* of the drafts you write, you are sadly mistaken. I am just not going to.' After which he muttered to me *sotto voce*, 'Now you know how he broke up the Labour Government in 1951, digging

[1] The National Insurance Bill was given a Third Reading by 309 votes to 248.

his toes in for £11 million in a £3,000 million rearmament scheme.' I must say I heartily concurred. Gaitskell was insane. He needed to get the draft through, yet he argued on this point till half-past twelve, when Nye said he had to go to lunch. Then when could we meet again? After twenty minutes we found the earliest moment possible is at two o'clock next Monday afternoon. We meet the T.U.C. at eleven o'clock on Tuesday morning. This means we shall give them no time beforehand and we have the whole risk of a leak over the weekend.

After the rest had gone, I stayed behind with Gaitskell and Sam and talked for twenty-five minutes. I put to him all my ideas about the second half of the paper. I pointed out that it was far too long and self-exculpatory and that the non-nuclear club proposal was spelt out at such length and with so many conditions that it was quite obviously something we were proposing because it was impossible. I suggested putting this as the most we could expect, pointing out that, at the other extreme, it might be possible to get an agreement of those producing, or nearly producing, nuclear weapons for a standstill of, say, two or three years, while a genuine effort was made for world disarmament.

First Hugh objected that this was technically impossible. 'Plowden told me yesterday', he said, 'that it's impossible to suspend nuclear production without stopping it altogether.' However, I wore him down and he finally said, 'You and David [Ennals] draft something.' 'I can't draft,' I said, 'I've no copy of the document.' He would have given me one but I wasn't having any and shall spend some time tomorrow in Transport House. What on earth we shall do on Monday, God only knows, since the second half is really in a lamentable state and needs drastic revision, and there's no time for it. Maybe David and I will do a complete redraft tomorrow, hoping that, as nobody has a copy, nobody will notice!

Sydney came to lunch today. I said the interesting thing is that for twenty years everybody had known Eden would fail as Premier. 'The same is true of Gaitskell,' Sydney said. 'If you got to power, you would have to ditch him within a year.' This is a remarkable confession from someone who was one of the main promoters of Gaitskell against both Hugh Cudlipp and myself. Hugh certainly isn't very good at keeping friends or influencing people, except against him.

Monday, June 22nd
In the intervals of writing a radio talk, I dictated a redraft of the second half of the Party statement on the H-bomb. I saw Gaitskell again on Thursday evening and he suggested that I should work with David Ennals on Friday morning. I told him the main idea I had was to loosen up the paragraphs on the nuclear bomb and to drastically shorten the document, cutting out its ruffled sense of apologia. He didn't seem very enthusiastic but that was that.

That evening I got hold of Nye, who sat with me in the Smoking Room and talked. First of all he said, 'Can I talk really freely to you? Sometimes, when I've talked to you in the past, things have got back to Gaitskell.' I said, 'You can say whatever you like,' and he began: 'That man is totally impossible – utterly, hopelessly impossible. You saw it yourself at the International. He's not the only person who can draft. I can draft, too, but it's not our job to draft and he kills himself with niggling away at the details and clinging to his own phrases. There's one particular thing I'm worried about – his continual emphasis that we don't abandon the use of the bomb. I've told him this is a detestable way of putting it, which I object to. I got it removed from the text but it's still there in one place. As you work it over, get rid of it. He's mad about it.' I then explained to Nye my idea for loosening up and, as Jennie took him away for his weekend in Paris, he concluded: 'All right, boy, I'll back you. That's a deal.' I'm not at all sure that he knew what he was backing, but we'll see today.

On Friday, when I'd finished my piece in a great rush I took it round to Transport House, where work had not been rendered easier by security requirements, which forbade us to have copies of the draft at home. (I was working on one provided by David Ennals.) I worked away with him quite happily, getting a finished document. At a quarter past four Hugh Gaitskell came in – as I now know, flushed from lunching with Woodrow Wyatt, who produced a not very helpful article in *Reynolds* as a result. We worked down in Morgan's room. I was due to catch the ten past six train to Banbury.

After Hugh had read my draft through, he said, 'Yes, that's pretty good and, apart from details, I buy it.' We then began to work through it and the first part was pretty acceptable to him, with minor changes. Then suddenly he said, 'You've left out all the passages I put most emphasis on. Anyway, I told you to confine yourself to redrafting and not to make any policy changes.' 'In that case,' I said, 'you will have to rely on your paid officials. I'm not here for that kind of job. I told you that if I set to work I would make some pretty radical changes, both in the length, the emphasis and also in the policy with regard to the non-nuclear club.'

From this point we had a terrible row. At twenty to six a message came in from Rose that I should catch my train, so I rose to go. But David Ennals made his sole remark in the three hours: 'But you've already done so much good to the draft. Can't we finish the job?' Hugh was now spending his time spatchcocking in whole paragraphs of the previous drafts and he kept on ejaculating, 'I've got to be frank, I've got to be honest. That's why you've got to put in that passage. This is something I've said and anyway they'll attack us for it.' I'm still wondering whether this was the flush of Woodrow's wine or sheer overwrought neurosis, but he was in fact in a terrible state of alarm, feeling he was going to be accused of ratting, and rightly so, feeling he must cover this up by insisting on his phrases.

After a long period of work, I finally lifted my head and said, 'It's no good,

Hugh. You're now putting everything back where it was before and it's a waste of time. Why can't you realize you are the worst person of all to draft this document because you are so deeply and personally engaged? I can do this far better, not only because I am a better drafter but because I am less engaged. Why can't you let your friends help you? You should never have touched this draft but should have come in, as a Leader, at a critical point in the discussion. I am no good to you unless I can talk to you like this.' I read him a long lecture, to which he immediately replied that of course I had the right to talk to him in this way but didn't I see that he had to make sure that we emphasized again and again the sacrifice involved in giving up the British H-bomb, because he had been its chief protagonist for seven years?

I think what had really angered him was that I said at the beginning that I had had a talk to Nye and he had told me his objection to the word 'use'. 'But he agreed a draft. He has no right to go back on his word,' Gaitskell shouted angrily. 'Anyway, we must be prepared to use the bomb. Yes, we must use it, use it! Otherwise we are abandoning our whole position.' Never have I met a more terrible example of the 'nuclear obsession'. He's just like a pacifist in his inability to see nothing but nuclear bombs. I tried to get him to see that, if we were dealing at all with this question of use, we must have some reference to the need to balance our strategy by greater emphasis on conventional weapons. That he would have nothing to do with. 'Not relevant,' he said, to which I replied, 'Well, in that case we should leave out all strategy and deal only with politics.'

In the course of our three hours, for it lasted until a quarter past seven, a message came in that George Brown was waiting at home and would come straightaway to help, if required. Brown had told me the day before that he was going to see Gaitskell in the afternoon and look at my draft. I had taken the precaution of telling this to three people, as of course Gaitskell has no right to show Brown the draft, and I had also telephoned David Ennals, telling him to tell Gaitskell that, if the draft were submitted to Brown, I would report the fact to the Executive. Ennals said he couldn't do this but I have a shrewd guess he did, because Brown wasn't consulted. I checked this morning that it is our draft, finally botched together at a quarter past seven, which is to be circulated today. Of course it's a frightful mess now, with Gaitskell's insertions, and, since this may give quite an interesting elucidation of Gaitskell's mind, I put all this in the diary for the record.

Tuesday, June 23rd

Every paper this morning has had a very competent survey of the main policy points in our document. Assuming there had been a press release, I rang up Sydney, who said there hadn't. 'There were no leaks from the Committee,' he said, 'and the lobby had a hard job building a story from secondary sources.' So much for the decision that we should never have a copy of our document except actually in the Committee, a decision which prevented anyone except me from doing any serious work between the meetings.

It was a hot, stenchy day and when I had walked across the Park, up St Martin's Lane and through Seven Dials to Bloomsbury, I was sweating, all the more so when pushed info a small waiting room, where we were all massed, hurriedly scanning our document for the first time since yesterday. The poor T.U.C. had only been given it at ten o'clock this morning – ten pages of it – but at a quarter past eleven we were duly ushered in. [Reg] Willis, who is running the big printers' strike[1] at the moment, had on his right Tewson, Webber and Birch of USDAW. On his left were Tom O'Brien, Frank Cousins and Hayday[2] of the Municipal and General Workers.

Nye started with a long harangue, which was quite good, but Willis immediately replied by saying that he couldn't see what sacrifice there was in the non-nuclear club, since we would be protected by America. Then, having shown himself hostile to the document, he suggested questions and discussion. After this there was a long silence, as the rest of the T.U.C. waited for Cousins and Cousins waited for them.

At last Cousins said he appreciated Nye's aim of unifying the Movement but this document would divide and demoralize it. In particular, he had three questions. First, if we meant stopping tests, why not say so? He had heard rumours of a row about 'suspend' or 'stop'. Why this phrase 'refrain from resuming'? Secondly, why not say frankly we shall never use these terrible weapons first? Thirdly, why pretend that a non-nuclear club was anything but a tricky manoeuvre, when any fool would see that China would anyway refuse to join?

There followed a long, animated altercation between Nye and Cousins, until Nye, timing it nicely, burst out that trade unions have useful functions but were a poor place for making serious political decisions. He would rather get out than be told by the trade unions what to do in the Foreign Office. Anyway, the way union delegates voted at their conferences bore no relation to the way their members voted at the Elections. The history of our Movement was the story of unions striking revolutionary postures at Conferences and then failing to carry them out. Moreover, the fact was that we were just before an Election and, if Frank Cousins carried this division further, he would make defeat certain. 'I have led more controversies and rebellions than anyone else here, but whenever Elections approach I call for unity against the common foe.'

---

[1] At the beginning of June ten printing unions had struck over a claim for a 10 per cent wage increase and a forty-hour week. More than 100,000 workers in 4,000 printing firms and 1,000 provincial and London suburban newspapers were out for six and a half weeks. London daily newspapers continued publication but some of the leading weeklies were obliged to appear in emergency form. The strike lasted until July 30th.

[2] Frederick Hayday, National Industrial Officer of the N.U.G.M.W. 1946–71. He was a member of the General Council of the T.U.C. 1950–72 and its Chairman 1962–3, and was also Chairman of the T.U.C. International Committee. He was knighted in 1969.

Cousins replied that there had been a strong shift of opinion in the Movement and they must be given something to settle it with, something definite, clear-cut, moral. When challenged to say what it was, he said it was the answer to his three questions. Nye replied that the first two were mere questions of nomenclature, on which there was no serious controversy. This was pretty cool, since two years ago, when we met the T.U.C., Nye supported Cousins for an hour on Question 2 and, as for Question 1, I heard him and Hugh Gaitskell arguing ferociously on it for an hour last week!

After this, each member of the General Council in turn stated his support for the document, starting with Birch, then Webber, Tewson and Ernest Jones of the Miners,[1] whom I forgot to mention. Hayday made it clear that his union's so-called decision was not very firm and would never have taken place if our document had come out in time. Only O'Brien prevaricated. So Cousins was completely isolated. We filed out to leave them to deliberate on advice they would give their colleagues tomorrow. We left at ten minutes to one and at five minutes past they had finished their business.

I walked all the way back with Hugh and mentioned Cousins's attitude. 'Power,' said Hugh. 'Power is all he wants. It's as simple as that.' Of course it isn't as simple as that. However, I learnt the incredible – that no one had bothered to see Cousins during the last ten days, except for Barbara. We all agreed that she had given him the three questions to put on her behalf. I also said, with hindsight, 'We can now see. Once the spring Election was off, we were bound to require a new statement before Conference. So that dreadful paper we got from the T.U.C. was a merciful deliverance after all, since it spurred us to action.' Hugh Gaitskell testily disagreed and as he left us in Parliament Square David Ennals, who had come along with us, said, 'He'll never admit that. Indeed, he never admits anything and you are the only man I've ever seen get the better of him because you are the only person who goes on and on even more obstinately than he does.'

This afternoon Ennals and I went into Hugh Gaitskell's room at a quarter past four to tidy the draft. We found Nye there lolling in a chair and discovered that none of us had a copy, because they had all been locked up except the one Ennals had brought. 'Nothing but drafting points,' pleaded Hugh, but, perversely, Nye had just begun to read the document for the first time and hit on my paragraph suggesting, as a first stage, a provisional moratorium. I was horrified, since I knew that he was suddenly remembering telling Harold Davies last night that a provisional moratorium was utterly useless. The old mind began to work and we hurriedly began to introduce some 'possiblys' and 'ifs', staving off a major change illicitly introduced out of school. As I left, Hugh called out, 'And thanks for all your help.'

I dined with Nye, John Strachey, Ungoed-Thomas and Hugh Dalton

[1] Ernest Jones, a member of the T.U.C. General Council 1950–60 and President of the N.U.M. 1954–60. He was Chairman of the Southern Regional Board for Industry 1961–5 and a member of the Monopolies Commission 1959–69. He died in 1973.

before the Party Meeting at half-past seven. Suddenly, over dinner, we discovered that Dalton, mumbling about his memoirs, is now deaf and hardly articulate. Nye thought him drunk but he is only, quite suddenly, gaga.

Nye predicted that the Meeting wouldn't last an hour. Actually it lasted nearer two, in Room 14, for once packed. Nye began with over half an hour of real old-fashioned oration, spiced with gleams of his best humour and charged with plenty of emphatic emotion. In the afternoon Hugh Gaitskell had said that much would depend on who was called after Nye and he would do his best to call a damper. So I was amused when he called my Coventry neighbour Maurice Edelman, who made a long, quite able, moral abolitionist speech, arguing that nuclear weapons are wicked and one must fight in future only with conventional ones.

Maurice was answered by Peart, who rebuked us for surrendering too far to the Left. Denis Healey then made the only really good speech for the non-nuclear club, after which Mayhew followed Peart's line and was himself followed in much the same vein by Herbert Morrison, who had announced his resignation from Parliament yesterday. Harold Davies clowned, Tony Wedgwood Benn wanted unilateral inspection of Britain, and then there were shouts of 'Time, time', so Hugh Gaitskell summed up much as usual.

Of course M.P.s always know better. On this occasion they were irritated that the N.E.C. had already decided and also by the appearance of surrender to the Municipal and General Workers. So they came in ultra-suspicious mood, assuming that we were fixing a tactical deal. My guess is that they will be agreeably surprised because the document is, in fact, a good deal better than they rate it and the non-nuclear club, as Hugh pointed out, will be highly relevant after the French bomb explodes this summer. This meeting was useful in letting the M.P.s release all their frustrations and suspicions. The leadership, I hope, will seem better in retrospect. If leadership means reacting to opportunities for changing policy rather than creating them, this has been quite good leadership. To do nothing would have split the Movement. So would any surrender to abolitionists. We have seized the opportunity to introduce a new idea and, if that's not popular now, well, the Labour Party never does like a new idea at first.

Wednesday, June 24th
I had assumed that last Wednesday's Executive would be flat and a foregone conclusion and that we should get through the discussion of the document quickly. But no! Immediately we got there, someone moved that we should do all the other business first and take the document at the end. Crazy as we are, this was not agreed and we finally sat for twenty minutes while non-International members, spiritually headed by James Callaghan, read with patient indignation. He and Alice Bacon made it very clear that they thought it scandalous that the Executive should only have the chance to state a view after the decision had virtually been taken and when any substantial change

would involve our going back to the T.U.C., who were simultaneously meeting in their offices in Bloomsbury.

Our meeting and theirs in fact, had to be pure formalities, unless we were prepared for the sensation of either of us repudiating our own International Committee. But this didn't stop our having some three hours on it. I had underestimated the determination of some of my colleagues to go on the record. Of course, in this case, if the Executive had been confidential, the record would have been off the record and they could only have registered their protest in the strictest confidence. But each of them knew well that they would be on the record in both senses, in that their votes, too, would be known outside.

What happened, briefly, was that Tony Greenwood raised again precisely the three points Frank Cousins had raised at the meeting with the T.U.C. Stop tests, not suspend them; pledge ourselves not to use nuclear weapons first; anyway, the thing was futile because of China. He also proposed that the non-nuclear club could be made good by offering a unilateral two-year British moratorium as an encouragement to others to join it. In the course of the discussion Tony's only active supporters were Mikardo and Harry Nicholas, who moved one resolution on behalf of the T. & G. Greenwood was finally persuaded not to press his motion to a vote, on the ground that it would scarcely do much good to compel the Executive to vote against it! Alice Bacon, on the whole, represented those who disliked the policy as a concession to the Left, here allying herself closely with Sam Watson, who expressed silent indignation throughout the meeting.

By the end of the morning I had heard Nye's case pretty often and was pretty sick of it, but what struck me again was his great buoyancy and good humour and the way he was standing by Gaitskell, even on points where he could well have extorted a concession from his Leader. I suppose he realized he and Gaitskell must stand together, whatever happens, and take a simple, sensible position against Frank Cousins and the unilateralists.

I spent the rest of the day partly on the Front Bench dealing with the National Assistance Bill. As I was leaving the Commons, I ran into Nicky Kaldor, who motored me home and gossiped about the Party. He had been dining with the XYZ Club, where Hugh Gaitskell had been addressing them on the Party policy and telling them once again that pensions was our best thing. Kaldor's impression is that the Party has no kind of economic policy, mainly because, for the last year or so, Hugh Gaitskell has taken little interest in economics and Wilson has completely failed to lead and has retired into himself, losing even the support he had once gained from Patrick Gordon Walker and Roy Jenkins. Kaldor was utterly contemptuous of the politicians' attitude to his taxation proposals and had just the same impression as I had of Hugh Gaitskell's terrible inability to devolve work and avoid the scribbler's itch when he saw a draft.

Next evening I had Tony Crosland and Brian Abel-Smith to dinner, in fulfilment of a promise to Hugh Gaitskell that we would submit the finances of our pensions scheme to Crosland for approval. Crosland repeated a good deal of Kaldor's gossip verbatim – the absence of any economic policy, the obstinacy of the politicians about taxation, the vacuum of leadership created by Harold Wilson and by Hugh's retirement from the economic field. I found Crosland a good deal more pleasant and co-operative than usual but it was clear that he merely regarded our pensions scheme as a social service, that he didn't take the whole idea of saving and funding seriously and that for him – as, to be fair, for Brian too – contributions are merely a form of taxation and the fund is a myth. More interesting, Crosland repeated once or twice his doubt whether we needed a great deal of extra saving or capital investment, as Thomas Balogh had predicted that we would. He, too, surprisingly, repeated all Kaldor's criticisms of Gaitskell and ended by doubting whether we have a Chancellor of the Exchequer in Harold Wilson.

We had a lovely weekend at Prescote, with showers of rain to break the drought and save our grass. I've never enjoyed the farm more. What a subtly corrupting thing it is to marry into a farm! Slowly you start believing you have something to do with it!

Over the weekend it became clearer and clearer that at least the first round in this nuclear contest had gone to Hugh and Nye. The press had built up their leadership qualities, mostly involuntarily. I spoke to Hugh on Friday and again today on the phone and you can almost feel across the telephone wire – not that he is swollen (that would be unfair) – but that he has literally physically grown in stature and hasn't got to stretch to speak into it. He re-emphasized how genuinely Nye had made unnecessary concessions to his point of view and expressed a worry lest Nye should have been upset by the hecklers over the weekend. I gather he had a very rough meeting at Cardiff and he isn't good at tackling them.

For those who have seen the inside, it's clear that, in fact, Hugh has almost exactly repeated his Suez performance. His, and Nye's, first stand on the H-bomb was as chauvinist as their first stand at Suez. Then, as circumstances change and pressure grows, they have been forced, scandalously late but not too late for the public, into a much more reasonable position. In this case, however, it's fair to say that Nye was more reasonable in the first instance and that, from the inside, the new document is a concession on the big issue by Hugh to Nye and only on small issues by Nye to Hugh. Yet, from the public's point of view, Gaitskell comes out as the strong, resolute Leader. Most papers seem to believe he wrote the whole document himself.

The joint Labour Party–T.U.C. document was called Disarmament and Nuclear War: The Next Step. *It set out the case against unilateral action and proposed*

> *an agreement, preferably under the auspices of the United Nations, signed by*

every nation with the exception of the U.S.A. and the U.S.S.R. Under this agreement, each nation would pledge itself not to test, manufacture or possess nuclear weapons, and the agreement would be subject to full and effective international control to ensure that it was carried out. The Government should be prepared to announce now that, if such an agreement could be successfully negotiated, Great Britain would not only cease the manufacture of nuclear weapons but would also deprive herself of their possession.

What will happen next? Frank Cousins has certainly put himself out on a limb and is now being pressed by all the nuclear disarmers to stay out on it. Michael Foot came out in this week's *Tribune* for a fight to the death and for the campaign to go on throughout the Election. Silverman launched another attack, calling us all frauds and deceivers. All this is a bit odd, since the nuclear disarmers agreed a few weeks ago that the non-nuclear club was a first-rate idea, though not enough. But, as so often happens, anything which is accepted by the Establishment becomes unacceptable to the opposition inside the Labour Party.

Nevertheless I have no doubt that electorally we are gaining from this. There is a printing strike to make us unpopular and the picture of Bevan and Gaitskell fighting Frank Cousins is something really useful to counteract it. All this Gaitskell understands well and so does Nye. But we have to face it that something over 70 per cent of our active Party workers are probably against us on this issue and, if there weren't an Election, we might all lose our seats on the Executive in another sweep. The Gallup Poll last week showed only 15 per cent of the public in favour of unilateral repudiation. It is clear that the Movement, though intensifying its fervour and probably winning active adherents, is not gaining much ground in terms of votes or mass opinion. What it is doing is creating another fervent Left, half in, half out of the Labour Party, to replace Bevanism — and that, in a normal period, would be no bad thing.

Friday, July 3rd
I had Taper (Bernard Levin),[1] Tony Howard[2] of the *Manchester Guardian* and

---

[1] Bernard Levin joined the *Spectator* in January 1957, as their Political Correspondent, writing under the name Taper. Though he ceased to write their regular parliamentary column in 1960, he remained with the *Spectator* until 1962, when he moved to the *Daily Mail*, first as Drama Critic and then as a daily columnist. In 1971 he became a regular columnist for *The Times* and from 1976 he also wrote for the *Sunday Times*, as Drama Critic from 1976 to 1979 and from 1979 as Chief Fiction Reviewer. He has published two collections of articles, *The Pendulum Years* (London: Cape, 1970) and *Taking Sides* (London: Cape, 1979).

[2] Anthony Howard, a journalist, was Political Correspondent of *Reynolds News* 1958–9, a member of the editorial staff of the *Guardian* 1959–61, and Political Correspondent of the *New Statesman* 1961–4. He was Whitehall Correspondent of the *Sunday Times* 1965, Washington Correspondent of the *Observer* 1966–9 and returned to the *New Statesman* as Assistant Editor 1970–2 and as Editor 1972–8. In 1979 he became Editor of the *Listener*.

Sunday Pictorial and Michael Howard[1] to dinner last night and we were joined later by Wayland Young and his wife Elizabeth.[2] What did I learn? Bernard Levin, whom I had just met at the *Spectator* party, turned out, as might have been expected, to be as unlike Taper as Michael Foot's private self is unlike his public persona. He is not even untidily dressed — a neat little man with gold in his spectacles and a very slight accent, very careful of what he said and what he drank, reserved, but, when pressed, in no way concealing his views.

By far the most exciting part of the evening came at the end, when we began to discuss nuclear weapons and the Labour Party. Wayland Young's position is extremely similar to the kind of thing which George Wigg and I have been thinking about. But when we started discussing, he and his wife both expressed the most violent views about the hypocrisy of the Labour leadership in its new statement and asserted that there would be a tremendous blow-up when it was revealed that our new policy statement still permitted the British use of American nuclear weapons. I said this seemed to me absolutely clear from the statement. We were concerned to establish an organization to prevent the spread of manufacture and made it clear that this had not affected strategy or use for the time being.

At this point Tony Howard interjected that he also disliked the document but he had to admit, in his own words, that there was nothing to be found wrong with the document itself. What was wrong was the motives of the leaders in putting it forward, since everyone knew they didn't believe it. Wayland Young's point was that the leaders were deliberately deceiving the rank and file. I pointed out that Wayland Young's own position was, from the point of view of most people, identical with that of the Executive. What real difference was there between a plan under which the British did not manufacture their own weapons but used American weapons, and a plan under which the British did not manufacture or use them but had Americans in Britain to use them on our behalf?

On all this I found Taper and Michael Howard altogether on my side, with Anthony Howard and the Youngs representing very fairly the antagonisms felt for us in the leadership by a very large number of young left-wingers today. At one point I said rather angrily, 'The definition of the Left is a group of people who will never be happy unless they can convince themselves that they are about to be betrayed by their leaders.' Levin smiled, as though this was something new to him, but I must say the behaviour of the young people

[1] Lecturer in War Studies, University of London 1953–61, Professor 1963–8. In 1968 he became a Fellow of All Souls College, Oxford; he was Chichele Professor of the History of War 1977–80 and became Regius Professor of History 1980. His books include *The Franco-Prussian War* (London: Hart-Davis, 1961), *The Continental Commitment* and *War and The Liberal Conscience* (London: Temple Smith, 1972 and 1978).

[2] Wayland Young succeeded his father as the 2nd Baron Kennet in 1960. He was Parliamentary Secretary at the Ministry of Housing and Local Government 1966–70. An author, he was Director of Europe Plus Thirty for the European Commission 1974–5 and a Member of the European Parliament 1978–9. In 1948 he married Elizabeth Adams, who, as Elizabeth Young, has written on marine affairs and disarmament.

throughout the evening completely confirmed my views. What they objected to was not the policy statement, which they admitted was pretty good, but the leadership which had issued it and which was, in their view, suspect.

It looks as though, throughout a very large segment of the kind of keen, young, educated people who should be our most enthusiastic workers, there is a really deep malaise about the Party and the leadership, which is finding a convenient expression in this nuclear controversy. They used to think the non-nuclear club an excellent idea when it was put forward by Bertie Russell and Nehru. But the moment we adopt it, they feel it has been corrupted because they don't trust us. What they are looking for is an undefiled cause with undefiled leaders.

I must say that talk and all that has been happening in the last fortnight have left me extremely depressed. If we lose the Election, as we very well may, there will be a period of nauseating infighting on the Executive. I can see that Barbara, Ian, Tony Greenwood, Tom Driberg and Harold Wilson are all carefully preparing their positions to blame others for the defeat and to prove that they themselves were pure and undefiled. My trouble is that I have rather less confidence in them than I have in Gaitskell and Bevan. At least these two, on this issue, have faced it with intellectual honesty and have worked out what is pretty well the best policy they can. What is depressing is that they get no kind of credit for doing so from their closest colleagues or from the Left, although it is not denied that public opinion would sweep away any Labour Party which conceded the Left unilateralist position. But of course the nuclear controversy doesn't really interest the public, which is going to vote, as usual, on bread-and-butter issues.

My own feeling is that, outside in the country, the Labour Party is now doing rather better — we certainly are in Coventry — with slightly more organization, slightly more canvassing and much less backbiting than in 1955. For this reason I am pretty sure that there will be no great disaster in the Election, nor landslide, and there might well be a victory. But the more I reflect, the more I am convinced that this is the last normal Election of this kind, with the present two-party system, since, whatever comes after it, either a weak Labour Government or a Tory Government and a self-accusing Opposition, is going to accelerate the process of disintegration. And the more I look at the inside of the Labour Party, the less I can find any side I want to be on in the kind of dirty fighting which will ensue. So let's hope we win and I can do my little Pensions Bill quietly in the corner, because, if we don't, even our pension scheme will quietly fade out, as people get tired of it.

Tuesday, July 7th
Throughout the weekend I was brooding over the situation in the leadership and the threat of trouble from the Isle of Man,[1] where the Transport Workers

[1] The T.G.W.U. annual conference was held in Douglas, Isle of Man, in the week ending Saturday, July 11th.

are meeting this week. I have now had it confirmed that, before the famous meeting with the T.U.C., neither Gaitskell nor Bevan had any informal connection with any members of the T.U.C., including Frank Cousins. We simply presented an ultimatum and told them to accept it without any effort whatsoever to take the advice of some of the important ones or stroke their ruffled pride. Then, on the day after the meeting, Gaitskell and Bevan spent three hours on the Commons Terrace trying to soothe Frank Cousins down. This is the kind of conduct which makes one suicidal. Think how much wiser Hugh would have been to let Ennals and me do the drafting, while he did some contacts. Or think how Bevan went away to Paris that weekend instead of seeing Cousins, as he could have done.

Friday, July 17th
This, of course, was the weekend of the Cousins/Gaitskell row,[1] with Cousins on the telly on Friday and Gaitskell covering most of the front page of all the Sunday papers with his reply, delivered, as Dora told me, in a cold wind to about 100 people at Workington. There is no doubt that Gaitskell's speech was an immense success. Indeed, a telegram was sent to Hamburg from the Shadow Cabinet, congratulating him.

On Wednesday I was asked to appear on 'This Week' with George Brown, under Ludo Kennedy's[2] lead, to discuss the relations of the trade unions and the Labour Party. I found George Brown rather sullen but when he discovered that I wasn't there to savage him in public, he had supper with me and told me something fascinating. At an early stage of the drafting, George had taken a draft to Cousins with, inserted into it, a form of words to meet Cousins's requirements about our not using thermo-nuclear weapons first. George brought this back to Gaitskell and Gaitskell had turned it down flat, as the kind of concessions he didn't want to make. 'From the first, Hugh manoeuvred to isolate Cousins. He didn't want an agreement. I can tell you that. After all, on this issue I am not likely to offer Cousins compromises which are very extreme. I warned Cousins he was going out on a limb and Hugh would lick him but he wouldn't listen. Hugh has certainly won. But will it pay him in the long run, if he loses the Election? I think he's started something, something very serious indeed, with Cousins leading a new Left.'

George and I agreed that Nye has been quite soft and ineffective throughout the crisis. We also agreed that he had done nothing to put Cousins's points to Hugh and that during this crisis Nye could quite easily have overthrown

[1] On July 7th Frank Cousins delivered a speech attacking the Labour leadership for departing from traditional doctrines of public ownership. On July 9th he condemned the Labour Party–T.U.C. policy document on *Disarmament and Nuclear War*, securing an overwhelming majority for a policy of unilateral cessation of the testing and production of nuclear weapons.

[2] Ludovic Kennedy, the writer and broadcaster of current affairs programmes. He contested Rochdale for the Liberal Party at the 1958 by-election and in 1959.

Hugh by insisting on having his way on the two points Cousins wanted. 'But he hasn't the strength left,' said George.

One other little episode. I met Callaghan in the lobby this week and he said, 'You hit Frank Cousins very hard in your column.[1] I'll give you credit for courage, Dick. It's something you've never lacked.' 'Why courage?' I asked. 'Well, it's certainly risking your long-term prospects to antagonize someone like that.' This conversation explains a lot about my top-level colleagues. It is not an accident that, of the seven constituency members, four — Barbara, Tom, Tony Greenwood and Ian Mikardo — all voted against the official line. Of the others, Harold Wilson has been discreet, Jim Callaghan talked as he did, I am the remainder. If I were seriously concerned to remain a constituency member of the Executive, I should certainly be advised to trim my language. So much for the idea of free speech on the Executive.

Thursday, August 13th

A whole month without diary, and why? Partly, no doubt, because Rose insisted on taking a week off in the summer, in fact, the last week of Parliament. True, there was no prospect of her having any summer holiday without it but, in my view, when the Crossmans are preparing to have an August baby, everybody else falls into line! But there was a profounder reason, I suspect, for not writing and that was sheer lack of interest.

I spent the first part of the Recess struggling with Party propaganda. The printers' strike came to an end before the Bank Holiday. At a party on the Thursday, Hugh Cudlipp said to me, 'I've got good news for you. You and Sydney will have to finish the text by next Thursday.' As the baby kept us in London, this was not, in one sense, too disastrous but it did mean slaving away over Monday and Tuesday of Bank Holiday, in perfect summer weather. We finished on Thursday morning. Simultaneously I've had to do nearly all the work on our new popular pamphlet on pensions, which should be going to press this week. I felt rather self-righteous and rather injured at having to do all this, though of course the proper answer is that you don't have to do it at all if you don't want to!

Last week I went out to lunch with Hugh Gaitskell and Tony Crosland, whom he had instructed to carry out a new analysis of our pensions scheme. Hugh turned to the draft of the popular pamphlet[2] and complained that there was too much about poverty and prosperity and that we couldn't concede so much about Tory prosperity. I said you couldn't make the moral point except by stressing that poverty was amid plenty, to which he said once again, 'I shouldn't worry about morals if I were you. What people want to hear is how little they will pay and how much they will get from our scheme.' I came back

---

[1] On July 10th and 14th. As a result of the second article Frank Cousins wrote Crossman a letter complaining of misrepresentation; Crossman replied on July 16th.

[2] *Members of One Another*, published on August 25th.

profoundly depressed and finally decided to ask Hugh to come to a drink. This occurred yesterday.

He came in a bit late because, as he told me quite frankly, he had been lunching until four o'clock with the London editors. He sat from six o'clock till a quarter to eight, drinking Anne's father's best whisky. One tiny thing tickled me. We were discussing Harold Wilson and he said something about Harold's liking the drink rather too much. But later, having had two very large whiskies, Hugh said, 'Do give me another whisky, old boy.' Three double whiskies, after having lunch till four o'clock, is quite a lot. This was all the more striking since I know Harold far better than Hugh does and though Harold quite likes a drink he is nothing like the drinker Hugh himself is. While I'm on the subject, I did say to Hugh that I was sick of all the anti-Harold talk by Tony, Roy, Nicky Kaldor and Patrick Gordon Walker. 'It's really an academic matter,' Hugh replied. 'They don't trust his intellectual integrity. They think all his judgments are political.' This again was a little unselfconscious from a man whose judgments on pensions I had been listening to and I had to remind him that, on my pensions plan, Harold had shown absolute integrity and no interest in votes – no doubt because he is going to be Chancellor of the Exchequer.

I told Hugh of my intention, if we lost the Election, of resigning from the Executive and writing a serious book. What was really interesting was that, in replying, he didn't repudiate the likelihood of our losing. Indeed, we discussed it with an extraordinary quietness and objectivity. 'If we lose by a little,' he said, 'I don't see how you could possibly get out. If the Tories increased their majority, it would only prove that we were even more out of touch with the electorate than you and I now think we are and that our renovation of the Party hasn't gone fast or far enough. In that case I should want you there. Frankly, apart from Harold, there's no one else on the Executive but you to do the work.'

Then Hugh turned to the Cabinet and said that he could just about fill it, but only just. There are quite a number of people like George Strauss who can be given a place safely, but men of outstanding ability are desperately short. This was the first occasion on which Hugh had quite clearly implied that he regarded me as a man of outstanding ability and of the inner circle. He finally said he would like me to stay on the Executive *and* write the book but, when I asked about the trade unions, Hugh at once agreed that this was impossible. 'Your writing of the last three years', he said, 'has proved that you can do both.' I replied, 'For a time, yes. But then, my writing for the last three years has been extremely safe and careful and limited and I doubt whether papers will take it for ever.' Again he didn't dissent.

Hugh is getting really fond of Aneurin, whose loyalty and basic integrity he stresses, in sharp contrast with Harold. Of Roy Jenkins, he said, 'He is very much in the social swim these days and I am sometimes anxious about him and young Tony. We, as middle-class Socialists, have got to have a profound humility. Though it's a funny way of putting it, we've got to know that we lead them because they can't do it without us, with our abilities, and yet we must feel humble to working people. Now that's all right for us in the upper middle class, but Tony and Roy are not upper and I sometimes feel they don't have a proper humility to ordinary working people.'

The whole talk was that of a man who is rather rapidly growing up, growing tougher and growing stronger. We talked about George Brown's efforts to mediate between him and Cousins. He didn't deny it and made it quite clear that he is determined to smash Cousins and that he has accepted the Municipal and General Workers reversing themselves, though he wasn't formally asked whether he wanted it.

Tuesday, August 25th

Since I last wrote Virginia[1] has safely arrived. She was born at thirty-five minutes past five last Thursday morning. I celebrated her birthday by going to Camberley, to the Staff College, with Bob Boothby, a jaunt we had done before. On the way down, Bob told me about the House of Lords. Of course, he's always one for thinking that what he has got is the best but I think in this case there is something to what he was saying. He and Eddie Shackleton, Victor Collins[2] and Stephen Taylor[3] all genuinely feel that life is more interesting, the debates are better and the whole atmosphere more real politically in the Lords than in the Commons this year.[4] We agreed about the decline in the quality of the Commons and I mentioned that Gaitskell had said he would be able, just but only just, to select a Cabinet. At this Bob said, 'Curiously enough, Lady Dorothy[5] told me of an almost exactly similar remark by Harold Macmillan a few days ago: " 'You have no idea how the quality of the Conservative Party will decline in the next Parliament, whatever happens. I shall only just be able to pull a Cabinet together if we win.' " '

Lady Dorothy had also told Bob that Macmillan said he expected to win, though he's by no means sure. 'If we do, it will be largely luck,' he had said, 'particularly the luck of the economic situation. But the one thing I can take credit for and which will probably win me the Election is Ike's invitation to

---

[1] The Crossmans' second child, born on August 20th, 1959.

[2] Conservative M.P. for the Taunton division of Somerset 1945–50. In 1958 he became a life peer, taking the title of Lord Stonham. He died in 1971.

[3] Labour M.P. for the Barnet division of Hertfordshire 1945–50 and P.P.S. to the Lord President of the Council 1947–50. A doctor, he had been Director of the Home Intelligence and Wartime Social Survey at the Ministry of Information 1941–5 and was Medical Director of Harlow Industrial Centre 1955–64. He became a life peer in 1958 and served as Under-Secretary of State for Commonwealth Relations and the Colonies in 1965. He returned to his post at Harlow 1965–7 and in 1973 became Visiting Professor of Medicine at the Memorial University of Newfoundland.

[4] Edward Shackleton, Victor Collins and Stephen Taylor had all been introduced in the House of Lords in October 1958. Robert Boothby had been introduced in November 1958.

[5] Lady Dorothy Cavendish, the daughter of the 9th Duke of Devonshire, married Harold Macmillan in 1920. She became a G.B.E. in 1964. She died in 1966.

Khrushchev.[1] No one can take away from me now the fact that I started this whole process by going to Moscow, when it was extremely unpopular.' Macmillan had also, apparently, indicated that in his view it was not so much bad leadership from which the Labour Party was suffering as the luck of the game. Finally, he had also said that, if he won, he certainly wouldn't stay P.M. for more than two years. The awful example of Ramsay MacDonald, Stanley Baldwin and Clem Attlee was always present for him and he was going to resign while he was still young and vigorous and able to enjoy life. He is the first Prime Minister this century who really has a life outside politics to enjoy.

Wednesday, August 26th
Hugh came in yesterday on his way to lunch with Tony Crosland. The main thing he wanted to say to me was that he would like me, during the Election campaign, to be available to steer the propaganda war. He was extremely vague about where and how it would be done and he was equally vague about drafting the Election manifesto, which he also wanted me to try. Once again he seemed sensible and thoroughly competent but he is obviously worried about Nye, who has sat in the country, taking no part whatsoever in anything.

This afternoon we made the first attempts to draw up a propaganda directive for the Party under the title, which I invented, *Aide-mémoire of the Chief Whip to the Leader*. This is the only formula under which we can do such a thing without causing somebody offence. Harold Wilson may have improved the organization of the electoral machine but, as a publicity machine, Transport House is a very puzzling thing. It contains any number of able young men and women but nothing comes out of it and nothing gets done. I should be quite willing to help them in concerting and controlling central propaganda during the campaign if I saw any way of doing so. Maybe this little committee and directive we have started to run in this week may give us a chance. But what a puny little thing it is, compared to the colossal propaganda machine of the Tories, with its huge advertising campaign, bill-posting campaign, with its press relations officers in all the regions and, of course, the Establishment and most of the press on its side.

Thursday, August 27th
Sydney rang up this morning, saying he wanted to see me extremely urgently and couldn't talk on the phone. I finished my column, reflecting on what he could want. It was either that Hugh Cudlipp had resigned or something about the column and me, more probably the latter. So I was not surprised when Sydney arrived and said, 'Hugh is sending you a letter about your future and

---

[1] The Foreign Ministers' Conference had adjourned, after making little progress, on August 5th. On August 3rd Mr Khrushchev had been invited to visit the United States; he arrived on September 15th. On August 27th President Eisenhower had come to Britain for a five-day visit.

I said I wanted to talk to you first. He is going to tell you that the column will come to an end some time after the Election, because the paper isn't going to be as Labour as all that.'

Sydney added that in his view the real reason was the purchase of various magazines which had been overpriced and lost £1 million already, apparently owing to the printers' strike. In order to break even, the *Mirror* would have to make even more money, and anyway Hugh was getting impatient with its present form and with the Labour Party. So he wasn't going to have a political columnist.

Sydney told me that he had told Hugh that the first three months after the Election would be fascinating and he would be insane to get rid of me then. So the tentative arrangement would be that I should be sent a letter, warning me that the column would end some time but not saying when, offering me double money for the Election (when I shan't be writing at all!) and continuing me for three months afterwards, and then *Schluss*. Sydney was obviously terribly anxious lest this should prove my financial ruin. But I really felt quite elated at the idea that my mind had been made up for me about writing a book and also at the thought that the investment in the farm had been well timed.

'Of course,' Sydney added, 'I shan't stay myself. The *Herald* has been trying to get me for a year but I am nearly fifty-one and this was my last job before retirement. If I stay with the *Mirror*, it gives me a pension and Hugh might ask me to be Deputy Editor. But how miserable if everything we stood for is destroyed!' He also revealed that Hugh had got more and more dubious about all-out support of Labour during the Election campaign itself. Sydney had warned him how fatal it would be, even in his own interest, to go back on his support till after the Election, but Hugh apparently varies from day to day and from hour to hour. The whole pressure on Hugh will now be to keep him steady till the Election and, even in the three months afterwards, to see the paper gradually, and if possible with some decency, shift its line.

I told Sydney that, in my own interest, it would be better to have a clean break at the Election. Financially, what I would like would be a clean break plus a capital sum equivalent to six months' salary, since this would be tantamount to a year's salary when you take income tax into consideration. Sydney said he thought this could be arranged quite easily and I was to see Hugh privately about it. Meanwhile no one, least of all Hugh Gaitskell, is to be informed of what could be a terribly damaging anti-*Mirror* story if Sydney and I chose to make it so.

Throughout the talk it was clear that Sydney was much more worried than I was (maybe about himself), as I had always assumed, since a conversation some time ago, that the Election would end it for me. I would either be a Minister in a successful Labour Government or Cudlipp would be tired of the Labour Party. I suppose the explanation is that this solution is much more acceptable to me than it is to Sydney. I care much less, partly because of the farm but partly because I love having decisions taken for me by fate, so that I don't have to worry. I also know Anne will be absolutely delighted and maybe so will Rose.

What a classic Marxist story about the capitalist press! This is the only thing which makes me sad. We had tried, with considerable success, to make the *Mirror* into a semi-serious popular paper, to build up confidence in it. Now all this is to be destroyed because of a loss on some magazines. But even that isn't true. One of the factors, as I pointed out to Sydney, was Hugh's increasing disillusion with the Labour Opposition, a disillusion partly fed by Sydney and myself. If Labour had been a real going concern, on the up grade, the coming idea, Hugh Cudlipp and Cecil King would not have pulled out on it or at least they would not have pulled out without much more compunction.

One last thought. Sydney and I agree that Cudlipp may well change his mind again in the three months after the Election, particularly if we take up Jack Nener's suggestion and have the column only once a week, much more prominent. So, as nearly always happens in life, in that case there would not be a nice, simple, clear-cut decision but another piece of compromise and drift – of course, in financial comfort.

Last night, in an appalling heatwave, I went up to Hugh Gaitskell's party. He had invited the General Council and the Executive. I had a long, pleasant talk with Edna Healey back from a camping tour with her children, and with Audrey Gordon Walker,[1] entirely concerned about how to look after dying grandmas and grandpas at home, with Alf Robens, smooth as ever, and, at the last moment, with Tom Williamson and Harry Douglass, who suddenly and expectedly blew up over my head about a recent column of mine. They could hardly have been more violent. 'It's always the right-wing which comes to the rescue of the Labour Party and what thanks do we get from people like yourself, working in a rich capitalist paper, etc., etc.' It's really impossible to reason with Tom and Harry Douglass and, when I told them that I thought the Labour Party would do better with a narrow majority, they were obviously feeling this was another proof that intellectual, middle-class Socialists are utterly impossible. But, characteristically, Tom Williamson took me and Alice Bacon back home in his chauffeur-driven car.

On September 7th the Prime Minister visited the Queen at Balmoral and shortly afterwards announced the date of the General Election. It was to be on October 8th. The news coincided with the Trades Union Congress at Blackpool, which on September 9th rejected by a 2 to 1 majority the policy of unilateral cessation of nuclear weapons testing and production, advocated by Mr Cousins. Just before the Conference, Gaitskell and Bevan had visited Moscow, as members of a

[1] Edna Edmunds married Denis Healey in 1945. Audrey Rudolf married Patrick Gordon Walker in 1934.

Labour Party delegation. Bevan succeeded in taking with him, as interpreter and adviser, K. S. Karol (see Michael Foot, Aneurin Bevan, *London: Davis-Poynter, 1973, pp. 617–20). The visit was cut short by the announcement of the Election; Bevan, a sick man, returned to a full campaign tour.*

Crossman, meanwhile, was preparing to leave the Mirror.

Tuesday, September 15th

Directly he returned from his holiday, Hugh Cudlipp asked me to lunch. As I couldn't go he asked me to a drink at 6 o'clock and I said I couldn't do that because I had our gynaecologist coming. Hugh arrived here at a quarter past seven in a bad temper in his Bentley, because he doesn't like being said no to and because he was uncomfortable. I made things easy for him by explaining, before he did, why the *Mirror* was going to get rid of me and why it was inevitable that after the Election they wouldn't want to be tied to the Labour Party. We got on fine, agreeing with each other about everything, until his car failed to return at about a quarter past eight, after we had chatted for an hour.

Then he suddenly attacked my column of that Friday.[1] What I was doing, in fact, was making everything of the column which he wanted it to be two years ago and which he didn't want it to be today. Suddenly we had flared into one of those blazing rows and finally he said he had to get a taxi. We couldn't get a taxi and he started rushing out. 'Well, I'm glad it's all cleared up,' I said. 'You will pay me compensation, lump sum, capital gain, equivalent to six months' earnings. But I'd like to make sure with my lawyer and accountant of the form of words you use.' 'I'm not going to have any of your damn lawyers again,' he said. 'Once again you can't trust me. What do you think I'm paid my salary for, except to know how to settle these things?' And he flared out in a flaming row. Next morning a quiet little voice rang up and said that he would send me a draft letter after the Election, which I could show to my lawyer. He hoped that was all right. And that's the last I've heard of it, except that, ironically enough, since then, with the General Election my column has become very prominent and I've gained Hugh some kudos by being made the chairman of the Campaign Committee to run Transport House.

But that's jumping things. I must first describe those odd ten days when Hugh and Nye went to Russia to see Khrushchev, the T.U.C. conference took place at Blackpool and Macmillan announced the Election. The visit to Russia started very queerly, with no assurance even of an interview. But it actually turned out a great success.

Meanwhile I went to Blackpool to the T.U.C. and had a fantastically

---

[1] 'Will This Tory Stunt Succeed?', *Daily Mirror*, September 4th. Crossman had attacked the way in which President Eisenhower's visit had 'been turned into a pre-Election publicity stunt' for the Conservatives, something for which 'Mr Harold Macmillan must take full responsibility'.

funny time. I got there on Monday evening, just after Barbara had brought the fraternal greetings from the Labour Party, on the day when everybody knew the Election was coming, though not the date. Of course she is nervy about her 400 majority at Blackburn and nervy full stop, too. And she was fussing to have her speech put forward for the press, etc. Finally Willis, the Chairman, said, as she rose to speak, 'Mind, only ten minutes.' She gave a vibrant, rabble-rousing, shrill speech, saying the reason to vote Labour was because we didn't dare trust the Tories. She got a formal reception, though many of the delegates liked her speech, but that evening, as I went round the General Council from table to table in the Imperial Hotel, chatting, they all felt she had struck a discordant, jarring note in their proceedings. The atmosphere was complacent, detached and completely defeatist about Labour's chances. They all seemed to think a third Tory victory was a bad thing but something inevitable you had to come to terms with, in a placid kind of way.

On Tuesday came the formal announcement of the Election, and Willis rose and said it was something which couldn't pass completely unnoticed. Once again there was only a ripple. However, that evening Harold Hutchison[1] and I got to work on the obvious thought that, now the Labour Party Conference was cancelled and the Election was on, Gaitskell must be invited to this conference. We talked it all round the Imperial and made sure that every paper carried the story that Gaitskell would be invited.

At tea-time George Woodcock came up to me and I asked what he thought. 'Well, it's a very careful balance,' he said, 'from your point of view as well as ours. Suppose Gaitskell were photographed between Cousins and Haxell[2] of the E.T.U.! It might lose you a million votes.' And Woodcock wasn't laughing. He added, 'And the General Council must consider its position. It's unprecedented you know, to ask the Opposition Leader to interrupt our proceedings. And suppose you lose the Election — where would the General Council then be?' I said I thought it possible for them each to cut Gaitskell dead for six months and so regain the good favours of Mr Macmillan.

It was obvious that George Woodcock hated the whole idea and later that

---

[1] Political Editor of the *Daily Mirror* and, later, Political Columnist of the *Sunday Mirror*.

[2] Frank Haxell, a Communist, was elected to the Executive Council of the Electrical Trades Union in January 1938 and became Assistant General Secretary in October 1948 and General Secretary in April 1955. The union had been dominated by its Communist members since the Second World War but, after the Hungarian invasion of 1956, some leading E.T.U. members made vigorous attempts at reform. From 1958 to 1960 the T.U.C. General Council sought to investigate accusations of fraud in E.T.U. elections. Meanwhile, Frank Haxell retained the post of General Secretary in the E.T.U. elections of 1959. His defeated opponent, John Byrne, a Roman Catholic from Glasgow, and Frank Chapple, another leading E.T.U. member, issued writs against the union and its officers for alleged fraud. On June 28th 1961 Frank Haxell and Frank Foulkes, E.T.U. President since 1945, were found guilty of conspiracy to prevent Byrne's election 'by fraudulent and unlawful devices' and Haxell was declared defeated by Byrne.

evening I found even old Ted Hill,[1] a left-winger and a good friend of Gaitskell, equally reluctant. 'Why shouldn't we on the General Council do the job of arousing our people, without inviting somebody else?' he asked — and here was half the rub. For what Gaitskell would do would be to get all the applause and all the publicity and steal attention from these old gentlemen on the platform.

When I got home from a longish walk along the beach on Wednesday, I found a message to ring Hugh Gaitskell, just back from Russia. I did this. By then he had been invited and had decided to come on Thursday for an afternoon speech. I told him about the atmosphere and that it would be a good thing to get there as early as possible for the local press. He said that as he had a private aeroplane he could perfectly well lay it on an hour earlier. He also said, when I asked him, that he thought it would be a good idea not to go straight to the conference hall as proposed, but to come to the Imperial for half an hour, to wash and relax. This was all the more necessary as he had just got home from Russia, starting at four o'clock in the morning. 'Would you go down and see Tewson,' Hugh said, 'and check this?'

All unwitting, I proceeded to do so, finding Sir Vincent at dinner with his wife[2] and Sir Thomas Yates,[3] the Vice-President. I said, quite politely but breezily, that Hugh had rung me up, wondered whether he should come earlier to get a better press and whether he shouldn't come to the Imperial first. Tewson said at once, 'No. We want him on the platform at half-past three,' but he agreed the second proposal about coming to the Imperial. He then said to me, 'Are you going out to meet him at the airport?' 'Well,' I said, 'he suggested this to me because he wanted a chat on the way in.' At this, Sir Thomas Yates said, 'Well in that case I needn't go.' I said, 'But I can't substitute for the Vice-President. That's the last thing I would like to do.' 'No, no,' said Yates, 'you go and meet him and I'll stay in the hotel.' And that's just what he meant. After that I met Tom O'Brien, who saw the point and also saw that he himself was missing publicity. So he proposed that the four Labour M.P.s there, led by himself, should join the crowd at the airport.

At one o'clock in the morning I was still chatting to him when Victor Feather, the Assistant General Secretary, came along to solicit my support for his taking Morgan Phillips's place as General Secretary of the Labour Party. As Victor was getting up, I mentioned that Hugh had telephoned me. 'Oh, that's all fixed,' he said. 'I telephoned him after you.' Then I men-

---

[1] General Secretary of the United Society of Boilermakers 1948–63 and President of the Amalgamated Society of Boilermakers, Shipwrights, Blacksmiths and Structural Workers 1963–5. He was a member of the T.U.C. General Council 1948–65 and its Chairman in 1961 and Vice-Chairman in 1962. In 1967 he became a life peer, taking the title Lord Hill of Wivenhoe. He died in 1969.

[2] Florence Moss married Vincent Tewson in 1929.

[3] General Secretary of the National Union of Seamen 1947–60 and Chairman of the T.U.C. 1957–8. He was knighted in 1969. He died in 1978.

tioned my talk with Tewson and the new arrangements about Hugh's coming to the Imperial. Feather said, 'Do you think Tewson runs anything round here? I'm doing these arrangements. If he comes to the Imperial, I walk out. The drama is to put him straight on the platform from the aeroplane. And anyway, I won't stand people like you going out to the airport on a T.U.C. occasion.' He got up to go and I caught him and shook him and said, 'Don't be a bloody fool. In that case I wouldn't dream of going to the airport or doing anything whatsoever.' Next morning at eight o'clock I came downstairs and saw Tewson, who turned away. I went up to him and said, 'I shan't be at the airport,' whereupon he turned to Sir Thomas Yates and said, 'So you'll be going to the airport, Tom, after all.'

This is a very good illustration of the mentality of the T.U.C. bureaucrats. I kept out of the way throughout Hugh's stay. Actually they did take my advice. The three Knights — Sir Alf Roberts, Sir Tom Williamson and Sir Thomas Yates — all went to the airport to receive him, brought him to the Imperial and stayed with him all day, and all three gave him dinner in the best dining room, with me sitting a little way away, dining alone. I had taken the precaution of putting my bag with the hall porter and telling him to get it on to Gaitskell's car. As I was trying to get in with Gaitskell for the journey back to London, I was told there was no room and that I'd better get a taxi. So I went in the police car. As we were climbing into the plane, Victor Feather boomed up to me and said, 'All forgiven and forgotten?' 'Forgiven by me,' I said, 'but not forgotten. It's in my diary.'

On the way down, Hugh pulled out the draft of the manifesto and asked me to read it. A fortnight ago he had told me to get hold of it but Morgan had denied its existence. I read it and told him it was a non-starter. He looked at it and agreed. He then said he wanted me to run Transport House. So I said that Tom Driberg must write the manifesto, since I couldn't do both without offence. Hugh agreed and proposed this at the campaign committee on Friday morning.

That morning at two o'clock I had been telephoned by David Ginsburg, saying that a delegation would attend me with the manifesto, which I had to rewrite, since Tom Driberg was in Rome. This was to have been my first weekend in Prescote and I was furious. I spent Friday finishing my Election address and a host of other things and spent fourteen hours on Saturday redrafting, with shifts of Transport House secretaries, nice girls. We resumed at ten on Sunday and finished by lunch-time in time for Tony Wedgwood Benn to take me up to Hugh Gaitskell's for a first talk about television shows, another matter which has been sedulously kept-from me until this week.

There was some tension in the air with those three stars — Benn, Wyatt and Mayhew — seeing Crossman at last getting in on their racket but, when I went over to Transport House on Saturday and Sunday for the drafting, we had a perfectly reasonable discussion. Then Hugh had an hour to look at the manifesto and, as I expected, began to tear apart all the economic paragraphs.

Before we had the manifesto, Gaitskell had announced to the N.E.C. that there must be a campaign committee in Transport House throughout the Election. He did it very artfully. 'We should have London Members,' he said, 'Tom Driberg and Ray Gunter. Then there's Alice [Bacon] and Dick, who has a safe seat in Coventry and has written the manifesto. I think Dick will have to be chairman,' he added, 'because he's the only one who wouldn't have to be in his constituency at all.' It turned out, of course, that both Tom and Gunter couldn't be there every day, Alice can't be there at all and I will have to be in Coventry for at least a week. But Hugh had got me made chairman and that was all that mattered.

Today I had the first delicate job of getting into Transport House. I started in the morning, finishing the manifesto with the help of the young officials, who all knew which way the wind was blowing and couldn't have been nicer. Then I went round to see Morgan and told him that of course I would have nothing to do with organization or press and our main job (note 'our') would be to keep the television boys under control and just tick along on publicity.

Morgan couldn't have been more co-operative. I went back to give Hugh lunch and go through the whole manifesto with him. At three points he repudiated what the Executive had wanted, in particular writing in all sorts of qualifications on further nationalization, which would have taken months of debate before the Election. I think he was impressed by the way the job had been done, but he still read every page and made about twenty amendments. He kept on saying I should go back to Transport House and leave him to follow but I clung to him like a leech till it was through.

Meanwhile, thanks to Albert Rose,[1] Coventry has shown itself quite amenable and was obviously proud that its Member was so busy in the stratosphere. As for the sunshine, it goes on and on and on, unbelievably – Macmillan weather, which makes it impossible for the public to take politics seriously. So we are left with an awkward predicament. In order to destroy a complacent mood of euphoria, we need thunder, rain and hail. But will thunder, rain and hail deter the Labour voters? There's a nice choice for you.

Tuesday, September 22nd

All through the week we have had great reports of great vitality in the constituencies – not big public meetings but our few workers keen, more people coming in than we've seen since '45 and a sudden, quite unexpected feeling that we had really better win. The general view in the country is that everything is over bar the shouting, and that after the defeat there will be a split in the Labour Party. However the Gallup Poll shows that, while the overwhelming majority of Labour voters think the Tories will win, nearly as many are convinced they themselves are going to win in their own constituency.

[1] Crossman's new Constituency Secretary.

This indicates the power of propaganda. Although each thinks he can win, they think that collectively we have no chance.

Inside Transport House Morgan Phillips has been quiet and perfectly amiable, at least on the surface. All through last week he was trying to get a Derbyshire constituency, for which he was duly defeated on Saturday by the Miners' candidate.[1] There can seldom have been a greater humiliation for the Secretary of the Party just before an Election, but somehow or other it didn't seem to damage us at all—I suspect because all the industrial correspondents have known for years that he is half-way out and hadn't the heart to strike him. When I was working with Hugh for an hour yesterday in Morgan's room, I saw him sitting at his desk and the whole time he sat with the newspaper in front of him doing nothing, absolutely nothing. Yet, whenever you ask him something, he is shrewd and I think he still handles the daily press conference with the very greatest skill.

All I have been doing, in collaboration with Tom Driberg, is to take direct charge of the Research Department, which issues campaign notes, and of the television and radio and the leaflets, as well as trying to impose the general policy direction on the campaign. We meet every morning at half-past ten. At the first meeting, yesterday, David Ennals put forward the basic directive composed after long consultations with me, and on the basis of it we worked out a tentative fill-in, with themes and names, for all the television and radio programmes. Today we did the same thing for the series of *Speakers' Notes*. I found the Research Department intolerably opinionated and I was amused when Morgan said to me, 'Of course they can put the *Notes* out but no candidate reads them.' But, if so, what has he been doing, letting them go out in that form in Election after Election?

Meanwhile there in the background has been Hugh Gaitskell, whose personality has so far completely dominated the campaign. Since he came back from Russia, everybody has noticed that he has suddenly become a television star, a political personality in his own right—confident, relaxed, a Leader—with Nye as a rather faded elder statesman behind him. In private Gaitskell is much the same. Once he has given me this job, he relies on me and he has some justification, since the manifesto came out not too badly in the end and certainly no one else would push and shove and be unpleasant enough to get things done in the appallingly short space of time required.

Yesterday we were discussing the last television programme, alone. Gaitskell had just come back from lunch with Hugh Cudlipp and Sydney and he said, 'We might answer the Tories not with the Shadow Cabinet—that would be a mistake—but with me and my inner group coming on, each saying in a minute what he stood for. Let's see who it would be.' 'Oh,' I said, 'brood on that one. It's delicate.' But he began to write. 'Bevan, Wilson, Callaghan,

[1] He sought the Labour nomination for the North-East Derbyshire seat and, with Edward Castle, was among the short-listed candidates. The nomination went to Thomas Swain, who won the seat at the General Election with a majority of 15,332 votes.

Brown. You on pensions, of course.' 'What about Barbara?' I said. 'No, she can't go anywhere near that programme,' he replied very testily, 'not even at the beginning.' Gaitskell has obviously got a very clear idea of who he thinks of these days as his inner group of advisers.

Thursday, September 24th
What is fascinating me is that never in Labour history has any committee of this sort sat each day; nor has any common strategy or tactics been organized before. In fact, previous campaigns have been played by ear, in the sense that there hasn't been a strategy from the moment the campaign started. Everybody has been saying and doing what they felt like in the constituencies, with a few tours of famous speakers. It is only the emergence of television which has changed it. With sound, right up to the end the time is allocated between half a dozen prominent personalities, who merely make speeches on the radio. It's the television magazine programme which has changed all this and brought about the possibility of really answering quickly at the last moment. This requires central direction and control.

In the last two days the Gaitskell boom has been rapidly swelling. How strange political leadership is! For months he was no bloody good because everyone said he was no bloody good. Now everybody says that Gaitskell is very good indeed and he becomes very good indeed, so that I can watch the godhead emerging from the man. Yes, one can actually watch it. The Leader emerges from the husk of the ordinary politician. I went up to Hampstead yesterday with half a dozen items on the agenda – all cleared in twenty minutes and I was out of the house without more than a cursory goodbye. He hadn't wasted any time and that was that. Yesterday evening we had a sandwich together at seven o'clock before he went off on a round of meetings in South London and I found him really buoyant, genial and self-confident. It must be quite nice to feel one's a man emerging into a god. But I am fully content to remain a man and even an acolyte.

One final conclusion, already noted in today's *Mail*. Up till a week ago it was assumed that a Labour defeat would all be blamed on Gaitskell and the Labour propaganda. Now Gaitskell is superb in the public eye and second only to Gaitskell is the brilliance of the Labour propaganda. If we lose, it will be despite, not because of, ourselves at Transport House.

Monday, September 28th
Transport House is on top of the world. As we go through the corridors now, you can feel the girls proud that they have typed the communiqué which they read on the tape half an hour later and next day in the press. The winning mood, following a mood of complacent defeatism, is exhilarating and probably intoxicating. Anyway, it's enjoyable at the moment.

Further complications have arisen from Gaitskell, who has sent a message via Woodrow that he wants to cut his Inner Group presentation on the last television programme to four people—Griffiths, Bevan, Wilson and, of course, Crossman, the architect of the pensions scheme and of our psychological warfare. What terrible jealousies and envies are being brewed by this I cannot conceive but at present it's roughly true that, because Hugh's Chief of Staff is in an absolutely key position, I am having the time of my life and regretfully, reluctantly, Transport House staff say, 'Well, it's better to win and have decisions taken and have leadership.' But, oh, the moment the battle is over, if I were to postpone my retirement for a second, the mood would turn to sourest hatred.

However, why think of this when the thing is on? Even George Hutchinson[1] of the *Evening Standard* rings me to say that all Fleet Street is greatly enjoying watching the show. The only people who are not enjoying it, I suspect, are Hugh Cudlipp and Cecil King, who have decided to sack me in such a way that I shall leave not with a whimper but with a resounding bang, which will make it even more difficult to explain why they have sacked me. And they will have to sack me because otherwise I don't get my capital gain. And, if they don't sack me, I shall go on writing. Therefore the only hope of deliverance for the *Mirror* now is the Labour victory which only ten days ago they ruled out as totally impossible.

Wednesday, September 30th
Since I last wrote the Tories have launched their first big counter-attack. It was the result of the first slip-up by Hugh Gaitskell.[2] To my amazement, yesterday's papers carried as their main story a speech by him, pledging that there will be no increase in income tax under the next Labour Government. Nothing could be more foreign to Hugh's nature or more unlike what Harold Wilson has been saying for years about not making specific tax commitments for the next Labour Chancellor. I discovered that Hugh had rung Harold, who was in London yesterday, and they had fixed it between them. I also discovered, because Woodrow told me, that on the television next Thursday Harold proposes to go one further and say we hope to reduce tax for everyone, including high business executives.

Yesterday Nye Bevan had telephoned in righteous indignation. He pointed out that this would tie the hands of the next Labour Government and, though

---

[1] George Hutchinson was Political Correspondent of the *Evening Standard* 1953–60 and Director of Publicity for the Conservative Party 1961–4. He returned to journalism in 1964, to write a column in *The Times* and as a Director and Deputy Editor of the *Spectator*. He published *Edward Heath: A Personal and Political Biography* (London: Longmans, 1970) and, just before his death in 1980, *The Last Edwardian at No. 10: An Impression of Harold Macmillan* (London: Quartet Books).

[2] In a speech at Newcastle on September 28th Gaitskell had stated that there would be 'no increase in the standard or other rates of income tax under the Labour Government so long as normal peacetime conditions continue'. At Glasgow the next day Mr Macmillan reminded his audience of Mr Gaitskell's record as Chancellor: '[He] introduced only one Budget, fortunately for you. He was faced with having to raise something like £400 million in extra taxation ... What did he do? ... He put 6*d*. [2·5 new pence] on the income tax ... and for good measure he put a charge on spectacles and teeth under the Health Service.'

he didn't say so, it was clear that what he meant was to warn us against the threat of another Bevanite split. When he was told that Hugh had consulted Harold Wilson before saying it, his anger was hardly appeased. Indeed, this convinced Nye that there was a real conspiracy going on to strangle the last traces of Socialism.

I must say, on this I wholly sympathize with Nye. Moreover, I had smelt something of this in the first draft broadcast sent down to me by train to Coventry on the day before I was adopted, which included a promise to reduce taxation. I learnt from John Harris[1] that the idea of the whole thing was to anticipate the Tories, who were apparently planning to accuse us of having to raise taxation. If that was the object, it has succeeded, but only at the cost of producing much greater difficulties, particularly for Hugh, who as an ex-Chancellor should really know better.

How rapidly moods in an Election change! Last Monday evening, when we completed our television show, we really felt on top of the world. All the B.B.C. technicians there admitted it was more packed and more polished than any edition of 'Tonight' had ever been. Aneurin Bevan had finally been allocated only four and a half minutes and had then run half a minute short but, even so, he had seemed extremely nice and we all felt wonderful. Then, on Tuesday, began the Tory counter-attack, which is mounting up. Quite clearly the policy of playing the Election down and maintaining a small vote has been abandoned and now each side is outbidding the other in a frantic effort to achieve the initiative. Old Morgan, who really is a hardened campaigner, agreed with me this morning that the Election will be decided over this weekend. We have been temporarily driven on the defensive and, if the Tories can maintain this, they will probably draw away slightly.

After Nye's blast of anger he disappeared to Newbury and I've been telephoning to Harold Wilson and Hugh throughout the last twenty-four hours. Harold at once agreed to scrap all the questions he had previously worked out with Woodrow Wyatt, including the one on lower taxation, and to go in for the kind of hard-hitting tough line which is the only way of beating the Tories towards the end of this week. Harold rang me to propose only two questions, one enabling him to answer Iain Macleod's challenge on how much our total costs would be, and the other on Macmillan's effort to create a panic about a flight from the pound if Labour won. 'I shall answer that,' he said, 'by asking what right Macmillan has to talk, when he was Chancellor at the time of Suez and nearly caused a devaluation.' I must say this took my breath away.

At our meeting this morning most people felt that a personal attack on

---

[1] A journalist, he was personal assistant to Gaitskell 1959–62 and Director of Publicity for the Labour Party 1962–4. He was Special Assistant to the Foreign Secretary 1964–5 and acted as adviser to Roy Jenkins at the Home Office 1965–7 and at H.M. Treasury 1967–70. After working for *The Economist* 1970–4, he served as Minister of State in the Home Office (again with Roy Jenkins) 1974–9. He became a life peer in 1974, taking the title Lord Harris of Greenwich. In 1979 he became Chairman of the Parole Board.

Macmillan would be a mistake, but we also agreed that it was wise to anticipate the Tories' secret weapon and thus immunize it to some extent. I have a strong suspicion that they will run the line of the runaway inflation, the runaway Government and the flight from the pound, as well as trying to arrange that the date of the summit conference should be announced early next week. So what we tentatively agreed was that Harold should not attack Macmillan but should bring the subject into the open and make Macmillan seem anti-patriotic in his effort to exploit financial panic.

Then I got another message from Gaitskell saying that he felt he ought to spend his time on Thursday defending his position as Chancellor, an idea which John Harris agreed with me was fatal and indicated that Hugh was losing his nerve. I replied with our ideas and heard after lunch that Hugh ruled out any reference to the flight from the pound before the Tories delivered the attack. This will have to be argued out tomorrow, before the programme goes on the air. Hugh has been extremely good, up to two days ago, and we are all obviously a bit anxious lest over-exhaustion and over-strain will have weakened his will. Morgan said to me today that the trip Hugh had undertaken was one he wouldn't have advised, since it was too heavy. Let's hope he's wrong.

Monday, October 5th
I wish I had kept this diary throughout last week. Nevertheless, I don't think I shall be twisting anything or committing hindsight in these notes.

Our initiative went at a tremendous pace until the morning when we read in the *Herald* Hugh Gaitskell's income tax pledge.[1] I should add that all of us on the Committee, without exception, were appalled at what we felt was a breach in Gaitskell's intellectual integrity. The last thing I would have expected from him, as an ex-Chancellor and an economist, was a commitment of this kind. Moreover, it wasn't very popular. I said all this to John Harris, trying to get him to impress on Hugh the danger with Nye and the damage he was doing to the television image of his integrity. Immediately the Tory counter-attack began and reached full fury when, at his press conference, Morgan Phillips nonchalantly let out, on a background paper on the cost of living, a firm pledge to reduce purchase tax on essentials.

At our daily conference Morgan had been called out to talk with Nye and I assumed this had been provoked by the *Daily Herald* front page running, for the second time, Hugh's income tax pledge. But when Morgan came back he said it was a different subject. So I left for Coventry and it was only that night, when I got back to Prescote, that I heard about the purchase tax furore. John Harris rang me, telling me of Hugh's violent indignation and I had to tell him in reply that the pot could hardly call the kettle black! Hugh thought Morgan had done this deliberately. I thought it was a mistake and next day began to investigate.

[1] Describing how he would avoid tax increases.

It was true that Morgan hadn't said a word about it at the press conference and that the paper in which it occurred was only issued at the end and wasn't received by all the correspondents. The pledge was an odd sentence in the middle. I therefore concluded that what had really happened was a sheer error in the Research Department, which had issued a paper Morgan hadn't read. Then, when the furore occurred, I talked to Morgan, who is a vain virtuoso and wasn't going to admit a clerical error but took credit for yet another front-page coup.

This may indeed be the explanation. Yesterday he suddenly got pally with me and said, 'Of course I had to do it, as Nye insisted on a diversionary tactic.' On reflection, I find it difficult to believe this story. How could the document have been drafted and roneo-ed in time for a press conference, when Nye's telephone conversation only occurred in the middle of our conference, twenty minutes before the press conference? On the other hand, it is just possible that Morgan was fly enough to do this and I must put it down on the record.

Curiously enough, as Morgan himself said to me, the purchase tax offer greatly improved the situation, since ordinary people felt it was quite normal for Labour to reduce purchase tax on essentials, unlike their reaction to our income tax pledge. Moreover, Morgan could show that Harold Wilson had made this pledge frequently in the House, that it was in Harold's Election address and that the actual words Morgan used had been taken from an article by Harold in the last week's *News of the World*.

All through last week and the weekend we on the inside, when we had a moment off, were discussing the effects. We all agreed that, after marching forward for ten days, Hugh had tripped over his own feet and given the Tories a magnificent occasion for launching their counter-offensive. But, as Morgan observed to me yesterday, they were going to launch it anyway and it was anyway going to be on the line that the country can't afford Labour's programme· and there would be runaway inflation. Harold and Hugh apparently had advance information that the Tories' plan was to announce 2s. 6d. (12·5 new pence) a week income tax as necessary to pay for Labour's programme. Our side made the pledge in order to anticipate and kill this attack. It certainly killed the attack but, according to Anthony Howard, it caused grave damage in the West, where he and practically every Labour person who rang me up was uncomfortable and ill at ease about it, including such varied people as George Wigg, Patricia Llewelyn-Davies and Sydney. David Ennals and Tom Driberg both thought it had lost us the Election. We were all waiting spellbound for the Gallup Poll. Actually, Woodrow rang me up at midnight to tell me that in today's Gallup Poll, though the Don't Knows have again increased, we are now dead level with the Tories.

I myself remain in two minds. I deeply dislike Hugh's behaviour, particularly as he hadn't consulted his own chief of propaganda and had been in cahoots with Wilson, who has been slippery on this. On the other hand, nothing I saw in Coventry, where I have been each afternoon and evening, gave me any indication that, on that level, anybody was noticing what was going on! Of course, you can say that, in a local battle, you never see the Don't Knows or the other side—and that is true.

But I must add here that since 1945 I have never known Coventry in such good heart. I am cheered in the streets and last night in the Club I got a very warm reception—so different from the chilly, reserved atmosphere of '55. If the Midlands is any test, we should be getting a very good vote, though I suspect there are a large number of Labour-minded people who are doubtful or apathetic and for whom the weather or a T.V. film may make all the difference. But there's no doubt that, trade union-wise or Labour-wise, the Midlands are in good heart and the trouble, if there is any, is in the marginal constituencies.

All last week we were struggling to maintain the image of the Party and to rebuild the image of integrity. Last Thursday's programme was quite a strain. Hugh, who had lost his nerve a little, let me know that he was going to spend his time defending his position as Chancellor in 1951. John Harris and I struggled with him and turned him down and, though a little smug, I thought he was first-rate in rather a flat programme, whose virtue was its flatness because it wasn't too flashy. He also did extremely well on sound radio on Saturday and we are preparing a programme of the same tone for this evening. This could possibly be decisive, since the Tories are lashing out more and more wildly and losing their temper.

I still don't, in my inmost heart, believe in victory, but I must concede the possibility that I may not get a week's holiday on Friday after all. All the way through, just as during a Session of the House of Commons, I feel that I am participating in something which isn't my affair. Here I am and, if we win, I really shall be the chief of staff who has been the architect of victory. Yet I've seldom felt more detached or less convinced that the whole show is real. Possibly that makes me quite good at the job and certainly it will prevent any undue disappointment if I have my holiday after all. But really—to think that what we are now doing could decide not only British history but world history! That I can't swallow.

In the Election the Conservatives again increased their majority, securing 108 seats more than the Labour Party and 102 over both Opposition parties combined. The figures were: Conservatives 366, Labour 258 and Liberals 6.

Crossman's majority at Coventry East rose by 0·5 per cent to 7,762 votes; Maurice Edelman's majority at Coventry North fell by 2·1 per cent to 1,241 votes, while at Coventry South Elaine Burton lost the seat to P. N. Hocking, Conservative, by 1,830 votes, the Labour proportion of the poll falling by 3·6 per cent and the Conservatives making a 2·3 per cent gain.

Friday, October 9th

I have come up from the country partly to see Hugh and partly to write this diary before I pervert it too much in hindsight.

The last days of the campaign were lovely weather, it was enormously enjoyable and I think the Coventry Labour Party put up far the best fight I have ever seen. Yet I did notice, on the eve of poll, that suddenly there was a sense of hush. At my meetings the questions were almost formal and I knew that people had already made up their minds at last. Moreover, I also noticed that, in most areas where one dished out window cards, they tended to disappear by next day, though this wasn't true of those in Willenhall, which is, in a slummy way, solid for me. But in all those big lines of semi-detached houses up behind Wyken and Stoke Heath there were ominous gaps and even in the workingmen's clubs, which I visited on Sunday, there was a good deal of friendliness but nothing approaching enthusiasm. As for the factory-gate meetings which I did at G.E.C., Humber and Courtaulds, there were a couple of hundred men at each, which was considered quite a good attendance, but what percentage was it of the thousands in the shops?

Nevertheless, I did feel very enthusiastic, and all the more so at the end of polling day, when I found that almost everybody had voted by eight o'clock and the committee rooms were empty. Of course it had been ominous that there had been 50 per cent polling before six o'clock and many women had gone down on their own. That should have tipped me off. But I persuaded myself it was the young wives going so that they could look after the children while their husbands went later on. Actually, I'm sure it was wives going to vote against their husbands' wishes.

We had decided to dine in the Leofric Hotel and sat with the television set by the dance band. Within twenty minutes of starting dinner I realized things were very bad. They didn't get any better. The real crash came when the first Midlands results were announced — a big fall in the majority at Wolverhampton and 10,000 down at Leamington. Poor Maurice took it very well and we tottered down to the hall to find Elaine comfortably out and Maurice just through. The actual announcement took place about forty minutes after we got there.

The more I reflect on this Election, the more I feel that we came quite near to winning it and that the tactics we employed were the only ones possible under prosperity. The image we presented was quite right. The policies were quite interesting and all we were dogged by was the simple truth: Tory voters are far more afraid of another Labour Government than Labour voters are afraid of another Tory Government. The Tories were able to exploit fear of nationalization, inflation, flight from the pound, trade unions, and so on. We could do the same with the men. I think the trade unions were magnificent but I am sure we failed to get the women and we may have failed to get some of the young men.

What puzzles me, however, is the amazing difference of atmosphere between 1955 and '59. The last campaign was terrible, with people turning thumbs down at us and complete awareness that the Tories were jubilant and we were defeated and divided. This one was a splendid campaign, with the Tories extremely nervous, ourselves attacking all the time and with a tremendous sense of unity and idealism. Yet, at first sight, the results of 1959 aren't appreciably better than those of 1955. Let's modify that about Coventry (I think I shall be proved right by detailed figures). It looks as though in fact we did very well in Coventry compared with the swing all round us, so that our improved morale and hard fighting had some effect.

Nevertheless, in the country as a whole it will be said very quickly that Labour did no better in 1959 than in 1955 and that therefore Gaitskell's whole tactic and leadership were wrong. What I personally believe is that we started the campaign magnificently and, as I have described in this diary, Gaitskell made that fatal stumble which enabled the Tories to revive all the suspicion of our disunity, insincerity, financial dishonesty, and so tip the Don't Knows back into the Government camp.

I can't help believing that, if we had gone ahead on the line of our first days, honestly emphasizing that we couldn't promise any tax reductions and that we couldn't carry the programme out unless we got the expansion, we could probably have got quite near beating the Government and could at least have reduced the Tory majority. What undid us was the fatal step that enabled them to accuse us of an auction and thereby to revive all the other fears. For there is no doubt there are other fears. Nationalization of steel, for instance, very nearly cost James Callaghan his seat, and Eirene White's as well. Also, surprisingly to me, the Tories were able to play on our disunity about foreign affairs and, even more important, our lack of patriotism as the result of Suez.

Moreover, another trouble is that our whole attack was so desperately brief. After months and months of lethargy and inactivity and ineffectiveness we suddenly started off with a bang on September 14th. It was too sudden a job to be really convincing. The fact is that the image we put over on our television shows seemed to many people far removed from the realities of the Labour Party they knew in their own district. We are paying a tremendous price for the appalling public relations of Labour groups, Labour parties and so on all over the country. However, in an hour's time, I hope, I shall be seeing Gaitskell and I shall be able to report more in this diary.

The composition of the new Cabinet was announced on October 14th. Selwyn Lloyd remained at the Foreign Office, Derick Heathcoat Amory at the Treasury and R. A. Butler at the Home Office and as Leader of the House of Commons. Iain Macleod became Colonial Secretary, while his place at the Ministry of Labour went to Edward Heath, the former Chief Whip. Reginald Maudling took over the Board of Trade, replacing Sir David Eccles, who returned to Education. The former Postmaster-General, Ernest Marples, went to the Ministry of Transport, which Harold Watkinson left for the Ministry of Defence. Lord Hailsham became Lord Privy Seal and occupied a new post as Minister for Science. He was succeeded as Chairman of the Party by Mr Butler.

The Opposition, meanwhile, were preoccupied with internal disputes over the cause of their defeat.

Monday, October 19th

Once again the gap is far too long and a great deal has happened. Above all, after three weeks of exciting action and organization we are right back in that terrible slough of despond where one is on one's own and everybody is intriguing against everybody else. 'Things fall apart. The centre cannot hold.'

But let's start where I left off. When I got round to Transport House, I found that Hugh had just arrived. My first job was to help him to draft his statement for the waiting press men. He was obviously dead tired and on the edge of an emotional collapse. John Harris told me that on Monday night, when Hugh couldn't go to sleep, he had been making his Cabinet, confident that he could win. And on Thursday night, when he was told the news of the poll, he very nearly broke down with shock and disappointment.

Certainly on the Friday he was over-quiet, not tense but somehow slumped, and the draft he produced consisted of double negatives. 'It isn't true that we shall not go forward', and suchlike. I substituted a few positives and a last sentence saying we shall fight and fight and fight again until we win, which he used straightaway in the press conference upstairs and also on the television that night. The poor man was subjected to that strain, too. I had a good many words with Dora while we were waiting, as well as with him, and they obviously felt quite a considerable amount of personal gratitude to me. Dora said she must get him away overseas if possible and I said, 'Why not bring him down to us in the country?'

I caught the train back that night in time to help with the preparation for Virginia's christening on Saturday. Over the weekend I talked to a very few people, including George Wigg, and it seemed clear to me that it was vital to avoid for as long as possible a renewed Left/Right clash. What was needed, it seemed to me was, first and foremost, to try to make the administration our organization required to keep the campaign going in peacetime.

When Woodrow rang me up, I deterred him from writing an article for the *Sunday Express* but I was a little disconcerted to hear that he was giving Hugh dinner on Sunday night. On Monday I learnt that all the gang – Gordon Walker, Douglas Jay, Tony Crosland, Roy Jenkins – had been with Hugh on Sunday morning before the dinner with Woodrow. I now believe that he didn't discourage them and probably positively assented to their flying kites about the need to drop nationalization and to rewrite the Party constitution. On the other hand, I have no reason to doubt Hugh's word that the kind of kites flown in succession were not to his taste and that he himself does not agree with Douglas and Roy about dropping steel nationalization.

It seems I have already plunged away from the proper narrative order. So let me now short-circuit. On Sunday night, Kingsley rang me and I agreed to do an article for the *Statesman*,[1] not discussing policy but proposing that the Leader's authority should be increased by a nominated Shadow Cabinet and, in return, Standing Orders should be suspended. I knew this was something which even Roy and Tony would support and I was hoping it could be got through before the Left/Right storm broke and everybody started voting merely for a faction. However, on Monday night (though I myself didn't see it), Roy Jenkins appeared on 'Panorama' along with Shirley Williams, Reg Prentice and one other, discussing what went wrong, and Roy made an all-out attack of an extreme form on nationalization.

By Tuesday morning everybody was telephoning to tell me about it and all were assuming Hugh was responsible. So I was all agog when Dora rang up to say that Hugh would like to come and spend the night at Prescote after lunching with Nye, before he went for a walk on the Downs. George also rang up and agreed that we should go for administrative strengthening of the Centre and no discussion of policy. By the time Hugh arrived I was suffering from acute duodenitis, so I couldn't eat or drink anything while he was there. But he talked to me at length from six to eleven o'clock and then again in the morning when he could get a word in after our walk round the farm and discussion of cows. So he must have had six hours.

First of all, he made it clear that in his view we couldn't afford to lose the next Election again. Then there would really be a growth of a Liberal Party and a split. We must let the pendulum take us in and carry nothing which stops it swinging our way. It wasn't iron and steel and road haulage, the specific pledges, but the general threat to nationalize 600 firms[2] which lost us votes this time. 'Douglas Jay and Roy want to drop all nationalization. I am not in favour of dropping iron and steel and road haulage. That is why I propose a complete rewriting of the Party constitution, defining our name and our aims in modern terms and introducing a federal structure, with indirect election to the N.E.C. for all. This means the Parliamentary Party will elect its representatives as the trade unions do and the constituency parties will elect rank-and-file members, as they will be forbidden to choose M.P.s.' I was at first very surprised by this constitutional reform but Hugh told me that Morgan long ago recommended it and Jim Griffiths was keenly in favour. Nye Bevan had also concurred during lunch.

The lunch had apparently been heavy, with a lot of drink, and Hugh was still very torpid when he got to me. I pressed him quite a lot but suspect that very little serious discussion had taken place. Nye had made it clear that he would like to succeed Jim Griffiths as Deputy Leader[3] and he had shown no

---

[1] Crossman's post-Election analysis, 'The Stimulus of Defeat', appeared in the *New Statesman* on October 17th.

[2] Implied in *Industry and Society*.

[3] Griffiths had just resigned the deputy leadership. Bevan was appointed in his place.

signs whatsoever of wanting to lead a Left attack on moderate policies. I said this was a bit new to me. In my view, any constitutional reform or moderation of our attitude to public ownership should not split the Party and I would only support formulae to which Nye concurred. Nye must have the veto. Hugh looked a bit surprised but, on reflection, saw this was sensible. I said, 'This means that you and Roy Jenkins will not be able to have what you want. You will have to argue it out on equal terms with Nye and Harold and myself.'

Hugh began to talk of Harold. 'I am going to make a lot of Shadow Cabinet changes and I'm thinking of moving Harold.' I outlined my ideas, which were that Hugh required a number of officers with functions. In addition to the Chief Whip he needed a Shadow Leader of the House, a Secretary of the Shadow Cabinet to prepare its papers and two co-ordinators, one a co-ordinator of publicity and the other of research, with no administrative powers but with policy control. Since Nye was Deputy Leader and wouldn't do it, I suggested that he should have Harold as Shadow Leader of the House, 'if he would regard that as promotion'. Hugh was obviously a bit sceptical. He was very anti-Harold but didn't disclose whom he thought of putting in his place.

I then said bluntly that my most useful job would be to co-ordinate research. 'Yes,' Hugh said, 'I'd like to make you chairman of the Policy Committee.' But I insisted that what was really necessary was for me to be in the Shadow Cabinet but in a nominated capacity. Hence my desire that he should nominate at least half its members. He said this was something which Nye had also proposed but he wasn't at all keen on it himself, since he somehow felt that he would get his way without it and that nomination would make him too open to blame for everything that went wrong.

I then said that the morale of the Parliamentary Party and the improvement of its fight was all-important. Hugh said, 'You can do nothing about this. Half of them are hopeless anyway. Moreover, most of the time there's no activity in Parliament. So how can you keep it lively?' At the time I found his attitude horrifying, since it's true enough that the rot starts in Westminster and seeps to the constituencies. Since we can't run advertising and billposting, our main means of continuing the fight between Elections must be in Parliament, and to say that we can't do anything better than we did in the last three years is to admit defeat.*

I argued round and round with Hugh, he always insisting on the improvement of the Party constitution immediately after the conference on

---

* I must say that in later talks, particularly with Jim Callaghan and Harold Wilson, the two other prominent members of the Shadow Cabinet, I found the same complacency. They all want to reform Transport House but they don't find there's much wrong at Westminster. This is exactly the reverse of the truth. Or am I also being prejudiced, since I am on the Executive and I am a backbencher and agin the Shadow Cabinet?

December 5th,[1] I insisting that he should try to get the administrative reorganization in the Parliamentary Party straightaway, while tempers were still good. Last Tuesday, of course, I didn't know of Douglas Jay's famous article, due to appear on Friday in *Forward*.[2] By itself, Roy Jenkins's 'Panorama' appearance hadn't created more than a minor ripple.

On Wednesday, after lunch, Hugh drove on to the Downs and on Thursday I came up to do another dry run for my new Granada television programme.[3] I was clear by lunch-time and then I had Harold Wilson in, furious and insecure and even more furious at the suggestion he should be promoted to Leader of the House. He regarded this as a conspiracy to chase him out of the Shadow Chancellorship and stood pat, with the only expression of anger and passion I've ever heard him use. He also defended the elective principle to the Shadow Cabinet. In fact he wasn't prepared for any kind of reforms, for the obvious reason that he wasn't going to be in charge of them. On this occasion he was bound to regard me as a dangerous rival. However, we managed to keep on close terms and I told him that it was his duty to go to see Gaitskell about it.

After this I gave Tony Wedgwood Benn dinner at the Athenaeum. He's as keen as anyone on a sensible reorganization, including effective co-ordination of Parliament and Transport House. He pullulates with proposals, including the names of the people to fill every job, from top to bottom. His enthusiasm is, for me, the reverse of infectious. The more names he names, the more cautious I get. I also saw Peter Shore, now promoted to Head of Research and desperately anxious for my help. I talked too to David Ennals, who, under my direction, was preparing the analysis of how the Election went and the report on our campaign committee. I gave him the most careful instructions that the report should contain no institutional recommendations and conclude only with suggestions of subjects for further research. On the other hand, I told Peter Shore of the idea for my place as co-ordinator, which Hugh and I had worked out, and he seemed delighted and wholly discreet.

Then on Saturday came the storm in every morning paper, as a result of Douglas Jay's article in *Forward*, demanding a wholesale rejection of 'the myth of nationalization', including steel nationalization, and suggesting a change in the name of the Labour Party.[4] It was the exact equal and opposite

[1] It was to be announced on October 28th that at the end of November some 2,000 trade union and constituency party delegates would spend a weekend at Blackpool reviewing the position. Proceedings, which would be public, would be opened by Gaitskell and closed by Bevan and there would be no motion.

[2] In the issue of October 16th, Mr Jay wrote that 'the better-off wage earners and numerous salary earners are tending to regard the Labour Party as associated with a class to which they themselves do not belong … we are in danger of fighting under the label of a class which no longer exists'. He argued, too, that the word 'nationalization' had become a liability and that 'we must destroy this myth decisively; otherwise we may never win again'.

[3] In 'Who Goes Next?', a television programme broadcast by Granada from its Manchester studios, Richard Crossman, Peter Thorneycroft and Malcolm Muggeridge discussed subjects prepared by the producer, Milton Shulman.

[4] He suggested 'Labour and Radical' or 'Labour and Reform'.

to Friday's extreme nationalizing article in *Tribune*[1] but on this occasion the right-wing was even sillier. The net result, of course, was to knock stone dead any idea that one could get some sensible administrative changes before the controversy about policy broke. Indeed, over the weekend my perfectly decent article in the *Statesman* has, of course, been associated with all the other intellectual friends of Gaitskell and my own position as an independent, and certainly not an anti-nationalizer, has been seriously impaired. I shouldn't be surprised if my chances of being elected to the Shadow Cabinet have been greatly reduced, though of course they may go up again during the events of the next ten days, before the ballot papers are issued.

I was so disturbed that I rang up and insisted that I should go to see Gaitskell last night. I arrived at half-past nine. We went through the argument over again, this time with me much more positively critical of the right-wing anti-nationalizers and Gaitskell somewhat more positively arguing their case. Once again, however, he was extremely careful not to associate himself with them. I was also extremely careful not to assent in any way to anything that Hugh said. It was a perfectly friendly talk and he made me postpone my going, until, when I got to the Tube at half-past eleven, I found the last train had gone at twenty-three minutes past, and it cost me twelve bob [12*s*.] to get home, thus breaking my post-*Mirror* resolution to stop taxis and restaurants.

I don't think yesterday's talk with Hugh added anything at all. It was simply that each of us got a little more set in our positions, from which the manoeuvring will start. He seems to feel quite confident that he will have no difficulty at the Party Meeting on Wednesday morning and that the vote of confidence in him will be sufficiently fervent to prevent any Left/Right rows. Maybe it will on that morning, but I am pretty sure that already the 100 trade unionists are burning with anger against the intellectuals, not unreasonably, for having started this row within a few hours of polling day. As for the Party, I shall be very surprised if Hugh hasn't overestimated the number of M.P.s who are prepared to throw nationalization so gaily overboard in the full public eye.

This morning we had our Election committee to consider Ennals's paper. The meeting was really excellent, with everybody present who had been there during the campaign. But I was horrified to find that David had put at the end of the draft a series of administrative resolutions, including proposals for publicity and research co-ordination between Parliament and Transport House, which could only have derived from me and only been suggested in order to give me the job! Morgan slipped out before we got to them and Ray Gunter at once expressed disapproval. I'm afraid I did the only thing possible and disowned them, rebuking David publicly. I'm sure he did it with the very finest motives, probably being prompted by Peter Shore. But it probably put me in filthily with a lot of people.

So the net result of the whole thing is that ten days of busy-bodying by

[1] Which that week demanded 'a return to Socialist principles'.

myself with Hugh, Harold and others have achieved precisely nothing, except the charge that I am a busybody. Maybe I shall learn soon to leave well alone.

Wednesday, October 21st
Our first Granada television show has passed off, with us, as you might say, sneaking into the world without too much harm. But meanwhile we are back in Parliament and I will report today's Party Meeting.

Yesterday we were there for the election of the Speaker[1] and I went in the morning to a Party Meeting and a great deal of talk. About my own personal position I was profoundly depressed, since I had realized that it had been deeply prejudiced by the performance of Jay and Jenkins. As another intellectual friend of Gaitskell, I was tarred with their brush. However, I may have over-simplified somewhat and I was careful on Monday on the television to dissociate myself entirely from Douglas Jay, something which was noted by three or four Labour Members who came up to me in the lobby.

Yesterday evening I got Roy Jenkins to come in and found him in a state of neurotic frenzy. Or is that fair? Better say that he had worked himself up into a mood for heroic crusading. 'After all, you taught me', he said, 'that, in order to educate, one must shock. Shock tactics are required to shake the Party into dropping nationalization altogether. Nothing less.' Tony Wedgwood Benn had told me how odd he had found Roy and the sensation he had that Roy was frantic and he, Tony cool. I was even more surprised to find myself cool and reasonable, with Roy frantic. I warned him that he was narrowing Hugh's room for manoeuvre and making it even more difficult to drop nationalization, even if we want to. 'How can Mr Bevan', I said, 'drop nationalization because you and Jay order him to? And, anyway, what matters is not merely what we do but how we do it.' However, Roy stormed out, saying he would make a great speech this morning.

This conversation had occurred just after I had had an hour and a half with Aneurin, the first time I had spoken to him since the Election. I sat in the Smoking Room with him, Tom Driberg and Jack Mendelson, the other two, of course, lick-spittle toadies, confirming Nye in everything he said, which was plainly exaggerated. He spent a long time attacking leaderolatry, the way Hugh Gaitskell was built up in every television programme, and so on. Nye talked as though he himself had been only too anxious to collaborate, a point where even Tom Driberg had to protest!

Then Nye said, 'These outrageous intrigues have got to stop.' 'Not secret intrigues,' I said, 'very blatant and public kites. What intrigues have there been, Nye?' He talked vaguely of Sunday's meeting in Hampstead. He was obviously furious and moving into action against the idea of dropping nationalization. 'Gaitskell', Nye said, 'will never be a Leader because he can never leave anything alone. He's always personally interfering.' Nye also

---

[1] W. S. Morrison was succeeded by Sir Harry Hylton-Foster, Q.C., also a Conservative.

made it clear that his proposal to Gaitskell last Tuesday that the Shadow Cabinet should be nominated and not elected had been invalidated by what had happened. On the whole, he was less explosive than I had expected, but deeply injured and all the more formidable because he was relatively quiet. It was surprising how very frankly he talked to me, because he obviously considers me a pure agent of Gaitskell's. But I think Nye can't resist a good talk.

This, then, was my background for this morning's Party Meeting. It started with a speech from Gaitskell, so measured, so balanced, so indecisive that there was no suggestion of an ovation. His first main point was that everybody had the right to take part in the inquest on our defeat, but the discussion should take place within reasonable limits of good behaviour. Then he outlined the main problems in ways which I had heard before. He next said we shouldn't have an inquest but began to talk about how to make the Parliamentary Party better. But on this he could have hardly been less effective.

At once Bill Blyton, the old Durham miner, got up and denounced Douglas Jay and told him to join the Liberal Party if he wanted to sacrifice our principles. He was followed by Michael Stewart, who made a perfectly capable, sensible speech, as usual, stressing that our policy in the Election had been pretty good and suggesting that we should carry on with it but face certain problems.

Far the best speech came from Christopher Mayhew, who said that the image of the Labour Party at present was that it is the party of the working class, of the underdog and of nationalization. This was an image that would get us an ever declining number of votes. We must dissociate the Labour Party from this narrow class connection. I was struck by the way the trade unionists were willing to receive this speech in silence but I couldn't help feeling it was a pity that some of it was delivered by a middle-class Socialist. However, Fred Lee followed up with quite a good speech on the need to reform the trade unions and then Roy Jenkins weighed in with his great plea to cut away from nationalization. After this Zilliacus made a dreary left-wing reply, which nobody listened to.

It was then twenty to one and there were twenty or thirty people wanting to speak. But Hugh stopped the meeting and said it should resume in a fortnight, since next week we must discuss the Queen's Speech. This was characteristic of our Party leadership. There was no earthly reason why we shouldn't resume this afternoon or tomorrow morning, since it was an extremely good debate and we should have gained by it. But that's not the tempo of the parliamentary leadership.

Moreover, the net effect of this morning's meeting was to show that the Jenkins/Jay line has no chance whatsoever of being accepted. Even Christopher Mayhew said we must stand by our principles of Socialization and it was obvious that most of the Party were deeply shocked by what they felt was a betrayal by Gaitskell's closest friends. On the other hand, I must say that the speeches made by Mayhew and Jenkins were very well delivered and thoughtful and were received thoughtfully. It was the highest level of debate I have heard for a long time. But what on earth is the point of having this debate and starting this tremendous inquest? All Hugh has done, from his own point of view, is to make the job of changing the Party constitution far more difficult.

This was confirmed to me this evening when I had to go and check with Tom Driberg and Ray Gunter about our campaign report to the Executive, whose final draft was prepared by David Ennals on my instructions. I have sharpened it up a great deal, so that it shows that the turning-point of the campaign was the Leader's Speech on income tax and I have inserted the words, 'The Leader, after consultation with Harold Wilson ... ' Ray said, 'Hadn't you better leave out "after consultation with Harold Wilson?" Isn't that too damning to poor Harold?' Then Ray added, 'You realize that Hugh has made all the 100 trade union members here deeply suspicious by his behaviour and he will now find it very difficult to get any change in the constitution.'

I have let Gerry Reynolds, to my great surprise, nominate me for the Shadow Cabinet, but I shall not be in any way surprised if I do rather badly. A hundred trade unionists will certainly refuse to vote for me because I am an intellectual. Moreover, the fact that I am universally regarded as responsible for the Gaitskellites' campaign makes me doubly suspect as trying to reorganize the Parliamentary Party, and that's something nobody will ever forgive. So it looks as though I may be driven to writing a book, willy-nilly.

Friday, October 23rd
I have a feeling this section of my diary wound itself up when I went yesterday to be sworn in and walked behind the Speaker's chair to find Hugh Gaitskell going towards his room. Earlier on I had been half inclined to go in for a talk to him. I told him I thought the week had been wholly unsatisfactory and, whatever you thought of the content of Jay's article, the result had been devastating, particularly as it was closely connected with Hugh. 'One must never underestimate the value of courage,' Hugh replied. 'When I made my famous Stalybridge speech after the Morecambe Conference, all my friends told me it was extremist and dangerous.[1] Of course I can't do it now, but one must expect it in Roy and Douglas.' 'Your Stalybridge speech', I said, 'started two and a half years of the most disastrous in-fighting in the country and included a general impression that I was a Communist. One has to have fairly careful definitions of courage and distinguish it from folly. The main trouble is that, by letting all this happen, you have prevented yourself from carrying out the necessary reorganization of the Parliamentary Party.'

'But one can't stop a thing of this sort,' Hugh said. 'People have got to be allowed to discuss freely. And, anyway, sooner or later we shall have to

[1] See above, p. 154 and n.

change things.' 'Yet the net effect,' I said, 'as I heard from Nye, is that he is now asking for more public ownership.' 'Well, in that case, I walk out,' Hugh said. 'Oh no, you don't,' I said. 'You veto each other into total immobilism and that I don't think much of. But I can't blame Nye for being thoroughly suspicious of Douglas and Roy. I warn you that the activities of Douglas are making other people form left-wing groups.' 'I told them not to,' Hugh replied. 'Yes, you may have told them not to but you didn't stop Douglas and the others conspiring and you can't blame the Left if it responds.'

After this Hugh launched a great attack on the *Tribune* for totally irresponsible and malicious attacks on him. 'Nye has far less to do with *Tribune* than you have to do with *Forward*, Roy and Douglas,' I said. Hugh didn't say no. As I was going out I asked him whether the suspension of Standing Orders had been discussed in the Parliamentary Committee. 'No,' he said, 'nobody suggested nomination,' thinking I was talking about the proposal to nominate the Shadow Cabinet instead of electing it.[1] When I told him my meaning, he said Nye had mentioned it. 'I am still more in favour of it,' I said. 'I was against it,' Hugh said tersely. 'But if you want to change the image of the Party,' I said, 'surely here is where you start.' 'But we'll have them voting against us,' he said, 'and then there will be chaos.' After this I went away. I discovered that Tony Wedgwood Benn had rung him up the same morning, giving much the same message.

This week has done appalling damage to the Party. On the other hand, one can only say that we reached the end of week with the Hampstead poodles in complete rout. Gordon Walker has let it be known that the article he has published today in *Forward* has been watered down to suit Party policy.

I went to dinner with Barbara on Wednesday and found Mikardo there, as well as, strangely enough, Paul Johnson, Tony Wedgwood Benn and Peter Shore. We all began to discuss how to resist what had happened and soon fell into the attitude of the Bevanite Group, much to Tony Wedgwood Benn's disturbance. It was extraordinary how instinctively one moved back into old habits of mind. Whereas, only a fortnight ago, we were all united in a great campaign against the Tories, now the Hampstead group and the Bevanites were eyeing each other as the main enemies. I myself was doing it as well as everybody else, instinctively.

However, next day, when Ian Mikardo asked Nye to have a chat, Nye replied that he wasn't going to have anything corresponding to the Hampstead group, that they had been routed, that there was no danger of a change in the constitution and that everything was all right. I think Nye's attitude was very wise, but of course he loves just saying No to any change. What has really been achieved by this disastrous week is a terrible state of rigid inability, from which the Parliamentary Party, I fear, will relapse into the kind of demoralization we had last July. It couldn't really be much more depressing.

[1] See above, p. 790.

Tuesday, October 27th

Yesterday I dined at the French Embassy to meet Mendès France. I found my fellow guests were Jenkins and Gaitskell. After dinner Mendès France asked us for twenty minutes or so about our Election campaign. What interested me was, first, Hugh's deference to me, whom he described as his campaign manager, and, secondly, his admission that his income tax pledge may have been a very grave mistake. But he added, quite fairly, that it probably wasn't decisive. We then began to discuss the problem of all Socialist parties of the West — the decline of class-consciousness with rising prosperity. Jenkins was very snappy when I pointed out that Lord Woolton, about whom I had been writing, is a Keynesian Liberal, like the American Democrats.[1] At once Jenkins spotted what I was at when I added, 'What really distinguishes a Socialist is the belief in public ownership and State trading.' However, we soon switched to French affairs, on which Hugh Gaitskell showed great boredom by yawning all the time. This irritated me a good deal.

Driving me home, Jenkins admitted that there had been grave tactical errors in the activities of the Hampstead group. 'However,' he said, quite cheerfully, 'to judge from the press, you are part of it now!' This, I'm afraid, is true enough. As one of Gaitskell's close associates, I have been identified with Jay, Jenkins, and so on, in a way which could hardly be more damaging. I gather from Barbara today that Harold Wilson has convinced himself that I came to him as an emissary of Gaitskell, having agreed to help get rid of Harold from the Shadow Chancellorship in order to put Jenkins in his place. The idea that Gaitskell should send me as an emissary was a bit amusing but I can well understand Harold's point of view. Anyway, the situation is unspeakably dreary and I am looking forward with — no, dread would be too dynamic a word — with a dull, mulish apprehension to tomorrow's National Executive, where every effort will be made to postpone every kind of decision until after the Conference and the appointment of the new Executive.

Tony Howard, who dined with me yesterday, had just seen Gaitskell and found him a combination of listlessness and complacency. Once again he had repeated all his claptrap about Jay's courage and the Stalybridge speech. Once again he had said that no harm had been done and then had added, 'It won't matter who is elected to the Shadow Cabinet. I know Dick thinks this is of importance but it isn't.' My own impression is that Gaitskell is quite unrepentantly determined to get his way about dropping nationalization and cares about nothing else. All our ideas of making the Party a more efficient fighting instrument are to him quite unimportant. The fact that Douglas Jay's kite has been flown and vigorously bombarded merely indicates to Hugh that the fight will be longer and that he must keep up the pressure even more fiercely.

[1] Crossman's review of the *Memoirs of the Rt Hon. The Earl of Woolton* (London: Cassell, 1959) appeared as 'Uncle Fred' in the *New Statesman* of October 31st, 1959.

Meanwhile, on the floor of the Commons there isn't even a shambles. It's utterly lifeless and bloodless. I hear that forty-one people have been nominated for the Shadow Cabinet, including Barbara. I guess that George Brown, Charlie Pannell and Denis Healey will get on, in addition to Dick Mitchison and Frank Soskice. I guess that Edith Summerskill won't but that Healey will take her place. I guess I shall do worse than last time, possibly worse than Barbara.

What a mess we are in! Dear Thomas Balogh tries hard to placate Harold Wilson, who has convinced himself that I acted as an emissary for Hugh Gaitskell in the attempt to throw him out of the Shadow Chancellorship. Nye Bevan is absolutely aloof and won't work with anybody for fear of being accused of having a group. George Brown informed George Wigg that Hugh Gaitskell has sacked him from the Shadow Defence Ministry. I don't believe it, unless Hugh has changed his mind, since he told me that of course George would stay Shadow Defence Minister unless he could think of something better. I've never known such a fuming, senseless mood of frustration. And to think of fifty poor young new Members plunged into it as their first experience of Socialist politics at Westminster!

Friday, November 13th
I meet quite a number of people now in Parliament who, for the first time, see the importance of my column, now that it's dropped. It's a great loss to the Labour Party, for my column was one of the few places where a systematic attempt was made, year in, year out, to explain the Labour Party's policies to the masses in intelligible terms. Without the column there is virtually no means of communication still available between the leadership in Parliament and ordinary people outside. Hugh Gaitskell, I think, always appreciated this. But now, when it's too late, a few others are doing so.

The *Mirror* did itself a great deal of damage by backing the Labour Party heavily up to Election day and then going completely non-political two days later. Sydney described to me the terrible scenes among the staff. On Election night, 90 per cent had revealed their Tory prejudices and roared and cheered the results, to the fury of Cudlipp, who came down in evening dress, very drunk, with Malcolm Muggeridge and Alma Birk, both of whom had to be carried out, and Cecil King. Hugh, also drunk, bitterly attacked the British people and the Labour Party for letting the *Mirror* down by not voting the right way. As a result of all this, the switch became even more violent and all the serious reporters had all their stories spiked for ten days. It became impossible to keep this up because the paper had ceased to be a paper.

Moreover, in the Fleet Street pubs the *Mirror* men, though Tories, couldn't stand the jeers at the performance of their paper and many of them begged that the paper should become Labour again in self-respect. So duly, ten days later, Sydney Jacobson wrote a leader, saying they were still an independent paper of the Left.

During this fortnight we have seen the usual intrigues and lobbying which always precede the election of the Shadow Cabinet. On Thursday of last week, when the results were due to be announced at the six-thirty meeting, George Wigg blew in. He was full of first-hand information about how the whole Parliamentary Party had now turned against Gaitskell and against anybody and everybody, particularly with university education, who had ever associated with him. After listening to George, I felt sure that the vote I should get would be much less than last year. Walking into the Commons, I ran into Hugh Massingham. He too had been primed by George and was full of his not very sympathetic sympathy with the injustice which fate had done me. I was also quite full of it myself, since self-pity is something which grows on a politician with age.

However, when the results were read out, as usual I discovered I had over-estimated the emotionalism of the Parliamentary Party. In fact, the voting showed almost incredible conservatism. True enough, six of the twelve elected are members of the trade union group. That includes, by the way, Tony Greenwood, who, as I learnt from Charlie Pannell, is now a sponsored T. & G. candidate, at the insistence of Frank Cousins. But even this trade union group had not had a real ticket. Fred Lee doubled his vote but Charlie Pannell and Bob Mellish, two outstanding members of it, got under forty each. No, the Party had voted for the decent, hard-working middle-of-the-road parliamentarians like Fred Willey,[1] Fred Lee and Michael Stewart, who came just above me. Patrick Gordon Walker had his vote reduced from 140 to 100.[2] But still, despite the indignation against the Hampstead set, Patrick was comfortably elected, and so was Dick Mitchison.

Listening to the results, I sat between Charlie Pannell and Barbara Castle. I bet Charlie two bob [2s.] that he'd be elected and took the bet. As for Barbara, she had come, I suspect, with hopes that had grown into expectations. It was bitter for her to find she was five places below me and had been beaten by ten votes by Edith Summerskill. But one certainly couldn't draw the conclusion from this ballot either that the entire Parliamentary Party had turned against Gaitskell or that the trade union group had voted as a whole. Indeed, if I were sober I should say that probably next year and almost certainly the year after, if I stand regularly, I shall be elected in place, say, of Dick Mitchison but well below Gordon Walker or Fred Lee.

As soon as the new Committee had been elected, Gaitskell began the task

---

[1] Labour M.P. for Sunderland 1945–50 and for Sunderland North since 1950. He was P.P.S. to Chuter Ede 1946–50 and Parliamentary Secretary at the Ministry of Food 1950–1, and was Minister of Land and Natural Resources 1964–7 and Minister of State at the Ministry of Housing and Local Government 1967.

[2] Crossman again received 87 votes, coming second in the list of those not elected. Harold Wilson topped the poll with 167 votes. Fred Willey had 92 votes, Fred Lee 137 and Michael Stewart 89. Patrick Gordon Walker had 101 votes and Dick Mitchison 94. Neither Charles Pannell, with 33 votes, nor Barbara Castle, with 76, were elected.

of forming his Shadow Administration. A fortnight ago I had fondly believed that I had persuaded him to drop these vast paper Ministries in Opposition. I think I had, but he is a conscientious man and, once you put your hand to producing a Shadow Ministry, it is difficult to stop before you've manned up not only the top jobs but the joint under-secretaryships as well. I had my own little tiff. Hugh had rung me over the weekend and told me he wanted Barbara as my Number Two. I told him this was silly and that anyway Barbara wouldn't accept. It didn't occur to me that Hugh quite literally wanted her to match up to Patricia Hornsby-Smith,[1] who is Number Two on pensions for the Government.

When I spoke to Barbara, I found that she was certainly determined to be in any Shadow Administration but would like to get out of pensions if she could be sure of something else. After some to-ing and fro-ing, she got herself Ministry of Works, an excellent idea, since it puts her in the lead in the popular cause for better offices for M.P.s, a fact which Hugh Gaitskell had quite forgotten when he offered her the job. After Questions this Wednesday, I confirmed that she was off and then asked if I could have as my Number Two either Gerry Reynolds or Reg Prentice. 'Both are available,' Hugh said, 'but Gerry's too much a newcomer for any job. You'd better have Prentice.' I said that would be excellent, since he was a trade unionist with special knowledge of the subject, and when I ran into him an hour later I found him delighted.

I was therefore peeved when Gaitskell rang me up at five o'clock yesterday to say that my Number Two was Douglas Houghton, one of the most explosive, erratic men I know, quite apart from being a member of the General Council of the T.U.C., the last thing I want near me if I am going to reconstruct our health and unemployment insurance. I exploded down the phone, whereupon Gaitskell rapped, 'I must say, I don't know what you're grumbling at. I don't remember being consulted on who was my Number Two when I was offered a Cabinet job. Anyway, it's too late for a change.' 'Not too late for me to pull out,' I said. He said, 'That's impossible. You should consider such a step very seriously indeed.' Of course it was impossible, since I well knew that, if I did pull out, Hugh would let it be known that I objected to Douglas Houghton as my Number Two and then where would I be with the trade unions?

One other incident was illuminating. Owing to the Granada programme, I couldn't go to Home Policy on Monday and Hugh Gaitskell assured me that Barbara would take the chair, so as to leave next year's chairmanship open for me, something Peter Shore desperately wanted. However, according to Barbara afterwards, Harold Wilson rushed into the meeting to say that,

[1] Conservative M.P. for the Chislehurst division of Kent 1950–66 and from 1970 until February 1974, when she became a life peer. She was Parliamentary Secretary at the Ministry of Health 1951–7 and Joint Parliamentary Under-Secretary of State at the Home Office 1957–9, and also Joint Parliamentary Secretary at the Ministry of Pensions and National Insurance 1959–61. She became a D.B.E. in 1961.

19 At Transport House 1959 at work on the Manifesto: (*left to right*) Bevan, Castle, Ian Mikardo, Morgan Phillips, Peter Shore and Gaitskell

20 Crossman playing with his children

21 Gaitskell's 'fight, fight and fight again' speech at the 1960 Party
Conference, Scarborough

22 Michael Foot on a CND march

according to precedent, the man to follow Jim Griffiths, the Deputy Chairman of the Party, as chairman of Home Policy, was Nye Bevan, who was prepared to accept. Harold tried to get him elected and only Nye's absence made it impossible. Next day, I sat next to Harold at lunch in the Members' Dining Room. 'I was trying to get you all last week,' Harold said. 'There's a new contender for the chairmanship of Home Policy. I did my best for you but Nye Bevan was insistent.' Of course, if Nye does take the chair, there will be no kind of policy thinking in the next twelve months. I have no doubt that that is what he intended.

Nevertheless, when I look at the whole picture, things aren't quite so grim as I sometimes see them from my own point of view. The fact that all the gains of the Election campaign have been lost in Transport House is sad, but not fatal. The fact that the Parliamentary Party is still organized in precisely the same way is sad, but not fatal. It is my impression that the mood of the Party is still a good deal better than in July and that there are some excellent new Members. Moreover, the Parliament seems to be developing on slightly more liberal lines and with slightly more vitality. One certainly shouldn't write off everything as finished. But what a task we have!

Wednesday, November 25th
I suppose the questions I raise now will be answered by the Blackpool Conference next weekend. Meanwhile I have virtually nothing to report on the Labour Party, since I've hardly been in the Commons or had any talks. I doubt if I've ever been so isolated since I entered the House in 1945. It's not like the time when I was a social pariah, sent to Coventry by the trade unions. It's just that I live at home and don't talk to anybody much. George Wigg is in hospital and I have a chat with him from time to time but I feel very cut off and also, if I am honest with myself, I am very deeply chagrined by the treatment I have had from the Executive. It's not merely that I am suffering from guilt by association with the Leader, which I certainly am; but, as Peter Shore remarked to me the other day, 'After all, you did work out for them their only good policy. You were personally responsible for their only two successful propaganda pamphlets and you ran their campaign. But you are the only person they have deliberately not thanked. That's fairly tough.' And, curiously enough, it is. When I sat at the Executive this morning I couldn't help feeling sour and just refusing to have any part if they were such damn fools. At the end David Ennals came up and said, 'May I take it you have now retired from politics?' And I said, 'No, but I'm not going to help them when they behave like that.'

I dined on Monday with Alastair Hetherington, Editor of the *Guardian*,[1] having for the first time visited his august building with Anthony Howard. I

---

[1] Foreign Editor 1953–6 and Editor 1956–75 of the *Manchester Guardian* (later the *Guardian*). He was Controller of B.B.C. Scotland 1975–9. From September 1961 to February 1964 he lodged with Crossman at 9 Vincent Square.

found Hetherington much more interesting on this occasion. He first of all wanted to discuss the *Mirror*, by which he was fascinated. He held the view, like many others, that the *Mirror* had thrown away a good long-term asset for the sake of a short-term circulation it wouldn't get. This view, which Sydney and I discussed together four weeks ago, is now becoming prevalent among most journalists.

Then Hetherington turned to the Labour Party and said that in the last ten days he had been supporting it but he was finding it difficult going, since it was so fundamentalist in its thinking. Could anyone help? He quite agreed that one could not possibly abandon public ownership but he also saw that one had to have an independent philosophy of it.

The fact is, the whole leadership of the Party is now stinking with intrigue and suspicion, since everybody knows that Bevan is now manoeuvring against Gaitskell and that Harold Wilson, who doesn't forgive easily, is going to take his vengeance for Gaitskell's vague plot to oust him from the Shadow chancellorship. Everybody knows that the trade unions are now bitterly against what they call the right-wing intellectuals and that the left-wing intellectuals like Barbara and Ian are fiercely dissociating themselves from any responsibility for the campaign.

Wednesday, December 9th
I suppose, if I had written this diary immediately on our return from Blackpool, I would have remembered a great deal more vividly the successive episodes in which was, from a dramatic point of view, a vintage Conference.[1] All the journalists present loved it, because there was movement and a sense of unpredictability, owing to the failure of the Executive to make up its mind — or rather, the deliberate decision of Gaitskell that the Executive should not be allowed to make up its mind. I spent most of my evenings with the journalists, partly because they were staying in the better hotels, partly because I am used to being with the *Daily Mirror* at Conferences and partly because I am more ill at ease with my colleagues than ever before.

I shall not recount the story of the Conference, which was pretty accurately told in the press, except to say this. When I arrived at The Cliffs, I learnt that both Barbara's and Hugh's speeches would be ready and cyclostyled by nine o'clock in the morning and in fact one or two copies were available the night before. But neither had seen the other's speech and Nye had only seen Hugh's for the first time on the Friday evening. It really was true that the only Executive statements were to be three personal statements, deliberately uncorrelated and the first two highly competitive.

Hugh had at least had the sense to arrange that the first session before

---

[1] The Conference at Blackpool, on November 28th and 29th, was opened by the outgoing Chairman of the Party, Barbara Castle. In his own speech Hugh Gaitskell demanded the repeal of Clause 4 of the Labour Party constitution, which pledged the Party to 'the eventual nationalization of all the means of production, distribution and exchange'.

lunch should be on other business, but he was still determined to speak first in the debate and to leave Nye to wind up after two sessions. Hugh was also taking the risk of letting Barbara start off. I didn't speak to him at all in the Conference, except at the Mayor's Reception, when he came up to me and said, 'Cheer up! Don't look so gloomy!' or words to that effect. Dora talked chit-chat on one or two occasions. So I don't know for sure, but I strongly suspect, that, for the last eight days, Hugh had known at the bottom of his heart that he wasn't going to carry us with him or even get much of an ovation.

But what he didn't know was that Barbara would make a brilliant doctrinal speech and, more important, show how one can attack Tory prosperity in terms of the affluent society and show that it is riddled with inconsistencies, injustices and weaknesses. What really did Hugh down was the contrast between Barbara's attack on the Tory economy and his own apparent complacent acceptance of it as satisfactory and stable. Of course, the two attitudes are closely linked to corresponding attitudes to public ownership.

The common report is that the tide was all against Hugh on Saturday afternoon and Sunday morning and then turned suddenly after Benn Levy's speech, with courageous contributions from Denis Healey and Shirley Williams, so that in the end there were speeches in favour of Gaitskell. In my experience this was not the case. What did come was a strong tide of anti-split emotion and speakers who felt that, even if you disagreed with a Leader, you shouldn't treat him so rough and split the Party.

Certainly, on the Executive, there was virtually no enthusiasm for Hugh's speech or for his tactics. On my side of the rostrum the last two seats were filled by Eirene White and Ray Gunter. Both refused to clap and sat numb, and so did Tony Greenwood. Dai Davies, who came next, clapped fervently. Tom Driberg and I gave token applause and so did Nye, whereas Ian Mikardo did not. Most of the trade unionists felt, rightly enough, that Hugh's tactic was to commit them by a personal statement from which they could not withdraw and they didn't like the feeling of being treated in this way. I found his speech dull and prosaic and quite unsuited to carry the Conference – the culmination of eight of the dreariest weeks of my life.

But of course it's true that the antis, led by Michael Foot,[1] are completely antediluvian. What was really fantastic was staging a Conference without central direction or leadership and there's a very strong feeling on the Executive that this must never be allowed to happen again. The Executive is going to forbid its leaders the kind of authority they enjoyed in the Campaign Committee and the Chairmen's Committee and that means, next year, that Hugh Gaitskell will find it much more difficult to carry any changes at all.

Indeed, what amazes me, looking back, is the attitude of most of the press. Bob Mackenzie in the *Observer* is an extreme example, who holds that Gaitskell must win because we can't afford a split and because no sensible

---

[1] Who told the Conference that, as they obviously didn't want Mr Gaitskell any more, they had better choose someone else.

man can oppose him. This is not my impression. It certainly isn't the view of
Aneurin Bevan, with whom I have talked several times since the Conference
and who now thinks at least that he won't repeat his sloppy behaviour during
our discussion of the non-nuclear club. Never again will Nye let Hugh get
away with insisting on his personal prejudices.

This is felt even more strongly by Harold Wilson, who has now palled up
with me again, and proved his palliness when Ian Mikardo was knocked off
the Executive. Ian and I had observed early on that we had better push
George Brinham to follow Ian as Vice-Chairman, since the trade unionists
were restless. When Ian was knocked off, this meant that George was elected
as Chairman, leaving the vice-chairmanship open to Harold and me. Harold
took me off the stage and insisted that I should have it, which, indeed, was
not unreasonable in alphabetical terms (B,C,W). But all the same it was a
definite act on his part, after which he expressed the bitterest criticism of
Gaitskell's performance, though he never doubted that Nye would rescue
him.

But since the Conference Harold has been increasingly bitter, as the following episode will confirm. Last week the *Daily Mail* came out with a fantastic
story, 'WILSON LEADING LEFT AGAINST GAITSKELL'. Harold caught me in the
lobby and took me away for an hour's talk. 'I first got wind of it at half-past
eleven last night,' he said, 'thanks to my contacts in the press. I immediately
planted a counter-story in the *Daily Express*, which they have printed. This
morning I have contacted each of the main lobby correspondents to deny it.
But something more was needed and so I went to see Hugh and told him how
serious and absurd it was. I mentioned your name, by the way, at which Hugh
commented, "Dick's been saying some very queer things about you recently,
Harold".' Harold was clearly hinting that the whole story that he was due for
a shift from the Shadow Chancellorship had been invented by me. Indeed, he
diverted at this point to say that Hugh was putting the blame for all the things
that had happened in the last seven weeks either on Douglas Jay or on me.
'So,' said Harold, 'I insisted on a personal statement this evening, which I
have typed out and shall give to the press.'

As we went on talking, Harold's tone changed and he spent twenty
minutes telling me that it was impossible to conceive that Hugh would last
for two years as the Leader. 'He has committed himself too far. He's too
mulish and obstinate to give way. He can't be an Attlee, to do him justice,
and we won't let him move the constitution. It's essential that he shouldn't
stay too long if he is to go at all,' he concluded. 'Let's hope it's under twelve
months.' This episode is characteristic of Labour politics. Harold had come
to me indignantly denying a charge that he was leading an anti-Gaitskell
campaign but within half an hour he had said every single thing which would
fully justify anyone who overheard it concluding that he was! And when I
heard him reading aloud his long, laboured statement at the Party Meeting,
I felt even more strongly that he was protesting a bit too much. But he hadn't

misread the press, from which he got tremendous publicity for this attitude of characteristically Wilsonian nobility.

I haven't seen Hugh since the Conference and have only twice talked to Nye and twice to Harold. I haven't been in Parliament much either, now that I'm fairly busy writing my little book on Palestine,[1] which has interested me more and more. Since I stopped writing for the *Mirror*[2] I seem to enjoy writing more and have had a great success with my review of *F.E.* and of Strachey's book for the *Statesman*.[3] But this gets me further out of Party politics, despite my vice-chairmanship, which gives me all the robes of office and all contacts with power in the Party, if I want to use it. But what should I use it for? Even if one did work out a decent doctrine, I find it more and more difficult to see how, under Gaitskell and Bevan, we can recover, and what on earth we should do without them.

Never have I felt my colleagues more hostile. Harold dropped it out of the corner of his mouth that two trade unionists had approached him in a desperate effort to stop me being made Vice-Chairman. They were Walter Padley and, of course, Ray Gunter, who worked with me throughout the Election campaign. I should think by now I would get twenty fewer votes in elections to the Shadow Cabinet. What a relief it is to be connected with Prescote and to spend a whole day at the Smithfield Show, looking at the livestock and studying potato scrabblers and deciding what kind of deep freeze to buy! Moreover, the *Guardian* rang up today and asked me to review *Ernest Bevin*[4] by Alan Bullock when it comes out, and that's fun.

---

[1] *A Nation Reborn* (London: Hamish Hamilton, 1960).

[2] Crossman's legal adviser, Arnold Goodman, had pointed out to him that, since he didn't have a salary, he could not obtain any compensation for 'loss of office'. Instead, it was arranged in mid-November that Crossman should be retained as political adviser for three years at £1,000 a year.

[3] Crossman reviewed John Strachey's *The End of Empire* (London: Gollancz, 1959) in the *New Statesman* on November 28th, 1959. Lord Birkenhead had written the life of *F. E. Smith: First Earl of Birkenhead* (London: Eyre & Spottiswoode, 1959).

[4] *The Life and Times of Ernest Bevin: I: Trade Union Leader 1881–1940* (London: Heinemann, 1960). Fellow, Dean and Tutor in Modern History at New College, Oxford, 1945–52, Censor of St Catherine's Society, Oxford, 1952–62 and Master of St Catherine's College, Oxford, since 1960, Alan Bullock was Vice-Chancellor of Oxford University 1969–73. In 1972 he was knighted and in 1976 he became a life peer. His other publications include *Hitler: A Study in Tyranny* (London: Odhams, 1952; revised edn 1964) and vol. II of *The Life and Times of Ernest Bevin: Minister of Labour 1940–45* (London: Heinemann, 1967).

1960

In early January Crossman was in Germany, staying with Lilo Milchsack, lecturing and covering a trial proceeding before the Fourth Chamber of the Landgericht in Düsseldorf, in which six leaders of the German Peace Movement were accused of 'endangering the State'. Crossman's articles on Germany appeared in the New Statesman *on January 23rd and 30th and February 6th.*

Wednesday, January 27th

I got back to Lilo's house last Wednesday to hear after a long day in Düsseldorf that I was wanted urgently by the *Daily Mirror*. I was rather puzzled and then Hugh Cudlipp's voice came through, saying that Nye would be dead by the end of the night.[1] Would I do five articles on him for a really good sum? I asked, 'How much?' and Hugh said, '£2,500.' I said that sounded all right. He said he would send over someone with the necessary books and cuttings to help me. Meanwhile Hugh agreed the articles shouldn't start before Monday. I said on those terms I would do them and made arrangements to fly home on Saturday morning. A young innocent duly arrived, carrying with him two little books and ten cuttings. He had been thirteen years a general reporter and this was his first day out of England. Poor young man! His second German meal made him very sick. He could give me no help and there was no point in his being there. However, I arranged for him to stay two days and come back with me.

Nye didn't die and on Saturday Hugh rang up and said he would pop round and see me on Sunday morning. I said I would pop round to him and walked in drenching rain to Chelsea, where I arrived at half-past eleven to find Hugh and Eileen having gins and tonics. We resumed our relationship as though the little gap since he came last August and told me he was getting rid of me had never occurred. Eileen complained that Sydney had gone round for three weeks after the Election defeat looking like a sourpuss and Hugh said, 'It only took me two days to throw off the little depression one naturally has.'

I said I assumed that the urgent idea for the Bevan article was off. Eileen said it would be far better if Nye died straightaway—how awful to hang on, since he is doomed. I had told Hugh on the phone that I couldn't start writing the articles before Nye died and now, whatever happened, he would have to give me two days between the death and the announcement of the series. Hugh had sounded reluctant on the phone but now he agreed. The truth, I think, is that the great idea is now beginning to look not quite such sensational journalism. I shall be most interested to see what does happen if Nye does die in the next four weeks. At present Hugh intends to have not five but four articles. And how much will he pay? My guess is less than half as much.

All this sounds terribly mercenary. Actually the news that Nye was dying came as a real national shock. George Wigg was not exaggerating when he said it was worse news for the Labour Party than the loss of the Election. I

---

[1] After a four-hour operation for cancer, Bevan had become very weak.

think I have probably written before in this diary that, since the Election, Nye has been the sheet anchor keeping this poor boat steady and, in particular, preventing the skipper turning it over in an attempt to reorganize it.

When Parliament resumed yesterday, the state of the Party was the only subject of conversation and nobody dared to think beyond Nye's death. I had Harold and Barbara to dinner. Harold came rushing in like a busy little bee and, when asked, said that, if the place were vacant, he would not only stand for the treasurership, as he decided some time ago, but also for Deputy Leader. I was very surprised, since he had never made this suggestion before, and said, almost involuntarily, 'What, you and Gaitskell, two Oxford economists? That won't do! It would be better to have Gaitskell and Robens.'

Then I realized that Harold was in deadly earnest and won't let anybody step ahead of him. I fear he expected Barbara and me to leap to it and offer him our devoted services in his bid for the leadership. But neither of us rose to the moment and I don't think either of us even said we would support him, at least not very enthusiastically, which put him off for the rest of the evening. Yet, the truth is that, if Nye is away, Gaitskell is intolerable, Robens is impossible and I would rather have Harold. But what I am not prepared to do is to start organizing and intriguing for it.

It was a funny, roundabout evening, not at all like old times, though we referred to them from time to time in the upstairs room. Harold is not prepared to consider any kind of policy issue and Barbara and I each have our own hobby-horses to ride, she Colonies and I, at the moment, Germany and defence. Whenever she talked about Colonies or I talked about Germany, however, Harold somehow got out of the way. All we could discuss was tactics for the Executive this morning. Like Hugh Gaitskell, Harold Wilson had been in America during the Recess. On his return he found a message saying that he should see Hugh. Hugh was all over him—very different from after the Election. On the other hand, not unexpectedly, I have had no contact with the Leader, apart from sitting next to him this morning.

I woke up to find in all this morning's papers a release saying that Hugh Gaitskell thought we should postpone discussion during Nye's illness. Directly we came to the item on the agenda, Hugh said he had told Jennie yesterday that, since a bitter row might endanger Nye's health, we should postpone things for a month. Jennie said she appreciated this and went on to argue that the whole constitutional issue should be postponed while we discussed our policies. Why a bitter argument about abstract words, she said, when what we need to decide is what we are going to do? This obviously disconcerted Hugh, who said he didn't want to enter into a discussion.

So we decided to postpone everything until next month's N.E.C., at which we shall decide the date for a special N.E.C., which will probably be on March 16th. At this meeting we shall have a general debate on the issue of whether or not to revise the Party constitution. Morgan pointed out, that, if we postpone our conclusions too long, all the unions will have had their annual conferences and will be unable to make up their minds. So it looks, anyway, as though, if the decision were taken to revise the constitution, the recommendations could not be made to this year's but only to next year's Conference, when Crossman will be in the chair, unless he can get off this frightful body[1] in time.

The atmosphere at the Executive was as dead and dreary and suspended-animation as ever. What Hugh apparently cannot understand is that his proposal to amend the constitution has really frozen us stiff, so that as a Party we are completely motionless and will go on being defeated in local elections and by-elections while this appalling process occurs at the top. But why worry about the Labour Party, with civil war in Algiers and with the kind of things I have been seeing in Germany, where I have just made my first expedition since Virginia arrived. Once again I find that, if I work sixteen hours a day, over-eat, over-drink, over-talk, I feel better and better, mainly because I am away, on the job, doing things I really can do and causing a commotion. It was a wonderful time and I've written three first-rate articles for Kingsley.

Thursday, February 4th

Because I happened to have the first Coventry East Dinner,[2] I decided to make a speech about Clause 4. George Wigg was rather against it, prophesying that people would regard it as a personal attack on Gaitskell. But I think I drafted it quite skilfully and certainly it went down wonderfully at Coventry, besides getting a very wide discussion in the press. Partly as an after effect, at the Party Meeting yesterday morning on nuclear weapons I for once got a very good reception.

Friday, February 12th

Harold Wilson has come out with a speech which he has been touting round the lobbies for ten days and which he finally delivered at the Press Gallery lunch.[3] I must give Harold credit for diligence, hard work—and success. Though a threatened rail strike was the main news, he certainly got prominence and two leaders for his moderate, middle-of-the-road proposal that, before discussing Clause 4, we should agree on our policy for national-

---

[1] I.e. the N.E.C.

[2] At the annual dinner of the Coventry East Labour Party on January 29th, Crossman stated that nothing he had heard at Blackpool had made him like any better the proposals originally put forward by Mr Jay. 'But I still thought that, since the proposals had been made, it should be argued to a conclusion. Since then, however, I have begun to wonder whether we can afford to enter on another, long, internal controversy.' Crossman preferred to 'drop the whole idea' of rewriting the constitution, concentrating instead on reviewing the policies on which the Party had fought the last Election, 'with the aim of presenting our cause more effectively to the electorate'.

[3] In a speech to the Parliamentary Press Gallery Luncheon Club on February 11th Harold Wilson said: 'We must settle the argument on policy first and then, and only then, decide what, if any, additions are necessary to Clause 4.'

ization, a job which could be done in ten minutes. In one sense his speech was a follow-up of mine last week, but Harold, who is fly, made sure that no one should feel this and that they should treat him as the great mediator – and also as the possible rival if things go wrong for Gaitskell. Harold discussed his speech at length with me on Tuesday, once again pouring out his venom against Gaitskell and not concealing his desire to get rid of him. But then I think he must have discussed his speech with at least fifty other people, treating each as his main adviser, and he told me he discussed it at length with Gaitskell, too.

This morning I went into the Commons to hear yet another statement on the railway strike.[1] I ran into Tony Wedgwood Benn. He said that the Party was just a mass of hopeless compromises and we must think all our policies through again. I said we had been doing that for the last four years and I just couldn't face another twenty working parties. Altogether we had a fine, muddled altercation, partly because both of us are so desperately angry with everything that we cannot be very sensible even to each other; partly, I think, because Tony has been partially nobbled about Clause 4 and is in a genuine confusion. To my amazement, he bitterly attacked Anthony Greenwood as the chief enemy of progress, though I can find nothing very different between the two of them – both rather nice, good-looking, success boys. But I think Tony Wedgwood Benn is nearer the truth when he says that he is beginning to doubt whether anybody can make anything of the Labour Party ever again.

Friday, February 26th

The boredom of Clause 4 has been gnawing my vitality away week by week. On Monday John Strachey, that arch middle-of-the-way conspirator, drew me aside and said he'd had a long talk to Gaitskell. The occasion for this was an article John had written for the *Spectator*.[2] 'Naturally, as I was trying to help the Leader, I submitted the article for his approval. It so happened Michael Stewart was there and we had an hour's discussion. Gaitskell objected to two passages. The first was where I said it was very unfair to accuse him of agreeing with Jay's original article:[3] "You must take that out," Gaitskell said. "I won't repudiate Douglas." The second was a sentence in

[1] As part of the settlement in avoidance of a strike in 1958, the British Transport Commission and the three railway unions had agreed on the establishment of a committee, with Mr Claude Guillebaud, a Cambridge economist, as chairman, to assess the 'comparability' of railway workers' wages with those paid in other industries. The committee's report was due in April 1960, with any awards to be backdated to January. The N.U.R. now demanded an immediate wage increase, but the two other railway unions, ASLEF and the T.S.S.A., dissociated themselves from the demand. The N.U.R. declared a strike on February 15th, even though the date of the Guillebaud report was advanced to early March. On February 12th the strike was called off after the Minister of Labour, Edward Heath, had intervened. The British Transport Commission's offer of an interim 5 per cent award was accepted by the railwaymen.

[2] Presumably unsigned, since nothing under his signature appears at this time.

[3] See above, p. 791.

which I said that those who made Clause 4 a life-and-death matter were doing us harm, whether they insisted on revising it or insisted in leaving it intact. Hugh imperiously said this was quite impossible and, much as Michael and I pleaded with him, would brook no word of it.'

I have also talked to one middle-of-the-roader and one right-winger, by chance. I sat next to Fred Mulley[1] at the Party Meeting on defence on Thursday morning, when he whispered to me, 'Of course the only thing is to leave Clause 4 alone. It's sheer craziness to touch it.' Again last night, Ernest Popplewell, a right-wing railwayman Whip, was equally violent in attacking the whole concept. I really think there is no one in favour of it. And yet – and this is the fascinating fact – the Leader can get his way.

Of course Harold Wilson had overdone his lobbying and conspiring before producing his speech. So had Tony Greenwood, who had leaked to all the press that he was going to try to get another postponement. By the way, I must add that I was ten minutes late for the N.E.C. meeting and I went out to lunch with Otto Preminger[2] at one o'clock and so missed the end. So all this is secondhand. But obviously Hugh had been able to persuade all the trade unionists that a conspiracy was taking place among the politicians against his leadership. Immediately all the trade-unionists' suspicion of change and dislike of his violation of the rules had been switched into a passionate anti-politician agitation, in which Hugh was also backed by all the women. It would be wrong to assume from this that he will not have a hard time on March 16th, but I am pretty sure that, unless Nye sends a letter, which he won't, we are bound to allow Hugh to submit his proposals and then we are bound to proceed. Of course, if this is all that happens, it won't really be very important, since in fact by now most of the content of his revisionism has been quietly jettisoned. I have summarized my views in an article in *Encounter*[3] and also sent a letter to Gaitskell.

Crossman's papers do not include a copy of this letter, to which Gaitskell did not reply. In a private letter to Crossman on March 19th, accompanying the official letter seeking assurances of Crossman's loyalty or his resignation from the Front Bench, Gaitskell described as greatly exaggerated Crossman's 'fears about a new statement of aims'. Gaitskell's letter continued:

Incidentally, I very well remember discussing the idea of a new statement

[1] Labour M.P. for the Park division of Sheffield since 1950. He was Deputy Secretary of State for Defence and Minister for the Army 1964–5, Minister of Aviation 1965–7, Joint Minister of State at the Foreign and Commonwealth Office, with responsibility for Disarmament, 1967–9 and Minister of Transport 1969–70. With the return of the Labour Government in February 1974, he served as Minister for Transport at the Department of the Environment 1974–5, Secretary of State for Education and Science 1975–6 and Secretary of State for Defence 1976–9. A member of the N.E.C. 1957–8, 1960–4 and since 1965, he was Chairman of the Labour Party 1974/75.

[2] A producer and director of films and plays. His films include *Forever Amber* (1947), *St Joan* (1957), *Exodus* (1960) and *Tell Me that You Love Me, Junie Moon* (1970).

[3] 'The Spectre of Revisionism', *Encounter*, April 1960.

with you at your farm after the Election. I actually suggested that you should take a hand at drafting. You did not seem to oppose this at the time though I admit that you did seem to associate it — not I think very logically — with the change in the method of appointment to the Parliamentary Committee.

On the personal side, I do not feel disposed to say much. I doubt if it would help. Of course, I do not object to being warned or advised but I have certainly had the impression since the Election that you were definitely on the side of those who would like to see me defeated in the present controversy — and this despite the fact that you thought no issue of principle was at stake. Perhaps it is just that I hope for what you would regard as an unreasonable degree of loyalty from my friends. I certainly regret that the close and happy relations existing between us before and during the Election do not seem to have continued in the last few months.

Meanwhile there blew up another split and crisis about defence.[1] For days I have been talking to George Wigg about the White Paper and I had agreed to support a resolution which he and Manny had drafted. Then we all went to the joint meeting of the defence and foreign affairs group, harangued by George Brown and Denis Healey, which really was a ghastly schemozzle, since all the speeches from the platform were concerned with forms of words, achieving formal unity, parrying the Government attack, etc., and not with policy.

Next day, on Thursday morning, we had the full Party Meeting. This went much better than I expected, though George Brown was again terrible. Zilliacus started by asking us to abandon NATO. I was called next and made a reasoned speech in favour of this year going forward to oppose nuclear strategy, which I defined as reliance on nuclear weapons as a substitute for rather than an addendum to conventional forces. It was this, I argued, that had got the whole West into trouble and against which we must fight. One should not be against a nuclear deterrent but against getting oneself into a position where one's conventional forces were so weak that one was bound to resort to it, even in a secondary action. Of course all this didn't impress the pacifists, though it did impress Stephen Swingler, George and Shinwell. Indeed, the whole debate went very well for us. Gaitskell made a very pleasant, reasoned reply, in which, however, he said that one must stand by the policy and not seem to be changing it.

However, by the evening meeting[2] at half-past six, when the final resolution was submitted for approval, Gaitskell had been got at. He tried to stop any

---

[1] The annual Defence White Paper (Cmnd 952) was to be debated on February 29th and March 1st. On February 17th it had been announced in the House of Commons that a missile warning station, costing £34 million (to which the American Government would contribute), was to be built at Fylingdales, near Whitby, on Government-owned land that was part of a national park. The public continued to be deeply anxious about nuclear weapons and there were intermittent demonstrations by protesters.

[2] I.e. of the defence and foreign affairs groups.

discussion of their final, hopelessly exposed wording, protesting against the evasions and confusions of the Government's nuclear policy. 'Evasions and confusions'! And for us to accuse the Government of that! I suggested a blunt protest against the Government's nuclear policy and Hugh again said, 'There can be no change of Party policy,' but this time angrily.

We were due to vote at seven o'clock, after which everybody would disperse, so there was a frantic rush to decide what to do. Should a rival back-bench resolution be tabled? We stood in the Central Lobby, rapidly discussing. Shinwell said he'd rather not table [a rival] resolution but was prepared to abstain on the Party resolution. Silverman was sharply insistent that a resolution must go down and so was George Wigg, who said he would sign it, if nobody else did. I had found that Tom Driberg's name had simply been appended because mine was there. In another corner of the Lobby was Barbara Castle, discussing her new job of Shadow Minister of Works and obsessed, with no time for nuclear weapons. In another corner were Harold Wilson and Tony Greenwood, obsessed with Clause 4 and the Executive and appalled by the idea that any member of the Executive should get into further trouble by signing a splitting resolution.

I took another look at the list of names. Did I want to be in with Zilliacus, Emrys Hughes, Stephen Swingler, Julius Silverman and Sydney Silverman? Reluctantly, but rather definitely, I ditched them—because of course, by taking my name and Tom Driberg's name off, I completely altered the whole balance. Even though Manny's name was on, this was an ultra-Left split and not a really major rebellion against the leadership.[1] But then, would it have been that if Tom and I had been on? Not really. And are we ready for it and can I really face it all over again? Anyhow, I said no and went into the dining room to help give the Israelis dinner, flushed with their electoral triumph.[2] We had a wonderful and tremendous argument with each other in front of the Labour M.P.s and then fell into each other's arms. I enjoyed myself immensely.

In the two-day defence debate the Opposition motion deplored the Government's inefficiency but assumed a bipartisan position on the need for nuclear armament. The Opposition Amendment was defeated by 330 votes to 197; the Government resolution approving the White Paper was carried by 329 votes to 245. The division lists showed that 43 Labour M.P.s had failed to support the Opposition Amendment. One of these was Crossman, whose speech attacked

[1] Shinwell's Amendment, which was not accepted, read: 'This House deplores a defence policy based upon a nuclear strategy which, since 1951, has involved an expenditure of over £13,000 million, which proposes to continue such expenditure at an even greater rate, and which affords to Her Majesty's subjects no effective defence.'

[2] In the General Election of November 3rd, 1959, the Mapai Party had increased its representation from 40 to 47 seats, a number greater than in any previous Knesset. Mr Ben-Gurion was now in a better position to select a new coalition Government. Among the successful Mapai candidates were Shimon Peres, General Moshe Dayan and Crossman's particular friend, Abba Eban.

the strategic, economic and political arguments for British nuclear strategy.
He concluded with a warning: 'We shall find it very difficult to vote for an
Amendment in which the Government nuclear strategy is not censured, but
only the confusions and evasions of that strategy.'

Wednesday, March 2nd

So the rebellion occurred after all! For once I have cheated in writing this
diary and read the last entry, otherwise I would have completely forgotten
that on Thursday evening I had decided that the rebellion was off because we
weren't ready for it. What has happened since then to alter my mind? Nothing
over the weekend. Anne and I went down to Prescote without the children
and I immersed myself in farm problems. Saturday was an absolutely perfect
spring morning and we walked the farm from end to end together, as Anne
can only do when the children are not there.

On Monday I got back from Manchester, where I was doing my Granada
television show, just in time to hear George Wigg and Nigel Birch in the
defence debate. George was very long and detailed and really very powerful,
if you understood the subject, and Nigel Birch said the same thing in eighteen
minutes, with caustic brevity. After that the debate petered out into inconceivable boredom.

I was determined to speak and that night the Speaker told me, to my
amazement, that he would put me in first, before Shinwell, on Tuesday
afternoon. I think that, probably because I hadn't put my name to Shinwell's
resolution, the Whips had wanted me, but I've no evidence of this and it may
have been the Speaker's own idea. Anyway, on Tuesday morning I read in the
Guardian a filthy leader,[1] which really infuriated me. I then knew that I
should abstain anyway and planned my speech as a statement of why I
should abstain. This was bound to make it highly political, although I realized
that Manny, who was speaking after me, would as the mover of the Amendment get most of the press — quite rightly since, as an ex-Minister of Defence,
he was bound to be long and insulting to Gaitskell, as he was.

However, what none of us had reckoned on was dear John Strachey.
Once again we had one of those difficult scenes, with Anne and Celia next to
each other in the Gallery looking down, as they did three years ago.[2] Once

---

[1] The leader, headed 'Labour Loyalists', began, 'The charms of discretion must seem
more than usually alluring, just now, to the Labour politicians'. It stated: 'At present, Mr
Gaitskell is the only man who could have any hope of leading the Party to victory, for he is
the only man who can appeal to uncommitted voters.' The piece did not mention Crossman
by name; in a letter to the Editor of the *Guardian*, Alastair Hetherington, on March 2nd,
Crossman said:

> more than half the article is concerned to smear anyone who dares to suggest, as I do,
> that Gaitskell's whole initiative is misconceived. You imply, in fact, that no one can
> oppose Mr Gaitskell on this issue unless he is one of those 'for whom mutiny has an
> appeal that no familiarity can dull'; or, alternatively (a few lines later), a member of 'a
> rebellious coalition determined to force Mr Gaitskell out of the leadership'.

[2] In fact, two years before. See above, p. 671.

again John rose, with that high-pitched, supercilious voice. Once again, recklessly, he decided to devote a large part of his speech to an arrogant, utterly opinionated, 100 per cent nuclear warrior attack on those of us who are not pacifists but support NATO while criticizing nuclear strategy. Actually, of course, John did not mention me by name, though he did insult Manny. But he had put an edge to the debate and, after Soames had made a soldierly, dull Government contribution, I was called and immediately answered Strachey.

I thought I was doing it rather nicely and gently but that was not Anne's impression. She said it was devastating. She tells me that throughout Strachey's speech the Front Bench, including Gaitskell, sat glum and silent, a glumness which continued through my speech. I did succeed in being short — twenty-two minutes compared with forty-five for George, forty-eight for Manny and fifty-seven for Zilliacus — and because I got in early I had quite a good House, with the Tories listening very intently.

The speech I made could have in fact been a leading article in *The Economist*, the *Observer*, or the *Financial Times*. This is what made the thing so dreadful, because well-informed opinion throughout the House was urging the Government to move away from the Sandys nuclear policy and the only people still defending that policy were Strachey and Brown. I don't think Strachey did what he did on Gaitskell's pressure but he certainly justified our being much sharper and more controversial, since we could say we didn't start it and that nothing had happened on the first day.

After me came Manny, who, by divine inspiration, remarked in the middle of his speech that Gaitskell, surprised at people wanting to alter the Party's defence policy, was himself wanting to alter the Party constitution. Manny said this blithely, advising Gaitskell to put his mind on the big, essential things, like disarmament. It was a brilliant performance but undoubtedly it infuriated most of those on our side who heard it.

What would Gaitskell do? I had written my letter to him on Friday, and he had received it on Saturday, just as all other members of the Executive received it. Just before the debate I got a short note, saying he would answer it afterwards. Now I am most curious to know how he will reply. In answering the debate, he was extremely conciliatory to me in manner, as well as to George, and was only slightly sharp to Manny. Gaitskell tried to suggest there wasn't much difference in our conclusions, but in fact in what he said he reverted to the most unrealistic and extreme arguments of Strachey's pamphlet three years ago and committed us as a Party to the permanent retention of British nuclear bombs. I suspect he was got at at the last moment by Strachey, who helped to write the speech.

When the vote was called, most people below the gangway stayed put. I had intended to slip out, since as Vice-Chairman[1] I didn't believe in ostentatious abstention. But at this moment Tom Driberg pushed along, in great

[1] Of the Party.

alarm. I hadn't revealed my plans to anyone around me but I had to say to
Tom, 'I think I'm abstaining,' and he said, 'But you took my name off the
resolution. What am I to do, when Harold, Tony and Barbara all say we
ought to vote, for the sake of Clause 4?' This was true. Harold had pushed
his way to me in the afternoon and said, 'What's this rumour I hear about
your abstaining? Put first things first. Clause 4 is what matters!' I had curtly
replied, 'You and Tony Greenwood remained silent in the Shadow Cabinet
when this monstrous resolution was drafted and of course you have got to
vote for it. I've spoken against it and am conscientiously abstaining. So
that's that, Harold.' Barbara was also in a great schemozzle. As Shadow
Minister of Works, her whole mind was on the Questions she had been putting
that afternoon on accommodation for the Commons, a campaign with which
she hopes to get herself elected to the Shadow Cabinet next October and
probably will. So there we all were in fine disarray.

At this point John Cronin,[1] a curious, wealthy surgeon and Whip, came up
and said, 'Isn't it pretty bad sitting about here like this?' I thought he had
been sent by the Whips to rebuke us and only noticed this morning that he
is an abstainer too but wanted to abstain, like I did, more privily. Outside,
however, I found Frank Bowles and Hugh Delargy, who had both voted
because they don't like Manny. The same, I think, is true of Jennie. Young
Mr Mendelson, too, was self-righteously refusing to associate with a vulgarian
like Manny and voted with Gaitskell, something I would have confidently
predicted, having watched his type.

Yes, it wasn't a good vote, since we got all the odds and sods and only, in
addition, Manny, George, myself and Cronin. Nevertheless it was a vote
which enormously mattered, for it broke the spell of artificial unity we had
imposed on ourselves for so long. It was a vote which mattered and a vote
in which the abstentionists were 100 per cent right and truly reflected the
opinion of the Commons, including most of the Tories.

I must admit I walked home feeling much better to be back in my old
galère as a free-thinker, as an awkward guy, as a Keep-Leftist or whatever
you like to call it, though by far the most accurate description would be that,
after three years of uncomfortable lodging in the Labour Establishment,
during which my talents have been mercilessly exploited, I am now back in
my natural habitat. I had a gorgeous long talk on the phone with Michael
Foot, as in the old days, when one could have friends in politics because we
were like-minded.

So when I get into the House this afternoon we shall be back in the old
atmosphere of mob hatred against the filthy minority which has been disloyal. On this topic, by the way, the letters I have received from my trade
union colleagues on the Executive, in response to my letter to them, are
extremely illuminating. 'One doesn't talk out of turn,' roughly sums up their
attitude. But I don't care a fig about Clause 4, more particularly as I hear

[1] Labour M.P. for Loughborough since 1955 and a Labour Whip 1959–62.

from Michael Foot that Gaitskell has got a very good complete redraft of
the whole Clause, which with a bit of amendment should be perfectly O.K.
If that is so, I will give it to him. But I care really about nuclear weapons.

Friday, March 4th
As we went into the Savoy together today, Sydney Jacobson said to me,
'Why are you looking so spry and gay and young and why have you got such
a photograph on the back of *The Times*?'[1] I said, 'Because I am back in the
wilderness and it's just flowering like a green bay tree.' I had had some
reason to enjoy myself. Yesterday morning I was in Oxford, where I had
motored with Pen Balogh to vote. It was a *Zuleika Dobson*[2] occasion — a pale
blue sky washed out with heavy rain, crocuses in the Parks, and a delicious
long queue of ancient dons, politicians and parsons in their unfamiliar gowns
and mortar boards, recognizing each other, hobnobbing, with the television
and the press cameras all round. This is the real Greek election, where one
really votes freely as one wishes, without obligation, without even responsibility, if by responsibility you mean being prevented by other reasons from
doing what you think right.

I found myself with Isaiah Berlin,[3] D'Avigdor-Goldsmid,[4] Edward Boyle,
Tommy Balogh and half a dozen others. As we went through those exquisite
buildings, we took up our ballot papers, put our cross on them, resting on
the back of our mortar boards, and presented them, face upwards, to Masterman, the Vice-Chancellor.[5] He took off his mortar board, bowed, took a

[1] He was photographed with others arriving in Oxford to vote for a new Chancellor of
the University, in succession to Lord Halifax, who had died on December 23rd, 1959. Sir
Oliver Franks had been nominated by a committee of Heads of Houses (i.e., Colleges);
others had nominated Harold Macmillan. The electorate consisted of all Oxford Masters
of Arts, appearing in person, wearing academic dress. Of some 7,000 who were qualified
to vote, nearly half took part. On March 5th Mr Macmillan was elected by 1,976 votes to
Sir Oliver's 1,697. It was said that Sir Oliver had a majority of the vote 'of resident and
working Oxford'.

[2] In *Zuleika Dobson* (London: Heinemann, 1911), Max Beerbohm describes the
conquest of Oxford by a beauty, who then moved on to Cambridge.

[3] Lecturer in Philosophy at New College, Oxford, 1932 and 1938–50 and a Fellow of All
Souls College, Oxford, 1932–8, 1950–66 and since 1975. He served with the Ministry of
Information in New York 1941–2, at H.M. Embassy in Washington 1942–6 and in Moscow
September 1945–January 1946. From 1957 to 1967 he was Chichele Professor of Social and
Political Theory at Oxford University and President of Wolfson College, Oxford, 1966–
March 1975. He was Professor of Humanities at the City University of New York 1966–71.
He was knighted in 1957 and became a member of the Order of Merit in 1971. His works
include *The Hedgehog and the Fox* (London: Weidenfeld & Nicolson, 1953), *Two Concepts
of Liberty* (Oxford: Clarendon Press, 1959) and *Russian Thinkers* (London: Hogarth Press,
1978).

[4] Sir Henry d'Avigdor-Goldsmid, Conservative M.P. for Walsall South 1955–74. He
succeeded to his father's baronetcy in 1940. He died in 1976.

[5] J. C. Masterman, a Student of Christ Church College, Oxford, 1919–46 and Provost of
Worcester College, Oxford, 1946–61. He represented England at lawn tennis and hockey.
His writings include *To Teach the Senators Wisdom* (London: Hodder & Stoughton,
1952), *XX (Doublecross) System in the War 1939–45* (New Haven: Yale University Press,
1972), such detective novels as *Fate Cannot Harm Me* (London: Gollancz, 1935), and an
autobiography, *On The Chariot Wheel* (Oxford University Press, 1975).

good look at mine and grinned in appreciation at finding a Socialist voting for Macmillan. I had been asked by the press outside how I would vote and had firmly said the ballot was secret. However, round the corner, without the press, were Isaiah and Boyle. 'What a delicious sense of irresponsibility,' said Isaiah. 'Yes,' I said, 'delicious.' 'Well, that's ended the secrecy of the ballot so far as you're concerned,' Isaiah replied. Afterwards I went to the revived dons' lunch club — sixty-five people gathered in an Elizabethan tithe barn in St Giles, having coffee and large ham rolls. They asked me to talk about Clause 4, which I did with an uninhibited raciness which I know captivated them. Afterwards, on the way to the station, Pen said to me, 'Of course, no one who can talk like that will ever be given political responsibility. All you get is the nickname "Double Crossman" from people who don't talk like that and get on.'

I took a wonderful diesel back to London and brooded on what I should say at the Party Meeting that evening. I only knew of its existence from the morning papers, which had told us that this would be the occasion when Gaitskell would chastise the rebels. I thought out my speech very precisely, got home in time to say goodnight to Patrick and walked across to sit behind George Wigg in Committee Room 10. I suppose there were 100 people present, as the press say, but I should have said eighty. I was expecting fireworks and got ultra-moderation from Gaitskell. Thank God, Manny wasn't there.

George started with a moving speech about his personal emotion and sincerity, which made it impossible to say he hadn't a conscience. I got away with it by saying that of course I would resign from my pensions Shadow job if required for the sake of the cause, and warning Hugh that the last occasion on which we were forced by a majority to swallow something impossible was German rearmament and we were going to be right again and go on fighting.[1] One or two virtuous people, like Bert Oram[2] and the new Judith Hart,[3] told us about their pacifist consciences, which did us all good. We had Alice Bacon and Jim Griffiths saying we'd betrayed the Party, but to much smaller cheers than you might have expected. George and I came out treading on high air. We had given nothing away.

This morning I read a highly angled account in the press and rang up Gaitskell to insist that I must have the right to speak in my constituency,[4]

[1] See above, pp. 309 ff.

[2] Labour and Co-operative M.P. for East Ham South 1955–February 1974. He was Parliamentary Secretary at the Ministry of Overseas Development 1964–9. In 1975 he became a life peer and served as a Lord-in-Waiting 1976–8.

[3] Labour M.P. for Lanark since 1959. She was Joint Parliamentary Under-Secretary of State for Scotland 1964–6, Minister of State at the Commonwealth Office 1966–7, Minister of Social Security 1967–8, Paymaster-General 1968–9, Minister of Overseas Development 1969–70 and 1974–5 and Minister for Overseas Development 1977–9. She became a D.B.E. in 1979.

[4] Crossman made his statement at a meeting of the Coventry Fabian Society on March 4th.

which I had anyway intended to do. I then got his approval of the relevant paragraphs but didn't tell him the rest. Gaitskell couldn't have been more conciliatory or personally friendly, trying to reason that George and I were acting from judgment, not from conscience. Mrs Skelly had let me know I was due to see Gaitskell and the Chief Whip, so I said I would see him on condition we had an agreed press statement on the meeting, to which he concurred.

Rightly or wrongly, I was gay and said, 'About that letter I wrote you. This is my first attempt to show that the Left can also have as bright ideas as Tony Crosland for a new image.' I heard Hugh laugh at the other end of the phone and then gulp it back and say, 'That wasn't what I meant. I'm hoping to write you an answer in due course. Meantime, for heaven's sake, don't say anything which makes things more difficult.'

My only other comment is about my colleagues on the Executive. Harold Wilson spent an hour with me on Wednesday, pacing up and down the corridors, asking what my real intentions were. When I said I hadn't got any except to enjoy the luxury of the wilderness, he was, I think, genuinely baffled at that concept and genuinely alarmed. Barbara, on the other hand, was positively envious of my brilliant acumen at seeing the political capital to be made out of the defence debate. And I? I am happy and had a wonderful lunch telling Sydney about how nice everything was.

Tuesday, March 8th

I duly attended on Mr Gaitskell yesterday afternoon. I got there at exactly five o'clock to find the Chief Whip with Mrs Skelly in the anteroom. We had a very pleasant conversation about the Gallup Poll and the terrible state of the Labour Party.[1] At twenty-five past five Gaitskell came back from the Home Policy Committee, which I should have attended but didn't, and we settled down round his table.

He started by saying that our purpose was to discuss my future activities but beforehand we might have a talk about nuclear weapons. I murmured that there was very little point but he proceeded to address me on the subject and soon indicated that in his view, whereas the pacifists could be said to have a conscience, I only had a judgment:

CROSSMAN: You mean that only people who, in your opinion, are silly and sentimental have a conscience whereas those of us who are intelligent and rational are excluded from that?

GAITSKELL: Well, you can put it that way, if you like, but I really think it's stretching a point to say that you and George Wigg acted on conscience.

CROSSMAN: Anyway, it's silly to accuse us of organizing a revolt. If we had,

[1] The February 1960 issue of the *Gallup Political Index* compared voting behaviour in the 1955 and 1959 General Elections. In Crossman's words, 'all we gained this time were the very old and the very poor. We lost heavily on the under-thirties and the well-to-do middle classes, but most of what we lost went Liberal [or] wouldn't vote. What a prospect for the future!'

it would have been 110, not 43, as you very well know. When we organize, we are efficient. But, to come back to conscience, George and I have a real conscience about consenting to policy which leaves this country defenceless.

GAITSKELL: That's the very point I'm making: it all goes back to conscription. What you are really demanding is that we should have conscription back and that's quite unreasonable. You can hardly pretend that we should have opposed the abolition of conscription in 1957.

CROSSMAN: Of course I can see your difficulty, since in 1956 we and the T.U.C. had advocated its abolition. But you will remember what I said at the time. I recommended you to go to Macmillan privately and offer a bipartisan policy, under which we wouldn't oppose the Government's prolonging the National Service Act until such time as it was sure that the minimum number of recruits were available.

GAITSKELL (crossly): Macmillan would have exploited that for his own purposes. It was totally impracticable.

CROSSMAN: It may be true. I am only interested in pointing out that I recommended it and that I think it would not have been impracticable. My views were dismissed within a few minutes, on the initiative of George Brown, as sheer intellectual lunacy. The view then was that the Party couldn't possibly oppose the abolition of conscription, even if the price of abolishing it was to make this country dependent on nuclear weapons and ultimately impotent.

GAITSKELL: Whatever you may say about your own position, as the Leader of the Party I could not consider the possibility of accepting your advice.

CROSSMAN: Well, what I am asking is the right to abstain conscientiously, not the right to take over the leadership of the Party. You may be right that the Party as such was bound to condone this wicked—

GAITSKELL: I wish you wouldn't use words like wicked. They're so emotional and extreme!

CROSSMAN: But I do think it was wicked, as wicked as Chamberlain's actions in the 1930s. At that time the official Conservative line was appeasement and all Winston Churchill demanded was the right to abstain and protest. I am not demanding that you should accept my view but that you should permit me to protest.

And so finally I said, 'But we shan't ever settle this argument,' and Gaitskell said, 'Now about the future. What are your intentions?'

CROSSMAN: I intend to continue this campaign until we reverse the Party policy and I have already made it clear that, if this is taken amiss, I am willing to resign from the Front Bench.

GAITSKELL: I accept the view that your position on the Executive is unaffected, though some people may take it amiss that the Vice-Chairman should behave in this way.

CROSSMAN: As you know, I didn't want to be Vice-Chairman. It was forced on me by the defeat of Mikardo.[1] There's nothing I want less than to be

[1] In the 1959 N.E.C. election.

muzzled all next year. So do remember that, if I have a reasonable chance, I am only too anxious to get out of it.

GAITSKELL (hurriedly): No, we're considering your position as an M.P. and I must warn you that, if you were to continue these public attacks, it might well make it impossible to let you stay on the Front Bench.

CROSSMAN: But I've already told you, in a public declaration on Saturday,[1] that I'll get off the Front Bench. Only I won't do it unless you actually expel me from it. It's for you to make up your minds.

GAITSKELL: Well, the Chief Whip and I will be reporting back to the Parliamentary Committee on Wednesday.

CROSSMAN: Well, I hope you will tell them that I meant what I said last Thursday — that they only have to say the word and say I've gone too far and I shall be glad to get back to my natural habitat on the backbenches.

During all this Gaitskell was looking uneasily out of the window and we never once let our eyes meet. I got up to go and as we were at the door I said, 'Remember I couldn't care less about the Vice-chairmanship or the Front Bench during the next twelve months. Of course, in the period immediately before an Election I will be good next time, as I was last. But this is the period for revising Party policy. Tony Crosland has put forward his ideas, which I disagree with, and I am determined to put forward my own.'

GAITSKELL: But if we are to revise, we have to agree them.

CROSSMAN: But we didn't agree Crosland's policies before they were announced. I am going to spend the next twelve months putting forward my ideas for the revising of the Party's policy. That's all I care about in the next next twelve months, Hugh. Nothing else matters.

At this point I was pushed out of the room.

I had to go through the lobby to get my coat and at the other end I was pursued by a journalist. 'I gather you have just been carpeted by Mr Gaitskell. Have you any statement?' he asked. I replied, 'You had better ask Gaitskell about that,' and fled to the Tube. I gather even this laconic interview provided sufficient material for some stories in the morning papers.

After lunch I brought Jennie Lee by taxi to the House. We have avoided asking her anything about Nye for all these weeks for fear of upsetting her. She told me of her own accord that she wasn't going to take him abroad until he could eat and drink what he liked, walk about on his own legs and enjoy it. 'Already he is eating and drinking,' she said, 'but the wound isn't fully healed. In a fortnight I shall be taking him to Brighton, in the hope that he will soon get bored with it and then I can take him off.' Somehow, as we neared the House, the conversation went back to defence problems. 'Remember,' she said, almost gaily, despite her arthritis and general tiredness, 'remember what Nye said. When you've taken a stand, go on standing. Don't give way. You were right to say what you said on Saturday. Keep it up.' On

[1] In his speech at Coventry.

the way she also said to me, 'Of course they're always trying to get hold of Nye and use him for the meeting on March 16th.[1] Whatever happens I shall stop them doing that. Until he is able to take his full part, these little men must take their own decisions.'

Tuesday, March 15th

Since I left Jennie Lee at the House that day, a lot seems to have happened. On Wednesday I rushed to Oxford to talk to David Butler's seminar[2] about the Parliamentary Labour Party. The discussion was led by young Peter Jay, young Miss Callaghan[3] and young Miss Kaldor.[4] Jay was extremely good in asking a series of questions, starting from inquiries about the frequency of meetings and culminating in questions about the exact power of the Leader. Then he toppled over into saying there was no Hampstead set and asking about Party discipline.

I answered it all as frankly as I could and got into an interesting discussion about whether a weak Labour Government is better than a strong Socialist Opposition.

JAY: But nothing can be worse than a Tory Government! Anyone is a traitor who wants that. You want to be in Opposition for ever.

CROSSMAN: I'm trying to analyse, as a social scientist, the connection between personal attitudes and political ideologies. You asked me about left-wingers and right-wingers. Right-wingers tend to be people who want office and who regard their main object as getting rid of the Tories. Left-wingers tend to be propagandists, for whom office is only secondary to pushing ideas. The Party needs a Left and a Right, a blend of both.

At dinner I sat next to Norman Chester, the Warden, and quite forgot myself in admitting that I had voted for Macmillan as Chancellor. Chester nearly blew up and I suddenly remembered he was the man who had proposed Franks.[5] 'You people call yourselves liberal-minded and then advertise all over Oxford your betrayal of the cause,' he said. But by the end of the evening, he and I walked out together. We had had a long session in the Common Room about the future of the Labour Party, our relationship with the trade

---

[1] At which the N.E.C. was to discuss the revision of the Party constitution.

[2] A weekly seminar at Nuffield College, Oxford, at which visiting politicians and men of affairs answered questions from graduate and undergraduate students.

[3] Margaret, the daughter of James Callaghan, married Peter Jay in 1961.

[4] Frances Kaldor, the second daughter of Nicholas and Clarissa Kaldor. She was a development economist who in 1975 became a Fellow of Somerville College, Oxford. Her works include *Technology and Underdevelopment* (London: Macmillan, 1977).

[5] In the election for Chancellor. Oliver Franks was a temporary civil servant at the Ministry of Supply 1939–46 and Permanent Secretary there 1945–6. He was Provost of The Queen's College, Oxford, 1946–8, British Ambassador to Washington 1948–52, a Director of Lloyd's Bank Ltd 1953–75 (Chairman 1954–62), a Director of Schroders, Chairman of the Committee of London Clearing Banks 1960–2 and Provost of Worcester College, Oxford, 1962–76. He became a life peer in 1962. He was Chairman of the Committee on the Reform of Section 2 of the Official Secrets Act 1971–2, and since 1976 has been a member of the Political Honours Scrutiny Committee.

unions and so on. At the end, Chester said, rather nicely, 'That's the finest tutorial I've ever heard. Your hand hasn't forgotten its cunning, my dear Crossman, at least as a tutor. Let these tutors take note of how it's really done, since you've done it to them.'

I got back to find a message that Gaitskell wanted to see me. Rose [? Cohen] said, 'I fear the worst.' I certainly didn't. I thought the whole thing had blown over and lunched with a gay heart before I went in at half-past two to see Gaitskell and the Chief Whip. This time he was far testier and far more careful to avoid discussing the issue. He asked me whether I would give an assurance and I said no. Then he said he would have to ask me formally. If I gave the assurance, nothing in writing would be required. If I didn't, he would put it in writing and ask me to submit my resignation.

I said all this would take a little time, since I would like to study his script, though I had little doubt what my answer would be. He said it would have to be hurried up because there was a pensions debate on Wednesday and he would have to announce to the Party Meeting in three hours' time who would be speaking.[1] I said, 'In that case you will have to announce that I am speaking and then I will sleep on it and let you know tomorrow morning.' 'I shall be away from tomorrow morning,' Gaitskell said, 'and won't be back till Monday.' This surprised me a bit. I said I would be in Manchester on Monday and would discuss the press release of the correspondence on Tuesday morning, so that it could come out on Tuesday evening.

In the course of this conversation Gaitskell had read aloud rather fast the draft statement.* As soon as I heard Gaitskell's draft I knew there was no chance of agreeing, but I got a copy of it from Mrs Skelly and took it home.

On Friday morning I sat down and wrote my reply very carefully and wondered what kind of an impact the whole thing would make. I read it aloud to George Wigg, who very wisely made me remove any reference to resignation and then I went off to Prescote, leaving Rose to finalize and post it. The whole thing was cloaked in secrecy, although Alf Robens was apparently tipped off that he might be required and this provided a hint to Peter Shore, who was there to do the document.

Crossman's letter to Gaitskell included the words: 'You now require me to give you an assurance that I will stop "persistent and public advocacy" of the revision of Labour Party defence policy which I have been urging for so long. This assurance I cannot conscientiously give.' He continued:

I do note with some alarm that the extension (with very minor concessions) of the doctrine of collective responsibility from the twelve members of the

[1] As the Front Bench spokesman in the pensions debate.

* I had heard a hint of this that morning from Tony Greenwood, who had rung me up and asked me to be reasonable and to give the assurance, since otherwise Clause 4 would be ruined on Wednesday. I had replied rather testily that I would wait and see what Gaitskell said.

Shadow Cabinet to a numerous Shadow Administration means that no less than 59 members of the Parliamentary Labour Party are now only permitted to express in private any deep-felt criticisms they may feel of the present Party line. It is no doubt essential to impose discipline of this kind on the members of a Government, but is it not possible that the establishment of a Shadow Administration, with the same kind of discipline, will weaken the vigour of our Opposition?

Crossman then spoke of the need for the Labour Party's great debate on the revision of its image and of its policies and concluded: 'It is clear to me from your letter that if I want, as I do, to make a vigorous and independent contribution to this debate, my proper place is on the backbenches.' *Crossman enclosed a personal letter to Gaitskell, regretting in his turn that*

we have not been able to carry on as we were doing in the months before and the weeks of the Election. They were a good time while they lasted – the first and only time in my adult life when my energies were fully employed in working for the Party. But the fact that you decided on a certain line, which ruled out any collaboration with me, should not turn us into personal enemies or members of warring cliques. I only hope that what comes out at the end of this argument will be a sufficiently constructive policy and a sufficient improvement on what we had in the Election to justify those who started it.

Prescote was wonderfully remote and quiet, with all our thoughts on whether the cattle were out too soon and whether the grass would hold out and who should have the new cottage. We motored back on Sunday night so that I could catch the half-past eleven night train. I still imagined I should be coming down on Monday to do the press release with the Chief Whip on Tuesday morning. At midday on Monday, while we were rehearsing our Granada programme, the Chief Whip came through on the phone and said Gaitskell wanted the announcement out that evening. I said I had no objection and we agreed that Transport House should give it to the press at half-past five for release at ten o'clock.

I had fixed lunch with Alastair Hetherington, Editor of the *Guardian*, and so, while the rest caught the plane back to London,[1] I stayed, quite relieved, since it stopped me going to the House. I told Alastair, who seemed a bit taken aback and, as usual, naïvely surprised by everything. 'Gaitskell hasn't got much out of Clause 4,' he said, and I replied, 'That's exactly what I said would happen in the speech you so much objected to.' 'But all of us wanted him to make a real break with nationalization,' he said. 'Yes,' I said, 'but it's very bad for you to advise him to go in for an enterprise on which he is bound to fail, as he was in this case.' My lunch was at least useful in

[1] From Manchester, where the Granada programme was produced.

holding Hetherington in,[1] as I saw from today's *Guardian*.[2] I had also rather ingeniously decided to give high praise to Lord Beaverbrook in the T.V. programme, knowing this would be spotted at the *Daily Express* and would for one day somewhat moderate the poison of their attack, which it actually did.

The train home from Manchester roared along and stopped at Watford, where it was boarded by a photographer and reporter from the *Express*. The reporter loomed up to me. I said I had agreed with Gaitskell to give no interviews, whereupon he sat opposite me and began to talk and talk and talk, poor young man. However, he tipped me off about what to expect at Euston, so I nimbly crossed to where a Post Office train was stopped and thus missed fifteen photographers and journalists. I got into the Tube before the *Daily Express* photographer, tipped off by my friend, caught up.[3] The *Daily Express* man offered me £200 for an article. The *Daily Herald* man demanded the articles that last week I agreed to do for them by tomorrow and they sat with me in the Tube, trying to have an interview. However, I threw them off at Victoria and got home to dinner with the telephone receiver off. I was still not sure what kind of effect the news would have but began to suspect the largest.

Tony Wedgwood Benn rang up, having heard the half-past ten news, terribly alarmed about his own position in the Shadow Admin. I rang up dear Peter Shore to explain what had happened and to ask him to dinner. Then the *Daily Herald* and the *News Chronicle* photographers and journalists arrived at regular five-minute intervals. The best trick was to let them ring the front-door bell and then to open the bottom door and make them come down in the dark to the basement entry. They were not sure who I was and it brought them into a mood in which they were ready to accept the view that I couldn't give an interview since I had promised Gaitskell that I wouldn't if he didn't.

Altogether the evening passed very amicably. It was an excellent dinner. During it I learnt that Harold Wilson hadn't been present at the famous Shadow Cabinet on Wednesday and that George Brown had been strongly supported by Robens and Callaghan in demanding action against me. Finally, dear George Wigg came in, smirking with the feeling that he had started the whole thing off, as he actually had.

---

[1] In a leader published on March 5th, the *Guardian* analysed 'Mr Crossman's apologia' in Coventry the night before and his abstention in the defence debate. 'Inevitably', the newspaper said, 'one suspects that Clause 4 is at the bottom of it.'

[2] The *Guardian* printed the text of Crossman's official reply to Gaitskell and their correspondent concluded:

Some Labour Members will regret that, once more, as in the days of the Labour Government, authority has found it impossible to use Mr Crossman's talents. He has a lively mind — too lively for orthodoxy perhaps — but it ought to be used for the Party as a whole.

[3] The *Express* printed a photograph of Crossman, 'The Man Who Said Too Much', on the train.

This morning, when I took up the papers at a quarter to seven, it really was front-page, double column in everything, including *The Times* and the *Guardian*. All the papers were as pro-Gaitskell as they could be in their editorials but my main achievement was that both Hugh's letter and my reply were printed in full, so that people could judge for themselves. This, of course, was largely the result of today being a day without much news. On the whole I think the impression created by the press was as unhelpful to Gaitskell and as helpful to me as one could possibly hope. Nevertheless, in net it was helpful to him, giving a picture of the strong man at last taking action against the rebels.

After lunch I strolled round the House. By and large, people smirked when they saw me, with such expressions as, 'Well, that's a blow-up!' or 'You certainly have done it!' or 'Whoopee!' Not very hostile, and somehow admiring the dimensions of the explosion. George came up, urgently saying that Manny insisted I must speak tomorrow.[1] I had a good talk with George about it. They think it is essential to make an appearance and so also said John Rankin, an amiable Scot: 'We shall all be expecting it. You shouldn't be kept out of the debate.' Unfortunately, on Albert Rose's suggestion, I had in the meantime arranged to attend the G.M.C. [General Management Committee] in Coventry and had got the Chief Whip's permission to be absent on a three-line whip.

Jo Grimond walked up and down the corridor discussing the vagaries of Gaitskell as a Leader, and the working of two-party politics and every five minutes a telegram or telephone message was pushed into my hand by an attendant. It was all moderately amusing. The evening papers, with the posters outside saying 'CROSSMAN SPEAKS', are unlikely to be repeated for some time. The Speaker agreed to let me have a short intervention but warned me that there might be some delay in the business before the pensions debate starts, so that proceedings may be held up for some time. I am still very much in two minds and anxious to have my cake and eat it by both speaking and getting down to Coventry to the meeting.

Tuesday, March 22nd
In the first part of last week time seemed to go very slowly but now I can hardly believe it's a week since I last wrote the diary.

I must go back to the meeting of the Executive last Wednesday, though I need hardly put it in this private and confidential diary, since within a few hours every detail had been leaked into the press. I went there with the gloomiest forebodings after a most unsatisfactory meeting the night before in Harold Wilson's room. With enormous precautions he had arranged that Tony Greenwood, Barbara, Tom Driberg and myself should meet him in the

---

[1] In the pensions debate on March 14th. Two Members had been appointed to take Crossman's place as Front Bench spokesman on pensions and national insurance: Douglas Houghton and William Ross.

room he has as chairman of the Public Accounts Committee. It was difficult to get there without being seen because it's on the top floor, past the Members' television room, and there were two divisions while we were talking on Tuesday evening.

Moreover, when we got together there was nothing to talk about, except that Harold had thought up an ingenious device for keeping Clause 4 and then inserting Hugh's draft by an amendment of Clause 5. All I think Harold wanted was that we should support him in this. On the other hand, we didn't discuss any amendments to Hugh's statement.

Barbara came in right at the end, when the rest had gone, and I took her down and gave her a cup of coffee, since she was too neurotic to eat or drink anything else and seemed to be entirely concerned with Members' accommodation. As for my plight that evening, my colleagues were detached but already sympathetic, since I had scored a partial success. When Harold had gone, Tom Driberg, Tony and I had revealed to each other that we would all prefer to keep Gaitskell rather than work for Harold Wilson. It was clear, however, that Barbara would work for Harold. I tentatively suggested we might start lunching together but they all thought this was terribly dangerous. None of them really seemed concerned in the least with any kind of policy issue.

So came Wednesday morning and we found ourselves in the fourth-floor room, with photographers climbing around outside to snap us through the windows.[1] I sat between Len Williams and Hugh Gaitskell and remained silent for the first hour and a half. Hugh started extremely soberly for half an hour and, very wisely, none of us constituency Members joined in at first, but left the running to the trade unionists.

Very soon it was clear that not one single trade unionist present was in favour of amending Clause 4. Indeed, I don't think a single person started his speech without saying, 'Of course I am against the idea of amending the Party objects, but, since it haś to be done … ' A Swedish friend had told me of the lunch at which Tony Crosland had told him they had the majority already fixed. Actually no work had been done and Boyd of the A.E.U. was one of the strongest objectors, along with Harry Nicholas, to any kind of amendment.

After an hour and a half it became clear that what we should discuss first was the bridge which would link the old statement of Party objects to Gaitskell's insert. At this point a long document was handed round with Morgan's solution, which used the words, 'this restatement and amplification'. Someone pointed out, rightly, that 'restatement' would mean that Clause 4 was embalmed, at which many trade unionists expressed their resentment that Tony Crosland had used this word on 'Panorama' on the previous Monday.

[1] The *Daily Express* photograph, taken through the fourth-floor windows, showed N.E.C. members eating sandwiches as they redrafted.

It became clear there could be no question of embalming Clause 4 or restating it. I then suggested 'clarification and amplification', which was immediately jumped on by Hugh, much to the distress of the left-wingers. Then Evans, of the Railwaymen, said 'reaffirmation' as well and we got all three, to satisfy everybody. I was surprised when Hugh accepted that and it was clear that it strained him a good deal to do so, since, after the word 'reaffirmation', he had to admit that he had not got rid of the phrase and there would now be a New Testament and an Old Testament and every justification for the Tories asking which we believed in.

After a lunch interval we went on to finish the job by amending Hugh's draft.[1] In my first contribution I had pointed out two things: first, that the draft as it stood substituted for a large increase of nationalization a picture of Big Brother interfering everywhere through State controls. I got the whole of the reference to control delated. I also pointed out there was no reference to the role of the voluntary organization in society or to the Socialist ideal of getting above economics to the good life, culture, etc. All this and a good many amendments with which I helped produced an astonishing atmosphere of billing and cooing between Hugh and myself. Seldom have I heaped coals of fire so mercilessly on an evil-doer! I really much enjoyed the six and a half hours.

Meanwhile I had definitely decided to speak in the pensions debate. I got a very good response from our side for being there at all and for speaking as I did,[2] and I am grateful to George and Manny for the advice they gave me because it made a great deal of difference to my relations with the Party.

Simultaneously the press had been on to the subject of how my expulsion had been arranged. George Hutchinson rang me up from the *Standard* on the Monday night with the rumour that George Brown had insisted on it. I said I knew nothing about it but it was my guess that George Brown, Alf Robens and Callaghan had been the ringleaders. I also told Hutchinson that I gathered Harold Wilson was away at the time and that Tony Greenwood was the only person to plead for me. I was amused that this story appeared intact in the next day's *Standard* and was transferred from there to the front page of the *Mail* and the *Express* on Wednesday. The Shadow Cabinet had a

---

[1] Gaitskell's new draft, the statement of the Party's aims and objects, declared that they could

be achieved only through extension of common ownership substantial enough to give the community power over the commanding heights of the economy, including State-owned industries and firms, producer and consumer co-operation, municipal ownership, and public participation in private concerns ... In recognizing that both public and private enterprise have a place in the economy, it believes that further extension of common ownership should be decided from time to time in the light of these objectives according to circumstances, with due regard to the views of the workers and consumers concerned.

[2] Crossman began his remarks in the debate on National Insurance benefits with the words, 'The fact that I am speaking from a position in the House different from that expected a few days ago will, I hope, make only one difference to what I say: it will be shorter and it will be sharper.'

long discussion of the leaks and I somewhat unwisely told Callaghan that there had been no leak — I had just invented the whole thing, since I usually found that imaginative fiction is closer to the truth than partial fact. This is the kind of joke one shouldn't make to Callaghan and no doubt he has passed it on in the form of saying that I deliberately misinformed the press. However, the story sustained itself throughout the week and right into the weeklies, and the longer it lasted the worse Gaitskell's position grew. He had made the mistake of claiming after the Executive an 80 per cent victory for himself and by the time the by-election results[1] were announced on Friday there was no doubt the leadership was what had come out worst.

The whole incident has been quite interesting. For the first time since my Amendment to the King's Speech in 1946 I really have been front-page news in the full sense of the word. Even in 1946 I didn't have quite this astonishing publicity. I still don't quite know how it happened. Partly it was that there was no news that day, partly because it was the day before the Executive meeting and partly, I like to think, the two letters between Hugh and me made a natural news story.

Sydney Jacobson, who was deeply shocked by the whole thing, told me on the phone that he had been with Gaitskell at five o'clock on the Monday, no doubt discussing Clause 4. As he was getting up to leave, Gaitskell said, 'You'd better know what's happened to Dick, since it will be out at ten o'clock tonight,' and told him the news. Sydney said, 'Well, I must get back to my office straightaway.' 'Why?' said Gaitskell. 'Oh, it's big news and I must do the front page.' 'No!' said Gaitskell, thereby revealing that he thought he could put me in my place without any difficulty.

In fact, of course, Gaitskell has given me publicity in a position which I have never had before. Although the press was unanimously pro-Gaitskell, congratulating him on his strength in dealing with an undisciplined character, I suspect the public was 90 per cent on my side. All sorts of people, including Mrs Meek[2] and all my family, have expressed strong support for the first time in my long and varied political life. Of course, anybody who says 'I'd rather resign than give up my principles' is fairly popular. Then there is the feeling that Gaitskell isn't very good and, further, that, on this issue, I happen to be right.

I had Pat Blackett to dinner with Peter and Liz Shore.[3] I find the Shores are now fanatically anti-Gaitskell, whereas Blackett is simply bewildered at

[1] L. J. Edwards, Labour M.P. for Brighouse and Spenborough, had died on November 23rd, 1959, and a by-election was held on March 17th. Michael Shaw (Liberal and Conservative) took the seat from Colin Jackson (Labour) with a majority of 666 votes. On the same day a by-election took place at Harrow West, where Sir Albert Braithwaite (Conservative) had died on October 19th, 1959. A. J. Page retained the seat for the Conservatives, with a majority of 11,426 over J. Wallbridge (Liberal). P. Jenkins (Labour) came third.

[2] The Crossmans' cleaner at Vincent Square.

[3] Dr Elizabeth Wrong married Peter Shore in 1948. She joined the Medical Civil Service in 1962 and since 1977 has been Deputy Chief Medical Officer at the Department of Health and Social Security.

the utter stupidity of the leadership on this issue. Dining with John Freeman on Sunday, I suggested that the *Statesman* might try to form a kind of XYZ dining club for a year at least, with Blackett, Titmuss, Tommy and myself as founding members, to try to work out some kind of policy, because what is really appalling in all this is that no one cares about policy or ideas. I suspect it's rather like Russian politics under Stalin, with everybody jostling and manoeuvring for power. We now have Alf Robens campaigning to get us all off the Executive by making M.P.s electable to it only through the Parliamentary Party, a proposal first put forward by Douglas Jay and specially mentioned to me by Gaitskell when he came to Prescote. 'Stop discussion at all costs' seems to be the present mood.

Wednesday, March 23rd
I went to Coventry last night to talk to the G.M.C. About thirty-five people turned up, which I suppose was not bad on a Tuesday, and I gave them an inside picture of life in the Labour Party since the Election. We had a whole number of questions, rising to a crescendo of anti-Gaitskell discussion. Madge Evans[1] said, 'There's no split in the Party. We just have a Leader who is trying to sabotage Socialism. Why should we put up with it?' Bob Ritchie[2] had warned me this mood would be there and had told me that, at Maurice Edelman's Precinct meeting last Saturday, there had been shouts from the general public of, 'Get rid of Gaitskell, that dirty man!'

I left this morning's Executive to have lunch with Sydney. There remained a mysterious item on the agenda — Mr Wilson's motion about the treasurership. I gather it has been postponed and that it consists of a proposal that, since we all love Nye so much and wish to keep him on the Executive, we should keep him as Treasurer, though completely inactive. 'And Harold will be Deputy,' we all murmured to ourselves. Talk about a man losing his touch! Two people had gone to Harold and said, 'The subject of the treasurership is not for you, Harold,' but nothing had deterred him. It would have been a nice laugh if we had got to that point at the meeting this morning.

On April 4th the Chancellor presented the Budget. There were several small concessions to the taxpayer: the abolition of cinema duty, reductions in some wine duties, increases in premium bond prizes and in the number of bonds which an individual could hold, larger tax allowances for dependent relatives and a reduction in death duties on gifts made in the third, fourth and fifth years before death.

These reductions were balanced by increases in tobacco duty and a rise from 10 to 12·5 per cent in profits tax. Loss relief for 'hobby farmers' was abolished

---

[1] Miss Madge Evans was a left-wing member of Coventry Labour Party and subsequently, as Mrs Madge Rosher, a member of Coventry City Council.

[2] Bob Ritchie, an agent, looked after Elaine Burton's constituency and worked with George Hodgkinson, Crossman's agent, taking responsibility for certain aspects of the multi-Member Coventry constituency's affairs.

23 Crossman, as Party Chairman, with Gaitskell and Wilson at Blackpool, 1961

24 Marcia Williams and Giles Wilson listen to Harold Wilson at a Press Conference, 1963

25 Election of the Oxford University Chancellor, 1963; Edward Boyle; Sir William Hayter; Crossman

26 Wilson, Crossman and Anthony Greenwood confer at the last Party Conference before Wilson comes to power

*and the company directors' 'golden handshake' was to be liable for income tax.
Wider powers were to be taken to prevent tax avoidance.*

Crossman does not mention the Budget in his diary; his preoccupation remained defence. On March 24th it had been announced that the Prime Minister would visit Washington to discuss with President Eisenhower the latest phase of the Geneva nuclear test negotiations. The U.S.S.R. had demanded a ban on all nuclear tests and the U.S.A. had in early February declared its readiness to ban all explosions that could be controlled (i.e., those below a seismic magnitude of 4·75). The Soviet Union accepted this, on condition that it be linked wiih a moratorium on small tests during further research. At Mr Macmillan's urging, the American Government now agreed to an announcement that, as soon as a nuclear treaty was signed banning all tests of weapons above a seismic magnitude of 4·75, it would agree to a moratorium of agreed duration on smaller detonations. This statement was made on March 29th in a joint communiqué by Mr Macmillan and President Eisenhower, issued from the President's Gettysburg farm. Mr Macmillan returned to Britain on April 1st.

On April 13th the Minister of Defence, Mr Harold Watkinson, informed the House of Commons that, owing to progress in techniques of nuclear warfare, the Government had decided to cease development of the Blue Streak missile. Between £65 million and £100 million had been spent on this military weapon, the protégé of Duncan Sandys, the previous Minister. Mr Gaitskell announced that the Opposition would move a vote of censure on April 27th, the day Parliament reassembled after the Easter Recess.

During the debate Mr Watkinson announced that the Admiralty had been urgently instructed to study the requirements for British-built submarines capable of carrying the American Polaris missile. This policy was criticized by Antony Head, Minister of Defence in the period immediately preceding Mr Macmillan's premiership. He warned the Government not to seek again enormously expensive and quickly obsolescent nuclear weapons, to the neglect of conventional forces.

The Opposition vote of censure was moved by George Brown, who indicated that the Labour Party might be about to change its defence policy and abandon its support for an independent British deterrent. 'Even I', he said, 'cannot be expected to go in for a policy that has no chance of ever being successful.' Mr Brown's remarks were underlined by those of Mr Shinwell; Mr Gaitskell, lecturing in Haifa, was absent from the debate. The Opposition motion of censure was defeated by 305 votes to 225.

Thursday, April 28th

When I last wrote in this diary, it was before the Easter holidays and the complete *bouleversement* of Labour's defence policy, which finally got under way yesterday. If one was ever wanting to write a political short story, here is a classic little instance of the way things happen and who gets the kudos. The defence debate was on March 1st and I had by no means made up my

27

mind on the first day whether on the second day I would actually make the speech which caused the row. On the Ides of March I was sacked by Gaitskell, under pressure from George Brown. Now, on April 27th, George Brown announces the Labour Party's intention of abandoning support for the independent British deterrent. Yet, when this happened yesterday, the newspapers only saw it as a Labour shift of policy and those who did look backwards described Mr Shinwell as the man who for years has been advocating the abandonment of the deterrent. In fact, of course, Manny was one of the great nuclear warriors until January of this year, when he was persuaded by George Wigg to join us, quite unexpectedly, in the revolt we had been staging since 1957. But I would be as ridiculously self-centred as the average politician if I tried to pretend that most of the credit for this belongs to me—because of course in this affair I have throughout been coasting along on the expert knowledge of George Wigg, every now and then slipping back into orthodoxy and then being prised or catapulted back by George into active revolt. Yet yesterday, in the great debate, he was not allowed to speak and all the credit went to others.

How did all this happen? Well, it all started before the Easter Recess with Watkinson's[1] announcement of the abandonment of Blue Streak. This occurred on a Thursday and that same evening the Parliamentary Party met. Gaitskell reaffirmed the decision to put a vote of censure and urged us all to put aside differences and concentrate on attacking the Government. At once George Wigg was up on his feet, giving warning that Tory memories were not as short as that. He reminded us that George Brown had been in favour of Blue Streak in a television interview in March 1957, etc., etc. George Wigg's speech was received with active hatred, so great that, when John Strachey rose and said we should unite to attack the enemy, he got an ovation; if Strachey gets an ovation from the Party, someone else must have promoted it.

What George did at that meeting was to scare the Shadow Cabinet's pants off. They met next day and decided to forestall an unpleasant debate and gag Manny, George and me by having a half-day's discussion, ending at seven o'clock, which would only give forty minutes for backbenchers. This was duly announced just before the Recess, when George had disappeared to the Canaries on a fruit boat. Of course, the rest of us took it phlegmatically, as a characteristic action.

I had just got back on Monday from ten days at Prescote, when the telephone rang, and it was George Wigg. 'I took a taxi from the docks. I've been thinking of nothing else since the wireless news arrived on board. Now we've

[1] Conservative M.P. for the Woking division of Surrey 1950–64. He was P.P.S. to the Minister of Transport and Civil Aviation 1951–2, Parliamentary Secretary at the Ministry of Labour and National Service 1952–5, Minister of Transport and Civil Aviation 1955–9, and Minister of Defence 1959–62. From 1957 to 1962 he sat in the Cabinet. In 1964 he was created 1st Viscount Watkinson. He was Chairman of Cadbury Schweppes Ltd 1969–74 and President of the C.B.I. 1976–7.

got them! We shall oppose the closure, or alternatively I will speak from 6.59 till ten o'clock without a break.' The old ram was battering once again at the bastions of Labour corruption and once again I was mildly, deliciously, familiarly captivated. More important, I was dragged into action.

'Dear me, that speck over there is beginning to look like young Healey!'

On Tuesday morning Manny, George, Stephen Swingler and Sydney Silverman went to the Speaker. They pointed out that the debate could not really be stopped at seven o'clock except by the closure and that they were going to make trouble. They were referred to Butler, who at once said that the Government didn't want to stop at seven o'clock; the Opposition had asked for a debate only up to seven. So, for convenience, the day of the Royal Academy Banquet had been chosen, so that everybody could go off to dine after the vote. Back it went to the Labour Chief Whip, who said this was sabotage and threatened that, if George Wigg was speaking, he would himself move the closure against him. This is the kind of idiotic bluff which Labour power politicians make and which is always being called by the facts.

I clocked in at half-past three on Tuesday to hear Manny Shinwell asking in his egregious manner about the business of the week. At once Mr Butler advertised that the Opposition had asked to stop the debate at seven. Then came the first surprise. During the Recess, Hugh Gaitskell has been in America. On arrival at London airport he waited two hours and took another plane to Israel, to the Socialist International. So Gaitskell was away and, after a long tussle in the Shadow Cabinet, Harold Wilson was in charge. Up he jumped on Tuesday, blandly asserting that the Opposition wanted a whole day, and within half a minute the whole elaborate plan for gagging us had been punctured, in the absence of Gaitskell and to the suppressed fury of the Chief Whip and most of the Parliamentary Labour Party. All round me there were mutters about these fellows trying to wreck things; why couldn't they be content with a well-organized half-day attack? They were out for their own ends, and so on. I realized that, if the half-day had really happened and we had opposed it, we would literally have been de-bagged or expelled. However, first victory went to the rebels.

Meanwhile I had written a note to the Speaker, saying I wanted a brief ten-minute intervention, as the Shadow Minister who got the sack. So I turned up to the debate to listen to George Brown make one of his grandiose exhibitions of candour, integrity and courage, in a carefully calculated concoction. But the main thing was that he indicated an abandonment of support for an independent British deterrent, which, he very reasonably argued, had now ceased to exist, if it ever existed before. What a cheer he got and with what eagerness I led that cheer from below the gangway, making sure the press observed my enthusiasm. And with George Wigg just in front of me and Manny to my right, we were all a united band of brothers, behind George Brown's abandoning his convictions for the sake of the Party.

The rest of the debate was not uninteresting. I missed the first hour and, in my absence, Antony Head spoke highly critically and Manny made the correct speech—lighthearted, supporting George Brown. This electrified our own side. Jack Mendelson had met me beforehand and blamed me bitterly for the shambles that was coming. He was certain that we would wreck our own people and he wouldn't believe my assurances. But nothing of the sort happened. The Government was under attack throughout, and Aubrey Jones, the ex-Minister of Supply,[1] made a most powerful, quiet indictment of the whole Tory method.*

I followed Manny with a pleasant little speech, of which the only point was that it was supporting George Brown, and then went out to give Anne a ten-minute supper. Harold Wilson wound up in his usual Oxford Union style but taking exactly the same policy line as Brown. Throughout, Dora Gaitskell

---

[1] Unionist M.P. for the Hall Green division of Birmingham 1960–5. He was Minister of Fuel and Power 1955–7 and Minister of Supply 1957–9. From 1965 to 1970 he was Chairman of the National Board for Prices and Incomes. His works include *The New Inflation: The Politics of Prices and Incomes* (London: Deutsch, 1973). The Ministry of Supply had been abolished on October 22nd, 1959.

* By the way, this sensation was simply not recorded in the daily press, which can only tell one story about a debate and for whom the story in this case was Labour's shift of policy.

had sat in the Speaker's Gallery, looking, poor woman, like an aged Medusa or Gorgon. She knew what was happening. Patricia [Llewelyn-Davies] had tea with Tony Greenwood just after George Brown's speech, and Tony was summoned to Dora's table. 'I'm surprised you didn't protest to Kingsley about his outrageous article this week.[1] You're not being exactly loyal to Hugh in his absence,' etc., etc. Of course, Dora was working off on Tony her feelings about George Brown, and I was sorry for her.

Since then I've tried to disentangle what happened. This story is from Harold Wilson who talked to me on the phone this morning. George Brown arrived back from Strasbourg[2] early in the morning and before this there had been no discussion between him, Gaitskell and Wilson. In the Reference Library of the House of Commons George discussed the situation and the line with Harold. Then they both prepared their speeches. Why did the line shift as much as it did? First, because of the Aldermaston marchers, who had held in Trafalgar Square the biggest demonstration ever known by the police, and got a very friendly press. Secondly, because USDAW had voted against the bomb the night before.[3] Thirdly, because both Harold and George felt the wind of change and were also anxious to show that other kinds of cats can play when the cat is away.

Here is a record of my conversation with Harold:

CROSSMAN: I was just ringing you, Harold, to tell you that I realize how entirely the whole wonderful thing is due to you personally and how unjustly the press treated you this morning by giving all the credit to George Brown.

WILSON: Ah, George has thoroughly deserved it. I have no ill feelings about him. We must all think of the Party.

CROSSMAN: But don't you think this may harm Gaitskell?

WILSON: Oh, it's greatly in his interest. This will strengthen him a great deal when he gets back, though he may not like it. The fact is, we could only do this in his absence. If he had been here, he and the Chief would have insisted that the debate should stop at seven and there would have been no change of line. Really he should be grateful to us for shifting the line in his absence and so holding the Party together.

CROSSMAN: That's what you meant in the lobby last night when you said to

[1] In 'The Leader', published on April 23rd, the *New Statesman* had discussed Gaitskell's alleged refusal to allow members of his Front Bench to support the Easter protest march from London to the Atomic Weapons Research Establishment at Aldermaston, and back. This had culminated in a rally in Trafalgar Square on April 18th, attended by a crowd estimated at between 60,000 and 100,000 people. Kingsley Martin's signed article ended: 'If the British Labour Party follows the dismal pattern of some Continental parties and breaks up into impotent groups, the responsibility will be Mr Gaitskell's.'

[2] From a meeting of the Consultative Assembly of the Council of Europe, which had been electing a new President.

[3] Both the Co-operative Party and USDAW had passed resolutions demanding an end to testing, production, stockpiling and the basing of nuclear weapons in Britain. On May 4th the A.E.U. was to do the same.

Anne, 'If only we can keep the Leader in Haifa for ever, we shall have a jolly fine fighting Opposition?'

WILSON: Well, it's true, you know. But still, even when he's back it will be a good thing to have got it over. We're doing it for the Party and for him. I assure you I have no ill feelings about the press.

Never in my life have I heard Harold be magnanimous before. As Sydney Jacobson said to me at lunch today, in the last three weeks Harold's conduct in his fight for the treasurership has been outrageous. He's been doing everything to defeat George Brown, including announcing that Harry Nicholas was going to be put up before Nicholas or Cousins had heard of it. The truth, I think, is that Harold knew he had lost the game and that he had to ally himself with Brown against the common enemy.

Be that as it may, the fact remains that the Party did get through yesterday's debate with enthusiasm, that an important shift of policy was taken, that it was a saving grace that Gaitskell was away and that it is now possible to look forward to the joint conversations between the T.U.C. and the Labour Party. But here there is a danger. I am sure the next disaster Hugh will instinctively drift into is support for the European nuclear weapon as an alternative to the independent British nuclear weapon. This is the kind of NATO or European claptrap to which they will all instinctively have recourse and which we must resist if we possibly can.

What about my own personal position? Well, over Easter I've been brooding over and working on my Fabian pamphlet, which will be Crossman's great manifesto, the first serious ideological document, apart from Crosland, on Labour's future. I suppose I have also been brooding with amusement on the obvious fact that Labour's nuclear policy was going to shift and that I would get no credit for it and that George Wigg, who is more responsible, would get even less. But even in my gloomiest moments I never anticipated my predictions would be fulfilled as rapidly as this or that George and I would be seen to be playing so small a role.

In the *Sunday Times* this week I was described by A Student of Politics as the leader of the Left against Gaitskell. That, no doubt, did me a great deal of harm.[1] It may also be true that, though it's not in the daily papers, the role we have played is in the minds of most of our colleagues and they are determined to see that we gain very little out of it. Finally, it's true that neither George nor I is trying to gain very much out of it or doing much about that kind of thing. So why should we bother?

Ten days at Prescote, in lovely sunny weather, with the whole Llewelyn-Davies family sitting down, ten to table, like Victorian families, is a great reducer of ambition. I enormously enjoy politics now because I need them less for self-esteem. I enjoy writing even more and, now that I'm free of the *Daily Mirror*, I'm writing much more of what I like. In fact, I'm lucky.

[1] James Margach also described Crossman as looking 'like a good-natured, ambling St Bernard who has found his brandy'.

Tuesday, May 3rd

On Thursday evening Roy Jenkins looked in. He had been charged by the Fabian Executive with vetting my manuscript for publication.[1] He told me he could find nothing unfair in my presentation of the revisionist case and then explained what his main arguments would be if he reviewed my pamphlet. Firstly, he would point out that no one has made such a ferocious cold war doctrine as I have. And that it is very extreme to stake everything on the danger of Communist expansion. Secondly, the argument seems contrived, as though I had said to myself, 'I must take it as an assumption that the Labour Party is pledged to nationalization and then erect an ideology to justify it.' Thirdly, Roy thought I had rather exaggerated the rate of progress of the Communists. I found all this not very helpful and was more interested when he told me that he had spoken to Gaitskell as he was passing through London on his way to Haifa on the previous Sunday—'a long telephone call on which I tried to tell him we ought to switch our policy from the great deterrent and also urged him to stay for the debate. As usual, I was successful in neither object.' Then Roy got up and left.

On Friday I set off for Oslo. Every Saturday during the winter and spring the students of Oslo have a distinguished foreigner and pay his expenses for getting there. My great occasion took place in a dark and gloomy beercellar, dominated by a student portrait of a pig and with all the appurtenances of beer tables, beer bars and general difficulty for a speaker. I should think they were disappointed by the turn-out, since the cellar can hold 700 and I doubt if they had more than 300 for me. Moreover, though they can claim to know English and do know a remarkable amount, I doubt if they find it really easy to follow.

However, I managed to give them a rip-roaring lecture, which had them all in a great peal of laughter and merriment at the beginning and spellbound with horror at the end. I had assumed that, since I had given a press conference on Friday and since the lecture took place at seven o'clock English time on Saturday, I needn't worry about British press coverage. So I was peeved to find that a joke that I had made about Tony Crosland and myself had been maliciously telegraphed. Trying to break the ice with these students on the internal workings of the Labour Party, I had said how little honour intellectuals had with us—so little, I said, warming to my theme, that there are only two great thinkers in the Labour Party, Anthony Crosland and Richard Crossman, and, spelling out the names, I then added, 'But people care so little that they can't distinguish between us, our names or our views.' On the front page of the *Sunday Express* Anne showed me, on my return, the report that I had stated there were only two great thinkers in the Party,

[1] *Labour in the Affluent Society* was published in early June. Crossman argued that the only way to remedy the maladies of capitalism was by increasing public ownership. If he did not believe that capitalism was doomed, Crossman stated, he would prefer to reconstruct the Liberal Party as 'the main alternative to Conservatism'.

Anthony Crosland and Richard Crossman, to which the reporter had added my statement that the workers had more luxuries than a Roman Emperor in his heyday, omitting the other half of my remark, where I said they were denying the essentials and public services for the sake of the luxuries. However, the whole lecture seemed to go all right.

I got back on Sunday, after an immense first-class lunch on the plane, to find Anne at the airport and everyone still talking about Gaitskell and nuclear weapons. On Monday it was clear that he was in his usual form, with a long speech attacking the pacifists.[1] I went into the House to pick up the atmosphere and found myself besieged with talkers, and Harold Wilson eager to tell me how he had gone to the airport with the Chief Whip to meet Gaitskell and help him to draft his skilful statement. 'But he spoilt it all with that terrible reactionary speech. If only he'd stay away and let us run things for him!' Harold had made a speech of his own in Hyde Park and had denounced the European bomb. He assured me he had Cabinet authority for doing so, which he believes but I don't. He also told me that Hugh was completely untruthful in asserting that his conversations with Tewson had begun already.

Antony Head was also anxious for a talk, telling me how superb Patrick Blackett is and discussing what form of collaboration we can best undertake to achieve our common aim. Then it was Jack Mendelson, anxious to clear up the terrible story in the *Express*. How did it happen? What did I mean by appeasing Crosland in that way? Then there was Crosland, for once quite breezy, though admitting that this was the final *coup de grâce* for his reputation. I realized, of course, that he felt I had linked my name with a serious thinker, whereas I am merely a vulgar journalist. Altogether it was a gay afternoon, in the sense that the Labour Party was once again the centre of the news, destroying itself by its appearance of division and aimlessness.

Wednesday, May 11th
The only real subject is still the nuclear row in the Party. Meanwhile I returned to Prescote for a long weekend, partly because I had agreed to help Coventry in the municipal elections this year. Last year they complained bitterly that the M.P.s had let them down, so this year I offered a good deal of time and, not unexpectedly, found they hardly knew how to use me.

The atmosphere is really terrifyingly apathetic — a few people struggling to get out the election addresses, absolutely no sign of life or vitality of any kind. This is very sad in Coventry, where the Council has done a really remarkable job and where, the more one looks at their record, the more

[1] At Leeds on May Day he had said that it would be 'quite wrong' of him, as Leader of the Labour Party, to commit himself to any one of the possible solutions arising from the abandonment of Blue Streak, until talks within the Party and with the T.U.C. had been completed. He continued, however: 'we must stand by our alliance and retain our defences ... the contrary policy — pacifist, neutralist, unilateralist — is in present conditions profoundly dangerous to our own security and that of the world.'

one feels that their one failure is the lack of public relations. But, if any group of citizens should be grateful to their councillors, it is those of Coventry, because the Council has shown an astonishing initiative, enterprise and verve. All of them there feel terribly downhearted, not unnaturally, at the general sense of depression at what has been happening at Westminster, with the newspapers day after day describing Gaitskell's rows and troubles. I don't think there is any doubt that the so-called image of the Labour Party has been getting more and more unattractive. Indeed, one of the most ironical facts of the situation is that Gaitskell and Crosland, whose main concern is to improve the electoral image, have since the Election done nothing but harden it catastrophically by every one of their actions and attitudes.

All this time, it was perfect, hot, sunshiny weather. The only trouble for Prescote was that we've had no rain for a month and the grass isn't growing high enough. On Monday the weather broke up, but God was unkind because at Prescote not a drop fell. I should, I suppose, mention that an extra reason for escaping from London last week was the Royal Wedding.[1] What a mercy it is that Anne hates public events even more than I do. Anyway there we were, I writing and she cooking and we all forgot to see it, though Nanny saw a résumé in the evening and thought it wonderful.

Now back to our Labour Party affairs. The B.B.C. asked me to appear on 'Panorama' on Monday, with Antony Head, George Brown and a dreary little Tory called Airey Neave.[2] After the broadcast, Brown talked to me about a NATO bomb or a European bomb. I indicated that I thought it was quite impracticable. He then tried the idea that we should join the whole Common Market, to which I replied that nobody would believe we were sincere about joining the Common Market, when all we were doing was trying to find some form of words to get the Shadow Cabinet out of a defence fix.

Over the weekend we had the usual barrage of inspired articles from the Gaitskell stable, this time all denouncing irresponsible trade union leaders and irresponsible constituency representatives on the N.E.C. and praising the parliamentary leadership as the only Labour leaders genuinely responsible to the people. Ironical to remember that Gaitskell got his leadership because he was shoved into it by the trade union leaders and how odd that he should think that the way to persuade them to change the Party constitution and get rid of constituency members is to have them all abused!

[1] On May 6th in Westminster Abbey Princess Margaret was married to Mr Anthony Armstrong-Jones, a professional photographer.

[2] Conservative M.P. for Abingdon from July 1953 until his murder in April 1979. He was Joint Parliamentary Secretary at the Ministry of Transport and Civil Aviation 1957–9 and Parliamentary Under-Secretary of State for Air 1959. A distinguished war record included his escape from Colditz. He later served as Commissioner for Criminal Organizations at the Nuremberg International Military Tribunal. His works include *They Have Their Exits* (London: Hodder & Stoughton, 1953) and *Nuremberg* (London: Hodder & Stoughton, 1978).

Yesterday, after George Wigg and I had finished our joint article for the *Statesman*,[1] I went and had lunch in the Commons. I found myself sitting with Frank Soskice and Reg Paget. At first we got on quite well, since I got myself on to the theme of Crosland versus Crossman, on which Soskice was perfectly rational. Then Paget said something about the suicidal mania of the Party, which attacks its leaders at the moment when they are going to knock out the Tories on defence. Within a minute there was a frightful row between us. At one point I said something about everybody now knowing that a British deterrent didn't exist, to which Paget replied, 'What nonsense, what complete nonsense! The case for it is stronger than ever.'

At this point Soskice said quietly, 'I agree with Reggie entirely on this.' I don't know what possessed me but I turned to Soskice and said, 'Well, fortunately, on these defence matters, Frank, your views don't count much.' 'You're talking to a member of the Shadow Cabinet,' said Reggie and I made it worse by saying, 'My God, I'd forgotten!' I've never in his life before seen Soskice really angry. He was hurt and withered through and through and he will never forgive me. But he had revealed some very important information, which I later confirmed when I found that he and Gordon Walker are the arch-priests of no change, Gaitskell standing firm, etc., whereas George Brown has ratted.

And so we come to yesterday's meeting of the International Sub. I had unsuccessfully tried to get Sam Watson to lunch beforehand but he had sent me an enigmatic letter. The meeting started with some routine business but the main item read: 'Joint discussions on defence (a) with the Parliamentary Committee (b) with the T.U.C.' Morgan read a letter from Frank Barlow,[2] saying that the Parliamentary Committee would like to be represented at these discussions and nominating three men, Robens, Brown and, I think, Callaghan. The letter made it fairly clear that they wanted these three to attend our meeting with the T.U.C. as full representatives and for this to be preceded by discussions between the International Sub. and the Parliamentary Committee.

At once I pointed out that we could either have tripartite discussions, with each of the three bodies formally represented, or two-way discussions, in which case we should only consult with the Parliamentary Committee before doing the job and taking our decisions. Walter Padley leapt in to support me on a matter of the greatest constitutional importance. It was clear that every trade unionist present had read in the press the inspired attacks on them. Barbara said she thought this was a dangerous predecent.

---

[1] In a *News Chronicle* article on Thursday, May 5th, Crossman had set out a five-point plan for combining loyalty to NATO with a non-nuclear Europe; George Wigg was now anxious to follow this with a joint article in the *New Statesman*. This was published as 'Defence After Blue Streak' in the issue of May 14th, 1960.

[2] He joined the Parliamentary Labour Party as an official in 1939 and was Assistant Secretary 1947 and Secretary from 1959 until his death in 1979, the year in which he was knighted.

Weren't we changing the constitution in suggesting that the Parliamentary Committee should act jointly with the N.E.C. and share responsibility?

At this point Hugh intervened with an explanation. 'It hasn't been thought out very exactly,' he said, 'but we've had several meetings about it and we feel very strongly that we want to be represented at these vital talks. As for Barbara's point, I thought we all agreed that, without formally changing the constitution, we did want a new position, in which, on all important statements, the Parliamentary Committee joined with the N.E.C. in preparing them.' This, Hugh added, warming to his topic, had been expressly laid down for the Parliamentary manifesto. Should we not now gradually move towards an informal recognition?

Oh dear, the fat was in the fire for him! Ray Gunter, right-wing to his last breath, is a procedural expert, like all trade union leaders. 'I'm afraid we can't have that, Hugh,' he said. 'We're responsible here on the executive and no one can take that responsibility from us. Of course, we can consult with other people but we must take our own decisions.' Hugh tried to breeze it off by saying once again that nothing very exact had been thought out. Ray said, 'Do you suggest that those three could come with us to meet the the T.U.C.?' Somebody else said, 'Should they have voting rights?' Gaitskell replied, 'I think it would be most unwise even to consider the possibility of voting in the kind of friendly discussion we shall have, but I can tell you that the Parliamentary Committee's recommendation is that these three should take full part in the discussions with the T.U.C.'

Once again I patiently pointed out that we could either have tripartite or two-way discussions and it was no good saying these things were informal or that votes might not take place. If they did occur, we should have to exclude from voting anybody who was a member of the N.E.C. By this time all the trade unionists were with me — Walter Padley on my left, Dan McGarvey[1] and Ray Gunter opposite me, with Tom Driberg apparently bewildered and not knowing what side he was on, and with Barbara freelancing on her own.

Morgan said, 'Surely the only sane way of doing it is to have the Parliamentary Committee in?' I replied, 'It can't really be the only sane thing to do, Morgan, because last year we didn't do it.[2] Last year we had two-way discussions after informal talks with some members of the Shadow Cabinet. Previously we had tripartite discussions on defence at a low level. Another way would be to call our defence sub-committee, to which no doubt we should be glad to co-opt Mr Brown and Mr Strachey.' Just to show how the mood was, this was greeted by a peal of merry laughter from the trade unionists, who knew I had scored off their enemies. I then said, 'Let's

[1] President of the Amalgamated Society of Boilermakers, Shipwrights, Blacksmiths and Structural Workers and a member of the T.U.C. General Council from 1965 until his death in 1977.

[2] See above, pp. 759 ff.

shorten the discussion (it had lasted fifty minutes by now) by my formally moving that we hold a special meeting next Tuesday and shall be glad to see any members of the Shadow Cabinet who like to attend. Let's send them our paper, which will form the basis of the meeting and suggest that they should submit any comments they think fit.'

Gaitskell drew himself up and said, 'I think I should warn you that, if that's the way the business is conducted, the Parliamentary Committee will have the freedom to disown your decisions.' There was a short pause. Dan McGarvey said, 'I think it is a pity you used language like that, Mr Gaitskell. It may be misunderstood. After all, a good many trade union leaders have had to accept the democratic decision of their union, even when they themselves have been against it. You wouldn't be the first person to have to do it.' I said I thought it was a pity to discuss such gloomy possibilities. We should know better after our first meeting on what basis agreement could be reached. Gaitskell said he wanted speed. The latest possible date was June 23rd and, after some discussion, we all agreed that we ought to get as much as possible of the discussion done before the end of this month.

Gaitskell went off with Sam Watson. Morgan Phillips, Dan McGarvey, Ray Gunter and I went and had a drink for an hour and a half. After I had jollied Morgan along about Cropredy[1] for a long time (a safe subject for him), I said something about Gaitskell. He replied, 'What an impossible man he is! That remark of his, threatening to turn the Parliamentary Committee against us! Every trade union official will hear about it by tomorrow. And he hasn't done his homework either—no preparation for that meeting. Ever since the Election we've done nothing right. Every single thing has been wrong, thanks to him. It can't go on much longer.'

The more I reflect on this extraordinary meeting, the more certain I become that Gaitskell is heading for disaster. I rang up Harold this morning, who told me they had had their fourth long meeting of the Shadow Cabinet and that Gaitskell was coming fast my way. But Soskice and Gordon Walker are holding out for the British deterrent and Gaitskell and George Brown had a flaming row for a long time. I told Harold what had happened at the International and he told me we ought to allow George Brown to attend the joint meetings. I pointed out that we were not likely to do this, in view of inspired leaks about changing the constitution. It became clear that Harold and I had drifted apart and we are meeting behind the Speaker's chair at three o'clock this afternoon to clear things up between us.

Harold also told me that Soskice yesterday tried to persuade the Shadow Cabinet to jump the gun and issue a policy statement next Monday as an ultimatum to the Executive. He agreed with me, however, that, if Gaitskell appeals to the Parliamentary Party, he may well get defeated or be forced by them in the same direction as ourselves. It's clear that yesterday Gaitskell went to our meeting without preparing anybody for it, without approaching

[1] The village near Banbury where the Crossmans had their farm, Prescote Manor.

a single one of the trade unionists and without facing in any way the kind of impression he created by threatening not to accept the decision of the Executive.

Another even more sardonic impression is that of my sudden popularity with the trade union leaders. They all know what I was sacked for. They all know that the line I am taking is the only line they can take in their unions and get away with. Therefore they are on my side. Therefore they think me fine. In fact, if there has got to be a clever intellectual drafting away, they prefer one who will draft the kind of document they can get away with rather than the kind of document which gets them into trouble.

When I think of Gunter's attitude to me even six weeks ago and his present beaming friendliness and good humour! But I am now seriously beginning to think that there may be a move to get rid of Gaitskell before the Conference.[1] For one of our problems is that, even if we adopt the Wigg/Crossman line, it would be voted down by Conference if Gaitskell were to move it, so great is the hatred and distrust of him. Morgan tells me that his hope is to prevent Nye from making a single speech before Conference and there to present him as the saviour and deliverer. Anyway, we shall see what happens.

Thursday, May 12th
I saw Harold Wilson yesterday, who said he had spent the morning sitting next to Frank Cousins at the T.U.C. Economic Committee. 'I had put down the seven essential points on a bit of notepaper and he agreed them straightaway.' 'What are they?' I said, and it was all right. Dear little Harold had got them right. It was the Crossman Plan, lifted from the *News Chronicle* and memorized. 'A few weeks ago,' said Harold, 'they were saying they would get rid of Gaitskell if there was an alternative. Now they are saying they must get rid of him, whoever takes his place. He can't last long now.'

Then there was a meeting of the defence group, at which some forty people turned up. It was opened by George Brown in his oiliest form, with the most moving speech about how a completely new situation had been created, in which we should never look back on the past or remind each other of things we had done or said. I kept wondering what would have happened if it had been my past which had gone wrong and not his! The noteworthy fact of the meeting was the unconscious collaboration in splitting the Party achieved between the nuclear warriors and the nuclear abolitionists.

As we were going along the passage to the meeting, George Brown said to me, 'I think you and I, Dick, could work out a policy pretty quickly if one man would let us prevent him from destroying himself.' After the meeting I met Strachey in the lobby and fell into conflict because he had

---

[1] The Labour Party Conference was to take place in Scarborough from October 3rd to October 7th.

been saying that we couldn't fulfil our duty to NATO if we abandoned nuclear weapons. 'Every other member of NATO does its duty with a conventional contribution,' I said, 'including the Germans.' 'But the Germans are forbidden nuclear weapons,' he said, 'whereas we would abandon them. To abandon them would be to betray NATO.' This was the line James Callaghan was also vaguely taking. It looks as though it's the Gaitskellite line at present. Jack Mendelson came to me in closest secrecy. He had just been asked by George Brown whether he would join a delegation of four — Brown, De Freitas, Mellish, Mendelson — to be flown over to Atlanta, Georgia, mainly to see the Lockheed transport aircraft, a rival to the Britannia but also to see Polaris. I said Mendelson ought to go as a spy but he felt it would be selling the pass and he's probably right. The delegation will set out on June 5th and what interests me is how George Brown is playing it double, since I have checked with George Wigg that this has been fixed by the American Embassy as a method of tying us to nuclear weapons.

Thursday, May 20th
On the night of Thursday, the 12th, it was a heavy, oppressive day, raining all over Britain and helping the disastrous results of our municipal elections.[1] In London the drought broke with rolling thunder. 'Not a thunderstorm,' Patrick said to me, 'only clouds banging each other.' That evening at a quarter past six I went into the Smoking Room with George Wigg. We found George Brown sitting there with Frank Tomney opposite him and Jack Mendelson. By the time I got there George Brown was rather high with dry Martinis, an Etruscan flushed with wine but by no means unfriendly, and we soon got a lively conversation about how 'That man down the passage' was making life totally impossible. 'Last year I spent five hours on end with him in Transport House drafting the non-nuclear club statement,' I said. 'You can have the job this year.' 'Never on my life! He's utterly impossible. Do you know what he's just done? He made Patrick Gordon Walker call a meeting of the Shadow Cabinet this afternoon, in which it was proposed that we should put out a statement on our defence policy, jumping the gun on the Executive and the Parliamentary Committee. The old guard was ardently supported by Frank Soskice, and people like Fraser and Willey were doubtful. I had to put a stop to the nonsense. Think of jumping the gun like that! It's sheer madness.'

Then George Brown reminisced on how it was Gaitskell who had vetoed an agreement about 'first-strike nuclear weapons', which would have avoided Frank Cousins's outbreak last year, and how it was Hugh who had vetoed this February the draft defence resolution Brown had agreed with Silverman. In his cups, at least, George Brown was extremely violent about the impossible, interfering leader we have and how he had had enough of it and how

[1] Municipal elections were held on May 12th in 363 English and Welsh boroughs. Labour lost 470 of its seats; the Conservatives gained 389, the Liberals 51 and Independents 30.

the job could be finished within a few hours if it was only left to Brown, Crossman and Wigg.

All this time, by the way, John Strachey had been sitting on the sofa opposite him, silent and anxious-looking, obviously embarrassed by Mr Brown's exuberance, as was Frank Tomney, by no means in his cups. Brown got so excited that George Wigg finally said, 'Well, I'll take you at your word. Let's reach an agreement before the defence group meets on Monday. Dick will make a draft tomorrow morning.' I said, 'You'd better bring Strachey along and I'll bring my George and we'll have little Harold Wilson as well and then we can do the job.'

It was agreed we should meet at a quarter to two in the Visitors' Dining Room to discuss my draft. It wasn't difficult to promise, since I had already written it that afternoon and sent a copy to Harold Wilson for his comments. So George Wigg and I drifted off home at a quarter past eight and on Friday morning I telephoned Harold. He had received my draft, was delighted with it and promised to discuss it with Denis Healey during the day and to bring him along on the Monday.

Anne set off for the country and I had scarcely got there when the telephone rang. It was Harold, to tell me that George Brown was in Westminster Hospital with a fractured skull, caused by a fall downstairs in the Commons. I hadn't much doubt how the fall had occurred but Harold, who is now a loyal Brownite, indignantly said, 'It was overstrain. He's been under great nervous strain recently.' He began to discuss the ghastly· problems which would arise as to who should share Monday's meeting, since George Wigg and John Strachey are joint vice-chairmen.

Throughout the weekend a good deal of telephoning went on. However, it finally became clear that George Brown could be brought in on Monday to chair the meeting, though with two black eyes, concussion and a very bad bruise on his forehead. He was determined to be the saviour of the Party. Harold decided to have him alone to lunch, to discuss my draft, and George Wigg and I had lunch together. This was before the defence group at four o'clock, which was in Committee Room 10 and even more largely attended.

This time George Brown behaved himself even better and the whole meeting went pretty well. It was even clearer, however, that, surprisingly enough, the serious opposition would come from people who used to be the moderate Centre of the Party—Michael Stewart, George Strauss, John' Strachey—all still believing in the independent British deterrent and, much more important, all able enough to realize that George Brown had leap-frogged them into his new alliance with us and left his old buddies in the lurch. It was clear enough at the end of this meeting that Brown had virtually accepted the Wigg/Crossman policy and he ostentatiously stressed during the meeting the mistakes he had made by not taking George Wigg's advice and by relying on non-existent weapons. The significance of the meeting was that, though the undoubted mood of the majority of those there was against my case for a non-nuclear NATO, George Brown had committed himself to our side and was willing to stand up for it.

Next day, Tuesday 17th, we had the first joint meeting of the International Sub. and the Parliamentary Committee, crowded together in one of the downstairs committee rooms. Previously we had had all the tremendous fuss about the constitutional rights of the International in which I had led the way. Now I was busily ensuring that George Brown and his colleagues should play a leading role. We had George Brown's speech repeated all over again with extremely little opposition. Gaitskell let Brown do most of the running and over half the time was spent on procedure—who should go to meet the T.U.C. International, whether spokesmen should be mandated from our side, etc., etc.

On Thursday, the 19th, I lunched with Geoffrey Goodman[1] of the *Herald* who told me that the *Herald* staff had finally been converted to the Crossman/Wigg line and who also began to discuss the eternal problem of Gaitskell's leadership. I don't know how many hours I've spent since I last wrote this diary, taking part in conversations which go round and round that central issue of Gaitskell's awfulness, how the Party is dying on its feet and how there is nobody to replace him.

In drenching rain that afternoon I then caught the train to Banbury in time for our clay-pigeon shoot, which took place on the coldest day of the year. But at least the rain held off and we sheltered under the big garden wall. The shoot took place across the Cherwell into the field. It took hours for the teams to shoot it out and afterwards they all came into the big panelled room for sandwiches and whisky. They really seemed rather pleased that Anne and I were maintaining the traditions of Prescote. There were forty people, the big farmers of Warwickshire and North Oxfordshire. Mr Pritchett was quite pleased, too, because he's a superb farmer but he can't run a party for forty people in a panelled room and he knows he can't and wants us there for it. Just imagine if we had a young gentleman with an agricultural degree from Reading who said to us, 'Don't worry to come down. Let me open up the house and give the party.' It's nice that there's something for which it's essential that we should be there and, with all the stalwart local ladies coming round and doing all the work, it's not a very heavy obligation, particularly as they are all extremely curious to chat with the Labour politician.

On Monday I had my social security working party. Quite literally, this is the only constructive thinking in the Labour Party that has taken place since the Election, apart from the nuclear weapon job we are now doing.

---

[1] A journalist, he worked on the *News Chronicle* 1949–59, the *Daily Herald* 1959–64, the *Sun* 1964–9 and then on the *Daily Mirror*, of which he became Industrial Editor in 1969 and Assistant Editor in 1976. He was head of the Government's Counter-Inflation Publicity Unit 1975–6. He wrote a biography of Frank Cousins, *The Awkward Warrior* (London: Davis-Poynter, 1979).

When we had finished, I took Peter Townsend, Tony Lynes[1] and Titmuss to the lower bar and was just giving them a drink when in walked George Brown, Frank Cousins and Harry Nicholas. Harry Nicholas had been at our committee. They sat down beside us and we were all beams and smiles, the first time Cousins had spoken to me since he had written a terrific blast about my articles in the *Mirror*.

At once I tackled George on the subject of Gaitskell's weekend speech, which got tremendous headlines, saying we must keep our NATO nuclear weapons. I had checked with David Ennals that he now thought it possible to have a NATO thermo-nuclear deterrent and joint NATO atomic weapons, as an alternative to our British bombs. 'I'll stop his nonsense,' said George. 'I'll make sure that doesn't go into the draft for tomorrow. I will promise you. What an impossible fellow he is!'

The summit meeting in Paris between President Eisenhower, President de Gaulle, Mr Macmillan and Mr Khrushchev was to begin on May 16th. On May 5th Mr Khrushchev had announced that a Lockheed U-2 unarmed single-seater reconnaissance aircraft had been shot down near Sverdlovsk in the Urals; two days later the U.S. State Department admitted that it had probably been on an Intelligence mission. Despite sending notes of protest to the American Government, Mr Khrushchev arrived in Paris on May 14th for discussions with President de Gaulle and Mr Macmillan, in preparation for the summit. On the opening day, however, Mr Khrushchev declared that as a condition of his attending the meeting the U.S.A. must stop all U-2 flights, apologize and punish those concerned. President Eisenhower said that flights had ended but that Mr Khrushchev's 'ultimatum' on Berlin (of November 20th, 1958) would never be acceptable to the U.S.A. Mr Macmillan sought to act as a mediator between his three colleagues; nevertheless the summit was abandoned. Mr Khrushchev left for East Germany on May 18th and Mr Macmillan and President Eisenhower departed the following day.

On Tuesday morning we had a Party Meeting, which was overshadowed by the news that Hugh had made a great speech to the General Workers at Yarmouth on Monday. It is symptomatic of how inward-thinking one is that I should say it was overshadowed by that. Of course, what cast the shadow was the break-up of the summit talks in Paris, which had been taking place during our endless intrigues and conversations. I don't think I

[1] A member of the Labour Party social policy group who worked with Richard Titmuss at the L.S.E. 1958–65 and in 1965 with Margaret Herbison as a temporary Principal at the Ministry of Pensions and National Insurance. He was Secretary of the Child Poverty Action Group 1966–9 and from 1969 a Consultant on Children to the Social Service Department of Oxfordshire County Council. From 1974 to 1979 he was Adviser on Social Security at the Department of Health and Social Security. His works include *French Pensions* (London: Bell, 1967) and the *Penguin Guide to Supplementary Benefits* (Harmondsworth: Penguin, 1972).

was nearly as shocked as most people, partly because Khrushchev seemed to behave on this occasion exactly the same way as he behaved at our Labour Party dinner four years ago and partly because I have been so busy writing my Fabian pamphlet,[1] in which the central theme is that the Russians are going to continue their pressure on the Western democracies, summit or no summit.

Nevertheless, there is no doubt that the shooting down of the American spy plane and Khrushchev's decision to use the occasion to smash up the Conference came at a wonderful moment for Gaitskell, since it seemed to put us right back into cold war and so to weaken the whole offensive launched by the pacifists, unilateralists and the people who generally wanted to get out of NATO or to be disloyal to it. These pacifists, unilateralists and anti-NATO-ists would have gained gigantically by the summit and the break-down certainly made Gaitskell's speech have more effect on the general public. But, in the inside struggle for the leadership, the pacifists and uni-lateralists are an insignificant minority and the real struggle is that between the nuclear warriors and the supporters of the Wigg/Crossman line. In this dispute, the failure of the summit made no difference whatsoever.

On Tuesday morning George Brown opened once again and this time made a really admirable exposé of the position, almost exactly as I had got it in my second amended draft. Significantly, Hugh took care to call after him three out-and-out right-wingers, headed by Roy Mason,[2] and two out-and-out pacifists, Frank Allaun[3] and Emrys Hughes. Finally Strachey made an impassioned appeal that the Party should stand by, first, the prin-ciple that Blue Streak had in fact been abandoned and, secondly, the prin-ciple that a Labour Government must be left free to select the right weapons appropriate to the occasion. However, he wrapped this up in a fifteen-minute speech of such fervour that most people were unaware that he wasn't sup-porting Brown. Emrys Hughes got a rough reception for his attack on Gait-skell, whom he described as a jumping flea and a Ramsay MacDonald. Manny Shinwell made a statesmanlike speech before Hugh Gaitskell wound up, fairly all right.

So at half-past five we moved to the International, where again George Brown started, outlining his seven points. Here the only opposition, again vague and emotional, was that of Barbara. Hugh looked a little puffy, inflated with the news that the General Workers had voted on his side and

---

[1] *Can Labour Win?*, published by the Fabian Society on May 4th.

[2] A former miner and branch official of the National Union of Mineworkers, he became Labour M.P. for Barnsley in March 1953. He was Minister of State (Shipping) at the Board of Trade 1964–7, Minister of Defence (Equipment) 1967–April 1968, Postmaster-General April–June 1968, Minister of Power 1968–9, President of the Board of Trade 1969–70 and Secretary of State for Northern Ireland 1976–9.

[3] Industrial Correspondent of the *Manchester Evening News* and the *Daily Herald* and Editor of *Labour's Northern Voice* 1951–67, he became Labour M.P. for East Salford in 1955. He was P.P.S. to the Secretary of State for the Colonies from October 1964 to March 1965.

yet uncertain of himself. This afternoon I pointed out that there were two issues on which we needed precise formulations—German nuclear weapons and a declaration that we should not use nuclear weapons first. At once Hugh was up in arms against anything so dangerous but George Brown backed me up on both.

Right at the end, it was decided that we might start drafting. As we were getting up, Hugh said, 'Well, I suppose we ought to have George and Denis and Morgan, and perhaps Dick as well.' I didn't have time to say that I should be on the car ferry next Tuesday and, since the T.U.C. couldn't meet us till then, it was no good putting me on the drafting committee. I muttered this to George a little later, who seemed disappointed, and Morgan had known all along. However, I felt I might help a bit over the week-end, so I didn't fuss.

Yesterday morning we had the N.E.C. and, as he sat down beside me, Hugh Gaitskell said, 'I think that this morning we shall have to have a serious discussion of the municipal defeats.' He said it was a pity that we hadn't followed up the researches on the causes of our unpopularity (he was thinking of Crosland's pamphlet) and he thought we should have a paper as soon as possible, analysing why the electorate was turning against us. He had come into the room flushed with pleasure, since every newspaper had as its main headline, 'Gaitskell's Double Victory' – over the General Workers and over the Parliamentary Party—and the second story was a verbatim account of exactly what had happened and how we had all unanimously adopted the Gaitskell line.[1]

But the moment he talked about municipals, Walter Padley said, 'Before you get to the electorate, what matters is the Party. There's a crisis of confidence in the Party. They are being driven mad by all this talk about the Parliamentary Committee overriding the Party or defying its decisions.' Greenwood followed up with a quotation in that morning's *Herald*, which said Gaitskell was conferring with four big trade union leaders on how to change the Party Constitution. I sit beside Gaitskell and I felt him start with righteous indignation. 'What concerns us is the electorate,' he said. 'Oh no, it isn't,' was chorused, 'first of all we've got to look after the Party. That's what we are responsible for on the Executive.' And Morgan Phillips strongly backed us up. Harold Wilson made an outright attack on Hugh, blaming him for sacking me in February and adopting my policy this week.

[1] Gaitskell's line was: no unilateral renunciation of nuclear weapons, pending multilateral, controlled disarmament; adequate arrangements for Britain's defence; continued NATO membership; and retention by NATO of nuclear weapons, under joint political control, for as long as the U.S.S.R. possessed them. Crossman's line was: provision, both strategic and tactical, of the Western nuclear deterrent to be left entirely to the U.S.A.; a purely 'conventional' contribution by Britain; a non-nuclear strategy for NATO, with the disappearance as soon as possible of American bases; and, unless Britain's defence commitments were ruthlessly pruned, the consideration of some form of selective National Service.

Others hinted more and more broadly that the Clause 4 row started by Hugh, and the timings of his actions, had been disastrous.

Finally Tony Benn made his first good intervention since he became a Member, saying we must have a meeting at which we decide on the themes we are going to run, the leadership we are going to give and how we are going to get the Party going again. Hugh picked this up and said we must have a meeting of the old Chairmen's Committee to work out a paper. What an idiot he is! This committee is detested, particularly by the trade unionists. So I very neatly suggested that our General Secretary should be entrusted with the job of preparing the paper. 'Not without consultation,' said Hugh *sotto voce*. 'We can't have that.' Informal consultations were then suggested and Hugh was finally defeated when Morgan said, 'I will take the job but of course it will be my draft and no one else's.'

When we came to defence, Sam Watson read aloud the report, Hugh and I added to it and I did just notice that the names of the drafting committee were in the minutes. So I mentioned to Hugh that I would have to leave on Tuesday. He thought it a great pity. But there was no real discussion. When I went into the Smoking Room that evening, I was greeted with quite a cheer by David Ormsby-Gore, Profumo and Selwyn Lloyd, who were all sitting having a drink. 'A new job for you,' said David. 'Shadow Defence Minister!' 'Nonsense,' I said, to which Profumo said, 'But it's on the tape,' and, blow me, it was. Morgan had had his revenge. Seeing how grossly Gaitskell-biased the new stories were, he had cut his account of the Executive, quite rightly omitting our real rows, and then dropped in the names of the four members of the defence drafting committee,[1] reckoning that the appetite of the press would be whetted. This morning I got almost as big a press for getting back into Labour's counsels as for being thrown out a few weeks ago. Of course, it hadn't been at all intended that I should be back in the inner counsels but, by giving all this to the press, Morgan undoubtedly gave the drafting committee a very great importance, if it wished to use it.

When we met this morning, I suggested two things to Morgan and George. First, I said I was postponing going away but wanted to get away soon and we agreed that Friday was the latest day by which we should be finished. Secondly, I said that, in view of the T.U.C.'s feelings, although we should actually be preparing a draft no one outside should be allowed to see it and, indeed, theoretically we should not exist. George immediately agreed and Morgan, coming in a little later, said when he was asked, 'And that means no one, David. You know what I mean.' And we all did. So we've decided to prepare our own draft secretly, without consulting Gaitskell.

At this point George Brown said he was rather disgusted at Gaitskell's discussing the morality of anyone who touches the press, considering his unrivalled network of informal press relations.

[1] Crossman, Denis Healey, George Brown and Morgan Phillips.

RETURN OF THE PRODIGAL

We then got down to the job, going through the trade union conference resolutions and noting the points which we would have to avoid if we were not to compel the union secretaries to vote against us. We got the order of the paragraphs right and formulated the vital sentence about not using the weapons first and not allowing the Germans weapons. We then decided that David Ennals and I should do the first draft, ready for ten o'clock tomorrow.

So I went off to give lunch to Tony Wedgwood Benn at the Athenaeum, he full of gaiety and excitement and pretty clear that Gaitskell couldn't last very long, enjoying the irony of the morning press. There's nothing more pleasurable in British politics than seeing a Leader made a fool of and poor Gaitskell, who has had everything his own way in the headlines yesterday, has now had the bubble pricked by Morgan today. Moreover, though he doesn't know it, Gaitskell has now got a drafting committee whose views could hardly be challenged even by him, providing they can put their draft to the committee without showing it to him first, as we intend shall be done. George Brown says that Frank Cousins is willing to join our drafting committee on Wednesday but I doubt if the T.U.C. will agree that he should go in alone. Anyway we're better without him.

Monday, May 30th
I spent Friday morning on our four-man drafting committee in Morgan's room. How like old times it was to enter his outside office and see his two plump secretaries beaming at me, when for months they have glowered if ever I came their way. During all this, we had quite a lot of chat. George

Brown had been telling me of how he had worked on his famous Blue Streak speech while at Strasbourg, and at one point I threw in, slightly maliciously, 'But I hear so little from you about that great conversation with Harold Wilson, in which you decided the whole policy together in the Library of the Commons.' 'Certainly I met Harold for a moment in the Library,' George said, 'but it was literally for a moment. If I remember right, Harold said to me, "Whatever line you take, George, I will back you up." Frankly I'm puzzled about that man. Whenever I open a paper I read how Harold and I have jointly been forming the new policy but I can't remember a single occasion when he has ever discussed it with me.'

'What about that Monday when you were due to lunch with me and discuss my draft and Harold rang me to say it was more important for him and you to agree it together?' 'Dammit, he certainly clung to me like a leech, coming right to my house with his car and getting himself asked in, but I don't remember discussing the policy at all. Indeed, I wondered why he was so solicitous.' 'Still,' I said, 'it's nice to know that he's going round saying that George Brown deserves at least half the credit for what has been achieved.' At this point Morgan chipped in with a sly allusion to Harold's power of priming the press. If there is one thing that is clear that is that these two men have a pestilential hatred and contempt for Harold Wilson and, if they have their way, he is going to be kept very far from the leadership. They were both very critical of Hugh but equally clear there was no one to replace him, although I daresay that, at the back of George Brown's mind, there was the idea of George Brown.

Wednesday, June 1st
On Monday evening we had Michael Howard dining and I went in before-hand to listen to a little of the post-summit debate. It was utterly flat, Denis Healey was dull and Selwyn Lloyd was dull on purpose. As I was going out, George Brown came up and said he had had a look at my draft and he was a bit upset. 'Very fluffy,' he said. 'Too long, a lot of things fudged.' That evening David Ennals also rang up because he hadn't seen it and he had obviously been spoken to at length by Brown.

It was with slight apprehension that I went to the meeting in Morgan's room at half-past ten yesterday morning. I deliberately got there five minutes late so that they would have had time to read and discuss the draft, only to find that Denis Healey hadn't yet arrived. However, the moment I came in and took the chair (as I have to do, as the only member of the Executive present), George Brown said, 'Well the others (i.e. Ennals and Phillips) tell me it's a good draft, so let's start by saying that I misjudged it yesterday.' I am so unused to this kind of behaviour from a colleague that I was absolutely bowled over by a display of chivalry unexampled in Labour history and, as a result, we finished considering the draft in just over an hour. Denis came in after a quarter of an hour and at a quarter past eleven we had reached unanimity on every word and comma, apart from the summary, which was left for David Ennals and myself to do. It was quite an achievement.

Tuesday was the day on which we were due to go to France but the postponement of the holiday was justified by my being able to attend the joint meeting with the T.U.C. at half-past four at Congress House. Nineteen people came from the Labour Party and ten from the T.U.C. It was a baking afternoon and, in that wonderful modern building with its wonderful large windows, we were grilled. On the other hand, the acoustics are exquisite and one can talk across a really big room as though one is conversing, which makes a great difference to one's temper.

I got there, with David Ennals, a few minutes early and stood outside in the sun, watching the others arrive, until a great black car drew up, out of which came Mr Robens, Mr Phillips, Mr Brown and Mr Gaitskell, the last three looking very black. Brown and Morgan both winked gloomily at me. Tom Williamson was voted into the chair and at once said that the T.U.C. had appointed a drafting committee of four to work with our drafting committee. At once Hugh Gaitskell said that ours, of course, was a purely temporary committee, which let the cat out of the bag all right. George Brown proceeded for forty minutes to read aloud our memorandum, sentence by sentence, interpersing explanations and notes. A masterly performance. At once Hugh Gaitskell followed up by saying it was masterly but adding that, of course, the draft was far too long and complicated to be put into the kind of document required. George Brown replied that the drafting committee had managed to get it into 1,600 words, a good deal less than the 1958 document we had been told to copy. One could feel the barbs shooting between the two of them.

After this there was a terribly desultory discussion, with Frank Cousins airing his problems about nuclear retaliation and George Brown and, to a lesser extent, myself explaining the document punctiliously. Suddenly Alfred Robens burst in, saying that, as chairman of the Parliamentary and Scientific Committee,[1] he could tell us that a European bomb was technically economically feasible, and, if we turned down making it, it must not be for reasons of practicality. All this was said very threateningly, clearly implying that he would like the idea.

Alan Birch made an odious speech. His union, of course, has voted pacifist and he advised us to be very statesmanlike and write a document which was noble, even if it got us defeated, like him. George Brown rebuked him rather severely, saying that the drafting committee would at least make some effort to win the support of Conference. Callaghan was at his most helpful, telling Frank Cousins all the things we could agree about, to which Frank replied that Callaghan wasn't a child and shouldn't talk to others as though they were. Of course we knew what we could agree about and we had come together to discuss what we disagreed about.

[1] An all-party committee of M.P.s, scientists, industrialists and others.

Right at the end it was agreed that the two drafting committees should meet at half-past two today. As we were rising to go, Sam Watson's voice could just be heard, saying, 'I'm sure you won't object if we add Hugh Gaitskell's name to the Committee.' Snap! So he had done it! Everybody knew that this meant partly that he didn't trust his own committee and partly that he was determined to get the credit for anything that was achieved. It was to be the Gaitskell line, not the Brown line or the Crossman/Wigg line. George and I fumed in the taxi on the way to the Commons and while we told the story to Harold Wilson and George Wigg over a drink. Who has ever heard of a Leader forcing himself into a drafting committee, just when its members have achieved unanimity? If the eight of us had met, we could have brought Frank Cousins over. Last night I said, 'But Hugh doesn't want to bring Frank Cousins over.' He wants to make sure that we fight with him in Conference, win or lose.' This afternoon I learnt how right I was. I lunched with Michael King[1] and Sydney Jacobson. Sydney had been lunching yesterday with Hugh, who had apparently been very polite about George Brown and myself but had expressed anxiety lest things were being cooked up behind his back.

The moment we got to today's meeting, Hugh got himself elected to the chair and said, 'Of course, you will appreciate this isn't a final document. It's merely some ideas put together by David Ennals.'

BROWN: In order to clear up any misunderstandings, I should inform the T.U.C. members that this document is a unanimously agreed document, over which we four members of the drafting committee have been slaving for four days.

GAITSKELL: Well, I haven't seen it before, so I can't possibly be bound by it. And, after all, I only set up the drafting committee to save trouble.

After this, Hugh virtually forced the meeting to have a Second Reading discussion rather than take the draft clause-by-clause. This line-by-line analysis took three and a half hours. Every word, every comma, was niggled at and disputed, either for minutiae of drafting points or, more often, in demand for a more nuclear-warrior-like presentation. Mostly it turned into a terrible, dreary triangular wrangle between Gaitskell and Brown and myself, interspersed with explosions from Frank Cousins and querulous complaints by the T.U.C. members. There was, however, a thirty-five-minute intermezzo where the T.U.C. members wrangled with each other, while we sat outside the ring as spectators.

George and I got angrier and angrier and George blew his top three or four times, after which a T.U.C. person would ask why on earth the Labour Party couldn't settle their disputes before coming to see them. Denis Healey wasn't a very loyal member of the Four Wise Men, and at one critical

---

[1] The son of Cecil King, he was Foreign Editor of the *Daily Mirror* 1952–67 and Director of Information at the C.B.I. from 1967 to 1972, when he joined the Imperial Group as the Group Public Affairs Adviser.

moment proposed an amendment which would have completely sold the pass to John Strachey.

At about half-past five we had done only the first two clauses of the defence part. George and I both pushed our chairs back and threatened to walk out, after Hugh had remarked that our draft had failed to represent faithfully the views agreed previously by the Committee. 'Since you have no confidence in our committee,' I observed, 'and since we have failed to do our job, we had better leave you to find somebody else.' Hugh said, 'Come, come, keep calm.' Twenty minutes later we had finished the draft. Our ultimatum had worked but both of us were so hot and bothered with it we didn't know it. We again repeated that, when the new draft was provided, we wouldn't do it. Gaitskell, genuinely surprised: 'But no new draft is required! We've agreed this one.' And, blow me, we had, with the tiniest modifications. All those four hours rowing, wrangling, for nothing, except to make sure Frank Cousins was against us.

I expect the T.U.C. people thought George Brown and myself unbearable prima donnas and pups and sympathized with Hugh in his dignified handling of us. Frankly, I couldn't care less. I am really quite pleased that my Fabian pamphlet is coming out this week to ensure that nobody suspects me of being in Gaitskell's fold. On the other hand, I have deterred George Brown from going to the press and spilling the whole story or talking about his resignation. My personal inclination is that each of us should send a letter to Gaitskell and threaten to publish it at a later date unless things go as we wish in the final document.

Crossman did write a 'private and personal' letter to Gaitskell, copying it to George Brown. Crossman urged Gaitskell 'to keep the document grey . . . verbally accurate, which can be presented with equal conscientiousness as a good document by a number of people at the head of our Movement whose feelings and views about nuclear warfare do not coincide'. He continued: 'If you personally are determined to present it with the bias that you were displaying throughout the meeting, I can predict that it will achieve none of the objects which George, Morgan and I set ourselves as your drafting committee.' Crossman concluded that, in that case, 'it is only fair to tell you that I should be among those who would feel in duty bound to oppose it publicly as well as privately'.

On June 3rd Mr Cousins announced that the Executive of his union, the T.G.W.U., had reaffirmed its support for unilateral nuclear disarmament. Gaitskell replied to Crossman's letter on June 13th, reiterating his belief that particularly at this stage, 'we should surely try ... not to hide *but to* narrow *points of difference, if this can possibly be done'. He denied deliberately picking a quarrel with Frank Cousins:*

On the contrary, sensing his personal antipathy to me, I kept, as you know, perfectly silent throughout the long exchange between Cousins on the one side and Bill Webber and the rest of you on the other which led to the ultimate declaration by Cousins that he was against NATO having any nuclear weapons at all ...

'Nevertheless,' he ended, 'apart from the bad feeling and unpleasant bickering which has been roused and which I intensely dislike, I do not feel too despondent.'

On June 22nd the N.E.C. unanimously agreed to 'express our full confidence in the elected leader of the Parliamentary Party'. They also gave 'general approval' to the defence policy statement, which reaffirmed the Party's belief in collective security alliances and allegiance to NATO and accepted American bases in Britain at least for the present. It left to the U.S.A. the development of the thermo-nuclear deterrent, opposed the establishment of Thor missile bases in Britain, insisted that no nuclear weapons be manufactured in Germany and that no German troops be armed with them, and urged a NATO strategic review to reduce dependence on nuclear weapons and to increase political control over the military commanders. The T.U.C. General Council, for its part, decided to defer until July 1st its consideration of the document.

Wednesday, June 22nd

We had a lovely fortnight in France. I rushed down to Prescote on Thursday, after our row with the T.U.C., and we left on Friday the 3rd to catch the evening car ferry. I was heartily glad to get away from the dissensions and destructions. But before I got to the Commons yesterday George Wigg came whirling round to warn me that for two days the B.B.C. and all the papers had been carrying inspired stories about drastic amendments to our draft statement. Some explanation of this was given to me by a letter from Hugh Gaitskell, in reply to mine, which showed that on the 13th he was still hopeful that the T.U.C. could be persuaded to insist on wrecking amendments. However, he apparently couldn't bring them up to scratch. When George Brown saw him yesterday morning he agreed to keep the draft pretty well intact.

At six o'clock yesterday the International Sub. started its meeting and went on for two hours and twenty minutes, with Hugh Gaitskell and Barbara Castle at the two extremes, egging each other on. George Brown and I fought like yoked brothers in a most extraordinary alliance, defending our draft iota by iota and I was even prepared to fight for writing 'will' instead of 'should', where it made complete nonsense, simply because George liked it that way three weeks ago. Hugh Gaitskell seemed perfectly friendly throughout but afterwards I met Harold Wilson in the lobby and he said that Hugh had already told one correspondent he was deeply dissatisfied.

This morning, at the N.E.C., the same kind of scene occurred all over again. I had given them a little warning yesterday that, if we made too many amendments to the draft as amended by the T.U.C., we might be in trouble with them. Gaitskell, most unwisely, nevertheless insisted on any number of amendments of his own. This gave Barbara a chance to insist on hers, so that, when the T.U.C. met this morning, they were confronted with a new draft of ours, incorporating some, but by no means all, of their amendments and a great many new ones of our own. This gave them the perfect excuse for referring the whole thing to their International in a fortnight's time, which they did despite telephoned bleats from us.

So, when we struggled through the draft once again and when we had once again had Tony Greenwood and Barbara Castle registering their protests and keeping their consciences clean and their votes for the Executive high, we were coolly informed by Morgan that a joint statement was impossible. Horror and consternation, in which Morgan Phillips, Ray Gunter and Charlie Evans of the Railwaymen[1] all said there was no chance; we had to go ahead with our Conference and get the T.U.C. to endorse what we had done in due course. I said to Hugh Gaitskell, sitting next to me, 'This should teach us a lesson never to have joint statements again.' To my surprise, he heartily concurred and said we should always do it on our own in the future.

Meanwhile the Party continues to die on its feet and I can see no way out. I don't see it recovering under present conditions, nor do I see how Hugh can pull it round. However, that's all that.

Tuesday, June 29th
This morning we spent voting confidence in Hugh Gaitskell. The whole situation has been worked up because Victory for Socialism, which includes six M.P.s, passed a resolution demanding his resignation. Nothing could have been more helpful to him, as Sam Watson frankly stated at the Executive last Wednesday, when a similar vote of confidence was passed under Any Other Business. (I had to leave before that vote.) Gaitskell took full advantage of this and insisted on a Full Party Meeting this morning, which was preceded by the usual intrigues and manoeuvres.

I got there at half-past ten to find the seats in Committee Room 10 all occupied. I was only able to share a table, squeezed between John Strachey and John Dugdale, where comfort required me to sit with my back to the front bench and face upwards at that ghastly Frank Salisbury picture of George V standing before the Tomb of the Unknown Soldier.[2] The debate started with the Chief Whip making what somebody described as his maiden speech to the Party Meeting, of which the theme was, whereas policy discussion was an excellent thing, all this personal wrangling was fatal. Actually, there have been very few personal attacks and what has really damaged us in the public mind and shattered the confidence of our members has been

---

[1] Charles Evans was President of the N.U.R. 1958–61.
[2] Frank Salisbury (1874–1962), an artist known for his treatment of historic and ceremonial subjects.

precisely the policy discussion which was said to be O.K. The blunt fact is that nine out of ten of our active members believe that Gaitskell is trying to ditch Socialism and, of those nine, at least seven think he ought not to do so. The crisis of confidence is a crisis of confidence in the line Gaitskell has taken, obstinately, since the Election. But the case argued this morning was quite simply that, if we all stopped personal attacks on each other and had our discussions without wrangling, everything would be O.K.

However, the next three speakers he called – Bill Blyton, David Griffiths[1] and Ray Gunter, all called as reliable, right-wing trade unionists – each devoted a considerable part of their speeches to telling Gaitskell what mistakes he had made last October, particularly on the subject of Clause 4 and Tony Crosland.[2]

By half-past eleven things were going very badly and there was a call for 'Vote! Vote! Vote!' Again any sane Leader would have acceded to the request to shorten our proceedings and get our defence debate started. For on this the leadership would do well. But Hugh wanted to make a great speech and he couldn't close the debate at that point without denying himself his own remarks. So things went on. Fortunately for him he was saved by a speech by Sydney Silverman, the Chairman of Victory for Socialism, who was trapped into a discussion of why he and his fellow M.P.s had put this out from outside Parliament instead of coming to the Parliamentary Party. How well I know the traps of procedure which are laid at the feet of left-wingers. The right-wing will always get you on procedure and Sydney was got. I have never heard an experienced politician collapse as abjectly as he did. His speech gave Hugh Gaitskell the assistance he needed. There was an odious, rousing appeal for loyalty from James Griffiths to a man of perfect integrity – that is, Hugh Gaitskell – and finally a longish speech by Hugh, in which he pleaded how difficult his job was, how decent he was, etc., etc. I found the speech tolerable but, talking to George Brown, found him contemptuous of it. The final vote was 179 to 8, which showed about 100 people either away or abstaining.

Thursday, August 4th

I thought it wasn't worth keeping this diary *seriatim* because so little was happening. But when I look back I find the period was more eventful than I expected, so I will write accounts for each day, but always remembering that my memory has rolled everything into one and in all likelihood done all sorts of distortions in the process.

Soon after the National Executive on June 22nd, I heard that Morgan had asked me to attend a drafting committee on the Friday morning. I got there to find it consisted of him, Peter Shore and myself, Peter having drafted

---

[1] Labour M.P. for the Rother Valley division of the West Riding of Yorkshire 1945–70. He died in 1977.
[2] See above, pp. 812–14 and 823.

the first document. We all agreed that it was vital to make this an Executive document, with as many action points as possible. We talked once again about the difficulties Gaitskell had made for himself. Morgan, too, had noticed how reluctant he was to see the defence turned into a policy document and how he isolated himself all over again. But Morgan was also extremely careful to abstain ostentatiously from any kind of anti-Gaitskell position. He discussed once again the tactics getting through this Conference without disaster. We agreed that Morgan would have to move this new document and that it should be wound up, if possible, by Walter Padley. 'At all costs we must avoid Gaitskell doing it,' Morgan observed. 'If we don't look out he'll be insisting on moving four documents and getting four defeats.'

I spent most of the following week doing my part of the draft, which we finally got together on Thursday. Quite literally, every word of it was written by Peter Shore and myself. Originally, there were two terse but powerful paragraphs of introduction, describing how a few voices had suggested the repudiation of Socialism and the Party had rejected them. When we first got together on Thursday I was surprised to find that Morgan liked this, though I had already warned Peter that they would probably have to be deleted, because Anne felt they shouldn't be there. On the other hand, Morgan was quick to smell out two other paragraphs as blatantly having been written by me. He wanted to make sure that nobody knew I had anything to do with the draft and I obliged by basing a large part of it on a speech of Harold Wilson's, made the previous week in the House, which in its turn had been based on my *Affluent Society*.

One evening in the Commons (I think it was Tuesday), I was talking to George Wigg and Mr James Margach (A Student of Politics in the *Sunday Times*), when I was called to the telephone to discuss the draft. I rather thoughtlessly mentioned this on my return. Margach pricked up his ears, especially when I said that this document, when approved by the N.E.C., might change the whole atmosphere of Conference by making it look forwards instead of backwards and giving it a positive outlook. 'And you're helping to draft that?' Margach said. 'I thought it was Morgan's.' 'Now, if you know what friendship means,' I said, 'you will get it into your head that Morgan has written every word of this draft, every single word. If you want to check on it, ring him up.' 'I'll go and do it straight away,' said Margach and apparently he did so, to judge from the *Sunday Times*. I had talked things over a good deal with Tony Wedgwood Benn who was later very disconcerted to read the *Sunday Times*. I explained to him that I was responsible for ensuring that Morgan drew all the credit and I think Tony had some idea about psychological warfare. The document had to be finished by Friday for distribution to the Executive on Monday, so that we could discuss it on Wednesday.

Meanwhile, on Tuesday, I had Michael and Jill Foot to dinner. I had thought it possible that I could write a quick portrait of Nye,[1] not a full-scale biography but the kind of thing Francis Williams did of Bevin.[2] Michael explained to me that Jennie said she wanted to do it but she had also agreed that, if she didn't, Michael should. I said we should get a young man from Nuffield College to do the spadework and Michael said he could do it all himself and wanted to spend two years on it. This finished any idea I had of butting in. If Michael really will do it, he can produce his one and only masterpiece, none the worse for its being the product of someone who adored and worshipped Nye.

On Monday evening of the next week we went to a farewell party for the Yugoslav ambassador. There I found myself in confab. with Reg Willis, last year's T.U.C. Chairman and Secretary of the Compositors. In a stentorian voice he shouted his attacks on Gaitskell, and his little wife, who I thought was prim, intervened at one point, saying, 'Mr Crossman, he won't do and you know it perfectly well.' Round us were gyrating Callaghans, Alma and Ellis Birk and others. Finally Ellis took us all off to dinner at a place called Ziggi in Charles Street, Mayfair, where the bill for quite a good three-course dinner with two bottles of claret was £27 for five people. At my end of the table I was talking to Ellis about my pamphlet and the future of the Party. At the other end the two girls were hearing from James Callaghan with coy admissions that, if he were drafted, he would lead the party. I agreed with them that Jim had at least one quality, a humble recognition that the Party had made him everything he was and that he would have to rely on other people to do the thinking for him. Comparing Jim with Harold Wilson, who is now becoming a podgy caricature of his self-important self, or with George Brown, who really is a bit of a thug, I realize that anything can happen.

Next day, the 26th, I went to the Abbey for the Bevan memorial service. I sat between Collison[3] and Jack Cooper of the Municipal and General Workers, with an empty row in front of me and, in front of that, six chairs with only Morgan Phillips and the Chairman of the Party.[4] We were right up under the pulpit and facing us were the relatives, headed by Jennie. It's so characteristic that one should have empty seats for the N.E.C. just opposite Jennie, when thousands whom she couldn't see were turned away. Anyway, our seats were empty because Hugh Gaitskell, Harold Wilson and so on preferred sitting in the choirstalls with the Rt. Hons.

I found the service unbearably sad — not moving, not stirring, just sad. As Mervyn Stockwood[5] frankly admitted, in a pretty good panegyric, Nye

---

[1] He had died on July 6th.

[2] *Ernest Bevin* (London: Hutchinson, 1952).

[3] Harold Collison, General Secretary of the National Union of Agricultural and Allied Workers 1953–69. In 1964 he became a life peer.

[4] George Brinham.

[5] Vicar of the University Church, Cambridge, from 1955 to 1959, when he became Bishop of Southwark.

wouldn't have thought much of being preached over by a bishop, and it was too grand a service for people to sing hymns properly. Yet I did feel a huge, gaping sadness. Also, although I knew it was irrational and silly, I couldn't help feeling terribly repentant that I should have ever quarrelled with Nye, in view of what everybody else in the Party was like. Yet I know that it was impossible to be with him without quarrelling, that he was a leader with feet of clay and that sometimes he was selfish and unrewarding. Nevertheless, oh dear, oh dear, oh dear, Parliament for me was over 60 per cent that corner of the Smoking Room. It would be a little brighter if Michael Foot were now back there but without Nye one feels very much alone.

That evening John Freeman came to dinner with his wife Catherine.[1] We talked politics the whole evening and I discovered, by the way, that he favours George Brown against Harold Wilson for the deputy leadership. But Catherine isn't really interested and I feel she is pulling him further and further away. And why shouldn't she, by God, considering how appalling politics are today?

On the 27th came our famous Executive, at which the new N.E.C. statement was to be agreed. At the previous meeting I had moved that it should be the first item on the agenda and it was disposed of before Harold Wilson came in. As we sat down, Hugh, who sits next to me, said, 'Of course there can't be any question of its being an N.E.C. document. I strongly disagree with a very great deal of it.'

Morgan was asked to introduce it and it was clear that most people there hadn't read it. Hugh barged in, saying it might shorten proceedings if we agreed it should not be an N.E.C. document but one signed by Morgan. I pointed out that this was not what had been decided at the previous meeting. It was extremely important for the N.E.C. to give a strong lead. Hugh said he couldn't be asked to agree every word of it, a view to which Tom Driberg immediately assented, and it was clear that most of the Parliamentarians there would feel comfier if it was by Morgan. Some of them felt this, no doubt, because they were anti-Hugh — Barbara, for instance — and didn't want him strengthened. But his few friends — Eirene White and Bessie Braddock, for instance — seemed totally unaware that, by making this a Morgan Phillips document, they were building up Morgan tremendously and leaving Hugh even more isolated. The Conference would have to approve the document if we commended it and the only difference in making it by Morgan Phillips was to make it clear that Hugh didn't stand by it, which couldn't do him much good. However, as a result of this device, the document was agreed without a single comment on its text, except a warm commendation by Barbara Castle.

Once again I felt a sense of absolute hopelessness in the presence, not of

[1] Catherine Dove was a producer with B.B.C. television 1954–8 and, from 1976, with Thames Television. She married John Freeman in 1962. The marriage was dissolved in 1976. Crossman was the godfather of their son, Matthew.

lack of leadership—for that is too negative an expression—but of the most positive unleaderly behaviour one could conceive. The whole atmosphere of the Executive is now that of a collection of company directors, trying to get through the day's business without touching on any serious issue for fear it might blow up on them.

That evening we had our end-of-term party at Vincent Square. Perhaps it was because I was tired and also because my leg was hurting that I got into a panic and went to see the doctor next door, who arranged for me to go to the Westminster Hospital and assured me I shouldn't die if I conducted our party before going. It was rather a good, mixed party, with Mervyn Stockwood, Philip Hendy[1] of the National Gallery, Patrick Blackett and Richard Titmuss to give it tone, as well as K. S. Karol, Clancy Sigal,[2] Brian Abel-Smith, Peter Townsend and Michael Howard to provide middle-aged youth. They all drank champagne for a very long time and the last one left at half-past nine. Harold Wilson came booming in at about eight o'clock and stayed till the end, exuding complacency, Barbara darted her looks round the party, stabbing at everyone in her great anti-Gaitskell campaign. God knows what she said to Hugh Massingham.

Meanwhile the B.B.C. came out with the news that the National Executive had decided to support Hugh Gaitskell in leading the Parliamentary Party in defiance of Conference if Conference goes unilateralist. When I looked at Thursday morning's papers, particularly the *News Chronicle* and the *Guardian*, I knew what had happened. Morgan had merely handed the document out, with virtually no questions asked, while John Harris, who is nothing more than Gaitskell's personal pressman, had briefed his friendly press. Hence the fact that the *Herald*, which relied on Morgan, had an accurate and totally different story from the *Chronicle* and the *Guardian*, which relied on Hugh.

I spent the day in bed and at the Westminster, writing an article for the *Statesman*, so angry was I made by this press treatment.[3] At five o'clock Barbara rang me up and asked me to sign a protest statement along with Tony Greenwood, Harry Nicholas and Tom Driberg. It took me forty-five minutes' telephoning to make her make the statement accurate.[4] She had got it into her head that Morgan was conspiring with Hugh and said to me

---

[1] A lecturer at the Wallace Collection 1927–30, and in Florence and the U.S.A., he became Director of Leeds City Art Gallery in 1934, serving in that capacity until 1945. He was Slade Professor of Fine Art at the University of Oxford 1936–46 and Director of the National Gallery 1946–67. He was knighted in 1950.

[2] An American writer and critic, who came to live in Britain in 1957.

[3] 'Labour's Constitutional Crisis' appeared in the *New Statesman* on August 6th.

[4] The statement, issued on Thursday, July 28th, said that press accounts had misunderstood the nature of the policy document. It was a purely factual background paper for the information of delegates to the annual Conference, who would be discussing resolutions on the subject. The Executive's attitude to the resolutions would be decided as usual at its pre-Conference meeting. The statement was signed by Barbara Castle, Crossman, Tom Driberg, Anthony Greenwood and Harry Nicholas of the T.G.W.U.

ferociously, 'There's no reason why those people, who treated us the way they did, shouldn't have a taste of their own medicine.'

However, the statement we signed came out with a bang and had its effect. I felt its tremors when I went in to vote on the three-line whip on Thursday. After the vote I ran into James Callaghan, who said he heard there was some document going round to sign. I explained what it was and said there was plenty of time to sign it, at which James flounced off, saying he wouldn't dream of doing so, because he was a good Executive man and knew how to behave. I said, 'My dear James, when other people use their press officers for deliberately distorting things, one is entitled to defend oneself.'

The three-line whip, by the way, was on the subject of Lord Home and Macmillan's Government reconstruction,[1] which had meanwhile been taking place. I had known for a fortnight that Peter Thorneycroft would be in the Government but it was nice to see that Enoch Powell was also there – two rebels who have not got their normal reward. But then Macmillan is not a normal Premier. He certainly makes the best of bad human material, combined with phenomenal good luck, in his handling of affairs. Nevertheless, if the Opposition hadn't ceased to exist, this Government would be getting into very rough weather at this moment. In inner circles the gilt is off Macmillan, though his mass popularity is higher than ever before.

What a strange, strange summer! Never since 1945 have my political activities and thinking been so introverted, so ingrowing, so frustrated, so frustrating. Whenever I read a book about politics and politicians – the recent Life of Lord Haldane,[2] for instance – it gives me a shock to realize how interesting, constructive, useful political activity can be, in contrast to the way we have to spend our time in this disintegrating Labour Party. Of course, George Wigg always says that it's not only the Labour Party that is disintegrating but the country and that our problems are merely a symptom of the fact that what Britain does no longer matters in the world. There's something in this but my temperamental optimism is strongly supported by my reason in the belief that one could transform the whole situation in Parliament with a different leadership of the Labour Party. And I am also now inclined to believe that this kind of transformation may well take place next October.

[1] Mr Heathcoat Amory had announced his retirement from the Treasury and Mr Derek Walker-Smith, Minister of Health, had resigned, in order to pursue his career at the Bar. In consequence a small Cabinet reshuffle was announced on July 27th. Lord Home became Foreign Secretary and Selwyn Lloyd Chancellor of the Exchequer. Edward Heath became Lord Privy Seal and Foreign Office representative in the House of Commons and his place as Minister of Labour was taken by John Hare. Christopher Soames became Minister of Agriculture and Duncan Sandys Secretary of State for Commonwealth Relations. Peter Thorneycroft and Enoch Powell returned to the Government, as Minister of Aviation and Minister of Health respectively.

[2] *Haldane of Cloan* by Dudley Sommer (London: Allen & Unwin, 1960).

28

When I had finished my article[1] I sent a copy to Peter Shore and to Morgan, for their private comments. Indeed, I had taken the precaution of saying to Morgan that I was thinking of writing it and of getting his warm support. Morgan rang me yesterday. I made some remark about Barbara's leaping to the conclusion that he was hand in glove with Hugh. He coughed angrily down the phone and said, 'As a matter of fact, it's my own view that the Party won't get out of its difficulties as long as Gaitskell's there.' This is the first time Morgan has ever committed himself to this view in my hearing. And the more I think about the autumn, the more exciting it may be. All these months of dreary committees and in-fighting may not really have been entirely wasted if they lead to a convulsion which changes the leadership.

Tuesday, August 30th

Politics resumed for me yesterday, when I gave dinner at the Athenaeum to Harold Wilson. He had rung me up and urgently said that it was high time we really had things out together. I went to the dinner with fairly clear ideas in my head. First, I had come to the conclusion that, in the interests of the Party, it would be a good thing if we were defeated at Conference so heavily and ignominiously that Gaitskell had to resign. Even so, to get a resignation would require an organization of the Parliamentary Party, such as George Wigg and I could possibly do. I had tried to prepare for that through my article in the *N.S.* Secondly, however, these things very rarely work out and one might well have to assume that there would be some fixing and further surrenders by Gaitskell, so that he would stay Leader, but on ignominious terms. In that case I had come to the conclusion that, whatever happened, I would take a leading part in forming a new Left, coherent and with a policy. I was sick and tired of a life in which each of us is a completely isolated, atomic individual, and the degeneration of the individual Bevanites that has taken place since the Bevanite Group was broken up is the proof of what I mean.

Harold came in, looking very brown and plump and immediately said he felt a new man and that he had been down and terribly bad at the end of the last Session, especially in the Common Market debate.[2] I put my two points to him and, when I reflect on the evening, I realize that he didn't precisely reply to either, even when I made it quite clear that in my view he was the only alternative to Gaitskell. He, on the other hand, is working on the assumption that Gaitskell will somehow survive Conference and that he must get himself elected Deputy Leader and then, from that position,

[1] For the *New Statesman*.

[2] On July 25th the House of Commons had debated a Government motion recognizing the need 'for political and economic unity in Europe' and expressing its readiness to welcome 'the conclusion of suitable arrangements to that end, satisfactory to all the Governments concerned'. The motion was approved by 215 votes to 4, with the Opposition abstaining.

carry out the *coup de grâce*. Obviously Harold's view is that he will then, as Deputy Leader, be the man who attacks Macmillan, takes the initiative, floors the Tories and generally shows up the deficiencies of Mr G. My thinking (Harold hadn't read my article) seemed to be new to him and he was not assuming nearly as confidently as I am that Gaitskell will be defeated at Conference.

What was healthy about our talk was that most of it was concerned with revitalizing the Parliamentary Party, arousing the attacking mood, and so on. A good deal of fixing has gone on already. Harold let me know that his idea is that he should become Deputy Leader, that George Brown should take his place, that Callaghan should take George Brown's place. And where did I fit in? 'The Board of Trade is the place for you,' said Harold, by which, of course, he meant that no one else was clever enough or disinterested enough to take over the Common Market, with all its intricacies.

In the course of the evening he talked a good deal, and I was pleased that he did, about the need to revise some kind of puritanism in the Party, some self-dedication, and he was careful to remind me twice that he couldn't tell the difference between hock and burgundy, though he is quite good at drinking either. As he was dropping me from his car at Vincent Square and I was looking across at the primary school behind Massingham's house, I told him of my problems about Patrick's education.[1] Suddenly Harold said, 'It was the worst mistake of my life when I sent my boys to University College School. You're right that we can't afford to sacrifice our principles.'

This morning I strolled round to Transport House at half-past ten for the meeting the press has been advertising for days with Gaitskell, Len Williams and George Brinham. I got there exactly at ten-thirty to find George and Len sitting at the long table at the far end of Morgan's room. 'Hello, Mr Chair,' I said, to which George replied, 'Not for much longer,' and once again I realized how people assume you mean things in the world of politics. Gaitskell came in a minute or two afterwards, sat down beside me, facing the other two, and without a word we all got down to the agenda—no greetings, no personal relations, though gradually it began to warm up a bit.

The main problem, of course, was the speakers for Conference. I had talked to George and Len at length on the phone from Prescote, when we had all agreed that there need not be a meeting of the Executive to discuss things but that Len would be well advised to get the backing of the officers for his speakers' selection. What we had in front of us, however, was a complete Conference agenda. Against the various items were the names Len had put down. (By the way, Harold Wilson told me he had seen him lunching with Hugh and Sam Watson yesterday.) In conversation with me, George has said that, on the key debate on *Labour in the Sixties*, there were

---

[1] Patrick Crossman eventually went to the local primary school in Oxfordshire. See *The Diaries of a Cabinet Minister* for Crossman's further opinions on this subject.

only four possible speakers now that Morgan had gone — Ray Gunter, Walter Padley, myself and Len. But as soon as I looked at the list I saw that the names were Gunter and Wilson. However, to my astonishment, the whole of Monday morning at Conference was devoted to Crossman and pensions.

I was careful to point out that a terrible lot of time had been devoted to pensions and myself and this was only practicable if I could say a good deal about our future policy. But they all seemed very firm. Well did I know that this was all an elaborate explanation of why I should not speak on *Labour in the Sixties*, although I had written it. Hugh rubbed it in by saying that of course, if I hadn't been the coming Chairman [of the Party] for the following year, they would have expected me to speak more than once! Considering that I usually don't open my mouth at Conference, this was quite a mouthful.

But most of the morning centred on the proposal to have the debate on the Parliamentary Party on Tuesday, before defence. I at once pointed out that, if we were defeated on defence, there would be a sense of crisis, which would be relieved if we had the debate on the Parliamentary Party the next morning, so that the answer could be officially given by the N.E.C. At once Hugh replied that the best thing to do was to have the answer on this constitutional issue given, 'with a clear, strong line', to use his own words, on the day before, not after, the debate. After all, he said, he knew Morgan's view on this. What was needed was simply to tell the Conference that, whatever happened, we could not give orders to the Parliamentary Party. On this he was supported by Len.

I then said that this made sense if a clear, decisive line was given on the day before, but would it be? Hugh replied, 'Well, Len's job is to put across Morgan's memorandum, already issued.' 'But the memorandum only gives the factual background,' I replied. 'The Executive line was what we had to decide afterwards. And that hasn't been decided.' To this Hugh replied that there was nothing to decide. All that was necessary was to tell the Conference that it could not interfere with the Parliamentary Party. And anyway, if we were defeated on defence, that is what Hugh, as leader, would have to say. I replied that the Chairman of the Party, representing the N.E.C., would also have to make a statement.

At first I thought that Hugh was bluffing but I gradually came to the conclusion that he was extraordinarily badly informed on this issue and genuinely thought there was nothing to discuss. I reminded him that a large part of *Labour in the Sixties* had been omitted because it was to be the brief for Morgan's speech. This part of the document said that some people had wanted to change the Party constitution and give the Parliamentary Party much more power, while others wanted to give the Conference more power, and the document had firmly stated that any change was thoroughly bad. 'Surely our spokesman will have to say that much,' I said, 'and will also have to point out that, if the Parliamentary Party constitutionally has the right to defy Conference, Conference and the N.E.C. equally have the constitutional right to expel from the Party any M.P. who preaches defiance outside Parliament.'

To this Hugh replied, 'But don't be ridiculous, M.P.s are constantly defying Conference and nothing happens to them.' 'But constitutionally,' I said, 'they can be expelled and a whole number of them have been, including Zilliacus and Platts-Mills.'[1] Hugh seemed to regard this as very theoretical, whereas the practical fact was that Conference could not order Parliament about.

The argument went on for over an hour, with Len Williams also suggesting that anyway it wasn't our job in this debate to look forward to the future or to anticipate the kind of crisis which might arise after a defeat on defence. He would limit himself to spelling out, in an uncontroversial way, the factual background. I agreed that, if the debate was put before defence, it might be somewhat more limited, but I warned them they wouldn't possibly get away with a factual statement. There would have to be a clear declaration by the Executive and the kind of declaration Hugh wanted was not one the Executive would make. So I concluded by saying that anyway we ought to have submitted to us for the next Executive meeting a draft of what Len was going to say. Hugh said this was impossible, as he would be answering a debate, but George Brinham supported me on this and it was left very much in suspense.

But the important thing, of course, is that this private argument between Hugh and me has tipped us all off. I passed it all on to Harold today and shall discuss it with him and Barbara when we dine together after a party at Hugh's tomorrow. When I proposed this to Harold yesterday, he said that we should all slip off separately so as not to be observed, since Ray Gunter would take it very ill if we were known to be colluding. Harold also let it out that he had seen Gunter the day before yesterday, just at the moment when he was telling me that I was the only man who ought to speak on *The Sixties*. I now realize that this was characteristic of Wilson. Having seen Gunter and got himself nominated to do the job, he was only too ready to urge my claim but then anxious that Gunter should not see him consorting with me.

[1] John Platts-Mills, Labour M.P. for Finsbury 1945–8 and Independent Labour M.P. for the same constituency 1948–50. He became a Q.C. in 1964. Mr Zilliacus had been expelled from the Labour Party on May 18th, 1949, for persistent opposition to the Government's foreign policy and Mr Platts-Mills was expelled in 1948 at the time of the incident over the 'Nenni telegram'. On June 21st, 1949, both Members, together with two colleagues, formed a Labour Independent Group in the House of Commons, stating that they would give general support to the Government but would oppose it 'in those fields where the Group regards it as abandoning a Socialist policy and collaborating with the Conservatives'. Zilliacus was readmitted to the Labour Party in February 1952. (The other two Members of this Group were D. N. Pritt and L. J. Solley. Pritt had been expelled in 1940 for his opposition to the Party's policy at the time of the Russo-Finnish war and Solley was expelled at the same time and for the same reason as Zilliacus.)

It is difficult to sum up how I found Hugh's mood today. He came in sheepish, embarrassed; he warmed up and we became quite friendly. Throughout we talked quite freely, on the assumption that he might be defeated on defence, but I got the impression that he somehow thinks that he is going to win through on the simple line that the Parliamentary Party has the right to lay down its own policy and that he, as elected by the Parliamentary Party, has the right to defy Conference and the N.E.C. I am quite sure that he is not going to get away with this as soon as the N.E.C. trade union members smell what is up.

Thursday, September 1st
Yesterday we came up to London to attend the Gaitskell party. Dora was extremely pally to me and explained that she had had to have three parties to get us all in and we were the left-overs. It was a strangely Gaitskellian mixed bag, with John Cronin, the Rolls-Royce doctor-Whip, a loyalist who spent the evening the other day at the French Embassy freely attacking Gaitskell to Anne; Desmond Donnelly, the only member of the Party of whom I am sure it can be said that he will leave it at the first opportunity; Bob Manning, the *Time/Life* correspondent;[1] Sydney Jacobson and the new Editor of the *Herald*, John Beavan,[2] a complacent sod with whom I had a talk and who at once concurred in the concept of the *Daily Herald* as the *Daily Mail* of the Left. He is, I am sure, a Gaitskell man. Then there were all the Bevanites — Wilsons, Castles, Greenwoods,[3] Crossmans and Dribergs. Then there were the Ray Gunters, the Browns, the Skeffingtons and that was about it.[4]

When eight o'clock came we all trooped out and Hugh said to me and Anne, 'Oh, do stay on, we haven't seen anything of you.' However, by an elaborate conspiracy we had agreed to dine with the Wilsons and the Castles but I had forgotten the name of the restaurant and was frantically trying to catch them up. As we got into our car, Tom Driberg asked us to give him a lift down towards Vincent Square and we looked extremely criminal when he drove off with Tony Greenwood, who also seemed hurt. Meanwhile Harold Wilson swept past in his car, breezily waving goodbye for keeps, in best conspiratorial style. However, he had chosen a small Polish restaurant

---

[1] Robert Manning, State Department and White House Correspondent for United Press 1944–6, Chief U.N. Correspondent for United Press 1946–9, *Time* Correspondent 1949–55 and Chief of the London Bureau of *Time* Inc. 1958–61. He was Assistant Secretary of State for Public Affairs from 1962 to 1964, when he became Executive Editor of *Atlantic Monthly*; in 1966 he became Editor-in-Chief.

[2] A journalist on the *Manchester Evening News*, of which he was Editor 1943–59. He was Editor of the *Daily Herald* 1960–2 and Political Adviser to the *Daily Mirror* Group 1962–76. In 1970 he became a life peer, taking the title of Lord Ardwick. He was a Member of the European Parliament 1975–9.

[3] Gillian Crawshay-Williams married Anthony Greenwood in 1940.

[4] Elsie Elkins married Ray Gunter in 1934; Sheila McKenzie married Arthur Skeffington in 1952.

in Heath Street, packed to the doors, where we sat in great prominence in the middle. So we had to leave and — miracle of miracles — I arrived inside the Wilson home! Another miracle of miracles — Harold had seized from my hand the bill for the dinner and himself paid £6. This makes me think that he is really seriously out for the leadership!

However, let's be fair. When we got in, the two boys, who were in bed, were brought down to see us — a great big, gangling handsome young man of seventeen, a pure mathematician, and a charming little boy of about twelve.[1] They couldn't have been nicer or funnier about their Pop, whom they adore and who is obviously great fun with them, as is Mary — a lovely family, all titillated at meeting the Crossmans and the Castles. After this Harold supplied us with drinks and we settled down to discuss The Situation.

As he had done with me, Harold tried to talk about the deputy leadership, whereat Castle said we must talk about replacing Gaitskell and the chances of it. Ted, by the way, was a great nuisance throughout the evening, shouting everybody else down. Harold was I think very pleased to have around him friends, who for the first time were committing themselves to backing him for the leadership. He pointed out that the little initiative in these matters he had taken during the summer[2] had done him no end of harm and the one clear thing was that there must be no effort to replace Gaitskell but merely to get rid of him. Any kind of conspiracy designed to back anybody against him would be fatal.

We then had a long discussion of the constitutional situation and all agreed that it would be essential to insist on a draft for Len Williams's speech. Harold was much less certain than the rest of us that Gaitskell was in for an actual defeat. We all agreed that, first, if Hugh is Leader and the fight is for the deputy leadership, Harold will have a very tough time, because many M.P.s, for instance Curly Mallalieu, say we can't have two Oxford dons. On the other hand, if Fred Lee and George Brown both run, Harold should get it. He is convinced he has got most of the Miners' votes already. Secondly, if Hugh resigned and the issue was who should be Leader, there would be much less difficulty in getting a majority vote for Harold. He himself would then like to have George Brown as the Deputy. Harold said that, until a few weeks ago, he had never considered himself for the leadership, since he knew he was young and his whole idea was centred on being the Labour Chancellor of the best Budget since Lloyd George. All this I believe to be true.

[1] Robin Wilson (born in 1943) read a mathematics degree at Balliol College, Oxford, and then gained a Ph.D. at the University of Pennsylvania. After further research at the University of Cambridge, he became Lecturer in Mathematics at Jesus College, Oxford, and then Senior Lecturer in Mathematics at the Open University and, simultaneously, Lecturer at Balliol College, Oxford. Giles Wilson (born in 1948), became a mathematics teacher at Wincanton, and took his degree at the Open University.

[2] Possibly his tactics during Gaitskell's absence in Haifa. See above, p. 836.

The most important change registered yesterday was Harold's determination to re-form a Group. We all agreed that, directly we get back, we must have another meeting, which will consist of a dinner at Vincent Square, this time including Tony Greenwood and Tom Driberg. Ted Castle wanted us to have Padley as well but it's too dangerous at present and, also, if we have Padley we ought to have others. I think this may be the beginning of quite a big change, since it has been the absence of any kind of corporate activity which has been half the trouble. It was extremely pleasant to work with one's friends again and the news that Michael Foot has allowed his name to go forward for Ebbw Vale also cheered us up.[1]

The Trade Union Congress opened on September 5th at Douglas, in the Isle of Man. At the preliminary meeting to discuss the agenda, the T.U.C. General Council agreed to put to the vote both the Transport and General Workers' Union motion demanding unilateral disarmament and the official proposals agreed with the Labour Party by the T.U.C.'s joint committee. Some union leaders, including the President of the A.E.U., William Carron, decided to vote for both. When defence policy was debated on September 7th, the Congress approved the T.G.W.U. motion by 4,356,000 votes to 3,213,000 and also accepted the joint T.U.C./Labour Party statement by 4,150,000 to 3,460,000 votes.

Tuesday, September 20th

We came back from our holiday in Scotland on Thursday and I came up to London on Friday. It was good luck that I did for I found myself in the middle of a new crisis. There waiting for me was a letter from David Ennals, stating that George Brown wanted to attend the meeting of the International tomorrow and to circulate a paper beforehand. Sam Watson, as chairman of the Committee, agreed in principle but wanted confirmation from the officers. George Brinham, he added, had concurred.

I rang Ennals to find that the letter had been overtaken by events. Already Hugh Gaitskell had demanded to see the paper George wanted to circulate before deciding whether he should himself attend. After seeing it Hugh had curtly told David that on no account should the paper be circulated and that he was amazed that Brown had put it forward. David Ennals then came round to show me the paper, which was an argument in favour of the Executive's accepting the T. & G.W. resolution on the grounds that it contained nothing incompatible with our own policy.

In fact we were back at the row we had when the drafting committee met the T.U.C., after George Brown had persuaded Frank Cousins that our draft was O.K. On that occasion Hugh Gaitskell, from the chair, had deliberately picked a quarrel with George Brown and myself and destroyed any

[1] On September 24th he was selected as Labour candidate for Bevan's former seat at Ebbw Vale.

chance of agreement with Frank Cousins. Now, logically enough, George Brown, who throughout the summer has been the only man valiantly going round the country defending our defence policy, is making one last effort to avoid confusion at Conference and to win, not by welshing or by compromising but by pointing out the truth, which is that Frank Cousins's Executive has not permitted him to put in a downright unilateralist resolution and that the generalities he has been allowed to put in are perfectly harmless.[1] I didn't like the part of George's argument about the A.E.U. but I immediately responded welcomingly when David said George would like me to put the document in, since he had been excluded. I said, however, that I would like to consult with Harold and Barbara first.

That evening I left by the night ferry for Paris, where I did a long interview for *L'Express*, which they want to publish on the Thursday of Conference, when it is presumed that I shall have been elected Chairman. By good luck, Barbara was there on the way back from Yugoslavia. She and I spent the afternoon looking at the print shops on the Left Bank in lovely sunshine and discussing the situation. To my surprise, she agreed with Harold's first reaction, namely that I should put in a paper arguing the case for accepting the T. & G. resolution.

I flew back on Sunday morning in time to prepare my Granada show and then had to rush off to Manchester on Monday, only getting back very late. So it was only this morning that I got another letter from David Ennals, saying that Mr Watson and Mr Gaitskell didn't think my paper should be distributed until they had seen it. There was also a telephone message requesting me to see them at two o'clock tomorrow afternoon.

I spent the morning writing the paper and then went to the Organization Sub this afternoon in order to meet Ray Gunter, who is on the Committee. I let him know what had happened and gave him a copy of my paper, while Harold Wilson was simultaneously briefing Skeffington. Ray was amazed that Gaitskell should choose to pick a quarrel with George Brown at this time. It had now been ruled that George Brown was not even going to be allowed to attend the meeting and Ray added that Hugh would never concede on this because he was neurotic about it. To this I replied that in that case there would have to be a vote and that tomorrow we would be in for a row.

Harold Wilson told me that there had been another minor but significant row between Gunter and Gaitskell on the subject of John Harris, the pleasant young P.R.O. Hugh had during the Election and who, after a great deal of opposition, he persuaded us to make P.R.O. to the Parliamentary Party, paid for by Transport House. Len Williams, on the instructions of Morgan, who is still in hospital, speechless and right out,[2] had vetoed Harris's going

---

[1] He had stated that 'by any unprejudiced judgment' Cousins was 'facing both ways to a far greater extent than was Bill Carron'.

[2] He had collapsed with a stroke on August 15th, shortly after recording a television interview in Scotland.

to Conference this year as part of the Transport House staff, whereat Hugh had issued an order that the veto was to be reversed, something he had no right to do, since the Leader cannot overrule the General Secretary and, to say the least of it, is doing something very unwise if he does that kind of thing at this kind of juncture. So it looks as if Hugh is as mad as ever.

One or two other small items on the same subject. Tony Wedgwood Benn, just back from ten days in Russia, is obviously in much the state of mind as I was after my Russia–China visit. Never much interested in public ownership before, he at last sees the point of it and he is now discussing quite openly how to get rid of Hugh because, with him as Leader, we can't get anything done.

I also talked to Denis Healey, who, with his wife, spent a fortnight in Yugoslavia with the Gaitskells and who, Benn had told me, is now fully lined up on their side. I did indeed find him fairly firm but, as usual, quite intelligent. We at once agreed that our aim must be not only to get a majority for our document but to defeat the unilateralists on a motion explicitly demanding withdrawal from NATO Denis then added, 'If we can do these two things, it seems to me quite unimportant what happens to the T. & G. resolution.' I said, 'Oh, that's wonderful, because, as long as you don't mind, you won't object to what those of us who think it important do, in order to deal with it.' 'Ah now,' Denis said, 'you're being too quick for me. I said it wouldn't matter even if it were passed, because we have the A.E.U.'

I replied, 'I hope to God this time the A.E.U. is going to vote one way and not both.' Denis said, 'We can't win without voting both.' I said that would bring our Conference into total disrepute. Denis replied, 'That wouldn't matter very much,' thus confirming what I have long suspected, namely, that it is now the tactic of Gaitskell deliberately to bring the Conference into disrepute, as the T.U.C. was brought into disrepute, so as to strengthen the case for concentrating the power of decision in the Parliamentary leadership.

I asked Denis whether he thought there was anything in the T. & G. resolution incompatible with our document. 'In a different situation,' he said, 'it would be perfectly harmless, but of course we have to see it in conjunction with Cousins's known views and speeches.' I replied that what binds Conference and the N.E.C. is simply and solely the text of resolutions, to which Denis replied, 'Well, if the T. & G. would vote for our document, we could vote for their resolution.' 'So you are willing to huckster?' I said, to which he replied, 'There's no chance of its coming off.' But of course, in saying this, he had conceded that there is nothing in the T. & G. resolution that is incompatible with ours.

Wednesday, September 21st
I am still no good at predicting politics, least of all inside-Labour politics. Last night and this morning we were full of ginger and delight. We dined

with the Benns and the Shores, all enthusiastic for the idea. I talked at length to George Wigg and this morning to George Brown. Of course, I knew in advance that Sam and Hugh would be against me but, quite wrongly, I assumed that I should get some support from the trade unions. I continued to think this even after lunching with Sydney Jacobson, who has been busy writing a series of huge *Daily Mirror* centre-page efforts to put over Hugh's policy.

Down to the International. There we are sitting round — Sam in the Chair, on his right Len Williams, so deaf he doesn't know what's going on, then Hugh Gaitskell, next George Brinham, with his hair coming out and smoothing his greying locks to conceal the baldness, then Ray Gunter, Arthur Skeffington and Dan McGarvey of the Boilermakers. On our side of Sam came David Ennals, implicated up to the neck in our conspiracy, as Sam and Hugh both knew, then Barbara, Eirene White, myself and, beyond me, the grey, ageing, tired, harassed and a little bewildered Jennie Lee.

The meeting started with Sam's taking the first item and asking us to turn to the memorandum, which selected for consideration half a dozen of the resolutions on the agenda. I know my Sam and, if I hadn't jumped in at this point, I would have been ruled out of order. So I immediately asked whether I should now raise my point on the resolution I wanted to discuss. Sam replied that we could only discuss the resolutions in the memorandum. I then began to talk about George Brown's being refused admission and Sam ruled that all this was out of order.

We then had forty-five minutes of procedural discussion, in which Sam and Hugh tried to prevent my raising the issue. My memorandum was there but of course not distributed. Sam reached a point when he said that it was not in order for the International to discuss resolutions for Conference, since this must be left to the Executive at Conference. Indeed, their whole objective was to postpone this discussion until then. The rest of the Committee got more and more uncomfortable, particularly when I pointed out that Sam and Hugh were trying to vote against me on a subject where they knew the facts and the rest of the Executive didn't. So I was to be condemned without the Executive's even hearing my case.

After forty minutes Ray Gunter said, 'Well, why can't we hear what Dick has to say? Once it has been ruled that George Brown isn't entitled to come if the officers are not unanimous in his favour, we must admit that Dick has a right to put his point to the Executive.' This took, as I say, forty-five minutes. So I said drily, 'I should like my memorandum to be distributed now and it might have been more convenient for you all if you could have read it quietly before, as the chairman prevented you from doing. Still you can have five minutes' silence to digest it now.'

So I had least won the procedural point, only to be annihilated afterwards, and by something I hadn't really thought of, namely, the fact that the General Council of the T.U.C. is already firmly committed to regarding

Cousins's motion as incompatible with our policy document and that for the Labour Party to reverse this would be a vote of no confidence in the General Council. Of course I pointed out that this argument implied that the Labour Party is the servant of the General Council and is not free to make up its own mind. But this hardly weighed with our trade union friends, who had been on the Isle of Man.[1]

Moreover, they were able to say that the incompatibility had been agreed to by Frank Cousins himself at the meeting of the General Council before the T.U.C. Conference began. At one point in the discussion Ray Gunter said, 'Of course, we've got a great deal of sympathy with what Dick is trying to do, but it's three months too late. This is something which should have been done before the T.U.C. met. It can't be done now.' Others also suggested that there would be no harm in informal talks with members of the T. & G.W. Executive, and Eirene White said that, if Dick and George Brown felt strongly about this, why didn't they make a public statement on the issue? I was careful to accept quickly the right to make a public statement on this subject but didn't commit myself to making one. Gaitskell was utterly scornful of the whole idea, which he described as one of the most ridiculous he had ever heard.

Gaitskell also, at one point, emphasized that in his view there was a difference of principle between the first clause of the T. & G. resolution and our document. I got a little support from Jennie and very much less than I had expected from Barbara. David Ennals sat numb and embarrassed. Finally, when I saw how things were going, I withdrew the document without a vote being taken. Of course, the decision to oppose the T. & G. resolution will have to be formally taken at the Executive.

I suppose I was fairly rude but the atmosphere was curiously dejected, with most of them sitting on the sidelines and feeling uneasy, as though we were drifting along and nothing could be done to stop it. I went out for a moment to have a word with Jennie and when I came back I heard Hugh Gaitskell rebuking George Brown's discourtesy, to which I replied that the real discourtesy was the way in which he had treated his Shadow Defence Minister. I received from across the room a funny kind of disapproving but sympathetic head-nod from Ray Gunter. Maybe they are right. Maybe it's too late to do anything. Maybe, moreover, if I tried to do anything now, particularly with George Brown, I should be completely misunderstood by the Conference delegates, who still don't understand what the score is inside. These are all things which we shall discuss when I go upstairs at this moment.

Wednesday, September 28th
I was sitting down that evening, just thinking about going to bed, when the telephone rang. It was Margaret Stewart of the *Chronicle*. 'I expect you

[1] At the T.U.C. annual Conference.

know what I am ringing about,' she said archly. 'Have you anything to say about this sensational story which the *Herald* has spread over its whole front page?'[1] So somebody had leaked the whole International story. She told me the headline was about my going out in a huff. Now, curiously enough, I had walked out in a huff, then met Jennie at the lift, talked to her for a moment and realized that it's always a mistake to leave in a huff, and walked back. So here we had a leaker for once caught *flagrante delicto*. Who was it?

Well I remembered going back and finding that Eirene White had left and I heard later that Dan McGarvey had also left at the same time, so the suspicion therefore rests on him.[*] I filled in Margaret Stewart, particularly on the fact that the whole thing arose out of the treatment of George Brown, and went to bed gloomily. Next morning I found it was true. The *Herald* had made a bombshell of it, Margaret had an extremely well-informed story in the *Chronicle* and every other paper had listed the story of the *Herald* first edition, a characteristic piece of British journalism.

I spent Thursday morning doing a press release and then went off to Prescote, where I found on Friday morning that very little had been made of my release. Most of the papers disregarded it altogether, mainly, I think, because they had got their story of a great contest between Keep-the-Bomb Gaitskell and Bust-up-NATO Cousins and they didn't want their story complicated by this confusing interruption in the Centre. As a result, when Tony Wedgwood Benn came out with wildly enthusiastic support for my proposal, he got no mention.

I had a lovely weekend without Nanny and with, for once, beautiful weather. Altogether the farm was lovely and Coventry was nice too. Everything was nice till I got back to the intrigues of London, which have been going all this week. Tony Wedgwood Benn has been making statements every day and has at last got one of them into the press today. I am quite pleased that at least I have forced *The Times* and the· *Guardian* to devote their first leaders to proving the T. & G.W. resolution is in some way out of harmony with our policy. Meanwhile, a surprising event has been the arrival at the *New Statesman* from George Brown in Strasbourg of a tremendous, hard-hitting article,[3] which should break through even the press reserve and make people realize that there's a real story about it.

[1] On September 22nd the *Daily Herald* published Geoffrey Goodman's story, with the headline 'Crossman's Bomb. He Quits Meeting After Shock for Gaitskell'.

[*] Curiously enough, John Cole,[2] who was dining with me last Monday night, explained to me at length that it is the Industrial Correspondents who cover the N.E.C. and the T.U.C., usually on the same day. 'It's a terrible rush,' he said, 'and our natural contacts are with the trade union members. Since we haven't got an entry into the House, we never have time, even if we wanted to, to make contact with the politicians. That is why our sources are trade union and nearly all of them are right-wing.' He went on naïvely, 'Wouldn't you like to provide me with regular information to counter-balance them?'

[2] Labour Correspondent for the *Manchester Guardian* (later the *Guardian*) 1957–63 and its News Editor 1963–9 and Deputy Editor 1969–75. In 1975 he became Assistant Editor of the *Observer* and in 1976 Deputy Editor of that paper.

[3] 'The Road to Trust', October 1st, 1960.

Meanwhile, of course, the other big event was the selection of Michael Foot as the candidate for Ebbw Vale. He was lunching with me on Thursday and I told him how much I personally wanted him back in the House, but we agreed his chances were a bit dim. Then, on Saturday night, came the news on the telly that he was in. He had romped home with a huge majority. His wife, Jill, told me on the phone that the selection had been by no means purely personal nor even on the issue of whether there should be a good local candidate or a national successor to Nye. Every candidate had been asked, as first question, to state his attitude to nuclear weapons. The constituency had passed their anti-nuclear resolution while their Member, Bevan, was ill, which shows how strongly they felt about it. Anyone who gave any kind of equivocating answer or any kind of support for the N.E.C. was at the bottom of the first Poll. Michael and Parry, who both promised to fight without compromise for total nuclear disarmament, were the two leading candidates.[1] Michael had also made no concessions about living in the constituency of being local or anything else.

Of course, one result of the Brown/Crossman/Benn initiative has been to infuriate the nuclear abolitionists and to embarrass Mr Cousins, who would like people to believe that his resolution is very different from N.E.C. policy. Indeed, we have the extraordinary situation of Mr Gaitskell wanting people to believe that N.E.C. policy is totally unlike what it is really and Mr Cousins wanting the same about his Union policy. As a result, the real issues have been entirely submerged and both sides are furious when some people in the middle are so old-fashioned as to say that we might consider the defence issues for a change and what the Party really stands for.

I am sure we are adding a great deal to the confusion and that, if one was thinking merely about one's vote at Conference, one should fight shy of any kind of course of this kind. But I agree with Tony and George that it's really intolerable to see the Party going on smashing itself to pieces. So I've been trying to keep Michael in line on the one side and I've even had some effect on Gaitskell, as can be seen from a letter, which I received this morning.[2] I had told Rose to send my press release to the members of the International, and I got this extraordinarily friendly reply. Contrast this with Hugh's infuriated denunciation of George Brown on the phone a week ago and his stern reprimand of me across the table last week for putting forward the most ridiculous and dangerous proposal he had ever heard. What one

[1] There had been three other candidates on the short-list for the Labour nomination at Ebbw Vale: R. Evans, Secretary of the divisional party and Bevan's former agent; Dr K. G. Pendse of Llanbradach; and Gordon Parry, a Pembrokeshire schoolteacher, who had been Labour candidate for Monmouth in 1959 and stood for Pembroke in 1970, February 1974 and October 1974. In 1975 he became a life peer.

[2] In an eight-line letter, Gaitskell said: 'I agree with a good deal of what you say though not, as you realize, with the particular proposals which you were putting to the Committee. I am afraid the consequences of our accepting them would be very different from what you suppose.'

can do from the middle is to make both extremes realize that they don't want to be presented to people as extremists or as itching for a battle.

Meanwhile a few little things were occurring outside the Labour Party. In the far, far distance a United Nations Assembly was taking place in New York, with all the stunt of Khrushchev's arrival.[1] Now we have Mr Macmillan flying over and seeking to mediate — not, I fear, with any hope of achieving anything but simply to satisfy the British people's egos and make us feel we are still in the centre of the picture.

More relevant to us is something I saw last night on television, the first hour-long debate between Nixon[2] and Kennedy[3] in the presidential contest.[4] Oh God it was dull! Nixon looked like a ratty lay preacher and Kennedy looked like a wealthy young man whom George Wigg was just training as a W.E.A. lecturer. If that had been what they were, you would have said they were good second-raters, whom we wouldn't have tolerated in the North Staffs District but who might have been good enough for Berks, Bucks and Oxon! But, as presidential candidates, these two tight-lipped, image-conscious, rigid, nervous, totally humourless young men—Oh dear, oh dear! Compare them with Mr Khrushchev or Colonel Nasser or Mr Ben-Gurion or Mao Tse-tung—Oh dear, oh dear! That's the ally we rely on.

The Labour Party Conference resulted in a defeat for Hugh Gaitskell. On October 6th he secured support for the compromise statement on Clause 4, which was unsuccessfully opposed by Mr Cousins, but in the defence debate on the previous day the unilateralist policy prevailed. Before the vote was taken Mr Gaitskell uncompromisingly rejected unilateralism and committed his position as Party Leader to the judgment of the Parliamentary Party. He

[1] Mr Khrushchev had announced on September 1st that he intended to visit New York during the session of the U.N. General Assembly. He arrived by sea on September 19th. Five days before, President Eisenhower had announced that he would address the General Assembly; Mr Macmillan declared that he, too, would attend. On September 23rd Mr Khrushchev gave a two-hour speech, attacking the Western World for aggression and colonialism and the United Nations for its 'unseemly work' in the Congo. He proposed that the Secretary-General's office should be abolished and the executive authority of the U.N. vested in three representatives, one each for the Communist group, the Western group and the 'uncommitted countries'. Mr Macmillan arrived in the United States by air on September 25th and four days later gave a quiet and soothing speech.

[2] Richard Nixon, Republican Senator from California 1950–3, Vice-President 1953–61, unsuccessful Republican candidate for the Presidency 1960, was elected President of the United States 1968 and again from 1972. In August 1974, facing impeachment, he resigned. He published *Six Crises* (New York: Doubleday, 1962) and *The Memoirs of Richard Nixon* (New York: Grosset & Dunlap, 1978).

[3] John F. Kennedy, a Democratic member of the House of Representatives 1947–53 and a Senator from Massachusetts 1952–60, was elected President of the United States in 1960 and was assassinated on November 22nd, 1963.

[4] The American presidential election was to take place on November 8th. On July 13th the Democratic Convention chose John Kennedy as its presidential candidate and on July 27th the Republican Convention nominated Richard Nixon. On September 26th these two contestants had the first of a series of four televised debates, before an audience of some 70 million.

referred to his opponents as 'pacifists, neutralists and fellow travellers'; these remarks aroused great resentment. In the vote itself the official policy was defeated by 297,000 votes, out of a total of more than 6 million. Mr Gaitskell declared: 'There are some of us, Mr Chairman, who will fight and fight and fight again to save the Party we love.'

Thursday, October 13th

My first job after the Conference was, as Chairman, to deliver a four-and-a-half-minute party political broadcast on the Light Programme on Tuesday.[1] I had been thinking about it for days. What line could I take which would establish my position as Chairman-moderator in the crisis and give the idea of the hard centre we have got to form between these yelping ideological phalanxes? I had told Hugh at Scarborough about the broadcast and suggested we should discuss it. But by Tuesday morning my mind was made up. I would discuss it with no one except Len Williams and the officials. I took my draft to Len at three o'clock and, as a result of his and Arthur Bax's advice, it was somehow toned down but, I'm sure, greatly improved. Moreover, as the afternoon went on I found that not only Len but Arthur Bax and Mollie Bell[2] of the Press Department had been horrified at Hugh's performance and were 100 per cent behind the line I was taking. It had quite a good press on Wednesday morning and I was touched when Morgan's secretary rang me up to say how good it was. This, from a loyal Morganite, would have been incredible a year ago.

I was also amused to find yesterday evening that Barbara and Co. had been pleasantly nonplussed by what they found its dazzling originality. I had actually said something new about the problem and something obviously true. Barbara had asked us to come and discuss action. There were present Jennie Lee, Barbara, Michael, Ian Mikardo, Lena Jeger,[3] Harold Wilson and myself. I had got Harold Wilson to come and pick me up and it was obvious that he was desperately worried. Poor little man, he has really cornered himself this time. He knew he would be pressed to stand against Hugh,[4] in which case he would be committing political suicide, and he wants to stand as Deputy Leader instead. But he also knows that, if he doesn't stand against Hugh, he will be accused of cowardice and he may well be defeated for Deputy Leader, now George Brown has jumped on the bandwagon again

[1] Crossman discussed the relationship of the annual Conference to the Parliamentary Labour Party, suggested that 'we all keep a sense of proportion' and emphasized that facts about nuclear warfare changed month by month. He concluded: 'How crazy it would be if, now we're agreed on every other major problem, we proceed to tear each other to pieces on an issue where the probability is that any defence policy we recommend today will be obsolete long before the General Election comes round.'

[2] Assistant Press Officer of the Labour Party in the 1950s and early 1960s.

[3] Labour M.P. for Holborn and St Pancras South November 1953–September 1959 and 1964–74, and for Camden, Holborn and St Pancras South 1974–9. In 1968 she became a member of the N.E.C. and in 1979 she was created a life peer.

[4] In the election at the beginning of the new parliamentary Session.

and has Hugh's backing. Here is an object lesson in the master-tactician and the super-opportunist, who is so clever that his tactics are disastrous and he destroys his opportunities. But what can I say about somebody who, throughout all these talks, has been utterly trivial, complacent and vain?

The evening started with Tony Greenwood saying he had decided to resign from the Shadow Cabinet and reading out a fine letter of resignation, protesting against Gaitskell's leadership during the last year. I said this made sense only if Tony were resigning in order to stand against Gaitskell, at which Barbara said, 'But Harold must do that.' Then the fat was in the fire. They all bullied Harold and threatened him and pushed at him and tugged at him and this little spherical thing kept twirling round in dismay until Ian Mikardo and I both said, 'What's the good of bullying him? Someone who doesn't want to stand can't stand. Leave him alone.'

After this it became clear that Tony Greenwood had wanted to resign in order to stand.[1] He really does know the consequences and the cynical say he is doing it because he would be driven off the Shadow Cabinet anyway. But on this occasion I have really respected him, since he hates unpopularity and knows exactly what he is in for. I came to the conclusion, as the evening went on, that Tony would actually be a better candidate than Harold because he is immolating himself sincerely for what he considers a cause.

Of course, Tony may gain by it. One never knows. But the point is, he's not doing it for that reason. But oh dear, dear, dear. Suddenly it became clear that Barbara's one ambition was to immolate herself and thereby to establish that women can be Leaders and Prime Ministers. She was nearly in tears insisting that she had the right, and later I went out into the kitchen and found Tony Greenwood with the uncomfortable job of deterring a termagant from suicide. If she had been the candidate, it would have been a farce.

I had gone to this meeting in some perturbation, for two reasons. In the first place, on the Friday we were leaving Scarborough I had had a frightful tiff with Jennie and Tony at our last lunch. Jennie had said twice that we must expect Dick to do a complete somersault in the next two months, by which she clearly meant my climbing back on the Gaitskell bandwagon, and Tony had said my fault was being too nice to everybody, including people like Gaitskell — a comment which Anne regarded as showing a greater ignorance of me than anything she had ever heard.

However, it was clear that they were all expecting me, as Chairman, to be very goody-goody. It's true enough that it would be crazy for me to destroy my position by taking part in a cabal against Gaitskell. What I have to do is to offer the best advice possible and to try to get the Executive to take a line which I think would be in the interests of the Party and to persuade

---

[1] He announced his resignation from the Shadow Cabinet on October 13th; on the following day he offered himself as a candidate for the leadership, a move that was widely interpreted as intended to induce Harold Wilson to come forward.

him to go along with it. But I wasn't cheerful about persuading the Bevanites that this was my duty, especially since, at the meeting when I was elected Chairman, Barbara jumped in to move Ian Mikardo without any kind of warning. Altogether we got rather edgy to each other and yet yesterday all this went away.

I told them exactly what I have told Sam and Ray in the letter I have written them. What I hope the officers will propose at the Executive is a meeting with a new Shadow Cabinet as soon as it is elected, to agree on the following points. First, no immediate attempt to patch up a new defence policy. Secondly, a period of several months, during which we have political education about defence and foreign policy and neither side tries to use the Party platform for propaganding against the other — standstill months, in fact, while we think rationally and sensibly about the matter. Thirdly, during this period the Parliamentary Party takes no disciplinary action against the unilateralist minority and the National Executive takes no disciplinary action against the anti-unilateralist minority. Fourthly, by-election candidates should make a virtue of necessity by emphasizing that the Labour Party gives them the conscientious right to what line they will take at Westminster, freely and without fear. Fifthly, to oppose the idea of a recall Conference and, without openly saying so, get rid of the notion that the Scarborough decision is simply to be reversed, by preparing the ground for a new and much wider statement on the broad principles of foreign and defence policy, as a result of which we rid the Party of its defence obsession.

I had talked all this over with Len Williams and this is what I put to the Bevanites last night. To my surprise, they all accepted it. No one proposed, as I feared they would, that the unilateralists should now exert their theoretical right to use the Party machine for Aldermaston propaganda. I must admit that, in order to discourage this, I pointed out that the Executive is not committed to unilateralism or to going out of NATO but only to two extremely vague and ambiguous resolutions, which don't comprise a policy, and, in order to get a policy which could be propaganda, we should have to sit down and think one out, with five unilateralists against twenty non-unilateralists, and the result would be what you would guess. Now it's my job to persuade Gaitskell and his friends that they also can't get things their own way.

In doing this I was greatly strengthened by visiting Morgan Phillips yesterday afternoon at his home. He is much thinner but extremely spry and cocky and enormously alert. He can laugh, he can smile, but he is totally speechless and completely paralysed down the right side, so that he can't write either. However, he was able to get across to me his determination that Gaitskell should not get control of the machine in Transport House, and I was able to assure Morgan that Transport House was following out his directive before he gave it. Now it's my job to deal with the Gaitskellites, I hope via Sam Watson. I have got to show them that the kind of campaign they are trying to wage just won't work, even in their own interests. At a recall Conference, for example, the Executive would not be able to propose a reversal and Hugh would not be able to speak, since we are pledged to the other policy. Moreover, it is quite impossible for us to permit Hugh to use the Party machinery to argue against Party policy. I was surprised and delighted yesterday when Arthur Bax told me he had already given instructions forbidding this to be done. The fact is that, naturally enough, the bureaucrats at Transport House take the party constitution in grim earnest and I fancy the twelve trade unionists[1] will, too.

This morning I spent going round Transport House. Everybody seemed enormously relieved and almost pleased to see me. The fact is that they want a steady central leadership there and I don't believe there is anybody in the place who is following Gaitskell's lead of 'Fight, fight, fight'. Three years ago it was 90 per cent Gaitskellite. Now he has lost every friend he had there.

Tuesday, October 18th
On Thursday afternoon I suddenly had an impulse, rang up Hugh, found Mrs Skelly only too anxious to arrange for me to see him and strolled over. I found that, owing to repairs, he had been moved out of his room and put downstairs into a kind of committee room. We started quite amicably by my putting to him some of the ideas Len and I had discussed for the N.E.C. meeting next Wednesday. On the subject of candidates — each must say what he would conscientiously do — we reached quick agreement, and also that we didn't want a speedy production of a new document on defence.

Then I outlined the idea that we should have an N.E.C./Shadow Cabinet discussion and that meanwhile we should have a self-denying ordinance, with nobody campaigning against anybody else and, so far as the subject of defence is treated, it should be devoted to education. 'No, no!' Hugh said, I must feel myself completely free to run my campaign as I wish.' And he added, 'If they* were to forbid me to use their platform for it, they would make themselves a laughing-stock in the country.' 'Not they — we,' I interjected. 'You are a member, you know.' Hugh looked up and said, 'Dick, you can come and talk to me but you must be polite.' I replied, 'Hugh, you must decide whether you think the Labour Party can be run by personal or collective leadership. That is the real issue — not defence.'

I began to discuss Sam Watson's idea of an apex of power. Hugh got very restless and said that all informal things were difficult. There used to be a Chairmen's Committee. I said the important thing was an agreed strategy at the centre and illustrated how Morgan and he had drifted apart. 'I used to consult with Morgan,' he said. 'I used to consult, too,' I replied, 'and I expect he said rather different things to you and to me,' to which Hugh curtly agreed.

[1] I.e. the twelve trade union members of the N.E.C.
* I.e. the N.E.C.

But I got nowhere on that line. Hugh said, 'But Dick, don't you realize? This issue of collective security versus neutralism is the greatest issue of our time and I am faced by a dangerous, malicious, underground conspiracy.' 'Fundamentally,' I replied, 'I don't accept your diagnosis. Defence is a most shifting subject and, as for the conspiracy, I see no evidence of it. The fact is that we mismanaged the Party last year and that's why we got defeated. If you allow us to manage the Party properly this year and say nothing at all, we can guarantee you a million and a half majority for a policy fully compatible with your ideals. But the kind of riproaring campaign you talk about might make things more difficult.' 'I see you are against me,' he said, 'not on my side.'

I didn't reply to that. We began to talk about the relations of the N.E.C. and the Parliamentary Party. 'Historically, in our Party the leadership has always been in Parliament,' Hugh said, 'and that's where it ought to be. You people on the N.E.C. should do as little as possible this year. You can spend some time in studying things like the land problem, for instance.' 'That kind of attitude', I said, 'is unworkable in our Party and it's not true that all leadership has been in Parliament. What about Ernest Bevin before the war or half a dozen other big trade union leaders? And anyway, there's a crisis of confidence in the leadership.' 'Not in the parliamentary leadership,' he said; 'I daresay there is in the N.E.C., but I doubt whether the relationship between the parliamentary leadership and the rank and file has ever been better. We have a splendid collective spirit in the Parliamentary Party, whereas the N.E.C. is hopelessly divided.'

For the last quarter of an hour I was trying to get out of the room, but the subject of Tony Greenwood came up. Hugh had just received his resignation letter. 'Did you know?' Hugh said. 'Yes', I said, 'I knew he was sending it.' 'What's his motive?' Hugh said. 'I presume so that he can stand against you.' 'But he could do that in the Shadow Cabinet.' 'Yes, but he couldn't state the reasons why he is standing against you unless he resigns.' 'Oh!' Hugh said, as though this came as a surprise.

The net impression of the interview was that Hugh is full of a divine afflatus and at that time was confident that he has the Parliamentary Party behind him and could afford to be fairly arrogant and contemptuous. Neither of us gave anything away and both knew that we were speaking for the record.

Wednesday, October 19th
All these last days inside the Labour Party have been spent — no, consumed, no, eaten up — by the most elaborate fencing and manoeuvring I have ever experienced in the long and dreary history of the last nine years. On one side Gaitskell has been inspiring various spontaneous offers of support for him — speeches from George Brown, safely back in the fold, from Reg Prentice, pledging the Burkean rights of M.P.s, a spontaneous manifesto

which came out this morning from Bill Rodgers[1] and Alderman Pickstock,[2] who once ran the Extra-Mural Department at Oxford and who now wants to run a Croslandite anti-Victory for Socialism group, a fervent speech from Jim Griffiths and so on.

On the other side, the most amusing moves have been taking place, centred round Mr Wilson. We had made it pretty clear at Barbara's house that most of us thought he ought to stand, but no one could make him. The prime result of Tony Greenwood's initiative was, of course, to smoke Harold out of his lair and make him realize two things: first, that if he tried to get Deputy Leader, he would now be defeated with certainty by the Right, and, secondly, that, if he failed to take an initiative now, he would be doomed for ever as the leader of the Left.

On Sunday at Prescote I was suddenly rung up by Tony Greenwood to tell me that Harold had been suggesting that he, Tony, should in due course stand down and Harold should take over the challenge. Harold had talked vaguely about a speech next Friday, followed by further manoeuvres before making up his mind. Tony, not unreasonably, felt this a pretty intolerable position for someone who had been pretty well crucified in the press for doing what he had done.

A few minutes later Harold rang up to say he had been talking to Tony. I indicated the gist of Tony's remarks and Harold said that he had got no impression of this from his talk. He had now checked with Jennie, Michael and Barbara and they were all enthusiastic for the idea that Tony should stand down. I said that, if this was to happen, it was vital that Harold should act quickly and decisively. He then insisted that he must see me that evening, even if it meant his coming to Paddington and crossing London to Euston with me, where I was taking the sleeper.[3] My train got to Paddington an hour late, thanks to fog, and to the wrong platform, where there was no Harold. So I took my time, went by underground to Euston, rang up Mary to say that I had missed Harold and then settled down in my sleeper.

At three minutes to eleven a voice whispered in my ear and it was Harold,

---

[1] William Rodgers, Labour M.P. for Stockton-on-Tees 1962–74 and for the Teesside division of Stockton since 1974. He served as General Secretary of the Fabian Society 1953–60. He was Parliamentary Under-Secretary of State at the D.E.A. 1964–7 and the Foreign Office 1967–8, Minister of State at the Board of Trade 1968–9, at H.M. Treasury 1969–70 and at the Ministry of Defence 1974–6, and was Secretary of State for Transport 1976–9.

[2] Frank Pickstock, a North Staffordshire railway clerk, who studied with the W.E.A. tutorial class and became a committee member of the Railway Clerks' Association. He was vice-chairman of the Stoke Divisional Labour Party and in 1934 studied P.P.E. at The Queen's College, Oxford, as an extra-mural scholar. He was treasurer of the Stockport Divisional Labour Party and, after the Second World War, moved to Oxford as secretary of the Tutorial Classes Committee. He was a Councillor on Oxford City Council from 1952, an Alderman from 1958 and became Lord Mayor in 1967. In 1962 he was appointed Deputy Director of the Department of External Studies of Oxford University, retiring in 1978. He published a Fabian pamphlet on the railways in 1950.

[3] On his way to Manchester for 'Who Goes Next?'

who had rushed round. I told him I had had yet another talk with Tony Greenwood and said it was vital that this issue should be settled on Wednesday at the latest. Why not accept the decision of those who were dining with me?[1] To this Harold cordially agreed, a fact which made Tony very surprised when I informed him by phone next morning. For the first time I am regarded as a great mediator and honest broker. But, oh dear, Harold's arrival on the train was comic! As Derek Walker-Smith[*][2] said drily, 'Usually people go to see the candidate for the leadership. The candidate doesn't go to see the people unless he's in great difficulty.' Next morning all the papers were full of the Wilson manoeuvres. The only thing which surprised us was that there was no communiqué from Euston platform!

I had been suffering from the return of old stomach trouble, due merely, I think, to a cold, and when I got back to London I went with reluctance to the London Labour Party annual dance. I found that I had been told to be there at nine, whereas Hugh Gaitskell was coming to speak a few words at quarter to eleven. I sat for an hour in a box adjoining the Attlees and other octogenarians, who looked very sourly at me. Just as I was slipping out I ran into Barbara in full evening dress and full of gaiety. So I told her I was bloody well off and Harold Wilson said, 'If it's necessary I'll say a few words on your behalf.' So I knew everybody was happy.

Meanwhile I have been working away in Transport House, trying to screw Len Williams up to the need for writing the briefest of agendas for next Wednesday's meeting there. I have also been preparing for this afternoon's Shadow Cabinet. My impression is that Hugh Gaitskell may well make a tactical withdrawal. Last night I had a long and very angry discussion with Jim Griffiths, an acolyte of Hugh's. Jim said that many Executive members had run away from the Executive defence statement, that anyway it had been defeated by dubious methods and it was a scandal that unions had made up their minds before they arrived at Conference. All this from Jim, who has been living on such Conference methods for thirty years! But it was useful, because it revealed to me Gaitskell's mind.

The Chief Whip came in and I told him, for some reason, quite laconically, what I thought ought to be done – an agreement for tripartite discussions, which would take at least two months; an agreement not to write another Defence White Paper and to concentrate on producing general principles: this period to be a cooling-off period, with no defiance of 'Fight, fight, fight'. To my surprise he agreed with all these points and added, 'What's

---

[1] On October 20th. See below, pp. 889 ff.

[*] He was appearing for the first time on the Granada programme and had been occupying the compartment next door.

[2] Conservative M.P. for the Hertford division of Hertfordshire 1945–55 and the East division since 1955. A lawyer, he was Parliamentary Secretary at the Board of Trade 1955–6, Economics Secretary at the Treasury November 1956–January 1957, Minister of State at the Board of Trade 1957 and Minister of Health 1957–60. He became a Q.C. in 1955 and was created a baronet in 1960. From 1973 to 1979 he was a Member of the European Parliament.

the good of agreeing a defence policy which will be out of date before the Election?' I somehow thought I had heard those words before![1] Has he given this advice to Gaitskell? I presume he has. If so, Harold Wilson's job this afternoon will be very difficult, for he has screwed himself up to the point of asking Gaitskell a number of questions and, if he gets unsatisfactory replies, announcing his decision to stand against him. I have a shrewd suspicion Gaitskell is not going to oblige Harold, even if I do my very best, as I must, in loyal support, prodding him and irritating him into saying what he really thinks. But I shall be surprised if we are successful.

Thursday, October 20th
Yesterday's Shadow Cabinet was a strange, and, for me, somewhat disconcerting affair. I strolled over in nice time to have five minutes before the meeting, presuming it to be in Gaitskell's temporary room, lost my way there and got there to find it had been changed to Room J. So I arrived when everybody else was seated, just in time to hear Gaitskell welcoming two new members. I sat at the end between A. V. Alexander[2] and Tom Fraser. What first struck me about the Shadow Cabinet is how aptly it is named. For here are people, all behaving like Shadow Ministers in an alternative Government, with quite a lot of parliamentary pomp and circumstance and very ostentatiously and self-consciously acting as Westminster characters as against Transport House.

The thing only got interesting because John Stonehouse[3] had sent in a resolution for the Party Meeting, in strict conformity with our Party constitution and the resolution we passed at Scarborough, and as a result the whole issue became relevant. Apparently the order of speaking follows the seating round the table in the sense that each person speaks once before anybody else speaks again. Affairs were started by James Callaghan, who said that we, the Shadow Cabinet, must give a lead to the Parliamentary Party in

[1] In Crossman's broadcast and in his conversation with Gaitskell (see above, pp. 880 and 883 ff).

[2] A. V. ('Albert') Alexander (1885–1965), Labour and Co-operative M.P. for the Hillsborough division of Sheffield 1922–31 and 1935–50. He was Parliamentary Secretary at the Board of Trade 1924, First Lord of the Admiralty 1929–31, 1940–5 and 1945–6, Minister of Defence 1947–50 and Chancellor of the Duchy of Lancaster 1950–1. In 1950 he was created 1st Viscount Alexander of Hillsborough and was Leader of the Labour Peers in the Lords 1955–64.

[3] Labour and Co-operative M.P. for Wednesbury 1957–74 and for Walsall North 1974–6 (from April to August 1976 as a member of the English National Party). He was Parliamentary Secretary at the Ministry of Aviation 1964–6, Parliamentary Under-Secretary of State for the Colonies 1966–7, Minister of Aviation 1967, Minister of State at the Ministry of Technology 1967–8, Postmaster-General 1968–9 and Minister of Posts and Telecommunications 1969–70. In December 1974 he disappeared, mysteriously, while swimming off the coast of Miami Beach, Florida, and was found in Australia. On his reappearance in 1975 he returned to the House of Commons, but in 1976 resigned the Labour whip and joined the English National Party. In August 1976 he was found guilty at the Central Criminal Court of eighteen out of nineteen charges involving theft and false pretences and he was sentenced to seven years' imprisonment. He was released from prison in 1979.

showing we shall have no nonsense with the Conference's unilateralism, etc. He wanted the meeting to prepare a resolution to this effect to put before the Party Meeting. At once George Brown intervened, urging caution and asking why we should gratuitously come into conflict with the Conference. Our views on defence were not to be doubted. What we had to consider were the feelings of our colleagues—a view supported by Fred Lee and strenuously opposed by Frank Soskice, who said we couldn't have any shilly-shallying on this great issue and must leave the country in no doubt that we would have no truck with the Conference.

At this point Harold Wilson weighed in. I had known before that it would be his greatest effort to issue challenges to Gaitskell, but this was none too easy in the circumstances and he got caught out when he referred to Gaitskell's announcing on behalf of the Parliamentary Party his determination to 'Fight, fight, fight'. 'Not on behalf of anybody,' said Gaitskell; 'I spoke for myself.' I then tried my first intervention and started demurely by saying that I would not have come in so early on my first meeting were it not that I thought we ought to consider the Executive's difficulties.

At this point Hugh said, 'This is out of order. We're not the Executive here,' and James Callaghan said, 'You don't seem quite at home yet in this meeting.' I replied that every other speaker had discussed the Executive's position, I didn't see why the Chairman should be excluded from doing so also and I intended to do so. I ploughed on. I supported George Brown, Fred Lee and Harold Wilson in urging that we in the Shadow Cabinet should at all costs avoid a direct confrontation with the Conference. Moreover, this was unnecessary, since it was quite wrong to state that the Executive was committed to a policy of withdrawing from NATO. If one studies the two resolutions we have accepted, what they really come to is the defeat of our own policy, with some vague flirtations with neutralism. But that doesn't constitute the kind of full commitment of which Frank Soskice was talking. I urged, therefore, that on no account should any resolution be put to the Party Meeting, even if unilateralists might try to put one.

It became clear that the meeting was divided, with only Fred Lee, Harold Wilson and myself and George Brown in the minority. Everybody else wanted to stand and fight, though, at my end of the table, Gavin Faringdon and Lucan[1], who are both unilateralists, retained unilateral silence.

Finally Hugh Gaitskell said it was his view that he should make the first statement at the Meeting, having first ruled out of order all motions, including that of Stonehouse. This we all agreed with, if it's possible. Hugh proceeded to read aloud very rapidly a kind of draft resolution which he now says will be the theme of his speech, reaffirming in general terms our exceptional

---

[1] After a distinguished Army career, George Bingham succeeded his father as 6th Earl of Lucan in 1949. He was Deputy Chief Whip in the Lords 1950–1, Parliamentary Under-Secretary of State for Commonwealth Relations June–October 1951 and Chief Opposition Whip in the Lords from 1954 until his death in 1964.

attitude on collective security. Then, also very rapidly, he read aloud a passage in which he stated that he was determined to reverse the Conference decision.

This gave me a chance of a second intervention. I said I could see no reason why George Brown and others, who are not members of the National Executive, should not personally urge such a view, but that was quite different from asking the Shadow Cabinet to stand collectively for reversing a Conference decision. In particular, it seemed to me impossible for those of us who are members both of the Shadow Cabinet and of the Executive to take this line. This applies particularly to the Leader, who clearly shares collective responsibility in both organizations. This time I wasn't ruled out of order until I had successfully made my point, which infuriated everybody. James Callaghan again said, 'All that is entirely irrelevant to our discussion here. This isn't the Executive.'

That night at half-past eight we had our dinner. Tom Driberg and Ian Mikardo were not there, so it consisted of Michael, Jennie, Harold, Barbara, Lena Jeger, Tony Greenwood and myself. Tony came first, speechless from an appalling cold, the same cold, presumably, which has roused my own stomach and made me unable to drink anything but milk for the last four days. Michael came with Jennie, slightly the worse for wear, and drank enormously until they all went at two o'clock in the morning. Old Lena Jeger had her share, too, and towards the end of the evening Harold swilled a good deal of whisky.

It was long, dramatic, exhausting, and in its way fascinating. We started with a report to them on the events in the Shadow Cabinet. Then we turned to the Executive and I repeated the procedures which they had agreed so easily last week and which I had now got agreed by Len. Immediately there was uproar. 'But Gaitskell will be able to accept this! Why on earth should we help him?' 'And what's all this about a new agreed statement?' shouted Mike. 'Agreed with whom? Is it clear that we are prepared to have an agreed statement with anyone except Gaitskell? Anyway, if the Executive gets into negotiation with the Shadow Cabinet, it will be outnumbered, whereas we have a clear majority on the Executive.' I pointed out that we only had a majority on the Executive for policies overwhelmingly proved to be reasonable, even though Gaitskell opposed them. The moment we seemed to be unreasonable or ourselves disregarding the Party constitution, we should lose the trade unionists.

I was irritated that Harold Wilson, who had agreed every detail of this, suddenly got cold feet and began to back the critics. I said, 'Look, any individual on the Executive can put down one of Michael's rumbustious motions, but I've got to try to prevent the crisis in the Party and not to split it. I thought our accusation against Gaitskell was that he's splitting the Party and our claim was that we were abiding by the Party constitution. If so, we must abide by it.' At this I was told that the constitution did not require these meetings and it was made quite clear by Michael, supported now by Barbara, that once again I was being too conciliatory. I said there were always two groups among us, those of us who were prepared to work with everybody, Centre and Left of Centre, and those who wanted a really Socialist policy. Neither could insist that the other should surrender.

After this Barbara said, 'Let's get on to the really important subject of the leadership, the issue, in fact, of whether Tony or Harold should stand.' Barbara decided to take the chair, which she didn't do for long, and suggested we should go round the room, starting with Michael Foot. He, to Harold's obvious consternation, made an extremely good case for Tony's standing and Harold's coming out with a statement supporting Tony and his resignation from the Shadow Cabinet. Lena Jeger, who was next, shirked anything very definite and Jennie made one of her long, confused orations. She wanted to see a new, revitalized Parliament, with a revitalized Left, and that should be our aim. She herself was anti-unilateralist but, on the other hand, she felt that Tony had got in first owing to Harold's refusal and this made it very difficult for Tony to withdraw. I wouldn't say Jennie balanced on the fence — she never does — but she roamed round the bush.

Harold intervened with a long speech, saying that what really mattered was getting votes, the votes of the Centre, and he could get more than Tony because he was a multilateralist, whereas Tony would only get the unilateralist votes. There was a good deal of discussion of this. Both Jennie and Michael repeated several times that of course Harold would get a few more votes, but only three or four, whereas he himself estimated that he might get thirty more. That's my estimate too.

It became pretty clear that Michael was uncompromisingly for Greenwood but that Jennie was hostile to Harold and only inhibited by her multilateralism from actively supporting Greenwood; that Lena detested Harold; and that Barbara and I were his only two supporters. We were both fairly judicious, pointing out that Tony Greenwood had staked a prior claim, that, whatever happened, we would have to explain away Harold's conduct and that the strongest case for Harold was that he was a multilateralist who could get the Centre.

Gradually, as the night wore on, Harold began to take over and say what he would do. It was obvious that he had prepared his *coup* down to the last detail, including the speech and the statement, both in his pocket, Walter Padley and Fred Lee as his whippers-up in the trade union group, etc., etc. But, when I remembered how he told me that Michael and Jennie had both eagerly approved his standing, I agreed with Barbara when she said to me that he had often got a false impression of people's unwillingness to say no.

Then suddenly, partly perhaps owing to whisky, the mood changed, when Harold told us the main points of his speech. I've heard him do it before and his speeches always sound even more terrible than they are. This time was no exception. It sounded dreadful and flat but what shocked Michael and Jennie above all was when he said that Britain needed defence and he stood by collective security, etc. 'How can I stand down for that?' cried Tony. 'I can only stand down on condition that Harold makes it clear that he accepts the Conference decision and will implement it—gradually, no doubt, but unequivocally.' I said, 'Don't be absurd. If Harold were to say that he would destroy any position he had at all. We've either got to have an honest-to-God unilateralist for whom multilateralists will vote or an honest-to-God multilateralist for whom unilateralists will vote. What we can't have is a compromise candidate, trying to ride both horses.'

At this point Harold suddenly became stubborn, rough and rude and said Tony could stand, because it was clear that what was wanted was not a Left-Centre candidate to win the confidence of the Party but a Left candidate, anti-Gaitskell, to be as extreme on one side as Gaitskell is on the other. Both Jennie and I pleaded that it was no good going on talking. It was clear we had given what advice we could. All that was possible now was that Harold and Tony should meet next morning and decide on their course of conduct.

Michael said they should toss up, since we couldn't have a majority vote, and I said, 'Don't be ridiculous. I don't agree that there's very little to choose and the more I hear of the argument the more vital it is that we should not have Tony, with his extreme unilateralism. I like everything about him except his views.' Well, it went round and round for a very long time and finally, at two o'clock, we pushed them out into the rain to drive up to Hampstead and Highgate. As they left, Lena Jeger said, 'I suppose all this means that Harold never wanted to stand at all,' which showed that she hadn't understood anything that was going on.

I rang Harold this morning and Tony rang me. I told Harold on no account to accept any conditions from Tony except the one we had agreed, that he should not stand for the deputy leadership or the Shadow Cabinet. But no policy conditions. He was perfectly all right on this. Tony then rang me and said it was impossible, after the morning papers, to accept Harold. I patiently explained that neither Harold nor I could compromise on the defence issue without ruining things. By eleven o'clock this morning the whole thing was agreed. In a sense, Harold had called Tony's bluff or, in another sense, had refused to succumb to the moral blackmail or threat from the Left that they wouldn't support him unless he became their prisoner. In many ways it was the most impressive performance I have ever seen from Harold, since he started from the impossible position into which he had got himself[1] and by the end had been behaving rather well.

Harold came round at lunch-time to show me his draft. I fancy that, now we've smoked him out and forced him into the open, he may not be too bad. There are quite a lot of signs that, with his fighting the leadership

[1] In the previous week. See above, p. 880.

and Fred Lee fighting the deputy leadership, this will be seen not to be a cabal, going for personal power, but a serious protest against the wrong kind of leadership.

On October 29th Harold Wilson announced that he would stand for the Party leadership. It was reported that Mr Greenwood had authorized him to say that he would withdraw. The next day Crossman wrote two letters, one to Anthony Greenwood, thanking him for what he had done and saying,

> *If personal integrity, comradeship and unswerving constancy to principle had been the only factors involved, you would have got my support. But at this moment I'm sure it was absolutely vital to prevent the formation of a smallish, isolated Left and to achieve a break-through towards the Centre.*

He concluded: 'Of course you will never get a tenth of the credit which you deserve.'

The other letter was to Harold Wilson. It began, 'So the first part of the operation is over. Magnificent.' He gave Harold Wilson suggestions from 'your old-hand psychological warfare adviser', asked whether he agreed that Crossman should come out openly in support of Wilson's candidacy and offered congratulations and

> *also to Mary for tolerating the politician who is driving her to distraction as patiently as my Anne, who, I suspect, feels much the same way as she does. What fun it is to be on the warpath together again. And, by Jove, haven't we learnt something since that first time we bearded Nye together alone [sic].'*

Wednesday, October 26th
Next day, I looked at the press and knew Harold had done a first-rate job. The difference between his standing and Tony's standing was bigger than even I had guessed. Now it was a serious challenge.

That Thursday evening I had an engagement at Oxford which was a little painful. Last July Julia Gaitskell[1] had asked me to address the post-graduate Voltaire Society and I had chosen the subject 'The Intellectual In Politics'. She gave me dinner. I was unable to eat or drink much owing to a bad stomach and this restricted conversation. But she's a charming little thing and I was at my breeziest and jolliest, though I ruined things for her telling her Harold had decided to stand. I could feel the bottom fall out of her stomach. The meeting was a bit painful, since somehow the whole room seemed to be interested in whether Gaitskell was an intellectual and whether what I was saying about the intellectual in Labour politics was being applied to him. I made a list of people:

---

[1] Julia, the elder daughter of Hugh Gaitskell, was then reading P.P.E. She became Mrs McNeal in 1969.

Intellectual	Non-intellectual
Lenin	Stalin
Nehru	Gandhi
Woodrow Wilson	F.D.R.[1]
Stafford Cripps	Beveridge
Balogh	Kaldor
Crossman	Gaitskell

It was a good joke but as the evening wore on no one believed it and, when I was asked to have a drink, Julia said she could take no more and had to be taken home.

I had to spend the whole of Monday in the train to Manchester and back and arrived late at Barbara Castle's party. Sydney Jacobson and Cassandra were both there. Otherwise it was a Wilsonite party, with Lynn Ungoed-Thomas voicing strong views — but whether he will actually vote for Harold I am not sure. During the evening the news came that Dalton and Attlee were both supporting Gaitskell. I also heard that George Wigg had taken over the organization of Harold's campaign, with the terse observation to me on the phone, 'He's not up to it,' which I'm afraid is true enough. Altogether, though it started with a bang, I now feel we've settled down to what one might have expected. Harold will get up to eighty votes and the only thing of doubt is the number of abstentions and the effect which the campaign will have on Hugh.

This morning's Executive has some bearing on this. I had very carefully prepared with Len his short paper on our procedures and our aim was to get this through, and nothing else. We started with quite a lot of routine business, but at the very beginning, on the minutes of the meeting at Scarborough, Tony Greenwood raised the issue of whether we had agreed to make no statement for the duration of the Scarborough Conference or, as Jim Matthews[2] had stated, up to the next Executive. Immediately, Bessie Braddock bashed in, 'Of course it was up to today's meeting that we were to make no statements and if Tony Greenwood wants a row I can bash him.'

But, curiously enough, after this ominous spark the meeting subsided until we reached Len's note. Len explained it quite competently and ponderously, whereupon Danny McGarvey immediately said that he wanted to ask, speaking as a democrat, not as a unilateralist, whether we couldn't pass a resolution resolving to carry out Conference instructions. At once Jim Matthews said, 'Not on your life,' and Sam Watson said, 'Well if Danny

[1] Franklin Delano Roosevelt (1882–1945), a Democratic Member of the New York State Senate 1910-13 and from 1913 to 1920 Assistant Secretary for the Navy, was Governor of New York State 1928–32 and was elected President of the United States in 1932. Twice re-elected, he remained President until his death on April 12th, 1945.

[2] James Matthews, National Officer of the General and Municipal Workers' Union 1947–62 and President of the Federation of Shipbuilding and Engineering Unions 1960–2. He joined the N.E.C. in 1956. He died in 1969.

puts a resolution I shall put another resolution and mine will be carried.'
I ruled them both out of order, since we were discussing a narrow procedural
issue. This shows the advantage of putting something down on paper first.
It does enable you to keep the debate to what you want, if you are the
person who puts it on paper! Barbara pointed out that we should talk about
talks with the Parliamentary Committee, whereas the Party constitution
mentioned only the Parliamentary Party. At this Jim Callaghan immediately
seconded her proposal, much to her embarrassment, and it was carried
unanimously.

Hugh Gaitskell, meanwhile, had been relatively quiet. On the Braddock/
Greenwood interlude, he had intervened with a laboured self-defence of his
television appearance on the Friday of the Conference, which I thought
unfortunate but in this other part of our discussion, no one could have been
more conciliatory or careful. Hugh welcomed tripartite talks and welcomed
the approach to the Parliamentary Party. Tony Greenwood said he couldn't
agree to all this until we had some assurance that the Parliamentary Party
would not pre-judge the issue before the talks, at which Hugh Gaitskell
gave the assurance that the Shadow Cabinet had unanimously decided
against putting any resolution at the evening meeting, since, as a dying
Shadow Cabinet, it would be improper for it to commit the Party. I suppose
the whole discussion lasted about forty minutes, but it went relatively
amicably.

So we passed over the danger point and came to a special recommendation
of the Publicity Committee that we should have a Party emblem, which
should be on all our posters and which Alice Bacon exhibited for us. This
produced a most fascinating reaction. Sensibly, the Publicity Committee
had got the best British designer to do something voluntary for us and had
taken a great deal of trouble. Hugh Gaitskell took one look at it, said it
looked like L for Learner and that it wouldn't do. Harold Wilson disliked
it and also tried to get it knocked out. Eirene White and Tom Driberg, who
had been on the Committee, pleaded. Of course, when Alice Bacon proposes
anything it's difficult to like it but I was fascinated by Hugh's committing
himself once again, within two minutes of a new subject being raised and,
in this case, infuriating Alice Bacon, who is one of his loyal supporters, and,
incidentally, upsetting Transport House, which feels that, if someone has
been working for three months on something, it shouldn't be dismissed in
three seconds.

The meeting ended at about ten minutes to twelve, to everybody's amazement, and I received quite a share of congratulations. But, after all, all that
had happened had been that we had postponed a row. Well, postponement
is gained time.

I went downstairs and had a long talk to Sam, who was baffling and
baffled, trying to persuade himself that he is entitled to stay as chairman
of the International and fight the Scarborough decision. The excuse he was

giving himself was that they were Communist-inspired or that the unions had decided beforehand. I tried to make him see that his job was not to fight the decision but to hold our hand and work for a new policy which explicitly re-emphasized the principles we stood for but which didn't reaffirm every detail of the defence paper.

At the beginning of our talk Sam said, 'For heaven's sake get it clear, Dick, you've got Gaitskell as your leader and nothing will change it, whatever you think of him.' To this I replied, 'Very well. In that case you have got to handle him, since I can't and he may listen to you.' Sam didn't dissent. He also told me that he had strongly disliked the end of Gaitskell's Conference speech and had no warning of it from Gaitskell before it was made. However, it had had an astonishingly good response among the Durham miners, who obviously respected Gaitskell's demagogic skill in doing it. We fenced around a good deal. Sam obviously doesn't know what to do on the International and is determined not to come down to London until the day of the meeting. So that leaves us down here to try and get a paper out with David Ennals.

I then strolled home to lunch. Home is now very empty because Nanny's mother is ill, Anne is staying in the country with the children and everything is being made slowly clean by dear Mrs Meek, now back with us at a great increase of wages, as I discovered when I paid her this week.

Thursday, October 27th
After lunch yesterday and the press conference at Transport House, I went after an interval into the Shadow Cabinet, where we were immediately presented with the text of a declaration that Hugh Gaitskell wanted to make on behalf of the dying Parliamentary Committee. At the last meeting I had been entirely aware of the difficulties presented. We had managed to see that there would be no resolution of any kind put to the Party, no defiance of Scarborough — whereat Hugh said he wanted to make a statement on our behalf, and, as the statement contained nothing I could possibly object to, it was difficult to object to it. I think I can see now that Harold and I should have made a row about it but if we had voted against it we would have been accused of being unilateralists and it would have taken five minutes to explain that we weren't.

Moreover, from the Executive's point of view, I was mainly concerned to rule out references to Scarborough or a resolution committing the Party before the talks. This we did achieve, since this statement merely expressed the opinion of the Shadow Cabinet and no consent to it was demanded by the Party. This formal separation of the Executive and the Parliamentary Committee is obviously of great importance to Hugh and he made it clearer than ever that he regards himself as the Leader of the Shadow Cabinet and merely as looking in on the Executive to make sure it doesn't do any harm.

All the lobbies were full of to-ings and fro-ings, with George Wigg running round organizing everybody. The party Meeting started at seven, with Gaitskell reading out the statement. He inserted at the beginning, 'As a result of the Scarborough decisions ... ', but otherwise left it unchanged.

But what he did omit was his reference to the fact that this was a statement of a dying Shadow Cabinet, which by no means bound the Party, and that the Executive discussions would take place with a new Shadow Cabinet, completely uncommitted. As a result, I could feel that the Left had been terribly upset by the unanimous declaration and, always eager to think of betrayal, began to think it of Harold and, I suppose, me.

After Hugh's brief statement he called Fred Peart, who made an odious anti-Left speech, and then there was a whole series of anti-Leftists — including Bill Blyton and Ted Short,[1] all standing for loyalty to the Leader and stating that, on this great fundamental issue, there can be no papering over cracks but there must be a fight to the death. In reply to these Hugh called William Warbey, Sydney Silverman and — well, I've forgotten the others. What I did notice, however, was that Lynn Ungoed-Thomas, Jennie Lee, Walter Padley and Tony Benn were all standing up during the two hours of the Meeting and not being seen. What Hugh called, in fact, was the extreme Left and the stalwarts, knocking out all Harold's supporters. It was a dirty, stormy, vulgar meeting, full of great moral principles and interspersed with personal innuendoes and, of course, with constant reminders that on no account must it be turned into a husting.

Poor old Harold, when he rose, spent about four minutes telling us he wasn't a unilateralist and added that he had helped George Brown draft the defence statement. It took my breath away and didn't do Harold much good. But when he at last got on to the subject of unity and the danger of tearing the Party apart and that what mattered was whether one's attitude to the problem was a divisive or a unifying one, he got a deep growl of approval. The fact is that all Harold can do is to corrode the fundamentalist crusading of Gaitskell with anxious doubts as to whether it is really sincere and whether it won't destroy the Party. There is, of course, no way in a great public meeting of discussing in a serious way the defence issues involved.

In terms of the actual meeting, it was clear that Gaitskell was going to get a triumph, even before he rose and made another 'Fight, fight, fight' appeal. Anyway, he had well over 100 people baying for him. Nevertheless, the Left is far more divided and scattered than the Right, and anyway the whole press and radio have been rooting for him and building things up for so long that he starts with an enormous advantage.

Finally, after Harold, Hugh called on George Brown, who performed one

---

[1] Edward Short, Labour M.P. for Newcastle-upon-Tyne Central 1951–7. A Whip 1955–1962, Deputy Chief Opposition Whip 1962–4 and Government Chief Whip 1964–6, he was Postmaster-General 1966–8, Secretary of State for Education and Science 1968–70, and Lord President and Leader of the House of Commons 1974–6. In 1977 he became a life peer, taking the title of Lord Glenamara, and in 1976 became Chairman of Cable and Wireless Ltd.

half of a pincer movement by dissociating himself from Harold and asserting that, though he had thought there was a compromise possible before Conference, he now saw it was completely impossible. I've never seen a neater movement of re-securing one's position on the bandwagon and at the same time neatly scuppering your other bandwagon rival, James Callaghan, who couldn't get a word in. Altogether the whole atmosphere was so redolent of the hustings that, sitting there on the platform for the first time, just behind Harold, and looking down on the sweaty faces below, I realized what elections must have looked like before 1832,[1] and that's about the value of the Parliamentary Party today.

Within a few minutes of getting out I realized that the Left were furious with Harold and me. People were now starting to say that there should have been a row at the Executive, which had been deliberately stopped by me, that Harold and I had sold out in the Shadow Cabinet and even, finally, that by refusing to come out for Harold I was wavering in my support.

Today's papers looked terrible but I agree with George Wigg that they've probably overdone it. There may well be a reaction against what was an outrageously fixed meeting. Just imagine one of the candidates being in the chair and selecting all the speakers! And that's the Labour Party. It is probably true that little damage has been done to Harold, though Jennie has issued a blistering attack. I still think we shall get our 80 votes and possibly 20 abstentions. This may be sufficient to box Hugh and prevent his going the whole hog and trying to force an expulsion of the Left.

Thursday, November 3rd

Well, it's just a week since I last wrote in this diary and, while we are awaiting the results of the poll, I may as well commit my guess in writing. I guess Harold will get 80 votes and Hugh 160, with 10 abstentions (I am told that 250 is the total available vote).[2] On the whole I get the impression that middle-of-the-road opinion, led by Eirene White, Ray Gunter and so on, has settled down to voting for Gaitskell, on the understanding that he should really make peace this year, and I wouldn't be too surprised if Harold got less than 80. But I am quite sure the whole operation has achieved its main purpose of providing a protest so formidable that it has to be taken notice of and, secondly, getting out into the open serious criticisms of Gaitskell's leadership.

I went to Prescote last Thursday and spent most of Friday in Birmingham. I became very clear at both my meetings there that what seems obvious in Westminster is by no means obvious outside. On the way down I had been thinking that, after Hugh's behaviour, I should make a statement myself — as M.P., of course, not as Chairman. These two meetings completely clinched this view, since most of these people seemed to feel vaguely that I must be

[1] When the first Reform Act widened the franchise.
[2] In the leadership election Hugh Gaitskell obtained 166 votes and Harold Wilson 81.

29

on Gaitskell's side and, at the end of the meetings, begged me to speak out. So on Saturday morning I roughed out the thing and dictated it to Rose, without seeing it typed. I had considered rather carefully and realized that Saturday midday is the ideal time to launch a statement if you want publicity, since you get it in the Saturday evening papers, the Sunday papers and the Monday papers, if it's any good.

That evening we had our harvest dinner and Mr Pritchett and all the men were agog, because they had seen me on the telly. The whole village felt that their boy was now in the fight some way or other, they weren't quite sure how. Pritchett, who never talks politics to me, said on Sunday, 'We're very interested because we naturally want our boss to get to the top of his own particular tree and our conclusion is that you're out for the leadership now. That's the only sense we can make of your actions. Clearly Wilson stands no chance in the long run and someone else will have to replace Gaitskell.' I said rather priggishly that I had no ambitions, to which Pritchett replied, 'Well, you ought to have, if you're serious at the job. You ought to want to do it.'

Meanwhile the Sunday press had certainly given the whole thing headlines. On the way to Manchester on Sunday night and down on Monday afternoon I began to have some qualms and second thoughts about whether it had really helped Harold to have the Chairman coming out in this way. Of course I've had an extraordinary protest from Sam Watson and a milder one from Eirene White but by and large I believe that what I did succeeded, in two ways.

First of all it undoubtedly helped Harold because, by sheer accident, the timing was perfect, coming on the tape just before the announcement that twenty of the T.U.C. were supporting Gaitskell and effectively countering it. By pushing the issue away from defence and on to Party unity, I had helped Harold. But, secondly, I had certainly helped myself in this extraordinary atmosphere of Labour politics. Though Nye didn't practise what he preached, he was right to tell me that it pays to attack and not to be mealy-mouthed. If I hadn't said it, all sorts of people would have accused me of secretly supporting Harold but without the courage of my convictions. And, although I might well have been behaving with perfect moderation, fairness and impartiality, I would have been suspected of facing both ways.

Now, curiously enough, even one's opponents give one credit for a good bash. Ray Gunter was very characteristic. He came up to me in the lobby with a broad grin on his face and said, very seriously, 'Dick, you shouldn't have done it. You've undermined your own position as Chairman and you'll make things more difficult for yourself. I've been preaching to all of them for the past three weeks that we could rely on you to be a real peace-maker and we've been relying on your coming in and saying what was necessary — not now, but months ahead.' I pointed out that there would never come a time when I could speak out, as Chairman. This contest was my one opportunity and as an M.P. I had the right to do it. 'Oh, I don't dispute your rights for a moment,' Ray said, 'especially the way the others are behaving. It's just that I wish you hadn't.' He said much the same to Harold about standing, yet it's perfectly clear to me that, by all coming out in this way, we've enabled people like Ray Gunter and Eirene White to say to Gaitskell much more strongly the warnings which they would only have whispered if we hadn't been opposed. Even George Wigg, who was fulminating last week about war to the death, said to me this week that he thinks that after the leadership election Gaitskell will be forced into a compromise.

Meanwhile it's certainly true that the atmosphere in the Parliamentary Party, which on our return was poisonous, has been cleared by having things out publicly. Nevertheless, the hatchet men are out. I went to a most characteristic meeting of the Shadow Cabinet last night. (By the way, I have much pleasure in always sitting on the backbenches in the House, which slightly baffles our frontbenchers, who don't know what I am at.) At this meeting we discussed forthcoming parliamentary business. There was a tiny amusing episode when we came to Friday's Queen's speech debate, of which the topic is to be foreign policy and defence. Noel-Baker, who is due to wind up, is ill. Hugh said he wanted somebody to take his place. Who on earth was available? Patrick Gordon Walker? Tom Fraser? 'I can't see any-body,' Hugh said. At this point Dick Mitchison blurted out, 'Why not Dick Crossman?' Hugh said hotly, 'With all respect, I think that's a lot to ask in the present state of the Party.' Curiously enough, he knew that he had misbehaved because, for the rest of the meeting, he had to treat me with quite unusual respect.

Tuesday, November 8th

Yesterday I went to the Bolton by-election[1] and in the evening I got Reg Wallis[2] to drive me back to Manchester. We had a long wrangle, at the end of which he agreed that the Party was being destroyed by the fighting and that a three-month self-denying ordinance would do good. Just as I was getting out to catch the train, I said, 'Well, there's no doubt Gaitskell's the best leader we've got at present,' to which, to my astonishment, Reg replied, 'You've said something very important. The best Leader we've got at present. The fact is that we haven't got an adequate Leader and that's that.'

Wednesday, November 23rd

If I ask myself what has happened since I last wrote in my diary, the answer is that it has rained! Indeed, it seems to have been raining all this autumn, or, to be more exact, it started raining when the harvest began. My own life has more and more shifted its centre of balance to Prescote, and this has

---

[1] The Bolton East by-election, caused by the appointment of Philip Bell, Conservative, as a county court judge, was to take place on November 16th. See below, p. 900.
[2] The Area Agent for the Labour Party.

been an interesting event, which has influenced my politics as well. Where you live matters terribly. Up to this summer we lived in London and had weekends in the country. As a result, we decided to spend several hundred pounds repairing our home in London and now we've finished we find we've only repaired our office.

What was the cause of the move? Undoubtedly, Nanny, the London girl who now gets a headache after half an hour in the foetid atmosphere of the metropolis. She has blossomed out, her hair is glossier, her eyes brighter – and all from having the Methodist chapel, sixteen children on the farm, in fact the community in the country, plus, to do her justice, the obvious truth that children in the country have a better life than in the town. However, at long last Anne is bringing them back to this house tomorrow where I've been camping at midweek and gazing out of my bath at our blue roses and the tiles which were meant for the children and are hardly suitable for a grown man.

Still, I must come back to politics, which in my case means the dreary and ever more dreary top-level row in the Labour Party. I suppose I can say that, purely personally, I have had good fortune, since in some strange way I am emerging as the patron saint of the constituency parties outside, who look up to their Chairman like sheep waiting to be fed and for whom I issue a fortnightly bleat on the subject of unity, no wrangling and peace, which is largely bromidic and which is yet regarded as the most deadly attack on Gaitskell. That, of course, has been the weakness of his position. It is awkward for a Leader that, when the Chairman of the Party says we shouldn't wrangle and should fight the Tories, this is interpreted as a bitter attack on the Party Leader! And even more irritating for him, no doubt, is that he knows that I know how funny all this is and how irritating it must be for him.

I have, by the way, also discovered that the way to get publicity is not to write a column twice a week in the *Mirror* but to make a speech once every five weeks at three o'clock on a Saturday afternoon, with a hand-out from Transport House in time to get the Saturday evening press, the Sunday press *and* the Monday Press. Mind you, it is important that your hand-out should be readable and here is where columnizing is so important. For I can now write a hand-out which is a little jewel of a column in the sense that it is nothing like a speech. It is undeliverable as a speech, because it begins with those two sentences which sum up the guts of the thing and then repeats it all over again in detail. Hence each paper can leave out the detail if it hasn't got space.

I did this, backing Harold Wilson, during the contest with Hugh, I did it again last Saturday after the Little General Election.[1] I attended three of the

---

[1] Seven by-elections were held on November 16th. In Bolton East, Edwin Taylor (Conservative) had a majority of 641 over R. L. Howarth (Labour). At Carshalton Captain Walter Elliott (Conservative) had a majority of 8,925 over Gordon Browne (Liberal); at

by-elections—my afternoon at Bolton, Mid-Bedfordshire and, finally, my eve-of-poll at Ebbw Vale, which was warm and memorable. Of course it was raining when I was there. It had rained, apparently, day and night throughout the whole campaign, but one basked in the sunshine of an old-fashioned Socialist campaign, with everybody happy and with one's driver saying, 'You know, Dick, we've been able to meet all the famous Socialists and hear them speak. Isn't it wonderful?' It's a tremendous tribute to Michael that, despite the Welsh resistance to foreigners, he managed to have this effect and it was excitement itself when the news was telephoned to me last Friday afternoon from Transport House. 'I've had three double whiskies to celebrate,' said Mollie Bell. And Arthur Bax is just the same: 'We'll have the Red Flag out for Michael at Transport House when he comes and I don't mind whether Hugh Gaitskell hears it or not.' So much for the neutrality of Transport House in the Party Conflict. They're all Crossmanites now and that means three-quarters of the way to being Footites too.

But I can't paint a very encouraging picture of the Left as one sees it from the inside. We are all still fragmented, at sixes and sevens, actuated by personal motives, without any coherent policy—because I don't regard a dislike of Gaitskell as a coherent policy. Even that dislike is shared in very varying degrees. Nevertheless, today's Executive, for which I have been waiting in grievous suspense for a fortnight, went off surprisingly well. I had had many preliminary discussions. All the old Bevanites were here on Monday night. I had long talks with Len on Tuesday morning. I had Harold and Harry Nicholas to lunch on Tuesday at the Athenaeum and in the afternoon I talked to Ray Gunter. Mostly I was concerned to try to get them to insist that the Executive is instructed by Conference and must go to the talks with the Parliamentary Party as the spokesman of Conference decisions, that we must try to curb Hugh's activities on the platform without overtly controlling the Leader etc. Once again I had completely failed to predict what would actually happen. We had agreed that Jennie should put the central idea forward when the right moment came. The moment came somewhat later than I had expected.

After one or two very amusing little rows we came to the big discussion. Jennie put her point very well and there was complete silence. No one wanted to speak. Then Charlie Evans said there could be no question about it. Our Executive was instructed by the Conference and we must go to the talks instructed by the Conference. Man after man followed this up. True, Alice

---

Ludlow, Jasper More (Conservative) had a majority of 5,650 over Dai Rees (Liberal); in the Mid-Bedfordshire constituency Stephen Hastings (Conservative) had a majority of 6,222 over Bryan Magee (Labour); at Petersfield Miss Joan Quennell (Conservative) had a majority of 7,303 over Lt Colonel Michael Digby (Liberal); and at Tiverton Robin Maxwell-Hyslop (Conservative) had a majority of 3,040 over James Collier (Liberal). At Carshalton, Ludlow, Petersfield and Tiverton the Labour candidates all came third. In the Ebbw Vale by-election on the same day, Michael Foot (Labour) had a majority of 16,729 over Sir Brandon Rhys-Williams (Conservative).

Bacon and Jim Callaghan made some kind of noises about two-thirds majorities, which took a long time, but George Brown was very careful to accept the trade union view and only to add, very sensibly, that, though we must enter the talks instructed, we were free, as the talks went on, to help evolve a new policy. In fact, we are captives of the Conference until we have a new policy. Now this is something I have known for months but it hadn't dawned on poor Gaitskell that, unless he got a new policy, the Executive would enter next year's Conference committed to last year's resolutions. Now that it has dawned on him, whether he likes it or not he will find himself committed to yet another dreary document, just like last year's.

So really there wasn't a great deal of sting in the discussion, particularly when Harold Wilson reminded George Brinham of his brilliant formulation at the International that the Executive were the 'custodians' of the Scarborough decision. How we love a good word! This word was as intoxicating today as 'the commanding heights of the economy' had been during our Clause 4 debate. We savoured it. We chewed it. And the more we chewed it, the better we liked it.

There was a ridiculous altercation about resolutions when Barbara wanted our representatives to 'advocate' the Scarborough resolutions and George Brinham moved that we should 'present' them. Once again Barbara insisted on a vote, which only meant a gratuitous victory for the other side. But then I suspect that her aim was to get defeated and leak the villainy of those who defeated her, a tactic which may please her but makes any kind of work on the Executive a bit difficult.

Of course the whole thing lasted an interminable time but Hugh's friends had at least persuaded him to stay quiet. The only time tempers rose at all was when Tony Greenwood made a resolution proposing that, wherever Hugh spoke on defence, there should be another Executive spokesman representing Scarborough. It was not difficult for Len Williams to defeat this on purely practical grounds and once again the Left had laid itself open to a gratuitous defeat. But in terms of Party unity, it wasn't a bad day and we are obviously moving towards what I had expected.

Thursday, December 8th
Today was the great day for the joint meeting of the N.E.C. and the Parliamentary Committee. I had been thinking about it for a long time but it is characteristic of our present plight that neither the Executive nor the Parliamentary Committee as such made any preparations. Yesterday afternoon I rang Len Williams and told him to go to the Shadow Cabinet and tell them that we assumed I should be in the chair, since it was our initiative, and that I would present our position as concisely as possible, in three main points. I suggested Len should say all this to Bert Bowden and try to get him to clear it with Hugh. This was the first action anybody on either side took to prepare, as I found out later.

Apparently Hugh refused to settle this and made Len put it all to the Shadow Cabinet, which then discussed it for an hour and a quarter – or rather, they discussed whether I should be chairman, Hugh saying it was impossible. All this infuriated not only Ray Gunter but even Jim Callaghan. I was giving the Meeks and Nanny a great dinner in the House and, as I came in, Ray and Len came out. Ray took me aside and said, 'You bloody Winchester boys! Have you heard what that bugger has been doing for the last hour and a half? He's digging his own grave, with all of us. What you've got to do is to capture the chair, capture it, and we'll back you to the hilt.' Of course the story was soon all round the lobby.

This morning I got up and prepared my speech very carefully. I arrived at ten to two in Committee Room 12. This has a dais where the chairman and officials usually are and below that two facing ranks of seats, one for the Government and the other for the Opposition. The seat where the Minister sits is at the end, by the dais, facing the Opposition spokesman on any Bill. It was the room where Boyd-Carpenter and I had faced each other for so many weeks. The Executive had occupied the Government seats and put me in the Minister's Seat, scoring the first point. The dais, of course, was empty. The second point was scored when Hugh Gaitskell arrived at one minute past ten and was forced to sit in the Opposition seat opposite me, to wave his hand and say, 'You start.' I not only started but took over the meeting, selecting the speakers, leading the discussion and making no comment when Hugh three times addressed me as 'Mr Chairman'. It was a great victory, for which I received handshakes all round. Almost as noteworthy was the fact that Callaghan, who came in late, ostentatiously sat on the Executive side, while Alice Bacon, though not a member of the Shadow Cabinet, sat behind Hugh.

I started extremely carefully, quoting the Party constitution, emphasizing our standing as custodians of Scarborough and that we must remain in that standing until we ourselves issued a new policy statement or the Conference changed its mind. Hugh had not prepared his reply, started by agreeing with me that we should not discuss the substance of the issue, and proceeded to do so at length for fourteen minutes, babbling on nuclear weapons. I had put three questions, stressing that we had come to listen to their suggestions before we made up our mind on our course of action, with particular relationship to our conduct during the deadlock, a possible *modus vivendi* and a possible new statement. As soon as Hugh had finished, I pointed out that he had not answered the questions, whereupon George Brown[1] leapt in and said there were four possible courses of action. First, to do nothing and let things take their course, with each side maintaining its views. Secondly, do nothing but seek to have the official policy reinstated intact at the next Conference. Thirdly, to seek to have a version, amended in relation to

---

[1] Who had been elected as Deputy Leader on November 10th, in preference to Fred Lee. Harold Wilson did not stand.

Scarborough, accepted. Fourthly, to have a new statement but absolutely brand-new.

Once George had said this, there was a great deal of support for the idea of a new statement. Tom Driberg talked about reconciliation, whereat Gaitskell intervened to say that the Shadow Cabinet had gone to the very limit of concession and there could be no question of its going any further. At this point Jennie Lee made a stalwart protest that the new statement should be made regardless of personal prestige and Tony Greenwood chipped in on intransigence.

George Brown firmly took over and said of course this was the kind of argument which was hopeless, but people were looking behind and not forward. He meant a really new statement, and that would require everybody to think afresh and be new. There were quite sensible interventions by Douglas Houghton about the timetable, after which Hugh Gaitskell moved his position and talked about a short new statement limited to principles. Denis Healey pointed out, rightly, that such a statement would not help in any way, since we have to have something which deals practically with the problems raised at Scarborough.

When I suggested we should come to an end, Hugh summed up his own views, reiterating that we could not make up our minds and that there was quite a lot to be said for doing nothing, since we were getting on quite well despite the so-called conflict, which had not had the untoward consequences people anticipated. He once again insisted that, if there was a new statement, it should only be a short statement of principle. I said I took what he said as representing his personal point of view and that we listened to it with interest, since we had come to hear their opinions before we made up our minds. It was agreed that we should then approach the T.U.C. straightaway.

It was also agreed that Hugh and I should have a press conference, which we did with the lobby, much to his advantage, since they are his boys. Once again he wasn't very skilful. Instead of asking me to tell them what happened, he did so himself, at quite inordinate length, once again with all his own views emphasized, so that, very mildly but firmly, I had to correct him point by point – or rather, put the Executive point of view, all done with deadly politeness, showing very clearly where the rifts were and also showing the two of us speaking on terms of complete equality.

As we walked home towards Transport House, Len Williams said to me, 'He's hopeless, you know, absolutely hopeless. He antagonizes everybody. You're difficult enough but at least you have some idea of what other people are thinking and when you're annoyed you do it on purpose.'

This afternoon, after the Publicity Committee, I saw George Brown, who said to me eagerly, 'Hugh's digging his own grave all right, isn't he? Absolutely impossible fellow. And I spend my time hearing long warnings from him that we shouldn't do this and we shouldn't trust anybody.'

Altogether from my point of view it was a very successful day. At my first direct confrontation with Hugh Gaitskell, I undoubtedly scored a victory on points, in the view of virtually everybody present, mainly because I represented my side to their satisfaction, whereas he seemed to be representing no one but himself. But it is also a significant victory for peace-making in the Party. No more talk of 'Fight, fight, fight'. No more rampaging public meetings. Once again Gaitskell is doing a backcrawl. As Len Williams said to me, 'He's obstinate as hell on the small points and surrenders on all the major issues, until he suddenly, at the last moment, hits back, as he did at Scarborough.'

One other incident worth noting was Tawney's[1] eightieth birthday. We had arranged a little N.E.C. party at the House for him on the Tuesday. Twenty-eight people could have turned up; eight did. Not Harold Wilson, not Barbara Castle. But, thank God, Eirene White, daughter of Tom Jones,[2] was there to help me. She, I think, was the only other person who had read a book of Tawney's. Dear Ray Gunter hadn't but was there. Nor had Alice Bacon. And Len Williams boasted that he hadn't. But they also admitted that Tawney's our greatest Socialist fighter. But why bother about reading books? Hugh Gaitskell came in forty minutes late. I had received Tawney outside and he had said, as people always do, 'Of course, you don't want a speech from me?' And I had said, 'No, but I'll say a few words to toast you and then you'll say a few words back.' I couldn't, of course, make a speech to eight people but I said a few words to toast him and then the dear old man said, 'Now do I say my piece?', to which Gaitskell replied, condescendingly and kindly, 'Oh no, no speeches here!' and Tawney was denied the words he would have liked to say to us and we were denied hearing them.

In the course of a speech on November 1st the Prime Minister had told the Commons that a floating base for the American Polaris missile-firing submarines was to be established in Holy Loch, a small inlet off Firth of Clyde, twenty-five miles below Glasgow. The first Polaris was expected to arrive in March 1961. Mr Gaitskell preferred not to move an Amendment condemning the proposal and, as the Speaker indicated that he was unable to accept Amendments to the Address from Members other than the accredited leaders of

---

[1] R. H. Tawney (1880–1962), the Socialist historian, whose thinking deeply influenced the Labour movement. He was Professor of Economic History at the University of London 1931–49 and from 1949 Professor Emeritus. His works include *Religion and the Rise of Capitalism* (London: Murray, 1926), *Equality* (London: Allen & Unwin, 1931) and *The Radical Tradition* (edited by R. Hinden and published posthumously, London: Allen & Unwin, 1964).

[2] Thomas Jones (1870–1955), a Special Investigator for the Poor Law Commission 1906–9, Professor in Economics at Queen's University, Belfast, 1909–10, Secretary of the Welsh National Campaign Against Tuberculosis 1910–11 and of the National Health Insurance Commissioners (Wales) 1912–16, and a member of the Unemployment Assistance Board 1934–40. A friend and confidant of Lloyd George, he became Deputy Secretary to the Cabinet and Secretary to the Economic Advisory Council. His *Whitehall Diary*, covering the years 1916–29, was edited in three volumes by Keith Middlemas and was published by Oxford University Press in 1969 and 1970.

parties, no Amendment was proposed. The division in the Labour Party was
exposed once more in the defence debate on December 13th.

Wednesday, December 14th

Quite suddenly politics has become dramatic and exciting again, at least for
me. For some weeks I have been looking forward to a visit to Rome, to do
some interviewing, and I had decided to fly yesterday afternoon, until I heard
that the big defence debate was that day. It was clear from the first that there
could be no question of not abstaining in this three-line whip, since I realized
it was bound to re-create the crisis of last February in a new form. I doubt
whether anybody will disentangle the to-ing and fro-ing which preceded it.
As long ago as when I was on the Shadow Cabinet, the issue of a debate on
Polaris was raised and when we were leaving my last Shadow Cabinet
George Brown said to me, 'No, no, there can be no question of a resolution.
We will see that the debate takes place on the Adjournment, since anything
else would merely advertise our divisions and make them worse.'[1]

But since then a lot has happened and, in particular, Gaitskell and his
friends had got the impression, for which there was some support in fact,
that they were getting away with things very easily in the Parliamentary
Party and that no very formidable opposition was being manifested to their
campaign for reversing Scarborough or writing a new statement that was
tantamount to reversal. Nevertheless, they were obviously in two minds, or
at least there were two pressures, as was made clear enough in our joint
meeting last Thursday.

That meeting had been preceded on Monday by a joint meeting of the
defence and foreign affairs groups, which had been all sweetness and light
and about which there is now a great deal of controversy. George Brown put
a very moderate point of view and gave the impression that, having heard the
views of his colleagues, he would go to the Shadow Cabinet on Tuesday with
a resolution which would hurt nobody. It now transpires that a resolution,
prepared in the previous week, was in his pocket when he was saying this.
When he was attacked with this this morning, he did not deny it. As for
George's going to the Shadow Cabinet, no meeting took place on the Tuesday,
so that, when the Party met on the Wednesday morning and the resolution
was read out, it was the first that either Harold Wilson, or I for that matter,
had heard of it. That meeting also went very quietly, largely because Hugh
refused to call either Barbara, Michael or myself, though we stood up throughout the meeting.

As a result, Hugh got the impression that there was no serious opposition
to the Amendment. Its text was harmless enough, apart from the concluding

---

[1] On December 13th George Brown moved a motion of censure, asserting 'the para-
mount need for multilateral disarmament'. Sydney Silverman and Emrys Hughes moved
Amendments supporting the unilateralist position. George Brown's motion was defeated
by 318 votes to 163.

clause, which I had questioned at the meeting in an interruption of Hugh's speech and got short shrift for my suggestion that it should be rephrased to regret the Government's Polaris agreement. Certainly only twelve people did raise their hands against it. Why? I really don't know. But by the weekend I myself was perfectly clear that there would be grave trouble when it came to a public debate and public testing of Members in the lobby — a very different thing from voting secretly in the Party Meeting. Scots and Welsh Members, in particular, are under tremendous pressure not to approve Polaris and, if they had voted for the Amendment, that is just what they would have done.

Since Saturday happened to be our Coventry East annual dinner, at which Michael was the guest of honour, I decided to make a speech, with a press release. Most of it was devoted to an account of our 'hit back' campaign, to be launched in January, and a discussion of the role of youth in that campaign. Only at the end did I insert a couple of paragraphs on the chances of reaching agreement, in the course of which I expressed my disappointment at the official motion and suggested there should be no public disagreements of this kind while unity talks were proceeding. Once again my device of a press release on Saturday afternoon worked. I have no doubt that everybody in the Parliamentary Party knew that I had made a speech and that all the Gaitskellites were furious and all the anti-Gaitskellites jubilant.

The dinner, by the way, was a great success. I made my speech, as planned, and Michael then spoke, I thought a little monotonously and extremely intransigently. On the way to Coventry I had Michael to myself for forty minutes and discussed our tactics. I told him I wasn't going to draft a compromise document for Gaitskell this time and could give as excuse for not doing so the fact that I am Chairman. On the other hand, I was anxious to get out a document of the kind which we could say afterwards could have united the Party if Hugh had agreed it. I wanted to do this with two or three other people in close confidence, including Michael and George. Michael greatly liked the idea and I got the impression from him that his commitment to C.N.D. is a bit of an embarrassment, since he really knows in his heart of hearts that the Party can't be a completely unilateralist Party.

On Tuesday the chaps came to the first of our new regular lunches and it was like old times. Everything was pretty sensible. Harold couldn't be there and Michael was suddenly away because his father had died.[1] On Tuesday afternoon, when I had finally decided to go to Rome the following day, I had a message not to come as my interviews had been cancelled. In the afternoon I had to go to the Org. Sub. for over two hours, from four o'clock till quarter past six, so I missed George Brown's and Michael Foot's speeches. I got into the Chamber to find the debate very well attended, but incredibly dim. The impression given me, particularly by Patricia Llewelyn-Davies, who was in

---

[1] Isaac Foot (1880–1960), Liberal M.P. for the Bodmin division of Cornwall 1922–4 and 1929–35. He was Secretary for Mines 1931–2. He had seven children, among whom were John, Dingle, Hugh and Michael Foot.

the Gallery, was that Michael had started well but had become diffuse and a little vague. However he had certainly been pretty self-controlled, though he had made it clear that abstention was required by anybody who respected the Scarborough decision.

I took Pat for a short dinner at a quarter to seven and we got back in time to hear Tony Greenwood make what I thought was a first-rate speech, which was scandalously neglected in this morning's press, in comparison with Michael. Then there was a knockabout by Manny which ended disastrously. The whole atmosphere of the debate was very curious, since there was no issue and certainly no issue between the two Front Benches. Gaitskell, remembering last year, took the greatest care not to debate with his own side. In the new circumstances, this didn't make any sense, since the motion had been put down in a debate with his own side and no one could make it a motion of censure on the Government. However, he got through his speech without any great disasters and was followed by Ted Heath, previously the Tory Chief Whip, now a most bromidic kind of junior Foreign Secretary,[1] who burbled along.

It was quite clear that the tactic of both Front Benches was to play it soft and spongy and so to avert a crisis. Right through, George Wigg had been unwilling to prophesy what abstention we should get and I had been telling him it would be far bigger than anybody guessed. So we came to the critical moment and, sure enough, there were four solid benches of abstentionists, with me sitting in my commanding position on the gangway, not having said a word in the whole debate — not, indeed, having spoken since we came back last summer — but obviously in control of the proceedings of the abstentionists and particularly infuriating the others.

When the result was announced — 163 votes for the official Opposition Amendment — you could hear the crack of doom.[2] I have never really heard it before. It's a really ear-splitting moment of silence — and then life goes on again. How exhilarating such moments are, when for the moment one forgets the consequences in the pleasure of victory. We had brought it off.

[1] Edward Heath, Conservative M.P. for Bexley 1950–74 and for the Bexley division of Sidcup since 1974. From February 1951 to October 1959 he served in the Whips' Office, becoming Government Chief Whip in December 1955. He was Minister of Labour 1959–60 and Lord Privy Seal with Foreign Office responsibilities (which included the direction of the British attempt to join the E.E.C.) 1960–3 and was Secretary of State for Industry, Trade and Regional Development 1963–4. Elected Leader of the Conservative Party in 1965, he led the Opposition until 1970, when he became Prime Minister. He was Leader of the Opposition from 1974 to 1975, when the Conservatives elected a new Leader and he returned to the backbenches. He is National President of the European Community Youth Orchestra. His works include *Sailing* (London: Sidgwick & Jackson, 1975), *Music* (London: Sidgwick & Jackson, 1976) and *Travels* (London: Sidgwick & Jackson, 1977).

[2] The Opposition motion was defeated by 318 votes to 163. Five Liberal M.P.s and some 68 Labour Members abstained, among them Anthony Greenwood, Emanuel Shinwell, Michael Foot, Barbara Castle, Sydney Silverman and Crossman himself, the Party Chairman.

Afterwards I went up to have a talk with Harold, who was obviously highly uncomfortable, poor man. Here, after all, is the alternative Leader to Mr Gaitskell, but one who has simply disappeared into obscurity. I have been seeing Harold fairly often and throughout this crisis he has always managed to be absent from the Shadow Cabinet when the decisions were taken. When I asked his advice, he had strongly advised me to go to Rome and stay away, so as to remain arbitrator and conciliator-in-chief. However, we were friendly enough, discussing what should be done in the new situation, though I have an uncomfortable feeling that he feels my shadow.

As a result of not going to Rome, I quite unexpectedly found myself able to attend this morning's Party Meeting. What accidents there are in politics! I strolled along and on the way thought over a short speech I could make. I had got my mind a little clearer when I sat down. The Right was there in full force, sombre and vengeful. Ernest Popplewell, the old Deputy Chief Whip who led the attack on me about my famous trade union article and is one of the most personally unpleasant men in the House, rose with a long and carefully prepared brief in his hand. He soon pointed out that this was not merely an issue of personal abuse. Even worse were the kind of speeches attacking the parliamentary leadership which the Chairman of the Party had been making week after week. At this there was one of those sullen deep-throated roars of applause of which our trade union group is uniquely capable. Ernest was speaking for the whole mob. He then accused me of raising the issue of Clause 4, although in the past I had never been keen on nationalization, and accused me of something even worse, telling the parliamentary leadership last Saturday not to rock the boat.[1] I told him to quote in full what I had said and he said he hadn't got it there. He went on to attack more and more people and even our Party began to realize that, in a debate on stopping personal abuse, his was a strange speech, although he pointed out that he made his personal attacks in the privacy of the Parliamentary Party Meeting, whereas we did it as highly paid journalists in the press and on television.

I at once rose to reply. Hugh Gaitskell called Dick Marsh,[2] who made a not very effective speech, lashing at anonymous journalists and people hating each other, but evading the central issue. And then, because Hugh couldn't stop it, I had my go. I shall no doubt read in tomorrow's press what I actually said. All I know is that I forgot myself, plunged into it and said that I agreed with Ernest Popplewell, that he had every right to attack me and

---

[1] In his speech at the Coventry East dinner.

[2] Richard Marsh, Labour M.P. for Greenwich 1959–April 1971. He was Parliamentary Secretary at the Ministry of Labour 1964–5, Joint Parliamentary Secretary at the Ministry of Technology 1965–6, Minister of Power 1966–8 and Minister of Transport 1968–9. From 1971 to 1976 he was Chairman of British Rail. In 1976 he was knighted. He became Chairman of the Newspaper Publishers' Association in 1976 and of the Iron and Steel Consumers' Council in 1977. He wrote an autobiography, *Off The Rails* (London: Weidenfeld & Nicolson, 1978).

that the issue was not personal abuse but the conflict in the Party, in which I was on one side and he on the other.

I said that nothing anybody else had said had done more than a tiny particle of the damage of Hugh's 'Fight, fight, fight' at Scarborough. That was the beginning of the whole catastrophe and Hugh had followed it by making an unheard-of claim that, as an *ex officio* member of the Executive he was relieved of collective responsibility for the Scarborough decisions. I said he was leading the Parliamentary Party into headlong collision with the Party outside, which those of us elected by the constituencies had the honour to represent. I said that it was this collision, started entirely by the parliamentary leadership, which was the cause of all evil. I had been challenged on my right to criticize the decision to put down an amendment but, as Chairman of the N.E.C., I had a duty to those who had voted for me and in my view it was reckless, irresponsible and provocative to put down an amendment when the unity talks were proceeding. I said this could only be ended by an agreed solution, in which everybody would have to make sacrifices, and the kind of intransigence exhibited last summer would have to stop.

In fact, I said a packet and I am told by those who watched Gaitskell's face that he looked groggy under it. I was so excited that, although I was constantly interrupted with demands that I should give way, I waved them all down. Thank God I did, because, for the first time in my fifteen years in the Party Meeting, I got across what I had to say. It was, of course, the first occasion on which there has been a direct challenge to Gaitskell on the constitutional issue. The drama was that it took the form of a confrontation between the Chairman of the Parliamentary Party and the Chairman of the N.E.C.

I was followed by Mayhew, who attacked me for joining in intrigues to get rid of Gaitskell and said that as Chairman of the Party I had failed in my trust and not played the role of conciliator. Then Gaitskell rose to reply to the debate. In a sanctimonious voice he said that, when he had used the words 'Fight, fight, fight', he had meant, 'Fight for the Party we all love.' He raised one or two issues with me, very mildly indeed and in no way challenging my right to say what I had said. There was one of those awful wrangles, with people interrupting him, especially Manny Shinwell, and he wound up completely ineffectively. He was knocked groggy when the vote was taken.[1]

Outside I found everybody — no, by no means everybody! — shaking my hand and went and had a drink in the Smoking Room before lunching with Manny, who, for the first time in his life, was really civil to me. Then, to cool my temper, I went off with John Mackie to a lecture by the greatest grass

[1] The whip could not be withdrawn from the large number of M.P.s who had abstained in the previous day's division. It was reported that by 114 votes to 2 the Party Meeting passed a resolution condemning personal attacks and affirming the P.L.P.'s right to deal with them. There were some 6 abstentions.

expert in the world, which was absolutely fascinating and which I must discuss at length with Mr Pritchett.

I went back to the House and wandered round the lobbies, picking up gossip. Of course the whole press has the speech and not one journalist has rung me or asked me what I said, because apparently they know it already. Perhaps the most interesting comment was from Frank Barlow, our senior paid official. He took me into his room. 'Well, Dick,' he said, 'I thought I heard half a dozen more nails hammered into the coffin this morning. I'm not blaming you but I've known for years the problem is leadership. We haven't a leadership in this Party now.' I replied with Butler's *mot* that he's the best Leader we have[1] and Frank said, 'Exactly.' It was clear he wouldn't possibly challenge the position I had adopted, nor did he want to do so. He just didn't see what was to happen next. That was the view of one or two other people. This would make an agreement more unlikely, they said sadly. But on that I am sure they are wrong. The only chance of making Gaitskell agree is to squeeze him so tight that he is compelled to do so. Any sign of weakness, any trace of conciliation, will be exploited by him to try and get his way.

So there it is. I have now emerged as one of the most powerful figures in the Party, using my position as Chairman to be the first man with an open and unchallengeably justifiable challenge to Hugh Gaitskell. But let's see what tomorrow's papers say.

Monday, December 19th
The Party Meeting was still front-page news on Thursday. It was obvious from *The Times* and the *Guardian*, in particular, that the press had been briefed by the Chief Whip or someone near him. I had actually gone to Frank Barlow and asked that John Harris, who is supposed to be the Parliamentary Party press officer and actually is P.R.O. to Gaitskell, should give me a fair deal. Frank said, 'But he's not supposed to tell anyone anything about Party Meetings and I'll make sure he doesn't this time.' I'm sure Frank was as good as his word but the only visible result next morning was that the *Daily Mail*, which is usually extremely well-informed about Party Meetings, didn't print a single word.

I went into the House that evening for the normal Thursday Party Meeting, which was doleful in the extreme. It was as though people were recovering from a heavy cannonade. Looking at it now, I can see that a large section of the Party did not realize what had hit them until after I spoke on Wednesday. Up till that time they had managed to convince themselves that Gaitskell would see them through and that it was safe enough to shout that they wouldn't be dictated to by the Conference and that M.P.s must make up

[1] In an interview at London Airport in December 1955 a Press Association reporter asked R. A. Butler if he 'would say that this is the best Prime Minister we have?' R. A. Butler: 'Yes.'

their own minds. After Wednesday they had begun to realize that this just won't work, that Gaitskell may not be able to persuade the Conference, that, in defying Conference, they will be defying their own constituency parties and that anyway it's uncomfortable to be defying Conference decisions. Of course, they dislike me intensely for usurping, as they feel I have done, the status of custodian of the Party spirit, and they think that what I am really after is the leadership. There's no doubt that, by the end of last week, I had suddenly been jumped up to the status of a contender.

On Friday, Harold Davies's Polaris motion was moved.[1] I had heard that George Brown was making a speech that night, inquesting on the debate, and thought this justified another round from me on Saturday afternoon. Having finished my press release, I sent it round to Transport House. I went into the Chamber, where the debate was quite vigorous, and heard Reg Prentice, one of the earnest right-wingers, saying, 'To vote for this motion is to vote against any kind of defence.' I came back from lunch just in time to hear Reggie Paget make his first Front Bench appearance and, in an unguarded moment, express enthusiasm for Polaris as the ideal weapon and his grudge that the Americans wouldn't let us have enough of them. After him the debate petered out and, since the closure was not refused by the Tories, a vote was taken. I was so angry with Reggie that I changed my mind and voted for the motion, when I had intended to abstain. In a way I ought not to have done this if I want to be impeccable as Chairman but Reggie's outrageous speech had provided a beautiful cover, and anyway the motion was perfectly in accord with Scarborough, so it came out all right.

After I had voted, Ray Gunter caught me and asked me to come and have a drink. I said I had to go back for my birthday tea with my family but Ray held me in the lobby like the Ancient Mariner. He started by saying he had better warn me that he was going to make an all-out attack on me on Wednesday for my abuse of the chairmanship. I said that would give me an opportunity for raising the issue of how members of the Executive, who pledge themselves to be custodians of Scarborough, could, as members of the Shadow Cabinet, put up a motion in defiance of it and blame those of us who abstain. 'You're being too literal-minded,' Ray said. 'We expected you to be neutral and retiring and then in due course you would have had Gaitskell where you wanted him and you would have had us with you in enforcing our terms upon him.'

I told Ray this was all a myth and that, if he had had his way and I had done nothing, Gaitskell would have imposed his will on the Executive without resistance. I explained that every word I had spoken had been based on two principles: first, upholding the authority of the Conference and accepting its decisions as instructions, and, secondly, pleading that we should not be intransigent in this custodianship of Scarborough but be ready to meet others in a reasonable spirit of reconciliation. 'And how,' I asked, 'can you tell me that, in doing this, I am not discharging my functions as Chairman?

[1] This motion, debated on Friday, December 16th, was defeated by 164 votes to 46.

You ask me to be neutral but no custodian can be neutral when what he is guarding is attacked, even if the attacker is the Party Leader.'

Poor old Gunter heard all this with dismay and said to me, 'The trouble about you is that you've no sense of timing. I agreed with 99 per cent of what you said to Gaitskell last Wednesday but you said it at the wrong time and anyway discredited it by signing your name to Foot's motion on defence.'[1] 'It's not Foot's motion,' I said, 'it was George Wigg's and mine, and I signed it because it was both compatible with Party policy and with Scarborough and indicated a way to unification. Of course, if you think anything Michael Foot can sign must be wrong, you're showing a spirit of intransigence, which is completely at variance with your responsibilities as a member of the N.E.C. Anyway, I'm delighted you should raise all this issue on the N.E.C., since I can repeat there the speech I made to the Party Meeting and I hope it goes down as well.' 'Oh Dick,' Ray said, 'you're a terrible fellow. I don't know what to do with you.' Poor Mr Gunter. He's a great watery slob, who drinks a bit too much and whose statesmanship consists of being two-faced and backing the winning side. However, we parted in the firm conviction that we were two disinterested men, with no ambitions whatsoever, and I went back to have my fifty-third birthday tea at Vincent Square, before Patrick took Nanny back to the country, where they now belong, on Saturday.

Though I talked quite jovially to Ray Gunter, I was a bit shaken by it, since I really hate rows. I reconsidered my press release, a rethinking which was first encouraged by Arthur Bax's refusal to put it out, so as to keep out of the controversy. However, one glance at George Brown's speech in the Saturday morning papers showed that I was lucky again and had been justified in another piece of high-minded unity lecturing.[2]

Wednesday, December 21st
Well, the Executive is just over and, from the point of view of the Chairman, it was quite a meeting. Last night I had run into Gunter again in the House and he had been his usual convivial two-faced self, but slightly more withdrawn. I had also had it confirmed by Len Williams that they were likely to raise my record as Chairman but he wouldn't define who 'they' were.

This morning trouble started when we came to the report of our conversations with the Parliamentary Committee. I said we should postpone it until we heard from the T.U.C., who were then in session, and George Brown said very innocently that he had two little points to raise. The first was a leak in

---

[1] The amendment to the official Opposition motion, on December 13th.

[2] In a speech at Wandsworth South-West on the evening of December 16th, Mr Brown had referred to the Labour Members who had abstained from the division on the Opposition motion on defence, debated on December 13th. He said he hoped the rank and file in the Party and the unions would make their disapproval known 'to those who, by their refusal to work with their colleagues, turned what should have been a demonstration against the Government on issues we all care deeply about into such a sad display of Party disunity'. Crossman himself issued a press release before his speech at Matlock, on Saturday, December 17th.

a Liverpool paper, which he blatantly but not directly attributed to Harold Wilson, and the second, to my great surprise, was my speech at Matlock last weekend, or rather a *Sunday Times* version of it, which I had noticed with some mild annoyance, since, where I had written 'conflict between two constituency bodies', they had rewritten it 'conflict between the Shadow Cabinet and the N.E.C.'. I said mildly that it was a pity George hadn't mentioned this to me before, since I could have cleared up the confusion. Hugh intervened very quietly to say that it was a little bad luck that he should have 'Fight, fight, fight' tagged on to him like that when he had already declared that he was 'Fight, fight, fighting' for the Party. At this Bessie Braddock chipped in and said she had the speech before her and it was an outrage how Hugh had been maligned now one saw the text for it. It should be reprinted, so that everybody could see.

The storm had very nearly passed, but it was suddenly blown up when Mr Ray Gunter said that, unlike George Brown, he had mentioned the thing to me before. He proceeded to make a great, carefully prepared oration, ending, to my great surprise, with the phrase, 'No, Dick, you can't ride two horses.' I said we were getting somewhat wide of the subject but, since it was about me, I would give them the benefit of the doubt for a moment or two. Eirene White, I think, said that she found what I was saying very difficult to swallow and James Callaghan made a nice, sour-sweet speech in a semi-affectionate tone, ending that I had no right to claim that the Chairman was in any special sense custodian of the Conference.

I said we must now stop. What had so far been said would of course be leaked without any adequate reply from me and, if another word was said, I would insist on the subject's being down on the agenda for the next meeting, in which case I would circulate the document and make a long and reasoned statement. All I would say now was that nothing I had said and nothing I had done had been anything but carefully considered and I would not excuse anything as thoughtlessness. Indeed, I would not apologize for anything and would, on reflection, do it again, since I had been acting strictly in my capacity as a member of the N.E.C., responsible for carrying out Party decisions. There was then a bit more discussion but not much. It was agreed that Harold's leak should be referred to the usual Leak Committee and meanwhile Hugh Gaitskell proposed that we should not discuss the talks while they were still on. James Callaghan said, 'Yes, the Chairman shouldn't,' and I said, 'No, every member of the Executive is bound by this, Hugh, isn't he?' And Hugh said, 'Yes, but only the talks. We must be free to defend ourselves.' I said, 'Certainly.'

We passed to ordinary business. Towards the end of the meeting a message came through from the T.U.C. They had changed the recommendation of the International, which was that the two Internationals should meet. Instead, they recommend that there should be a tripartite meeting between the full General Council, the full Parliamentary Committee and the full National

Executive. I said I hoped we could find an adequate hall to hire and asked
whether anybody had any suggestions to make about procedure. Gaitskell
was ruffled. 'Oh no,' he said, 'we can't discuss that now.' I said, 'What, then,
are we going to talk about?' And he said, 'We know we want a new statement but we mustn't go to the Conference as though we have made up our
mind. In this first talk with them we must leave things open.' So the snail
procedure continues and they're going to run out of time.

After the meeting I went downstairs with Callaghan, who, when I pressed
him on majority decisions, said that he agreed it was a difficult question for
him now but it is only when defence is at stake that one is justified in defying
majority decisions. These are such grave issues that one's conscience must
prevail and he would fight Gaitskell or anybody else who tried to work out a
mere verbal compromise that sacrificed the principle of multilateralism. He is
now in pretty violent mood.

1961

From January 7th to 22nd Crossman was in the United States, where on November 9th Richard Nixon had conceded the presidential victory to John Kennedy. Mr Kennedy's majority in the popular vote was very small: 34,221,531 votes to Mr Nixon's 34,108,474. In the electoral college, however, Mr Kennedy secured 303 votes and Mr Nixon 219. In the Congress the Democrats lost seats. They had 262 in the House of Representatives, compared with 283 before, while the Republicans gained 174, compared with 154 before. In the Senate the Democrats lost 1 seat, giving them 65, and there were now 35 Republicans. (One seat was in doubt.)

Among the problems which awaited the new President's attention was a domestic economic crisis. The United States had become particularly concerned at the drain on its gold reserves; by the end of the year they had declined by $17,837 million: Foreign affairs were also worrying, especially the activities in Cuba of Dr Fidel Castro, who had by October nationalized virtually all American property and assets in the island. On October 28th the United States formally accused the Soviet bloc of secretly sending thousands of tons of new arms to Dr Castro and on November 1st President Eisenhower reaffirmed that the U.S. held its Guantanamo base in Cuba under treaty rights and 'would take whatever steps may be appropriate to defend that base'. On January 3rd, 1961, the American Government severed diplomatic relations with Cuba.

President Kennedy's inauguration took place on January 20th. He had invited to join his Administration a number of 'intellectuals', many of them friends or acquaintances of Crossman, who wrote from Cambridge, Massachusetts, on January 8th, 'Everything was agog with excitement about moving to Washington. The tents were being packed as Cambridge moved in.' Crossman conducted several interviews and broadcasts and devoted a morning to investigating actual and potential sales of the Sulgrave honey produced by his neighbour at Cropredy, Major Donner.

Friday, January 27th

I got back on Monday morning and was home by ten o'clock. In the afternoon I tottered up to Barbara's, where the gang had agreed to meet to discuss our long-term parliamentary policy. We agreed to have, every Thursday, in addition to our Tuesday lunches, a four o'clock meeting of an informal non-Group, which would somehow keep contact with people and get things going. The first meeting duly took place yesterday and was quite successful, since George Wigg agreed to be chief of staff.

Meanwhile Parliament has started again at its old clogged pace. I was in the Tea Room yesterday when Frank Tomney, who is one of my main haters, remarked sardonically, 'So there goes our Chairman, after five years of wrecking the Party.' I got into some kind of conversation with him, George Jeger[1]

---

[1] Labour M.P. for the Winchester division of Hampshire 1945–50 and for the Goole division of the West Riding of Yorkshire from 1950 until his death in 1971. He had been Mayor of Shoreditch 1937–8 and was a member of Shoreditch Borough Council 1926–40.

and George Deer[1] and gradually, within forty minutes, they were sitting round questioning me anxiously about the prospects of reaching agreement among the Twelve.[2] What they revealed was an intense anger that I should have misbehaved as Chairman by openly supporting Harold and attacking Hugh. But they also revealed no kind of enthusiasm for Hugh and a frank recognition that the place from which most of the poison enters the Party is the Parliamentary Party.

On Tuesday we had our mass meeting at Congress House. I got there in good time, to find that special seating arrangements had been made for the eighty-six people due to attend. I think I counted sixty-eight there. It had been arranged to have Ted Hill as chairman, with Gaitskell next to him, Len Williams next to him and me beyond, with George Woodcock on the other side, pushing the Chairman of the Labour Party as far from the centre as possible. I changed places with Len, thus sitting next to Gaitskell.

Ted started by reading aloud incoherently a typed statement. Bill Webber, obviously on a pre-concerted plan, said, 'We'll now hear the Party Leader,' and Hugh addressed us for twenty-five minutes. To my great surprise, he at once launched into a proposal for the content of a new joint statement. This was a little boring but all he did was to repeat last year's official policy, point by point, every now and then assuring us that what we needed was to cut out the details and have a short statement of principle.

When Hugh had finished, Ted Hill said he suggested there should now speak a member of the General Council, so that each side would speak alternately. At this, Jennie said that it might be a good idea if the Chairman of the N.E.C. spoke. I found myself in some difficulty, since I wasn't prepared to comment on the content of Hugh's speech but, on the other hand, I didn't feel like pretending that it wasn't my own policy. However, I managed to outline the four alternatives and to emphasize the need for speed. Then we had a wrangling, random oration from Frank Cousins, who, however, was careful to deny that he was against NATO or against the West's having nuclear weapons, two of the chief points which the multilateralists have been making against the unilateralists.

The debate lasted about two hours. In my view the most noteworthy feature was a longish speech by George Brown, which, though it purported to support Gaitskell, was in fact a strong indication that we could get agreement once again with Cousins, after his two denials. We also had a speech from Callaghan, blustering about how we must stand up against the unilateralist sob-sisters and not give way an inch. Then suddenly Alfred Roberts got up and proposed a committee of twelve, obviously pre-agreed. It looks as though Gaitskell had got all this carefully worked out with the General

---

[1] George Deer (1890–1974), Labour M.P. for Lincoln 1945–50 and for the Newark division of Nottinghamshire from 1950 until his death.
[2] The representatives of the T.U.C., the N.E.C. and the Parliamentary Committee.

Council. When I said rather impatiently, after half an hour during which nothing but opponents had spoken, that I wondered how long we should let this go on, Gaitskell whispered to me loudly, 'Oh, we shall carry on for an hour and a half but it's in the bag by 27 to 9. The General Council has decided to draft a statement with us, whatever happens.'

When the figure of twelve had been fixed — four from each body — I asked Gaitskell who he thought we should have. He readily replied, 'Chairman, Vice-Chairman, Chairman of International Sub. (Sam Watson) and Chairman of Defence Sub. (Brinham).' I said I thought the Defence Sub. had lapsed over six months ago and he said, 'Well then, let's have Brinham. He's a good chap.' I said I thought it was important to have a balanced team, which showed some respect for the Scarborough decisions. At this Gaitskell bristled and walked off. So I immediately saw George Brown, who at once saw the point.

Next day, Wednesday, was the N.E.C. — as usual a detestable atmosphere. Indeed, though not as unpleasant for me, it was worse than last time, since nobody wanted to discuss any major issues and the only items of interest were personal scores. When we came to the job of selecting our four, Alice Bacon at once suggested the four Hugh had named the previous day. I said, 'I'm afraid the Chairman can't be assumed to be a member unless it were a reasonably well-balanced team.' This aroused great fury from Callaghan, Bacon, etc., with Callaghan shouting, 'Are you impugning my good faith?' I said no, but I just wanted to say that I would not be a member unless all points of view were fairly represented, at least that of the Scarborough decision. Gaitskell said, 'But you're not being selected for yourself but as Chairman.' I replied, 'Could I be reassured by the Executive that it would be purely as Chairman, i.e. as a person with no personal views at all and bound by Scarborough?' This didn't go down very well. But I had made my point and both Walter Padley and George Brown said they thought it was essential to have somebody who believed in Scarborough.

After some discussion they voted me and Sam Watson unanimously, but agreement couldn't be reached on the other two. Someone then suggested that we should simply have the Chairman, the Vice-Chairman, the Treasurer and the Chairman of the International, to which Hugh Gaitskell said he couldn't permit such an unfair weighting against him. 'Unfair?' I said. 'But you've got three multilateralists to one!' 'Well,' said Hugh, 'you may be a multilateralist but you and Harold have wide differences from me and I couldn't accept you as being on my side, with the best will in the world.'

So the wrangle went on until we got into a ballot with seven names proposed — and the rest was in the papers. All, that is, except for one very comic item. The score announced was: Padley 11, Wilson 10, Driberg 10. Then we had to vote on the two 10s and Wilson lost. Last night I pulled out of my pocket the paper on which the score had been recorded by Frank

Gomersall.[1] I noticed that Walter Padley, who had scored 11, seemed to have very few ticks. I added up and found he actually had 9. If Padley had been rightly counted there would have been no second count. Barbara would think this was a criminal conspiracy but, if it had been, the paper would hardly have been handed over to me. It was just one of those wonderful accidents, which Harold Wilson must never know about.

Wednesday, February 8th
I spent the weekend with the Pakenhams after doing a World Government Rally for them at Brighton. Frank and Elizabeth motored me back to their home, a comfortable Victorian house, where the last two of their children[2] were home from school for the weekend. They had the people from the village — the parson, the doctor and so on — in for drinks, and Wolf Mankowitz,[3] plus Collins the publisher and his wife,[4] for dinner. I found Wolf rather nice. He spent most of his time explaining that people like himself had lost interest in the Party after Nye's Brighton speech.[5] That was the turning point. Since then they couldn't care less about the parliamentary leadership or see any great distinction, indeed, between Gaitskell, Wilson and Crossman, all intriguing against each other. What he would like to see would be some of us coming out clear and profound against Gaitskell and the bomb. 'But you know,' I said, 'Gaitskell last year accepted the policy of abandoning the British deterrent.' Quite literally, Wolf had no idea of this and said that the truth is that they never would bother to read any policy associated with Gaitskell or with the rest of the people, who were just politicians.

In long private talks Elizabeth and Frank were even more surprising. Both repeatedly emphasized that I was the only possible Leader of the Party now that Hugh had proved himself incapable of unifying it. I pointed out the absurdity of this. While admitting that I had every possible qualification, I added that the one difficulty was my inability to get more than thirty votes from the Parliamentary Party or to obtain any confidence from the trade unions!

I discovered, to my amazement, that the Pakenhams have only seen Hugh once at Scarborough and once since then. I had imagined them his closest confidants, since they are among his oldest personal friends and supporters. But, as we talked, it became clear that Frank's experience was the same as

[1] Frank Gomersall was the Labour Party's Administrative Officer until 1965. One of the Administrative Officer's duties is to count votes at N.E.C. meetings; lately it has been found necessary for him to be aided in this task by the Secretary of the P.L.P.

[2] The youngest two Pakenhams were the Hon. Michael, born in 1943, and the Hon. Kevin, born in 1947.

[3] Honorary Consul to the Republic of Panama in Dublin 1971 and a novelist, playwright and author of television and film scripts.

[4] William Collins, the Chairman and Managing Director of William Collins Sons & Co., the London publishing house, until his death in 1976. He was awarded a C.B.E. in 1966 and knighted in 1970. He married Priscilla Lloyd in 1924.

[5] See above, pp. 619 ff.

the rest of us. He just couldn't take Hugh's inability ever to thank him or to show any appreciation for what he has been doing. 'I know the House of Lords doesn't matter but it would have been nice if Hugh could, once even, be aware that I have been opening debates there for him for three years.'

I asked Frank whether he had ever tried to put his views across to Hugh in talk and he told me he found it quite impossible. The visor comes down and he won't listen. I got the impression that he had managed to get across to Hugh even less than I had.

I came back on Sunday afternoon in order to dine with Peter Shore and go on working with the Titmuss group on our social security programme. We worked hard for three hours and sketched out a draft of what should be inserted in this year's home policy document. But, when I began to talk freely of the atmosphere at the top, I realized how depressing it was to these young people.

On Tuesday, the 31st, we had the first meeting of the Twelve. Beforehand we had a long discussion on tactics, at lunch here, but the meeting itself was all sweetness and light. This was partly due to a very odd incident with George Brown. In the afternoon I had a talk to the four N.E.C. delegates. Sam was quite agreeable that we should all act as individuals, recommending that majority decisions be taken by the Twelve, who would also report back to the Executive any differences of opinion. We finished this discussion by twenty-five to seven and went for a drink to the lower bar, where we found that George Brown and Ted Hill had been standing drinking whisky since a quarter to five. At seven we went up to the meeting and at five past George hadn't turned up. So I proposed Alf Roberts for the chair and we got going, with Hugh Gaitskell looking rather uncomfortable. No wonder, since it had leaked that George was to come with a draft in his pocket and produce it bashfully when requested. At a quarter past seven he came bouncing in, flopped himself down in the front and immediately got into an altercation with Frank Cousins, disregarding Alf Roberts's feeble protest from the chair. Tom Driberg then shouted 'Chair!', at which George shouted across, 'Shut up! You haven't got the votes!'

George then began to rehearse what I take to be the headings of the document in his pocket, which ran rather like: (a) We are in favour of peace. (b) We are against war. And so it went to (f) The Western alliance must have whatever weapons are required. At this point I protested that this just wouldn't do. George replied in his most lordly manner, 'Well, if you think you can do it yourself better than I can, have it your own way,' and swept out. It was a terribly embarrassing exhibition, which makes it difficult to conceive of him as a substitute for Hugh.

After he went, we all got on like a house on fire and real progress was made, with Frank Cousins repeating that he had never said we should leave NATO and never said the Western alliance should get rid of nuclear weapons before the Russians did so. I insisted on the importance of NATO's non-nuclear strategy, whereat Denis said that, though this phrase was attributed to him, it had actually been added to his article in the *New Léader* by a sub-editor.[1]

Hugh, who had been silent on instructions, came in saying of course he agreed with what I was saying and it was all a matter of emphasis. I said that, if they wanted principles, the principles would have to be rather sharper, because it was the qualifications and particular details which blunted them. The principle, therefore, must be that we stood for a non-nuclear strategy for our European forces, though we realized we could not get it straightaway. There was quite an atmosphere of everybody genuinely contributing. We all agreed that it was most important to get away from details and from a Defence White Paper atmosphere. At the end it was suddenly proposed that Denis should write a draft and that we should meet this Wednesday and Thursday.

I went away quite cheered up but next morning David Ennals told me that Denis's draft wouldn't be ready till Wednesday morning. I said this was absurd, since we must have time. I also had a word with George about the problem of conscription since Hugh had said at the meeting, not unreasonably, that the Party couldn't be expected to go out on a line on that issue, even though it did recognize the need for strengthening conventional weapons.

I managed to see Hugh for a moment that afternoon and said, 'There seems to be a chance of a unanimous report.' He replied, 'Oh, not unanimous! There's no chance of Frank Cousins.' I said, 'Chance? If we really want it, we can get it.' Hugh said, 'Oh no, no chance at all.' I mentioned how silly it would be for him and George and Denis to cook up a draft without showing it to me in time for my comments and he said he would see what he could do. Actually he did nothing and after the International yesterday George Brown very ostentatiously shouted to Sam that he should go up to his room as he wanted to show him something. My impression is that what they want is agreement, excluding Cousins and the unilateralists, since this is the only way to achieve the reversal of Scarborough, or what looks like it. If last year Hugh was in the minority in the voting, this year Cousins must be in the minority in the voting and at least they must be on opposing sides.

Now, this morning, the draft has come. It fulfils my worst expectations, except that it avoids the missile bases issue by saying we must be free to decide each particular case on its merits. But the whole document is utterly jejune from the moment it touches defence. It doesn't clearly state what the principles of our strategy should be and how we should get it. It's just an odd collection of negative points and the only warmth in it is in its insistence on our NATO obligation. At our gang lunch yesterday we decided that Tom and I would go to the meeting this afternoon with no draft amendments and leave

[1] In an article entitled 'Non-Atomic Strategy for NATO', which Denis Healey had written for the *New Leader*, published in New York on March 7th, 1960 (vol. 34, no. 10).

that till tomorrow. The whole atmosphere is more depressing than ever, if that is possible.

Monday, February 13th

Since I wrote last a great deal seems to have happened inside the Labour Party. First of all, the two meetings of the Twelve took place on Wednesday and Thursday last week. Both were in Room J and were somewhat disturbed by the riproaring debate on health charges[1] going on upstairs on the Wednesday, which anyway delayed George Brown from coming down.

At the Wednesday meeting Denis Healey's draft was discussed. We had only received it that morning and the discussion centred, as always, on the problem of nuclear strategy and whether we could pledge ourselves to use nuclear weapons first. After two hours we agreed to meet again next day, when Denis would try a redraft to meet our objections. I said I also would like to prepare a draft.

I worked hard on Thursday to do my draft and cleared with Harold Wilson that it was compatible with his six points. At the meeting, consideration of this took the whole time and it was now that the conversations really woke up and got keen. Denis Healey had only inserted six lines of change in his, which left it virtually the same, though one might say that a very slight concession had been made by an admission that ultimately it was the aim of the West not to rely on any nuclear weapons in Europe. But when Frank Cousins, at the beginning, started by asking what exactly the difference was and what concessions had been made, the answer given was that our job was not to consider Scarborough but to draft the best document.

They then turned to my document, where everything centred on Clause 6.[2] It was very amusing, since the more they looked at this, compared with Denis's draft, the less difference in policy they seemed to find. Yet the whole tone and attitude could hardly have been more different and that is what they all felt. There was no doubt in the meeting that Brown and Healey were acting as lieutenants to Hugh and were not free agents. There was also no doubt that three of the T.U.C. — Webber, Hayday and Roberts, the very weak chairman — were prepared to accept the Healey draft without question.

[1] The National Health estimates for 1960/61 had been more than 8 per cent higher than those of the previous year and they were likely to increase by a further 11 per cent in 1961/62. On February 1st the Minister of Health announced that he intended to raise practically all the 11 per cent in increased Health Service charges. These included the doubling of the prescription charge, increases of 5s. (25 new pence) to 11s. (55 new pence) in dental charges and an additional £49 million in a full year to be raised by increased weekly N.H.S. contribution. An Opposition motion of censure, debated on February 8th, was defeated by 321 votes to 231.

[2] Crossman's Clause 6 stated that they must

call attention to the disastrous effects of the nuclear strategy of massive retaliation ... While we agree that the Americans must certainly retain nuclear weapons so long as the Russians possess them, we reject absolutely a Western strategy based on the threat to use them first and a defence policy which compels NATO's forces to rely on these weapons in the field ...

It was also clear from very early on that Frank Cousins was prepared to accept my draft. (I had taken the precaution of going to see him at Transport House first and we had spent an hour together going through it and making sure it conformed with Wilson's six points.) Once this was obvious, the political problem came to this. I had produced a draft which would get acceptance from the Left. (A letter in the *New Statesman*, signed by Kingsley and members of the C.N.D. had also broadly supported this line as a compromise.) My draft, in fact, was the only possible compromise which the Left would consider. Denis Healey's rival draft was not a compromise but an assertion of the Right position, virtually unchanged.

All the sparring, therefore, was motivated by that single thought. To turn my draft down was to turn down a compromise acceptable to the Left. But to accept my draft as it stood was to make a very large concession, which Gaitskell was simply not prepared to do. But the difficulty he and George Brown had was in justifying their opposition to it, since very few people round the table knew enough about the subject to know what the difference was. George and I found ourselves, time after time, in agreement that there really was a difference between us which others wouldn't admit and we were also agreed that what I was putting forward was the line I had put forward last year in my first draft, which had been watered down later to meet his objections.

At one point I said, 'But why let this happen year after year – that we're always lagging behind and only catching up with events at the last moment? This year, if you don't take care, Kennedy and Macmillan will accept the strategy I am proposing while you're still opposing it.' James Callaghan replied, 'You're a journalist, Dick, whose profession makes him want to be ahead of events. We're responsible politicians.'

As the evening wore on it became clear that they were desperately anxious to persuade me to settle, i.e. to be allowed my draft if the policy was emasculated. But it was also clear that, if this happened, the draft would be of no value because Cousins wouldn't support it. Finally, time was running on, we weren't getting forward and I said, 'Why not vote on my draft? That would clear one thing out of the way.' The vote was 7 to 4, with Walter Padley as well as Tom Driberg and Frank Cousins supporting me. This was as good as I could possibly hope, since Walter Padley is a confirmed anti-unilateralist and would only vote for something which, as he told me before, was unequivocally standing by the multilateral position. I really had, therefore, got a bridge between the multilateralists and the unilateralists. Last year, after all, we couldn't prove our assertion that we could have had a reasonable compromise, under which Frank Cousins supported a multi-lateralist draft. This year I have actually got it and moreover I have got it down as a whole, so that it will have to be reported as a whole to our Executive on the 22nd.

Then Frank Cousins suddenly said that he wanted to put in a draft but couldn't do so until next week. This was a confounded nuisance for every-body. Moreover, it would have been far better if there had only been two and not three drafts. At first Hugh Gaitskell, who had been quiet throughout, said it wouldn't be allowed, but George Brown saw danger there. Think of the rumour that Frank had been forbidden to submit a draft! So they agreed to meet next Wednesday, finalize their own draft and hear Cousins's. I was left with the decision whether or not to go to Copenhagen this week. On balance I decided to do so, partly because I don't want to be present, voting against Frank Cousins, and partly because I hate changing plans.

Afterwards I told Harold Wilson what had happened and tried to make sure there were no leaks. There weren't any which showed great knowledge but there was a very silly article in *Reynolds News*, entirely on Harold Wilson, the thirteenth man, who is really running the committee from outside!

At the end of 1960 an abortive conference had met in London to decide on the future of the Central African Federation. A new constitution had already been agreed, in August 1960, for Nyasaland and in 1961 that country was to imple-ment the new arrangements smoothly.

Northern and Southern Rhodesia remained the outstanding problem and it was agreed in December 1960 that further discussion must await the outcome of constitutional conferences in the two territories. Talks on Northern Rhodesia, with the Colonial Secretary, Iain Macleod, as chairman, proceeded slowly and ended without agreement. On February 21st the Government published a White Paper (Cmnd 1295) setting out its proposals for the form of a Northern Rhodesian legislature; these were instantly rejected by Sir Roy Welensky, the Prime Minister of the Federation, and by the United Federal Party. He was supported by Lord Salisbury.

The talks on Southern Rhodesia, with the Secretary of State for Common-wealth Relations, Duncan Sandys, as chairman, ended on February 7th, having apparently proceeded easily. However, immediately the results of the con-ference were announced, the sections dealing with the franchise and allocation of parliamentary seats were rejected by the National Democratic Party and the Dominion Party. The issue was left to a referendum, to be held in July.

Meanwhile the other great item of news is that apparently a serious split about Rhodesia is now developing in the Tory Party. For quite a long time I had been predicting that this was the area which really might break the Tories. Now it does look as if the Government and sixty-five of its back-benchers are in a crisis, where an open revolt may be forced on them. The fact is that politics are now moving rapidly into a situation where the Opposition could seize the leadership in the country, win by-elections and really see the Government on the run. I suppose it's just possible we shall do it, despite our differences about defence. Of course we're faced with terrible problems in the Labour Party but they are all soluble in terms of a Party happily on the offensive, with confidence in itself. Equally, they are insoluble in terms of a Party gloomy, divided and unsure of itself.

Tuesday, February 21st
I got back from Denmark to find that on the defence issue people had been very busy behind my back. Already last Thursday's and Friday's papers had been full of inspired reports that the Twelve Wise Men had reached agreement and that the only obstacle to unity was Mr Cousins. Yesterday *The Times* had on its front page the virtual text of the manifesto and on another page an inspired article that Padley and I alone could wreck unity.

Meanwhile the Parliamentary Party had been busily fed with the idea that unity was possible if only it wasn't wrecked by us. Quite skilful use had, of course, been made of my absence in Denmark and of Frank Cousins's flu. Yesterday, with George's help, I got to work and gave the *Guardian* the truth to put on their front page, namely that there is a minority report, a fact which had been virtually obscured for the past week. We also gave it to *The Times*, which refused to publish it, since it didn't square with their yesterday's story. We also alerted our friends.

Meanwhile some quite comic manoeuvrings are going on. I found that Len Williams had only circulated the majority draft to the Executive. Yesterday, when I rang him, he told me he couldn't circulate mine until he had my consent and, arriving on Saturday, I hadn't been able to give it. But Walter Padley had written on my behalf to the Parliamentary Committee asking them to report our minority findings.

Yesterday I went to see Frank Barlow, who told me that the only report made by their four was the majority finding. True enough, the Shadow Cabinet had not been apprised that there was a minority report or of anything really that had happened. I said to Frank it would be a bit silly if I stood outside the door when the Party Meeting discussed it tomorrow evening, doling out our memorandum! He agreed that that was a fact but said that the Parliamentary Committee took a different view. So late last night I saw the Chief Whip, who also agreed with me but told me they were being difficult. This morning he rang to say that he still felt bound to abide by the decision of the Committee of Twelve that there should be only one report of its proceedings. Of course he recognized that each of the constituent bodies would have the right to make any report it liked.

I may be exaggerating but I think all this means is that Gaitskell and Brown have been desperately anxious to conceal the existence of a compromise draft which could have created unanimity. They probably realized that they could not do this entirely and that the only other method available was to discredit it, on the ground that I was absent when the committee came to its conclusions. However, my draft has now been circulated to the Executive. I find that Frank Cousins's draft, which he put forward last week in my absence, is perfectly all right, since it includes the vital decisions about NATO.

But how important are these incredibly dreary manoeuvrings? There is no doubt that the political situation is making this Labour Party conflict more and more insignificant in the public eye and also making our own Party people more and more impatient of those of us who seem to be squabbling at the top. That is why they are so desperately anxious to prove that somebody else is to blame for disunity. I too would like nothing better than to see our defence squabble pushed out of the centre, because other politics are really getting more and more interesting. There is no doubt now that the Government is faced in Central Africa with far the gravest crisis of its history, much graver than Suez. Suez was a folly into which it jumped and from which it could extricate itself in a matter of days. But if war breaks out in Central Africa we are in there with whole divisions of troops or, alternatively, if the Government hesitates to send them, I believe it will be faced with a split Party.

Africa seems to me far more important than the Health Service charges. But there's no doubt that, while I've been in Denmark this week, the morale of the Parliamentary Party has been enormously improved by all-night sittings on the Health Service. Even more remarkable, the prestige of the Party outside Parliament has been greatly improved by the same thing. There is no doubt that people now think that the Labour Party has begun to do its job as a fighting Opposition.

Thursday, February 23rd

One can never predict the mood of the Executive. I had, what is very unusual for me, a bad night before it, which means that I woke up constantly and only snoozed. But actually the meeting couldn't have been easier. There was virtually no other business apart from the defence problem. When we got to it there was some rather silly bickering about whether Frank Cousins's document could legitimately be on the agenda. (At the T.U.C. they managed to keep mine off the agenda.) However, we got round this by the device of saying there were three documents being presented by the four N.E.C. representatives of the Twelve—the majority document, presented by Mr Watson, the minority report by Mr Crossman and Mr Padley, while Tom Driberg would move Frank Cousins's draft.

George Brown made a long speech, which surprised me by emphasizing throughout how much had been conceded for the cause of unity. Indeed, his main point was that the Right had made larger concessions than were perhaps responsible, particularly on the subject of nuclear strategy. Their sticking point, however, was the pledge not to use nuclear weapons first, and the matter of bases.

I asked the Executive whether I should move out of the chair to put my amendment and there was quite a murmur of dismay at the prospect—

30

pleasurable for me but it didn't suit Harold Wilson very well. There is no doubt they like me in the chair, whatever else, simply because business gets done. I moved the compromise, first of all by stressing that, whereas my resolution, if carried, would get 80 per cent of the vote of Conference, Hugh's resolution, if carried, would doom us to certain defeat. I repeated that I believed it was hopeless to try to achieve victory on defence in the Party. One's aim must be reconciliation and this was what we had tried by putting forward a compromise resolution to the Twelve, which Cousins said he could acquiesce in if it was accepted.

I argued in some detail on George's two points and then pointed out that, on the issue of conscription, I had merely repeated last year's document and could not see why that was not satisfactory. At one point I made a slip, when I got worked up about the responsibility of those who rejected my compromise for, as I put it, splitting the Party. This was objected to loudly by George Brown and Hugh and gave me the opportunity for an unconditional apology and withdrawal, which always does one good in the Executive, on a point of no importance.

Walter Padley seconded me in an extremely good speech. First he pointed out, that, by rejecting our compromise amendment, Hugh and George might quite likely ensure that Conference committed the Party to full-blooded unilateralism. He took up one point of George's on tactical weapons, where George had said one must rely on these while conventional weapons were in short supply. 'I am willing to commit a lot for NATO,' said Padley, 'but I am not willing to commit national suicide for NATO and that's what George Brown's policy implies.' At this point Eirene White asked George some very searching questions. At lunch on Tuesday Harold Wilson had said we might get thirteen votes, including Eirene White, and I had laughed him off about her. I still thought she would only abstain – but we will come to that later.

The debate was conducted with greatest sobriety. Hugh Gaitskell said very little at the beginning. Tom Driberg, who had moved the Cousins thing quite well, made it clear that he had been stretching his conscience to support me, and so had Tony Greenwood, who, Patricia [Llewelyn-Davies] tells me, really found it very difficult to support my resolution. The trade unionists played very little part, being obviously extremely uncomfortable.

Towards the end Hugh made a speech, in which he did not bother about the Cousins draft. He had three objections to mine. In the first place, he did not like the way it was written and quoted a number of my more stirring sentences, which he felt had false emotional overtones. He then objected on the issue of nuclear weapons and bases, as George had. His speech was very quiet. Harold Wilson reserved himself for the end and was completely ineffective.

We voted first on the Cousins resolution, which was defeated 16 to 7, with me, as Chairman, abstaining. Then came mine and I asked if I could vote. To my amazement I was at once told by Sam that the Chairman could always vote if he wished, as well as giving his casting vote. When the result, 15 to 13, was announced, there was very nearly an audible whistle. Yet there was only one vote on our side more than one could reckon on in advance. The truth is that Hugh can't count. Or is it that, having got Mr John Harris to leak into all the newspapers his optimistic versions, he then believes what has been leaked. On the report itself, Eirene White also voted with us, making 10 against 16.

There came an amusing incident when I raised the issue of press statements. Hugh Gaitskell solemnly proposed that, since this was unusual, we should authorize the Deputy Leader and the chairman of the International to attend the press conference. I am now very good-tempered, so I laughed and said, 'That would be rather invidious after your decision a few weeks ago, Hugh, that no member of the Executive should be present at press conferences, including the Chairman.' Hugh was completely silent, since the Executive roared its applause.

I then said that, in addition to the votes, I presumed that all three drafts would be released. At once Alice Bacon said this would be breaking precedent; only the one approved by the N.E.C. should be released. Hugh added, 'The other two are entirely a matter for the individuals concerned.' This, of course, is totally untrue, since no individual on the Executive is entitled to leak whatever amendments he may have put forward at a meeting. However it enabled Tom to walk down to the journalists and hand over our draft to them in time for the evening papers.

I learnt from Tony Benn that he had travelled to Oxford immediately afterwards with Eirene. She explained to him that she had voted for my draft because it was warm and persuasive, whereas Hugh's was cold and provocatively bleak. She had also been put off by his rigidity and George's bogus punditry about nuclear weapons. He thought they were far too right-wing to carry the Movement with them but guessed that George would succeed Hugh somehow or other after the next Conference. 'George Brown is playing the role of Churchill in 1940,' she said. 'He will loyally carry out the Norwegian campaign for his Chamberlain before replacing him.'

At seven o'clock we all went in for the Parliamentary Party Meeting on defence, to find Room 14 snowed under with literature – three documents for each of us lying waiting on the desk. I had been putting on great pressure that the discussion should be postponed till this morning to give people time to read and Frank Barlow tipped me off that the Committee had concurred. Immediately we started Hugh Gaitskell rose to make this suggestion. It was a little difficult for him to explain why he hadn't thought of the documents, when, on the previous Thursday, he had announced the whole thing would be got through that evening without difficulty. As usual, Alice Bacon managed to make it more difficult for her boss by getting up and pointing this out, saying that, if we had only had the one we expected there would have been no difficulty at all. Anyway, she was puzzled why we had one from the T.U.C.

At this point Shinwell made one of his most brilliant interruptions. He concurred in the postponement and pointed out that Thursday morning was very bad, since there were four Standing Committees and, anyway, with the defence debate on Monday and Tuesday[1] and the spirit of unity manifest in the defence group on the previous day, it would be a tragedy if this should be marred by an acrid debate on defence problems. Better postpone things till Wednesday morning of next week, when everyone could be present, when there would have been time for reflection and when the defence debate would be over.

To my amazement, Bill Blyton, a stalwart right-winger, strongly supported Manny and it became clear that the whole meeting was pulsating with unity on defence. They even listened with tolerance to John Rankin prosing away on this subject and he was supported by such right-wingers as George Chetwynd[2] and Christopher Mayhew. Even Tony Crosland was nodding his head. You would have thought that anyone on the platform must have felt the atmosphere.

On the other hand, I knew what Gaitskell and Brown were feeling. Give the Party five days to look at these documents, go back to their constituencies, read the Sunday papers, and it was doubtful if they could get them through. George Brown got up and in his most portentous and verbose style tried to hammer home the point that the Parliamentary Party must decide the same day as the N.E.C. and the T.U.C., that their role as a joint policy-maker would be impaired if they didn't and that any delay would be misinterpreted by the press as a sign of weakness.

The more George shouted, the more the meeting murmured against him. Lynn Ungoed-Thomas upped to say that the last time there were so-called tripartite consultations the Parliamentary Party had been treated in the same way and been told to give its approval one evening, without any time. After all, he urged, the Parliamentary Party had been advised by its leaders recently of its importance and its independent role. It should take this seriously. Postponement for a week would merely add to the interest the public would feel and show a sense of responsibility before a great decision. There seemed to be a dangerous assumption among some people that the decision had already been taken. But the Party was a sovereign body etc., etc. Gaitskell at one point tried to stem this by saying, 'Really, you don't understand, we've got to get our decision as soon as possible.' This produced a howl of anger.

This went on for more than an hour. A leadership which had begun to build up confidence on the floor of the House in the Health Service debates and so on which are now raging every night managed to dissipate the goodwill in a few minutes. Finally the vote was taken on a proposal to hold the Meeting

[1] To discuss the defence White Paper (Cmnd 1288). In the debate on February 28th the White Paper was approved by 338 votes to 231.

[2] Labour M.P. for Stockton-on-Tees 1945-62. He was Deputy Chairman of the Land Commission 1967-70 and its Chairman 1970-1, and in 1978 became Chairman of the Northern Regional Health Authority.

at half-past six tonight. This has every disadvantage, since it empties the House during our Health Service demonstration for at least three hours, but it was carried by 73 to 65, with many abstentions and Crosland voting against. Many people think the vote was rigged. I've seldom seen a more fantastic scene. Tom Driberg and I kept whispering to each other that we must contain ourselves and show no pleasure on our faces. Poor Gaitskell looked more and more buttoned up, tight and miserable. He had had a rough morning and now everything was going wrong, since the Parliamentary Party, which he relied on as his cohort of praetorian guards, was now out of control and asserting its democratic rights against him.

Another advantage of the postponement yesterday was that the morning papers could devote themselves to the N.E.C., on which, on the whole, they gave a pretty good report. The line of the leaders in the *Guardian* and *The Times*, as well as the comment in the *Herald*, was that the differences between my version and the official one were so fine that it was outrageous to have a split, whereas Cousins's version was miles away. But, in the narrative reports, most papers have admitted that my compromise document was backed by Cousins. This therefore made the reader wonder why Gaitskell couldn't accept it. He and George will be in great difficulty tonight.

So once again, by trying to slap me down and push me out, Gaitskell has bobbed me up like a jack-in-the-box as the leader of the opposition to him. The Crossman amendment is now the unifying compromise which Gaitskell has turned down. I have succeeded in my manoeuvre of demonstrating with proof what I asserted last summer, namely that a compromise was possible between Frank Cousins and the Executive. On the other hand, I have to be very careful not to misuse Cousins or make him fire off in the wrong direction.

Meanwhile all this has been going on as a sideshow, while a colossal crisis develops over Northern Rhodesia and while the parliamentary footlights display the scenes of obstruction in the Chamber to which the Opposition is now committed. We have an all-night sitting tonight, which I must duly attend. It would be excellent if all this were done by backbenchers. But George Brown and Hugh are both now playing the backbench guerrilla role from the Front Bench. Just think that six months ago they were claiming that one must play the dignified role of an alternative Government and not sink to the level of a fighting Opposition.

Friday, March 3rd
Let me start with the Party Meeting on Thursday night of last week. It took place in the first four hours of the all-night sitting, roughly from half-past six to eleven, with, I think, two breaks for double divisions. On the whole, it was relatively well conducted. Each person was provided with his documents and at the end, when the vote was to be taken, there were just over 200 present, which means there could have been at most some twenty deliberate

abstentions. I went into the meeting, I remember, with the very definite hope
— almost with the expectation — that we would put on a really good vote and,
for the first time in our lives, win over the Centre of the party to the Left
point of view.

What was the actual debate like? It started with George Brown, not very
exciting. Then followed Tony Greenwood, speaking instead of Tom Driberg
on the Cousins motion and putting the case very extremely. This made it
much easier for me to show my draft as a genuine compromise and it was
generally agreed that I had made a very powerful case, not merely on the
defence problems involved but, much more, on the fact that this was a
compromise, supported by Cousins, which could carry the Conference, I
said, with 80 per cent behind it, whereas the Gaitskell motion had no chance
of success.

I was strongly and well backed by Walter Padley, who has throughout been
a very loyal, if discreet, friend. As President of USDAW, he wants to use the
draft he did jointly with me to unhook his union from unilateralism. But, in
order to do this, he cannot associate too closely with a maverick like me.
Michael Foot also spoke well for us. It was obvious that the Whips had been
very busy telling people there was no reason to believe Frank was genuinely
with me. Hugh Gaitskell at the end made a great deal of emphasis on the
difference between his draft and mine, in that mine could only be carried out
with recourse to conscription, while theirs did not require it.

Actually the voting, superficially at least, was very much as before. I got
69 votes to 133 for my amendment and there were only 61 votes against the
substantive resolution. This compared with 70 abstentions last December.
But, then, how much easier it is to be absent, not so very ostentatiously, than
to stand in a meeting with your hand up, being counted by the Whips, on
whose favour you depend not merely for a Shadow job but for one of those
endless little expeditions, abroad or at home, which make a modern M.P.'s
life worth living. In retrospect, I regard the vote as very satisfactory. We got
69 positive votes for my amendment and probably another dozen or so
abstentions.

Right up to the vote I hoped for a better result. There is something intensely
depressing in feeling that, even at a Party Meeting, hardly a vote changes as a
result of the argument. But in this case, though votes were not changed,
minds, I think, were. Quite a number of people admitted that they voted for
Gaitskell while thinking it crazy to turn down our compromise. For example,
Eric Fletcher said to me, leaning across to where I was dozing on a bench at
one o'clock in the morning, 'Well done, Dick, you put up a jolly good show.'
'But you didn't vote for me,' I said. He replied, 'No, of course not, but I
thought you did very well.' In his own way John Strachey was equally
characteristic. 'After talking to you the other day,' he said, 'I went straight
in to Gaitskell and pleaded with him to consider the compromise. But he
won't move an inch because he doesn't trust Cousins. It doesn't matter what

compromise you produce; with Cousins's name on it he would distrust it just the same.' I said wasn't this a pity, but John shrugged his shoulders in the way I presume everyone does if they've been cured by psychoanalysis of their convictions.

The morning papers showed a fairly full report of the so-called private Party Meeting and in every report I read that Gaitskell had attacked my compromise as involving conscription. He and Brown were both said to have made magnificent speeches, which were given at some length, and so was George Thomas. I was given very little but embarrassment at having my suggestions about Cousins exposed. I thought this gave me a chance of reply in my weekend speech. If I had been attacked about conscription in every newspaper, I had the right to answer back. So I spent the morning in bed, preparing a draft press release, giving at some length my answer on conscription.

At half-past six I went to King's Cross to address a railway workers' meeting. When I got back, Hugh Massingham came across, as he wanted my press release. He took a look and said, 'Look, Dick, this is terribly complicated and, if I may say so, you must make up your mind. Either you do come out and say something or you don't. This is neither one thing or the other.' Looking at it, I knew he was right, so when he had left at eleven I knocked out a new statement with Anne. I took this with me to Cardiff,[1] when I caught the 7.55 on Saturday morning.

On arrival I was taken straight from the station to the meeting at eleven o'clock. Some 200 delegates were gathered and there I found James Callaghan on the platform. I made a reasoned, all-round speech on *Labour in the Sixties* and the Health Service, introducing, about a third of the way through, my passage on defence. I could feel an electrical thrill of awed silence as I said it and there's no doubt people knew at once it was something important.

When the press had withdrawn, we started questions and somebody asked me why the Parliamentary Party was behaving in the way it was. I made a very brief reply and said I thought they should ask Callaghan. He spoke for twenty-two minutes, accusing me of telling lies and asserting that I had publicly stated my approval of the majority draft, from which I did not seriously disagree. I could feel there was a struggle for men's souls. Callaghan had not only had his clique, but he had a fraction of each heart of these present. In the course of an hour's discussion, I should say that 55 per cent to 60 per cent were with me, but it was by no means an easy meeting.

---

[1] Where he was addressing a Labour Party conference. Crossman said, 'I feel it a tragedy that Hugh Gaitskell found it impossible in all conscience to accept the proposals made by me together with Walter Padley and for which Frank Cousins voted.' Crossman declared that the Conservative defence programme of 1957 was in ruins and the country in a crisis. 'I am convinced', he said, 'that the right way to solve this is to cut NATO and imperial defence commitments even though this may finally involve withdrawal from most of our overseas stations east of Gibraltar.'

Inside myself I was shaken because Callaghan knows how to lambast and assault and create a foul impression of his opponent.

When I got back to Cardiff station platform, a professor from Swansea came up to speak to me and I was so distrait that he had to crawl away. I had just an hour on the train to eat lunch and was sitting down when a young man came up and said, 'I'm the *Observer* correspondent. Can I sit with you?' I let him sit there and hear my depression about the Party. I suppose before the meeting I hadn't fully realized the electric effect of what I would say. Certainly, if somebody had said to me, 'Why not insert the words "Gaitskell and the majority" or even "The majority"?' I should have done so without a second thought. What I felt was that though, as Chairman, I was bound to accept the majority decision, I had the right to express on at least one occasion my profound regret that it had been taken, the reasons why I disagreed and my view that my own amendment was still open for the Movement to adopt. Further than that I felt I could not go without abusing the principle of the majority decision. I don't think it entered my head that I was attacking Gaitskell. Mainly I had assumed that everybody knew that the Leader of the Party had played a determining role in getting my compromise voted down and therefore there was nothing particularly damaging in asserting the obvious. If somebody had pointed it out to me, I think I would have replied, 'Yes, I can see that the others would feel offended, so I will certainly mention them.' But it wouldn't have occurred to me that Gaitskell would be more offended than he anyway was with my determination to fight for my compromise. After the Cardiff meeting, though, I did know that thunder was in the air.

I had a more successful meeting at Swansea, where the whole atmosphere was different. Nothing could have been nicer and friendlier and no support more enthusiastic. I travelled back to London in a somewhat more cheerful mood and had a lovely Sunday alone with Anne and the children, but on Monday morning I knew what was up. John Harris had gone to work. *The Times*, the *Guardian*, the *Telegraph* and the *Herald* all carried obviously inspired stories that Crossman had once again outraged the majority of Labour leaders and was in for serious trouble. Fortunately for me, these stories indicated that I had made false claims about Cousins, as well as personalizing the issue in an attack on Gaitskell. I rang Cousins at home, to find he was in Liverpool without a telephone number. So I had a couple of hours to meditate on whether he would stand by me. Neither Tony Greenwood nor Michael Foot seemed too sure but when Cousins came through on the phone he was perfectly O.K. Half an hour later Harry Nicholas rang me to read aloud Cousins's draft statement, which I approved with one or two modifications.[1] It was out by midday and forced Hugh and his eight friends,

---

[1] On March 27th Mr Cousins issued a press statement declaring unequivocally that he had supported Mr Crossman's draft statement on defence. On the same evening the eight supporters of Mr Healey's draft declared their astonishment 'at Mr Crossman's suggestion that only the obstinacy of the Party Leader prevented unanimous agreement'.

who were drafting their denunciation, to start their work again, since one of the two pillars of their argument had been knocked away.

I went down to the lobby to prime the correspondents and then went in to the first day of the defence debate. Denis Healey made a speech which, in every possible detail, conformed with my compromise amendment and not with Hugh's. I led the cheering from behind.

Late that night I was rung up by Tom Driberg and told that the eight had, at ten o'clock, issued their blast against me and he had issued a blast against them. I didn't realize the size of the storm until I opened Tuesday's papers, with banner headlines as big as when Gaitskell sacked me a year ago. But this time the atmosphere was more unpleasant, since I was accused of being a bloody liar. It's true that, in the latter part of their stories, the papers carried Cousins's support for me. If it hadn't been for this, I should indeed have been in a desperate way. I had at least cauterized half the poison. But it was extremely unpleasant.

I worked all Tuesday morning on a short reply, shortening it all the time and then discussing it with our Tuesday lunch. People were pleasant enough but, oh dear, why should they trouble terribly about my troubles, which they don't feel to be very closely related to themselves? By Tuesday evening the atmosphere was very unpleasant. Both I.T.V. and B.B.C. were asking me to appear. I turned down I.T.V.'s insult (one minute, with one minute to Denis Healey) but considered an offer by the B.B.C. of seven minutes each. But by Wednesday evening I concluded that this also was too dangerous and turned it down, a decision wholly justified by what happened on Thursday.

On Thursday afternoon I got a note from Bill Hamilton[1] quite civilly saying he was going to raise my Saturday speech[2] at that evening's Party Meeting. So I went along and found some thirty to forty stalwarts left in an empty House. Apart from George Wigg, there was no other left-winger. Hamilton raised his point, first mildly and then suddenly launching into a violent attack. Hugh Gaitskell rose and said he proposed to call Denis Healey and George Brown, then he would say something and presumably I would like to reply. I suddenly realized it was a most carefully prepared affair and that they had decided not to drop things but to continue the vendetta.

Healey expressed deep moral disapprobation of revelations about all the secrets of the Committee of Twelve and all the lies I told about Cousins. Healey added that the theological arguments were nothing; the truth was that I was organizing an anti-Gaitskell conspiracy, a personal vendetta against the Leader. George Brown took much the same line but added, rather unwisely, that I had no right to think I had Cousins's support, since Cousins would have to answer for his departure from the unilateral line to his own union executive.

[1] This can only be William Hamilton, Labour M.P. for the Central division of Fife since 1950, but always referred to as 'Willie'. He was Chairman of the House of Commons Estimates Committee 1960–70.
[2] At Cardiff.

I replied simply by quoting the speech but couldn't get through a sentence without howling and jeering from an audience possessed by the conviction that it had caught a sinner out and was going to burn him alive. I got a little angry and told them that what was wrong with them was that they hated people and imputed motives to me which were utterly remote. I had never run personal vendettas nor cared about personalities. I was fighting for a compromise, without which the Party would fall to pieces, and I should go on fighting for it. As for the charge that the point of my speech was an attack on Gaitskell, I rejected it entirely. I was merely indicating the obvious fact that, with the Executive voting 15 to 13, the Leader's influence had been decisive. But what I said made no difference. It was the ugliest meeting I have ever experienced and I came home extremely depressed and only too anxious to get away to the country today.

Wednesday, March 8th
One item which surprised and disconcerted me on Monday was to open *The Times* and discover a very strange article by the Political Correspondent.[1] On the previous Monday I had asked him to talk and, as usual, he had sent his Number Two—a good, decent, uninspired journalist called George Clark.[2] I had briefed him on the situation, along with the other journalists and then (I think at ten o'clock) Wood himself came up to me in the lobby. As everything was over at that moment, I sat with him and talked completely freely about the situation. I told him frankly that there seemed to me no prospect in a change in the leadership next October, since Harold Wilson had more enemies than Hugh. Indeed, the only possible chance was a *coup d'état* by George Brown and that could cost us a million votes. I said a number of fairly free and easy things, assuming, as always, that everything said in the lobby was off the record unless one says it is on.

I was astonished, therefore, to find that Wood had quoted me direct, taking the sentence about Gaitskell out of context. At first I was very angry but when I read the article[3] more carefully I realized it had certainly been

[1] David Wood, who had joined the parliamentary staff of *The Times* in 1948 and in 1951 worked as a correspondent for *The Times* at home and abroad. He was Political Correspondent 1957–67, Political Editor 1967–77 and in 1977 became European Political Editor. He published THE TIMES *Guide to the European Elections*, edited by Alan Wood (London: Times Books Ltd, 1980).

[2] Apprenticed to the *Bedfordshire Times* 1934–9, from 1939 to 1947 George Clark served in the Navy as a Writer, in Naval Intelligence and subsequently as an interpreter in Germany. He was Senior Reporter on the *Bedfordshire Times* in 1947 and then moved to the *Daily Express* in Glasgow as Senior Reporter. He was East of Scotland Correspondent for the *Sunday Express* 1947–50 and in February 1950 joined *The Times* as Gallery Reporter. In 1957 he became *The Times*'s Assistant Political Correspondent and in 1976 its Political Correspondent.

[3] 'Mr Crossman Names a Vote Millionaire' included the following passage:

In other words, Mr Crossman believes that (or, to be fair, believed last week) if there were to be a general election now, even after any damage inflicted by an 18-month campaign against the public image of the leadership, Mr Gaitskell could save the

written with the best of intentions. I had obviously convinced Mr Wood that I was not a mere conspirator against Gaitskell but was working for a compromise and for reconciliation as an end in itself. It was only a sign of Wood's naïveté that he had believed that this article would be so helpful that I could excuse him for quoting me without asking my leave.

However, I was a bit apprehensive when we met for the group lunch on Tuesday, but everybody there was discreet enough to say nothing. Indeed it was a difficult article to discuss, either for the Right, where it demolished the main charge against me, or for the Left, which was terrified it was true. This afternoon I went into the Smoking Room and found two stalwart Gaitskellites, John Strachey and Kenneth Robinson. We discussed the situation in the Party with no new gambits, until John airily asked me about *The Times* article and I told him the story. 'It was intended to do good,' I said. Kenneth Robinson replied, 'Well, it has done a great deal of good, you know, in the Parliamentary Party. It has certainly removed a lot of the poison.'

Though I had a streaming cold, I came back for supper and then went out to Hendon to listen to the Young Socialists there complaining about the National Executive's banning their Trotskyite organ, *Keep Left*. Even in this diary I can't dilate at length on Labour's failure to organize a youth movement.

The meeting went quite well and at ten o'clock the chairman, trying to be friendly, thanked me and said, 'Well, at least we've saved the Party Chairman from having to attend his all-night sitting tonight.' I replied, without thinking, 'Well, as a matter of fact, I've an all-night standing to do from two to four o'clock in the morning outside Lancaster House.'[1] It was like an electric spell. You could hear the thrilled silence. Then the chairman said, 'You?' I said, 'Yes, of course.' He said, 'That makes a difference! Well good luck, comrade!' and I went out in the odour of sanctity, with all the young people thinking I was splendid.

We drove back and I stayed up reading until I walked across the park at

---

Parliamentary Labour Party in the Commons from facing a Conservative majority of much more than 150, compared with 100 today.

Crossman's papers include copies of a courteous and conciliatory exchange of letters between himself and David Wood.

[1] The Commonwealth Prime Ministers' Conference had opened in London on March 8th. South Africa had decided, in a referendum in October 1960, to become a republic. That decision would not be implemented until May 31st and, if South Africa wished to remain a member of the Commonwealth after that date, she would now have to apply for acceptance as a republic. It was known that South Africa wished to remain in the Commonwealth but she was first anxious to hear the views of her fellow members about her racial policy before deciding whether or not to apply for Commonwealth membership. These discussions lasted from March 13th to 15th and, meanwhile, demonstrators wearing black sashes stood outside Lancaster house, where the conference took place, in a silent vigil of protest against South Africa's Apartheid policy. At the end of the talks the South African Prime Minister, Dr Hendrik Verwoerd, announced that he would withdraw his application for membership, as it had been shown that his country 'was not welcome'.

2 a.m. to Lancaster House, where I found John Freeman and others putting on their sashes. This is a seventy-two-hour vigil, which started at midnight — naturally with Carol[1] and Tony Wedgwood Benn ready for the photographers — and we were the second shift, eight of us standing there in sashes. It is by no means a silly idea. What interested me was that every one of those young people in Hendon knew about the vigil. This is exactly the kind of activity which really excites them when we do it as well. If only Hugh and George Brown would see this kind of thing not as a trick but as one of the ways of building up the Party! All-night sittings they have accepted, because this is an established parliamentary procedure, but vigils in sashes are something which they, and I as well, feel a little off-colour. That's one of the reasons we fail with young people.

One advantage of the vigil was that I could talk at length to John Freeman. He told me he had interviewed Gaitskell on Thursday morning for an hour and a half, one hour off the record.[2] Gaitskell had been obsessed with three themes. First, there were only two people he had mentioned personally, Frank Cousins and myself, as men possessed with the desire to overthrow him. He also saw every move in politics as a conspiracy against him personally. Secondly, time after time he reverted to the theme of how outrageous I had been to suggest that it was he who had turned my compromise down, when in fact George Brown and Denis Healey had played a far more prominent part. Thirdly, he had also said how terrible it was for me to personalize the issue in this way.

'But surely you personalized it yourself at Scarborough,' John had said, at which Hugh's visor had fallen and he had replied, 'That's totally different.' Hugh had spent most of his time discussing what happened at the Committee of Twelve and insisting that I had been a complete liar about Cousins. John had argued more than once that surely this was now irrelevant, if, whatever happened there, Cousins now supported my draft. That changed the whole situation. But Hugh had refused to admit this in any way. This interview had occurred a few hours before the Party Meeting at which he had organized a demonstration against me.

But has anything happened since then? There is a strong feeling in the House, according to George Wigg, that compromise is again in the air. It is certainly true that Hugh's weekend speech at a Hull regional conference could not have been more conciliatory. Moreover, a very queer incident occurred yesterday when the International met to discuss Polaris. I had insisted on this and at once George Brown listed the points he had made in Parliament — that it wasn't for the Opposition to give its blessing, that we opposed bases in principle, that we objected to features of the agreement and that we thought the site was too near Glasgow.

I then reminded George that we should also complain that the agreement

[1] Caroline de Camp married Anthony Wedgwood Benn in 1950.
[2] The interview appeared in the *News of the World* on March 5th.

should not have been signed permitting Polaris without a clause agreeing to the removal of the Thor bases. Jennie added, 'I think we should insist on a joint Macmillan/Kennedy declaration that Polaris is a second-strike weapon, which will never be used unless the Russians fire first.' Gaitskell said this was perfectly acceptable and could be worked up, whereat Tom Driberg said that we had to refuse all nuclear weapons equally, since all are equally evil.

Altogether we reached, as we always do, a great deal of agreement. George Brown was then instructed to draft. He turned to me and said, 'Will you be in the House tomorrow? I'll let you see the draft.' I said, 'I shall have to consider it very carefully.' How different from the behaviour when the Committee of Twelve met and I asked to see the draft and was refused! This difference seemed to indicate that, at least on the Polaris issue, they were all extremely anxious to reach an agreed statement. I am also aware that, if I agree with them on this too easily, my whole position will disappear. The Left will think I have sold out, at which point *The Times* correspondent will be recognized as the cleverest and best-informed man in the lobby. I must, of course, be in the House, so that I can be given the draft and I shall then toughen it up and make it acceptable to myself and send it back to George. This is the most treacherous and tricky period. As George Wigg says, one should fear one's comrades most when they are being comradely. Altogether we are going through a particularly violent spasm now. I think it is due to the complete lack of any clear strategy by the present leadership. They veer between a determination to fight Conference and a regretful realization that they have got to seek a reconciliation with it; between a determination to get on with the Left and a determination to knock us on the head.

Crossman spent late March and the first part of April travelling, as Party Chairman, to various Labour Party conferences. He spent the Easter weekend with his family at Prescote, resting.

Meanwhile the Labour Party was preparing its draft document on domestic policy, ready for presentation at the autumn Conference. Harold Wilson gave a glimpse of some of his own ideas for a 'Four-Year Plan for Britain', published in the New Statesman *on March 24th.*

Monday, April 24th
The first event after Easter week was the meeting of Home Policy on the 10th. It was an astonishingly friendly and helpful meeting, with Gaitskell falling over backwards to be conciliatory. We managed to isolate a number of policy points which needed more attention and we also agreed that in its present form the draft was an office document, not a pamphlet. This was already a great difficulty because it is clear that Peter Shore and his staff just can't write anything except office documents. However, it was also clear that Hugh Gaitskell was willing to go a long way in concessions on home policy, in order not to have to fight on two fronts.

Next day at our group lunch, which occurs every Tuesday, Ian Mikardo
was determined to produce a draft on nationalization that Hugh couldn't
accept. I told him he would find it difficult to achieve this but he tried his best.
On Thursday morning we had another fascinating Home Policy meeting.
On public ownership, Mikardo's extreme draft, in which he was going to be
so firm, ceased to be so extreme when he knocked out the commitment of
the next Labour Government to carry out his large-scale takeover. After all,
it was easy to point out that the inclusion of margarine and detergents as the
'commanding heights of the economy' was a bit comic. Harold Wilson said
with conspicuous skill how much he liked this draft, apart from the only
passage with teeth in it, and asked whether he should rewrite it. All through,
the only real opposition came from Fred Mulley, who might be said to be
representing the old Gaitskellite point of view in insisting that we should say
nothing which would commit us to anything about extensions of power.
But the atmosphere couldn't have been much more amiable.

Thursday, May 11th
My main concern has been the Home Policy draft, which was considered
from four o'clock on Monday. It was an absolutely terrible meeting. Of
course the draft is second-rate and Peter Shore will not let anything be done
to it. The truth is, you can't solve Labour's problems by writing documents
and no serious thinking or work has been done. In the last six months the
Left has had a tremendous chance, with Gaitskell distracted, to work hard
and produce a really powerful reapplication of Socialist principle to the
1960s. But the Left on the Executive has done absolutely nothing and Harold
Wilson has left it to Peter Shore, concerning himself, apparently, chiefly with
press relations in order to pile up his own position.

On Tuesday, at our lunch, it was obvious that our Left group is in the
process of breaking up again, with most of them only concerned to be anti-
Gaitskell and openly saying they are not prepared for unity if it strengthens
him, while Harold and I, as in the old Bevanite days, say we must consider
the Party and that, since they agree there is no chance of getting rid of
Gaitskell, we must go ahead and do the best we can with him.

I was so appalled by Monday's meeting and the chaos it left in the document that on Tuesday morning I rang Gaitskell. Characteristically, he and
George Brown had both spent Monday debating Wedgy Benn[1] in the House

---

[1] His father, Lord Stansgate, had died on November 17th, 1960, and Anthony Wedgwood
Benn sought to renounce the peerage he thus inherited. The Labour constituency party of
South-East Bristol, Mr Benn's former seat, readopted him as its candidate and in a by-
election on May 4th he doubled his majority. On May 8th Mr Benn returned to Westminster;
he was excluded from the House of Commons, in accordance with a vote taken on
April 13th. Mr Gaitskell moved that he be admitted and heard; this motion was defeated
by 73 votes. Mr Benn's Conservative opponent in the by-election, Malcolm St Clair, discharged his duty of claiming the Bristol seat and the Government carried a motion
remitting the decision to a court of two judges. For the passage of the Act which eventually
enabled Mr Benn to keep his seat, see below, p. 1004 and n. and see *The Table*, 1961.

"If only it was someone else out of harm's way in the Lords . . ."

so that I was likely to be faced at next Tuesday's Executive with a document which neither the Leader nor the Deputy Leader had discussed. Meanwhile, day by day, the press has been pouring out details—on Monday the *Daily Mail*, slanted to Harold Wilson; on Tuesday the *Herald*, re-slanted to Gaitskell; and on Thursday an exclusive scoop by the *Guardian* on all the latest changes. It really is intolerable. However, there is to be a meeting on Monday morning between Hugh, George Brown, Harold and myself. Hugh said he was bound to take up the press with Harold and I fear the worst, since what really matters is not the leaking in the press but what on earth we are to do when the Executive meets on Tuesday evening.

Monday, May 15th
Over the weekend the flood of leaks about the Home Policy document continued. Today we had the meeting between Hugh, George, Harold and myself. I was fascinated to know what would take place. I got there, with Harold, a few minutes early. Harold, by the way, had rung me up in high alarm last night. No doubt he had been informed by Peter Shore of my more drastic comments on the draft. I allayed Harold's fears by first agreeing that the analysis and then the part on public ownership at the end were all right and that only the middle part was squashy. That's well over half of it. Harold said we could try to get Hugh and George to agree Parts I and III and allow redrafting of the middle. He also said that they would want to postpone it till after Conference.

Hugh came in next and George and I expected a blazing row about the leaks, with George accusing Harold, but everything was sweetness and light. Hugh asked George to give his view and at once he said that he thought Parts I and III were all right, broadly speaking. I checked with George very carefully to make sure and, true enough, all the part about public ownership and so on is undisputed. Then George said, quite wittily, that it contained so much that the gaps were even more obvious. If one tries to write about everything, one notices what one leaves out. Harold at once agreed and blamed Peter Shore. 'That boy is trying to put in everything, including a passage on Wolfenden,[1] which would cost us, at a rough estimate, 6 million votes. It's these young people trying to deal with modern problems.' Hugh said, 'Can't we be sure this time not to say things which are going to lose us votes?' I

---

[1] In September 1957 the Report was published of a departmental committee, with Sir John Wolfenden as chairman, to advise on possible changes in the laws relating to homosexuality and prostitution. On homosexuality, the report (Cmnd 247) recommended that homosexual behaviour between consenting adults in private should no longer be a criminal offence. In November 1958 the House of Commons at last debated the Report's recommendation. There was no vote. In mid-December of that year the Government introduced a Bill dealing with the subject of prostitution. Wolfenden's recommendations regarding homosexuality were again discussed on June 29th, 1960, when a Labour Member's motion supporting the Report's recommendations was defeated by 213 votes to 99, on a free vote. Legislation reforming the laws relating to homosexuality was eventually passed in 1967, as a result of sustained efforts in the House of Lords.

A philosophy don, John Wolfenden was a Fellow of Magdalen College, Oxford, 1929–34, Headmaster of Uppingham School 1934–44 and of Shrewsbury School 1944–50, and Vice-Chancellor of the University of Reading 1950–64. In addition to serving as Chairman of the Departmental Committee on Homosexual Offences and Prostitution 1954–7, he was Chairman of the University Grants Committee 1963–8 and Director and Principal Librarian of the British Museum 1969–73. In 1974 he became a life peer. He published a volume of memoirs, *Turning Points* (London: The Bodley Head, 1976).

said the most important thing was to know what to do tomorrow. Hugh said he would like the officers to be instructed to draft it all over again. Of course I knew this was going to come in the end. It always does.

We then looked at one or two of the controversial passages. We all thought that all the proposals for the public schools were far too detailed and George Brown made the sensible comment that more emphasis should go on primary and secondary education, possibly by reversing the order and starting with the schools, going on to the universities and ending with the public schools. Hugh said he hadn't been able to check on the passage about land and indeed I got the impression that none of them had had time to look at it properly. We then had George Brown saying he thought the whole thing should be postponed till after Conference.

Harold and I pointed out that this would only be interpreted in one way and that it didn't matter what we said – that interpretation would hold. On the other hand, it seemed to me impossible to get an agreed version by tomorrow or even by the June meeting. The one possibility was to get the officers instructed to do a draft of their own. This would keep it out of the hands of the Home Policy Committee and in fact meant that I should have to draft it. There were some quite friendly facetious references to leaks but in the course of an hour and a half no one said an angry word. The moment Harold objected to postponement, George gave way. Then we had a long discussion whether we shouldn't have a draft published in September, submitted to Conference and then finally commended as a finished document in the following year. The snag about this, as Harold pointed out, was that Conference would then have twelve months to amend it. How fatal that would be.

Hugh then said, quite well, 'Look, there are five subjects we have to deal with: control of the economy, including public ownership; land values; education; social security; taxation. Let's just have five chapters on those and let's have the analysis of the Affluent Society by somebody who can write it amusingly and not gloomily.' Harold said we should have an Executive weekend, to which Hugh replied that we would want the officers to come for a weekend or for a day. I said, 'Well, I'm away on holiday. You make all your policy decisions and when I come back I'll write it for you – that is, if you can get all this through the Executive tomorrow.' And that was about it. I could feel Hugh was longing to have me stay on talking to him and be reconciled – but not I. I went off with Harold to talk about the Common Market, which, of course, is the real political problem threatening Westminster.

On May 17th a two-day debate on foreign affairs opened in the Commons. Edward Heath, Lord Privy Seal and Commons spokesman for the Foreign Office, devoted the greater part of his speech to setting out the advantages of British membership of the Common Market. The Opposition had no collective policy on this issue. Indeed, all parties contained both opponents and supporters of an application for Britain to join. On May 26th it was announced that an all-party committee of eminent men and women called upon the Government 'formally and explicitly to declare their readiness in principle' to join the Common Market. On June 13th Mr Macmillan stated that the Government had as yet taken no decision and that, first, they would have full discussions with Commonwealth Governments. Mr Sandys, Mr Thorneycroft and Mr John Hare accordingly set off to visit Commonwealth capitals.

I was at Oxford on Thursday, debating at the Union[1] with Julian Amery, and found myself dining next to his wife,[2] who is a young Macmillan. She was quite frank and interesting about the crisis in the Tory Party on the Common Market and the danger that all the agricultural constituencies would get upset and the Party be split. Here, for once, the Labour Party is being canny. Just imagine if for the last two years we had discussed the Common Market as we've been discussing nuclear weapons! Instead we've had the sense to stand on the side and wait for the Government to commit itself.

Wednesday, May 17th
So once again this curious kaleidoscope has shaken the pieces of glass into another pattern and we are all back collaborating once again on a new document. It all happened roughly as I wanted. We sat down yesterday at five o'clock and started, of course, with a complaint about leaks. After three hours, I proposed an adjournment until half-past eight. Anne came at eight and I took her and Peter Shore and Harry Nicholas down to the Visitors' Dining Room, where I had taken the precaution of ordering a table for four, and had the pleasure of seeing Hugh Gaitskell and Sam Watson come in and be turned away because there was no place. Indeed, they had to go down to the bar.

We resumed the meeting and by ten o'clock we had got through the main policy points and there came the question as to who was to do the work. Someone breathed the word 'officers', there was a sigh of relief and that was that. Nobody suggested referring the document back to the Home Policy Committee or setting up a special drafting committee. So we had our way. It was a five-hour show and at the end of it that awful Callaghan said, 'I think we should move a vote of thanks to our Chairman.' There was a hum of applause. They had been pushed and shoved and bullied along and at one point Ian Mikardo had shouted back that they knew the business wouldn't have got done without it.

At twelve o'clock this morning the officers went down to Morgan's room,

---

[1] The motion was 'That this House has no confidence in Her Majesty's Government's defence policy'. Richard Crossman spoke third, for the motion, and Julian Amery spoke fourth, in opposition. The motion was carried by 161 votes to 96.
[2] Catherine, daughter of the Rt Hon. Harold Macmillan, married Julian Amery in 1950.

where the Chairman presided and allocated work to his boys. Gaitskell, Brown and Wilson are to jointly work away on first drafts of the two sections Public Ownership and Finance. Gaitskell, because he is gifted, is to have a personal shot at the part on land. Crossman will do the rest. 'And where does the office come in?' asked Peter Shore plaintively. 'At this stage,' Hugh Gaitskell remarked firmly, 'you should sit back and let somebody else have a go.' It was a very strange atmosphere of reconciliation, especially when Hugh invited me to spend the whole of one Saturday at Frognal Gardens. What will Dora think? And will she put arsenic in the tea? No. Because, in politics, friendships change with political constellations and the wife of a Labour Leader must accept it.

I very much suspect that this means the end of our Tuesday lunches. It was very much dying yesterday. Harold Wilson failed to turn up and told me blandly that he had forgotten. Barbara was busy elsewhere, Jennie was in Canada, Tom was at a service in the Kingsway Hall and there we were with no common denominator, since we are still divided on defence and on this domestic policy I am sure we shall find Foot and Mikardo will attack it, whatever it now says.

Meanwhile, one little anecdote from Michael Foot. He sat with me in the Smoking Room on Tuesday evening, after the N.E.C. 'I've just been giving Kingsley a drink,' he said, 'and was tactful enough to make the kind of comments on the *Statesman* which he would like. Then Kingsley said, "You know, I had to let John Freeman take over at that moment, because otherwise we would have lost him for good to television and if that had happened Dick Crossman would have been bound to get it." ' I find this an extremely interesting observation and I would like to know precisely why Kingsley would like at any price to keep me out. I think he never really forgave me for going to the *Daily Mirror*. Nevertheless, there is little doubt that the *Statesman* is now getting very much duller. John Freeman has brought in a young Scot called Karl Miller[1] from the *Spectator*, and to Paul Johnson he has added Anthony Howard so that the bright young men are in the ascendant, but in both cases young men without any very strong convictions or balance. Balance John himself provides — or over-provides.

The other night I had the Freemans and Llewelyn-Davies to dinner. As so often happens when one carefully arranges a meeting, it didn't at all come off. Patricia arrived half an hour late and immediately assaulted John for destroying the mag. To my astonishment, John replied, 'You don't seem to realize that 40 per cent of our readership are Tories and we can't disregard their views altogether.' Then, under my prompting I'm afraid, John went on to say, 'The truth is that Kingsley had to go, largely because that absurd

---

[1] Karl Miller worked in H.M. Treasury 1956–7 and at the B.B.C. 1957–8 and was Literary Editor of the *Spectator* 1958–61 and of the *New Statesman* 1961–7. He was Editor of the *Listener* 1967–73 and in 1974 became Northcliffe Professor of English Literature at University College, London.

anti-Gaitskell campaign caused a dangerous sag in circulation. The *New Statesman* shouldn't get involved in these intra-Party personal, factional disputes. We must show a certain detachment and balance.' When he said all this, I felt he was making a desperately poor appearance, and yet he was bridling and genuinely nettled by the attack.

Anne's friend Celia Gimpel[1] told an amusing story today. She had been staying with an old friend who is a manufacturer in Leicester, a Tory, who has read the *Statesman* for years. 'What's gone wrong with it?' he asked her. 'For three months now I've found nothing to be angry at and I only bought it to get angry.' I ought to tell John this story as a reminder that Tories may want some Socialist material in the paper. This is the same kind of mistake that Hugh Gaitskell makes about the Labour Party.

Well, we're off to Greece tonight, so this part of the season ends. What a strange one it has been! The defence controversy burnt itself out – or rather, to change the metaphor, the fire of wrangling was hurriedly quenched when it was felt that the Movement was getting sick of all the leadership, irrespective of Left and Right. But I think there's no doubt that this episode has taught Hugh and George quite a lot. They're obviously desperately anxious to get an agreed domestic policy for Conference and to get personal relations a little better.

On the other hand, I, too, have learnt a good deal. Compared to a year ago, I am seriously sceptical now about the limits of policy formation by party democracy. Certainly the committee machinery of the Executive is becoming completely unworkable in its waste of time and this unworkability is made intolerable by the leaks from Left, Right and Centre by everyone concerned. Compared with this, a coherent parliamentary leadership, grouped round a Leader, is a much more feasible centre of power.

I suppose the truth is as I said it a year ago. The effect on party democracy of the deadlock has been to make all the machinery creak even worse and worse. You certainly can't have the Party legislature functioning well, with our division of powers, unless the Executive is in the hands of a strong Leader, with the confidence of the rank and file. Anyhow, whatever the truth of these reflections, a great deal will be decided by my success with this policy draft. If one could bring off something that the Executive accepts and which gets a good press, the Conference may be enthusiastic and we may start next year in quite a different mood.

Wednesday, June 14th
It's just a week since we got back from our lovely Greek holiday and I am still pining for it. I found myself at once submerged in the Executive affairs, for the first meeting of the officers for finalizing the Home Policy document had been fixed for Sunday and, to my horror, I discovered that the drafts I had

---

[1] Joseph and Celia Gimpel, an old friend of Anne Crossman, lived at No. 9 Vincent Square for a time.

promised to write were expected for circulation on Friday. I found it hard going getting my mind down to this drafting job, which is a slogging kind of work. It requires a lot of skill and, I suppose, a spark of inspiration. But it is one of the kinds of writing in which, in my experience, sheer hard work, trying, re-trying and trying again, is the only way to success.

On Saturday I took the last train to London and on Sunday morning Peter Shore took me up to Frognal at a quarter to eleven. I hadn't been to the Gaitskell house since the fracas started after Scarborough and it was sign indeed of new times that Harold and I were asked for the day, including a lunch provided by Dora, who for months past has been burning candles and sticking pins in them in order to contrive my death by slow torture. However, throughout Sunday all was sunshine and light and we worked steadily away. Harold's draft on public ownership, as I had told him before, was verbose in its analysis and totally inadequate in its conclusions. In the end, while I chatted, I drafted a new last paragraph, which I think is pretty good.

On the other hand, Hugh's chapter on building land gets stronger, more radical and more interesting each time he redrafts it. George Brown, who turned up half an hour late of course, hadn't done any drafting and was intellectually out of his element, since he cannot keep up with us three at this particular kind of work. However, he managed to throw his weight about satisfactorily from time to time, at least sufficiently to deceive himself about his own importance. At the end of the day I felt really sorry for Hugh in having to rely on George Brown as his Deputy. He is not only superficial and lightweight intellectually; he is not only vain and vulgar; he is not only drunken; he is also a little cad. However, in the new spirit of unity, such words should not be recorded, even in a diary. But I do record them, because this day spent with the leadership reconvinced me of my rightness in asserting that I would never lift a finger to replace Gaitskell by George Brown.

Throughout the day it was clear that Gaitskell was not going to try to go back on the policies we had agreed before his defence triumphs. Most of my left-wing friends confidently predicted that this would happen and I have no doubt that George Brown and some of Gaitskell's right-wing advisers would have liked him to try and welsh. But, on Sunday at least, he was scrupulously careful to preserve all the policy decisions and merely to concentrate on presenting them in a palatable and convincing form, convincing both to the Party and to the voter. To achieve that combination is no mean thing.

In the Budget, introduced on April 17th, the Chancellor proposed to raise the starting-point of surtax from £2,000 to £4,000 earned income, to encourage 'initiative and enterprise'. This measure was to be introduced in a year's time. An extra £80 million in taxation was to be obtained by an increase of 2·5 per cent in profits tax, an extra 2d. (0·8 new pence) a gallon on fuel, gas and lubricating oil and paraffin, a 10 per cent duty on television advertisements and an increase from £12 10s. (£12·50 new pence) to £15 in vehicle licences. Mr

Lloyd also sought power to introduce 'regulators'. He asked for authority to add up to 4s. (20 new pence) a week to the employer's National Insurance contribution, as a temporary expedient, if it should be necessary to economize in the use of manpower, and to vary by 10 per cent, up or down, purchase tax and certain duties, including those on tobacco, petrol and alcohol.

This week, with the Committee Stage of the Finance Bill going on and with Anne at Prescote looking after Virginia, I have spent much more time and eaten more meals in the House and so talked to more Labour Members. With every day, Gaitskell's defence triumph becomes clearer. Before I left for Greece it was obvious he would not need the Crossman/Padley amendment and I therefore wasn't really surprised when yesterday on the tape appeared the news that Walter Padley and the USDAW Executive had decided not to put the amendment as a resolution to the Labour Party Conference. This doesn't mean that they have gone back on it. If anybody else puts it down they would have to support it. What it does mean is that Walter, probably correctly, calculates that there isn't a majority for it and that therefore it can hardly be described as a compromise document.

In the lobby last night the Left was very bitter about this, arguing that it was a complete sell-out, and some of them suggested that Walter had been guilty of a lovely machiavellian manoeuvre. One person said that the whole USDAW conference was staged as a breakthrough, with the express intention later of going back on the resolution. All this, of course, is the sheerest nonsense. I think Walter would have been wiser to make USDAW put the resolution on the agenda and stand by it, but to suggest there is anything machiavellian is absurd. In fact, he has been hoist by his own petard. No man has more pedantically insisted on accepting Conference as the final authority and obeying majority decisions. He and I are therefore bound, as members of the Executive, to accept the Executive decision and he is bound to accept Conference's support for Gaitskell when it takes place.

The bitterness of the Left reaction, therefore, has nothing to do with the facts. Indeed, the people who are attacking Walter most bitterly are those who detested our resolution and have never spoken in its favour. If the Left had strongly supported it, Walter's position would have been easier. But the truth is that the Left disliked it even more than the Right and that is something we had to face. Fortunately, however, I had nothing to do with this and could look on at the whole affair with relative detachment.

I slogged away at the redrafting, which I have been carrying on all this week. I have done the preface, the introductory analysis of Toryism, social security and education and after tomorrow evening's meeting I shall have to take the whole thing in hand on Friday and shape it round. Then we see it again on the following Tuesday, after which there will be a final revision before it is circulated to the Executive. At the present stage I feel that we are in the process of turning out a pretty good document but one can never be sure, because sometimes succeeding revisions make a document worse and worse.

Everything will depend on tomorrow evening, when the other officers come to Vincent Square for supper, prepared by Anne. So you see what a love feast there will be. Of course it's great good luck that we can rely on the officers on this occasion. It so happens that, if we had wanted to select four men to do the draft, it should have been Gaitskell, Brown, Wilson and myself, and here we are, all officers, with Harry Nicholas, the fifth officer, having carefully chosen this fortnight to be absent in Brittany.

Meanwhile, slowly but steadily, the issue of the Common Market is over-shadowing the House of Commons, rather like an eclipse of the moon. I have spent many hours discussing it privately with Tommy Balogh and others and formally in the home policy, foreign policy and Commonwealth meetings of the N.E.C., as well as listening to the first of a series of debates in the Parliamentary Party. Hugh Gaitskell and Harold Wilson are firmly determined to avoid making the mistake with this issue that we made on nuclear weapons by trying to work out a detailed Party policy that only splits us. On this occasion we are letting the Government make all the running and we are assisted in this by the fact that the *Daily Mirror* has plumped for the Common Market and is doing an extremely good job of attacking Macmillan for his indecision.

But this fence-sitting may well become increasingly difficult in the next fortnight, because, slowly, Labour M.P.s are lining up in new constellations. Everybody says that one cannot predict who is for entering and who is against it and that this has little to do with Left and Right. This is a very misleading statement. Crosland and Jenkins are the leading adherents of entry, while the Left (Barbara Castle, Michael Foot, and so on) are leading against it, with such congenital left-wingers as Manny Shinwell and John Dugdale also taking the pro-Commonwealth line. Basically, therefore, this is a Left/Right issue, though there are some unusual divergences. Douglas Jay, for example, is on this occasion against entry. So are Michael Stewart and Bill Blyton, while, to my amazement yesterday evening, I found Richard Llewelyn-Davies, now Professor of Architecture at London, vigorously for it, though I have always regarded him as extremely left-wing.

I suppose the truth is that we are bound to be a bit divided in ourselves on this issue, for the following reasons. The fact that Britain must now consider entering the Market is a demonstration that the attempt to maintain our-selves as an independent Great Power, which all parties have been making since the war, has come unstuck. Even three years ago, no one was dreaming of proposing such a thing. Everybody not only underestimated the likelihood of the Common Market's coming off but overestimated our capacity to stay out if it did. In fact, despite all pretensions, for fifteen years we have been going downhill, while France and Germany have been overtaking us and forging ahead. All parties have blinded themselves to this awkward fact.

Now, of course, it is true, as I pointed out in my Fabian pamphlet,[1] that the real case for an out-and-out Socialist policy is that without it 50 million people cannot survive as a separate economy. From this point of view, in fact, entry to the Common Market is a substitute for Socialism. It is hoped that, if the British economy is pushed inside Europe, the necessity of competing within the tariff wall will provide the shock required to shake British industry out of its apathy.

Tommy Balogh said that going in would mean devaluation and the 10 per cent cut in our standard of living which we need, unless we are prepared to impose upon ourselves the same degree of austerity by Socialist means. The trouble is that all of us know that, if we stay out of the Common Market, it will not be in order to have an extremely austere Socialist economy but to go on drifting along in our usual provincial, insular way. Talking to Llewelyn-Davies last night, I said at least staying out would enable us to go neutral, in the event of the Kennedy regime going wrong and war coming in Berlin. 'Not at all,' he replied. 'Britain outside the Common Market will become an appendage of America, a mere anchored aircraft carrier, if I know anything about it. No, the only kind of unit which could become a third force is a federal Europe and that is one reason why we ought to get inside.'

At the three Executive meetings I have attended, I have been shocked by Harold Wilson's bumbling fence-sitting and by his anxiety to postpone decisions by any kind of excuse. The paper which was produced by his committee[2] was deplorable and I find Hugh Gaitskell on this occasion far more sensible. While I have been supporting Hugh and Harold in avoiding a precise commitment too early, I've been trying to insist that we should publicly, as well as privately, insist on listing the questions that have got to be answered and so formulating minimum conditions of entry. These must surely include, first, treatment of our overseas Commonwealth at least as favourable as that conceded to the French overseas territories; secondly, detailed safeguards for British agriculture (this will be a great deal more difficult to work out than most people imagine); thirdly, assurances that we can carry out Socialist planning and extensions of public ownership within the Market just as freely as we do outside it — i.e. a careful study of the Rome Treaty to ensure that it doesn't forbid the kind of policies we have been working out in *Signposts for the Sixties*; fourthly, assurances that we are not committed to a federal union; last, assurances that in our foreign policy, particularly with regard to Berlin, we should not be committed to the Germans by going in.

Wednesday, June 28th
Since I last wrote I seem to have been doing nothing except prepare for the launching of *Signposts for the Sixties*, which took place at Transport House

---

[1] *A Neutral Belt in Europe?* (London: Fabian Society, January 1958).
[2] The domestic policy document.

at three o'clock this afternoon.[1] We met last Tuesday morning and again on Thursday at midday. By now time was getting very short, since we had to roll off the stencils on Friday afternoon. On Friday Rose at last got a day off and Anne and I went in lovely weather to Hampton Court while the roneos were running. At four o'clock I went into Transport House to O.K. the finished job. Owing to Executive leaks, we had decided to issue the document to members by special messenger on Saturday afternoon, to prevent it getting to the Sunday press. As I left Transport House I said to the girl there, 'Thank God this is over.' 'No,' she said. 'I'm spending Saturday afternoon driving round London delivering copies. It doesn't give me great confidence in the Executive that I have to spend my Saturday afternoon this way because they can't be trusted not to leak to the press.' It is indeed humiliating and I wasn't surprised to find that by Monday morning the *Daily Mirror* had a copy.

On Monday morning I went into Hugh's room at four o'clock, when we had agreed just to have a last look at the draft and make a list of our official amendments, if any. One never knows. Suddenly Hugh was back in the worst of his moods and proposed six amendments, two of them major ones, on the first two pages. Fortunately this took thirty-five minutes and he had a Shadow Cabinet at five o'clock. So we got through the rest, though, dear, oh dear, I was very angry and showed it. What made him in that mood? I don't know. It may be the Sunday press. Some of it was talking a lot about the Big Four who were working miracles for unity, including Harold Wilson and myself. Nevertheless, Hugh has been incredibly well behaved ånd, miraculous to say, at the end of one of my many sessions with him, thanked me profoundly and sincerely — the first time in his whole life he has ever done such a thing, to me at least.

The Executive meeting took place at five o'clock on Tuesday and lasted until twenty past eight, with intervals for two divisions. Again, I judged it wrong. I rather thought that, in its present mood, the Executive would let us have the document. Partly, I think, because we had so many official amendments, it wasn't in that mood. We spent forty-five minutes on the first four pages, with twenty or thirty amendments, most of them minor and literary, but one or two of them quite sensible. Hugh Gaitskell was consecrating the new Archbishop at Canterbury[2] and arrived an hour and a half late, but this didn't make any difference. The Executive just can't keep its hands off a thing like this.

However, I had taken the precaution of first discussing the uncontroversial passages. After one division we had got to Public Ownership and I got it through in six minutes, simply by psychological steam-rollering. 'Page 21', was said so ominously that nobody dared move an amendment, so to speak.

[1] It was published on June 28th.

[2] On January 17th it had been announced that Dr Fisher, who would be seventy-four in May, had tendered his resignation, to take effect on May 31st. His successor was Dr Michael Ramsey, then Archbishop of York.

The Left produced no serious resistance. I'm told my performance as Chairman was outrageous but essential. They really got quite scared of the headmaster.

And so to the press conference, for which Harold Wilson had been preparing by constantly urging that he had to speak as well as Hugh. Actually, very sensibly, none of us spoke. I made a few purely introductory remarks and so did Hugh and we had questions for forty-five minutes.

So that's that. I realize now on reflection, that I must have drafted most of the important documents, unofficial or official, which the Labour Party has had since 1945. My own feeling is that this in its way, is an improvement on *Labour in the Sixties*. It does what it sets out to do. It shows how to apply Socialist principles to the changed conditions. It sets a tone and gives the Party its new posture. But how will the press receive it? In the preparatory leaks, some, like the *Express*, have been talking of Gaitskell's tremendous victory over the Left, others of unity. I am fascinated to see what happens tomorrow.

Meanwhile there is no doubt that once again, in this strange political quadrille, we have moved into the Centre and are bowing and cooing at each other like turtle-doves. This document, like the *The Future Labour Offers You*, is to be launched by a television show, in which, once again, as one of the inner group, I am taking part, along with Harold, George and Hugh. The Left, headed by Michael and Barbara, are, of course, intensely suspicious and on one issue they know that I let down their principles. I was always against municipalization and in this draft I backed Hugh in knocking the doctrinaire guts out of it and making it only one of the jobs local authorities can do in their own time. The Left will certainly describe this as a great betrayal. Dining with Michael last night, I said I had calculated that in advance. It is always a good thing to have a topic where the Left can feel betrayed and concentrate their attacks. Since all their efforts were concentrated on municipalization, everything else had gone through much more easily. Michael thought this was very clever but it was sheer common sense. I think it will probably apply to the Conference as well.

Thursday, June 29th

The Party Meeting this morning was almost embarrassing. Person after person got up to say what a splendid document it was, after Hugh had prosed along for far too long. Then up stood Anthony Crosland and overflowed with praise — the finest document produced since the war, with exactly the right attitude to public ownership. This praise was interspersed with a number of asides, such as that the introduction was brilliantly written but was clearly by someone who had no understanding of the crisis. Nevertheless it was all praise from everyone there. Each person said that they thoroughly approved of not going into too much detail and then asked for detail on his own subject.

On the whole, the Left wasn't there, apart from Harold Davies, and I think it's characteristic that Barbara, Tony, Tom are all notably absent when the document they have shared in producing, but on which they have agreed with Gaitskell, is being put to the Party. Each is busily preparing a position from which he can say that he did his best valiantly, month after month, but was defeated.

Crosland had started with a complaint that the Parliamentary Party had not been consulted and that such documents should in future be prepared with full representation from the Parliamentary Committee. In reply, George Brown, not unreasonably, pointed out that, of the four people who drafted, all were M.P.s, two elected by the Parliamentary Party and two by the Conference, and then he added, 'One shouldn't mention names but I can't help paying special tribute to Dick Crossman, who not only did most of the drafting but contributed so much to the discussion of policy throughout our sessions.' So that was the culmination of the love duet. When I recall that, a few months ago, I was being denounced in the Party Meeting by George Brown for unforgivable, irresponsible lying about the Leader and that roughly the same people were booing me then as now warmly cheered me, I realized the full unpredictability of Labour politics.

Thursday, July 13th
After a weekend in the Northern Region[1] I came back on the night sleeper to King's Cross, looking forward to Monday's Home Policy meeting on the Common Market. This proved to be extremely interesting. Peter Shore and David Ennals had both prepared quite good office papers and, when Harold Wilson opened the meeting and asked who would start, there was complete silence. So Barbara breezed in. I was sitting close to her and had discussed with her what line we should take. She put forward the idea that, while remaining carefully uncommitted on the big issue, we should propose to the T.U.C. that, in any joint statement, we should outline the basic conditions necessary for Labour support for going in; namely: full satisfaction of the Commonwealth claims; a clear understanding that we were not committed to federal union; meeting the requirements of EFTA and of British agriculture.

When she finished I was most unwilling to speak but literally nobody else would say anything. They were all so scared of disunity. So I took much the same line as Barbara, though I pointed out that the threat of immediate entry seemed somewhat reduced by the tremendous storm of opposition in Australia and New Zealand. I threw out the idea, which I knew would cause some alarm, that, if we had offered Malta integration,[2] I couldn't see how, in the event of our going in, we could deny the right of integration to any Commonwealth country which wanted it. This would bring them inside the Common Market and put them on a level with Algeria.

[1] Addressing Labour Party regional conferences.
[2] See above, pp. 440 and 449 ff.

My poor colleagues' breath was taken away by such an original idea and that warmed my heart, so I added that I thought we ought to look ahead and see the kind of job Labour would have if Britain joined the Common Market. Clearly we should have to become federalists and see our Socialism in terms of strengthening a federal State. Clearly, also, most of our energies for the next ten years would be spent on organizing the European Labour Movement, since we would be bound to be leading an Opposition. I added that this was a role which I could well appreciate but I was surprised that some of my colleagues seemed to acquiesce in the notion of permanent Opposition, which would undoubtedly be our fate inside the Common Market.

The moment I had finished Hugh weighed in and said he disagreed with everything I had said and it was foolish and irresponsible. He was as determined as ever to say absolutely nothing either way. Any kind of attempt to lay down conditions would split the Movement from top to bottom. Anyway, conditions would either be platitudinous or too detailed to carry conviction before we knew what Macmillan was up to. Of course, once Hugh had spoken, everybody else weighed in. Alice Bacon, who is a firm anti-Common Marketeer, still supported Hugh by saying there could be no thought of Labour's making any statement until the negotiations were over. Fred Mulley was appalled by another of my ideas, namely that we should insist that the Government should seek a fresh mandate before any treaty was signed. To fight an Election on that, he said, would be to split the Party. 'But surely,' I remarked, 'the whole future of British democracy and sovereignty is something which requires M.P.s to show a certain responsibility.'

Hugh was terribly nettled, rough, hasty and back in his old form of plunging far too soon. However, it was universally agreed that nothing whatsoever should be said or done by the joint meeting with the T.U.C. on Friday, which will obviously be the sheerest waste of time. Harold Wilson closed the meeting by what I would describe – I must say people laughed – as his best completely impartial summing-up against the Common Market.

On June 4th President Kennedy and Mr Khrushchev had met in Vienna and the Soviet leader had handed the President two memoranda. One proposed a conference to conclude a German peace treaty and to establish West Berlin as a demilitarized free city; the other suggested that nuclear test negotiations should be merged with discussions on disarmament. On July 17th, after obtaining the approval of the NATO Council, America, Britain and France rejected the Soviet proposal on Germany and West Berlin. Acrimonious exchanges continued between the U.S.S.R. and the West over the future of the city. On August 13th the authorities in East Berlin closed the frontier between that part of the city and West Berlin.

The Common Market issue continues to dominate everybody's thinking and indeed dominates my thinking now. Today's *Times* is indicative of the mood I found with Pam Berry[1] and her friends, when I lunched with them a few days ago. Pam had had the Prime Minister to lunch last week and he had drunk six brandies after lunch. In the course of the meal, he had twice referred to the danger of World War III starting over Berlin and the desperate plight of this country. Apparently he had sounded like Ramsay MacDonald in reverse — down and down and down.[2] But there's no doubt there's now a deep and profound mood of defeatism in the London Establishment and that Hugh Gaitskell shares it.

On July 20th the Prime Minister announced in the House of Commons that on Monday, July 31st, he would make a Statement on the European Economic Community and that there would be a debate later in the week, before Parliament rose for the summer Recess. The Prime Minister's Statement emphasized his belief that it was 'both our duty and our interest' to contribute towards the strength of the free world 'by securing the greatest unity in Europe', while maintaining 'long-standing and historic ties' between the United Kingdom and other Commonwealth nations. He concluded:

> *We have now reached the stage where we cannot make further progress without entering into formal negotiations ... with a view to joining the Community, if satisfactory arrangements can be made to meet the special needs of the United Kingdom, of the Commonwealth, and of the European Free Trade Association.*

The House held a two-day debate on August 2nd and 3rd. The Opposition offered an Amendment to the Government's policy, declaring that Great Britain should enter the European Economic Community only if 'this House gives its approval and if the conditions negotiated are generally acceptable to a Commonwealth Prime Ministers' Conference and accord with our obligations and pledges to other members of the EFTA'. In the division, the Opposition Amendment was defeated by 318 votes to 209. The Government's proposals were approved by 313 votes to 5, with rather more than 20 Conservatives abstaining and a slightly smaller number of Labour M.P.s refraining from supporting the Opposition Amendment. On August 10th Britain's formal application for membership of the E.E.C. under Article 237 of the Treaty of Rome was lodged with the Brussels headquarters of the Council of Ministers.

---

[1] Pamela Berry, the second daughter of the 1st Earl of Birkenhead. In 1954 she became President of the Incorporated Society of London Fashion Designers and in 1979 a Trustee of the British Museum. Her husband, Michael Berry, was Chairman and Editor-in-Chief of the *Daily Telegraph* and the *Sunday Telegraph*. He was Chairman of Amalgamated Press Ltd 1954–9 and became a life peer in 1968, taking the title of Lord Hartwell.

[2] A reference to a speech, celebrated for its vague and rambling style, which Ramsay MacDonald made in 1935, when he proclaimed, 'Society goes on and on and on. It is the same with ideas.'

At the Trades Union Congress, on September 5th, a motion of approval of the Government's decision was carried by the show of hands. On the last day of the Congress, September 7th, delegates decisively repudiated the unilateral disarmament policy they had supported the year before. Mr Cousins declared that 'this struggle will go on'.

The Labour Party Conference met at Blackpool from October 2nd to 6th. On the first day delegates endorsed the N.E.C. decision to expel the Communist-controlled Electrical Trades Union, by a majority of roughly 9 to 1. On October 3rd a proposal by Mr Cousins that Signposts for the Sixties *should contain more precise pledges of further nationalization was defeated by 3,759,000 to 2,453,000 votes and on the next day the unilateralists were defeated by 4,526,000 to 1,756,000 votes. On October 5th the Conference discussed entry to the E.E.C.; no decision was taken.*

On October 9th, two days before the Conservative Party Conference, the Prime Minister announced a Cabinet reshuffle. R. A. Butler retained the office of Home Secretary and assumed, in addition, the task of co-ordinating the work of Ministers concerned with E.E.C. negotiations. His posts as Leader of the House of Commons and Chairman of the Conservative Party Organization passed to Iain Macleod. The Colonial Office went to Reginald Maudling, who was succeeded as President of the Board of Trade by Frederick Erroll, a new Cabinet Minister. Henry Brooke became Chief Secretary to the Treasury and Paymaster-General, with a seat in the Cabinet. (A Mrs Margaret Thatcher became Joint Parliamentary Secretary to the Ministry of Pensions and National Insurance.)

At the Conservative Party Conference, held at Brighton from October 11th to 14th, delegates approved of the decision to apply for E.E.C. membership. On October 10th Edward Heath made his opening statement to E.E.C. Ministers in Paris.

Crossman kept no diary during this period.

Tuesday, November 28th

Why did I stop writing this diary last July? Partly, no doubt, I just stopped for a week and then it became a second week and so on. Partly it was the long Recess. But I suspect there was another motive — the sense that one's political life was so useless and, even worse, so trivial, that the idea of leaving a record of it was purely horrific. Certainly, when I look back on what has happened since last summer and imagine myself recording it spasmodically so that it unreeled in thousands and thousands of words, it's profoundly depressing. So let's have the pleasure of abridging into three or four paragraphs what might have been half a volume of diary.

Last summer I was completely intent on the job that Harold Wilson and I had set ourselves. We were determined to create, if it was possible, a Centre of the Party and we were convinced that we could only do this from our position of Left of Centre. For this purpose it seemed to us absolutely necessary to produce a home policy on which everybody agreed and then to ensure that the Blackpool Conference, in which I was Chairman and Harold was Vice-Chairman, should be a Unity Conference, in which we put divisions behind us and, even though the leadership was far from perfect, we all decided to back them, at least up till the next Election.

When I got down to the job of writing my Chairman's address, this was my theme. At the time I thought that the appalling difficulty I found in composition was due simply and solely to the fact that this was quite literally the first occasion in my whole life in which I had written out a speech verbatim. I have no doubt that had a lot to do with it but in retrospect I can see a second cause of my difficulties. What I was trying to do was to think up synthetically the basis of unity and express it in a speech which would make the Left feel that its views and feelings were being respected, without giving the Right a sense of provocation. The real truth is that the message I brought them was a Centre message, which neither the Right nor the Left wanted to hear and which, to some extent at least, was actively resented, on the grounds that I had no right to use my position to put that sort of thing over on them.

In the early part of the Conference the three sessions on *Signposts for the Sixties* were dreary in the extreme. Delegates were restless and for some reason all the trade union leaders had decided to boycott the debate, so as to leave Frank Cousins the only one speaking — a nice idea for private warfare against Cousins but a bad idea if our aim was to put *Signposts* over. Indeed, alas, the Conference really only woke up for the defence debate on Wednesday.

We ended, with some difficulty, at twelve o'clock on the last morning and had the normal votes of thanks, to which I replied. I again stressed the theme of unity for the two years before the Election and. threw into a quite impromptu speech the phrase, 'The policy and the leadership issue are settled'. I didn't think very much about it until I noticed that the left-wing table in the dining room had disappeared at lunch-time without saying goodbye. After that Anne and I went to Portmeirion, so it wasn't for ten days that I discovered that this sentence had been regarded as the great betrayal by a Left which had been looking very hard for some excuses for its total ineffectiveness.

But all that is unimportant. What was important, to me at least, when we resumed this October was the quick realization that Harold and I had achieved exactly nothing, except to infuriate the Left and to isolate ourselves even more completely. All this summer, despite the fact that I had worked quite happily with Hugh, I hadn't talked to him privately. I had one talk with him shortly before we went to the Socialist International at Rome.[1] I formally asked to see him to talk about the general secretaryship. Morgan Phillips's determination to appear at Blackpool had been useful in making

[1] Where the Seventh Congress opened on October 23rd.

everybody, including his wife,[1] realize that he would have to retire, poor man. So there the post was, open.

I went to tell Hugh that in my view the appointment of Len Williams would be utterly disastrous. At this time Hugh was open to the thought but obviously deeply committed the other way. I explained why I thought this and then told him that, if he had wanted, I would have retired from Parliament to do the job, but I gathered there was no chance of this. Hugh looked relieved at my letting him out of saying no and then said he wanted me to concentrate this year on Transport House preparations for the next Election. He told me he was putting George Brown in charge by making him chairman of Organization.

I then said I couldn't be a member of the campaign committee or indeed do anything effective unless I were the chairman and that Harold Wilson had proposed that Alice should move to Home Policy to make way for me at Publicity. To this Hugh replied, rather tesily, 'That's asking a lot of me, you know, to move poor Alice after the work she's done. No, I couldn't do that. I must find room for you some other way if possible.'

I said I wasn't particularly sorry not to do too much in Transport House because I'd been out of Parliament for a year and would like to become active there once again. What did Hugh think of that? To this he replied hastily, 'Oh, there'll be no promotions to the Front Bench, you know. One has to get there by one's own efforts. But', he added, 'I wouldn't advise you to stand this year, since there's no chance of your getting on. They've decided to have the present team re-elected. No, you keep out of it this year. Do your *Guardian* column[2] and make a few speeches and concentrate on Transport House.' Then, my official half-hour being up, he thanked me and I withdrew.

I wasn't a bit surprised by this talk, though I would have been if Anne hadn't been so firm and correct in her predictions. It was clear then that Hugh had quite deliberately pushed aside any idea of forming a Centre, that he was relying on the Right of the Party, that he was allowing Harold to work with him because he was indispensable on the Front Bench and that I could work on the same terms in Transport House. But, as allies, he didn't want us. Indeed, I forgot to mention that at one point in our talk he said, 'I can do nothing whatsoever for you. Don't you realize that last year, when you and I were quarrelling and I was seeing you, all my friends were accusing me of being far too close to you? The same would happen this year.' This conversation had taken place just after it had been announced that Tony Greenwood would be standing for the leadership, an announcement Lynn Ungoed-Thomas and I opposed.

[1] Norah Lusher married Morgan Phillips in 1930. She became a life peer in 1964 and was a Government Whip in the Lords 1965–70. In 1978 she became Lord-Lieutenant of Greater London.

[2] Crossman had first discussed with Alastair Hetherington in June 1960 the suggestion that he should write a weekly *Guardian* column. 'Left of Centre' began on October 20th, 1961.

After this I went to Rome for the Socialist International and had five days working on a delegation with Hugh, which made me realize once and for all that I just can't work in the same committee with him. So I came back not too depressed at the prospect of opting out for a year. However, then came the elections to the Shadow Cabinet. The Left wanted a slate and right at the last moment I agreed to stand and then carefully wrote a column in the *Guardian* which lost me a lot of votes. Even so, apart from Harold and Fred Lee, who were members before, I came top of the Left — above Alice Bacon, to my surprise and everybody else's by the way, but showing, I suppose, that some thirty people in addition to the fifty basic Left supporters wanted me on the Front Bench.

So here we are, more polarized than ever and with the situation in the country going steadily further and further against the Government. What is the net result? Well, one thing's certainly been achieved. Hugh Gaitskell and George Brown are together taking complete responsibility for leadership and they will take the full credit for any success we have. There is no question of any joint efforts. The Party is to be led by the right-wing, the election plans are to be drawn up by the right-wing. Indeed, they have excluded from the campaign committee any except the chairmen of active committees, thus making it consist of Harry Earnshaw, George Brinham, Alice Bacon and George Brown.

All this, as I say, means that this year the Right will take all the credit or all the blame for everything up to the Election. Harold Wilson has taken the line that, though we should never rock the boat and always do our duty, we need not over-exert ourselves. 'This year I shall be playing golf on Sundays, not taking regional conferences,' he has said more than once. And that is the sensible line to take. We have tried our level best to create a situation where Hugh can be in the Centre, working with people on the Left as well as on the Right. Our overtures have been refused.

At the end of 1961, on December 21st and 22nd, President Kennedy and Mr Macmillan met in Bermuda, to plan the next stage of Western relations with the U.S.S.R. The Soviet Union had resumed the testing of nuclear weapons and it seemed plain that the U.S.A. must now do likewise. On Berlin, it was decided that diplomatic contacts should once more begin in Moscow.

The 1962 Defence White Paper, The Next Five Years *(Cmnd 1639), was published on February 20th. It indicated that the existing deterrent, the V-bomber force, would be retained for the remainder of the decade, its striking power assisted further by the Blue Steel stand-off bomb and, later, by the American-manufactured air-to-ground missile, Skybolt. Britain would maintain all its existing overseas alliances and every effort would be made to continue with all-Regular forces, without resort to selective military service. The Government were, it appeared, pressing the West German Government to make a larger contribution to the maintenance of the 51,000 troops stationed in the Rhine.*

31

These cost £73 million a year in foreign exchange. The total defence budget for 1962/63 was to be £1,721 million, 7 per cent of gross national product.

In the defence debate on August 5th and 6th, Harold Wilson referred to dwindling American faith in the British nuclear deterrent; Harold Watkinson, the Minister, did not concede this, though he did reveal his own doubts on the political stability of Aden and Singapore, where there were British bases.

On April 1st Mr Thorneycroft, now Minister of Defence, announced in the Commons the end of the agreement with the United States for the stationing of sixty Thor intermediate-range missiles in Britain. These weapons were too vulnerable to be used for more than a first strike and they were rapidly becoming obsolete. On August 10th the English Electric Company, manufacturers of the short-range Army missile, Blue Water, learnt that this project was to be scrapped. NATO allies had decided to purchase a similar U.S. missile, the Sergeant, so that Blue Water would be too expensive for Britain to manufacture alone. Moreover, Mr Thorneycroft had been obliged to make drastic savings in defence expenditure to avoid the estimates rising to £200 million a year. This episode emphasized that U.S./U.K. interdependence had not been entirely successful and, indeed, seemed to have been largely at Britain's expense. From September 9th to 16th Mr Thorneycroft visited Washington to make this point.

A month later the Americans faced a major crisis in foreign policy. On October 22nd President Kennedy announced that the Soviet Union was building missile bases in Cuba and that the United States intended to impose a blockade on all military supplies approaching the island. Offensive weapons already installed there must be dismantled. British reaction was ambivalent, especially on the part of Labour's N.E.C., which pressed for a U.N. investigation. On October 25th the Prime Minister emphasized in the Commons that there should be 'no wavering or break among the Allies. That is perhaps the main purpose of the Russian initiative'. Three days later Mr Khrushchev agreed to withdraw the missiles.

Meanwhile, on October 20th, the Chinese launched an attack on Indian military posts along the Himalayan border. The Chinese announced a ceasefire on November 21st; six days later after much delay, agreement was officially signed in Delhi for the despatch of British arms to India. The British Foreign Secretary declared that Mr Khrushchev should now be persuaded to see the developing common interest between the Soviet Union and the West, in the face of Chinese intransigence.

In December it became known that the U.S. Government no longer intended to develop the Skybolt missile and, when the American Secretary of State for Defence, Robert McNamara, visited London on December 11th, Mr Thorneycroft stressed the British commitment to this weapon, originally negotiated in 1960, at the time of the abandonment of Blue Streak. Four days later Mr Macmillan set out on a series of crucial diplomatic visits, beginning with a call on President de Gaulle. On December 19th he arrived at Nassau, in the

Bahamas, for a meeting with President Kennedy. By this time more than 120 Conservative backbenchers had signed a motion insisting that Britain should retain its independent nuclear status. President Kennedy first offered to hand over the Skybolt programme to Britain, with joint financing; this the Prime Minister refused. On December 21st the President offered to supply both Britain and France with Polaris missiles, to be fired from nuclear submarines, provided the European contribution was earmarked for a new NATO force. It was conceded that, in a major emergency affecting Britain alone, the British submarines could still operate under orders from London. Mr Macmillan accepted these arrangements, though President de Gaulle remained suspicious.

In domestic affairs, too, Mr Macmillan was in difficulty. The Budget presented on April 9th had been neutral; it did little to ameliorate the worsening economic situation. The Treasury's Economic Survey *(Cmnd 1678), published five days before, had warned that Britain's export goods were not competitive and that pressures of home demand on the economy were becoming too great. In the previous year, at the end of July, the Chancellor had introduced a 'pay pause'. This was intended to allow production to catch up with incomes and, in the longer term, a National Economic Development Council was to be established, to assist in planning the economy. Bank rate had been increased from 5 to 7 per cent, credit became more difficult to obtain for personal consumption and property development, and the Treasury had issued an Order, using the 'regulator', making the full 10 per cent surcharge on customs duties and purchase tax.*

In February 1962 the Government published a White Paper, Incomes Policy: The Next Step *(Cmnd 1626), setting out the criteria by which future wage demands would be judged. The pay pause came to an end, officially, on April 1st; henceforth normal arbitration procedures were resumed but the Government expected that a 2·5 per cent 'guiding light' would be observed. Neither employers nor the T.U.C. received these exhortations with enthusiasm. In late July the Government also established a National Incomes Commission, to inquire into and express views on important wage claims, in the light of the national interest.*

Throughout the year the decline in the Government's popularity showed itself in by-elections and local elections. Mr Macmillan's grip seemed to be slipping and on July 13th he implemented an extensive Cabinet reshuffle. Seven out of twenty-one Cabinet Ministers were dismissed: the Lord Chancellor, Lord Kilmuir; the Chancellor of the Exchequer, Selwyn Lloyd; the Secretary of State for Scotland, John Maclay; the Minister of Defence, Harold Watkinson; the Minister of Housing and Local Government, Charles Hill; the Minister of Education, Sir David Eccles; and the Minister without Portfolio, Lord Mills.

Mr Butler, with a title of First Secretary of State, retained responsibility for both Central African affairs and for the E.E.C. negotiations; his place as Home Secretary was taken by Henry Brooke. Mr Sandys added the Colonial Office to his responsibilities as Commonwealth Secretary, Reginald Maudling became Chancellor of the Exchequer, Peter Thorneycroft Minister of Defence, Sir Edward Boyle Minister of Education and Sir Keith Joseph Minister of Housing and Local Government.

On July 16th the Prime Minister dismissed a further nine junior Ministers. Among those who were newly introduced to office were Edward Du Cann, as Economic Secretary to the Treasury, Nigel Fisher, to a position at the Colonial Office, and Christopher Chataway and David Price at the Ministry of Education and the Board of Trade. Selwyn Lloyd's abrupt dismissal was much deplored and the manner of Lord Kilmuir's departure greatly lamented.

Meanwhile the Conservative Party awaited the outcome of Britain's negotiations over entry to the E.E.C. While the Prime Minister engaged in private talks with his European counterparts, Edward Heath conducted the laborious technical discussions in Brussels. Mr Macmillan also sought to placate Britain's Commonwealth partners. On August 5th the French Foreign Minister, M. Couve de Murville, presented Mr Heath and the other negotiators of the Six in Brussels with a document laying down the French version of the import levies falling on all foodstuffs entering the E.E.C. from outside. At the Commonwealth Prime Ministers' Conference in September it was clear that neither the 'old Dominions' nor the 'new Commonwealth' were happy with recent developments in the negotiations.

Within the Conservative Party there was similar anxiety. In June Mr Sandys had again pledged himself as 'the Commonwealth's watchdog'; on June 14th Sir Derek Walker-Smith and Mr Peter Walker, claiming the sympathy of sixty fellow Conservative backbenchers, published a pamphlet, A Call to the Commonwealth, which presented an alternative solution to E.E.C. entry. On July 30th forty Conservative rebels tabled a motion reminding the Prime Minister of his promises the previous year to the Commonwealth, British agriculture and the partners in the EFTA.

On the same day an Anti-Common Market Committee led by Bill Blyton, Edwin Gooch, John Stonehouse, Barbara Castle and Douglas Jay asserted that they had the backing of a majority of the P.L.P. They were opposed by another group, led by Roy Jenkins and John Diamond, including a large number of young supporters of Hugh Gaitskell and claiming the support of up to ninety members of the P.L.P. Mr Gaitskell continued to strike a balance.

However, on September 9th, the eve of the meeting of the Commonwealth Conference, Mr Gaitskell joined with Commonwealth Labour leaders in a statement opposing Britain's E.E.C. entry on the basis of what had so far been agreed. Labour policy was now that the Government had no mandate to enter Europe. Mr Macmillan broadcast on the next evening his most positive opinion yet in favour of entry.

A few days earlier, at their meeting in Blackpool, the T.U.C. had decided to follow the direction of the General Council and sit on the fence over the E.E.C. issue. Labour's annual Conference, at Brighton from October 2nd to 5th, *with Harold Wilson as Chairman, was expected to close ranks and unite on the demand that a General Election should be held before any irrevocable agreement was reached with the Six at Brussels. But, speaking on October 3rd, Mr Gaitskell asserted that, while on economic grounds the arguments for and against entry were 'no more than evenly balanced', politically a federal Europe would be the end of an independent Britain and of the Commonwealth, the end 'of a thousand years of history'. At the end of the debate George Brown attempted to redress the balance on the pro-European side; he seemed to have support not just from committed pro-Marketeers, but also from right-wing trade union leaders unhappy about Britain's economic prospects.*

Short shrift was given to the anti-Marketeers at the Conservative Conference at Llandudno a week later. Mr Macmillan had already presented his E.E.C. policy in a pamphlet, Britain, the Commonwealth and Europe, *published on October 7th; he now roused the Conference to enthusiastic expectation that Mr Heath would return from Brussels with acceptable terms.*

In the first fortnight of January negotiations resumed in Brussels. But on January 14th President de Gaulle gave a press conference in Paris at which he cast doubt on the Atlantic Alliance and on Britain's capacity to keep pledges she might make in the Brussels negotiations. Britain, he suggested, might better enter into some form of 'association' with the E.E.C.; as for the American offer of Polaris missiles, France preferred to remain independent. When the six E.E.C. partners met again on January 17th to continue their discussions with Mr Heath, the French demanded the indefinite suspension of talks. Protesting, the Five, who had given private assurances to Britain, decided that negotiations would begin again on January 28th. Meanwhile, however, President de Gaulle conferred at the Elysée with Dr Adenauer, who preferred to settle for Franco-German reconciliation. The Six reassembled in Brussels on January 28th; the next day Mr Heath was summoned to the conference room and told that no agreement could be reached on further procedure.

It seemed that the hopes of Mr Macmillan and his Cabinet were dashed. The Opposition saw electoral success approaching—but at this moment they were plunged once more into internal confusion. On December 15th Mr Gaitskell, who had been ill for some time with what seemed to be a form of rheumatism, had gone into hospital to nurse an apparent attack of influenza. He was discharged on December 23rd but shortly afterwards his condition worsened. On January 4th he entered the Middlesex Hospital, where he showed acute symptoms of pleurisy and pericarditis. His doctors diagnosed a severe virus infection of both heart and lungs but they remained unsure about the exact nature of his illness. He was suffering from an obscure immunological disease, Lupus erythematosus, *which had probably been caused by a viral infection. (At the time, Gaitskell's friends believed, incorrectly, that he might have contracted his illness on one of his recent visits to India, Warsaw or Paris and, subsequently, the security services suspected that Gaitskell might have been given a drug while he was in Poland.) By January 17th Gaitskell's condition had so gravely deteriorated that he required an artificial kidney; on January 18th, at the age of fifty-six, he died.*

There were three candidates for the succession: George Brown, supported by the right-wing, including almost all the Shadow Cabinet and trade union M.P.s; Harold Wilson, the candidate of the Left; and James Callaghan, the Shadow Chancellor.

During the whole of 1962 and January 1963 Crossman had kept no diary. Now he took it up once more.

1963

Friday, February 8th

Today I start my diary once more because it looks as though, quite unpredictably, my political life is beginning again. The diary faded off, if I remember rightly, in the summer of 1961 when my year of chairmanship was drawing to a close. At that time I had an ever-increasing feeling that Labour politics were becoming unbearable. Incidentally, though I did not know it at the time, the sheer worry and frustration of that year of chairmanship was stimulating the growth of the ulcer which put me out of action in January 1962. Anyhow, I felt less and less inclination to continue to record trivial details of frustration. Life at Prescote and the farm were becoming more and more important to me and, with the best will in the world, I could not see that, even if we did win an Election and Gaitskell became Prime Minister, he would be heading the kind of Labour Government that I believed in or would give me the kind of scope which I needed to do a job.

Then quite suddenly this Christmas came Gaitskell's illness and death. The whole situation inside the Party was transformed and overnight I was chucked into a battle to elect Harold Wilson. I found myself watching George Wigg at work, being rung up by him every day, ringing up Harold most days, but really leaving George with all the work while I did the talking. Or, if I am very vain, while I fed George and Harold with ideas on how to handle it.

From the day Hugh died, it seemed to me, first, that we should not win if George Brown was our only opponent, getting the Establishment vote as acting Leader of the Party, and, secondly, that in view of Harold's reputation for shiftiness and manoeuvring his best campaign was to have no campaign at all and to be seen studiously doing nothing with closed eyes, while leaving the Party to make up its mind.

On these points at least I think I was proved right. At first George Wigg was afraid of Callaghan's candidature and thought we should do better on a straight vote. But actually the Callaghan candidature was precipitated by the strong-arm methods of the Brownites, combined with the agonized awareness of some of Gaitskell's closest friends that, if Harold Wilson was an odious and impossible man, George Brown was plain impossible.

Watching this from the point of view of my book on democratic politics,[1] I have once again been impressed by the extraordinarily *little* that actually happens in an election of this kind. Certainly, on the Wilson side, there was an absolute minimum of organization, almost as little as the Bevanites used to have. As far as I know, George Wigg[2] relied on Judith Hart and Stephen Swingler to be responsible for the sixty or seventy leftists and on John Stonehouse, John Dugdale and Ben Parkin to tackle all the other possibles George did not tackle himself. But he did at least make a very careful list, first of those of whom we were absolutely certain — not more than seventy —

[1] Which he hoped to write and for which the diaries were to be the raw material.
[2] George Wigg's account of the campaign may be found in *George Wigg* (London: Michael Joseph, 1972), pp. 255-9.

then of the probables and then of the possibles. In the final count George's calculation of the absolute certainties for Harold was 118. The actual figure was 115, confirming that at least a dozen people had solemnly sworn to George that they were voting for Harold when they were actually voting for someone else.[1] He got the George Brown vote fairly accurate but underestimated the Callaghan vote.

Brown's campaign seems to have been run chiefly by Charles Pannell, Desmond Donnelly and such lieutenants as Roy Mason and Frank Tomney. George himself did a good deal of talking in the bars and lobbies and apparently some crude appeals were made to honour, some fairly rough threats were issued, that men would lose their Shadow jobs and chance of office if they voted wrong, but I do not think it came to more than that. What really happened was an inordinate amount of gossiping, gossiping, gossiping among the Labour M.P.s.

Right at the beginning, on the Monday after Hugh's death to be exact, I appeared on 'Panorama' with Charlie Pannell. On the way down, he told me he was campaign manager for George Brown and suggested a pact under which George and Harold would each agree to be Deputy Leader to the other if either one was not successful. This obviously paid Harold as being sense and I concurred. I also concurred that we should only do the broadcast on the understanding that neither of us lobbied for his man. We merely discussed how the Labour Party elected its Leader. Rather characteristically, however, Harold gave this to the press on the Tuesday evening, with the result that he had a furious row with George Brown at the National Executive on Wednesday morning and Brown equally characteristically disowned the pact in the press, thereby cutting off his nose to spite Harold Wilson.

During this period I suppose I have seen more of Wilson than ever before, at least more concentratedly. He has talked to me much more freely about the future. Right at the beginning he suggested that if he won there would be two changes in the Shadow Cabinet. He would give Charles Pannell a job and he would make me spokesman for Science, in fact the head of his private brains trust. I suppose the idea is to do a balancing act by appointing one of his own and one of Brown's men. But I fancy that by now the idea of appointing Pannell is less attractive, though I think Harold has rather the same ideas for me as before.

Throughout George Wigg and I tried to keep Harold from talking to the press but he was constantly eluding us. One thing I did discover is how assiduously he works his press relations, so that he now does it almost by habit. However, as time went on and particularly as George Wigg and I succeeded in getting a wonderful press last Sunday, Harold got more confidence in our efforts.

---

[1] In the first ballot by the P.L.P. on February 7th Harold Wilson secured 115 votes, George Brown 88 and James Callaghan 41. There were 5 abstentions.

We had some difficulty in deciding what to do last night, since we did not know what the result of the first ballot would be. I suggested having a party here for Harold's main workers but he felt this might leak and do damage in the second ballot. Finally we decided that Mary and her son should come down here at six o'clock, to see the telly and hear the result, and that only a few personal friends should come over to supper. I was interested to find who Harold meant by personal friends. Those finally chosen were Harold's secretary, Marcia (who was previously Morgan Phillips's secretary until she changed sides and came over to Harold with all her files and secrets), George Wigg, Leslie Plummer, Tony Greenwood and ourselves.

Tony Greenwood had to be included for very good political reasons. He could have stood himself and, if he had done so and become the fourth candidate, he would almost certainly have scored between 50 and 60 votes, putting Harold third in the ballot and almost certainly ensuring George Brown's victory. A Greenwood candidature would have been as fatal to Harold as a Callaghan proved to George Brown. Harold therefore owes Tony Greenwood a lot and the debt is all the greater when one remembers those awful scenes in my house in 1961,[1] when Tony decided to challenge Hugh, and Harold, when he found the challenge a success, insisted that Tony should stand down for him. Tony is a bit of a fuddy-duddy but he is also a very good man and, as always, behaved impeccably on this occasion and indeed has done so throughout the campaign. But I suspect he didn't much like it when Harold suddenly said last night, 'There is one toast we must drink, to the man who is not here, the man who should have done it, Nye Bevan.' Not that Tony himself was a very loyal Bevanite. When he was elected to the Executive he tried to strengthen his position by refusing to join our Group, but he regards himself as the keeper of the conscience of the Left and resented Harold's attitude to Nye.

I found Harold himself extremely impressive last night. At ten past six I went up to the room he has as chairman of the Public Accounts Committee and found him frantically nervous. Leslie Plummer and George Wigg joined us and we all went downstairs together. In the meeting Harold sat there impeccably imperturbable and after the result we went upstairs again and agreed that, though it was not the best we could hope for, it was the best we could possibly expect. George Wigg had hoped to scrape home with a clear majority in the first ballot but now Harold only required to win 7 of Callaghan's 40-odd votes to achieve a clear majority in the second ballot. He was quite quiet and when we went across to supper he remained cool and collected. He went across our sitting room and said, 'That's my chair', taking the small green one by the fire, where he had always sat at the Bevanite meetings.

[1] See above, pp. 881 ff.

We first discussed the week ahead and the need to continue to prevent any suggestion of deals or collusion, but we also added up and made sure that at the very least Harold has 10 or 12 votes, which is more than is required. After a time we found ourselves discussing the future, on the assumption that Harold will be elected next Thursday. What was to be done about Party publicity? He saw straightaway that he should make a virtue of necessity by refusing to have a personal publicity officer, such as he had attacked Gaitskell for demanding. As for John Harris, Head of Publicity at Transport House, he obviously cannot be sacked but he might become the candidate to take Hugh's place in Leeds. In this case Anthony Wedgwood Benn might be put in, at least until the Election. 'One thing I am going to change,' Harold said, 'is Hugh's habit of wasting his time on the press. Two press conferences a week but no special interviews unless you choose to tell me that they are important.' 'And no social life either,' he added. 'That was another of Hugh's mistakes. A leader cannot afford it. Mary and I will have none of it whatsoever. We have a serious job to do.'

Of course Harold was exhilarated and excited but he was also extraordinarily professional and sensible. Though vain, he is certainly not conceited. Though enormously intelligent, he is certainly not an intellectual. He is a supremely professional politician – in this he resembles Kennedy. But he is also an agile manoeuvrer and something of the demagogue, and therefore a wonderful listener who can pick the brains of skilful people, qualities he shares with Lloyd George. I have a strong feeling that he will make a far better Leader than Gaitskell.

But then, of course, I am prejudiced because of all the 249 Members of the Parliamentary Labour Party Harold is the one person closest to me, the one I get on with best, the one whose relationships with me have been tested over twelve years by some fairly trying times. I think he was really touched by our determination to get his wife Mary down here and look after her yesterday. I think he really does rely on me personally and is probably the only member of the Parliamentary Labour Party who is not afraid of my brutal brain power.

'One change I shall make,' he said to me, I have forgotten when, 'is in the Party's view of science. The scientists, the technologists, and their like felt excluded by the Gaitskell leadership, left out, not wanted. But if I get the job, I shall want to create an atmosphere where they all feel wanted in the Labour Party.' What he aims at, in fact, is the British equivalent of Kennedy's New Frontier, with a professional politician at the centre, hard-boiled, ruthless but with a basic inner drive and integrity, and round him a galaxy of talented, able, brilliant men. In this Harold sees me as the head of his brains trust, with a not too important job which keeps me near him.

This morning I was so excited that I woke up early and started reading at five o'clock. At eight o'clock, the telephone started. Elizabeth Pakenham rang up to congratulate me on Harold's success. She and Frank had dined here last week and revealed that, whereas she is a Wilsonite, Frank is not, but a lukewarm Brownite. Patricia Llewelyn-Davies told me that Tony Greenwood had looked in on her on his return from the House and seemed quite contented. She, too, could hardly believe the incredible truth. Tony Wedgwood Benn had caught a virus in Poland and is in bed with flu but he is thrilled that at last the Labour Party is an open society, not a closed Gaitskell clique.

I rang Harold to emphasize the enormous importance of keeping things absolutely clean for the next five days. 'There must not be a rumour that you are offering anybody anything, let alone doing any deals. There must not be a whisper that anybody, friend or enemy, has been given a job or a promise. There must not be any publicity if we can avoid it.' In the course of the morning, I turned down the *Sunday Pictorial*'s request for a big feature article by me. I stopped the *Observer* publishing this week a profile based on information that Harold and I had given them on the understanding that it would only be used after he had been elected Leader.

Then I went into the House and into an empty Chamber. I ran into Michael Foot. He, too, had this wonderful sense that the incredible has happened and that all kinds of things which had been impossible before Gaitskell's illness are now possible again. Of course, there will be moments of appalling disillusion and depression, but it is my settled conviction that Harold Wilson would be a far better Prime Minister than Hugh would have been, far less autocratic and imperious, far less impulsive and, above all, open to ideas in a way Hugh was not.

Tuesday, February 12th
It was a very pleasant sensation, retreating from the Labour Party election into farming at Prescote. Not that the farm is making much progress when the sun never shines, the sky trails over us and every now and then it sleets or snows a little. I kept on reflecting over the weekend on the unpredictability of politics. During Christmas, I was more than ever brooding over the possibility of semi-retirement, even to accepting a life peerage, since I so much disliked the notion of working with a Gaitskell/Brown Government. But this weekend, I had to assume the near-inevitability of a Wilson Government and to realize that my whole life might well be transformed by it. Harold himself was up in Lancashire with Barbara Castle, George Brown was up in Huddersfield and the West Riding and both men were on their best behaviour, being carefully covered by the press.

In the debate on February 11th and 12th the Prime Minister moved that the House had full confidence 'in the determination and ability of Her Majesty's Government to deal with the political and economic situation arising from the breakdown of the Brussels negotiations'. The Prime Minister set out the changes ahead in the 'Kennedy round', negotiated with the GATT. He forecast a new policy for agricultural support, now running at £342 million a year. Harold Wilson moved an Opposition Amendment calling for changes in Britain's policies in international trade and for economic and political co-operation. It spoke of the need for a sense of urgency and national purpose to meet the situation caused by the breakdown of the Brussels negotiations. Mr Wilson attacked the Government for concentrating on Europe at the expense of Commonwealth trade in the preceding eighteen months; he urged a Commonwealth development programme, which would also help British capital goods industries. The Amendment was defeated by 333 votes to 227 and the Government motion was carried by 330 votes to 227.

I came back to London on Monday and, after lunch, I had to spend the afternoon on the N.E.C. Home Policy Committee, which was going on simultaneously with the big Common Market debate up above in the Commons. Harold, George and James Callaghan were all absent and in their absence I was of course able to get what I wanted about social security. Then I went upstairs to hear the end of Harold's speech. Oh dear, oh dear! He had given me the headings of the speech to include in my *Guardian* column a fortnight ago[1] and, spun out at great length, they sounded even worse. Moreover, he seemed physically tired. Apparently he had diarrhoea in the North and, when he complained to Barbara, she had said to him sweetly, 'The result, my dear Harold, of Anne Crossman's food,' revealing her knowledge that he had been invited to 9 Vincent Square, while she hadn't! So mean are people.

This was having an effect on Harold yesterday. I found the speech pawky but during the evening I discovered that it had had an excellent effect on my colleagues. They found Harold statesmanlike whereas I found him dull. They found that he was at last speaking for the whole Party while I found that he had relapsed into clichés. I suppose I must get used to this now. Certainly George Wigg was right in telling me that I must now not make critical comments, not even *sotto voce*, on my Leader[2] when sitting in the Chamber. But later in the evening Jeremy Bray,[3] our new Member for Middlesbrough, who voted for Callaghan, was telling me how fine he found Harold's speech.

Just when I was going out to give the Baloghs dinner, Dick Mitchison held

---

[1] 'Mr Macmillan's Choice', in the *Guardian*, January 25th, 1963.

[2] Crossman and Wigg were anticipating Harold Wilson's victory, now inevitable, in the second ballot on Thursday, February 14th.

[3] On June 6th a by-election had been held at Middlesbrough West, where the former Conservative M.P., Sir Jocelyn Simon Q.C., had been appointed a judge of the High Court. Dr Jeremy Bray had won the seat for Labour, with a majority of 2,270 over the Conservative candidate, Bernard Connelly. An econometrician, Jeremy Bray sat as Labour M.P. for that constituency 1962–70 and has represented Motherwell and Wishaw since October 1974. He was Parliamentary Secretary at the Ministry of Power 1966–7 and Joint Parliamentary Secretary at the Ministry of Technology 1967–9. He was Chairman of the Fabian Society 1971–2.

me with a beady eye in the inner lobby. 'Sit down and talk to me,' he said, pointing to the bench in the corner by the Opposition Whips. This was something Dick has never done before in seventeen years. I obeyed the Ancient Mariner and his tale began. 'You probably know what I want to ask you. What am I to do, faced by three people, none of whom I much want? Tell me, my dear Dick, what am I to do?' 'Oh, my answer is easy. Your vote no longer matters. We have got Harold in, so you can abstain. We have won it for you, my dear Dick, and you will be able to feel a pleasant surprise at how good Harold is as Leader, knowing that you did not help to elect him.' 'That is not the answer I wanted from you. And anyway why did you assume that I voted for Brown?' 'I make no such assumption but I am saying don't worry about your vote. The issue is decided for the best. Providence this time has been on our side.' 'Well, maybe you are right, and in that case no doubt you will be the Party spokesman on Science. Be sure I bear you no ill-will if you take it over from me. At my age, what can I expect from a young man like Harold?' I quote this conversation to illustrate what George Wigg meant when he said to me, 'On a rough calculation, 250 out of 248 Labour M.P.s voted for Harold on the first ballot!'

Today I went to Morgan Phillips's memorial service[1] in the Kingsway Hall, with Donald Soper[2] presiding and James Griffiths giving what I must reluctantly admit was an admirable and decently modulated address. Of course Harold was there with Mary, looking stunning in black and singing like the Methodist she is. George Brown was not there. He forgot, no doubt, and was preparing his speech for this evening. Whereas the Westminster Abbey service for Hugh Gaitskell was a piece of Anglican ritual, loosely attached to the name of a dead man, Donald Soper's show was a real memorial to a real man. But, alas, Westminster Abbey was packed with all the Establishment and all those who wished to be members of the Establishment, whereas for an infinitely superior memorial the Kingsway Hall was half-empty.

Friday, February 15th
When I asked Jennie[3] about the diary, I was amazed to discover that I last dictated on Tuesday. It only seems a day ago but the fact is that these last days of Harold's campaign have been a curiously intense kind of living. Nevertheless when one adds up what one actually has done to help him, it comes to very little. Indeed, when I look back on the whole four weeks of the campaign, I realize that most of my activity has consisted of talking to Harold once or twice a day, talking to George Wigg every morning on the

[1] He had died on January 15th, 1963.
[2] A Methodist Minister, Donald Soper was Superintendent of the West London Mission at the Kingsway Hall 1936–78. He became a life peer in 1965 and sat on the Labour benches.
[3] Jennie Hall, Crossman's indispensable personal secretary from 1962 to 1966. She later worked in Harold Wilson's Private Office from 1973 to 1974 and for a short time during James Callaghan's premiership, in 1978.

phone and four or five times a day, and having a number of chance conversations with members of the Party. The truth about this election is not how much happened but how little. Or rather, how little happened of organized canvassing. The fascination of it was that, for once, 248 politicians had to make up their minds and take a decision and were left with several weeks in which to discuss how they should vote with each other, with their friends outside and with the press.

On Tuesday evening I went straight back to the House to see Harold, who wanted to discuss future plans. Sitting on his little sofa, he told me that he intended to make Patrick Gordon Walker his Shadow Foreign Minister and Denis Healey Shadow Defence. After discussing this with George Wigg, I told Harold we agreed, more particularly since from early on Denis had with some courage opposed the independent deterrent. 'Not much courage on that occasion,' Harold noted carefully, 'since he did not say so publicly. Nevertheless I agree that he would do well and George would work well with him.' Harold went on, 'As for Gordon Walker, he is so stupid that, by appointing him Shadow Foreign Secretary, I need not commit myself to my real Foreign Secretary when I form my Government. Of course I shall keep my two present P.P.S.s, Slater[1] and Hayman, though Hayman will go in April.' 'But shouldn't you train up one of these bright new men to be your P.P.S.?' I asked. 'Which one?' Harold said, looking at me sharply. I thought rather desperately and said, 'Dick Taverne[2] is voting for you in the second ballot.' 'But what reason have I to think he is trustworthy?' Harold said sharply. 'Oh, no reason at all, but what reasons have you to think him untrustworthy?' 'I don't give people jobs if I don't know whether they are trustworthy,' he said.

After dinner I rushed back in time for the vote on the second day of the second Common Market debate. This had been opened by Harold in a dull, competent speech on Monday afternoon and was wound up by George Brown in what was apparently quite a sporting, rumbustious performance. I came in to hear Maudling reading an uninspired brief. The whole debate had been curiously flat because the Government clearly has no policy now that the negotiations have broken down and the Labour spokesmen's efforts

[1] Joseph Slater, a Lodge Official of the Miners' Union since 1930 and a member of the Durham Miners' Union Executive 1940 and 1947. He was Labour M.P. for the Sedgefield division of Durham from 1950 until 1970, when he became a life peer. He was a member of the Council of Europe and the Western European division in 1958 and served as P.P.S. to the Leader of the Opposition 1960–4 and Assistant Postmaster-General 1964–9.

[2] Labour M.P. for Lincoln from March 1962 until October 1972, when he left the Labour Party and announced his intention of resigning his parliamentary seat. He successfully contested Lincoln as a Democratic Labour M.P. on March 1st, 1973, but was defeated at the General Election in October 1974. He was Parliamentary Under-Secretary of State at the Home Office 1966–8, Minister of State at H.M. Treasury 1968–9 and Financial Secretary to the Treasury 1969–70. In 1970 he became Director-General of the Institute for Fiscal Studies. An account of his break with the Labour Party appears in his book *The Future of the Left: Lincoln and After* (London: Cape, 1973). He has also written *Reform of the Tax Laws* (Manchester Statistical Society, 1978).

to make it sound as if we have a policy were not very convincing. That evening I said to Harold that I was a bit worried about the content of his own speech. 'But I can't reveal all our policy,' he replied, assuring me; 'but we have one, all right.' 'Have we?' I asked. George Wigg and I knew that in the nuclear debate where we briefed Harold he talked jolly good sense. We both feel worried because we are not sure that the briefing of the economists is very good and we are not at all sure that he really knows what a Labour Government would do.

Immediately after the vote, I took a taxi over to Long Acre to see Sydney. He was with Dick Dinsdale[1] and at once said that the *Mirror* had made arrangements for a special feature treatment of Harold. 'But he wants to offer you an exclusive front-page interview, only with the *Herald*.'[2] They were not very keen at first but saw it was a decent thing for Harold to give the *Herald* and accepted. Sydney and I got down to drafting the questions and making the arrangements. I told him that Harold was very unwilling to follow Hugh's example and accept invitations to eat and drink heavily with Hugh Cudlipp and Cecil King. Couldn't I do this job for him? Sydney explained that they are both reformed characters who don't drink so much and would not resent Harold drinking nothing. But he would have to have relations with them himself, Sydney said, and he then went on to discuss press relations and especially the need for the *Mirror* to get special news from the Party in Westminster. It was a nice businesslike talk and Sydney laughed at how unpredictable fate is and that I should be talking on behalf of the Leader.

On Wednesday morning I got down reluctantly to working on a draft of our policy statement on social security. Then I went off to see Harold again. I reported on Sydney and we discussed arrangements for news and the press. 'I can't rely on Leslie Plummer,' Harold said. 'He isn't trusted by the Party or the press and he did a bad job for me in my campaign for Deputy Leader.[3] I know that now when I compare it with the job you and George Wigg are doing.' Harold outlined his plan to use the Chief Whip and make him devolve his own routine duties on the Deputy Chief. Harold would send John Harris back to Transport House, where Anthony Wedgwood Benn and I could run publicity. The organization would be left to George Brown.

We once again discussed my job. I said George Wigg and I wanted no jobs, least of all Shadow jobs. 'But there must be some good reason for my seeing

[1] A journalist, he worked on the *Daily Mirror* 1940–2 and 1946–61, from 1955 as Deputy Editor. He became Editorial Adviser to the *Daily Herald* in 1961 and was its Deputy Editor 1962–3. The following year he became Deputy Editor of the *Sun* and from 1965 to 1969 was Editor of that paper. He was Chairman of West of England Newspapers Ltd 1969–72.

[2] The *Mirror* Group had taken over Odhams Press early in 1961. On March 1st, at a private meeting with members of the trade union group of the P.L.P., Cecil King had pledged that no question of merging the *Daily Herald* with the *Daily Mirror* would be raised during the next seven years.

[3] See above, p. 810.

you so often,' Harold said. 'If there isn't, people will get jealous. That's why I will make you spokesman on Science and also chairman of the Policy Committee.' I said that the Policy Committee was a first-rate idea because I was the only person who could intellectually succeed Harold, as the others must recognize. But what if they did not? 'I'm afraid they will have to take orders after Thursday,' he said, 'or there'll be trouble. We'll see to it at the next meeting.'

Watching Harold in all these talks, I keep on noticing his unruffled inner composure and self-confidence. 'It'll be easier to sleep properly,' I said to him, and he replied, truthfully, I think, 'I haven't lost a moment's sleep in this contest, though Mary has.' We discussed whether George Brown would remain Deputy Leader and Harold made it clear that he would do everything to encourage this. 'Would you even consider making him Shadow Foreign Minister?' I asked. 'No, that would be going too far. Besides I don't trust him on foreign policy and I know Gordon Walker would do as he's told, once I am Leader. I must keep George as Deputy but I haven't got to do more than that for him.'

I had a drink with Michael Foot, who with the four other rebels who have lost the whip[1] is without a vote on Thursday. George and I were trying to get them back by persuading each of them to send a letter asking for readmission to the Party. Silverman of course wants a joint action but this will lead to a procedural wrangle, since the Chief Whip has the right to treat each rebel individually. I was interested to find that Michael Foot is genuinely and enormously excited by the prospect of Harold's victory. He sees this as changing the whole political situation, just like Patrick Blackett, who rang me up this morning with a schoolboyish excitement that we were coming to the end of the tunnel and that soon scientists would have a chance in the Party.

Yesterday was column day but I took an hour and a half off with Roy and Jennifer Jenkins[2] to lunch at the Athenaeum. I particularly wanted to find out what they were thinking. Both of them were completely knocked out by Gaitskell's death. It makes a huge gap in their personal lives, bigger even than the gap in Crosland's. I felt them to be generally in mourning for Gaitskell and not particularly enthusiastic for Brown. Jenkins had only got back from America on the Sunday before the first ballot, too late to play any part in the Brown campaign. Nevertheless Roy was as implacable as ever and I spent most of lunch trying to make him say what makes him support a thug like Brown against a man of Wilson's quality. Jenkins found it surprisingly difficult. First he tried to call Harold intellectually dishonest but he really couldn't pretend that Douglas Jay or Patrick Gordon Walker show greater

---

[1] Over the issue of nuclear disarmament.

[2] Jennifer Morris married Roy Jenkins in 1945. She was a member of the Council of the Consumers' Association from 1958 to 1976 and its Chairman 1965–76. In 1975 she became Chairman of the Historic Buildings Council for England.

intellectual integrity. All Roy could say was that it was worse in Harold's case because he was more gifted.

Roy also indignantly denied the charge of jealousy, though I don't think he quite convinced himself on that score. I said, 'But wasn't it a hallmark of a Gaitskellite to be anti-Wilson? Wasn't a condition of your group to jump on Harold, ever since Hugh Dalton called him Nye's little dog? And wasn't Hugh the cause of all the trouble?' Roy at once denied this about Hugh. 'Indeed,' he said, 'at one of his last talks with me, he said that at least Harold was predictable, whereas Callaghan was completely unpredictable in seeking his personal self-interest.' Finally Roy said, 'The fact is that Harold is a person no one can like, a person without friends.' 'So much the better for him as a Leader,' I replied. 'You admired Attlee. That loneliness was Attlee's quality.' Roy was indignant at the comparison and both of us finished lunch genuinely baffled as to what it was that caused the revulsion in each of us that the other didn't share.

This was the final election day.[1] I hung about in the Central Lobby in an atmosphere of suspense. It's really astonishing how this election has dominated Westminster for weeks on end, so that the Tories are just as interested in the result as we are. It is also astonishing how the election has impressed the voters outside. We all assumed that it would do us terrible damage and spoil our image. But, as I wrote in my column, the fact that in the Gallup Poll our lead has risen from 9·5 per cent under Gaitskell to 18 per cent under Harold Wilson shows that the three weeks of the election have actually done us good.

George Wigg came rushing up to say that the Brownites had been in conclave all afternoon with Herbert Morrison and Dora Gaitskell. There was a rumour that Brown was throwing his hand in because he was desperately short of cash. If he didn't get 100 votes he would regard this as a vote of no confidence and walk out of the meeting. Later we confirmed that Herbert Morrison had advised him to do this and that Dora advised him to stay on. George Wigg reckoned that we should get 145 votes and that George Brown would get round about 100. George Wigg's very last act before half-past six was to bet Harold Wilson a pound – and win!

I went up to Harold's room once again and found him alone with Marcia. We were soon joined by Mary and Giles and had a rather nice family party as we waited to go down. After all, we all knew the result and our whole minds were now concentrated on George Brown and what Harold should do. 'If he walks out, what will you do?' I asked. Harold replied at once, 'I shall call him back. I shall get up and call him back and then if he goes out he will have finished himself ... but he won't.'

As I sat by Mary, I told her the most important thing she could do in Downing Street was to keep Harold's home life absolutely separate in the top flat and feel no compunction about not doing much social activity. Then

[1] I.e. Thursday, February 14th, the day of the second and final ballot for the leadership.

I said, 'Did you expect this when you married him?' 'I wouldn't tell anybody else this but I wanted to marry an Oxford don and the only thing I have ever dreamt of is living as the wife of an Oxford don and that is the only thing I want today.' I tried to tell her how awful the lives of dons' wives really are. I had been in Oxford for seven years. 'Oh, I know you were. How lovely it must have been.' Then I knew she really would have liked it, even if Harold went off to dinner in college, leaving her at home with a supper of cold sausage. 'After all,' she said, 'he leaves me now, oftener than that.'

When the result was announced,[1] Harold tried to speak but George Brown waved him down and read aloud his written announcement that he wanted time to think things over. Since this was completely unexpected, it was the first test of Harold's leadership. He made a really superb spontaneous gesture, warmly and with apparent magnanimity, begging George on behalf of the whole Party to remember that he had been elected Deputy Leader for the whole year, that he was needed by the Party in the country and that he couldn't pack it in. Though George didn't realize it, his own gesture and Harold's reply had boxed him in completely.

After this I went upstairs to Harold's room to telephone Anne. In due course he and I went across to Transport House where I wanted to listen to his press conference before I appeared on the B.B.C.'s television show 'Gallery'. At the press conference Harold repeated almost verbatim and not nearly so convincingly the speech of the Party Meeting. He was pretty flat in answering questions, until somebody ribaldly inquired, whether, like Stanley Baldwin in a similar situation, he would ask for their prayers. Harold took the question seriously and, completely sincerely, said, 'Yes, of course,' in such a way that for the first time I believed that he is still a Nonconformist believer.

At Lime Grove I had the usual interminable wait but this gave me a chance to see all the television shows, news and programmes on which Harold was appearing and to see what a composed, competent performer he is and how he was putting himself over in his new character with complete self-assurance. I had come to talk about Harold's career since 1951. I found that Norman St John Stevas[2] was there. After all the waiting, the conversation on the programme went off quite well, though, in order to defend Harold from charges of treachery and ambiguity, I found myself compelled to attack

[1] Harold Wilson had 144 votes and George Brown 103.

[2] Conservative M.P. for Chelmsford since October 1964. He was Parliamentary Under-Secretary of State at the D.E.S. 1972–3 and Minister of State for the Arts 1973–4. In 1979 he became Chancellor of the Duchy of Lancaster and Leader of the House of Commons, with ministerial responsibility for the Arts. An author, barrister and journalist, his publications include *The Biography of Walter Bagehot* (London: Eyre & Spottiswoode, 1959), an eleven-volume edition of *The Works of Walter Bagehot* (London: *The Economist*, 1966, 1968, 1974, 1978), and two books on law and morals: *Obscenity and the Law* (London: Secker & Warburg, 1956) and *The Right to Life* (London: Hodder & Stoughton, 1963).

Gaitskell on 'Fight, fight, fight', and on the Common Market. After the show, Robin Day[1] said to me over a drink, 'So you are taking a hack at the image of Gaitskell, are you?' I was a little uneasy whether Harold would really approve. But this morning he rang up, saying how wonderful he had heard the broadcast had been. I explained that I had been chipping off a flake or so from the plaster cast in the Pantheon. 'That's all right,' he said, 'After all, the election is over.' I asked about the situation with George Brown and he replied, 'We've got him just where we want him. If he resigns now, it is a private decision of no political significance.' That statement is worth reflecting on. It shows that we now have as our Leader a very different kind of man from either Gaitskell or Attlee. I lunched with John Freeman today and found myself discussing this fascinating topic. I pledged myself to dictate to Jennie an analysis of Wilson as I see him after the contest and I will do this early next week and look at it once every twelve months to see how foolish I have been, or how wise.[2]

Tuesday, February 19th

I was rather scared about the Sunday press when Patricia Llewelyn-Davies rang and told me that the *Observer* had a wonderful story about my running Harold's campaign, with a photograph entitled 'Crossman the Kingmaker'. To my great relief I saw when I got my copy that my only activity in the story was a report that I had given Harold dinner one night and that the picture caption bore no relation to the words. None the less it caused quite a flurry. George Hodgkinson rang me up in delight and, to take the other side of the picture, when I strolled into the Chamber on Monday, Dick Marsh sat beside me and said, 'Well, they scarcely had space to talk about the new Leader.' Actually I was greatly relieved that there was virtually nothing about me in the Sunday press, far less indeed than would have been printed by anyone who really knew what happened. But it shows how quick M.P.s are to sense that a man in the background is shoving himself forward. Nevertheless my first afternoon in the House was quite amusing from another point of view. All sorts of people come up to one now or are anxious to have a friendly smile when they meet a member of the new Establishment.

Harold asked to see me and I went in just as Gordon Walker came out, after being offered the Shadow foreign secretaryship. Harold told me first that George Brown had disappeared and was incommunicado. He was

---

[1] A distinguished television political journalist, with a reputation for incisive interviewing. He was a newscaster and Parliamentary Correspondent for Independent Television News from 1955 to 1959, and in 1959 wrote a column in the *News Chronicle*. He joined B.B.C. Television's current affairs programme 'Panorama' in 1959 and introduced it from 1967 to 1972. He contested Hereford, as a Liberal candidate, in 1959. His publications include *The Troubled Reflections of a Television Journalist* (London: Kimber, 1973), republished as *Day by Day: or A Dose of My Own Hemlock* (London: Kimber, 1975).

[2] He did not.

probably staying with one of the friends of Bustani,[1] the Arab millionaire, in Scotland. But hints were being made that George would only come back as Shadow Foreign Secretary. In order to confirm this, he had already resigned the chairmanship of the Organization Sub-Committee. 'There could be no question of my taking that deal,' Harold said, 'and I have already appointed Gordon Walker to succeed George, so that the Right can't really object in terms of policy. Anyway, I'm not going to be blackmailed by his going away like this.'

Harold then turned to my job and explained the top priority was to prepare the series of studies the Government would do in power, that is, advance Socialist planning, particularly in science and higher education. 'I shall need you on the Front Bench,' he said. I said it wasn't worth my being there for a couple of speeches a year. 'But it's one of the most important jobs and I shall have to have you on the Front Bench beside me.' He said so, so I supposed that was that. 'Of course, if you insist on doing pensions, I can't say no. And I am not saying that in the Government you would be Minister of Science.' 'No,' I chipped in, 'Minister of Social Security of course, far the most important thing to push through.' 'Oh,' Harold said, 'I should have thought you wanted something more important than that,' and I noticed a surprised look in those grey eyes which made me realize he had something much more important for me. It may have been sheer imagination, but Harold's consistently saying that he was holding the Foreign Office down by having Gordon Walker there made me wonder how much wiser I would be to do the job of pensions.

Wednesday, February 20th

Last night I was giving Wilfred Cave[2] dinner to discuss agricultural policy. The Harcourt Room [in the House of Commons] was full when I arrived and Harold Wilson called me across to his table. During the afternoon I had read the banner headlines in the *News* and the *Standard* reporting George Brown's activities. This was a very obvious attempt to dominate Harold Wilson by telephone and press leaks. In the Tea Room it had had an appalling effect but there were a number of left-wing M.P.s who were anxious lest Harold should surrender. Knowing that he had not been prepared to give way to George before the election results were announced, I was certain that this behaviour afterwards would only strengthen his resolve. So I was not in the least surprised when Harold said to me at once that he was insulted that the

---

[1] Emile Bustani, a Lebanese businessman. The company which he founded prospered during the war and he won large War Department contracts. He entered the Lebanese Parliament in 1951 and was briefly Minister of Public Works in 1956. He was killed in an air crash in 1963.

[2] Wilfred Cave was one of the biggest and most successful farmers in the South-West and an enthusiastic supporter of land nationalization. An ardent Socialist, he failed to get into Parliament in 1964 as candidate for Devizes but continued to work throughout the Labour Government on Labour's policy committees.

question was even being asked. 'I have had no conversation on the telephone with George except about the time of his return,' Harold told me. 'Otherwise, all I know is that Desmond Donnelly came to me and began to say, "I have come as George Brown's broker".' Harold had replied, 'I don't deal with brokers,' and that had been the end of the conversation.

When this had been reported to the Chief Whip, it had stiffened him. Anyway he was infuriated that Donnelly had previously leaked to the press the text of a private letter George had sent him. Harold told me that he would show George Brown the list of the Shadow Cabinet he and the Chief Whip had agreed on Thursday and that he had called a press conference at five o'clock, so that the names would be on the wireless at six o'clock, half an hour before the Party Meeting. 'That will prevent our friend George from staging any argument,' he said. He then referred to my television show last Thursday, when I had said that, if he was flexible, he was also tough. 'Many people have commented on that,' he said. 'You were right. And you were also right to say last week that he whom the gods want to destroy, they first make blind [*sic*]. Everything George Brown has done has played into my hands.'

At this point Wilfred Cave and John Mackie came over and we discussed agriculture. Harold was at his briefest. 'If you can't write a long policy,' he said, 'tell the farmers in a couple of pages that you promise them security. And remember what the Premier of Saskatchewan, Bill Douglas,[1] once told me, "One year, we had a long, detailed programme for the farmers and lost. The next year we promised them security in a couple of paragraphs and won our biggest majority ever." ' We tried to reason a little with Harold but that was the total directive he gave us. Afterwards we three sat and discussed it at some length but it was clear that Harold had given me a mandate to get on with the job of producing a short but not too precise policy.

Tuesday, March 5th

It is nearly a fortnight since I last wrote in this diary, so it cannot pretend to be that but only a composite impression of how the first fortnight of Harold's leadership has gone, and, incidentally, how I have fared. Well, there is no doubt that, compared with what I expected, he has started at a far faster pace, has gone on making the running and has produced something like a psychological revolution in the Parliamentary Party and in the Party in the country. How do I know that? By the number of people who in their different ways tell one what a wonderful sense of freedom they have now that the Party is going ahead. All the scientists with whom I am now having to

---

[1] Presumably Thomas C. Douglas (known as 'Tommy' Douglas, not 'Bill'), Premier of Saskatchewan from July 1944 until he resigned in November 1961 to assume new duties as Leader of the New Democratic Party. Although defeated as an N.D.P. candidate at the 1962 Canadian General Election, he was returned as Member for a different constituency in a by-election later that year and continued to lead the New Democratic Party until the early 1970s.

work as Shadow spokesman had found Hugh terribly stick-in-the-mud. Indeed, one of them said to me when we were dining at the Reform Club, 'Gaitskell was more like Hailsham. Hailsham treats us as technicians whose specialist advice must be asked but who, of course, know nothing about how to run the country, manage the economy or decide great issues of state. In Hailsham's mind the kind of people who could do that are those with a First in Greats.[1] Well, change from a First in Greats to a First in P.P.E. and you have Hugh Gaitskell's view.'

All these people feel an astonishing sense of liberation and in talking to them one finds oneself irresistibly driven to clichés of the New Frontier and comparisons of Harold with Kennedy. Of course, the difference in their private lives and cultural interests could not be greater, but there is the resemblance that both men are extremely professional, egotistical, self-seeking and ruthless politicians who are also men of immense public spirit, because they identify their careers with the good of their party and the good of their country. What further unites them is that both feel a need to gather round them the most brilliant brains they can get. Unlike Aneurin Bevan or Ernest Bevin, neither of them has any chip on his shoulder when dealing with intellectuals. But, equally, neither feels haughty about them, like Hugh Gaitskell. They quite naturally want a galaxy of talent and they are the kind of men who can with great rapidity extract information from clever people.

That explains Harold's success with the scientists, but I do not think that there is any doubt that he has also been pretty successful with the Parliamentary Party. Why? Because, first, he is a really demagogic party Leader and does not play the role of non-party statesman that Gaitskell liked so much. In his first weekend, Harold's speeches sounded astonishingly left-wing. A number of Tory papers accused him of swinging away from the Gaitskell line, until they looked up their references and found that little Harold had religiously copied out the Party policy on Berlin, on land nationalization, on leasehold reform. Until that weekend no one had any idea that the Labour Party had quite radical policies on every topic under the sun. When we worked out *Signposts for the Sixties*, Hugh Gaitskell quite obviously wanted it not as a policy to put to the nation but as a document to settle the intra-Party dispute. Once that dispute had been settled and the Left had been humbled, he played the policy down and then when he became Prime Minister he would have forgotten everything about it that was out of step with his own ideas. I have no doubt whatsoever that this was Hugh's plan. Once he got to power he was going to be immensely autocratic. It was going to be a Gaitskell Government, hand-picked by him and woe betide anyone who did not toe the line.

In just the same way, he was making the Party into the Gaitskell Party,

[1] The Oxford University four-year degree course in philosophy, combined with classical literature and ancient history; philosophy, politics and economics (P.P.E.) was sometimes known as 'Modern Greats'.

forcing it to suppress its nature and straitjacketing it under his leadership. What has happened since his death is that we all feel that this strait-jacket has dropped off our shoulders and that the Labour Party is free to be itself again. Maybe in certain ways it is a silly and a demagogic self, a senti-mental self, but as a Party it's a personality that we have had for a long time, a personality which Gaitskell disliked and manoeuvred for his own purposes. Whatever one says about Harold, he doesn't want to exercise that kind of leadership. It is not just cleverness or expediency that makes him hew to the agreed Party line. I think he genuinely feels that, when policies are worked out and compromises are agreed, that line must be observed by everyone including the Leader.

One Sunday paper described it as Bevanite policy to be executed by a Bevanite Shadow Cabinet. This is true enough if one looks back to the draft-ing of the *Signposts for the Sixties* and realizes that most of the content was put into it by Harold, Tommy Balogh and myself, with Hugh Gaitskell only yielding what was necessary to get the document through.

I asked Harold last week about that first afternoon when Gerald Nabarro[1] baited him about nationalization and he rose to the bait.[2] I knew that this was an entirely extempore answer because I had asked Marcia whether Harold was going into the House that afternoon and she had said no. Harold admitted this but added, 'My instinct wasn't too bad. I had a feeling that we ought to get this nationalization issue into the open as soon as possible. But having done so, let's be sensible about it and keep very carefully to the policies in *Signposts for the Sixties*.'

This last week I have been immersed in doing the final draft of the new social security policy statement. We reached the issue of whether the funding proposals of National Superannuation should be included in the new draft and, after talks with Tommy, I strongly felt that they should. In the early years of the Labour Government we shall need to save and the National Insurance Fund in its new form will be a demonstration of saving. I put this to Harold this morning and he agreed to the Fund, but immediately added: 'But be careful about talk of investing in equities. We don't want to resurrect the trouble we had with the 600 firms.' It was a sign of how quick and careful he is that I only had to ask him this for him to spot what I was *really* asking beneath my simple questions.

So far Harold has been extremely faithful to his friends, seeking them out for advice, giving them his time and even taking care to smooth down

---

[1] Conservative M.P. for Kidderminster 1950–64 and for South Worcestershire from 1966 until his death in 1973. Beginning as a sawmill hand, he eventually became Managing Director of two engineering companies in the Midlands. He was one of the most con-spicuous and independent of Conservative backbenchers, promoting a Private Members' Bill which led to the passage of the Government's Clean Air Act 1955. He also championed the series of attempts to rationalize purchase tax. In 1958 he fought a long action in the High Court, concerning his alleged slander of Randolph Churchill. He lost the case and the plaintiff received £1,500 damages.

[2] In the debate on the steel industry on February 18th.

Barbara Castle and Tony Greenwood, who have been given the strong impression that next October their turn will come. But while Harold has kept his anchor out to the Left, he has been quietly consolidating his position in the Centre along with the Chief Whip, and he is not prepared to let Tony Wedgwood Benn and me, for example, insert ourselves and reorganize the Shadow Security or even organize any political warfare. He will do nothing that disturbs the Chief Whip and he is quite frank that on certain issues he won't alienate the Right. For instance, Michael Foot, Emrys Hughes and the others who lost the whip have asked to get it back and Harold said, 'The Shadow Cabinet are being extremely difficult and it won't be at all easy, since this is something where I am not prepared to lead them. Anyway, it is their own fault that the rebels are in their present position.'

Out in the country, as far as I can judge, Harold's impact has been the same. His first party political television show was verbose and ham-handed but it was perfectly all right because it was so solid and unclever and confidence-building. It is trivial that he was awkward with his hands and his movements. That kind of stiffness is automatically removed by repetition. Every indication suggests that in his first fortnight he has quite quietly established himself as the new Leader with his own quite distinct personality, with a far more polemical attachment to Socialist policy and with the grammar school boy's curious classlessness which makes him belong to a younger generation than Gaitskell. How terrible it must be for Dora, with the sense of Hugh's indispensability entirely disissipated by the man Hugh despised and maligned to all his friends.

Of course it is early yet to judge of Harold's leadership. It takes many months before the Gallup Poll registers a change of Leader. It is the same with newspapers. It's months after you have run into a thoroughly bad editorial patch that this reflects itself, if it ever does, in circulation. It is years after a school has started going downhill that its reputation is affected. We shall therefore have to wait and see what in the long run the British people really think of Harold. But the first impression is that he has regenerated the Labour Party, given it a fine springtime fighting spirit, made it feel happy and itself and natural and liberated.

He has done all this although he is not young or natural or liberated but is a tight, little, careful, calculating man. I must admit that in the formation of his image what I have been saying and writing has had quite an influence. It was fun to be a kingmaker. It is just as much fun to take part in creating a political image and building up a Leader.

So there he is. Whenever I go to see him and we sit on that stiff horsehair sofa side by side I look into those grey eyes and see nothing. But he could not be cosier with me or more confidential or indeed more grateful. What I don't like at all is the job he has given me. I feel no kind of self-confidence that I shall feel at home as spokesman for Science and I have an extraordinary reluctance to get down to reading any of the stuff. This is partly because I am still immersed in social security but it is also I think a sense of fear and anxiety about going on to the Front Bench. When one has been away from it for so long or, rather, denied it for so long, the pose of not wanting it becomes, to one's amazement, a reality. In a deep sense, I really don't want to sit there at Question Time, particularly because I am scared of doing something that I haven't done before. It is a scare I have to get over but it would have been far easier if Harold had let me do pensions and let poor Dick Mitchison—who will never forgive me for replacing him—carry on with science.

Tuesday, March 12th
We had a most interesting evening last Sunday when Barbara Castle invited Harold Wilson to supper to meet Judith Hart, Michael Foot, George Wigg, Tony Greenwood and myself. It was an interesting test of how Harold would behave to his old friends of the Left. He could not have been nicer, more natural or more shrewd. He was relaxed, completely frank and easy and yet careful not to promise more than he could fulfil. 'You must understand that I am running a Bolshevik Revolution with a Tsarist Shadow Cabinet,' he remarked, and explained how bitterly hostile and suspicious most of these miserable creatures are. They were causing every kind of difficulty about the readmission of the rebels. They obviously also resented Harold's strong personal line and the appearance which he has publicly shown of giving a Socialist slant, merely by faithfully repeating parts of the Party policy which Gaitskell and Brown had left virtually unmentioned.

Harold made it pretty clear that he felt terribly boxed in at the moment but that directly he dug himself in he was determined to start cleaning up the Augean stables. Apparently his intention is to start with the Number Twos in the Shadow Administration, the people he has so far left alone. But his main problem is that he is a general without any chief of staff and indeed without any structure of command. This was the old problem that I pointed out to Gaitskell just after the Election. He wouldn't listen and was concerned only to drop nationalization. Harold now feels this far more than he did three weeks ago. He hasn't even a secretarial staff to answer his letters but above all he has no right-hand man to plan his political strategy and to put up suggestions to him. Therefore he is in a weak position inside his hostile Shadow Cabinet, despite his overwhelming strength in the country.

During the evening we went through all the current topics of the day and also discussed proposals for electoral strategy. He had just succeeded in getting Tony Wedgwood Benn put in charge again of our Election preparations for radio and T.V., a job which the campaign committee has completely neglected for a year. We now agreed that Harold might take two further steps. First, he should make the campaign committee instruct Peter Shore to draw up a directive and, secondly, reactivate the old Liaison Committee[1]

---

[1] As a channel of communication between the Parliamentary Committee and the P.L.P.

which works under the Chief Whip, so that later on he could turn it into the kind of campaign committee I was running during the last Election. Harold seemed anxious that we should not exclude the possibility of a May or October Election, though I think both are extremely unlikely.

The Government was in some difficulty over security matters. In November 1962 a tribunal had been established under the chairmanship of Lord Radcliffe to investigate the case of William Vassall, an Admiralty clerk sentenced to eighteen years' imprisonment for spying for the Soviet Union. The tribunal's Report (Cmnd 2009) to be published on April 25th, 1963, cleared of inefficiency the First Lord of the Admiralty, Lord Carrington, and of complicity in Vassall's espionage and homosexual activities the former Civil Lord, Thomas Galbraith. Despite the tribunal's criticism of lapses by those responsible for security at the Admiralty, Mr Macmillan was to stand by his Ministers and officials. On May 3rd Mr Galbraith was restored to the Government as Joint Parliamentary Secretary at the Ministry of Transport.

The Report also censured the press; two reporters, Reginald Foster of the Daily Sketch *and Brendon Mulholland of the* Daily Mail, *had already been imprisoned by the High Court on March 7th for failing to disclose to the tribunal their sources of information. On March 21st their imprisonment was discussed in the House of Commons. During the debate George Wigg, Barbara Castle and Crossman referred, under privilege, to rumours which had for weeks been circulating in Westminster and Fleet Street, regarding the Secretary of State for War, John Profumo.*

According to these stories, Mr Profumo had been sharing with a Captain Eugene Ivanov, an Attaché at the Soviet Embassy, the favours of Miss Christine Keeler, a model. On March 14th Miss Keeler had failed to appear as a prosecution witness at the trial at the Old Bailey of John Edgecombe, a West Indian accused of shooting at her out of jealousy at her preference for another West Indian, 'Lucky' Gordon. It was rumoured that Miss Keeler had left the country.

In a personal statement made in the Commons on the morning of March 22nd, Mr Profumo stated that he had met Captain Ivanov only twice and Miss Keeler on half a dozen occasions, socially, at the London flat of a Dr Stephen Ward. The Secretary of State denied any impropriety and announced that he would take legal action if such allegations were repeated outside the House. Mr Macmillan sat beside Mr Profumo as he spoke and warmly patted him on the back when he sat down.

Wednesday, March 27th
I have been working very hard on my social security draft[1] and at this morning's National Executive the policy statement came up for final approval. It should have been a formal approval but I had suspected that a counter-attack

[1] *New Frontiers for Social Security* was published on April 1st.

was brewing and I was right. The debate lasted an hour and a half, with Callaghan leading off against publication and George Brown winding up by coming off the fence on Callaghan's side. I moved the document and wound up and we carried publication by 18 to 8. But they only carried non-publication of the figures by 14 votes to 13.

Meanwhile I got my science panel together a fortnight ago, on March 13th. Everyone turned up as keen as mustard and we divided up into three working parties, exactly as Pat Blackett wished. It was a really wonderful atmosphere of goodwill and the air was full of compliments for the chairman, though quite literally all I had done was to call a meeting. Why is it that one really works hard? I have visited Shirley Williams of the Fabian Group and I am now getting rather more at home in science. I have the impression that the older generation, headed by Blackett, have extremely clear-cut, precise, limited solutions and that my job will be to try to have them fertilized by some younger and fresher people without upsetting the older ones.

The other political sensation was of course, the story of Jack Profumo and the disappearing model. I first heard of it at Barbara's dinner party when George Wigg blurted it all out and we told him to stay quiet.[1] Ever since then the story has been building up in the papers, with no direct allusion to Profumo but with talk from one side about his possible resignation and from the other talk of the witness who disappeared. Last Thursday evening there was a debate on the jailed journalists and I went in to listen. Barbara came in saying she was going to blow the gaff on Profumo, under the protection of parliamentary privilege. George Wigg and I thought we had better get in first and we did so, using fairly careful language. Even so I was interrupted by Reggie Paget, who mentioned Profumo's name and so on. Then Barbara took off about the perversion of justice.[2] Next day it was front-page news in every paper, including *The Times*, which followed this report with a leader saying that we had used privilege justifiably, but ...

The real interest of the affair is the hostility between the press and the Government, which makes the press willing to leap at anything. A secondary interest is the sleaziness of those Tories who get mixed up with this kind of society. I had sworn never to speak on this from the Front Benches and had intended to make only a non-political speech on such matters as the freedom of the press. Suddenly I found my good resolutions dissipated by front-page prominence with Wigg and Castle.

When Harold arrived at midnight from dinner with Lynn Ungoed-Thomas and I told him what we had done, he was as cool as a cucumber. He went in and made a long speech in the debate, brilliantly defining press freedom, and has since then made three further speeches, using the occasion to put Labour formally on the side of the press against the Government. By so doing, he has

[1] George Wigg's account of these events may be found in Chapter 13 of his *George Wigg* (London: Michael Joseph, 1972).
[2] She referred to Miss Keeler's disappearance.

done more for our public relations than Gaitskell ever did in his whole leadership.

On Friday morning I had to rush into the House at eleven, to hear Profumo's denial. This has been followed by a lot more material on call girls.[1] Meanwhile, the pimp, Dr Ward, the osteopath with a cottage in the park at Cliveden and his new Cliveden set,[2] has spent hours with George Wigg. George has scared Ward by saying on 'Panorama' that this really is a security issue since Ward had been friendly with a Russian naval attaché, Ivanov,[3] and had introduced him to Profumo.

George Wigg later wrote that in the late afternoon on Tuesday, March 26th, he was handed a telephone message by a Commons official, asking him to ring Stephen Ward at a Paddington number. He did so, with Wilfred Sendall, the political journalist, as witness, and from six to nine o'clock that evening interviewed Ward at the House. He recorded their conversation and immediately afterwards showed it to Harold Wilson, who asked for an 'appreciation to be made for his information'. This Wigg did, completing it on March 29th. (A summary of Dr Ward's remarks may be found on pp. 270–73 of Lord Wigg's book, George Wigg.*)*

George Wigg's document was, he maintained, sent to the Government Chief Whip, with a covering letter, dated April 9th, from Harold Wilson to the Prime Minister.

Sunday, June 2nd to Sunday, June 9th[4]

I think it might be interesting if, over Whitsuntide, I try to make a record of my memories of the whole Profumo affair as I saw it. I have for this purpose checked through my previous entries and done a little bit of initial spadework.

The story starts on March 10th, when Barbara had arranged a party for Harold at supper with some of his left-wing friends. There were present, as far as I remember, Barbara and Ted Castle, Michael Foot, George Wigg, myself, Peter Shore and possibly one other. Actually the meeting wasn't really a great success and afterwards Harold certainly agreed with George and me that there was too great a risk of its being leaked

---

[1] Miss Keeler and a Miss Mandy Rice-Davies had allegedly been selling their stories to newspapers.

[2] A term invented by the left-wing weekly newssheet *The Week* to describe the habitués in the 1930s of Lady Astor's weekend house-parties at Cliveden, near Marlow. *The Week* alleged that these meetings were the centre of a web of pro-appeasement influence within political and press circles. Many individual members of the 'Set' were indeed appeasers, but many were not and the notion of a conscious movement was an oversimplification. Dr Ward had a cottage on the Cliveden estate, where, it was said, he had introduced Mr Profumo to Miss Keeler.

[3] Captain Eugene Ivanov was Assistant Naval Attaché at the Soviet Embassy in London. He was recalled to Moscow in December 1962.

[4] This section of the diary was dictated at various times throughout the week.

that he was associating with left-wing friends in a secret clique, creating another kind of Gaitskell Hampstead set. But that's not the point of this story.

George drove me to the party and on the way he said, 'I suppose you know about the Profumo scandal?' I said I knew nothing and George said, 'Where do you live? Every Tory I know is talking about the scandal of Profumo and the call girl.' I had heard absolutely nothing of this, nor had I read the sensational stories in the newspapers. However, when we arrived at the party, George outlined the story to us and we emphatically and unanimously repudiated it. We all felt that, even if it was true and Profumo was having an affair with a call girl and that some Russian diplomat had been mixed up in it, the Labour Party simply shouldn't touch it. I remember that we all advised Harold very strongly against it and in a way rather squashed George. Nevertheless George maintained that the honour of the Army was at stake, that the Secretary of State for War couldn't be allowed to behave in this way and that – and I remember this – he himself was going to charge Profumo with it next day.

Why were we so sensitive about the whole thing? The Vassall[1] affair was still hanging over us, when we'd had the experience of the effect on the Labour Front Bench of George Brown's trying to exploit the charge that Thomas Galbraith[2] had had homosexual relations with Vassall. We had seen how unfortunate this was. We'd had the debate when the tribunal was established and, having been through this, I think we were aware that the tribunal was just about to report, that the press was extremely frightened of what the Report was going to be and knew quite well that, in view of the impression the journalists had made when they had appeared in court, the tribunal's Report was hardly likely to be very favourable to the press. For all these reasons, when George Wigg first discussed this whole idea, which was, I am pretty sure, news to Harold Wilson as well as to the rest of us, we all unanimously turned it down.

As we left the party at the end of the evening, George deliberately stayed behind in order to brief Harold even more fully on what he kept on repeating was the security aspect of the affair. It seemed that there really was something rather fishy and dangerous about Profumo and the Russian Naval Attaché Ivanov having the same girl as their girlfriend.

After that, the story jumps to the evening of March the 21st, when it was decided to raise in the House the case of the imprisoned journalists. These are the two, Mulholland and Foster, who refused to reveal their sources to

[1] William Vassall, the Admiralty clerk convicted on October 22nd, 1962, of spying for the Soviet Union. He was sentenced to eighteen years' imprisonment, but was released in 1973.

[2] Unionist M.P. for the Hillhead division of Glasgow since 1948. A Whip 1951–7, he then became Civil Lord of the Admiralty 1957–9 and was subsequently Joint Parliamentary Under-Secretary of State at the Scottish Office 1959–62 and Joint Parliamentary Secretary at the Ministry of Transport 1963–4.

the Radcliffe tribunal[1] and who had been imprisoned. Peter Kirk, a very nice progressive Tory, decided to raise this issue in the House. I had rather wanted to speak in the debate but I had agreed to give dinner to Nigel Balchin,[2] the novelist, who wanted to help me with my new job as Shadow spokesman for science. So I came in very late, after the debate had started, assuming that I couldn't speak. As I sat there listening to a very, very boring speech by Leslie Hale, George Wigg came to me on the fourth bench towards the back and said, 'I hear that Barbara has been briefed by the *Daily Herald* to spill the Profumo scandal during this debate. She's bound to do it wrong. Dick, you and I must get in first. If the story is to be broken we must break it in a reasonable way.'

The debate had started just before nine and its whole tone was very different from the previous Vassall debate, very quiet and very correct, pleading for the journalists. At 10.40 things suddenly woke up. George Wigg got up and, after using the argument which he and I had used regularly together, that the investigative machinery of the tribunal was the wrong kind of machinery and that the worst of the British system of concealment was that rumours were spread by it, he then suddenly said, 'Aren't we now in the middle of a new rumour campaign?' As you'll find in Hansard, George then asked the Home Secretary to deny the rumours relating to Christine Keeler and the shooting of [sic] the West Indian. He went on to say that, if there was anything in these rumours, he urged the Prime Minister not to repeat the tribunal procedure but to set up a Select Committee to deal with them.

I immediately followed George with my speech and said that *Paris Match* was printing a full account of the whole Profumo/Keeler scandal.[3] Reggie Paget bobbed up from the Front Bench and made a remark that I was using privilege in a wrong kind of way. He said, 'I should 'have thought that this was using a privileged occasion greatly to enlarge rumours. What do the rumours amount to? They amount to the fact that a Minister is said to be acquainted with an extremely pretty girl. As far as I am concerned, I should have thought that that was a matter for congratulation rather than inquiry.'

[1] Which investigated the Vassall case, under the chairmanship of Lord Radcliffe. Cyril Radcliffe was Director-General of the Ministry of Information 1941–55 and from 1949 to 1964 was a Law Lord (he had been created a baron in 1949 and a viscount in 1962). He was chairman of many other important Government inquiries, including those on the Monetary and Credit System 1957–9, on Security Procedure and Practices 1961 and on D-Notices 1967, and, following the announcement of the publication of the first volume of Richard Crossman's *Diaries of a Cabinet Minister*, he was chairman of the Privy Councillor's Committee on Ministerial Memoirs 1975. He died in 1977.

[2] An author whose work in the Second World War included service as Deputy Scientific Adviser to the Army Council. His novels, some of which were published under the pseudonym Mark Spade, include *How To Run a Bassoon Factory* (London: Hamish Hamilton, 1934) and the novels *The Small Back Room* (London: Collins, 1943), *Mine Own Executioner* (London: Collins, 1945) and *The Fall of a Sparrow* (London: Collins, 1955).

[3] Mr Profumo launched a successful action against *Paris Match* and on April 11th was awarded damages and costs against the distributors of *Tempo Illustrato*.

That put the fat in the fire. I went on and pointed out that this was spreading the rumours. After me, Barbara Castle got up and specifically suggested that Miss Keeler might have been spirited off to Spain because she was a witness who could have done damage. Barbara's actual words were, 'What if it is the question of the perversion of justice that is at stake? The Clerk of the Central Criminal Court, Mr Leslie Boyd,[1] is reported in *The Times* today as saying that, if any member of the public did know where Miss Keeler was, it was his or her duty to inform the police. If accusations are made that there are people in high places who *do* know and who are not informing the police is it not a matter of public interest?'

I think Barbara Castle's was the last reference to Profumo in the course of the debate, which then went back to the two imprisoned journalists. We had an absolutely formal winding-up from the Home Secretary, Henry Brooke, who specifically refused to deal with the rumours which he said that George and Barbara had been spreading under the cloak of privilege. The only surprise was that after Brooke[2] had sat down Harold Wilson got up at 12.56 in the morning and made a very long and able speech. Harold had come back from a dinner with Lynn Ungoed-Thomas and, before he got up, George and I got to him and warned him that we had blown the story. All this Harold took in extremely quickly in his usual way. As always, he didn't express approval or disapproval, didn't commit himself, but was simply prepared to back his friends in what they had done. Therefore when he got up to speak he was extremely careful not to refer to the rumours in any way but the fact that he spoke in that debate and that he had been seen talking to us had its significance.

Of course, between the meeting at Barbara's house and this debate on March 21st, there hadn't been a day in which the rumours had not been alluded to in the press. At this time, too, Profumo had given out a statement that he had no thoughts of resignation. So everybody in the House of Commons and in Fleet Street knew that the rumours had been thickening steadily, linking Profumo's name with that of Miss Keeler. But though there was hardly anybody on the Tory side who didn't seem to assume that the stories were true and that it was a blazing scandal that Profumo should be involved; on the other hand, the fact that we had blown the gaff in the course of this debate had as its first result the rallying of the Tories. A great deal of ill-feeling was expressed, although I think that a number of Tories certainly felt a great respect for George Wigg, because they couldn't

[1] He joined the staff of the Central Criminal Court in 1951, serving as Clerk of the Court 1955–71 and the Court's Administrator 1972–7.

[2] Henry Brooke, Conservative M.P. for West Lewisham 1938–45 and for Hampstead 1950–6. He was Financial Secretary to the Treasury 1954–7, Minister of Housing and Local Government and Minister for Welsh Affairs 1957–61, Chief Secretary to the Treasury and Paymaster-General 1961–2 and Home Secretary 1962–4. In 1966 he became a life peer, taking the title of Lord Brooke of Cumnor. His wife Barbara also became a life peer, in 1964, taking the title of Baroness Brooke of Ystradfellte.

possibly deny that he had raised the issue both because of his passionate concern for the War Office and the Army and because of his disgust at the notion that the Secretary of State for War should be involved in this.

Not surprisingly, the next morning's papers had headlined the whole affair. Nor was it the least surprising that we were rung up by the Chief Whip to be told that Profumo would make a Statement when the House met at eleven o'clock, as it always does on Friday mornings. So we rushed in, sat there together and heard Profumo's Statement explicitly attacking us for attacking him under the cloak of privilege. I must say both George and I felt at the time that this was a very remarkable *kind* of personal statement because it involved not merely a personal explanation but an attack on colleagues. George and I thought that it was pretty scandalous that the Speaker had allowed it. However, the atmosphere of the House was icy, as it always is on these occasions. We were extremely isolated. I think the people on our own side much disliked what we had done. Anne is always a fair test of these things and, though she hadn't quite gathered what had happened the night before, when she saw the papers that morning she also felt a keen distaste that I should be muddled up in what looked like mud-slinging against a man who simply threatened us with action if we dared to say these things outside Parliament.

As a matter of fact there was an important distinction here. What Barbara said was clearly actionable in the courts and she would have been quite unable to repeat it outside. But there was no word in what George Wigg and I said which was in any sense actionable. Indeed, we had phrased it most carefully so that we *could* repeat it outside. But of course, the fact that at eleven o'clock on Friday morning Profumo had categorically denied it absolutely shut our mouths. We would have been in a very bad way and even inside the Party we would have been very unpopular, had it not been for a remarkable leading article in *The Times* in which this issue of privilege was taken up. *The Times* most emphatically asserted that the three M.P.s had not only had the right to do this but that it was their duty to use privilege for this specific purpose. If for weeks on end the press was inhibited in talking about a matter of public interest, it was precisely then that M.P.s should use privilege. This defence of us by *The Times* stood us in good stead.

However George and I both felt that it was now absolutely vital to lie low. We had made ourselves unpopular and we had launched the idea publicly. However, something remarkable happened because, to everybody's surprise and certainly to mine, George Wigg was invited to appear on 'Panorama' the following Monday. The whole issue was discussed and he was able to make it clear once again that his sole concern was security. He discussed it quite publicly on television and he referred quite publicly to Ivanov and to this Dr Ward. Within forty-eight hours of George's appearance on 'Panorama', Dr Ward was asking to see him. Some time that week, I'm not sure on which day, with the assistance of Wilf Sendall,[1] George took Ward to a downstairs room in the basement of the House of Commons and interviewed him for more than two hours. He got a long, elaborate statement which he immediately wrote out and presented to Harold Wilson. In this way, we were able to put the thing on an even keel because, from that moment on, the Labour Party line was, 'Well, we're not attacking Profumo's private life. We are only stating that there do seem to us to be security matters to be probed here and we in the Labour Party, through the Leader Harold Wilson, present our information to the Prime Minister.'

This is what happened. On the basis of what George had given him, Harold prepared a memorandum, which was duly sent to the Prime Minister. After that, through the weeks, considerable correspondence piled up between the P.M. and Harold Wilson.[2] At some much more recent date (I'm not quite sure when), Harold Wilson actually received a letter from Ward as well. Meanwhile, the following Sunday (I think it must have been March 31st) we dined at Oving with Pamela Berry on our way back from Banbury to London. This little dinner had its importance in the whole episode and I must record it here.

The Berrys have a most wonderful house with a view over the whole plain of Aylesbury. It was a perfect evening, with the setting sun. We found we were dining alone with Pam and Michael. She said how marvellous George and I had been and how superb it was and then said, 'What are you going to do now?' I said, 'Nothing. The fact is we've done quite enough. There is nothing more we can do now that Profumo has denied it.' 'But that's intolerable,' she said. 'That's impossible. How can you hold back now the whole press is waiting for you to go ahead? As you have privilege you must speak on.' I said, 'There's nothing whatever we can do. In fact, we have done all we could. We've collected our information.' Then, unwisely perhaps – but it didn't do any harm then – I let out that George Wigg had interviewed Ward and that the memorandum had been passed to the Prime Minister by Harold Wilson. In the course of saying this, I actually said we had taken a tape-recording of Ward. This I said half-consciously, knowing that it would be passed on and would be regarded as a sign of the serious weight of the information we were giving. In fact *no* tape-recording was taken. George Wigg had merely made a note immediately after his interview with Ward.

Miss Keeler returned to the United Kingdom and appeared at the Old Bailey on April 1st; on April 8th she was attacked by her West Indian friend 'Lucky' Gordon, who on May 3rd was committed for trial. Dr Ward meanwhile sought an interview with the Prime Minister. At a meeting with the Prime Minister's

[1] Wilfred Sendall wrote the Crossbencher column in the *Sunday Express* from 1956 until 1963, when he moved to the *News of the World*. From September 1965 until his retirement in 1973 he was Chief Political and Diplomatic Correspondent for the *Daily Express*.

[2] According to Wigg, the Prime Minister replied to letters from Harold Wilson, sent on April 9th and 13th, saying that no further action seemed necessary.

Private Secretary and a representative of the Security Service, Ward apparently persistently declared that Mr Profumo's statement had been untrue.

On May 19th, George Wigg stated, Dr Ward wrote to the Home Secretary and to his local M.P., Sir Wavell Wakefield. He also issued a statement to the press and, on May 24th, wrote to Harold Wilson. The Leader of the Opposition arranged to see the Prime Minister on May 27th and a note of their conversation was sent to the Security Service the next day. On May 30th the Prime Minister wrote to Harold Wilson, stating that he had decided that an inquiry should be conducted by Lord Dilhorne, the Lord Chancellor. Despite Mr Wilson's request on the eve of the Whitsun recess that the inquiry should be announced, the Prime Minister did not refer to the matter.

The following week I flew out on Thursday to Königswinter. I won't record here at length all the misfortunes that fell upon me this year. But it's necessary to mention one minor incident. On the last Sunday evening, I was talking with John Beavan of the *Daily Mirror* and with Peregrine Worsthorne of the *Sunday Telegraph*.[1] All I need record here is that we were discussing the Profumo affair, as everybody was, and I repeated to them the statement I had made on the previous Sunday to Pamela Berry. It was extremely interesting to observe that the *Sunday Telegraph* and the *Daily Telegraph* duly reported and were the first to report that Labour backbenchers had collected information about Ward and that Harold Wilson had provided a memorandum. This was a leak which George Wigg observed and reported to me and, strangely enough, attributed to George Brown, who Wigg thought had given it to John Beavan. As a matter of fact it was a half-deliberate passing of information. I thought at the time that as I had already given it to Pamela, I would give it to them, because it wouldn't do any harm to warn people that the Labour Party was well informed about this, was in contact with Ward and was duly passing the information to the P.M.

The next stage, I suppose, is the debate on the report of the Vassall tribunal, on May 25th. In this we all spoke again and I made one of my better speeches, more amusing this time, and it was a great success. George Wigg's speech was not as good but in the course of it he once again referred to the Keeler scandal and gave due warning that he was still on the job of chasing it. The more I think about this whole affair, the clearer it becomes to me that one man can do incredible things if he works hard enough and is sufficiently tenacious and unrelenting and single-minded. I think it is perfectly true to say that, if it wasn't for George Wigg, Profumo would still be Secretary of State for War. Even more certainly, if the Labour Party had had anything to do with the affair, it would have sullied its hand with it and totally discredited itself. It was George who first got hold of Harold Wilson early and, by his steadying

[1] A journalist, he was on the staff of *The Times* 1948–53 and the *Daily Telegraph* 1953–61. He was Deputy Editor of the *Sunday Telegraph* 1961–76 and in 1976 became Associate Editor.

influence, confirmed Harold's natural intuition that here we must be strictly concerned not with Profumo's private life, but with security. On this there was quite a lot of disagreement, with people like Frank Soskice expressing keen moral disgust at the revelations about Profumo. Secondly, of course, George's contacts in the Tory Party and his appearance on 'Panorama' enabled him to keep tags on Ward and to build up the position.

I remember that while the Vassall debate was going on, we all agreed that one of the reasons why the press had so carefully pulled its punches about the Profumo scandal was precisely because of the disastrous appearance it had made in the Vassall affair. Undoubtedly, as Macmillan intended it to do, the Vassall debate did inhibit the press from probing and printing as it would normally have done. One can really say that the whole Establishment did everything possible to rally round the Profumos and to try and save them from their fate. For some weeks I must say I assumed absolutely, and I think probably George Wigg did too, that the affair was closed. When we were asked what we could do, we knew perfectly well we couldn't possibly say any of this outside the House of Commons because Ward and the girl were such hopeless witnesses that any cross-examination would break them down and make them seem totally unreliable in comparison with the word of Profumo. That was why we couldn't go any further.

In the first week of June the Prime Minister and his wife left for their Whitsun holiday on Iona. Mr Profumo and his wife had gone to Venice but on Whit Monday, June 3rd, he returned to London. On Tuesday morning he saw the Prime Minister's Private Secretary and the Chief Whip and on the same day sent the Prime Minister a letter, recalling his personal statement on March 22nd and admitting that he had misled the Prime Minister, his Cabinet colleagues and the House. Though, he said, 'there is no truth in the other charges', he felt that he could not remain a member of the Administration or of the House of Commons.

The press received a copy of this letter and of Mr Macmillan's brief reply, in which he accepted Mr Profumo's resignation.

On Saturday, June 8th, Dr Ward was arrested and charged with living on immoral earnings. (His trial opened at the Old Bailey on June 22nd; he died from an overdose of a sleeping drug three days after being found guilty.) On June 9th the News of the World *began a serialization of Miss Keeler's life story, for which she had been paid £23,000; the* Sunday Mirror *printed a letter to her from Mr Profumo which it had earlier acquired.*

Mr Macmillan returned to London on June 10th. Though Mr Wilson had announced that the Opposition would concentrate on the security aspect of the episode, the Conservative Party was restless. This mood was reflected in, and exacerbated by, a Times *leader on June 11th, headed 'It* Is *A Moral Issue'. That day, the Prime Minister presented a group of senior Ministers with Lord Dilhorne's report, which was then put before a two-hour Cabinet meeting on*

June 12th. Three Ministers stayed behind for half an hour that morning — Lord Dilhorne, Henry Brooke and Enoch Powell. According to rumours in The Times *and the* Daily Express *next morning, there was a ministerial revolt, said to be led by Mr Powell, with Mr Brooke, Sir Keith Joseph and Sir Edward Boyle. All but Mr Powell denied this allegation.*

On May 13th the Cabinet met again and that evening a deputation from the National Union of Conservative and Unionist Associations called on the Prime Minister. Still later that night, Lord Hailsham appeared on B.B.C. television, it was said to calm Conservative fears. In fact, he castigated both Mr Profumo and The Times *and declared that the Government's hands were clean.*

The Commons was to reassemble on June 17th and the Opposition used a Supply Day to discuss the Profumo affair as the opening debate. On June 16th the Prime Minister was visited at Chequers by the Chief Whip, Martin Redmayne. The day before, in a speech at Narborough, in Norfolk, Mr Powell had stated that he would be in his place to support the Prime Minister. Before the House met Mr Redmayne saw the 1922 Committee; a number of backbenchers there declared that, though they would vote for Mr Macmillan that evening, this must not be understood as a sign of confidence in his continued leadership.

What then was it that finally brought matters to a head so that this week, when the P.M. was on holiday, Profumo was forced, apparently very suddenly, to issue this astonishing statement that he had lied to the House of Commons and had had this association with Christine Keeler? We don't know yet. But it is almost certain that it was the fear that otherwise Ward would come clean. You see, after all, Ward had been ruined by the whole affair and the publicity. I suppose Ward was the kind of man who felt that if he'd been ruined there was no reason why he should go on protecting and preserving Profumo. So it was perhaps the knowledge that Ward was going to reveal what he knew that forced Profumo to save what little he could from the wreck by getting in first.

So we come to this week's account. I was here at Prescote for the Whitsun holiday when I was rung by young Douglas-Home[1] of the *Daily Express*. He said, 'You've heard the news that Profumo has made a statement and resigned already. Have you any statement to make?' Immediately I heard this, I said, because I knew this was for the record, that George Wigg and I had no interest at all in the personal publicity. We originally raised this matter because it wanted clearing up. We were justified in our position and all we cared about was that the truth should be known. I then repeated to Douglas-Home very carefully that all the information had been passed to the

---

[1] Charles Douglas-Home. A journalist on the *Daily Express* 1961–4, he was Defence Correspondent of *The Times* 1965–70, Features Editor 1970–3, Home Editor 1973–8 and in 1978 became Foreign Editor. His publications include a life of *Evelyn Baring: The Last Proconsul* (London: Collins, 1978).

P.M. by Harold Wilson, in a memorandum. Once all this was published I was sure everything would be clear.

An hour later George Wigg was on the phone, to say that he had also been approached. We agreed that we would make no formal statement under our own names, though naturally it was our job to ensure that the press was all right. I got on to Monkhouse[1] of the *Guardian* (Alastair Hetherington wasn't there) and to Sydney Jacobson, just to make sure that they got it clear that the Opposition was solely concerned with security. Harold Wilson had passed on the information but had been brushed off by Macmillan and here we were, as an Opposition, completely justified.

The news first came out on the wireless and T.V. on Wednesday night and I had my column to write on Thursday.[2] I decided, and I'm sure I was right, not to make any reference to the affair. However, I got Anne to go into Banbury to buy up all the papers and see what they had made of it. I also contacted Transport House to hear that Harold Wilson was flying back from some engagement he had been keeping in Toronto and would arrive on Thursday morning. I was rung up by I.T.V. to ask whether I would appear on 'This Week' on Thursday evening at half-past nine. I wasn't keen to do so and I pointed out that George Wigg and I should appear together. However, they wanted me alone — I don't quite know why. I then said I must wait until Harold Wilson came back and take his advice.

George Wigg and I had one of our usual altercations on the phone. I said that we must weigh up the decision whether, if I refused to appear, others would go on instead of me. There was Barbara, for instance (I didn't know at the time that she was safely away in Italy). Finally, Harold Wilson telephoned at lunch-time and we agreed that I shouldn't go on television. Meanwhile, I had heard from I.T.V. that Gordon Walker, who had also flown in that morning from Washington, had been approached and was willing to go on. After giving a couple of press conferences on exactly the right line Harold Wilson apparently spent the afternoon preventing Gordon Walker, preventing Shinwell, preventing any Labour Member from appearing. So last night's 'This Week' programme had a devastating account of the whole affair with a long personal interview with Dr Ward, but the Labour Party kept itself absolutely clear from incrimination, George Wigg was again right on this.

Yesterday I telephoned Harold. He was just listening to the 'This Week' programme and I got him afterwards. We agreed that we should keep to the line that George Wigg and I had decided. Harold was, as usual, absolutely cool and collected. The main aim now is to ensure that when the House reconvenes on Monday week the P.M. should be compelled to make a Statement on the affair.

Let me now try to put down my impression of what the effect of the episode has been. I should think that the whole account in yesterday's papers of the

[1] P. J. Monkhouse, Northern Editor of the *Guardian*. He retired in 1969.
[2] In the *Guardian*.

trial of Keeler and her Negro friends must have been the biggest shock to public morality which has been known in this century. I can't think of a more humiliating and discrediting story than that of the Secretary of State for War's being involved with people of this kind. It has social seediness and some fairly scabrous security background concerning Ivanov, the lying, the collusion, and, the fact that Royalty and the Establishment back Profumo.[1] Now the Queen will see him next week when he hands over his seals of office. I would think this would do the Establishment enormous harm. I would say that, handled as George advised Harold to handle it, this will in fact enormously undermine the Government and so assist in creating the conditions for a Labour Party victory at the next Election.

Saturday, June 22nd

We made the preparations for the debate on Profumo and decided that George Wigg and I would speak. I was allotted the role of raising the issue of press participation in the affair. I didn't mention this in the last slab of diary I did on this subject because the issue only really emerged last Sunday, when the *Sunday Mirror* suddenly published the text of a letter Profumo had sent to Christine Keeler. They had obtained this letter from her along with her story and had handed the letter back to Profumo on April 3rd, ten days after the debate in which George, Barbara and I pitted our honour against Profumo's honour. Now, of course, when George and I saw from the *Sunday Mirror* article that they had handed back to Profumo through Ward's solicitors a letter that had become a vital piece of evidence in the dispute, we were furious. Our suspicions were aroused that during this period the *Daily Mirror* Group — that is, Cecil King — had been colluding with Macmillan. At the time this looked very important because, if we could prove collusion and could prove the P.M. knew in advance, we thought we could probably bring about his downfall. So I was put up to ask in the debate four very carefully drafted questions relating first to the *Daily Mirror* and Cecil King and then to the *News of the World* and Mark Chapman Walker,[2] who was previously in the Conservative Party Office.

In the afternoon at four o'clock George Wigg came round and we talked things over and made our preparations more carefully. He was then assuming that he would have to tell the whole story. He had been through Harold's speech and I checked it. Then I went to dinner with Thomas Balogh and his wife at Hampstead and we discussed it again there.

On Monday morning there were more preparations for the debate and it duly took place that afternoon. Of course, as always happens, our prepara-

[1] On the afternoon of March 22nd, when he had made his Commons Statement, Mr Profumo and his wife, the actress Valerie Hobson, had joined the Queen Mother at Sandown Park races.

[2] Mark Chapman Walker joined the staff of Conservative Central Office in 1946 as Personal Assistant to Lord Woolton. He was Chief Publicity Officer there from 1949 until 1955, when he left to become Managing Director of the *News of the World*.

tions were knocked sideways. Harold made an absolutely magnificent speech, the best I've ever heard him make, better than I thought possible. It was really annihilating, a classical prosecution speech, with weight and self-control. However, to my great surprise the P.M. conceded in his reply most of the points which were the object of my questions. Meanwhile, Harold had discovered that the *Daily Mirror* had *not* had any contact with the P.M. Since the P.M. said officially that he had first heard of the thing from Mark Chapman Walker,[1] that took away one of my main sensational disclosures. Macmillan's speech was very long and very effective, though very plaintive. He admitted that he had been told of this by Mark Chapman Walker, that Norman Brook[2] had warned Profumo the year before[3] without bothering to inform him, the P.M., and that the Secret Service knew nothing about the Keeler/Profumo/Ward triangle before the newspapers did. It was a sort of devastating speech and it was followed by Nigel Birch's expected attack, demanding Macmillan's resignation.

The Prime Minister told the House that Sir Norman Brook, the Secretary to the Cabinet, had warned Mr Profumo against Dr Ward in 1961 but word of this had not passed to Mr Macmillan. He had not himself tackled Mr Profumo personally about the rumours but some of his ministerial colleagues had done so.

At the end of the debate Nigel Birch suggested that the Prime Minister should make way for 'a much younger colleague' and quoted Browning's poem 'The Lost Leader':

> *Let him never come back to us!*
> *There would be doubt, hesitation and pain,*
> *Forced praise on our part, the glimmer of twilight,*
> *Never glad confident morning again!*

Then came George, who wasn't by any means in his best form. He had also had to scrap all his narrative but of course he had built up his position to a point where his speech was a major sensation. When it was my turn, I made a pretty good speech. Looking back, it was one of my better ones and everybody there thought so, too. It was therefore rather disconcerting when I discovered next morning that my speech wasn't even mentioned in *The Times* and though there was a line in the *Guardian*, it had no mention in any other paper. I read it again in Hansard and it was good, one of the shrewdest analyses, with as its central point that it was not Macmillan's honour that was affected. What had gone wrong had been that the P.M. had not wanted to know and had turned a half-blind eye to Profumo's failings. It was that he had not really wanted to investigate that was his crime.

[1] Harold Macmillan referred only to 'a general manager of a national newspaper'.

[2] A civil servant who was Secretary to the Cabinet 1947–62. He was knighted in 1946 and raised to the peerage, as 1st Baron Normanbrook, in 1963. He died in 1967.

[3] But see below.

In one's own diary one is bound to ask why one's own speech wasn't mentioned. I think the answer was partly technical. Apparently the Press Association got jammed between five and seven o'clock and the tape room was two or three hours behind, which meant that the newspaper offices had no time to digest the speeches between seven and eight o'clock before the winding-up speeches came. These, made between nine and ten o'clock, were of course compulsorily digested. The second reason, which hadn't occurred to me, was that no newspaper would want to print my discussion of the role of the *Mirror* and the *News of the World*, particularly with the edge that had been taken off the stories by Macmillan. Nevertheless, it was a bit disconcerting. In terms of the House of Commons I had done well. Nevertheless it was a humbling experience.

In the division, the Opposition motion of censure was defeated by 321 votes to 252, with 27 Conservative abstentions. The 1922 Committee met on the night of June 20th and decided that any demand for Mr Macmillan's resignation should be deferred. Backbenchers, particularly those with marginal seats, were in no mood for the dissolution that resignation might entail. On June 1st the Prime Minister announced that a judicial inquiry would be conducted by Lord Denning, the Master of the Rolls, into the security and other aspects of the case. On June 28th Mr Macmillan reaffirmed that he hoped to lead the Party into the next Election, 'All being well and if I keep my health and strength.' He added that Mr Wilson should not 'try on the crown early in his life'.

By the end of the debate, what the Labour Party said was relatively unimportant because what mattered now was the Tory crisis. Looking back and reflecting on it, this crisis was a most extraordinary affair. Why was it that, on this single episode of security, suddenly the whole Tory Party was on the edge of dissolution? That is no exaggeration. On the Monday, after the debate, and on the Tuesday it is literally true that the Tory Party was on the edge, or seemed to be, of tearing itself to pieces. I put some reflections on this in my column in the *Guardian*.[1] I'm sure George Wigg is right in stressing that the officer class who were the centre of this revolt were not going along with the idea of a Maudling succession all that easily. That's why I wasn't myself the least bit surprised when the news came through late on Thursday evening that the 1922 Committee had shown itself perfectly amenable to the chairman, John Morrison,[2] and to the devices of the Chief Whip in postponing the event.

Nevertheless it was a very astonishing experience to see this absolutely suicidal mania. The real explanation is that the Profumo debate was the *occasion* for the expression of the fury and discontent which have been piling

[1] 'The Tory Stampede', published on June 21st.
[2] Conservative M.P. for Salisbury 1942–64, he was Chairman of the 1922 Committee 1955–64. In 1965 he was created 1st Baron Margadale.

up ever since the July massacre last year when Macmillan got rid of Selwyn Lloyd and Watkinson. I think that from that moment Macmillan's touch has failed and that since then the Tories realize that under his leadership they really have no chance. Once he had made the mistake of not taking his time and resigning after the failure of the Common Market negotiations, it was inevitable that a moment would come when this fury and violence and dissatisfaction would be expressed.

Of course it's true that in Tory terms failures about security and the Armed Services are failures against the sacred cow. The Services and security are a subject on which the Tories feel they must be able to do far better than us. So the appalling disclosure of incompetence and laxity has had its effect. Personally George Wigg and I did feel fairly proud that for ten years now, since the Burgess and MacLean episode,[1] we have been preaching the lessons of security and exposing the effects on the British ruling class of this deep inner laxity which is constantly mistaken for genuine freedom and tolerance.

One other amusing incident occurred this week. Of course, the *Daily Mirror* people read Hansard and didn't at all like the way that I supported Francis Williams in saying they had shown a dereliction of journalistic duty in suppressing the Profumo letter.[2] It was highly characteristic that Hugh Cudlipp should have rung me up urgently on Wednesday to ask me to lunch the next day and to take part in a special stunt they were doing the following Sunday. It was a terrible rush because Thursday is my *Guardian* column day, but I decided to do it, as it was 100 guineas [£105] a time and I was curious to find out what had really happened.

I duly attended at a private room in the Café Royal and found Hugh surrounded by four of his minions, plus James Cameron and Malcolm Muggeridge. The idea was to swing from the one fact that Norman Brook had warned Profumo about Ward without telling the P.M. and to ask how England is governed.[3] I suppose the *Mirror* wanted me to do it because of my introduction on prime ministerial Government to the new edition of Bagehot.[4] I agreed but in the course of our lunch we had a pretty edgy time. At one moment, I don't know why, I said to Hugh, 'Well, how are those photographs which the Secret Service took?' This was because I had been told by George that, in addition to obtaining the Keeler articles and letters, Odhams Press had somehow got hold of a whole number of Ward's obscene

[1] See above, pp. 440 and n. and 443.

[2] Crossman quoted a statement made by Lord Francis-Williams in the *New Statesman* on June 14th, saying of the *Sunday Pictorial* that 'Not to have published this letter at the time Profumo made his first personal statement in the Commons, thus forcing the real issue, the security issue, into the open, seems to me to be a dereliction of journalistic responsibility.'

[3] The article, in the *Sunday Mirror* of June 23rd, 1963, was headlined 'Who Runs This Country, Anyway?' Malcolm Muggeridge wrote on 'The Slow, Sure Death of the Upper Classes', James Cameron on 'Why the World is Mocking Britain' and Richard Crossman on 'The Peril of the Whitehall Mandarins'. The *Sunday Mirror* included its own list of 'The 20 Most Powerful People in Britain Today'.

[4] Published in paperback by Fontana. See above, pp. 733 n. and 740 n.

photographs. When Scotland Yard had received the information from George, these had been taken back as evidence for the case. I rather breezily made this remark and suddenly realized that what I had said was true. Hugh Cudlipp was indignantly saying that George Wigg had talked nonsense and every one of Hugh's staff around the room was uneasily aware that I was on to something about them that was not too reputable. However, we got through the lunch and the article was duly done, though I don't know what has happened because I haven't yet seen this morning's papers.

Well, having said all this, let me now try to sum up my impression of the present situation. I was not one of those who ever really believed, even at the height of last week's excitement, that the Tories would literally overthrow Macmillan in a week. Certainly the crisis is settling down and the P.M. has regained control with the help of the Whips, the chairman of the 1922 Committee and Lord Poole. It looks to me as though Macmillan will now be able to choose his time. He could theoretically stay on but from his own point of view I can see no point in that. Why should he now involve himself in what is almost certainly the inevitable defeat of the Tory Party? It now looks as though he can gracefully accede to the demands of the rebels and, before the new Session begins in the autumn, say in September, before the party Conferences, let a younger man take over. Of course if the rebels had had their way last week, no doubt Maudling would have been the immediate choice of the backbenchers. But I am not so sure Maudling will get it so easily. There is now time to think, time for Butler to strengthen his position more and more and, of course, there is also the possibility of the Lords Hailsham and Home taking their chance, because they will soon be free to become members of the Commons.[1]

So the situation is pretty open. I would still bet that Maudling would get in in the end but it wouldn't be nearly as certain as the rebels guessed last week. What I would bet for the future is a change of Tory leadership in September, duly carried out in time for the Party Conference, and then an effort to play the new man in and have the Election next May or June. If that happens, our majority might be considerably reduced because there doesn't seem to be any doubt that, by all normal prognostications, the economic situation should get better during the next year and thereby slightly improve the Tory Government's chances.

I was very amused this week when I was discussing my article with Harold

[1] The Peerage Bill, permitting hereditary peers to renounce their titles for life and to stand for election as commoners, was passed by the Commons on May 30th. It was the culmination of Mr Wedgwood Benn's efforts, begun some ten years before. (See above, p. 942 n.) The Government had announced that the Act would come into force at the dissolution of the present Parliament but Mr Gordon Walker moved an Amendment in the Commons to make it operative from the day of Royal Assent. This was rejected in the House of Commons but carried by 105 to 25 votes in the Lords, on July 16th, and the Bill's sponsor in the Commons, Iain Macleod, gave way. On July 31st Royal Assent was given; Mr Wedgwood Benn (closely followed by John Grigg, 2nd Baron Altrincham) presented his instrument of disclaimer. Mr Wedgwood Benn was re-elected at Bristol on August 20th.

Wilson to hear him say, 'Well, you know what our directive is — to keep Macmillan as our most valuable asset.' He added, 'The one thing I am really frightened of is Maudling.' I know very well why. Maudling is Harold's own age, a figure comparable to him. As long as he has Macmillan opposite him, old, effete, worn out, a cynical dilettante, the contrast between Harold's character and Macmillan's is an overwhelming advantage to Harold and the Labour Party. There would be no such sharp contrast between Harold Wilson and young Maudling.

Wednesday, June 26th

All last weekend, or rather, all the time I had on Sunday, apart from the children and people coming to see me, I spent struggling to get a draft of our paper on science and government. We are now nearing the time of the science debate in the House and of our science conference on July 20th.[1] All the work of various groups is having to be summed up with papers and documents. On Monday evening we had the dinner for the older scientists, a group who worked for years with Mr Gaitskell and who, with Bronowski[2] as emissary, had finally in desperation written a letter telling him they would rather resign than be going on as uselessly and underemployed as they had been. It was a very nice evening, although Harold turned up an hour late and we had to dine without him. But all of them were delighted with the transformation of the situation since I took over, and some very nice things were said to Harold when he arrived, in my presence.

The really important thing which happened was Harold's own disquisition, as he leant back in his chair, on his intentions. To my amazement he laid out before us a fairly complete survey of his intentions for reconstructing Whitehall. Of course it all started from the old problem of the Ministry of Science and the proposal of our Higher Education working party that there should be a Minister of Education who would include in his realm not only the schools, but all the universities and Colleges of Advanced Technology. One of the first things Harold had done when he took over, in a speech at Imperial College with Blackett in the chair, was to disown this proposition. He had suggested that we should not have an all-embracing Minister of Education, but, on the one hand, a Minister of Education and, on the other hand, a Minister of Science and Research and Higher Education. I must say that the more I reflected on this proposal, the greater difficulties I found in it. This was partly because I was scared of having two Ministers of Education

[1] The conference, organized by the Fabian Society, was to take place on July 20th and 21st.

[2] Jakob Bronowski. A former university lecturer in Science, he worked for various Government Departments during the war and for the Ministry of Works 1946–50, and was Director of the National Coal Board's Coal Research Establishment 1950–9 and Director-General of its Process Development Department from 1959 to 1964, when he moved to the United States. He was a gifted popular writer on the sciences; his books include, for example, *The Western Intellectual Tradition* (London: Allen Lane, 1960); and his 'The Ascent of Man', for the B.B.C., was a notable television series.

in the Cabinet and partly because I didn't see how one could call the Ministry in charge of the Universities dominated by the arts and humanities a Ministry of Science and Higher Education. I honestly felt that if you were going to do it this way, you had better drop the title Science altogether.

However it was perfectly clear that on this point not only was I against the scientists but Harold was overwhelmingly against me. He built up his picture of what he was going to do roughly as follows. He made it clear that the central and most important Minister on the home front would be the Minister of Production, or he might be called Minister of Planning. This would be a new Ministry and the cadre on which it would be built would be the present staff of N.E.D.C. That is Number One, the Minister of Planning. Next to him would be, equally important, the Minister of Science and Higher Education, who would be in charge of all the grants for research, for research councils, who would be in charge of scientific Intelligence and, with the Minister of Planning, would jointly do the planning. As for the Chancellor of the Exchequer, in Harold's actual words, he would be downgraded to a secondary Minister in charge of a secondary Ministry.

Patrick Blackett said that he felt it was important to have a Ministry of Industry, something parallel to the Ministry of Supply during the war, which would be responsible for pushing science and scientific development in the private sector of industry. Harold resisted this very strongly. He thought it was the job of the Minister of Science and I think Blackett was very largely persuaded. We had considerable talk about the importance of getting new people into Whitehall. Harold said the whole point was that, if you created the new Ministries of Science, of Planning and of Industry, you could much more easily get the new blood, instead of trying to push it into the old Ministries.

At one point Harold made a reference to steel. He said that his friend Charlie de Peyer[1] had been prematurely sacked from the Ministry of Power and had agreed to spend the next four months actually drafting the measure for nationalizing steel. Harold said he is one of the ablest men and it was a wonderful gift that he was doing this. He also added that the bill would have to be ready for the first Session and that the idea that we had last time, of merely setting up holding companies, would not be possible. This news was of the very greatest interest because I had known that we were making no preparations for what to do about steel. Up till now this was a gaping hole in our preparations for taking power. I think that the way Harold is handling this is very indicative. Preparation does not take the form of setting up a committee or an N.E.C. working party or a parliamentary working party but of appointing *Harold's* man to do it. I think there is a great deal to be said for this Rooseveltian method of *ad hoc* work. But of course the decisions to put

[1] Charles de Peyer became a civil servant in 1930, retiring in 1964 as Under-Secretary of the Ministry of Fuel and Power. From 1952 to 1956 he was Minister in the U.K. delegation to the European Coal and Steel Community.

everything in the hands of the individuals—letting me do science, Charlie de Peyer steel, George Wigg defence—means that everyone has to report direct to Harold, because he has no office, no organization and no chief of staff. The pressure on him becomes overwhelming.

After the dinner Harold offered to take me home and in the car I briefly told him about the problem of the handbook. This is something which each of the main political parties always produces for the General Election. It is a great round-up of all the propaganda nuggets, with chapters about the record of the other side, suitable for quotations. At Monday's Home Policy Committee meeting, George Brown had said that we shouldn't give hostages to fortune and that he had already glanced at the *Speaker's Handbook* and found it packed full of extensions of Labour policy which would be quoted against us by the Tories. I had expressed a little surprise and said that both last October and the previous October I had pointed out that the amount of time and manpower devoted to preparing the *Speaker's Handbook* was out of all proportion greater than its value to our candidates and I had been strongly in favour of the office not doing it. But here I have been overruled, the work had been done, the whole handbook was already in galley proof and part of it in page proof. If we scrapped it, all the money, more than £1,000, would be wasted and the office would have wasted its time.

George Brown had said it was insufferable to be told by a man like me that we couldn't change our minds. Peter Shore had spoken up and pointed out that nine-tenths of the material in the handbook was in fact an account of twelve years of Tory rule and was providing the kind of anti-Tory ammunition which George Brown's own view of how to fight the Election requires us to give our candidates. I had said that it was absolutely ludicrous to take any decision until people had read the handbook. We left the matter open for this morning's Executive. When I told Harold about this and said I thought it was a terrible thing to scrap it, he expressed the same view as George Brown. So George hadn't been cheating when he said that he had Harold on his side. I also mentioned the problem of the agricultural policy document which George Brown had also wanted us not to publish as a policy statement, but simply to present in a speech to Conference next September. George had argued that we had had too many policy statements and that telling people things only caused trouble. Here again, Harold backed George Brown in a perfectly friendly way.

So we came to this morning's meeting and these subjects came up. First of all George Brown explained how the Executive felt for electoral reasons that we didn't want any more policy statements and that it would appear that we were handing hostages to fortune and giving the Tories propaganda which they could exploit. Quite fairly Harold immediately said we should take the issues one by one, beginning with agriculture. Again George Brown said what he wanted and Harold discussed it. I said, 'Surely, before we come to the presentation of this document, the Executive has got to consider it page by page, because it's a most important document.' But there was not a single comment because no one on the Executive had read any of the six pages. This is extremely revealing. We have now reached a point where nobody bothers about policy. The Executive all feel that this has slipped out of their hands and they felt embarrassed when I demonstrated that they hadn't bothered to read it. Then I made my speech, a good speech, in which my main point was that we have to remember not only the voter but the confidence, morale and democratic nature of our own Party. We pride ourselves on being different from the Tories, who just say, 'Let's win power, having promised as little as possible. Then we shall be free to do what we like.' I said we had always contrasted with theirs our democratic constitution, where our rank and file really participate in policy-making.

My speech was listened to in extremely uneasy silence. It's striking that after I had finished not a single person there, not one of the left-wingers, said a word in favour of my argument that the Conference should be consulted. In a second speech, about publication, I pointed out that you are really less liable to be caught out by the Tories with a carefully written, printed document than you are with a version of it fluffed by George Brown in a speech. Harold Wilson had earlier on admitted that this was an absolutely first-rate policy statement and I think he had been half convinced that he had made a mistake in this case in backing George Brown. But of course I didn't blame Harold, he couldn't go back on this.

So we came to the other question, that of the handbook. Here again we had the same argument: it would be terribly dangerous. We reached a compromise and got our way. The handbook is going to have all the policy taken out of it and is going to be 'twelve years wasted under the Tories' — a collection of anti-Tory propaganda. Something will be saved. But it's an extraordinary thing that people should be thinking of getting rid of a handbook which will be essential in the education of our own people.

Strangely enough, there came up a few minutes later yet another example of the same tendency among our leadership, now, to think solely in terms of winning votes and to run away from all their democratic responsibilities. As it was revealed in N.E.C. this morning, we have now committed ourselves to £160,000 for an advertising campaign. It was solemnly proposed to save £337 by cutting off the supply of 'Speakers' Notes', our little weekly propaganda thing from Transport House. I pointed out that for £337 we were cutting off some of the vital education of our political officers, and our constituencies. I was told that Len Williams had observed that these things were being wasted when they were sent out free and that, in order to save money, we shouldn't send them out to people who didn't read them. I said that, if they didn't read them, what we wanted to make sure of was to send them and make sure they did read them — it was fantastic that at this moment, when we needed to build up the politically educated Party, we should be cutting them out. I was then told that this economy had taken place because of a concession—concession!—that M.P.s should be supplied free with policy statements. I didn't know it, but when our new policy statement on social security came out, it didn't go to a single M.P. because they had to pay in order to get them.

Both Tony Wedgwood Benn and I made a speech about how terribly dangerous it was to rely on propaganda to the mass electorate and to starve the Party of vital political education. I must admit I was very, very disturbed by what has happened in the last few days and by the conversations we have had in off-moments. It is quite clear that Harold and George Brown have it in their heads and have a passion for feeling that they must avoid Election defeat by the Tory exploitation of Labour policy. They feel that *everything* must be done to prevent the Tories getting at it. As for the arguments about party democracy and party political education, they don't take these seriously. It seems to me that the leadership now is making exactly the same mistake that the Attlee leadership made in 1944 and 1945. They are thinking solely in terms of the electorate, not at all in terms of building up a politically educated cadre of trained Party workers, to stand by them when they are in Government.

It is depressing to me that within so few weeks of assuming the leadership Harold should have so 100 per cent sided with George Brown in this terribly shortsighted cynicism. After all, it is in fact a democratic duty for a left-wing Party to lay before the electorate the policies we shall carry out. Frankly, however, the view of our leadership is that we should welsh on that demo-cratic responsibility as far as we possibly can in order to avoid a possible electoral defeat.

What is so ironical is that this terror of losing votes is infecting our leader-ship at a time when the Gallup Poll shows us 20 per cent in the lead over the Tories and when the Profumo affair has utterly discredited the Tory leader-ship. The problem is not whether we shall win but the size of our majority. Possibly the greatest problem that faces Harold Wilson is that he may have too great a majority and will have his hands full.

Well, those are my thoughts now and I wanted to record them while they were still fresh in my mind.

On July 1st it was announced by Edward Heath that Harold ('Kim') Philby, a former Foreign Office official recently employed as Correspondent in Beirut for the Observer *and* The Economist, *had been the 'third man' who had warned the defecting diplomats Burgess and MacLean in 1951 (see above, p. 1003 n.). Philby had himself disappeared in January. On July 30th* Izvestia *revealed that Philby had been given asylum and citizenship in the Soviet Union (where, in October, he was to be joined by his wife). On November 15th, 1979, it was announced in the House of Commons by the Prime Minister, Mrs Margaret Thatcher, that the 'fourth man' associated with the three defectors was Sir Anthony Blunt, a former Security Service officer and a distinguished art historian, who had been*

Surveyor of the King's Pictures 1945–52, Surveyor of the Queen's Pictures 1952–72 and Adviser for the Queen's Pictures and Drawings from 1972 until his retirement in 1978. On the following day, November 16th, his knighthood was cancelled and annulled.

Monday, July 1st

In the House of Commons yet another security scandal has broken, with the admission by Ted Heath to a totally surprised House that Philby, the *Observer* Correspondent for the Middle East in Beirut, who disappeared months ago, was the third man in the Burgess/MacLean case and that he has really gone across to the other side. This of course has great political importance, because in 1955, when Macmillan was Foreign Secretary and we debated the report on Burgess and MacLean, Marcus Lipton,[1] who is a terribly silly Labour M.P., said that Philby was the third man. In the course of that debate, we had compelled Lipton to get up and make a personal statement to withdraw such an accusation.

So Macmillan is now really in trouble again, with yet another security scandal, yet another lapse. It will be interesting to see how he handles this, because Philby was a high Foreign Office official in Washington and was Burgess's superior officer in 1954, and, though when he retired from the Foreign Office many people suspected he was the third man, Macmillan denied it. This is another example of Macmillan's not knowing because he didn't want to know. Did he take the kind of tolerant lackadaisical attitude to Philby which we found he had taken to Profumo? If he did, will that cause him more trouble?

Wednesday, July 17th

This time the slab really does seem to be a concentrated period, in which my mind has been completely dominated by a single topic — the science debate. In the course of my whole life in Parliament, nearly eighteen years, I don't remember a single period when I've worried and concerned myself more with a debate than this, or indeed, have done more work or preparation for it. Of course I'd known that this debate was coming on and also, in a strange way, known that this would be a terrific test for me, not only a test in Parliament, in the Parliamentary Party and in the press outside (which is bad enough, by the way, since so many people would have liked to see me fail), but also a test in Harold's mind, though I myself don't think for a moment that he doubted the rightness of his choice. Nevertheless, this feeling of test and of passing an examination was a bit of a nightmare. I don't have many nightmares when I sleep. Indeed, almost the only one I've had consecutively during my adult life is to wake up, as I think I wake up during the dream, to find myself just going in for Greats at Oxford, though I'm a fully-fledged M.P. and I've totally

[1] Labour M.P. for the Brixton division of Lambeth 1945–74 and for Lambeth Central from 1974 until his death in 1978.

forgotten all the work I've done. So it looks as though examinations have made some kind of searing wound on my unconscious. Certainly this sense of being examined is one of those which frightens me most and I suppose also puts me on my mettle.

Well, I can trace this back and it all starts at the first moment of real shock when I knew the exam was *on* and could no longer be postponed. This was when the Chief Whip met me in the lobby and said, 'Would you take next Thursday, July 4th, for your science debate?' I said, 'Oh heavens, God forbid. We're not ready.' He said, 'Well, on the 4th you could have a whole day and a vote. If you put it off longer, it won't be nearly as good.' I said, 'Can you give me half an hour?' I went to see Harold and asked him what he thought. He agreed the 4th would be a bit close, considering none of my scientists had finished their homework, but he wasn't sure if the Shadow Cabinet would allow us to have the 17th, when he would be free. He added that, even if the 4th were possible, he wasn't very hopeful that he himself would speak. Now of course our great scheme for this debate was that I should start and, to give it importance, Harold would wind up. It had always been very clear in my mind that you can't make a debate in the Commons really important unless the winder-up is the Leader at least. So it was a bit of a blow to me that Harold seemed doubtful and of course I began to realize that people in the Shadow Cabinet were manoeuvring. Some people imagine that owing to his enormous success Harold now has all the power in the world inside his Shadow Cabinet. This is by no means true. It is still the case that only one of them, Fred Lee, voted for Harold against George Brown. Above all, it's still true that they suspect his relationships with old friends. On this occasion I'm quite sure that they were determined to prevent our plan to have me starting and Harold winding up.

So when I had this news and Harold's word I had to make up my mind what to do. It became quite clear that if I agreed to have the debate on the 4th, before any of our science papers for the conference came in, I would deeply upset the scientists. I would also do it without very much gain, because it was doubtful whether I would have Harold with me. There was also the point that I just wanted to postpone my examination.

So I said no to the Chief Whip and felt better about it but I knew that I would now have to start working. In due course (it must have been on Wednesday, the 3rd) Fred Lee met me in the lobby and said, 'Well, it's fixed for the 15th and you are to start and I am to wind up.' Then I knew the worst and knew that they had done what they wanted — they had put the science debate on the 15th, a Monday, with a cold House, an empty House, Harold away. They had gone further and put a higher education debate on Wednesday, by which time Harold would be available, and they had given Fred Lee and Eirene White a chance on the Wednesday. They had also in some way circumscribed me, by putting a higher education debate after my science debate.

As I dictate all of these things on to my tape-recorder, I begin to realize how fantastically egocentric the whole thing sounds. How can I be fussing in this way, worrying about the right order of debate? Well, that's the politician. One does fuss about oneself, partly because the self one's fussing about also involves an issue and, indeed, it is difficult to remember sometimes that what one is fussing about is not merely personal issues but issues of state and politics. One has something at stake in the matter and I think it's fair that throughout these months I've had the growing feeling that the science debate might matter.

Actually it wasn't only my personal success or failure that was at stake, but also the future of Britain and science — all the things I was working up. As the weeks have turned into months my work with the science groups and our preparations for the conference on July 20th/21st have increasingly convinced me that Harold is on to something completely real. His intuition was profoundly right that a science policy for Labour and a new attitude to scientists and technology is the coming thing. Though I was against it, the fact that he'd dragooned me into this and said, 'You've finished social security. Get off that and I'll put you on a new topic,' was not only understanding my psychology but understanding the real issues involved in a Wilson Government.

From the moment on the 3rd that I heard the news I had this frantic sense of oppression. I had been reading every single piece, article, White Paper, etc., that had piled on my desk, as part of my science reading. In the early months of this, I felt an extraordinarily reluctance to read anything and actually to get down to it. I had been content to go to the groups and pick up what I could by discussion. Now, however, that I was coming to the debate, I began to be uneasily aware that I normally speak on things I know something about, things I have worked on for years. I didn't speak in the House on social security until at least three or four years after we started our working party and I had made myself quite an expert. Apart from social security, I speak on defence, Germany, on things that I really naturally and instinctively *know*, where I have something to *say*.

Here, however, I was bound to speak to a brief, provided by other people. The vast majority of our Front Bench people are perfectly used to speaking to a brief — there they are, this year's Shadow Minister of this, next year's Shadow Minister of that, speaking to a Shadow brief just as Ministers are trained to move from Department to Department and speak to Government briefs. As a long-standing backbencher with an academic background, I haven't got that habit. I felt a profound sense of insecurity that I would be caught out and that I must try to know enough about the subject to try to absorb it, so that it would come out of me by nature. That is something which I was doing throughout all those ten days.

I also knew that on this occasion I would have to write the speech out, and learn to be a Minister. I found this quite extraordinarily difficult. In my mind, writing and speaking are two completely different things. I write with great difficulty now and with very great care, draft after re-draft, working across the table with Jennie. I don't do it as most people think, easily, but with infinite trouble, smoothing it out. I think the great art is to get the guts of it down and then to give it fluidity and apparent informality so that it seems quite easy. This sense of ease in what I write is all being artificially injected in working it over. My speaking in the House of Commons is exactly the opposite. For years now I've had the habit of merely making a few notes to remind me of the order. This is because I am speaking on something I know about. I don't think that on any occasion I have ever found that I turn over the first page of notes because, the moment I arrive, I get a tremendous intensity of interest and 100 per cent involved in the debate. In a curious way, discretion, no, not discretion, inhibition, goes to the wind. I'm *there* debating and I think my power in the House is my complete involvement in the debate – but it's an impromptu involvement. Here is a quality which, I think, to compare very, very small things with big things, I share to an extent with Aneurin Bevan. He was a spontaneous debater and, however much he prepared beforehand, the way his speech went was in the debate. He was involved and it was the debate which brought his speech out. So I'm maximum impromptu in debates and maximum hard-working and worked-out in writing.

So, when I try to write a speech, it's the one thing I can't do. I can write an article but I find this other task extraordinarily difficult. I worked away trying to actually write down words I could use in the speech. I realized that, as I wrote it all down, then memorized it, there was extreme difficulty in actually making it sound all right on the day. Indeed, I was so worried about it that I managed to get an interview with Harold on the 11th, the Thursday before the debate, in order to check over with him the policy statement I was to make but *really* in order to discuss these things with him.

Well, Harold and I had our meeting at seven o'clock and the policy statement only took a few minutes to check over. He said, 'Be careful about the commitment to a Ministry of Science and Higher Education[1] because you may upset Fred Willey and Eirene White, who are members of the working party which recommended quite different arrangements. Otherwise everything is O.K.' Obviously Harold wanted to talk about other things. I held on a bit and then said, 'Harold, I am terribly worried about how I do this. Do I write it all out?' He said (very interesting), 'I usually write everything out.' I said, 'How do you manage all this?' 'Well,' he said, 'in my last week's speech it took me two to two and a half hours straight. I write it down in my own kind of shorthand.' 'Don't you have it typed out by Marcia?' 'No, I write it down in my own shorthand on pieces of large House of Commons paper and then there is the speech and I read it aloud.'

Well! Two to two and a half hours for a major speech! But I had already spent about sixteen hours on writing the first twenty to twenty-five minutes

[1] See above, pp. 1005–6.

of a minor speech. There one realizes what I am practised and skilled at, which Harold is very moderately good at: article-writing; and what he is practised and good at: speech-writing and preparation. In the course of the last ten years each man has specialized on a certain thing and therefore has a completely different aptitude.

I ought to note here how that conversation with Harold continued. When he had said that 'the great thing you must do is to write down your notes, then don't use them,' he said, 'Now let's talk about other things — what would you like, Dick, in my Government?' 'Harold, I really don't like discussing that kind of thing.' He insisted. So I said, 'Well, I'd really like pensions, of course, because I would like to get that job done properly. It's not easy.' Here, Harold was quite impatient. 'Pensions? That's all finished. You've done that. No, no, that's not a job worth your while. I'll give that to somebody quite junior. Try again.' 'Well, Tommy Balogh,' I said rather cautiously, 'Tommy Balogh said I ought to be your Minister of Planning.' 'No,' Harold said, 'that's no good, that's for somebody else. That can't be for you.'

Then he said, 'But of course I could make you my Minister of Industry.' (Planning, by the way, will be the top man to replace the Chancellor; Industry will be the reconstituted Board of Trade, carrying out the application of science to industry.) 'No,' I said, 'no good at all, I know nothing about it, Harold. I wouldn't want to feel the lack of self-confidence which I'm feeling about this debate.' 'Well,' he said, 'would you like Colonies?' 'No, no,' I said, 'no. In that case I would rather have Higher Education, which I know something about. But you've booked that for Blackett.' 'Yes, I have, but what about making you Minister of Education?' And I suddenly realized that the artful old bugger had organized the conversation to put into my mind the idea that Blackett and I should work together for him. I immediately said, 'Well, of course, that's something I could *do*. There is no doubt about whether I could do it.' 'Well,' Harold said, 'if you and Blackett were there, I could leave that to you. And heaven knows there are very few jobs where I feel any confidence that I can get men really to do it without my interfering.'

Harold went on to make his usual comments on James Callaghan, who is his Shadow Chancellor and who during the last weeks has developed in a most extraordinary way that kind of parliamentary softening of the brain which seems to occur so very often in frontbenchers both in Government and in Shadow Government. Men who are vigorous and alert but who are mere professional politicians reach a point where they suddenly become relaxed public figures, members of an Establishment, who manage to formulate the most safe comments on every subject and who are the kind of people who are simply the playthings of their Departments. Every time I've watched James Callaghan sitting in the Committee and enunciating his platitudes and pointing issues and more and more expressing the doubts of the Establishment about Labour, I've realized that from Harold's point of view he is a disaster.

I said to Harold, 'Well, how will James react to being down-graded to

Chancellor, if you make the Minister of Planning the real thing?' (By the way, Harold had not indicated who he was making Minister of Planning. It could really only be one person—George Brown.)[1] He then made the devastating comment that, of course, if James didn't want to stay Chancellor, he could always be Minister of Defence, showing the small esteem in which he holds the Minister of Defence, as well as the Foreign Secretary, who in his mind is still Gordon Walker.

Harold went over things with me about education and said frankly that Fred Willey was not up to this. It's obviously true that Harold felt that the Blackett/Crossman team would be the right thing to have. By this time, the interview was over. I had not really wanted this but realized Harold had been very clever about it. Provided I was a success in the debate on Monday, this would then consolidate it in his mind.

On Tuesday I went to see Ted Heath about my negotiations for a memorial in Dresden, to be presented by Coventry Cathedral, to commemorate the Germans killed in the air raid. Heath, poor man, was absolutely overwhelmed at the latest part of the security scandal. We discussed the memorial and, as we were going out of the room, I thought I would ask him a great question. This was in the very week when the troubles about Philby were being discussed in the House. 'Ted, why on earth doesn't the Prime Minister agree about our proposal that there should be in the P.M.'s office a Minister of Security, who would take all these responsibilities off his own shoulders and off you?' Heath looked at me and said, 'Well, look, Dick, I'll ask you a question. Does your friend George Brown *understand* about security?'[2] 'Why do you ask?' 'Well,' Heath said, 'from the Questions he put yesterday in the House, he didn't understand the real situation, which is that the F.O. isn't in his sense of the word in charge of security. We don't have any control over the secret organizations but only over the imposition of certain security measures in our Office.' I said, 'I understand that all right and I fancy George Brown does in a way.' 'Well,' said Heath, 'if he understands it, how can he blame me?' So I said, 'That's a different question. What I was asking was, why you don't get out of this by having a Minister in charge?'

'Well, it would be a Minister just to take the kicks, wouldn't it? Who in our situation is willing to do *that*?' Of course that threw a flood of light on the whole crisis about the P.M., which has been going on all through these past weeks. There has been this amazing situation where, ever since the Profumo debate, the majority of Tory backbenchers now in the House have been declaring to the nation that they should get rid of their P.M. and, if possible, substitute Maudling. I do see that in such a situation the proposal that a particular Minister should expose his political future for the sake of saving Mr Macmillan doesn't sound very attractive. So I laughed and said to Heath, 'Why don't we put such a Minister in the House of Lords?' He replied, 'That

[1] It was.
[2] George Brown had asked a Supplementary Question on July 2nd.

would be no good at all, because after all the whole point is that he should subject himself to the House of Commons. No, it would have to be done there and frankly I don't see anybody ever being ready to be something so absolutely blighted. There would be no kind of future for a Minister who took on that particular job.' At this point I dropped off for lunch.

So I finally come to last weekend—rather like preparing for a major operation. I arrived home, worked all Friday on the written text of my speech and got out after a desperate rush with Jennie something like a text, twenty-five long pages. Then I caught the 7.15 train to Prescote.

At home the corn looked all right and the potatoes too, though the rain was hanging round the farm still and there were only patches of sunshine. The children were in particularly nice form that weekend. They are growing now and the result of Nanny's being away is that they are really much more endearing, though less well behaved. It's not only that they are not kept dolled-up and clean when they go down to the village, but they tend to shout a great deal more and leave their nursery untidier and express themselves more violently. Both are tremendous extroverts, great, crashing, decisive, pushing personalities, both knowing what they want to do, both growing, thrusting themselves into life, each in its own way. Wonderfully different. They get on quite well together. Patrick knocks Virginia about but also reads to her and she adores playing with him. He allows her to join in his games. One of his games, like one I used to play, is building with the bricks I had myself as a child. I used to have them mostly for forts and soldiers but he is more creative and constructs a great story and calls it a film show. I'm brought in every now and then to see a film which consists of a story invented by Patrick about something which has happened. Virginia is sometimes allowed to play but more often sits there. Patrick can now read, pretty well, and every morning I go into his bedroom and find him reading away. Last week I found him reading the Prayer Book and he said, in answer to my question, 'Oh all ye works of the Lord, Bless ye the Lord; Praise Him and magnify Him for ever.' I said, 'All ye whales ... ' and he said, 'No, that's on the next page.' It was pretty clear that, having read it, he had practically memorized the whole of the Benedicite.

Virginia is very different. She is not interested in reading so much and she reads in bed, as she puts it, only because her brother does. For her, this means looking at the pictures. She already sews neatly and is wonderfully nimble as a person, tough, vital and practical. I have already got there one theoretical, thoughtful, strong, violent boy and one unspeculative, practical, loving, flirtatious, vigorous, sporting girl. Patrick is now old enough not to want me to be a Minister because he wants to see more of me. We now have arranged that when his school is over they are all coming up to London, when the science conference is on next Saturday. Of course, Prescote has in the last year made more difference to me, a growing difference. I now really genuinely begrudge every moment I spend in London. When I get back to

Prescote, I feel I can relax, that I'm really there, living and growing and I
think in a way keeping young with the children.

Of course, there is another thing about it, I don't do anything at Prescote.
True, I read a bit and am now slowly learning to use my tape-recorder. But
frankly, if I were to be at Prescote, I would be retired and not do a day's
work, because I don't know enough about farming and I can't do the kind of
work I'm good at. So, in order to be a person, I really have to work in
London. I have to have this split life, which is much more of a split for Anne
living in Prescote with the children than it is for me. I don't much like these
days of being a grass widower here in London but, on the other hand, Anne
doesn't like entertaining and it isn't as bad as it might be, as I am intent on
work and life in Parliament. I can live life in Parliament and I can live that
kind of life fairly well without her because she doesn't really like it. This
means that the time we have together at Prescote is even more our own.

On this occasion Anne wanted to come and hear the debate and we had
quite a discussion about it. I said I didn't want her to but I knew perfectly
well that if I said I didn't want her to she would get in on her own. I knew
over the weekend she was making preparations with Jennie for coming.
I had had to arrange to go up to London on Sunday, which I *hate* doing, to
see Pat Blackett whom I wanted to read through my speech.

On Saturday afternoon our old friend Captain Bob Maxwell[1] suddenly
rang up from Bletchley, where he had been rained out of a fête. He asked
whether he could come over on his way to Oxford, to discuss my speech.
Maxwell is a very strange fellow — a Czech Jew with a perfect knowledge of
Russian, who has an infamous reputation in the publishing world as the
creator of the Pergamon Press. Throughout this work on science, where I
regretfully let him set up a group of very powerful scientists, he has been
unfaultable. I can't find him putting a foot wrong. The paper he and his
group have produced is by far the best of the four. When he came over I ran
right through the speech with him and he was in fact more helpful,
constructive and sensible in his criticism than I had thought possible.

So next day up I went to London to go through my speech with Blackett —
think of my going through a speech twice! Never done such a thing in my
life. When I got on to the train at Leamington and walked into the restaurant
car, there sitting by himself was Peter Thorneycroft and he asked me to sit
with him. I found myself having lunch with the Minister of Defence two days
before his big Statement in the Commons on the reorganization of the
Defence Ministry.[2] Well, I knew I must be careful about my conversation. I

---

[1] Robert Maxwell, Labour M.P. for Buckingham 1964–70, a seat he also contested in the
General Elections of February and October 1974. He was founder and Chairman of
Pergamon Press and from 1960 to 1969 Chairman of the Labour Party National Fund-
Raising Foundation.

[2] On March 4th the Government had announced its decision to establish a unified
Ministry of Defence, integrating the three Service Ministries with the Ministry itself. On
July 16th Mr Thorneycroft gave full details in a White Paper (Cmnd 2097). A single

told him a little about what I was going to do on Monday. He told me about his preparations about his big Statement.

Then we talked about security. I put my ideas to him. 'Well,' he said, 'you had better wait until after next Tuesday, because you will find we are centralizing a great deal in the Ministry of Defence.' I said, 'But do you want to be the fall guy?' He said, 'Well, it looks as though the Minister of Defence has to be.' We had a little discussion about Government research and development and I found a fact he didn't know. It was extremely disturbing. As I suspected, Thorneycroft is another man suffering from political softening of the brain. He is just Minister, he's got a job, things are quite out of his control. He must have the feeling of being on the edge of retirement and that he is not really an effective Minister any more. He couldn't have been nicer that day and we had a pleasant time.

When I got down off the train, I took a bus down to Chelsea and then ran into Lord Salter,[1] who asked me what I was doing in Chelsea on Sunday afternoon and showed an interest in science. A hundred yards further on I ran into Cecil King, proprietor of the *Daily Mirror*, out for a walk with Ruth Railton, his wife,[2] the dynamic organizer of the Youth Orchestra. He told me he was due to see the P.M. next day. We had a little chat. Then round the corner to Pat Blackett's, where again we went through this speech very carefully. I told Blackett how Harold was designating us to run education together and I suspect that he would like it. He's a bit nervous and I am not absolutely sure he is the right man for it. I think myself that in the scientific world he is a bit passé and that plenty of younger men would think him too old. However, he might do as an image. I think myself he is extremely nice and somehow belongs to an older generation and is a little bit rigid. However, it's Harold's affair. Or is it? Is it? I can't make up my mind about this and I have talked over with George Wigg whether or not I should express

---

Secretary of State for Defence would sit in Whitehall, with three Ministers of State and all the planning chiefs of the Services. The Minister of Aviation would also be in the same building. The Admiralty, War Office and Air Ministry would disappear, being replaced by Service Boards of Management. Three men would be particularly powerful: the Chief of the Defence Staff, the Permanent Under-Secretary and the Chief Scientific Adviser.

[1] The distinguished civil servant, politician and academic Arthur Salter (1881–1975). He had served as Director of the Economic and Finance Section of the League of Nations June 1919–January 1920 and 1922–31 and from 1934 to 1944 was Gladstone Professor of Political Theory and Institutions at Oxford University. In the mid-1930s he entered politics, and sat as Independent M.P. for Oxford University 1937–50 and, subsequently, as Conservative M.P. for the Ormskirk division of Lancashire 1951–3. He was Parliamentary Secretary to the Ministry of Shipping 1939–41, Joint Parliamentary Secretary at the Ministry of War Transport 1941, Chancellor of the Duchy of Lancaster 1945, Minister of State for Economic Affairs 1951–November 1952 and Minister of Materials November 1952–3. He was also Head of the British Merchant Shipping Mission to Washington 1941–3, Senior Deputy Director-General of UNRRA 1944, and Chairman of the Advisory Council of the International Bank 1947–8. He was knighted in 1922 and in 1953 created a baron.

[2] Founder and Musical Director of the National Youth Orchestra 1947–65. In 1962 she married Cecil King. She became a D.B.E. in 1966.

my doubts on this matter to Harold Wilson. Would it be so terribly disloyal to Pat? I think what I'll do is to wait until after this science conference next weekend and on the basis of that decide whether or not I do so.

However, last Sunday Pat couldn't have been more helpful. After I left him I went home and washed and had then arranged for Pat Llewelyn-Davies to let me take her out that evening. Her husband is in Greece and I wanted to take my mind off science. I had really been brooding over it far too long. I now had these twenty-five messed about pages of the text of the speech and I had to form them into some sort of notes on Monday morning. But I wasn't going to do it on Sunday night. I took Pat down to the Café Royal. I ordered melon and they asked, 'Do you want Israeli melon?' I said yes and found it cost us 15s. 6d. each. But it was superb. The other contretemps was when we got outside the restaurant and found the car key wouldn't work for her husband's new Mercedes. We spent an hour wandering round Piccadilly trying to find a policeman or somebody to rescue us. Finally the R.A.C. rescue car turned up, a strange young man with a beard got out and within five minutes had broken his way with a piece of wire through the front window, put the wire through, made the wire turn the wheel, which opened the window, and then said to us, as we drove away, 'Well, I've never done a Mercedes before. That leaves only the Rover 3-litre and I'm longing to do that as well.'

I got back at midnight and on Monday morning Jennie came. I had to work hard to get the whole thing shaped round and put on large sheets of ordinary House of Commons paper in note form but with odd quotations. It turned out as some twenty-four pages plus quotations and, when we got this done, I got Helga Greene to take me out to lunch to take my mind off things again. I took her to the House of Commons and we had a quiet chat.

When she had driven me back to Vincent Square Thomas Balogh very sweetly came in and then drove me back to the House again. I got there about three o'clock. Oh dear, half an hour too early. I can't go and sit on the Front Bench in a half-empty House, so I strolled down the lobby, into the Smoking Room, I wander round and finally at twenty-past three I get on the Front Bench. There are some sixty to seventy people there. The Chief Whip comes and sits behind me. Is the Speaker going to be there? No, he will move out of the chair and the House will be in Committee. I'm desperate because I may not know the name of the Chairman of Committee. One has to say not Mr Deputy Speaker, but 'Sir Robert', or whatever the case may be. Patrick Gordon Walker, beside me, reminds me it *is* Sir Robert[1] and then at 3.33 I am up on my feet and I start slowly and collectedly.

Gradually, as the House of Commons came over me, I began, not departing

[1] Sir Robert Grimston, National Conservative M.P. for the Westbury division of Wiltshire from 1931 until 1964. He was a junior Whip 1937–42, Assistant Postmaster-General 1942–5 and Parliamentary Secretary at the Ministry of Supply 1945 and was Deputy Chairman of Ways and Means 1962–4. In 1952 he was created a baronet and in 1964 became 1st Baron Grimston of Westbury.

from the manuscript but inserting a sentence here and another there. Everything went pretty well until I wanted a quotation, looked down and found
that I had somehow confused the two piles of paper, the ones I had already
used and the ones I hadn't. I couldn't find the quotation. Well, Denzil Freeth[1]
helped me out and actually gave me the wrong one. But from that moment I
had to *ad lib* the rest of the speech and it became much more my old backbench style, as one sees from the *Daily Telegraph* account which, although a
bit guying and harsh, has some strong element of truth.[2]

When I sat down, I knew I had done fairly well but I was by no means sure
whether it was a success. As the evening went on and the debate petered
along, with no significance apart from a speech by Aubrey Jones, and the
wind-up occurred and the House was still empty, I felt profoundly depressed.
However when I looked at the papers on Tuesday morning, it was clear that
the speech had been a success in the sense that it had been a great occasion.
I had broken through the sound barrier and put science on the map in the
way Harold wanted. I was pleased but not surprised when he rang me up and
congratulated me. We had a talk and I immediately took the occasion to say,
'Look, Harold, this is the moment. We've got through this science barrier.
Let's have a morning at Conference.[3] You make your big speech on Labour
in the Science Age; I will wind up the debate. We've got a parcel of resolutions to do it on.' 'Ah,' Harold said quickly, 'we can't do that unless we've
got an Executive statement.' I said, 'Let's *have* an Executive statement, which
we will do as a result of our science conference.' I think I've got him warmed
to the notion that the really big occasion for the Labour Party will be that
morning at the Party Conference. It was also clear that he was terribly pleased
with me and with himself in backing me and deciding this was the thing to do.
It became pretty clear that this had really been quite a success.

That morning I had to go in to take Mrs Meek's friends around the House.
The Commons is an amazing place. People came up to me, saying, 'Wonderful speech, marvellous speech'. I bet you that not more than one in three of
them had been present. The debate was quite well attended but I should say
there were no more than 120 people there. When it is a success, they all think
they have attended it. I don't even think they had read it in Hansard, but they
had simply got the smell of success, whereupon they smile at you, talk, are
friends and there you are.

[1] A member of the Stock Exchange, he was Conservative M.P. for the Basingstoke
division of Hampshire 1955–64. He was P.P.S. to the Minister of State at the Board of
Trade 1956, to the President of the Board of Trade 1957–9 and to the Minister of Education
1959–60, and was Parliamentary Secretary for Science 1960–3.

[2] The column, by Colin Welch, called Crossman 'the erratic sage' and reported that,

As his oration proceeded, Mr Crossman gained in confidence and vehemence what he lost
in coherence and intelligibility ... By the end Mr Crossman appeared almost intoxicated
and carried away by visions of gigantic programmes, vast sums, strong Ministers ... total
reorganization of the economy and stupendous efforts of the collective will.

[3] The Labour Party Conference was to be at Scarborough from September 30th to
October 4th.

Friday, July 26th
One thing running through last week has been the spate of rumours about the future of the Labour Government and how it will be constructed. I think the source of these rumours has been the way Harold has been talking, both in press conferences and at dinners. I have recorded his dinner with our older scientists' group and, the other day, coming back from the Socialist International with George Brown, I heard, and there is no reason to disbelieve him on this score, that Harold has talked just as freely and in just the same vein to a group of editors.

There has been a good deal of tension behind the scenes, with James Callaghan feeling he hasn't got Harold's confidence—which he certainly hasn't—and with George Brown getting into more and more trouble. George Brown, of course, is a key issue. He is certainly much abler than Callaghan and he is like the little girl. When he is good, he is very, very good and, when he's bad, he's horrid. He's good oftener than bad. When he's good, he's frightfully good. In the last ten days, for instance, he was entrusted with launching our agricultural policy and he made two superb speeches. Yet, in Friday morning's *Telegraph* last week, there was a tiny notice that he had lunched with David Browns[1] at Huddersfield and assured them that they wouldn't be affected by Labour plans. He had apparently told the press that he couldn't see the difference between sensible Labour and the Conservatives. When you recall that David Browns employ Desmond Donnelly, you see how idiotic George Brown was to talk like that and you see the difficulties we are in. This followed on two lunch parties which leaked to the *Daily Express*, where George Brown gave assurances to property owners, headed by a fellow called Sunley.[2] This week there were two further scandals, one which George Wigg told me about D-Notices,[3] which I needn't put into the diary here, and one which Harold Wilson told me about last night.

Last night I went in to see Harold because I wanted to check with him about the science conference. We didn't take long to deal with that and our talk was not very satisfactory because he is set on believing that there are immediate sensational things to be achieved by giving development contracts to private industry and pushing them ahead. By the way, somebody remarked to me that the only disadvantage of Harold Wilson is that he once was President of the Board of Trade. There is a great deal of truth in that because he has a rather mythical memory of his great things in the Board of Trade and this makes him believe what I think to be wrong, that you can get sensational

[1] A major specialist engineering and fabricating company, registered in 1864 and quoted on the London Stock Exchange.
[2] The property developer Bernard Sunley, known in his later years for his charitable work, especially for boys' clubs, alcoholics and in the field of education. He stood, unsuccessfully, as Conservative candidate for Ealing West in the 1945 General Election. He died in 1964.
[3] According to Crossman he had been rebuked about a D-Notice, issued to editors, embargoing publication of a story on housing scandals.

results from Government assistance in private sectors of science, through the National Research Development Council and development contracts.

Harold turned to the problem of George Brown. I had sent him the cutting from the *Telegraph* about the meeting at David Brown's. 'Oh, it's been an impossible week with him,' Harold said. 'He's been drunk constantly and he's been raving round. I must tell you about one incident. I came in through the inner court the other day and saw a black car there. I happened to see something sticking out that looked like the last Fabian pamphlet. I looked at it and there was a bit of paper, with the name of M.I.6 with C.'s name, which you know.'[1] I said I didn't. 'Well, I didn't know it until yesterday. There it is in George's car and that was the kind of security he was keeping. Well, I sent Marcia down and she checked again and we gave instructions to get the car open and got this thing taken out. I wrote a letter to George Brown, sending the paper back to him and telling him he was no good at security!' Well, there was the second thing. We've already had the D-Notice scandal and now this scandal about M.I.6. Really, the fact is, George is really impossible.

In the middle of the week, the *Daily Express* had on the front page a sardonic and extremely bitter comment by Ian Aitken,[2] leaking Harold's thinking. George Brown was to be fixed up as Minister of Planning and Callaghan is to be down-graded. This caused great ill-feeling. Callaghan spent an hour with Harold Wilson, who said to me, 'I'm getting quite good. These chaps come and bleat to me and talk to me and I send them away consoled. But really this life is impossible.' I can feel Harold is getting pretty desperate about the lack of confidence in Brown and his great problem will be whether or not to deal with it during the Recess. I have little doubt that, if there were a candidate put up against Brown for the deputy leadership, Brown would be removed. But the opposition would not come from the Left because this is now rallying to his support. It's from the Right that it is coming.

As for Callaghan, he is quite a different case. He is really a rather feeble creature. Then, in addition, you have Gordon Walker, who is very different, absolutely competent but totally undistinguished. On the far side, you have Denis Healey, a very lone mover, completely on his own, running his own ideas. He, by the way, went to the Institute of Strategic Studies yesterday, and delivered a fifty-minute lecture on Labour defence policy, in which he insisted that the Minister of Defence should make it. Ordinarily speaking, of course, the border line should be laid down in the Foreign Office. This shows that Denis is now regarding it as possible to achieve his ambition and become Minister of Defence.

[1] Sir Dick White, described in *Who's Who* as 'formerly attached to the Foreign and Commonwealth Office'. He was knighted in 1955 and became a K.C.G.B. in 1960. From 1953 to 1956 he was head of M.I.5, the Security Service, and from 1956 to 1967 of M.I.6, the Intelligence Service, whose director is known as 'C'. He retired in 1972.

[2] Ian Aitken started his journalistic career by working as Industrial Editor for *Tribune*. He then worked for *Reynolds News* and after that for the *Daily Express*, where he was Political Editor in 1963–4. He is now Political Editor of the *Guardian*.

Those are the inner four. Harold knows he can't really rely on any of them. On the other hand, it's doubtful whether he can take people like myself and put them in commanding positions, even if he wants to do so. I got the impression yesterday that I'm not as intimate with him as I used to be. I can't help it. We never see each other. Just as I was going, I asked him what he was doing in the first week of August. I said, 'Shall we see each other!' 'Oh well,' he said, 'let's make an appointment. The diary is getting full.' Obviously I had wondered about the chance of a meeting. But no. I certainly don't let him down and he knows I've done a good job on science. He's absolutely loyal to me but he is removing himself inevitably into a professional stratosphere.

Meanwhile we've had an astonishing summer with the Ward case going on in the courts and now the Rachman scandal.[1] Then last night the test-ban agreement was signed, which Macmillan looks on as his great achievement.[2] It has certainly saved him from being got rid of by the Tories.

Thursday, October 8th
Since I've come back from Russia[3] this diary has really consisted of trying to catch up with the Russian diary day after day. So, long afterwards, I'm sitting down to recap, what happened in the period before Conference and at Conference itself.

In July the Executive had agreed in principle to the idea of a brief policy statement on science, since without it we should not be committed procedurally to have two Executive speakers — Harold Wilson at the beginning and myself concluding. But this notion of Harold's had not been taken very seriously and everybody was assuming that he would like to take part in the debate on the need for a Labour Government. However, Harold had been quite clear that he wanted to go into the science debate. Directly I got back from Russia I rang him up and found that he was O.K., that he had cleared

---

[1] The Labour M.P. for North Paddington, Ben Parkin, had been campaigning against rapacious landlords in his constituency and particularly against a Polish property dealer, Peter Rachman. Both Christine Keeler and Mandy Rice-Davies had apparently lived at one period with Rachman; this attracted special attention to Mr Parkin's allegation that Rachman had not, as reported, died in Edgware Hospital in November 1962 but was still alive. On July 18th the Opposition tabled a motion, condemning 'intolerable extortion, evictions and profiteering', which it attributed to the 1957 Rent Act, which had removed rent control. The motion was debated on July 22nd and defeated, with a Government majority of 97. Sir Keith Joseph announced that he had asked Sir Milner Holland, Chairman of the General Council at the Bar, to lead an independent committee of inquiry into housing, especially rented property, in London.

[2] An Anglo-American team led by Averell Harriman and Lord Hailsham had been sent to Moscow in July to negotiate with Mr Gromyko a treaty banning nuclear tests in the atmosphere, in outer space and under water. It was initialled in Moscow on July 25th and formally signed by Dean Rusk, Lord Home and Mr Gromyko on August 5th. The treaty came into effect on October 15th, and was by that time signed by more than 100 countries, with the significant exceptions of Communist China and France.

[3] Where he had spent part of the early autumn.

the new draft science policy statement that I had left with Peter Shore before I went away. Though I didn't terribly like what they had done, naturally I was not going to complain.

On Tuesday, September 17th, we had a very characteristic meeting on home policy. Harold Wilson had gone out and not come back and George Brown was away at Strasbourg. Tony Greenwood was in the chair, and the document came up straightaway with nobody to move it.

Peter Shore said a few words about it and Ian Mikardo said that he really didn't agree and thought it was quite good in substance although very poorly written. At this point Harold Wilson entered the room and it was quite clear that things were decided by his determination to have the document in order to be able to speak at Conference. There was a little more discussion. Harold made one or two comments, especially wanting to firm up the references to competitive public enterprise, and it was agreed that drastic redrafting should take place and that the document should be presented to Conference in galley proof.

After the meeting, Harold stayed behind and I said to him, 'Look, I'm not too sure about these two paragraphs you want redrafted. Would you like to have a go?' 'Not on your life,' he said. 'That's you and Peter.' I thought to myself, 'There's the difference between Harold and Hugh. Hugh Gaitskell was a man who could never keep his fingers off any document you were drafting and was constantly interfering. Harold Wilson is the supreme delegator, never doing the job if he can leave it to someone else.'

After that we came to chatting about the Denning Report,[1] which Harold had been reading that morning but which was not yet published. He was very discreet but he said he thought it would make no difference. In this he was proved wrong, since the Report, as interpreted by the press two days later, was far more hostile to the Government than anyone expected.[2]

On Thursday, September 26th, I did my column and then caught the five o'clock train to Scarborough, finding myself in the same compartment as

---

[1] Lord Denning's Report (Cmnd 2152), on the security aspect of the Profumo affair, was published on September 26th. He had seen 116 witnesses and investigated many rumours. His verdict was that there had been no security breach, but the report revealed failure of co-ordination between the police departments in their earlier inquiries into Miss Keeler's activities. Lord Denning had also discovered that not the Prime Minister but the Home Secretary was the Minister officially responsible for security; his summing-up stated:

> The fact remains that the conduct of Mr Profumo was such as to create, amongst an influential section of the people, a reasonable belief that he had committed adultery with such a woman in such circumstances as the case discloses. It was the responsibility of the Prime Minister and his colleagues, and of them only, to deal with this situation; and they did not succeed in doing so.

Alfred Denning was a High Court Judge 1944–8 and a Lord Justice of Appeal from 1948 until 1957, when he became a life peer. From 1957 to 1962 he was a Lord of Appeal in Ordinary and in 1962 he became Master of the Rolls. His publications include *The Discipline of Law* (London: Butterworth, 1979).

[2] Mr Macmillan did not consent to the Opposition's demand for an early recall of Parliament to debate the issue.

Eirene White and James Callaghan. I talked a little to them both about the policy statement on science and generally pulled them along in the right direction. Because the children hadn't had a holiday this year, we had accepted a very kind offer from Alec Spearman to borrow his flat on the Esplanade. When I got to Scarborough at ten o'clock that night Anne met me at the station and drove me back through a lovely, fine starry night. I found that the flat was on the most beautiful point looking right across the bay, with a magnificent view of the castle and the little port underneath. Immediately below, just a minute or two's walk away, was the Spa where Conference took place. As Conference went on I did find it extremely difficult to combine active work, preparing speeches, with sharing a small sitting-room with our children and also trying to share their holiday. It was a strain for all of us. On the other hand, it was overwhelmingly worth while and we found that Scarborough as a holiday place is better than Broadstairs and Margate. It has really one of the best beaches for children that I've ever seen. When the tide is down, there is a wonderful beach, and we spent the time digging sand-castles and creating canals linking one rock pool to another and, above all, wandering round the pools collecting sea worms, snails, crabs and starfish. The weather was very kind to us but with a lot of strong wind and some rain. There was a great deal of sunshine and the holiday side was an immense success.

This was the background to the most successful Labour Conference I've ever attended. It started on Friday, September 27th, with the N.E.C. meeting at ten o'clock in the morning. Here of course my major interest was the policy statement. One can hardly blame the N.E.C. Most of them were seeing for the first time a brand new policy document, when the N.E.C. had pledged itself to issue no policy statements. Moreover, it was on an entirely new subject with new ideas in it, they were asked to accept it in galley and told they could hardly change anything. There were some fairly awkward nasty moves, and, frankly, I doubt whether two or three people on the Executive, if that, were in favour of issuing the statement or did anything but suspect that it was a Wilson/Crossman gimmick foisted upon them.

Moreover, they were all extremely mystified by Harold's insistence on speaking in the debate and they realized that the only justification for the policy statement was his insistence. Just as we were formalizing it George Brown, who as the chairman of Home Policy had to produce the document, though he hadn't even read it, remarked *sotto voce*, 'Frankly, it's a complete flop. It has no intellectual cutting edge.' That was more or less the Executive view of our science policy. If Harold or I had even suggested to them what we were going to say on the following Tuesday, I can feel their horror.

By the end of Sunday I was beginning to wonder when I was going to hear something about Harold's science speech. But there wasn't much chance to talk to him and I didn't really worry much when Conference began on

33

Monday morning and I still had no news. Monday was a deadly day. I felt by the end of the afternoon that it was essential to talk to Harold and I was suddenly given a message that, though he really had no time, I could walk with him from the Spa to a Fabian tea meeting and we could talk on the way. I caught him at five o'clock. It was soon obvious we couldn't walk along the front because of autograph hunters, so we walked up and down a very steep hillside path for thirty-five minutes, while he outlined to me very accurately the sections of his speech and how they were going to be delivered. The whole thing was satisfactorily agreed. I was still worrying about timing. I was aware that Harold's speech would scoop the headlines and that I couldn't achieve much in the winding-up, yet I also knew there must *be* a winding-up and that I must have enough time to do it. So I went to the Chairman and Len Williams and got them to agree that I should speak for ten to fifteen minutes.

I didn't sleep much that night. When I sat down to work with Anne, I completely failed to produce any kind of a draft speech before we went to bed. Finally I got up at half-past six in the morning, prepared a speech and got Anne to come down and take my dictated notes. I had pretty full notes by eight o'clock and it was all ready.

I needn't describe here the effect of Harold's speech, which followed a very satisfactory Executive election — especially for me, going up a place and getting 1,000 votes. I was able to sit back and watch his tremendous performance. He had been up until half past three in the morning and later told me he was so tired when he started that it was quite a pleasure to wake himself up by speaking. He spoke beautifully, completely collectedly, carrying the whole Conference with him. When he sat down, it was wonderful to see how the trade unions had opened up at his rather surprising proposal that apprenticeship must be modernized and perhaps taken over by the State. I never heard such a proposal and he told me afterwards that it only occurred to him while he was on his feet. Instead of producing horror in the mind of Bill Carron, Frank Cousins and Ted Hill, who all spoke, Harold had obviously swept them into his view and made the trade unions feel they must modernize themselves. In fact of course he had provided the revision of Socialism and its application to modern times which Gaitskell and Crosland had tried and completely failed to do. Harold had achieved it.

I dutifully got up and, at five to twelve, managed to make what was probably the most skilful and effective Conference speech of my life. I managed to put across the problem that, if we just substitute a scientific élite for an oligarchy of old boys, we should be destroying democracy. The whole Movement had to take part, we had to give people a chance to decide for themselves. Education had to be mass education and we had to have apprenticeship and training and a university of the air. I got a tremendous ovation. I was also a little disappointed, though not surprised, that all I had done scarcely registered. However, the morning was a tremendous success. I also got my share of thanks and applause and in the afternoon I was able to sit back and relax. Then I went down to the *Daily Mirror* party where again, if one has been a success, it is a real pleasure to wander round.

We came back yesterday after what has been on the whole a successful Conference, one which completely consolidated the Labour Party and makes the contrast even more severe between our own unity behind Harold and the tremendous disunity in the Tories, now desperately trying to change their leadership. Of course, underneath our unity there is a good deal of disgruntlement. Peter Shore told me yesterday that at Conference he had been invited by Dai Davies to the Steelworkers' dinner. He was one of seven guests and the six others, including Jim Matthews, George Brown and Mrs Brown,[1] were all ardent Gaitskellites and made speeches about Gaitskell and how wonderful George Brown is. This reminds one of how much there is this kind of disgruntlement on the Right of the Party and, as George Wigg says, how many enemies we have. Nevertheless I don't rate all this too badly.

The Conservatives were holding their Conference in Blackpool from October 8th to 11th, under the chairmanship of the Earl of Home. Mr Macmillan spent the preceding weekend at Chequers, where Lord Home drove to see him. At Cabinet on October 8th some of the Prime Minister's colleagues noticed that he seemed to be in some discomfort but at seven o'clock that evening Mr Macleod, who had just arrived in Blackpool, announced that the Prime Minister would 'speak to the point' when he addressed the mass rally on the Saturday.

At 9.30 p.m., however, news arrived from London that Mr Macmillan had been taken to the King Edward VII Hospital for Officers, for an urgent operation on his prostate gland. During the course of the Conference, it was announced that, before entering the operating theatre on October 10th, Mr Macmillan had given to Lord Home a message for the delegates at Blackpool. On behalf of Mr Macmillan, the Foreign Secretary stated that 'it will not be possible for me to carry out the physical burden of leading the Party at the next General Election ... Nor could I hope to fulfil the tasks of Prime Minister for an extended period, and I have so informed the Queen'.

Three candidates immediately appeared: Mr Butler, Mr Maudling and Lord Hailsham, who declared that evening his intention, 'after deep thought', to disclaim his peerage. On Monday, October 14th, the 'usual process of consultation' began. From his hospital bed Mr Macmillan asked the Lord Chancellor to take individual soundings from members of the Cabinet, and asked the Chief Whip to consult M.P.s. Other views were to be taken from among the Conservative peers, the constituencies and the prospective parliamentary candidates.

Tuesday, October 15th
I had a tremendous job to get last Thursday's *Guardian* column done. I was writing it after the first day of the Tory Party Conference, which had started with Macmillan absent and with keen expectations that sooner or later the

[1] Sophie Levene married George Brown in 1937.

announcement would be made on choice of the new Leader. By Wednesday there seemed to be clear indications of this. Then, on Wednesday evening, came the sensational news that the Prime Minister was not going to go on Saturday to deliver the closing speech. This made it difficult to write a column. I sat down on Thursday morning, with some apprehension, to slave out a column on the Tory Conference. Rather cautiously, I chose as my subject Mr Butler because there was enough news about him. I started the column by saying that Butler's worst enemy in preventing him succeeding Macmillan would be not one of his rivals but himself and his own indiscretion. I then quoted an outrageous interview which Henry Fairlie published in that morning's *Express* and also Butler's behaviour on 'Panorama' the previous day. After that I had a very nice tailpiece on Lord Hailsham.

It was in fact a pretty ingenious column, in view of the situation as I saw it. Things were obviously always changing but what I wrote assumed that Macmillan was completely out, of course not officially admitted at the time, that there would be a fight for the succession and that Butler was in the running to win. I only just got this column finished, before I rushed to catch the ten past five train to Banbury, where, on behalf of the county, I was to move the toast to the N.U.T. at their annual county dinner.

The moment I arrived at the hotel where the dinner was taking place and where I was to change into evening dress, a message was given to me to ring the *Guardian*. They gave me the news that Macmillan had not only been unable to go to the Conference but had announced that, as a result of his operation, he was not going to continue to be Prime Minister. It was about the only occasion when I haven't had my column with me, but after some thought I rang back the *Guardian* and gave them the necessary changes which still kept it pretty topical, including the lead on Butler being his own worst enemy. It was still pretty good.

Next morning, Friday, October 11th, Jennie rang me to ask if I had seen the *Guardian*. I said no. 'Well,' she said, 'they've taken your column out and say it has been postponed.' I told her to ring up Alastair immediately and to ask him to ring me back. Soon he was on the phone, saying, 'Sorry, Dick, It was entirely my decision. I found there was such pressure on the paper that we had to leave your column out, in order to give room for Mackintosh.'[1] Now Mackintosh is the fellow who wrote the book on Cabinet Government which I have often quoted, and apparently he was about and had provided the *Guardian* with an article on how Premiers are selected. Alastair has then calmly knocked my column out.

---

[1] John Mackintosh, Labour M.P. for Berwick and East Lothian 1966–February 1974 and from October 1974 until his death in 1978. A political scientist, he was Senior Lecturer at the University of Glasgow 1963–5 and Professor of Politics at the University of Strathclyde 1965–6. He was part-time Professor of Politics at the University of Edinburgh 1977–8. His publications include *The British Cabinet* (Edinburgh: Stevens, 1962), *The Devolution of Power* (Harmondsworth: Penguin, 1968) and *Government and Politics in Britain* (London: Hutchinson, 1970).

At the time when I had first heard the news about Macmillan, I thought Alastair would have had the column sent to him at Manchester, been through it and thought it a bit dated, which it was by this time. It would have been clear enough to any reader on Friday morning that I had written it before the news that the P.M. was clean out. So I thought it was an intelligible thing to do and Alastair assured me he had tried to ring me at the hotel and at Prescote. Nevertheless, it did drive me mad to think this little jackass had treated me in this way. All the time I had worked on the *Sunday Pic* and the *Mirror*, Hugh Cudlipp had never dreamed of knocking out a column of mine without discussing it with me. Indeed, he had never knocked one out during the whole time. He had often asked me to recast it but had always assumed that the column has to stay in. But here was Alastair just saying, 'Sorry about this, but it was a decision.' I was furious and, after he had rung off, the more I thought it over, the more I felt that this was my opportunity to drop it.

When I had been dining with Pen and Tommy Balogh, Pen had talked of the column and said it was a damn nuisance and high time I finished writing it. I suppose I had begun to realize that, with my present standing as one of the half-dozen top Opposition leaders, a column which had to be churned out each week was becoming an increasing embarrassment not only to myself but to my friends. So I had, I suppose, underneath been wondering whether it wasn't really time to drop it. In a way this behaviour of Alastair's clicked.

So I knocked off a letter to him, saying that I took this to mean he wanted to get rid of me and I certainly would not write for him again. Next day, on Saturday, I received a letter from him explaining his action and saying possibly it was a mistake. I wrote a second letter to him, patiently telling him that his columnists have to write every week, even when it is highly inconvenient to do so, and that editors must agree to publish every week. This was my personal reaction to the P.M.'s news.

Meanwhile, off I went to Ditchley Park for the second of two Anglo-Polish conferences. The first one had taken place in Poland in February but I hadn't gone because the Wilson election had been just at its height and I felt I must stay to help Harold. I had heard vaguely of Ditchley Park and knew it as Churchill's hide-out during the war. Until I turned up there last Friday evening, I had no idea what an astonishing place it is. It is one of the good second-class, small, stately houses, with lovely gardens, a beautiful view over a lake, beech trees and nice country all around. But it's a stately home with all twentieth-century American luxuries. I had a bedroom, with a bathroom attached which I shared with one other person. There were butlers, a huge staff, magnificent food and drink served in a marvellous dining room. There was simultaneous translation laid on for the thirty-five or so members of the conference. Anne drove me over and left me there at seven o'clock. A butler received me at the door and I went into this great big place, with fires and cocktails, before dinner by candlelight. Here, then, was the place where I was to have the impact of Macmillan's news. On the first evening this wasn't very acute because all the Tories except one had failed to arrive. It was a jolly good thing I turned up because otherwise the British would have been a bit thin on the ground.

The whole weekend was perfect October weather. The summer which we didn't get was followed now by a good autumn. It had started at Scarborough and now these Poles were given a sight of perfect British countryside, with clear, pale blue skies, the trees just beginning to change colour, the shrubs and bushes by the lake brilliant red. Lawns and statues and the pale grey house. Inside were great wood fires, warmth and comfort. Altogether I enjoyed the conference. As it went on there was this constant background of reading in the papers about the Tories' leadership struggle. I didn't see much of the television coverage but it did strike me that the struggle to appoint a new Leader in the Tory Party was much more like a struggle inside a Communist Party than inside the Labour Party. We have a constitution under which this struggle is resolved in quite an overt battle, with a Left and a Right and voting at the end. By avoiding a vote as the Tory Party and as all C.P.s do, you push the struggle behind the scenes and make it murky. If it works, it looks lovely; if it is difficult, terrible conflict breaks out.

Meanwhile my little tiff with the *Guardian* has continued. When Alastair rang me up during the Ditchley Park weekend, I told him it was inconvenient to speak to him then. I said he had better wait for my second letter and ring me on Tuesday morning when I was back at Prescote. He did so and I was amazed to find that he was ringing from a call-box near Coventry on his way back to Manchester from house-hunting in London. Now he was prepared to apologize for what was a terrible mistake. I rather weakly talked as if I was going to resume work this Thursday. I had my doubts and immediately went and wrote a letter to the Deputy Editor telling him I wanted to postpone things until we had clarified the issue and that I would therefore not write this week. I then got Jennie to ring up Hugh Cudlipp to tell him I was having a tiff.

This morning I had a telephone message from Hugh, who wanted to give me a firm contract to write a weekly article for the *Sunday Mirror* from now until the Election. Well, that's that. The *Sunday Mirror* will pay me £100 an article instead of the 20 guineas I earn from Alastair. However, I'm going to tell Hugh tomorrow that I don't want to write regularly but that I should like to write pretty often but irregularly, on subjects I choose. This will not be a regular routine. Now I am ceasing to be primarily a journalist and writer, for the time being becoming primarily a politician. I now want to move to occasional journalism, that is, I really am becoming front-bench. What would suit me down to the ground would be to be elected to the Front Bench this time so I could be predominantly a politician until the Election.

While I was waiting for Anne at Ditchley on Tuesday morning, I had a long talk with Marcus Worsley,[1] a young Tory and a very nice man. I had got to know him a bit during the weekend and he had talked quite frankly about his ghastly anxieties. He is one of the people who doesn't really know what he wants. On the whole he isn't in favour of Butler. He had been in favour of Hailsham until his speech at Conference when he threw his hat in the ring and shocked Worsley by the obvious demagogy. Now Worsley is convinced that Hailsham with his hands on the nuclear button would be a menace to world peace and he is determined to try and prevent this. There is no doubt that there will be a large number of Tories who hold this view. In the last few days the general impression I have got is that Hailsham can be kept out.

On the other hand the Hailshamites consist, I should think chiefly, of people who think that Butler is the devil incarnate and that everything must be done to prevent Butler from taking over. There will be powerful people in the Tory Party who will take that view. There are Hailshamites possessed by determination to keep Butler out; Butlerites possessed to keep Hailsham out. Macleod is clearly committing himself to the Butler line. Most people at Ditchley thought the result would be that Lord Home would be the new man but I think this strange because he is utterly remote from the Commons. He may have been there for eleven years but he was inconspicuous and unsuccessful. I find it difficult to see that he will be the *tertium quid*. I would have thought that, if Butler doesn't make it against Hailsham or Hailsham against Butler, it would not be impossible that Macleod would be in the running. Anyway, it should be Macleod or Heath—they would be the most formidable antagonists to Harold Wilson.

On the evening of October 17th the Chief Whip, Martin Redmayne, visited Lord Home. Meanwhile a group had emerged of those opposed to the succession of Lord Home. A midnight meeting at Enoch Powell's house was attended by Iain Macleod, Reginald Maudling, Frederick Erroll and Lord Aldington, with the Chief Whip calling as a messenger. Lord Hailsham now got in touch with Mr Butler.

But early on the morning of October 18th Mr Macmillan sent his resignation to Buckingham Palace. The Queen came to his bedside, where he advised her to send for Lord Home, who carefully agreed only to try to form a Government. First Mr Butler was offered the Foreign Office and on Saturday, October 19th, he agreed to serve. Mr Maudling was invited to remain Chancellor of the Exchequer. On that day Lord Home returned to the Palace to formally kiss hands.

On October 20th the first list of Cabinet appointments was published. Neither Mr Macleod nor Mr Powell took office. Selwyn Lloyd replaced Mr Macleod as

[1] Conservative M.P. for Keighley 1959–64 and for Chelsea 1966–September 1974. He was P.P.S. to the Minister of Health 1960–1, to the Minister without Portfolio 1962–4 and to the Lord President of the Council 1970–2. He was Second Church Estates Commissioner 1970–4. In 1973 he succeeded his father to become the 5th Baronet.

Leader of the House of Commons and Mr Powell was succeeded as Minister of Health by Anthony Barber. Edward Heath became Secretary of State for Industry, Trade and Regional Development and Maurice Macmillan Economic Secretary to the Treasury. At the Conservative Central Office John Hare, the Minister of Labour, became Chairman, going to the House of Lords as Lord Blakenham. Lord Poole stepped down to be Vice-Chairman.

The new Prime Minister advised the Queen to prorogue the new parliamentary Session until November 12th, giving him time to renounce his title and win a Commons seat. On October 23rd he disclaimed his several peerages, becoming Sir Alec Douglas-Home. After a brief campaign in the vacant and safe Scottish constituency of Kinross and West Perthshire, where the Conservative M.P., W. G. Lieburn, had died on August 19th, Sir Alec was elected as Member for that constituency on November 8th.

Thursday, November 7th

I don't know whether it is more or less truthful to do one's diary in this way, not doing it every day as I used to when I started but doing it in solid slabs on the tape-recorder, when I feel inclined. Of course, in one sense, a daily diary is more faithful. Every time I do it now I telescope, distort, forget, remember falsely. Nevertheless, it's the way I do it.

I had agreed with David Butler to go over to Nuffield on Wednesday, October 16th, and do his seminar there. I chose as my subject the problem of parliamentary reform and democracy. The only importance of the evening was that David had been at Blackpool, watching the whole Tory Conference and seeing the struggle for power. He was quite clear (and was correct on that) that Lord Hailsham had no chance of being elected. Already on that day the anti-Hailsham front had been formed and by his very success at the Conference Hailsham had created sufficient opposition to prevent his getting in. Of course what I didn't know then was that Rab Butler had created sufficient force against himself (David Butler didn't know this then, either) to force a *tertium quid* on the Party. I must admit that right up to the end I remained very difficult to convert to the view that Alec Home would be the final man to be projected into Downing Street as a result of this double veto. It was an interesting evening but once again my whole experience at Nuffield made me realize how antipathetical to the Nuffield tradition I am, and how odious I find that particular kind of academic.

The next day I dined with Sydney Jacobson. Everyone was now committing themselves to Butler, as the next Tory Prime Minister. Meanwhile I was continuing my row with Alastair. I had decided not to write my column that week but I had also decided to leave it open and give Alastair a chance. On Thursday afternoon I went to see Hugh Cudlipp, my first time in the *Daily Mirror* building in Holborn Circus. It was a pleasant, friendly interview. Hugh saw my point about turning down his offer of a weekly column and straightaway offered me the job of being his main writer whenever I liked. I must say I felt a great relief returning to the *Mirror*. Moreover, the more I thought about it, the more I discovered the extraordinary relief and enjoyment at not having to write a weekly column. This was the first Thursday that I hadn't done the *Guardian* and almost the first week in seventeen years when I had not had the chore of a weekly piece.

Of course, I'm a regular worker and a chore has its advantages and attractions, skills and charms. But it had been growing ever more clear to me that I had now become primarily a politician and not a journalist. This has made as much difference to me as the politicians said it would. I do see that for years I have been first a political journalist and only secondarily a parliamentary politician. It's only now that I am close to Harold and want him to be a Prime Minister and really believe in my Leader that I feel the burden of a weekly column. Alastair had played into my hands, Anne was keen I shouldn't do it and, by the time I left for Nottingham to address the Fabian Society and the University Socialist Group, I knew I wouldn't be doing that column again.

Friday morning's papers revealed the sensation of a late-night meeting in Powell's house, and the attempt to block Home at the last moment. The Butlerites had made fantastic efforts to get him in but, when I heard the news, Home had gone to the Palace. I suppose, for the sake of the record, I should say that I actually heard this from a little transistor wireless in the Friends' Meeting House, near Euston, where I was giving a lunch-time talk. By the time I got to Nottingham on Friday night, Home had kissed hands and was trying to form a Cabinet.

Directly I heard Home had been appointed, though I found it hard to believe, I characteristically began to see the advantages to the Tories. I think I was correct that, the moment this decision was taken, Macmillan's falling off the back of the Tory Party was an enormous relief, that anybody was better than he was, that Home would have a good television personality and that probably he would be good on the hustings, too. This was the kind of picture I put to a packed meeting at Nottingham.

Friday, November 1st
Yesterday evening, we were invited to the Melchetts'. Julian Melchett,[1] the present Lord, is a very pleasant young man, active in the House of Lords, an ardent Conservative and Common Marketeer whom I had met at the Aidan Crawleys'. His wife is a Gentile — a handsome-looking girl. They were obviously curious to meet me. I found I was there with Eddie Shackleton and Frank Giles,[2] the Foreign Editor of the *Sunday Times*, and his rather snooty,

---

[1] A banker and industrialist, he succeeded his father to become 3rd Baron Melchett in 1949 and was appointed Chairman of the British Steel Corporation in 1967, serving until his death in 1973. His family, the Monds, had been prominent in the development of the British heavy chemical industry. In 1947 he married Sonia Graham.

[2] Chief Correspondent of *The Times* in Italy 1950–3 and in Paris 1953–61. He was Foreign Editor of the *Sunday Times* 1961–78 and in 1967 became Deputy Editor. He married, in 1946, Lady Katharine Sackville, the only daughter of the 9th Earl De La Warr.

horsey wife, and the female editor of the *Queen*,[1] a mere hack working under Jocelyn Stevens,[2] the proprietor, *and* the proprietor of the *Spectator* and his titled wife.[3] Well, frankly, ever since we got the money out of Gilmour I have been pretty careful to avoid him and since he has been elected to the Commons we have avoided each other. He is just the same as when I saw him in Court being cross-examined by the Lord Chief Justice, when he made a so-called brilliant speech. He also had a sensational success in his maiden speech, because he contributed to the Vassall debate a bitter attack on the press, which was enormously popular with the Commons which, I must say I thought was like biting the hand which, well, didn't feed him, but it seemed to be indecent.

When I arrived at the Melchetts', Gilmour was outside the dining room, telephoning. Through the whole of dinner he seemed to be putting in an appearance every three-quarters of an hour. It soon came out that it was the big news, breaking unexpectedly that evening, that he had made the scoop of getting Macleod to be Editor of the *Spectator*. Throughout the whole evening of course I didn't have any notion of what we later knew, that Gilmour had done this without consulting his present editor, Hamilton.[4] None at all. All I knew was that there was a frightful fuss on, that he had to rush to the B.B.C. and appear on the ten o'clock programme and that the news had unexpectedly leaked. That was the reason why he kept saying that he would have to make a full statement next day, and that unfortunately he was dealing with a crisis. Luckily I didn't know the nature of the crisis. All I knew was that he was tremendously excited by the news that he had got Macleod for the paper.

The other thing was that Gilmour had been a great Hailshamite. There was no doubt that the *Spectator* and he himself played a leading role at the Blackpool Conference. Gilmour regards himself as a progressive Tory who backed Hailsham in order to renovate and revive the Party. He wanted the kind of rabble-rousing Hailshamite leadership as the only possibility for defeating Labour. So the fact that he had taken Macleod for the paper meant

[1] The Editor of *Queen* in 1963 was Miss Beatrix Miller.

[2] A journalist with the Hulton Press, 1955–6, he owned and edited *Queen* magazine 1957–68. In 1968 he joined Beaverbrook Newspapers Ltd and from May to December acted as Personal Assistant to the Chairman. He was appointed Managing Director of the *Evening Standard* in 1969, serving until 1972, when he became Managing Director of the *Daily Express*. From 1974 to 1977 he was Managing Director of Beaverbrook Newspapers, of which he had become a Director in 1971. In 1977 he was appointed Managing Director of *Express* Newspapers and Deputy Chairman of the same company.

[3] Ian Gilmour and his wife, Lady Caroline.

[4] Iain Hamilton, a journalist and publisher, worked on the *Daily Record* 1944–5, the *Manchester Guardian* 1945–52 and the *Spectator* 1952–6. Moving to publishing, he worked as Editor-in-Chief for the Hutchinson Group and then as Editorial Director 1957–62 before returning to journalism as Editor of the *Spectator* 1962–3. He was Director of Studies for the Institute for the Study of Conflict 1957–77. His publications include *Scotland the Brave* (London: Michael Joseph, 1957) and *Embarkation for Cythera* (London: Martin Brian & O'Keefe, 1975).

that he sought to rally both kinds of anti-Home forces. As a Hailshamite he couldn't have disagreed more profoundly with Macleod during the battle, when, after flirting with the notion of Home, Macleod resolutely came down for Butler as a lesser evil than Hailsham. Macleod, as Party Chairman, had backed Butler, whereas Poole, as the other Party Chairman, had backed Hailsham. This split, which had gone right up and down the Tory Central Office, had of course been the reason why in the final resort Macleod and Powell had refused to take part in the Government.

I still don't know, though I've tried to find out, exactly why they refused to take part. I suspect both men committed themselves or felt themselves so committed in the battle and had said such strong things that even when Butler caved in they felt themselves unable to cave in with him. Anyway at dinner that night, Gilmour used the wildest language and one concludes that appointing Macleod was, on Gilmour's part, a political appointment. He hoped not only that Macleod would increase the paper's circulation, but that he would use it for maintaining the progressive Tory tradition and a leadership to take over when the appalling ineptitude of Home had been demonstrated.

The Melchetts' house is very nice, rather like Pam Berry's house, and I stayed on for some time. George Weidenfeld[1] was also there, and Eddie, and we had a mild talk after the others had gone. I got back home to discover in the morning papers the sensational news that Gilmour had not only had this thing blurted out too soon but had actually fixed Macleod's takeover without mentioning it to the existing Editor who, ironically, had himself been brought in to take over from another person whom Gilmour had turned out.

By some strange good fortune I had accepted an invitation to lunch on Friday, the next day, with Lady Pam. I found the other guest was Perry Worsthorne and, after lunch, Hugh Massingham and Henry Fairlie came in. So we gained a new aspect of the affair. A spice was added by the further news that David Astor[2] had decided to substitute Randolph Churchill for Mark Arnold-Forster as his Chief Political Correspondent.[3] Worsthorne told us that during the morning Arnold-Forster had been on the phone to him asking what chances there were of a job with the *Sunday Telegraph*. I don't say that is exactly what happened but apparently he had been making inquiries. It isn't by any means clear that David Astor has *literally* made the substitution

[1] A publisher who fled to Britain from his native Austria immediately before the Second World War. He worked for the B.B.C. 1939–46 and also contributed a weekly column on foreign affairs to the *News Chronicle* 1943–4. In 1948 he founded the publishing house of Weidenfeld & Nicolson Ltd, of which he is Chairman. He was made a life peer in 1976. A celebrated host, his parties are described in Crossman's *The Diaries of a Cabinet Minister*.

[2] The Hon. David Astor, heir to the 4th Viscount Astor, was Foreign Editor of the *Observer* 1946–8 and Editor 1948–75. He has been a Director of the paper since 1976. With Valerie Yorke, he wrote *Peace in the Middle East* (London: Corgi, 1978).

[3] On the *Observer*. Mark Arnold-Forster was a Night Editor at I.T.N. in 1957–8 and then worked as Chief Reporter, News Editor and then Lobby Correspondent for the *Observer* 1958–63, before moving to the *Guardian* in 1964; he is now Diplomatic Editor there.

but he has certainly added Churchill to his staff with the intention of using him very prominently as a political writer. That is a fantastic decision. Almost as silly as Alastair Hetherington's attitude to me, because to take Randolph Churchill,[1] when he was really suffering from debility from over-drinking, really utterly past it, when the *News of the World* can't take him any more, when Charles Wintour[2] had to tell Lord Beaverbrook that he just couldn't take Randolph Churchill and that even Dick Crossman would be preferable,* shows a chronic instability and fear. This is of course what has been wrong with the *Observer* ever since the *Sunday Telegraph* came along. I find the *Sunday Telegraph* pretty odious, too, and it's not doing too well but the battle between the *Observer* and the *Sunday Telegraph* for the conscience of the nation is something worth watching.

We all discussed at great length the possibilities of Macleod as an Editor and the significance of this appointment. I said that Macleod had probably accepted the job largely for financial reasons, because he didn't want to take directorships in the normal Tory way but wanted £5,000 a year for himself, his ill family and his standard of living. Probably, it was also to fill in time and I wasn't so sure it would become all that political. He might just take the cash and Gilmour would be disappointed.

Henry Fairlie disagreed with this and made it quite clear he thought it tremendously important politically. He is a passionate Butlerite and had almost burst into tears when Butler had failed. He also felt that as Editor of the *Spectator* Macleod would enable him, Henry, to come back into that paper and exert enormous influence. He had clearly been talking to Macleod about his role as Editor and feeling confident that it would have an enormous effect inside the Tory Party.

If that is true, something like Tory Bevanism might emerge, on condition of course that the Tories lose the Luton by-election[3] and the new leadership can't get a good jumping-off ground. If they really get off to a good start, they might well recover over the winter. If Luton knocks them, I think it is possible that they may disagree within the Party and then this Tory Bevanism might really begin to grow. I must add, though, that all the evidence so far is slightly against it. Macleod has made the most idiotic speech at Luton, or rather, in answer to a question has said that he had undiluted admiration for

---

[1] Randolph Churchill had returned from the United States in the middle of the Conservative Party Conference, declaring himself ready to support Lord Hailsham's campaign.

[2] A journalist, whose career started on the *Evening Standard* in 1946. He became Political Editor in 1952 and then moved to the *Sunday Express* as Assistant Editor. He returned to the *Evening Standard* in 1954 as its Deputy Editor. In 1957 he moved to the *Daily Express* as Managing Editor and in 1959 came back to the *Evening Standard* as Editor, a post he held until 1976. He was Managing Director of the *Daily Express* 1977–8.

* That contract was offered to me. Wintour said this to Beaverbrook, who said that, if he couldn't have anyone really good and he couldn't have Randolph because he wasn't any good, he could have me!

[3] A by-election was held at Luton, where the Liberal and Conservative M.P. Dr Charles Hill had become a life peer. Will Howie won the seat for Labour, with a majority of 3,749 over Sir John Fletcher-Cooke, Conservative.

the P.M. Why, then, isn't he in the Government? Equally, Enoch Powell has made a speech to his constituency, making it meaningless that he isn't in the Government. This is the great problem of Tory loyalty. In the Labour Party, with its Left and Right, you feel entitled to speak up for yourself and stand for a line. With the Tories, it's impossible to resign and really lead a faction. You can only stand in the wings, waiting for fate to bring you back again either, like Thorneycroft, on the bandwagon you have left, or as a leader because the bandwagon collapses and another vehicle is required.

Wednesday, November 13th
After lunch today I walked across to 2 Richmond Terrace, to the office of the Minister for Science, to see Quintin Hogg. We had a talk about whether or not the P.M. should grant the special security permission to all the Shadow Ministers, including the Minister for Science, which might allow me special access to security establishments. However, Quintin suggested I should go to his Ministry and be briefed by the officials, to find out whether they would tell me enough to satisfy me, and then we could have further discussion.

Quintin was his usual boisterous self. We discussed public schools for a short time and I said I thought the Robbins Report[1] and the expansion of university places would produce one major reason for sending your children to them. Quintin roared at me, 'That's not the major reason. The major reason is that middle-class people find their children unbearable at home and need to send them away before they are fourteen. Ah, my dear Dick, you will soon discover that.' Quintin, I think, has five children.

I also asked him about his future and what the Government was going to do about the Ministries. He said, curiously, 'One of the reasons why I decided to move from the House of Lords was that my advisers felt that this subject is better tackled in the House of Commons and I assure you I shall tackle it.' So it looks as though he thinks he is going to be the big boss on this thing and will bring the battle against Edward Boyle, who is controlling the situation. The other amusing thing was that he talked as if I would still be going to do the job. 'Well, you'll find this ... it will seem to you ... ' was the tenor of his remarks.

After I had finished with him and had my hair cut I came back, walked across the Park and into the House of Commons. Oh dear, that Queen's Speech debate was as dreary and boring and unutterable as it has ever been. I had come back to take Harold out to dinner. This morning I had looked things up and seen that the P.M.'s reply to Harold had had only one successful point in it—the central theme of the British independent deterrent

---

[1] The Report of the Committee on Higher Education (Cmnd 2154), published on October 23rd, declared that higher education should be open to all who qualified for it. A firm target was set for 1973/74 of 390,000 full-time places, with a formation of six new universities, the accession to degree-giving status of colleges of advanced technology, the development of new institutions for scientific and technological education and research and the close association of teacher training colleges with neighbouring universities.

as the challenge to the Labour Party to explain its position. It is obvious that the P.M.'s speech had been ruled out by the Labour Party as idiotic but even the Tories hadn't been too happy about it. I shouldn't think they will be pleased about the press, which was also pretty chilly. They said that the P.M. would survive but admitted he was not exactly expert on the home side and had only been at all convincing on foreign affairs.

This statement of Home's came home to George Wigg and me and immediately confirmed what we had said for many months: that, of all the Labour Party policies, our defence policy is the weakest and, with Denis Healey there, who is not interested in defence policy but is a rather adventurous young man who sensationalizes everything, we are in a weak position. George and I both thought that we must get on to Harold and insist that there should be some kind of job done now, to work out a defence policy to be valid over a period of time.

I rang Harold and asked if I could see him today. I found he would be in the House and after the Parliamentary Committee would be free, so I said I would take him out to dinner. I felt sure he wouldn't want to go outside so I fixed a table for us in the Visitors' Dining Room. Sure enough, when he arrived, he said there was a crisis and he had to go back to his room after a quick dinner. Marcia came along too.

We had a pleasant dinner. On the phone this morning Harold had again said that George Wigg and I should knock out something on defence like the brilliant things we have done before. He said, 'Of course, George is a marvellous chap but he doesn't really have a political sense or a psychological warfare sense like you do, Dick. You must do it together.' 'Well,' I replied, 'it's no good our knocking things out. What the Party needs is to sustain itself for an eight-month campaign. On this issue we shall always be on the defensive; it is always the attractive thing for the ordinary man for Britain to have a deterrent. We shall always be in an uncomfortable position. The only defence of our policy is in terms of the outcome on Germany and in presenting this as a political stunt of the Tories.'

Harold continued to say that this policy should be my responsibility. 'Well,' I said, 'what's really wrong is having Denis Healey as Shadow Defence Minister. Why not throw him out and put George Brown in?' 'You can't possibly do that,' said Harold, 'because if I change to George Brown everyone will say Callaghan has won in the battle between the two of them on who is going to control the economy in our planning.'

I laughed and agreed. Harold said he couldn't shift any of the top people now. They must stay as they are. 'By the way, I thought once of shifting you and making you Minister of Defence, but after five minutes I realized I couldn't possibly let the scientists down.' I entirely agreed. I asked him about my future. What about making me the opposite number to Quintin Hogg, whatever happens? Harold said, 'But wait until that comes.' He made it absolutely clear to me that he doesn't think anything of the Shadow Cabinet and he doesn't care whether people are in it or not. 'Well, this Shadow Cabinet — they don't count. They have got the better of me on only one occasion.' He also made it clear that he doesn't really expect a change in the Shadow Cabinet in the elections this week. (I have got myself nominated.) I think we shall find much the same people are returned. Tam Dalyell[1] is going to canvass for me but I shall be surprised if I get more than twelve extra votes this time and that isn't nearly enough to get me in. I have talked to Anne today and seen how things are at Prescote. On the whole this life is pretty interesting, though I don't really care much about Parliament and still feel very insecure on the Front Bench. But I can't deny I have a feeling now of extreme well-being and interest in life and enjoyment.

Monday, December 2nd

On Thursday, November 21st, came the results of the election for the Shadow Cabinet. I went upstairs after spending the whole day writing and got there just in time to stand at the back and hear the results read aloud. Once again I was runner-up. Yes, I had done slightly better and got 100 votes.[2] But Dick Mitchison, senile at seventy-three, got 132. Mr Willey got 131. So I came home and I sat in front of the fire and I thought. I had the job, that evening, of appearing on the 'Gallery' television programme on education. I had been selected by the B.B.C. as the Labour Party person to appear, even though this was strictly the job of Eirene White and Fred Willey.

What kind of an impression I made was pretty important and I thought fairly carefully about what I should do. I had been put on to debate with Edward Boyle and had been told that, after a film, we should have ten minutes of discussion which, by B.B.C. standards, is quite a lot. I decided before the car came to fetch me that the best thing I could do was at all costs to avoid being rude or insulting to Edward Boyle and that I had to give an impression of somebody who cared about education, not Party polemics. The whole programme was made as namby-pamby as possible. I behaved in a namby-pamby way. I was careful, statesmanlike, I twice called Boyle charming, not once, but twice, and twice was too much. At the end I talked to Boyle and we drove home together in his ministerial car.

Now, funnily enough, when I got home Anne told me that this was the best performance I had ever given on television. Maybe that was what steadied me, because I very soon got a lot of letters saying how namby-pamby I had

---

[1] A schoolteacher who was elected Labour M.P. for West Lothian at a by-election in 1962. A member of the Public Accounts Committee 1962–6, he was P.P.S. to Richard Crossman during his period as a Cabinet Minister (1964–70), with one short interval. One of Crossman's closest and most loyal friends, he lodged for a time at 9 Vincent Square. A firm opponent of devolution, he expounded his views in *Devolution: The End of Britain?* (London: Cape, 1977).

[2] In the election to the Parliamentary Committee on November 21st, Crossman, with 102 votes, headed the list of those not elected.

been, saying how schoolteachers had expected me to attack the Minister. I felt a bit shaken by these until I talked to Harold Wilson. He said that he and the Chief Whip had watched the programme and had been delighted because they thought I had given the image of a Labour Minister of Education.

Oh dear! Oh dear! I must admit that, half inside me, I had been conscious of this, conscious that I wasn't just debating or discussing, conscious that what mattered was that I should present myself to the world, present an image of a potential Minister of Education. Why am I ashamed of this? I *am* half ashamed and I think I am deeply divided in my mind between my role as a rebel and provoker and my desire to do a decent job of work.

Next morning when I woke, George Wigg rang me up and said, 'You looked pretty grim on "Gallery". You didn't smile at all. Was it that you were really thinking about those Shadow Cabinet election results?' Curiously enough, I could answer with a good conscience, 'They never occurred to me.' Nevertheless, that morning, I was pretty angry about the election. I tried to steel myself, as I do each year, and to say I know I can't win. Yet when I saw in the paper the miserable show I had made, considering what I had done, I was really boiling.

However I settled down to write my *Sunday Mirror* article and George Wigg came in to help me. Then I caught the train to Rugby, where I had agreed to talk to the boys about Labour politics, as I regularly do.

It's always the same housemaster who asks me to his house for tea beforehand. He is a real, absolutely pukkah, 100 per cent British public school housemaster and he has a very correct little wife who reads the right books, rather modern and progressive. I suppose they are the kind of people housemasters have to be. This time I gave the talk in the presence of the headmaster, who thought it was a superb political performance, as indeed it was! Then we came down to the housemaster's drawing room for drinks before dinner. Suddenly in rushed the maid and said, 'Mr Kennedy has been assassinated.'[1]

It was an odd sensation. In came the headmaster. I was sorry for the hostess. He kept on demanding to see the television and the soup got cold. The whole evening was dominated by the thought of the assassination. There was no doubt it was a tremendous shock. I remember thinking during dinner about the comparison between the death of Kennedy and the death of Roosevelt. I had been in Paris when I heard of the death of Roosevelt and I must admit that this was a far greater shock because, after all, I had followed Kennedy's life. I knew that this brilliant, starry, gritty, young man was a tremendous performer, a tremendous professional politician, but it was also a great demonstration that the most perfect politician with perfect staff doesn't

[1] On a visit to Dallas, Texas, with his wife, John Kennedy was shot in the head. He died about half an hour later. Lee Harvey Oswald, a young ex-Marine, was arrested that day. In the aircraft taking the late President's body back to Washington, Lyndon Baines Johnson took the oath of Office as President.

get much further than the amateur. So I felt the tragedy of it. When Anne said, 'Oh, his poor wife,' I couldn't help saying, 'Dora Gaitskell is much worse off than Jackie[1] because Jackie had three years and Dora didn't have a day of it.' That made me sound very tough.

Anyhow, we started off home pretty soon. As we got into the kitchen at Prescote I switched on the television and was just in time to see an I.T.V. Kennedy programme, obviously put together at the last moment, with an American of some kind talking of Kennedy's death. Then on came George Brown. At the first moment I saw that he was pissed and he was pretty awful. He jumped up and down and claimed a very intimate relationship with Kennedy. He said, 'Jack Kennedy was one of my best friends,' and I knew quite well that George had only seen him twice in his life, in formal interviews. Then he said how he'd discussed the whole Labour Party programme with Kennedy, walking up and down the lawn at the White House, and how he didn't know Lyndon[2] so well and how he would have to go over to America to discuss things with Lyndon. I turned to Anne and said, 'Pretty dreadful.' The programme ended and a few minutes later we were hearing the formal tributes from the Prime Minister, from Harold and from Grimond.

I thought Harold was absolutely first-class. I didn't think very much more about the Brown thing, except how terrible he was and how bad it was that it should happen again. At this moment there came a telephone message from London. The article I had done for the *Daily Mirror* this week was O.K. but they were asking me for a special Kennedy article. 'Well,' I said, 'I can't possibly do it. I've got the Coventry bazaar tomorrow.' The idea that I, a Member for Coventry, should miss the bazaar which I've never missed in my life, was more than I could take. However, I then thought again and said I would think it over. Sure enough, by next morning I had come to the conclusion that it was worth doing a big Kennedy article for the *Sunday Mirror*. So I sent Anne and the children off to the bazaar and sat down to rough out an article and dictate it, straight off the cuff, so to speak. I knew quite well as I dictated it that it was a far better article than if I had been able to work away at it with my secretary, as I usually do.

That was November 23rd, the day after Kennedy's death. Already the orgy of British lamentations was getting going. I am not surprised to record here that I take against the British public when it gets into a lamenting frame of mind. That weekend, though I was deeply shocked by Kennedy's death and in one sense appalled by it, I was also thinking not only of what to write about Lyndon Johnson to counter-balance the general tendency but I was also pretty clear that there was nothing very disastrous about this, that the main

---

[1] Jacqueline Bouvier married John Kennedy in September 1953. Her second husband was Aristotle Onassis, whom she married in October 1968.

[2] Lyndon Baines Johnson. Democratic Congressman from Texas 1937–48 and Senator from Texas 1948–60, he was Vice-President of the U.S.A. from 1961 until November 1963, when he succeeded John Kennedy. He was himself elected President in 1964 but in 1968 announced that he would not seek a further term of office.

thing was a drama of a young man. I was also clear that these feelings of mine were alienating me from any ordinary normal people.

On Sunday the Kennedy thing went on. The whole of the wireless and television were doing nothing but Kennedy programmes. I had a long talk with George Wigg because I had heard on the news that Harold was going to Washington for the funeral. Was it something he was forcing his way into, I felt? I was greatly relieved to hear that the British plane was hired by the P.M. to take him and the Duke of Edinburgh and that Harold and Jo Grimond were both to go. I now, later, hear that Harold's going was almost entirely due to a good friend in the press, who constantly asked in the White House whether there was a place for Wilson, forcing a reply. However, I was very relieved to hear that Harold had actually been invited and that there was no question about its being in order. He hadn't pushed his way in.

On Tuesday, the 26th, I went back to London. I had really rather forgotten about George Brown and everything else but I found that the affair was warming up. The newspapers had begun to have little stories about George Brown's behaviour and, at the Banbury farmers' dinner the night before, the Tory farmers had been asking me what on earth was wrong. People had just thought George was very much himself. However, I didn't think much about it. On Thursday evening there was a Party Meeting, which I missed because I was speaking in Cambridge. On Friday, when I opened the papers, I found banner headlines, 'Brown Carpeted at the Party Meeting'. Apparently, and I picked this up afterwards, Harold Wilson, who had in fact told me he was very angry with Brown, had summoned him and really carpeted him in the presence of the Chief Whip. The fact is that Brown had given Harold a solemn promise that he would never again drink before a television show. It wasn't any good Brown explaining the truth, which was that the I.T.V. had had to razzle round for a programme at two hours' notice. They had called George out of a Labour Party dinner, when he was half-seas-over, and his breaking the promise was involuntary. None of this made any difference. Harold had to discipline him.

However, Brown had been smart enough to say, 'But you can't discipline me here. I am bound to make my apology to the Party Meeting.' This reminded me of what I had done to Hugh, when Hugh said he wanted my resignation and I had the sense to force him to sack me and get the initiative on my side. Well, Brown had done the same thing. He had gone to the Party Meeting, had leaked to the press and so turned the whole thing round, so that here he was, poor old Brown, being carpeted in this way by Harold, as a result of a Left conspiracy. I have no doubt that this has done a great deal of damage because, ever since that Friday morning, nearly a week ago now, we have had newspaper stories every day and a mounting volume of criticism, with the result that Harold Wilson has, I think, suffered. The view is now held that for the first time he has really misbehaved.

Thursday, December 19th

On Tuesday evening I had dinner with Harold Wilson. I at last persuaded him to join me in the Strangers' Dining Room and reported to him on my latest science conference. He was very pleased with the press we had got and my press release and statement. He then turned to defence, which he had wanted to discuss with me for a long time, and told me that his aim was that George Wigg and I should prepare him a key speech on this subject. This fitted with something which Tony Wedgwood Benn had also told me. Harold has now decided that Tony shall be chairman of a group which includes Tommy Balogh, Peter Shore and myself, to work up six keynote speeches which he is to deliver roughly once a fortnight during January, February and March next year. The one George and I are to work up is the seventh in this series.

Harold keeps on repeating that he doesn't want everybody to know that we are ghost-writing his speeches for him, since he doesn't like the idea of ghost-writing. But he is sensible enough to see that he simply hasn't got the time to do it. Indeed, when he saw my press releases, he said, 'This is the kind of thing which you can do, Dick. I haven't been able to do that kind of serious thinking and writing since I became Leader.' This is going to be Harold's biggest contribution to the build-up in the spring. These are going to be positive, creative speeches, under the headline, 'Purpose in Politics'. We really had an extremely cosy and pleasant evening. Harold came straight from the Whips' party and had a little bit to drink and was cheerful. But he was terribly concerned all the time about payment. He doesn't want to take even from me a single meal, though I insisted on paying. After the meal was finished we went back to his room, brandy was poured out and we really had a kind of cheerful conviviality together which I haven't known for a long time.

Throughout the meal he had talked to me once again very carefully, assuming that I would like to be Minister of Education. We discussed the position of the Lord President and we also discussed the whole George Brown affair. Since the episode of George Brown's appearance on the I.T.V. programme and the carpeting at the Party Meeting the whole thing has surged along in a very dreary kind of way. Of course, people outside didn't know what had happened, what Harold had had to suffer from George Brown in security lapses, drunkenness, and really, the degree of irresponsibility which it is difficult to tolerate in a Deputy Leader. One knew how tempted Harold had been to treat George Brown in the way he actually treated him on this occasion. Nevertheless, it is clear that this has made its mark. It did in fact prevent Harold from doing his Cabinet reshuffle and, though he may have his own view of what he will do with George Brown afterwards, and though now George Brown has gone sick and is in hospital, it's true that, as I felt at dinner that night, the whole affair has clouded Harold's position. Apart from that, he is friendly enough with me and Tony and George Wigg and gradually he is forming round him his group of men whom he really trusts to do a job of work with him.

As for the rest of politics, it's just been routining along. The Conservative Party has now accepted the new Prime Minister. The Election boom is proceeding rather more rapidly than the Conservatives themselves had wanted. There is a certain danger coming into the economy, since it looks as though there are too many imports and new increases are always being announced in Government expenditure. My strong impression, and this is now Harold's impression, too, is that the Tories will find it better to go to the country quickly in March or April rather than taking the risk of waiting until July or August.

Today I've just done my Christmas shopping in the usual places, Hatchards in Piccadilly and Fortnum & Mason. I brought the shopping home across St James's Park and, when I was crossing the little bridge, I saw a sight which excited me more than anything I've seen for a very long time. It is just a year ago since I took Anne to New York and saw that beautiful view from Central Park across to the Plaza Hotel, with the ice-rink in front. Now here I was looking down towards the new War Office and behind it Whitehall Court. Suddenly this became one of those romantic views. On the left was that great new building, New Zealand House, at the bottom of the Haymarket. Then came the trees, and, in the background, a fantastic arrangement, a fairy castle rising behind the modern structure. As I turned round to face Buckingham Palace, there was a crescent moon and behind it the new brilliantly illuminated skyscraper. It was really my first sight of the new London, with the old behind it. I was reminded once again that, in some mysterious way, in a living city the old and the new do blend together.

Members of the Cabinet 1951–63

Members of the Cabinet October 26th–28th, 1951

Prime Minister	Winston Churchill
Lord President	Lord Woolton
Lord Chancellor	Lord Simonds
Lord Privy Seal	Marquess of Salisbury
Chancellor of the Exchequer	R. A. Butler
Foreign Office	Anthony Eden
Home Office	Sir David Maxwell-Fyfe
Colonial Office	Oliver Lyttelton
Commonwealth Relations Office	Lord Ismay
Defence	Winston Churchill
Health	Harry Crookshank
Housing and Local Government	Harold Macmillan
Labour and National Service	Sir Walter Monckton
Paymaster-General	Lord Cherwell
Scottish Office	James Stuart
Board of Trade	Peter Thorneycroft

Changes in 1952

On March 1st Earl Alexander of Tunis became Minister of Defence, in place of Sir Winston Churchill. On March 12th the Marquess of Salisbury replaced Lord Ismay at the Commonwealth Relations Office. On May 7th Harry Crookshank became Lord Privy Seal, an office which the Marquess of Salisbury had held until then. The Ministry of Health became a non-Cabinet post. On November 24th the Marquess of Salisbury succeeded Lord Woolton as Lord President of the Council and was himself followed at the Commonwealth Relations Office by Viscount Swinton. Lord Woolton became Chancellor of the Duchy of Lancaster.

Changes in 1953

On November 11th the Earl of Selkirk became Paymaster-General; the office was no longer a Cabinet post.

Changes in 1954

On July 28th Alan Lennox-Boyd succeeded Oliver Lyttelton at the Colonial Office. On October 18th Sir David Maxwell-Fyfe, now Viscount Kilmuir, became Lord Chancellor; his post at the Home Office went to Gwilym Lloyd George. Harold Macmillan became Minister of Defence, while his former place at the Ministry of Housing and Local Government was taken by Duncan Sandys. Oswald Peake became Minister with responsibility for Pensions and National Insurance, a new office.

Members of the Cabinet April 6th, 1955

Prime Minister	Sir Anthony Eden
Lord President	Marquess of Salisbury
Lord Chancellor	Viscount Kilmuir
Lord Privy Seal	Harry Crookshank
Chancellor of the Exchequer	R. A. Butler
Foreign Office	Harold Macmillan
Home Office	Gwilym Lloyd George
Colonial Office	Alan Lennox-Boyd
Commonwealth Relations Office	Earl of Home
Defence	Selwyn Lloyd
Housing and Local Government	Duncan Sandys
Scottish Office	James Stuart
Board of Trade	Peter Thorneycroft

Changes in 1955

On December 20th R. A. Butler became Lord Privy Seal. Harold Macmillan succeeded him at the Treasury and was himself followed by Selwyn Lloyd at the Foreign Office. Sir Walter Monckton became Minister of Defence and Iain Macleod Minister for Labour and National Service. John Boyd-Carpenter became Minister of Pensions and National Insurance, an office no longer in the Cabinet.

Changes in 1956

On October 18th Antony Head succeeded Sir Walter Monckton as Minister of Defence.

Members of the Cabinet January 13th–14th, 1957

Prime Minister	Harold Macmillan
Lord President of the Council	Marquess of Salisbury
Lord Chancellor	Viscount Kilmuir
Lord Privy Seal and Home Secretary	R. A. Butler
Chancellor of the Exchequer	Peter Thorneycroft
Foreign Office	Selwyn Lloyd
Agriculture, Fisheries and Food	Derick Heathcoat Amory

Colonial Office	Alan Lennox-Boyd
Commonwealth Relations Office	Earl of Home
Defence	Duncan Sandys
Education	Viscount Hailsham
Housing and Local Government	Henry Brooke
Labour and National Service	Iain Macleod
Duchy of Lancaster	Charles Hill
Power	Lord Mills
Scottish Office	John Maclay
Board of Trade	Sir David Eccles
Transport and Civil Aviation	Harold Watkinson

Changes in 1957

On March 29th the Earl of Home succeeded the Marquess of Salisbury as Lord President. On September 17th that office was taken by Viscount Hailsham, who was succeeded at the Ministry of Education by Geoffrey Lloyd. The Earl of Home became Leader of the House of Lords.

Changes in 1958

On January 6th Derick Heathcoat Amory succeeded Peter Thorneycroft as Chancellor of the Exchequer. John Hare became Minister of Agriculture, Fisheries and Food.

Changes in 1959

On October 14th the Earl of Home succeeded Viscount Hailsham as Lord President of the Council. Lord Hailsham became Lord Privy Seal and, in a new office, Minister for Science. The Ministry of Transport and Civil Aviation was divided: Ernest Marples became Minister of Transport and Duncan Sandys of Aviation. Iain Macleod became Colonial Secretary, Harold Watkinson Minister of Defence and David Eccles Minister of Education. Edward Heath took the Ministry of Labour and National Service (after November 12th, it was the Ministry of Labour only). Reginald Maudling became President of the Board of Trade.

Changes in 1960

On July 27th Viscount Hailsham returned to the office of Lord President of the Council, retaining his responsibility for Science. The Earl of Home became Foreign Secretary, succeeding Selwyn Lloyd, the new Chancellor of the Exchequer. Edward Heath became Lord Privy Seal. Christopher Soames succeeded John Hare as Minister of Agriculture, while Mr Hare became Minister of Labour. Duncan Sandys went to the Commonwealth Relations Office.

Changes in 1961
On October 9th Reginald Maudling became Colonial Secretary, in succession to Iain Macleod, who became Chancellor of the Duchy of Lancaster. Frederick Erroll followed Mr Maudling at the Board of Trade.

Changes in 1962
On July 13th R. A. Butler became First Secretary of State, a new office. Lord Dilhorne became Lord Chancellor, Reginald Maudling Chancellor of the Exchequer, Henry Brooke Home Secretary and Julian Amery Minister of Aviation. Peter Thorneycroft became Minister of Defence, Sir Edward Boyle Minister of Education, Sir Keith Joseph Minister of Housing and Local Government and Michael Noble Secretary of State for Scotland. The Colonial Office was merged with the Commonwealth Relations Office.

Members of the Cabinet October 16th–20th, 1963

Prime Minister	Sir Alec Douglas-Home (formerly the Earl of Home)
Lord President and Minister for Science	Quintin Hogg (formerly Viscount Hailsham)
Lord Chancellor	Lord Dilhorne
Lord Privy Seal	Selwyn Lloyd
Chancellor of the Exchequer	Reginald Maudling
Foreign Office	R. A. Butler
Home Office	Henry Brooke
Agriculture, Fisheries and Food	Christopher Soames
Aviation	Julian Amery
Colonial Office and Commonwealth Relations	Duncan Sandys
Defence	Peter Thorneycroft
Education	Sir Edward Boyle
Housing and Local Government	Sir Keith Joseph
Labour	Joseph Godber
Duchy of Lancaster	Viscount Blakenham (formerly John Hare)
Scottish Office	Michael Noble
Board of Trade and Secretary of State for Industry, Trade and Regional Development	Edward Heath
Transport	Ernest Marples

The office of First Secretary of State, headed by R. A. Butler, was abolished.

Speakers of the House of Commons and Government and Opposition Whips 1951–63
During the period covered by this volume, the Speakers of the House of

Commons were William Morrison (November 1951–October 1959) and Sir Harry Hylton-Foster (October 1959–October 1965).

The Government Chief Whips in the House of Commons were Patrick Buchan-Hepburn (until 1955), Edward Heath (1955–9) and Martin Redmayne (1959–64). The Deputy Government Chief Whips were Cedric Drewe (1951–2), Harry Mackeson (1951–3), Herbert Butcher (1952–4) Edward Heath (1954–5), Martin Redmayne (1955–9) and Michael Hughes-Young (1960–2).

The Opposition Chief Whips in the House of Commons were William Whiteley (until 1955) and Herbert Bowden (1955–64). The Deputy Opposition Chief Whips were Herbert Bowden (1951–5), Ernest Popplewell (1955–9), John Taylor (1959–62) and Edward Short (1962–4).

Biographical Notes

ATTLEE, Clement (1883–1967). Labour M.P. for the Limehouse division of Stepney 1922–50 and for West Walthamstow 1950–5. Leader of the Opposition 1935–40, he served in the wartime coalition Government as Lord Privy Seal 1940–2, Secretary of State for the Dominions 1942–3 and Lord President 1943–5. Attlee became Prime Minister on July 26th, 1945, and resigned on October 26th, 1951. He retired from politics at the end of 1955, when he was raised to the peerage as an earl. An account of his political life is given in his autobiography, *As It Happened* (London: Heinemann, 1954). He married Violet Millar in 1922. She died in 1964.

BALOGH, Thomas. A fellow of Balliol College, Oxford, 1945–73 (now an Emeritus Fellow), he was Reader in Economics at Oxford University 1960–73 and was Leverhulme Fellow there 1973–6. From 1964 to 1967 he acted as Economic Adviser to the Cabinet and, in 1968, as the Prime Minister's own consultant. On leaving No. 10 in 1968 he became a life peer. From 1974 to 1975 he was Minister of State at the Department of Energy. He was Deputy Chairman of the British National Oil Corporation 1976–7 and from 1978 to 1979 Adviser to the Corporation. His first marriage, to Mrs Penelope Gatry in 1945, was dissolved in 1970. She died in 1975.

BENN, Tony. Anthony Wedgwood Benn was President of the Oxford Union in 1947 and a producer for the B.B.C.'s North American Service in 1949 and 1950. He was Labour M.P. for Bristol South-East 1950–60 and, after a successful battle to disclaim the title inherited from his father, Viscount Stansgate, again from 1963. He was Postmaster-General 1964–6 and Minister of Technology 1966–70. In 1974 he became Secretary of State for Industry and from 1975 to 1979 served as Secretary of State for Energy.

BEVAN, Aneurin (1897–1960). Labour M.P. for Ebbw Vale from 1929 until his death, he was founder of *Tribune*, which he edited from 1942 to 1945 and to which he was a regular contributor. He was Minister of Health and Housing in Attlee's Government and was responsible for the nationalization of the Health Service and the National Assistance Act of 1948. He became increasingly opposed to the escalation of armaments and to the Government's alignment with the United States. Transferred to the Ministry of Labour in January 1951, he resigned in April of that year over Gaitskell's proposal to introduce Health Service charges. In 1951 and 1952 Bevan headed the poll for the N.E.C. and the Shadow Cabinet, from which he resigned in April 1954 over SEATO. On Attlee's resignation he challenged Gaitskell unsuccessfully for the Party leadership in December 1955. Nine months later he was elected as Party Treasurer. Labour spokesman on foreign affairs, he became Deputy Leader of the Party in October 1959. See Michael Foot, *Aneurin Bevan*: vol. 1 (1897–1945) (London: Paladin, new edn 1975); vol. 2 (1945–60) (London: Davis-Poynter, 1973).

BEVIN, Ernest (1881–1951). Trade union leader and Labour politician. A dockers' leader, he became Secretary of the Transport and General Workers' Union in 1921. He was Labour M.P. for Central Wandsworth 1940–50 and for East Woolwich 1950–1. Minister of Labour and National Service in the wartime coalition, he was Attlee's Foreign Secretary from 1945 until March 1951 and Lord Privy Seal from March 1951 until his death on April 14th of that year. A two-volume biography has been written by Alan Bullock: *The Life and Times of Ernest Bevin* (London: Heinemann, 1960, 1967).

BING, Geoffrey (1909–77). He was called to the Bar in 1934 and practised in Gibraltar in 1937, the Gold Coast 1950 and Nigeria 1954. He was Labour M.P. for the Hornchurch division of Essex 1945–50 and for Hornchurch 1950–5. He was an Assistant Government Whip 1945–6, Constitutional Adviser to the Prime Minister of Ghana 1956–7, Attorney General in the Government of Ghana 1957–61 and Adviser to President Nkrumah of Ghana 1961–6.

BOOTHBY, Robert. Conservative M.P. for East Aberdeen 1924–58, he was Parliamentary Private Secretary to Winston Churchill 1926–9, Parliamentary Secretary at the Ministry of Food 1940–1 and British delegate to the Council of Europe 1945–57. He was Rector of St Andrew's University 1958–61 and in 1958 became a life peer. Like Crossman, Boothby made frequent radio and television broadcasts. He published an autobiography in 1978: *Boothby: Recollections of a Rebel* (London: Hutchinson).

BOYD-CARPENTER, John. Conservative M.P. for Kingston-upon-Thames 1945–72, he was Financial Secretary to the Treasury 1951–4, Minister of Transport and Civil Aviation 1954–5, Minister of Pensions and National Insurance 1955–62 and Chief Secretary to the Treasury and Paymaster-General 1962–4. He was also chairman of the Public Accounts Committee 1964–70 and in 1972 he became a life peer. A Director of Rugby Portland Cement 1970–6, since 1976 he has been the company's Chairman. His autobiography, *Way of Life* (London: Sidgwick & Jackson), as published in 1980.

BROWN, George. Labour M.P. for Belper 1945–70; in 1970 he became a life peer, taking the title of Lord George-Brown. He served as P.P.S. to the Minister of Labour and National Service 1945–7 and in 1947 to the Chancellor of the Exchequer, and was Parliamentary Secretary to the Ministry of Agriculture and Fisheries 1947–51 and Minister of Works from April to October 1951. In 1963 he was an unsuccessful candidate for the leadership of the Labour Party. In 1964 he became First Secretary of State at the newly created Department of Economic Affairs and in 1966 Foreign Secretary. After his resignation from that office in 1968 he remained Deputy Leader of the Labour Party until 1970 and his elevation to the Upper House. He resigned his membership of the Labour Party in 1976. He has published a volume of memoirs, *In My Way* (London: Gollançz, 1971).

BUTLER, Richard Austen. Conservative M.P. for Saffron Walden 1929–65. He was Under-Secretary of State at the India Office 1932–7, Parliamentary Secretary at the Ministry of Labour 1937–8, Under-Secretary of State for Foreign Affairs 1938–41, Minister of Education 1941–5, Minister of Labour June–July 1945, Chancellor of the Exchequer 1951–5, Lord Privy Seal 1955–9 and Leader of the House of Commons 1955–61, Home Secretary 1957–62, First Secretary of State July 1962–October 1963, Minister in Charge of the Central African Office 1962–October 1963 and Secretary of State for Foreign Affairs 1963–4. He was Chairman of the Conservative Party Research Department and of the Conservative Party Organization 1959–61. He was created a life peer in 1965 and in that year became Master of Trinity College, Cambridge. He has published a volume of memoirs, *The Art of the Possible* (London: Hamish Hamilton, 1971).

CALLAGHAN, James. Labour M.P. for South Cardiff 1945–50 and for South-East Cardiff since 1950. He was Parliamentary Secretary at the Ministry of Transport 1947–50 and at the Admiralty 1950–1. A member of the Labour Party N.E.C. since 1957, from 1967 to 1976 he was Treasurer of the Party. From 1955 to 1964 he was consultant to the Police Federation. In 1964 he became Chancellor of the Exchequer and in 1967 Home Secretary, holding that office until 1970. He became Foreign Secretary in 1974 and was Prime Minister from April 1976 until May 1979, when he became Leader of the Opposition after the Conservative Party's victory in the General Election. He married Audrey Moulton in 1938.

CASTLE, Barbara. Labour M.P. for Blackburn 1945–79 and a member of the Labour Party's N.E.C. since 1950. In 1946, the year she married Edward Castle, she became Minister of Overseas Development, and in 1965 Minister of Transport, an office she held until 1968, when she became First Secretary of State at the newly created Department of Employment and Productivity, holding that office until Labour's defeat in 1970. From 1974 to

1976 she was Secretary of State for Social Services. In 1979 she became a member of the European Parliament.

CHURCHILL, Winston Spencer (1874–1965). Cavalryman, journalist, politician, historian, and statesman. He sat as Conservative M.P. for Oldham 1900–4; as Liberal M.P. for the same constituency 1904–6, for North-West Manchester 1906–8, for Dundee 1908–18 and for the City of London 1918–22; as Constitutional M.P. for the Epping division of Essex 1924–31; and as Conservative M.P. for that constituency 1931–45, and for Woodford 1945–61, during which period he was Prime Minister and wartime coalition leader 1940–5, Leader of the Opposition 1945–51, and Prime Minister October 1951–April 1955. In 1953 he became a Knight of the Garter. His publications include a variety of memoirs, a Life of Marlborough and a six-volume *History of the Second World War* (London: Cassell 1948–52, 1954). His speeches, edited by Robert Rhodes James, were published in 1974 (London: Bowker), and significant biographies include those by H. Pelling (London: Macmillan, 1974), by Randolph Churchill and Martin Gilbert (London: Heinemann, five volumes to date: 1966–7, 1971, 1975–6) and by Lord Moran: *Winston Churchill: The Struggle for Survival: 1940–65* (London: Constable, 1966).

CRIPPS, Stafford (1889–1952). The nephew of Beatrice Webb and the son of Lord Parmoor, Cripps's first career was as a chemist, and he discovered the inert gas xenon in 1922. His father and uncle were in Ramsay MacDonald's 1929 Cabinet. Encouraged by Morrison to join the Labour Party, Cripps became Solicitor-General in 1930 (he became the youngest K.C. in 1927) and Labour M.P. for East Bristol in 1931, but was expelled from the Party in 1939. He served as Ambassador to Moscow in 1940, as Leader of the House of Commons and Lord Privy Seal in 1942, as Minister for Aircraft Production 1942–5 and as President of the Board of Trade 1945. In October 1947 he was made Minister for Economic Affairs and became Chancellor of the Exchequer after Dalton's resignation. From the stringency of his fiscal measures he became known as the Iron Chancellor. He retired, exhausted, in October 1950. He was knighted in 1930 and in 1951 he became a Companion of Honour. A man of the highest ideals and frugal personal habits, he was not likely 'to be amused'.

CROSLAND, Anthony (1918–77). Labour M.P. for South Gloucestershire 1950–5 and for Grimsby from 1959 until his death. He was Minister of State for Economic Affairs 1964–5, Secretary of State for Education and Science 1965–7, President of the Board of Trade 1967–9 and Secretary of State for Local Government and Regional Planning from 1969 until 1970. In 1974 he became Secretary of State for the Environment and in 1976 Foreign Secretary. He was the author of a number of books on the theory of

Socialism, notably *The Future of Socialism* (London: Cape, 1956) and *Socialism Now* (London: Cape, 1974).

CROSSMAN, Anne. Richard Crossman's third wife, Anne McDougall, whom he married in 1954. Their son, Patrick, was born in 1957 and died in 1975 and their daughter, Virginia, was born in 1959.

CROSSMAN, Richard Howard Stafford (1907–74). Labour M.P. for Coventry East from 1945 until his death. He was Fellow and Tutor at New College, Oxford, from 1930 to 1937, Assistant Editor of the *New Statesman & Nation* 1938–55, Lecturer for the Oxford University Delegacy for Extra-Mural Studies and the Workers' Educational Association 1938–40 and Leader of the Labour Group on Oxford City Council 1934–40. He served as Deputy Director of Psychological Warfare at Allied Forces Headquarters, Algiers, 1943, and as Assistant Chief of the Psychological Warfare Division of SHAEF 1944–5. He was a member of the Anglo-American Palestine Commission in 1946 and of the Malta Round Table Conference in 1955 and was a member of the National Executive Committee of the Labour Party from 1952 until 1967. From 1964 to 1966 he was Minister of Housing and Local Government, from 1966 to 1968 Lord President of the Council and Leader of the House of Commons and from 1968 to 1970 Secretary of State at the Department of Health and Social Security. He returned to the *New Statesman* as Editor in 1970, remaining there until 1972.

CROSSMAN, Zita. Inezita Davis married John Baker, a colleague of Crossman's at New College, Oxford, in 1923. After her divorce from John Baker in 1939, she became Crossman's second wife. She died in 1952.

CUDLIPP, Hugh. A journalist since 1927, he was Features Editor of the *Sunday Chronicle* 1932–5 and of the *Daily Mirror* 1935–7; Editor of the *Sunday Pictorial* 1937–40 and 1946–9; Managing Editor of the *Sunday Express* 1950–2; Editorial Director of the *Daily Mirror* and the *Sunday Pictorial* 1952–63; and Joint Managing Director of the *Daily Mirror* and *Sunday Pictorial* 1959–63. He was Chairman of Odhams Press Ltd 1961–3, Chairman of *Daily Mirror* Newspapers Ltd 1963–8, Deputy Chairman of the International Publishing Corporation 1964–8, Chairman of the Corporation 1968–73, and from 1970 to 1973 Chairman of the I.P.C. Newspaper Division and Deputy Chairman (Editorial) of the Board of Reed International. He was a Director of Associated Television Limited 1956–73. He was knighted in 1973 and became a life peer in 1974. His second wife, Eileen Ascroft, whom he married in 1945, died in 1962. He has published two volumes of autobiography, *Publish and Be Damned!* (London: Dakers, 1953) and *Walking on the Water* (London: The Bodley Head, 1977).

DALTON, Hugh (1887–1962). Labour M.P. for the Camberwell division of Peckham 1924–9, and for Bishop Auckland 1929–33 and 1935–59. He was Minister for Economic Warfare 1940–2, President of the Board of Trade 1942–5 and Chancellor of the Exchequer 1945–7, resigning after an indiscreet Budget leak. He was Chancellor of the Duchy of Lancaster 1948–50, Minister of Town and Country Planning 1950–1 and of Local Government Planning 1951. His Memoirs were published in London in three volumes by Muller: *Call Back Yesterday: 1887–1931* (1953); *The Fateful Years: 1931–45* (1957); and *High Tide and After: 1945–60* (1962). His *Principles of Finance* went through numerous editions (including London: Routledge, revised edn 1954). A selection from his diaries is in the course of preparation under the editorship of Dr Ben Pimlott.

DAVENPORT, Nicholas (1893–1979) and Olga. A wartime civil servant, Nicholas Davenport went into the City and worked with J. M. Keynes, becoming Deputy Chairman of the Mutual Life Assurance Society in 1960. In 1923 he became Financial Correspondent of the *Nation* and wrote the City column of the *New Statesman & Nation* 1930–53, when he became the Financial Correspondent of the *Spectator*, writing a weekly column until his death. He served on the National Investment Council from 1946 until its abolition in October 1947 and, briefly, on the National Film Finance Corporation established by Harold Wilson. Olga Davenport was a ballet dancer and actress and is a professional painter. Their life is described in *Memoirs of a City Radical* (London: Weidenfeld & Nicolson, 1974) and their home Hinton Manor and its history in *The Honour of St Valery: The Story of an English Manor* (London: Scolar Press, 1978).

DEAKIN, Arthur (1890–1955). General Secretary of the Transport and General Workers' Union from 1946 until his death while addressing a May Day rally in Leicester. He was Chairman of the T.U.C. 1951–2 and a Director of the *Daily Herald*.

DONNELLY, Desmond (1920–74). A journalist, he was Labour M.P. for Pembroke 1950–68 and Independent M.P. for the same constituency 1968–70. He was Director of the Town and Country Planning Association 1948–50. His expulsion from the Labour Party in 1968 provoked him to publish *Gadarene '68: The Crimes, Follies and Misfortunes of the Wilson Government* (London: Kimber, 1968) and *The Nearing Storm* (London: Hutchinson, 1968).

DOUGLAS HOME, Alec. Unionist M.P. for South Lanark 1931–45 and Conservative M.P. for the Lanark division of Lanarkshire 1950–1; in 1951 he succeeded his father and became the 14th Earl of Home, but in 1963 he disclaimed his peerages and became Unionist M.P. for Kinross and West Perthshire in November that year, serving in that capacity until September 1974, when he returned to the Lords as a life peer, with the title of Lord Home of the Hirsel. He was P.P.S. to the Prime Minister (Neville Chamberlain) 1937–40, Joint Parliamentary Under-Secretary at the Foreign Office 1945, Minister of State at the Scottish Office 1951–5, Secretary of State for Commonwealth Relations 1955–60, Deputy Leader of the House of Lords 1956–7 and Leader 1957–60, and from 1957 to 1960 also Lord President of the Council. He was Foreign Secretary 1960–3, Prime Minister October 1963 to October 1964, Leader of the Opposition 1964–July 1965 and Secretary of State for Foreign Affairs 1970–4. He was knighted in 1962. He has written two volumes of autobiography: *The Way the Wind Blows* (London: Collins, 1976) and *Border Airs* (London: Collins, 1979).

DRIBERG, Tom (1905–76). Independent M.P. for Maldon division of Essex 1942–5, and its Labour M.P. 1945–55, and for Barking 1959–74. A noted journalist and broadcaster, he wrote for the *Daily Express* 1928–43, for *Reynolds News* 1943—55 and for the *New Statesman & Nation* (later the *New Statesman*) 1955–61. A member of the N.E.C. 1949–72, he was Chairman of the Party 1957/58. He became a life peer in 1976, taking the title of Lord Bradwell. His various books include a biography of Beaverbrook: *Beaverbrook: A Study in Power and Frustration* (London: Weidenfeld & Nicolson, 1956) and a posthumous volume of reminiscences: *Ruling Passions* (London: Cape, 1977). He married Mrs Ena Binfield in 1951.

DULLES, John Foster (1888–1959). U.S. Senator from New York in 1949. As special representative of the President, with the rank of Ambassador 1950–1, he negotiated and signed for the United States the Japanese Peace Treaty and the Australian, New Zealand, Philippine and Japanese Security Treaties. He was Secretary of State from January 1953 to April 1959. He died the following month.

EDEN, Anthony (1897–1977). Conservative M.P. for Warwick and Leamington 1923–57. After holding a variety of junior ministerial posts in foreign affairs he was Secretary of State for Foreign Affairs 1935 to 1938. He then became Secretary of State for Dominion Affairs 1939–40, for War 1940 and for Foreign Affairs 1940–5. He was Leader of the Opposition 1945–51, Foreign Secretary and Deputy Prime Minister 1951–5 and Prime Minister from April 1955 until his resignation in January 1957. He was knighted in 1954 and in 1961 he was created 1st Earl of Avon. He wrote an autobiography, *The Eden Memoirs* (London: Cassell: *Full Circle*, 1960; *Facing the Dictators*, 1962; *The Reckoning*, 1965; *Towards Peace in Indo-China*, 1966).

EISENHOWER, Dwight David (1890–1969). An American general, he was

Supreme Commander in Western Europe 1944–5 and, later, Co-ordinator of the Allied Supreme Command of NATO 1950–2. He was President of the United States 1953–61, as a member of the Republican Party.

FOOT, Michael. Labour M.P. for the Devonport division of Plymouth 1945–1955 and since November 1960 for Ebbw Vale. He was Editor of *Tribune* 1948–52 and 1955–60, and Managing Director 1945–74. From 1974 to 1976 he was Secretary of State for Employment and from 1976 to 1979 Lord President of the Council and Leader of the House of Commons. Since 1976 he has been Deputy Leader of the Labour Party. An author and journalist, his works include a two-volume biography of Aneurin Bevan (see above) and a study of Swift, *The Pen and the Sword* (London: MacGibbon & Kee, 1966). He married Jill Craigie, a television producer, in 1949.

FREEMAN, John. Labour M.P. for the Watford division of Hertfordshire 1945–50 and for Watford 1950–5. He was Financial Secretary at the War Office 1946, Parliamentary Under-Secretary of State for War 1947 and Parliamentary Secretary at the Ministry of Supply from 1947 until 1951, when he resigned his post at the same time and on the same issue as Bevan (see above). Like Crossman, he was a *New Statesman* journalist and in 1951 he became Assistant Editor. He was Deputy Editor 1958–60, succeeding as Editor 1961–5. He served as High Commissioner in India 1965–8 and as Ambassador in Washington 1969–71. He has been Chairman of London Weekend Television since 1971 and Chairman of Independent Television News since 1976. As presenter of the B.B.C. television programme 'Face to Face', he achieved a considerable public following during the early 1960s. During the period of the *Backbench Diaries*, he was married to Margaret Kerr (his second wife) from 1948 until her death in 1957 and from 1962 until the dissolution of the marriage in 1976 to Catherine Dove.

GAITSKELL, Hugh (1906–63). Labour M.P. for South Leeds from 1945 until his death, he was Minister of Fuel and Power 1947–50, Minister of State for Economic Affairs 1950, Chancellor of the Exchequer 1950–1, and Leader of the Labour Party from December 1955 until he died. A biography has been written by Philip Williams: *Hugh Gaitskell* (London: Cape, 1979).

GREENE, Helga. Helga Guinness married Hugh Carleton Greene in 1934. The marriage was dissolved in 1948 and in 1963 she married Stuart Connolly. She was Crossman's literary agent.

GREENWOOD, Anthony. Labour M.P. for Heywood and Radcliffe 1946–50 and for Rossendale from 1950 until he became a life peer in 1970, taking the title of Lord Greenwood of Rossendale. He was Vice-Chairman of the Parliamentary Labour Party 1950–1, a member of the Parliamentary Committee of the Labour Party 1951 and 1955–60, and a member of the N.E.C. 1954–70. He served as Secretary of State for Colonial Affairs 1964–5, Minister for Overseas Development 1965–6, and for Housing and Local Government 1966–70. From 1977 to 1979 he was Chairman of the House of Lords Select Committee on the European Communities and Principal Deputy Chairman of the House of Lords.

HEALEY, Denis. Labour M.P. for South-East Leeds 1952–5 and for Leeds East since 1955. From 1945 until 1952 he was Secretary of the International Department of the Labour Party. He was Secretary of State for Defence 1964–70 and Chancellor of the Exchequer 1974–9. In 1945 he married Edna Edmunds, the author of *Lady Unknown: The Life of Angela Burdett-Coutts* (London: Sidgwick & Jackson, 1978). His book *Healey's Eye: a photographic memoir* was published in 1980 (London: Cape).

HODGKINSON, George and Carrie. During the First World War George Hodgkinson worked as a skilled man at the Daimler Company, where he became a steward and took part in a strike over the recognition of shop stewards. After the First World War he spent a year at Ruskin College, Oxford. He became the first paid Secretary of the Coventry Borough Labour Party and a member of Coventry City Council, when the Labour Party gained control in 1937. In 1945 he was Lord Mayor. As Agent for the multi-Member Coventry constituency, he was Crossman's agent and, later, devoted much of his time to the affairs of Coventry East. He and Carrie Wilson, whom he married in 1927, were two of Crossman's most trusted and loyal friends.

HOGG, Quintin. Conservative M.P. for Oxford City from 1938 until 1950, when he succeeded to his father's viscountcy. In 1963, after disclaiming his peerage, he was elected Conservative M.P. for St Marylebone and represented that constituency from 1963 until 1970, when he became a life peer, taking the title of Lord Hailsham of St Marylebone. He was Joint Parliamentary Under-Secretary for Air in 1945, First Lord of the Admiralty 1956–7 and Minister of Education in 1957. From 1960 to 1963 he was Leader of the House of Lords and held various offices while he was there, including that of Secretary of State for Education and Science April–October 1964. From September 1957 to October 1959 he was Chairman of the Conservative Party Organiza-tion. When he returned to the House of Commons in 1963 he stood, un-successfully, as a candidate for the leadership of his Party. He was Lord Chancellor from 1970 to February 1974, when the Conservatives lost office and he returned to the Bar. In 1979 he became Lord Chancellor once more. His publications include *The Case for Conservatism* (Harmondsworth: Penguin, 1947), a volume of memoirs, *The Door Wherein I Went* (London: Collins, 1975) and *The Dilemma of Democracy* (London: Collins, 1978).

JAY, Douglas. Labour M.P. for Battersea North since July 1946. He was Economic Secretary to the Treasury 1947–50, Financial Secretary 1950–1, and President of the Board of Trade 1964–7. A staunch anti-Marketeer, he was Chairman of the Common Market Safeguards Campaign 1970–7. His first marriage, in 1933, to Margaret ('Peggy') Garnett was dissolved in 1972. His autobiography, *Change and Fortune* (London: Hutchinson), was published in 1980.

JENKINS, Roy. Labour M.P. for Central Southwark 1948–50 and for the Stetchford division of Birmingham 1950–76. He was a member of the Executive of the Fabian Society 1949–61 and served as Minister of Aviation 1964–5, Home Secretary 1965–7, Chancellor of the Exchequer 1967–70 and again as Home Secretary from 1974 until 1976, when he became President of the Commission of the European Communities. He was Deputy Leader of the Labour Party 1970–2. An author, his biographies include *Sir Charles Dilke* (London: Collins, 1958) and *Asquith* (London: Collins, 1964).

KALDOR, Nicholas. A Fellow of King's College, Cambridge, since 1949, he was Reader in Economics at the University of Cambridge 1964–5 and Professor of Economics 1966–75. An Economic Adviser to many foreign Governments, he was Special Adviser to the Chancellor of the Exchequer from 1964 to 1968 and from 1974 to 1976. He became a life peer in 1974. He married Clarissa Goldschmidt in 1934.

KING, Cecil Harmsworth. The nephew of Lord Harmondsworth and Lord Northcliffe, he was Chairman of *Daily Mirror* Newspapers Ltd and *Sunday Pictorial* Newspapers Ltd 1951–63 and of the International Publishing Corporation and the Reed Paper Group 1963–8. The two-volume *The Cecil King Diary: 1967–70* and *1970–74* (London: Cape) was published in 1972 and 1975.

LEE, Jennie. She married Aneurin Bevan in October 1934 and was herself a Labour M.P., representing North Lanark 1929–31 and Cannock 1945–70. She was a member of the National Executive Committee of the Labour Party 1958–70 and served as Parliamentary Secretary at the Ministry of Public Building and Works 1964–5 and Parliamentary Under-Secretary at the Department of Education and Science 1965–7; in 1967 she became Minister of State at that Department, with special responsibility for the Arts, holding office until 1970, when she was created a life peer, taking the title of Baroness Lee of Asheridge. She was instrumental in founding the Open University. Her book *My Life with Nye* was published in 1980 (London: Cape).

LENNOX-BOYD, Alan. Conservative M.P. for mid-Bedfordshire 1931–60, he was Parliamentary Secretary at the Ministry of Labour 1938–9, the Ministry of Home Security 1939, the Ministry of Food 1939–40 and the Ministry of Aircraft Production 1943–5. With the return of the Conservatives to office, he served as Minister of State for Colonial Affairs 1951–2, Minister of Transport and Civil Aviation 1952–4, and Secretary of State for the Colonies 1954–October 1959. He was Managing Director of Arthur Guinness, Son & Co. Ltd 1960–7 and became Joint Vice-Chairman of the company in 1967; he was also a Director of the Royal Exchange 1962–70, of Tate & Lyle 1966–74 and of ICI 1967–75. In 1960 he was created 1st Viscount Boyd of Merton.

LLEWELYN-DAVIES, Patricia. Chairman of the Board of Governors of Great Ormond Street Hospital for Sick Children 1967–9 and Director of the African Educational Trust 1960–9, she became a life peer in 1967 and was a Government Whip in the Lords 1969–70, Deputy Opposition Chief Whip 1972–3 and Opposition Chief Whip 1973–4. She became Captain of the Gentlemen At Arms (Government Chief Whip in the Lords) in 1974 and, when the Labour Party lost office in 1979, Opposition Chief Whip once again. She married Richard Llewelyn-Davies in 1943.

LLEWELYN-DAVIES, Richard. Senior Partner of Llewelyn-Davies, Weeks, Forestier-Walker & Bor. He was Professor of Architecture at University College, London, 1960–9, Professor of Urban Planning 1969–75 and subsequently Emeritus Professor. In 1967 he became Chairman of the Centre for Environmental Studies. He was created a life peer in 1963.

LLOYD, Selwyn (1904–78). Conservative M.P. for the Wirral 1945–70 and, after his election as Speaker of the House of Commons, M.P. for the Wirral 1970–6. He was Minister of State at the Foreign Office 1951–4, Minister of Supply 1954–5, Minister of Defence April–December 1955, Secretary of State for Foreign Affairs 1955–60, Chancellor of the Exchequer 1960–2, Lord Privy Seal and Leader of the House of Commons 1963–4 and Speaker 1970–6. In 1976 he became a life peer, taking the title of Lord Selwyn-Lloyd. He wrote a volume of memoirs, *Mr Speaker, Sir* (London: Cape, 1976), and in his last years wrote *Suez 1956: A Personal Account* (London: Cape), which was published shortly after his death.

MACMILLAN, Harold. Conservative M.P. for Stockton-on-Tees 1924–9 and 1931–45, and for Bromley November 1945–September 1964. He was Parliamentary Secretary at the Ministry of Supply 1940–2, Parliamentary Under-Secretary of State at the Colonial Office 1942, Minister Resident at Allied Headquarters in North-West Africa 1942–5, Secretary for Air 1945, Minister of Housing and Local Government 1951–4, Minister of Defence October 1954–April 1955, Secretary of State for Foreign Affairs April–December 1955, Chancellor of the Exchequer December 1955–January 1957 and Prime Minister January 1957–October 1963. He was Chairman of the publishing house Macmillan & Co and of Macmillan (Journals) 1963–7 and then of Macmillan Ltd from 1963 to 1974, when he became President of the company. Since 1960 he has been Chancellor of the University of Oxford. He became an O.M. in 1976. His publications include six volumes of Memoirs (London: Macmillan, 1966–7, 1969, 1971–3) and *Past Masters* (London: Macmillan, 1975).

MALLALIEU, J. P. W. ('Curly') (1908–80). Labour M.P. for Huddersfield 1945–50 and for Huddersfield East 1950–79. He came from a long-serving political family, and his father and his brother, Lance, were also both M.P.s. He was P.P.S. to John Strachey in 1945 and again in 1946–9 and held posts in Harold Wilson's first Government as a Navy Minister, and later as Minister of State at the Department of Trade. He married Harriet Tinn in 1945.

MARTIN, Kingsley (1897–1969). Editor of the *New Statesman & Nation* (later the *New Statesman*) 1930–60. He published two volumes of autobiography: *Father Figures* (London: Constable, 1966) and *Editor* (London: Constable, 1968). C. H. Rolph's biography, *Kingsley* (London: Gollancz), was published in 1973.

MENDELSON, John Jakob (1917–78). Labour M.P. for the Penistone division, West Riding of Yorkshire, from 1959 until his death. From 1949 to 1959 he was Lecturer in Economics and Public Administration at the University of Sheffield.

MIKARDO, Ian. Labour M.P. for several Reading constituencies 1945–59, for Poplar 1964–74 and for Tower Hamlets, Bethnal Green and Bow since 1974. A member of the N.E.C. 1950–9 and 1960–78, from February to November 1974 he was Chairman of the Parliamentary Labour Party.

MITCHISON, (Gilbert) Richard (1890–1970) and Naomi. Richard Mitchison was Labour M.P. for the Kettering division of Northamptonshire 1945–64, when he became a life peer. He was Joint Parliamentary Secretary at the Ministry of Land and National Resources 1964–6. In 1916 he married Naomi Haldane, the daughter of J. S. Haldane. She was a member of the Argyll County Council 1945–65, the Highland & Islands Advisory Panel 1947–65 and the Highlands & Islands Development Consultative Council 1966–76. In 1963 she became Tribal Adviser to the Bakgatia in Botswana. A prolific writer of both fiction and non-fiction, her works include three volumes of autobiography, *Small Talk: Memoirs of an Edwardian Childhood* (London: The Bodley Head, 1973), *All Change Here* (London: The Bodley Head, 1975) and *You May Well Ask: A Memoir: 1920–40* (London: Gollancz, 1979).

MORRISON, Herbert (1888–1965). Labour M.P. for South Hackney 1923–4,

1929–31 and 1935–45, for East Lewisham 1945–51 and for South Lewisham 1951–9. Morrison was a key figure in the London Labour Party and Leader of the L.C.C. from 1934 to 1940. He served as Minister of Transport 1929–31, Minister of Supply 1940, Home Secretary 1940–5 and as Deputy Prime Minister from 1945 to 1951, when he became First Lord President and Leader of the Commons, and from March to October 1951 Foreign Secretary. In 1959 he was created a life peer, taking the title Lord Morrison of Lambeth. His writings include *How Greater London is Governed* (London: Lovat Dickson & Thompson, 1935), *Government and Parliament* (Oxford University Press, 1954) and *An Autobiography* (London: Odhams, 1960). A biography, *Herbert Morrison: Portrait of a Politician*, by Bernard Donoughue and George Jones (London: Weidenfeld & Nicolson), was published in 1973.

PHILLIPS, Morgan (1902–63). Secretary of the Bargoed Labour Party 1923–5, he was Chairman of the Bargoed Steam Coal Lodge of the South Wales Miners' Federation 1924–6, Secretary and Agent of the West Fulham Constituency Labour Party 1928–30 and of the Whitechapel Constituency Party 1934–7. In 1937 he joined the staff of Transport House and was the Labour Party's Propaganda Officer 1937–40, Eastern Counties Organizer 1940–1 and Secretary of the Research Department 1941–4. He was General Secretary of the Labour Party from 1944 until his retirement in 1962 and Chairman of the Socialist International 1948–57.

ROBENS, Alfred. Labour M.P. for Wansbeck 1945–50 and for Blyth 1950–60. He was Parliamentary Secretary at the Ministry of Fuel and Power 1947–51, Minister of Labour and National Service April–October 1951 and Chairman of the National Coal Board 1961–71. He became a life peer in 1961 and in 1971 Chairman of Vickers Ltd.

SANDYS, Duncan. Conservative M.P. for the Norwood division of Lambeth 1935–45 and for Streatham from 1950 to February 1954. He was Financial Secretary at the War Office 1941–3, Parliamentary Secretary at the Ministry of Supply 1943–4, Minister of Works 1944–5, Minister of Supply 1951–4, Minister of Housing and Local Government 1954–7, Minister of Defence 1957–9, Minister of Aviation 1959–60 and Secretary of State for Commonwealth Relations 1960–4. In 1947 he founded the European Movement. He became a life peer in 1974, taking the title of Lord Duncan-Sandys. He married Winston Churchill's daughter Diana in 1935. The marriage was dissolved in 1960.

SHACKLETON, Edward. The son of the polar explorer and an explorer himself, Edward Shackleton was Labour M.P. for Preston 1946–50 and for Preston South 1950–5. In 1958 he became a life peer and in 1964 Minister of Defence for the R.A.F. He was Minister without Portfolio and Deputy Leader of the

House of Lords 1967–8, Lord Privy Seal January–April 1968, Paymaster-General April–October 1968 and Leader of the House of Lords and Minister in charge of the Civil Service Department April 1968–70. He was Leader of the Opposition in the House of Lords 1970–4. Since 1975 he has been Deputy Chairman of the Rio Tinto Zinc Corporation.

SHINWELL, Emanuel (born 1884). Labour M.P. for Linlithgow 1922–4 and 1928–31 and for the Seaham and later the Easington divisions of Durham 1935–70. He was Minister of Fuel and Power 1945–7 and of Defence 1950–1 and was Chairman of the Parliamentary Labour Party from October 1964 until his resignation in 1967. In 1970 he became a life peer.

SHORE, Peter. Labour M.P. for Stepney 1964–74 and for Tower Hamlets, Stepney and Poplar since 1974. Head of the Research Department of the Labour Party 1959–64, he was P.P.S. to the Prime Minister 1965–6, Joint Parliamentary Secretary at the Ministry of Technology 1966–7 and at the Department of Economic Affairs 1967, Secretary of State for Economic Affairs 1967–9 and Minister without Portfolio and Deputy Leader of the House of Commons 1969–70. He was Opposition spokesman on Europe 1971–4, Secretary of State for Trade 1974–6 and for the Environment 1976–9. In 1979 he was appointed Shadow Foreign Secretary.

STRACHEY, John (1901–63). Labour M.P. for Aston 1929–31 and for West Dundee 1950 until his death. He was Parliamentary Under-Secretary of State for Air 1945–6, Minister of Food 1946–50 and Secretary of State for War 1951. Co-founder of the Left Book Club and himself a prolific writer, his works include the two-volumes *Principles of Democratic Socialism* (London: Gollancz, 1956, 1959). Earlier, he had collaborated with Aneurin Bevan and George Strauss in *What We Saw in Russia* (London: Leonard and Virginia Woolf, 1931). A biography, *John Strachey*, was written by Hugh Thomas (London: Eyre Methuen, 1973).

STRAUSS, George. Labour M.P. for North Lambeth 1929–31 and 1934–50 and for Lambeth Vauxhall 1950–79. He was Parliamentary Secretary at the Ministry of Transport 1945–7 and Minister of Supply 1947–51, during which time he introduced the Iron and Steel Nationalization Bill 1949. 'Father of the House of Commons' 1974–9, he became a life peer in 1979.

SUMMERSKILL, Edith (1901–80). Labour M.P. for West Fulham 1938–55 and for Warrington 1955–61. She was Parliamentary Secretary at the Ministry of Food 1945–50, Minister for National Insurance 1950–1, and was Chairman of the Labour Party 1954/55. In 1961 she became a life peer. She wrote an autobiography, *A Woman's World* (London: Heinemann), in 1967.

THORNEYCROFT, Peter. A barrister, painter and politician, he was Conservative M.P. for Stafford 1938–45 and for Monmouth 1945–66. He was Parliamentary Secretary at the Ministry of War Transport 1945, President of the Board of Trade October 1951–January 1957, Chancellor of the Exchequer from January 1957 until his resignation in January 1958, Minister of Aviation July 1960–July 1962, Minister of Defence 1962–4 and Secretary of State for Defence April–October 1964. In 1975 he became Chairman of the Conservative Party. He was created a life peer in 1967. He was Chairman of the Simplification of International Trade Procedures 1968–75 and of the British Overseas Trade Board 1972–5 and is now Chairman of Pye Holdings, Pye of Cambridge Ltd, Pirelli General Cable Works Ltd, Pirelli Ltd and Trust Houses Forte Ltd. He is also a Director of Securicor Ltd.

WATSON, Sam (1898–1967). A miner, he became Secretary of the Durham Miners' Association in 1936, serving until his retirement in 1963. He was a member of the Council of the University of Durham, from which he received an honorary D.C.L. in 1955, and a member of the Board of the National Health Service, as well as a part-time member of the National Coal Board and of the Central Electricity Generating Board.

WIGG, George. Labour M.P. for Dudley 1945–67. He was Shinwell's P.P.S. in the Attlee Government, an Opposition Whip 1951–4 and Paymaster-General 1964–7. In 1967 he became a life peer. He was Chairman of the Horserace Betting Levy Board 1967–72. He has written an autobiography, *George Wigg* (London: Michael Joseph, 1972).

WILSON, Harold. Labour M.P. for Ormskirk 1945–50 and for Huyton since 1950. He joined the Civil Service in 1943 as an economist and statistician. From 1945 to 1947 he was Parliamentary Secretary to the Ministry of Works, from March to October 1947 Secretary for Overseas Trade and from October 1947 until his resignation in April 1951 President of the Board of Trade. From 1959 to 1963 he was Chairman of the Public Accounts Committee. He was Chairman of the N.E.C. of the Labour Party 1961–2, and in 1963 he succeeded Hugh Gaitskell as Leader of the Party. When Labour won the 1964 General Election he became Prime Minister and First Lord of the Treasury; after 1970 he continued to lead the Party in Opposition, becoming Prime Minister once more in February 1974. He held that office until his resignation and return to the backbenches, as Sir Harold Wilson, in April 1976. He has written *The Labour Government 1964–70: A Personal Record* (London: Weidenfeld & Nicolson and Michael Joseph, 1971), *The Governance of Britain* (London: Michael Joseph, 1976), *A Prime Minister on Prime Ministers* (London: Michael Joseph, 1977), and *Final Term: The Labour Government 1974–6* (London: Weidenfeld & Nicolson and Michael Joseph, 1979). He married in 1940 Mary Baldwin, who has written two volumes of poetry:

Selected Poems (London: Hutchinson, 1970) and *New Poems* (London: Hutchinson, 1979).

WYATT, Woodrow. Labour M.P. for the Aston division of Birmingham 1945–1955 and for the Bosworth division of Leicester 1959–70. He was Parliamentary Under-Secretary of State and Financial Secretary at the War Office, May–October 1951. From 1965 to 1973 he was a *Daily Mirror* columnist, and since 1976 he has been Chairman of the Horserace Totalizator Board. His writings include *Turn Again Westminster* (London: Deutsch, 1973) and *What's Left of the Labour Party?* (London: Sidgwick & Jackson, 1977).

Abbreviations

A.E.U.	Amalgamated Engineering Union
ASLEF	Associated Society of Locomotive Engineers and Firemen
A.U.E.F.W.	Amalgamated Union of Engineering and Foundry Workers
A.U.E.W.	Amalgamated Union of Engineering Workers
B.B.C.	British Broadcasting Corporation
C.B.E.	Commander of the British Empire
C.B.I.	Confederation of British Industry
C.N.D.	Campaign for Nuclear Disarmament
C.O.	Constituency Organization
C.P.S.U.	Communist Party of the Soviet Union
D.B.E.	Dame Commander Order of the British Empire
D.C.L.	Doctor of Civil Law
D.C.M.G.	Dame Commander of St Michael and St George
D.E.A.	Department of Economic Affairs
D.E.S.	Department of Education and Science
E.D.C.	European Defence Community
EFTA	European Free Trade Association
EOKA	Ethniki Organisis Kyprion Agoniston (National Organization of Cypriot Combatants)
E.P.U.	European Payments Union
E.T.U.	Electrical Trades Union
GATT	General Agreement on Tariffs and Trade
G.B.E.	Knight or Dame Grand Cross Order of the British Empire
G.E.C.	General Electric Company
G.M.C.	General Management Committee
G.M.W.U.	General and Municipal Workers' Union
G.O.C.	General Officer Commanding
GOSPLAN	Gosudarspvennaia Planovaia Komissia (State Planning Office)
I.B.A.	Independent Broadcasting Authority
I.C.B.M.	Intercontinental Ballistic Missile
I.L.P.	Independent Labour Party
I.M.F.	International Monetary Fund

I.O.M.	Isle of Man
I.P.C.	International Publishing Corporation
I.R.B.M.	Intermediate-Range Ballistic Missile
I.T.A.	Independent Television Authority
I.T.N.	Independent Television News
I.T.V.	Independent Television
K.C.	King's Counsel
L.W.T.	London Weekend Television
MEDO	Middle East Defence Organization
M.R.P.	Mouvement Républicain Populaire
NATO	North Atlantic Treaty Organization
N.B.C.	National Broadcasting Company
N.E.C.	National Executive Committee
N.E.D.C.	National Economic Development Committee
N.K.V.D.	Narodny komissariat vnutrennik del (People's Commissariat for Internal Affairs)
N.U.G.M.W.	National Union of General and Municipal Workers
N.U.P.E.	National Union of Public Employees
N.U.R.	National Union of Railwaymen
N.U.T.	National Union of Teachers
O.E.E.C.	Organization of European Economic Co-operation
OGPU	Obyedinyonnoe gosudarstrevennoe politicheskoe upravlenie (Unified State Political Directorate)
O.M.	Order of Merit
P.C.I.	Partito Comunista Italiano
P.E.P.	Political and Economic Planning
P.L.P.	Parliamentary Labour Party
P.P.E.	Philosophy, Politics and Economics
P.P.S.	Parliamentary Private Secretary
P.S.D.I.	Partito Socialista Democratico Italiano
P.S.I.	Partito Socialista Italiano
P.Z.P.R.	Polska Zjednoczona Partia Robotnicza (Polish United Workers Party)
Q.C.	Queen's Counsel
R.D.C.	Rural District Council
R.I.I.A.	Royal Institute of International Affairs
SCUA	Suez Canal Users' Association
SEATO	South-East Asia Treaty Organization
SHAPE	Supreme Headquarters Allied Powers in Europe
S.P.D.	Sozialdemokratische Partei Deutschlands
T.G.W.U./T.&G.	Transport and General Workers Union
T.N.T.	Trinitrotoluene
T.S.S.A.	Transport and Salaried Staff Association
T.U.C.	Trades Union Congress

U.K.A.E.A.	United Kingdom Atomic Energy Authority
U.N.	United Nations
UNEF	United Nations Emergency Force
UNESCO	United Nations Educational, Scientific and Cultural Organization
U.N.O.	United Nations Organization
UNRRA	United Nations Relief and Rehabilitation Administration
USDAW	Union of Shop, Distributive and Allied Workers
U.S.D.R.	Union Démocratique et Socialiste de la Résistance
U.S.E.	United States of Europe
W.E.A.	Workers' Educational Association

The Bevanites

As the *Backbench Diaries* show, the 'Bevanites' were a loose group, whose members did not always agree on every issue. Nor did they all meet regularly at Vincent Square or elsewhere. It was after the rebellion over the 1952 Defence Estimates (see pp. 86 ff.), when fifty-seven M.P.s (one-fifth of the P.L.P.) voted against their own Front Bench, that the Bevanite Group was labelled 'a party within a party'. The Government sought approval for the Statement on Defence (Cmd 8475) but the Shadow Cabinet, while approving the defence programme, put down an Amendment noting the Government's incapacity to carry it out. Bevan and his associates, defying a three-line whip, first abstained on the Labour Amendment and, on the main Question, voted against the Estimates. Those who seek a list of 'Bevanites' will therefore find it helpful to examine the records of the divisions on March 5th, 1952 (see *H. C. Debates*, vol. 497, col. 522 ff.), particularly that of the opponents of the Estimates:

Acland, Sir Richard
Baird, J.
Bence, C. R.
Bevan, Rt Hon. A. (Ebbw Vale)
Bing, G. H. C.
Bowles, F. G.
Brockway, A. F.
Carmichael, J.
Castle, Mrs B. A.
Cove, W. G.
Craddock, George (Bradford, S.)
Crossman, R. H. S.
Davies, Harold (Leek)
Davies, Stephen (Merthyr)
Delargy, H. J.
Donnelly, D. L.
Driberg, T. E. N.
Evans, Edward (Lowestoft)
Fernyhough, E.

Foot, M. M.
Freeman, John (Watford)
Grenfell, Rt Hon. D. R.
Griffiths, William (Exchange)
Hale, Leslie (Oldham, W.)
Hughes, Cledwyn (Anglesey)
Hughes, Emrys (S. Ayrshire)
Irvine, A. J. (Edge Hill)
Jones, Frederick Elwyn (West
    Ham, S.)
Lee, Miss Jennie (Cannock)
Lever, Harold (Cheetham)
Lewis, Arthur
Lipton, Lt.-Col. M.
Longden, Fred (Small Heath)
McGovern, J.
MacMillan, M. K. (Western Isles)
Mallalieu, J. P. W. (Huddersfield, E.)
Manuel, A. C.

Mikardo, Ian
Orbach, M.
Padley, W. E.
Poole, C. C.
Rankin, John
Roberts, Goronwy (Caernarvonshire)
Silverman, Julius (Erdington)
Silverman, Sydney (Nelson)
Smith, Ellis (Stoke, S.)
Snow, J. W.
Stross, Dr Barnett

Swingler, S. T.
Thomas, George (Cardiff)
Timmons, J.
Williams, David (Neath)
Williams, W. T. (Hammersmith, S.)
Wilson, Rt Hon. Harold (Huyton)
Yates, V. F.

TELLERS FOR THE NOES:
Mr Monslow and
Mr Tudor Watkins

Index

165, 167–8; disbandment of the Bevanites, 175; voting system for Parliamentary Committees, 181, 182, 249; and the end of the Bevanite feud, 187; Dec. 1952 weekend conference, 189; and the *Tribune*'s attack on Lincoln Evans, 197; and the *Tribune* brains trusts, 204; and journalists on the N.E.C., 204, 206; and abstention on a three-line Whip, 211–12; April 1953 N.E.C. policy meeting, 225; 1953 policy document, 232, 234; 1953 Party Conference, 266, 269; calls for Party unity, 329, 330; 1954 Party Conference, 348, 349, 350; and *Tribune*'s attack on Deakin, 364; withdraws Whip from Bevan, 398; and Bevan's possible expulsion, 402, 403, 405, 406, 407, 408, 409, 411–12, 413; Party more centred on, 420; 'Report on Party Organization', 441, 442; 1955 Party Conference, 445, 449

personal life: after-dinner speeches, 42; and King George VI's death, 70, 71, 72; and Zita Crossman's death, 126; and Queen Mary's death, 213; illness, 439; senility, 771; biographical note, 1051

relationship with colleagues: rebukes Bevan for constitutional impropriety, 132–4; Morrison's relations with, 159, 746; Bevin's support for, 197; rebukes Mallalieu, 277, 279–80; Bevan wishes to destroy reputation of, 315, 317, 318; Wilson joins Parliamentary Committee, 320; and Morrison's attack on Bevan in *Socialist Commentary*, 325; King's attitude to, 399, 422; no personal differences with Bevan, 400; Bevan pledges loyalty to, 413; on Harry Truman, 442; supports Gaitskell against Wilson, 893; Jenkins's admiration for, 979

other topics: and the 1951 election of the Speaker, 29; 1951 King's Speech, 31; and George VI's preference for Bevin, 79; 1946 King's Speech debate, 86; and journalists, 204, 206, 277; West Midlands Rally, 208; misses Königswinter Conference, 217; M.P.'s salaries, 333, 335; influence of internal politics on, 338; and the *New Statesman*, 360; speech for Eden's takeover, 416, 417; and *The Road to Brighton Pier*, 746

Attlee, Violet, 128, 147, 209, 417, 447
Auden, Wystan, 498–9 and n
Australia, 1951 Japanese Peace Treaty, 41; and British membership of E.E.C., 955
Austria, peace treaty, 37, 255
Ayr Burghs, 247

Bacon, Alice, 431, 459, 773, 960; biographical note, 104n; and Council of Europe, 104; 1952 Party Conference, 146;

and the *Tribune* brains trusts, 204, 205; 1953 policy document, 232–3; and Morrison's standing for Party Treasurer, 254; 1953 Party Conference, 264, 270; and Organization Sub-Committee, 454; Attlee's retirement, 456; and Khrushchev's visit, 489; Middle East crisis, 501, 502; 1958 Party Conference, 714; 1959 election campaign, 747, 778; and Labour nuclear policy, 761, 762; and the 1960 Defence debate rebellion, 820; and a Party emblem, 894; 1960 Conference defence debate defeat, 901–2, 903; and Tawney's 80th birthday, 905; tripartite defence talks, 921, 931–2; and E.E.C. membership, 956; 1961 Shadow Cabinet elections, 961; 1964 election campaign, 961

Bagehot, Walter, 733 and n, 737 and n, 740, 1003
Baghdad Pact, 464–5, 466, 472, 474, 475, 491, 586, 614, 751
Baird, John, 151 and n, 397, 417, 428, 1071
Baker, Gilbert, 121 and n, 122, 123, 237, 240, 248
Baker, John, 124 and n
Baker, Liena, 124
balance of payments: 1951 crisis, 32; 1952 situation, 162
Balchin, Nigel, 992 and n
Baldwin, Stanley, 181 and n, 416, 726, 771, 980
Balfour, Honour, 395 and n
Balogh, Pen, 154, 177, 240, 282, 298, 299, 384, 819, 820, 974, 1000, 1029; at Zita Crossman's funeral, 124; period of National Service, 178; trip to Workington, 215; goes to *The Apple Cart*, 237
Balogh, Stephen, 215
Balogh, Thomas, 65, 154, 174, 177, 180, 196, 262, 298, 299, 328, 341, 384, 392, 398, 424, 798, 819, 832, 974, 1014, 1019, 1029; speech to Keep Left Group, 31; 1951 Bevanite Group conference at Buscot, 51–3; rearmament, 52; on the 1951 economic situation, 52; and nationalized industries, 53; 1952 defence expenditure, 80–1; 1952 Party crisis, 90; at Zita Crossman's funeral, 124; 1952 balance of payments report, 162; and the debate on groups within the Party, 162; anxious about Bevan, 175; 1952 U.S. presidential election, 176; nationalization, 184; and the importance of foreign affairs, 187; hopes to influence defence policies, 187; N.E.C. weekend conferences, 188; and the absence of Bevanite policy, 206; trip to Workington with RC, 215; 1953 Budget, 221; takes RC to Cambridge, 239–40; and Pompeiian art,

35

36